D0164063

LIFT TAKE YOUR STUDYING TO THE NEXT LEVEL.

This book comes with 1-year digital access to the *Examples & Explanations* for this course.

Step 1: Go to **www.CasebookConnect.com/LIFT** and redeem your access code to get started.

Access Code:

Step 2: Go to your BOOKSHELF and select your online *Examples & Explanations* to start reading, highlighting, and taking notes in the margins of your e-book.

Step 3: Select the STUDY tab in your toolbar to access the questions from your book in interactive format, designed to give you extra practice and help you master the course material.

Is this a used casebook? Access code already scratched off?

You can purchase the online *Examples & Explanations* and still access all of the powerful tools listed above. Please visit CasebookConnect.com/Catalog to learn more about Connected Study Aids.

PLEASE NOTE: Each access code provides 12 month access and can only be used once. This code will also expire one year after the discontinuation of the corresponding print title and must be redeemed before then. CCH reserves the right to discontinue this program at any time for any business reason. For further details, please see the Casebook Connect End User Agreement.

PIN: 9111149620   04398

ADMINISTRATIVE LAW

ASPEN CASEBOOK SERIES

ADMINISTRATIVE LAW
Fourth Edition

John M. Rogers

Judge, U.S. Court of Appeals for the Sixth Circuit
Thomas P. Lewis Professor of Law Emeritus
University of Kentucky College of Law

Michael P. Healy

Senator Wendell H. Ford Professor of Law
University of Kentucky College of Law

Ronald J. Krotoszynski, Jr.

John S. Stone Chair, Director of Faculty Research, and Professor of Law
University of Alabama School of Law

 Wolters Kluwer

Published by Wolters Kluwer in New York.

Wolters Kluwer Legal & Regulatory U.S. serves customers worldwide with CCH, Aspen Publishers, and Kluwer Law International products. (www.WKLegaledu.com)

To contact Customer Service, e-mail customer.service@wolterskluwer.com, call 1-800-234-1660, fax 1-800-901-9075, or mail correspondence to:

Wolters Kluwer
Attn: Order Department
PO Box 990
Frederick, MD 21705

Printed in the United States of America.

2 3 4 5 6 7 8 9 0

ISBN 978-1-4548-7878-0

Library of Congress Cataloging-in-Publication Data

Names: Rogers, John M. (John Marshall), 1948- author. | Healy, Michael P., 1956- author. | Krotoszynski, Ronald J., 1967- author.
Title: Administrative law / John M. Rogers, Judge, U.S. Court of Appeals for the Sixth Circuit, Thomas P. Lewis Professor of Law Emeritus University of Kentucky College of Law; Michael P. Healy, Senator Wendell H. Ford Professor of Law, University of Kentucky College of Law; Ronald J. Krotoszynski, Jr., John Stone Chair, Director of Faculty Research and Professor of Law, University of Alabama School of Law.
Description: Fourth edition. | New York : Wolters Kluwer, [2017] | Series: Aspen casebook series
Identifiers: LCCN 2016055799 | ISBN 9781454878780
Subjects: LCSH: Administrative law — United States — Cases. | Administrative procedure — United States — Cases. | LCGFT: Casebooks.
Classification: LCC KF5402.R64 2017 | DDC 342.73/06 — dc23
LC record available at https://lccn.loc.gov/2016055799

About Wolters Kluwer Legal & Regulatory U.S.

Wolters Kluwer Legal & Regulatory U.S. delivers expert content and solutions in the areas of law, corporate compliance, health compliance, reimbursement, and legal education. Its practical solutions help customers successfully navigate the demands of a changing environment to drive their daily activities, enhance decision quality and inspire confident outcomes.

Serving customers worldwide, its legal and regulatory portfolio includes products under the Aspen Publishers, CCH Incorporated, Kluwer Law International, ftwilliam.com and MediRegs names. They are regarded as exceptional and trusted resources for general legal and practice-specific knowledge, compliance and risk management, dynamic workflow solutions, and expert commentary.

For Ying Juan.

John M. Rogers

For Carol.

Michael P. Healy

In memory of my mother, Barbara Carol Jamison Krotoszynski (1949-2013).

Ronald J. Krotoszynski, Jr.

SUMMARY OF CONTENTS

CONTENTS

CHAPTER 4

CHAPTER 5

PREFACE

The fourth edition of the *Administrative Law* casebook is intended to meet several objectives. First, we hope to accomplish the core goal of the first edition of the text. That goal was described in the preface to the first edition:

> This book is designed to serve as a streamlined workhorse for professors who like to teach out of cases and to focus on the principles underlying core doctrines. It lets the cases speak for themselves, with a minimum of editorializing text. This approach gives professors and students alike the opportunity to reconcile the principles of the case, each in his or her own way.

The fourth edition accordingly retains the organizational structure of the first edition. That structure is dictated by the four fundamental components of administrative law: (1) procedural requirements for agency adjudication; (2) procedural requirements for, and other issues related to, agency rulemaking; (3) separation-of-powers issues related to administrative agencies; and (4) judicial review of agency action. The authors' experience is that the course is most successful when taught in this order and the fourth edition of the text adheres to this order for presenting the materials. The four components are, however, presented in chapters that are largely independent. Instructors may change the order of presentation to conform to their own judgment about the optimal order of presentation.

Although adhering to the organizing principles and structure of the first edition, this new edition has been revised to account for developments in administrative law that have occurred since the third edition was published. The revised text includes as lead cases the recent Supreme Court decisions in *Kerry v. Din, Wellness International Network, Ltd. v. Sharif, NLRB v. Noel Canning, Decker v. Northwest Environmental Defense Center, King v. Burwell,* and *United States Army Corps of Engineers v. Hawkes Co.* A new note addresses the issue of delegation of governmental power to a private entity. Throughout the text, questions and notes for students have been added to reflect the insights of decisions in recent cases, including *Perez v. Mortgage Bankers Ass'n, City of Arlington v. FCC, Department of Transportation v. Association of American Railroads, T-Mobile South, LLC v. City of Roswell, Young v. United Parcel Service, Inc., University of Texas Southwestern Medical Center v. Nassar, Michigan v. EPA, Cuozzo Speed Technologies, LLC v. Lee, Christopher v. SmithKline Beecham Corp., Encino Motorcars, LLC v. Navarro,* and *Lexmark Int'l, Inc. v. Static Control Components, Inc.* The third objective of the new text is to provide opportunities for students to apply their understanding of administrative law principles in new legal contexts. The fourth edition retains the series of "Theory Applied Problems" at the conclusion of different sections of the text. These problems allow students to test their understanding of the principles of administrative law.

Although the text includes significant changes with new lead cases, we have sought to ensure that the materials included in the fourth edition may be taught in a three-hour course. Meeting this objective has meant that some materials have been removed from previous editions. Finally, we wish to acknowledge in this preface the debt that we also acknowledged in the preface to the earlier editions. That debt is owed to the teachers of administrative law and authors of administrative law texts who have affected our understanding of this subject. That group of law professors has grown since the date of publication of the first edition, because we are now indebted to the adopters of the text who have helped us to revise and, we hope, improve it in this fourth edition.

John M. Rogers
Michael P. Healy
Ronald J. Krotoszynski, Jr.

January 2017

ACKNOWLEDGMENTS

Bybee, Jay S., Agency Expertise, ALJ Independence, and Administrative Courts: The Recent Changes in Louisiana's Administrative Procedure Act, 59 Louisiana Law Review 431, 434-41 (1999). Copyright © 1999 Louisiana Law Review. Reprinted by permission. All rights reserved.

Uniform Law Commissioners' Model State Administrative Procedure Act (1981), §§ 1-101, 1-102, 2-104, 3-103, 3-104, 3-105, 3-106, 3-107, 3-108, 3-109, 3-110, 3-111, 3-112, 3-113, 3-114, 3-115, 3-116, 3-117, 3-201, 3-202, 3-203, 3-204, 4-101, 4-102, 4-103, 4-104, 4-105, 4-201, 4-202, 4-203, 4-204, 4-207, 4-208, 4-209, 4-210, 4-211, 4-212, 4-213, 4-214, 4-215, 4-216, 4-217, 4-218, 4-219, 4-220, 4-221, 4-301, 4-401, 4-402, 4-403, 4-501, 4-502, 4-503, 4-504, 4-505, 4-506, 5-101, 5-102, 5-103, 5-104, 5-105, 5-106, 5-107, 5-108, 5-114, 5-116. Copyright © 1981 National Conference of Commissioners on Uniform State Laws. Reprinted by permission. All rights reserved.

ADMINISTRATIVE LAW

CHAPTER

1

Introduction

A. OVERVIEW OF THE WORK AND PLACE OF ADMINISTRATIVE AGENCIES IN OUR SYSTEM OF GOVERNMENT

Administrative law involves the study of the place of administrative agencies in the American legal system. Agencies, of course, do what government does. Government taxes, spends, builds, paves, educates, punishes, regulates, and so on. Those who actually do this work are agents of the government, hence the word *agencies.* In a sense, they are necessary if government is to do anything.

The need for government action, at all, and the appropriate government agent to take action when warranted, may vary in different contexts. Should government do a lot or leave most matters to the market and thereby preserve more freedom? When government does not leave something to the market, why not? What theory or theories justify changing what otherwise would be the market result?

When matters are not best left to the market, why not legislate a general standard and simply let courts enforce civil liability, without creating agencies? If there are good reasons not to leave the details to the courts, why can't Congress just set specific and detailed requirements in areas where regulation is warranted?

The following case excerpts introduce the principal public-policy contexts in which a need has been recognized for specialized agencies to undertake government action. These selections also raise, in a preliminary way, some of the important legal themes that will be developed through the remainder of the course.

INTERSTATE COMMERCE COMMISSION v. CINCINNATI, NEW ORLEANS AND TEXAS PACIFIC RAILWAY CO.
167 U.S. 479 (1897)

MR. JUSTICE BREWER . . . delivered the opinion of the court.

. . . In view of its importance, and the full arguments that have been presented, we have deemed it our duty to re-examine the question [of the powers of the Interstate Commerce Commission under the Interstate Commerce Act] in its entirety, and to determine what powers congress has given to this commission in respect to the matter of rates. The importance of the question cannot be overestimated. Billions of dollars are invested in railroad properties. Millions of passengers, as well as millions of tons of freight, are moved each year by the railroad companies, and this transportation is carried on by a multitude of corporations working in different parts of the country, and subjected to varying and diverse conditions.

Before the passage of the act it was generally believed that there were great abuses in railroad management and railroad transportation, and the grave question which Congress had to consider was how those abuses should be corrected, and what control should be taken of the business of such corporations. The present inquiry is limited to the question as to what it determined should be done with reference to the matter of rates. There were three obvious and dissimilar courses open for consideration. Congress might itself prescribe the rates, or it might commit to some subordinate tribunal this duty, or it might leave with the companies the right to fix rates, subject to regulations and restrictions, as well as to that rule which is as old as the existence of common carriers, to wit, that rates must be reasonable. There is nothing in the act fixing rates. Congress did not attempt to exercise that power, and, if we examine the legislative and public history of the day, it is apparent that there was no serious thought of doing so. The question debated is whether it vested in the commission the power and the duty to fix rates, and the fact that this is a debatable question, and has been most strenuously and earnestly debated, is very persuasive that it did not. The grant of such a power is never to be implied. The power itself is so vast and comprehensive, so largely affecting the rights of carrier and shipper, as well as indirectly all commercial transactions, the language by which the power is given had been so often used, and was so familiar to the legislative mind, and is capable of such definite and exact statement, that no just rule of construction would tolerate a grant of such power by mere implication. . . .

It is one thing to inquire whether the rates which have been charged and collected are reasonable — that is a judicial act; but an entirely different thing to prescribe rates which shall be charged in the future — that is a legislative act. *Chicago, Milwaukee &c. Railway v. Minnesota,* 134 U.S. 418, 458.

It will be perceived that in this case the interstate commerce commission assumed the right to prescribe rates which should control in the future, and their application to the court was for a mandamus to compel the companies to comply with their decision; that is, to abide by their legislative determination as to the maximum rates to be observed in the future. Now, nowhere in the interstate commerce act do we find words similar to those in [some state statutes], giving to the commission power to "increase or reduce any of the rates"; "to establish rates of charges"; "to make and fix reasonable and just rates of freight and passenger tariffs"; "to make a schedule of reasonable maximum rates of charges"; "to fix tables of maximum charges"; to compel the carrier "to adopt such rate, charge or classification as said commissioners shall declare to be equitable and reasonable." The power, therefore, is not expressly given. Whence then is it deduced? In the first section it is provided that "all charges . . . shall be reasonable and just; and every unjust and unreasonable charge for such service is prohibited and declared to be unlawful." Then follow sections prohibiting discrimination, undue preferences, higher charges for a short than for a long haul, and pooling, and also making provision for the preparation by the companies of schedules of rates, and requiring their publication. Section 11 creates the Interstate Commerce Commission. Section 12, as amended March 2, 1889, (25 Stat. 858), gives it authority to inquire into the management of the business of all common carriers, to demand full and complete information from them, and adds, "and the commission is hereby authorized to execute and enforce the provisions of this act." And the argument is that, in enforcing and executing the provisions of the act, it is to execute and enforce the law as stated in the first section, which is that all charges shall be reasonable and just, and that every unjust and unreasonable charge is prohibited; that it cannot enforce this mandate of the law without a determination of what are reasonable and just charges, and, as no other tribunal is created for such determination, therefore it must be implied that it is authorized to make the determination, and, having made it, apply to the courts for a mandamus to compel the enforcement of such determination. In other words, that though Congress has not in terms given the commission the power to determine what are just and reasonable rates for the future, yet as no other tribunal has been provided, it must have intended that the commission should exercise the power. We do not think this argument can be sustained. If there were nothing else in the act than the first section, commanding reasonable rates, and the twelfth, empowering the commission to execute and enforce the provisions of the act, we should be of the opinion that Congress did not intend to give to the commission the power to prescribe any tariff, and determine what for the future should be reasonable and just rates. The power given is the power to execute and enforce, not to legislate. The power given is partly judicial, partly executive and administrative, but not legislative. . . .

Our conclusion, then, is that Congress has not conferred upon the commission the legislative power of prescribing rates, either maximum or minimum or absolute. As it did not give the express power to the commission it did not intend to secure the same result indirectly by empowering that tribunal to determine what in reference to the past was reasonable and just, whether as maximum, minimum, or absolute, and then enable it to obtain from the courts a peremptory order that in the future the railroad companies should follow the rates thus determined to have been in the past reasonable and just. . . .

[Justice Harlan dissented without opinion.]

QUESTIONS

1. Professor White describes the Interstate Commerce Commission (ICC) as "[t]he first modern federal regulatory agency," modeled upon state special study commissions established to regulate the railroads. G. Edward White, *Allocating Power Between Agencies and Courts: The Legacy of Justice Brandeis*, 1974 Duke L.J. 195, 197. Why should railroad rates be regulated?
2. How would you characterize the attitude of the Supreme Court toward the scope of authority granted to the ICC by Congress? Congress delegated power to the ICC to define "just and reasonable" maximum rates in the Hepburn Act of 1906. *See* 34 Stat. 584.
3. What are the relative advantages and disadvantages of the "three obvious and dissimilar courses" open to Congress?

PENNSYLVANIA v. WEST VIRGINIA
262 U.S. 553 (1923)

[The majority in an opinion written by Justice Van Devanter invalidated a West Virginia statute that restricted the ability of pipeline companies to sell natural gas produced in the state to consumers out of the state. Justice Brandeis dissented and declined to reach the constitutional issue of whether the state law failed under the interstate commerce clause. He identified several reasons why the Court should decline to decide the case, including the following rationale.]

. . . [I]f all other obstacles could be overcome, this Court, sitting as a court of equity, should dismiss the bills, because it would be unable to grant the only relief appropriate. This Court, sitting in equity, clearly should not lend its aid to enable West Virginia public service corporations to discriminate against West Virginia consumers in the interest of Ohio and Pennsylvania consumers. Therefore an appropriate decree should be framed so as to require each of the West Virginia corporations to treat West Virginia customers at least as well as it does those outside of the State and the decree should not leave any West Virginia public service corporation free to export gas in disregard of the duty not to discriminate against the public of that State. But natural gas is produced also in Pennsylvania and Ohio; and the local production furnishes a large part of the supplies consumed in those States. Furthermore, West Virginia gas is exported also to Maryland, Indiana, and Kentucky; and in two of those states natural gas is produced in quantity. Clearly the court should, in no event, go further than to compel West Virginia to share its production equitably with other States now dependent upon it for a part of their gas supply. But in order to determine what is equitable (that is, what part of the West Virginia production that State might require its public service corporations to retain and what part they should be free to export to other States) it would obviously be necessary to marshal the resources and the demands, or needs, of the six States, and to consider, in respect to each, both the conduct of the business therein and the circumstances attending its development. The factors necessary to be considered in determining what division of the West Virginia production would be fair, the conditions under which the determination would have to be made, and the character of the questions to be decided are such that this Court would be obliged to refuse to undertake the task. For this reason, the bills should be dismissed. . . . To do justice as between the several States the following inquiries would be essential:

(a) The potential as well as the actual production in each State would have to be ascertained. The actual production during earlier years, and approximately the current production, could be ascertained from data which are regularly collected by the United States Geological Survey and by the public utility commissions of the several States. But to ascertain the potential production, searching inquiry would have to be made into the methods of production pursued, and, among other things, to what extent recent production has been secured by forcing the wells; what the likelihood is that production lessened by forcing wells will be restored by allowing periods of rest; and to what extent recent reduced outputs may have been attributable to failure to sink enough wells or to open additional territory. . . .

(b) The demand, actual and potential, in each State would have to be determined. In determining the demand, the Court could not confine its inquiry to ascertaining the amount then used or called for. The rates charged in the several communities must also be considered. For upon these, as well as upon the relative cost of other kinds of fuel, would depend in large part the extent of the demand; particularly by the industries. The character of the use and the circumstances under which it had been developed would likewise be important factors in deciding what distribution would be equitable. . . .

(c) No determination concerning production and none concerning demand could afford a stable basis for future action, for no factor entering into the determination would be constant. Investigations into supply and demand would have to be pursued continuously; and recurrent decisions as to distribution would be required. Thus, the estimate of the undeveloped gas territory must be ever changing; for new discovery may open territory theretofore unknown; and the sinking of test wells may establish the fact that territory previously deemed valuable will be wholly unproductive. In no other field of public service regulation is the controlling body confronted with factors so baffling as in the natural gas industry, and in none is continuous supervision and control required in so high a degree.

(d) The decisions to be made would be of the character which calls for the informed judgment of a board of experts. The tribunal would have to determine, among other things, whether inadequate service was due in the several States to inadequate supply or to improvident use by some consumers; whether to overcome inadequacy of supply new territory should be developed or more wells be sunk in old territory; whether, in view of prospective needs of the several communities, it would not be better that the reserves should be husbanded and that the uses to which gas may be put be curtailed. It would, thus, be called upon to review — and perhaps to control — the business judgment of those managing the companies. Pro rata distribution among all users of the gas from time to time available would obviously not result in equitable distribution. For domestic users, and also many industrial ones, would, if their gas supply were uncertain, find it necessary to assure themselves of an adequate supply, for heating, cooking, and power, of either oil or some other kind of fuel, and the expense of producing the necessary alternative appliances would be large. The tribunal would have to decide, also, many other serious questions of the character usually committed for determination to public utility commissions, and the difficulties involved in these decisions would be much enhanced by differences in the laws, rules, and practices of the several States regarding the duties of natural gas companies to furnish adequate service.

Clearly this Court could not undertake such determinations. To make equitable distribution would be a task of such complexity and difficulty that even an interstate public service commission with broad powers, perfected administrative machinery, ample resources, practical experience, and no other duties, might fail to perform it satisfactorily. As this Court would be powerless to frame a decree and provide machinery by means of which such equitable distribution of the available supply could be effected, it should, according to settled practice, refuse to entertain the suits.

[Justices Holmes and McReynolds also wrote separate dissents.]

QUESTIONS

1. Why does Justice Brandeis view the Supreme Court as institutionally incompetent to provide a remedy in the dispute between West Virginia

and Pennsylvania? The concerns that Justice Brandeis raised about the judiciary's institutional competence were recently echoed by the Supreme Court. In *American Elec. Power Co. v. Connecticut*, 564 U.S. 410 (2011), the Court held that the federal Clean Air Act had preempted the federal common law of nuisance regarding the effects of emissions of greenhouse gases. Writing for a unanimous Supreme Court, Justice Ginsburg explained that:

> It is altogether fitting that Congress designated an expert agency, here, EPA, as best suited to serve as primary regulator of greenhouse gas emissions. The expert agency is surely better equipped to do the job than individual district judges issuing ad hoc, case-by-case injunctions. Federal judges lack the scientific, economic, and technological resources an agency can utilize in coping with issues of this order. See generally *Chevron U.S.A. Inc. v. Natural Resources Defense Council, Inc.*, 467 U.S. 837, 865-866 (1984). Judges may not commission scientific studies or convene groups of experts for advice, or issue rules under notice-and-comment procedures inviting input by any interested person, or seek the counsel of regulators in the States where the defendants are located. Rather, judges are confined by a record comprising the evidence the parties present. Moreover, federal district judges, sitting as sole adjudicators, lack authority to render precedential decisions binding other judges, even members of the same court.

Id. at 428.

2. What would be the institutional competence of the legislature to perform the tasks identified by Justice Brandeis?
3. Are there some types of public policy questions that lend themselves best to administrative — as opposed to legislative or judicial — determination? If so, which?
4. Is Justice Brandeis naïve to believe that an agency can act solely in an apolitical, expert fashion? Is that how other government entities, like courts and legislatures, work? If not, why should we expect administrative officials selected by elected officeholders, perhaps for political reasons, to cease taking the political implications of agency decisions into account?
5. At the same time, isn't expertise a substantial potential benefit associated with creating a specialized entity to address a particular set of problems? The question then becomes: How do we distinguish questions of scientific fact from questions of public policy (or even politics)? Moreover, should courts reviewing administrative actions be more deferential to agency decisions that plainly rest on scientific or technical expertise?

NATIONAL BROADCASTING CO. v. UNITED STATES
319 U.S. 190 (1943)

[The Court, in an opinion by Justice Frankfurter, reviewed the legality of the Chain Broadcasting Regulations that the Federal Communications Commission (FCC) adopted in 1941. The FCC enacted these regulations in response to the growing importance of national networks in radio broadcasting and followed the agency's three-year investigation of the influence of the national networks on local affiliate radio stations. The regulations governed the treatment to be accorded agreements with national networks in the licensing of broadcast stations. The national networks challenged the regulations as beyond the power of the FCC.]

Federal regulation of radio begins with the Wireless Ship Act of June 24, 1910, which forbade any steamer carrying or licensed to carry fifty or more persons to leave any American port unless equipped with efficient apparatus for radio communication, in charge of a skilled operator. The enforcement of this legislation was entrusted to the Secretary of Commerce and Labor, who was in charge of the administration of the marine navigation laws. But it was not until 1912, when the United States ratified the first international radio treaty, that the need for general regulation of radio communication became urgent. In order to fulfill our obligations under the treaty, Congress enacted the Radio Communications Act of August 13, 1912. This statute forbade the operation of radio apparatus without a license from the Secretary of Commerce and Labor; it also allocated certain frequencies for the use of the Government, and imposed restrictions upon the character of wave emissions, the transmission of distress signals, and the like.

The enforcement of the Radio Act of 1912 presented no serious problems prior to the World War I. Questions of interference arose only rarely because there were more than enough frequencies for all the stations then in existence. The war accelerated the development of the art, however, and in 1921 the first standard broadcast stations were established. They grew rapidly in number, and by 1923 there were several hundred such stations throughout the country. The Act of 1912 had not set aside any particular frequencies for the use of private broadcast stations; consequently, the Secretary of Commerce selected two frequencies, 750 and 833 kilocycles and licensed all stations to operate upon one or the other of these channels. The number of stations increased so rapidly, however, and the situation became so chaotic, that the Secretary, upon the recommendation of the National Radio Conferences which met in Washington in 1923 and 1924, established a policy of assigning specified frequencies to particular stations. The entire radio spectrum was divided into numerous bands, each allocated to a particular kind of service. The frequencies ranging from 550 to 1500 kilocycles (96 channels in all, since the channels were separated from each other by 10 kilocycles) were assigned to the standard broadcast stations. But the problems created by the enormously rapid development of radio were far from solved. The increase in the number of channels was not enough to take care of the constantly growing number of stations. Since there were more stations than available frequencies, the Secretary of Commerce attempted to find room for everybody by limiting the power and hours of operation of stations in order that several stations might use the same channel. The number of stations multiplied so rapidly, however, that by November, 1925, there were almost 600 stations in the country, and there were 175 applications for new stations. Every channel in the standard broadcast band was, by that time, already occupied by at least one station, and many by several. The new stations could be accommodated only by extending the standard broadcast band, at the expense of the other types of services, or by imposing still greater limitations upon time and power. The National Radio Conference which met in November, 1925, opposed both of these methods and called upon Congress to remedy the situation through legislation.

The Secretary of Commerce was powerless to deal with the situation. It had been held that he could not deny a license to an otherwise legally qualified applicant on the ground that the proposed station would interfere with existing private or Government stations. *Hoover v. Intercity Radio Co.,* 286 F. 1003. . . . This was followed on July 8, 1926, by an opinion of Acting Attorney General Donovan that the Secretary of Commerce had no power, under the Radio Act of 1912, to regulate the power, frequency, or hours of operation of stations. 35 Ops. Atty. Gen. 126. The next day the Secretary of Commerce issued a statement abandoning all his efforts to regulate radio and urging that the stations undertake self-regulation.

But the plea of the Secretary went unheeded. From July 1926, to February 23, 1927, when Congress enacted the Radio Act of 1927, 44 Stat. 1162, almost 200 new stations went on the air. These new stations used any frequencies they desired, regardless of the interference thereby caused to others. Existing stations changed to other frequencies and increased their power and hours of operation at will. The result was confusion and chaos. . . .

The plight into which radio fell prior to 1927 was attributable to certain basic facts about radio as a means of communication — its facilities are limited; they are not available to all who may wish to use them; the radio spectrum simply is not large enough to accommodate everybody. There is a fixed natural limitation upon the number of stations that can operate without interfering with one another. Regulation of radio was therefore as vital to its development as traffic control was to the development of the automobile. In enacting the Radio Act of 1927, the first comprehensive scheme of control over radio communication, Congress acted upon the knowledge that if the potentialities of radio were not to be wasted, regulation was essential.

The Radio Act of 1927 created the Federal Radio Commission, composed of five members, and endowed the Commission with wide licensing and regulatory powers. We do not pause here to enumerate the scope of the Radio Act of 1927 and of the authority entrusted to the Radio Commission, for the basic provisions of that Act are incorporated in the Communications Act of 1934, 48 Stat. 1064, 47 U.S.C. §151 *et seq.,* the legislation immediately before us. As we noted in *Federal Communications Comm. v. Pottsville Broadcasting Co.,* 309 U.S. 134, 137, "In its essentials the Communications Act of 1934 [so far as its provisions relating to radio are concerned] derives from the Federal Radio Act of 1927. . . . By this Act Congress, in order to protect the national interest involved in the new and far-reaching science of broadcasting, formulated a unified and comprehensive regulatory system for the industry. The common factors in the administration of the various statutes by which Congress had supervised the different modes of communication led to the creation, in the Act of 1934, of the Communications Commission. But the objectives of the legislation have remained substantially unaltered since 1927."

Section 1 of the Communications Act states its "purpose of regulating interstate and foreign commerce in communication by wire and radio so as to make available, so far as possible, to all the people of the United States a rapid, efficient, Nation-wide, and world-wide wire and radio communication service with adequate facilities at reasonable charges." Section 301 particularizes this general purpose with respect to radio: "It is the purpose of this Act, among other things, to maintain the control of the United States over all the channels of interstate and foreign radio transmission; and to provide for the use of such channels, but not the ownership thereof, by persons for limited periods of time, under licenses granted by Federal authority, and no such license shall be construed to create any right, beyond the terms, conditions, and periods of the license." To that end a Commission composed of seven members was created, with broad licensing and regulatory powers. . . .

The criterion governing the exercise of the Commission's licensing power is the "public interest, convenience, or necessity." §§ 307(a)(d), 309(a), 310, 312. In addition, § 307(b) directs the Commission that "In considering applications for licenses, and modifications and renewals thereof, when and insofar as there is demand for the same, the Commission shall make such distribution of licenses, frequencies, hours of operation, and of power among the several States and communities as to provide a fair, efficient, and equitable distribution of radio service to each of the same."

The Act itself establishes that the Commission's powers are not limited to the engineering and technical aspects of regulation of radio communication. Yet we are asked to regard the Commission as a kind of traffic officer, policing the wave lengths to prevent stations from interfering with each other. But the Act does not restrict the Commission merely to supervision of the traffic. It puts upon the Commission the burden of determining the composition of that traffic. The facilities of radio are not large enough to accommodate all who wish to use them. Methods must be devised for choosing from among the many who apply. And since Congress itself could not do this, it committed the task to the Commission.

The Commission was, however, not left at large in performing this duty. The touchstone provided by Congress was the "public interest, convenience, or necessity," [§ 303] a criterion which "is as concrete as the complicated factors for judgment in such a field of delegated authority permit." *Federal Communications Comm. v. Pottsville Broadcasting Co.,* 309 U.S. 134, 138. "This criterion is not to be interpreted as setting up a standard so indefinite as to confer an unlimited power. Compare *N.Y. Cent. Securities Corp. v. United States,* 287 U.S. 12, 24. The requirement is to be interpreted by its context, by the nature of radio transmission and reception, by the scope, character, and quality of services. . . ." *Federal Radio Comm. v. Nelson Bros. Bond & Mortgage Co.,* 289 U.S. 266, 285.

The "public interest" to be served under the Communications Act is thus the interest of the listening public in "the larger and more effective use of radio." § 303(g). The facilities of radio are limited and therefore precious; they cannot be left to wasteful use without detriment to the public interest. "An important element of public interest and convenience affecting the issue of a license is the ability of the licensee to render the best practicable service to the community reached by his broadcasts." *Federal Communications Comm. v. Sanders Bros. Radio Station,* 309 U.S. 470, 475. The Commission's licensing function cannot be discharged, therefore, merely by finding that there are no technological objections to the granting of a license. If the criterion of "public interest" were limited to such matters, how could the Commission choose between two applicants for the same facilities, each of whom is financially and technically qualified to operate a station? Since the very inception of federal regulation by radio, comparative considerations as to the services to be rendered have governed the application of the standard of "public interest, convenience, or necessity." *See Federal Communications Comm. v. Pottsville Broadcasting Co.,* 309 U.S. 134, 138 n. 2.

The avowed aim of the Communications Act of 1934 was to secure the maximum benefits of radio to all the people of the United States. To that end Congress endowed the Communications Commission with comprehensive powers to promote and realize the vast potentialities of radio. Section 303(g) provides that the Commission shall "generally encourage the larger and more effective use of radio in the public interest"; subsection (i) gives the Commission specific "authority to make special regulations applicable to radio stations engaged in chain broadcasting"; and subsection (r) empowers it to adopt "such rules and regulations and prescribe such restrictions and conditions, not inconsistent with law, as may be necessary to carry out the provisions of this Act."

These provisions, individually and in the aggregate, preclude the notion that the Commission is empowered to deal only with technical and engineering impediments to the "larger and more effective use of radio in the public interest." We cannot find in the Act any such restriction of the Commission's authority. Suppose, for example, that a community can, because of physical limitations, be assigned only two stations. That community might be deprived of effective service in any one of several ways. More powerful stations in nearby cities might blanket out the signals of the local stations so that they could not be heard at all. The stations might interfere with each other so that neither could be clearly heard. One station might dominate the other with the power of its signal. But the community could be deprived of good radio service in ways less crude. One man, financially and technically qualified, might apply for and obtain the licenses of both stations and present a single service over the two stations, thus wasting a frequency otherwise available to the area. The language of the Act does not withdraw such a situation from the licensing and regulatory powers of the Commission, and there is no evidence that Congress did not mean its broad language to carry the authority it expresses.

In essence, the Chain Broadcasting Regulations represent a particularization of the Commission's conception of the "public interest" sought to be safeguarded by Congress in enacting the Communications Act of 1934. The basic consideration of policy underlying the Regulations is succinctly stated in its Report: "With the number of radio channels limited by natural factors, the public interest demands that those who are entrusted with the available channels shall make the fullest and most effective use of them. If a licensee enters into a contract with a network organization which limits his ability to make the best use of the radio facility assigned him, he is not serving the public interest. . . . The net effect [of the practices disclosed by the investigation] has been that broadcasting service has been maintained at a level below that possible under a system of free competition. Having so found, we would be remiss in our statutory duty of encouraging 'the larger and more effective use of radio in the public interest' if we were to grant licenses to persons who persist in these practices."

We would be asserting our personal views regarding the effective utilization of radio were we to deny that the Commission was entitled to find that the large public aims of the Communications Act of 1934 comprehend the considerations which moved the Commission in promulgating the Chain Broadcasting Regulations. True enough, the Act does not explicitly say that the Commission shall have power to deal with network practices found inimical to the public interest. But Congress was acting in a field of regulation which was both new and dynamic. "Congress moved under the spur of a widespread fear that in the absence of governmental control the public interest might be subordinated to monopolistic domination in the broadcasting field." *Federal Communications Comm. v. Pottsville Broadcasting Co.,* 309 U.S. 134, 137. In the context of the developing problems to which it was directed, the Act gave the Commission not niggardly but expansive powers. It was given a comprehensive mandate to "encourage the larger and more effective use of radio in the public interest," if need be, by making "special regulations applicable to radio stations engaged in chain broadcasting." § 303(g)(i).

Generalities unrelated to the living problems of radio communication of course cannot justify exercises of power by the Commission. Equally so, generalities empty of all concrete considerations of the actual bearing of regulations promulgated by the Commission to the subject-matter entrusted to it, cannot strike down exercises of power by the Commission. While Congress did not give the Commission unfettered discretion to regulate all phases of the radio industry, it did not frustrate the purposes for which the Communications Act of 1934 was brought into being by attempting an itemized catalogue of the specific manifestations of the general problems for the solution of which it was establishing a regulatory agency. That would have stereotyped the powers of the Commission to specific details in regulating a field of enterprise the dominant characteristic of which was the rapid pace of its unfolding. And so Congress did what experience had taught it in similar attempts at regulation, even in fields where the subject-matter of regulation was far less fluid and dynamic than radio. The essence of that experience was to define broad areas for regulation and to establish standards for judgment adequately related in their application to the problems to be solved. . . .

We conclude, therefore, that the Communications Act of 1934 authorized the Commission to promulgate regulations designed to correct the abuses disclosed by its investigation of chain broadcasting. . . .

[Justices Murphy and Roberts dissented.]

QUESTIONS

1. What motivated Congress to regulate the radio broadcasting industry? Was it necessary for Congress to establish the FCC as part of that regulatory scheme? Or was the problem of interference the opportunity that justified comprehensive governmental regulation of the broadcast media? Some commentators suggest that, over time, a property rights regime created by state courts would have resolved the interference problems without any need for comprehensive national regulations. *See* Thomas W. Hazlett, *Physical Scarcity, Rent Seeking, and the First Amendment,* 97 Colum. L. Rev. 905 (1997); Thomas W. Hazlett, *The Rationality of U.S. Regulation of the Broadcast Spectrum,* 33 J. L. & Econ. 133 (1990). Before creating a new government agency, one question usually worth considering is whether administrative regulations, as opposed to reliance on market forces, would provide the best means of approaching a social problem.

2. The problem of interference among radio stations can be thought of as one example of the more general problem of how to allocate scarce resources. In a sense, the problem of "externalities" that provides a justification for much

environmental legislation is analogous. The concern about "externalities" arises when industrial producers emit the waste resulting from their productive processes into the air and water without bearing the costs imposed upon others by such emissions. This use of air and water adversely affects, for instance, those who breathe the air or use the waters for recreation. Without government regulation, such adversely affected persons bear the cost that should, under some sense of fairness, be borne by the producer. The problems relating to inconsistent use of these resources arise because air and water have a finite capacity to absorb the emissions of waste products without adversely affecting other users. The result has been government regulation pursued at the federal level by the U.S. Environmental Protection Agency. The Supreme Court has described the development of federal regulation of air and water in *Train v. Natural Resources Defense Council, Inc.,* 421 U.S. 60 (1975) (air) and *Environmental Protection Agency v. California ex rel. State Water Resources Control Board,* 426 U.S. 200 (1976) (water). For a famous elaboration of the need to rely upon "mutual coercion, mutually agreed upon" to protect the commons, see Garrett Hardin, *The Tragedy of the Commons,* 162 Science 1243 (1968).

3. Has the Supreme Court's attitude toward regulatory agencies in *National Broadcasting Co.* changed since the *Cincinnati Railway* case, or is the result in this case driven by a clearer statute?

4. Did the election (and subsequent reelection) of FDR, who championed a "New Deal" featuring a vastly expanded federal role in regulating the economy, have anything to do with the Supreme Court's change in attitude? Consider that by 1943, President Roosevelt had selected several members of the Supreme Court including Justice Hugo Black (previously a New Deal senator from Alabama) and William O. Douglas (previously head of one of FDR's new "alphabet soup" agencies, the Securities and Exchange Commission). Would judges with such backgrounds be more or less likely to view administrative agency powers sympathetically? Expansively?

UNITED STATES v. SOUTHWESTERN CABLE CO.
392 U.S. 157 (1968)

[This case involved a claim that the Federal Communications Commission lacked statutory authority to regulate community antenna television (CATV) systems. "CATV systems receive the signals of television broadcasting stations, amplify them, transmit them by cable or microwave, and ultimately distribute them by wire to the receivers of their subscribers. CATV systems characteristically do not produce their own programming, and do not recompense producers or broadcasters for use of the programming which they receive and redistribute. Unlike ordinary broadcasting stations, CATV systems commonly charge their subscribers installation and other fees." Justice Harlan wrote the opinion for the Court.]

The Commission's authority to regulate broadcasting and other communications is derived from the Communications Act of 1934, as amended. The Act's provisions are explicitly applicable to "all interstate and foreign communication by wire or radio. . . ." 47 U.S.C. § 152(a). The Commission's responsibilities are no more narrow: it is required to endeavor to "make available . . . to all the people of the United States a rapid, efficient, Nationwide, and world-wide wire and radio communication service. . . ." 47 U.S.C. § 151. The Commission was expected to serve as the "single Government agency"[25] with "unified jurisdiction" and "regulatory power over all forms of electrical communication, whether by telephone, telegraph, cable, or radio." It was for this purpose given "broad authority."[28] As this Court emphasized in an earlier case, the Act's terms, purposes, and history all indicate that Congress "formulated a unified and comprehensive regulatory system for the [broadcasting] industry." *F.C.C. v. Pottsville Broadcasting Co.*, 309 U.S. 134, 137.

Respondents do not suggest that CATV systems are not within the term "communication by wire or radio." Indeed, such communications are defined by the Act so as to encompass "the transmission of . . . signals, pictures, and sounds of all kinds," whether by radio or cable, "including all instrumentalities, facilities, apparatus, and services (among other things, the receipt, forwarding, and delivery of communications) incidental to such transmission." 47 U.S.C. §§ 153(a), (b). These very general terms amply suffice to reach respondents' activities. . . .

Nonetheless, respondents urge that the Communications Act, properly understood, does not permit the regulation of CATV systems. First, they emphasize that the Commission in 1959 and again in 1966 sought legislation that would have explicitly authorized such regulation, and that its efforts were unsuccessful. In the circumstances here, however, this cannot be dispositive. The Commission's requests for legislation evidently reflected in each instance both its uncertainty as to the proper width of its authority and its understandable preference for more detailed policy guidance than the Communications Act now provides. We have recognized that administrative agencies should, in such situations, be encouraged to seek from Congress clarification of the pertinent statutory provisions. *Wong Yang Sung v. McGrath*, 339 U.S. 33, 47. . . .

Second, respondents urge that § 152(a)[34] does not independently confer regulatory authority upon the Commission, but instead merely prescribes the forms of communication to which the Act's other provisions may separately be made applicable. Respondents emphasize that the Commission does not contend either that CATV systems are common carriers, and thus within Title II of the Act, or that they are broadcasters, and thus within Title III. They conclude that CATV, with certain of the characteristics both of broadcasting and of common carriers, but with all of the characteristics of neither, eludes altogether the Act's grasp.

We cannot construe the Act so restrictively. Nothing in the language of § 152(a), in the surrounding language, or in the Act's history or purposes limits the Commission's authority to those activities and forms of communication that are specifically described by the Act's other provisions. The section itself states

25. The phrase is taken from the message to Congress from President Roosevelt, dated February 26, 1934, in which he recommended the Commission's creation. *See* H.R. Rep. No. 1850, 73d Cong., 2d Sess., 1.

28. The phrase is taken from President Roosevelt's message to Congress. H.R. Rep. No. 1850, *supra*, at 1. The House Committee added that "the primary purpose of this bill (is) to create such a commission armed with adequate statutory powers to regulate all forms of communication. . . ." *Id.*, at 3.

34. 47 U.S.C. § 152(a) provides that "[t]he provisions of this chapter shall apply to all interstate and foreign communication by wire or radio and all interstate and foreign transmission of energy by radio, which originates and/or is received within the United States, and to all persons engaged within the United States in such communication or such transmission of energy by radio, and to the licensing and regulating of all radio stations as hereinafter provided. . . ."

merely that the "provisions of (the Act) shall apply to all interstate and foreign communication by wire or radio. . . ." Similarly, the legislative history indicates that the Commission was given "regulatory power over all forms of electrical communication. . . ." S. Rep. No. 781, 73d Cong., 2d Sess., 1. Certainly Congress could not in 1934 have foreseen the development of community antenna television systems, but it seems to us that it was precisely because Congress wished "to maintain, through appropriate administrative control, a grip on the dynamic aspects of radio transmission," *F.C.C. v. Pottsville Broadcasting Co., supra,* 309 U.S. at 138, that it conferred upon the Commission a "unified jurisdiction" and "broad authority." Thus, "[u]nderlying the whole [Communications Act] is recognition of the rapidly fluctuating factors characteristic of the evolution of broadcasting and of the corresponding requirement that the administrative process possess sufficient flexibility to adjust itself to these factors." *F.C.C. v. Pottsville Broadcasting Co., supra,* at 138. Congress in 1934 acted in a field that was demonstrably "both new and dynamic," and it therefore gave the Commission "a comprehensive mandate," with "not niggardly but expansive powers." *National Broadcasting Co. v. United States,* 319 U.S. 190, 219. We have found no reason to believe that § 152 does not, as its terms suggest, confer regulatory authority over "all interstate . . . communication by wire or radio."

Moreover, the Commission has reasonably concluded that regulatory authority over CATV is imperative if it is to perform with appropriate effectiveness certain of its other responsibilities. Congress has imposed upon the Commission the "obligation of providing a widely dispersed radio and television service," with a "fair, efficient, and equitable distribution" of service among the "several States and communities." 47 U.S.C. § 307(b). The Commission has, for this and other purposes, been granted authority to allocate broadcasting zones or areas, and to provide regulations "as it may deem necessary" to prevent interference among the various stations. 47 U.S.C. §§ 303(f), (h). The Commission has concluded, and Congress has agreed, that these obligations require for their satisfaction the creation of a system of local broadcasting stations, such that "all communities of appreciable size [will] have at least one television station as an outlet for local self-expression." In turn, the Commission has held that an appropriate system of local broadcasting may be created only if two subsidiary goals are realized. First, significantly wider use must be made of the available ultra-high-frequency channels. Second, communities must be encouraged "to launch sound and adequate programs to utilize the television channels now reserved for educational purposes." These subsidiary goals have received the endorsement of Congress.

The Commission has reasonably found that the achievement of each of these purposes is "placed in jeopardy by the unregulated explosive growth of CATV." H.R. Rep. No. 1635, 89th Cong., 2d Sess., 7. Although CATV may in some circumstances make possible "the realization of some of the [Commission's] most important goals," First Report and Order, *supra,* at 699, its importation of distant signals into the service areas of local stations may also "destroy or seriously degrade the service offered by a television broadcaster," *id.,* at 700, and thus ultimately deprive the public of the various benefits of a system of local broadcasting stations.

The Commission has been charged with broad responsibilities for the orderly development of an appropriate system of local television broadcasting. The significance of its efforts can scarcely be exaggerated, for broadcasting is demonstrably a principal source of information and entertainment for a great part of the Nation's population. The Commission has reasonably found that the successful performance of these duties demands prompt and efficacious regulation of community antenna television systems. We have elsewhere held that we may not, "in the absence of compelling evidence that such was Congress' intention . . . prohibit administrative action imperative for the achievement of an agency's ultimate purposes." *Permian Basin Area Rate Cases,* 390 U.S. 747, 780. Compare *National Broadcasting Co. v. United States, supra,* 319 U.S. at 219-220; *American Trucking Assns. v. United States,* 344 U.S. 298, 311. There is no such evidence here, and we therefore hold that the Commission's authority over "all interstate . . . communication by wire or radio" permits the regulation of CATV systems.

[Justices Douglas and Marshall did not participate. Justice White concurred.]

QUESTIONS

1. How does the statutory basis for the regulatory authority that the FCC exercised in this case differ from the one at issue in *National Broadcasting Co., supra,* p. 6. In what respects does the Court's decision indicate even greater tolerance of agency regulatory power than *National Broadcasting Co., supra,* p. 6.
2. Should courts creatively and expansively interpret organic acts, the statutes that create federal agencies and empower them to act? Or should the burden of inertia fall on Congress to expand or clarify the scope of an agency's authority with respect to a gray area? What risks are associated with permitting federal agencies to creatively interpret (or reinterpret) the scope of their regulatory authority? Consider these issues carefully as you read the next case.

FDA v. BROWN & WILLIAMSON TOBACCO CORP.
529 U.S. 120 (2000)

JUSTICE O'CONNOR delivered the opinion of the Court.

This case involves one of the most troubling public health problems facing our Nation today: the thousands of premature deaths that occur each year because of tobacco use. In 1996, the Food and Drug Administration (FDA), after having expressly disavowed any such authority since its inception, asserted jurisdiction to regulate tobacco products. *See* 61 Fed. Reg. 44619-45318. The FDA concluded that nicotine is a "drug" within the meaning of the Food, Drug, and Cosmetic Act (FDCA or Act), 52 Stat. 1040, as amended, 21 U.S.C. § 301 *et seq.,* and that cigarettes and smokeless tobacco are "combination products" that deliver nicotine to the body. 61 Fed. Reg. 44397 (1996). Pursuant to this authority, it promulgated regulations intended to reduce tobacco consumption among children and adolescents. *Id.,* at 44615-44618. The agency believed that, because most tobacco consumers begin their use before reaching the age of 18, curbing tobacco use by minors could substantially reduce the prevalence of addiction in future generations and thus the incidence of tobacco-related death and disease. *Id.,* at 44398-44399. . . . This is hardly an ordinary case.

Contrary to its representations to Congress since 1914, the FDA has now asserted jurisdiction to regulate an industry constituting a significant portion of the American economy. In fact, the FDA contends that, were it to determine that tobacco products provide no "reasonable assurance of safety," it would have the authority to ban cigarettes and smokeless tobacco entirely. Owing to its unique place in American history and society, tobacco has its own unique political history. Congress, for better or for worse, has created a distinct regulatory scheme for tobacco products, squarely rejected proposals to give the FDA jurisdiction over tobacco, and repeatedly acted to preclude any agency from exercising significant policymaking authority in the area. Given this history and the breadth of the authority that the FDA has asserted, we are obliged to defer not to the agency's expansive construction of the statute, but to Congress' consistent judgment to deny the FDA this power.

Our decision in *MCI Telecommunications Corp. v. American Telephone & Telegraph Co.,* 512 U.S. 218 (1994), is instructive. That case involved the proper construction of the term "modify" in § 203(b) of the Communications Act of 1934. The FCC contended that, because the Act gave it the discretion to "modify any requirement" imposed under the statute, it therefore possessed the authority to render voluntary the otherwise mandatory requirement that long distance carriers file their rates. *Id.,* at 225. We rejected the FCC's construction, finding "not the slightest doubt" that Congress had directly spoken to the question. *Id.,* at 228. In reasoning even more apt here, we concluded that "[i]t is highly unlikely that Congress would leave the determination of whether an industry will be entirely, or even substantially, rate-regulated to agency discretion — and even more unlikely that it would achieve that through such a subtle device as permission to 'modify' rate-filing requirements." *Id.,* at 231.

As in *MCI,* we are confident that Congress could not have intended to delegate a decision of such economic and political significance to an agency in so cryptic a fashion. To find that the FDA has the authority to regulate tobacco products, one must not only adopt an extremely strained understanding of "safety" as it is used throughout the Act — a concept central to the FDCA's regulatory scheme — but also ignore the plain implication of Congress' subsequent tobacco-specific legislation. It is therefore clear, based on the FDCA's overall regulatory scheme and the subsequent tobacco legislation, that Congress has directly spoken to the question at issue and precluded the FDA from regulating tobacco products. . . .

By no means do we question the seriousness of the problem that the FDA has sought to address. The agency has amply demonstrated that tobacco use, particularly among children and adolescents, poses perhaps the single most significant threat to public health in the United States. Nonetheless, no matter how "important, conspicuous, and controversial" the issue, and regardless of how likely the public is to hold the Executive Branch politically accountable, an administrative agency's power to regulate in the public interest must always be grounded in a valid grant of authority from Congress. And "[i]n our anxiety to effectuate the congressional purpose of protecting the public, we must take care not to extend the scope of the statute beyond the point where Congress indicated it would stop." *United States v. Article of Drug . . . Bacto-Unidisk,* 394 U.S. 784, 800 (1969) (quoting *62 Cases, More or Less, Each Containing Six Jars of Jam v. United States,* 340 U.S. 593, 600 (1951)). Reading the FDCA as a whole, as well as in conjunction with Congress' subsequent tobacco-specific legislation, it is plain that Congress has not given the FDA the authority that it seeks to exercise here. For these reasons, the judgment of the Court of Appeals for the Fourth Circuit is affirmed. It is so ordered.

[Justices Breyer, Stevens, Souter, and Ginsburg dissented.]

QUESTIONS

1. Does the Court's decision limiting the scope of the FDA's regulatory authority reflect an attitude toward regulatory agencies that differs from the Court's attitude in *National Broadcasting Co.* and *Southwestern Cable?* Is the Court returning to the approach of *Cincinnati Railway* in requiring an express delegation of regulatory authority?

2. How workable is the Court's requirement that Congress delegate regulatory authority expressly when the underlying subject involves a matter "of such economic and political significance"? In 2001, Justice Scalia, writing for the Court in *Whitman v. American Trucking Associations*, 531 U.S. 457 (2001) (*infra* p. 380), relied upon Justice O'Connor's decision in *Brown & Williamson* and christened this canon of interpretation with a new name, the "elephants in mouseholes" canon, which reflects Justice Scalia's view that Congress does not hide policy elephants in the mouseholes of statutory detail. The effect of the canon is that an agency must have clear statutory power when it exercises great administrative power. Chief Justice Roberts, writing for the Court in *King v. Burwell*, 135 S. Ct. 2480 (2015) (*infra* p. 609), relied on this principle in deciding that the Internal Revenue Service had not been delegated great administrative power under the Patient Protection and Affordable Care Act (often referred to as Obamacare). More questions about this doctrine are raised following *King v. Burwell.* Would the application of the "elephants in mouseholes" canon have yielded a different result in *National Broadcasting Co.* and *Southwestern Cable?*

3. Did the Court properly reject the agency's argument that the exercise of regulatory jurisdiction should be upheld because voters would have the opportunity to hold the executive branch politically accountable for the regulatory decision?

4. Should the failure to enact specific regulations of tobacco preclude the FDA from acting if regulating tobacco as a "drug" otherwise seems to come within the terms of the organic act? On the other hand, should reviewing courts be more or less deferential when an agency seeks to abandon a longstanding interpretation of a law, seeks to expand its own jurisdiction, or, as in this case, seeks to do both at the same time?

5. Are agencies ever likely to argue that they have less, rather than more, power to regulate? If so, under what circumstances? Have you ever heard of an agency arguing that it no longer serves any useful purpose and should be abolished? If not, what does this suggest about how courts should review agency claims of suddenly discovered expanded powers? If an agency seeks an expanded jurisdiction, should the burden of going forward lie with the agency, the courts, or the Congress?

6. Should an agency be bound to follow a longstanding interpretation of its organic act? Under what circumstances should an agency be permitted to change its mind on a matter of fundamental importance?

THEORY APPLIED PROBLEM

In the year 2025, it becomes obvious that the world's supply of fossil fuels is no longer sufficient to meet existing energy demands. You work as a Special Assistant to the President for energy policy. The President asks you to advise her about how best to address the crisis. Several alternatives exist: the Administration could seek new legislation from Congress, it could use existing administrative entities, like the Department of Energy and the Nuclear Regulatory Commission, or it could seek action at the international level (perhaps through the United Nations). What are the advantages and disadvantages of each potential approach? Could any single approach provide the best response to the problem?

B.   ADJUDICATION AND RULEMAKING

The study of American administrative law is helpfully preceded not only by the foregoing overview of the role of administrative agencies, but also by an introduction to the two broad categories into which agency actions are almost always divided: adjudication and rulemaking. The following classic pair of cases, *Londoner* and *Bi-Metallic,* reflects these categories in one particular context, thereby allowing an initial understanding of the legal and practical differences between these two types of agency action. Although the line between the categories may shift in different contexts, much of American administrative law depends on which side of the line an agency action falls.

LONDONER v. CITY AND COUNTY OF DENVER
210 U.S. 373 (1908)

MR. JUSTICE MOODY delivered the opinion of the court.

The plaintiffs in error began this proceeding in a state court of Colorado to relieve lands owned by them from an assessment of a tax for the cost of paving a street upon which the lands abutted. The relief sought was granted by the trial court, but its action was reversed by the Supreme Court of the State, which ordered judgment for the defendants. The case is here on writ of error. The [Colorado] Supreme Court held that the tax was assessed in conformity with the constitution and laws of the State, and its decision on that question is conclusive.

[Petitioners relied on the Fourteenth Amendment to challenge the Colorado Supreme Court's decision upholding the assessments.]

The tax complained of was assessed under the provisions of the charter of the city of Denver, which confers upon the city the power to make local improvements and to assess the cost upon property specially benefited. It does not seem necessary to set forth fully the elaborate provisions of the charter regulating the exercise of this power, except where they call for special examination. The board of public works, upon the petition of a majority of the owners of the frontage to be assessed, may order the paving of a street. The board must, however, first adopt specifications, mark out a district of assessment, cause a map to be made and an estimate of the cost, with the approximate amount to be assessed upon each lot of land. Before action notice by publication and an opportunity to be heard to any person interested must be given by the board. . . .

It appears from the charter that, in the execution of the power to make local improvements and assess the cost upon the property specially benefited, the main steps to be taken by the city authorities are plainly marked and separated: 1. The board of public works must transmit to the city council a resolution ordering the work to be done and the form of an ordinance authorizing it and creating an assessment district. This it can do only upon certain conditions, one of which is that there shall first be filed a petition asking the improvement, signed by the owners of the majority of the frontage to be assessed. 2. The passage of that ordinance by the city council, which is given authority to determine conclusively whether the action of the board was duly taken. 3. The assessment of the cost upon the landowners after due notice and opportunity for hearing.

In the case before us the board took the first step by transmitting to the council the resolution to do the work and the form of an ordinance authorizing it. It is contended, however, that there was wanting an essential condition of the jurisdiction of the board, namely, such a petition from the owners as the law requires. . . . The state Supreme Court held that the determination of the city council was conclusive that a proper petition was filed, and that decision must be accepted by us as the law of the State. The only question for this court is whether the charter provision authorizing such a finding, without notice to the landowners, denies to them due process of law. We think it does not. The proceedings, from the beginning up to and including the passage of the ordinance authorizing the work did not include any assessment or necessitate any assessment, although they laid the foundation for an assessment, which might or might not subsequently be made. Clearly all this might validly be done without hearing to the landowners, provided a hearing upon the assessment itself is afforded. The legislature might have authorized the making of improvements by the city council without any petition. If it chose to exact a petition as a security for wise and just action it could, so far as the Federal Constitution is concerned, accompany that condition with a provision that the council, with or without notice, should determine finally whether it had been performed. This disposes of the first assignment of error, which is overruled. The second assignment is that the court erred in deciding that the city council had determined that the board of public works had complied with the conditions of its jurisdiction to order the work done. It is enough to say that this is not a Federal question. . . .

The ninth assignment questions the constitutionality of that part of the law which authorizes the assessment of benefits. It seems desirable, for the proper disposition of this and the next assignment, to state the construction which the Supreme Court gave to the charter. This may be found in the judgment under review and two cases decided with it. From these cases it appears that the lien upon the adjoining land arises out of the assessment; after the cost of the work and the provisional apportionment is certified to the city council and landowners affected are afforded an opportunity to be heard upon the validity and amount of the assessment by the council sitting as a board of equalization; if any further notice than the notice to file complaints and objections is required, the city authorities have the implied power to give it; the hearing must be before the assessment is made; this hearing, provided for by § 31, is one where the board of equalization "shall hear the parties complaining and such testimony as they may offer in support of their complaints and objections as would be competent and relevant"; and that the full hearing before the board of equalization excludes the courts from entertaining any objections which are cognizable by this board. The statute itself therefore is clear of all constitutional faults. It remains to see how it was administered in the case at bar.

The fifth assignment, though general, vague and obscure, fairly raises, we think, the question whether the assessment was made without notice and opportunity for hearing to those affected by it, thereby denying to them due process of law. The trial court found as a fact that no opportunity for hearing was afforded, and the [Colorado] Supreme Court did not disturb this finding. The record discloses what was actually done, and there seems to be no dispute about it. After the improvement was completed the board of public works, in compliance with § 29 of the charter, certified to the city clerk a statement of the cost, and an apportionment of it to the lots of land to be assessed. Thereupon the city clerk, in compliance with § 30, published a notice stating, *inter alia*, that the written complaints or objections of the owners, if filed within thirty days, would be "heard and determined by the city council before the passage of any ordinance assessing the cost." Those interested, therefore, were informed that if they reduced their complaints and objections to writing, and filed them within thirty days, those complaints and objections would be heard, and would be heard before any assessment was made. The notice given in this case, although following the words of the statute, did not fix the time for hearing, and apparently there were no stated sittings of the council acting as a board of equalization. But the notice purported only to fix the time for filing the complaints and objections, and to inform those who should file them that they would be heard before action. . . . Resting upon the assurance that they would be heard, the plaintiffs in error filed within the thirty days the following paper:

Denver, Colorado, January 13, 1900.

To the Honorable Board of Public Works and the Honorable Mayor and City Council of the City of Denver:

The undersigned, by Joshua Grozier, their attorney, do hereby most earnestly and strenuously protest and object to the passage of the contemplated or any assessing ordinance against the property in Eighth Avenue Paving District No. 1, so called, for each of the following reasons, to wit:

1st. That said assessment and all and each of the proceedings leading up to the same were and are illegal, voidable and void, and the attempted assessment if made will be void and uncollectible.

2nd. That said assessment and the cost of said pretended improvement should be collected, if at all, as a general tax against the city at large and not as a special assessment.

3d. That property in said city not assessed is benefited by the said pretended improvement and certain property assessed is not benefited by said pretended improvement and other property assessed is not benefited by said pretended improvement to the extent of the assessment; that the individual pieces of property in said district are not benefited to the extent assessed against them and each of them respectively; that the assessment is arbitrary and property assessed in an equal amount is not benefited equally; that the boundaries of said pretended district were arbitrarily created without regard to the benefits or any other method of assessment known to law; that said assessment is outrageously large.

4th. That . . . the 1893 city charter was not properly passed and is not a law of the State of Colorado. . . .

5th. Because the pretended notice of assessment is invalid and was not published in accordance with the law, and is in fact no notice at all; because there was and is no valid ordinance creating said district; because each notice required by the 1893 city charter to be given, where it was attempted to give such notice, was insufficient, and was not properly given or properly published.

6th. Because of non-compliance by the contractor with his contract and failure to complete the work in accordance with the contract; because the contract for said work was let without right or authority; because said pretended district is incomplete and the work under said contract has not been completed in accordance with said contract; because items too numerous to mention, which were not a proper charge in the said assessment, are included therein. . . .

9th. Because of delay by the board of public works in attempting to let the contract and because the said pretended improvement was never properly nor sufficiently petitioned for; because the contracts were not let nor the work done in accordance with the petitions, if any, for the work, and because the city had no jurisdiction in the premises.

10th. Because before ordering the pretended improvement full details and specifications for the same, permitting and encouraging competition and determining the number of installments and time within which the costs shall be payable, the rate of interest on unpaid installments, and the district of lands to be assessed, together with a map showing the approximate amounts to be assessed, were not adopted by the board of public works before the letting of the contract for the work and furnishing of material; . . .

11th. Because the attempted advertisement for bids on the contract attempted to be let were not properly published . . .

Wherefore, because of the foregoing and numerous other good and sufficient reasons, the undersigned object and protest against the passage of the said proposed assessing ordinance.

This certainly was a complaint against and objection to the proposed assessment. Instead of affording the plaintiffs in error an opportunity to be heard upon its allegations, the city council, without notice to them, met as a board of equalization, not in a stated but in a specially called session, and, without any hearing, adopted the following resolution:

Whereas, complaints have been filed by the various persons and firms as the owners of real estate included within the Eighth Avenue Paving District No. 1, of the city of Denver against the proposed assessments on said property for the cost of said paving, the names and description of the real estate respectively owned by such persons being more particularly described in the various complaints filed with the city clerk; and

Whereas, no complaint or objection has been filed or made against the apportionment of said assessment made by the board of public works of the city of Denver, but the complaints and objections filed deny wholly the right of the city to assess any district or portion of the assessable property of the city of Denver; therefore, be it

Resolved, by the city council of the city of Denver, sitting as a board of equalization, that the apportionments of said assessment made by said board of public works be, and the same are hereby, confirmed and approved.

Subsequently, without further notice or hearing, the city council enacted the ordinance of assessment whose validity is to be determined in this case. The facts out of which the question on this assignment arises may be compressed into small compass. The first step in the assessment proceedings was by the certificate of the board of public works of the cost of the improvement and a preliminary apportionment of it. The last step was the enactment of the assessment ordinance. From beginning to end of the proceedings the landowners, although allowed to formulate and file complaints and objections, were not afforded an opportunity to be heard upon them. Upon these facts was there a denial by the State of the due process of law guaranteed by the Fourteenth Amendment to the Constitution of the United States?

In the assessment, apportionment and collection of taxes upon property within their jurisdiction the Constitution of the United States imposes few restrictions upon the States. In the enforcement of such restrictions as the Constitution does impose this court has regarded substance and not form. But where the legislature of a State, instead of fixing the tax itself, commits to some subordinate body the duty of determining whether, in what amount, and upon whom it shall be levied, and of making its assessment and apportionment, due process of law requires that at some stage of the proceedings before the tax becomes irrevocably fixed, the taxpayer shall have an opportunity to be heard, of which he must have notice, either personal, by publication, or by a law fixing the time and place of the hearing. It must be remembered that the law of Colorado denies the landowner the right to object in the courts to the assessment, upon the ground that the objections are cognizable only by the board of equalization.

If it is enough that, under such circumstances, an opportunity is given to submit in writing all objections to and complaints of the tax to the board, then there was a hearing afforded in the case at bar. But we think that something more than that, even in proceedings for taxation, is required by due process of law. Many requirements essential in strictly judicial proceedings may be dispensed with in proceedings of this nature. But even here a hearing in its very essence demands that he who is entitled to it shall have the right to support his allegations by argument however brief, and, if need by, by proof, however informal. It is apparent that such a hearing was denied to the plaintiffs in error. The denial was by the city council, which, while acting as a board of equalization, represents the State. The assessment was therefore void, and the plaintiffs in error were entitled to a decree discharging their lands from a lien on account of it. . . .

Judgment reversed.

[Chief Justice Fuller and Justice Holmes dissented without opinion.]

QUESTIONS

1. Were the plaintiffs challenging the decision to pave, the amounts of the assessment, or both decisions?
2. What would have been at issue in the requested hearing?
3. Why was an oral hearing necessary?
4. Would the result have been the same in this case if a legislative body had been the sole decision maker?

BI-METALLIC INVESTMENT CO. v. STATE BOARD
OF EQUALIZATION

239 U.S. 441 (1915)

MR. JUSTICE HOLMES delivered the [unanimous] opinion of the court.

This is a suit to enjoin the State Board of Equalization and the Colorado Tax Commission from putting in force, and the defendant Pitcher as assessor of Denver from obeying, an order of the boards increasing the valuation of all taxable property in Denver forty per cent. The order was sustained and the suit directed to be dismissed by the Supreme Court of the State. The plaintiff is the owner of real estate in Denver and brings the case here on the ground that it was given no opportunity to be heard and that therefore its property will be taken without due process of law, contrary to the Fourteenth Amendment of the Constitution of the United States. That is the only question with which we have to deal. There are suggestions on the one side that the construction of the state constitution and laws was an unwarranted surprise and on the other that the decision might have been placed, although it was not, on the ground that there was an adequate remedy at law. With these suggestions we have nothing to do. They are matters purely of state law. The answer to the former needs no amplification; that to the latter is that the allowance of equitable relief is a question of state policy and that as the Supreme Court of the State treated the merits as legitimately before it, we are not to speculate whether it might or might not have thrown out the suit upon the preliminary ground.

For the purposes of decision we assume that the constitutional question is presented in the baldest way — that neither the plaintiff nor the assessor of Denver, who presents a brief on the plaintiff's side, nor any representative of the city and county, was given an opportunity to be heard, other than such as they may have had by reason of the fact that the time of meeting of the boards is fixed by law. On this assumption it is obvious that injustice may be suffered if some property in the county already has been valued at its full worth. But if certain property has been valued at a rate different from that generally prevailing in the county the owner has had his opportunity to protest and appeal as usual in our system of taxation, so that it must be assumed that the property owners in the county all stand alike. The question then is whether all individuals have a constitutional right to be heard before a matter can be decided in which all are equally concerned — here, for instance, before a superior board decides that the local taxing officers have adopted a system of undervaluation throughout a county, as notoriously often has been the case. The answer of this court in the *State Railroad Tax Cases,* 92 U.S. 575, at least as to any further notice, was that it was hard to believe that the proposition was seriously made.

Where a rule of conduct applies to more than a few people it is impracticable that every one should have a direct voice in its adoption. The Constitution does not require all public acts to be done in town meeting or an assembly of the whole. General statutes within the state power are passed that affect the person or property of individuals, sometimes to the point of ruin, without giving them a chance to be heard. Their rights are protected in the only way that they can be in a complex society, by their power, immediate or remote, over those who make the rule. If the result in this case had been reached as it might have been by the State's doubling the rate of taxation, no one would suggest that the Fourteenth Amendment was violated unless every person affected had been allowed an opportunity to raise his voice against it before the body entrusted by the state constitution with the power. In considering this case in this court we must assume that the proper state machinery has been used, and the question is whether, if the state constitution had declared that Denver had been undervalued as compared with the rest of the State and had decreed that for the current year the valuation should be forty per cent higher, the objection now urged could prevail. It appears to us that to put the question is to answer it. There must be a limit to individual argument in such matters if government is to go on. In *Londoner v. Denver,* 210 U.S. 373, 385, a local board had to determine "whether, in what amount, and upon whom" a tax for paving a street should be levied for special benefits. A relatively small number of persons was concerned, who were exceptionally affected, in each case upon individual grounds, and it was held that they had a right to a hearing. But that decision is far from reaching a general determination dealing only with the principle upon which all the assessments in a county had been laid.

Judgment affirmed.

QUESTIONS

1. What happened to the "political delegation" theory of *Londoner?* Is it carried through in *Bi-Metallic?*
2. How is *Bi-Metallic* different from *Londoner?* Does the different result in *Bi-Metallic* turn on the type of determination being made by the government? Professor Kenneth Culp Davis, a well-known administrative law scholar, distinguished between "adjudicative facts" and "legislative facts." Professor Davis stated that "[a]djudicative facts usually answer the question of who did what, where, when, how, why, with what motive or intent. . . . Legislative facts do not usually concern the immediate parties but are the general facts which help the tribunal decide questions of law and policy and discretion." 2 Kenneth Culp Davis, Administrative Law Treatise § 12:3, at 413 (2d ed. 1978). He then advocated that the category of facts being determined by the agency should dictate the procedural requirements:

    > [Adjudicative facts] are intrinsically the kind of facts that ordinarily ought not to be determined without giving the parties a chance to know and to meet any evidence that may be unfavorable to them. . . . The reason is that the parties know more about the facts concerning themselves and their activities than anyone else is likely to know. . . . Because the parties may have little or nothing to contribute to the development of legislative facts, the method of trial often is not required for the determination of disputed issues about legislative facts.

    Id. Are you persuaded by the approach advocated by Professor Davis? Is it ultimately circular?
3. Does the Court's decision in *Bi-Metallic* mean that the right to a hearing is just a numbers game? *See Anaconda Co. v. Ruckelshaus,* 482 F.2d 1301, 1306 (10th Cir. 1973) (Court rejected company's claim that, as an affected class of one, the Due Process Clause required adjudicative proceedings, stating that "[t]he fact that Anaconda alone is involved is not conclusive on the question

as to whether the hearing should be adjudicatory, for there are many other interested parties and groups who are affected and are entitled to be heard").

THEORY APPLIED PROBLEM

In May 2018, the Transportation Security Administration (TSA) adopted new regulations that established a comprehensive passenger screening program for commercial airline passengers in the United States. The regulations list various specific factors that will trigger enhanced security screening for persons holding tickets for commercial flights originating in the United States. A special computer program will conduct a security search applying these factors at the time a ticket is purchased and will code each purchaser as "green light," "yellow light," or "red light." Green light passengers will not be subject to any special screening procedures at TSA airport security checkpoints; yellow light passengers will be subject to enhanced screening procedures; red light passengers will not be permitted to proceed through the TSA security check point. On which side of the *Londoner/Bi-Metallic* dichotomy does the creation of this new program fall? Why?

On August 1, 2020, the TSA stops Fred Mertz from proceeding beyond the TSA security checkpoint at the LAX airport. The computer program that implements the screening protocols established in 2018 has flagged Mertz as a "red light" passenger; because of this, he was not permitted to proceed through security and, accordingly, missed his flight. On which side of the *Londoner/Bi-Metallic* dichotomy does this TSA action fall? Why?

1) everybody — more legislative, authority and no due process hearing
+ prospective, applies to everyone

2) Londoner — affecting one person in specific way, applies to something in the past

CHAPTER

2

Adjudication

A. CONSTITUTIONAL RIGHT TO A HEARING

A Brief Introduction to Procedural Due Process

Suppose that you have a good friend who teaches in a local public elementary school funded with local property taxes and maintained by a local school district organized under the laws of the state. Suppose further that she assigns a *Harry Potter* novel to her sixth grade English class for a routine book report assignment. Finally, suppose that a number of angry parents object to the use of novels containing sorcery, witchcraft, and other story lines associated with the occult. In order to mollify the angry parents, the principal summarily fires your friend, without any warning, process, or provision for severance pay. Your friend immediately calls you, angry and upset, in hopes of obtaining sound legal advice about how best she should proceed.

As an initial matter, you might wish to research whether any state law sets forth the procedures associated with the suspension or discharge of a public school teacher (or other state or local government employee). Alternatively, you might want to determine if the city or the school district maintains written procedures that govern the discharge of an employee. In some states and localities, such a written policy might well exist. In at least some cases, however, no such statute or formal policy would be available to provide guidance to you or your friend.

Indeed, one might imagine the school district taking the view that government employment as a public school teacher is merely a privilege, and not a right. Accordingly, the government retains for itself precisely the same authority to fire at will that a private employer in an employment-at-will jurisdiction would enjoy. As Justice Holmes once observed:

> There are few employments for hire in which the servant does not agree to suspend his constitutional right of free speech, as well as of idleness, by the implied terms of his contract. The servant cannot complain, as he takes the employment on the terms which are offered him.

McAuliffe v. Mayor of New Bedford, 29 N.E. 517, 518 (Mass. 1892). From this perspective, a public school teacher enjoys only such procedural rights as the local school district deigns to offer him or her; because such employment is merely a "privilege" and not a "right," a discharged public school employee simply has no cause to complain if the district terminates her employment. *See generally,* Kathleen M. Sullivan, "Unconstitutional Conditions," 102 Harv. L. Rev. 1415 (1989). If an employee holds merely a "privilege" and the state has an unfettered discretion to fire for a good reason, a bad reason, or no reason at all, your friend's situation would appear, at least from a legal perspective, rather grim.

But, before one abandons all hope and advises the friend to consider seeking alternative employment, it might be worth a close second look at the basic text of the federal Constitution. Perhaps a provision exists that would offer the prospect of some relief from the principal's rather arbitrary actions.

As it happens, the Fifth and Fourteenth Amendments contain virtually identical "due process" clauses that purport to hold the government to a standard of basic fairness. In relevant part, the clauses provide that no person shall be "deprived of life, liberty, or property, without due process of law." This language would seem to demand at least minimal process of some sort from the government whenever it acts in a way to deprive a citizen of "life, liberty, or property." *Cf.* William W. Van Alstyne, "Cracks in the 'New Property': Adjudicative Due Process in the Administrative State," 62 Cornell L.J. 445 (1977) (arguing that the Due Process Clauses should be understood to guarantee a right to be free from arbitrary or irrational government actions as a general matter, regardless of the precise interests at stake). Thus, as a matter of textual logic, if your friend can claim a property or liberty interest in her employment as an elementary school teacher at a public school, she has a right to demand "due process of law" before being denied that interest (i.e., before being fired).

As you will learn in the cases that follow, whether your friend would have a viable due process claim will ultimately depend on whether she had more than a unilateral expectation of continued employment. If she can show a "legitimate claim of entitlement" to her job as an elementary school teacher, then the school district owed her some kind of hearing and associated process.

Presenting evidence that your friend has a legitimate claim of entitlement to continued employment would, of course, only begin the inquiry. How much process did the school district owe her? When was it due? To what extent can the district provide process only *after* it has acted adversely to your friend's interest in continued employment (and a steady paycheck)?

In many respects, the cases that follow raise more questions than they answer: due process analysis is almost always highly context specific. Accordingly, the ability of the government to act summarily and without full trial-type procedures before adversely affecting a property or liberty interest will vary depending on the precise circumstances presented.

For example, if a police officer or FBI agent faces charges of using excessive force or a government hospital doctor is accused of practicing while drunk, the government might be able to act quickly and without providing substantial predeprivation process to the adversely affected individual. On the other hand, if the need for speed is less than self-evident, or the citizen's interest in the liberty or property interest is particularly acute, the government may be required to undertake extensive predeprivation investigations, i.e., investigate before acting.

In general, cases arising under the procedural aspect of the Due Process Clauses require consideration of two basic questions: (1) is process due? and

(2) if so, how much process is due? Both of these questions require close attention to the timing of the procedural protections that are sought. The following Supreme Court cases take up some aspect of each of these questions. In thinking about procedural due process, they provide a useful analytical framework.

One should always remember that, in many circumstances, procedural due process will represent a *floor* and not a *ceiling.* For example, in the case of federal agencies, the procedural guarantees of sections 554, 556, and 557 of the Administrative Procedure Act (APA), when applicable, will invariably afford parties to such proceedings more process than the Fifth Amendment Due Process Clause would require. Similarly, a state APA, local ordinance, school board policy, or the regulations of a federal agency might set forth procedures that greatly exceed the requirements of procedural due process. Only when such statutes, ordinances, or regulations provide less protection than procedural due process might require will one find it necessary to argue about the vagaries of procedural due process. In this sense, concerns about procedural due process will arise in a relatively limited subset of cases.

In those cases governed by the Due Process Clauses, the amount of procedure a reviewing court will require an agency to provide might vary from minimal process to a mini-trial. For a thoughtful discussion of the kinds of procedural protections that one might wish to demand from an agency as incidents of the due process of law, *see* Henry J. Friendly, *Some Kind of Hearing,* 123 U. Pa. L. Rev. 1267 (1975).

BAILEY v. RICHARDSON
182 F.2d 46 (D.C. Cir. 1950)

PRETTYMAN, Circuit Judge.

This is a civil action brought in the United States District Court for the District of Columbia for a declaratory judgment and for an order directing plaintiff-appellant's reinstatement in Government employ. [The district court granted summary judgment to the federal officials that Bailey had sued, and Bailey appealed this adverse ruling. The Secretary of Labor was added as a party appellee.]

THE FACTS

Appellant Bailey was employed in the classified civil service of the United States Government from August 19, 1939, to June 28, 1947. Upon the latter date she was separated from the service due to reduction in force. On March 25, 1948, she was given a temporary appointment, and on May 28, 1948, she was reinstated under circumstances to be related. . . .

[Two months after Bailey returned to government employment, the Regional Loyalty Review Board informed Bailey, by letter, that she was under investigation for suspicion of being disloyal to the United States. Bailey denied the charges categorically and presented extensive evidence of her loyalty at a hearing conducted before the regional board. The government did not contest this evidence and "[n]o person other than presented by her testified." Nevertheless, the regional board found her to be disloyal and a security risk. Bailey "appealed [the adverse decision] to the Loyalty Review Board and requested a hearing," which was granted. Once again, "[n]o person other than Miss Bailey testified, and no affidavits other than hers were presented on the record."]

On February 9, 1949, the Chairman of the Loyalty Review Board advised the Federal Security Agency that the finding of the Regional Board was sustained, and he requested that the Agency remove Miss Bailey's name from the rolls. Notice to that effect was sent to counsel for Miss Bailey on the same day. The full Board subsequently declined to review the conclusions of its panel.

Miss Bailey's position from May 28, 1948, to November 3, 1948, was that of a training officer (general fields) CAF-13.

THE QUESTION

The rights claimed by and for appellant must be discovered accurately and defined precisely. The events with which we are concerned were not accidental, thoughtless, or mere petty tyrannies of subordinate officials. They were the deliberate design of the executive branch of the Government, knowingly supported by the Congress.

The case presented for Miss Bailey is undoubtedly appealing. She was denied reinstatement in her former employment because Government officials found reasonable grounds to believe her disloyal. She was not given a trial in any sense of the word, and she does not know who informed upon her. Thus viewed, her situation appeals powerfully to our sense of the fair and the just. But the case must be placed in context and in perspective.

The Constitution placed upon the President and the Congress, and upon them alone, responsibility for the welfare of this country in the arena of world affairs. It so happens that we are presently in an adversary position to a government whose most successful recent method of contest is the infiltration of a government service by its sympathizers. This is the context of Miss Bailey's question. . . .

[The D.C. Circuit first held that the agency's action conformed with statutory requirements and requirements of the relevant Executive Order.]

III. VALIDITY OF THE BAR TO EMPLOYMENT

Appellant [argues] that the order of the Board which barred her from the federal service for three years, was constitutionally invalid under the decision of the Supreme Court in the *Lovett* case [*United States v. Lovett,* 328 U.S. 303 (1946)]. We agree with that contention. The Court in that case clearly held that permanent proscription from Government service is "punishment" and that punishment can be inflicted only upon compliance with the Sixth Amendment. . . . We hold that the portions of the orders and directions of the defendants-appellees which purported to bar Miss Bailey from federal employ for three years, are invalid.

IV. CONSTITUTIONALITY OF THE DISMISSAL

We did not understand appellant to urge the unconstitutionality of her dismissal, apart from the three-year bar. But there is a difference of opinion among us in that respect, and we, therefore, state our views upon the point. First we consider the contentions respecting the constitutionality of the procedure pursued, and then we consider the constitutionality of the condition imposed upon the reinstatement. For the first purpose, we must assume that Miss Bailey was in the classified service without condition at the time of her removal from the rolls and that she was, therefore, dismissed from employment and not merely denied appointment; although, as we have indicated, we do not agree with that view of her status. If her status was merely that of an applicant for appointment, as we think it was, her nonappointment involved no procedural constitutional rights. Obviously, an applicant for office has no constitutional right to a hearing or a specification of the reasons why he is not appointed. We, therefore, consider the constitutionality of the procedure followed in this case upon the assumption that a Government employee in the classified service is being dismissed because her superiors have grounds, which to them are reasonable, to believe that she is disloyal. . . .

FIFTH AMENDMENT

It is next said on behalf of appellant that the due process clause of the Fifth Amendment requires that she be afforded a hearing of the quasi-judicial type before being dismissed. The due process clause provides: "No person shall . . . be deprived of life, liberty, or property, without due process of law;. . . ." It has been held repeatedly and consistently that Government employ is not "property" and that in this particular it is not a contract. We are unable to perceive how it could be held to be "liberty." Certainly it is not "life." So much that is clear would seem to dispose of the point. In terms the due process clause does not apply to the holding of a Government office.

Other considerations lead to the same conclusion. Never in our history has a Government administrative employee been entitled to a hearing of the quasi-judicial type upon his dismissal from Government service. That record of a hundred and sixty years of Government administration is the sort of history which speaks with great force. It is pertinent to repeat in this connection that the Lloyd-Lafollette Act, sponsored and enacted by advocates of a merit classified government service, expressly denies the right to such a hearing. Moreover, in the acute and sometimes bitter historic hundred-year contest over the wholesale summary dismissal of Government employees, there seems never to have been a claim that, absent congressional limitation, the President was without constitutional power to dismiss without notice, hearing or evidence; except for the question as to officials appointed with the advice and consent of the Senate. That history has been told many times and need not be repeated here. The controversy concerning the removal power began when the First Congress considered the establishment of the first executive department. Since then the subject has involved many colorful events and personalities over the years, including such as Presidents Jefferson, Jackson, Lincoln, Cleveland, Hayes, Theodore Roosevelt and Woodrow Wilson. The effort to establish a degree of stability in Government employ, tempestuous though that effort has been at time, has been made in the Congress and before the Presidents and their advisers, as a legislative and executive problem. . . .

In the absence of statute or ancient custom to the contrary, executive offices are held at the will of the appointing authority, not for life or for fixed terms. If removal be at will, of what purpose would process be? To hold office at the will of a superior and to be removable therefrom only by constitutional due process of law are opposite and inherently conflicting ideas. Due process of law is not applicable unless one is being deprived of something to which he has a right.

Constitutionally, the criterion for retention or removal of subordinate employees is the confidence of superior executive officials. Confidence is not controllable by process. What may be required by acts of the Congress is another matter, but there is not requirement in the Constitution that the executive branch rely upon the services of persons in whom it lacks confidence. . . .

We hold that the due process of law clause of the Fifth Amendment does not restrict the President's discretion or the prescriptive power of Congress in respect to executive personnel. . . .

Conclusion

It is our clear opinion that the President, absent congressional restriction, may remove from Government service any person of whose loyalty he is not completely convinced. He may do so without assigning any reason and without giving the employee any explanatory notice. If, as a matter of policy, he chooses to give the employee a general description of the information which concerns him and to hear what the employee has to say, he does not thereby strip himself of any portion of his constitutional power to choose and to remove. . . .

Reversed in part, affirmed in part, and remanded with instructions.

EDGERTON, Circuit Judge (dissenting).

Without trial by jury, without evidence, and without even being allowed to confront her accusers or to know their identity, a citizen of the United States has been found disloyal to the government of the United States.

For her supposed disloyal thoughts she has been punished by dismissal from a wholly nonsensitive position in which her efficiency rating was high. The case received nation-wide publicity. Ostracism inevitably followed. A finding of disloyalty is closely akin to a finding a treason. The public hardly distinguishes between the two.

No charges were served on appellant. The chairman of the Regional Board said "Nobody has presented any charges." The Board told appellant it was inquiring whether there were reasonable grounds for believing she was disloyal to the government of the United States. The Federal Bureau of Investigation had reported that informants believed to be reliable had made general statements purporting to connect her with the Communist Party. These reports were not disclosed to the appellant and have not been disclosed in court. The informants were not identified to the appellant or even to the Board. Their statements were admittedly not made under oath. The appellant denied under oath any membership in and any relationship or sympathy with the Communist Party, any activities connected with it or with communism, and any affiliation with any organization that advocated overthrow of the government of the United States. She asserted her loyalty to the government of the United States. She admitted attending one Communist meeting in 1932 in connection with a seminar study of the platforms of the various parties while she was a student at Bryn Mawr.

Appellant had no power to subpoena witnesses. Though it takes courage to appear as a voluntary defense witness in a loyalty case, four appeared. One was the pastor of the Methodist church of which appellant is an active member. He testified: "When this charge or information came to me I was not only surprised, I was dumfounded. . . . People in our community and in our church think of her and her family in the highest terms." Three officials of appellant's government agency, the United States Employment Service, who had known appellant professionally and socially for years, testified respectively that they were "extremely shocked" by the suggestion of her being disloyal, that it was "inconceivable" and "out of reason." Persons prominent in business, government and education who knew appellant but could not be present submitted affidavits.

No witness offered evidence, even hearsay evidence, against appellant. No affidavits were introduced against her. The record consists entirely of evidence in her favor. Yet the Board purported to find "on all the evidence" that there were reasonable grounds for believing she was disloyal to the government of the United States. Appellees admit the Board made this finding "after considering all the evidence, including the confidential reports of the Federal Bureau of Investigation." The Board directed the Federal Security Agency to suspend appellant pending her appeal to the Loyalty Review Board, and told her she was barred from civil service examinations for three years.

Appellant appeared and testified before a panel of the Loyalty Review Board. She submitted her own affidavit and the affidavits of some 70 persons who knew her, including bankers, corporate officials, federal and state officials, union members, and others. Again no one testified against her. She proved she had publicly and to the knowledge of a number of the affiants taken positions inconsistent with Communist sympathies. She showed not only by her own testimony but by that of other persons that she favored the Marshall Plan, which the Communist Party notoriously opposed, and that in 1940, during the Nazi-Soviet Pact, she favored Lend-Lease and was very critical of the Soviet position. In her union she urged its officers to execute non-communist affidavits, opposed a foreign policy resolution widely publicized as pro-Russian, and favored what was then the official CIO resolution on foreign policy.

Against all this, there were only the unsworn reports in the secret files to the effect that unsworn statements of a general sort, purporting to connect appellant with Communism, had been made by unnamed persons. Some if not all of these statements did not purport to be based on knowledge, but only on belief. Appellant sought to learn the names of the informants or, if their names were confidential, than at least whether they had been active in appellant's union, in which there were factional quarrels. The Board did not furnish or even have this information. Chairman Richardson said: "I haven't the slightest knowledge as to who they were or how active they have been in anything." All that the Board knew or we know about the informants is that unidentified members of the Federal Bureau of Investigation, who did not appear before the Board, believed them to be reliable. . . .

Appellant's dismissal violates both the Constitution and the Executive Order. . . .

QUESTIONS

1. Where does the conclusion come from that government employment is neither life, liberty, nor property?

2. Is there a balancing here? Of what?
3. Is the theory of the case defensible as a matter of constitutional policy?
    a. If not, is it because of the stigma resulting from the government's action? What if we hypothesize away any stigma?
    b. If not, is it because there is really punishment here? What if we hypothesize away any punishment?
    c. If employment was at will, what purpose would a hearing have served?
4. This case was affirmed by an equally divided Supreme Court. 341 U.S. 918 (1951). What does that mean? What does it imply?

GOLDBERG v. KELLY
397 U.S. 254 (1970)

Mr. Justice Brennan delivered the opinion of the Court.

The question for decision is whether a State that terminates public assistance payments to a particular recipient without affording him the opportunity for an evidentiary hearing prior to termination denies the recipient procedural due process in violation of the Due Process Clause of the Fourteenth Amendment.

This action was brought in the District Court for the Southern District of New York by residents of New York City receiving financial aid under the federally assisted program of Aid to Families with Dependent Children (AFDC) or under New York State's general Home Relief program.[1] Their complaint alleged that the New York State and New York City officials administering these programs terminated, or were about to terminate, such aid without prior notice and hearing, thereby denying them due process of law.[2] At the time the suits were filed there was no requirement of prior notice or hearing of any kind before termination of financial aid. However, the State and city adopted procedures for notice and hearing after the suits were brought, and the plaintiffs, appellees here, then challenged the constitutional adequacy of those procedures. . . .

Pursuant to [state regulations], the New York City Department of Social Services promulgated Procedure No. 68-18. A caseworker who has doubts about the

1. AFDC was established by the Social Security Act of 1935, 49 Stat. 627, as amended, 42 U.S.C. §§ 601-610 (1964 ed. and Supp. IV). It is a categorical assistance program supported by federal grants-in-aid but administered by the States according to regulations of the Secretary of Health, Education, and Welfare. . . .

Home Relief is a general assistance program financed and administered solely by New York State and local governments. N.Y. Social Welfare Law §§ 157-165 (1966), since July 1, 1967, Social Services Law §§ 157-166. It assists any person unable to support himself or to secure support from other sources. Id., § 158.

2. Two suits were brought and consolidated in the District Court. The named plaintiffs were 20 in number, including intervenors. Fourteen had been or were about to be cut off from AFDC, and six from Home Relief. During the course of this litigation most, though not all, of the plaintiffs either received a "fair hearing" . . . or were restored to the rolls without a hearing. However, even in many of the cases where payments have been resumed, the underlying questions of eligibility that resulted in the bringing of this suit have not been resolved. For example, Mrs. Altagracia Guzman alleged that she was in danger of losing AFDC payments for failure to cooperate with the City Department of Social Services in suing her estranged husband. She contended that the departmental policy requiring such cooperation was inapplicable to the facts of her case. The record shows that payments to Mrs. Guzman have not been terminated, but there is no indication that the basic dispute over her duty to cooperate has been resolved, or that the alleged danger of termination has been removed. Home Relief payments to Juan DeJesus were terminated because he refused to accept counseling and rehabilitation for drug addiction. Mr. DeJesus maintains that he does not use drugs. His payments were restored the day after his complaint was filed. But there is nothing in the record to indicate that the underlying factual dispute in his case has been settled.

recipient's continued eligibility must first discuss them with the recipient. If the caseworker concludes that the recipient is no longer eligible, he recommends termination of aid to a unit supervisor. If the latter concurs, he sends the recipient a letter stating the reasons for proposing to terminate aid and notifying him that within seven days he may request that a higher official review the record, and may support the request with a written statement prepared personally or with the aid of an attorney or other person. If the reviewing official affirms the determination of ineligibility, aid is stopped immediately and the recipient is informed by letter of the reasons for the action. Appellees' challenge to this procedure emphasizes the absence of any provisions for the personal appearance of the recipient before the reviewing official, for oral presentation of evidence, and for confrontation and cross-examination of adverse witnesses. However, the letter does inform the recipient that he may request a post-termination "fair hearing." This is a proceeding before an independent state hearing officer at which the recipient may appear personally, offer oral evidence, confront and cross-examine the witnesses against him, and have a record made of the hearing. If the recipient prevails at the "fair hearing" he is paid all funds erroneously withheld. HEW Handbook, pt. IV, §§ 6200-6500; 18 NYCRR §§ 84.2-84.23. A recipient whose aid is not restored by a "fair hearing" decision may have judicial review. N.Y. Civil Practice Law and Rules, Art. 78 (1963). The recipient is so notified, 18 NYCRR § 84.16.

I

The constitutional issue to be decided, therefore, is the narrow one whether the Due Process Clause requires that the recipient be afforded an evidentiary hearing *before* the termination of benefits. The District Court held that only a pre-termination evidentiary hearing would satisfy the constitutional command, and rejected the argument of the state and city officials that the combination of the post-termination "fair hearing" with the informal pre-termination review disposed of all due process claims. The court said: "While post-termination review is relevant, there is one overpowering fact which controls here. By hypothesis, a welfare recipient is destitute, without funds or assets. . . . Suffice it to say that to cut off a welfare recipient in the face of . . . 'brutal need' without a prior hearing of some sort is unconscionable, unless overwhelming considerations justify it." The court rejected the argument that the need to protect the public's tax revenues supplied the requisite "overwhelming consideration." "Against the justified desire to protect public funds must be weighed the individual's overpowering need in this unique situation not to be wrongfully deprived of assistance. . . . While the problem of additional expense must be kept in mind, it does not justify denying a hearing meeting the ordinary standards of due process. Under all the circumstances, we hold that due process requires an adequate hearing before termination of welfare benefits, and the fact that there is a later constitutionally fair proceeding does not alter the result." Although state officials were party defendants in the action, only the Commissioner of Social Services of the City of New York appealed. We noted probable jurisdiction . . . . We affirm.

Appellant does not contend that procedural due process is not applicable to the termination of welfare benefits. Such benefits are a matter of statutory entitlement for persons qualified to receive them.[8] Their termination involves state action that adjudicates important rights. The constitutional challenge cannot be answered by an argument that public assistance benefits are "a 'privilege' and not a 'right.'" *Shapiro v. Thompson,* 394 U.S. 618, 627 n. 6 (1969). Relevant constitutional restraints apply as much to the withdrawal of public assistance benefits as to disqualification for unemployment compensation, *Sherbert v. Verner,* 374 U.S. 398 (1963); or to denial of a tax exemption, *Speiser v. Randall,* 357 U.S. 513 (1958); or to discharge from public employment, *Slochower v. Board of Higher Education,* 350 U.S. 551 (1956). The extent to which procedural due process must be afforded the recipient is influenced by the extent to which he may be "condemned to suffer grievous loss," *Joint Anti-Fascist Refugee Committee v. McGrath,* 341 U.S. 123, 168 (1951) (Frankfurter, J., concurring), and depends upon whether the recipient's interest in avoiding that loss outweighs the governmental interest in summary adjudication. Accordingly, as we said in *Cafeteria & Restaurant Workers Union v. McElroy,* 367 U.S. 886, 895 (1961), "consideration of what procedures due process may require under any given set of circumstances must begin with a determination of the precise nature of the government function involved as well as of the private interest that has been affected by governmental action."

It is true, of course, that some governmental benefits may be administratively terminated without affording the recipient a pre-termination evidentiary hearing.[10] But we agree with the District Court that when welfare is discontinued, only a pre-termination evidentiary hearing provides the recipient with procedural due process. *Cf. Sniadach v. Family Finance Corp.,* 395 U.S. 337 (1969). For qualified recipients, welfare provides the means to obtain essential food, clothing, housing, and medical care. . . . Thus the crucial factor in this

8. It may be realistic today to regard welfare entitlements as more like "property" than a "gratuity." Much of the existing wealth in this country takes the form of rights that do not fall within traditional common-law concepts of property. It has been aptly noted that

"[s]ociety today is built around entitlement. The automobile dealer has his franchise, the doctor and lawyer their professional licenses, the worker his union membership, contract, and pension rights, the executive his contract and stock options; all are devices to aid security and independence. Many of the most important of these entitlements now flow from government: subsidies to farmers and businessmen, routes for airlines and channels for television stations; long term contracts for defense, space, and education; social security pensions for individuals. Such sources of security, whether private or public, are no longer regarded as luxuries or gratuities; to the recipients they are essentials, fully deserved, and in no sense a form of charity. It is only the poor whose entitlements, although recognized by public policy, have not been effectively enforced." Reich, Individual Rights and Social Welfare: The Emerging Legal Issues, 74 Yale L.J. 1245, 1255 (1965). *See also* Reich, The New Property, 73 Yale L.J. 733 (1964).

10. One Court of Appeals has stated: "In a wide variety of situations, it has long been recognized that where harm to the public is threatened, and the private interest infringed is reasonably deemed to be of less importance, an official body can take summary action pending a later hearing." *R. A. Holman & Co. v. SEC,* 299 F.2d 127, 131 (D.C. Cir.), cert. denied, 370 U.S. 911 (1962) (suspension of exemption from stock registration requirement). *See also,* for example, *Ewing v. Mytinger & Casselberry, Inc.,* 339 U.S. 594 (1950) (seizure of mislabeled vitamin product); *North American Cold Storage Co. v. Chicago,* 211 U.S. 306 (1908) (seizure of food not fit for human use); *Yakus v. United States,* 321 U.S. 414 (1944) (adoption of wartime price regulations); *Gonzalez v. Freeman,* 334 F.2d 570 (D.C. Cir. 1964) (disqualification of a contractor to do business with the Government). In *Cafeteria & Restaurant Workers Union v. McElroy, supra,* at 896, summary dismissal of a public employee was upheld because "in [its] proprietary military capacity, the Federal Government . . . has traditionally exercised unfettered control," and because the case involved the Government's "dispatch of its own internal affairs." *Cf. Perkins v. Lukens Steel Co.,* 310 U.S. 113 (1940).

context — a factor not present in the case of the blacklisted government contractor, the discharged government employee, the taxpayer denied a tax exemption, or virtually anyone else whose governmental entitlements are ended — is that termination of aid pending resolution of a controversy over eligibility may deprive an eligible recipient of the very means by which to live while he waits. Since he lacks independent resources, his situation becomes immediately desperate. His need to concentrate upon finding the means for daily subsistence, in turn, adversely affects his ability to seek redress from the welfare bureaucracy.

Moreover, important governmental interests are promoted by affording recipients a pre-termination evidentiary hearing. From its founding the Nation's basic commitment has been to foster the dignity and well-being of all persons within its borders. We have come to recognize that forces not within the control of the poor contribute to their poverty. This perception, against the background of our traditions, has significantly influenced the development of the contemporary public assistance system. Welfare, by meeting the basic demands of subsistence, can help bring within the reach of the poor the same opportunities that are available to others to participate meaningfully in the life of the community. . . .

Appellant does not challenge the force of these considerations but argues that they are outweighed by countervailing governmental interests in conserving fiscal and administrative resources. These interests, the argument goes, justify the delay of any evidentiary hearing until after discontinuance of the grants. Summary adjudication protects the public fisc by stopping payments promptly upon discovery of reason to believe that a recipient is no longer eligible. Since most terminations are accepted without challenge, summary adjudication also conserves both the fisc and administrative time and energy by reducing the number of evidentiary hearings actually held.

We agree with the District Court, however, that these governmental interests are not overriding in the welfare context. The requirement of a prior hearing doubtless involves some greater expense, and the benefits paid to ineligible recipients pending decision at the hearing probably cannot be recouped, since these recipients are likely to be judgment-proof. But the State is not without weapons to minimize these increased costs. Much of the drain on fiscal and administrative resources can be reduced by developing procedures for prompt pre-termination hearings and by skillful use of personnel and facilities. Indeed, the very provision for a post-termination evidentiary hearing in New York's Home Relief program is itself cogent evidence that the State recognizes the primacy of the public interest in correct eligibility determinations and therefore in the provision of procedural safeguards. Thus, the interest of the eligible recipient in uninterrupted receipt of public assistance, coupled with the State's interest that his payments not be erroneously terminated, clearly outweighs the State's competing concern to prevent any increase in its fiscal and administrative burdens. . . .

II

We also agree with the District Court, however, that the pre-termination hearing need not take the form of a judicial or quasi-judicial trial. We bear in mind that the statutory "fair hearing" will provide the recipient with a full administrative review.[14] Accordingly, the pre-termination hearing has one function only: to produce an initial determination of the validity of the welfare department's grounds for discontinuance of payments in order to protect a recipient against an erroneous termination of his benefits. Cf. *Sniadach v. Family Finance Corp.*, 395 U.S. 337, 343 (1969) (Harlan, J., concurring). Thus, a complete record and a comprehensive opinion, which would serve primarily to facilitate judicial review and to guide future decisions, need not be provided at the pre-termination stage. We recognize, too, that both welfare authorities and recipients have an interest in relatively speedy resolution of questions of eligibility, that they are used to dealing with one another informally, and that some welfare departments have very burdensome caseloads. These considerations justify the limitation of the pre-termination hearing to minimum procedural safeguards, adapted to the particular characteristics of welfare recipients, and to the limited nature of the controversies to be resolved. We wish to add that we, no less than the dissenters, recognize the importance of not imposing upon the States or the Federal Government in this developing field of law any procedural requirements beyond those demanded by rudimentary due process.

"The fundamental requisite of due process of law is the opportunity to be heard." *Grannis v. Ordean,* 234 U.S. 385, 394 (1914). The hearing must be "at a meaningful time and in a meaningful manner." *Armstrong v. Manzo,* 380 U.S. 545, 552 (1965). In the present context these principles require that a recipient have timely and adequate notice detailing the reasons for a proposed termination, and an effective opportunity to defend by confronting any adverse witnesses and by presenting his own arguments and evidence orally. These rights are important in cases such as those before us, where recipients have challenged proposed terminations as resting on incorrect or misleading factual premises or on misapplication of rules or policies to the facts of particular cases.

We are not prepared to say that the seven-day notice currently provided by New York City is constitutionally insufficient per se, although there may be cases where fairness would require that a longer time be given. Nor do we see any constitutional deficiency in the content or form of the notice. New York employs both a letter and a personal conference with a caseworker to inform a recipient of the precise questions raised about his continued eligibility. Evidently the recipient is told the legal and factual bases for the Department's doubts. This combination is probably the most effective method of communicating with recipients.

The city's procedures presently do not permit recipients to appear personally with or without counsel before the official who finally determines continued eligibility. Thus a recipient is not permitted to present evidence to that official orally, or to confront or cross-examine adverse witnesses. These omissions are fatal to the constitutional adequacy of the procedures.

The opportunity to be heard must be tailored to the capacities and circumstances of those who are to be heard. It is not enough that a welfare recipient may present his position to the decision maker in writing or secondhand through his caseworker. Written submissions are an unrealistic option for most recipients, who lack the educational attainment necessary to write effectively and who cannot obtain professional assistance. Moreover, written

---

14. Due process does not, of course, require two hearings. If, for example, a State simply wishes to continue benefits until after a "fair" hearing there will be no need for a preliminary hearing.

submissions do not afford the flexibility of oral presentations; they do not permit the recipient to mold his argument to the issues the decision maker appears to regard as important. Particularly where credibility and veracity are at issue, as they must be in many termination proceedings, written submissions are a wholly unsatisfactory basis for decision. The secondhand presentation to the decision maker by the caseworker has its own deficiencies; since the caseworker usually gathers the facts upon which the charge of ineligibility rests, the presentation of the recipient's side of the controversy cannot safely be left to him. Therefore a recipient must be allowed to state his position orally. Informal procedures will suffice; in this context due process does not require a particular order of proof or mode of offering evidence. Cf. HEW Handbook, pt. IV, § 6400(a).

In almost every setting where important decisions turn on questions of fact, due process requires an opportunity to confront and cross-examine adverse witnesses. What we said in *Greene v. McElroy,* 360 U.S. 474, 496-497 (1959), is particularly pertinent here:

> "Certain principles have remained relatively immutable in our jurisprudence. One of these is that where governmental action seriously injures an individual, and the reasonableness of the action depends on fact findings, the evidence used to prove the Government's case must be disclosed to the individual so that he has an opportunity to show that it is untrue. While this is important in the case of documentary evidence, it is even more important where the evidence consists of the testimony of individuals whose memory might be faulty or who, in fact, might be perjurers or persons motivated by malice, vindictiveness, intolerance, prejudice, or jealousy. We have formalized these protections in the requirements of confrontation and cross-examination. They have ancient roots. They find expression in the Sixth Amendment. . . . This Court has been zealous to protect these rights from erosion. It has spoken out not only in criminal cases, . . . but also in all types of cases where administrative . . . actions were under scrutiny."

Welfare recipients must therefore be given an opportunity to confront and cross-examine the witnesses relied on by the department.

"The right to be heard would be, in many cases, of little avail if it did not comprehend the right to be heard by counsel." *Powell v. Alabama,* 287 U.S. 45, 68-69 (1932). We do not say that counsel must be provided at the pre-termination hearing, but only that the recipient must be allowed to retain an attorney if he so desires. Counsel can help delineate the issues, present the factual contentions in an orderly manner, conduct cross-examination, and generally safeguard the interests of the recipient. We do not anticipate that this assistance will unduly prolong or otherwise encumber the hearing. Evidently HEW has reached the same conclusion. See 45 CFR § 205.10, 34 Fed. Reg. 1144 (1969); 45 CFR § 220.25, 34 Fed. Reg. 13595 (1969).

Finally, the decision maker's conclusion as to a recipient's eligibility must rest solely on the legal rules and evidence adduced at the hearing. *Ohio Bell Tel. Co. v. PUC,* 301 U.S. 292 (1937); *United States v. Abilene & S. R. Co.,* 265 U.S. 274, 288-289 (1924). To demonstrate compliance with this elementary requirement, the decision maker should state the reasons for his determination and indicate the evidence he relied on, *cf. Wichita R. & Light Co. v. PUC,* 260 U.S. 48, 57-59 (1922), though his statement need not amount to a full opinion or even formal findings of fact and conclusions of law. And, of course, an impartial decision maker is essential. Cf. *In re Murchison,* 349 U.S. 133 (1955); *Wong Yang Sung v. McGrath,*

339 U.S. 33, 45-46 (1950). We agree with the District Court that prior involvement in some aspects of a case will not necessarily bar a welfare official from acting as a decision maker. He should not, however, have participated in making the determination under review. *Affirmed.*

[Chief Justice Burger, Justice Stewart, and Justice Black filed separate dissents.]

MR. JUSTICE BLACK, dissenting.

In the last half century the United States, along with many, perhaps most, other nations of the world, has moved far toward becoming a welfare state, that is, a nation that for one reason or another taxes its most affluent people to help support, feed, clothe, and shelter its less fortunate citizens. The result is that today more than nine million men, women, and children in the United States receive some kind of state or federally financed public assistance in the form of allowances or gratuities, generally paid them periodically, usually by the week, month, or quarter. Since these gratuities are paid on the basis of need, the list of recipients is not static, and some people go off the lists and others are added from time to time. These ever-changing lists put a constant administrative burden on government and it certainly could not have reasonably anticipated that this burden would include the additional procedural expense imposed by the Court today. . . .

The more than a million names on the relief rolls in New York, and the more than nine million names on the rolls of all the 50 States were not put there at random. The names are there because state welfare officials believed that those people were eligible for assistance. Probably in the officials' haste to make out the lists many names were put there erroneously in order to alleviate immediate suffering, and undoubtedly some people are drawing relief who are not entitled under the law to do so. Doubtless some draw relief checks from time to time who know they are not eligible, either because they are not actually in need or for some other reason. Many of those who thus draw undeserved gratuities are without sufficient property to enable the government to collect back from them any money they wrongfully receive. But the Court today holds that it would violate the Due Process Clause of the Fourteenth Amendment to stop paying those people weekly or monthly allowances unless the government first affords them a full "evidentiary hearing" even though welfare officials are persuaded that the recipients are not rightfully entitled to receive a penny under the law. In other words, although some recipients might be on the lists for payment wholly because of deliberate fraud on their part, the Court holds that the government is helpless and must continue, until after an evidentiary hearing, to pay money that it does not owe, never has owed, and never could owe. I do not believe there is any provision in our Constitution that should thus paralyze the government's efforts to protect itself against making payments to people who are not entitled to them.

Particularly do I not think that the Fourteenth Amendment should be given such an unnecessarily broad construction. . . . It somewhat strains credulity to say that the government's promise of charity to an individual is property belonging to that individual when the government denies that the individual is honestly entitled to receive such a payment. . . .

The Court apparently feels that this decision will benefit the poor and needy. In my judgment the eventual result will be just the opposite. While today's decision requires only an administrative, evidentiary hearing, the inevitable logic of the approach taken will lead to constitutionally imposed, time-consuming delays of a full adversary process of administrative and judicial review. In the next case the welfare recipients are bound to argue that cutting off benefits before judicial review of the agency's decision is also a denial of due process. Since, by hypothesis, termination of aid at that point may still "deprive an eligible recipient of the very means by which to live while he waits," I would be surprised if the weighing process did not compel the conclusion that termination without full judicial review would be unconscionable. After all, at each step, as the majority seems to feel, the issue is only one of weighing the government's pocketbook against the actual survival of the recipient, and surely that balance must always tip in favor of the individual. Similarly today's decision requires only the opportunity to have the benefit of counsel at the administrative hearing, but it is difficult to believe that the same reasoning process would not require the appointment of counsel, for otherwise the right to counsel is a meaningless one since these people are too poor to hire their own advocates. *Cf. Gideon v. Wainwright,* 372 U.S. 335, 344 (1963). Thus the end result of today's decision may well be that the government, once it decides to give welfare benefits, cannot reverse that decision until the recipient has had the benefits of full administrative and judicial review, including, of course, the opportunity to present his case to this Court. Since this process will usually entail a delay of several years, the inevitable result of such a constitutionally imposed burden will be that the government will not put a claimant on the rolls initially until it has made an exhaustive investigation to determine his eligibility. While this Court will perhaps have insured that no needy person will be taken off the rolls without a full "due process" proceeding, it will also have insured that many will never get on the rolls, or at least that they will remain destitute during the lengthy proceedings followed to determine initial eligibility.

For the foregoing reasons I dissent from the Court's holding. The operation of a welfare state is a new experiment for our Nation. For this reason, among others, I feel that new experiments in carrying out a welfare program should not be frozen into our constitutional structure. They should be left, as are other legislative determinations, to the Congress and the legislatures that the people elect to make our laws.

QUESTIONS

1. What is taken by the government here? Would it traditionally have been considered a "privilege"?
2. How did the Court come to the conclusion that procedural due process applied? Does the *Goldberg* Court reject the right/privilege distinction? Does the Court use a "grievous loss" and/or a "balancing" test? Is the analysis coherent? Logical?
3. How does the Court reach the conclusion that an oral predeprivation hearing is required? How does it determine the required characteristics of the hearing?
4. What is the purpose of the hearing required by the Court? To increase the accuracy of the decision making? To afford dignity to the welfare recipient? Perhaps both?

5. *Goldberg* is difficult to translate into "tests" for determining if process is constitutionally due and how much is due. The "tests" to answer these questions have been developed in the cases that follow. Do the following cases constitute refinements of the *Goldberg* holding, or departures from it?

BOARD OF REGENTS v. ROTH

408 U.S. 564 (1972)

Mr. Justice Stewart delivered the opinion of the Court.

In 1968 the respondent, David Roth, was hired for his first teaching job as assistant professor of political science at Wisconsin State University-Oshkosh. He was hired for a fixed term of one academic year. The notice of his faculty appointment specified that his employment would begin on September 1, 1968, and would end on June 30, 1969.[1] The respondent completed that term. But he was informed that he would not be rehired for the next academic year.

The respondent had no tenure rights to continued employment. Under Wisconsin statutory law a state university teacher can acquire tenure as a "permanent" employee only after four years of year-to-year employment. Having acquired tenure, a teacher is entitled to continued employment "during efficiency and good behavior." A relatively new teacher without tenure, however, is under Wisconsin law entitled to nothing beyond his one-year appointment.[2] There are no statutory or administrative standards defining eligibility for re-employment. State law thus clearly leaves the decision whether to rehire a nontenured teacher for another year to the unfettered discretion of university officials.

The procedural protection afforded a Wisconsin State University teacher before he is separated from the University corresponds to his job security. As a matter of statutory law, a tenured teacher cannot be "discharged except for cause upon written charges" and pursuant to certain procedures. A nontenured teacher, similarly, is protected to some extent during his one-year term. Rules promulgated by the Board of Regents provide that a nontenured teacher "dismissed" before the end of the year may have some opportunity for review of the "dismissal." But the Rules provide no real protection for a nontenured teacher who simply is not re-employed for the next year. He must be informed by February 1 "concerning retention or nonretention for the ensuing year." But "no reason for non-retention need be given. No review or appeal is provided in such case."

1. The respondent had no contract of employment. Rather, his formal notice of appointment was the equivalent of an employment contract.

The notice of his appointment provided that: "David F. Roth is hereby appointed to the faculty of the Wisconsin State University Position number 0262. (Location:) Oshkosh as (Rank:) Assistant Professor of (Department:) Political Science this (Date:) first day of (Month:) September (Year:)1968." The notice went on to specify that the respondent's "appointment basis" was for the "academic year." And it provided that "regulations governing tenure are in accord with Chapter 37.31, Wisconsin Statutes. The employment of any staff member for an academic year shall not be for a term beyond June 30th of the fiscal year in which the appointment is made." See n. 2, *infra.*

2. Wis. Stat. § 37.31(1) (1967), in force at the time, provided in pertinent part that: "All teachers in any state university shall initially be employed on probation. The employment shall be permanent, during efficiency and good behavior after 4 years of continuous service in the state university system as a teacher."

I

The requirements of procedural due process apply only to the deprivation of interests encompassed by the Fourteenth Amendment's protection of liberty and property. When protected interests are implicated, the right to some kind of prior hearing is paramount.[7] But the range of interests protected by procedural due process is not infinite.

The District Court decided that procedural due process guarantees apply in this case by assessing and balancing the weights of the particular interests involved. It concluded that the respondent's interest in re-employment at Wisconsin State University-Oshkosh outweighed the University's interest in denying him re-employment summarily. Undeniably, the respondent's re-employment prospects were of major concern to him — concern that we surely cannot say was insignificant. And a weighing process has long been a part of any determination of the form of hearing required in particular situations by procedural due process.[8] But, to determine whether due process requirements apply in the first place, we must look not to the "weight" but to the nature of the interest at stake. We must look to see if the interest is within the Fourteenth Amendment's protection of liberty and property.

"Liberty" and "property" are broad and majestic terms. They are among the "great [constitutional] concepts . . . purposely left to gather meaning from experience. . . . They relate to the whole domain of social and economic fact, and the statesmen who founded this Nation knew too well that only a stagnant society remains unchanged." *National Ins. Co. v. Tidewater Co.*, 337 U.S. 582, 646 (Frankfurter, J., dissenting). For that reason, the Court has fully and finally rejected the wooden distinction between "rights" and "privileges" that once seemed to govern the applicability of procedural due process rights.[9] The Court has also made clear that the property interests protected by procedural due process extend well beyond actual ownership of real estate, chattels, or money. By the same token, the Court has required due process protection for

7. Before a person is deprived of a protected interest, he must be afforded opportunity for some kind of a hearing, "except for extraordinary situations where some valid governmental interest is at stake that justifies postponing the hearing until after the event." *Boddie v. Connecticut*, 401 U.S. 371, 379. "While 'many controversies have raged about . . . the Due Process Clause,' . . . it is fundamental that except in emergency situations (and this is not one) due process requires that when a State seeks to terminate [a protected] interest . . . , it must afford 'notice and opportunity for hearing appropriate to the nature of the case' before the termination becomes effective." *Bell v. Burson*, 402 U.S. 535, 542. For the rare and extraordinary situations in which we have held that deprivation of a protected interest need not be preceded by opportunity for some kind of hearing, see, *e.g.*, *Central Union Trust Co. v. Garvan*, 254 U.S. 554, 566; *Phillips v. Commissioner*, 283 U.S. 589, 597; *Ewing v. Mytinger & Casselberry, Inc.*, 339 U.S. 594.

8. "The formality and procedural requisites for the hearing can vary, depending upon the importance of the interests involved and the nature of the subsequent proceedings." *Boddie v. Connecticut, supra*, at 378. *See*, e.g., *Goldberg v. Kelly*, 397 U.S. 254, 263; *Hannah v. Larche*, 363 U.S. 420. The constitutional requirement of opportunity for some form of hearing before deprivation of a protected interest, of course, does not depend upon such a narrow balancing process.

9. In a leading case decided many years ago, the Court of Appeals for the District of Columbia Circuit held that public employment in general was a "privilege," not a "right," and that procedural due process guarantees therefore were inapplicable. *Bailey v. Richardson*, 182 F.2d 46, *aff'd* by an equally divided Court, 341 U.S. 918. The basis of this holding has been thoroughly undermined in the ensuing years. For, as Mr. Justice Blackmun wrote for the Court only last year, "this Court now has rejected the concept that constitutional rights turn upon whether a governmental benefit is characterized as a 'right' or as a 'privilege.'" *Graham v. Richardson*, 403 U.S. 365, 374.

deprivations of liberty beyond the sort of formal constraints imposed by the criminal process.

Yet, while the Court has eschewed rigid or formalistic limitations on the protection of procedural due process, it has at the same time observed certain boundaries. For the words "liberty" and "property" in the Due Process Clause of the Fourteenth Amendment must be given some meaning.

II

"While this Court has not attempted to define with exactness the liberty . . . guaranteed [by the Fourteenth Amendment], the term has received much consideration and some of the included things have been definitely stated. Without doubt, it denotes not merely freedom from bodily restraint but also the right of the individual to contract, to engage in any of the common occupations of life, to acquire useful knowledge, to marry, establish a home and bring up children, to worship God according to the dictates of his own conscience, and generally to enjoy those privileges long recognized . . . as essential to the orderly pursuit of happiness by free men." *Meyer v. Nebraska,* 262 U.S. 390, 399. In a Constitution for a free people, there can be no doubt that the meaning of "liberty" must be broad indeed.

There might be cases in which a State refused to reemploy a person under such circumstances that interests in liberty would be implicated. But this is not such a case.

The State, in declining to rehire the respondent, did not make any charge against him that might seriously damage his standing and associations in his community. It did not base the nonrenewal of his contract on a charge, for example, that he had been guilty of dishonesty, or immorality. Had it done so, this would be a different case. For "where a person's good name, reputation, honor, or integrity is at stake because of what the government is doing to him, notice and an opportunity to be heard are essential." *Wisconsin v. Constantineau,* 400 U.S. 433, 437. In such a case, due process would accord an opportunity to refute the charge before University officials.[12] In the present case, however, there is no suggestion whatever that the respondent's "good name, reputation, honor, or integrity" is at stake.

Similarly, there is no suggestion that the State, in declining to re-employ the respondent, imposed on him a stigma or other disability that foreclosed his freedom to take advantage of other employment opportunities. The State, for example, did not invoke any regulations to bar the respondent from all other public employment in state universities. Had it done so, this, again, would be a different case. For "to be deprived not only of present government employment but of future opportunity for it certainly is no small injury. . . ." *Joint Anti-Fascist Refugee Committee v. McGrath, supra,* at 185 (Jackson, J., concurring). The Court has held, for example, that a State, in regulating eligibility for a type of professional employment, cannot foreclose a range of opportunities "in a manner . . . that contravene[s] . . . Due Process," *Schware v. Board of Bar Examiners,* 353 U.S. 232, 238, and, specifically, in a manner that denies the right to a full

---

12. The purpose of such notice and hearing is to provide the person an opportunity to clear his name. Once a person has cleared his name at a hearing, his employer, of course, may remain free to deny him future employment for other reasons.

prior hearing. *Willner v. Committee on Character,* 373 U.S. 96, 103. *See Cafeteria Workers v. McElroy, supra,* at 898. In the present case, however, this principle does not come into play.[13]

To be sure, the respondent has alleged that the nonrenewal of his contract was based on his exercise of his right to freedom of speech. But this allegation is not now before us. The District Court stayed proceedings on this issue, and the respondent has yet to prove that the decision not to rehire him was, in fact, based on his free speech activities.[14]

Hence, on the record before us, all that clearly appears is that the respondent was not rehired for one year at one university. It stretches the concept too far to suggest that a person is deprived of "liberty" when he simply is not rehired in one job but remains as free as before to seek another. *Cafeteria Workers v. McElroy, supra,* at 895-896.

III

The Fourteenth Amendment's procedural protection of property is a safeguard of the security of interests that a person has already acquired in specific benefits. These interests — property interests — may take many forms.

Thus, the Court has held that a person receiving welfare benefits under statutory and administrative standards defining eligibility for them has an interest in continued receipt of those benefits that is safeguarded by procedural due process. *Goldberg v. Kelly,* 397 U.S. 254. Similarly, in the area of public

13. The District Court made an *assumption* "that non-retention by one university or college creates concrete and practical difficulties for a professor in his subsequent academic career." And the Court of Appeals based its affirmance of the summary judgment largely on the premise that "the substantial adverse effect non-retention is likely to have upon the career interests of an individual professor" amounts to a limitation on future employment opportunities sufficient to invoke procedural due process guarantees. But even assuming, arguendo, that such a "substantial adverse effect" under these circumstances would constitute a state-imposed restriction on liberty, the record contains no support for these assumptions. There is no suggestion of how nonretention might affect the respondent's future employment prospects. Mere proof, for example, that his record of nonretention in one job, taken alone, might make him somewhat less attractive to some other employers would hardly establish the kind of foreclosure of opportunities amounting to a deprivation of "liberty."

14. *See* n. 5, *supra.* The Court of Appeals, nonetheless, argued that opportunity for a hearing and a statement of reasons were required here "as a *prophylactic* against non-retention decisions improperly motivated by exercise of protected rights" (emphasis supplied). While the Court of Appeals recognized the lack of a finding that the respondent's nonretention was based on exercise of the right of free speech, it felt that the respondent's interest in liberty was sufficiently implicated here because the decision not to rehire him was made "with a background of controversy and unwelcome expressions of opinion." *Ibid.*

When a State would directly impinge upon interests in free speech or free press, this Court has on occasion held that opportunity for a fair adversary hearing must precede the action, whether or not the speech or press interest is clearly protected under substantive First Amendment standards. Thus, we have required fair notice and opportunity for an adversary hearing before an injunction is issued against the holding of rallies and public meetings. *Carroll v. Princess Anne,* 393 U.S. 175. Similarly, we have indicated the necessity of procedural safeguards before a State makes a large-scale seizure of a person's allegedly obscene books, magazines, and so forth. *A Quantity of Books v. Kansas,* 378 U.S. 205; *Marcus v. Search Warrant,* 367 U.S. 717. *See Freedman v. Maryland,* 380 U.S. 51; *Bantam Books v. Sullivan,* 372 U.S. 58. *See generally* Monaghan, First Amendment "Due Process," 83 Harv. L. Rev. 518.

In the respondent's case, however, the State has not directly impinged upon interests in free speech or free press in any way comparable to a seizure of books or an injunction against meetings. Whatever may be a teacher's rights of free speech, the interest in holding a teaching job at a state university, *simpliciter,* is not itself a free speech interest.

employment, the Court has held that a public college professor dismissed from an office held under tenure provisions, *Slochower v. Board of Education,* 350 U.S. 551, and college professors and staff members dismissed during the terms of their contracts, *Wieman v. Updegraff,* 344 U.S. 183, have interests in continued employment that are safeguarded by due process. Only last year, the Court held that this principle "proscribing summary dismissal from public employment without hearing or inquiry required by due process" also applied to a teacher recently hired without tenure or a formal contract, but nonetheless with a clearly implied promise of continued employment. *Connell v. Higginbotham,* 403 U.S. 207, 208.

Certain attributes of "property" interests protected by procedural due process emerge from these decisions. To have a property interest in a benefit, a person clearly must have more than an abstract need or desire for it. He must have more than a unilateral expectation of it. He must, instead, have a legitimate claim of entitlement to it. It is a purpose of the ancient institution of property to protect those claims upon which people rely in their daily lives, reliance that must not be arbitrarily undermined. It is a purpose of the constitutional right to a hearing to provide an opportunity for a person to vindicate those claims.

Property interests, of course, are not created by the Constitution. Rather, they are created and their dimensions are defined by existing rules or understandings that stem from an independent source such as state law — rules or understandings that secure certain benefits and that support claims of entitlement to those benefits. Thus, the welfare recipients in *Goldberg v. Kelly, supra,* had a claim of entitlement to welfare payments that was grounded in the statute defining eligibility for them. The recipients had not yet shown that they were, in fact, within the statutory terms of eligibility. But we held that they had a right to a hearing at which they might attempt to do so.

Just as the welfare recipients' "property" interest in welfare payments was created and defined by statutory terms, so the respondent's "property" interest in employment at Wisconsin State University-Oshkosh was created and defined by the terms of his appointment. Those terms secured his interest in employment up to June 30, 1969. But the important fact in this case is that they specifically provided that the respondent's employment was to terminate on June 30. They did not provide for contract renewal absent "sufficient cause." Indeed, they made no provision for renewal whatsoever.

Thus, the terms of the respondent's appointment secured absolutely no interest in re-employment for the next year. They supported absolutely no possible claim of entitlement to re-employment. Nor, significantly, was there any state statute or University rule or policy that secured his interest in re-employment or that created any legitimate claim to it.[16] In these circumstances, the respondent surely had an abstract concern in being rehired, but he did not have a property interest sufficient to require the University authorities to give him a hearing when they declined to renew his contract of employment.

---

16. To be sure, the respondent does suggest that most teachers hired on a year-to-year basis by Wisconsin State University-Oshkosh are, in fact, rehired. But the District Court has not found that there is anything approaching a "common law" of re-employment, see *Perry v. Sindermann, post,* so strong as to require university officials to give the respondent a statement of reasons and a hearing on their decision not to rehire him.

IV

Our analysis of the respondent's constitutional rights in this case in no way indicates a view that an opportunity for a hearing or a statement of reasons for nonretention would, or would not, be appropriate or wise in public colleges and universities. For it is a written Constitution that we apply. Our role is confined to interpretation of that Constitution.

We must conclude that the summary judgment for the respondent should not have been granted, since the respondent has not shown that he was deprived of liberty or property protected by the Fourteenth Amendment. The judgment of the Court of Appeals, accordingly, is reversed and the case is remanded for further proceedings consistent with this opinion.

[Justices Douglas and Marshall filed dissents; Justice Powell did not participate, and Chief Justice Burger filed a concurrence.]

MR. JUSTICE MARSHALL, dissenting.

Respondent was hired as an assistant professor of political science at Wisconsin State University-Oshkosh for the 1968-1969 academic year. During the course of that year he was told that he would not be rehired for the next academic term, but he was never told why. In this case, he asserts that the Due Process Clause of the Fourteenth Amendment to the United States Constitution entitled him to a statement of reasons and a hearing on the University's decision not to rehire him for another year. This claim was sustained by the [courts below]. I dissent.

While I agree with Part I of the Court's opinion, setting forth the proper framework for consideration of the issue presented, and also with those portions of Parts II and III of the Court's opinion that assert that a public employee is entitled to procedural due process whenever a State stigmatizes him by denying employment, or injures his future employment prospects severely, or whenever the State deprives him of a property interest, I would go further than the Court does in defining the terms "liberty" and "property."

The prior decisions of this Court, discussed at length in the opinion of the Court, establish a principle that is as obvious as it is compelling — i.e., federal and state governments and governmental agencies are restrained by the Constitution from acting arbitrarily with respect to employment opportunities that they either offer or control. Hence, it is now firmly established that whether or not a private employer is free to act capriciously or unreasonably with respect to employment practices, at least absent statutory or contractual controls, a government employer is different. The government may only act fairly and reasonably. . . .

Employment is one of the greatest, if not the greatest, benefits that governments offer in modern-day life. When something as valuable as the opportunity to work is at stake, the government may not reward some citizens and not others without demonstrating that its actions are fair and equitable. And it is procedural due process that is our fundamental guarantee of fairness, our protection against arbitrary, capricious, and unreasonable government action. . . .

We have often noted that procedural due process means many different things in the numerous contexts in which it applies. *See*, e.g., *Goldberg v. Kelly*, 397 U.S. 254 (1970); *Bell v. Burson*, 402 U.S. 535 (1971). Prior decisions have held that an applicant for admission to practice as an attorney before the United

States Board of Tax Appeals may not be rejected without a statement of reasons and a chance for a hearing on disputed issues of fact; that a tenured teacher could not be summarily dismissed without notice of the reasons and a hearing; that an applicant for admission to a state bar could not be denied the opportunity to practice law without notice of the reasons for the rejection of his application and a hearing; and even that a substitute teacher who had been employed only two months could not be dismissed merely because she refused to take a loyalty oath without an inquiry into the specific facts of her case and a hearing on those in dispute. I would follow these cases and hold that respondent was denied due process when his contract was not renewed and he was not informed of the reasons and given an opportunity to respond.

It may be argued that to provide procedural due process to all public employees or prospective employees would place an intolerable burden on the machinery of government. Cf. *Goldberg v. Kelly, supra.* The short answer to that argument is that it is not burdensome to give reasons when reasons exist. Whenever an application for employment is denied, an employee is discharged, or a decision not to rehire an employee is made, there should be some reason for the decision. It can scarcely be argued that government would be crippled by a requirement that the reason be communicated to the person most directly affected by the government's action.

Where there are numerous applicants for jobs, it is likely that few will choose to demand reasons for not being hired. But, if the demand for reasons is exceptionally great, summary procedures can be devised that would provide fair and adequate information to all persons. As long as the government has a good reason for its actions it need not fear disclosure. It is only where the government acts improperly that procedural due process is truly burdensome. And that is precisely when it is most necessary.

It might also be argued that to require a hearing and a statement of reasons is to require a useless act, because a government bent on denying employment to one or more persons will do so regardless of the procedural hurdles that are placed in its path. Perhaps this is so, but a requirement of procedural regularity at least renders arbitrary action more difficult. Moreover, proper procedures will surely eliminate some of the arbitrariness that results, not from malice, but from innocent error. "Experience teaches . . . that the affording of procedural safeguards, which by their nature serve to illuminate the underlying facts, in itself often operates to prevent erroneous decisions on the merits from occurring." *Silver v. New York Stock Exchange,* 373 U.S. 341, 366 (1963). When the government knows it may have to justify its decisions with sound reasons, its conduct is likely to be more cautious, careful, and correct.

Professor Gellhorn put the argument well:

> "In my judgment, there is no basic division of interest between the citizenry on the one hand and officialdom on the other. Both should be interested equally in the quest for procedural safeguards. I echo the late Justice Jackson in saying: "Let it not be overlooked that due process of law is not for the sole benefit of an accused. It is the best insurance for the Government itself against those blunders which leave lasting stains on a system of justice" — blunders which are likely to occur when reasons need not be given and when the reasonableness and indeed legality of judgments need not be subjected to any appraisal other than one's own. . . ."

Summary of Colloquy on Administrative Law, 6 J. Soc. Pub. Teachers of Law 70, 73 (1961).

Accordingly, I dissent.

PERRY v. SINDERMANN
408 U.S. 593 (1972)

MR. JUSTICE STEWART delivered the opinion of the Court.

From 1959 to 1969 the respondent, Robert Sindermann, was a teacher in the state college system of the State of Texas. After teaching for two years at the University of Texas and for four years at San Antonio Junior College, he became a professor of Government and Social Science at Odessa Junior College in 1965. He was employed at the college for four successive years, under a series of one-year contracts. He was successful enough to be appointed, for a time, the cochairman of his department.

During the 1968-1969 academic year, however, controversy arose between the respondent and the college administration. The respondent was elected president of the Texas Junior College Teachers Association. In this capacity, he left his teaching duties on several occasions to testify before committees of the Texas Legislature, and he became involved in public disagreements with the policies of the college's Board of Regents. In particular, he aligned himself with a group advocating the elevation of the college to four-year status — a change opposed by the Regents. And, on one occasion, a newspaper advertisement appeared over his name that was highly critical of the Regents.

Finally, in May 1969, the respondent's one-year employment contract terminated and the Board of Regents voted not to offer him a new contract for the next academic year. The Regents issued a press release setting forth allegations of the respondent's insubordination.[1] But they provided him no official statement of the reasons for the nonrenewal of his contract. And they allowed him no opportunity for a hearing to challenge the basis of the nonrenewal.

The respondent then brought this action in Federal District Court. He alleged primarily that the Regents' decision not to rehire him was based on his public criticism of the policies of the college administration and thus infringed his right to freedom of speech. He also alleged that their failure to provide him an opportunity for a hearing violated the Fourteenth Amendment's guarantee of procedural due process. The petitioners — members of the Board of Regents and the president of the college — denied that their decision was made in retaliation for the respondent's public criticism and argued that they had no obligation to provide a hearing.[2] On the basis of these bare pleadings and three brief affidavits filed by the respondent, the District Court granted summary judgment for the petitioners. It concluded that the respondent had "no cause of action against the [petitioners] since his contract of employment terminated May 31, 1969, and Odessa Junior College has not adopted the tenure system."

---

1. The press release stated, for example, that the respondent had defied his superiors by attending legislative committee meetings when college officials had specifically refused to permit him to leave his classes for that purpose.

2. The petitioners claimed, in their motion for summary judgment, that the decision not to retain the respondent was really based on his insubordinate conduct. See n. 1, *supra*.

The Court of Appeals reversed the judgment of the District Court. First, it held that, despite the respondent's lack of tenure, the nonrenewal of his contract would violate the Fourteenth Amendment if it in fact was based on his protected free speech. Since the actual reason for the Regents' decision was "in total dispute" in the pleadings, the court remanded the case for a full hearing on this contested issue of fact. Second, the Court of Appeals held that, despite the respondent's lack of tenure, the failure to allow him an opportunity for a hearing would violate the constitutional guarantee of procedural due process if the respondent could show that he had an "expectancy" of re-employment. It, therefore, ordered that this issue of fact also be aired upon remand. We granted a writ of certiorari, and we have considered this case along with *Board of Regents v. Roth, ante.*

I

The first question presented is whether the respondent's lack of a contractual or tenure right to re-employment, taken alone, defeats his claim that the nonrenewal of his contract violated the First and Fourteenth Amendments. We hold that it does not.

For at least a quarter-century, this Court has made clear that even though a person has no "right" to a valuable governmental benefit and even though the government may deny him the benefit for any number of reasons, there are some reasons upon which the government may not rely. . . .

. . . [T]his Court has held that a teacher's public criticism of his superiors on matters of public concern may be constitutionally protected and may, therefore, be an impermissible basis for termination of his employment.

For this reason we hold that the grant of summary judgment against the respondent, without full exploration of this issue, was improper.

II

The respondent's lack of formal contractual or tenure security in continued employment at Odessa Junior College, though irrelevant to his free speech claim, is highly relevant to his procedural due process claim. But it may not be entirely dispositive.

We have held today in *Board of Regents v. Roth,* that the Constitution does not require opportunity for a hearing before the nonrenewal of a nontenured teacher's contract, unless he can show that the decision not to rehire him somehow deprived him of an interest in "liberty" or that he had a "property" interest in continued employment, despite the lack of tenure or a formal contract. In *Roth* the teacher had not made a showing on either point to justify summary judgment in his favor.

Similarly, the respondent here has yet to show that he has been deprived of an interest that could invoke procedural due process protection. As in *Roth,* the mere showing that he was not rehired in one particular job, without more, did not amount to a showing of a loss of liberty. Nor did it amount to a showing of a loss of property.

But the respondent's allegations — which we must construe most favorably to the respondent at this stage of the litigation — do raise a genuine issue as to his interest in continued employment at Odessa Junior College. He alleged that this interest, though not secured by a formal contractual tenure provision, was secured by a no less binding understanding fostered by the college administration. In particular, the respondent alleged that the college had a *de facto* tenure program, and that he had tenure under that program. He claimed that he and others legitimately relied upon an unusual provision that had been in the college's official Faculty Guide for many years:

> "*Teacher Tenure:* Odessa College has no tenure system. The Administration of the College wishes the faculty member to feel that he has permanent tenure as long as his teaching services are satisfactory and as long as he displays a cooperative attitude toward his co-workers and his superiors, and as long as he is happy in his work."

Moreover, the respondent claimed legitimate reliance upon guidelines promulgated by the Coordinating Board of the Texas College and University System that provided that a person, like himself, who had been employed as a teacher in the state college and university system for seven years or more has some form of job tenure.[6] Thus, the respondent offered to prove that a teacher with his long period of service at this particular State College had no less a "property" interest in continued employment than a formally tenured teacher at other colleges, and had no less a procedural due process right to a statement of reasons and a hearing before college officials upon their decision not to retain him.

We have made clear in *Roth, supra,* that "property" interests subject to procedural due process protection are not limited by a few rigid, technical forms. Rather, "property" denotes a broad range of interests that are secured by "existing rules or understandings." A person's interest in a benefit is a "property" interest for due process purposes if there are such rules or mutually

---

6. The relevant portion of the guidelines, adopted as "Policy Paper 1" by the Coordinating Board on October 16, 1967, reads:

"A. Tenure

"Tenure means assurance to an experienced faculty member that he may expect to continue in his academic position unless adequate cause for dismissal is demonstrated in a fair hearing, following established procedures of due process.

"A specific system of faculty tenure undergirds the integrity of each academic institution. In the Texas public colleges and universities, this tenure system should have these components:

"(1) Beginning with appointment to the rank of full-time instructor or a higher rank, the probationary period for a faculty member shall not exceed seven years, including within this period appropriate full-time service in all institutions of higher education. This is subject to the provision that when, after a term of probationary service of more than three years in one or more institutions, a faculty member is employed by another institution, it may be agreed in writing that his new appointment is for a probationary period of not more than four years (even though thereby the person's total probationary period in the academic profession is extended beyond the normal maximum of seven years). . . .

"(3) Adequate cause for dismissal for a faculty member with tenure may be established by demonstrating professional incompetence, moral turpitude, or gross neglect of professional responsibilities."

The respondent alleges that, because he has been employed as a "full-time instructor" or professor within the Texas College and University System for 10 years, he should have "tenure" under these provisions.

explicit understandings that support his claim of entitlement to the benefit and that he may invoke at a hearing.

A written contract with an explicit tenure provision clearly is evidence of a formal understanding that supports a teacher's claim of entitlement to continued employment unless sufficient "cause" is shown. Yet absence of such an explicit contractual provision may not always foreclose the possibility that a teacher has a "property" interest in re-employment. For example, the law of contracts in most, if not all, jurisdictions long has employed a process by which agreements, though not formalized in writing, may be "implied." 3 A. Corbin on Contracts §§ 561-572A (1960). Explicit contractual provisions may be supplemented by other agreements implied from "the promisor's words and conduct in the light of the surrounding circumstances." *Id.*, at § 562. And, "the meaning of [the promisor's] words and acts is found by relating them to the usage of the past." *Ibid.*

A teacher, like the respondent, who has held his position for a number of years, might be able to show from the circumstances of this service — and from other relevant facts — that he has a legitimate claim of entitlement to job tenure. Just as this Court has found there to be a "common law of a particular industry or of a particular plant" that may supplement a collective-bargaining agreement, so there may be an unwritten "common law" in a particular university that certain employees shall have the equivalent of tenure. This is particularly likely in a college or university, like Odessa Junior College, that has no explicit tenure system even for senior members of its faculty, but that nonetheless may have created such a system in practice.

In this case, the respondent has alleged the existence of rules and under-standings, promulgated and fostered by state officials, that may justify his legit-imate claim of entitlement to continued employment absent "sufficient cause." We disagree with the Court of Appeals insofar as it held that a mere subjective "expectancy" is protected by procedural due process, but we agree that the respondent must be given an opportunity to prove the legitimacy of his claim of such entitlement in light of "the policies and practices of the institution." Proof of such a property interest would not, of course, entitle him to reinstate-ment. But such proof would obligate college officials to grant a hearing at his request, where he could be informed of the grounds for his nonretention and challenge their sufficiency.

Therefore, while we do not wholly agree with the opinion of the Court of Appeals, its judgment remanding this case to the District Court is *Affirmed.*

[Chief Justice Burger filed a concurring opinion; Justices Brennan and Mar-shall filed opinions dissenting in part, and Justice Powell did not participate in the decision.]

QUESTIONS

1. Now what is the first step in determining whether there is a constitutional procedural due process right?
2. Is this the only way to make sense of *Goldberg?* Is it the best way? Does it lead to no protection whatsoever in some cases?
3. What would amount to a liberty interest according to the Court?
4. What amounts to a property interest according to the Court?

5. If state law determines whether or not there is a property interest, does this permit states to circumvent procedural due process requirements by not conferring the entitlement in the first place? Can a state do this by leaving a state agency or officer with broad discretion?

6. Should state courts have the final word on the meaning of state law in this regard? In *Bishop v. Wood*, 426 U.S. 341 (1976), the Supreme Court deferred to a federal trial court's refusal to read a city ordinance to create a property interest under North Carolina law. In a 2-1 decision in *Brotherton v. Cleveland*, 923 F.2d 477 (6th Cir. 1991), a widow was held to have a protected property interest in her deceased husband so as to require some kind of process before his corneas were removed by the county coroner. The majority explained:

> [W]e do not need to determine whether the Supreme Court of Ohio would categorize the interest in the dead body granted to the spouse as property, quasi-property or not property. Although the existence of an interest may be a matter of state law, whether that interest rises to the level of a "legitimate claim of entitlement" protected by the due process clause is determined by federal law. This determination does not rest on the label attached to a right granted by the state but rather on the substance of that right. [Ohio law grants a right to the wife to control the disposal of the husband's body, recognizes that she has a possessory right to his body, and allows a claim for disturbance of his body.] [T]hese rights form a substantial interest in the dead body, regardless of Ohio's classification of that interest. We hold the aggregate of rights granted by the state of Ohio . . . rises to the level of a "legitimate claim of entitlement."

923 F.2d at 481-82.

7. The Supreme Court has not extended procedural due process rights to *applicants* for, as opposed to recipients of, government benefits. In *American Manufacturers Mutual Insurance Co. v. Sullivan*, 526 U.S. 40 (1999), the Court held that an applicant for benefits under Pennsylvania's workers' compensation scheme lacked procedural due process protection. The Court contrasted the case with *Goldberg*, where "the question presented was whether predeprivation notice and a hearing were required before the individual's interest in *continued* payment of benefits could be terminated." *Id.* at 60.

> Respondents' property interest in this case, however, is fundamentally different [from the interest in *Goldberg*]. Under Pennsylvania law, an employee is not entitled to payment for *all* medical treatment once the employer's initial liability is established, as respondents' argument assumes. Instead, the law expressly limits an employee's entitlement to "reasonable" and "necessary" medical treatment, and requires that disputes over the reasonableness and necessity of particular treatment must be resolved *before* an employer's obligation to pay — and an employee's entitlement to benefits — arise. *See* 77 Pa. Stat. Ann. §531(1)(i) (Purdon Supp. 1998) ("The employer shall provide payment . . . for *reasonable* surgical and medical services" (emphasis added)); §531(5) ("All payments to providers for treatment . . . shall be made within thirty (30) days of receipt of such bills and records *unless the employer or insurer disputes the reasonableness or necessity of the treatment*" (emphasis added)). Thus, for an employee's property interest in the payment of medical benefits to attach under state law, the employee must clear two hurdles: First, he must prove that an employer is liable for a work-related injury, and second,

he must establish that the particular medical treatment at issue is reasonable and necessary. Only then does the employee's interest parallel that of the beneficiary of welfare assistance in *Goldberg*. . . .

Respondents obviously have not cleared both of these hurdles. While they indeed have established their initial *eligibility* for medical treatment, they have yet to make good on their claim that the particular medical treatment they received was reasonable and necessary. Consequently, they do not have a property interest — under the logic of their own argument — in having their providers paid for treatment that has yet to be found reasonable and necessary. To state the argument is to refute it, for what respondents ask in this case is that insurers be required to pay for patently unreasonable, unnecessary, and even fraudulent medical care without any right, under state law, to seek reimbursement from providers. Unsurprisingly, the Due Process Clause does not require such a result. [We] conclude[] that respondents' due process claim falters for lack of a property interest in the payment of benefits. . . .

Id. at 60-61. Does the applicant/recipient distinction make sense in light of *Roth?*

8. *Wisconsin v. Constantineau*, 400 U.S. 433 (1971), involved a Wisconsin statute under which a city police chief, without notice or hearing, ordered a notice to be posted in all the liquor stores in the city warning that a particular individual could not buy liquor for a year. The Supreme Court found this to be a violation of procedural due process, noting that "[w]here a person's good name, reputation, honor, or integrity is at stake because of what the government is doing to him, notice and an opportunity to be heard are essential." 400 U.S. at 437. Compare the next case.

9. What should one make of Justice Thurgood Marshall's argument (in dissent) that "every citizen who applies for a government job is entitled to it unless the government can establish some reason for denying the employment"? Given the tens of thousands of positions that the federal, state, and local governments must fill each year, is this a realistic approach? If not, why does Justice Marshall propose such a rule? Could he be concerned not so much about process, but rather about ferreting out invidious government decisions (*e.g.*, refusals to hire based on discriminatory reasons such as race, gender, or religion)? Justice Marshall served as the lead litigator for the NAACP during the height of the civil rights movement and was a tireless advocate for advancing racial equality. He appears to believe that absent a duty to provide every applicant who asks with a statement of reasons, government might act for bad reasons.

PAUL v. DAVIS
424 U.S. 693 (1976)

MR. JUSTICE REHNQUIST delivered the opinion of the Court.

We granted certiorari in this case to consider whether respondent's charge that petitioners' defamation of him, standing alone and apart from any other governmental action with respect to him, stated a claim for relief under 42 U.S.C. § 1983 and the Fourteenth Amendment. For the reasons hereinafter stated, we conclude that it does not.

Petitioner Paul is the Chief of Police of the Louisville, Ky., Division of Police, while petitioner McDaniel occupies the same position in the Jefferson County, Ky., Division of Police. In late 1972 they agreed to combine their efforts for the purpose of alerting local area merchants to possible shoplifters who might be operating during the Christmas season. In early December petitioners distributed to approximately 800 merchants in the Louisville metropolitan area a "flyer," which began as follows:

To: Business Men in the Metropolitan Area

> The Chiefs of The Jefferson County and City of Louisville Police Departments, in an effort to keep their officers advised on shoplifting activity, have approved the attached alphabetically arranged flyer of subjects known to be active in this criminal field.
>
> This flyer is being distributed to you, the business man, so that you may inform your security personnel to watch for these subjects. These persons have been arrested during 1971 and 1972 or have been active in various criminal fields in high density shopping areas.
>
> Only the photograph and name of the subject is shown on this flyer, if additional information is desired, please forward a request in writing. . . .

The flyer consisted of five pages of "mug shot" photos, arranged alphabetically. Each page was headed: "NOVEMBER 1972 CITY OF LOUISVILLE & JEFFERSON COUNTY POLICE DEPARTMENTS ACTIVE SHOPLIFTERS." In approximately the center of page 2 there appeared photos and the name of the respondent, Edward Charles Davis III.

Respondent appeared on the flyer because on June 14, 1971, he had been arrested in Louisville on a charge of shoplifting. He had been arraigned on this charge in September 1971, and, upon his plea of not guilty, the charge had been "filed away with leave [to reinstate]," a disposition which left the charge outstanding. Thus, at the time petitioners caused the flyer to be prepared and circulated respondent had been charged with shoplifting but his guilt or innocence of that offense had never been resolved. Shortly after circulation of the flyer the charge against respondent was finally dismissed by a judge of the Louisville Police Court.

At the time the flyer was circulated respondent was employed as a photographer by the *Louisville Courier-Journal* and *Times*. The flyer, and respondent's inclusion therein, soon came to the attention of respondent's supervisor, the executive director of photography for the two newspapers. This individual called respondent in to hear his version of the events leading to his appearing in the flyer. Following this discussion, the supervisor informed respondent that although he would not be fired, he "had best not find himself in a similar situation" in the future.

Respondent thereupon brought this § 1983 action in the District Court for the Western District of Kentucky, seeking redress for the alleged violation of rights guaranteed to him by the Constitution of the United States. Claiming jurisdiction under 28 U.S.C. § 1343 (3), respondent sought damages as well as declaratory and injunctive relief. Petitioners moved to dismiss this complaint. The District Court granted this motion, ruling that "[t]he facts alleged in this case do not establish that plaintiff has been deprived of any right secured to him by the Constitution of the United States."

Respondent appealed to the Court of Appeals for the Sixth Circuit which recognized that, under our decisions, for respondent to establish a claim cognizable under § 1983 he had to show that petitioners had deprived him of a right secured by the Constitution of the United States, and that any such deprivation was achieved under color of law. The Court of Appeals concluded that respondent had set forth a § 1983 claim "in that he has alleged facts that constitute a denial of due process of law." In its view our decision in *Wisconsin v. Constantineau,* 400 U.S. 433 (1971), mandated reversal of the District Court.

I

Respondent's due process claim is grounded upon his assertion that the flyer, and in particular the phrase "Active Shoplifters" appearing at the head of the page upon which his name and photograph appear, impermissibly deprived him of some "liberty" protected by the Fourteenth Amendment. His complaint asserted that the "active shoplifter" designation would inhibit him from entering business establishments for fear of being suspected of shoplifting and possibly apprehended, and would seriously impair his future employment opportunities. Accepting that such consequences may flow from the flyer in question, respondent's complaint would appear to state a classical claim for defamation actionable in the courts of virtually every State. Imputing criminal behavior to an individual is generally considered defamatory *per se,* and actionable without proof of special damages.

Respondent brought his action, however, not in the state courts of Kentucky, but in a United States District Court for that State. He asserted not a claim for defamation under the laws of Kentucky, but a claim that he had been deprived of rights secured to him by the Fourteenth Amendment of the United States Constitution. Concededly if the same allegations had been made about respondent by a private individual, he would have nothing more than a claim for defamation under state law. But, he contends, since petitioners are respectively an official of city and of county government, his action is thereby transmuted into one for deprivation by the State of rights secured under the Fourteenth Amendment. . . . We . . . pause to consider the result should respondent's interpretation of § 1983 and of the Fourteenth Amendment be accepted.

If respondent's view is to prevail, a person arrested by law enforcement officers who announce that they believe such person to be responsible for a particular crime in order to calm the fears of an aroused populace, presumably obtains a claim against such officers under § 1983. And since it is surely far more clear from the language of the Fourteenth Amendment that "life" is protected against state deprivation than it is that reputation is protected against state injury, it would be difficult to see why the survivors of an innocent bystander mistakenly shot by a policeman or negligently killed by a sheriff driving a government vehicle, would not have claims equally cognizable under § 1983.

It is hard to perceive any logical stopping place to such a line of reasoning. Respondent's construction would seem almost necessarily to result in every legally cognizable injury which may have been inflicted by a state official acting under "color of law" establishing a violation of the Fourteenth Amendment. We think it would come as a great surprise to those who drafted and shepherded the adoption of that Amendment to learn that it worked such a result, and a study of our decisions convinces us they do not support the construction urged by respondent.

II

The result reached by the Court of Appeals, which respondent seeks to sustain here, must be bottomed on one of two premises. The first is that the Due Process Clause of the Fourteenth Amendment and § 1983 make actionable many wrongs inflicted by government employees which had heretofore been thought to give rise only to state-law tort claims. The second premise is that the infliction by state officials of a "stigma" to one's reputation is somehow different in kind from the infliction by the same official of harm or injury to other interests protected by state law, so that an injury to reputation is actionable under § 1983 and the Fourteenth Amendment even if other such harms are not. We examine each of these premises in turn.

A

The first premise would be contrary to pronouncements in our cases on more than one occasion with respect to the scope of § 1983 and of the Fourteenth Amendment. In the leading case of *Screws v. United States,* 325 U.S. 91 (1945), the Court considered the proper application of the criminal counterpart of § 1983, likewise intended by Congress to enforce the guarantees of the Fourteenth Amendment. In his opinion for the Court plurality in that case, Mr. Justice Douglas observed:

> "Violation of local law does not necessarily mean that federal rights have been invaded. The fact that a prisoner is assaulted, injured, or even murdered by state officials does not necessarily mean that he is deprived of any right protected or secured by the Constitution or laws of the United States." 325 U.S., at 108-109.

... Respondent ... apparently believes that the Fourteenth Amendment's Due Process Clause should *ex proprio vigore* extend to him a right to be free of injury wherever the State may be characterized as the tortfeasor. But such a reading would make of the Fourteenth Amendment a font of tort law to be superimposed upon whatever systems may already be administered by the States. We have noted the "constitutional shoals" that confront any attempt to derive from congressional civil rights statutes a body of general federal tort law, a fortiori, the procedural guarantees of the Due Process Clause cannot be the source for such law.

B

The second premise upon which the result reached by the Court of Appeals could be rested—that the infliction by state officials of a "stigma" to one's reputation is somehow different in kind from infliction by a state official of harm to other interests protected by state law—is equally untenable. The words "liberty" and "property" as used in the Fourteenth Amendment do not in terms single out reputation as a candidate for special protection over and above other interests that may be protected by state law. While we have in a number of our prior cases pointed out the frequently drastic effect of the "stigma" which may result from defamation by the government in a variety of contexts, this line of cases does not establish the proposition that reputation alone, apart from some more tangible interests such as employment, is either "liberty" or "property" by itself sufficient to invoke the procedural protection of the Due Process Clause. As we have said, the Court of Appeals, in reaching a contrary conclusion, relied primarily upon *Wisconsin v. Constantineau*, 400 U.S. 433 (1971). We think the correct import of that decision, however, must be derived from an examination of the precedents upon which it relied, as well as consideration of the other decisions by this Court, before and after *Constantineau*, which bear upon the relationship between governmental defamation and the guarantees of the Constitution. While not uniform in their treatment of the subject, we think that the weight of our decisions establishes no constitutional doctrine converting every defamation by a public official into a deprivation of liberty within the meaning of the Due Process Clause of the Fifth or Fourteenth Amendment.

In *United States v. Lovett*, 328 U.S. 303 (1946), the Court held that an Act of Congress which specifically forbade payment of any salary or compensation to three named Government agency employees was an unconstitutional bill of attainder. The three employees had been proscribed because a House of Representatives subcommittee found them guilty of "subversive activity," and therefore unfit for Government service. The Court, while recognizing that the underlying charges upon which Congress' action was premised "stigmatized [the employees'] reputation and seriously impaired their chance to earn a living," *id.*, at 314, also made it clear that "[w]hat is involved here is a congressional proscription of [these employees], prohibiting their ever holding a government job." *Ibid.* . . .

Two things appear from the line of cases beginning with *Lovett*. The Court has recognized the serious damage that could be inflicted by branding a government employee as "disloyal," and thereby stigmatizing his good name. But the Court has never held that the mere defamation of an individual, whether by branding him disloyal or otherwise, was sufficient to invoke the guarantees of procedural due process absent an accompanying loss of government employment. . . .

It was against this backdrop that the Court in 1971 decided *Constantineau*. There the Court held that a Wisconsin statute authorizing the practice of "posting" was unconstitutional because it failed to provide procedural safeguards of notice and an opportunity to be heard, prior to an individual's being "posted." Under the statute "posting" consisted of forbidding in writing the sale or delivery of alcoholic beverages to certain persons who were determined to have become hazards to themselves, to their family, or to the community by reason of their "excessive drinking." The statute also made it a misdemeanor to sell or give liquor to any person so posted.

There is undoubtedly language in *Constantineau*, which is sufficiently ambiguous to justify the reliance upon it by the Court of Appeals:

> "Yet certainly where the state attaches 'a badge of infamy' to the citizen, due process comes into play. *Wieman v. Updegraff*, 344 U.S. 183, 191. '[T]he right to be heard before being condemned to suffer grievous loss of any kind, even though

it may not involve the stigma and hardships of a criminal conviction, is a principle basic to our society.' [sic] *Anti-Fascist Committee v. McGrath,* 341 U.S. 123, 168 (Frankfurter, J., concurring).

"Where a person's good name, reputation, honor, or integrity is at stake *because of what the government is doing to him,* notice and an opportunity to be heard are essential." [400] U.S., at 437 (emphasis supplied).

The last paragraph of the quotation could be taken to mean that if a government official defames a person, without more, the procedural requirements of the Due Process Clause of the Fourteenth Amendment are brought into play. If read that way, it would represent a significant broadening of the holdings of *Wieman v. Updegraff,* 344 U.S. 183 (1952), and *Joint Anti-Fascist Refugee Comm. v. McGrath,* 341 U.S. 123 (1951), relied upon by the *Constantineau* Court in its analysis in the immediately preceding paragraph. We should not read this language as significantly broadening those holdings without in any way adverting to the fact if there is any other possible interpretation of *Constantineau's* language. We believe there is.

We think that the italicized language in the last sentence quoted, "because of what the government is doing to him," referred to the fact that the governmental action taken in that case deprived the individual of a right previously held under state law — the right to purchase or obtain liquor in common with the rest of the citizenry. "Posting," therefore, significantly altered her status as a matter of state law, and it was that alteration of legal status which, combined with the injury resulting from the defamation, justified the invocation of procedural safeguards. The "stigma" resulting from the defamatory character of the posting was doubtless an important factor in evaluating the extent of harm worked by that act, but we do not think that such defamation, standing alone, deprived Constantineau of any "liberty" protected by the procedural guarantees of the Fourteenth Amendment.

This conclusion is reinforced by our discussion of the subject a little over a year later in *Board of Regents v. Roth,* 408 U.S. 564 (1972). There we noted that "the range of interests protected by procedural due process is not infinite," *id.,* at 570, and that with respect to property interests they are

"of course, . . . not created by the Constitution. Rather, they are created and their dimensions are defined by existing rules or understandings that stem from an independent source such as state law — rules or understandings that secure certain benefits and that support claims of entitlement to those benefits." *Id.,* at 577.

While *Roth* recognized that governmental action defaming an individual in the course of declining to rehire him could entitle the person to notice and an opportunity to be heard as to the defamation, its language is quite inconsistent with any notion that a defamation perpetrated by a government official but unconnected with any refusal to rehire would be actionable under the Fourteenth Amendment:

"The state, *in declining to rehire the respondent,* did not make any charge against him that might seriously damage his standing and associations in his community. . . . [sic]

"Similarly, there is no suggestion that the State, *in declining to re-employ the respondent,* imposed on him a stigma or other disability that foreclosed his freedom to take advantage of other employment opportunities." *Id.,* at 573 (emphasis supplied).

Thus it was not thought sufficient to establish a claim under § 1983 and the Fourteenth Amendment that there simply be defamation by a state official; the defamation had to occur in the course of the termination of employment. Certainly there is no suggestion in *Roth* to indicate that a hearing would be required each time the State in its capacity as employer might be considered responsible for a statement defaming an employee who continues to be an employee. . . .

III

It is apparent from our decisions that there exists a variety of interests which are difficult of definition but are nevertheless comprehended within the meaning of either "liberty" or "property" as meant in the Due Process Clause. These interests attain this constitutional status by virtue of the fact that they have been initially recognized and protected by state law, and we have repeatedly ruled that the procedural guarantees of the Fourteenth Amendment apply whenever the State seeks to remove or significantly alter that protected status. In *Bell v. Burson,* 402 U.S. 535 (1971), for example, the State by issuing drivers' licenses recognized in its citizens a right to operate a vehicle on the highways of the State. The Court held that the State could not withdraw this right without giving petitioner due process. In *Morrissey v. Brewer,* 408 U.S. 471 (1972), the State afforded parolees the right to remain at liberty as long as the conditions of their parole were not violated. Before the State could alter the status of a parolee because of alleged violations of these conditions, we held that the Fourteenth Amendment's guarantee of due process of law required certain procedural safeguards.

In each of these cases, as a result of the state action complained of, a right or status previously recognized by state law was distinctly altered or extinguished. It was this alteration, officially removing the interest from the recognition and protection previously afforded by the State, which we found sufficient to invoke the procedural guarantees contained in the Due Process Clause of the Fourteenth Amendment. But the interest in reputation alone which respondent seeks to vindicate in this action in federal court is quite different from the "liberty" or "property" recognized in those decisions. Kentucky law does not extend to respondent any legal guarantee of present enjoyment of reputation which has been altered as a result of petitioners' actions. Rather his interest in reputation is simply one of a number which the State may protect against injury by virtue of its tort law, providing a forum for vindication of those interests by means of damages actions. And any harm or injury to that interest, even where as here inflicted by an officer of the State, does not result in a deprivation of any "liberty" or "property" recognized by state or federal law, nor has it worked any change of respondent's status as theretofore recognized under the State's laws. For these reasons we hold that the interest in reputation asserted in this case is neither "liberty" nor "property" guaranteed against state deprivation without due process of law.

Respondent in this case cannot assert denial of any right vouchsafed to him by the State and thereby protected under the Fourteenth Amendment. That being the case, petitioners' defamatory publications, however seriously they may have harmed respondent's reputation, did not deprive him of any "liberty" or "property" interests protected by the Due Process Clause. . . .

None of respondent's theories of recovery were based upon rights secured to him by the Fourteenth Amendment. Petitioners therefore were not liable to him under § 1983. The judgment of the Court of Appeals holding otherwise is *Reversed.*

MR. JUSTICE STEVENS took no part in the consideration or decision of this case. [Justices Brennan, Marshall and White dissented.]

NOTE

The D.C. Circuit has more recently found that the U.S. Secretary of State violated the procedural due process rights of two Iranian groups that the Secretary had designated as "foreign terrorist organizations" without giving the groups notice of the impending designation or a chance to respond. *Nat'l Council of Resistance of Iran v. Dep't of State,* 251 F.3d 192 (D.C. Cir. 2001). The court rejected the government's argument that the designation process and its consequences did not deprive the groups of life, liberty, or property:

> Like the parties in *Constantineau,* and unlike the parties in *Paul,* petitioners here have suffered more than mere stigmatization. Rather than being posted as drunkards, the petitioners have been designated as foreign terrorist organizations under the [statute]. Rather than being deprived of the previously held right to purchase liquor, they have been deprived of the previously held right to — for example — hold bank accounts, and to receive material support or resources from anyone within the jurisdiction of the United States. Many people . . . would consider these to be rights more important than the right to purchase liquor. We consider at least one of them equally entitled to constitutional protection.
>
> The most obvious rights to be impaired by the Secretary's designation are the petitioners' property rights. Specifically, there is before us at least a colorable allegation that at least one of the petitioners has an interest in a bank account in the United States.

251 F.3d at 204.

QUESTIONS

1. Is the Court's opinion in *Paul v. Davis* persuasive?
2. What about an employee who is dischargeable at will (and who therefore has no property interest under *Roth*) who is fired and slandered at the same time? Would a liberty interest exist on these facts?
3. In *Owen v. City of Independence,* 445 U.S. 622 (1980), a case dealing primarily with the scope of municipal immunity under 42 U.S.C. § 1983, the Supreme Court appeared to answer the question in a footnote. In *Owen,* a city council had released police department investigative reports on the city's police department to the news media, and told the city manager to take action against persons involved in illegal, wrongful, or inefficient activities brought out in the investigative reports. The city manager discharged the city's chief

of police, giving no reason for the dismissal, but merely sending the chief a notice stating that his employment was terminated under the provisions of the city's charter giving the city manager sole authority to remove city employees "when deemed necessary for the good of the service." The Eighth Circuit had held that a "name-clearing" hearing was required by procedural due process, but that the city was immune from liability, since its officials acted in good faith and without malice.

In the Supreme Court, the police chief successfully argued that the city was not immune. In footnote 13, the Court stated,

> Although respondents did not cross petition on this issue, they have raised a belated challenge to the Court of Appeals' ruling that petitioner was deprived of a protected "liberty" interest. We find no merit in their contention, however, and decline to disturb the determination of the court below.
>
> *Wisconsin v. Constantineau* held that [where] a person's good name, reputation, honor, or integrity is at stake because of what the government is doing to him, notice and an opportunity to be heard are essential." In *Board of Regents v. Roth,* we explained that the dismissal of a government employee accompanied by a "charge against him that might seriously damage his standing and associations in his community" would qualify as something "the government is doing to him," so as to trigger the due process right to a hearing at which the employee could refute the charges and publicly clear his name. In the present case, the city — through the unanimous resolution of the City Council — released to the public an allegedly false statement impugning petitioner's honesty and integrity. Petitioner was discharged the next day. The Council's accusations received extensive coverage in the press, and even if they did not in point of fact "cause" petitioner's discharge, the defamatory and stigmatizing charges certainly "[occurred] in the course of the termination of employment." Cf. *Paul v. Davis.* Yet the city twice refused petitioner's request that he be given written specification of the charges against him and an opportunity to clear his name. Under the circumstances, we have no doubt that the Court of Appeals correctly concluded that the city's actions deprived petitioner of liberty without due process of law.

445 U.S. at 633. Four justices explicitly dissented on this issue. 445 U.S. at 659-65 (Powell, J., dissenting). What would be the point of a hearing required in these circumstances?

B.   HOW MUCH PROCESS IS DUE?

MATHEWS v. ELDRIDGE
424 U.S. 319 (1976)

Mr. Justice Powell delivered the opinion of the Court.

The issue in this case is whether the Due Process Clause of the Fifth Amendment requires that prior to the termination of Social Security disability benefit payments the recipient be afforded an opportunity for an evidentiary hearing.

I

Cash benefits are provided to workers during periods in which they are completely disabled under the disability insurance benefits program created by the 1956 amendments to Title II of the Social Security Act. 70 Stat. 815, 42 U.S.C. § 423.[1] Respondent Eldridge was first awarded benefits in June 1968. In March 1972, he received a questionnaire from the state agency charged with monitoring his medical condition. Eldridge completed the questionnaire, indicating that his condition had not improved and identifying the medical sources, including physicians, from whom he had received treatment recently. The state agency then obtained reports from his physician and a psychiatric consultant. After considering these reports and other information in his file the agency informed Eldridge by letter that it had made a tentative determination that his disability had ceased in May 1972. The letter included a statement of reasons for the proposed termination of benefits, and advised Eldridge that he might request reasonable time in which to obtain and submit additional information pertaining to his condition.

In his written response, Eldridge disputed one characterization of his medical condition and indicated that the agency already had enough evidence to establish his disability.[2] The state agency then made its final determination that he had ceased to be disabled in May 1972. This determination was accepted by the Social Security Administration (SSA), which notified Eldridge in July that his benefits would terminate after that month. The notification also advised him of his right to seek reconsideration by the state agency of this initial determination within six months.

Instead of requesting reconsideration Eldridge commenced this action challenging the constitutional validity of the administrative procedures established by the Secretary of Health, Education, and Welfare for assessing whether there exists a continuing disability. He sought an immediate reinstatement of benefits pending a hearing on the issue of his disability. The Secretary moved to dismiss on the grounds that Eldridge's benefits had been terminated in accordance with valid administrative regulations and procedures and that he had failed to exhaust available remedies. In support of his contention that due process requires a pretermination hearing, Eldridge relied exclusively upon this Court's decision in *Goldberg v. Kelly,* 397 U.S. 254 (1970), which established a right to an "evidentiary hearing" prior to termination of welfare benefits. The Secretary contended that *Goldberg* was not controlling since eligibility for disability benefits, unlike eligibility for welfare benefits, is not based on financial need and

1. The program is financed by revenues derived from employee and employer payroll taxes. 26 U.S.C. §§ 3101(a), 3111(a); 42 U.S.C. § 401(b). It provides monthly benefits to disabled persons who have worked sufficiently long to have an insured status, and who have had substantial work experience in a specified interval directly preceding the onset of disability. 42 U.S.C. §§ 423(c)(1)(A) and (B). Benefits also are provided to the worker's dependents under specified circumstances. §§ 402(b)(d). When the recipient reaches age 65 his disability benefits are automatically converted to retirement benefits. §§ 416(i)(2)(D), 423(a)(1). In fiscal 1974 approximately 3,700,000 persons received assistance under the program. Social Security Administration, The Year in Review 21(1974).

2. Eldridge originally was disabled due to chronic anxiety and back strain. He subsequently was found to have diabetes. The tentative determination letter indicated that aid would be terminated because available medical evidence indicated that his diabetes was under control, that there existed no limitations on his back movements which would impose severe functional restrictions, and that he no longer suffered emotional problems that would preclude him from all work for which he was qualified. In his reply letter he claimed to have arthritis of the spine rather than a strained back.

since issues of credibility and veracity do not play a significant role in the disability entitlement decision, which turns primarily on medical evidence.

The District Court concluded that the administrative procedures pursuant to which the Secretary had terminated Eldridge's benefits abridged his right to procedural due process. The court viewed the interest of the disability recipient in uninterrupted benefits as indistinguishable from that of the welfare recipient in *Goldberg*. It further noted that decisions subsequent to *Goldberg* demonstrated that the due process requirement of pretermination hearings is not limited to situations involving the deprivation of vital necessities. *See Fuentes v. Shevin*, 407 U.S. 67, 88-89 (1972); *Bell v. Burson*, 402 U.S. 535, 539 (1971). Reasoning that disability determinations may involve subjective judgments based on conflicting medical and nonmedical evidence, the District Court held that prior to termination of benefits Eldridge had to be afforded an evidentiary hearing of the type required for welfare beneficiaries under Title IV of the Social Security Act. Relying entirely upon the District Court's opinion, the Court of Appeals for the Fourth Circuit affirmed the injunction barring termination of Eldridge's benefits prior to an evidentiary hearing. We reverse. . . .

III

A

Procedural due process imposes constraints on governmental decisions which deprive individuals of "liberty" or "property" interests within the meaning of the Due Process Clause of the Fifth or Fourteenth Amendment. The Secretary does not contend that procedural due process is inapplicable to terminations of Social Security disability benefits. He recognizes, as has been implicit in our prior decisions, that the interest of an individual in continued receipt of these benefits is a statutorily created "property" interest protected by the Fifth Amendment. Rather, the Secretary contends that the existing administrative procedures, detailed below, provide all the process that is constitutionally due before a recipient can be deprived of that interest.

This Court consistently has held that some form of hearing is required before an individual is finally deprived of a property interest. *Wolff v. McDonnell*, 418 U.S. 539, 557-558 (1974). The "right to be heard before being condemned to suffer grievous loss of any kind, even though it may not involve the stigma and hardships of a criminal conviction, is a principle basic to our society." *Joint Anti-Fascist Comm. v. McGrath*, 341 U.S. 123, 168 (1951) (Frankfurter, J., concurring). The fundamental requirement of due process is the opportunity to be heard "at a meaningful time and in a meaningful manner." *Armstrong v. Manzo*, 380 U.S. 545, 552 (1965). Eldridge agrees that the review procedures available to a claimant before the initial determination of ineligibility becomes final would be adequate if disability benefits were not terminated until after the evidentiary hearing stage of the administrative process. The dispute centers upon what process is due prior to the initial termination of benefits, pending review.

In recent years this Court increasingly has had occasion to consider the extent to which due process requires an evidentiary hearing prior to the deprivation of some type of property interest even if such a hearing is provided thereafter. In only one case, *Goldberg v. Kelly*, 397 U.S., at 266-271, has the Court held that a hearing closely approximating a judicial trial is necessary. In other cases requiring some type of pretermination hearing as a matter of constitutional right the Court has spoken sparingly about the requisite procedures. *Sniadach v. Family Finance Corp.,* 395 U.S. 337 (1969), involving garnishment of wages, was entirely silent on the matter. In *Fuentes v. Shevin,* 407 U.S., at 96-97, the Court said only that in a replevin suit between two private parties the initial determination required something more than an ex parte proceeding before a court clerk. Similarly, *Bell v. Burson, supra,* at 540, held, in the context of the revocation of a state-granted driver's license, that due process required only that the pre-revocation hearing involve a probable-cause determination as to the fault of the licensee, noting that the hearing "need not take the form of a full adjudication of the question of liability." More recently, in *Arnett v. Kennedy, supra,* we sustained the validity of procedures by which a federal employee could be dismissed for cause. They included notice of the action sought, a copy of the charge, reasonable time for filing a written response, and an opportunity for an oral appearance. Following dismissal, an evidentiary hearing was provided. 416 U.S. at 142-146.

These decisions underscore the truism that "'[d]ue process,' unlike some legal rules, is not a technical conception with a fixed content unrelated to time, place and circumstances." *Cafeteria Workers v. McElroy,* 367 U.S. 886, 895 (1961). "[D]ue process is flexible and calls for such procedural protections as the particular situation demands." *Morrissey v. Brewer,* 408 U.S. 471, 481 (1972). Accordingly, resolution of the issue whether the administrative procedures provided here are constitutionally sufficient requires analysis of the governmental and private interests that are affected. More precisely, our prior decisions indicate that identification of the specific dictates of due process generally requires consideration of three distinct factors: First, the private interest that will be affected by the official action; second, the risk of an erroneous deprivation of such interest through the procedures used, and the probable value, if any, of additional or substitute procedural safeguards; and finally, the Government's interest, including the function involved and the fiscal and administrative burdens that the additional or substitute procedural requirement would entail. See, e.g., *Goldberg v. Kelly, supra,* at 263-271.

We turn first to a description of the procedures for the termination of Social Security disability benefits, and thereafter consider the factors bearing upon the constitutional adequacy of these procedures.

B

The disability insurance program is administered jointly by state and federal agencies. State agencies make the initial determination whether a disability exists, when it began, and when it ceased. 42 U.S.C. § 421 (a). The standards applied and the procedures followed are prescribed by the Secretary, see § 421 (b), who has delegated his responsibilities and powers under the Act to the SSA. See 40 Fed. Reg. 4473 (1975).

In order to establish initial and continued entitlement to disability benefits a worker must demonstrate that he is unable

"to engage in any substantial gainful activity by reason of any medically determinable physical or mental impairment which can be expected to result in death or which has lasted or can be expected to last for a continuous period of not less than 12 months. . . ." 42 U.S.C. § 423(d)(1)(A).

To satisfy this test the worker bears a continuing burden of showing, by means of "medically acceptable clinical and laboratory diagnostic techniques,"§ 423 (d)(3), that he has a physical or mental impairment of such severity that

> "he is not only unable to do his previous work but cannot, considering his age, education, and work experience, engage in any other kind of substantial gainful work which exists in the national economy, regardless of whether such work exists in the immediate area in which he lives, or whether a specific job vacancy exists for him, or whether he would be hired if he applied for work." § 423 (d)(2)(A).

The principal reasons for benefits terminations are that the worker is no longer disabled or has returned to work. As Eldridge's benefits were terminated because he was determined to be no longer disabled, we consider only the sufficiency of the procedures involved in such cases.

The continuing-eligibility investigation is made by a state agency acting through a "team" consisting of a physician and a nonmedical person trained in disability evaluation. The agency periodically communicates with the disabled worker, usually by mail — in which case he is sent a detailed questionnaire — or by telephone, and requests information concerning his present condition, including current medical restrictions and sources of treatment, and any additional information that he considers relevant to his continued entitlement to benefits.

Information regarding the recipient's current condition is also obtained from his sources of medical treatment. DISM [Disability Insurance State Manual] § 353.4. If there is a conflict between the information provided by the beneficiary and that obtained from medical sources such as his physician, or between two sources of treatment, the agency may arrange for an examination by an independent consulting physician. *Ibid.* Whenever the agency's tentative assessment of the beneficiary's condition differs from his own assessment, the beneficiary is informed that benefits may be terminated, provided a summary of the evidence upon which the proposed determination to terminate is based, and afforded an opportunity to review the medical reports and other evidence in his case file. He also may respond in writing and submit additional evidence. *Id.,* § 353.6.

The state agency then makes its final determination, which is reviewed by an examiner in the SSA Bureau of Disability Insurance. 42 U.S.C. § 421 (c); CM §§ 6701 (b), (c). If, as is usually the case, the SSA accepts the agency determination it notifies the recipient in writing, informing him of the reasons for the decision, and of his right to seek de novo reconsideration by the state agency. 20 CFR §§ 404.907, 404.909 (1975). Upon acceptance by the SSA, benefits are terminated effective two months after the month in which medical recovery is found to have occurred. 42 U.S.C. § 423 (a) (1970 ed., Supp. III).

If the recipient seeks reconsideration by the state agency and the determination is adverse, the SSA reviews the reconsideration determination and notifies the recipient of the decision. He then has a right to an evidentiary hearing before an SSA administrative law judge. 20 CFR §§ 404.917, 404.927 (1975). The hearing is nonadversary, and the SSA is not represented by counsel. As at all prior and subsequent stages of the administrative process, however, the claimant may be represented by counsel or other spokesmen. § 404.934. If this hearing results in an adverse decision, the claimant is entitled to request discretionary review by the SSA Appeals Council, § 404.945, and finally may obtain judicial review. 42 U.S.C. § 405(g); 20 CFR § 404.951 (1975). Should it be determined at any point after termination of benefits, that the claimant's disability extended beyond the date of cessation initially established, the worker is entitled to retroactive payments. 42 U.S.C. § 404. If, on the other hand, a beneficiary receives any payments to which he is later determined not to be entitled, the statute authorizes the Secretary to attempt to recoup these funds in specified circumstances. 42 U.S.C. § 404.

C

Despite the elaborate character of the administrative procedures provided by the Secretary, the courts below held them to be constitutionally inadequate, concluding that due process requires an evidentiary hearing prior to termination. In light of the private and governmental interests at stake here and the nature of the existing procedures, we think this was error.

Since a recipient whose benefits are terminated is awarded full retroactive relief if he ultimately prevails, his sole interest is in the uninterrupted receipt of this source of income pending final administrative decision on his claim. His potential injury is thus similar in nature to that of the welfare recipient in *Goldberg*, see 397 U.S., at 263-264, the nonprobationary federal employee in *Arnett*, see 416 U.S., at 146, and the wage earner in *Sniadach*. See 395 U.S., at 341-342.

Only in *Goldberg* has the Court held that due process requires an evidentiary hearing prior to a temporary deprivation. It was emphasized there that welfare assistance is given to persons on the very margin of subsistence:

> "The crucial factor in this context — a factor not present in the case of . . . virtually anyone else whose governmental entitlements are ended — is that termination of aid pending resolution of a controversy over eligibility may deprive an *eligible* recipient of the very means by which to live while he waits." 397 U.S., at 264 (emphasis in original).

Eligibility for disability benefits, in contrast, is not based upon financial need. Indeed, it is wholly unrelated to the worker's income or support from many other sources, such as earnings of other family members, workmen's compensation awards, tort claims awards, savings, private insurance, public or private pensions, veterans' benefits, food stamps, public assistance, or the "many other important programs, both public and private, which contain provisions for disability payments affecting a substantial portion of the work force. . . ." *Richardson v. Belcher*, 404 U.S., at 85-87 (Douglas, J., dissenting). *See* Staff of the House Committee on Ways and Means, Report on the Disability Insurance Program, 93d Cong., 2d Sess., 9-10, 419-429 (1974) (hereinafter Staff Report).

As *Goldberg* illustrates, the degree of potential deprivation that may be created by a particular decision is a factor to be considered in assessing the validity of any administrative decisionmaking process. The potential deprivation here is generally likely to be less than in *Goldberg*, although the degree of difference can be overstated. As the District Court emphasized, to remain eligible for benefits a recipient must be "unable to engage in substantial gainful activity." 42 U.S.C. § 423. Thus, in contrast to the discharged federal employee in *Arnett*, there is little possibility that the terminated recipient will be able to find even temporary employment to ameliorate the interim loss.

As we recognized last Term in *Fusari v. Steinberg,* 419 U.S. 379, 389 (1975), "the possible length of wrongful deprivation of . . . benefits [also] is an important factor in assessing the impact of official action on the private interests." The Secretary concedes that the delay between a request for a hearing before an administrative law judge and a decision on the claim is currently between 10 and 11 months. Since a terminated recipient must first obtain a reconsideration decision as a prerequisite to invoking his right to an evidentiary hearing, the delay between the actual cutoff of benefits and final decision after a hearing exceeds one year.

In view of the torpidity of this administrative review process and the typically modest resources of the family unit of the physically disabled worker, the hardship imposed upon the erroneously terminated disability recipient may be significant. Still, the disabled worker's need is likely to be less than that of a welfare recipient. In addition to the possibility of access to private resources, other forms of government assistance will become available where the termination of disability benefits places a worker or his family below the subsistence level. In view of these potential sources of temporary income, there is less reason here than in *Goldberg* to depart from the ordinary principle, established by our decisions, that something less than an evidentiary hearing is sufficient prior to adverse administrative action.

D

An additional factor to be considered here is the fairness and reliability of the existing pretermination procedures, and the probable value, if any, of additional procedural safeguards. Central to the evaluation of any administrative process is the nature of the relevant inquiry. *See Mitchell v. W. T. Grant Co.,* 416 U.S. 600, 617 (1974); Friendly, Some Kind of Hearing, 123 U. Pa. L. Rev. 1267, 1281 (1975). In order to remain eligible for benefits the disabled worker must demonstrate by means of "medically acceptable clinical and laboratory diagnostic techniques," 42 U.S.C. §423(d)(3), that he is unable "to engage in any substantial gainful activity by reason of any *medically determinable* physical or mental impairment. . . ." §423(d)(1)(A) (emphasis supplied). In short, a medical assessment of the worker's physical or mental condition is required. This is a more sharply focused and easily documented decision than the typical determination of welfare entitlement. In the latter case, a wide variety of information may be deemed relevant, and issues of witness credibility and veracity often are critical to the decisionmaking process. *Goldberg* noted that in such circumstances "written submissions are a wholly unsatisfactory basis for decision."

By contrast, the decision whether to discontinue disability benefits will turn, in most cases, upon "routine, standard, and unbiased medical reports by physician specialists," *Richardson v. Perales,* 402 U.S., at 404, concerning a subject whom they have personally examined.[28] In *Richardson* the Court recognized the

---

28. The decision is not purely a question of the accuracy of a medical diagnosis since the ultimate issue which the state agency must resolve is whether in light of the particular worker's "age, education, and work experience" he cannot "engage in any . . . substantial gainful work which exists in the national economy. . . ." 42 U.S.C. § 423(d)(2)(A). Yet information concerning each of these worker characteristics is amenable to effective written presentation. The value of an evidentiary hearing, or even a limited oral presentation, to an accurate presentation of those factors to the decision maker does not appear substantial. Similarly, resolution of the inquiry as to the types of employment opportunities that exist in the national economy for a physically impaired worker

"reliability and probative worth of written medical reports," emphasizing that while there may be "professional disagreement with the medical conclusions" the "specter of questionable credibility and veracity is not present." *Id.*, at 405, 407. To be sure, credibility and veracity may be a factor in the ultimate disability assessment in some cases. But procedural due process rules are shaped by the risk of error inherent in the truthfinding process as applied to the generality of cases, not the rare exceptions. The potential value of an evidentiary hearing, or even oral presentation to the decision maker, is substantially less in this context than in *Goldberg*.

The decision in *Goldberg* also was based on the Court's conclusion that written submissions were an inadequate substitute for oral presentation because they did not provide an effective means for the recipient to communicate his case to the decision maker. Written submissions were viewed as an unrealistic option, for most recipients lacked the "educational attainment necessary to write effectively" and could not afford professional assistance. In addition, such submissions would not provide the "flexibility of oral presentations" or "permit the recipient to mold his argument to the issues the decision maker appears to regard as important." 397 U.S., at 269. In the context of the disability-benefits-entitlement assessment the administrative procedures under review here fully answer these objections.

The detailed questionnaire which the state agency periodically sends the recipient identifies with particularity the information relevant to the entitlement decision, and the recipient is invited to obtain assistance from the local SSA office in completing the questionnaire. More important, the information critical to the entitlement decision usually is derived from medical sources, such as the treating physician. Such sources are likely to be able to communicate more effectively through written documents than are welfare recipients or the lay witnesses supporting their cause. The conclusions of physicians often are supported by X-rays and the results of clinical or laboratory tests, information typically more amenable to written than to oral presentation. Cf. W. Gellhorn & C. Byse, Administrative Law — Cases and Comments 860-863 (6th ed. 1974).

A further safeguard against mistake is the policy of allowing the disability recipient's representative full access to all information relied upon by the state agency. In addition, prior to the cutoff of benefits the agency informs the recipient of its tentative assessment, the reasons therefor, and provides a summary of the evidence that it considers most relevant. Opportunity is then afforded the recipient to submit additional evidence or arguments, enabling him to challenge directly the accuracy of information in his file as well as the correctness of the agency's tentative conclusions. These procedures, again as contrasted with those before the Court in *Goldberg,* enable the recipient to "mold" his argument to respond to the precise issues which the decision maker regards as crucial.

Despite these carefully structured procedures, *amici* point to the significant reversal rate for appealed cases as clear evidence that the current process is inadequate. Depending upon the base selected and the line of analysis followed,

---

with a particular set of skills would not necessarily be advanced by an evidentiary hearing. Cf. 1 K. Davis, Administrative Law Treatise § 7.06, p. 429 (1958). The statistical information relevant to this judgment is more amenable to written than to oral presentation.

the relevant reversal rates urged by the contending parties vary from a high of 58.6% for appealed reconsideration decisions to an overall reversal rate of only 3.3%.[29] Bare statistics rarely provide a satisfactory measure of the fairness of a decisionmaking process. Their adequacy is especially suspect here since the administrative review system is operated on an open file basis. A recipient may always submit new evidence, and such submissions may result in additional medical examinations. Such fresh examinations were held in approximately 30% to 40% of the appealed cases in fiscal 1973, either at the reconsideration or evidentiary hearing stage of the administrative process. In this context, the value of reversal rate statistics as one means of evaluating the adequacy of the pretermination process is diminished. Thus, although we view such information as relevant, it is certainly not controlling in this case.

E

In striking the appropriate due process balance the final factor to be assessed is the public interest. This includes the administrative burden and other societal costs that would be associated with requiring, as a matter of constitutional right, an evidentiary hearing upon demand in all cases prior to the termination of disability benefits. The most visible burden would be the incremental cost resulting from the increased number of hearings and the expense of providing benefits to ineligible recipients pending decision. No one can predict the extent of the increase, but the fact that full benefits would continue until after such hearings would assure the exhaustion in most cases of this attractive option. Nor would the theoretical right of the Secretary to recover undeserved benefits result, as a practical matter, in any substantial offset to the added outlay of public funds. The parties submit widely varying estimates of the probable additional financial cost. We only need say that experience with the constitutionalizing of government procedures suggests that the ultimate additional cost in terms of money and administrative burden would not be insubstantial.

Financial cost alone is not a controlling weight in determining whether due process requires a particular procedural safeguard prior to some administrative decision. But the Government's interest, and hence that of the public, in conserving scarce fiscal and administrative resources is a factor that must be weighed. At some point the benefit of an additional safeguard to the individual affected by the administrative action and to society in terms of increased assurance that the action is just, may be outweighed by the cost. Significantly, the cost of protecting those whom the preliminary administrative process has identified as likely to be found undeserving may in the end come out of the pockets of the deserving since resources available for any particular program of social welfare are not unlimited. See Friendly, *supra*, 123 U. Pa. L. Rev., at 1276, 1303.

But more is implicated in cases of this type than ad hoc weighing of fiscal and administrative burdens against the interests of a particular category of claimants.

---

29. By focusing solely on the reversal rate for appealed reconsideration determinations amici overstate the relevant reversal rate. As we indicated last Term in *Fusari v. Steinberg,* 419 U.S. 379, 383 n. 6 (1975), in order fully to assess the reliability and fairness of a system of procedure, one must also consider the overall rate of error for all denials of benefits. Here that overall rate is 12.2%. Moreover, about 75% of these reversals occur at the reconsideration stage of the administrative process. Since the median period between a request for reconsideration review and decision is only two months, the deprivation is significantly less than that concomitant to the lengthier delay before an evidentiary hearing. Netting out these reconsideration reversals, the overall reversal rate falls to 3.3%.

The ultimate balance involves a determination as to when, under our constitutional system, judicial-type procedures must be imposed upon administrative action to assure fairness. We reiterate the wise admonishment of Mr. Justice Frankfurter that differences in the origin and function of administrative agencies "preclude wholesale transplantation of the rules of procedure, trial, and review which have evolved from the history and experience of courts." *FCC v. Pottsville Broadcasting Co.*, 309 U.S. 134, 143 (1940). The judicial model of an evidentiary hearing is neither a required, nor even the most effective, method of decisionmaking in all circumstances. The essence of due process is the requirement that "a person in jeopardy of serious loss [be given] notice of the case against him and opportunity to meet it." *Joint Anti-Fascist Comm. v. McGrath*, 341 U.S., at 171-172 (Frankfurter, J., concurring). All that is necessary is that the procedures be tailored, in light of the decision to be made, to "the capacities and circumstances of those who are to be heard," *Goldberg v. Kelly*, 397 U.S., at 268-269 (footnote omitted), to insure that they are given a meaningful opportunity to present their case. In assessing what process is due in this case, substantial weight must be given to the good-faith judgments of the individuals charged by Congress with the administration of social welfare programs that the procedures they have provided assure fair consideration of the entitlement claims of individuals. See *Arnett v. Kennedy*, 416 U.S., at 202 (White, J., concurring in part and dissenting in part). This is especially so where, as here, the prescribed procedures not only provide the claimant with an effective process for asserting his claim prior to any administrative action, but also assure a right to an evidentiary hearing, as well as to subsequent judicial review, before the denial of his claim becomes final. Cf. *Boddie v. Connecticut*, 401 U.S. 371, 378 (1971).

We conclude that an evidentiary hearing is not required prior to the termination of disability benefits and that the present administrative procedures fully comport with due process. The judgment of the Court of Appeals is *Reversed*.

[Justice Stevens took no part in the consideration or decision of this case.]

MR. JUSTICE BRENNAN, with whom MR. JUSTICE MARSHALL concurs, dissenting.

For the reasons stated in my dissenting opinion in *Richardson v. Wright*, 405 U.S. 208, 212 (1972), I agree with the District Court and the Court of Appeals that, prior to termination of benefits, Eldridge must be afforded an evidentiary hearing of the type required for welfare beneficiaries under Title IV of the Social Security Act, 42 U.S.C. § 601 *et seq.* See *Goldberg v. Kelly*, 397 U.S. 254 (1970). I would add that the Court's consideration that a discontinuance of disability benefits may cause the recipient to suffer only a limited deprivation is no argument. It is speculative. Moreover, the very legislative determination to provide disability benefits, without any prerequisite determination of need in fact, presumes a need by the recipient which is not this Court's function to denigrate. Indeed, in the present case, it is indicated that because disability benefits were terminated there was a foreclosure upon the Eldridge home and the family's furniture was repossessed, forcing Eldridge, his wife, and their children to sleep in one bed. Tr. of Oral Arg. 39, 47-48. Finally, it is also no argument that a worker, who has been placed in the untenable position of having been denied disability benefits, may still seek other forms of public assistance.

QUESTIONS

1. The government conceded in this case that some amount of process was constitutionally required. Why?
2. What did Goldberg get that Eldridge did not? What are the process rights that Eldridge wanted?
3. What exactly does the Court say should be balanced in determining the extent of process due?
4. In applying the first factor, the private interest, does the Court adequately distinguish *Goldberg*?
5. How should the increase in accuracy be measured? Are medical determinations really as easy to make, and objective, as Justice Powell suggests? On the other hand, how expensive would it be to have a witness room full of medical professionals waiting to testify in Eldridge's benefits hearing? If the net budget for the program is fairly inelastic, would it be a wise use of resources to allocate them to oral testimony and cross examination in appeals, rather than for payments to persons found eligible? Does Justice Powell confuse the interest in accuracy with the cost/benefit analysis of providing oral testimony from medical professionals?
6. How should the governmental interest be judged? Is the government's interest avoiding the payment of benefits to unqualified persons? If so, what happened to the *Goldberg* notion that the government has a significant interest in distributing benefits to needy persons? Is the government's interest the efficient administration of a vast social insurance program? If so, would direct consideration of the cost/benefit effects of more process be appropriate?
7. Does the analysis required by *Eldridge* assume that accuracy in decision making is the primary (or only) goal of procedural due process? Does the analysis minimize the value of preserving personal dignity, power, or good feelings as goals of procedural due process? On the other hand, if the cost of getting every decision exactly right radically increases the cost of administering the program, perhaps it would be more sensible to accept some erroneous decisions if the system works well in the vast run of cases. How does this kind of reasoning compare to *Goldberg*?
8. Is the test too vague? Does it give too much leeway to the courts? Would a set package of constitutional due process procedures be preferable?

CLEVELAND BOARD OF EDUCATION v. LOUDERMILL
470 U.S. 532 (1985)

JUSTICE WHITE delivered the opinion of the Court.

In these cases we consider what pretermination process must be accorded a public employee who can be discharged only for cause.

In 1979 the Cleveland Board of Education, petitioner in No. 83-1362, hired respondent James Loudermill as a security guard. On his job application, Loudermill stated that he had never been convicted of a felony. Eleven months later, as part of a routine examination of his employment records, the Board discovered that in fact Loudermill had been convicted of grand larceny in 1968. By letter dated November 3, 1980, the Board's Business Manager informed

Loudermill that he had been dismissed because of his dishonesty in filling out the employment application. Loudermill was not afforded an opportunity to respond to the charge of dishonesty or to challenge his dismissal. On November 13, the Board adopted a resolution officially approving the discharge.

Under Ohio law, Loudermill was a "classified civil servant." Ohio Rev. Code Ann. § 124.11 (1984). Such employees can be terminated only for cause, and may obtain administrative review if discharged. § 124.34. Pursuant to this provision, Loudermill filed an appeal with the Cleveland Civil Service Commission on November 12. The Commission appointed a referee, who held a hearing on January 29, 1981. Loudermill argued that he had thought that his 1968 larceny conviction was for a misdemeanor rather than a felony. The referee recommended reinstatement. On July 20, 1981, the full Commission heard argument and orally announced that it would uphold the dismissal. Proposed findings of fact and conclusions of law followed on August 10, and Loudermill's attorneys were advised of the result by mail on August 21.

Although the Commission's decision was subject to judicial review in the state courts, Loudermill instead brought the present suit in the Federal District Court for the Northern District of Ohio. The complaint alleged that § 124.34 was unconstitutional on its face because it did not provide the employee an opportunity to respond to the charges against him prior to removal. As a result, discharged employees were deprived of liberty and property without due process. The complaint also alleged that the provision was unconstitutional as applied because discharged employees were not given sufficiently prompt postremoval hearings.

Before a responsive pleading was filed, the District Court dismissed for failure to state a claim on which relief could be granted. *See* Fed. Rule Civ. Proc. 12(b)(6). It held that because the very statute that created the property right in continued employment also specified the procedures for discharge, and because those procedures were followed, Loudermill was, by definition, afforded all the process due. The post-termination hearing also adequately protected Loudermill's liberty interests. Finally, the District Court concluded that, in light of the Commission's crowded docket, the delay in processing Loudermill's administrative appeal was constitutionally acceptable.

The other case before us arises on similar facts and followed a similar course. Respondent Richard Donnelly was a bus mechanic for the Parma Board of Education. In August 1977, Donnelly was fired because he had failed an eye examination. He was offered a chance to retake the examination but did not do so. Like Loudermill, Donnelly appealed to the Civil Service Commission. After a year of wrangling about the timeliness of his appeal, the Commission heard the case. It ordered Donnelly reinstated, though without backpay. In a complaint essentially identical to Loudermill's, Donnelly challenged the constitutionality of the dismissal procedures. The District Court dismissed for failure to state a claim, relying on its opinion in *Loudermill*.

The District Court denied a joint motion to alter or amend its judgment, and the cases were consolidated for appeal. A divided panel of the Court of Appeals for the Sixth Circuit reversed in part and remanded. After rejecting arguments that the actions were barred by failure to exhaust administrative remedies and by res judicata—arguments that are not renewed here—the Court of Appeals found that both respondents had been deprived of due process. It disagreed with the District Court's original rationale. Instead, it concluded that the compelling private interest in retaining employment, combined with the value of presenting evidence prior to dismissal, outweighed the added administrative burden of a pretermination hearing. With regard to the alleged deprivation of liberty, and Loudermill's 9-month wait for an administrative decision, the court affirmed the District Court, finding no constitutional violation.

The dissenting judge argued that respondents' property interests were conditioned by the procedural limitations accompanying the grant thereof. He considered constitutional requirements satisfied because there was a reliable pretermination finding of "cause," coupled with a due process hearing at a meaningful time and in a meaningful manner.

Both employers petitioned for certiorari. In a cross-petition, Loudermill sought review of the rulings adverse to him. We granted all three petitions and now affirm in all respects.

II

Respondents' federal constitutional claim depends on their having had a property right in continued employment. *Board of Regents v. Roth,* 408 U.S. 564, 576-578 (1972); *Reagan v. United States,* 182 U.S. 419, 425 (1901). If they did, the State could not deprive them of this property without due process.

Property interests are not created by the Constitution, "they are created and their dimensions are defined by existing rules or understandings that stem from an independent source such as state law. . . ." *Board of Regents v. Roth, supra,* at 577. *See also Paul v. Davis,* 424 U.S. 693, 709 (1976). The Ohio statute plainly creates such an interest. Respondents were "classified civil service employees," Ohio Rev. Code Ann. § 124.11 (1984), entitled to retain their positions "during good behavior and efficient service," who could not be dismissed "except . . . for . . . misfeasance, malfeasance, or nonfeasance in office," § 124.34.[4] The statute plainly supports the conclusion, reached by both lower courts, that respondents possessed property rights in continued employment. Indeed, this question does not seem to have been disputed below.

The Parma Board argues, however, that the property right is defined by, and conditioned on, the legislature's choice of procedures for its deprivation. The Board stresses that in addition to specifying the grounds for termination, the statute sets out procedures by which termination may take place.[6] The procedures were adhered to in these cases. According to petitioner, "[to] require additional procedures would in effect expand the scope of the property interest itself."

4. The relevant portion of § 124.34 provides that no classified civil servant may be removed except "for incompetency, inefficiency, dishonesty, drunkenness, immoral conduct, insubordination, discourteous treatment of the public, neglect of duty, violation of such sections or the rules of the director of administrative services or the commission, or any other failure of good behavior, or any other acts of misfeasance, malfeasance, or nonfeasance in office."

6. After providing for dismissal only for cause, see n. 4, *supra,* § 124.34 states that the dismissed employee is to be provided with a copy of the order of removal giving the reasons therefor. Within 10 days of the filing of the order with the Director of Administrative Services, the employee may file a written appeal with the State Personnel Board of Review or the Commission. "In the event such an appeal is filed, the board or commission shall forthwith notify the appointing authority and shall hear, or appoint a trial board to hear, such appeal within thirty days from and after its filing with the board or commission, and it may affirm, disaffirm, or modify the judgment of the appointing authority." Either side may obtain review of the Commission's decision in the State Court of Common Pleas.

This argument, which was accepted by the District Court, has its genesis in the plurality opinion in *Arnett v. Kennedy,* 416 U.S. 134 (1974). *Arnett* involved a challenge by a former federal employee to the procedures by which he was dismissed. The plurality reasoned that where the legislation conferring the substantive right also sets out the procedural mechanism for enforcing that right, the two cannot be separated:

> "The employee's statutorily defined right is not a guarantee against removal without cause in the abstract, but such a guarantee as enforced by the procedures which Congress has designated for the determination of cause. . . .
>
> "[Where] the grant of a substantive right is inextricably intertwined with the limitations on the procedures which are to be employed in determining that right, a litigant in the position of appellee must take the bitter with the sweet." *Id.,* at 152-54.

This view garnered three votes in *Arnett,* but was specifically rejected by the other six Justices. *See id.,* at 166-167 (Powell, J., joined by Blackmun, J.,); *id.,* at 177-178, 185 (White, J.,); *id.,* at 211 (Marshall, J., joined by Douglas and Brennan, JJ.). Since then, this theory has at times seemed to gather some additional support. More recently, however, the Court has clearly rejected it. In *Vitek v. Jones,* 445 U.S. 480, 491 (1980), we pointed out that "minimum [procedural] requirements [are] a matter of federal law, they are not diminished by the fact that the State may have specified its own procedures that it may deem adequate for determining the preconditions to adverse official action." This conclusion was reiterated in *Logan v. Zimmerman Brush Co.,* 455 U.S. 422, 432 (1982), where we reversed the lower court's holding that because the entitlement arose from a state statute, the legislature had the prerogative to define the procedures to be followed to protect that entitlement.

In light of these holdings, it is settled that the "bitter with the sweet" approach misconceives the constitutional guarantee. If a clearer holding is needed, we provide it today. The point is straightforward: the Due Process Clause provides that certain substantive rights — life, liberty, and property — cannot be deprived except pursuant to constitutionally adequate procedures. The categories of substance and procedure are distinct. Were the rule otherwise, the Clause would be reduced to a mere tautology. "Property" cannot be defined by the procedures provided for its deprivation any more than can life or liberty. The right to due process "is conferred, not by legislative grace, but by constitutional guarantee. While the legislature may elect not to confer a property interest in [public] employment, it may not constitutionally authorize the deprivation of such an interest, once conferred, without appropriate procedural safeguards." *Arnett v. Kennedy, supra,* at 167 (Powell, J., concurring in part and concurring in result in part); *see id.,* at 185 (White, J., concurring in part and dissenting in part).

In short, once it is determined that the Due Process Clause applies, "the question remains what process is due." *Morrissey v. Brewer,* 408 U.S. 471, 481 (1972). The answer to that question is not to be found in the Ohio statute.

III

An essential principle of due process is that a deprivation of life, liberty, or property "be preceded by notice and opportunity for hearing appropriate to the nature of the case." *Mullane v. Central Hanover Bank & Trust Co.,* 339 U.S. 306, 313 (1950). We have described "the root requirement" of the Due Process Clause as being "that an individual be given an opportunity for a hearing *before* he is deprived of any significant property interest."[7] *Boddie v. Connecticut,* 401 U.S. 371, 379 (1971) (emphasis in original); *see Bell v. Burson,* 402 U.S. 535, 542 (1971). This principle requires "some kind of a hearing" prior to the discharge of an employee who has a constitutionally protected property interest in his employment. *Board of Regents v. Roth,* 408 U.S., at 569-570; *Perry v. Sindermann,* 408 U.S. 593, 599 (1972). . . . Even decisions finding no constitutional violation in termination procedures have relied on the existence of some pretermination opportunity to respond. For example, in *Arnett* six Justices found constitutional minima satisfied where the employee had access to the material upon which the charge was based and could respond orally and in writing and present rebuttal affidavits. *See also Barry v. Barchi,* 443 U.S. 55, 65 (1979) (no due process violation where horse trainer whose license was suspended "was given more than one opportunity to present his side of the story").

The need for some form of pretermination hearing, recognized in these cases, is evident from a balancing of the competing interests at stake. These are the private interest in retaining employment, the governmental interest in the expeditious removal of unsatisfactory employees and the avoidance of administrative burdens, and the risk of an erroneous termination. *See Mathews v. Eldridge,* 424 U.S. 319, 335 (1976).

First, the significance of the private interest in retaining employment cannot be gainsaid. We have frequently recognized the severity of depriving a person of the means of livelihood. *See Fusari v. Steinberg,* 419 U.S. 379, 389 (1975); *Bell v. Burson, supra,* at 539; *Goldberg v. Kelly,* 397 U.S. 254, 264 (1970); *Sniadach v. Family Finance Corp.,* 395 U.S. 337, 340 (1969). While a fired worker may find employment elsewhere, doing so will take some time and is likely to be burdened by the questionable circumstances under which he left his previous job. *See Lefkowitz v. Turley,* 414 U.S. 70, 83-84 (1973).

Second, some opportunity for the employee to present his side of the case is recurringly of obvious value in reaching an accurate decision. Dismissals for cause will often involve factual disputes. Cf. *Califano v. Yamasaki,* 442 U.S. 682, 686 (1979). Even where the facts are clear, the appropriateness or necessity of the discharge may not be; in such cases, the only meaningful opportunity to invoke the discretion of the decision maker is likely to be before the termination takes effect. See *Goss v. Lopez,* 419 U.S., at 583-584; *Gagnon v. Scarpelli,* 411 U.S. 778, 784-786 (1973).[8]

---

7. There are, of course, some situations in which a postdeprivation hearing will satisfy due process requirements. See *Ewing v. Mytinger & Casselberry, Inc.,* 339 U.S. 594 (1950); *North American Cold Storage Co. v. Chicago,* 211 U.S. 306 (1908).

8. This is not to say that where state conduct is entirely discretionary the Due Process Clause is brought into play. See *Meachum v. Fano,* 427 U.S. 215, 228 (1976). Nor is it to say that a person can insist on a hearing in order to argue that the decision maker should be lenient and depart from legal requirements. *See Dixon v. Love,* 431 U.S. 105, 114 (1977). The point is that where there is an entitlement, a prior hearing facilitates the consideration of whether a permissible course of action is also an appropriate one. This is one way in which providing "effective notice and informal hearing permitting the [employee] to give his version of the events will provide a meaningful hedge against erroneous action. At least the [employer] will be alerted to the existence of disputes about facts and arguments about cause and effect. . . . [His] discretion will be more informed and we think the risk of error substantially reduced." *Goss v. Lopez,* 419 U.S., at 583-584.

The cases before us illustrate these considerations. Both respondents had plausible arguments to make that might have prevented their discharge. The fact that the Commission saw fit to reinstate Donnelly suggests that an error might have been avoided had he been provided an opportunity to make his case to the Board. As for Loudermill, given the Commission's ruling we cannot say that the discharge was mistaken. Nonetheless, in light of the referee's recommendation, neither can we say that a fully informed decision-maker might not have exercised its discretion and decided not to dismiss him, notwithstanding its authority to do so. In any event, the termination involved arguable issues, and the right to a hearing does not depend on a demonstration of certain success.

The governmental interest in immediate termination does not outweigh these interests. As we shall explain, affording the employee an opportunity to respond prior to termination would impose neither a significant administrative burden nor intolerable delays. Furthermore, the employer shares the employee's interest in avoiding disruption and erroneous decisions; and until the matter is settled, the employer would continue to receive the benefit of the employee's labors. It is preferable to keep a qualified employee on than to train a new one. A governmental employer also has an interest in keeping citizens usefully employed rather than taking the possibly erroneous and counterproductive step of forcing its employees onto the welfare rolls. Finally, in those situations where the employer perceives a significant hazard in keeping the employee on the job,[10] it can avoid the problem by suspending with pay.

IV

The foregoing considerations indicate that the pretermination "hearing," though necessary, need not be elaborate. We have pointed out that "[the] formality and procedural requisites for the hearing can vary, depending upon the importance of the interests involved and the nature of the subsequent proceedings." *Boddie v. Connecticut*, 401 U.S., at 378. *See Cafeteria Workers v. McElroy*, 367 U.S. 886, 894-N95 (1961). In general, "something less" than a full evidentiary hearing is sufficient prior to adverse administrative action. *Mathews v. Eldridge*, 424 U.S., at 343. Under state law, respondents were later entitled to a full administrative hearing and judicial review. The only question is what steps were required before the termination took effect.

In only one case, *Goldberg v. Kelly*, 397 U.S. 254 (1970), has the Court required a full adversarial evidentiary hearing prior to adverse governmental action. However, as the *Goldberg* Court itself pointed out, see *id.*, at 264, that case presented significantly different considerations than are present in the context of public employment. Here, the pretermination hearing need not definitively resolve the propriety of the discharge. It should be an initial check against mistaken decisions — essentially, a determination of whether there are

---

10. In the cases before us, no such danger seems to have existed. The examination Donnelly failed was related to driving school buses, not repairing them. As the Court of Appeals stated, "[n]o emergency was even conceivable with respect to Donnelly." As for Loudermill, petitioner states that "to find that we have a person who is an ex-felon as our security guard is very distressful to us." But the termination was based on the presumed misrepresentation on the employment form, not on the felony conviction. In fact, Ohio law provides that an employee "shall not be disciplined for acts," including criminal convictions, occurring more than two years previously. Petitioner concedes that Loudermill's job performance was fully satisfactory.

reasonable grounds to believe that the charges against the employee are true and support the proposed action. See *Bell v. Burson,* 402 U.S., at 540.

The essential requirements of due process, and all that respondents seek or the Court of Appeals required, are notice and an opportunity to respond. The opportunity to present reasons, either in person or in writing, why proposed action should not be taken is a fundamental due process requirement. *See* Friendly, "Some Kind of Hearing," 123 U. Pa. L. Rev. 1267, 1281 (1975). The tenured public employee is entitled to oral or written notice of the charges against him, an explanation of the employer's evidence, and an opportunity to present his side of the story. See *Arnett v. Kennedy,* 416 U.S., at 170-171 (opinion of Powell, J.); *id.,* at 195-196 (opinion of White, J.); see also *Goss v. Lopez,* 419 U.S., at 581. To require more than this prior to termination would intrude to an unwarranted extent on the government's interest in quickly removing an unsatisfactory employee.

V

Our holding rests in part on the provisions in Ohio law for a full post-termination hearing. In his cross-petition Loudermill asserts, as a separate constitutional violation, that his administrative proceedings took too long. The Court of Appeals held otherwise, and we agree. The Due Process Clause requires provision of a hearing "at a meaningful time." At some point, a delay in the post-termination hearing would become a constitutional violation. In the present case, however, the complaint merely recites the course of proceedings and concludes that the denial of a "speedy resolution" violated due process. This reveals nothing about the delay except that it stemmed in part from the thoroughness of the procedures. A 9-month adjudication is not, of course, unconstitutionally lengthy *per se.* Yet Loudermill offers no indication that his wait was unreasonably prolonged other than the fact that it took nine months. The chronology of the proceedings set out in the complaint, coupled with the assertion that nine months is too long to wait, does not state a claim of a constitutional deprivation.[13]

VI

We conclude that all the process that is due is provided by a pretermination opportunity to respond, coupled with post-termination administrative procedures as provided by the Ohio statute. Because respondents allege in their complaints that they had no chance to respond, the District Court erred in dismissing for failure to state a claim. The judgment of the Court of Appeals is affirmed, and the case is remanded for further proceedings consistent with this opinion. *So ordered.*

[Justice Marshall concurred in part and concurred in the judgment. Justice Brennan concurred in part and dissented in part.]

13. The cross-petition also argues that Loudermill was unconstitutionally deprived of liberty because of the accusation of dishonesty that hung over his head during the administrative proceedings. As the Court of Appeals found the failure to allege that the reasons for the dismissal were published dooms this claim. *See Bishop v. Wood,* 426 U.S. 341, 348 (1976).

JUSTICE REHNQUIST, dissenting.

In *Arnett v. Kennedy,* 416 U.S. 134 (1974), six Members of this Court agreed that a public employee could be dismissed for misconduct without a full hearing prior to termination. A plurality of Justices agreed that the employee was entitled to exactly what Congress gave him, and no more. The CHIEF JUSTICE, JUSTICE STEWART, and I said:

> "Here appellee did have a statutory expectancy that he not be removed other than for "such cause as will promote the efficiency of [the] service." But the very section of the statute which granted him that right, a right which had previously existed only by virtue of administrative regulation, expressly provided also for the procedure by which "cause" was to be determined, and expressly omitted the procedural guarantees which appellee insists are mandated by the Constitution. Only by bifurcating the very sentence of the Act of Congress which conferred upon appellee the right not to be removed save for cause could it be said that he had an expectancy of that substantive right without the procedural limitations which Congress attached to it. In the area of federal regulation of government employees, where in the absence of statutory limitation the governmental employer has had virtually uncontrolled latitude in decisions as to hiring and firing, *Cafeteria Workers v. McElroy,* 367 U.S. 886, 896-897 (1961), we do not believe that a statutory enactment such as the Lloyd-La Follette Act may be parsed as discretely as appellee urges. Congress was obviously intent on according a measure of statutory job security to governmental employees which they had not previously enjoyed, but was likewise intent on excluding more elaborate procedural requirements which it felt would make the operation of the new scheme unnecessarily burdensome in practice. Where the focus of legislation was thus strongly on the procedural mechanism for enforcing the substantive right which was simultaneously conferred, we decline to conclude that the substantive right may be viewed wholly apart from the procedure provided for its enforcement. The employee's statutorily defined right is not a guarantee against removal without cause in the abstract, but such a guarantee as enforced by the procedures which Congress has designated for the determination of cause." *Id.,* at 151-152.

In these cases, the relevant Ohio statute provides in its first paragraph that

> "[the] tenure of every officer or employee in the classified service of the state and the counties, civil service townships, cities, city health districts, general health districts, and city school districts thereof, holding a position under this chapter of the Revised Code, shall be during good behavior and efficient service and no such officer or employee shall be reduced in pay or position, suspended, or removed, except . . . for incompetency, inefficiency, dishonesty, drunkenness, immoral conduct, insubordination, discourteous treatment of the public, neglect of duty, violation of such sections or the rules of the director of administrative services or the commission, or any other failure of good behavior, or any other acts of misfeasance, malfeasance, or nonfeasance in office." Ohio Rev. Code Ann. § 124.32 (1984).

The very next paragraph of this section of the Ohio Revised Code provides that in the event of suspension of more than three days or removal the appointing authority shall furnish the employee with the stated reasons for his removal. The next paragraph provides that within 10 days following the receipt of such a statement, the employee may appeal in writing to the State Personnel Board of Review or the Commission, such appeal shall be heard within 30 days from the time of its filing, and the Board may affirm, disaffirm, or modify the judgment of the appointing authority.

Thus in one legislative breath Ohio has conferred upon civil service employees such as respondents in these cases a limited form of tenure during good behavior, and prescribed the procedures by which that tenure may be terminated. Here, as in *Arnett,* "[the] employee's statutorily defined right is not a guarantee against removal without cause in the abstract, but such a guarantee as enforced by the procedures which [the Ohio Legislature] has designated for the determination of cause." 416 U.S., at 152 (opinion of Rehnquist, J.). We stated in *Board of Regents v. Roth,* 408 U.S. 564, 577 (1972):

> "Property interests, of course, are not created by the Constitution. Rather, they are created and their dimensions are defined by existing rules or understandings that stem from an independent source such as state law — rules or understandings that secure certain benefits and that support claims of entitlement to those benefits."

We ought to recognize the totality of the State's definition of the property right in question, and not merely seize upon one of several paragraphs in a unitary statute to proclaim that in that paragraph the State has inexorably conferred upon a civil service employee something which it is powerless under the United States Constitution to qualify in the next paragraph of the statute. This practice ignores our duty under *Roth* to rely on state law as the source of property interests for purposes of applying the Due Process Clause of the Fourteenth Amendment. While it does not impose a federal definition of property, the Court departs from the full breadth of the holding in *Roth* by its selective choice from among the sentences the Ohio Legislature chooses to use in establishing and qualifying a right.

Having concluded by this somewhat tortured reasoning that Ohio has created a property right in the respondents in these cases, the Court naturally proceeds to inquire what process is "due" before the respondents may be divested of that right. This customary "balancing" inquiry conducted by the Court in these cases reaches a result that is quite unobjectionable, but it seems to me that it is devoid of any principles which will either instruct or endure. The balance is simply an ad hoc weighing which depends to a great extent upon how the Court subjectively views the underlying interests at stake. The results in previous cases and in these cases have been quite unpredictable. To paraphrase Justice Black, today's balancing act requires a "pretermination opportunity to respond" but there is nothing that indicates what tomorrow's will be. *Goldberg v. Kelly,* 397 U.S. 254, 276 (1970) (Black, J., dissenting). The results from today's balance certainly do not jibe with the result in *Goldberg* or *Mathews v. Eldridge,* 424 U.S. 319 (1976).[*] The lack of any

---

[*] Today the balancing test requires a pretermination opportunity to respond. In *Goldberg* we required a full-fledged trial-type hearing, and in *Mathews* we declined to require any pretermination process other than those required by the statute. At times this balancing process may look as if it were undertaken with a thumb on the scale, depending upon the result the Court desired. For example, in *Mathews* we minimized the importance of the benefit to the recipient, stating that after termination he could always go on welfare to survive. 424 U.S., at 340-343; see also *id.,* at 350 (Brennan, J., dissenting). Today, however, the Court exalts the recipient's interest in retaining employment; not a word is said about going on welfare. Conversely, in *Mathews* we stressed the interests of the State, while today, in a footnote, the Court goes so far as to denigrate the State's interest in firing a school security guard who had lied about a prior felony conviction.

Today the Court purports to describe the State's interest, but does so in a way that is contrary to what petitioner Boards of Education have asserted in their briefs. The description of the State's

principled standards in this area means that these procedural due process cases will recur time and again. Every different set of facts will present a new issue on what process was due and when. One way to avoid this subjective and varying interpretation of the Due Process Clause in cases such as these is to hold that one who avails himself of government entitlements accepts the grant of tenure along with its inherent limitations.

Because I believe that the Fourteenth Amendment of the United States Constitution does not support the conclusion that Ohio's effort to confer a limited form of tenure upon respondents resulted in the creation of a "property right" in their employment, I dissent.

QUESTIONS

1. Does Justice White's summary rejection of the "bitter with the sweet" approach advocated by then-Justice Rehnquist — namely permitting government to define a property interest by including specific procedures associated with its protection — represent a cramped view of legislative power?
2. Is it really possible to distinguish between substance and procedure when more procedures mean less money for substantive purposes?
3. Or is there "differential reliance" in the sense that people rely more on substantive provisions than procedural provisions of statutory schemes? If so, how do we know?
4. Is it perhaps sufficient just to say that there is intrinsic value in process? Moreover, would the Due Process Clause give *any* effective protection to state-created property rights if the states enjoyed plenary power to define the procedures associated with their termination?
5. Under the rule announced in *Loudermill,* a government entity is free to create — or not create — a property interest, but it cannot preclude federal court expansion of the procedures associated with burdening or terminating the newly created property interest. Even so, should reviewing courts give any deference to such state-created procedures when considering requirements of procedural due process? Perhaps such procedures could have the power to persuade, if not the power to compel, when analyzing procedural due process claims. Would this constitute a workable compromise approach between the polar approaches advocated by Justice White and Justice Rehnquist?
6. In *State ex rel. Kilburn v. Guard,* 448 N.E.2d 1153 (Ohio 1983), the Ohio Supreme Court found, over a dissent, that an evidentiary hearing was required to determine whether "the deliberate silence of the city and its officials concerning the reasons for Kilburn's dismissal may constitute an employer-created and disseminated false and defamatory impression about Kilburn in connection with his termination, so as to infringe on his right to

---

interests looks more like a makeweight to support the Court's result. The decision whom to train and employ is strictly a decision for the State. The Court attempts to ameliorate its ruling by stating that a State may always suspend an employee with pay, in lieu of a predischarge hearing, if it determines that he poses a threat. This does less than justice to the State's interest in its financial integrity and its interest in promptly terminating an employee who has violated the conditions of his tenure, and ignores Ohio's current practice of paying back wages to wrongfully discharged employees.

liberty." Is this possibility precluded by footnote 13 of the later *Loudermill* decision?

NOTE ON TOWN OF CASTLE ROCK v. GONZALES,
545 U.S. 748 (2005)

In *Town of Castle Rock*, the Supreme Court had to decide whether a Colorado law requiring state and local law enforcement officers to enforce restraining orders in domestic violence cases gave rise to a procedural due process claim when local law enforcement officers failed to enforce such an order and failed to provide predeprivation notice to the person covered by the restraining order at issue. Jessica Gonzales argued successfully before the U.S. Court of the Appeals for the Tenth Circuit that Colorado state law guaranteed enforcement of such orders, thereby creating a legitimate claim of entitlement to enforcement, a kind of property interest. (Gonzales could not argue a substantive due process claim because the Supreme Court, in *DeShaney v. Winnebago County Department of Social Services*, 489 U.S. 189 (1989), had held that substantive due process does not impose any affirmative duty of care on government officials to protect citizens from private acts of violence.) The facts giving rise to the case are horrifying: Jessica Gonzales's husband kidnapped and killed their three daughters; even though Ms. Gonzales contacted local police well before the murders, and even though a valid restraining order prohibited her husband from taking custody of the children, the police did nothing for several hours after she reported to the local police that her children were missing from her home.

Writing for the majority, Justice Scalia rejected the argument that Colorado law created a property interest in enforcement of temporary restraining orders issued in domestic abuse cases:

> Our cases recognize that a benefit is not a protected entitlement if government officials may grant or deny it in their discretion. . . . The Court of Appeals concluded that [a Colorado law, Colo. Rev. Stat. § 18-6-803.5(3)] — especially taken in conjunction with a statement from its legislative history, and with another statute restricting criminal and civil liability for officers making arrests — established the Colorado Legislature's clear intent "to alter the fact that the police were not enforcing domestic abuse restraining orders," and thus its intent "that the recipient of a domestic abuse restraining order have an entitlement to its enforcement." 366 F.3d, at 1108. Any other result, it said, "would render domestic abuse restraining orders utterly valueless." *Id.*, at 1109.
>
> This last statement is sheer hyperbole. Whether or not respondent has a right to enforce the restraining order, it rendered certain otherwise lawful conduct by her husband both criminal and in contempt of court. The creation of grounds on which he could be arrested, criminally prosecuted, and held in contempt was hardly "valueless" — even if the prospect of those sanctions ultimately failed to prevent him from committing three murders and a suicide.
>
> We do not believe that these provisions of Colorado law truly made enforcement of restraining orders *mandatory*. A well established tradition of police discretion has long co-existed with apparently mandatory arrest statutes. . . . Against this backdrop, a true mandate of police action would require some stronger indication from the Colorado Legislature than "shall use every reasonable means to enforce a restraining order" (or even "shall arrest . . . or . . . seek a warrant"), §§ 18-6-803.5(3)(a), (b). . . .

Even if the statute could be said to have made enforcement of restraining orders "mandatory" because of the domestic violence context of the underlying statute, that would not necessarily mean that state law gave *respondent* an entitlement to *enforcement* of the mandate. Making the actions of government employees obligatory can serve various legislative ends other than the conferral of a benefit on a specific class of people. . . .

Respondent's alleged interest stems only from a State's *statutory* scheme — from a restraining order that was authorized by and tracked precisely the statute on which the Court of Appeals relied. She does not assert that she has any common-law or contractual entitlement to enforcement. If she was given a statutory entitlement, we would expect to see some indication of that in the statute itself. Although Colorado's statute spoke of "protected person[s]" such as respondent, it did so in connection with matters other than a right to enforcement. . . .

The creation of a personal entitlement to something as vague and novel as enforcement of restraining orders cannot "simply g[o] without saying." *Post,* at 788 n.16 (STEVENS, J., dissenting). We conclude that Colorado has not created such an entitlement.

Even if we were to think otherwise concerning the creation of an entitlement by Colorado, it is by no means clear that an individual entitlement to enforcement of a restraining order could constitute a "property" interest for purposes of the Due Process Clause. Such a right would not, of course, resemble any traditional conception of property. Although that alone does not disqualify it from due process protection, as *Roth* and its progeny show, the right to have a restraining order enforced does not "have some ascertainable monetary value," even as our "*Roth*-type property-as-entitlement" cases have implicitly required. Merrill, The Landscape of Constitutional Property, 86 Va. L. Rev. 885, 964 (2000). Perhaps most radically, the alleged property interest here arises *incidentally,* not out of some new species of government benefit or service, but out of a function that government actors have always performed — to wit, arresting people who they have probable cause to believe have committed a criminal offense. . . .

We conclude, therefore, that respondent did not, for purposes of the Due Process Clause, have a property interest in police enforcement of the restraining order against her husband.

545 U.S. at 756, 759-61, 764-68.

Justice Souter, joined by Justice Breyer, concurred in Justice Scalia's opinion for the majority. Although he "agree[d] with the Court that Jessica Gonzales has shown no violation of an interest protected by the Fourteenth Amendment's Due Process Clause," *Id.* at 769 (Souter, J. concurring), he wrote separately to emphasize that, in addition to the majority's argument premised on the traditional discretion police have enjoyed to enforce (or not enforce) restraining orders, "a further reason appears for rejecting [the plaintiff's] call to apply *Roth,* a reason that would apply even if the statutory mandates to the police were absolute, leaving the police with no discretion when the beneficiary of a protective order insists upon enforcement." *Id.* at 771.

Justice Souter explained that:

The Due Process Clause extends procedural protection to guard against unfair deprivations by state officials of substantive state-law property rights or entitlements; the federal process protects the property created by state law. But Gonzales claims a property interest in a state-mandated process in and of itself. This argument is at odds with the rule that "[p]rocess is not an end in itself. Its constitutional purpose is to protect a substantive interest to which the individual has a legitimate claim of entitlement." . . . Just as a State cannot diminish a property right, once conferred, by attaching less than generous procedure to its deprivation, neither does a state create a property right merely by ordaining beneficial procedure unconnected to some articulable substantive guarantee. This is not to say that state rules of executive procedure may not provide some significant reasons to infer an articulable property right meant to be protected; but it is to say that we have not identified property with procedures as such. State rules of executive procedure, however important, may be nothing more than rules of executive procedure. . . .

Finally, Justice Stevens, joined by Justice Ginsburg, dissented. Justice Stevens argued that the real issue was "whether the restraining order entered by the Colorado trial court on June 4, 1999, created a 'property' interest that is protected from arbitrary deprivation by the Due Process Clause of the Fourteenth Amendment." *Id.* at 773 (Stevens, J., dissenting). With respect to this question, Justice Stevens argued that:

Police enforcement of a restraining order is a government service that is no less concrete and no less valuable than other government services, such as education. The relative novelty of recognizing this type of property interest is explained by the relative novelty of the domestic violence statutes creating a mandatory arrest duty; before this innovation, the unfettered discretion that characterized police enforcement defeated any citizen's "legitimate claim of entitlement" to this service. Novel or not, respondent's claim finds strong support in the principles that underlie our due process jurisprudence. In this case, Colorado law *guarantees* the provision of a certain service, in certain defined circumstances, to a certain class of beneficiaries, and respondents reasonably relied on that guarantee. . . . Surely, if respondent had contracted with a private security firm to provide her and her daughters with protection from her husband, it would be apparent that she possessed a property interest in such a contract. Here, Colorado undertook a comparable obligation, and respondent—with restraining order in hand—justifiably relied on that undertaking. Respondent's claim of entitlement to this promised service is no less legitimate than the other claims our cases have upheld, and no less concrete than a hypothetical agreement with a private firm. The fact that it is based on a statutory enactment and a judicial order entered for her special protection, rather than on a formal contract, does not provide a principled basis for refusing to consider it "property" worthy of constitutional protection.

Because respondent had a property interest in the enforcement of the restraining order, state officials could not deprive her of that interest without observing fair procedures. Her description of the police behavior in this case and the department's callous policy of failing to respond properly to reports of restraining order violations clearly alleges a due process violation. At the very least, due process requires that the relevant state decision maker *listen* to the claimant and then *apply the relevant criteria* in reaching his decisions. The failure to observe these minimal procedural safeguards creates an unacceptable risk of arbitrary and "erroneous deprivation[s]," *Mathews*, 424 U.S., at 335.

Id. at 790-93.

QUESTIONS

1.   Does Justice Scalia's argument that Gonzales lacked a valid property interest rest on the text of the relevant Colorado statute? The tradition of police discretion to act (or not)? Both?
2.   What kind of legislative language would Colorado's legislature be required to use in order to create a legitimate claim of entitlement to enforcement of domestic violence-related restraining orders? Must Colorado legislate a tort action against police officers directly? What language short of an overt cause of action would meet Justice Scalia's concerns?
3.   Is Justice Souter correct to argue that Gonzalez was essentially claiming a property interest in process itself? If the state creates a legitimate claim of entitlement to specific consideration of certain requests of its officers, why can't a citizen claim a legitimate claim of entitlement in process? Or does this sort of claim completely collapse the *Roth/Perry* prerequisite?
4.   Is Justice Stevens persuasive when he argues in dissent that Colorado created a legitimate claim of entitlement to security services? If this is what Colorado did (or intended to do), should the statute look more like a social welfare program (e.g., the Social Security Act or the Medicare Act) than a police procedural regulation?
5.   If Colorado expressly created an entitlement to police protection for battered spouses (rather than an obligation to enforce certain judicial restraining orders), would this meet Justice Scalia's and Justice Souter's concerns? Would such an approach better comport with what Justice Steven's seems to have in mind?

INGRAHAM v. WRIGHT
430 U.S. 651 (1977)

Mr. Justice Powell delivered the opinion of the Court.

This case presents questions concerning the use of corporal punishment in public schools: First, whether the paddling of students as a means of maintaining school discipline constitutes cruel and unusual punishment in violation of the Eighth Amendment; and second, to the extent that paddling is constitutionally permissible, whether the Due Process Clause of the Fourteenth Amendment requires prior notice and an opportunity to be heard.

I

Petitioners James Ingraham and Roosevelt Andrews filed the complaint in this case on January 7, 1971, in the United States District Court for the Southern District of Florida. At the time both were enrolled in the Charles R. Drew Junior High School in Dade County, Fla., Ingraham in the eighth grade and Andrews in the ninth. The complaint contained three counts, each alleging a separate cause of action for deprivations of constitutional rights, under 42 U.S.C. §§ 1981-1988. Counts one and two were individual actions for damages by Ingraham and Andrews based on paddling incidents that allegedly occurred in October 1970 at Drew Junior High School. Count three was a class action for declaratory and injunctive relief filed on behalf of all students in the Dade County schools. Named as defendants in all counts were respondents Willie J. Wright (principal at Drew Junior High School), Lemmie Deliford (an assistant principal), Solomon Barnes (an assistant to the principal), and Edward L. Whigham (superintendent of the Dade County School System). [Following a week long trial the] District Court granted [defendants'] motion [to dismiss] as to all three counts, and dismissed the complaint without hearing evidence on behalf of the school authorities.

Petitioners' evidence may be summarized briefly. In the 1970-1971 school year many of the 237 schools in Dade County used corporal punishment as a means of maintaining discipline pursuant to Florida legislation and a local School Board regulation. The statute then in effect authorized limited corporal punishment by negative inference, proscribing punishment which was "degrading or unduly severe" or which was inflicted without prior consultation with the principal or the teacher in charge of the school. Fla. Stat. Ann. § 232.27 (1961). The regulation, Dade County School Board Policy 5144, contained explicit directions and limitations. The authorized punishment consisted of paddling the recalcitrant student on the buttocks with a flat wooden paddle measuring less than two feet long, three to four inches wide, and about one-half inch thick. The normal punishment was limited to one to five "licks" or blows with the paddle and resulted in no apparent physical injury to the student. School authorities viewed corporal punishment as a less drastic means of discipline than suspension or expulsion. Contrary to the procedural requirements of the statute and regulation, teachers often paddled students on their own authority without first consulting the principal.

Petitioners focused on Drew Junior High School, the school in which both Ingraham and Andrews were enrolled in the fall of 1970. In an apparent reference to Drew, the District Court found that "[t]he instances of punishment which could be characterized as severe, accepting the students' testimony as credible, took place in one junior high school." The evidence, consisting mainly of the testimony of 16 students, suggests that the regime at Drew was exceptionally harsh. The testimony of Ingraham and Andrews, in support of their individual claims for damages, is illustrative. Ingraham was subjected to more than 20 licks with a paddle while being held over a table in the principal's office. The paddling was so severe that he suffered a hematoma requiring medical attention and keeping him out of school for several days. Andrews was paddled several times for minor infractions. On two occasions he was struck on his arms, once depriving him of the full use of his arm for a week.

A panel of the Court of Appeals voted to reverse [the district court's decision]. The panel concluded that the punishment was so severe and oppressive as to violate the Eighth and Fourteenth Amendments, and that the procedures outlined in Policy 5144 failed to satisfy the requirements of the Due Process Clause. Upon rehearing, the en banc court rejected these conclusions and affirmed the judgment of the District Court. The full court held that the Due Process Clause did not require notice or an opportunity to be heard. . . .

We granted certiorari, limited to the questions of cruel and unusual punishment and procedural due process.

[In Sections II and III, both omitted, Justice Powell discussed and rejected the Petitioners' Eighth Amendment arguments.]

IV

The Fourteenth Amendment prohibits any state deprivation of life, liberty, or property without due process of law. Application of this prohibition requires the familiar two-stage analysis: We must first ask whether the asserted individual interests are encompassed within the Fourteenth Amendment's protection of "life, liberty or property"; if protected interests are implicated, we then must decide what procedures constitute "due process of law." *Morrissey v. Brewer,* 408 U.S., at 481; *Board of Regents v. Roth,* 408 U.S. 564, 569-572 (1972). *See* Friendly, Some Kind of Hearing, 123 U. Pa. L. Rev. 1267 (1975). Following that analysis here, we find that corporal punishment in public schools implicates a constitutionally protected liberty interest, but we hold that the traditional common-law remedies are fully adequate to afford due process.

A

"[T]he range of interests protected by procedural due process is not infinite." *Board of Regents v. Roth, supra,* at 570. We have repeatedly rejected "the notion that *any* grievous loss visited upon a person by the State is sufficient to invoke the procedural protections of the Due Process Clause." *Meachum v. Fano,* 427 U.S., at 224. Due process is required only when a decision of the State implicates an interest within the protection of the Fourteenth Amendment. And "to determine whether due process requirements apply in the first place, we must look not to the 'weight' but to the *nature* of the interest at stake." *Roth, supra,* at 570-571.

The Due Process Clause of the Fifth Amendment, later incorporated into the Fourteenth, was intended to give Americans at least the protection against governmental power that they had enjoyed as Englishmen against the power of the Crown. The liberty preserved from deprivation without due process included the right "generally to enjoy those privileges long recognized at common law as essential to the orderly pursuit of happiness by free men." *Meyer v. Nebraska,* 262 U.S. 390, 399 (1923); *see Dent v. West Virginia,* 129 U.S. 114, 123-124 (1889). Among the historic liberties so protected was a right to be free from, and to obtain judicial relief for, unjustified intrusions on personal security.

While the contours of this historic liberty interest in the context of our federal system of government have not been defined precisely, they always have been thought to encompass freedom from bodily restraint and punishment. *See Rochin v. California,* 342 U.S. 165 (1952). It is fundamental that the state cannot hold and physically punish an individual except in accordance with due process of law.

This constitutionally protected liberty interest is at stake in this case. There is, of course, a *de minimis* level of imposition with which the Constitution is not concerned. But at least where school authorities, acting under color of state law, deliberately decide to punish a child for misconduct by restraining the child and inflicting appreciable physical pain, we hold that Fourteenth Amendment liberty interests are implicated.[43]

---

43. Unlike *Goss v. Lopez,* 419 U.S. 565 (1975), this case does not involve the state-created property interest in public education. The purpose of corporal punishment is to correct a child's behavior without interrupting his education. That corporal punishment may, in a rare case, have the unintended effect of temporarily removing a child from school affords no basis for

B

"[T]he question remains what process is due." *Morrissey v. Brewer, supra,* at 481. Were it not for the common-law privilege permitting teachers to inflict reasonable corporal punishment on children in their care, and the availability of the traditional remedies for abuse, the case for requiring advance procedural safeguards would be strong indeed.[44] But here we deal with a punishment—paddling—within that tradition, and the question is whether the common-law remedies are adequate to afford due process.

> "'[D]ue process,' unlike some legal rules, is not a technical conception with a fixed content unrelated to time, place and circumstances . . . Representing a profound attitude of fairness . . . 'due process' is compounded of history, reason, the past course of decisions, and stout confidence in the strength of the democratic faith which we profess . . ." *Anti-Fascist Comm. v. McGrath,* 341 U.S. 123, 162-163 (1951) (Frankfurter, J., concurring).

Whether in this case the common-law remedies for excessive corporal punishment constitute due process of law must turn on an analysis of the competing interests at stake, viewed against the background of "history, reason [and] the past course of decisions." The analysis requires consideration of three distinct factors: "First, the private interest that will be affected . . . second, the risk of an erroneous deprivation of such interest . . . and the probable value, if any, of additional or substitute procedural safeguards; and finally, the [state] interest, including the function involved and the fiscal and administrative burdens that the additional or substitute procedural requirement would entail." *Mathews v. Eldridge,* 424 U.S. 319, 335 (1976). Cf. *Arnett v. Kennedy,* 416 U.S. 134, 167-168 (1974) (Powell, J., concurring).

1

Because it is rooted in history, the child's liberty interest in avoiding corporal punishment while in the care of public school authorities is subject to historical limitations. . . .

The concept that reasonable corporal punishment in school is justifiable continues to be recognized in the laws of most States. It represents "the balance struck by this country," *Poe v. Ullman,* 367 U.S. 497, 542 (1961) (Harlan, J., dissenting), between the child's interest in personal security and the traditional view that some limited corporal punishment may be necessary in the course of a child's education. Under that longstanding accommodation of interests, there can be no deprivation of substantive rights as long as disciplinary corporal punishment is within the limits of the common-law privilege.

This is not to say that the child's interest in procedural safeguards is insubstantial. The school disciplinary process is not "a totally accurate, unerring

---

concluding the practice itself deprives students of property protected by the Fourteenth Amendment.

Nor does this case involve any state-created interest in liberty going beyond the Fourteenth Amendment's protection of freedom from bodily restraint and corporal punishment. Cf. *Meachum v. Fano,* 427 U.S. 215, 225-227 (1976).

44. If the common-law privilege to inflict reasonable corporal punishment in school were inapplicable, it is doubtful whether any procedure short of a trial in a criminal or juvenile court could satisfy the requirements of procedural due process for the imposition of such punishment. See *United States v. Lovett,* 328 U.S., at 317-318; cf. *Breed v. Jones,* 421 U.S. 519, 528-529 (1975).

process, never mistaken and never unfair ..." *Goss v. Lopez*, 419 U.S. 565, 579-580 (1975). In any deliberate infliction of corporal punishment on a child who is restrained for that purpose, there is some risk that the intrusion on the child's liberty will be unjustified and therefore unlawful. In these circumstances the child has a strong interest in procedural safeguards that minimize the risk of wrongful punishment and provide for the resolution of disputed questions of justification.

We turn now to a consideration of the safeguards that are available under applicable Florida law.

2

Florida has continued to recognize, and indeed has strengthened by statute, the common-law right of a child not be subjected to excessive corporal punishment in school. Under Florida law the teacher and principal of the school decide in the first instance whether corporal punishment is reasonably necessary under the circumstances in order to discipline a child who has misbehaved. But they must exercise prudence and restraint. For Florida has preserved the traditional judicial proceedings for determining whether the punishment was justified. If the punishment inflicted is later found to have been excessive — not reasonably believed at the time to be necessary for the child's discipline or training — the school authorities inflicting it may be held liable in damages to the child and, if malice is shown, they may be subject to criminal penalties.

Although students have testified in this case to specific instances of abuse, there is every reason to believe that such mistreatment is an aberration. ... Moreover, because paddlings are usually inflicted in response to conduct directly observed by teachers in their presence, the risk that a child will be paddled without cause is typically insignificant. In the ordinary case, a disciplinary paddling neither threatens seriously to violate any substantive rights nor condemns the child "to suffer grievous loss of any kind."

In those cases where severe punishment is contemplated, the available civil and criminal sanctions for abuse — considered in light of the openness of the school environment — afford significant protection against unjustified corporal punishment. Teachers and school authorities are unlikely to inflict corporal punishment unnecessarily or excessively when a possible consequence of doing so is the institution of civil or criminal proceedings against them.[46]

It still may be argued, of course, that the child's liberty interest would be better protected if the common-law remedies were supplemented by the administrative safeguards of prior notice and a hearing. We have found frequently that some kind of prior hearing is necessary to guard against arbitrary impositions on interests protected by the Fourteenth Amendment. ... But where the State

46. The low incidence of abuse, and the availability of established judicial remedies in the event of abuse, distinguish this case from *Goss v. Lopez*, 419 U.S. 565 (1975). The Ohio law struck down in *Goss* provided for suspensions from public school of up to 10 days without "any written procedure applicable to suspensions." *Id.*, at 567. Although Ohio law provided generally for administrative review, Ohio Rev. Code Ann. § 2506.01 (Supp. 1973), the Court assumed that the short suspensions would not be stayed pending review, with the result that the review proceeding could serve neither a deterrent nor a remedial function. 419 U.S., at 581 n. 10. In these circumstances, the Court held the law authorizing suspensions unconstitutional for failure to require "that there be at least an informal give-and-take between student and disciplinarian, preferably prior to the suspension. . . ." *Id.*, at 584. The subsequent civil and criminal proceedings available in this case may be viewed as affording substantially greater protection to the child than the informal conference mandated by *Goss*.

has preserved what "has always been the law of the land," *United States v. Barnett*, 376 U.S. 681 (1964), the case for administrative safeguards is significantly less compelling. . . .

3

But even if the need for advance procedural safeguards were clear, the question would remain whether the incremental benefit could justify the cost. Acceptance of petitioners' claims would work a transformation in the law governing corporal punishment in Florida and most other States. Given the impracticability of formulating a rule of procedural due process that varies with the severity of the particular imposition, the prior hearing petitioners seek would have to precede *any* paddling, however moderate or trivial.

Such a universal constitutional requirement would significantly burden the use of corporal punishment as a disciplinary measure. Hearings — even informal hearings — require time, personnel, and a diversion of attention from normal school pursuits. School authorities may well choose to abandon corporal punishment rather than incur the burdens of complying with the procedural requirements. Teachers, properly concerned with maintaining authority in the classroom, may well prefer to rely on other disciplinary measures — which they may view as less effective — rather than confront the possible disruption that prior notice and a hearing may entail.[50] Paradoxically, such an alteration of disciplinary policy is most likely to occur in the ordinary case where the contemplated punishment is well within the common-law privilege. . . .[51]

. . . In view of the low incidence of abuse, the openness of our schools, and the common-law safeguards that already exist, the risk of error that may result in violation of a schoolchild's substantive rights can only be regarded as minimal. Imposing additional administrative safeguards as a constitutional requirement might reduce that risk marginally, but would also entail a significant intrusion into an area of primary educational responsibility. We conclude that the Due Process Clause does not require notice and a hearing prior to the imposition of corporal punishment in the public schools, as that practice is authorized and limited by the common law. *Affirmed.*

Mr. Justice White, with whom Mr. Justice Brennan, Mr. Justice Marshall, and Mr. Justice Stevens join, dissenting.

Today the Court holds that corporal punishment in public schools, no matter how severe, can never be the subject of the protections afforded by the Eighth Amendment. It also holds that students in the public school systems are not constitutionally entitled to a hearing of any sort before beatings can be inflicted on them. Because I believe that these holdings are inconsistent with the prior decisions of this Court and are contrary to a reasoned analysis of the constitutional provisions involved, I respectfully dissent. . . .

---

50. If a prior hearing with the inevitable attendant publicity within the school, resulted in rejection of the teacher's recommendation, the consequent impairment of the teacher's ability to maintain discipline in the classroom would not be insubstantial.

51. The effect of interposing prior procedural safeguards may well be to make the punishment more severe by increasing the anxiety of the child. For this reason, the school authorities in Dade County found it desirable that the punishment be inflicted as soon as possible after the infraction.

II

The majority concedes that corporal punishment in the public schools implicates an interest protected by the Due Process Clause — the liberty interest of the student to be free from "bodily restraint and punishment" involving "appreciable physical pain" inflicted by persons acting under color of state law. The question remaining, as the majority recognizes, is what process is due.

The reason that the Constitution requires a State to provide "due process of law" when it punishes an individual for misconduct is to protect the individual from erroneous or mistaken punishment that the State would not have inflicted had it found the facts in a more reliable way. *See,* e.g., *Mathews v. Eldridge,* 424 U.S. 319, 335, 344 (1976). In *Goss v. Lopez,* 419 U.S. 565 (1975), the Court applied this principle to the school disciplinary process, holding that a student must be given an informal opportunity to be heard before he is finally suspended from public school.... To guard against this risk of punishing an innocent child, the Due Process Clause requires, not an "elaborate hearing" before a neutral party, but simply "an informal give-and-take between student and disciplinarian" which gives the student "an opportunity to explain his version of the facts." *Id.,* at 580, 582, 584.

The Court now holds that these "rudimentary precautions against unfair or mistaken findings of misconduct," *id.,* at 581, are not required if the student is punished with "appreciable physical pain" rather than with a suspension, even though both punishments deprive the student of a constitutionally protected interest. Although the respondent school authorities provide absolutely *no* process to the student before the punishment is finally inflicted, the majority concludes that the student is nonetheless given due process because he can later sue the teacher and recover damages if the punishment was "excessive."

This tort action is utterly inadequate to protect against erroneous infliction of punishment for two reasons. First, under Florida law, a student punished for an act he did not commit cannot recover damages from a teacher "proceeding in utmost good faith ... on the reports and advice of others," the student has no remedy at all for punishment imposed on the basis of mistaken facts, at least as long as the punishment was reasonable from the point of view of the disciplinarian, uninformed by any prior hearing.[11] The "traditional common-law remedies" on which the majority relies, thus do nothing to protect the student from the danger that concerned the Court in *Goss*—the risk of reasonable, good-faith mistake in the school disciplinary process.

Second, and more important, even if the student could sue for good-faith error in the infliction of punishment, the lawsuit occurs after the punishment has been finally imposed. The infliction of physical pain is final and irreparable; it cannot be undone in a subsequent proceeding. There is every reason to require, as the Court did in *Goss,* a few minutes of "informal give-and-take between student and disciplinarian" as a "meaningful hedge" against the erroneous infliction of irreparable injury. 419 U.S. at 583-584.

---

11. The majority's assurances to the contrary, it is unclear to me whether and to what extent Florida law provides a damages action against school officials for excessive corporal punishment. Giving the majority the benefit of every doubt, I think it is fair to say that the most a student punished on the basis of mistaken allegations of misconduct can hope for in Florida is a recovery for unreasonable or bad-faith error. But I strongly suspect that even this remedy is not available.

The majority's conclusion that a damages remedy for excessive corporal punishment affords adequate process rests on the novel theory that the State may punish an individual without giving him any opportunity to present his side of the story, as long as he can later recover damages from a state official if he is innocent. The logic of this theory would permit a State that punished speeding with a one-day jail sentence to make a driver serve his sentence first without a trial and then sue to recover damages for wrongful imprisonment. . . . There is no authority for this theory, nor does the majority purport to find any, in the procedural due process decisions of this Court. . . .

The majority emphasizes, as did the dissenters in *Goss,* that even the "rudimentary precautions" required by that decision would impose some burden on the school disciplinary process. But those costs are no greater if the student is paddled rather than suspended; the risk of error in the punishment is no smaller; and the fear of "a significant intrusion" into the disciplinary process, is just as exaggerated. The disciplinarian need only take a few minutes to give the student "notice of the charges against him and, if he denies them, an explanation of the evidence the authorities have and an opportunity to present his side of the story." 419 U.S. at 581. In this context the Constitution requires, "if anything, less than a fair-minded school principal would impose upon himself" in order to avoid injustice. *Id.,* at 583.

I would reverse the judgment below.

Mr. Justice Stevens, dissenting.

. . . The constitutional prohibition of state deprivations of life, liberty, or property without due process of law does not, by its express language, require that a hearing be provided *before* any deprivation may occur. To be sure, the timing of the process may be a critical element in determining its adequacy — that is, in deciding what process is due in a particular context. Generally, adequate notice and a fair opportunity to be heard in advance of any deprivation of a constitutionally protected interest are essential. The Court has recognized, however, that the wording of the command that there shall be no deprivation "without" due process of law is consistent with the conclusion that a postdeprivation remedy is sometimes constitutionally sufficient.

When only an invasion of a property interest is involved, there is a greater likelihood that a damages award will make a person completely whole than when an invasion of the individual's interest in freedom from bodily restraint and punishment has occurred. In the property context, therefore, frequently a postdeprivation state remedy may be all the process that the Fourteenth Amendment requires. It may also be true — although I do not express an opinion on the point — that an adequate state remedy for defamation may satisfy the due process requirement when a State has impaired an individual's interest in his reputation. On that hypothesis, the Court's analysis today gives rise to the thought that *Paul v. Davis,* 424 U.S. 693, may have been correctly decided on an incorrect rationale. Perhaps the Court will one day agree with Mr. Justice Brennan's appraisal of the importance of the constitutional interest at stake in *id.,* at 720-723, 734 (dissenting opinion), and nevertheless conclude that an adequate state remedy may prevent every state-inflicted injury to a person's reputation from violating 42 U.S.C. § 1983.

QUESTIONS

1.   What precisely is the rationale of Justice Powell's decision? Have the plain-
     tiffs established the existence of a liberty or property interest? If so, why is the
     state free to abrogate it without any predeprivation process?
2.   If a postdeprivation remedy — in this case a common law tort suit — consti-
     tutes sufficient process for wrongly administered corporal punishment, why
     shouldn't a postdeprivation remedy also be sufficient for a terminated
     public employee?
3.   Is Justice Stevens correct to distinguish between liberty interests and prop-
     erty interests when considering the necessity of predeprivation process? Are
     liberty interests inevitably more incommensurable than property interests?
4.   Is this case really about who should run the schools? Is the majority's
     decision driven by the adequacy of the postdeprivation remedy or concerns
     about turning the federal courts into a super-school board?
5.   Contrast *Paul v. Davis* with *Ingraham*. Did Justice Rehnquist offer the wrong
     rationale for the right substantive result? If a postdeprivation tort remedy
     provides sufficient process to a paddled student, why shouldn't a postdepri-
     vation tort suit against the Louisville police chief also satisfy procedural due
     process concerns? Does Justice Powell's approach of recognizing a liberty
     interest but granting the state great leeway in establishing the procedures
     that will safeguard that interest effectively respond to Justice Rehnquist's
     concern in *Paul* that procedural due process not be turned into a "font of
     tort law"?

NOTE ON GOSS v. LOPEZ, *419 U.S. 565 (1975)*

Some critics of Justice Powell's approach in *Ingraham v. Wright* point to *Goss v.
Lopez* as providing a better general approach for applying the requirements of
procedural due process in the public schools. *Goss* involved the decision of the
Columbus, Ohio Public School System (CPSS) to suspend several students from
school without providing any predeprivation process (not even an informal give-
and-take with a school administrator or teacher). The lower federal court, a
three judge district court, held in the plaintiffs' favor, finding that the CPSS
had failed to provide adequate process before suspending the students. On
direct appeal to the Supreme Court, the questions presented were whether
the students had a cognizable liberty or property interest in attending the public
schools and, if so, whether the CPSS had provided adequate procedural safeguards before suspending the students.

With respect to the first question, whether the students possessed a cognizable
liberty or property interest, Justice White, writing for the majority, concluded
that under Ohio law the students did possess a legitimate claim of entitlement to
a free public education:

> Here, on the basis of state law, appellees plainly had legitimate claims of entitle-
> ment to a public education. Ohio Rev. Code Ann. §§ 3313.48 and 3313.64 (1972
> and Supp. 1973) direct local authorities to provide a free education to all residents
> between five and 21 years of age, and a compulsory-attendance law requires atten-
> dance for a school year of not less than 32 weeks. Ohio Rev. Code Ann. § 3321.04

(1972). It is true that § 3313.66 of the Code permits school principals to suspend students for up to 10 days; but suspensions may not be imposed without any grounds whatsoever. All of the schools had their own rules specifying the grounds for expulsion or suspension. Having chosen to extend the right to an education to people of appellees' class generally, Ohio may not withdraw that right on grounds of misconduct, absent fundamentally fair procedures to determine whether the misconduct has occurred. *Arnett v. Kennedy, supra,* at 164 (Powell, J., concurring), 171 (White, J., concurring and dissenting), 206 (Marshall, J., dissenting). . . .

The Due Process Clause also forbids arbitrary deprivations of liberty. "Where a person's good name, reputation, honor, or integrity is at stake because of what the government is doing to him," the minimal requirements of the Clause must be satisfied. *Wisconsin v. Constantineau,* 400 U.S. 433, 437 (1971); *Board of Regents v. Roth, supra,* at 573. School authorities here suspended appellees from school for periods of up to 10 days based on charges of misconduct. If sustained and recorded, those charges could seriously damage the students' standing with their fellow pupils and their teachers as well as interfere with later opportunities for higher education and employment. It is apparent that the claimed right of the State to determine unilaterally and without process whether that misconduct has occurred immediately collides with the requirements of the Constitution.

Appellants proceed to argue that even if there is a right to a public education protected by the Due Process Clause generally, the Clause comes into play only when the State subjects a student to a "severe detriment or grievous loss." The loss of 10 days, it is said, is neither severe nor grievous and the Due Process Clause is therefore of no relevance. Appellants' argument is again refuted by our prior decisions; for in determining "whether due process requirements apply in the first place, we must look not to the 'weight' but to the *nature* of the interest at stake." *Board of Regents v. Roth, supra,* at 570-571. Appellees were excluded from school only temporarily, it is true, but the length and consequent severity of a deprivation, while another factor to weigh in determining the appropriate form of hearing, "is not decisive of the basic right" to a hearing of some kind. *Fuentes v. Shevin,* 407 U.S. 67, 86 (1972). The Court's view has been that as long as a property deprivation is not *de minimis,* its gravity is irrelevant to the question whether account must be taken of the Due Process Clause. *Sniadach v. Family Finance Corp.,* 395 U.S. 337, 342 (1969) (Harlan, J., concurring); *Boddie v. Connecticut,* 401 U.S. 371, 378-379 (1971); *Board of Regents v. Roth, supra,* at 570 n. 8. A 10-day suspension from school is not *de minimis* in our view and may not be imposed in complete disregard of the Due Process Clause.

Having concluded that the students possessed valid liberty and property interests sufficient to trigger the application of procedural due process rights, Justice White turned to the issue of when and how much process the CPSS owed the suspended students on the facts at bar:

We do not believe that school authorities must be totally free from notice and hearing requirements if their schools are to operate with acceptable efficiency. Students facing temporary suspension have interests qualifying for protection of the Due Process Clause, and due process requires, in connection with a suspension of 10 days or less, that the student be given oral or written notice of the charges against him and, if he denies them, an explanation of the evidence the authorities have and an opportunity to present his side of the story. The Clause requires at least these rudimentary precautions against unfair or mistaken findings of misconduct and arbitrary exclusion from school.

There need be no delay between the time "notice" is given and the time of the hearing. In the great majority of cases the disciplinarian may informally discuss the alleged misconduct with the student minutes after it has occurred. We hold only that, in being given an opportunity to explain his version of the facts at this discussion, the student first be told what he is accused of doing and what the basis of the accusation is. Lower courts which have addressed the question of the *nature* of the procedures required in short suspension cases have reached the same conclusion. Since the hearing may occur almost immediately following the misconduct, it follows that as a general rule notice and hearing should precede removal of the student from school. We agree with the District Court, however, that there are recurring situations in which prior notice and hearing cannot be insisted upon. Students whose presence poses a continuing danger to persons or property or an ongoing threat of disrupting the academic process may be immediately removed from school. In such cases, the necessary notice and rudimentary hearing should follow as soon as practicable, as the District Court indicated.

In holding as we do, we do not believe that we have imposed procedures on school disciplinarians which are inappropriate in a classroom setting. Instead we have imposed requirements which are, if anything, less than a fair-minded school principal would impose upon himself in order to avoid unfair suspensions. Indeed, according to the testimony of the principal of Marion-Franklin High School, that school had an informal procedure, remarkably similar to that which we now require, applicable to suspensions generally but which was not followed in this case. Similarly, according to the most recent memorandum applicable to the entire CPSS, school principals in the CPSS are now required by local rule to provide at least as much as the constitutional minimum which we have described.

Justice Powell filed a dissent joined by Chief Justice Burger and Justices Blackmun and Rehnquist. In *Ingraham v. Wright*, however, Justice Powell was able to secure a majority of five Justices to support the conclusion that even though procedural due process rights attach to corporal punishment, postdeprivation process was a sufficient procedural protection against erroneous decisions.

Obviously *Goss* reflects greater skepticism of the abilities and good faith of public school personnel than does *Ingraham*. The tension between the two cases is clear: Why should a ten-day suspension (at issue in *Goss*) trigger predeprivation procedural due process rights, when a beating with a large wooden paddle (at issue in *Ingraham*) does not? Nevertheless, *both* cases remain good law. Corporal punishment triggers only a postdeprivation hearing requirement, whereas a suspension or expulsion usually triggers a duty to provide some sort of predeprivation hearing.

QUESTIONS

1. Does the *Goss* analysis trivialize procedural due process? Or is Justice White correct to suggest that if cognizable liberty or property rights are at stake, no de minimis exceptions to providing procedural due process should apply?
2. Does *Goss* show that the *Roth* analysis is unsound?
3. Should the federal courts stay out of school altogether? Does Justice Powell (author of *Ingraham*) or Justice White (author of *Goss*) have the better view of how to approach the question of applying procedural due process principles to discipline in the public schools?

4. Does *Goss* show that *Eldridge* is unsound? Does (or should) a mere face-to-face meeting satisfy procedural due process? Does this holding permit or invite minimal due process in more significant areas?

5. Is the analysis so squishy as to be totally unpredictable? Are the facts in *Goss v. Lopez* really distinguishable from the facts in *Ingraham*? If not, what does this say about the ability of *Eldridge* balancing to provide consistent results across cases with similar facts?

KERRY v. DIN
135 S. Ct. 2128 (2015)

JUSTICE SCALIA announced the judgment of the Court and delivered an opinion, in which THE CHIEF JUSTICE and JUSTICE THOMAS join.

Fauzia Din is a citizen and resident of the United States. Her husband, Kanishka Berashk, is an Afghan citizen and former civil servant in the Taliban regime who resides in that country. When the Government declined to issue an immigrant visa to Berashk, Din sued [on behalf of her husband and her own behalf because the decision precluded them from residing together in the United States despite being married].

For the reasons given in this opinion and in the opinion concurring in the judgment, we vacate and remand.

I

Under the Immigration and Nationality Act (INA), 66 Stat. 163, as amended, 8 U.S.C. § 1101 et seq., an alien may not enter and permanently reside in the United States without a visa. § 1181(a). The INA creates a special visa-application process for aliens sponsored by "immediate relatives" in the United States. §§ 1151(b), 1153(a). Under this process, the citizen-relative first files a petition on behalf of the alien living abroad, asking to have the alien classified as an immediate relative. *See* §§ 1153(f), 1154(a)(1). If and when a petition is approved, the alien may apply for a visa by submitting the required documents and appearing at a United States Embassy or consulate for an interview with a consular officer. *See* §§ 1201(a)(1), 1202. Before issuing a visa, the consular officer must ensure the alien is not inadmissible under any provision of the INA. § 1361. . . .

Fauzia Din came to the United States as a refugee in 2000, and became a naturalized citizen in 2007. She filed a petition to have Kanishka Berashk, whom she married in 2006, classified as her immediate relative. The petition was granted, and Berashk filed a visa application. The U.S. Embassy in Islamabad, Pakistan, interviewed Berashk and denied his application. A consular officer informed Berashk that he was inadmissible under § 1182(a)(3)(B) but provided no further explanation.

Din then brought suit in Federal District Court seeking a writ of mandamus directing the United States to properly adjudicate Berashk's visa application; a declaratory judgment that 8 U.S.C. § 1182(b)(2)-(3), which exempts the Government from providing notice to an alien found inadmissible under the terrorism bar, is unconstitutional as applied; and a declaratory judgment that the denial violated the Administrative Procedure Act. App. 36-39, Complaint ¶ ¶ 55-68. The District Court granted the Government's motion to dismiss, but the Ninth Circuit reversed. The Ninth Circuit concluded that Din "has a protected liberty interest in marriage that entitled [her] to review of the denial of [her] spouse's visa," 718 F.3d 856, 860 (2013), and that the Government's citation of § 1182(a)(3)(B) did not provide Din with the "limited judicial review" to which she was entitled under the Due Process Clause, id., at 868. This Court granted certiorari.

II

The Fifth Amendment provides that "[n]o person shall be . . . deprived of life, liberty, or property, without due process of law." Although the amount and quality of process that our precedents have recognized as "due" under the Clause has changed considerably since the founding, it remains the case that no process is due if one is not deprived of "life, liberty, or property[.]" The first question that we must ask, then, is whether the denial of Berashk's visa application deprived Din of any of these interests. Only if we answer in the affirmative must we proceed to consider whether the Government's explanation afforded sufficient process. . . .

[T]his Court has seen fit on several occasions to expand the meaning of "liberty" under the Due Process Clause to include certain implied "fundamental rights." (The reasoning presumably goes like this: If you have a right to do something, you are free to do it, and deprivation of freedom is a deprivation of "liberty" — never mind the original meaning of that word in the Due Process Clause.) These implied rights have been given more protection than "life, liberty, or property" properly understood. While one may be dispossessed of property, thrown in jail, or even executed so long as proper procedures are followed, the enjoyment of implied constitutional rights cannot be limited at all, except by provisions that are "narrowly tailored to serve a compelling state interest." *Reno v. Flores*, 507 U.S. 292, 301-302 (1993). Din does not explicitly argue that the Government has violated this absolute prohibition of the substantive component of the Due Process Clause, likely because it is obvious that a law barring aliens engaged in terrorist activities from entering this country is narrowly tailored to serve a compelling state interest. She nevertheless insists that, because enforcement of the law affects her enjoyment of an implied fundamental liberty, the Government must first provide her a full battery of procedural-due-process protections. . . .

Din describes the denial of Berashk's visa application as implicating, alternately, a "liberty interest in her marriage," Brief for Respondent 28, a "right of association with one's spouse," *id.*, at 18, "a liberty interest in being reunited with certain blood relatives," *id.*, at 22, and "the liberty interest of a U.S. citizen under the Due Process Clause to be free from arbitrary restrictions on his right to live with his spouse," *ibid.* To be sure, this Court has at times indulged a propensity for grandiloquence when reviewing the sweep of implied rights, describing them so broadly that they would include not only the interests Din asserts but many others as well. For example: "Without doubt, [the liberty guaranteed by the Due Process Clause] denotes not merely freedom from bodily restraint but also the right of the individual to contract, to engage in any of the common occupations of life, to acquire useful knowledge, to marry, establish a home and bring up children, [and] to worship God according to the dictates of his own conscience" *Meyer v. Nebraska*, 262 U.S. 390, 399 (1923). But this Court is not bound by dicta, especially dicta that have been repudiated by the holdings of our subsequent cases. And the actual holdings of the cases Din relies upon hardly establish the capacious right she now asserts.

Unlike the States in *Loving v. Virginia*, 388 U.S. 1 (1967), *Zablocki v. Redhail*, 434 U.S. 374 (1978), and *Turner v. Safley*, 482 U.S. 78, the Federal Government here has not attempted to forbid a marriage. Although Din and the dissent borrow language from those cases invoking a fundamental right to marriage, they both implicitly concede that no such right has been infringed in this case. Din relies on the "associational interests in marriage that necessarily are protected by the right to marry," and that are "presuppose[d]" by later cases establishing a right to marital privacy. The dissent supplements the fundamental right to marriage with a fundamental right to live in the United States in order to find an affected liberty interest. Post, at 2142-2143 (BREYER, J., dissenting).

Attempting to abstract from these cases some liberty interest that might be implicated by Berashk's visa denial, Din draws on even more inapposite cases. . . . [But] [n]othing in the cases Din cites establishes a free-floating and categorical liberty interest in marriage (or any other formulation Din offers) sufficient to trigger constitutional protection whenever a regulation in any way touches upon an aspect of the marital relationship. Even if our cases could be construed so broadly, the relevant question is not whether the asserted interest "is consistent with this Court's substantive-due-process line of cases," but whether it is supported by "this Nation's history and practice." *Glucksberg*, 521 U.S., at 723-724 (emphasis deleted). Even if we might "imply" a liberty interest in marriage generally speaking, that must give way when there is a tradition denying the specific application of that general interest. . . .

Here, a long practice of regulating spousal immigration precludes Din's claim that the denial of Berashk's visa application has deprived her of a fundamental liberty interest. Although immigration was effectively unregulated prior to 1875, as soon as Congress began legislating in this area it enacted a complicated web of regulations that erected serious impediments to a person's ability to bring a spouse into the United States. See Abrams, What Makes the Family Special?, 80 U. CHI. L. REV. 7, 10-16 (2013). . . .

Although Congress has tended to show "a continuing and kindly concern . . . for the unity and the happiness of the immigrant family," E. Hutchinson, Legislative History of American Immigration Policy 1798-1965, p. 518 (1981), this has been a matter of legislative grace rather than fundamental right. Even where Congress has provided special privileges to promote family immigration, it has also "written in careful checks and qualifications." *Ibid*. This Court has consistently recognized that these various distinctions are "policy questions entrusted exclusively to the political branches of our Government, and we have no judicial authority to substitute our political judgment for that of the Congress." *Fiallo v. Bell*, 430 U.S. 787, 798 (1977). Only by diluting the meaning of a fundamental liberty interest and jettisoning our established jurisprudence could we conclude that the denial of Berashk's visa application implicates any of Din's fundamental liberty interests. . . .

III

Neither Din's right to live with her spouse nor her right to live within this country is implicated here. There is a "simple distinction between government action that directly affects a citizen's legal rights, or imposes a direct restraint on his liberty, and action that is directed against a third party and affects the citizen only indirectly or incidentally." *O'Bannon v. Town Court Nursing Center*, 447 U.S. 773, 788 (1980). The Government has not refused to recognize Din's marriage to Berashk, and Din remains free to live with her husband anywhere in the world that both individuals are permitted to reside. And the Government has not expelled Din from the country. It has simply determined that Kanishka Berashk engaged in terrorist activities within the meaning of the Immigration and Nationality Act, and has therefore denied him admission into the country. This might, indeed, deprive Din of something "important," *post*, at 2142, but if that is the criterion for JUSTICE BREYER'S new pairing of substantive and procedural due process, we are in for quite a ride. . . .

Because Fauzia Din was not deprived of "life, liberty, or property" when the Government denied Kanishka Berashk admission to the United States, there is no process due to her under the Constitution. To the extent that she received any explanation for the Government's decision, this was more than the Due Process Clause required. The judgment of the Ninth Circuit is vacated, and the case is remanded for further proceedings. *It is so ordered.*

JUSTICE KENNEDY, with whom JUSTICE ALITO joins, concurring in the judgment.

The respondent, Fauzia Din, is a citizen and resident of the United States. She asserts that petitioner Government officials (collectively, Government) violated her own constitutional right to live in this country with her husband, an alien now residing in Afghanistan. She contends this violation occurred when the Government, through State Department consular officials, denied her spouse's immigrant visa application with no explanation other than that the denial was based on 8 U.S.C. § 1182(a)(3)(B), the statutory provision prohibiting the issuance of visas to persons who engage in terrorist activities.

The plurality is correct that the case must be vacated and remanded. But rather than deciding, as the plurality does, whether Din has a protected liberty interest, my view is that, even assuming she does, the notice she received regarding her husband's visa denial satisfied due process.

Today's disposition should not be interpreted as deciding whether a citizen has a protected liberty interest in the visa application of her alien spouse. The Court need not decide that issue, for this Court's precedents instruct that, even assuming she has such an interest, the Government satisfied due process when it notified Din's husband that his visa was denied under the immigration statute's terrorism bar, § 1182(a)(3)(B). See ante, at 2131-2132. . . .

Here, the consular officer's determination that Din's husband was ineligible for a visa was controlled by specific statutory factors. The provisions of § 1182(a)(3)(B) establish specific criteria for determining terrorism-related inadmissibility. The consular officer's citation of that provision suffices to show that the denial rested on a determination that Din's husband did not satisfy the statute's requirements. Given Congress' plenary power to "suppl[y] the conditions of the privilege of entry into the United States," *United States ex rel. Knauff v. Shaughnessy*, 338 U.S. 537, 543 (1950), it follows that the Government's decision to exclude an alien it determines does not satisfy one or more of those conditions is facially legitimate under *Mandel.*

The Government's citation of §1182(a)(3)(B) also indicates it relied upon a bona fide factual basis for denying a visa to Berashk. Cf. *United States v. Chemical Foundation, Inc.,* 272 U.S. 1, 14-15 (1926). Din claims due process requires she be provided with the facts underlying this determination, arguing *Mandel* required a similar factual basis. It is true the Attorney General there disclosed the facts motivating his decision to deny Dr. Mandel a waiver, and that the Court cited those facts as demonstrating "the Attorney General validly exercised the plenary power that Congress delegated to the Executive." 408 U.S., at 769. But unlike the waiver provision at issue in *Mandel,* which granted the Attorney General nearly unbridled discretion, §1182(a)(3)(B) specifies discrete factual predicates the consular officer must find to exist before denying a visa. Din, moreover, admits in her Complaint that Berashk worked for the Taliban government, App. 27-28, which, even if itself insufficient to support exclusion, provides at least a facial connection to terrorist activity. Absent an affirmative showing of bad faith on the part of the consular officer who denied Berashk a visa — which Din has not plausibly alleged with sufficient particularity — *Mandel* instructs us not to "look behind" the Government's exclusion of Berashk for additional factual details beyond what its express reliance on §1182(a)(3)(B) encompassed. See 408 U.S., at 770.

The Government, furthermore, was not required, as Din claims, to point to a more specific provision within §1182(a)(3)(B). To be sure, the statutory provision the consular officer cited covers a broad range of conduct. And Din perhaps more easily could mount a challenge to her husband's visa denial if she knew the specific subsection on which the consular officer relied. Congress understood this problem, however. The statute generally requires the Government to provide an alien denied a visa with the "specific provision or provisions of law under which the alien is inadmissible," §1182(b)(1); but this notice requirement does not apply when, as in this case, a visa application is denied due to terrorism or national security concerns. §1182(b)(3). Notably, the Government is not prohibited from offering more details when it sees fit, but the statute expressly refrains from requiring it to do so.

Congress evaluated the benefits and burdens of notice in this sensitive area and assigned discretion to the Executive to decide when more detailed disclosure is appropriate. This considered judgment gives additional support to the independent conclusion that the notice given was constitutionally adequate, particularly in light of the national security concerns the terrorism bar addresses. *See Fiallo v. Bell,* 430 U.S. 787, 795-796 (1977); *see also INS v. Aguirre-Aguirre,* 526 U.S. 415, 425 (1999). And even if Din is correct that sensitive facts could be reviewed by courts in camera, the dangers and difficulties of handling such delicate security material further counsel against requiring disclosure in a case such as this. Under *Mandel,* respect for the political branches' broad power over the creation and administration of the immigration system extends to determinations of how much information the Government is obliged to disclose about a consular officer's denial of a visa to an alien abroad.

For these reasons, my conclusion is that the Government satisfied any obligation it might have had to provide Din with a facially legitimate and bona fide reason for its action when it provided notice that her husband was denied admission to the country under §1182(a)(3)(B). By requiring the Government to provide more, the Court of Appeals erred in adjudicating Din's constitutional claims.

JUSTICE BREYER, with whom JUSTICE GINSBURG, JUSTICE SOTOMAYOR, and JUSTICE KAGAN join, dissenting.

Fauzia Din, an American citizen, wants to know why the State Department denied a visa to her husband, a noncitizen. She points out that, without a visa, she and her husband will have to spend their married lives separately or abroad. And she argues that the Department, in refusing to provide an adequate reason for the denial, has violated the constitutional requirement that "[n]o person . . . be deprived of life, liberty, or property, without due process of law." U.S. Const., Amdt. 5.

In my view, Ms. Din should prevail on this constitutional claim. She possesses the kind of "liberty" interest to which the Due Process Clause grants procedural protection. And the Government has failed to provide her with the procedure that is constitutionally "due." See *Swarthout v. Cooke*, 562 U.S. 216, 219 (2011) (*per curiam*) (setting forth the Court's two-step inquiry for procedural due process claims). Accordingly, I would affirm the judgment of the Ninth Circuit.

The plurality opinion (which is not controlling) concludes that Ms. Din lacks the kind of liberty interest to which the Due Process Clause provides procedural protections. Ante, at 2132-2138. JUSTICE KENNEDY's opinion "*assum[es]*" that Ms. Din possesses that kind of liberty interest. Ante, at 2131 (opinion concurring in judgment) (emphasis added). I agree with JUSTICE KENNEDY's assumption. More than that, I believe that Ms. Din possesses that kind of constitutional interest.

The liberty interest that Ms. Din seeks to protect consists of her freedom to live together with her husband in the United States. She seeks procedural, not substantive, protection for this freedom. Compare *Wilkinson v. Austin*, 545 U.S. 209, 221 (2005) (Due Process Clause requires compliance with fair procedures when the government deprives an individual of certain "liberty" or "property" interests), with *Reno v. Flores*, 507 U.S. 292, 302 (1993) (Due Process Clause limits the extent to which government can substantively regulate certain "fundamental" rights, "no matter what process is provided"). Cf. *Smith v. Organization of Foster Families For Equality & Reform*, 431 U.S. 816, 842, n. 48 (1977) (liberty interests arising under the Constitution for procedural due process purposes are not the same as fundamental rights requiring substantive due process protection).

Our cases make clear that the Due Process Clause entitles her to such procedural rights as long as (1) she seeks protection for a liberty interest sufficiently important for procedural protection to flow "implicit[ly]" from the design, object, and nature of the Due Process Clause, or (2) nonconstitutional law (a statute, for example) creates "an expectation" that a person will not be deprived of that kind of liberty without fair procedures. *Wilkinson, supra*, at 221.

The liberty for which Ms. Din seeks protection easily satisfies both standards. As this Court has long recognized, the institution of marriage, which encompasses the right of spouses to live together and to raise a family, is central to human life, requires and enjoys community support, and plays a central role in most individuals' "orderly pursuit of happiness," *Meyer v. Nebraska*, 262 U.S. 390, 399 (1923). . . . Similarly, the Court has long recognized that a citizen's right to live within this country, being fundamental, enjoys basic procedural due process protection. *See Ng Fung Ho v. White*, 259 U.S. 276, 284-285 (1922); *Baumgartner v. United States*, 322 U.S. 665, 670 (1944).

At the same time, the law, including visa law, surrounds marriage with a host of legal protections to the point that it creates a strong expectation that government will not deprive married individuals of their freedom to live together without strong reasons and (in individual cases) without fair procedure. Cf. *Turner v. Safley*, 482 U.S. 78, 95-96 (1987) (noting various legal benefits of marriage); 8 U.S.C. § 1151(b)(2)(A)(i) (special visa preference for spouse of an American citizen). JUSTICE SCALIA's response — that nonconstitutional law creates an "expectation" that merits procedural protection under the Due Process Clause only if there is an unequivocal statutory right, ante, at 2136-2137 — is sorely mistaken. His argument rests on the rights/privilege distinction that this Court rejected almost five decades ago, in the seminal case of *Goldberg v. Kelly*, 397 U.S. 254, 262 (1970). See generally *Board of Regents of State Colleges v. Roth*, 408 U.S. 564, 571 (1972) ("[T]he Court has fully and finally rejected the wooden distinction between 'rights' and 'privileges' that once seemed to govern the applicability of procedural due process rights"); *id.*, at 572 ("In a Constitution for a free people, there can be no doubt that the meaning of 'liberty' must be broad indeed").

JUSTICE SCALIA's more general response — claiming that I have created a new category of constitutional rights, ante, at 2136-2138 — misses the mark. I break no new ground here. Rather, this Court has already recognized that the Due Process Clause guarantees that the government will not, without fair procedure, deprive individuals of a host of rights, freedoms, and liberties that are no more important, and for which the state has created no greater expectation of continued benefit, than the liberty interest at issue here. *See*, e.g., *Wolff v. McDonnell*, 418 U.S. 539, 556-557 (1974) (prisoner's right to maintain "goodtime" credits shortening term of imprisonment; procedurally protected liberty interest based on nonconstitutional law); Paul v. Davis, 424 U.S. 693 (1976) (right to certain aspects of reputation; procedurally protected liberty interest arising under the Constitution); Goss v. Lopez, 419 U.S. 565, 574-575 (1975) (student's right not to be suspended from school class; procedurally protected liberty interest arising under the Constitution); Vitek v. Jones, 445 U.S. 480, 491-495 (1980) (prisoner's right against involuntary commitment; procedurally protected liberty interest arising under the Constitution); Washington v. Harper, 494 U.S. 210, 221-222 (1990) (mentally ill prisoner's right not to take psychotropic drugs; procedurally protected liberty interest arising under the Constitution); see generally *Goldberg*, *supra*, at 262-263 (right to welfare benefits; procedurally protected property interest based on nonconstitutional law). But cf. *ante*, at 2136-2138 (plurality opinion) (making what I believe are unsuccessful efforts to distinguish these cases). How could a Constitution that protects individuals against the arbitrary deprivation of so diverse a set of interests not also offer some form of procedural protection to a citizen threatened with governmental deprivation of her freedom to live together with her spouse in America? As compared to reputational harm, for example, how is Ms. Din's liberty interest any less worthy of due process protections?

II

The more difficult question is the nature of the procedural protection required by the Constitution. . . .

Here, we need not consider all possible procedural due process elements. Rather we consider only the minimum procedure that Ms. Din has requested — namely, a statement of reasons, some kind of explanation, as to why the State Department denied her husband a visa.

We have often held that this kind of statement, permitting an individual to understand why the government acted as it did, is a fundamental element of due process. . . .

I do not deny the importance of national security, the need to keep certain related information private, or the need to respect the determinations of the other branches of Government in such matters. But protecting ordinary citizens from arbitrary government action is fundamental. Thus, the presence of security considerations does not suspend the Constitution. *Hamdi*, 542 U.S., at 527-537 (plurality opinion). Rather, it requires us to take security needs into account when determining, for example, what "process" is "due." *Ibid.*

Yet how can we take proper account of security considerations without knowing what they are, without knowing how and why they require modification of traditional due process requirements, and without knowing whether other, less restrictive alternatives are available? How exactly would it harm important security interests to give Ms. Din a better explanation? Is there no way to give Ms. Din such an explanation while also maintaining appropriate secrecy? I believe we need answers to these questions before we can accept as constitutional a major departure from the procedural requirements that the Due Process Clause ordinarily demands. . . .

QUESTIONS

1. The Supreme Court divided 3-2-4 in *Din*. How do the Justices divide on the essential preliminary question of whether the plaintiffs possessed a liberty interest?
2. Did the Department of State provide an adequate explanation for the denial of the visa, particularly in light of the fact that that the government cited Berashk's participation as an officer in the Taliban-run government of Afghanistan before 9/11?
3. Justice Scalia, joined by Chief Justice Roberts and Justice Thomas, argues that government action that affects interests recognized as constituting fundamental liberty interests does not automatically trigger procedural due process protections. Does this approach make sense? Assuming that marriage, procreation, and child rearing are fundamental liberty interests for purposes of the so-called "substantive" aspect of the Due Process Clauses, how could they not also constitute constitutional "liberty" interests that enjoy the protection of procedural due process? Is Justice Scalia's position internally consistent or coherent? Or is he simply attempting to limit the potential scope of application of substantive due process rights?
4. Should the government have an obligation to provide detailed reasons for denial of a visa when the question implicates national security and anti-terrorism programs? Or is a context of this sort precisely one in which federal courts should be more, rather than less, vigilant?
5. Should the context matter in assessing whether particular procedures meet the requirements of procedural due process? The Supreme Court has

regularly held that Congress has "plenary power" over immigration and naturalization. With this being so, should an assessment of procedural due process take this into account? Should it be relevant to applying *Mathews v. Eldridge* balancing? *See supra* pp. 62-71.

NOTE ON SUMMARY DEPRIVATIONS OF PROPERTY

Cases like *Din* and *Ingraham* involved the deprivation of protected liberty interests. A majority in *Din* found that either no liberty interest existed or, alternatively, that the procedures used to safeguard it met the requirements of procedural due process; under either approach, the government did not fail to provide required predeprivation process. On the other hand, *Ingraham* involved postdeprivation process for the loss of a constitutionally protected liberty interest. The adequacy of a postdeprivation hearing arises more frequently in the context of emergency deprivations of property than in the context of government actions burdening deprivations of liberty interests. In *Goldberg v. Kelly,* the Supreme Court stated that under some circumstances the government could deprive a person of property and provide a hearing after the deprivation without violating the due process clause, and listed several examples. *See* fn. 10 of *Goldberg*, p. 36, *supra.*

In *United States v. James Daniel Good Real Property,* 510 U.S. 43 (1993), the Court employed the *Eldridge* test to address the adequacy of summary deprivations of property subject only to a postdeprivation hearing. In that case the United States had filed an in rem action in the federal district court, seeking to forfeit the house of Good, a drug criminal defendant. In an ex parte proceeding, a United States Magistrate Judge found that the government had established probable cause to believe Good's property was subject to forfeiture under 21 U.S.C. § 881(a)(7). A warrant of arrest in rem was issued, authorizing seizure of the property, based on an affidavit recounting the fact of Good's conviction and on evidence discovered during a search of his home by state police. The government seized the property, without prior notice to Good or an adversary hearing. At the time of the seizure, Good was renting his home to tenants for $900 per month.

In an opinion written by Justice Kennedy, five members of the Court decided that this forfeiture of real property violated the due process clause. The Court first found easily that there had been a deprivation of a property interest. The Court also rejected the government's argument that, because the civil forfeiture of property served a law enforcement function, the government procedures were required only to conform to the fourth amendment's requirements for a reasonable search and seizure.

The Court then evaluated the sufficiency of the procedures under *Eldridge*. First, the private interest was strong ("Good's right to maintain control over his home, and to be free from governmental interference, is a private interest of historic and continuing importance. The seizure deprived Good of valuable rights of ownership, including the right of sale, the right of occupancy, the right to unrestricted use and enjoyment, and the right to receive rents. All that the seizure left him, by the Government's own submission, was the right to bring a claim for the return of title at some unscheduled future hearing"). Second, "[t]he practice of ex parte seizure, moreover, creates an unacceptable risk of error." ("The ex parte preseizure proceeding affords little or no protection to the innocent owner. . . . The Government is not required to offer any evidence on the question of innocent ownership or other potential defenses a claimant might have.")

Applying the third *Eldridge* factor, the Court then found that Government interests did not justify summary procedures:

> This brings us to the third consideration under *Mathews,* "the Government's interest, including the function involved and the fiscal and administrative burdens that the additional or substitute procedural requirement would entail." 424 U.S., at 335. The governmental interest we consider here is not some general interest in forfeiting property but the specific interest in seizing real property before the forfeiture hearing. The question in the civil forfeiture context is whether ex parte seizure is justified by a pressing need for prompt action. We find no pressing need here.
>
> This is apparent by comparison to *Calero-Toledo,* where the Government's interest in immediate seizure of a yacht subject to civil forfeiture justified dispensing with the usual requirement of prior notice and hearing. Two essential considerations informed our ruling in that case: First, immediate seizure was necessary to establish the court's jurisdiction over the property, 416 U.S., at 679, and second, the yacht might have disappeared had the Government given advance warning of the forfeiture action, *ibid.* Neither of these factors is present when the target of forfeiture is real property.
>
> Because real property cannot abscond, the court's jurisdiction can be preserved without prior seizure. . . .
>
> . . . In the case of real property, the res may be brought within the reach of the court simply by posting notice on the property and leaving a copy of the process with the occupant. In fact, the rules which govern forfeiture proceedings under § 881 already permit process to be executed on real property without physical seizure. . . .
>
> Nor is the ex parte seizure of real property necessary to accomplish the statutory purpose of § 881(a)(7). The Government's legitimate interests at the inception of forfeiture proceedings are to ensure that the property not be sold, destroyed, or used for further illegal activity prior to the forfeiture judgment. These legitimate interests can be secured without seizing the subject property.
>
> Sale of the property can be prevented by filing a notice of lis pendens as authorized by state law when the forfeiture proceedings commence. 28 U.S.C. § 1964; and see Haw. Rev. Stat. § 634-51 (1985) (lis pendens provision). . . .
>
> In the usual case, the Government thus has various means, short of seizure, to protect its legitimate interests in forfeitable real property. There is no reason to take the additional step of asserting control over the property without first affording notice and an adversary hearing.
>
> Requiring the Government to postpone seizure until after an adversary hearing creates no significant administrative burden. A claimant is already entitled to an adversary hearing before a final judgment of forfeiture. No extra hearing would be required in the typical case, since the Government can wait until after the forfeiture judgment to seize the property. From an administrative standpoint it makes little difference whether that hearing is held before or after the seizure. And any harm that results from delay is minimal in comparison to the injury occasioned by erroneous seizure.
>
> C. It is true that, in cases decided over a century ago, we permitted the ex parte seizure of real property when the Government was collecting debts or revenue. *See, e.g., Springer v. United States,* 102 U.S. 586, 593-594 (1881); *Murray's Lessee v. Hoboken*

Land & Improvement Co., 18 How. 272 (1856). Without revisiting these cases, it suffices to say that their apparent rationale — like that for allowing summary seizures during wartime, *see Stoehr v. Wallace*, 255 U.S. 239 (1921); *Bowles v. Willingham*, 321 U.S. 503 (1944), and seizures of contaminated food, *see North American Cold Storage Co. v. Chicago*, 211 U.S. 306 (1908) — was one of executive urgency. . . .

A like rationale justified the ex parte seizure of tax-delinquent distilleries in the late 19th century, *see*, e.g., *United States v. Stowell*, 133 U.S. 1 (1890); *Dobbins's Distillery v. United States*, 96 U.S. 395 (1878), since before passage of the Sixteenth Amendment, the Federal Government relied heavily on liquor, customs, and tobacco taxes to generate operating revenues. . . .

. . . Although the Government relies to some extent on forfeitures as a means of defraying law enforcement expenses, it does not, and we think could not, justify the prehearing seizure of forfeitable real property as necessary for the protection of its revenues.

D. The constitutional limitations we enforce in this case apply to real property in general, not simply to residences. That said, the case before us well illustrates an essential principle: Individual freedom finds tangible expression in property rights. At stake in this and many other forfeiture cases are the security and privacy of the home and those who take shelter within it.

Finally, the suggestion that this one claimant must lose because his conviction was known at the time of seizure, and because he raises an as applied challenge to the statute, founders on a bedrock proposition: Fair procedures are not confined to the innocent. The question before us is the legality of the seizure, not the strength of the Government's case.

In sum, based upon the importance of the private interests at risk and the absence of countervailing Government needs, we hold that the seizure of real property under § 881(a)(7) is not one of those extraordinary instances that justify the postponement of notice and hearing. Unless exigent circumstances are present, the Due Process Clause requires the Government to afford notice and a meaningful opportunity to be heard before seizing real property subject to civil forfeiture.

To establish exigent circumstances, the Government must show that less restrictive measures — i.e., a lis pendens, restraining order, or bond — would not suffice to protect the Government's interests in preventing the sale, destruction, or continued unlawful use of the real property. We agree with the Court of Appeals that no showing of exigent circumstances has been made in this case, and we affirm its ruling that the ex parte seizure of Good's real property violated due process. . . .

For other cases permitting summary procedures prior to deprivation, with elaborate procedures delayed until after the deprivation, *see*, e.g., *Lowery v. Faires*, 57 F. Supp. 2d 483 (E.D. Tenn. 1998) (allowing seizure of cattle); *Contreras v. City of Chicago*, 920 F. Supp. 1370 (N.D. Ill. 1996) (allowing closure of restaurant).

THEORY APPLIED PROBLEM

Let us return to Fred Mertz, first introduced in Chapter 1, who wishes to travel by plane on August 1, 2020. Mertz holds a valid one-way ticket to travel from LAX to JFK on JetBlue. When Mertz presents his boarding pass at the Transportation Security Administration (TSA) checkpoint, a TSA employee informs him that the TSA's screening program has given him a "red light" and that he will not be permitted to proceed through the checkpoint to catch his flight because he presents "a terroristic threat to airline security." Mertz volunteers to undergo heightened security screening, but is told that "red lighted" passengers are simply not permitted to board any commercial flight originating in the United States. The TSA agent suggests that Mertz consider driving to New York City instead of flying. Mertz asks for a formal statement of reasons for his "red light" status; the TSA employee tells him that the classification took place shortly after Mertz purchased his ticket twelve weeks earlier and that she cannot provide any additional information. The TSA agent gives Mertz a slip of paper entitled "Denial of Boarding: Know Your Rights." According to the paper, Mertz may write to an appeals panel to seek review of his denial of boarding.

Mertz writes to the TSA appeals panel contesting his designation as a "terroristic threat" to commercial airline flights, seeking a statement of reasons for the TSA's designation, and asking for some assurance that, should he book another airline ticket, he will be permitted to fly. In response to his letter, the TSA writes back saying that "we have enclosed our file materials regarding your denial of boarding on August 1, 2020. Our computer system does not save any of the information used to determine security status; all such information is destroyed immediately after the classification decision." In addition to the letter, Mertz receives a copy of his JetBlue airline ticket (which he already possessed).

Mertz then does some online research and learns that the TSA relies on a complicated computer program to assess passenger security risk; the program makes a determination shortly after a person purchases a plane ticket originating in the United States. Although the program banned Mertz from his flight mere seconds after he purchased his ticket, this information was not conveyed to Mertz until he appeared at the TSA security check point on the date of his flight (for security reasons). All of these procedures were established under regulations adopted by the TSA to govern passenger screening procedures for domestic airline passengers.

You work as a staff attorney in the Los Angeles branch of the American Civil Liberties Union (ACLU). Mr. Mertz has scheduled a consultation with you to discuss the possibility of suing the TSA for a violation of his procedural due process rights. On September 12, 2020, you meet with Mr. Mertz. How do you advise him? Does he have a liberty or property interest sufficient to trigger procedural due process rights? And, if so, under *Eldridge* balancing did the TSA provide acceptable process at an appropriate time?

C. STATUTORY HEARING RIGHTS: TRIGGERING APA REQUIREMENTS

The Due Process Clause is of course not the only source of adjudicatory hearing rights. Indeed, other sources of law — statutes and regulations — may impose procedural requirements for agency adjudications. The statutes that set agencies up and give them powers, often called "organic statutes" or "enabling acts," may impose procedural requirements, as well as generic statutes, often called "administrative procedure" acts. Procedures imposed by such statutes, and by regulations that implement them, will often exceed the minimum procedures that would be necessary to conform to the requirements of due process.

NOTE ON THE FEDERAL APA

The federal Administrative Procedure Act of 1946, commonly referred to as the "APA," sets forth the basic procedural rules governing the work of administrative agencies. The APA represents to administrative law practice what the Federal Rules of Civil Procedure represent to federal civil litigation practice: the basic blueprint that sets the background rules that generically govern agency proceedings.

A Brief History of the APA

One should keep in mind that there were administrative agencies long before the enactment of the APA. Although Congress created the Interstate Commerce Commission in 1887, it did not see fit to establish a generic set of operating procedures for federal administrative agencies for almost sixty years. Indeed, even with the coming of President Franklin D. Roosevelt's "New Deal" program, including the creation of dozens of new federal administrative agencies, Congress did not enact generic agency procedural requirements. To the extent that Congress regulated agency procedures, it imposed agency-specific requirements in the agencies' organic statutes.

The explosive growth of the administrative state after 1933 gave some observers pause. Opponents of President Roosevelt's new administrative state worried that agencies would exercise both judicial and legislative functions without meaningful accountability either to Congress or the federal courts. Exercising broad delegations set forth in vaguely worded statutes, these new agencies arguably constituted a new "Fourth Branch" of the federal government.

Many of the organic statutes creating these agencies authorized the agencies to enact rules supplementing the substantive provisions of those statutes. *See,* e.g., 47 U.S.C. § 156 (authorizing the Federal Communications Commission to establish rules to effectuate its policies under the Communications Act). Similarly, the agencies possessed authority to adjudicate claims arising from the administration and enforcement of these federal statutes. The creation of these powers squarely presented the question of *how* the agencies would go about exercising these adjudicatory and legislative powers.

Of course, the Fifth Amendment guarantees "due process of law" whenever government acts in a way that constitutes a deprivation of "life, liberty, or property." In theory, the federal courts could have fashioned common law rules that governed the exercise of agency power. This approach, however, would likely have placed only very minimal constraints on the exercise of agency power. Constitutional due process represents a minimum, or floor, of procedural rights that government cannot deny the citizenry. Moreover, in light of the principle of the *Bi-Metallic* case, *supra,* p. 23, procedural due process does not mandate minimum procedural requirements in the context of quasi-legislative rulemaking activity.

Opponents of the New Deal hoped to enact legislation severely restricting the agencies' ability to write quasi-legislative rules and conduct quasi-judicial adjudications. If Congress imposed burdensome procedures on the agencies, federal agencies might be significantly impeded in their efforts to regulate the national economy effectively. Supporters of the New Deal reflexively opposed efforts to place the new administrative agencies in burdensome procedural straitjackets. Consequently, the creation of myriad new federal agencies was not accompanied by the adoption of any generalized procedural requirements defining and delimiting the methods and procedures by which the agencies would act.

Nevertheless, there was a growing consensus that something had to be done.[1] A patchwork of procedural due process precedents, developed over time in the various federal courts, was not an effective means of ensuring that agencies acted fairly and rationally. Although the New Deal supporters of the Fourth Branch placed far more faith in the newly minted agencies — with their growing expertise over their respective regulatory empires — than in the federal courts,[2] even they conceded the need to have a single set of baseline procedures governing the exercise of regulatory power.

World War II made the enactment of a generic statute governing federal administrative procedures a rather low legislative priority. Once the war ended, however, the need to establish some basic guidelines to govern the exercise of administrative power remained. By this juncture, even supporters of the New Deal were prepared to concede some role for the federal judiciary in supervising federal agencies in the exercise of their delegated powers. The question facing Congress was how to strike the appropriate balance between protecting regulated industries from poorly conceived agency policies and protecting agencies from judicial usurpation of their powers.

The Administrative Procedure Act was an attempt to accomplish this objective by setting forth minimum procedures and by striking a compromise between proponents and opponents of judicial review of agency action. In large part it codified what was already perceived to be the law. On the one hand, virtually all agency actions are reviewable in the federal courts. This represented a concession to those who questioned whether agencies would invariably exercise their delegated powers wisely absent some sort of review process.

On the other hand, judicial review of agency action would occur, for the most part, under a highly deferential "arbitrary and capricious" standard of review. The federal courts were not to substitute their own views for those of the federal agencies, but rather were to ascertain whether a particular federal administrative agency's work-product regarding a specific matter was minimally rational. The deferential standard of review set forth in section 706 virtually ensured that most agency decisions would survive the judicial review process. For a comprehensive review of the history of the APA and the cross-cutting policy objectives that Congress sought to accommodate, *see* George B. Shepherd, *Fierce Compromise:*

---

1. Justice Jackson summarized the history of the enactment of the APA in his opinion for the Court in *Wong Yang Sung v. McGrath,* 339 U.S. 33, 36-41 (1950). For further background on the politics and policies informing the enactment of the APA, *see* Reuel E. Schiller, *The Era of Deference: Courts, Expertise, and the Emergence of New Deal Administrative Law,* 106 Mich. L. Rev. 399 (2007).

2. Remember that the Supreme Court of the United States was perceived as an opponent of the New Deal program from 1933 to 1937. *See, e.g., Retirement Board v. Alton R.R. Co.,* 295 U.S. 330 (1935); *A.L.A. Schechter Poultry Co. v. United States,* 295 U.S. 495 (1935); *United States v. Butler,* 297 U.S. 1 (1936); *Carter v. Carter Coal Co.,* 298 U.S. 238 (1936). Using the concept of liberty of contract, coupled with a limited reading of congressional commerce powers, the Supreme Court struck down many important pieces of New Deal legislation. Supporters of the New Deal, then, viewed the federal judiciary with great suspicion (if not outright hostility). *See* William E. Leuchtenburg, Franklin D. Roosevelt and the New Deal: 1932-1940 (1963); William E. Leuchtenburg, *The Origins of Franklin D. Roosevelt's "Court-Packing" Plan,* 1966 Sup. Ct. Rev. 347.

The APA Emerges from New Deal Politics, 90 Nw. U. L. Rev. 1557 (1996); Martin Shapiro, *APA: Past, Present, Future,* 72 Va. L. Rev. 447 (1986).

The Basic Structure of the APA's Procedural Requirements

As *Londoner* and *Bi-Metallic* illustrated, the work of agencies falls into the broad categories of adjudication and rulemaking. Section 551 of the APA, which provides definitions that govern all aspects of the APA, draws a line that is roughly equivalent to (but not necessarily identical with) the *Londoner/Bi-Metallic* line. Section 551 provides that "adjudication" is the "agency process for the formulation of an order," 5 U.S.C. § 551(7), while "rule making" is the "agency process for formulating, amending, or repealing a rule." *Id.* § 551(5). The scope of these two types of agency action thus turns on the APA definitions of "rule" and "order." The APA defines a "rule" as "the whole or a part of an agency statement of general or particular applicability and future effect designed to implement, interpret, or prescribe law or policy . . . bearing on any of the foregoing [listed agency objects of rulemaking]." *Id.* § 551(4). On the other hand, the APA defines an "order" as "the whole or part of a final disposition . . . of an agency in a matter other than rule making but including licensing." *Id.* § 551(6). The APA thus includes all agency actions within one of these two categories.

The differences between a rule and an order are thus critical to the structure and applicability of the Administrative Procedure Act. One can think of a rule as like a statute or code provision. Similarly, one could analogize an order in an adjudication to a common law precedent that tinkers with the substantive rules governing the case even as the court purports to apply the rules to the parties before it. The Department of Justice offered the following description of the important differences:

> [T]he entire [APA] is based upon a dichotomy between rule making and adjudication. . . . Rule making is agency action which regulates the future conduct of either groups of persons or a single person; it is essentially legislative in nature, not only because it operates in the future but also because it is primarily concerned with policy considerations. The object of the rule making proceeding is the implementation or prescription of law or policy for the future, rather than the evaluation of a respondent's past conduct. Typically, the issues relate not to evidentiary facts, as to which the veracity and demeanor of witnesses would often be important, but rather to the policy-making conclusions to be drawn from the facts. Conversely, adjudication is concerned with the determination of past and present rights and liabilities. Normally, there is involved a decision as to whether past conduct was unlawful, so that the proceeding is characterized by an accusatory flavor and may result in disciplinary action. Or, it may involve the determination of a person's right to benefits under existing law so that the issues relate to whether he is within the established category of persons entitled to such benefits. In such proceedings, the issues of fact are often sharply controverted.

Attorney General's Manual on the Administrative Procedure Act 14-15 (1947). Of course, an order might have precedential value in a future case presenting similar facts, but it would not have the same generic prospective effect associated with a rule. You might want to think preliminarily about how the APA approach to the distinction between adjudication and rulemaking compares to the Supreme Court's approach in *Londoner* and *Bi-Metallic.*

The APA prescribes the procedures that an agency must follow when it engages in rulemaking or adjudication. At this point you should examine APA sections 553; 554(a), (b), (c), and (d); 556; 557; and 706(2)(E). APA requirements for rulemaking are addressed in Chapter 3 of this book.

With respect to adjudications, the APA prescribes detailed requirements only for "formal" adjudications. The APA does not establish requirements for the huge residual category of "informal" adjudications, apart from the "ancillary matters" provided by § 555. We look first, in *Seacoast* and later cases, at how the APA distinguishes between formal and informal adjudications for purposes of imposing procedural requirements. With respect to the minimal requirements for informal adjudications, compare *Pension Benefit Guarantee Corp. v. LTV Corp.*, 496 U.S. 633 (1990) (holding that section 555 of the APA governs informal adjudications conducted by federal administrative agencies) with *The Federal Administrative Procedure Act: Codification or Reform?*, 56 Yale L.J. 670, 705 (1947) (omitting "informal adjudications" from a chart showing the procedural provisions of the APA applicable to agency adjudications and rulemakings). Section 555(e) provides that denial of an application must generally "be accompanied by a brief statement of the grounds for denial."

Requirements for formal APA adjudications are, in contrast, quite detailed, as the D.C. Circuit has summarized:

> APA section 554 "applies . . . in every case of adjudication required by statute to be determined on the record after opportunity for an agency hearing" with some enumerated exceptions not applicable here. 5 U.S.C. § 554. If an adjudication is governed by section 554, it must feature the following procedural components: an impartial and unbiased presiding officer, *id.* § 556(b); notice and an opportunity to participate in the hearing, *id.* § 554(c); the right of the parties to appear with counsel, *id.* [§ 555(b)]; the right to present oral and written evidence (including rebuttal evidence) and to conduct such cross-examination as is required for a full and true disclosure of the facts, *id.* § 556(d); the right to submit proposed findings, conclusions and exceptions, *id.* § 557(c); the compilation of an exclusive record upon which the agency must base its decision, *id.* § 556(e); and limitations on *ex parte* communications and on the combination of prosecutorial and adjudicative functions, *id.* § 554(d).

St. Louis Fuel & Supply Co. v. FERC, 890 F.2d 446, 448 (D.C. Cir. 1989).

The cases and materials that follow in this chapter and the next explore in some detail the procedural requirements that the APA imposes on agencies when they engage in adjudication and rulemaking. The judicial review provisions of the APA, §§ 701 *et seq.*, are covered in Chapter V, along with other topics relating to court review of agency action. Although the APA provides the basic procedural framework that agencies must observe when regulating, there are many questions that the APA, on its face, does not address, such as whether reviewing courts or administrative agencies should enjoy principal responsibility for construing ambiguous statutory text. Although the APA is the most important federal statute governing the operation of federal administrative agencies, you will discover that it does not address in detail all aspects of agency operation or define with precision all matters associated with federal court review of agency action. *See* APA § 559 (noting that the APA does "not limit or repeal additional requirements imposed by statute or otherwise recognized by law").

State Administrative Procedure Acts are a more recent phenomenon. Many were influenced by the Model State Administrative Procedure Acts of 1961 and 1981. The 1981 Model State APA is included in Appendix B. You should familiarize yourself with the APA of the state in which you are most likely to practice, if that state has an APA.

SEACOAST ANTI-POLLUTION LEAGUE v. COSTLE
572 F.2d 872 (1st Cir. 1978)

COFFIN, CHIEF JUDGE.

This case is before us on a petition by the Seacoast Anti-Pollution League and the Audubon Society of New Hampshire (petitioners) to review a decision by the Administrator of the Environmental Protection Agency (EPA). We have jurisdiction under 33 U.S.C. § 1369(b)(1). The petition presents several important issues relating to the applicability and effect of the Administrative Procedure Act (APA), 5 U.S.C. §§ 501 *et seq.*, and the interpretation of the Federal Water Pollution Control Act of 1972 (FWPCA), 33 U.S.C. §§ 1251 *et seq.* In order to place those issues in context we set forth the procedural and factual background of the case.

The Public Service Company of New Hampshire (PSCO) filed an application with the EPA for permission to discharge heated water into the Hampton-Seabrook Estuary which runs into the Gulf of Maine. The water would be taken from the Gulf of Maine, be run through the condenser of PSCO's proposed nuclear steam electric generating station at Seabrook, and then be directly discharged back into the Gulf at a temperature 39 degrees F higher than at intake. The water is needed to remove waste heat, some 16 billion BTU per hour, generated by the nuclear reactor but not converted into electrical energy by the turbine. Occasionally, in a process called backflushing, the water will be recirculated through the condenser, and discharged through the intake tunnel at a temperature of 120 degrees F in order to kill whatever organisms may be living in the intake system.

Section 301(a) of the FWPCA, 33 U.S.C. § 1311(a), prohibits the discharge of any pollutant unless the discharger, the point source operator, has obtained an EPA permit. Heat is a pollutant. 33 U.S.C. § 1362(6). Section 301(b) directs the EPA to promulgate effluent limitations. The parties agree that the cooling system PSCO has proposed does not meet the EPA standards because PSCO would utilize a once-through open cycle system — the water would not undergo any cooling process before being returned to the sea. Therefore, in August, 1974, PSCO applied not only for a discharge permit under § 402 of the FWPCA, 33 U.S.C. § 1342, but also an exemption from the EPA standards pursuant to § 316 of the FWPCA, 33 U.S.C. § 1326. Under § 316(a) a point source operator who "after opportunity for public hearing, can demonstrate to the satisfaction of the Administrator" that the EPA's standards are "more stringent than necessary to assure the projection [*sic*] and propagation of a balanced, indigenous population of shellfish, fish, and wildlife in and on the body of water" may be allowed to meet a lower standard. Moreover, under § 316(b) the cooling water intake structure must "reflect the best technology available for minimizing adverse environmental impact."

In January, 1975, the Regional Administrator of the EPA held a non-adjudicatory hearing at Seabrook. He then authorized the once-through system in June, 1975. Later, in October, 1975, he specified the location of the intake structure. The Regional Administrator granted a request by petitioners that public adjudicative hearings on PSCO's application be held. These hearings were held in March and April, 1976, pursuant to the EPA's regulations establishing procedures for deciding applications for permits under § 402 of the FWPCA, 40 C.F.R. § 125.36. The hearings were before an administrative law judge who certified a record to the Regional Administrator for decision. The Regional Administrator decided in November, 1976, to reverse his original determinations and deny PSCO's application.

PSCO, pursuant to 40 C.F.R. § 125.36(n), appealed the decision to the Administrator who agreed to review it. Thereafter, a new Administrator was appointed, and he assembled a panel of six in-house advisors to assist in his technical review. This panel met between February 28 and March 3, 1977, and submitted a report finding that with one exception PSCO had met its burden of proof. With respect to that exception, the effect of backflushing, the Administrator asked PSCO to submit further information, offered other parties the opportunity to comment upon PSCO's submission, and stated that he would hold a hearing on the new information if any party so requested and could satisfy certain threshold conditions (set out below). Petitioners did request a hearing, but the Administrator denied the request.

The Administrator's final decision followed the technical panel's recommendations and, with the additional information submitted, reversed the Regional Administrator's decision, finding that PSCO had met its burden under § 316. It is this decision that petitioners have brought before us for review.

APPLICABILITY OF THE ADMINISTRATIVE PROCEDURE ACT

Petitioners assert that the proceedings by which the EPA decided this case contravened certain provisions of the APA governing adjudicatory hearings, 5 U.S.C. §§ 554, 556, and 557. Respondents answer that the APA does not apply to proceedings held pursuant to § 316 or § 402 of the FWPCA, 33 U.S.C. §§ 1326, 1342.

The dispute centers on the meaning of the introductory phrases of § 554(a) of the APA:[4] This section applies . . . in every case of adjudication required by statute to be determined on the record after opportunity for an agency hearing. . . .

Both § 316(a) and § 402(a)(1) of the FWPCA provide for public hearings, but neither states that the hearing must be "on the record." We are now the third court of appeals to face this issue. The Ninth Circuit and the Seventh Circuit have each found that the APA does apply to proceedings pursuant to § 402.

---

4. The determination that the EPA must make under § 316 of the FWPCA is not a rule because it is not "designed to implement, interpret, or prescribe law or policy." 5 U.S.C. § 551(4). Rather the EPA must decide a specific factual question already prescribed by statute. Since the determination is not a rule, it is an order. 5 U.S.C. § 551(6). The agency process for formulating an order is an adjudication. 5 U.S.C. § 551(7). Therefore, § 554 rather than § 553 of the APA is the relevant section. The same result is dictated because § 316(a) of the FWPCA is a licensing, 5 U.S.C. § 551(9), since it results in the granting or denial of a form of permission. See 5 U.S.C. § 551(8). A license is an order. 5 U.S.C. § 551(6).

Marathon Oil Co. v. EPA, 564 F.2d 1253 (9th Cir. 1977); *United States Steel Corp. v. Train,* 556 F.2d 822 (7th Cir. 1977). We agree.

At the outset we reject the position of intervenor PSCO that the precise words "on the record" must be used to trigger the APA. The Supreme Court has clearly rejected such an extreme reading even in the context of rule making under § 553 of the APA. *See United States v. Florida East Coast Ry. Co.,* 410 U.S. 224, 245 (1973); *United States v. Allegheny-Ludlum Steel Corp.,* 406 U.S. 742, 757 (1972). Rather, we think that the resolution of this issue turns on the substantive nature of the hearing Congress intended to provide.

We begin with the nature of the decision at issue. The EPA Administrator must make specific factual findings about the effects of discharges from a specific point source. On the basis of these findings the Administrator must determine whether to grant a discharge permit to a specific applicant. Though general policy considerations may influence the decision, the decision will not make general policy. Only the rights of the specific applicant will be affected. "As the instant proceeding well demonstrates, the factual questions involved in the issuance of section 402 permits will frequently be sharply disputed. Adversarial hearings will be helpful, therefore, in guaranteeing both reasoned decisionmaking and meaningful judicial review. In summary, the proceedings below were conducted in order 'to adjudicate disputed facts in particular cases,' not 'for the purposes of promulgating policy-type rules or standards.'" *Marathon Oil Co., supra,* at 1262.

This is exactly the kind of quasi-judicial proceeding for which the adjudicatory procedures of the APA were intended. As the Supreme Court has said, "Determination of questions of [the Administrative Procedure Act's] coverage may well be approached through consideration of its purposes as disclosed by its background." *Wong Yang Sung v. McGrath,* 339 U.S. 33, 36 (1950). One of the developments that prompted the APA was the "multiplication of federal administrative agencies and expansion of their functions to include adjudications which have serious impact on private rights." *Id.,* 339 U.S. at 36-37. This is just such an adjudication. The panoply of procedural protections provided by the APA is necessary not only to protect the rights of an applicant for less stringent pollutant discharge limits, but is also needed to protect the public for whose benefit the very strict limitations have been enacted. If determinations such as the one at issue here are not made on the record, then the fate of the Hampton-Seabrook Estuary could be decided on the basis of evidence that a court would never see or, what is worse, that a court could not be sure existed. We cannot believe that Congress would intend such a result.

Our holding does not render the opening phrases of § 554 of the APA meaningless. We are persuaded that their purpose was to exclude "governmental functions, such as the administration of loan programs, which traditionally have never been regarded as adjudicative in nature and as a rule have never been exercised through other than business procedures." Attorney General's Manual on the Administrative Procedure Act 40 (1947). Without some kind of limiting language, the broad sweep of the definition of "adjudication," defined principally as that which is not rule making, 5 U.S.C. §551(6), (7), would include such ordinary procedures that do not require any kind of hearing at all. In short, we view the crucial part of the limiting language to be the requirement of a statutorily imposed hearing. We are willing to presume that, unless a statute otherwise specifies, an adjudicatory hearing subject to judicial review must be on the record. The legislative history of the APA and its treatment in the courts bear us out.

This rationale and conclusion also are supported by our holding in *South Terminal Corp. v. EPA*, 504 F.2d 646, 660 (1st Cir. 1974) ("public hearing" not tantamount to "on the record"), and the other rule making cases cited to us for similar propositions. The presumption in rule making cases is that formal, adjudicatory procedures are not necessary. A hearing serves a very different function in the rule making context. Witnesses may bring in new information or different points of view, but the agency's final decision need not reflect the public input. The witnesses are not the only source of the evidence on which the Administrator may base his factual findings. For these reasons, we place less importance on the absence of the words "on the record" in the adjudicatory context.

> It is believed that with respect to adjudication the specific statutory requirement of a hearing, without anything more, carries with it the further requirement of decision on the basis of the evidence adduced at the hearing. With respect to rule making, it was concluded, *supra,* that a statutory provision that rules be issued after a hearing, without more, should not be construed as requiring agency action "on the record," but rather as merely requiring an opportunity for the expression of views. That conclusion was based on the legislative nature of rule making, from which it was inferred, unless a statute requires otherwise, that an agency hearing on proposed rules would be similar to a hearing before a legislative committee, with neither the legislature nor the agency being limited to the material adduced at the hearing. No such rationale applies to administrative adjudication. In fact, it is assumed that where a statute specifically provides for administrative adjudication (such as the suspension or revocation of a license) after opportunity for an agency hearing, *such specific requirement for a hearing ordinarily implies the further requirement of decision in accordance with evidence adduced at the hearing.* Of course, the foregoing discussion is inapplicable to any situation in which the legislative history or the context of the pertinent statute indicates a contrary congressional intent.

Attorney General's Manual, *supra,* 42-43 (footnote and citation to statutory history omitted) (emphasis added).

Here the statute certainly does not indicate that the determination need *not* be on the record, and we find no indication of a contrary congressional intent. Therefore, we will judge the proceedings below according to the standards set forth in §§ 554, 556, and 557 of the APA.

Compliance with the Administrative Procedure Act

Petitioners contend that two steps in the EPA's proceedings in this case violated the APA. We will look at each in turn.

1. the post-hearing submissions; the request for information

The Regional Administrator, in his initial decision, had determined that the record was insufficient to properly evaluate the environmental effects of backflushing. The Administrator's technical panel agreed. The Administrator asked PSCO to submit supplemental information on that subject. Other parties were given permission to comment on PSCO's submission. In addition, the Administrator provided that a hearing with respect to the submission would be held if four conditions designed to guarantee that the hearing could resolve a substantial issue of fact were met. PSCO submitted the requested information. Other parties, including petitioners, submitted comments, and petitioners requested a hearing. The Administrator denied the hearing because petitioners had failed to meet the threshold conditions.

Petitioners argue, first, that the Administrator could not rely on this information because it was not part of the exclusive record for decision. 5 U.S.C. § 556(e). Second, petitioners argue that even if the information was legitimately part of the record, the Administrator was obligated to provide an opportunity for cross-examination pursuant to 5 U.S.C. § 556(d).

Section 556(e) provides that "the transcript of testimony and exhibits, together with all papers and requests filed in the proceeding, constitutes the exclusive record for decision. . . ." The first point to make about this section is that it does not limit the time frame during which any papers must be received. Certainly the submissions at issue were "filed in the proceeding." Moreover, 5 U.S.C. § 557(b) provides that "on appeal from or review of the initial decision, the agency has all the powers which it would have in making the initial decision. . . ." One of those powers is the power to preside at the taking of evidence. 5 U.S.C. § 556(b)(1). For these reasons we can find no fault with the Administrator's decision to seek further evidence. Indeed we think this procedure was a most appropriate way to gather the necessary information without the undue delay that would result from a remand.

The question remains, however, whether the procedures by which the Administrator gathered the information conformed to the governing law. The first point is whether the Administrator was empowered to require that the new evidence be submitted in written form. The Administrator may, under 5 U.S.C. § 556(d), so require in cases of initial licensing. This is an initial licensing. But just as the APA does not impose procedures excused by a governing statute, so the APA does not excuse procedures compelled by the governing statute. In this case § 316(a) of the FWPCA requires the EPA to afford an opportunity for a *public hearing*. We do not believe that an opportunity to submit documents constitutes a public hearing. Nor do we believe that the Administrator can comply with the statute merely by taking some evidence at a public hearing and then taking the rest in written form. If that were the law, nothing would prevent the Administrator from holding a ten minute hearing to establish compliance and then requiring the submission of the rest of the evidence. Therefore, we interpret the closing lines of § 556(d) of the APA to mean that the Administrator can require evidence to be submitted in written form in initial licensings unless the governing statute requires a public hearing. The public hearing can be especially important in cases such as this one which turn not so much upon the actual baseline data (which presumably all parties will be happy to have submitted in written form) as upon experts' interpretation of the data. The experts' credibility is, therefore, very much at issue here. *See* Attorney General's Manual, *supra*, at 78.

While we believe that it was error for the Administrator not to hold a hearing to receive the responses to his request for Information, and that therefore the submission was not properly part of the record, we cannot be sure that any purpose would be served by ordering a hearing on this issue at this stage in these proceedings. Petitioners' principal complaints are that either the Administrator could not take any evidence or that he was required to afford an opportunity for cross-examination. The latter complaint has no more basis than the former. A party to an administrative adjudicatory hearing does not have an absolute right to cross-examine witnesses. The plain language of 5 U.S.C. § 556(d) limits that right to instances where cross-examination is "required for a full and true disclosure of the facts."

We will order a remand for the limited purpose of allowing the Administrator to determine whether cross-examination would be useful. This remand is necessary because the Administrator's threshold conditions were designed to determine whether a hearing was necessary, not how that hearing should be conducted. The parties' submissions likewise went to that somewhat distinct question. Ordinarily we might well overlook what appears to be a more theoretical than practical distinction, but we are influenced here by the fact that a remand is necessary anyway for reasons discussed below. If the Administrator finds that cross-examination would help disclose the facts a hearing must be provided at which cross-examination would be available. If, however, the Administrator concludes that cross-examination would not serve any useful purpose then we will not require him to hold a hearing merely to have the already submitted statements read into the record.

2. PARTICIPATION OF THE TECHNICAL REVIEW PANEL

Petitioners object to the Administrator's use of a panel of EPA scientists to assist him in reviewing the Regional Administrator's initial decision. The objection is two-fold: first, that the Administrator should not have sought such help at all; and, second, that the panel's report (the Report) to the Administrator included information not in the administrative record.

Petitioners point out that by the EPA's own regulations "*the Administrator shall decide* the matters under review on the basis of the record presented and any other consideration he deems relevant." 40 C.F.R. § 125.36(n)(12) (emphasis added). It is true that when a decision is committed to a particular individual that individual must be the one who reviews the evidence on which the decision is to be based, *See Morgan v. United States*, 298 U.S. 468, 481 (1936). But it does not follow that all other individuals are shut out of the decision process. That conclusion runs counter to the purposes of the administrative agencies which exist, in part, to enable government to focus broad ranges of talent on particular multi-dimensional problems. The Administrator is charged with making highly technical decisions in fields far beyond his individual expertise. "The strength [of the administrative process] lies in staff work organized in such a way that the appropriate specialization is brought to bear upon each aspect of a single decision, the synthesis being provided by the men at the top." 2 K. Davis, Administrative Law Treatise 84 (1958). Therefore, "evidence . . . may be sifted and analyzed by competent subordinates." *Morgan v. United States, supra,* at 481. *Cf.* 5 U.S.C. § 557(d) (forbidding *ex parte* communications only with persons outside the agency). The decision ultimately reached is no less the Administrator's simply because agency experts helped him to reach it.

A different question is presented, however, if the agency experts do not merely sift and analyze but also add to the evidence properly before the Administrator. The regulation quoted above cannot allow the Administrator to consider evidence barred from consideration by the APA, 5 U.S.C. § 556(e), "The transcript of testimony and exhibits, together with all papers and requests filed in the proceeding, constitutes the exclusive record for decision. . . ." To the extent the technical review panel's Report included information not in the record on which the Administrator relied, §556(e) was violated. In effect the agency's staff would have made up for PSCO's failure to carry its burden of proof.

Our review of the Report indicates that such violations did occur. The most serious instance is on page 19 of the Report where the technical panel rebuts the Regional Administrator's finding that PSCO had failed to supply enough data on species' thermal tolerances by saying:

> There is little information in the record on the thermal tolerances of marine organisms exposed to the specific temperature fluctuation associated with the Seabrook operation. However, the scientific literature does contain many references to the thermal sensitivity of members of the local biota.

Whether or not these references do exist and whether or not they support the conclusions the panel goes on to draw does not concern us here. What is important is that the record did not support the conclusion until supplemented by the panel. The panel's work found its way directly into the Administrator's decision at page 27 where he discusses the Regional Administrator's concerns about insufficient data but then precipitously concludes, "On the recommendation of the panel, however, I find that . . . local indigenous populations will not be significantly affected." This conclusion depends entirely on what the panel stated about the scientific literature.

Similar, though less egregious, examples occur in the Report at pages 13-14 ("Thus, while it is true that the applicant did not perform exhaustive studies on all [Representative Important Species] it is not true that nothing is known about these species, their biology, distribution or value to the ecosystem."); page 27 ("We concur . . . that there was no evidence on the question of whether there will be any impact on wildlife, such as birds. . . . Since we conclude that holoplankton . . . are not likely to be adversely affected, it is unlikely that there would be any conceivable impact at the top of the food chain."); and page 30 ("We agree that only limited data exist on the migratory pathways of fish to and from Hampton Harbor. . . . Nevertheless there have been substantial studies performed on fish migratory behavior; some of these have been done at power plant sites.") These find their way into the Administrator's decision at pages 25-26, 33-34, and 37, respectively.

We do not challenge the reliability of the panel, nor do we question the principle that informed opinion may be able to determine that information the Regional Administrator found lacking was either unavailable or irrelevant. On such issues the Administrator would be free to reverse the Regional Administrator. But the instances pointed to above, with the possible exception of page 27 of the Report, are of a different sort. The panel did not say that the information missing was unavailable or irrelevant; instead they supplied the information. They are free to do that as witnesses, but not as deciders.

The appropriate remedy under these circumstances is to remand the decision to the Administrator because he based his decision on material not part of the record. We are compelled to treat the use of the Report more severely than the use of the PSCO post-hearing submission because no party was given any opportunity to comment on the panel's Report. By contrast, all parties were given the opportunity to comment on PSCO's submission, and these comments were considered equally part of the record by the Administrator. We did hold that it was error to let the submission become part of the record, unless at an adjudicatory hearing. At such a hearing, however, the Administrator would have discretion to refuse cross-examination. 5 U.S.C. § 556(d). The remand on the point was to let the Administrator decide how he would use his discretion, assuming that all the materials in fact submitted had been in conjunction with an adjudicatory hearing. If the Administrator still would not allow cross-examination, then it would be pointless to require a hearing for the sole purpose of reading written statements into the record.

The Administrator will have the options of trying to reach a new decision not dependent on the panel's supplementation of the record; of holding a hearing at which all parties will have the opportunity to cross-examine the panel members and at which the panel will have an opportunity to amplify its position; or of taking any other action within his power and consistent with this opinion.

CONCLUSION

Because of this resolution, we do not reach the question of whether the Administrator's opinion was supported by substantial evidence. 5 U.S.C. § 706(2)(E). The Administrator must first set the record in order and reach his own conclusions on the state of the record as it will then stand.

So ordered.

QUESTIONS

1. Is the statute fairly read to trigger the formal rulemaking requirements of the federal APA? Does this case reflect a "tilt" toward environmentalists?
2. The 1981 Model State APA (MSAPA) takes an alternative approach to determining whether formal adjudication is required. *See* § 4-201. What triggers formal adjudication under that scheme? What triggers formal adjudication under your state's APA?
3. Review the provisions of sections 554, 556, and 557 of the APA, which appear in the Appendix. What are the main requirements of a formal adjudication that distinguish it from an informal adjudication? Why might an agency seek to avoid having to observe sections 554, 556, and 557?
4. What was wrong with the proceedings, assuming the APA applies? Why didn't the court rely upon 557(d)? 554(d)?
5. In March 2006, a panel of the First Circuit abandoned *Seacoast*'s rule that a hearing requirement in an organic act should be presumed to trigger formal adjudication. *Dominion Energy Brayton Point v. Johnson*, 443 F.3d 12, 17-18 (1st Cir. 2006). Instead of applying a presumption that the Clean Water Act's hearing requirement triggers formal adjudication, "we must defer to the EPA's interpretation of the CWA as long as that interpretation is reasonable." *Id.* at 18. For more general information on when a federal administrative agency must use the formal adjudication procedures set forth in sections 554, 556, and 557 of the APA, see the following note.

NOTE ON WHEN AGENCIES MUST OBSERVE FORMAL ADJUDICATION PROCEDURES

The question remains open whether a public hearing requirement in an organic act, without "on the record" language, triggers formal adjudication. To date, the Supreme Court has not issued a definitive ruling on this issue. In *Steadman v. SEC, infra,* p. 133, the Supreme Court in 1981 appeared to assume that a public hearing requirement, in the context of a statute providing for an agency adjudication, triggers formal adjudication procedures under sections 556 and 557 of the APA. *See* pp. 133-135 and especially fn. 13. However, the fact that the statute at issue in *Steadman* clearly required formal adjudication in certain proceedings, although not in others, arguably undercuts the inference that a public hearing requirement, without more, automatically triggers formal adjudication.

The *Steadman* Court also relied on a statutory provision that called for judicial review under a "substantial evidence" test, which presupposes a formal record. This assumption makes a great deal of sense. When Congress requires review of an adjudication under the substantial evidence test, one could logically view this requirement as presupposing formal, as opposed to informal, adjudication. But, even if this is so, *Steadman* fails to answer completely the larger question. The presence of a public hearing requirement, when joined with substantial evidence review, might trigger formal adjudication as a matter of course. This would still leave open the question of what happens when a statute requires a public hearing in the context of an adjudication, but fails to specify substantial evidence review of the facts.

The U.S. Court of Appeals for the District of Columbia Circuit squarely rejected the *Seacoast Anti-Pollution League* approach in *Chemical Waste Management, Inc. v. U.S. Environmental Protection Agency,* 873 F.2d 1477 (D.C. Cir. 1989). In relevant part, the court explained that:

> We will henceforth make no presumption that a statutory "hearing" requirement does or does not compel the agency to undertake a formal "hearing on the record," thereby leaving it to the agency, as an initial matter, to resolve the ambiguity. Instead of engaging in a general presumption in favor of formal adjudication, "the court will evaluate the reasonableness of the agency's interpretation [of the hearing requirement] using the normal tools of statutory interpretation — such as legislative history, structural inferences, or exceptional circumstances of the type presented in *UCS* [an earlier D.C. Circuit case requiring use of formal adjudication to satisfy a statutory public hearing requirement]."

The D.C. Circuit relied in this case on the deference to agency interpretation of statutes required by *Chevron U.S.A. v. NRDC,* 467 U.S. 837 (1984), deference that is treated extensively in the chapter on judicial review, *infra,* at pp. 507 *et seq. See also St. Louis Fuel & Supply Co. v. FERC,* 890 F.2d 446 (D.C. Cir. 1989) (finding that a statute that afforded "an opportunity for a hearing" but did not expressly state that the hearing must be "on the record" did not require formal adjudication where other prescriptions in the same act expressly invoked the APA, and where congressional floor statements had expressly disavowed formal adjudication). Subsequent decisions of the D.C. Circuit reflect the case-by-case approach that *Chemical Waste Management* adopted. In *Western*

Resources, Inc. v. Surface Transportation Board, 109 F.3d 782 (D.C. Cir. 1997), the court explained the rule as follows:

> Challenge to commission's procedure
>
>   Western Resources contends that the Commission violated its procedural rights when it (1) failed to provide for an oral hearing before the Commission, a member of the Commission, or an ALJ (other than four hours of oral argument before the Commission) or for cross-examination of witnesses before such officer; and (2) did not allow in-house counsel access to certain highly confidential materials.
>
>   Western Resources argues that the Commission's procedures were deficient in light of the requirements of APA formal adjudication, 5 U.S.C. §§ 554, 556, 557, and constitutional due process. According to petitioner, the statutory hook that imports formal adjudication into railway merger proceedings, is former 49 U.S.C. § 11344(a), new 49 U.S.C. § 11324(a). It states, in relevant part, that the agency "shall hold a public hearing . . . unless [it] determines that a public hearing is not necessary in the public interest." In view of the statute's express grant of discretion not to hold the public hearing at all, as well as the statistical and predictive nature of the issues before the Board, it seems doubtful that this language could require a full-fledged formal adjudicative hearing. *See generally Chemical Waste Management, Inc. v. EPA,* 873 F.2d 1477, 1482 (D.C. Cir. 1989) (stating that a statutory requirement of a "hearing" does not give rise to a presumption of formal adjudication and that it is necessary to look to other factors). [The court ultimately declined to reach the merits of this question "because Western Resources failed to raise either its APA or its constitutional argument before the Commission."]

Western Resources v. Surface Transp. Bd., 109 F.3d 782, 793 (D.C. Cir. 1997).

The District Court for the District of Columbia has explained the rule as follows:

> In a formal adjudication, the burden of proof is on "the proponent of the rule or order," in this case OSHA. 5 U.S.C. § 556(d). Despite plaintiffs' arguments to the contrary, however, OSHA's decision to approve Proposition 65 was not a formal adjudication. An adjudication is formal only when the decision "is required by statute on the record after opportunity for agency hearing." 5 U.S.C. § 554(a). While it is not clear what specific statutory language is required by the APA to trigger a formal adjudication, there must at least be some language instructing the agency to conduct some sort of hearing. *See United States v. Florida East Coast Railway Co.,* 410 U.S. 224, 241 (1973) (formal rulemaking required only when the specific phrase "on the record after opportunity for an agency hearing" is contained in statute); *Western Resources, Inc. v. Surface Transp. Bd.,* 109 F.3d 782, 793 (D.C. Cir. 1997) (court found it "doubtful" that statutory requirement to "hold a public hearing" required formal adjudicative procedures); *Chemical Waste Management, Inc. v. U.S. E.P.A.,* 873 F.2d 1477, 1482 (D.C. Cir. 1989) (statutory requirement for a "hearing" does not give rise to a presumption of formal adjudication).
>
>   Section 18 of the OSH Act provides that "[i]f the Secretary *rejects a plan* . . . , he shall afford the state submitting the plan due notice and opportunity for a hearing before so doing." 29 U.S.C. § 667(d) (emphasis added). The OSH Act does not require a hearing if the Secretary *approves* a plan (or amendment thereto). As the OSH Act does not contain the statutory language necessary to trigger formal adjudicative procedures, the decision in this case was not a formal adjudication and OSHA appropriately placed the burden of proof on the persons challenging the amendment.

Shell Oil Co. v. U.S. Dep't of Labor, 106 F. Supp. 2d 15, 19 (D.D.C. 2000).

These three cases stand for the proposition that absent a clearly expressed congressional intent, a statutory requirement for a public hearing *does not* automatically trigger formal adjudication procedures. Instead, the agency has discretion to use — or not use — such procedures as it thinks best.

In 2006, the United States Court of Appeals for the First Circuit abandoned *Seacoast* and adopted the *Chemical Waste Management* approach to determining whether an organic act that, in the context of an adjudicatory proceeding, contains a hearing requirement, but does not use the magic words "on the record," triggers the formal adjudication provisions of sections 554, 556, and 557 of the APA. *Dominion Energy Brayton Point v. Johnson*, 443 F.3d 12, 17-18 (1st Cir. 2006). "Although we in no way disparage the soundness of *Seacoast's* reasoning, the *Chevron* and *Brand X* opinions and the interposition of a new and reasonable agency interpretation of the disputed statutory language have changed the picture. Because we, like the *Seacoast* court, cannot discern a clear and unambiguous congressional intent behind the words 'public hearing' in the [Clean Water Act] and because the EPA's interpretation of that term constitutes a reasonable construction of the statute, deference is due." *Id.* at 18-19.

The *Dominion Energy* decision leaves the U.S. Court of Appeals for the Ninth Circuit as the only remaining U.S. Court of Appeals that adheres to the *Seacoast* presumption that a hearing requirement, in the context of an adjudicatory proceeding, triggers sections 554, 556, and 557 of the APA. *See Marathon Oil Co. v. EPA*, 564 F.2d 1253, 1262-64 (9th Cir. 1977) ("In summary, the crucial question is not whether particular talismanic language was used but whether the proceedings under review fall within that category of quasi-judicial proceedings deserving of special procedural protections"); *see also Portland Audubon Soc'y v. Oregon Lands Coalition*, 984 F.2d 1534, 1540-41 (9th Cir. 1993) (citing with approval and applying the *Marathon Oil Company* presumption that a hearing requirement in an organic act, in the context of an adjudication, triggers the formal adjudication provisions of the APA). Thus, at least for now, the Ninth Circuit's position is that "[c]ertain administrative decisions closely resemble judicial determinations and, in the interests of fairness, require similar procedural protections." *Portland Audubon Soc'y*, 984 F.2d at 1540. *See* Mila Sohoni, *Agency Adjudication and Judicial Nondelegation: An Article III Canon*, 107 Nw. U. L. Rev. 1569, 1605 & 1605-06 n.201 (2013) (noting that today "the predominant view is that agencies get *Chevron* deference as to whether the requirement for a hearing means a formal hearing or not," but also observing that "[t]he Ninth Circuit, however, has never overruled *Marathon Oil Co. v. EPA*").

With a 13-1 verdict against the Ninth Circuit's position among the U.S. Courts of Appeals, one might think that the Ninth Circuit's position lacks merit. From a purely numerical perspective, perhaps this is so. Viewed from the perspective of the *Londoner/Bi-Metallic* dichotomy, however, the Ninth Circuit's position has much to recommend it: what is the point of holding a hearing, in the context of an adjudication, if the agency is in no way bound to base its decision on materials adduced at the hearing? Unlike a congressional committee hearing, a hearing in the context of an adjudication looks more than a little like a kind of quasi-trial; a presumption in favor of applying procedural protections aimed at ensuring a decision supported by the record makes a great deal of sense when viewed in this light. Moreover, in an adjudicatory context, ascertaining facts correctly should constitute an important institutional goal; more formal procedures are likely to result in more accurate factual determinations.

Perhaps the best case for the Ninth Circuit's position flows from commentary in the ATTORNEY GENERAL'S MANUAL ON THE ADMINISTRATIVE PROCEDURE ACT (1947). The federal courts, including the Supreme Court, have afforded persuasive status to this guidebook, written by Attorney General (and soon-to-be Justice) Tom C. Clark and published immediately after the adoption of the APA in 1946. Consider the following excerpt:

> Other statutes authorizing agency action which is clearly adjudicatory in nature, such as the revocation of licenses, specifically require the agency to hold a hearing but contain no provision expressly requiring decision "on the record." . . . It seems clear that administrative adjudication exercised in this context is subject to sections 5, 7 and 8 [sections 554, 556, and 557].
>
> A further group of statutes merely authorizes adjudicatory action after hearing, and contain no reference to decision "on the record" nor any specific provision for judicial review. . . . It is believed that with respect to adjudication the specific statutory requirement of a hearing, without anything more, carries with it the further requirement of decision on the basis of the evidence adduced at the hearing. With respect to rule making, it was concluded, *supra*, that a statutory provision that rules be issued after a hearing, without more, should not be construed as requiring agency action "on the record", [sic] but rather as merely requiring an opportunity for the expression of views. That conclusion was based on the legislative nature of rule making, from which it was inferred, unless a statute requires otherwise, that an agency hearing on proposed rules would be similar to a hearing before a legislative committee, with neither the legislature nor the agency being limited to the material adduced at the hearing. No such rationale applies to administrative adjudication. In fact, it is assumed that where a statute specifically provides for administrative adjudication (such as the suspension of revocation of a license) after opportunity for agency hearing, such specific requirement for a hearing ordinarily implies the further requirement of decision in accordance with evidence adduced at the hearing. Of course, the foregoing discussion is inapplicable to any situation in which the legislative history or the context of the pertinent statute indicates a contrary congressional intent.

ATTORNEY GENERAL'S MANUAL ON THE ADMINISTRATIVE PROCEDURE ACT 42-43 (1947).

Obviously, this excerpt strongly supports the position of the Ninth Circuit and the First Circuit in *Seacoast.* Moreover, the *Marathon Oil Company* court expressly relied on this language in concluding that a presumption in favor of formal adjudication exists whenever an organic act, in the context of adjudication, calls for a public hearing. *See Marathon Oil Co.,* 564 F.2d at 1263-1264 & 1263 n.31. In sum, if one views the ATTORNEY'S GENERAL'S MANUAL as possessing persuasive force, it lends significant support to the Ninth Circuit's contrarian position.

Until the United States Supreme Court provides an authoritative answer, one rule will apply in the Ninth Circuit (encompassing most of the western United States) and another will apply in the rest of the country (including the Federal Circuit).

QUESTIONS

1. In determining whether formal adjudication is triggered, should a court look to the intent of the Congress that enacted the organic statute, or the intent of the Congress that enacted the APA? Can we assume the intent is the same?

2. In *Friends of the Earth v. Reilly,* 966 F.2d 690, 693-94 (D.C. Cir. 1992), the court
    had to determine whether an adjudication by the EPA was subject to the
    formal adjudication requirements of § 554. In making that determination,
    the court considered, *inter alia,* the nature of the facts that the agency had to
    consider in reaching its decision. The court stated that:

    > A section 554 hearing, with its attendant procedural protections, has as its
    > primary purpose the determination of "adjudicative facts," i.e., those facts
    > which "usually answer the questions of who did what, where, when, how,
    > why, with what motive or intent . . . [and] are roughly the kind of facts that
    > go to a jury in a jury case." 2 Kenneth Culp Davis, Administrative Law Treatise
    > § 12.3, at 413 (2d ed. 1979). A section 554 hearing is, in short, like a trial
    > proceeding. . . .
    >   The North Carolina [withdrawal] proceeding [whose status as a formal APA
    > adjudication was at issue in the case] demonstrates that the primary issues in a
    > withdrawal proceeding frequently involve legal issues such as whether the state
    > program is "equivalent to the Federal [RCRA] program" or is "consistent with
    > the Federal or State programs applicable in other States." 42 U.S.C. § 6926(b).
    > While factual issues may arise in the course of addressing these issues, these
    > factual issues can be classified as involving "legislative facts" — those "general
    > facts which help the tribunal decide questions of law and policy." Davis § 12:3,
    > at 413. A section 554 hearing is rarely necessary to determine such facts. As
    > Professor Davis notes: "Because the parties may often have little or nothing to
    > contribute to the development of legislative facts, the method of trial often is
    > not required for the determination of disputed issues about legislative facts."
    > *Id.* In short, neither the interests involved nor the issues likely to arise in a
    > withdrawal proceeding suggest that a section 554 hearing is required. We thus
    > conclude that Congress, in providing for a "public hearing," did not intend
    > that the withdrawal hearing be "'subject to' or 'governed by' section 554."

    Should a court consider the nature of the factual issues that an agency must
    decide in the adjudication when determining whether an organic statute has
    triggered a formal APA adjudication?
3. Does the APA prescribe any procedures for an informal adjudication? *See*
    § 555(e). To what sources of law should a party look for procedural require-
    ments for an informal adjudication?
4. Consider the alternatives to formal adjudication provided by the 1981
    MSAPA conference adjudicative hearings (§§ 4-401 to 4-403), emergency
    adjudicative proceedings (§ 4-501), and summary adjudicative proceedings
    (§§ 4-502 to 506).
5. Cases like *Seacoast* should be contrasted with the stricter requirement for
    "hearing on the record" language before formal *rulemaking* will be required
    under the federal APA. *See* the *Florida East Coast Railway* case, *infra,* p. 246.

D. PARTIES AND INTERVENTION

Compare APA §§ 551(3), 554(c), 555(b) with MSAPA § 4-209, and with Calif.
Govt. Code 11440.50:

(a) This section applies in adjudicative proceedings of an agency if the agency by regulation provides that this section is applicable in the proceedings.

(b) The presiding officer shall grant a motion for intervention if all of the following conditions are satisfied:

(1) The motion is submitted in writing, with copies served on all parties named in the agency's pleading.

(2) The motion is made as early as practicable in advance of the hearing. If there is a prehearing conference, the motion shall be made in advance of the prehearing conference and shall be resolved at the prehearing conference.

(3) The motion states facts demonstrating that the applicant's legal rights, duties, privileges, or immunities will be substantially affected by the proceeding or that the applicant qualifies as an intervenor under a statute or regulation.

(4) The presiding officer determines that the interests of justice and the orderly and prompt conduct of the proceeding will not be impaired by allowing the intervention.

(c) If an applicant qualifies for intervention, the presiding officer may impose conditions on the intervenor's participation in the proceeding, either at the time that intervention is granted or at a subsequent time. Conditions may include the following:

(1) Limiting the intervenor's participation to designated issues in which the intervenor has a particular interest demonstrated by the motion.

(2) Limiting or excluding the use of discovery, cross-examination, and other procedures involving the intervenor so as to promote the orderly and prompt conduct of the proceeding.

(3) Requiring two or more intervenors to combine their presentations of evidence and argument, cross-examination, discovery, and other participation in the proceeding.

(4) Limiting or excluding the intervenor's participation in settlement negotiations.

(d) As early as practicable in advance of the hearing the presiding officer shall issue an order granting or denying the motion for intervention, specifying any conditions, and briefly stating the reasons for the order. The presiding officer may modify the order at any time, stating the reasons for the modification. The presiding officer shall promptly give notice of an order granting, denying, or modifying intervention to the applicant and to all parties.

(e) Whether the interests of justice and the orderly and prompt conduct of the proceedings will be impaired by allowing intervention is a determination to be made in the sole discretion, and based on the knowledge and judgment at that time, of the presiding officer. The determination is not subject to administrative or judicial review.

(f) Nothing in this section precludes an agency from adopting a regulation that permits participation by a person short of intervention as a party, subject to Article 7 (commencing with Section 11430.10) of Chapter 4.5.

QUESTIONS

1. Which is the best approach? Are they really any different?
2. Do these statutory provisions confirm in your mind that "standing" to appear before an agency is not "standing" in the Article III case-or-controversy sense? *See Envirocare of Utah v. NRC,* 194 F.23d 72 (D.C. Cir. 1999),

discussed in William S. Jordan III, Envirocare v. NRC, *Increases Agency Discretion to Deny Administrative Intervention: Right Result — Wrong Reason,* 30 ELR News & Analysis 10597 (2000).

E. EVIDENCE AND PROOF ISSUES

RICHARDSON v. PERALES
402 U.S. 389 (1971)

MR. JUSTICE BLACKMUN delivered the opinion of the Court.

In 1966 Pedro Perales, a San Antonio truck driver, then aged 34, height 5 feet 11 inches, weight about 220 pounds, filed a claim for disability insurance benefits under the Social Security Act. Sections 216 (i)(1) and 223 (d)(1) both provide that the term "disability" means "inability to engage in any substantial gainful activity by reason of any medically determinable physical or mental impairment which [meets certain duration requirements]." Section 205 (g), 42 U.S.C. § 405 (g), relating to judicial review, states, "The findings of the Secretary as to any fact, if supported by substantial evidence, shall be conclusive. . . ."

The issue here is whether physicians' written reports of medical examinations they have made of a disability claimant may constitute "substantial evidence" supportive of a finding of nondisability, within the § 205 (g) standard, when the claimant objects to the admissibility of those reports and when the only live testimony is presented by his side and is contrary to the reports.

I

In his claim Perales asserted that on September 29, 1965, he became disabled as a result of an injury to his back sustained in lifting an object at work. [Five different medical doctors separately examined Mr. Perales, but they reached different medical conclusions regarding whether his back injuries were sufficiently severe to render him unable to work (and therefore legally disabled) because of severe back pain. The physicians each prepared formal written diagnoses of Mr. Perales' back condition; in turn, these written reports were entered into the formal hearing record that the hearing examiner compiled as the factual basis for his benefits decision. The hearing examiner placed substantial reliance on these medical reports, despite their hearsay status, in reaching the conclusion that Perales was not eligible for Social Security disability benefits.]

The hearing examiner, in reliance upon the several medical reports and the testimony of Dr. Leavitt, observed in his written decision, "There is objective medical evidence of impairment which the heavy preponderance of the evidence indicates to be of mild severity. . . . Taken altogether, the Hearing Examiner is of the conclusion that the claimant has not met the burden of proof." . . . The hearing examiner's decision, then, was that the claimant was not entitled to a period of disability or to disability insurance benefits.

It is to be noted at this point that § 205(d) of the Act, 42 U.S.C. § 405(d), provides that the Secretary has power to issue subpoenas requiring the attendance and testimony of witnesses and the production of evidence and that the Secretary's regulations, authorized by § 205(a), 42 U.S.C. § 405(a), provide that a claimant may request the issuance of subpoenas, 20 CFR § 404.926. Perales, however, who was represented by counsel, did not request subpoenas for either of the two hearings.

The claimant then made a request for review by the Appeals Council and submitted as supplemental evidence a judgment dated June 2, 1967, in Perales' favor against an insurance company for workmen's compensation benefits aggregating $11,665.84, plus medical and related expenses, and a medical report letter dated December 28, 1966. . . . The Appeals Council ruled that the decision of the hearing examiner was correct.

Upon this adverse ruling the claimant instituted the present action for review pursuant to § 205(g). Each side moved for summary judgment on the administrative transcript. The District Court stated that it was reluctant to accept as substantial evidence the opinions of medical experts submitted in the form of unsworn written reports, the admission of which would have the effect of denying the opposition an opportunity for cross-examination; that the opinion of a doctor who had never examined the claimant is entitled to little or no probative value, especially when opposed by substantial evidence including the oral testimony of an examining physician; and that what was before the court amounted to hearsay upon hearsay. The case was remanded for a new hearing before a different examiner. On appeal the Fifth Circuit noted the absence of any request by the claimant for subpoenas and held that, having this right and not exercising it, he was not in a position to complain that he had been denied the rights of confrontation and of cross-examination. It held that the hearsay evidence in the case was admissible under the Act; that, specifically, the written reports of the physicians were admissible in the administrative hearing; that Dr. Leavitt's testimony also was admissible; but that all this evidence together did not constitute substantial evidence when it was objected to and when it was contradicted by evidence from the only live witnesses.

On rehearing, the Court of Appeals observed that it did not mean by its opinion that uncorroborated hearsay could never be substantial evidence supportive of a hearing examiner's decision adverse to a claimant. It emphasized that its ruling that uncorroborated hearsay could not constitute substantial evidence was applicable only when the claimant had objected and when the hearsay was directly contradicted by the testimony of live medical witnesses and by the claimant in person. Certiorari was granted in order to review and resolve this important procedural due process issue.

II

We therefore are presented with the not uncommon situation of conflicting medical evidence. The trier of fact has the duty to resolve that conflict. We have, on the one hand, an absence of objective findings, an expressed suspicion of only functional complaints, of malingering, and of the patient's unwillingness to do anything about remedying an unprovable situation. We have, on the other hand, the claimant's and his personal physician's earnest pleas that significant and disabling residuals from the mishap of September 1965 are indeed present.

The issue revolves, however, around a system which produces a mass of medical evidence in report form. May material of that kind ever be "substantial evidence" when it stands alone and is opposed by live medical evidence and the client's own contrary personal testimony? The courts below have held that it may not.

IV

With this background and this atmosphere in mind, we turn to the statutory standard of "substantial evidence" prescribed by § 205(g). The Court has considered this very concept in other, yet similar, contexts. The National Labor Relations Act, § 10(e), in its original form, provided that the NLRB's findings of fact "if supported by evidence, shall be conclusive." 49 Stat. 454. The Court said this meant "supported by substantial evidence" and that this was

> "more than a mere scintilla. It means such relevant evidence as a reasonable mind might accept as adequate to support a conclusion." *Consolidated Edison Co. v. NLRB,* 305 U.S. 197, 229 (1938).

The Court has adhered to that definition in varying statutory situations. See *NLRB v. Columbian Enameling & Stamping Co.,* 306 U.S. 292, 300 (1939); *Universal Camera Corp. v. NLRB,* 340 U.S. 474, 477-487 (1951); *Consolo v. Federal Maritime Comm'n,* 383 U.S. 607, 619-620 (1966).

V

We may accept the propositions advanced by the claimant, some of them long established, that procedural due process is applicable to the adjudicative administrative proceeding involving "the differing rules of fair play, which through the years, have become associated with differing types of proceedings," *Hannah v. Larche,* 363 U.S. 420, 442 (1960); that "the 'right' to Social Security benefits is in one sense 'earned,'" *Flemming v. Nestor,* 363 U.S. 603, 610 (1960); and that the

> "extent to which procedural due process must be afforded the recipient is influenced by the extent to which he may be 'condemned to suffer grievous loss'. . . . Accordingly . . . 'consideration of what procedures due process may require under any given set of circumstances must begin with a determination of the precise nature of the government function involved as well as of the private interest that has been affected by governmental action.'" *Goldberg v. Kelly,* 397 U.S. 254, 262-263 (1970).

The question, then, is as to what procedural due process requires with respect to examining physicians' reports in a social security disability claim hearing.

We conclude that a written report by a licensed physician who has examined the claimant and who sets forth in his report his medical findings in his area of competence may be received as evidence in a disability hearing and, despite its hearsay character and an absence of cross-examination, and despite the presence of opposing direct medical testimony and testimony by the claimant himself, may constitute substantial evidence supportive of a finding by the hearing examiner adverse to the claimant, when the claimant has not exercised his right to subpoena the reporting physician and thereby provide himself with the opportunity for cross-examination of the physician.

We are prompted to this conclusion by a number of factors that, we feel, assure underlying reliability and probative value:

1. The identity of the five reporting physicians is significant. Each report presented here was prepared by a practicing physician who had examined the claimant. . . .

2. The vast workings of the social security administrative system make for reliability and impartiality in the consultant reports. We bear in mind that the agency operates essentially, and is intended so to do, as an adjudicator and not as an advocate or adversary. This is the congressional plan. We do not presume on this record to say that it works unfairly.

3. One familiar with medical reports and the routine of the medical examination, general or specific, will recognize their elements of detail and of value. The particular reports of the physicians who examined claimant Perales were based on personal consultation and personal examination and rested on accepted medical procedures and tests. . . .

These are routine, standard, and unbiased medical reports by physician specialists concerning a subject whom they had seen. That the reports were adverse to Perales' claim is not in itself bias or an indication of nonprobative character.

4. The reports present the impressive range of examination to which Perales was subjected. A specialist in neurosurgery, one in neurology, one in psychiatry, one in orthopedics, and one in physical medicine and rehabilitation add up to definitive opinion in five medical specialties, all somewhat related, but different in their emphases. It is fair to say that the claimant received professional examination and opinion on a scale beyond the reach of most persons and that this case reveals a patient and careful endeavor by the state agency and the examiner to ascertain the truth.

5. So far as we can detect, there is no inconsistency whatsoever in the reports of the five specialists. Yet each result was reached by independent examination in the writer's field of specialized training.

6. Although the claimant complains of the lack of opportunity to cross-examine the reporting physicians, he did not take advantage of the opportunity afforded him under 20 CFR § 404.926 to request subpoenas for the physicians. . . . This inaction on the claimant's part supports the Court of Appeals' view that the claimant as a consequence is to be precluded from now complaining that he was denied the rights of confrontation and cross-examination.

7. Courts have recognized the reliability and probative worth of written medical reports even in formal trials and, while acknowledging their hearsay character, have admitted them as an exception to the hearsay rule. . . .

8. Past treatment by reviewing courts of written medical reports in social security disability cases is revealing. Until the decision in this case, the courts of appeals, including the Fifth Circuit, with only an occasional criticism of the medical report practice, uniformly recognized reliability and probative value in such reports. The courts have reviewed administrative determinations, and upheld many adverse ones, where the only supporting evidence has been reports of this kind, buttressed sometimes, but often not, by testimony of a

medical adviser such as Dr. Leavitt. In these cases admissibility was not contested, but the decisions do demonstrate traditional and ready acceptance of the written medical report in social security disability cases.

9. There is an additional and pragmatic factor which, although not controlling, deserves mention. This is what Chief Judge Brown has described as "the sheer magnitude of that administrative burden," and the resulting necessity for written reports without "elaboration through the traditional facility of oral testimony." *Page v. Celebrezze*, 311 F.2d 757, 760 (CA5 1963). With over 20,000 disability claim hearings annually, the cost of providing live medical testimony at those hearings, where need has not been demonstrated by a request for a subpoena, over and above the cost of the examinations requested by hearing examiners, would be a substantial drain on the trust fund and on the energy of physicians already in short supply.

VI

1. Perales relies heavily on the Court's holding and statements in *Goldberg v. Kelly, supra,* particularly the comment that due process requires notice "and an effective opportunity to defend by confronting any adverse witnesses. . . ." 397 U.S., at 267-268. *Kelly,* however, had to do with termination of AFDC benefits without prior notice. It also concerned a situation, the Court said, "where credibility and veracity are at issue, as they must be in many termination proceedings." 397 U.S., at 269.

The *Perales* proceeding is not the same. We are not concerned with termination of disability benefits once granted. Neither are we concerned with a change of status without notice. Notice was given to claimant Perales. The physicians' reports were on file and available for inspection by the claimant and his counsel. And the authors of those reports were known and were subject to subpoena and to the very cross-examination that the claimant asserts he has not enjoyed. Further, the specter of questionable credibility and veracity is not present; there is professional disagreement with the medical conclusions, to be sure, but there is no attack here upon the doctors' credibility or veracity. *Kelly* affords little comfort to the claimant.

2. Perales also . . . would describe the medical reports in question as "mere uncorroborated hearsay" and would relate this to Mr. Chief Justice Hughes' sentence in *Consolidated Edison Co. v. NLRB,* 305 U.S., at 230: "Mere uncorroborated hearsay or rumor does not constitute substantial evidence."

Although the reports are hearsay in the technical sense, because their content is not produced live before the hearing examiner, we feel that the claimant and the Court of Appeals read too much into the single sentence from *Consolidated Edison.* The contrast the Chief Justice was drawing, at the very page cited, was not with material that would be deemed formally inadmissible in judicial proceedings but with material "without a basis in evidence having rational probative force." This was not a blanket rejection by the Court of administrative reliance on hearsay irrespective of reliability and probative value. The opposite was the case. . . .

3. The claimant, the District Court, and the Court of Appeals also criticize the use of Dr. Leavitt as a medical adviser. Inasmuch as medical advisers are used in approximately 13% of disability claim hearings, comment as to this practice is

indicated. We see nothing "reprehensible" in the practice, as the claimant would describe it. The trial examiner is a layman; the medical adviser is a board-certified specialist. He is used primarily in complex cases for explanation of medical problems in terms understandable to the layman-examiner. He is a neutral adviser. This particular record discloses that Dr. Leavitt explained the technique and significance of electromyography. He did offer his own opinion on the claimant's condition. That opinion, however, did not differ from the medical reports. Dr. Leavitt did not vouch for the accuracy of the facts assumed in the reports. No one understood otherwise. . . . We see nothing unconstitutional or improper in the medical adviser concept and in the presence of Dr. Leavitt in this administrative hearing.

4. Finally, the claimant complains of the system of processing disability claims. He suggests, and is joined in this by the briefs of amici, that the Administrative Procedure Act, rather than the Social Security Act, governs the processing of claims and specifically provides for cross-examination, 5 U.S.C. § 556(d) (1964 ed., Supp. V). The claimant goes on to assert that in any event the hearing procedure is invalid on due process grounds. He says that the hearing examiner has the responsibility for gathering the evidence and "to make the Government's case as strong as possible"; that naturally he leans toward a decision in favor of the evidence he has gathered; that justice must satisfy the appearance of justice, . . . ; and that an "independent hearing examiner such as in the" Longshoremen's and Harbor Workers' Compensation Act should be provided.

We need not decide whether the APA has general application to social security disability claims, for the social security administrative procedure does not vary from that prescribed by the APA. Indeed, the latter is modeled upon the Social Security Act. The cited § 556(d) provides that any documentary evidence "may be received" subject to the exclusion of the irrelevant, the immaterial, and the unduly repetitious. It further provides that a "party is entitled to present his case or defense by oral or documentary evidence . . . and to conduct such cross-examination as may be required for a full and true disclosure of the facts" and in "determining claims for money or benefits . . . an agency may, when a party will not be prejudiced thereby, adopt procedures for the submission of all or part of the evidence in written form."

These provisions conform, and are consistent with, rather than differ from or supersede, the authority given the Secretary by the Social Security Act's §§ 205(a) and (b) "to establish procedures," and "to regulate and provide for the nature and extent of the proofs and evidence and the method of taking and furnishing the same in order to establish the right to benefits," and to receive evidence "even though inadmissible under rules of evidence applicable to court procedure." Hearsay, under either Act, is thus admissible up to the point of relevancy. . . . The matter comes down to the question of the procedure's integrity and fundamental fairness. We see nothing that works in derogation of that integrity and of that fairness in the admission of consultants' reports, subject as they are to being material and to the use of the subpoena and consequent cross-examination. This precisely fits the statutorily prescribed "cross-examination as may be required for a full and true disclosure of the facts." That is the standard. It is clear and workable and does not fall short of procedural due process. . . .

Neither are we persuaded by the advocate-judge-multiple-hat suggestion. It assumes too much and would bring down too many procedures designed, and working well, for a governmental structure of great and growing complexity. The social security hearing examiner, furthermore, does not act as counsel. He acts as an examiner charged with developing the facts. The 44.2% reversal rate for all federal disability hearings in cases where the state agency does not grant benefits attests to the fairness of the system and refutes the implication of impropriety.

We therefore reverse and remand for further proceedings. We intimate no view as to the merits. It is for the District Court now to determine whether the Secretary's findings, in the light of all material proffered and admissible, are supported by "substantial evidence" within the command of § 205(g). *It is so ordered.*

[Justices Douglas, Black, and Brennan dissented.]

QUESTIONS

1. What is the source of the asserted procedural right?
2. Compare the way in which the 1981 MSAPA regulates the admissibility of evidence. *See* § 4-212(a).
3. Why should hearsay be more admissible in an agency hearing than in a court?
4. Distinguish between (a) the issue of whether evidence is admissible in a hearing and (b) whether a decision may be based on that kind of evidence alone.
5. A "residuum rule" requires at least some evidence that would be admissible in court for an order based upon the evidence to be upheld on review. Does it make sense to have a residuum rule? If evidence is admissible, why can't an agency rely upon it? With *Perales,* compare 1981 MSAPA § 4-215(d), and Cal. Govt. Code 11513(c)-(f), which provides:

    (c) The hearing need not be conducted according to technical rules relating to evidence and witnesses, except as hereinafter provided. Any relevant evidence shall be admitted if it is the sort of evidence on which responsible persons are accustomed to rely in the conduct of serious affairs, regardless of the existence of any common law or statutory rule which might make improper the admission of the evidence over objection in civil actions.
    (d) Hearsay evidence may be used for the purpose of supplementing or explaining other evidence but over timely objection shall not be sufficient in itself to support a finding unless it would be admissible over objection in civil actions. An objection is timely if made before submission of the case or on reconsideration.
    (e) The rules of privilege shall be effective to the extent that they are otherwise required by statute to be recognized at the hearing.
    (f) The presiding officer has discretion to exclude evidence if its probative value is substantially outweighed by the probability that its admission will necessitate undue consumption of time.

6. Would it make sense to apply a residuum rule to state agencies but not federal agencies?
7. Is *Perales* really a cost/benefit decision masquerading as a highly technical burden of proof decision? Would it be a prudent expenditure of government resources to require all treating physicians to testify in person at

contested benefits hearings? To put the matter starkly, would the increase in accurate decisions be sufficient to offset the tremendous increase in the cost of appeals? As one commentator has explained, "Agencies generally shy away from acknowledging that they are making value judgments, claiming that the values they apply are specified in their statutes. Yet, cost/benefit analysis is an attempt to increase social welfare by crafting a rule properly." Jacqueline Fox, *Medicare Should, but Cannot, Consider Cost: Legal Impediments to a Sound Policy*, 53 Buff L. Rev. 577, 630 (2005). Thus, "[a] decision to limit the availability of medical technology because of its cost is clearly a value judgment. Somewhere in this specific decision is a more broad determination that at a certain point in medical care, the cost is more than the country should spend." *Id.* at 630-31. If additional process cannot be justified in cost/benefit terms, should an agency be permitted to not provide it? Should it depend on the terms of the organic act? Or should courts permit agencies to imply cost/benefit analysis, even if the organic act in question does not speak directly to the issue?

8. If Perales were a white collar worker, like a lawyer or an accountant, complaining of chronic lower back pain, would the benefits system likely be more or less skeptical about the merits of the claim? For one perspective on how issues of race and class can affect the delivery of government benefits, *see* Dorothy A. Brown, *Race and Class Matters in Tax Policy*, 107 Colum. L. Rev. 790 (2007).

STEADMAN v. SECURITIES AND EXCHANGE COMMISSION
450 U.S. 91 (1981)

Justice Brennan delivered the opinion of the Court.

In administrative proceedings, the Securities and Exchange Commission applies a preponderance-of-the-evidence standard of proof in determining whether the antifraud provisions of the federal securities laws have been violated. The question presented is whether such violations must be proved by clear and convincing evidence rather than by a preponderance of the evidence.

I

In June 1971, the Commission initiated a disciplinary proceeding against petitioner and certain of his wholly owned companies. The proceeding against petitioner was brought pursuant to §9(b) of the Investment Company Act of 1940[1] and §203(f) of the Investment Advisers Act of 1940.[2] The Commission alleged that petitioner had violated numerous provisions of the federal

1. Section 9(b) of the Investment Company Act of 1940, 15 U.S.C. §80a-9(b), empowers the Commission, in specified circumstances, "after notice and opportunity for hearing . . . [to] prohibit, conditionally or unconditionally, either permanently or for such period of time as it in its discretion shall deem appropriate in the public interest, any person from serving or acting as an employee, officer, director, member of an advisory board, investment adviser or depositor of, or principal underwriter for, a registered investment company or affiliated person of such investment adviser, depositor, or principal underwriter. . . ."

2. Section 203(f) of the Investment Advisers Act of 1940, 15 U.S.C. §80b-3(f), empowers the Commission, in specified circumstances, after notice and opportunity for hearing "on the record" to "censure or place limitations on the activities of any person associated or seeking to become

securities laws in his management of several mutual funds registered under the Investment Company Act.

After a lengthy evidentiary hearing before an Administrative Law Judge and review by the Commission in which the preponderance-of-the-evidence standard was employed, the Commission held that between December 1965 and June 1972, petitioner had violated antifraud, reporting, conflict of interest, and proxy provisions of the federal securities laws. Accordingly, it entered an order permanently barring petitioner from associating with any investment adviser or affiliating with any registered investment company, and suspending him for one year from associating with any broker or dealer in securities.

Petitioner sought review of the Commission's order in the United States Court of Appeals for the Fifth Circuit on a number of grounds, only one of which is relevant for our purposes. Petitioner challenged the Commission's use of the preponderance-of-the-evidence standard of proof in determining whether he had violated antifraud provisions of the securities laws. He contended that, because of the potentially severe sanctions that the Commission was empowered to impose and because of the circumstantial and inferential nature of the evidence that might be used to prove intent to defraud, the Commission was required to weigh the evidence against a clear-and-convincing standard of proof. The Court of Appeals rejected petitioner's argument [and we] affirm.

II

Where Congress has not prescribed the degree of proof which must be adduced by the proponent of a rule or order to carry its burden of persuasion in an administrative proceeding, this Court has felt at liberty to prescribe the standard, for "[it] is the kind of question which has traditionally been left to the judiciary to resolve." *Woodby v. INS,* 385 U.S. 276, 284 (1966). However, where Congress has spoken, we have deferred to "the traditional powers of Congress to prescribe rules of evidence and standards of proof in the federal courts" absent countervailing constitutional constraints. For Commission disciplinary proceedings initiated pursuant to 15 U.S.C. § 80a-9(b) and § 80b-3(f), we conclude that Congress has spoken, and has said that the preponderance-of-the-evidence standard should be applied.

The securities laws provide for judicial review of Commission disciplinary proceedings in the federal courts of appeals and specify the scope of such review.[12] Because they do not indicate which standard of proof governs Commission adjudications, however, we turn to § 5 of the Administrative Procedure Act (APA), 5 U.S.C. § 554, which "applies . . . in every case of adjudication required by statute to be determined on the record after opportunity for an agency hearing," except in instances not relevant here.[13] Section 5(b), 5 U.S.C.

---

associated with an investment adviser, or suspend for a period not exceeding twelve months or bar any such person from being associated with an investment adviser. . . ."

12. Commission findings of fact are conclusive for a reviewing court "if supported by substantial evidence." 15 U.S.C. §§ 78y, 80a-42, and 80b-13; cf. § 77i (Commission findings conclusive "if supported by evidence").

13. This disciplinary proceeding, brought by the Commission pursuant to 15 U.S.C. § 80a-9(b) and § 80b-3(f), is clearly a "case of adjudication" within 5 U.S.C. § 554. Both § 80a-9(b) and § 80b-3(f) also explicitly require an "opportunity for [an agency] hearing." Moreover, the disciplinary proceeding must be conducted "on the record." The phrase "on the record" appears in § 80b-3(f),

§ 554(c)(2), makes the provisions of § 7, 5 U.S.C. [§ 556], applicable to adjudicatory proceedings. The answer to the question presented in this case turns therefore on the proper construction of § 7.

The search for congressional intent begins with the language of the statute. Section 7(c), 5 U.S.C. § 556(d), states in pertinent part:

> "Except as otherwise provided by statute, the proponent of a rule or order has the burden of proof. Any oral or documentary evidence may be received, but the agency as a matter of policy shall provide for the exclusion of irrelevant, immaterial, or unduly repetitious evidence. A sanction may not be imposed or rule or order issued except on consideration of the whole record or those parts thereof cited by a party and supported by and *in accordance with* the reliable, probative, and *substantial evidence.*" (Emphasis added.)

The language of the statute itself implies the enactment of a standard of proof. By allowing sanctions to be imposed only when they are "in accordance with . . . *substantial* evidence," Congress implied that a sanction must rest on a *minimum quantity* of evidence. The word "substantial" denotes quantity. The phrase "in accordance with . . . substantial evidence" thus requires that a decision be based on a certain quantity of evidence. Petitioner's contention that the phrase "reliable, probative, and substantial evidence" sets merely a standard of *quality* of evidence is, therefore, unpersuasive.

The phrase "in accordance with" lends further support to a construction of § 7(c) as establishing a standard of proof. Unlike § 10(e), the APA's explicit "Scope of review" provision that declares that agency action shall be held unlawful if "unsupported by substantial evidence,"[18] § 7(c) provides that an agency may issue an order only if that order is "supported by and *in accordance with . . .* substantial evidence" (emphasis added). The additional words "in accordance with" suggest that the adjudicating agency must weigh the evidence and decide, based on the weight of the evidence, whether a disciplinary order should be issued. The language of § 7(c), therefore, requires that the agency decision must be "in accordance with" the weight of the evidence, not simply supported by enough evidence "to justify, if the trial were to a jury, a refusal to direct a verdict

and while it does not appear in § 80a-9(b), *see* n. 1, *supra,* the absence of the specific phrase from § 80a-9(b) does not make the instant proceeding not subject to § 554. *See United States v. Florida East Coast R. Co.,* 410 U.S. 224, 238 (1973); *United States v. Allegheny-Ludlum Steel Corp.,* 406 U.S. 742, 757 (1972); *Seacoast Anti-Pollution League v. Costle,* 572 F.2d 872, 876 (CA1), cert. denied, 439 U.S. 824 (1978). Rather, the "on the record" requirement for § 80a-9(b) is satisfied by the substantive content of the adjudication. Title 15 U.S.C. § 80a-42 provides for judicial review of Commission orders issued pursuant to § 80a-9(b). Substantial-evidence review by the Court of Appeals here required a hearing on the record. See *Citizens to Preserve Overton Park, Inc. v. Volpe,* 401 U.S. 402, 415 (1971); *Seacoast Anti-Pollution League v. Costle,* 572 F.2d, at 877. Otherwise effective review by the Court of Appeals would have been frustrated. *Ibid.* In addition, the substantive violations to be proved pursuant to §§ 80a-9(b)(1)-(3) are virtually identical to the substantive violations stated in §§ 80b-3(e)(1), (4), and (5), which are incorporated by reference into § 80b-3(f). The only substantive difference between § 80b-3(f) and § 80a-9(b) is that the former permits the Commission to impose sanctions on persons affiliated with an investment adviser and the latter on persons affiliated with an investment company. In both statutes, the Commission is required to prove violations of the securities law provisions enumerated, precisely the type of proceeding for which the APA's adjudicatory procedures were intended. See generally 410 U.S., at 246.

18. Section 10(e) of the APA, 5 U.S.C. § 706, is entitled "Scope of review" and provides, in pertinent part, that "[the] reviewing court shall . . . hold unlawful and set aside agency action, findings, and conclusions found to be . . . unsupported by substantial evidence in a case subject to sections 556 and 557 of this title or otherwise reviewed on the record of an agency hearing provided by statute." § 706(2)(E).

when the conclusion sought to be drawn from it is one of fact for the jury." *Consolo v. FMC*, 383 U.S. 607, 620 (1966), quoting *NLRB v. Columbian Enameling & Stamping Co.*, 306 U.S. 292, 300 (1939). Obviously, weighing evidence has relevance only if the evidence on each side is to be measured against a standard of proof which allocates the risk of error. Section 10(e), by contrast, does not permit the reviewing court to weigh the evidence, but only to determine that there is in the record "such relevant evidence as a reasonable mind might accept as adequate to support a conclusion," *Consolo v. FMC, supra,* at 620, quoting *Consolidated Edison Co. v. NLRB*, 305 U.S. 197, 229 (1938). It is not surprising, therefore, in view of the entirely different purposes of § 7(c) and § 10(e), that Congress intended the words "substantial evidence" to have different meanings in context. Thus, petitioner's argument that § 7(c) merely establishes the scope of judicial review of agency orders is unavailing.[20]

While the language of § 7(c) suggests, therefore, that Congress intended the statute to establish a standard of proof, the language of the statute is somewhat opaque concerning the precise standard of proof to be used. The legislative history, however, clearly reveals the Congress' intent. The original Senate version of § 7(c) provided that "no sanction shall be imposed . . . except as supported by relevant, reliable, and probative evidence." S. 7, 79th Cong., 1st Sess. (1945). After the Senate passed this version, the House passed the language of the statute as it reads today, and the Senate accepted the amendment. Any doubt as to the intent of Congress is removed by the House Report, which expressly adopted a preponderance-of-the-evidence standard:

> "[Where] a party having the burden of proceeding has come forward with a prima facie and substantial case, he will prevail unless his evidence is discredited or rebutted. In any case the agency must decide "in accordance with the evidence." Where there is evidence pro and con, the agency must weigh it and decide *in accordance with the preponderance.* In short, these provisions require a conscientious and rational judgment on the whole record in accordance with the proofs adduced." H. R. Rep. No. 1980, 79th Cong., 2d Sess., 37 (1946) (emphasis added).

Nor is there any suggestion in the legislative history that a standard of proof higher than a preponderance of the evidence was ever contemplated, much less intended. Congress was primarily concerned with the elimination of agency decisionmaking premised on evidence which was of poor quality—irrelevant, immaterial, unreliable, and nonprobative—and of insufficient quantity—less than a preponderance.

---

20. It is true that the phrase "substantial evidence" is often used to denote the scope of judicial review. *See* n. 12, *supra.* But to conclude that the phrase "substantial evidence" in § 7(c) defines the scope of judicial review would make the "substantial evidence" language of § 10(e) redundant. Moreover, it is implausible to think that the drafters of the APA would place a scope-of-review standard in the middle of a statutory provision designed to govern evidentiary issues in adjudicatory proceedings. Section 7 is entitled "Hearings; presiding employees; powers and duties; burden of proof; evidence; record as basis of decision." It "is made up almost entirely of a specification of the various elements of trial procedure." 2 K. Davis, Administrative Law Treatise § 10:07, p. 332 (2d ed. 1979). More specifically, § 7(c) allocates the burden of proof (placing it on the proponent of a rule or order), provides for a broad rule governing admissibility of evidence, directs an agency to exclude "irrelevant, immaterial, or unduly repetitious evidence," and delineates the evidentiary basis on which a "sanction may . . . be imposed."

Petitioner's argument overlooks the different functions of initial decisionmaking and judicial review of it. As we recognized in *Consolo v. FMC*, 383 U.S. 607 (1966), the reviewing court is not to weigh the evidence, which *Consolo* assumed had already been done.

The language and legislative history of § 7(c) lead us to conclude, therefore, that § 7(c) was intended to establish a standard of proof and that the standard adopted is the traditional preponderance-of-the-evidence standard.[22]

III

Our view of congressional intent is buttressed by the Commission's longstanding practice of imposing sanctions according to the preponderance of the evidence. As early as 1938, the Commission rejected the argument that in a proceeding to determine whether to suspend, expel, or otherwise sanction a brokerage firm and its principals for, *inter alia,* manipulation of security prices in violation of § 9 of the Securities Exchange Act of 1934, 15 U.S.C. § 78i, a standard of proof greater than the preponderance-of-the-evidence standard was required. *In re White,* 3 S.E.C. 466, 539-540 (1938). Use of the preponderance standard continued after passage of the APA, and persists today. The Commission's consistent practice, which is in harmony with § 7(c) and its legislative history, is persuasive authority that Congress intended that Commission disciplinary proceedings, subject to § 7 of the APA, be governed by a preponderance-of-the-evidence standard.

. . . In § 7(c), Congress has similarly expressed its intent that adjudicatory proceedings subject to the APA satisfy the statute where determinations are made according to the preponderance of the evidence. Congress was free to make that choice, *Vance v. Terrazas,* 444 U.S., at 265-266, and, in the absence of countervailing constitutional considerations, the courts are not free to disturb it. *Affirmed.*

[Justices Powell and Stewart dissented.]

22. Petitioner's reliance on *Woodby v. INS, supra,* is misplaced. There the Court required the Immigration and Naturalization Service to establish facts in deportation proceedings by clear, unequivocal, and convincing evidence. The Court adopted this standard of proof because deportation proceedings were not subject to the APA, and the Immigration and Nationality Act (INA) did not prescribe a standard of proof, only the scope of judicial review. The Court reached this conclusion after examining the language, legislative history, and purpose of § 106(a)(4) and § 242(b)(4) of the INA. That both sections contained the words "reasonable, substantial, and probative evidence" has little bearing on the construction of somewhat different language in an entirely different statute. The language, purpose, and legislative history of these sections of the INA differ in material respects from the language, purpose, and legislative history of § 7(c). Section 106(a)(4) was explicitly labeled a judicial review provision. Section 242(b)(4) was also construed by the Court to be "addressed to reviewing courts," 385 U.S., at 283, in part because at the time that the provision was adopted, there was no other scope-of-judicial-review provision in the INA, *id.,* at 284. The APA, by contrast, was passed with an explicit judicial review provision, § 10(e), and with a provision explicitly governing evidentiary matters before the agency, § 7(c). To the extent § 242(b)(4) was viewed by the Court as representing a "yardstick for the administrative factfinder," the Court concluded that the provision was directed at the quality of evidence upon which an order could be based. *Id.,* at 283. The language of § 242(b)(4) differs from the language of § 7(c), which includes the additional phrase "in accordance with." Moreover, as explained above, the legislative history and purpose of § 7(c) make clear that it was not limited to quality-of-evidence concerns or directed at all at judicial review.

We thus accept Justice Clark's statement in dissent, with which the Court in *Woodby* did not disagree, that §§ 7(c) and 10(e) of the APA have "traditionally been held satisfied when the agency decides on the preponderance of the evidence." *Id.,* at 289, n. 1. Justice Clark's understanding of § 7(c), as expressed in *Woodby,* is entitled to particular respect. We have previously noted that the Attorney General's Manual on the Administrative Procedure Act (1947) has been "given some deference by this Court because of the role played by the Department of Justice in drafting the legislation," *Vermont Yankee Nuclear Power Corp. v. Natural Resources Defense Council, Inc.,* 435 U.S., at 546, and Justice Clark was Attorney General both when the APA was passed and when the Manual was published.

QUESTIONS

1. Distinguish among the *burden of going forward* (arguably dealt within the first sentence of § 556(d)), the *burden of persuasion* (the standard for which was at issue in *Steadman*), and the *scope of review* (§ 706(2)(e)).
2. How significant is the burden of going forward?
3. Note that the federal APA provisions for formal adjudication require findings. § 557(c)(A), as does 1981 MSAPA § 4-215(c). What about with respect to informal adjudications? There is no explicit requirement in the federal APA, *see Citizens to Preserve Overton Park v. Volpe*, p. 578, *infra*, but sometimes findings are in effect necessitated to permit the judicial review required by statute. *See Camp v. Pitts*, 411 U.S. 138 (1973). Courts have also generally required that agencies explain *inconsistent* determinations. *See UAW v. NLRB*, 802 F.2d 969 (7th Cir. 1986).

F. COMBINATIONS OF FUNCTIONS

WITHROW v. LARKIN
421 U.S. 35 (1975)

MR. JUSTICE WHITE delivered the [unanimous] opinion of the Court.

The statutes of the State of Wisconsin forbid the practice of medicine without a license from an Examining Board composed of practicing physicians. The statutes also define and forbid various acts of professional misconduct, proscribe fee splitting, and make illegal the practice of medicine under any name other than the name under which a license was issued if the public would be misled, such practice would constitute unfair competition with another physician, or other detriment to the profession would result. To enforce these provisions, the Examining Board is empowered under Wis. Stat. Ann. §§ 448.17 and 448.18 (1974) to warn and reprimand, temporarily to suspend the license, and "to institute criminal action or action to revoke license when it finds probable cause therefor under criminal or revocation statute. . . ."[1] When an investigative

---

1. "No person shall practice or attempt or hold himself out as authorized to practice medicine, surgery, or osteopathy, or any other system of treating the sick as the term 'treat the sick' is defined in § 445.01(1)(a), without a license or certificate of registration from the examining board, except as otherwise specifically provided by statute." Wis. Stat. Ann. § 448.02(1).

"The examining board shall investigate, hear and act upon practices by persons licensed to practice medicine and surgery under § 488.06, that are inimical to the public health. The examining board shall have the power to warn and to reprimand, when it finds such practice, and to institute criminal action or action to revoke license when it finds probable cause therefor under criminal or revocation statute, and the attorney general may aid the district attorney in the prosecution thereof." § 448.17.

"A license or certificate of registration may be temporarily suspended by the examining board, without formal proceedings, and its holder placed on probation for a period not to exceed 3 months where he is known or the examining board has good cause to believe that such holder has violated sub. (1). The examining board shall not have authority to suspend a license or certificate of registration, or to place a holder on probation, for more than 2 consecutive 3-month periods. All examining board actions under this subsection shall be subject to review under ch. 227." § 448.18 (7).

Section 448.18(1)(g) prohibits "engaging in conduct unbecoming a person licensed to practice or detrimental to the best interests of the public." Fee splitting is proscribed by § 448.23(1). Section

proceeding before the Examining Board was commenced against him, appellee brought this suit against appellants, the individual members of the Board, seeking an injunction against the enforcement of the statutes. The District Court issued a preliminary injunction, the appellants appealed, and we noted probable jurisdiction.

I

Appellee, a resident of Michigan and licensed to practice medicine there, obtained a Wisconsin license in August 1971 under a reciprocity agreement between Michigan and Wisconsin governing medical licensing. His practice in Wisconsin consisted of performing abortions at an office in Milwaukee. On June 20, 1973, the Board sent to appellee a notice that it would hold an investigative hearing on July 12, 1973, under Wis. Stat. Ann. § 448.17 to determine whether he had engaged in certain proscribed acts.[2] The hearing would be closed to the public, although appellee and his attorney could attend. They would not, however, be permitted to cross-examine witnesses. Based upon the evidence presented at the hearing, the Board would decide "whether to warn or reprimand if it finds such practice and whether to institute criminal action or action to revoke license if probable cause therefor exists under criminal or revocation statutes."

On July 6, 1973, appellee filed his complaint in this action under 42 U.S.C. § 1983 seeking preliminary and permanent injunctive relief and a temporary restraining order preventing the Board from investigating him and from conducting the investigative hearing. The District Court denied the motion for a temporary restraining order.

On July 12, 1973, appellants moved to dismiss the complaint. On the same day, appellee filed an amended complaint in which injunctive relief was sought on the ground that Wis. Stat. Ann. §§ 448.17 and 448.18 were unconstitutional and that appellants' acts with respect to him violated his constitutional rights. The District Court again denied appellee's motion for a temporary restraining order, but did not act upon appellants' motion to dismiss. On July 30, 1973, appellants submitted an amended motion to dismiss.

The Board proceeded with its investigative hearing on July 12 and 13, 1973; numerous witnesses testified and appellee's counsel was present throughout the proceedings. Appellee's counsel was subsequently informed that appellee could, if he wished, appear before the Board to explain any of the evidence which had been presented.

On September 18, 1973, the Board sent to appellee a notice that a "contested hearing" would be held on October 4, 1973, to determine whether appellee had engaged in certain prohibited acts[4] and that based upon the evidence adduced

---

448.02(4) regulates the use of a name by a physician in his practice other than the name under which he was licensed.

Appellee maintains that he has legal and factual defenses to all charges made against him.

2. The notice indicated that the hearing would be held "to determine whether the licensee has engaged in practices that are inimical to the public health, whether he has engaged in conduct unbecoming a person licensed to practice medicine, and whether he has engaged in conduct detrimental to the best interests of the public."

4. The notice stated that the hearing would be held "to determine whether the licensee has practiced medicine in the State of Wisconsin under any other Christian or given name or any other surname than that under which he was originally licensed or registered to practice medicine in this

at the hearing the Board would determine whether his license would be suspended temporarily under Wis. Stat. Ann. § 448.18(7). Appellee moved for a restraining order against the contested hearing. The District Court granted the motion on October 1, 1973. Because the Board had moved from purely investigative proceedings to a hearing aimed at deciding whether suspension of appellee's license was appropriate, the District Court concluded that a substantial federal question had arisen, namely, whether the authority given to appellants both "to investigate physicians and present charges [and] to rule on those charges and impose punishment, at least to the extent of reprimanding or temporarily suspending" violated appellee's due process rights. Appellee's motion to request the convening of a three-judge court was also granted, and appellants' motion to dismiss was denied.

The Board complied and did not go forward with the contested hearing. Instead, it noticed and held a final investigative session on October 4, 1973, at which appellee's attorney, but not appellee, appeared. The Board thereupon issued "Findings of Fact," "Conclusions of Law," and a "Decision" in which the Board found that appellee had engaged in specified conduct proscribed by the statute. The operative portion of its "Decision" was the following:

> "Within the meaning of sec. 448.17, Stats., it is hereby determined that there is probable cause to believe that licensee has violated the criminal provisions of ch. 448, Stats., and that there is probable cause for an action to revoke the license of the licensee for engaging in unprofessional conduct. [sic]
>
> "Therefore, it is the decision of this Board that the secretary verify this document and file it as a verified complaint with the District Attorney of Milwaukee County in accordance with sec. 448.18 (2), Stats., for the purpose of initiating an action to revoke the license of Duane R. Larkin, M.D., to practice medicine and surgery in the State of Wisconsin and initiating appropriate actions for violation of the criminal laws relating to the practice of medicine." App. 59-60.

On November 19, 1973, the three-judge District Court found (with an opinion following on December 21, 1973) that § 448.18(7) was unconstitutional as a violation of due process guarantees and enjoined the Board from enforcing it. Its holding was:

> "[F]or the board temporarily to suspend Dr. Larkin's license at its own contested hearing on charges evolving from its own investigation would constitute a denial to him of his rights to procedural due process. Insofar as § 448.18 (7) authorizes a procedure wherein a physician stands to lose his liberty or property, absent the intervention of an independent, neutral and detached decision maker, we concluded that it was unconstitutional and unenforceable."

---

state, which practicing has operated to unfairly compete with another practitioner, to mislead the public as to identity, or to otherwise result in detriment to the profession or the public, and more particularly, whether the said Duane Larkin, M.D., has practiced medicine in this state since September 1, 1971, under the name of Glen Johnson." It would also "determine whether the licensee has permitted persons to practice medicine in this state in violation of sec. 448.02 (1), Stats., more particularly whether the said Duane Larkin, M.D., permitted Young Wahn Ahn, M.D., an unlicensed physician, to perform abortions at his abortion clinic during the year 1972." Finally the Board would "determine whether the said Duane Larkin, M.D., split fees with other persons during the years 1971, 1972, and 1973 in violation of sec. 448.23 (1)."

Judgment was entered on January 31, 1974, by which it was "Ordered and Adjudged that § 448.18(7), Wis. Stats., is unconstitutional and that the defendants are preliminarily enjoined until further notice from utilizing the provisions of § 448.18(7), Wis. Stats."

Appellants took an appeal from that decision, and we noted probable jurisdiction on June 10, 1974. Subsequently, on July 25, 1974, the District Court, at the initial suggestion of appellants but joined in by a crossmotion of appellee, modified its judgment so as to withdraw its declaration of unconstitutionality and to enjoin the enforcement of § 448.18(7) against appellee only. The amended judgment declared that appellee would suffer irreparable injury if the statute were applied to him and that his challenge to the statute's constitutionality had a high likelihood of success. . . .

III

The District Court framed the constitutional issue, which it addressed as being whether "for the board temporarily to suspend Dr. Larkin's license at its own contested hearing on charges evolving from its own investigation would constitute a denial to him of his rights to procedural due process." The question was initially answered affirmatively, and in its amended judgment the court asserted that there was a high probability that appellee would prevail on the question. Its opinion stated that the "state medical examining board [did] not qualify as [an independent] decision maker [and could not] properly rule with regard to the merits of the same charges it investigated and, as in this case, presented to the district attorney." We disagree. On the present record, it is quite unlikely that appellee would ultimately prevail on the merits of the due process issue presented to the District Court, and it was an abuse of discretion to issue the preliminary injunction.

Concededly, a "fair trial in a fair tribunal is a basic requirement of due process." *In re Murchison,* 349 U.S. 133, 136 (1955). This applies to administrative agencies which adjudicate as well as to courts. *Gibson v. Berryhill,* 411 U.S. 564, 579 (1973). Not only is a biased decision maker constitutionally unacceptable but "our system of law has always endeavored to prevent even the probability of unfairness." *In re Murchison, supra,* at 136; cf. *Tumey v. Ohio,* 273 U.S. 510, 532 (1927). In pursuit of this end, various situations have been identified in which experience teaches that the probability of actual bias on the part of the judge or decision maker is too high to be constitutionally tolerable. Among these cases are those in which the adjudicator has a pecuniary interest in the outcome and in which he has been the target of personal abuse or criticism from the party before him.

The contention that the combination of investigative and adjudicative functions necessarily creates an unconstitutional risk of bias in administrative adjudication has a much more difficult burden of persuasion to carry. It must overcome a presumption of honesty and integrity in those serving as adjudicators; and it must convince that, under a realistic appraisal of psychological tendencies and human weakness, conferring investigative and adjudicative powers on the same individuals poses such a risk of actual bias or prejudgment that the practice must be forbidden if the guarantee of due process is to be adequately implemented.

Very similar claims have been squarely rejected in prior decisions of this Court. In *FTC v. Cement Institute*, 333 U.S. 683 (1948), the Federal Trade Commission had instituted proceedings concerning the respondents' multiple basing-point delivered-price system. It was demanded that the Commission members disqualify themselves because long before the Commission had filed its complaint it had investigated the parties and reported to Congress and to the President, and its members had testified before congressional committees concerning the legality of such a pricing system. At least some of the members had disclosed their opinion that the system was illegal. The issue of bias was brought here and confronted "on the assumption that such an opinion had been formed by the entire membership of the Commission as a result of its prior official investigations." *Id.*, at 700.

The Court rejected the claim, saying:

> "[T]he fact that the Commission had entertained such views as the result of its prior *ex parte* investigations did not necessarily mean that the minds of its members were irrevocably closed on the subject of the respondents' basing point practices. Here, in contrast to the Commission's investigations, members of the cement industry were legally authorized participants in the hearings. They produced evidence — volumes of it. They were free to point out to the Commission by testimony, by cross-examination of witnesses, and by arguments, conditions of the trade practices under attack which they thought kept these practices within the range of legally permissible business activities." *Id.*, at 701.

In specific response to a due process argument, the Court asserted:

> "No decision of this Court would require us to hold that it would be a violation of procedural due process for a judge to sit in a case after he had expressed an opinion as to whether certain types of conduct were prohibited by law. In fact, judges frequently try the same case more than once and decide identical issues each time, although these issues involve questions both of law and fact. Certainly, the Federal Trade Commission cannot possibly be under stronger constitutional compulsions in this respect than a court." *Id.*, at 702-703 (footnote omitted).

This Court has also ruled that a hearing examiner who has recommended findings of fact after rejecting certain evidence as not being probative was not disqualified to preside at further hearings that were required when reviewing courts held that the evidence had been erroneously excluded. *NLRB v. Donnelly Garment Co.*, 330 U.S. 219, 236-237 (1947). The Court of Appeals had decided that the examiner should not again sit because it would be unfair to require the parties to try "issues of fact to those who may have prejudged them. . . ." 151 F.2d 854, 870 (CA8 1945). But this Court unanimously reversed, saying:

> "Certainly it is not the rule of judicial administration that, statutory requirements apart . . . a judge is disqualified from sitting in a retrial because he was reversed on earlier rulings. We find no warrant for imposing upon administrative agencies a stiffer rule, whereby examiners would be disentitled to sit because they ruled strongly against a party in the first hearing." 330 U.S. at 236-237.

More recently we have sustained against due process objection a system in which a Social Security examiner has responsibility for developing the facts and making a decision as to disability claims, and observed that the challenge to this combination of functions "assumes too much and would bring down too many procedures designed, and working well, for a governmental structure of great and growing complexity." *Richardson v. Perales,* 402 U.S. 389, 410 (1971).[16]

That is not to say that there is nothing to the argument that those who have investigated should not then adjudicate. The issue is substantial, it is not new, and legislators and others concerned with the operations of administrative agencies have given much attention to whether and to what extent distinctive administrative functions should be performed by the same persons. No single answer has been reached. Indeed, the growth, variety, and complexity of the administrative processes have made any one solution highly unlikely. Within the Federal Government itself, Congress has addressed the issue in several different ways, providing for varying degrees of separation from complete separation of functions to virtually none at all. For the generality of agencies, Congress has been content with § 5 of the Administrative Procedure Act, 5 U.S.C. § 554(d), which provides that no employee engaged in investigating or prosecuting may also participate or advise in the adjudicating function, but which also expressly exempts from this prohibition "the agency or a member or members of the body comprising the agency."

It is not surprising, therefore, to find that "[t]he case law, both federal and state, generally rejects the idea that the combination [of] judging [and] investigating functions is a denial of due process. . . ." 2 K. Davis, Administrative Law Treatise § 13.02, p. 175 (1958). Similarly, our cases, although they reflect the substance of the problem, offer no support for the bald proposition applied in this case by the District Court that agency members who participate in an

---

16. The decisions of the Courts of Appeals touching upon this question of bias arising from a combination of functions are also instructive. In *Pangburn v. CAB,* 311 F.2d 349 (CA1 1962), the Civil Aeronautics Board had the responsibility of making an accident report and also reviewing the decision of a trial examiner that the pilot involved in the accident should have his airline transport pilot rating suspended. The pilot claimed that his right to procedural due process had been violated by the fact that the Board was not an impartial tribunal in deciding his appeal from the trial examiner's decision since it had previously issued its accident report finding pilot error to be the probable cause of the crash. The Court of Appeals found the Board's procedures to be constitutionally permissible:

> "[W]e cannot say that the mere fact that a tribunal has had contact with a particular factual complex in a prior hearing, or indeed has taken a public position on the facts, is enough to place that tribunal under a constitutional inhibition to pass upon the facts in a subsequent hearing. We believe that more is required. Particularly is this so in the instant case where the Board's prior contact with the case resulted from its following the Congressional mandate to investigate and report the probable cause of all civil air accidents." *Id.,* at 358.

. . .

Those cases in which due process violations have been found are characterized by factors not present in the record before us in this litigation, and we need not pass upon their validity. In *American Cyanimid Co. v. FTC,* 363 F.2d 757 (CA6 1966), one of the commissioners had previously served actively as counsel for a Senate subcommittee investigating many of the same facts and issues before the Federal Trade Commission for consideration. In *Texaco, Inc. v. FTC,* 336 F.2d 754 (D.C. Cir. 1964), vacated on other grounds, 381 U.S. 739 (1965), the court found that a speech made by a commissioner clearly indicated that he had already to some extent reached a decision as to matters pending before that Commission. See also *Cinderella Career & Finishing Schools, Inc. v. FTC,* 425 F.2d 583, 589-592 (D.C. Cir. 1970). *Amos Treat & Co. v. SEC,* 306 F.2d 260 (D.C. Cir. 1962), presented a situation in which one of the members of the Securities and Exchange Commission had previously participated as an employee in the investigation of charges pending before the Commission. In *Trans World Airlines v. CAB,* 254 F.2d 90 (D.C. Cir. 1958), a Civil Aeronautics Board member had signed a brief in behalf of one of the parties in the proceedings prior to assuming membership on the Board.

investigation are disqualified from adjudicating. The incredible variety of administrative mechanisms in this country will not yield to any single organizing principle.

Appellee relies heavily on *In re Murchison, supra,* in which a state judge, empowered under state law to sit as a "one-man grand jury" and to compel witnesses to testify before him in secret about possible crimes, charged two such witnesses with criminal contempt, one for perjury and the other for refusing to answer certain questions, and then himself tried and convicted them. This Court found the procedure to be a denial of due process of law not only because the judge in effect became part of the prosecution and assumed an adversary position, but also because as a judge, passing on guilt or innocence, he very likely relied on "his own personal knowledge and impression of what had occurred in the grand jury room," an impression that "could not be tested by adequate cross-examination." 349 U.S., at 138.

Plainly enough, *Murchison* has not been understood to stand for the broad rule that the members of an administrative agency may not investigate the facts, institute proceedings, and then make the necessary adjudications. The Court did not purport to question the *Cement Institute* case, *supra,* or the Administrative Procedure Act and did not lay down any general principle that a judge before whom an alleged contempt is committed may not bring and preside over the ensuing contempt proceedings. The accepted rule is to the contrary. *Ungar v. Sarafite,* 376 U.S. 575, 584-585 (1964); *Nilva v. United States,* 352 U.S. 385, 395-396 (1957).

Nor is there anything in this case that comes within the strictures of *Murchison.*[20] When the Board instituted its investigative procedures, it stated only that it would investigate whether proscribed conduct had occurred. Later in noticing the adversary hearing, it asserted only that it would determine if violations had been committed which would warrant suspension of appellee's license. Without doubt, the Board then anticipated that the proceeding would eventuate in an adjudication of the issue; but there was no more evidence of bias or the risk of bias or prejudgment than inhered in the very fact that the Board had investigated and would now adjudicate. Of course, we should be alert to the possibilities of bias that may lurk in the way particular procedures actually work in practice. The processes utilized by the Board, however, do not in themselves contain an unacceptable risk of bias. The investigative proceeding had been closed to the public, but appellee and his counsel were permitted to be present throughout; counsel actually attended the hearings and knew the facts presented to the Board. No specific foundation has been presented for suspecting that the Board had been prejudiced by its investigation or would be disabled from hearing and deciding on the basis of the evidence to be presented at the contested hearing. The mere exposure to evidence presented in nonadversary investigative procedures is insufficient in itself to impugn the fairness of the Board members at a later adversary hearing. Without a showing to the contrary, state administrators "are assumed to be men of conscience and intellectual

20. It is asserted by appellants and not denied by appellee that an agency employee performed the actual investigation and gathering of evidence in this case and that an assistant attorney general then presented the evidence to the Board at the investigative hearings. While not essential to our decision upholding the constitutionality of the Board's sequence of functions, these facts, if true, show that the Board had organized itself internally to minimize the risks arising from combining investigation and adjudication, including the possibility of Board members relying at later suspension hearings upon evidence not then fully subject to effective confrontation.

discipline, capable of judging a particular controversy fairly on the basis of its own circumstances." *United States v. Morgan*, 313 U.S. 409, 421 (1941).

We are of the view, therefore, that the District Court was in error when it entered the restraining order against the Board's contested hearing and when it granted the preliminary injunction based on the untenable view that it would be unconstitutional for the Board to suspend appellee's license "at its own contested hearing on charges evolving from its own investigation. . . ." The contested hearing should have been permitted to proceed.

IV

Nor do we think the situation substantially different because the Board, when it was prevented from going forward with the contested hearing, proceeded to make and issue formal findings of fact and conclusions of law asserting that there was probable cause to believe that appellee had engaged in various acts prohibited by the Wisconsin statutes. These findings and conclusions were verified and filed with the district attorney for the purpose of initiating revocation and criminal proceedings. Although the District Court did not emphasize this aspect of the case before it, appellee stresses it in attempting to show prejudice and prejudgment. We are not persuaded.

Judges repeatedly issue arrest warrants on the basis that there is probable cause to believe that a crime has been committed and that the person named in the warrant has committed it. Judges also preside at preliminary hearings where they must decide whether the evidence is sufficient to hold a defendant for trial. Neither of these pretrial involvements has been thought to raise any constitutional barrier against the judge's presiding over the criminal trial and, if the trial is without a jury, against making the necessary determination of guilt or innocence. Nor has it been thought that a judge is disqualified from presiding over injunction proceedings because he has initially assessed the facts in issuing or denying a temporary restraining order or a preliminary injunction. It is also very typical for the members of administrative agencies to receive the results of investigations, to approve the filing of charges or formal complaints instituting enforcement proceedings, and then to participate in the ensuing hearings. This mode of procedure does not violate the Administrative Procedure Act, and it does not violate due process of law.[24] We should also remember that it is not contrary to due process to allow judges and administrators who have had their initial decisions reversed on appeal to confront and decide the same questions a second time around. See *Cement Institute*, 333 U.S., at 702-703; *Donnelly Garment Co.*, 330 U.S., at 236-237.

Here, the Board stayed within the accepted bounds of due process. Having investigated, it issued findings and conclusions asserting the commission of

---

24. "The Act does not and probably should not forbid the combination with judging of instituting proceedings, negotiating settlements, or testifying. What heads of agencies do in approving the institution of proceedings is much like what judges do in ruling on demurrers or motions to dismiss. When the same examiner conducts a pre-hearing conference and then presides at the hearing, the harm, if any, is slight, and it probably goes more to impairment of effectiveness in mediation than to contamination of judging. If deciding officers may consult staff specialists who have not testified, they should be allowed to consult those who have testified; the need here is not for protection against contamination but is assurance of appropriate opportunity to meet what is considered." 2 K. Davis, Administrative Law Treatise § 13.11, p. 249 (1958).

certain acts and ultimately concluding that there was probable cause to believe that appellee had violated the statutes.

The risk of bias or prejudgment in this sequence of functions has not been considered to be intolerably high or to raise a sufficiently great possibility that the adjudicators would be so psychologically wedded to their complaints that they would consciously or unconsciously avoid the appearance of having erred or changed position. Indeed, just as there is no logical inconsistency between a finding of probable cause and an acquittal in a criminal proceeding, there is no incompatibility between the agency filing a complaint based on probable cause and a subsequent decision, when all the evidence is in, that there has been no violation of the statute. Here, if the Board now proceeded after an adversary hearing to determine that appellee's license to practice should not be temporarily suspended, it would not implicitly be admitting error in its prior finding of probable cause. Its position most probably would merely reflect the benefit of a more complete view of the evidence afforded by an adversary hearing.

The initial charge or determination of probable cause and the ultimate adjudication have different bases and purposes. The fact that the same agency makes them in tandem and that they relate to the same issues does not result in a procedural due process violation. Clearly, if the initial view of the facts based on the evidence derived from nonadversarial processes as a practical or legal matter foreclosed fair and effective consideration at a subsequent adversary hearing leading to ultimate decision, a substantial due process question would be raised. But in our view, that is not this case.[25]

That the combination of investigative and adjudicative functions does not, without more, constitute a due process violation, does not, of course, preclude a court from determining from the special facts and circumstances present in the case before it that the risk of unfairness is intolerably high. Findings of that kind made by judges with special insights into local realities are entitled to respect, but injunctions resting on such factors should be accompanied by at least the minimum findings required by Rules 52(a) and 65(d).

The judgment of the District Court is reversed and the case is remanded to that court for further proceedings consistent with this opinion. *So ordered.*

QUESTIONS

1. Are there situations where due process is violated by the potential for bias in the decision maker? Parse footnote 16 of the opinion.
2. Why did § 554(d) of the federal APA not apply in *Withrow?* Two well-known cases in which § 554(d) *was* applied are *Wong Yang Sung v. McGrath,* 339 U.S. 908 (1950), and *Grolier, Inc. v. FTC,* 615 F.2d 1215 (D.C. Cir. 1980).

---

25. Quite apart from precedents and considerations concerning the constitutionality of a combination of functions in one agency, the District Court rested its decision upon *Gagnon v. Scarpelli,* 411 U.S. 778 (1973), and *Morrissey v. Brewer,* 408 U.S. 471 (1972). These decisions, however, pose a very different question. Each held that when review of an initial decision is mandated, the decision maker must be other than the one who made the decision under review. *Gagnon, supra,* at 785-786; *Morrissey, supra,* at 485-486; see also *Goldberg v. Kelly,* 397 U.S. 254, 271 (1970). Allowing a decision maker to review and evaluate his own prior decisions raises problems that are not present here. Under the controlling statutes, the Board is at no point called upon to review its own prior decisions.

3. How does 1981 MSAPA § 4-214 deal with the *Withrow*-type situation? Compare your own state's APA.

4. To what extent should an objective and reasonable fear of bias in an adjudicator support the forced recusal of the decision maker or judge? In *Caperton v. A.T. Massey Coal Co.*, 556 U.S. 868 (2009), the Supreme Court ruled that the concept of due process requires an adjudicator to recuse herself if an objectively reasonable fear of bias exists. Writing for the 5-4 majority, Justice Kennedy explained that "The difficulties of inquiring into actual bias, and the fact that the inquiry is often a private one, simply underscore the need for objective rules. Otherwise there may be no adequate protection against a judge who simply misreads or misapprehends the real motives at work in deciding the case." *Id.* at 883. Moreover, "[j]ust as no man is allowed to be a judge in his own cause, similar fears of bias can arise when — without the consent of the other parties — a man chooses the judge in his own cause." *Id.* at 886. *Caperton* involved independent campaign expenditures that exceeded $3 million supporting the election of Brent Benjamin to a contested seat on the West Virginia Supreme Court. "To provide some perspective, Blankenship's [Massey's owner] $3 million in contributions were more than the total amount spent by all other Benjamin supporters and three times the amount spent by Benjamin's own committee." *Id.* at 873. On these facts, the Supreme Court held that a reasonably objective fear of bias existed and Justice Benjamin had a duty to recuse himself in a case involving Massey.

   The decision provoked a sharp dissent from Chief Justice Roberts, who objected to the majority's use of a "probability of bias" standard because "[u]nlike the established grounds for disqualification, a 'probability of bias' cannot be defined in any limited way." *Id.* at 890. In turn, Chief Justice Roberts feared that this approach "will inevitably lead to an increase in allegations that judges are biased, however groundless those charges may be." *Id.* at 891. To prove his point, Chief Justice Roberts raised a total of forty questions about the difficulties likely to arise from the "objectively reasonable" standard for bias — problems that, in his view, the majority simply failed to address. *See id.* at 893-99.

   In *Williams v. Pennsylvania*, 136 S. Ct. 1899 (2016), the Supreme Court reaffirmed its commitment to using an "objective standard" for assessing whether an unacceptable appearance of judicial bias exists that requires an adjudicator to recuse herself from a pending matter. Writing for a 6-3 majority, Justice Anthony Kennedy found that a state supreme court member's prior service as a prosecutor at the defendant's initial trial created an objective appearance of bias that, as a matter of procedural due process, required the judge's recusal from a subsequent appeal of the defendant's death sentence. *See id.* at 1905-09. Justice Kennedy explained that "[t]he Court now holds that under the Due Process Clause there is an impermissible risk of actual bias when a judge earlier had significant, personal involvement as a prosecutor in a critical decision regarding the defendant's case." *Id.* at 1905. Because Pennsylvania Supreme Court Chief Justice Ronald Castille had served as the prosecuting District Attorney at Terrence Williams's criminal trial, due process principles precluded him from hearing an appeal of Williams's death penalty sentence.

Should litigants before an Administrative Law Judge (ALJ), or other administrative decision maker, have the power to force the person's involuntary recusal based on reasonable "objective" evidence of bias? And, what precisely would constitute such evidence in the context of a formal adjudication before a federal agency? Whatever the practical difficulties of applying the objective appearance of bias standard, *Caperton* and *Williams* together stand for the proposition that a litigant is entitled to an adjudicator who does not labor under any obvious conflict of interest or "will to win." Accordingly, if objective and reasonable evidence of bias exists and can be proven by the litigant seeking the involuntary recusal of an adjudicator, then procedural due process principles require that the would-be adjudicator step aside and allow someone without an objective appearance of bias to hear and decide the matter.

NOTE ON "TOTAL QUALITY ASSURANCE" ("TQA") AND THE ADMINISTRATIVE LAW JUDGE

The APA takes great pains to insulate federal ALJs from undue influence within the agency for which they work. ALJs may not engage in prosecutorial functions within the agency, nor may they engage in ex parte contacts with staff members undertaking such functions. *See* 5 U.S.C. § 554(d) ("The employee who presides at the reception of evidence . . . may not . . . be responsible to or subject to the supervision or direction of an employee or agent engaged in the performance of investigative or prosecuting functions for an agency"); *id.* ("An employee or agent engaged in the performance of investigative or prosecuting functions for an agency in a case may not, in that or a factually related case, participate or advise in the decision, recommended decision or agency review pursuant to section 557 of this title, except as a witness or counsel in public proceedings"); *see also* 5 U.S.C. § 3105 ("Administrative law judges shall be assigned to cases in rotation so far as practicable, and may not perform duties inconsistent with their duties and responsibilities as administrative law judges"). Administrative agencies may not fire an ALJ except for "good cause," and only then after the Merit Systems Review Board reviews and endorses the agency's decision to discharge the judge. 5 U.S.C. § 7521(a). ALJs receive pay according to fixed statutory schedules, with regular salary increases based on seniority (subject to regulations established by the Office of Personnel Management). 5 U.S.C. § 5372(b) & (c).

Although most ALJs work for and within particular administrative agencies, they are not subject to the direct control of the agency policy makers. Instead, they conduct hearings and execute their judicial duties independent of the policy-making, investigative, and prosecutorial functions of the office.

Of course, an ALJ must apply the policies established by the agency for which she works, but the agency cannot attempt to control directly an ALJ's conduct or disposition of the case. And, an ALJ's fact findings are a significant part of the "whole record" that a reviewing court must look at on judicial review. *See Universal Camera, infra,* at p. 512. On the other hand, an agency may correct errors of law without giving deference to an ALJ's construction of a statute or an agency rule or policy statement.

Because ALJs exercise tremendous control over the disposition of fact-based disputes, agency heads sometimes wish to encourage ALJs to decide cases in particular ways or ensure that ALJs generally comply with agency rules and policies. When an ALJ denies a claim, it is highly likely that a disappointed applicant for benefits will appeal the adverse decision within the agency and, perhaps, to the federal courts. In the usual case, it is far less likely that a decision granting benefits will be appealed. Absent some sort of internal review process, a decision in favor of an applicant is likely to represent the end of the agency's consideration of the matter.

Accordingly, an agency administering a government benefits scheme is likely to see many appeals from adverse decisions, but relatively few appeals of favorable decisions. The economic effect of such a pattern should be obvious: the agency will pay more money out to program beneficiaries. In order to control costs, an agency administering such a program might wish to institute some kind of mandatory review protocol for ALJ decisions favorable to applicants.

Several federal agencies, most notably including the Social Security Administration, have established programs that require internal review of ALJ decisions favoring applicants for government benefits. The design of such programs can present delicate issues that directly relate to the decisional independence of ALJs in the discharge of their fact-finding duties.

A "Total Quality Assurance," or "TQA," program that randomly selects a certain percentage of ALJ decisions for internal review would not threaten the independence of ALJs. On the other hand, an agency might instead choose to target particular ALJs for special internal review—suppose that the agency subjects the decisions of ALJs with unusually high grant rates to automatic review for a certain time period. An ALJ approaching the targeted grant rate might attempt to decide a certain number of cases adversely to the claimant, in order to avoid such scrutiny. Moreover, an ALJ might resent having routine review of her decisions on the theory that she is improperly deciding too many cases in favor of claimants.

At the same time, of course, an agency has an absolute right, if not a duty, to ensure that the ALJs adjudicating claims arising under the programs that it administers are doing so correctly. Valid claims should be granted, while invalid claims should be denied.

A random system of checks would not be the most efficient means of enforcing the agency's policies. An ALJ with grant and denial rates that approximate the agency's own analysis of the percentage of meritorious and meritless applications would appear to be enforcing the agency's policies correctly (although correlation is not causation). ALJs with extreme grant (or denial) rates are more likely to be doing something unusual when deciding their cases. This is particularly likely if extreme disparities in grant and rejection rates persist over long periods of time. That said, an agency should be as concerned with unprincipled denials of benefits as it is with unprincipled grants of benefits. But, according to some observers, federal agencies are more concerned with benefits that are improperly paid than benefits that are improperly denied.

An additional agency concern might be the productivity of the ALJs conducting the agency's formal adjudications. If 90 percent of the ALJs working for the Social Security Administration can process and resolve 500 cases per month, an ALJ working for the agency who decides only 15 cases per month would appear to be shirking. Thus, as with unusual grant or denial rates, the overall case resolution rate might be a useful way of monitoring ALJ performance (particularly productivity rates over reasonably long periods of time, such as a year).

The problem, of course, is that agency efforts to quantify and review ALJ performance might adversely affect the independence and professionalism of ALJs. If an ALJ had decided only 300 cases in a particular month, she might rush to resolve as many cases as possible in the last week of the month. If she wanted to avoid appeals and possible reversals, she could simply grant large numbers of claims (assuming that her grant rate would not bring about undesired scrutiny). All of this is a rather roundabout way of noting that TQA programs can affect the behavior of ALJs in undesirable ways. The question for reviewing courts, then, is whether to allow agencies to establish TQA programs that might negatively impact the independence of the ALJs adjudicating claims within the agency.

In order to increase the independence of ALJ's, many states have created "central panels" or "central pools" of ALJ's. *See* 1981 MSAPA §§ 4-202, 4-301. A central panel is a corps of independent ALJ's who are assigned from a central state office to different state agencies on an ad hoc or temporary basis. The goal has generally been to increase the independence of ALJs and the quality of ALJ decisionmaking, and also to allocate more efficiently the work of ALJs. Opponents of central panel systems point to the potential loss of discretionary power by specialized agencies and the "overjudicialization" of agency process. *See generally* Allen Hoberg, *Administrative Hearings: State Central Panels in the 1990s*, 46 Admin. L. Rev. 75 (1994); Christopher B. McNeil, *Due Process and the Ohio Administrative Procedure Act: The Central Panel Proposal*, 23 Ohio N.U. L. Rev. 783, 810-814 (1997); Jay S. Bybee, *Agency Expertise, ALJ Independence, and Administrative Courts: The Recent Changes in Louisiana's Administrative Procedure Act*, 59 La. L. Rev. 431 (1999).

G. BIAS

ANTONIU v. SEC

877 F.2d 721 (8th Cir. 1989)

Lay, Chief Judge.

Adrian Antoniu (Antoniu) worked from August 1972 until May 1975 in the corporate finance department of Morgan Stanley & Co., Inc. (Morgan Stanley), a broker-dealer registered with the Securities and Exchange Commission (SEC or Commission). Antoniu entered into an insider trading conspiracy with James N. Newman (Newman), a securities trader. Antoniu would obtain the non-public information about imminent takeover bids by Morgan Stanley's clients. Newman would then buy large blocks of stock of the targeted companies and later sell the stock at a profit. Antoniu shared in the profits.

Morgan Stanley asked Antoniu to resign and he took a position at Kuhn, Loeb & Co. (Kuhn, Loeb) (later Lehman Brothers, Kuhn, Loeb, Inc.) in the newly established mergers and acquisitions department. Antoniu continued to receive market-sensitive non-public information from Morgan Stanley employee E. Jacques Courtois. While at Kuhn Loeb, Antoniu repeated the pattern: he misappropriated the information and passed it to Newman, who bought and sold stocks of target companies. The conspirators split the profits. Kuhn Loeb fired Antoniu in 1978 when he was investigated for insider trading violations. Antoniu then moved to Italy.

On November 13, 1980, Antoniu pled guilty to two counts of misappropriating information in securities markets in violation of 15 U.S.C. §§ 78j(b) and 78ff, and Rule 10b-5, 17 C.F.R. 240.10b-5 and 18 U.S.C. § 2, as part of a plea bargain. He was sentenced to three months' imprisonment, thirty-six months' suspended sentence and a $5000 fine, on August 11, 1982. On March 31, 1983, the sentence was reduced to thirty-nine months' unsupervised probation and a $5000 fine.

In 1984, Antoniu moved to Minnesota to take a job with M.H. Novick & Co. Due to Antoniu's criminal conviction, Antoniu and Novick sought approval for the employment from the National Association of Securities Dealers (NASD). After an evidentiary hearing, NASD approved the employment on June 3, 1985. Antoniu went to work for Novick later that summer.

On September 3, 1985, the SEC vetoed NASD's approval of that particular employment. (This set of proceedings is hereinafter referred to as *Antoniu I*). One of the participating commissioners was Charles C. Cox. On September 19, 1985, the SEC started a second set of proceedings (hereinafter referred to as *Antoniu II*). Commissioner Cox also took part in the SEC's decision to institute *Antoniu II*. The purpose of this second set of proceedings was to determine whether Antoniu should be subjected to sanctions due to his criminal conviction. In other words, the Commission was to determine whether it was in the public interest to exclude Antoniu from any employment in the securities business.

While *Antoniu II* was pending, on October 18, 1985, Commissioner Cox gave a speech in Denver entitled "Making the Punishment Fit the Crime — A Look at SEC Enforcement Remedies." The speech outlined two recent cases before the SEC in which the Commission had imposed sanctions on firms or persons. Commissioner Cox said that each of the sanctioned entities was an "indifferent violator" and further expounded:

> Mr. Antoniu, on the other hand, can be appropriately termed a violator, for he pled guilty to criminal violations of the federal securities laws. In his positions at Morgan Stanley and Kuehn [sic], Loeb and Company, he provided inside information on several occasions to accomplices who traded while in possession of that information. Although he was prosecuted for this conduct, Mr. Antoniu recently applied to become associated with a broker-dealer. Apparently, Mr. Antoniu believed that, since his rehabilitation was complete, there was no further reason to prevent his future dealings in the securities industry. In that case, the Commission responded by denying Mr. Antoniu's request for association.
>
> One issue that frequently arises with respect to individuals whom I call "indifferent violators" is the length of time that a Commission remedy should remain in effect. This may come up when originally structuring the settlement of an injunction or an administrative proceeding, or in later applications for relief from an injunction or Commission order. . . . *In the case of Mr. Antoniu, his bar from association with a broker-dealer was made permanent.*

(Emphasis added.)

Cox's words describing Antoniu's bar as permanent can only be interpreted as a prejudgment of the issue. We emphasize that the speech was made while the *Antoniu II* proceedings were pending. The text of the speech was also printed and distributed by the SEC. Following Cox's public denouncement of him,

Antoniu made multiple requests in the administrative proceedings for permission to develop the record on the issue of bias. His requests were denied. Antoniu also made a motion on April 6, 1986, to disqualify the whole Commission. The motion was denied and specifically, Commissioner Cox refused to recuse himself. He continued to participate in the *Antoniu II* proceedings, including the SEC's rejection of Antoniu's proposed settlement. Commissioner Cox did finally recuse himself, on December 3, 1987, the day the *Antoniu II* opinion of the Commission was handed down.

In the final *Antoniu II* opinion, the SEC found:

> Antoniu's misconduct could hardly be more serious. As the law judge observed, it was not the product of impulse or attributable to a temporary lapse in judgment or ethics. Rather, it arose from a carefully conceived scheme that Antoniu devised, using accomplices that he recruited. He engineered a protracted and complex operation to betray his employers' trust by misappropriating confidential information for personal gain. . . .
>
> As we have so often emphasized, the securities industry is heavily dependent upon the integrity of its participants. We must protect the public from persons like Antoniu whose demonstrated conduct falls so far below acceptable standards of honesty and trust. We recognize the serious effect of the sanction we are imposing. Yet we are convinced that a lesser remedy will not suffice. Under all the circumstances, particularly the egregious and protracted nature of Antoniu's misconduct, we conclude that the public interest requires that Antoniu be barred from association with any broker or dealer.

In the Matter of Adrian Antoniu, S.E.C. Rel. No. 25169, Admin. Proc. File No. 3-6566 at 7-8 (Dec. 3, 1987) (hereinafter *Antoniu II* opinion).

Antoniu appeals the SEC's orders, raising a number of arguments. After careful consideration, we find that only one of them merits our attention. Due in part to Commissioner Cox's remarks about Antoniu made in the Denver speech, Antoniu claims that the proceedings were biased or at least that they were impermissibly tainted with the appearance of impropriety. . . .

We begin with the fundamental premise that principles of due process apply to administrative adjudications. *See Amos Treat & Co. v. SEC*, 306 F.2d 260, 264 (D.C. Cir. 1962). The Supreme Court has described the requirements of due process: "A fair trial in a fair tribunal is a basic requirement of due process. Fairness of course requires an absence of actual bias in the trial of cases." *In re Murchison*, 349 U.S. 133, 136 (1955). The Court has demanded not only a fair proceeding, but also that "'justice must satisfy the appearance of justice.'" *Id., citing Offutt v. United States*, 348 U.S. 11, 14 (1954). The relevant inquiry is thus whether Commissioner Cox's post-speech participation in the *Antoniu II* proceedings comported with the appearance of justice.

A number of other courts have entertained similar questions. In *Staton v. Mayes*, 552 F.2d 908 (10th Cir.), a school superintendent was dismissed by a majority vote of the school board. The members comprising the majority had made statements about the superintendent, both in public and in private, prior to any sort of hearing on the matter. The Tenth Circuit reviewed the trial court's approval of the school board's actions. The court said:

> The firm public statements before the hearing by defendant Mayes for the removal of Dr. Staton, and the discussions by defendants Moore and Wade as admitted,

reveal a tribunal not meeting the demands of due process for a hearing with fairness and the appearance of fairness. These were not mere statements on a policy issue related to the dispute, leaving the decision maker capable of judging a particular controversy fairly on the basis of its own circumstances. Nor was this simply a case of the instigation of charges and a statement of them during an investigatory phase by the body that will later decide the merits of the charges.

Instead this case involves statements on the merits by those who must make factual determinations on contested fact issues of alleged incompetence and willful neglect of duty, where the fact finding is critical.

Id. at 914 (citations omitted). The court concluded:

We do not say that such statements in an election campaign or between members were unlawful or improper. However, a due process principle is bent too far when such persons are then called on to sit as fact finders and to make a decision affecting the property interests and liberty interests of one's reputation and standing in his profession.

Id. at 915. The court accordingly vacated the trial court's judgment and invalidated the superintendent's firing. The court directed that if it wished to do so, the board could make new findings on the matter.

The District of Columbia Circuit has produced two cases which provide us with further guidance.

In *Texaco, Inc. v. FTC,* 336 F.2d 754 (D.C. Cir. 1964), vacated on other grounds, 381 U.S. 739 (1965) (per curiam), the FTC had charged Texaco with unfair methods of competition in interstate commerce. After a lengthy set of adjudicative proceedings, the examiner found that Texaco had violated the Federal Trade Commission Act. While the case was pending before the examiner after remand Chairman Dixon made a speech castigating Texaco as one of a number of companies engaging in price fixing and price discrimination. Texaco's motion to disqualify Dixon was denied, and Dixon refused to recuse himself. The court admonished: "[A]n administrative hearing of such importance and vast potential consequences must be attended, not only with every element of fairness but with the very appearance of complete fairness. Only thus can the tribunal conducting a quasi-adjudicatory proceeding meet the basic requirement of due process." 336 F.2d at 760 (quoting *Amos Treat & Co. v. SEC,* 306 F.2d at 267). The court found that Chairman Dixon's speech revealed that he had prejudged the matter. Dixon's continued participation in the proceedings violated due process. The court therefore invalidated the FTC's order.

The District of Columbia Circuit again confronted the issue of Commissioner Dixon's behavior in *Cinderella Career and Finishing Schools, Inc. v. FTC,* 425 F.2d 583 (D.C. Cir. 1970). There, the court addressed a factual scenario very similar to the one at bar. Federal Trade Commission Chairman Dixon had given a speech in which (without naming the targeted business) he condemned certain advertising practices as deceptive. Dixon's speech was given while the business' appeal from the examiner's decision was still pending before the Commission (including Dixon). The court found that Chairman Dixon should have disqualified himself, saying:

The test for disquaification [sic] has been succinctly stated as being whether "a disinterested observer may conclude that [the agency] has in some measure

adjudged the facts as well as the law of a particular case in advance of hearing it."
Gilligan, Will & Co. v. SEC, 267 F.2d 461, 469 (2d Cir.), cert. denied, 361 U.S. 896
(1959).

Cinderella, 425 F.2d at 591. The court then remanded the case with instructions
"that the Commissioners consider the record and evidence in reviewing the
initial decision, without the participation of Commissioner Dixon." *Id.* at 592.
    We turn again to the case before us. . . .
    After reviewing the statements made by Commissioner Cox, we can come to
no conclusion other than that Cox had "in some measure adjudged the facts as
well as the law of a particular case in advance of hearing it." *Gilligan, Will & Co. v.
SEC,* 267 F.2d 461, 469 (2d Cir.1959). Even though Cox recused himself prior to
the filing of the SEC's final decision, there is no way of knowing how Cox's
participation affected the Commissioner's deliberations. Accordingly, we nullify
all Commission proceedings (including the Commission's rejection of Antoniu's proposed settlement) in which Commissioner Cox participated occurring
after Commissioner Cox's speech was given and remand the case to the
Commission with directions to make a de novo review of the evidence, without
any participation by Commissioner Cox. It is so ordered.

QUESTIONS

1. How is this case different from *Withrow v. Larkin?* See footnote 16 of *Withrow,
   supra* p. 143. For a case in which an ALJ who was a former "movement"
   lawyer was not found biased, see *Andrews v. Agricultural Labor Relations Board,*
   623 P.2d 151 (Cal. 1981). For a case in which a Social Security ALJ was found
   biased against disability claimants generally, see *Small v. Sullivan,* 820 F.
   Supp. 1098 (S.D. Ill. 1999).
2. Of course, there are usually two sides to every story. *See* Douglas C. Michael,
   "Prejudgment" Rejudgment: The True Story of Antoniu v. SEC, 61 Admin.
   L. Rev. 225 (2009). Professor Michael, who served as counsel to Commissioner Charles Cox and also drafted the speech at issue, argues that Cox, in
   the quoted part of the speech, did not prejudge the case but instead was
   simply describing the legal effect of the previously determined violation. *See
   id.* at 328-30. Moreover, with respect to the policy question in general,
   Michael argues that "[t]he statements in Commissioner Charles Cox's
   speech about Antoniu's case were precisely the kind of policy judgments —
   as opposed to 'adjudicative facts' — that agency members are entitled to
   make." *Id.* at 229. Second, Professor Michael states that Commissioner
   Cox had in fact already recused himself from the proceeding, but notes
   that this recusal was not noted in the record. *See id.* at 231-32.
3. Note that the court's standard, since it is based on due process, would apply
   to both state and federal adjudications. The *Antoniu* court did not consider
   whether this federal adjudication was formal and therefore subject to the
   APA's procedural requirements. If the adjudication had been subject to the
   APA's formal adjudication requirements, would a stricter requirement have
   applied? *See* APA § 556(b).
4. Disqualification of a presiding hearing officer is addressed in § 4-202 of the
   1981 MSAPA. Does your state's APA address agency bias, and if so, how?

5. Should the court have rejected the claim of bias because Commissioner Cox was only one member of a multi-member SEC? *See also McClure v. Independent School Dist. No. 16,* 228 F.3d 1205, 1216 n.8 (10th Cir. 2000) ("Litigants are entitled to an impartial tribunal whether it consists of one man or twenty and there is no way which we know of whereby the influence of one upon the others can be quantitatively measured" quoting *Hicks [v. City of Watonga],* 942 F.2d [737, 748 (10th Cir. 1991) (quoting *Cinderella Career & Finishing Sch., Inc. v. F.T.C.,* 425 F.2d 583, 592 (D.C. Cir. 1970)).

NOTES

1. Courts have recognized that a decision maker's bias may take different forms:

> There are two ways in which a plaintiff may establish that he has been denied his constitutional right to a fair hearing before an impartial tribunal. In some cases, the proceedings and surrounding circumstances may demonstrate actual bias on the part of the adjudicator. *See Taylor v. Hayes,* 418 U.S. 488, 501-04 (1974); *Cinderella Career and Finishing Schools, Inc. v. Federal Trade Comm'n,* 425 F.2d 583, 591 (D.C. Cir. 1970). In other cases, the adjudicator's pecuniary or personal interest in the outcome of the proceedings may create an appearance of partiality that violates due process, even without any showing of actual bias. *Gibson [v. Berryhill],* 411 U.S. [564, 578 (1973)]; *see also Exxon Corp. v. Heinze,* 32 F.3d 1399, 1403 (9th Cir. 1994) ("the Constitution is concerned not only with actual bias but also with 'the appearance of justice'").

Stivers v. Pierce, 71 F.3d 732, 741 (9th Cir. 1995).

2. For a discussion of the differing standard regarding bias in the rulemaking context, a standard that is considerably harder to satisfy because it requires proving an "unalterably closed mind" on a matter of central importance to the proceeding, *see* p. 216, *infra.*

THEORY APPLIED PROBLEM

The Occupational Safety and Health Act requires the Occupational Health and Safety Administration (OSHA) to establish regulations that will protect workers from a significant risk of material health impairment on the job. OSHA's organic act permits the agency to enforce its workplace safety rules, but requires that the agency provide "an opportunity for hearing" after citing an employer for a violation of an OSHA workplace safety regulation.

On May 5, 2017, OSHA cites the Del Mundo company for failing to comply with OSHA's field sanitation regulations. *See* 29 C.F.R. § 1928.110. These regulations exist "for the protection of the safety and health of agricultural workers" and "shall apply to any agricultural establishment where eleven (11) or more employees are engaged on any given day in hand-labor operations in the field." 29 C.F.R. § 1928.110(a). In relevant part, the field sanitation regulations require an employer to provide potable water, hand washing facilities, and no less than one toilet facility for every 20 agricultural workers or fraction thereof. 29 C.F.R. § 1928.110(c). On May 5, an OSHA inspector counts 21 agricultural workers at

Del Mundo's Salinas, California avocado farm, but finds only one field toilet. Because the regulation requires one field toilet for "each (20) employees or fraction thereof," the OSHA inspector deems Del Mundo to be in violation of the governing rule and issues a written citation to Del Mundo's local manager.

Del Mundo contests the citation and OSHA, consistent with its duty to provide "an opportunity for hearing," sets a hearing for June 1, 2017. Del Mundo argues that three of the 21 workers do not count under section 1928.110 because they work fewer than three hours per day. In relevant part, section 1928.110(c)(2)(5) provides that: "Toilet and handwashing facilities are not required for employees who perform field work for a period of three (3) hours or less (including transportation time to and from the field) during the day." Thus, if three workers were in fact employed for only three hours or less on May 5, 2017, Del Mundo would not be in violation of the regulations. OSHA contends that Del Mundo's own employment records show that the three workers in question were employed for more than three hours on May 4 and May 6-9, 2017, and that it would be reasonable to infer that the workers also worked more than three hours on May 5, 2017. (The hourly pay records for May 5, 2017 have gone missing and no one can seem to locate the workers themselves.)

OSHA proposes to have the supervisor of field inspectors for Region 7 (California, Oregon, and Washington) conduct the hearing; Del Mundo objects, but is overruled. Del Mundo argues that OSHA must prove by clear and convincing evidence that more than 20 workers worked for more than three hours on May 5, 2017, and that it has failed to meet this burden; OSHA contends that it must only provide substantial evidence to support this claim, and proffers the inspector's site report and the citation as prima facie evidence of a violation. The presiding officer holds that OSHA need only offer substantial evidence on the record as a whole to support its allegations. Finally, Del Mundo seeks to introduce four expert witnesses who would testify that even if, on May 5, 2017, 21 workers labored more than three hours each at the Del Mundo avocado farm, one field toilet was entirely sufficient to meet their hygienic needs and that a second toilet facility was not needed on the facts. The presiding officer (the Region 7 supervisor of field inspectors) refuses to permit more than one of these experts to testify. After the close of the hearing, the presiding officer makes an oral ruling in favor of OSHA and against Del Mundo. Del Mundo receives a $10,000 fine and is subjected to special reporting obligations related to its field sanitation practices for the next five years (the Occupational Safety and Health Act authorizes both penalties for a violation of a health and safety regulation). After reviewing a transcript of the hearing, OSHA's chief administrator affirms the decision of the presiding officer.

Del Mundo wishes to appeal this adverse decision. You work as general counsel to the Del Mundo Corporation. What arguments should you consider briefing in your petition for review of OSHA's adverse decision? Also, the organic act provides both venue and jurisdiction in either the U.S. Court of Appeals for the District of Columbia Circuit or in the Court of Appeals in the locality where the agency issued the citation (in this case, the Ninth Circuit). In which Court of Appeals should Del Mundo arguably file its petition for review? Why? Are you likely to prevail on appeal? Why or why not?

H.   EX PARTE CONTACTS

FIRST SAVINGS & LOAN ASSN. v. VANDYGRIFF
605 S.W.2d 740 (Tex. Civ. App. 1980)

Shannon, Justice.

. . . First Savings and Loan Association of Borger, Texas, has appealed from the judgment of the district court of Travis County sustaining the order of the Savings and Loan Commissioner of Texas granting a charter for Citizens Security Savings and Loan Association to be located in Borger. Appellant is First Savings and Loan Association, and appellees are the proposed association and L. Alvis Vandygriff, Savings and Loan Commissioner of Texas.

Appellant attacks the judgment by eight points of error. The crucial issue on appeal is stated in point of error two: the district court erred in failing to hold that the course of ex parte actions and conduct pursued by the organizers of the proposed association invalidated the Commissioner's order.

The Administrative Procedure and Texas Register Act, Tex. Rev. Civ. Stat. Ann. art. 6252-13a § 17 (1970), provides:

> Unless required for the disposition of ex parte matters authorized by law, members or employees of an agency assigned to render a decision or to make findings of fact and conclusions of law in a contested case may not communicate, directly or indirectly, in connection with any issue of fact or law with any agency, person, party, or their representatives, except on notice and opportunity for all parties to participate. An agency member may communicate ex parte with other members of the agency, and pursuant to the authority provided in Subsection (q) of Section 14, members or employees of an agency assigned to render a decision or to make findings of fact and conclusions of law in a contested case may communicate ex parte with employees of the agency who have not participated in any hearing in the case for the purpose of utilizing the special skills or knowledge of the agency and its staff in evaluating the evidence.

The organizers of the proposed association filed a charter application in 1978. The Commissioner heard the application in June and entered an order denying the application in August, 1978. The Commissioner overruled the applicant's motion for rehearing on August 17, 1978.

During the first week in September, 1978, and during the absence of counsel, five of the disappointed organizers came to Austin and visited with the Commissioner, giving him a "different view" of economic conditions of the Borger area than that reflected in the order denying the application. Those persons told the Commissioner that the economy of Borger was better at that time than it had been in thirty years. They suggested that two new shopping centers were going to be located in Borger and that such location would create a "real spurt in the economy." The organizers further told the agency head about the expansion of the Phillips Petroleum Company in the Borger area. No one representing appellant was advised of or was present at this parley with the Commissioner.

After their conference with the Commissioner, and in October, 1978, the organizers elected to refile the application with the Commissioner. In this connection, the charter applicants left the capital funds from the first application on deposit and used the stock subscription forms from the prior application. On cross-examination, Harold Orman, one of the organizing directors of the proposed association agreed that he viewed the entire proceeding "as just one ongoing application." In March, 1979, the Commissioner entered his order approving the charter application.

The Commissioner's order recited the fact that the organizers had met with him in September, 1978:

> [The] record forthrightly reflects that some of the charter applicants met with the Commissioner in September, 1978. That was a time when a previous application (which was turned down) had become final and prior to the filing of the present application. These applicants had nothing pending before the Commissioner at that time. The Commissioner would note the existence of that meeting only in order to say that his decision in this case was based only upon the record as compiled by all of the parties at the January 31 and February 1, 1979, hearing.

Appellees state that at the time of the discussion between the organizers and the Commissioner, the organizers had no application pending before the Commissioner. Accordingly, appellees argue that the ex parte communication could not and did not relate to a contested case or any matter pending before the Commissioner and, as such, was not prohibited by § 17.

An administrative order must be grounded upon evidence taken at the hearing and upon facts officially noticed by the hearings officer in the record of such hearing. Recognition of this fundamental rule necessarily means that *ex parte* communications may not be a basis for such order.

Section 17 codified the preexisting rule in Texas that condemned ex parte communications by parties with officials charged with the duty of deciding contested issues. *Lewis v. Guaranty Federal Savings and Loan Association*, 483 S.W.2d 837 (Tex. Civ. App.1972). The statutory prohibition against ex parte communications is, of course, consistent with the rules governing administrative hearings in this State, and, in addition, is recognition that such communications discredit the administrative process and undermine public confidence in government.

It is true, as urged by appellees, that at the time of the meeting the organizers had no formal contested case pending before the Commission. Nevertheless, it is also true that shortly after the parley with the Commissioner, the same organizers once again filed with the Commissioner their application for a charter for an association with the same name for the same location, Borger, Texas. The organizers placed in no new capital funds because the capital funds from the first application were still placed on account to the credit of the proposed association. The applicants also used the stock subscription forms from the prior application in the second application. This Court agrees with the organizers that, indeed, the first and second proceedings before the Commissioner were, in effect, "just one ongoing application," and concludes that the applicants acted contrary to the command of § 17.

On motion for rehearing, appellees insist that the holding of this Court places an unreasonable and unnecessary restraint upon communication between agencies and the public. To the contrary, the holding does not hinder proper communications between agencies and the public. Pursuant to § 17, the holding does inhibit communications of the character presented by the facts of this appeal.

It is not the burden of the complaining party to demonstrate harm by showing the extent, if any, to which the official was persuaded by the secret information. Instead, it is presumed that the separate meeting resulted in findings that precipitated the administrative order, *Lewis v. Guaranty Federal Savings and Loan Association, supra,* even though the administrative order may recite the opposite. One reason that the complaining party should not have the burden to show harm, is that it could be discharged only with great difficulty in view of the rule that the party may not probe the thought processes of the administrative officer. *United States v. Morgan,* 313 U.S. 409 (1940).

Appellees contend, finally, that any impropriety resulting from the *ex parte* communication was cured by the disclosure at the administrative hearing. Contrary to that argument, disclosure of the *ex parte* consultation does not somehow purge the parties' misconduct. Moreover, the opposing party is placed at a disadvantage in that an opportunity to controvert *ex parte* evidence afforded weeks or months after its communication to the decision maker is far less effective than timely cross-examination following the admission of evidence.

The judgment of the district court is reversed, and the judgment that the district court should have entered is here rendered that the order of the Commissioner be set aside and held for naught. Reversed and Rendered on Motion for Rehearing.

VANDYGRIFF v. FIRST SAVINGS & LOAN ASS'N
617 S.W.2d 669 (Tex. 1981)

Denton, Justice.

This is an appeal from an order of the Savings and Loan Commissioner of Texas granting a charter to Citizens Security Savings and Loan Association. The trial court upheld the order. The court of civil appeals reversed the judgment of the trial court and rendered judgment setting aside the order as void. We reverse the judgment of the court of civil appeals and remand the cause to that court for further consideration.

Early in 1978, the organizers of Citizens Security Savings and Loan Association, primarily residents of Borger, Texas, filed a charter application with the Savings and Loan Commission of Texas for a new savings and loan association to be located in Borger. The application was heard in June, and the Commissioner entered an order in August denying the charter. Thereafter, on August 17, the Commissioner overruled the applicants' motion for rehearing.

During the first week in September, five of the unsuccessful applicants came to Austin and, in the absence of counsel, met with the Commissioner "to find out what (they) had done wrong." They discussed economic conditions in Borger which indicated there was a public need for a new savings and loan association. After the meeting, counsel was contacted by the unsuccessful charter applicants. He recommended that no new application be filed until 1979 when complete economic data for 1978 would be available.

On September 15, 1978, North Plains Savings and Loan Association of Dumas, Texas, filed an application with the Commission to establish a branch office in Borger. This action precipitated filing of a second application by the organizers of Citizens Security Savings and Loan on October 31. The new charter application and branch application were consolidated and a single hearing was held on

January 31 and February 1, 1979. At the outset, the organizers of Citizens Security Savings and Loan testified about the meeting with the Commissioner and were cross-examined. On March 28, the Commissioner entered an order granting a charter to Citizens Security Savings and Loan and entered another order denying the North Plains Savings and Loan branch application.

The court of civil appeals held the meeting between the organizers of Citizens Security Savings and Loan and the Commissioner was an unlawful *ex parte* communication. We disagree. Section 17 of the Administrative Procedure and Texas Register Act, Article 6252-13a, provides in pertinent part:

> Unless required for the disposition of ex parte matters authorized by law, members or employees of an agency assigned to render a decision or to make findings of fact and conclusions of law in a contested case may not communicate, directly or indirectly, in connection with any issue of fact or law with any agency, person, party or their representatives, except on notice and opportunity for all parties to participate.

Section 17 prohibits *ex parte* communications during pendency of a contested case.[2] There is no contested case until an application for a savings and loan association charter is filed. See Texas Savings and Loan Act, Article 852a, section 2.01. When the unsuccessful charter applicants met with the Commissioner in September, 1978, a final order had been entered in Citizens' first application and the motion for rehearing had been overruled. Neither the branch application nor Citizens' second application had been filed. The opinion of the court of civil appeals correctly states "that at the time of the meeting the organizers had no formal contested case pending before the Commission."

Most of the capital funds on deposit from the first application were used for the second application. Similar stock subscription forms were used in both applications. Several of the organizers were the same. On cross-examination, one of the organizers testified that he considered the two applications one ongoing application. Because of these similarities and the short time that elapsed between denial of the first application and filing the second, the court of civil appeals concluded the organizers acted contrary to section 17. While these similarities exist, the applications were not the same. There are different organizers and stockholders and the location was different. This was stated in the Commissioner's order granting Citizens' charter. The organizers and stockholders not participating in the second application withdrew their money from the capital account. The new participants deposited new funds. The organizers paid a new and additional filing fee and new notices were given as required by statute and regulation. Article 852a, section 2.07. The hearing examiner refused to admit the record from the first application because it had no bearing on the record in the subsequent new application. The facts establish that no application was pending before the Savings and Loan Commission when the meeting between the Commissioner and the organizers occurred. There was no contested case at the time. We hold the meeting was not an *ex parte* communication prohibited by section 17 of Article 6252-13a.

---

2. Section 3(2) of Article 6252-13a defines "contested case" as "a proceeding, including but not restricted to ratemaking and licensing, in which the legal rights, duties, or privileges of a party are to be determined after an opportunity for an adjudicative hearing."

The court of civil appeals' opinion presumes that substantial harm resulted from the meeting. The court concludes the discussions with the Commissioner precipitated the order granting the charter. . . . Appeals are subject to review under the substantial evidence rule. Under substantial evidence review, the Commissioner's order may be overturned only upon showing that "substantial rights of the appellant have been prejudiced."[4] Denial of due process is one ground for finding substantial prejudice.

The court of civil appeals relies upon *Lewis v. Guaranty Federal Savings and Loan Association, supra,* in presuming harm occurred because of the meeting. In *Guaranty Federal* the Savings and Loan Commissioner and his deputy made an *ex parte* investigation four months after a charter application hearing to confirm or deny what was in the record. No written memorandum or findings developed by the investigation were placed in the official record. No notice was given of the investigation. Guaranty Federal learned of it eight months later while preparing for trial. The trial court set aside the order granting the charter as void. The court of civil appeals affirmed holding "due process is denied if the Commissioner considers, without notice and opportunity to be heard, evidentiary matters not introduced or not made a part of the record of hearing as otherwise permitted." The *ex parte* investigation occurred during pendency of a contested case and the appellants were clearly denied notice and opportunity to cross-examine and present rebuttal evidence. The present case is distinguishable from *Guaranty Federal.* There was no contested case pending when the meeting occurred. The content of the meeting was voluntarily disclosed at the outset of the hearing and First Savings and Loan had the opportunity to cross-examine and present evidence to the contrary. The Commissioner's order granting the Citizens Security Savings and Loan charter discloses the meeting and states that his order is based solely upon the record before the Savings and Loan Commission.

The Commissioner's order is presumed to be a valid exercise of his power and discretion. The court presumes the Commissioner performed his duties in compliance with the law, and the appellants have the burden to show he did not. We hold that the court of civil appeals erred in presuming harm resulted from the meeting and setting aside the order granting a charter to Citizens Security and Loan Association.

The petitioners raised other points of error. . . . We remand these points of error to the court of civil appeals for consideration. The judgment of the court of civil appeals is reversed and the cause is remanded to that court. [The court's decision was unanimous.]

---

4. Substantial prejudice may be found if the order is:

1. in violation of constitutional or statutory provisions,
2. in excess of the statutory authority of the agency,
3. made upon unlawful procedure,
4. affected by other error of law,
5. not reasonably supported by substantial evidence in view of the reliable and probative evidence in the record as a whole,
6. arbitrary or capricious or characterized by abuse of discretion or clearly unwarranted exercise of discretion.

Article 6252-13a § 19(e).

QUESTIONS

1. What policies support the Texas APA provision?
2. The Texas Supreme Court relied on two grounds for overturning the lower court's decision. Which is more persuasive? Why?
3. Compare federal APA §§ 551(14), 554(d), and 557(d). Also compare 1981 MSAPA § 4-213. Which best provides appropriate remedies for improper ex parte contacts?
4. Should there be limits on ex parte communications in *informal* adjudications?

I. ESTOPPEL AGAINST THE GOVERNMENT

SCHWEIKER v. HANSEN
450 U.S. 785 (1981)

Per Curiam.

On June 12, 1974, respondent met for about 15 minutes with Don Connelly, a field representative of the Social Security Administration (SSA), and orally inquired of him whether she was eligible for "mother's insurance benefits" under § 202(g) of the Social Security Act (Act), 42 U.S.C. § 402(g). Connelly erroneously told her that she was not, and she left the SSA office without having filed a written application. By the Act's terms, such benefits are available only to one who, among other qualifications, "has filed application." 42 U.S.C. § 402(g)(1)(D). By a regulation promulgated pursuant to the Act, only written applications satisfy the "filed application" requirement. 20 CFR § 404.601 (1974). The SSA's Claims Manual, an internal Administration handbook, instructs field representatives to advise applicants of the advantages of filing written applications and to recommend to applicants who are uncertain about their eligibility that they file written applications. Connelly, however, did not recommend to respondent that she file a written application; nor did he advise her of the advantages of doing so. The question is whether Connelly's erroneous statement and neglect of the Claims Manual estop petitioner, the Secretary of Health and Human Services, from denying retroactive benefits to respondent for a period in which she was eligible for benefits but had not filed a written application.

Respondent eventually filed a written application after learning in May 1975 that in fact she was eligible. She then began receiving benefits. Pursuant to § 202(j)(1) of the Act, she also received retroactive benefits for the preceding 12 months, which was the maximum retroactive benefit allowed by the Act. Respondent contended, however, that she should receive retroactive benefits for the 12 months preceding her June 1974 interview with Connelly. An Administrative Law Judge rejected this claim, concluding that Connelly's erroneous statement and neglect of the Claims Manual did not estop petitioner from determining respondent's eligibility for benefits only as of the date of respondent's written application. The Social Security Appeals Council affirmed.

Respondent then brought this lawsuit in the District Court for the District of Vermont, which held that the written-application requirement was "unreasonably restrictive" as applied to the facts of this case. A divided panel of the Court of Appeals for the Second Circuit affirmed. It agreed with petitioner as an initial matter that the regulation requiring a written application is valid and that the Claims Manual has no legally binding effect. But it considered the written-application requirement a mere "procedural requirement" of lesser import than the fact that respondent in June 1974 had been "substantively eligible" for the benefits. In such circumstances, the majority held, "misinformation provided by a Government official combined with a showing of misconduct (even if it does not rise to the level of a violation of a legally binding rule) should be sufficient to require estoppel." In summarizing its holding, the majority stated that the Government may be estopped "where (a) a procedural not a substantive requirement is involved and (b) an internal procedural manual or guide or some other source of objective standards of conduct exists and supports an inference of misconduct by a Government employee."

Judge Friendly dissented. He argued that the majority's conclusion is irreconcilable with decisions of this Court, e.g., *Federal Crop Insurance Corp. v. Merrill,* 332 U.S. 380 (1947); *Montana v. Kennedy,* 366 U.S. 308 (1961); *INS v. Hibi,* 414 U.S. 5 (1973) (*per curiam*), and with decisions of other Courts of Appeals, *Leimbach v. Califano,* 596 F.2d 300 (CA8 1979); *Cheers v. Secretary of HEW,* 610 F.2d 463 (CA7 1979).

We agree with the dissent. This Court has never decided what type of conduct by a Government employee will estop the Government from insisting upon compliance with valid regulations governing the distribution of welfare benefits. In two cases involving denial of citizenship, the Court has declined to decide whether even "affirmative misconduct" would estop the Government from denying citizenship, for in neither case was "affirmative misconduct" involved. *INS v. Hibi, supra,* at 8-9; *Montana v. Kennedy, supra,* at 314-315. The Court has recognized, however, "the duty of all courts to observe the conditions defined by Congress for charging the public treasury." *Federal Crop Insurance Corp. v. Merrill, supra,* at 385. Lower federal courts have recognized that duty also, and consistently have relied on *Merrill* in refusing to estop the Government where an eligible applicant has lost Social Security benefits because of possibly erroneous replies to oral inquiries. See *Leimbach v. Califano, supra,* at 304-305; *Cheers v. Secretary of HEW, supra,* at 468-469; *Goldberg v. Weinberger,* 546 F.2d 477, 481 (CA2 1976), cert. denied, 431 U.S. 937 (1977); *Simon v. Califano,* 593 F.2d 121, 123 (CA9 1979); *Parker v. Finch,* 327 F. Supp. 193, 195 (ND Ga. 1971); *Flamm v. Ribicoff,* 203 F. Supp. 507, 510 (SDNY 1961). This is another in that line of cases,[4] for we are convinced that Connelly's conduct—which the

---

4. Justice Marshall cites several cases in which federal courts have applied estoppel against the Government. In some of the cases, the Government had entered into written agreements which supported the claim of estoppel. E.g., *United States v. Lazy FC Ranch,* 481 F.2d 985, 990 (CA9 1973); *Walsonavich v. United States,* 335 F.2d 96, 100-101 (CA3 1964). In others, estoppel did not threaten the public fisc as estoppel does here. E.g., *Semaan v. Mumford,* 335 F.2d 704, 706, and n. 6 (D.C. Cir. 1964). In another, a bank claiming estoppel had erred in certain applications because it had to file before the Government would provide it with necessary information. *United States v. Fox Lake State Bank,* 366 F.2d 962 (CA7 1966). We need not consider the correctness of these cases. We do think that they are easily distinguishable from the type of situation presented in this case and the line of cases we rely upon above.

majority conceded to be less than "affirmative misconduct" — does not justify the abnegation of that duty.

Connelly erred in telling respondent that she was ineligible for the benefit she sought. It may be that Connelly erred because he was unfamiliar with a recent amendment which afforded benefits to respondent. Or it may be that respondent gave Connelly too little information for him to know that he was in error. But at worst, Connelly's conduct did not cause respondent to take action, cf. *Federal Crop Insurance Corp. v. Merrill, supra,* or fail to take action, cf. *Montana v. Kennedy, supra,* that respondent could not correct at any time.

Similarly, there is no doubt that Connelly failed to follow the Claims Manual in neglecting to recommend that respondent file a written application and in neglecting to advise her of the advantages of a written application. But the Claims Manual is not a regulation. It has no legal force, and it does not bind the SSA. Rather, it is a 13-volume handbook for internal use by thousands of SSA employees, including the hundreds of employees who receive untold numbers of oral inquiries like respondent's each year. If Connelly's minor breach of such a manual suffices to estop petitioner, then the Government is put "at risk that every alleged failure by an agent to follow instructions to the last detail in one of a thousand cases will deprive it of the benefit of the written application requirement which experience has taught to be essential to the honest and effective administration of the Social Security Laws." 619 F.2d, at 956 (Friendly, J., dissenting).

Finally, the majority's distinction between respondent's "substant[ive] eligib[ility]" and her failure to satisfy a "procedural requirement" does not justify estopping petitioner in this case. Congress expressly provided in the Act that only one who "has filed application" for benefits may receive them, and it delegated to petitioner the task of providing by regulation the requisite manner of application. A court is no more authorized to overlook the valid regulation requiring that applications be in writing than it is to overlook any other valid requirement for the receipt of benefits.

In sum, Connelly's errors "fal[l] far short" of conduct which would raise a serious question whether petitioner is estopped from insisting upon compliance with the valid regulation. *Montana v. Kennedy, supra,* at 314. Accordingly, we grant the motion of respondent for leave to proceed *in forma pauperis* and the petition for certiorari and reverse the judgment of the Court of Appeals. *It is so ordered.*

JUSTICE MARSHALL, with whom JUSTICE BRENNAN joins, dissenting.

A summary reversal is a rare disposition, usually reserved by this Court for situations in which the law is settled and stable, the facts are not in dispute, and the decision below is clearly in error. Because this is not such a case, I dissent from the majority's summary reversal of the judgment of the Court of Appeals, and would instead grant the petition and set the case for plenary consideration.

The issue here is important, not only in economic terms to respondent Hansen, but in constitutional terms as well. The question of when the Government may be equitably estopped has divided the distinguished panel of the Court of Appeals in this case, has received inconsistent treatment from other Courts of Appeals, and has been the subject of considerable ferment. *See, e.g., Corniel-Rodriguez v. INS,* 532 F.2d 301 (CA2 1976); *United States v. Lazy FC Ranch,* 481 F.2d 985 (CA9 1973); *United States v. Fox Lake State Bank,* 366 F.2d 962 (CA7 1966);

Walsonavich v. United States, 335 F.2d 96 (CA3 1964); *Simmons v. United States,* 308 F.2d 938 (CA5 1962); *Semaan v. Mumford,* 335 F.2d 704 (D.C. Cir. 1964); *Eichelberger v. Commissioner of Internal Revenue,* 88 F.2d 874 (CA5 1937). *See generally* K. Davis, Administrative Law of the Seventies § 17.01 (1976); Note, Equitable Estoppel of the Government, 79 Colum. L. Rev. 551 (1979). Indeed, the majority today recognizes that "[t]his Court has never decided what type of conduct by a Government employee will estop the Government from insisting upon compliance with valid regulations governing the distribution of welfare benefits." The majority goes on to suggest that estoppel may be justified in some circumstances. Yet rather than address the issue in a comprehensive fashion, the Court simply concludes that this is not such a case.[1] The apparent message of today's decision — that we will know an estoppel when we see one — provides inadequate guidance to the lower courts in an area of the law that, contrary to the majority's view, is far from settled. . . .

Moreover, in summarily reversing the judgment of the Court of Appeals, the majority glosses over the sorts of situations — such as that presented by this case — that have increasingly led courts to conclude that in some cases hard and fast rules against estoppel of the Government are neither fair nor constitutionally required. The majority characterizes Connelly's conduct in this case as little more than an innocent mistake, based possibly on his unfamiliarity with a "recent amendment" rendering respondent eligible for benefits, or possibly, the majority speculates, on respondent's failure to give Connelly sufficient "information . . . to know that he was in error." The majority further concludes that this error was essentially harmless, because, in the majority's view, it "did not cause respondent to . . . fail to take action . . . that respondent could not correct at any time."

While these characterizations certainly facilitate the summary disposition the majority seeks, they do not fit this case. The "recent amendment" had been in effect for a year and a half when respondent was incorrectly informed that she was not eligible. Moreover, it is quite clear that respondent provided Connelly with sufficient information on which to make a correct judgment, had he been so inclined. Finally, to conclude that Connelly's incorrect assessment of respondent's eligibility did not cause her to act to her detriment in a manner that she "could not correct at any time" is to blink in the face of the obvious. Connelly, and not respondent, had the legal duty to meet with Social Security applicants and advise them concerning their eligibility for benefits. While not necessarily free of error, such preliminary advice is inevitably accorded great weight by applicants who — like respondent — are totally uneducated in the intricacies of the Social Security laws. Hence, the majority's effort to cast respondent as the architect of her own predicament is wholly unpersuasive. Instead, the fault for respondent's failure to file a timely application for benefits that she was entitled to must rest squarely with the Government, first, because its agent

1. Ironically, the central case relied on by the majority today, *INS v. Hibi,* 414 U.S. 5 (1973), was also a *per curiam* decision rendered without the benefit of briefing and oral argument. Moreover, in that case the applicant applied for the sought-after benefit — naturalization — 20 years after his substantive eligibility had expired, and the claim of estoppel arose solely from an alleged general failure of the Government to adequately inform noncitizens who served with the Armed Services of the United States during World War II of their possible eligibility for naturalization. Here, in contrast, respondent was eligible for the benefits at the time of her interview with Connelly and the claim of estoppel here arises from Connelly's specific failures to answer correctly her questions concerning eligibility and to encourage her to file an application.

incorrectly advised her that she was ineligible for benefits, and, second, because the same agent breached his duty to encourage [her] to file a written application regardless of his views on her eligibility.

In my view, when this sort of governmental misconduct directly causes an individual's failure to comply with a purely procedural requirement established by the agency, it may be sufficient to estop the Government from denying that individual benefits that she is substantively entitled to receive. Indeed, in an analogous situation, we concluded that before an agency "may extinguish the entitlement of . . . otherwise eligible beneficiaries, it must comply, at a minimum, with its own internal procedures." *Morton v. Ruiz,* 415 U.S. 199, 235 (1974). At the very least, the question deserves more than the casual treatment it receives from the majority today.

QUESTIONS

1. Should the government be estopped just like a private citizen? Why or why not?
2. If not, are there exceptional situations where estoppel against the government is appropriate?
3. The special problem of estoppel against the government should not distract from the requirement that any case of estoppel must meet certain equitable requirements. The Supreme Court has stated that:

> [E]ven assuming that the Government is ever subject to estoppel, a "private party surely cannot prevail without at least demonstrating that the traditional elements of an estoppel are present." *Heckler v. Community Health Services of Crawford County, Inc.,* 467 U.S., at 61. An essential element of any estoppel is detrimental reliance on the adverse party's misrepresentations, *id.,* at 59; and neither the named plaintiffs, much less the 2,500 members of the class they represent, have sought to demonstrate such reliance. Moreover, the only misconduct specifically found by the District Court was the failure to give effective notice of information that, at least with respect to the second loan period, was concededly published in the Federal Register. Our cases leave no doubt that "failure to fully publicize the rights . . . accorded" by an Act of Congress does not "give rise to an estoppel against the Government." *INS v. Hibi,* 414 U.S. 5, 8-9 (1973) (*per curiam*). See also *Heckler v. Community Health Services of Crawford County, Inc., supra,* 467 U.S., at 63 ("[T]hose who deal with the Government are expected to know the law"); *Federal Crop Ins. Corp. v. Merrill,* 332 U.S. 380, 384 (1947).

Lyng v. Payne, 476 U.S. 926, 935-36 (1986).

J. DOCUMENT DISCLOSURE AND OPEN MEETINGS

The Freedom of Information Act

Since first enacting the APA in 1946, Congress has imposed additional generic requirements for federal agencies intended to ensure greater availability of information about agencies to the public. One such amendment was the Freedom of Information Act of 1966 (FOIA), Pub. L. No. 89-487, codified as amended at 5 U.S.C. § 552:

> This milestone law guarantees the right of persons to know about the business of their government. Subject to nine categories of exemptions, whose invocation in most cases is optional, the law provides that anyone may obtain reasonably identifiable records or other information from Federal agencies. Decisions by Government officials to withhold may be challenged in Federal court, and in such cases the burden of proof for withholding is placed on the Government.

H.R. Rep. No. 93-876, *reprinted in* 1974 U.S.C.C.A.N. 6267, 6269. The Supreme Court recently stated that:

> Upon request, FOIA mandates disclosure of records held by a federal agency, *see* 5 U.S.C. § 552, unless the documents fall within enumerated exemptions, *see* § 552(b). "[T]hese limited exemptions do not obscure the basic policy that disclosure, not secrecy, is the dominant objective of the Act," *Department of Air Force v. Rose,* 425 U.S. 352, 361 (1976); "[c]onsistent with the Act's goal of broad disclosure, these exemptions have been consistently given a narrow compass," *U.S. Department of Justice v. Tax Analysts,* 492 U.S. 136, 151 (1989); *see also FBI v. Abramson,* 456 U.S. 615, 630 (1982) ("FOIA exemptions are to be narrowly construed").

Department of the Interior v. Klamath Water Users Protective Ass'n, 532 U.S. 1, 7-8 (2001). Included among FOIA's exemptions from disclosure are (1) materials "to be kept secret in the interest of national defense or foreign policy" in accordance with an Executive order (§ 552(b)(1); see *Environmental Protection Agency v. Mink,* 410 U.S. 73 (1973)); (2) materials "related solely to the internal personnel rules and practices of an agency" (§ 552(b)(2); *see Rose, supra*); (3) certain materials "specifically exempted from disclosure by statute" (§ 552(b)(3); *see Students Against Genocide v. Department of State,* 257 F.3d 828 (D.C. Cir. 2001)); (4) certain trade-secret and commercial information (§ 552(b)(4); *see Center for Auto Safety v. National Highway Traffic Safety Admin.,* 244 F.3d 144 (D.C. Cir. 2001)); (5) certain "inter-agency or intra-agency memorandums or letters" (§ 552(b)(5); *see Klamath Water Users Protective Ass'n, supra*); (6) certain "personnel and medical files and similar files" (§ 552(b)(6); *see United States Department of Defense v. Federal Labor Relations Authority,* 510 U.S. 487 (1994)); and certain "records or information compiled for law enforcement purposes" (§ 552(b)(7); *see Department of Justice v. Reporters Comm. for Freedom of Press,* 489 U.S. 749 (1989)).

Consider the following early FOIA case and how the Supreme Court describes the purpose and effect of the statute, as well as how the Court applies the exemptions.

EPA v. MINK
410 U.S. 73 (1973)

MR. JUSTICE WHITE delivered the opinion of the Court.

The Freedom of Information Act of 1966, 5 U.S.C. § 552, provides that Government agencies shall make available to the public a broad spectrum of information, but exempts from its mandate certain specified categories of information, including matters that are "specifically required by Executive order to be kept secret in the interest of the national defense or foreign policy," §552(b)(1), or are "inter-agency or intra-agency memorandums or letters which would not be available by law to a party other than an agency in litigation with the agency," §552(b)(5). It is the construction and scope of these exemptions that are at issue here.

I

Respondents' lawsuit began with an article that appeared in a Washington, D.C., newspaper in late July 1971. The article indicated that the President had received conflicting recommendations on the advisability of the underground nuclear test scheduled for that coming fall and, in particular, noted that the "latest recommendations" were the product of "a departmental controversy." Two days later, Congresswoman Patsy Mink, a respondent, sent a telegram to the President urgently requesting the "immediate release of recommendations and report by inter-departmental committee. . . ." [sic] When the request was denied, an action under the Freedom of Information Act was commenced by Congresswoman Mink and 32 of her colleagues in the House.

[The district court granted summary judgment to the defendants because "each of the nine documents sought was exempted from compelled disclosure by §§ (b)(1) and (b)(5) of the Act." The U.S. Court of Appeals for the District of Columbia Circuit reversed the district court's decision granting the government summary judgment and remanded the case for *in camera* review of the nine contested documents to determine if they fell within subsection (b)(5) of FOIA, which exempts documents related to an agency's "decisional process." The Supreme Court then granted review of the D.C. Circuit's decision.]

II

The Freedom of Information Act, 5 U.S.C. §552, is a revision of §3, the public disclosure section, of the Administrative Procedure Act, 5 U.S.C. §1002 (1964 ed.). Section 3 was generally recognized as falling far short of its disclosure goals and came to be looked upon more as a withholding statute than a disclosure statute. The section was plagued with vague phrases, such as that exempting from disclosure "any function of the United States requiring secrecy in the public interest." Moreover, even "matters of official record" were only to be made available to "persons properly and directly concerned" with the information. And the section provided no remedy for wrongful withholding of information. The provisions of the Freedom of Information Act stand in sharp relief against those of §3. The Act eliminates the "properly and directly concerned" test of access, stating repeatedly that official information shall be made available "to the public," "for public inspection." Subsection (b) of the Act creates nine exemptions from compelled disclosures. These exemptions are explicitly made exclusive, 5 U.S.C. §552(c), and are plainly intended to set up concrete, workable standards for determining whether particular material may be withheld or must be disclosed. Aggrieved citizens are given a speedy remedy in district courts, where "the court shall determine the matter de novo and the burden is on the agency to sustain its action." 5 U.S.C. §552(a)(3). Non-compliance with court orders may be punished by contempt. *Ibid.*

Without question, the Act is broadly conceived. It seeks to permit access to official information long shielded unnecessarily from public view and attempts to create a judicially enforceable public right to secure such information from possibly unwilling official hands. Subsection (b) is part of this scheme and represents the congressional determination of the types of information that the Executive Branch must have the option to keep confidential, if it so chooses. As the Senate Committee explained, it was not "an easy task to balance the opposing interests, but it is not an impossible one either. . . . Success lies in providing a workable formula which encompasses, balances, and protects all interests, yet places emphasis on the fullest possible disclosure." S. Rep. No. 813, p. 3.

It is in the context of the Act's attempt to provide a "workable formula" that "balances, and protects all interests," that the conflict claims over the documents in this case must be considered.

[The Supreme Court went on to hold that any documents classified as secret by the President were entitled to a FOIA exemption under (b)(1): "We do not believe that Exemption 1 permits compelled disclosure of documents, such as the six here that were classified pursuant to this Executive Order. Nor does the Exemption permit *in camera* inspection of such documents to sift-out so-called 'nonsecret components.'" The Court characterized as "wholly untenable" the argument "that the Act intended to subject the soundness of executive security classifications to judicial review at the insistence of any objecting citizen." Accordingly, "[t]he Court of Appeals was thus in error" to order such *in camera* review of the six documents.

This left three additional documents to be considered. The government claimed that these documents, although unclassified, were nonetheless not subject to disclosure under section (b)(5)'s exemption for "inter-agency or intra-agency" communications. The Supreme Court ordered a remand for further consideration of whether these three documents contained merely factual material (which would be subject to mandatory disclosure) or advisory material (which could be withheld).

Justice Stewart concurred. Justice Brennan, joined by Justice Marshall, concurred in part and dissented in part. Justice Douglas dissented. Justice Rehnquist did not participate.]

QUESTIONS

1. Given Justice White's description of the predecessor provision to FOIA as an abject failure, are you surprised at the outcome of the case? Even with a much stronger presumption in favor of access, those seeking information from the government (who happen to all be members of Congress) do not get very far once the reviewing court applies the exemptions. This demonstrates one of the realities of the FOIA: even though it establishes a presumption in favor of disclosure, it is often not very difficult for the government to overcome (or attempt to overcome) that presumption by invoking one or more of the exemptions.

2. Contrast the result in *Mink* with the following statement from the Supreme Court in a subsequent FOIA case:

> There are, however, exemptions from compelled disclosure. They are nine in number and are set forth in § 552(b), but these limited exemptions do not obscure the basic point that disclosure, not secrecy, is the dominant objective of the Act. These exemptions are explicitly made exclusive and must be narrowly construed.

   Department of the Air Force v. Rose, 425 U.S. 352, 361 (1976). Does Justice White's approach reflect a "narrow construction" of the (b)(1) or (b)(5) exemptions?

3. Undoubtedly, some FOIA requests do seek highly sensitive information. In *CIA v. Sims*, 471 U.S. 159 (1985), for example, the Public Citizen Health Research Group, through attorney John C. Sims, sought disclosure of information related to MKULTRA, "a wide-ranging project" that undertook evaluation of "the research and development of chemical, biological, and radiological materials capable of employment in clandestine operations to control human behavior." *Id.* at 161. The question presented for review was whether the National Security Act of 1947 constituted an express exempting statute under the (b)(3) exemption. Writing for the majority, Chief Justice Burger held that "the Director of Central Intelligence was well within his statutory authority to withhold the names of the MKULTRA researchers from disclosure under the FOIA." *Id.* at 173. Should citizens have access to the names and institutional affiliations of persons researching brain-washing techniques for the CIA? What arguments exist in favor of mandatory disclosure? Against?

4. Government agencies routinely have claimed that the FOIA exempts disclosure of information otherwise available to the public, if the information, considered in tandem with other publicly available information, might fall within a FOIA exemption. This is called the "mosaic theory." As Professor Christina Wells explains:

> [M]osaic theory is a theory of informational synergy in which intelligence agencies convert independently innocuous information into potentially significant intelligence information. For national security purposes, United States intelligence agencies find construction of such mosaics particularly useful as they attempt to discover what others are doing. What can be done by United States intelligence agencies, however, can be done by hostile intelligence agencies. Thus, our government also sees mosaic theory as a justification for government secrecy.
>
> . . . In response to FOIA requests involving national security, government officials find mosaic theory particularly useful because it allows them to argue that information not evidently posing a threat to national security should nevertheless be considered appropriately classified or exempt. Their reasoning is that otherwise apparently innocuous information can be pieced together with other information to form part of a larger, more dangerous picture. Thus, the information, though admittedly innocuous in isolation, *could* prove to be dangerous and must be withheld. Accordingly, mosaic theory is an attempt to expand the government's ability to withhold information under existing law.

Christina E. Wells, CIA v. Sims: *Mosaic Theory and Government Attitude*, 58 Admin. L. Rev. 845, 853-54 (2008). Moreover, intelligence agencies commonly refuse to explain, even *in camera* to a federal district court judge, why the unclassified information should not be released. Instead, the government claims that simply explaining the "mosaic" would compromise national security. As Professor Wells observes, "[i]nvocation of mosaic theory thus creates a vacuum of knowledge that effectively paralyzes judicial assessment of the government's claims." *Id.* at 854. Beyond the FOIA context, the federal government has invoked mosaic theory to justify "closing deportation hearings, indefinitely detaining non-citizens, restricting dissemination of non-classified information, and secretly searching certain kinds of records, including library and Internet records." *Id.* at 872.

5. Section (b)(7), which among other things exempts disclosure of law enforcement information that "could reasonably be expected to constitute an unwarranted invasion of personal privacy," provides another important, and much litigated, exception from the general rule of mandatory disclosure of government information under FOIA. This exemption does not require a strong likelihood of an invasion of privacy; the language requires only that the information "could reasonably be expected to constitute" such an invasion. In *Department of Justice v. Reporters Committee for Freedom of the Press,* 489 U.S. 749 (1989), the Supreme Court had to decide if the "personal privacy" exemption to release of law enforcement materials extended to the contents of an FBI "rap sheet." 489 U.S. at 751, 757. "The Federal Bureau of Investigation (FBI) has accumulated and maintains criminal identification records, sometimes referred to as 'rap sheets,' on over 24 million persons." *Id.* at 751. "This case arose out of [FOIA] requests made by a CBS news correspondent and the Reporters Committee for Freedom of the Press (respondents) for information concerning the criminal records of four member of the Medico family," which the Pennsylvania Crime Commission had identified as participating in "organized crime." *Id.* at 757. The district court granted summary judgment for the FBI, but the D.C. Circuit reversed on appeal, ordering the FBI to release the rap sheet information.

Balancing the media's interest in disclosure against the privacy interests of the Medico family, the Supreme Court reversed the D.C. Circuit. "What we have said should make clear that the public interest in the release of any rap sheet on Medico that may exist is not the type of interest protected by FOIA." *Id.* at 775. "Accordingly, we hold as a categorical matter that a third party's request for law enforcement records or information about a private citizen can reasonably be expected to invade that citizen's privacy, and that when the request seeks no 'official information' about a Government agency, but merely records that the Government happens to be storing, the invasion of privacy is 'unwarranted.'" *Id.* at 780. *Reporters Committee* was a unanimous decision, although Justice Blackmun, joined by Justice Brennan, wrote a concurring opinion that noted he might find some rap sheet information subject to FOIA disclosure on different facts. *Id.* at 780-81 (Blackmun, J., concurring).

6. Section (b)(7) gave rise to another unanimous opinion involving a FOIA request seeking disclosure of death scene photographs taken of Vince

Foster, Jr., a Clinton Administration aide and friend of the Clintons, after he committed suicide in Fort Marcy Park, in metropolitan Washington, D.C. *See National Archives and Records Administration v. Favish,* 541 U.S. 157 (2004). Favish was "convinced that the Government's investigations were 'grossly incomplete and untrustworthy,'" and, invoking the FOIA, he sought disclosure of "among other things, 11 pictures, 1 showing Foster's eyeglasses and 10 depicting various parts of Foster's body." 541 U.S. at 161. Various government agencies, including the National Park Service, the Office of Independent Counsel Ken Starr, and the National Archives and Records Administration declined to provide the photographs, invoking the (b)(7)(C) exemption for law enforcement materials that could reasonably bring about an "unwarranted invasion of personal privacy." *Id.* at 161-63. Writing for a unanimous Supreme Court, Justice Kennedy reversed a decision of the Ninth Circuit ordering disclosure of all but one of the photographs sought by Favish. "Burial rites or their counterparts have been respected in almost all civilizations from time immemorial" and "this well-established cultural tradition acknowledging a family's control over the body and death images of the deceased has long been recognized at common law." *Id.* at 167-68. Justice Kennedy explained that "[w]e have long observed that the statutory privacy right protected by Exemption 7(C) goes beyond the common law and the Constitution. . . . It would be anomalous to hold in the instant case that the statute provides even less protection than does the common law." *Id.* at 170. Accordingly, the Supreme Court held that "FOIA recognizes surviving family members' right to personal privacy with respect to their close relative's death-scene images." *Id.* After balancing Favish's interest in obtaining the photographs against the Foster family's interest in privacy, Justice Kennedy concluded that Favish's interest in the information was not sufficient to justify the damage to the Foster family's privacy interests. *See id.* at 174-75. Once again, the "narrowly construed" FOIA exemption was sufficient to overcome the presumption in favor of mandatory disclosure.

7. If the net effect of FOIA exemptions is to severely curtail the practical utility of the statute, is the FOIA really a significant improvement over its predecessor, § 3? Or are the exceptions reasonable limits on an otherwise very generous policy favoring public disclosure of government information?

Note, however, that the government does not invariably win when it claims a FOIA exemption. Consider, for example, *Milner v. Department of the Navy,* 562 U.S. 562 (2011). In *Milner,* the Supreme Court rejected the Navy's attempt to invoke Exemption 2, which protects from involuntary disclosure materials "related solely to the internal personnel rules and practices of an agency," on facts involving a FOIA request for "explosives data and maps." Writing for the majority, Justice Kagan explained that "an agency's 'personnel rules and practices' are its rules and practices dealing with employee relations or human resources" and include material related to "pay, pensions, vacations, hours of work, lunch hours, parking" and the like. *Id.* at 570. Thus, materials subject to Exemption 2 "concern the conditions of employment in federal agencies, such as hiring and firing, work rules and discipline, compensation and benefits." *Id.* Consistent with this interpretation, the explosive maps and data sought in Milner's FOIA request did not fall within the claimed exemption to disclosure. *See id.* at 571-73.

The Supreme Court specifically considered and rejected a more generalized approach to construing and applying Exemption 2, in large part "because we have no warrant to ignore clear statutory language on the ground that other courts have done so." *Id.* at 576. The Supreme Court's decision rejected the D.C. Circuit's longstanding — and significantly more expansive — construction of Exemption 2 in *Crooker v. Bureau of Alcohol, Tobacco, and Firearms,* 670 F.2d 1051 (1981), which had garnered widespread acceptance within the lower federal courts prior to *Milner. Milner* demonstrates that the Supreme Court will not invariably construe FOIA exemptions broadly to permit the government to avoid disclosure.

8. Even if plaintiffs do not always prevail in FOIA litigation, what effect does the FOIA have on how agencies go about their business? Could this effect be as important, or even more important, than the win/loss ratio of FOIA plaintiffs?

9. Beyond the difficulty of overcoming exceptions, it is sometimes difficult to get an agency to respond to a FOIA request on a timely basis. A serious backlog exists at many federal agencies with respect to FOIA requests; some federal agencies have FOIA requests more than a decade old still pending and unanswered. Michael J. Sniffen, *Study: FOIA backlogs "out of control,"* *Seattle Times,* July 3, 2007, at A5 ("A new study released Monday found one requester has been waiting 20 years for the State Department to produce documents it has about the Church of Scientology"). The Governemnt Accountability Office found that twelve federal agencies had a ten year backlog of pending FOIA requests, ten agencies misreported their oldest pending FOIA requests to Congress, and 33 percent of federal agencies failed to respond to a FOIA archive request regarding the status of FOIA backlogs. On the bright side, "four agencies reported no backlog: the Small Business Administration, Army Department of Materiel Command, Naval Education and Training Command, and Labor Department Employee Benefits Security Administration." *Id.*

10. In addition to creating a presumption in favor of disclosure of government-held information and authorizing judicial review of denials of information requests, FOIA also "required agencies to publish their rules of procedure in the Federal Register, 5 U.S.C. § 552(a)(1)(C), and to make available for public inspection and copying their opinions, statements of policy, interpretations, and staff manuals and instructions that are not published in the Federal Register, § 552(a)(2)." *Reporters Committee,* 489 U.S. at 754.

NOTE ON THE GOVERNMENT IN THE SUNSHINE ACT

Ten years after first enacting the FOIA, Congress enacted the Government in the Sunshine Act, Pub. L. No. 94-409, codified as amended at 5 U.S.C. § 552b. Congress viewed this legislation as "a further, logical step in the continuing process of opening governmental decision making to the public at the Federal and State levels," building upon, *inter alia,* the requirements of FOIA. H.R. Rep.

No. 94-880 (Pt. 1), reprinted in 1976 U.S.C.C.A.N. 2183, 2186. The House committee stated that:

> The basic premise of the Sunshine legislation is that, in the words of Federalist No. 49, "the people are the only legitimate fountain of power, and it is from them that the constitutional charter . . . is derived." Government is and should be the servant of the people, and it should be fully accountable to them for the actions which it supposedly takes on their behalf.

Id. at 2184. The basic requirement of the Act is simple:

> The Sunshine Act provides, with ten specified exemptions, that "every portion of every *meeting of an agency* shall be open to public observation." 5 U.S.C. §552b(b) (emphasis added). It imposes procedural requirements to ensure, inter alia, that advance notice is given to the public before agency meetings take place. *See id.* §552b(e). It also imposes procedural requirements an agency must follow before determining that one of the ten exemptions from the openness requirement applies. *See id.* §552b(d), (f). However, neither the openness requirement, nor the related procedural requirements, are triggered unless the governmental entity at issue is an "agency," and unless the gathering in question is a "meeting" of that agency.

Natural Resources Defense Council, Inc., v. Nuclear Regulatory Commission, 216 F.3d 1180, 1182 (D.C. Cir. 2000).

The statute defines a "meeting" as "the deliberations of at least the number of individual agency members required to take action on behalf of the agency where such deliberations determine or result in the joint conduct or disposition of official agency business." §552b(a)(2). It defines the term "agency" to include "any agency . . . headed by a collegial body composed of two or more individual members . . . and any subdivision thereof authorized to act on behalf of the agency." §552b(a)(1). In one of its rare cases addressing the Sunshine Act, the Supreme Court sought to ensure that the Act did not intrude too greatly upon agency activities:

> Congress in drafting the Act's definition of "meeting" recognized that the administrative process cannot be conducted entirely in the public eye. "[I]nformal background discussions [that] clarify issues and expose varying views" are a necessary part of an agency's work. See S. Rep. No. 94-354, p. 19 (1975). The Act's procedural requirements effectively would prevent such discussions and thereby impair normal agency operations without achieving significant public benefit. Section 552b(a)(2) therefore limits the Act's application to meetings "where at least a quorum of the agency's members . . . conduct or dispose of official agency business." S. Rep. No. 94-354, at 2.

Federal Communications Commission v. ITT World Communications, Inc., 466 U.S. 463, 469-70 (1984). The Court accordingly concluded that the FCC was not required to comply with Sunshine Act requirements when members sufficient to comprise a quorum of its Telecommunications Committee attended sessions of the Consultative Process, a gathering of international regulatory agencies:

> [The Act] applies only where a subdivision of the agency deliberates upon matters that are within that subdivision's formally delegated authority to take official action

for the agency. . . . [I]t is clear that the Sunshine Act does not extend to deliberations of a quorum of the subdivision upon matters not within the subdivision's formally delegated authority. Such deliberations lawfully could not "determine or result in the joint conduct or disposition of official agency business" within the meaning of the Act. As the Telecommunications Committee at the Consultative Process sessions did not consider or act upon applications for common carrier certification—its only formally delegated authority—we conclude that the sessions were not "meetings" within the meaning of the Sunshine Act.

Id. at 472-73.

CHAPTER

3

Rulemaking

A. INTRODUCTION TO RULEMAKING

NATIONAL PETROLEUM REFINERS ASS'N v. FTC
482 F.2d 672 (D.C. Cir. 1973), cert. denied, 415 U.S. 951 (1974)

Opinion for the court filed by Circuit Judge Wright.

This case presents an important question concerning the powers and procedures of the Federal Trade Commission. We are asked to determine whether the Commission, under its governing statute, the Trade Commission Act, 15 U.S.C. § 41 *et seq.* (1970), and specifically 15 U.S.C. § 46(g), is empowered to promulgate substantive rules of business conduct or, as it terms them, "Trade Regulation Rules." The effect of these rules would be to give greater specificity and clarity to the broad standard of illegality — "unfair methods of competition in commerce, and unfair or deceptive acts or practices in commerce" — which the agency is empowered to prevent. 15 U.S.C. § 45(a). Once promulgated, the rules would be used by the agency in adjudicatory proceedings aimed at producing cease and desist orders against violations of the statutory standard. The central question in such adjudicatory proceedings would be whether the particular defendant's conduct violated the rule in question. *See* 16 C.F.R. § 1.12(c) (1973).

The case is here on appeal from a District Court ruling that the Commission lacks authority under its governing statute to issue rules of this sort. . . . Specifically at issue in the District Court was the Commission's rule declaring that failure to post octane rating numbers on gasoline pumps at service stations was an unfair method of competition and an unfair or deceptive act or practice.[1] The plaintiffs in the District Court, appellees here, are two trade associations

---

1. The rule provides:

In connection with the sale or consignment of motor gasoline for general automotive use, in commerce as "commerce" is defined in the Federal Trade Commission Act, it constitutes an unfair method of competition and an unfair or deceptive act or practice for refiners or others who sell to retailers, when such refiners or other distributors own or lease the pumps through which motor gasoline is dispensed to the consuming public, to fail to disclose clearly and conspicuously in a permanent manner on the pumps the minimum octane number or numbers of the motor gasoline being dispensed. In the case of those refiners or other distributors who lease pumps, the disclosure required by this section should be made as soon as it is legally practical; for example, not later than the end of the current

---

177

and 34 gasoline refining companies. Plaintiffs attacked the rule on several grounds, but the District Court disposed of the case solely on the question of the Commission's statutory authority to issue such rules. That is the only question presented for our consideration on appeal. We reverse and remand to the District Court for further consideration of appellees' challenge to the validity of the procedure before the Commission which resulted in the rule.

I

Our duty here is not simply to make a policy judgment as to what mode of procedure — adjudication alone or a mixed system of rule-making and adjudication, as the Commission proposes — best accommodates the need for effective enforcement of the Commission's mandate with maximum solicitude for the interests of parties whose activities might be within the scope of the statutory standard of illegality. The Federal Trade Commission is a creation of Congress, not a creation of judges' contemporary notions of what is wise policy. The extent of its powers can be decided only by considering the powers Congress specifically granted it in the light of the statutory language and background. The question to be answered is "not what the [Commission] thinks it should do but what Congress has said it can do."

As always, we must begin with the words of the statute creating the Commission and delineating its powers. Section 5 directs the Commission to "prevent persons, partnerships, or corporations . . . from using unfair methods of competition in commerce and unfair or deceptive acts or practices in commerce." Section 5(b) of the Trade Commission Act specifies that the Commission is to accomplish this goal by means of issuance of a complaint, a hearing, findings as to the facts, and issuance of a cease and desist order. The Commission's assertion that it is empowered by Section 6(g) to issue substantive rules defining the statutory standard of illegality in advance of specific adjudications does not in any formal sense circumvent this method of enforcement. For after the rules are issued, their mode of enforcement remains what it has always been under Section 5: the sequence of complaint, hearing, findings, and issuance of a cease and desist order. What rule-making does do, functionally, is to narrow the inquiry conducted in proceedings under Section 5(b). It is the legality of this practice which we must judge.

Appellees argue that since Section 5 mentions only adjudication as the means of enforcing the statutory standard, any supplemental means of putting flesh on that standard, such as rule-making, is contrary to the overt legislative design. But Section 5(b) does not use limiting language suggesting that adjudication alone is the only proper means of elaborating the statutory standard. It merely makes clear that a Commission decision, after complaint and hearing, followed by a

---

lease period. Nothing in this section should be construed as applying to gasoline sold for aviation purposes. NOTE: For the purposes of this section, "octane number" shall mean the octane number derived from the sum of research (R) and motor (M) octane numbers divided by 2; (R + M)/2. The research octane (R) and motor octane number (M) shall be as described in the American Society for Testing and Materials (ASTM) "Standard Specifications for Gasoline" D 439-70, and subsequent revisions, and ASTM Test Methods D 2699 and D 2700.

36 Fed. Reg. 23871 (1971).

cease and desist order, is the way to force an offender to halt his illegal activities. Nor are we persuaded by appellees' argument that, despite the absence of limiting language in Section 5 regarding the role of adjudication in defining the meaning of the statutory standard, we should apply the maxim of statutory construction *expressio unius est exclusio alterius* and conclude that adjudication is the *only* means of defining the statutory standard. This maxim is increasingly considered unreliable . . . for it stands on the faulty premise that all possible alternative or supplemental provisions were necessarily considered and rejected by the legislative draftsmen. *See American Trucking Assns v. United States,* 344 U.S. 298, 309-310 (1953). Here we have particularly good reason on the face of the statute to reject such arguments. For the Trade Commission Act includes a provision which specifically provides for rule-making by the Commission to implement its adjudicatory functions under Section 5 of the Act. Section 6(g) of the Act, 15 U.S.C. § 46(g), states that the Commission may "from time to time . . . classify corporations and . . . make rules and regulations for the purpose of carrying out the provisions of sections 41 to 46 and 47 to 58 of this title." . . .

Of course, it is at least arguable that . . . Section 6(g) [can be utilized only] to promulgate procedural, as opposed to substantive, rules for administration of the Section 5 adjudication and enforcement powers. But we see no reason to import such a restriction on the "rules and regulations" permitted by Section 6(g). On the contrary, as we shall see, judicial precedents concerning rule-making by other agencies and the background and purpose of the Federal Trade Commission Act lead us liberally to construe the term "rules and regulations." The substantive rule here unquestionably implements the statutory plan. Section 5 adjudications — trial type proceedings — will still be necessary to obtain cease and desist orders against offenders, but Section 5 enforcement through adjudication will be expedited, simplified, and thus "carried out" by use of this substantive rule. And the overt language of both Section 5 and Section 6, read together, supports its use in Section 5 proceedings.

II

Our belief that "rules and regulations" in Section 6(g) should be construed to permit the Commission to promulgate binding substantive rules as well as rules of procedure is reinforced by the construction courts have given similar provisions in the authorizing statutes of other administrative agencies. There is, of course, no doubt that the approved practices of agencies with similar statutory provisions is a relevant factor in arriving at a sound interpretation of the Federal Trade Commission's power here. In *National Broadcasting Co. v. United States,* 319 U.S. 190 (1943), for example, the Supreme Court upheld the Federal Communications Commission's chain broadcasting rules regulating programming arrangements between networks and affiliates, in part on the basis of the FCC's generalized rule-making authority in 47 U.S.C. § 303(r) (1970). *See* 319 U.S. at 217. It rejected arguments similar to those made here, ruling that this authority extended beyond specification of technical and financial qualifications to be used as guides in the administration of the Commission's license-granting power. *Id.* at 220. It permitted the FCC to use rule-making to elaborate the terms of its mandate to pursue the "public convenience, interest, or necessity," 47 U.S.C. § 303, by framing rules carrying out public policy objectives like affiliate independence and avoidance of undue network control over programming in the hope that listeners would be ensured a diversity of program offerings. . . .

This obvious judicial willingness to permit substantive rule-making to undercut the primacy of adjudication in the development of agency policy is not limited to cases involving the FCC. The Federal Power Commission has successfully utilized rules regulating practical business conduct to frame, and even to cut off, what were once thought to be certificate applicants' absolute rights to individualized adjudications. This practice was upheld in large part on the authority of *Storer* in *FPC v. Texaco, Inc., supra.* Similarly, this court has upheld the authority of the Civil Aeronautics Board to utilize substantive rules affecting allocation of air cargo business among different types of air carriers to modify existing certificates without the full adjudicatory hearing contemplated by the agency's statute. *See American Airlines, Inc. v. CAB,* 359 F.2d 624 (D.C. Cir. 1966) (*en banc*). And *see also Air Lines Pilots Assn, Int. v. Quesada,* 2 Cir., 276 F.2d 892 (1960), upholding a Federal Aviation Agency regulation barring pilots from service after their 60th birthday without providing for individualized hearings on the resultant modification of their pilots' licenses. The propriety of using rule-making rather than adjudication alone to set substantive regulatory standards has also been approved under the Poultry Products Inspection Act which, like the Federal Trade Commission Act, authorizes an agency, there the Secretary of Agriculture, to promulgate rules and regulations, 21 U.S.C. § 463 (1970), and also provides for specific adjudicatory procedures to determine the existence of misleading food labels, 21 U.S.C. § 457 (1970). *Borden Co. v. Freeman,* D. N.J., 256 F. Supp. 592, affirmed, 3 Cir., 369 F.2d 404 (1966) (*per curiam*).

Just as there has been little question of allowing substantive rule-making to intrude on asserted rights to a full hearing before an agency for a determination of a party's rights and liabilities, there has been a similar lack of hesitation in construing broad grants of rule-making power to permit promulgation of rules with the force of law as a means of agency regulation of otherwise private conduct. . . .

The need to interpret liberally broad grants of rule-making authority like the one we construe here has been emphasized time and again by the Supreme Court. . . .

Thus there is little question that the availability of substantive rule-making gives any agency an invaluable resource-saving flexibility in carrying out its task of regulating parties subject to its statutory mandate. More than merely expediting the agency's job, use of substantive rule-making is increasingly felt to yield significant benefits to those the agency regulates. Increasingly, courts are recognizing that use of rule-making to make innovations in agency policy may actually be fairer to regulated parties than total reliance on case-by-case adjudication.

The Supreme Court made this suggestion initially in *SEC v. Chenery Corp.,* 332 U.S. 194 (1947), where it dealt with an agency adjudication imposing novel restraints on the power of management of corporations to purchase stock during periods of reorganization under the Public Utility Holding Company Act of 1935. While the Court did not hold that the Securities and Exchange Commission was bound to follow rule-making procedures in making such a marked policy departure, it was clearly aware that exclusive reliance on adjudication could be criticized for unfairly focusing on a single defendant in a restricted proceeding when promulgating a new policy with industry-wide ramifications. The Court said:

> ... The function of filling in the interstices of the Act should be performed, as much as possible, through this quasi-legislative promulgation of rules to be applied in the future. ...

332 U.S. at 202. ...

This judicial trend favoring rule-making over adjudication for development of new agency policy does not, of course, directly dispose of the question before us. There was no question that the SEC in *Chenery* had substantive rule-making powers. See 332 U.S. at 20. ... Here we must decide just that question, whether Congress has given the FTC the same alternate means of proceeding, not whether the FTC should be required to use rule-making in some circumstances. ... [C]ontemporary considerations of practicality and fairness — specifically the advisability of utilizing the Administrative Procedure Act's rule-making procedures to provide an agency about to embark on legal innovation with all relevant arguments and information, 5 U.S.C. § 553 — certainly support the Commission's position here. [U]tilizing rule-making procedures opens up the process of agency policy innovation to a broad range of criticism, advice and data that is ordinarily less likely to be forthcoming in adjudication. Moreover, the availability of notice before promulgation and wide public participation in rule-making avoids the problem of singling out a single defendant among a group of competitors for initial imposition of a new and inevitably costly legal obligation.

Such benefits are especially obvious in cases involving initiation of rules of the sort the FTC has promulgated here. The Commission's statement on basis and purpose indicated that the decision to impose the obligation of octane rating disclosure on gasoline dealers entailed careful consideration of automobile engine requirements, automobile dealers' practices in instructing purchasers how to care for their engines, consumer gasoline purchasing habits, and costs to gasoline dealers. In addition, the Commission had to choose exactly what kind of disclosure was the fairest. In short, a vast amount of data had to be compiled and analyzed, and the Commission, armed with these data, had to weigh the conflicting policies of increasingly knowledgeable consumer decision-making against alleged costs to gasoline dealers which might be passed on to the consumer. True, the decision to impose a bright-line standard of behavior might have been evolved by the Commission in a single or a succession of adjudicatory proceedings, *see*, e.g., *FTC v. Texaco, Inc.*, 393 U.S. 223 (1968), much as the Supreme Court has imposed *per se* rules of business behavior in antitrust cases. But evolution of bright-line rules is often a slow process and may involve the distinct disadvantage of acting without the broad range of data and argument from all those potentially affected that may be flushed out through use of legislative-type rule-making procedures. And utilizing rule-making in advance of adjudication here minimizes the unfairness of using a purely case-by-case approach requiring "compliance by one manufacturer while his competitors [engaging in similar practices] remain free to violate the Act." *Weinberger v. Bentex Pharmaceuticals, Inc., supra*, U.S. at 653. ... [I]t is hard to escape noting that the policy innovation involved in this case underscores the need for increased reliance on rule-making rather than adjudication alone. . . .

IV

Although we believe there are thus persuasive considerations for accepting the FTC's view that the plain meaning of the statute supports substantive rule-making, the question is not necessarily closed. For appellees' contention — that the phrase "rules and regulations for the purpose of carrying out" Section 5 refers only to rules of procedure and practice for carrying out the Commission's adjudicatory responsibility — is not implausible. The opinion of the District Court argues forcefully that, in spite of the clear and unlimited language of Section 6(g) granting rule-making authority to the Commission, the Congress that enacted Section 5 and Section 6(g) gave clear indications of its intent to reject substantive rule-making, that the FTC's own behavior in the years since that time supports a narrow interpretation of its mandate to promulgate "rules and regulations," and that where Congress desired to give the FTC substantive rule-making authority in discrete areas it did so in subsequent years in unambiguous terms. Our own conclusion, based on an independent review of this history, is different. We believe that, while the legislative history of Section 5 and Section 6(g) is ambiguous, it certainly does not compel the conclusion that the Commission was not meant to exercise the power to make substantive rules with binding effect in Section 5(a) adjudications. We also believe that the plain language of Section 6(g), read in light of the broad, clearly agreed-upon concerns that motivated passage of the Trade Commission Act, confirms the framers' intent to allow exercise of the power claimed here. We do not find the District Court's reliance on the agency's long-standing practice, until 1962, of not utilizing rule-making or the District Court's reliance on enactment of specific grants of rule-making power in narrow areas sufficiently persuasive to override our view, and the Commission's view, that rule-making is not only consistent with the original framers' broad purposes, but appears to be a particularly apt means of carrying them out. [Discussion of legislative history omitted.]

The problems of delay and inefficiency that proponents of both a strong and a weak commission aimed to eliminate or minimize have plagued the Trade Commission down to the present. While the Commission has broad common law-like authority to delineate the scope of the statute's prohibitions, see *FTC v. Sperry & Hutchinson Co., supra,* 405 U.S. at 244, like the federal courts it was designed to supplement, it has remained hobbled in its task by the delay inherent in repetitious, lengthy litigation of cases involving complex factual questions under a broad legal standard. Close students of the agency agree that the historic case-by-case purely adjudicatory method of elaborating the Section 5 standard and applying it to discrete business practices has not only produced considerable uncertainty, but also has helped to spawn litigation the length of which has frequently been noted ruefully by commentators on the Commission's performance. We believe that, to the extent substantive rule-making to implement Section 5 proceedings is likely to deal with these problems given the statutory authority provided in Section 6(g), the Commission's position should be upheld as a reasonable means of attacking ills the Commission was created to cure.

There is little disagreement that the Commission will be able to proceed more expeditiously, give greater certainty to businesses subject to the Act, and deploy its internal resources more efficiently with a mixed system of rule-making and adjudication than with adjudication alone. With the issues in Section 5 proceedings reduced by the existence of a rule delineating what is a violation of the statute or what presumptions the Commission proposes to rely upon, proceedings will be speeded up. For example, in an adjudication proceeding based on a violation of the octane rating rule at issue here, the central question to be decided will be whether or not pumps owned by a given refiner are properly marked. Without the rule, the Commission might well be obliged to prove and argue that the absence of the rating markers in each particular case was likely to have injurious and unfair effects on consumers or competition. Since this laborious process might well have to be repeated every time the Commission chose to proceed subsequently against another defendant on the same ground, the difference in administrative efficiency between the two kinds of proceedings is obvious. Furthermore, rules, as contrasted with the holdings reached by case-by-case adjudication, are more specific as to their scope, and industry compliance is more likely simply because each company is on clearer notice whether or not specific rules apply to it.

Moreover, when delay in agency proceedings is minimized by using rules, those violating the statutory standard lose an opportunity to turn litigation into a profitable and lengthy game of postponing the effect of the rule on their current practice. As a result, substantive rules will protect the companies which willingly comply with the law against what amounts to the unfair competition of those who would profit from delayed enforcement as to them. This, too, will minimize useless litigation and is likely to assist the Commission in more effectively allocating its resources. In addition, whatever form rules take, whether bright-line standards or presumptions that are rebuttable, they are likely to decrease the current uncertainty many businesses are said to feel over the current scope and applicability of Section 5. But the important point here is not that rule-making is assuredly going to solve the Commission's problems. It is rather that recognition and use of rule-making by the Commission is convincingly linked to the goals of agency expedition, efficiency, and certainty of regulatory standards that loomed in the background of the 1914 passage of the Federal Trade Commission Act.

This relationship between rule-making's probable benefits and the broad concerns evident when the FTC was created, together with the express language of Section 6(g), help persuade us that any purported ambiguity of the statute must be resolved in favor of the Commission's claim. . . .

Any fears that the agency could successfully use rule-making power as a means of oppressive or unreasonable regulation seem exaggerated in view of courts' general practice in reviewing rules to scrutinize their statement of basis and purpose to see whether the major issues of policy pro and con raised in the submissions to the agency were given sufficient consideration. The Commission is hardly free to write its own law of consumer protection and antitrust since the statutory standard which the rules may define with greater particularity is a legal standard. Although the Commission's conclusions as to the standard's reach are ordinarily shown deference, the standard must "get [its] final meaning from judicial construction."

VII

In sum, we must respectfully register our disagreement with the District Court's painstaking opinion. Its result would render the Commission ineffective to do the job assigned it by Congress. Such a result is not required by the legislative history of the Act. We rely, therefore, on the plain language of Section 6(g) which gives the Commission the authority to "make rules and regulations for the purpose of carrying out the provisions of [Section 5]." We hold that under the terms of its governing statute, 15 U.S.C. § 41 *et seq.*, and under Section 6(g), 15 U.S.C. § 46(g), in particular, the Federal Trade Commission is authorized to promulgate rules defining the meaning of the statutory standards of the illegality the Commission is empowered to prevent. Thus we must reverse the District Court's judgment and remand this case for further proceedings.

QUESTIONS

1. Identify at least three policies that support giving agencies the power to promulgate substantive rules. How weighty are the policies?
2. Rulemaking by state agencies does not appear to be welcomed in the same way that the court in *National Petroleum Refiners* welcomed federal agency rulemaking. For example, the 1981 MSAPA indicates ambivalence toward rulemaking. The comment introducing its required rulemaking procedures states a concern that "[l]egislatures across the country have repeatedly delegated rule-making authority to agencies without providing detailed and specific substantive standards to guide them in the exercise of that authority." Comment to 1981 MSAPA Art. III. The MSAPA accordingly "highlights the importance of rule-making procedures that not only facilitate agency policy making that is technically sound, but also assure that such agency policy making is within the scope of agency authority and politically acceptable to the community at large." *Id.* Nevertheless, the 1981 MSAPA § 2-104 states that "each agency shall . . . to the extent practicable, adopt rules . . . embodying appropriate standards, principles, and procedural safeguards that the agency will apply to the law it administers." *Id.* § 2-104(3).

   The attitude of the Kentucky legislature toward rulemaking is not at all ambivalent. The following statutory provision reflects great suspicion of agency rulemaking:

   § 13A.120 Promulgation of Administrative Regulations; Prohibitions Concerning Promulgations

   (1)(a) An administrative body may promulgate administrative regulations to implement a statute only when the act of the General Assembly creating or amending the statute specifically authorizes the promulgation of administrative regulations or administrative regulations are required by federal law, in which case administrative regulations shall be no more stringent than the federal law or regulations.

   (b) An administrative body that promulgates an administrative regulation required by federal law or federal regulation shall comply with the provisions of this chapter.

(2) An administrative body shall not promulgate administrative regulations:

(a) When a statute prohibits the administrative body from promulgating administrative regulations;

(b) When the administrative body is not authorized by statute to promulgate administrative regulations;

(c) When a statute prohibits the administrative body from regulation of that particular matter;

(d) When the administrative body is not authorized by statute to regulate that particular matter;

(e) When a statute prescribes the same or similar procedure for the matter regulated;

(f) When a statute sets forth a comprehensive scheme of regulation of the particular matter;

(g) On any matter which is not clearly within the jurisdiction of the administrative body;

(h) On any matter which is beyond the statutory authorization of the administrative body to promulgate administrative regulations or which is not clearly authorized by statute; and

(i) Which modify or vitiate a statute or its intent.

(3) If a statute requires an administrative body or official to submit an administrative regulation to an official or administrative body for review or approval prior to filing the administrative regulation with the commission, the administrative body or official shall not file the administrative regulation without first having obtained the review or approval.

(4) Any administrative regulation in violation of this section or the spirit thereof is null, void, and unenforceable.

(5) No administrative body, other than the Court of Justice, shall issue rules.

(6) No administrative body shall issue standards or by any other name issue a document of any type where an administrative regulation is required or authorized by law.

Ky. Rev. Stat. § 13A.120. What might be the reason for the different attitudes toward rulemaking?

3. On the other hand, even when agencies receive clear legislative authority to engage in rulemaking, they do not always use this authority. At the federal level, the National Labor Relations Board did not engage in rulemaking for almost fifty years after Congress created the agency and, even today, uses rulemaking very sparingly. One commentator suggests that, in Florida, where state administrative agencies enjoy a broad mandate to engage in rulemaking, state agencies have failed to use this authority, instead using adjudication to establish major policies. *See* Johnny C. Burris, *The Failure of the Florida Judicial Review Process to Provide Effective Incentives for Agency Rulemaking*, 18 Fla. St. U.L. Rev. 661, 667-73 (1991) (noting that Florida state agencies often avoid the use of rulemaking because of the open nature of the process and various state procedural requirements applicable to rulemakings, but not adjudications, and suggesting that these factors produce a "net effect . . . that administrative agencies have engaged in a plethora of public policy development through adjudication" with "the net effect of this practice [being] that administrative agencies have functionally forsaken the rulemaking process in many important areas"). Professor Burris argues that

to combat this trend, the state judiciary should enforce the state APA's rule/ order dichotomy and create a requirement that certain major policies be undertaken by rule, rather than by an order established incident to an adjudication. *Id.* at 690-97.

4. An important point to keep in mind is that for an agency to adopt legislative rules, it must have some plausible claim to delegated authority for enacting rules. As a general matter, an agency may not issue legislative rules without a proper grant of authority in its organic act or some other statute. *See,* e.g., *EEOC v. Arabian American Oil Co.,* 499 U.S. 244, 257 (1991) (noting that "Congress, in enacting Title VII, did not confer upon the EEOC authority to promulgate rules or regulations" (internal quotations and citations omitted)). Moreover, even if an agency enjoys statutory authority to promulgate legislative rules, that authority must extend to the particular rules that the agency has adopted; the power to write rules with respect to one subject does not necessarily imply the right to create rules respecting another subject.

NOTE ON APA REQUIREMENTS FOR RULEMAKING

As we saw in *Seacoast* and the cases in the note following *Seacoast* (*supra* p. 112), the APA's procedural requirements for adjudications, found in §§ 554, 556, and 557, apply only in cases "of adjudication required by statute to be determined on the record after opportunity for an agency hearing" (§ 554(a)). Sections 554, 556, and 557 fully set out APA requirements for formal adjudications. But because the APA sets forth no procedures for *informal* adjudications (but *cf.* § 555(e)), such adjudications must only meet requirements mandated by the due process clause or established by the agency's organic statute or its regulations.

In contrast, when an agency engages in rulemaking, the APA provides procedural requirements for both informal and formal agency actions. The formal hearing requirements of §§ 556 and 557 — the same sections that apply to formal adjudications — apply as well to formal rulemaking when required by the last sentence in § 553(c). *See* §§ 556(a), 557(a). Section 553(c) requires formal rulemaking procedures "[w]hen rules are required by statute to be made on the record after opportunity for an agency hearing." (Compare this to the similar language in § 554(a) regarding adjudications.) Sections 556 and 557 impose largely the same procedural requirements for formal rulemaking as they do for formal adjudication, although under § 556(d) a party's right to present oral evidence is qualified with regard to formal rulemaking. When formal rulemaking is not required, the *informal* (notice and comment) requirements of § 553 apply, except to the extent the APA in § 553 exempts the rulemaking from even those requirements. Formal rulemaking is comparatively rare; the vast majority of federal rulemaking is informal notice and comment rulemaking. An agency's organic statute or its regulations may establish additional procedural requirements for informal rulemaking.

BOWEN v. GEORGETOWN UNIV. HOSPITAL
488 U.S. 204 (1988)

JUSTICE KENNEDY delivered the opinion of the Court.

Under the Medicare program, health care providers are reimbursed by the Government for expenses incurred in providing medical services to Medicare beneficiaries. *See* Title XVIII of the Social Security Act, 79 Stat. 291, as amended, 42 U.S.C. § 1395 *et seq.* (the Medicare Act). Congress has authorized the Secretary of Health and Human Services to promulgate regulations setting limits on the levels of Medicare costs that will be reimbursed. The question presented here is whether the Secretary may exercise this rulemaking authority to promulgate cost limits that are retroactive.

I

The Secretary's authority to adopt cost-limit rules is established by § 223(b) of the Social Security Amendments of 1972. This authority was first implemented in 1974 by promulgation of a cost-limit schedule for hospital services; new cost-limit schedules were issued on an annual basis thereafter.

On June 30, 1981, the Secretary issued a cost-limit schedule that included technical changes in the methods for calculating cost limits. One of these changes affected the method for calculating the "wage index," a factor used to reflect the salary levels for hospital employees in different parts of the country. Under the prior rule, the wage index for a given geographic area was calculated by using the average salary levels for all hospitals in the area; the 1981 rule provided that wages paid by Federal Government hospitals would be excluded from that computation.

Various hospitals in the District of Columbia area brought suit in United States District Court seeking to have the 1981 schedule invalidated. On April 29, 1983, the District Court struck down the 1981 wage-index rule, concluding that the Secretary had violated the Administrative Procedure Act (APA), 5 U.S.C. § 551 *et seq.*, by failing to provide notice and an opportunity for public comment before issuing the rule. The court did not enjoin enforcement of the rule, however, finding it lacked jurisdiction to do so because the hospitals had not yet exhausted their administrative reimbursement remedies. The court's order stated:

> "If the Secretary wishes to put in place a valid prospective wage index, she should begin proper notice and comment proceedings; any wage index currently in place that has been promulgated without notice and comment is invalid as was the 1981 schedule."

The Secretary did not pursue an appeal. Instead, after recognizing the invalidity of the rule, *see* 48 Fed. Reg. 39998 (1983), the Secretary settled the hospitals' cost reimbursement reports by applying the pre-1981 wage-index method.

In February 1984, the Secretary published a notice seeking public comment on a proposal to reissue the 1981 wage-index rule, retroactive to July 1, 1981. Because Congress had subsequently amended the Medicare Act to require significantly different cost reimbursement procedures, the readoption of the modified wage-index method was to apply exclusively to a 15-month period commencing July 1, 1981. After considering the comments received, the Secretary reissued the 1981 schedule in final form on November 26, 1984, and proceeded to recoup sums previously paid as a result of the District Court's ruling. In effect, the Secretary had promulgated a rule retroactively, and the net result was as if the original rule had never been set aside.

Respondents, a group of seven hospitals who had benefited from the invalidation of the 1981 schedule, were required to return over $2 million in reimbursement payments. After exhausting administrative remedies, they sought judicial review under the applicable provisions of the APA, claiming that the retroactive schedule was invalid under both the APA and the Medicare Act.

[When the case got to the D.C. Circuit, that court ruled for the hospitals] on the alternative grounds that the APA, as a general matter, forbids retroactive rulemaking, and that the Medicare Act, by specific terms, bars retroactive cost-limit rules. We granted certiorari, and we now affirm.

II

It is axiomatic that an administrative agency's power to promulgate legislative regulations is limited to the authority delegated by Congress. In determining the validity of the Secretary's retroactive cost-limit rule, the threshold question is whether the Medicare Act authorizes retroactive rulemaking.

Retroactivity is not favored in the law. Thus, congressional enactments and administrative rules will not be construed to have retroactive effect unless their language requires this result. By the same principle, a statutory grant of legislative rulemaking authority will not, as a general matter, be understood to encompass the power to promulgate retroactive rules unless that power is conveyed by Congress in express terms. Even where some substantial justification for retroactive rulemaking is presented, courts should be reluctant to find such authority absent an express statutory grant.

The Secretary contends that the Medicare Act provides the necessary authority to promulgate retroactive cost-limit rules in the unusual circumstances of this case. He rests on alternative grounds: first, the specific grant of authority to promulgate regulations to "provide for the making of suitable retroactive corrective adjustments," 42 U.S.C. § 1395x(v)(1)(A)(ii); and second, the general grant of authority to promulgate cost limit rules, §§ 1395x(v)(1)(A), 1395hh, 1395ii. We consider these alternatives in turn.

A

The authority to promulgate cost-reimbursement regulations is set forth in § 1395x(v)(1)(A). That subparagraph also provides that:

> "Such regulations shall ... (ii) provide for the making of suitable retroactive corrective adjustments where, for a provider of services for any fiscal period, the aggregate reimbursement produced by the methods of determining costs proves to be either inadequate or excessive." *Ibid.*

This provision on its face permits some form of retroactive action. We cannot accept the Secretary's argument, however, that it provides authority for the retroactive promulgation of cost-limit rules. To the contrary, we agree with the Court of Appeals that clause (ii) directs the Secretary to establish a procedure for making case-by-case adjustments to reimbursement payments where the regulations prescribing computation methods do not reach the correct result in individual cases. The structure and language of the statute require the conclusion that the retroactivity provision applies only to case-by-case adjudication, not to rulemaking. [Analysis of clause (ii) omitted.]

B

The statutory provisions establishing the Secretary's general rulemaking power contain no express authorization of retroactive rulemaking. Any light that might be shed on this matter by suggestions of legislative intent also indicates that no such authority was contemplated. In the first place, where Congress intended to grant the Secretary the authority to act retroactively, it made that intent explicit. As discussed above, § 1395x(v)(1)(A)(ii) directs the Secretary to establish procedures for making retroactive corrective adjustments; in view of this indication that Congress considered the need for retroactive agency action, the absence of any express authorization for retroactive cost-limit rules weighs heavily against the Secretary's position.

The legislative history of the cost-limit provision directly addresses the issue of retroactivity. In discussing the authority granted by § 223(b) of the 1972 amendments, the House and Senate Committee Reports expressed a desire to forbid retroactive cost-limit rules: "The proposed new authority to set limits on costs ... would be exercised on a prospective, rather than retrospective, basis so that the provider would know in advance the limits to Government recognition of incurred costs and have the opportunity to act to avoid having costs that are not reimbursable." H. R. Rep. No. 92-231, p. 83 (1971); see S. Rep. No. 92-1230, p. 188 (1972).

The Secretary's past administrative practice is consistent with this interpretation of the statute. The first regulations promulgated under § 223(b) provided that "[t]hese limits will be imposed prospectively. ..." 20 CFR § 405.460(a) (1975). Although the language was dropped from subsection (a) of the regulation when it was revised in 1979, the revised regulation continued to refer to "the prospective periods to which limits are being applied," and it required that notice of future cost limits be published in the Federal Register "[p]rior to the beginning of a cost period to which limits will be applied. ..." 42 CFR §§ 405.460(b)(2), (3) (1980). Finally, when the regulations were amended again in 1982, the Secretary reinserted the requirement that the limits be applied with prospective effect, noting that the language had been "inadvertently omitted" in the previous amendment but that the reinsertion would "have no effect on the way we develop or apply the limits." 47 Fed. Reg. 43282, 43286 (1982); see 42 CFR § 405.460(a)(2) (1983).

Other examples of similar statements by the agency abound. Every cost-limit schedule promulgated by the Secretary between 1974 and 1981, for example, included a statement that § 223 permits the Secretary to establish "prospective" limits on the costs that are reimbursed under Medicare. The Secretary's administrative rulings have also expressed this understanding of § 223(b).

The Secretary nonetheless suggests that, whatever the limits on his power to promulgate retroactive regulations in the normal course of events, judicial invalidation of a prospective rule is a unique occurrence that creates a heightened need, and thus a justification, for retroactive curative rulemaking. The Secretary warns that congressional intent and important administrative goals may be frustrated unless an invalidated rule can be cured of its defect and made applicable to past time periods. The argument is further advanced that the countervailing reliance interests are less compelling than in the usual case of retroactive rulemaking, because the original, invalidated rule provided at least some notice to the individuals and entities subject to its provisions.

Whatever weight the Secretary's contentions might have in other contexts, they need not be addressed here. The case before us is resolved by the particular statutory scheme in question. Our interpretation of the Medicare Act compels the conclusion that the Secretary has no authority to promulgate retroactive cost-limit rules.

The 1984 reinstatement of the 1981 cost-limit rule is invalid. The judgment of the Court of Appeals is *Affirmed.*

JUSTICE SCALIA, concurring.

I agree with the Court that general principles of administrative law suggest that § 223(b) of the Medicare Act, 42 U.S.C. § 1395x(v)(1)(A), does not permit retroactive application of the Secretary of Health and Human Service's 1984 cost-limit rule. I write separately because I find it incomplete to discuss general principles of administrative law without reference to the basic structural legislation which is the embodiment of those principles, the Administrative Procedure Act (APA), 5 U.S.C. §§ 551-552, 553-559, 701-706, 1305, 3105, 3344, 5372, 7521. I agree with the District of Columbia Circuit that the APA independently confirms the judgment we have reached.

The first part of the APA's definition of "rule" states that a rule

> "means the whole or a part of an agency statement of general or particular applicability *and future effect* designed to implement, interpret, or prescribe law or policy or describing the organization, procedure, or practice requirements of an agency. . . ." 5 U.S.C. § 551(4) (emphasis added).

The only plausible reading of the italicized phrase is that rules have legal consequences only for the future. It could not possibly mean that merely *some* of their legal consequences must be for the future, though they may also have legal consequences for the past, since that description would not enable rules to be distinguished from "orders," see 5 U.S.C. § 551(6), and would thus destroy the entire dichotomy upon which the most significant portions of the APA are based. (Adjudication — the process for formulating orders, see § 551(7) — has future as well as past legal consequences, since the principles announced in an adjudication cannot be departed from in future adjudications without reason.)

Nor could "future effect" in this definition mean merely "*taking effect* in the future," that is, having a future effective date even though, once effective, altering the law applied in the past. That reading, urged by the Secretary of Health and Human Services (Secretary), produces a definition of "rule" that is meaningless, since obviously *all* agency statements have "future effect" in the sense that they do not take effect until after they are made. (One might argue, I suppose, that "future effect" excludes agency statements that take effect immediately, as opposed to one second after promulgation. Apart from the facial silliness of making the central distinction between rulemaking and adjudication hang upon such a thread, it is incompatible with §553(d), which makes clear that, if certain requirements are complied with, a rule can be effective immediately.) Thus this reading, like the other one, causes §551(4) to fail in its central objective, which is to distinguish rules from orders. All orders have "future effect" in the sense that they are not effective until promulgated.

In short, there is really no alternative except the obvious meaning, that a rule is a statement that has legal consequences only for the future. If the first part of the definition left any doubt of this, however, it is surely eliminated by the second part (which the Secretary's brief regrettably submerges in ellipsis). After the portion set forth above, the definition continues that a rule

> "includes the approval or prescription *for the future* of rates, wages, corporate or financial structures or reorganizations thereof, prices, facilities, appliances, services or allowances therefor or of valuations, costs, or accounting, or practices bearing on any of the foregoing." 5 U.S.C. §551(4) (emphasis added).

It seems to me clear that the phrase "for the future"—which even more obviously refers to future operation rather than a future effective date—is not meant to add a requirement to those contained in the earlier part of the definition, but rather to repeat, in a more particularized context, the prior requirement "of future effect." And even if one thought otherwise it would not matter for purposes of the present case, since the HHS "cost-limit" rules governing reimbursement are a "prescription" of "practices bearing on" "allowances" for "services."

The position the Secretary takes in this litigation is out of accord with the Government's own most authoritative interpretation of the APA, the 1947 Attorney General's Manual on the Administrative Procedure Act (AG's Manual), which we have repeatedly given great weight. That document was prepared by the same Office of the Assistant Solicitor General that had advised Congress in the latter stages of enacting the APA, and was originally issued "as a guide to the agencies in adjusting their procedures to the requirements of the Act." AG's Manual 6. Its analysis is plainly out of accord with the Secretary's position here:

> "Of particular importance is the fact that "rule" includes agency statements not only of general applicability but also those of particular applicability applying either to a class or to a single person. In either case, they must be of *future effect,* implementing or prescribing future law. . . . [sic]
>
> "[T]he entire Act is based upon a dichotomy between rule making and adjudication. . . . Rule making is agency action which regulates the future conduct of either groups of persons or a single person; it is essentially legislative in nature, not only because it operates in the future but also because it is primarily concerned with policy considerations. . . . Conversely, adjudication is concerned with the determination of past and present rights and liabilities." *Id.*, at 13-14.

These statements cannot conceivably be reconciled with the Secretary's position here that a rule has future effect merely because it is made effective in the future. Moreover, the clarity of these statements cannot be disregarded on the basis of the single sentence, elsewhere in the Manual, that "[n]othing in the Act precludes the issuance of retroactive rules when otherwise legal and accompanied by the finding required by section 4(c)." *Id.*, at 37. What that statement means (apart from the inexplicable reference to §4(c), 5 U.S.C. §553 (d), which would appear to have no application, no matter which interpretation is adopted), is clarified by the immediately following citation to the portion of the legislative history supporting it, namely, H. R. Rep. No. 1980, 79th Cong., 2d Sess., 49, n.1 (1946). That Report states that "[t]he phrase 'future effect' does not preclude agencies from considering and, so far as legally authorized, dealing with past transactions in prescribing rules for the future." *Ibid.* The Treasury Department might prescribe, for example, that for purposes of assessing future income tax liability, income from certain trusts that has previously been considered nontaxable will be taxable — whether those trusts were established before or after the effective date of the regulation. That is not retroactivity in the sense at issue here, *i.e.*, in the sense of altering the *past* legal consequences of past actions. Rather, it is what has been characterized as "secondary" retroactivity, see McNulty, Corporations and the Intertemporal Conflict of Laws, 55 Cal. L. Rev. 12, 58-60 (1967). A rule with exclusively future effect (taxation of future trust income) can unquestionably *affect* past transactions (rendering the previously established trusts less desirable in the future), but it does not for that reason cease to be a rule under the APA. Thus, with respect to the present matter, there is no question that the Secretary could have applied her new wage-index formulas to respondents in the future, even though respondents may have been operating under long-term labor and supply contracts negotiated in reliance upon the pre-existing rule. But when the Secretary prescribed such a formula for costs reimbursable while the prior rule was in effect, she changed the *law* retroactively, a function not performable by rule under the APA.

A rule that has unreasonable secondary retroactivity — for example, altering future regulation in a manner that makes worthless substantial past investment incurred in reliance upon the prior rule — may for that reason be "arbitrary" or "capricious," *see* 5 U.S.C. § 706, and thus invalid. In reference to such situations, there are to be found in many cases statements to the effect that "[w]here a rule has retroactive effects, it may nonetheless be sustained in spite of such retroactivity if it is reasonable." *General Telephone Co. of Southwest v. United States,* 449 F.2d 846, 863 (CA5 1971). *See also National Assn. of Independent Television Producers and Distributors v. FCC,* 502 F.2d 249, 255 (CA2 1974) ("Any implication by the FCC that this court may not consider the reasonableness of the retroactive effect of a rule is clearly wrong"). It is erroneous, however, to extend this "reasonableness" inquiry to purported rules that not merely affect past transactions but change what was the law in the past. Quite simply, a rule is an agency statement "of future effect," not "of future effect and/or reasonable past effect." . . .

Although the APA was enacted over 40 years ago, this Court has never directly confronted whether the statute authorizes retroactive rules. This in itself casts doubt on the Secretary's position. If so obviously useful an instrument was available to the agencies, one would expect that we would previously have had occasion to review its exercise. The only Supreme Court case the Government cites, however, is the *pre*-APA case of *Addison v. Holly Hill Fruit Products, Inc.,* 322 U.S. 607 (1944). [Discussion distinguishing *Holly Hill* omitted.]

This case cannot be disposed of, as the Secretary suggests, by simply noting that retroactive rulemaking is similar to retroactive legislation, and that the latter has long been upheld against constitutional attack where reasonable. *See,* e.g., *Pension Benefit Guaranty Corp. v. R. A. Gray & Co.,* 467 U.S. 717 (1984); *Baltimore & Susquehanna R. Co. v. Nesbit,* 10 How. 395 (1851). The issue here is not constitutionality, but rather whether there is any good reason to doubt that the APA means what it says. For purposes of resolving that question, it does not at all follow that, since Congress itself possesses the power retroactively to change its laws, it must have meant agencies to possess the power retroactively to change their regulations. Retroactive legislation has always been looked upon with disfavor, *see* Smead, The Rule Against Retroactive Legislation: A Basic Principle of Jurisprudence, 20 Minn. L. Rev. 775 (1936); 2 J. Story, Commentaries on the Constitution of the United States § 1398, p. 272 (5th ed. 1891), and even its constitutionality has been conditioned upon a rationality requirement beyond that applied to other legislation, see *Pension Benefit Guaranty Corp., supra,* at 730; *Usery v. Turner Elkhorn Mining Co.*, 428 U.S. 1, 16-17 (1976). It is entirely unsurprising, therefore, that even though Congress wields such a power itself, it has been unwilling to confer it upon the agencies. Given the traditional attitude towards retroactive legislation, the regime established by the APA is an entirely reasonable one: Where quasi-legislative action is required, an agency cannot act with retroactive effect without some special congressional authorization. That is what the APA says, and there is no reason to think Congress did not mean it.

The dire consequences that the Secretary predicts will ensue from reading the APA as it is written (and as the Justice Department originally interpreted it) are not credible. From the more than 40 years of jurisprudence since the APA has been in effect, the Secretary cites only one holding and one alternative holding (set forth in a footnote) sustaining retroactive regulations. They are evidently not a device indispensable to efficient government. It is important to note that the retroactivity limitation applies *only* to rulemaking. Thus, where legal consequences hinge upon the interpretation of statutory requirements, and where no preexisting interpretive rule construing those requirements is in effect, nothing prevents the agency from acting retroactively through adjudication. *See NLRB v. Bell Aerospace Co.*, 416 U.S. 267, 293-294 (1974); *SEC v. Chenery Corp.*, 332 U.S., at 202-203. Moreover, if and when an agency believes that the extraordinary step of retroactive rulemaking is crucial, all it need do is persuade Congress of that fact to obtain the necessary ad hoc authorization. It may even be that implicit authorization of particular retroactive rulemaking can be found in existing legislation. If, for example, a statute prescribes a deadline by which particular rules must be in effect, and if the agency misses that deadline, the statute may be interpreted to authorize a reasonable retroactive rule despite the limitation of the APA. . . .

I need not discuss what other exceptions, with basis in the law, may permit an agency to issue a retroactive rule. The only exception suggested by the Secretary to cover the present case has no basis in the law. The Secretary contends that the evils generally associated with retroactivity do not apply to reasonable "curative" rulemaking — that is, the correction of a mistake in an earlier rulemaking proceeding. Because the invalidated 1981 wage-index rule furnished respondents with "ample notice" of the standard that would be applied, the Secretary asserts that it is not unfair to apply the identical 1984 rule retroactively. I shall assume that the invalidated rule provided ample notice, though that is not at all clear. It makes no difference. The issue is not whether retroactive rulemaking is fair; it undoubtedly may be, just as may prospective adjudication. The issue is whether it is a permissible form of agency action under the particular structure established by the APA. The Secretary provides nothing that can bring it within that structure. I might add that even if I felt free to construct my own model of desirable administrative procedure, I would assuredly not sanction "curative" retroactivity. I fully agree with the District of Columbia Circuit that acceptance of the Secretary's position would "make a mockery . . . of the APA," since "agencies would be free to violate the rulemaking requirements of the APA with impunity if, upon invalidation of a rule, they were free to 'reissue' that rule on a retroactive basis."

For these reasons in addition to those stated by the Court, I agree that the judgment of the District of Columbia Circuit must be affirmed.

QUESTIONS

1. What was the original procedural deficiency in this case? What is the statutory basis for the procedural requirement? What does "notice and comment" amount to? How is it different from an adjudicatory hearing?
2. Does the rule in this case (i.e., the product of the agency's rulemaking) affect anyone's rights? How?
3. Track the definitions in §551(8), (7), (6), (5), (4). How does the 1981 MSAPA definition of a rule differ from the APA definition? *See* MSAPA §1-102(10).
4. What is the statutory relevance under the federal APA of whether something is a "rule" or not? I.e., what difference does it make under the APA?
5. In light of your answer to 4, does Justice Scalia's concurrence make any sense? Is he arguing that statements of retroactive effect are *not* subject to the procedural requirements of §553? If not, where is the operative statutory language banning retroactive rules? Does anything in §551(4)'s definition of a "rule" preclude a rule from having both future and retroactive effect? Clearly Justice Scalia is correct in arguing that the APA's definition of a "rule" requires a "rule" to have prospective effect. Is it so clear that a "rule" may not have *both* prospective and retroactive effect?

B. NOTICE AND COMMENT: "INFORMAL" RULEMAKING

CHOCOLATE MANUFACTURERS ASS'N v. BLOCK
755 F.2d 1098 (4th Cir. 1985)

SPROUSE, Circuit Judge: Chocolate Manufacturers Association (CMA) appeals from the decision of the district court denying it relief from a rule promulgated by the Food and Nutrition Service (FNS) of the United States Department of Agriculture (USDA or Department). CMA protests that part of the rule that prohibits the use of chocolate flavored milk[1] in the federally funded Special Supplemental Food Program for Women, Infants and Children (WIC Program). Holding that the Department's proposed rulemaking did not provide adequate notice that the elimination of flavored milk would be considered in the rulemaking procedure, we reverse.

---

1. Referred to hereafter as "flavored milk."

I

Since 1946 USDA has administered a variety of child nutrition programs under the National School Lunch Act and the Child Nutrition Act of 1966. Besides the WIC Program, these programs are the National School Lunch Program, the Special Milk Program for Children, the School Breakfast Program, the Summer Food Service Program, and the Child Care Food Program.

The WIC Program was established by Congress in 1972 to assist pregnant, postpartum, and breastfeeding women, infants and young children from families with inadequate income whose physical and mental health is in danger because of inadequate nutrition or health care. Under the program, the Department designs food packages reflecting the different nutritional needs of women, infants, and children and provides cash grants to state or local agencies, which distribute cash or vouchers to qualifying individuals in accordance with Departmental regulations as to the type and quantity of food.

In 1975 Congress revised and extended the WIC Program through fiscal year 1978 and, for the first time, defined the "supplemental foods" which the program was established to provide. The term:

> shall mean those foods containing nutrients known to be lacking in the diets of populations at nutritional risk and, in particular, those foods and food products containing high-quality protein, iron, calcium, vitamin A, and vitamin C. . . . The contents of the food package shall be made available in such a manner as to provide flexibility, taking into account medical and nutritional objectives and cultural eating patterns.

Pub. L. No. 94-105, § 17(g)(3), 89 Stat. 511, 520 (1975).

Pursuant to this statutory definition, the Department promulgated new regulations specifying the contents of WIC Program food packages. These regulations specified that flavored milk was an acceptable substitute for fluid whole milk in the food packages for women and children, but not infants. This regulation formalized the Department's practice of permitting the substitution of flavored milk, a practice observed in the WIC Program since its inception in 1973 as well as in several of the other food programs administered by the Department.

In 1978 Congress, in extending the WIC Program through fiscal year 1982, redefined the term "supplemental foods" to mean:

> those foods containing nutrients determined by nutritional research to be lacking in the diets of pregnant, breastfeeding, and postpartum women, infants, and children, as prescribed by the Secretary. State agencies may, with the approval of the Secretary, substitute different foods providing the nutritional equivalent of foods prescribed by the Secretary, to allow for different cultural eating patterns.

Pub. L. No. 95-627, § 17(b)(14), 92 Stat. 3603, 3613 (1978). Congress stated further:

> The Secretary shall prescribe by regulation supplemental foods to be made available in the program under this section. To the degree possible, the Secretary shall assure that the fat, sugar, and salt content of the prescribed foods is appropriate.

Id. at § 17(f)(12), 92 Stat. at 3616. To comply with this statutory redefinition, the Department moved to redraft its regulations specifying the WIC Program food packages. In doing so it relied upon information collected during an extensive investigative effort which had begun in 1977. In June 1977 the Department held public hearings in seven cities and elicited testimony on the structure and administration of the WIC Program. The Department invited many interested and informed parties to attend these hearings — the governor and chief health officer of every state, the House Education and Labor Committee, the Senate Select Committee on Nutrition Evaluation, state WIC coordinators, industry representatives, and professional and advocacy groups. In addition to information gathered at the public hearings, the Department received periodic reports from the National Advisory Council on Maternal, Infant, and Fetal Nutrition, as well as recommendations from a Food Package Advisory Panel convened in October 1978.

Using this information as well as its own research as a basis, the Department in November 1979 published for comment the proposed rule at issue in this case. 44 Fed. Reg. 69254 (1979). Along with the proposed rule, the Department published a preamble discussing the general purpose of the rule and acknowledging the congressional directive that the Department design food packages containing the requisite nutritional value and appropriate levels of fat, sugar, and salt. *Id.* at 69254. Discussing the issue of sugar at length, it noted, for example, that continued inclusion of high sugar cereals may be "contrary to nutrition education principles and may lead to unsound eating practices." *Id.* at 69263. It also noted that high sugar foods are more expensive than foods with lower sugar content, and that allowing them would be "inconsistent with the goal of teaching participants economical food buying patterns." *Id.*

The rule proposed a maximum sugar content specifically for authorized cereals. The preamble also contained a discussion of the sugar content in juice, but the Department did not propose to reduce the allowable amount of sugar in juice because of technical problems involved in any reduction. Neither the rule nor the preamble discussed sugar in relation to flavoring in milk. Under the proposed rule, the food packages for women and children without special dietary needs included milk that could be "flavored or unflavored." *Id.*

The notice allowed sixty days for comment and specifically invited comment on the entire scope of the proposed rules: "The public is invited to submit written comments in favor of or in objection to the proposed regulations or to make recommendations for alternatives not considered in the proposed regulations." *Id.* at 69255. Over 1,000 comments were received from state and local agencies, congressional offices, interest groups, and WIC Program participants and others. Seventy-eight commenters, mostly local WIC administrators, recommended that the agency delete flavored milk from the list of approved supplemental foods.

In promulgating the final rule, the Department, responding to these public comments, deleted flavored milk from the list, explaining:

> In the previous regulations, women and children were allowed to receive flavored or unflavored milk. No change in this provision was proposed by the Department. However, 78 commenters requested the deletion of flavored milk from the food packages since flavored milk has a higher sugar content than unflavored milk. They indicated that providing flavored milk contradicts nutrition education and

the Department's proposal to limit sugar in the food packages. Furthermore, flavored milk is more expensive than unflavored milk. The Department agrees with these concerns. There are significant differences in the sugar content of fluid whole milk and low fat chocolate milk. Fluid whole milk supplies 12.0 grams of carbohydrate per cup compared to 27.3 grams of carbohydrate per cup provided by low fat chocolate milk. If we assume that the major portion of carbohydrate in milk is in the form of simple sugar, fluid whole milk contains 4.9% sugar contrasted with 10.9% sugar in low fat chocolate milk. Therefore, to reinforce nutrition education, for consistency with the Department's philosophy about sugar in the food packages, and to maintain food package costs at economic levels, the Department is deleting flavored milk from the food packages for women and children. Although the deletion of flavored milk was not proposed, the comments and the Department's policy on sugar validate this change.

45 Fed. Reg. 74854, 74865-66 (1980).

After the final rule was issued, CMA petitioned the Department to reopen the rulemaking to allow it to comment, maintaining that it had been misled into believing that the deletion of flavored milk would not be considered. In a letter to CMA dated November 18, 1981, the Department indicated that it would reopen the issue of flavored milk for "further public comments" and would request "rationale[s] both supporting and opposing the disallowance of flavored milk in the WIC Program." It subsequently reversed this position, however, and declined to reopen the rulemaking procedure.

On this appeal, CMA contends first that the Department did not provide notice that the disallowance of flavored milk would be considered, and second that the Department gave no reasoned justification for changing its position about the nutritional value of chocolate in the food distributed under its authority. The Department responds to the first contention by arguing that its notice advised the public of its general concern about high sugar content in the proposed food packages and that this should have alerted potentially interested commenters that it would consider eliminating any food with high sugar content. It also argues in effect that the inclusion of flavored milk in the proposed rule carried with it the implication that both inclusion and exclusion would be considered in the rulemaking process. Because we agree with CMA that the Department provided inadequate notice and, therefore, that it must reopen the comment period on the rule, we do not reach the issue of the reasonable justification for its change of position.

II

The requirement of notice and a fair opportunity to be heard is basic to administrative law. *See* 1 K. Davis, *Administrative Law Treatise* § 6.1 at 450 (2d ed. 1978). Our single chore is to determine if the Department's notice provided interested persons, including CMA, with that opportunity. We must decide whether inclusion of flavored milk in the allowable food packages under the proposed rule should have alerted interested persons that the Department might reverse its position and exclude flavored milk if adverse comments recommended its deletion from the program.

Section 4 of the Administrative Procedure Act (APA) requires that the notice in the Federal Register of a proposed rulemaking contain "either the terms or substance of the proposed rule or a description of the subjects and issues involved." 5 U.S.C. § 553(b)(3) (1982). The purpose of the notice-and-comment procedure is both "to allow the agency to benefit from the experience and input of the parties who file comments . . . and to see to it that the agency maintains a flexible and open-minded attitude towards its own rules." *National Tour Brokers Ass'n v. United States*, 591 F.2d 896, 902 (D.C. Cir. 1978). The notice-and-comment procedure encourages public participation in the administrative process and educates the agency, thereby helping to ensure informed agency decisionmaking.

The Department's published notice here consisted of the proposed rule and a preamble discussing the negative effect of high sugar content in general and specifically in relation to some foods such as cereals and juices, but it did not mention high sugar content in flavored milk. The proposed rule eliminated certain foods with high sugar content but specifically authorized flavored milk as part of the permissible diet. In a discussion characterized by pointed identification of foods with high sugar content, flavored milk was conspicuous by its exclusion. If after comments the agency had adopted without change the proposed rule as its final rule, there could have been no possible objection to the adequacy of notice. The public was fully notified as to what the Department considered to be a healthy and adequate diet for its target group. The final rule, however, dramatically altered the proposed rule, changing for the first time the milk content of the diet by deleting flavored milk. The agency concedes that the elimination of flavored milk by the final rule is a complete reversal from its treatment in the proposed rule, but it explains that the reversal was caused by the comments received from 78 interested parties—primarily professional administrators of the WIC Program.

This presents then not the simple question of whether the notice of a proposed rule adequately informs the public of its intent, but rather the question of how to judge the adequacy of the notice when the proposal it describes is replaced by a final rule which reaches a conclusion exactly opposite to that proposed, on the basis of comments received from parties representing only a single view of a controversy. In reviewing the propriety of such agency action, we are not constrained by the same degree of deference we afford most agency determinations. "Though our review of an agency's final decision is relatively narrow, we must be strict in reviewing an agency's compliance with procedural rules." *BASF Wyandotte Corp. v. Costle*, 598 F.2d at 641; *see also Weyerhaeuser Co. v. Costle*, 590 F.2d 1011, 1025-28 (D.C. Cir. 1978) (whereas a court defers to an agency's technical judgments, it is less hesitant to reject the agency's interpretation of statutes, and in reviewing an agency's procedural integrity, the court relies on its own independent judgment). "The question of adequacy of notice where a proposed rule is changed after comment . . . requires careful consideration on a case-by-case basis." *BASF*, 598 F.2d at 642.

There is no question that an agency may promulgate a final rule that differs in some particulars from its proposal. Otherwise the agency "can learn from the comments on its proposals only at the peril of starting a new procedural round of commentary." An agency, however, does not have carte blanche to establish a rule contrary to its original proposal simply because it receives suggestions to alter it during the comment period. An interested party must have been alerted by the notice to the possibility of the changes eventually adopted from the comments. *Wagner Electric Corporation v. Volpe*, 466 F.2d 1013, 1019 (3rd Cir.

1972). Although an agency, in its notice of proposed rulemaking, need not identify precisely every potential regulatory change, the notice must be sufficiently descriptive to provide interested parties with a fair opportunity to comment and to participate in the rulemaking.

As we have indicated, appellate review of changes in a proposed rule after comments is more specifically controlled by the circumstances of each case than most administrative appeals. Nevertheless, a review of decisions of our sister circuits performing similar tasks is helpful. In *BASF Wyandotte Corp. v. Costle*, 598 F.2d 637 (1st Cir. 1979), the court considered an EPA regulation controlling the discharge of pollutants into navigable waters by the pesticide industry. The EPA originally proposed dividing the organic pesticide industry into three subcategories, setting different pollutant standards for each one. The industry, arguing for expansion of the number of subcategories and, therefore, pollutant standards, submitted comments demonstrating that the proposed three subcategories were indistinguishable. The EPA, while agreeing with the comments, chose a different solution: it altered its initial rule by eliminating the subcategories and applying uniform standards throughout the entire organic pesticide industry. The industry complained that the EPA's decision to contract rather than expand the number of subcategories took them entirely by surprise. "The essential inquiry," the court said, "is whether the commentators have had a fair opportunity to present their views on the contents of the final plan." *Id.* at 642. The First Circuit reasoned that even if the initial rule had proposed uniform standards, the content of petitioner's comments would not have been different for they still would have argued, albeit more voluminously and vociferously, for more subcategories. *Id.* at 644. The petitioners, therefore, "had a fair opportunity to present their views." *Id.*

In *International Harvester Co. v. Ruckelshaus*, 478 F.2d 615 (D.C. Cir. 1973), the court considered an EPA decision to deny applications by vehicle manufacturers for a one-year suspension of the emission standards for light-duty vehicles. The court upheld the agency's denial even though the petitioners were precluded from commenting on the methodology that the EPA had used to determine that compliance with the emission standards was technologically possible. The court based this holding on the fact that the methodology in question was developed in part on the basis of the petitioners' submissions at prior hearings. The court stated that "the requirement of submission of a proposed rule for comment does not automatically generate a new opportunity for comment merely because the rule promulgated by the agency differs from the rule it proposed, partly at least in response to submissions." *Id.* at 632 (footnote omitted).

In *South Terminal Corp. v. EPA*, 504 F.2d 646 (1st Cir. 1974), the court considered an air quality transportation control plan for Boston, Massachusetts, which varied substantially from the proposal described in the notice. The petitioners contended that they had no meaningful notice of the substance of the plan. The *South Terminal* court identified two factors of primary importance in determining whether a substantially revised final rule is promulgated in accordance with the APA: the changes in the original rule must be "in character with the original scheme" and "a logical outgrowth" of the notice and comment already given. *Id.* at 658, 659; *see also BASF Wyandotte Corp. v. Costle*, 598 F.2d at 642. In rejecting the petitioners' claim, the court stated: "Although the changes were substantial, they were in character with the original scheme and were additionally foreshadowed in proposals and comments advanced during the rulemaking.

[In addition, the parties] had been warned that strategies might be modified in light of their suggestions." 504 F.2d at 658. A proposed rule, therefore, must fairly apprise interested parties of the potential scope and substance of a substantially revised final rule and, under this approach, a substantial change must relate in part to the comments received.

While considering factors similar to those applied in the above cases, the Third Circuit, in *Wagner Electric Corporation v. Volpe,* 466 F.2d 1013 (3rd Cir. 1972), found notice inadequate where a final rule had been substantially altered from the one described in the initial notice. The National Highway Traffic Safety Administration had published a proposed rule governing hazard warning flashers. The proposed rule would have eliminated the permissible failure rate for flashers, but it said nothing about changing the pertinent performance criteria. The final rule substantially downgraded the performance criteria for flashers. Despite the fact that several comments by manufacturers suggested downgrading the performance criteria, the court concluded that the agency's proposed rule provided inadequate notice of its final rule because it failed to apprise all interested parties of the issue of performance criteria. *Id.* at 1019-20. In support of this conclusion, the court noted the absence of comments from groups which could be expected to oppose downgrading the performance criteria, for example, consumer groups and state highway agencies. *Id.*

The test devised by the First Circuit for determining adequacy of notice of a change in a proposed rule occurring after comments appears to us to be sound: notice is adequate if the changes in the original plan "are in character with the original scheme," and the final rule is a "logical outgrowth" of the notice and comments already given. Other circuits also have adopted some form of the "logical outgrowth" test. *See,* e.g., *Sierra Club v. Costle,* 657 F.2d 298, 352 (D.C. Cir. 1981) (logical outgrowth of the notice and comments); *Taylor Diving & Salvage Co. v. Dept. of Labor,* 599 F.2d 622, 626 (5th Cir. 1979) (logical outgrowth of the standard originally proposed). Stated differently, if the final rule materially alters the issues involved in the rulemaking or, as stated in *Rowell v. Andrus,* 631 F.2d 699, 702 n.2 (10th Cir. 1980), if the final rule "substantially departs from the terms or substance of the proposed rule," the notice is inadequate.

There can be no doubt that the final rule in the instant case was the "outgrowth" of the original rule proposed by the agency, but the question of whether the change in it was in character with the original scheme and whether it was a "*logical* outgrowth" is not easy to answer. In resolving this difficult issue, we recognize that, although helpful, verbal formulations are not omnipotent talismans, and we agree that in the final analysis each case "must turn on how well the notice that the agency gave serves the policies underlying the notice requirement." Under either view, we do not feel that CMA was fairly treated or that the administrative rulemaking process was well served by the drastic alteration of the rule without an opportunity for CMA to be heard.

It is apparent that for many years the Department of Agriculture has permitted the use of chocolate in some form in the food distribution programs that it administers. The only time the Department has proposed to remove chocolate in any form from its programs was in April 1978 when it sought to characterize chocolate as a candy and remove it from the School Lunch Program. That proposal was withdrawn after CMA commented, supporting chocolate as a part of the diet. Chocolate flavored milk has been a permissible part of the

WIC Program diet since its inception and there have been no proposals for its removal until the present controversy.

The Department sponsored commendable information-gathering proceedings prior to publishing its proposed rule. Together with its own research, the information gathered in the pre-publication information solicitations formed the basis for the proposed rule. Most of the same information was presented to Congress prior to enactment of the 1978 statute that precipitated the 1979 rulemaking here in controversy. The National Advisory Council on Maternal, Infant, and Fetal Nutrition provided information and advice. Regional council meetings were open to the public and held in diverse areas of the country. Department of Agriculture personnel attended a number of regional, state, and local meetings and gathered opinions concerning possible changes in the food packages. The agency also gathered a food package advisory panel of experts seeking their recommendations. Food packages were designed based on the information and advice gleaned from these sources. In all of these activities setting out and discussing food packages, including the proposed rule and its preamble, the Department never suggested that flavored milk be removed from the WIC Program.

The published preamble to the proposed rule consisted of twelve pages in the Federal Register discussing in detail factors that would be considered in making the final rule. Two pages were devoted to a general discussion of nutrients, including protein, iron, calcium, vitamin A, vitamin C, folic acid, zinc, and fiber, and the dangers of overconsumption of sugar, fat, and salt. The preamble discussed some foods containing these ingredients and foods posing specific problems. It did not discuss flavored milk.

In the next eight pages of the preamble, the nutrition content of food packages was discussed — under the general headings of "cereal" and "juice" for infants; and "eggs," "milk," "cheese," "peanut butter and mature dried beans and peas," "juice," "additional foods," "cereals," "iron," "sugar," "whole grain cereals," "highly fortified cereals," and "artificial flavors and colors" for women and children. The only reference to milk concerned the correct quantity to be provided to children, i.e., 24 quarts per month instead of 28 quarts. Although there was considerable discussion of the sugar content of juice and cereal, there was none concerning flavored milk. Likewise, there was considerable discussion of artificial flavor and color in cereal but none concerning flavored milk. The only reference to flavored milk was in the two-page discussion of the individual food packages, which noted that the proposed rule would permit the milk to be flavored or unflavored. The proposed rule which followed the preamble expressly noted that flavored or unflavored milk was permitted in the individual food packages for women and children without special dietary needs.

At the time the proposed rulemaking was published, neither CMA nor the public in general could have had any indication from the history of either the WIC Program or any other food distribution programs that flavored milk was not part of the acceptable diet for women and children without special dietary needs. The discussion in the preamble to the proposed rule was very detailed and identified specific foods which the agency was examining for excess sugar. This specificity, together with total silence concerning any suggestion of eliminating flavored milk, strongly indicated that flavored milk was not at issue. The proposed rule positively and unqualifiedly approved the continued use of flavored milk. Under the specific circumstances of this case, it cannot be said that the ultimate changes in the proposed rule were in character with the original scheme or a logical outgrowth of the notice. We can well accept that, in general, an approval of a practice in a proposed rule may properly alert interested parties that the practice may be disapproved in the final rule in the event of adverse comments. The total effect of the history of the use of flavored milk, the preamble discussion, and the proposed rule, however, could have led interested persons only to conclude that a change in flavored milk would not be considered. Although ultimately their comments may well have been futile, CMA and other interested persons at least should have had the opportunity to make them. We believe that there was insufficient notice that the deletion of flavored milk from the WIC Program would be considered if adverse comments were received, and, therefore, that affected parties did not receive a fair opportunity to contribute to the administrative rulemaking process. That process was ill-served by the misleading or inadequate notice concerning the permissibility of chocolate flavored milk in the WIC Program and "does not serve the policy underlying the notice requirement."

The judgment of the district court is therefore reversed, and the case is remanded to the administrative agency with instructions to reopen the comment period and thereby afford interested parties a fair opportunity to comment on the proposed changes in the rule.

QUESTIONS

1. What are the contending interests here?
2. Who has the better of the disputed issue on appeal?
3. After an agency considers comments pursuant to APA § 553(c), there are several possible outcomes, including (1) discontinuing the rulemaking; (2) starting over; (3) going ahead exactly as proposed; (4) going ahead with minor changes; and (5) going ahead with major changes. The last option is legally problematic. Do you see why?
4. In *Long Island Care at Home, Ltd. v. Coke*, 551 U.S. 158 (2007), the Supreme Court emphatically rejected a claim that an agency's final regulations were not a "logical outgrowth" of the notice-and-comment informal rulemaking proceeding and endorsed the "logical outgrowth" test previously adopted in the lower federal courts. Justice Breyer, writing for a unanimous Supreme Court, explained that "[t]he Administrative Procedure Act requires an agency conducting notice-and-comment rulemaking to publish in its notice of proposed rulemaking 'either the terms or substance of the proposed rule or a description of the subject and issues involved.' 5 U.S.C. § 553(b)." *Id.* at 174. The Court went on to hold that if a final rule is the "logical outgrowth" of the proposed rule, this requirement has been met. *See id.* When applying this test, a reviewing court should ascertain whether the final rule would have been "reasonably foreseeable" to the parties affected by the proceeding. *Id.* at 175. As Justice Breyer observed, "[t]he object, in short, is one of fair notice." *Id.* at 174.
5. Compare the 1981 MSAPA provisions addressing the notice of a proposed rule adoption (§ 3-103) and the permissible changes in a final regulation (§ 3-107). Do these provisions serve one or more of the three purposes for

imposing MSAPA procedural requirements on rulemaking: (a) facilitation of technically sound rules; (b) insuring that rulemaking is authorized by statute; and (c) insuring that rulemaking determinations are politically acceptable?

UNITED STATES v. NOVA SCOTIA FOOD PRODUCTS CORP.

568 F.2d 240 (2d Cir. 1977)

GURFEIN, Circuit Judge. This appeal involving a regulation of the Food and Drug Administration is not here upon a direct review of agency action. It is an appeal from a [district court] judgment . . . enjoining the appellants, after a hearing, from processing hot smoked whitefish except in accordance with time-temperature-salinity (T-T-S) regulations contained in 21 C.F.R. Part 122 (1977). . . .

Appellant Nova Scotia receives frozen or iced whitefish in interstate commerce which it processes by brining, smoking and cooking. The fish are then sold as smoked whitefish.

The regulations cited above require that hot-process smoked fish be heated by a controlled heat process that provides a monitoring system positioned in as many strategic locations in the oven as necessary to assure a continuous temperature through each fish of not less than 180°F. for a minimum of 30 minutes for fish which have been brined to contain 3.5% water phase salt or at 150°F. for a minimum of 30 minutes if the salinity was at 5% water phase. Since *each* fish must meet these requirements, it is necessary to heat an entire batch of fish to even higher temperatures so that the lowest temperature for *any* fish will meet the minimum requirements.

Government inspection of appellants' plant established without question that the minimum T-T-S requirements were not being met. There is no substantial claim that the plant was processing whitefish under "insanitary conditions" in any other material respect. Appellants, on their part, do not defend on the ground that they were in compliance, but rather that the requirements could not be met if a marketable whitefish was to be produced. They defend upon the grounds that the regulation is invalid (1) because it is beyond the authority delegated by the statute; (2) because the FDA improperly relied upon undisclosed evidence in promulgating the regulation and because it is not supported by the administrative record; and (3) because there was no adequate statement setting forth the basis of the regulation.[4] We reject the contention that the regulation is beyond the authority delegated by the statute, but we find serious inadequacies in the procedure followed in the promulgation of the regulation and hold it to be invalid as applied to the appellants herein.

The hazard which the FDA sought to minimize was the outgrowth and toxin formation of *Clostridium botulinum* Type E spores of the bacteria which sometimes inhabit fish. There had been an occurrence of several cases of botulism traced to consumption of fish from inland waters in 1960 and 1963 which stimulated considerable bacteriological research. These bacteria can be present in the soil and water of various regions. They can invade fish in their natural

---

4. Appellants contend further that the regulation should be treated as merely interpretive rather than substantive and hence as an insufficient basis for the granting of injunctive relief. They also argue that the injunction is harsh and oppressive because it would destroy the whitefish business of appellants, and is unfair as selective enforcement against appellants alone.

habitat and can be further disseminated in the course of evisceration and preparation of the fish for cooking. A failure to destroy such spores through an
adequate brining, thermal, and refrigeration process was found to be dangerous
to public health.

The Commissioner of Food and Drugs ("Commissioner"), employing informal "notice-and-comment" procedures under 21 U.S.C. § 371(a), issued a proposal for the control of *C. botulinum* bacteria Type E in fish. [21 U.S.C. § 371(a)
provides: "(a) Authority to promulgate regulations. The authority to promulgate regulations for the efficient enforcement of this Act, except as otherwise
provided in this section, is hereby vested in the Secretary."] For his statutory
authority to promulgate the regulations, the Commissioner specifically relied
only upon § 342(a)(4) of the Act which provides:

> "A food shall be deemed to be adulterated —
>   (4) if it has been prepared, packed, or held under insanitary conditions whereby
> it may have become contaminated with filth, or whereby it may have been rendered
> injurious to health;"

Similar guidelines for smoking fish had been suggested by the FDA several years
earlier, and were generally made known to people in the industry. At that stage,
however, they were merely guidelines without substantive effect as law. Responding to the Commissioner's invitation in the notice of proposed rulemaking,
members of the industry, including appellants and the intervenor-appellant,
submitted comments on the proposed regulation.

The Commissioner thereafter issued the final regulations in which he
adopted certain suggestions made in the comments, including a suggestion
by the National Fisheries Institute, Inc. ("the Institute"), the intervenor herein.
35 F.R. 17,401 (Nov. 13, 1970). The original proposal provided that the fish
would have to be cooked to a temperature of 180°F. for at least 30 minutes, if the
fish have been brined to contain 3.5% water phase salt, with no alternative. In
the final regulation, an alternative suggested by the intervenor "that the param-
eter of 150°F. for 30 minutes and 5% salt in the water phase be established as an
alternate procedure to that stated in the proposed regulation for an interim
period until specific parameters can be established" was accepted, but as a
permanent part of the regulation rather than for an interim period.

The intervenor suggested that "specific parameters" be established. This
referred to particular processing parameters for different species of fish on a
"species by species" basis. Such "species by species" determination was proposed not only by the intervenor but also by the Bureau of Commercial Fisheries
of the Department of the Interior. That Bureau objected to the general application of the T-T-S requirement proposed by the FDA on the ground that application of the regulation to all species of fish being smoked was not commercially
feasible, and that the regulation should therefore specify time-temperature-
salinity requirements, as developed by research and study, on a species-by-
species basis. The Bureau suggested that "wholesomeness considerations
could be more practically and adequately realized by reducing processing temperature and using suitable concentrations of nitrite and salt." The Commissioner took cognizance of the suggestion, but decided, nevertheless, to impose
the T-T-S requirement on *all* species of fish (except chub, which were regulated
by 21 C.F.R. 172.177 (1977) [dealing with food additives]).

He did acknowledge, however, in his "basis and purpose" statement required by the Administrative Procedure Act ("APA"), 5 U.S.C. § 553(c), that "adequate times, temperatures and salt concentrations have not been demonstrated for each individual species of fish presently smoked." 35 F.R. 17,401 (Nov. 13, 1970). The Commissioner concluded, nevertheless, that "the processing requirements of the proposed regulations are the safest now known to prevent the outgrowth and toxin formation of *C. botulinum* Type E." He determined that "the conditions of current good manufacturing practice for this industry should be established without further delay." *Id.*

The Commissioner did not answer the suggestion by the Bureau of Fisheries that nitrite and salt as additives could safely lower the high temperature otherwise required, a solution which the FDA had accepted in the case of chub. Nor did the Commissioner respond to the claim of Nova Scotia through its trade association, the Association of Smoked Fish Processors, Inc., Technical Center that "the proposed process requirements suggested by the FDA for hot processed smoked fish are neither commercially feasible nor based on sound scientific evidence obtained with the variety of smoked fish products to be included under this regulation."

Nova Scotia, in its own comment, wrote to the Commissioner that "the heating of certain types of fish to high temperatures will completely destroy the product." It suggested, as an alternative, that "specific processing procedures could be established for each species after adequate work and experimention [sic] has been done—but not before." (*Id.*). We have noted above that the response given by the Commissioner was in general terms. He did not specifically aver that the T-T-S requirements as applied to whitefish were, in fact, commercially feasible.

When, after several inspections and warnings, Nova Scotia failed to comply with the regulation, an action by the United States Attorney for injunctive relief was filed on April 7, 1976, six years later, and resulted in the judgment here on appeal. The District Court denied a stay pending appeal, and no application for a stay was made to this court. . . .

The formal rulemaking with its concomitant standard of "substantial evidence of record," *see United States v. Florida East Coast Railway Co.*, 410 U.S. 224 (1973), is limited, however, to rulemaking under specific enumerated sections of the Act. Section 342, the "adulteration" section upon which the Commissioner relied for his statutory authority is not one of these. The section dealing with temporary permits for micro-organisms, § 344, is. *See* § 371(e)(1). Thus, a *temporary* suspension because of the presence of micro-organisms in food merits a formal procedure while *permanent* regulation of micro-organisms is achievable by informal "notice-and-comment" procedure. If we read the statute § 342(a)(4) broadly in terms of the authority delegated to the agency, we must, nevertheless, view with some strictness the minimal requirements for the informal "notice and comment" procedure that follows as of course—a matter we shall discuss below. . . .

II

Appellants contend that there is an inadequate administrative record upon which to predicate judicial review, and that the failure to disclose to interested persons the factual material upon which the agency was relying vitiates the element of fairness which is essential to any kind of administrative action. Moreover, they argue that the "concise general statement of . . . basis and purpose" by the Commissioner was inadequate. 5 U.S.C. §553.

The question of what is an adequate "record"[11] in informal rulemaking has engaged the attention of commentators for several years. The extent of the administrative record required for judicial review of informal rulemaking is largely a function of the scope of judicial review. Even when the standard of review is whether the promulgation of the rule was "arbitrary, capricious, an abuse of discretion, or otherwise not in accordance with law," as specified in 5 U.S.C. §706(2)(A), judicial review must nevertheless be based on the "whole record" (*id.*). Adequate review of a determination requires an adequate record, if the review is to be meaningful. Davis, *Administrative Law in the Seventies, supra,* at 669-71. What will constitute an adequate record for meaningful review may vary with the nature of the administrative action to be reviewed. Friendly, *"Some Kind of Hearing,"* 123 U. Pa. L. Rev. 1267, 1291-92 (1975). Review must be based on the whole record even when the judgment is one of policy, except that findings of fact such as would be required in an adjudicatory proceeding or in a formal "on the record" hearing for rulemaking need not be made. *Overton Park, supra,* 401 U.S. at 416-18 (1971). Though the action was informal, without an evidentiary record, the review must be "thorough, probing, [and] in depth." *Id.,* 401 U.S. at 415. *See* Scalia & Goodman, *Procedural Aspects of the Consumer Product Safety Act,* 20 U.C.L.A.L. Rev. 899, 934-35 (1973).

This raises several questions regarding the informal rulemaking procedure followed here: (1) What record does a reviewing court look to? (2) How much of what the agency relied on should have been disclosed to interested persons? (3) To what extent must the agency respond to criticism that is material?

A

With respect to the content of the administrative "record," the Supreme Court has told us that in informal rulemaking, "the focal point for judicial review should be the administrative record already in existence, not some new record made initially in the reviewing court." *See Camp v. Pitts,* 411 U.S. 138 (1973).

No contemporaneous record was made or certified.[13] When, during the enforcement action, the basis for the regulation was sought through pretrial discovery, the record was created by searching the files of the FDA and the memories of those who participated in the process of rulemaking. This resulted in what became Exhibit D at the trial of the injunction action. Exhibit D consists of (1) Tab A containing the comments received from outside parties during the administrative "notice-and-comment" proceeding and (2) Tabs B through L

11. Even under the standard of "arbitrary, capricious, an abuse of discretion or otherwise not in accordance with law," §706(2)(A), generally used in informal rulemaking review, "the court shall review *the whole record* . . . and due account shall be taken of the rule of prejudicial error."

13. A practice developed in the early years of the APA of not making a formal contemporaneous record, but rather, when challenged, to put together a historical record of what had been available for agency consideration at the time the regulation was promulgated. "One can conclude that 'record' now means whatever the agency produces on review." Verkuil, *supra,* 60 Va. L. Rev. at 204. *And see Deutsche Lufthansa, A.G. v. CAB,* 479 F.2d 912 ([D.C. Cir.] 1973) (record unchallenged). Professor Davis in a balanced review, has stated: "When the facts are of central importance and might be challenged, parties adversely affected by them should have a chance to respond to them." Clearly, whatever "factual information the agency has considered should be a part of the record for judicial review." K. Davis, *supra,* §29.01-6, pp. 672-73.

consisting of scientific data and the like upon which the Commissioner now says he relied but which was not made known to the interested parties.

Appellants object to the exclusion of evidence in the District Court "aimed directly at showing that the scientific evidence relied upon by the FDA was inaccurate and not based upon a realistic appraisal of the true facts. Appellants attempted to introduce scientific evidence to demonstrate that in fixing the processing parameters FDA relied upon tests in which ground fish were injected with many millions of botulism [sic] spores and then tested for outgrowth at various processing levels whereas the spore levels in nature are far less and outgrowth would have been prevented by far less stringent processing parameters." (Br. p. 33). The District Court properly excluded the evidence.

In an enforcement action, we must rely exclusively on the record made before the agency to determine the validity of the regulation. The exception to the exclusivity of that record is that "there may be independent judicial fact-finding when issues that were not before the agency are raised in a proceeding to *enforce* non-adjudicatory agency action." *Overton Park, supra,* 401 U.S. at 415. (Emphasis added.)

Though this is an enforcement proceeding and the question is close, we think that the "issues" *were* fairly before the agency and hence that *de novo* evidence was properly excluded by Judge Dooling. *Camp v. Pitts, supra.* Our concern is, rather, with the manner in which the agency treated the issues tendered.

B

The key issues were (1) whether, in the light of the rather scant history of botulism in whitefish, that species should have been considered separately rather than included in a general regulation which failed to distinguish species from species; (2) whether the application of the proposed T-T-S requirements to smoked whitefish made the whitefish commercially unsaleable; and (3) whether the agency recognized that prospect, but nevertheless decided that the public health needs should prevail even if that meant commercial death for the white-fish industry. The procedural issues were whether, in the light of these key questions, the agency procedure was inadequate because (i) it failed to disclose to interested parties the scientific data and the methodology upon which it relied; and (ii) because it failed utterly to address itself to the pertinent question of commercial feasibility.

1. The History of Botulism in Whitefish

The history of botulism occurrence in whitefish, as established in the trial record, which we must assume was available to the FDA in 1970, is as follows. Between 1899 and 1964 there were only eight cases of botulism reported as attributable to hot-smoked whitefish. In all eight instances, vacuum-packed whitefish was involved. All of the eight cases occurred in 1960 and 1963. The industry has abandoned vacuum-packing, and there has not been a single case of botulism associated with commercially prepared whitefish since 1963, though 2,750,000 pounds of whitefish are processed annually. Thus, in the seven-year period from 1964 through 1970, 17.25 million pounds of whitefish have been commercially processed in the United States without a single reported case of botulism. The evidence also disclosed that defendant Nova Scotia has been in business some 56 years, and that there has never been a case of botulism illness from the whitefish processed by it.

2. The Scientific Data

Interested parties were not informed of the scientific data, or at least of a selection of such data deemed important by the agency, so that comments could be addressed to the data. Appellants argue that unless the scientific data relied upon by the agency are spread upon the public records, criticism of the methodology used or the meaning to be inferred from the data is rendered impossible.

We agree with appellants in this case, for although we recognize that an agency may resort to its own expertise outside the record in an informal rulemaking procedure, we do not believe that when the pertinent research material is readily available and the agency has no special expertise on the precise parameters involved, there is any reason to conceal the scientific data relied upon from the interested parties. As Judge Leventhal said in *Portland Cement Ass'n v. Ruckelshaus*, 486 F.2d 375, 393 (1973): "It is not consonant with the purpose of a rulemaking proceeding to promulgate rules on the basis of inadequate data, or on data that [in] critical degree, *is known only to the agency*." (Emphasis added.) This is not a case where the agency methodology was based on material supplied by the interested parties themselves. *Cf. International Harvester Co. v. Ruckelshaus*, 478 F.2d 615, 632 (1973). Here all the scientific research was collected by the agency, and none of it was disclosed to interested parties as the material upon which the proposed rule would be fashioned.[15] Nor was an articulate effort made to connect the scientific requirements to available technology that would make commercial survival possible, though the burden of proof was on the agency. This required it to "bear a burden of adducing a reasoned presentation supporting the reliability of its methodology." *International Harvester, supra*, 478 F.2d at 643.

Though a reviewing court will not match submission against counter-submission to decide whether the agency was correct in its conclusion on scientific matters (unless that conclusion is arbitrary), it will consider whether the agency has taken account of all "relevant factors and whether there has been a clear error of judgment." *Overton Park, supra*, 401 U.S. at 415-16; *Appalachian Power Co. v. Environmental Protection Agency*, 477 F.2d 495, 507 (4th Cir. 1973). In this circuit we have said that "it is 'arbitrary or capricious' for an agency not to take into account all relevant factors in making its determination." *Hanly v. Mitchell*, 460 F.2d 640, 648 (2d Cir. 1972) (an enforcement action under NEPA).

If the failure to notify interested persons of the scientific research upon which the agency was relying actually prevented the presentation of relevant comment, the agency may be held not to have considered all "the relevant factors." We can think of no sound reasons for secrecy or reluctance to expose to public view (with an exception for trade secrets or national security) the ingredients of the deliberative process. *Cf. Mobil Oil Corp. v. FPC*, 483 F.2d 1238, 1259-61 (1973). Indeed, the FDA's own regulations now specifically require that every notice of proposed rulemaking contain "references to all data and information on which the Commissioner relies for the proposal (copies or a full list of which shall be a part of the administrative file on the matter . . .)." 21 C.F.R. § 10.40 (b)(1)

---

15. We recognize the problem posed by Judge Leventhal in *International Harvester, supra*, that a proceeding might never end if such submission required a reply *ad infinitum, ibid.* Here the exposure of the scientific research relied on simply would have required a single round of comment addressed thereto.

(1977). And this is, undoubtedly, the trend. *See*, e.g., *National Nutritional Foods v. Weinberger*, 512 F.2d 688 (2d Cir. 1975).

We think that the scientific data should have been disclosed to focus on the proper interpretation of "insanitary conditions." When the basis for a proposed rule is a scientific decision, the scientific material which is believed to support the rule should be exposed to the view of interested parties for their comment. One cannot ask for comment on a scientific paper without allowing the participants to read the paper. Scientific research is sometimes rejected for diverse inadequacies of methodology; and statistical results are sometimes rebutted because of a lack of adequate gathering technique or of supportable extrapolation. Such is the stuff of scientific debate. To suppress meaningful comment by failure to disclose the basic data relied upon is akin to rejecting comment altogether. For unless there is common ground, the comments are unlikely to be of a quality that might impress a careful agency. The inadequacy of comment in turn leads in the direction of arbitrary decision-making. We do not speak of findings of fact, for such are not technically required in the informal rulemaking procedures. We speak rather of what the agency should make known so as to elicit comments that probe the fundamentals. Informal rulemaking does not lend itself to a rigid pattern. Especially, in the circumstance of our broad reading of statutory authority in support of the agency, we conclude that the failure to disclose to interested persons the scientific data upon which the FDA relied was procedurally erroneous. Moreover, the burden was upon the agency to articulate rationally why the rule should apply to a large and diverse class, with the same T-T-S parameters made applicable to *all* species. *Cf. Associated Industries of N.Y.S., Inc. v. U.S. Dept. of Labor*, 487 F.2d 342, 352-53 (2d Cir. 1973). And *cf. Industrial Union Dept. AFL-CIO v. Hodgson*, 499 F.2d 467 (1974).

C

Appellants additionally attack the "concise general statement" required by APA, 5 U.S.C. § 553, as inadequate. We think that, in the circumstances, it was less than adequate. It is not in keeping with the rational process to leave vital questions, raised by comments which are of cogent materiality, completely unanswered. The agencies certainly have a good deal of discretion in expressing the basis of a rule, but the agencies do not have quite the prerogative of obscurantism reserved to legislatures. "Congress did not purport to transfer its legislative power to the unbounded discretion of the regulatory body." *F.C.C. v. RCA Communications, Inc.*, 346 U.S. 86, 90 (1953) (Frankfurter, J.). As was said in *Environmental Defense Fund, Inc. v. EPA*, 465 F.2d 528, 540-51 (1972): "We cannot discharge our role adequately unless we hold EPA to a high standard of articulation. *Kennecott Copper Corp. v. EPA*, . . . 462 F.2d 846 (1972)."

The test of adequacy of the "concise general statement" was expressed by Judge McGowan in the following terms:

> We do not expect the agency to discuss every item of fact or opinion included in the submissions made to it in informal rulemaking. We do expect that, if the judicial review which Congress has thought it important to provide is to be meaningful, the "concise general statement of . . . basis and purpose" mandated by Section 4 will enable us to see what major issues of policy were ventilated by the informal proceedings and why the agency reacted to them as it did.

Automotive Parts & Accessories Ass'n v. Boyd, 407 F.2d 330, 338 (D.C. Cir. 1968).

And Judge Friendly has noted that "in a case where a proposed standard under OSHA [Occupational Safety and Health Act] has been opposed on grounds as substantial as those presented here, the Department has the burden of offering *some* reasoned explanation." *Associated Industries of New York State, Inc. v. U.S. Department of Labor, supra,* 487 F.2d at 352 (emphasis in original).

The Secretary was squarely faced with the question whether it was necessary to formulate a rule with specific parameters that applied to all species of fish, and particularly whether lower temperatures with the addition of nitrite and salt would not be sufficient. Though this alternative was suggested by an agency of the federal government, its suggestion, though acknowledged, was never answered.

Moreover, the comment that to apply the proposed T-T-S requirements to whitefish would destroy the commercial product was neither discussed nor answered. We think that to sanction silence in the face of such vital questions would be to make the statutory requirement of a "concise general statement" less than an adequate safeguard against arbitrary decision-making.

We cannot improve on the statement of the District of Columbia Circuit in *Industrial Union Dep't, AFL-CIO v. Hodgson,* 499 F.2d 467, 475 (D.C. Cir. 1974).[17]

> What we are entitled to at all events is a careful identification by the Secretary, when his proposed standards are challenged, of the reasons why he chooses to follow one course rather than another. Where that choice purports to be based on the existence of certain determinable facts, the Secretary must, in form as well as in substance, find those facts from evidence in the record. By the same token, when the Secretary is obliged to make policy judgments where no factual certainties exist or where facts alone do not provide the answer, he should so state and go on to identify the considerations he found to be persuasive.

One may recognize that even commercial unfeasibility cannot stand in the way of an overwhelming public interest. Yet the administrative process should disclose, at least, whether the proposed regulation is considered to be commercially feasible, or whether other considerations prevail even if commercial infeasibility is acknowledged. This kind of forthright disclosure and basic statement was lacking in the formulation of the T-T-S standard made applicable to whitefish. It is easy enough for an administrator to ban everything. In the regulation of food processing, the worldwide need for food also must be taken into account in formulating measures taken for the protection of health. In the light of the history of smoked whitefish to which we have referred, we find no articulate balancing here sufficient to make the procedure followed less than arbitrary.

After seven years of relative inaction, the FDA has apparently not reviewed the T-T-S regulations in the light of present scientific knowledge and experience. In the absence of a new statutory directive by Congress regarding control of microorganisms, which we hope will be worthy of its consideration, we think that the T-T-S standards should be reviewed again by the FDA.

We cannot, on this appeal, remand to the agency to allow further comments by interested parties, addressed to the scientific data now disclosed at the trial below. We hold in this enforcement proceeding, therefore, that the regulation,

---

17. There informal agency procedure was followed, though with a standard of review traditionally conceived of as suited to formal adjudication or rulemaking.

as it affects non-vacuum-packed hot-smoked whitefish, was promulgated in an arbitrary manner and is invalid.

When the District Court held the regulation to be valid, it properly exercised its discretion to grant the injunction. In view of our conclusion to the contrary, we must reverse the grant of the injunction and direct that the complaint be dismissed.

QUESTIONS

1.   What is the procedural context for the challenge to the regulation? Notice the alternative grounds asserted for challenging the regulation.
2.   Is this a substantive challenge to the regulation, or a procedural one, or both? *See* federal APA §706(2). Does one affect the other here? Would the court make the same procedural decision if it were not so sure of the substantive answer? Why does the court not rely totally on its power to review the agency's decision substantively?
3.   What are the procedural bases for reversal? Are they technically sound?
4.   Compare 1981 MSAPA §3-110 (concise explanatory statement requirement). Does §3-110(b) give greater significance to the statement than is given by the federal APA?
5.   The APA imposes a non-waivable duty on an agency to publish a final rule *before* the rule becomes operative. *See* 5 U.S.C. §552(a)(1). As Professor Jack Beerman explains, "[a]gencies must publish rules that affect the public in the Federal Register" and "a rule not properly published may not be used against a person lacking actual notice of the rule." Jack M. Beermann, *Privatization and Public Accountability*, 28 Fordham Urb. L.J. 1507, 1553 n.151 (2001); *Morton v. Ruiz*, 415 U.S. 199, 232-36 (1974); *see also Kennecott Utah Copper Corp. v. U.S. Dep't of Interior*, 88 F.3d 1191, 1203 (D.C. Cir. 1996) ("As amended in 1974, §552(a)(1) protects a person from being 'adversely affected by' a regulation required to be published in the Federal Register unless an agency either published the regulation or the person had actual and timely notice of it. 5 U.S.C. §552(a)(1); *see also*[*Morton*]. This gives agencies a powerful incentive to publish any rules that they expect to enforce. See *Morton*, 415 U.S. at 233 n.27"). This requirement does not apply, however, when a statute or treaty itself directly establishes the underlying rule. *See*, e.g., *Malkan FM. Assoc. v. FCC*, 935 F.2d 1313, 1318 (D.C. Cir. 1991) (rejecting the claim that an FCC regulation was invalid, despite the agency's failure to publish it in the Federal Register, "because the [rule] is set by international agreement, binding upon the Commission, and not by 'rule' of the FCC"); *United States v. Hicks*, 947 F.2d 1356, 1360 (9th Cir. 1991) (rejecting the defendant's "meritless" claim that IRS Form 1040 is invalid, and therefore unenforceable against him, because the agency failed to publish it in the Federal Register, and explaining that "[i]t is the tax code itself, without reference to regulations, that imposes the duty to file a tax return"). Thus, an administrative regulation is invalid and unenforceable because of nonpublication *only if* the "unpublished rules [impose] substantive obligations beyond those created by the statute itself." *United States v. Bowers*, 920 F.2d 220, 222 n.2 (4th Cir. 1990).

NOTE ON THE "CONCISE GENERAL STATEMENT" REQUIREMENT

Section 553(c) of the APA requires an administrative agency to provide a "concise general statement" of the basis and purpose of new rules. Section 555(e) of the APA also creates an obligation to provide reasons in support of an agency action (not limited necessarily to a rule making):

> Prompt notice shall be given of the denial in whole or in part of written application, petition, or other request of an interested person made in connection with any agency proceeding. Except in affirming a prior denial or when the denial is self-explanatory, the notice shall be accompanied by a brief statement of the grounds for the denial.

Section 555(e) appears in the generic, catch-all "Ancillary Matters" section of the APA. Accordingly, its provisions would apply to any and all agency actions denying, in whole or in part, a written request by an "interested person."

The requirement to provide a "concise general statement," appears to demand more than the generic duty to provide "a brief statement" set forth in § 555(e). An agency always labors under a duty of explanation when it takes adverse action (section 555(e)). The obvious question for the student of the APA then becomes: "To what degree does section 553(c) impose a duty of explanation that goes beyond the 'brief statement' mandated by section 555(e)?" Reviewing courts have wrestled with this question since Congress enacted the APA in 1946.

On the one hand, absent any duty of explanation, it would be difficult for a reviewing court to ascertain whether the agency has complied with the other procedural requirements of section 553(c). For example, an agency must "consider[] the relevant matter presented" incident to the notice and comment proceedings. If an agency adopted rules without any explanation of precisely why it chose to do so, and without any effort to relate the final rules to the comments and reply comments in the public record, it would be difficult, if not impossible, for a reviewing court to ensure that the agency had, in fact, considered the filings. The concise general statement requirement also facilitates judicial enforcement of the "arbitrary and capricious" standard of review in section 706(2)(A). In sum, a duty to explain, at least to some degree, final agency rules directly facilitates judicial enforcement of both procedural and substantive statutory requirements.

Observing that the concise general statement requirement facilitates judicial review does not answer the larger question of how "concise" a "concise general statement" may be and still satisfy the requirements of section 553(c). In *Automotive Parts and Accessories Ass'n v. Boyd*, 407 F.2d 330 (D.C. Cir. 1968), Judge Carl McGowan explained what the concise general statement requires of an administrative agency:

> it is appropriate for us to remind the Administrator of the ever present possibility of judicial review, and to caution against an overly literal reading of the statutory terms "concise" and "general." These adjectives must be accommodated to the realities of judicial scrutiny, which do not contemplate that the court itself will, by a laborious examination of the record, formulate in the first instance the significant

issues faced by the agency and articulate the rationale of their resolution. We do not expect the agency to discuss every item of fact or opinion included in the submissions made to it in informal rule making. We do expect that, if the judicial review which Congress has thought it important to provide is to be meaningful, the "concise general statement of . . . basis and purpose" mandated by [APA § 553] will enable us to see what major issues of policy were ventilated by the informal proceedings and why the agency reacted to them as it did.

Because the "concise general statement" envisaged by the Congress is something different from the detailed "findings and conclusions" on all "material issues of fact, law or discretion" referred to in [APA § 557], there will inevitably be differences of emphasis and approach in the application of the judicial review standards prescribed in [APA § 706]. An adversary lawsuit, which most closely resembles the formal hearing of [APA §§ 556 & 557], throws up issues of law and fact in a form quite unlike those which take shape in informal rule making, which has many analogies to a legislative committee hearing. When the issue on appeal is whether a rule made in informal proceedings meets the criteria of [APA § 706], the court must necessarily go about the application of that standard in a manner unlike its review of findings of fact and conclusions of law compiled in a formal proceeding.

This exercise need be no less searching and strict in its weighing of whether the agency has performed in accordance with the Congressional purposes, but, because it is addressed to different materials, it inevitably varies from the adjudicatory model. The paramount objective is to see whether the agency, given an essentially legislative task to perform, has carried it out in a manner calculated to negate the dangers of arbitrariness and irrationality in the formulation of rules for general application in the future. . . .

Judge Robert Bork has described the concise general statement requirement as follows:

Under the Administrative Procedure Act, when an agency initiates a rulemaking that the governing statute does not require to be undertaken "on the record," the agency is nonetheless bound to comply with the requirements for "notice and comment" rulemaking set out in 5 U.S.C. § 553. One requirement is that after the agency considers the comments presented by the participating parties, it "shall incorporate in the rules adopted a concise general statement of their basis and purpose." 5 U.S.C. § 553(c). This statement need not be an exhaustive, detailed account of every aspect of the rulemaking proceedings; it is not meant to be the more elaborate document, complete with findings of fact and conclusions of law, that is required in an on-the-record rulemaking. *See id.* § 557(c). On the other hand, this court has cautioned against "an overly literal reading of the statutory terms 'concise' and 'general' [which] must be accommodated to the realities of judicial scrutiny." At the least, such a statement should indicate the major issues of policy that were raised in the proceedings and explain why the agency decided to respond to these issues as it did, particularly in light of the statutory objectives that the rule must serve.

Independent U.S. Tankers Owners Committee v. Dole, 809 F.2d 847, 852 (D.C. Cir. 1987). In *Tankers Owners Committee,* Judge Bork found that the Department of Transportation had failed to provide an adequate explanation for the rules that the agency had adopted regarding the use of certain subsidized tankers for domestic, as opposed to international, routes. The agency appeared to substitute its own objectives, including putting the tankers to an economically efficient use, for those that Congress established (which related to having U.S. flagged vessels plying foreign routes). In effect, Judge Bork used a procedural argument to engage a substantive deficiency; although he couched his decision in the language of a procedural failure (the agency's failure to proffer an adequate explanation), his real complaint was the inconsistency of the agency's objectives with the statutory scheme it purported to implement.

Reviewing courts can couch concerns with the substance of agency action in procedural language, in effect inviting the agency to try again. Had Judge Bork simply applied the arbitrary and capricious standard of review to the Department of Transportation regulations, they would undoubtedly have failed to pass muster. By recharacterizing the court's objection as a failure to observe an APA requirement, Judge Bork presented the agency with an opportunity to justify its rules in terms that were more consistent with the statutory objectives that Congress had established.

A clever lawyer representing a client in a challenge to an agency rule should always consider the desirability of couching a substantive objection in process terms. An agency decision might be arbitrary and capricious on the merits, but such a decision would probably also lack an adequate explanation. If the case is close, a reviewing court might be more willing to credit the procedural argument (failure to explain the decision adequately) than the substantive argument (the final rules are irrational).

QUESTIONS

1. Does Judge McGowan require too much of an agency in the guise of requiring a concise general statement? Judge Bork?
2. Compare the effect on agency rulemaking of the judicial elaboration of the requirements of §553 with 1981 MSAPA §3-112, which requires maintenance of "an official rule-making record." Has the federal judiciary effectively subjected federal agencies to the same requirement? Note that the MSAPA provides that the official rulemaking record "need not constitute the exclusive basis for agency action on that rule or for judicial review thereof." §3-112(c).
3. Remember that, in a notice and comment rule making proceeding, a federal agency is not bound to anchor all of its decisions on the paper record developed through the notice and comment process. Instead, an agency should be free to rely upon internal expertise to justify a rule (subject, of course, to the section 553 obligation to permit fair comment by members of the public). The Attorney General's Manual on the Administrative Procedure Act (1947) (at 31-32) states that, since APA §553 "does not require the formulation of rules upon the exclusive basis of any 'record' made in informal rule making proceedings, . . . an agency [in informal rulemaking] is free to formulate rules upon the basis of materials in its files and the knowledge and experience of the agency, in addition to the materials adduced in public rule making proceedings." Compare 1981 MSAPA §3-106(d) (allowing agency to rely on its own expertise when adopting a rule).

THEORY APPLIED PROBLEM

The Occupational Health and Safety Administration (OSHA) writes and enforces "air contaminant standards," regulations designed to protect workers from exposure to substances and conditions in the workplace that represent a significant risk of material health impairment. *See* 29 U.S.C. §§ 652(8), 655(b)(5) (2006). OSHA's enabling act permits the agency to use notice and comment rulemaking to establish workplace health and safety standards; however, on judicial review, the agency's factual findings are subject to "substantial evidence" review (rather than arbitrary and capricious review). Perchloroethylene ("Perc") is an industrial solvent widely used in dry cleaning operations and for industrial degreasing operations. Reliable studies show that at concentrations of 50 parts per million (ppm) in the air, perc can cause cancer and OSHA's current workplace Air Contaminants Standard, 29 C.F.R. § 1910.1000 *et seq.* (2007), establishes a permissible exposure limit (PEL) of 50 ppm over an eight-hour exposure period, with a peak concentration exposure limit of 100 ppm over 15 minutes or less (a "short term exposure limit," or "STEL"). New studies suggest that this 50/100 ppm PEL/STEL might leave workers exposed to a significant risk of material health impairment (namely leukemia and other cancers). OSHA has come to question the reliability of the existing standard and issues a Notice of Proposed Rulemaking (NPRM) seeking comments on a revised 25/50 ppm PEL/STEL standard. OSHA gives interested parties 54 days after the NPRM appears in the Federal Register to file comments and another 30 days to file reply comments. OSHA is inundated with comments: over 1,238 persons, organizations, and entities file comments and reply comments in the rulemaking docket. Among these comments are 26 studies considering the dose/response effects of perc: 19 of the studies, mostly submitted by industry, show no adverse health effects in mice exposed to 25/50 ppm concentrations of perc. On the other hand, however, 5 studies, mostly submitted by labor unions, indicate that mice exposed to 25/50 ppm concentrations of perc have a significantly elevated risk of contracting leukemia or other blood disorders. The remaining study, conducted by researchers at Johns Hopkins Medical School, found the data inconclusive regarding the 25/50 ppm standard.

Despairing of analyzing all of the submissions in a timely fashion, OSHA contracts with Healthy Workplaces, Inc. (HWI), a consulting firm, to analyze the submissions and to review and summarize all the scientific studies contained in the comments and reply comments. (The OSH Act expressly authorizes OSHA to employ expert consultants. *See* 29 U.S.C. § 656(c) (2006).) HWI concludes that both the industry and labor union sponsored studies are, for the most part, unreliable because of methodological flaws. HWI endorses the Johns Hopkins Medical School submission, but this submission did not reach a definitive conclusion regarding the risk of worker exposure to perc at the 25/50 levels. Based on its review of the record, HWI suggests that OSHA should adopt a 35/65 ppm standard for perc, rather than retaining the existing 50/100 ppm standard or adopting the proposed 25/50 ppm standard.

OSHA's Administrator reviews the HWI summary of the docket as well as a summary of the docket materials prepared by her Special Assistant. The Administrator also "dips" into the record and reviews some of the comments and reply comments directly. Based on her review of the summaries and the record, the

Administrator decides to adopt a new PEL/STEL of 35/65 ppm for perc. Using the record established in the rulemaking, staff documents prepared internally, and the HWI report, she and OSHA staff prepare a report and order demonstrating that the perc exposures at the revised 35/65 ppm level constitute a significant risk of material health impairment, that the new standard is both technologically and economically feasible, and that the new standards should take effect 180 days after the report and order containing the new Air Contaminant Standard for perc appears in the Federal Register.

You work as an assistant counsel to the International Fabricare Institute (IFI). The IFI's internal analysis estimates that compliance with the new perc standards will be bankruptingly expensive for many smaller dry cleaning businesses. Accordingly, the IFI is strongly inclined to seek judicial review of the revised perc standards. The General Counsel, your boss, asks you to advise her as to how the IFI might bring a successful challenge to the new perc regulations. In particular, she wishes to know if OSHA violated any substantive or procedural requirements in the rulemaking. Ideally, she would like to obtain a judicial decision not merely remanding the revised regulations back to OSHA, but rather an order vacating the entire proceeding and forcing the agency to start over from scratch. How do you advise your boss?

NOTE ON BIAS IN RULEMAKING

Recall that in the context of agency adjudications, due process provides some protection against bias on the part of agency decision makers. See *supra* p. 153. Must an agency be unbiased when it engages in rulemaking? The Court's decision in *Bi-Metallic Investment Co.* would suggest that due process does not provide such protection. In *Association of National Advertisers, Inc. v. Federal Trade Commission*, 627 F.2d 1151 (D.C. Cir. 1979), the court reversed a district court decision that the Chair of the FTC was barred from participating in a rulemaking because he had prejudged and given the appearance of having prejudged the merits of the rulemaking. The court held, *id.* at 1171 (footnote omitted), that a less strict standard applied to determine whether a Commission member had to be disqualified for bias:

> a Commissioner should be disqualified only when there has been a clear and convincing showing that the agency member has an unalterably closed mind on matters critical to the disposition of the proceeding. The "clear and convincing" test is necessary to rebut the presumption of administrative regularity. *See,* e.g., *Withrow v. Larkin,* 421 U.S. 35, 55 (1975); *Hercules, Inc. v. EPA,* 598 F.2d 91, 123 (D.C. Cir. 1978). The "unalterably closed mind" test is necessary to permit rulemakers to carry out their proper policy-based functions while disqualifying those unable to consider meaningfully a section 18 [rulemaking] hearing.

C. EXCEPTIONS TO INFORMAL RULEMAKING REQUIREMENTS

During the 1970s and 1980s, courts interpreted §553 to subject informal rulemaking to significant procedural requirements, many of which agencies viewed as burdensome. Professor Thomas McGarity has argued that because agencies viewed the requirements for informal rulemaking as burdensome, they developed ways to avoid the need to comply with the requirements of § 553. Agencies, according to McGarity, "engage in 'nonrule rulemaking' through relatively less formal devices such as policy statements, interpretive rules, manuals, and other informal devices." Thomas O. McGarity, *Some Thoughts on "Deossifying" the Rulemaking Process*, 41 Duke L.J. 1385, 1386, 1393, & 1443 (1992). The exceptions from the requirements of § 553 have accordingly become increasingly important and have been the subject of extensive litigation and scholarship. For some recent examples of the latter, *see* Peter L. Strauss, *Publication Rules in the Rulemaking Spectrum: Assuring Proper Respect for an Essential Element*, 53 Admin. L. Rev. 803 (2001); Richard J. Pierce, Jr., *Distinguishing Legislative Rules from Interpretative Rules*, 52 Admin. L. Rev. 547 (2000); Robert A. Anthony, *Interpretive Rules, Policy Statements, Guidances, Manuals, and the Like — Should Federal Agencies Use Them to Bind the Public?*, 41 Duke L.J. 1311 (1992).

MADA-LUNA v. FITZPATRICK

813 F.2d 1006 (9th Cir. 1987)

Fletcher, Circuit Judge: Eugene Fitzpatrick, an acting district director of the Immigration and Naturalization Service (INS), appeals from the district court's order directing him to reconsider Miguel Mada-Luna's application for deferred action status under INS Operating Instruction 103.1(a)(1)(ii). The district court ruled that Fitzpatrick improperly reviewed Mada's application under the 1981 version of the Operating Instruction. The court held the 1981 instruction invalid because the INS promulgated it without the notice-and-comment procedures required by the Administrative Procedure Act (APA), 5 U.S.C. § 553(b)-(d) (1982), and without publishing it in the Federal Register, as required by the Freedom of Information Act (FOIA), 5 U.S.C. § 552(a)(1)(D)-(E) (1982). The district court ruled that, as a result, the original, 1978 version of the Operating Instruction was never validly superseded, and that Fitzpatrick was required to review Mada's application under its more "generous" standard.[2] The court therefore granted Mada's habeas petition and

---

2. [T]he focus of the 1978 version of the Operating Instruction is thus significantly different from that of the 1981 version. The 1981 version is concerned first and foremost with the effect of deporting or excluding a particular alien upon the administration, management, and public image of the INS: it requires the district director to evaluate such factors as the "likelihood of ultimately removing the alien," the possibility that deportation proceedings will become "protracted" or that the law will be "distort[ed]," the likelihood of "adverse publicity" that will require a time-consuming response by the INS, and the "enforcement priority" given to the particular alien in question. In contrast, the 1978 version focuses upon the effect of deportation or exclusion upon the individual alien himself: it requires the district director to consider such issues as the potential "unconscionab[ility]" or the "undue hardship" that may result to the alien, his age and length of stay in the United States, his physical and mental condition and family situation, and his other recent conduct.

Because of these differences in the two versions of the Operating Instruction, our court has held that they differ in the extent to which they establish judicially enforceable rights. We held in *Nicholas v. INS*, 590 F.2d 802 (9th Cir. 1979), that "rather than merely providing internal procedural guidelines to the INS," the 1978 version of the Operating Instruction established a judicially enforceable right for deportable and excludable aliens applying for deferred action status to have their applications reviewed on an equal basis with those of similarly-situated applicants, and held that aliens' claims based on the 1978 Operating Instruction must be reviewed by courts under

remanded his application to the INS. Fitzpatrick appeals. We have jurisdiction under 28 U.S.C. § 1291 (1982).

In light of our recent decision in *Romeiro De Silva v. Smith*, 773 F.2d 1021 (9th Cir. 1985), issued after the district court's decision, we must reverse and remand. We reject Mada's claim that the INS's promulgation of the 1981 version of the Operating Instruction violated the notice-and-comment requirements of the APA, because the amended Operating Instruction qualifies under the APA's exception for "general statements of policy." We also reject Mada's claim that the application of the 1981 Instruction in his case violated the FOIA's publication requirements. Therefore, we conclude that the district court had no authority to overturn Fitzpatrick's decision.

FACTUAL BACKGROUND

Mada is a Mexican alien, convicted in 1981 for a narcotics violation. He was incarcerated for one year and then paroled. When he was released, the INS initiated deportation proceedings against him based upon his conviction, and he was ordered deported in 1983. Mada then applied to Fitzpatrick, as the acting district director, for deferred action status under the 1978 version of Operating Instruction 103.1(a)(1)(ii). Fitzpatrick denied the application in November, 1983, and in December, 1983, denied a supplemental application.

To support his application for deferred action, Mada stated that he had resided in the United States for seventeen years, and had no criminal record other than his single narcotics conviction. He submitted letters from prison officials and his parole officer characterizing him as a model prisoner and an outstanding parolee. Moreover, Mada stated that between the time of his narcotics arrest and trial, he had worked as an undercover operative for the United States Drug Enforcement Agency (DEA), and furnished evidence that this involvement has subjected him and his family to significant danger. While working for the DEA in Sonora, Mexico, Mada and his wife allegedly were kidnapped by drug traffickers, held at gunpoint, and released only when they promised to pay a ransom of about $20,000. According to Mada, he has not paid the ransom, and has, as a result, received a series of telephone calls from Mexico threatening his life if he returns there, several of which he transcribed and submitted to the INS. Finally, Mada indicated in his applications that both his wife and daughter are United States citizens.

Fitzpatrick rejected both of Mada's applications for deferred action status, concluding that besides his narcotics conviction, Mada had been "a habitual violator of the Immigration laws" and had lied to the INS under oath on at least two occasions. Furthermore, Fitzpatrick concluded, based on the evidence presented to him, that the death threats against Mada did not result directly from

---

the abuse-of-discretion standard. *Romeiro De Silva v. Smith*, 773 F.2d 1021, 1024-25 (9th Cir. 1985); *Nicholas*, 590 F.2d at 807-08. In contrast, we recently held that based upon the new language in the 1981 Operating Instruction, "'it is no longer possible to conclude that [the Instruction] is intended to confer any benefit upon aliens, rather than [to operate] merely for the INS's own convenience,'" and concluded that courts have no jurisdiction to review denials of applications for deferred action status under the 1981 Instruction. *Romeiro*, 773 F.2d at 1024 (quoting *Wan Chung Wen v. Ferro*, 543 F. Supp. 1016, 1018 (W.D.N.Y. 1982)). Thus, the resolution of which version of the Operating Instruction is applicable in Mada's case will determine whether or not he has a right to judicial review and may affect his entitlement to deferred action status.

his work for DEA, but instead were made by his former criminal associates who are now seeking repayment for the narcotics seized from Mada when he was arrested in 1981. For all these reasons, Fitzpatrick chose not to defer action on Mada's deportation.

Mada initiated the present action for habeas relief in district court. The court granted his petition, concluding that application of the 1981 Operating Instruction in Mada's case violated the APA and FOIA. The court remanded Mada's case to the INS for consideration of his deferred action application pursuant to the original, 1978 Operating Instruction.

Analysis

Mada's challenge to Fitzpatrick's denial of his application for deferred action status focuses exclusively upon the *validity* of the 1981 Operating Instruction and its *applicability to his petition*. Mada contends that the 1981 Operating Instruction was never validly promulgated because of the INS's failure to comply with the APA's notice-and-comment requirements and the FOIA's publication requirements, and that it therefore never validly superseded the original, 1978 Operating Instruction. He maintains that as a result, he is entitled to have his petition reviewed under the 1978 Operating Instruction, and that based upon our decision in *Nicholas v. INS,* 590 F.2d 802 (9th Cir. 1979), he is entitled to judicial review of that determination. See footnote 2, *supra.*

Mada does not challenge the manner in which Fitzpatrick applied the 1981 Operating Instruction in his case or the decision that Fitzpatrick reached based upon it. Mada conceded at the district court that he would have "no claim of entitlement nor substantive rights" if the 1981 Operating Instruction applied to his petition. Moreover, any challenge to the merits of Fitzpatrick's determination under the 1981 Operating Instruction would be foreclosed by our decision in *Romeiro,* where we held that courts have no authority to review denials of deferred action status petitions under the 1981 version of the Instruction. See *Romeiro,* 773 F.2d at 1024-25; *see also* 5 U.S.C. § 701(a)(2) (limiting judicial review of agency actions where they have been "committed to agency discretion by law" — presumably, the provision applied in *Romeiro*).

We conclude that Mada's challenges based on the APA and the FOIA to the application of the 1981 Operating Instruction in his case are without merit. We conclude that Fitzpatrick properly applied the amended Operating Instruction in reviewing Mada's petition, and that the district court had no authority to remand Mada's petition to the INS for review under the 1978 Operating Instruction.

A. Standard of Review

We review de novo the district court's decision on Mada's petition for writ of habeas corpus. We also review de novo the district court's determinations on issues of statutory interpretation, including the scope of the notice-and-comment and publication requirements imposed by the APA and the FOIA.

B. Mada's Challenge Under the APA

Mada challenges the validity of the 1981 Operating Instruction based on the INS's failure, when it promulgated the amended Instruction, to follow the notice-and-comment procedures prescribed in APA section 553. The INS's replacement of the original, 1978 version of the Operating Instruction with the 1981 version involves two separate procedural aspects: (1) the repeal of the 1978 Instruction; and (2) the promulgation of the 1981 Instruction. Each of these two agency "actions" constitutes "rulemaking" under the APA, and therefore each action independently triggers section 553's notice-and-comment requirements unless it qualified for one of the exceptions contained in that provision. *See* 5 U.S.C. §§ 551(5) (defining "rule making" under the APA as "agency process for formulating, amending, or *repealing* a rule") (emphasis added), 553(b)-(d). . . .

Fitzpatrick maintains that both the 1978 and the 1981 Operating Instructions qualify for the "general statements of policy" exception contained in section 553. We agree. 5 U.S.C. §§ 553(b)(A), 553(d)(2); *Romeiro*, 773 F.2d at 1025. Therefore, we conclude that the INS was not required under section 553 to conduct notice-and-comment proceedings either to repeal the 1978 Operating Instruction or to promulgate the 1981 Operating Instruction. *Romeiro*, 773 F.2d at 1025.

1. THE GENERAL STATEMENT OF POLICY EXCEPTION

The APA does not define the term "general statements of policy" as it is used in section 553. However, it is defined in the *Attorney General's Manual on the Administrative Procedure Act,* which was issued in 1947, just after the APA's enactment, as "statements issued by an agency *to advise the public prospectively of the manner in which the agency proposes to exercise a discretionary power.*" When officials or agencies have been delegated discretionary authority over a given area, such as the Attorney General and the INS in the field of immigration, such policy statement serves a dual purpose. Besides informing the public concerning the agency's future plans and priorities for exercising its discretionary power, they serve to "educate" and provide direction to the agency's personnel in the field, who are required to implement its policies and exercise its discretionary power in specific cases. *See* H. Friendly, *The Federal Administrative Agencies* 145-46 (1962) ("one of the values of the policy statement [is] the education of agency members in the agency's work"), *quoted in Noel v. Chapman,* 508 F.2d 1023, 1030 (2d Cir.), *cert. denied,* 423 U.S. 824 (1975); Bonfield, *Some Tentative Thoughts on Public Participation in the Making of Interpretative Rules and General Statements of Policy Under the APA,* 23 Admin. L. Rev. 101, 115 (1970-71) ("It may be that 'general statements of policy' are rules directed primarily at the staff of an agency describing how it will conduct agency discretionary functions, while other rules are directed primarily at the public in an effort to impose obligations on them"), *quoted in Noel,* 508 F.2d at 1030.

When a federal agency issues a directive concerning the future exercise of its discretionary power, for purposes of APA section 553, its directive will constitute either a substantive rule, for which notice-and-comment procedures are required, or a general statement of policy, for which they are not. *See Pacific Gas,* 506 F.2d at 38; 5 U.S.C. § 553 (b)-(d). The critical factor to determine whether a directive announcing a new policy constitutes a rule or a general statement of policy is "the extent to which the challenged [directive] leaves the agency, or its implementing official, free to exercise discretion to follow, or not to follow, the [announced] policy in an individual case." *Jean [v. Nelson],* 711 F.2d at 1481 . . . .

To the extent that the directive merely provides *guidance* to agency officials in exercising their discretionary power while preserving their flexibility and their opportunity to make "individualized determination[s]," it constitutes a general statement of policy. *Guardian Federal,* 589 F.2d at 666-67; *Noel,* 508 F.2d at 1030; see *Ryder,* 716 F.2d at 1377; *Jean,* 711 F.2d at 1481. In such cases, Congress has determined that notice-and-comment rulemaking would be of limited utility, *see* 5 U.S.C. §§ 553(b)(A), 553(d)(2), and parties can challenge the policy determinations made by the agency only if and when the directive has been applied specifically to them. See *Jean,* 711 F.2d at 1481-82 & n.23; *Pacific Gas,* 506 F.2d at 38. In contrast, to the extent that the directive "narrowly limits administrative discretion" or establishes a "*binding norm*" that "so fills out the statutory scheme that upon application one need only determine whether a given case is within the rule's criterion," it effectively replaces agency discretion with a new "binding rule of substantive law." *Ryder,* 716 F.2d at 1377 (emphasis added); *Jean,* 711 F.2d at 1481; *Guardian Federal,* 589 F.2d at 666-67. In these cases, notice-and-comment rulemaking proceedings are required, as they would be for any other substantive rule, *see* 5 U.S.C. § 553(b), (d), and they will represent the only opportunity for parties to challenge the policy determinations upon which the new rule is based. See *Pacific Gas,* 506 F.2d at 38.[9]

Thus, for the 1978 and 1981 Operating Instructions to qualify under section 553's "general statement of policy" exception, as Fitzpatrick contends, they must satisfy two requirements. First, they must operate only prospectively. Second, they must not establish a "binding norm" or be "finally determinative of the issues or rights to which [they are] addressed," but must instead leave INS officials "free to consider the individual facts in the various cases that arise." We conclude that the 1978 and 1981 Operating Instructions satisfy both these requirements.

We note that two considerations that Mada relies upon to establish that the 1978 and 1981 Operating Instructions do not constitute general statements of policy are not determinative of the issue. [The court concluded first that its earlier decision in *Nicholas,* holding determinations made pursuant to the

---

9. In *Pacific Gas and Electric Co. v. Federal Power Commission,* 506 F.2d 33 (D.C. Cir. 1974), the D.C. Circuit explained the difference between substantive rules and general statements of policy as follows:

> A properly adopted substantive rule establishes a standard of conduct which has the force of law. In subsequent administrative proceedings involving a substantive rule, the issues are whether the adjudicated facts conform to the rule and whether the rule should be waived or applied in that particular instance. The underlying policy embodied in the rule is not generally subject to challenge before the agency.
>
> A general statement of policy, on the other hand, does not establish a "binding norm." It is not finally determinative of the issues or rights to which it is addressed. The agency cannot apply or rely upon a general statement of policy as law because a general statement of policy only announces what the agency seeks to establish as policy. A policy statement announces the agency's tentative intentions for the future. When the agency applies the policy in a particular situation, it must be prepared to support the policy just as if the policy statement had never been issued.

Id. at 38 (citations omitted).

1978 Operating Instruction judicially reviewable, "does not foreclose the possibility that the 1978 Instruction constitutes a general statement of policy for purposes of section 553."]

Second, Mada apparently assumes that the 1978 Instruction cannot constitute a general statement of policy under section 553 because the INS's replacement of the 1978 Operating Instruction with the 1981 Instruction diminishes the likelihood that he and other similarly situated aliens will be granted deferred action status, and eliminates their opportunity to obtain judicial review. In essence, Mada suggests that if the repeal of an agency directive will cause a "substantial impact" to the rights of a specific class it cannot be exempt from section 553's notice-and-comment requirements. However, we have expressly "rejected the argument that, for the purposes of imposing notice-and-comment requirements on [an] agency for a particular rule, [courts should] look to the 'substantial impact' of the rule." *Alcaraz v. Block,* 746 F.2d 593, 613 (9th Cir. 1984) (citations omitted); *accord Rivera v. Becerra,* 714 F.2d 887, 890-91 (9th Cir. 1983), *cert. denied,* 465 U.S. 1099 (1984); *see Southern California Edison Co. v. FERC,* 770 F.2d 779, 783 (9th Cir. 1985). We have concluded that "simply because agency action has substantial impact does not mean it is subject to notice and comment if it is otherwise expressly exempt under the APA." *Alcaraz,* 746 F.2d at 613 (citations omitted); *accord Rivera,* 714 F.2d at 890-91 (citing the Supreme Court's admonition in *Vermont Yankee Nuclear Power Corp. v. Natural Resources Defense Council,* 435 U.S. 519 (1978), that courts should not impose procedural requirements upon agencies beyond those expressly provided in the APA); *contra United States Department of Labor v. Kast Metals Corp.,* 744 F.2d 1145, 1153-54 & n.19 (5th Cir. 1984) (adopting a more limited interpretation of *Vermont Yankee's* admonition).

In determining whether particular regulations or directives qualify for one of section 553's exemptions from notice-and-comment requirements, we have focussed upon the effect of the regulation or directive upon *agency decisionmaking,* not the public at large. See, e.g., *Southern California Edison,* 770 F.2d at 783 (discussing "rules of agency organization, procedure, or practice"); *Alcaraz,* 746 F.2d at 613 (discussing interpretative rules); *but cf.* Note, *An Analysis of the General Statement of Policy Exception to Notice and Comment Procedures,* 73 Georgetown L.J. 1007 (1985) (arguing that "substantial impact" test should be applied in conjunction with the "binding norm" test to determine whether a directive constitutes a general statement of policy). Therefore, to the extent that the 1978 and 1981 Operating Instructions satisfy the two requirements noted above — operating prospectively and not establishing a "binding norm" they constitute general statements of policy for purposes of section 553.

2. THE 1978 OPERATING INSTRUCTION

Applying these two requirements to the 1978 Operating Instruction, we conclude that it constituted a general statement of policy, and thus could be validly repealed and superseded without notice-and-comment proceedings. The 1978 Instruction operated only prospectively, and did not establish a "binding norm" that would limit the district director's discretion. The Instruction expressly authorizes the district director "to consider [any] individual facts" that he may feel appropriate in addition to the five enumerated factors in the instruction. See *Ryder,* 716 F.2d at 1377. It requires him to evaluate whether deporting or excluding an individual petitioning for deferred action status "would be *unconscionable* or result in *undue hardship* because of the existence of *appealing humanitarian factors*": these terms allow for great agency latitude and discretion, and cannot be viewed as establishing a "binding norm." See *Jean,* 711 F.2d at 1482 n.23 (suggesting that a standard that permits the granting of relief in cases where there are "significant humanitarian reasons" is "so broad that the agency official is free to grant relief" and is not constrained in his discretion). As a result, we conclude that the 1978 Operating Instruction constitutes a general statement of policy under section 553, and could be repealed validly without notice-and-comment proceedings.

3. THE 1981 AMENDED OPERATING INSTRUCTION

We conclude that the 1981 Operating Instruction presents even a clearer case of a general statement of policy. Like the 1978 Operating Instruction, it operates only prospectively. Moreover, the wording and structure of the amended Instruction emphasizes the broad and unfettered discretion of the district director in making deferred action determinations. None of the factors listed in the 1981 Instruction establishes a "binding norm": they require the district director to evaluate the "sympathetic" appeal of the deferred action applicant and to surmise the possible internal agency reaction and publicity that would result from his deportation and exclusion. The Instruction leaves the district director "free to consider the individual facts" in each case. *Ryder,* 716 F.2d at 1377. We conclude as a result, that the 1981 Operating Instruction constitutes a general statement of policy, and was validly promulgated without notice-and-comment proceedings. *See* 5 U.S.C. §§ 553(b)(A), 553(d)(2).

Because we conclude that notice-and-comment proceedings were not required under section 553 either to repeal the original, 1978 Operating Instruction or to promulgate the 1981 Operating Instruction, we reject Mada's challenge to the denial of his deferred action petition based upon the APA.

C. MADA'S CHALLENGE UNDER THE FOIA

Mada also contends that the 1981 version of the Operating Instruction is invalid, or at least should not be applied in his case, because the INS failed to publish it in the Federal Register, as required under FOIA sections 552(a)(1)(D) and (E). We rejected this precise claim in *Romeiro,*[14] concluding that the 1981 Operating Instruction "clearly does not create substantive rights" for aliens, *Romeiro,* 773 F.2d at 1025 n.3, and therefore the failure to publish it did not "'adversely affect a member of the public.'" *Zaharakis v. Heckler,* 744 F.2d 711, 714 (9th Cir. 1984) (citation omitted), *accord Cubanski v. Heckler,* 781 F.2d 1421, 1428-29 (9th Cir. 1986). As a result, we held that no individual, including the plaintiff in *Romeiro,* can challenge the INS's failure to publish the 1981 Instruction under the FOIA.

---

14. The fact that the 1981 amended Operating Instruction constitutes a "general statement of policy" under the APA does not exempt it from the FOIA's publication requirement. The FOIA explicitly requires that agencies publish their "statements of general policy" in the Federal Register. 5 U.S.C. § 552(a)(1)(D); *Cubanski v. Heckler,* 781 F.2d 1421, 1428 (9th Cir. 1986); *Zaharakis v. Heckler,* 744 F.2d 711, 714 (9th Cir. 1984).

See *Romeiro,* 773 F.2d at 1025 n.3; see also *Cubanski,* 781 F.2d at 1428-29; *Zaharakis,* 744 F.2d at 714. The FOIA explicitly provides that an individual cannot object to the application of an unpublished rule in his case if he has "actual and timely notice of [its] terms." 5 U.S.C. § 552(a)(1). We have previously held that an individual may not raise an FOIA claim based on an agency's failure to publish a rule or regulation, unless he makes an "initial showing" that "he was adversely affected by the lack of publication or that he would have been able to pursue an alternate course of conduct" had publication occurred. *Zaharakis,* 744 F.2d at 714; *accord Cubanski,* 781 F.2d at 1428-29; *see also United States v. Hall,* 742 F.2d 1153, 1155 (9th Cir. 1984). The record indicates that Mada was aware of the precise language of the 1981 Operation Instruction when he first petitioned for deferred action status in October, 1983. His petition expressly quoted the "sympathetic factors" language contained in the 1981 Instruction. Moreover, he has not alleged that he could somehow have altered his conduct in a material way had he been aware of the amended Instruction sooner. Thus, for all these reasons we must reject Mada's claim that the 1981 Operating Instruction should not be applied in his case because of the INS's failure to publish it in the Federal Register. See *Romeiro,* 773 F.2d at 1025 n.3; *Zaharakis,* 744 F.2d at 714; see also *Cubanski,* 781 F.2d at 1428-29.

CONCLUSION

We reject Mada's challenges to the promulgation and application of the 1981 Operating Instruction in his case based on the APA and FOIA. We conclude that Fitzpatrick properly reviewed Mada's petition for deferred action status under the 1981 Operating Instruction. As a result, we reverse the district court's grant of Mada's habeas petition, and remand this action to the district court for proceedings consistent with this opinion. REVERSED and REMANDED. (District Judge Hill concurred specially in the result only.)

QUESTIONS

1. Why have an exception for general statements of policy? How does the court determine that the exception applies? Note that the 1981 MSAPA does not include any specific exception from rulemaking for general statements of policy.
2. Note: *Mada-Luna* is a good case to consider for the importance of the Statement of Facts in appellate briefing. Here, the record showed that the alleged threats to Mada-Luna grew out of the original trafficking. In addition, Mada-Luna had actually returned to Mexico once on his own.
3. In *Mada-Luna* the lower court had conflated two administrative law principles: the requirements for notice and comment rulemaking, and the requirement that an agency must follow its own rules. The government was able to succeed on appeal by distinguishing the two principles.
4. Even though statements of general policy, interpretative rules, and rules of agency procedure are exempted from the notice and comment requirements of APA § 553, they are subject to the "publication" requirements of APA § 552(a)(1).

WARDER v. SHALALA
149 F.3d 73 (1st Cir. 1998)

CAMPBELL, Senior Circuit Judge. This appeal relates to the classification, for Medicare Part B reimbursement purposes, of medical equipment made for persons suffering from severe musculoskeletal problems. Produced by Appellees OrthoConcepts and used by Appellee Warder, the equipment consists of braces, fitted to the individual patient, on a wheeled base. The district court upheld OrthoConcepts' challenge to an administrative ruling ("the Ruling" or "HCFAR 96-1") from the Health Care Financing Administration ("HCFA") that classifies this equipment as "durable medical equipment" rather than as "braces." The former classification limits Medicare reimbursement to devices used at home, precluding reimbursement for such devices when used in certain hospital and institutional settings.

Holding that HCFAR 96-1 was a substantive, or legislative, rule requiring notice and comment, the court ruled it to be invalid because notice and comment procedures had not been followed prior to its issuance. The court also found that the equipment in dispute was not "durable medical equipment," and enjoined HCFA from treating it as such.

We disagree. We hold that HCFAR 96-1 is an interpretive rule, and was not invalidated by HCFA's failure to have adopted notice and comment procedures. We vacate the injunction on the ground that HCFA's interpretation was a permissible one.

BACKGROUND

1. STATUTORY AND REGULATORY BACKGROUND
A. Part B of the Medicare Act

The Medicare Act, 42 U.S.C. § 1395 et seq., establishes a national health insurance program for the elderly and the disabled. Congress authorized Appellant Secretary of Health and Human Services to implement the Medicare statute by issuing both substantive regulations and interpretive rules. *See* 42 U.S.C. § 1395hh. The Secretary has in turn delegated this authority to the HCFA Administrator.

Part B of the Medicare Act, 42 U.S.C. § 1395j et seq., establishes a voluntary supplemental insurance program. Eligible individuals enrolled in the program pay a monthly premium that, along with congressionally appropriated funds, finances physicians' and other health services. *See id.* § 1395j. Part B has been referred to as "a private medical insurance program that is subsidized in major part by the Federal Government."

Part B benefits are administered by private insurance carriers under contract with HCFA. *See* 42 U.S.C. § 1395u. HCFA reimburses a carrier for the costs of administering claims, and the carriers act as HCFA's agents. *See id.* § 1395u(a); 42 C.F.R. § 421.5(b). The carrier bears the initial responsibility for determining whether an item or service billed to the Part B program is covered and, if so, the amount to be paid. *See* 42 U.S.C. § 1395u.

B. Part B Coverage of DME and Braces

Medicare Part B provides coverage for "medical and other health services," 42 U.S.C. § 1395x(s), that are "reasonable and necessary for the diagnosis or treatment of illness or injury or to improve the functioning of a malformed body member," *id.* § 1395y(a)(1)(A). The statute expressly covers braces, including "leg, arm, back, and neck braces." *Id.* § 1395x(s)(9).

Ordinarily, coverage will extend to any piece of equipment that is reasonable and necessary for the treatment of an eligible patient regardless of the place where it is used. However, Part B reimburses devices classified as "durable medical equipment" ("DME") only when provided at the patient's "home" or other "institution used as [the patient's] home," and not in a hospital or skilled nursing facility ("SNF"). 42 U.S.C. § 1395x(n) (citing §§ 1395x(e)(1) (defining hospital), 1395i-3(a)(1) (defining SNF)). In other words, DME is reimbursable only when used in a patient's home, with "home" being defined to exclude hospitals and SNFs.

No similar restriction relates to "braces." *See* 42 U.S.C. § 1395x(s)(9). Hence if a piece of medical equipment used in a hospital or SNF is a "brace," it is reimbursable — but not if deemed to be DME.

C. DME and Braces Defined

The medical device here, intended for persons with severe musculosekeletal failure, includes a set of connected braces attached to a wheeled base. While various provisions define braces and DME, no single provision concisely differentiates the two, leaving it open which category is implicated when, as here, a brace-like device is used as part of a wheeled item that might be classified as DME.

The principal statutory definition of DME states that "[DME] includes iron lungs, oxygen tents, hospital beds, and *wheelchairs*." 42 U.S.C. § 1395x(s)(6) (emphasis supplied). . . .

In 1990, Congress amended § 1395m(a)(4) to add a provision — which ultimately, by its own terms, was superseded by a HCFA regulation — expressly providing that customized wheelchairs were DME. P.L. 101-508, § 4152(c)(4)(B).[2] The amendment provided that it would become effective on January 1, 1992, unless HCFA developed its own criteria for the treatment of customized wheelchairs as DME. In December, 1991, HCFA addressed customized wheelchairs in a regulation that substantially tracked the language of the amendment, providing that a wheelchair is DME if "uniquely constructed or substantially modified for a specific beneficiary" and "so different from another item used for the same purpose that the two items cannot be grouped together for pricing purposes." 42 C.F.R. § 414.224. In effect, Congress, and subsequently HCFA, treated as DME any wheelchair modified in light of an individual patient's disability, per a physician's instructions.

The regulatory definition of DME focuses not on examples, but rather on qualitative criteria, including the equipment's durability:

---

2. The amended definition of DME included any wheelchair "measured, fitted, or adapted in consideration of the patient's body size, disability, period of need, or intended use, and . . . assembled by a supplier . . . who makes available customized features, modifications, or components for wheelchairs that are intended for an individual patient's use in accordance with instructions from the patient's physician." P.L. 101-508, § 4152(c)(4)(B).

equipment, furnished by a supplier or a home health agency that—

   (1) Can withstand repeated use;

   (2) Is primarily and customarily used to serve a medical purpose;

   (3) Generally is not useful to an individual in the absence of an illness or injury; and

   (4) Is appropriate for use in the home [citing 42 C.F.R. § 410.38, which in turn cites statutory provisions defining "home" to exclude hospitals and SNFs].

42 C.F.R. § 414.202.

The manual HCFA prepares for its carriers repeats the regulatory criteria. Another provision in the manual goes farther, explaining that DME includes "supplies and accessories" that are "necessary for the effective use of [DME]."

The statutory definition of "brace" is ostensive, listing the sorts of braces that are covered. *Id.* § 1395x(s)(9) (defining orthotics as "leg, arm, back, and neck braces, and artificial legs, arms, and eyes, including requirements if required because of a change in the patient's physical condition"). The accompanying regulation, 42 C.F.R. § 414.202, tracks the statutory language.

2. THE ORTHOCONCEPTS PRODUCT

Due to illness, injury, and in some cases old age, thousands of Medicare beneficiaries suffer from musculoskeletal failure so severe as to render them incapable of moving or supporting their own limbs. These catastrophically crippled patients are vulnerable to numerous painful conditions. One of the most serious is contractures, a condition in which muscles become rigid and resistant to elongation following a long period of disuse. Other complications include the development of pressure sores, circulatory problems, and infections.

To manage the condition of patients with grave musculoskeletal failure, OrthoConcepts designed what it has marketed as the "OrthoConcepts Seating System." The Seating System consists of a set of connected braces — the number and type depending on the patient's condition — attached to a wheeled base. The patient sits, or reclines, on the Seating System, and the component braces maintain the patient in a position designed to reduce the weight borne by weaker extremities and to prevent contractures. Since 1989, OrthoConcepts has supplied the Seating System to more than 2700 patients.

3. HCFA'S CLASSIFICATION OF THE ORTHOCONCEPTS SEATING SYSTEM

On December 7, 1989, OrthoConcepts informed a regional HCFA office that OrthoConcepts would soon begin marketing the Seating System nationwide. OrthoConcepts' letter inquired about the Medicare coverage status of the Seating System and asked HCFA to establish a new billing code (known as a "L code," a standardized billing classification for "orthotics," or braces) that would allow the Seating System to be reimbursed as a brace. The regional office replied in January of 1990, advising OrthoConcepts that Part B covered the Seating System as DME, not as orthotics, and that it would provide no L Code for billing the Seating System as an orthotic.

The regional office also wrote its private carriers regarding the Seating System, instructing them to treat the device as DME. By letter dated February 21, 1990, the carrier then responsible for OrthoConcepts' claims, Nationwide

Insurance, notified OrthoConcepts of the HCFA regional office's letter and informed it that its products "are classified as [DME]; not orthotics." . . .

Despite HCFA's 1990 letter declaring the Seating System DME, OrthoConcepts, through its corporate affiliates, continued to bill Seating Systems supplied to patients at SNFs as an orthotic. [Three regional carriers denied reimbursement.]

OrthoConcepts appealed from the carriers' denials of their Part B claims.[3] [In Region A, an ALJ ruled that "the Seating Systems '[were] orthotic braces and not wheelchairs,'" and the Appeals Board denied HCFA's petition to review the ALJ's decision.] The Region B and Region C appeals were consolidated before a carrier fair hearing officer. On February 9, 1996, the hearing officer decided that the Seating System was an orthotic device rather than DME. This ended the matter, as the statute gives HCFA no administrative appeal from a hearing officer's adverse decision.

The net result of these proceedings was that by early 1996, HCFA's view of the Seating System as DME — as expressed in its 1990 letter to OrthoConcepts and its 1994 notice to its carriers — was at odds with the decisions of an ALJ and a hearing officer.

These decisions prompted HCFA to issue HCFAR 96-1, which became effective September 18, 1996. Noting the above-mentioned decisions classifying the Seating System as an orthotic, the Ruling's stated purpose is "to provide clarification and guidance regarding the scope and meaning of the statutory benefits for 'orthotics' and '[DME].'" HCFAR 96-1 at 2. The Ruling discusses the relevant statutes, regulations, legislative history, and administrative materials before reaching its conclusion: the definition of "orthotics" "is limited to leg, arm, back, and neck braces that are used independently [of], rather than in conjunction with, or as components of, other kinds of medical equipment." The Ruling also provides several illustrations of DME, one of which unmistakably refers to the OrthoConcepts Seating System.

On February 26, 1997, two Medicare beneficiaries who used the Seating System in SNFs and three OrthoConcepts suppliers (hereinafter, Appellees will be referred to collectively as "OrthoConcepts") brought the present district court action challenging HCFAR 96-1. Appellees advanced the procedural claim that HCFAR 96-1 was invalid, having been adopted without compliance with the notice-and-comment procedures of the Administrative Procedure Act ("APA"), 5 U.S.C. §553, and the Medicare statute, 42 U.S.C. §1395hh. Appellees also made the substantive claim that HCFAR 96-1 was arbitrary and capricious, see 5 U.S.C. §706(2)(A). Appellees sought a declaration that the Ruling was void and that the Seating System was reimbursable as a brace. They also requested a preliminary injunction blocking HCFA from enforcing the Ruling.

---

3. To receive reimbursement of past medical expenditures or pre-payment of expected costs, the beneficiary of the expenditures (or a "supplier of services" that has accepted assignment of the beneficiary's claim) must request payment from HCFA's designated carrier. *See* 42 U.S.C. §1395u(a) (granting authority to utilize private insurance carriers for administration of Part B claims). Each carrier contract must require the carrier to provide a "fair hearing" for suppliers whose claims are denied and that meet an amount-in-controversy requirement. *See id.* §1395u(b)(3)(C).

If dissatisfied with the result of the fair hearing, the beneficiary or supplier may appeal to an Administrative Law Judge and, if necessary, to the Departmental Appeals Board. *See id.* §1395ff(b)(2)(B). Judicial review of an adverse Appeals Board decision may be obtained if the amount in controversy is one thousand dollars or more and the beneficiary or supplier files a district court action within sixty days. *See id.* §1395ff(b)(1), (b)(2)(B).

After holding a hearing on Appellees' motion for a preliminary injunction, the district court notified the parties that it would issue a final determination on the merits of Appellees' claims. On March 7, 1997, the district court ruled that HCFAR 96-1 is a substantive rule and, therefore, invalid because HCFA issued it without following notice and comment procedures. The court went on to hold that, the definitions of DME and orthotics in effect prior to the Ruling prevented HCFA from treating the Seating System as DME. (The court left open the possibility that HCFA could validly re-enact the Ruling after using notice and comment procedures.) The court also enjoined HCFA from denying Appellees reimbursement for the Seating System.

This appeal followed.

DISCUSSION

1. THE INTERPRETATIVE RULE EXCEPTION TO THE REQUIREMENT OF NOTICE AND COMMENT

Whether an administrative ruling is substantive or interpretative is a question of law that this court reviews de novo. *See La Casa Del Convaleciente v. Sullivan*, 965 F.2d 1175, 1177 (1st Cir. 1992) ("*Convaleciente*").

The APA exempts "interpretative rules" from its notice and comment procedures. 5 U.S.C. § 553(b)(B). The Medicare Act expressly incorporates the APA's exemption for interpretive rules. *See* 42 U.S.C. § 1395hh(b)(2)(C) (1994).[4]

The line between a legislative or substantive rule and an interpretative one is, as many courts have noted, far from clear. The APA itself does not define "substantive" and "interpretive" (or, in the APA's nomenclature, "interpretative") rules. Moreover, courts and other authorities have provided any number of definitions, lending further imprecision to the field. Nevertheless, a few reasonably clear principles have emerged, leading us to conclude that HCFAR 96-1 is interpretative, and could be promulgated without notice and comment procedures.

The most authoritative explanation of the substantive/interpretative distinction is that provided by the Attorney General's Manual on the Administrative Procedure Act (1947). The Attorney General's Manual described an interpretive rule as one "issued by an agency to advise the public of the agency's construction of the statutes and rules which it administers." Courts have routinely quoted this definition with approval. *See Shalala v. Guernsey Memorial Hosp.*, 514 U.S. 87, 99 (1995); *Chrysler Corp. v. Brown*, 441 U.S. 281, 302; *Convaleciente*, 965 F.2d at 1178. The Attorney General's Manual defines substantive, or legislative, rules as those that

> are issued by an agency pursuant to statutory authority and which implement the statute [such as the Securities and Exchange Commission's proxy rules issued pursuant to the Securities Exchange Act of 1934, 15 U.S.C. § 78n(b)]. Such rules have the force and effect of law.

---

4. The Social Security Act ("SSA"), of which the Medicare statute is part, phrases the distinction between substantive and interpretative rules slightly differently from the APA, requiring notice and comment procedures for any rule "that establishes or changes a substantive legal standard governing the scope of benefits," 42 U.S.C. § 1395hh(a)(2), but exempting by implication, *inter alia*, "interpretive rules," *id.* § 1395hh(c) (requiring periodic publication of "interpretive rules" that have not been issued as regulations).

We proceed herein as if the SSA's exemption for interpretative rules were identical to the APA's. The SSA's language, drafted after the APA's, can fairly be read to duplicate the APA on this score. . . . OrthoConcepts has not argued that the two standards are materially different.

Id. These definitions have caused us to observe "that the distinction between legislative and interpretative rules has to do in part with the authority" — law-making versus law-interpreting — "under which the rule is promulgated." *Levesque v. Block,* 723 F.2d 175, 182 (1st Cir. 1982). The Seventh Circuit has stated that "rules are legislative when the agency is exercising delegated power to make law through rules, and rules are interpretative when the agency is not exercising such delegated power in issuing them." *Metropolitan Sch. Dist. v. Davila,* 969 F.2d 485, 490 (7th Cir. 1992).

Where a rule falls along the interpretative/legislative spectrum will turn in many cases on the novelty of a rule's substantive content. "If a rule creates rights, assigns duties, or imposes obligations, *the basic tenor of which is not already outlined in the law itself,* then it is substantive." *Convaleciente,* 965 F.2d at 1178 (emphasis supplied); *see also American Mining Congress v. Mine Safety & Health Admin.,* 995 F.2d 1106, 1112 (D.C. Cir. 1993) (stating that a rule is legislative if "in the absence of the rule there would not be an adequate legislative basis for enforcement action or other agency action to confer benefits or ensure the performance of duties"). Put more succinctly, a rule is exempt from notice and comment as an interpretative rule if it does not "effect a substantive change in the regulations." *Guernsey,* 514 U.S. at 100 (internal quotation marks and citation omitted).

On its face, HCFAR 96-1 appears to satisfy the criteria for an interpretive rule. We have said that an important factor in determining whether a rule is interpretive is the agency's own characterization. See *Convaleciente,* 965 F.2d at 1178; *Levesque,* 723 F.2d at 182. It is not disputed that HCFA intended HCFAR 96-1 to be interpretative. The Ruling itself purports only to "clarify" the proper application of existing statutory and regulatory definitions to a particular case.[6]

More importantly, the Ruling does not establish any new standard. Rather, it addresses an area of ambiguity: whether a device comprising both orthotic and DME components should be reimbursed as a brace or as DME. The statutory and regulatory definitions of DME and orthotics predated the Ruling, but neither was so complete as to provide an unambiguous answer to the question of the Seating System's classification.[7]

---

6. In *Levesque* we stated that the impact of a rule on the regulated parties "may be relevant in construing the intent of the agency in issuing the rule." 723 F.2d at 182. Both sides have acknowledged that the Seating System's reimbursement classification has public importance. However, where, as here, the agency's intent is unambiguous, a rule's impact on the public ceases to be of possible significance in construing agency intent.

Indeed, this Circuit's law regarding the relevance of a rule's public impact is in doubt. We did not give the substantial impact factor any weight in *Convaleciente, see* 965 F.2d at 1178 (noting that other circuits have treated public impact as irrelevant), and the Supreme Court wholly ignored it in *Guernsey* and in *Reno v. Koray,* 515 U.S. 50 (1995) (characterizing as interpretative a rule affecting prisoners' credit for time served), two cases that each involved a rule with an apparently substantial public impact.

7. The pre-Ruling ambiguity of the Seating System's proper classification is what distinguishes this case from *Linoz v. Heckler,* 800 F.2d 871 (9th Cir. 1986), upon which OrthoConcepts relies heavily. In *Linoz,* the court considered a change to the MCM instructing carriers that coverage of ambulance trips to the "nearest hospital with appropriate facilities" did not include trips "solely to avail a patient of the service of . . . a physician in a specific specialty." The *Linoz* court held that the limitation imposed by the new provision "withdrew coverage previously provided," therefore changing substantive law.

Unlike the rule in *Linoz,* which altered rather than clarified the coverage of ambulance trips, HCFAR 96-1 does not "carve out a per se exception" to a rule that previously contained no exceptions. Instead, the Ruling explicates the view that the existing statutory and regulatory definitions place certain equipment in one existing category instead of another.

These definitions created the need for clarification — precisely the function of an interpretative rule — and they provided an "adequate legislative basis for [the agency action]." *American Mining Congress,* 995 F.2d at 1112. The Ruling does not stake out any ground "the basic tenor of which [was] not already outlined in the law itself." *Convaleciente,* 965 F.2d at 1178.

We find guidance in the Supreme Court's recent *Guernsey* decision. There, the Court considered whether the interpretative rule exemption applied to an accounting provision in HCFA's Provider Reimbursement Manual ("PRM"). Like HCFAR 96-1, the PRM provision at issue in Guernsey "[did] not purport to be a regulation and [had] not been adopted pursuant to the notice-and-comment procedures of the [APA]." 514 U.S. at 90. The Court determined that the PRM provision concerned "the only question unaddressed by the otherwise comprehensive regulations on this particular subject." The Court concluded that the measure "[was] a prototypical example of an interpretive rule" because the PRM provision merely applied existing law, and was not "inconsistent with any of the Secretary's existing regulations."

The reasoning in *Guernsey* applies here. The Medicare statute and regulations provide a comprehensive classification of equipment as DME or orthotics. The Ruling addresses a small overlap in this scheme. The answer the Ruling provides is consistent with the existing definitions. The statute and regulations define braces only by referring to particular types of braces, none of which would have to include a system of braces attached to a wheeled base. *See* 42 U.S.C. § 1395x(s)(9). But clearly the Seating System fits within one category or the other, so HCFA was acting in an interpretive, rather than legislative, capacity. *See United Technologies Corp. v. EPA,* 821 F.2d 714, 719-20 (D.C. Cir. 1987) ("If the rule is based on specific statutory provisions, and its validity stands or falls on the correctness of the agency's interpretation of those provisions, it is an interpretative rule.").

By the same token, the Ruling is not inconsistent with existing law because the statutory and regulatory definitions of DME are broad enough to include the Seating System. It is conceded that the Seating System "can withstand repeated use," 42 C.F.R. § 414.202, a principal regulatory criterion differentiating DME from other equipment. Moreover, it is not inconsistent to treat the Seating System — which is, after all, a wheeled device in which a patient sits — as a customized wheelchair, a piece of equipment specifically identified as DME. *See* 42 U.S.C. § 1395x(n); 42 C.F.R. § 414.224. Nothing in any of the existing statutory or regulatory definitions is inconsistent with HCFAR 96-1. Together, the extant definitions were ambiguous in respect to the category within which the Seating System best fit, and "the quintessential example of an interpretive rule" is "[a] statement seeking to interpret a statutory or regulatory term." *Orengo Caraballo v. Reich,* 11 F.3d 186, 195 (D.C. Cir. 1993).

OrthoConcepts' main contention both in the district court and on appeal was that HCFAR 96-1 was legislative because it changed HCFA's policy of reimbursing the Seating System as DME. This argument rests on erroneous views of both the law and the facts.

The legal point is clear enough: in order for notice and comment to be necessary, "the [later] rule would have to be inconsistent with another rule having the force of law, not just any agency interpretation regardless of whether it had been codified." *Chief Probation Officers v. Shalala,* 118 F.3d 1327, 1337 (9th Cir. 1997) (White, J. (Retired, sitting by designation)). The Supreme Court in *Guernsey* intimated this much, concluding that the provision there was interpretive because it did not contradict "any of the Secretary's existing regulations." 514 U.S. at 100 (emphasis supplied); see also *id.* at 111 (O'Connor, J., dissenting) (observing that interpretive rules "must explain existing law and not contradict what the [extant] regulations require"). The lower federal courts are in agreement on this score. *See,* e.g., *Orengo,* 11 F.3d at 196 (explaining that a subsequent rule is legislative "only where [the] second rule repudiates or is irreconcilable with [a prior legislative rule]"); *White v. Shalala,* 7 F.3d 296, 304 (2d Cir. 1993) ("If the rule is an interpretation of a statute rather than an extra-statutory imposition of rights, duties or obligations, it remains interpretive even if the rule embodies the Secretary's changed interpretation of the statute"); *Davila,* 969 F.2d at 492 ("An agency's change in its reading of the statute does not necessarily make the rule announcing the change legislative"). As already stated, nothing in the statute or regulations addresses the precise issue decided in HCFAR 96-1. Thus, even supposing HCFA's pre-Ruling policy was different, the earlier policy would not prevent HCFA from adopting a contrary new interpretative rule.

However, we very much doubt that the Ruling, by limiting the coverage of braces to devices used independently of DME, added something new to HCFA's policies. In siding with OrthoConcepts, the district court concluded that the agency's informal pronouncements and practices regarding the reimbursement of the Seating System indicated a pre-Ruling policy to treat the Seating System as an orthotic. A number of factors, however, suggest the opposite conclusion.

First, the HCFA regional office's 1990 letter to OrthoConcepts specifically stated that the Seating System was DME. The district court disregarded this letter because a former OrthoConcepts attorney submitted an unsworn affidavit stating that the office promised to issue a letter rescinding the corresponding order instructing its carriers to treat the Seating System as DME. However, as the district court found, "there is no evidence that HCFA ever sent such a letter," nor is there any evidence corroborating the unsworn affidavit.

Second, HCFA instructed its carriers on three separate occasions that devices quite similar to the Seating System should be treated as DME. The first two memoranda, issued in 1987 and 1989, dealt with "contoured corrective seats," and concluded, as the 1989 memorandum put it, that the "only statutory provision that could apply to such equipment" was DME. The district court dismissed these memoranda on the ground that, by questioning whether the devices served a medical purpose, they relied on an alternative basis for denying the contoured corrective seats coverage. However, we cannot see how the inclusion of this complementary argument contradicts or negates the independent conclusion that the equipment at issue was DME.

A further manifestation of HCFA's earlier policy was its 1994 instruction to treat as DME equipment designated by the K-codes 0115 and 0116. The district court dismissed the 1994 instruction as "not directly on point," but the instruction set out a policy for equipment that, like the Seating System and the first illustration given in HCFAR 96-1, contained orthotic attachments. While the 1994 instruction addressed equipment with a different technical design, it implicitly contained the same principle as the Ruling: DME includes orthotic components that cannot be used independently of attached DME. That the 1994 instruction (as well as the 1987 and 1989 memoranda) did not address the precise equipment at issue here does not mean that HCFA had no relevant policy: "an interpretive statement may 'supply crisper and more detailed lines than the authority being interpreted.'" *Orengo,* 11 F.3d at 195 (*quoting American Mining Congress,* 995 F.2d at 1112). Thus, we reject OrthoConcepts' contention that HCFAR 96-1 effected a substantive change in the regulations.

As a fallback position, OrthoConcepts argues that HCFAR 96-1 could not be valid without notice-and-comment rulemaking because it has a binding effect on agency personnel. This argument confuses two senses in which a rule may bind. Of course, a rule with the force and effect of law — binding not only the agency and regulated parties, but also the courts — is by definition a substantive rule. However, a rule may lack this force and still bind agency personnel. Accordingly, "an interpretative rule binds an agency's employees, including its ALJs, but it does not bind the agency itself." Kenneth C. Davis & Richard J. Pierce, Jr., Administrative Law Treatise § 6.3 at 104 (3d ed. 1996 & Supp. 1997). In other words, a rule may be "binding" but not, for purposes of notice and comment, "substantive," or legislative. We rejected an argument almost identical to Ortho-Concepts' in *Levesque:* "If plaintiffs mean that any rule that an agency intends to be effective must be legislative, they are plainly wrong. Every rule is intended to have some effect." 723 F.2d at 181-82; see also *American Mining Congress,* 995 F.2d at 1111 ("Restricting discretion tells one little about whether a rule is interpretive"); *Davila,* 969 F.2d at 493 ("All rules which interpret the underlying statute must be binding because they set forth what the agency believes is congressional intent"). The fact that the Ruling binds HCFA carriers and ALJs is entirely consistent with its status as an interpretative rule.

We therefore reject OrthoConcepts' argument that HCFAR 96-1 was not legally adopted because of the absence of notice and comment procedures.

[Applying the deference required by *Skidmore v. Swift & Co.,* 323 U.S. 134, reproduced *infra* at 494, the court went on to hold that HCFAR 96-1 was substantively an appropriate construction of the statute.]

QUESTIONS

1. Why would Congress provide an exception for "interpretative rules"? Does such an exception make sense as a policy matter?
2. Why does the court reject "substantial impact" as a test for determining whether a rule is interpretive or legislative (see fn. 6)?
3. Why does the Medicare Act independently require notice and comment for substantive rules (see discussion at fn. 4)? See APA at § 553(a)(2).
4. May an agency rely upon the interpretive rule exception to rulemaking requirements to promulgate an interpretation, the effect of which is to change the substance of an agency regulation?
5. The D.C. Circuit has identified and criticized a "tendency of courts and litigants to lump interpretative rules and policy statements together in contrast to substantive rules, a tendency to which we have ourselves succumbed on occasion." *Syncor International Corp. v. Shalala,* 127 F.3d 90,

94-95 (D.C. Cir. 1997), citing *Community Nutrition Inst. v. Young*, 818 F.2d 943, 946 (D.C. Cir. 1987):

> That causes added confusion because interpretative rules and policy statements are quite different agency instruments. An agency policy statement does not seek to impose or elaborate or interpret a legal norm. It merely represents an agency position with respect to how it will treat—typically enforce—the governing legal norm. By issuing a policy statement, an agency simply lets the public know its current enforcement or adjudicatory approach. The agency retains the discretion and the authority to change its position—even abruptly—in any specific case because a change in its policy does not affect the legal norm. We thus have said that policy statements are binding on neither the public, nor the agency. The primary distinction between a substantive rule—really any rule—and a general statement of policy, then, turns on whether an agency intends to bind itself to a particular legal position.
>
> An interpretative rule, on the other hand, typically reflects an agency's construction of a statute that has been entrusted to the agency to administer. The legal norm is one that Congress has devised; the agency does not purport to modify that norm, in other words, to engage in lawmaking. To be sure, since an agency's interpretation of an ambiguous statute is entitled to judicial deference . . . , it might be thought that the interpretative rule—particularly if it changes a prior statutory interpretation as an agency may do without notice and comment—is, in reality, a change in the legal norm. Still, in such a situation the agency does not claim to be exercising authority to itself make positive law. Instead, it is construing the product of congressional lawmaking "based on specific statutory provisions." That is why we have said that "[t]he distinction between an interpretative rule and substantive rule . . . likely turns on how tightly the agency's interpretation is drawn linguistically from the actual language of the statute."[The court added in a footnote: "If the statute . . . to be interpreted is itself very general, using terms like 'equitable' or 'fair,' and the 'interpretation' really provides all the guidance, then the latter will more likely be a substantive regulation," because then the agency's rule gives content to the legal norm in question.]
>
> We should note, in order to be complete . . . , that an interpretative rule can construe an agency's substantive regulation as well as a statute. In that event, the interpretative rule is, in a sense, even more binding on the agency because its modification, unlike a modification of an interpretative rule construing a statute, will likely require a notice and comment procedure. Otherwise, the agency could evade its notice and comment obligation by "modifying" a substantive rule that was promulgated by notice and comment rulemaking.
>
> A substantive rule has characteristics of both the policy statement and the interpretative rule; it is certainly in part an exercise of policy, and it is a rule. But the crucial distinction between it and the other two techniques is that a substantive rule *modifies* or *adds* to a legal norm based on the agency's *own authority*. That authority flows from a congressional delegation to promulgate substantive rules, to engage in supplementary lawmaking. And, it is because the agency is engaged in lawmaking that the APA requires it to comply with notice and comment.

Are there reasons, other than purely academic, for distinguishing carefully between whether the agency is relying on the interpretive rule exception or the general statement of policy exception to § 553?

6. Consider Judge Starr's proposed solution to the problem of defining the scope of the exceptions to the procedural requirements for informal rule-making. In *Community Nutrition Institute v. Young,* 818 F.2d 943 (D.C. Cir. 1987), the court addressed whether action levels for contaminants identified by the Food and Drug Administration were legislative rules subject to notice-and-comment requirements. In an opinion concurring and dissenting in part, Judge Starr suggested the following approach:

> The majority is quite correct when it chronicles the difficulty courts have found in attempting to fathom the distinction between legislative or substantive rules on one hand, and interpretative rules or policy statements on the other. Inasmuch as our decisional law over the last decade avowedly reflects considerable uncertainty in discerning the line between agency pronouncements that are "law" and those that are "policy," it seems advisable to return to the pristine teaching of *Pacific Gas* [relied upon by the court in *Mada-Luna*]. In that case, this court articulated a rule which is clearly preferable to the present muddy state of the law. . . . As I read the case, *Pacific Gas* deems as "critical" the effect of the agency pronouncement in future proceedings.
>
> This is as it should be, . . . it is this element that is the essence of "law." Not only is the *Pacific Gas* approach therefore the most principled manner in which to draw the legislative-interpretative line (in view of the fact that the determination is whether a pronouncement is "law" or not), but it has the not insignificant practical benefit in an unclear world of providing great clarity where previously there has been "considerable smog."
>
> We should reembrace our *Pacific Gas* test as the determinative factor in analyzing whether a particular pronouncement is legislative or interpretative in nature. If the pronouncement has the force of law in future proceedings, it is a legislative rule. Unless that critical feature is present, however, the agency statement should be considered to be a lower form of pronouncement, a "non-law" as it were, or in APA terms an "interpretative rule" or "general statement of policy." The correct measure of a pronouncement's force in subsequent proceedings is a practical one: must the agency merely show that the pronouncement has been violated or must the agency, if its hand is called, show that the pronouncement itself is justified in light of the underlying statute and the facts.
>
> Application of this test can readily be illustrated by the case at hand. Action levels offer guidance to the regulated community with respect to what products FDA deems adulterated within the meaning of the FDC Act. But in an enforcement proceeding in which FDA seeks either to impose sanctions for shipment of an adulterated product or to enjoin shipment of an adulterated product, the agency must prove the product is "adulterated." That is, FDA cannot merely show that the product at issue fails to comply with the action level. Rather, FDA must offer scientific or other probative evidence to support its contention that the product is adulterated. Thus, the action level does not have the force of law in the subsequent proceeding. Indeed, it has no "force" at all. . . .
>
> . . . I recognize a potential danger lurking in the embrace of a single-factor, *Pacific Gas* test. Agencies may yield to temptation and seek to shield their regulations from the scrutiny occasioned by notice-and-comment procedures, choosing instead to cast would-be regulations as interpretative rules. The rule would still, of course, be subject to scrutiny in a subsequent proceeding, but this fact may be of little comfort to prospective commentors, given the deference accorded agency views in any such proceedings. But

upon analysis, the danger is more theoretical than real. Indeed, Congress not atypically provides agencies with a direct command to promulgate regulations, thereby imposing a duty that would not be satisfied with issuance of an humble interpretative rule. . . .

Does the *Warder* opinion persuasively refute Judge Starr's suggestion? Compare with Judge Starr's suggested approach the exception for interpretive rules adopted by the 1981 MSAPA. Notice and comment is not required for "a rule that only defines the meaning of a statute or other provision of law or precedent if the agency does not possess delegated authority to bind the courts to any extent with its definition." § 3-109(a). Moreover, the 1981 MSAPA provides that, in the event of judicial review of such an interpretive rule, "[a] reviewing court shall determine wholly de novo the validity of" such a rule. § 3-109(b).

7. A decision of the U.S. Court of Appeals for the Sixth Circuit thoroughly explored the question of when an agency is excused from using notice and comment rulemaking because the rule is interpretive. *See Dismas Charities, Inc. v. U.S. Dep't of Justice*, 401 F.3d 666 (6th Cir. 2005). The case involved a Department of Justice (DOJ) Memorandum, issued by the Deputy Attorney General, Larry Thompson, that prohibited the placement of federal prisoners in community correction centers (CCCs) rather than in traditional prisons. The DOJ relied on an opinion from the Office of Legal Counsel that found the practice of placing federal prisoners in CCCs violated federal law (specifically 18 U.S.C. § 3624(c) (2006)). See *id.* at 669-70. On December 20, 2002, the Bureau of Prisons (BOP) implemented the Thompson Memorandum and ceased placing federal prisoners in CCCs. *Id.* at 670-71. The plaintiff, Dismas Charities, operated 18 CCCs in seven different states and objected to the new policy; the organization faced significant financial losses if the policy remained in place. Among other arguments, Dismas Charities objected that the BOP failed to use notice and comment rulemaking to establish the new policy prohibiting the placement of federal prisoners in CCCs. *Id.* at 677. The merits of this claim turned on whether the BOP policy was a legitimate "interpretive rule" or, instead, a legislative rule requiring the use of notice and comment proceedings. Writing for the panel, Judge John M. Rogers (one of this casebook's co-authors) concluded that the BOP did not have to engage in notice and comment rulemaking to establish the new policy:

> The rulemaking requirements of § 553 of the APA do not apply to "interpretive rules." Both the Thomson [DOJ] and Sawyer [BOP] memoranda, assuming that either may be characterized as a "rule," clearly fall in the category of interpretative rule. The Attorney General's Manual on the Administrative Procedure Act, persuasive authority on the meaning of the APA, describes an interpretive rule as one "issued by an agency to advise the public of the agency's construction of the statutes and rules which it administers." The difference between legislative and interpretive rules "has to do in part with the authority — law-making versus law-interpreting — under which the rule is promulgated." *Warder v. Shalala*, 149 F.3d 73, 80 (1st Cir. 1998). "For purposes of the APA, substantive rules are rules that create law," while in contrast "[i]nterpretive rules merely clarify or explain existing law or regulations and go to what the administrative officer thinks the statute

or regulation means." *First National Bank v. Sanders*, 946 F.2d 1185, 1188-89 (6th Cir. 1991).

The distinction reflects the primary purpose of Congress in imposing notice and comment requirements for rulemaking — to get public input so as to get the wisest rules. That purpose is not served when the agency's inquiry or determination is not "what is the wisest rule," but "what is the rule." The interpretive rule exception reflects the idea that public input will not help an agency make the legal determination of what the law already is. The D.C. Circuit, for instance, in applying the interpretive rule exception, has "generally sought to distinguish cases in which an agency is merely explicating Congress' desires from those cases in which the agency is adding substantive content of its own."

It follows that the Thompson and Sawyer memoranda, assuming that either is a rule otherwise subject to the notice and comment requirements of the APA, are paradigm examples of interpretive rules. The memoranda each state that the statutory interpretation by the OLC will henceforth be implemented. The Thompson memorandum in its operative language relies specifically and directly on the unlawfulness of its previous practice as determined by the OLC. Even more clearly, the Sawyer memorandum does not make any kind of policy analysis or determine what is the better, or more effective, rule. Instead, the BOP changed its procedure because the "OLC . . . determined that the [BOP's] practice of using CCCs as a substitute for imprisonment contravenes well-established case law, and is inconsistent with U.S.S.G. § 5C1.1." Clearly, the memo simply determines what the law is, and does so by reliance upon a legal interpretation by the OLC. Notice and comment rulemaking proceedings are simply not designed as a means for agencies to improve their legal analysis. And it is the agency's legal analysis that Dismas challenges.

We recognize that some district courts have found that the BOP policy required notice and comment. Some of these cases rely on the idea that a rule is legislative rather than interpretive if it is "binding" or "nondiscretionary," and that the BOP policy, since binding, is not interpretive. The argument mistakes the extent to which a reviewing *court* is bound by a regulation with the extent to which an *agency* is bound. It is true that an interpretive rule is not binding upon a court, whereas a properly authorized legislative rule is so binding. But using that distinction, the BOP policy is interpretive, because the BOP's interpretation is not binding on reviewing courts, which may of course disagree with the government's statutory interpretation (as many have already done, see *Goldings*, 383 F.3d at 28-29, *Elwood*, 386 F.3d at 847). An interpretive regulation is binding on an *agency*, on the other hand, not by virtue of the promulgation of the regulation (as in the case of a legislative regulation), but by virtue of the binding nature of the interpreted statute. Such a binding nature cannot render a rule legislative, else every interpretive rule would become legislative.

Nor does the BOP memorandum lose its interpretive nature because of its substantial impact. The policies underlying the notice and comment requirement, and the apparent reasons for the exception for interpretive rules, are unrelated to the substantial impact of a rule. A pure statutory interpretation can have an enormous impact, yet be based entirely on statutory analysis for which public input would be of minimal value. Our court has accordingly rejected substantial impact as a basis for determining the applicability of the interpretive rule exception.

Finally, the rule is not legislative simply because it departs from the BOP's prior interpretation of § 3621. . . . Other circuits agree that "a new position does not necessarily make a rule legislative rather than interpretive." *Metro-politan School Dist. v. Davila*, 969 F.2d 485, 490 (7th Cir. 1992). This court accordingly has held that certain provisions of the Medicare Provider Reimbursement Manual were interpretive and therefore not subject to notice and comment despite the plaintiff's argument in that case that the provisions had changed. . . .

We take no position on the merits of Dismas's legal challenge to the BOP policy. We hold only that, under the interpretive rule exception, a rule that embodies a pure legal determination of what the applicable law already is does not require notice and comment under APA § 553(b).

Id. at 679-82.

Does the distinction between the mere interpretation of a statute and the creation of a legal norm or policy really work? How can you tell if a rule flows from a statute itself or rather reflects an agency's policy decision? Does it depend on whether the statute is vague?

8. There are (at least) two distinct approaches to the question of the permissible scope of interpretative rules and general statements of policy. One creates a strong bias in favor of forcing agencies to use notice and comment rulemaking whenever they create a binding norm (i.e., a norm that binds the agency, regardless of its effect on the courts). The best argument for this approach is that any less demanding standard will encourage agencies to establish poorly conceived policies through interpretive rules and general statements of policy. If an agency intends to create a binding norm with the force of law *within the agency*, it must use notice and comment rulemaking (or adjudication). From this perspective, both *Warder* and *Dismas Charities* are wrongly decided because both cases involve an agency creating a binding norm with the force of law without using notice and comment proceedings. There is also the question of providing significantly affected parties with prior notice of a change in policy and with an opportunity to share their views with an agency before the agency commits itself to a particular policy — whether that is classifying a device as "DME" rather than "braces" or prohibiting federal prisoners from serving time in community correction centers.

From the other perspective, however, agencies should be encouraged to create binding internal norms that arguably simply clarify what a statute already says without resorting to often cumbersome notice-and-comment informal rulemaking proceedings; this is the approach of *Warder* and *Dismas Charities*. From this perspective, forcing frequent recourse to informal rulemaking for small points of clarification has the effect of severely restricting the ability of agencies to use interpretive rules and general statements of policy to clarify how *existing* laws or regulations will apply to particular factual scenarios. If an agency is not creating a new legal norm, but simply announcing how it will apply existing legal norms in gray areas, the agency should not be required to engage in a duplicative notice and comment proceeding that does not change or modify any existing regulation. Moreover, as the *Dismas Charities* court points out, a reviewing court is not bound by an interpretive rule, even if the interpretive rule or general statement of policy binds the agency; accordingly, adversely affected parties are free to challenge the interpretation in court. Thus, if the BOP simply incorporates the Executive Branch's new interpretation of a statute, that decision should not trigger an obligation to provide opportunity for notice and comment.

9. Should the importance of the policy question affect the ability of an agency to establish ("clarify") how it will enforce a statute? Or if a policy question has a major impact on a nation-wide basis, should courts force agencies to use notice and comment rulemaking and disallow use of an interpretative rule to establish the policy? For example, the Fifth Circuit affirmed a federal district court order that rejected the Obama Administration's efforts to establish a major new immigration policy through an interpretative rule and required the administration to use notice and comment rulemaking proceedings instead. *See* Texas v. United States, 809 F. 3d 134 (5th Cir. 2015), *aff'd by an equally divided court*, 136 S. Ct. 2271 (2016). Writing for the majority, Judge Jerry Smith found that the DHS had adopted, in the guise of issuing interpretative rules, binding legislative rules that had the effect of establishing a brand new immigration program. The agency's new policy therefore constituted a legislative, rather than an interpretative, rule. See *id.* at 170-78. He added that "[w]e expect Congress to speak clearly if it wishes to assign to an agency decisions of vast economic and political significance" and that "[a]gency announcements to the contrary are greet[ed] . . . with a measure of skepticism." *Id.* at 188 (internal citations and quotations omitted).

A federal district court adopted a very similar approach to a new Department of Education policy regarding the ability of transgender persons to use bathrooms that correspond to their gender identity, rather than their cisgender, in public schools, colleges, and universities. *See* Texas v. United States, 2016 U.S. Dist. LEXIS 113459 (N.D. Tex. Aug. 21, 2016). District Judge Reed O'Connor explained that "[t]he Guidelines are, in practice, legislative rules — not just interpretations or policy statements because they set clear legal standards." *Id.* at *46. Accordingly, the Department of Education "should have complied with the APA's notice and comment requirement." *Id.* By way of contrast, the Department of Education argued that it was simply providing a gloss on the word "sex" as used in Title IX. The new interpretation of "sex" would have required all public schools receiving federal funds to permit transgender students to use a single-sex bathroom facility of their choice — on pain of losing all federal education funds for failure to comply with this policy requirement.

Should the potential scope of a policy "clarification" determine whether or not an agency may forgo notice and comment rulemaking? To be sure, the Supreme Court has not yet weighed in on this issue. However, decisions involving whether to apply *Chevron* deference to questions that have major economic effects could suggest that the Justices may, in the future, take the overall impact and importance of an agency policy into account when considering whether an agency may issue an interpretative rule rather than a legislative rule to establish how it will implement a particular statutory power. *See infra* pp. 609-619.

10. Even with the ambiguities that haunt this area of administrative law, there *are* cases that fall clearly on one side of the line or the other. If an agency

announces action levels at which it will bring enforcement proceedings to enforce a statute, the declaration qualifies as a general statement of policy. Under either *Mada-Luna* or *Warder,* the result is the same. Similarly, if the Federal Communications Commission is considering whether to authorize a new wireless broadcasting service, the agency would have to resort to notice and comment proceedings, rather than issue an interpretive rule, because the statute's "public interest" standard does not, of its own force, either require or prohibit the licensing of new services.

THEORY APPLIED PROBLEM

For each of the following hypotheticals, determine whether the agency could adopt the policy in question by using an interpretive rule or a general statement of policy, or rather whether a court would force the agency to use notice and comment rulemaking. Apply both the test from *Mada-Luna* and the test from *Warder* and *Dismas Charities.*

The Internal Revenue Service issues a general statement of policy that announces that persons who deduct more than 10 percent of their adjusted gross income for charitable donations on their federal income taxes will run a significantly higher risk of audit than those who deduct 10 percent or less of their adjusted gross income for charitable deductions.

The Federal Trade Commission issues an interpretive rule that declares the sale of repainted, but never titled, automobiles will constitute an "unfair or deceptive" trade practice in violation of the FTC Act unless the seller clearly marks the vehicle as "repainted" on the car itself in conspicuous print.

The EPA issues an interpretive rule declaring that the term "polluter" as used in several important sections of the Clean Water Act includes a supplier of toxic substances to a site where water pollution occurs, even if the supplier is not directly responsible for the release of the polluting substance into the water, thereby making the supplier of toxics liable for civil and criminal penalties under the Clean Water Act.

NOTE ON OTHER APA EXCEPTIONS FROM THE REQUIREMENTS FOR NOTICE-AND-COMMENT RULEMAKING

In addition to the APA's exceptions from the notice-and-comment requirements for statements of policy and for interpretive rules, the APA includes several other exceptions from the requirements of §553. These exceptions are less often litigated than the exceptions for statements of policy and for interpretive rules.

The first two of these exceptions are applicable when the regulations have a specific subject matter. The APA exempts from the applicability of §553 any regulation that "involve[s] — (1) a military or foreign affairs function of the United States." §553(a). In *Independent Guard Ass'n of Nevada, Local No. 1 v. O'Leary,* 57 F.3d 766 (9th Cir. 1995), the court considered whether the Department of Energy ("DOE") properly relied on the military function part of this exception when it adopted by regulation:

a Personnel Assurance Program ("PAP") applicable to all DOE and contractor employees assigned nuclear explosive duties. The PAP provides detailed certification requirements for the DOE and its contractor personnel who are certified to guard nuclear explosive devices in Nevada. For example, PAP disqualifies persons from such duties who fail to comply with any of its provisions, which include submission to laboratory testing, random drug testing, and a certification review procedure. PAP also provides for permanent disqualification from duty for any employee who has ever used hallucinogens, regardless of quantity consumed or remoteness in time.

Id. at 768. The court concluded, *id.* at 770, that the APA "exception can be invoked only where the activities being regulated directly involve a military function," and that there was no such direct involvement at issue in DOE's regulation:

contractor employees could perform a military function within the meaning of the APA. For example, if they were making military weapons, they might well be performing such a function. The record in this case, however, does not contain any evidence that the military has ever exercised any direct supervisorial control over the activities of these civilian contract guards. The record shows that the guards [at issue] were performing duties similar to those performed by civilian security guards everywhere. They were no more performing a "military function" than civilian contract guards employed to guard judges are performing a "judicial function." The exemption should not be stretched to encompass civilian support services.

The foreign affairs function part of the exception was applied by the court in *International Broth. of Teamsters v. Pena,* 17 F.3d 1478 (D.C. Cir. 1994). There, the court held that the Department of Transportation was permitted to forgo compliance with § 553 because the regulation implemented an international agreement between the United States and Mexico. See *id.* at 1486. *See also Zhang v. Slattery,* 55 F.3d 732, 744 (2d Cir. 1995) (rejecting applicability of the foreign affairs function exception because public consideration of the regulation would not result in "the public airing of matters that might enflame or embarrass relations with other countries").

The second subject-matter exception from the applicability of § 553 arises when "there is involved . . . (2) a matter relating to agency management or personnel or to public property, loans, grants, benefits, or contracts." § 553(a). This exception may reflect the acceptance of a right/privilege distinction by Congress when it enacted the APA in 1946 and its view that public involvement was not needed in the dispensation of government benefits. As illustrated by *National Wildlife Federation v. Snow,* 561 F.2d 227 (D.C. Cir. 1976), this exception can be quite broad in its application. There, the court concluded, *id.* at 234, that:

there can be no doubt that the regulations challenged in this case are both clearly and directly related to a federal grant program. One changes the approval process necessary to maintain state highway department eligibility for federal funds; the other allows federal funds to be used for right-of-way acquisitions before the normal location and design approvals have been given. These regulatory decisions go beyond mere managerial mechanics. They directly affect the general public's hearing and participation rights in the administration of the federal grant-in-aid program. However, there is a clear and direct connection with an exempted "proprietary" subject, and this excuses the [Federal Highway Administration] from an overall statutory obligation to comply with notice and comment procedures in promulgating the challenged regulations.

The potential breadth of the §553(a)(2) exception has caused both the judiciary and, more importantly, the executive to act to limit its applicability and thereby increase public involvement in government grant programs:

> the exceptions for grants, benefits, and contracts have met substantial criticism and we believe they should be narrowly construed. In 1970 the Administrative Conference of the United States recommended that governmental agencies agree to follow rulemaking procedures even if the subject matter would fall within the APA's exceptions for grants, benefits, and contracts. *See Rodway v. USDA,* 514 F.2d 809, 814 (D.C. Cir. 1975). Many agencies adopted this recommendation as an agency requirement. *See,* e.g., 29 C.F.R. §2.7 (1981) (Department of Labor); 36 Fed. Reg. 13,804 (1971) (Department of Agriculture); 36 Fed. Reg. 2,532 (1971) (Department of Health, Education and Welfare). Of special significance to this case is that on May 14, 1971, the Department of the Interior adopted the same requirement for it and its agencies, including the [Bureau of Indian Affairs], to follow in their subsequent actions. 36 Fed. Reg. 8,336 (1971). By adopting this requirement, the Department of the Interior has expressly recognized that the advantages of public participation in policy decisions affecting public benefits outweigh the disadvantages. This buttresses our conclusion that the exceptions do not apply here.

Vigil v. Andrus, 667 F.2d 931, 937 (10th Cir. 1982).

In addition to exempting regulations with a defined substantive content from its requirements, §553 also exempts "rules of agency organization, procedure, or practice" from its requirements. The D.C. Circuit has applied the exception for "rules of agency procedure" to permit the FHWA to issue a Motor Carrier Administrative Training Manual, that was "used to train FHWA investigative staff." *Aulenback, Inc. v. Federal Highway Administration,* 103 F.3d 156, 163 (D.C. Cir. 1997). Parties challenging the agency's decision to issue "out-of-service" orders claimed that the manual had changed the statutory requirements for issuing those administrative orders and that, even if the statutory requirements had not been changed, the manual could be issued only in accordance with APA requirements for notice-and-comment rulemaking. The court held that the claim that the manual had changed the statute's requirements for "out-of-service" orders was not ripe for review. (The question of ripeness for judicial review is addressed in Chapter 5, *infra* at p. 507.) The court then rejected the claim, *id.* at 168-69, that issuance of the manual without notice and comment violated the APA:

> The exception that is relevant here applies to "interpretive rules, general statements of policy, or rules of agency organization, procedure, or practice." §553(b)(3)(A). The FHWA maintains that the "rules" contained in the Manual could be described as falling into any of these three categories. We conclude that, if the guidelines in the Manual do not impermissibly alter statutory definition of an "imminent hazard," they are merely rules of agency procedure and practice, and that the FHWA was, therefore, not required to provide notice and an opportunity for public comment before issuing the Manual to its staff.

The primary purpose of the procedural rules exemption in § 553 is "to ensure 'that agencies retain latitude in organizing their internal operations.'" *American Hospital Ass'n v. Bowen*, 834 F.2d 1037, 1047 (D.C. Cir. 1987) (quoting *Batterton v. Marshall*, 648 F.2d 694, 707 (D.C. Cir. 1980)). In *American Hospital Association*, the court recognized that "enforcement plans developed by agencies to direct their enforcement activity warrant considerable deference" and are typically exempt from notice and comment requirements. *Id.* at 1050. Consequently, the court held that two manuals issued by the Department of Health and Human Services to govern the manner in which "peer review organizations" monitored the activities of Medicare providers were procedural rules exempt from § 553. *Id.* at 1049-51. Similarly, in *United States Department of Labor v. Kast Metals Corp.*, 744 F.2d 1145 (5th Cir. 1984), the Fifth Circuit held that an agency rule used to target employers for routine health and safety inspections was an exempt procedural rule. *Id.* at 1151-56. That the FHWA's Manual gives Regional Directors "crisper and more detailed" guidance on the identification of carriers whose operations pose imminent hazards than that provided by 49 U.S.C. § 521(b)(5)(B) does not render the Manual's provisions subject to notice and comment requirements. *American Mining Congress v. Mine Safety & Health Admin.*, 995 F.2d 1106, 1112 (D.C. Cir. 1993). The court has recognized that agencies do not "develop written guidelines to aid their exercise of discretion only at the peril of having a court transmogrify those guidelines into binding norms" subject to notice and comment strictures. *Community Nutrition Inst. v. Young*, 818 F.2d 943, 949 (D.C. Cir. 1987) (*per curiam*).

The guidelines in the Manual fit comfortably within the analytical framework of *American Hospital Association* and *Kast Metals*. They do not impose new substantive burdens, in the sense that they either require or prohibit any particular actions on the part of motor carriers. Carriers are obliged to comply with all valid and applicable federal safety rules, regardless of whether the FHWA has authority to suspend their operations for non-compliance. Nor does the Manual mandate that the FHWA take action upon making certain findings. The Manual simply provides guidance for FHWA administrators seeking to identify motor carrier operations that pose a potential danger to public safety. We hold, therefore, that the Manual's guidelines are procedural rules that are exempt from the APA's notice and comment requirements, 5 U.S.C. § 553.

The 1981 MSAPA includes an analogous exception for rules "concerning only the internal management of an agency." § 3-116(1).

The final exemption from the requirements of § 553 applies "when the agency for good cause finds (and incorporates the finding and a brief statement of reasons therefor in the rules issued) that notice and public procedure thereon are impracticable, unnecessary, or contrary to the public interest." § 553(b)(3)(B). This "good cause" exception thus itself identifies the broad limits on its application: the exception applies only when compliance with procedures is "impracticable, unnecessary, or contrary to the public interest." In *Hawaii Helicopter Operators Association v. Federal Aviation Administration*, 51 F.3d 212, 213 (9th Cir. 1995), the Ninth Circuit upheld the agency's reliance on the good cause exception in its "issuance of Special Federal Aviation Regulation ("SFAR") No. 71 establishing special operating rules, procedures and limitations for airplane and helicopter air tour operators in Hawaii."

This court has said that our "inquiry into whether the Secretary properly invoked 'good cause' proceeds case-by-case, sensitive to the totality of the factors at play." *Alcaraz v. Block,* 746 F.2d 593, 612 (9th Cir. 1984). We have observed that notice and comment procedures should be waived only when "delay would do real harm." *Buschmann v. Schweiker,* 676 F.2d 352, 357 (9th Cir. 1982).

In this case the FAA based its invocation of the "good cause" exception on Hawaii's "recent escalation of fatal air tour accidents." The FAA further explained that the problem was urgent:

"Despite voluntary measures, the cooperation of the Hawaii air tour operators, and the FAA's inspections, the accident data show that voluntary measures and existing regulations are insufficient to ensure safe air tour operations in Hawaii. The recent accidents . . . indicate an urgent safety problem that cannot be adequately addressed solely by enforcement of existing regulations."

Air Tour Operators in the State of Hawaii, 59 Fed. Reg. 49138, 49145 (Sept. 26, 1994). The FAA listed specific facts supporting its reasons for issuing SFAR No. 71. These facts included: (1) there had been 20 air tour accidents between 1991 and 1994, including 24 fatalities; (2) among the 20 accidents, seven had occurred in 1994; (3) the most recent fatal accident had occurred on July 14, 1994; (4) the most recent non-fatal accident had occurred on September 4, 1994, only three weeks before SFAR No. 71 was promulgated.

We perceive no indication in this record that the FAA waived notice and comment for any reasons other than its concern about the threat to public safety reflected in an increasing number of helicopter accidents. The FAA adequately explained the basis for taking emergency action without waiting for public participation. Compare *San Diego Air Sports Center, Inc. v. FAA,* 887 F.2d 966, 970 (9th Cir. 1989) (FAA did not comply with provisions of § 553 when it issued letter disallowing parachuting without any explanation of why it felt emergency action was needed and where only known accident had occurred two years earlier).

Compare the Sixth Circuit's rejection of an agency's reliance on the good cause exception in *United States v. Cain,* 583 F.3d 408, 420-23 (6th Cir. 2009) (rejecting the Attorney General's invocation of the "good cause" exception because "the Attorney General gave no specific evidence of actual harm to the public in his conclusory statement of reasons, and gave no explanation for why he could act in an emergency fashion when Congress had not deemed the situation so critical seven months earlier" and contrasting these facts from circumstances in which an "agency ha[s] specific reasons to conclude that its existing regulations insufficiently protected public safety, and those reasons arose after the existing regulations went into effect," which constitute "reasons [that] justif[y] issuing an emergency regulation") and the Second Circuit's similar conclusion in *Zhang v. Slattery,* 55 F.3d 732, 746 (2d Cir. 1995) ("The [challenged interim] rule itself contains a largely conclusory statement that its immediate promulgation is necessary in order to benefit the greatest number of aliens. That is not enough. Presumably, agencies deem all their rules beneficial; the notice and comment requirement would be a dead letter if compliance could be excused whenever the beneficial effect would thereby be accelerated"). *But cf.* Electronic Privacy Information Ctr. v. U.S. Dep't of Homeland Security, 653 F.3d 1 (D.C. Cir. 2011) (upholding deployment of nude full body scanners at some TSA checkpoints in U.S. airports under regulations adopted without *any* opportunity for public notice and comment, even though "the TSA has advanced no justification for having failed to conduct notice-and-comment rulemaking," because "vacating the present rule would severely disrupt an essential security operation" and "the rule is . . . otherwise lawful," noting that "we do nonetheless expect the agency to act promptly on remand to cure the defect in its promulgation," and expressly declining to reach the TSA's argument that the regulations are exempt from notice-and-comment rulemaking procedures under the "good cause" exception).

Keep in mind that Congress may authorize agencies to regulate before providing an opportunity for notice and comment. If Congress authorizes an exception to the generic rulemaking requirements of the APA, then an agency may act consistently with the authorization. The IRS, for example, has express statutory authority to adopt so-called "interim-final" regulations and to apply these regulations to taxpayers *before* providing interested parties with notice and an opportunity for comment. *See* 26 U.S.C. § 7805(b) (2016); *see also* James M. Puckett, *Embracing the Queen of Hearts: Deference to Retroactive Tax Rules*, 40 FLA. ST. U.L. REV. 349, 366-73 (2013) (describing and discussing the use of so-called "interim-final" regulations by the IRS); James M. Puckett, *Structural Tax Exceptionalism*, 49 GA. L. REV. 1067, 1094-1100 (2015) (discussing the IRS's use of interim-final regulations and the IRS's routine use of retroactive rulemaking more generally). Subject to the constraints of procedural due process — which are few and very limited in the context of quasi-legislative rulemaking — Congress is free to authorize agencies to regulate first and provide an opportunity for notice and comment after the fact. Of course, whether an agency is truly open to considering public comment after it has already adopted and begun to enforce a regulation is open to serious question — if not outright doubt. See Brief of Amicus Curiae Professor Kristin E. Hickman in Support of Respondents, at 14-19, United States v. Home Concrete & Supply, LLC, 132 S. Ct. 1836 (2012) (No. 11-139) (arguing that interim-final regulations unlawfully deny interested parties a meaningful opportunity to comment on binding new IRS regulations without a sufficient legal justification).

The 1981 MSAPA § 3-108 defines a good-cause exception to its procedural rulemaking requirements. That statute also includes a provision allowing the governor or an administrative rules committee to compel adoption of the rule in accordance with normal procedural requirements. *See* § 3-108(c).

D. BEYOND NOTICE AND COMMENT: "FORMAL," "HYBRID," AND NEGOTIATED RULEMAKING

In 1972, Professor Robert W. Hamilton wrote two law review articles that described the difficulties that formal rulemaking posed for agencies. In summarizing formal rulemaking proceedings administered by the Food and Drug Administration, Professor Hamilton wrote that the formal rulemakings "var[ied] from unnecessarily drawn out proceedings to virtual disasters." Robert W. Hamilton, *Procedures for the Adoption of Rules of General Applicability: The Need for Procedural Innovation in Administrative Rulemaking*, 60 Cal. L. Rev. 1276, 1287 (1972). These formal proceedings had an average length of "roughly four years." *Id.* (footnote omitted). Moreover, they yielded records that "tended to be drawn out, repetitious and unproductive." *Id.* Professor Hamilton described how one FDA formal "proceeding involving the standard of identity for peanut butter developed a transcript of over 7,700 pages, largely directed to the question of whether the product peanut butter should consist of 90 percent peanuts or 87 percent peanuts [see 32 Fed. Reg. 17,482 (1967)]." *Id.* at 1287-88 (footnote omitted). He concluded that: "The actual agency experience with [formal rulemaking] requirements raises serious doubts about their desirability. . . . In practice, . . . the principal effect of imposing rulemaking on a record has often been the dilution of the regulatory process rather than the protection of persons from arbitrary action." *Id.* at 1312-13. *See also* Robert W. Hamilton, *Rulemaking on a Record by the Food and Drug Administration,* 50 Tex. L. Rev. 1132 (1972).

UNITED STATES v. FLORIDA EAST COAST RAILWAY CO.
410 U.S. 224 (1973)

MR. JUSTICE REHNQUIST delivered the opinion of the Court.

Appellees, two railroad companies, brought this action in the District Court for the Middle District of Florida to set aside the incentive per diem rates established by appellant Interstate Commerce Commission in a rulemaking proceeding. *Incentive Per Diem Charges — 1968, Ex parte No. 252 (Sub-No. 1),* 337 I. C. C. 217 (1970). They challenged the order of the Commission on both substantive and procedural grounds. The District Court sustained appellees' position that the Commission had failed to comply with the applicable provisions of the Administrative Procedure Act, 5 U.S.C. § 551 *et seq.,* and therefore set aside the order without dealing with the railroads' other contentions. The District Court held that the language of § 1 (14)(a)[1] of the Interstate Commerce Act, 24 Stat. 379, as amended, 49 U.S.C. § 1 (14)(a), required the Commission in a proceeding such as this to act in accordance with the Administrative Procedure Act, 5 U.S.C. § 556 (d), and that the Commission's determination to receive submissions from the appellees only in written form was a violation of that section because the appellees were "prejudiced" by that determination within the meaning of that section.

Following our decision last Term in *United States v. Allegheny-Ludlum Steel Corp.,* 406 U.S. 742 (1972), we noted probable jurisdiction and requested the parties to brief the question of whether the Commission's proceeding was governed by 5 U.S.C. § 553, or by §§ 556 and 557, of the Administrative Procedure Act. We here decide that the Commission's proceeding was governed only by § 553 of that Act, and that appellees received the "hearing" required by § 1 (14)(a) of the Interstate Commerce Act. We, therefore, reverse the judgment of the District Court and remand the case to that court for further consideration of appellees' other contentions that were raised there, but which we do not decide.

---

1. Section 1 (14)(a) provides:

   The Commission may, after hearing, on a complaint or upon its own initiative without complaint, establish reasonable rules, regulations, and practices with respect to car service by common carriers by railroad subject to this chapter, including the compensation to be paid and other terms of any contract, agreement, or arrangement for the use of any locomotive, car, or other vehicle not owned by the carrier using it (and whether or not owned by another carrier), and the penalties or other sanctions for nonobservance of such rules, regulations, or practices. . . .

I. Background of Chronic Freight Car Shortages

This case arises from the factual background of a chronic freight-car shortage on the Nation's railroads, which we described in *United States v. Allegheny-Ludlum Steel Corp., supra.* Judge Simpson, writing for the District Court in this case, noted that "for a number of years portions of the nation have been plagued with seasonal shortages of freight cars in which to ship goods." Judge Friendly, writing for a three-judge District Court in the Eastern District of New York in the related case of *Long Island R. Co. v. United States*, 318 F. Supp. 490, 491 (EDNY 1970), described the Commission's order as "the latest chapter in a long history of freight-car shortages in certain regions and seasons and of attempts to ease them." Congressional concern for the problem was manifested in the enactment in 1966 of an amendment to § 1(14)(a) of the Interstate Commerce Act, enlarging the Commission's authority to prescribe per diem charges for the use by one railroad of freight cars owned by another. Pub. L. 89-430, 80 Stat.168. The Senate Committee on Commerce stated in its report accompanying this legislation:

> "Car shortages, which once were confined to the Midwest during harvest seasons, have become increasingly more frequent, more severe, and nationwide in scope as the national freight car supply has plummeted." S. Rep. No. 386, 89th Cong., 1st Sess., 1-2.

The Commission in 1966 commenced an investigation, *Ex parte* No. 252, Incentive Per Diem Charges, "to determine whether information presently available warranted the establishment of an incentive element increase, on an interim basis, to apply pending further study and investigation." 332 I. C. C. 11, 12 (1967). Statements of position were received from the Commission staff and a number of railroads. Hearings were conducted at which witnesses were examined. In October 1967, the Commission rendered a decision discontinuing the earlier proceeding, but announcing a program of further investigation into the general subject.

In December 1967, the Commission initiated the rulemaking procedure giving rise to the order that appellees here challenge. It directed Class I and Class II line-haul railroads to compile and report detailed information with respect to freight-car demand and supply at numerous sample stations for selected days of the week during 12 four-week periods, beginning January 29, 1968.

Some of the affected railroads voiced questions about the proposed study or requested modification in the study procedures outlined by the Commission in its notice of proposed rulemaking. In response to petitions setting forth these carriers' views, the Commission staff held an informal conference in April 1968, at which the objections and proposed modifications were discussed. Twenty railroads, including appellee Seaboard, were represented at this conference, at which the Commission's staff sought to answer questions about reporting methods to accommodate individual circumstances of particular railroads. The conference adjourned on a note that undoubtedly left the impression that hearings would be held at some future date. A detailed report of the conference was sent to all parties to the proceeding before the Commission.

The results of the information thus collected were analyzed and presented to Congress by the Commission during a hearing before the Subcommittee on

Surface Transportation of the Senate Committee on Commerce in May 1969. Members of the Subcommittee expressed dissatisfaction with the Commission's slow pace in exercising the authority that had been conferred upon it by the 1966 Amendments to the Interstate Commerce Act. Judge Simpson in his opinion for the District Court said:

> "Members of the Senate Subcommittee on Surface Transportation expressed considerable dissatisfaction with the Commission's apparent inability to take effective steps toward eliminating the national shortage of freight cars. Comments were general that the Commission was conducting too many hearings and taking too little action. Senators pressed for more action and less talk, but Commission counsel expressed doubt respecting the Commission's statutory power to act without additional hearings."

Judge Friendly, describing the same event in *Long Island R. Co. v. United States, supra,* said:

> "To say that the presentation was not received with enthusiasm would be a considerable understatement. Senators voiced displeasure at the Commission's long delay at taking action under the 1966 amendment, engaged in some merriment over what was regarded as an unintelligible discussion of methodology . . . and expressed doubt about the need for a hearing. . . . But the Commission's general counsel insisted that a hearing was needed . . . and the chairman of the commission agreed. . . ." 318 F. Supp., at 494.

The Commission, now apparently imbued with a new sense of mission, issued in December 1969 an interim report announcing its tentative decision to adopt incentive per diem charges on standard boxcars based on the information compiled by the railroads. The substantive decision reached by the Commission was that so-called "incentive" per diem charges should be paid by any railroad using on its lines a standard boxcar owned by another railroad. Before the enactment of the 1966 amendment to the Interstate Commerce Act, it was generally thought that the Commission's authority to fix per diem payments for freight car use was limited to setting an amount that reflected fair return on investment for the owning railroad, without any regard being had for the desirability of prompt return to the owning line or for the encouragement of additional purchases of freight cars by the railroads as a method of investing capital. The Commission concluded, however, that in view of the 1966 amendment it could impose additional "incentive" per diem charges to spur prompt return of existing cars and to make acquisition of new cars financially attractive to the railroads. It did so by means of a proposed schedule that established such charges on an across-the-board basis for all common carriers by railroads subject to the Interstate Commerce Act. Embodied in the report was a proposed rule adopting the Commission's tentative conclusions and a notice to the railroads to file statements of position within 60 days, couched in the following language:

> "That verified statements of facts, briefs, and statements of position respecting the tentative conclusions reached in the said interim report, the rules and regulations proposed in the appendix to this order, and any other pertinent matter, are hereby invited to be submitted pursuant to the filing schedule set forth below by an

interested person whether or not such person is already a party to this proceeding. . . ."

"That any party requesting oral hearing shall set forth with specificity the need therefore and the evidence to be adduced."

Both appellee railroads filed statements objecting to the Commission's proposal and requesting an oral hearing, as did numerous other railroads. In April 1970, the Commission, without having held further "hearings," issued a supplemental report making some modifications in the tentative conclusions earlier reached, but overruling *in toto* the requests of appellees.

The District Court held that in so doing the Commission violated § 556 (d) of the Administrative Procedure Act, and it was on this basis that it set aside the order of the Commission.

II. APPLICABILITY OF ADMINISTRATIVE PROCEDURE ACT

In *United States v. Allegheny-Ludlum Steel Corp., supra,* we held that the language of § 1 (14)(a) of the Interstate Commerce Act authorizing the Commission to act "after hearing" was not the equivalent of a requirement that a rule be made "on the record after opportunity for an agency hearing" as the latter term is used in § 553 (c) of the Administrative Procedure Act. Since the 1966 amendment to § 1 (14)(a), under which the Commission was here proceeding, does not by its terms add to the hearing requirement contained in the earlier language, the same result should obtain here unless that amendment contains language that is tantamount to such a requirement. Appellees contend that such language is found in the provisions of that Act requiring that:

"[T]he Commission shall give consideration to the national level of ownership of such type of freight car and to other factors affecting the adequacy of the national freight car supply, and shall, on the basis of such consideration, determine whether compensation should be computed. . . ."

While this language is undoubtedly a mandate to the Commission to consider the factors there set forth in reaching any conclusion as to imposition of per diem incentive charges, it adds to the hearing requirements of the section neither expressly nor by implication. We know of no reason to think that an administrative agency in reaching a decision cannot accord consideration to factors such as those set forth in the 1966 amendment by means other than a trial-type hearing or the presentation of oral argument by the affected parties. Congress by that amendment specified necessary components of the ultimate decision, but it did not specify the method by which the Commission should acquire information about those components.

Both of the district courts that reviewed this order of the Commission concluded that its proceedings were governed by the stricter requirements of §§ 556 and 557 of the Administrative Procedure Act, rather than by the provisions of § 553 alone. The conclusion of the District Court for the Middle District of Florida, which we here review, was based on the assumption that the language in § 1 (14)(a) of the Interstate Commerce Act requiring rulemaking under that section to be done "after hearing" was the equivalent of a statutory requirement that the rule "be made on the record after opportunity for an agency hearing." Such an assumption is inconsistent with our decision in *Allegheny-Ludlum, supra.*

The District Court for the Eastern District of New York reached the same conclusion by a somewhat different line of reasoning. That court felt that because § 1 (14)(a) of the Interstate Commerce Act had required a "hearing," and because that section was originally enacted in 1917, Congress was probably thinking in terms of a "hearing" such as that described in the opinion of this Court in the roughly contemporaneous case of *ICC v. Louisville & Nashville R. Co.,* 227 U.S. 88, 93 (1913). The ingredients of the "hearing" were there said to be that "all parties must be fully apprised of the evidence submitted or to be considered, and must be given opportunity to cross-examine witnesses, to inspect documents and to offer evidence in explanation or rebuttal." Combining this view of congressional understanding of the term "hearing" with comments by the chairman of the commission at the time of the adoption of the 1966 legislation regarding the necessity for "hearings," that court concluded that Congress had, in effect, required that these proceedings be "on the record after opportunity for an agency hearing" within the meaning of § 553 (c) of the Administrative Procedure Act.

Insofar as this conclusion is grounded on the belief that the language "after hearing" of § 1 (14)(a), without more, would trigger the applicability of §§ 556 and 557, it, too, is contrary to our decision in *Allegheny-Ludlum, supra.* The District Court observed that it was "rather hard to believe that the last sentence of § 553 (c) was directed only to the few legislative sports where the words 'on the record' or their equivalent had found their way into the statute book." This is, however, the language which Congress used, and since there are statutes on the books that do use these very words, *see,* e.g., the Fulbright Amendment to the Walsh-Healey Act, 41 U.S.C. § 43a, and 21 U.S.C. § 371 (e)(3), the regulations provision of the Food and Drug Act, adherence to that language cannot be said to render the provision nugatory or ineffectual. We recognized in *Allegheny-Ludlum* that the actual words "on the record" and "after . . . hearing" used in § 553 were not words of art, and that other statutory language having the same meaning could trigger the provisions of §§ 556 and 557 in rulemaking proceedings. But we adhere to our conclusion, expressed in that case, that the phrase "after hearing" in § 1 (14)(a) of the Interstate Commerce Act does not have such an effect.

III. "Hearing" Requirement of § 1 (14)(a) of the Interstate Commerce Act

Inextricably intertwined with the hearing requirement of the Administrative Procedure Act in this case is the meaning to be given to the language "after hearing" in § 1 (14)(a) of the Interstate Commerce Act. Appellees, both here and in the court below, contend that the Commission procedure here fell short of that mandated by the "hearing" requirement of § 1 (14)(a), even though it may have satisfied § 553 of the Administrative Procedure Act. The Administrative Procedure Act states that none of its provisions "limit or repeal additional requirements imposed by statute or otherwise recognized by law." 5 U.S.C. § 559. Thus, even though the Commission was not required to comply with §§ 556 and 557 of that Act, it was required to accord the "hearing" specified in § 1 (14)(a) of the Interstate Commerce Act. Though the District Court did not pass on this contention, it is so closely related to the claim based on the Administrative Procedure Act that we proceed to decide it now.

If we were to agree with the reasoning of the District Court for the Eastern District of New York with respect to the type of hearing required by the Interstate Commerce Act, the Commission's action might well violate those requirements, even though it was consistent with the requirements of the Administrative Procedure Act.

The term "hearing" in its legal context undoubtedly has a host of meanings. Its meaning undoubtedly will vary, depending on whether it is used in the context of a rulemaking-type proceeding or in the context of a proceeding devoted to the adjudication of particular disputed facts. It is by no means apparent what the drafters of the Esch Car Service Act of 1917, 40 Stat. 101, which became the first part of § 1 (14)(a) of the Interstate Commerce Act, meant by the term. Such an intent would surely be an ephemeral one if, indeed, Congress in 1917 had in mind anything more specific than the language it actually used, for none of the parties refer to any legislative history that would shed light on the intended meaning of the words "after hearing." What is apparent, though, is that the term was used in granting authority to the Commission to make rules and regulations of a prospective nature.

Appellees refer us to testimony of the chairman of the commission to the effect that if the added authority ultimately contained in the 1966 amendment were enacted, the Commission would proceed with "great caution" in imposing incentive per diem rates, and to statements of both Commission personnel and Members of Congress as to the necessity for a "hearing" before Commission action. Certainly, the lapse of time of more than three years between the enactment of the 1966 amendment and the Commission's issuance of its tentative conclusions cannot be said to evidence any lack of caution on the part of that body. Nor do generalized references to the necessity for a hearing advance our inquiry, since the statute by its terms requires a "hearing"; the more precise inquiry of whether the hearing requirements necessarily include submission of oral testimony, cross-examination, or oral arguments is not resolved by such comments as these.

Under these circumstances, confronted with a grant of substantive authority made after the Administrative Procedure Act was enacted, we think that reference to that Act, in which Congress devoted itself exclusively to questions such as the nature and scope of hearings, is a satisfactory basis for determining what is meant by the term "hearing" used in another statute. Turning to that Act, we are convinced that the term "hearing" as used therein does not necessarily embrace either the right to present evidence orally and to cross-examine opposing witnesses, or the right to present oral argument to the agency's decisionmaker.

Section 553 excepts from its requirements rulemaking devoted to "interpretative rules, general statements of policy, or rules of agency organization, procedure, or practice," and rulemaking "when the agency for good cause finds . . . that notice and public procedure thereon are impracticable, unnecessary, or contrary to the public interest." This exception does not apply, however, "when notice or hearing is required by statute"; in those cases, even though interpretative rulemaking be involved, the requirements of § 553 apply. But since these requirements themselves do not mandate any oral presentation, see *Allegheny-Ludlum, supra,* it cannot be doubted that a statute that requires a "hearing" prior to rulemaking may in some circumstances be satisfied by procedures that meet only the standards of §553. The Court's opinion in *FPC v. Texaco Inc.*, 377 U.S. 33 (1964), supports such a broad definition of the term "hearing."

Similarly, even where the statute requires that the rulemaking procedure take place "on the record after opportunity for an agency hearing," thus triggering the applicability of §556, subsection (d) provides that the agency may proceed by the submission of all or part of the evidence in written form if a party will not be "prejudiced thereby." Again, the Act makes it plain that a specific statutory mandate that the proceedings take place on the record after hearing may be satisfied in some circumstances by evidentiary submission in written form only.

We think this treatment of the term "hearing" in the Administrative Procedure Act affords a sufficient basis for concluding that the requirement of a "hearing" contained in §1 (14)(a), in a situation where the Commission was acting under the 1966 statutory rulemaking authority that Congress had conferred upon it, did not by its own force require the Commission either to hear oral testimony, to permit cross-examination of Commission witnesses, or to hear oral argument. Here, the Commission promulgated a tentative draft of an order, and accorded all interested parties 60 days in which to file statements of position, submissions of evidence, and other relevant observations. The parties had fair notice of exactly what the Commission proposed to do, and were given an opportunity to comment, to object, or to make some other form of written submission. The final order of the Commission indicates that it gave consideration to the statements of the two appellees here. Given the "open-ended" nature of the proceedings, and the Commission's announced willingness to consider proposals for modification after operating experience had been acquired, we think the hearing requirement of §1 (14)(a) of the Act was met.

Appellee railroads cite a number of our previous decisions dealing in some manner with the right to a hearing in an administrative proceeding. Although appellees have asserted no claim of constitutional deprivation in this proceeding, some of the cases they rely upon expressly speak in constitutional terms, while others are less than clear as to whether they depend upon the Due Process Clause of the Fifth and Fourteenth Amendments to the Constitution, or upon generalized principles of administrative law formulated prior to the adoption of the Administrative Procedure Act. . . .

ICC v. Louisville & Nashville R. Co., 227 U.S. 88 (1913), involved what the Court there described as a "quasi-judicial" proceeding of a quite different nature from the one we review here. The provisions of the Interstate Commerce Act, 24 Stat. 379, as amended, and of the Hepburn Act, 34 Stat. 584, in effect at the time that case was decided, left to the railroad carriers the "primary right to make rates," 227 U.S., at 92, but granted to the Commission the authority to set them aside, if after hearing, they were shown to be unreasonable. The proceeding before the Commission in that case had been instituted by the New Orleans Board of Trade complaint that certain class and commodity rates charged by the Louisville & Nashville Railroad from New Orleans to other points were unfair, unreasonable, and discriminatory. 227 U.S., at 90. The type of proceeding there, in which the Commission adjudicated a complaint by a shipper that specified rates set by a carrier were unreasonable, was sufficiently different from the nationwide incentive payments ordered to be made by all railroads in this proceeding so as to make the *Louisville & Nashville* opinion inapplicable in the case presently before us.

The basic distinction between rulemaking and adjudication is illustrated by this Court's treatment of two related cases under the Due Process Clause of the Fourteenth Amendment. In *Londoner v. Denver,* cited in oral argument by appellees, 210 U.S. 373 (1908), the Court held that due process had not been accorded a landowner who objected to the amount assessed against his land as its share of the benefit resulting from the paving of a street. Local procedure had accorded him the right to file a written complaint and objection, but not to be heard orally. This Court held that due process of law required that he "have the right to support his allegations by argument however brief, and, if need be, by proof, however informal." *Id.,* at 386. But in the later case of *Bi-Metallic Investment Co. v. State Board of Equalization,* 239 U.S. 441 (1915), the Court held that no hearing at all was constitutionally required prior to a decision by state tax officers in Colorado to increase the valuation of all taxable property in Denver by a substantial percentage. The Court distinguished *Londoner* by stating that there a small number of persons "were exceptionally affected, in each case upon individual grounds." *Id.,* at 446.

Later decisions have continued to observe the distinction adverted to in *Bi-Metallic Investment Co., supra.* In *Ohio Bell Telephone Co. v. Public Utilities Comm'n,* 301 U.S. 292, 304-305 (1937), the Court noted the fact that the administrative proceeding there involved was designed to require the utility to refund previously collected rate charges. The Court held that in such a proceeding the agency could not, consistently with due process, act on the basis of undisclosed evidence that was never made a part of the record before the agency. The case is thus more akin to *Louisville & Nashville R. Co., supra,* than it is to this case. *FCC v. WJR,* 337 U.S. 265 (1949), established that there was no across-the-board constitutional right to oral argument in every administrative proceeding regardless of its nature. While the line dividing them may not always be a bright one, these decisions represent a recognized distinction in administrative law between proceedings for the purpose of promulgating policy-type rules or standards, on the one hand, and proceedings designed to adjudicate disputed facts in particular cases on the other.

Here, the incentive payments proposed by the Commission in its tentative order, and later adopted in its final order, were applicable across the board to all of the common carriers by railroad subject to the Interstate Commerce Act. No effort was made to single out any particular railroad for special consideration based on its own peculiar circumstances. Indeed, one of the objections of appellee Florida East Coast was that it and other terminating carriers should have been treated differently from the generality of the railroads. But the fact that the order may in its effects have been thought more disadvantageous by some railroads than by others does not change its generalized nature. Though the Commission obviously relied on factual inferences as a basis for its order, the source of these factual inferences was apparent to anyone who read the order of December 1969. The factual inferences were used in the formulation of a basically legislative-type judgment, for prospective application only, rather than in adjudicating a particular set of disputed facts.

The Commission's procedure satisfied both the provisions of §1 (14)(a) of the Interstate Commerce Act and of the Administrative Procedure Act, and were not inconsistent with prior decisions of this Court. We, therefore, reverse the judgment of the District Court, and remand the case so that it may consider those contentions of the parties that are not disposed of by this opinion. *It is so ordered.*

[Justice Powell did not participate, and Justices Douglas and Stewart filed a dissent with the following opening summary:

> The present decision makes a sharp break with traditional concepts of procedural due process. The Commission order under attack is tantamount to a rate order. Charges are fixed that nonowning railroads must pay owning railroads for boxcars of the latter that are on the tracks of the former. These charges are effective only during the months of September through February, the period of greatest boxcar use. For example, the charge for a boxcar that costs from $15,000 to $17,000 and that is five years of age or younger amounts to $5.19 a day. Boxcars costing between $39,000 and $41,000 and that are five years of age or younger cost the nonowning railroad $12.98 a day. The fees or rates charged decrease as the ages of the boxcars lengthen. 49 CFR § 1036.2. This is the imposition on carriers by administrative fiat of a new financial liability. I do not believe it is within our traditional concepts of due process to allow an administrative agency to saddle anyone with a new rate, charge, or fee without a full hearing that includes the right to present oral testimony, cross-examine witnesses, and present oral argument. That is required by the Administrative Procedure Act, 5 U.S.C. § 556 (d); § 556 (a) states that § 556 applies to hearings required by § 553. Section 553 (c) provides that § 556 applies "when rules are required by statute to be made on the record after opportunity for an agency hearing." A hearing under § 1 (14)(a) of the Interstate Commerce Act fixing rates, charges, or fees is certainly adjudicatory, not legislative in the customary sense. . . .]

QUESTIONS

1. The railroads wanted the ICC to hold an oral hearing. Why? Would an oral hearing be useful? What would transpire?
2. Distinguish among three bases for the procedural challenges raised in this case. How was each decided?
3. Are "magic words" required for formal rulemaking? Should they be?
4. The comment to 1981 MSAPA § 3-112 rejects formal rulemaking under the APA, cites the Hamilton article quoted above, and concludes that the burden of on-the-record requirements is "far too great to justify such a requirement."
5. Has the judicial elaboration of § 553 notice-and-comment requirements undone the efficiency that presumably was the goal of the *Florida East Coast* holding? Professor Johnson has argued:

> Today, the informal rulemaking process is almost as time consuming and expensive as the formal rulemaking process. A recent study estimated that it generally takes more than three years for an agency to comply with the informal rulemaking procedures of the APA, excluding the time the agency takes to develop the rule before it begins the APA procedures. . . .

Stephen M. Johnson, *The Internet Changes Everything: Revolutionizing Public Participation and Access to Government Information Through the Internet,* 50 Admin. L. Rev. 277, 282 (1998) (footnote omitted). *See generally* Thomas

O. McGarity, *Some Thoughts on "Deossifying" the Rulemaking Process,* 41 Duke L.J. 1385 (1992).

6. One agency response to the time and cost associated with notice and comment rulemaking has been to promulgate "best practices" standards that encourage voluntary compliance with "norms," perhaps developed by the agency, but as likely developed by regulated entities. *See* David Zaring, *Best Practices,* 81 N.Y.U. L. Rev. 294 (2006). Professor Zaring explains that:

> The vilification [of notice and comment rulemaking] has produced a series of uneven efforts at rulemaking reform over the years. Agencies have sought consensus for new rules through negotiated regulation. They have tried to implement programs through contract and privatization instead of rulemaking. They have turned to the President to set their regulatory agendas. And they have sought to handle the increasingly international aspects of their purviews through informal agreements with regulatory counterparts abroad.
>
> Perhaps more important, and more vibrant, than any of these new approaches to rulemaking is the recent turn to "best practices" instead of rules to ensure the success of regulatory programs. Although best-practice rulemaking has been largely ignored by the legal literature, regulation through best practices has increased seven-fold in the past ten years in the federal government alone, touching every aspect of administrative law.

Id. at 295. Zaring argues that agencies adopt best practices rulemaking "when coordination is more important than any particular statutory outcome." *Id.* at 296. And, what exactly are "best practices?" Zaring defines them as:

> [A] method of regulation in which central administrators provide advice and disseminate information, instead of mandating a one-size-fits-all regulatory scheme. Indeed it might suggest a rather democratic form of regulatory experimentalism, in which regulated entities experiment with best practices as a way of vindicating the broad principles of various regulatory programs, while the regulators keep track of their progress and help to celebrate and publicize particularly successful local initiatives.

Id. at 297-98. He adds that best practices "proceed without judicial supervision and they operate outside the familiar framework of the Administrative Procedure Act." *Id.* at 299. Zaring concedes that "[b]est practices are no doubt strange beasts. As nonmandatory rules capable of securing widespread compliance, their effectiveness calls sharp distinctions between hard and soft law—let alone public and private law—into question." *Id.* at 301-02. Are voluntary "best practices" encouraged, but not mandated, by agencies capable of replacing mandatory regulatory duties? Are regulated entities likely to be as responsive to securing public goods as a government agency? And who precisely would be accountable for the substantive content of "best practices"? The agency? The regulated entities? Both? Neither?

In any event, Congress often requires agencies to write regulations implementing specific laws (particularly in the environmental area). Accordingly, the question of whether or not to use notice and comment rulemaking to implement a statute is not always entirely up to the agency to decide for itself. Notice and comment rulemaking, warts and all, is a critically important means of implementing federal statutes.

7. Where an organic statute passed by *Congress* requires procedures beyond
    notice and comment, but does not trigger the full requirements of formal
    rulemaking, the rulemaking procedure has been called "hybrid" rulemak-
    ing. *See* APA §559. The next case deals with whether such additional
    procedural requirements can be imposed by a *court* without express
    provision in the organic statute.

VERMONT YANKEE NUCLEAR POWER CORP. v. NRDC

435 U.S. 519 (1978)

MR. JUSTICE REHNQUIST delivered the opinion of the Court.

In 1946, Congress enacted the Administrative Procedure Act, which as we
have noted elsewhere was not only "a new, basic and comprehensive regulation
of procedures in many agencies," *Wong Yang Sung v. McGrath*, 339 U.S. 33
(1950), but was also a legislative enactment which settled "long-continued
and hard-fought contentions, and enacts a formula upon which opposing social
and political forces have come to rest." *Id.*, at 40. Section 4 of the Act, 5 U.S.C.
§553 (1976 ed.), dealing with rulemaking, requires in subsection (b) that
"notice of proposed rule making shall be published in the Federal
Register . . . ," describes the contents of that notice, and goes on to require in
subsection (c) that after the notice the agency "shall give interested persons an
opportunity to participate in the rule making through submission of written
data, views, or arguments with or without opportunity for oral presentation.
After consideration of the relevant matter presented, the agency shall incorporate in the rules adopted a concise general statement of their basis and
purpose." Interpreting this provision of the Act in *United States v. Allegheny-
Ludlum Steel Corp.*, 406 U.S. 742 (1972), and *United States v. Florida East Coast
R. Co.*, 410 U.S. 224 (1973), we held that generally speaking this section of the
Act established the maximum procedural requirements which Congress was
willing to have the courts impose upon agencies in conducting rulemaking
procedures.[1] Agencies are free to grant additional procedural rights in the
exercise of their discretion, but reviewing courts are generally not free to impose
them if the agencies have not chosen to grant them. This is not to say necessarily
that there are no circumstances which would ever justify a court in overturning
agency action because of a failure to employ procedures beyond those required
by the statute. But such circumstances, if they exist, are extremely rare.

Even apart from the Administrative Procedure Act this Court has for more
than four decades emphasized that the formulation of procedures was basically
to be left within the discretion of the agencies to which Congress had confided
the responsibility for substantive judgments. In *FCC v. Schreiber*, 381 U.S. 279, 290
(1965), the Court explicated this principle, describing it as "an outgrowth of the
congressional determination that administrative agencies and administrators
will be familiar with the industries which they regulate and will be in a better
position than federal courts or Congress itself to design procedural rules

---

1. While there was division in this Court in *United States v. Florida East Coast R. Co.* with respect to
the constitutionality of such an interpretation in a case involving ratemaking, which Mr. Justice
Douglas and Mr. Justice Stewart felt was "adjudicatory" within the terms of the Act, the cases in the
Court of Appeals for the District of Columbia Circuit which we review here involve rulemaking
procedures in their most pristine sense.

adapted to the peculiarities of the industry and the tasks of the agency involved." The Court there relied on its earlier case of *FCC v. Pottsville Broadcasting Co.*, 309 U.S. 134, 138 (1940), where it had stated that a provision dealing with the conduct of business by the Federal Communications Commission delegated to the Commission the power to resolve "subordinate questions of procedure . . . [such as] the scope of the inquiry, whether applications should be heard contemporaneously or successively, whether parties should be allowed to intervene in one another's proceedings, and similar questions."

It is in the light of this background of statutory and decisional law that we granted certiorari to review two judgments of the Court of Appeals for the District of Columbia Circuit because of our concern that they had seriously misread or misapplied this statutory and decisional law cautioning reviewing courts against engrafting their own notions of proper procedures upon agencies entrusted with substantive functions by Congress. We conclude that the Court of Appeals has done just that in these cases, and we therefore remand them to it for further proceedings. We also find it necessary to examine the Court of Appeals' decision with respect to agency action taken after full adjudicatory hearings. We again conclude that the court improperly intruded into the agency's decision-making process, making it necessary for us to reverse and remand with respect to this part of the cases also.

I

A

Under the Atomic Energy Act of 1954, 68 Stat. 919, as amended, 42 U.S.C. § 2011 *et seq.*, the Atomic Energy Commission[2] was given broad regulatory authority over the development of nuclear energy. Under the terms of the Act, a utility seeking to construct and operate a nuclear power plant must obtain a separate permit or license at both the construction and the operation stage of the project. In order to obtain the construction permit, the utility must file a preliminary safety analysis report, an environmental report, and certain information regarding the antitrust implications of the proposed project. This application then undergoes exhaustive review by the Commission's staff and by the Advisory Committee on Reactor Safeguards (ACRS), a group of distinguished experts in the field of atomic energy. Both groups submit to the Commission their own evaluations, which then become part of the record of the utility's application. The Commission staff also undertakes the review required by the National Environmental Policy Act of 1969 (NEPA), 42 U.S.C. § 4321 *et seq.*, and prepares a draft environmental impact statement, which, after being circulated for comment, 10 CFR §§ 51.22-51.25 (1977), is revised and becomes a final environmental impact statement. § 51.26. Thereupon a three-member Atomic Safety and Licensing Board conducts a public adjudicatory hearing, and reaches a decision which can be appealed to the Atomic Safety and Licensing Appeal Board, and currently, in the Commission's discretion, to the Commission itself. 10 CFR §§ 2.714, 2.721, 2.786, 2.787 (1977). The final agency decision may be

2. The licensing and regulatory functions of the Atomic Energy Commission (AEC) were transferred to the Nuclear Regulatory Commission (NRC) by the Energy Reorganization Act of 1974, 42 U.S.C. § 5801 *et seq.* (1970 ed., Supp. V). Hereinafter both the AEC and NRC will be referred to as the Commission.

appealed to the courts of appeals. 42 U.S.C. § 2239; 28 U.S.C. § 2342. The same sort of process occurs when the utility applies for a license to operate the plant, 10 CFR § 50.34(b) (1977), except that a hearing need only be held in contested cases and may be limited to the matters in controversy.

These cases arise from two separate decisions of the Court of Appeals for the District of Columbia Circuit. In the first, the court remanded a decision of the Commission to grant a license to petitioner Vermont Yankee Nuclear Power Corp. to operate a nuclear power plant. In the second, the court remanded a decision of that same agency to grant a permit to petitioner Consumers Power Co. to construct two pressurized water nuclear reactors to generate electricity and steam.

B

In December 1967, after the mandatory adjudicatory hearing and necessary review, the Commission granted petitioner Vermont Yankee a permit to build a nuclear power plant in Vernon, Vt. Thereafter, Vermont Yankee applied for an operating license. Respondent Natural Resources Defense Council (NRDC) objected to the granting of a license, however, and therefore a hearing on the application commenced on August 10, 1971. Excluded from consideration at the hearings, over NRDC's objection, was the issue of the environmental effects of operations to reprocess fuel or dispose of wastes resulting from the reprocessing operations.[6] This ruling was affirmed by the Appeal Board in June 1972.

In November 1972, however, the Commission, making specific reference to the Appeal Board's decision with respect to the Vermont Yankee license, instituted rulemaking proceedings "that would specifically deal with the question of consideration of environmental effects associated with the uranium fuel cycle in the individual cost-benefit analyses for light water cooled nuclear power reactors." The notice of proposed rulemaking offered two alternatives, both predicated on a report prepared by the Commission's staff entitled Environmental Survey of the Nuclear Fuel Cycle. The first would have required no quantitative evaluation of the environmental hazards of fuel reprocessing or disposal because the Environmental Survey had found them to be slight. The second would have specified numerical values for the environmental impact of this part of the fuel cycle, which values would then be incorporated into a table, along with the other relevant factors, to determine the overall cost-benefit balance for each operating license.

Much of the controversy in this case revolves around the procedures used in the rulemaking hearing which commenced in February 1973. In a supplemental notice of hearing the Commission indicated that while discovery or cross-examination would not be utilized, the Environmental Survey would be available to the public before the hearing along with the extensive background documents cited therein. All participants would be given a reasonable opportunity to

6. The nuclear fission which takes place in light-water nuclear reactors apparently converts its principal fuel, uranium, into plutonium, which is itself highly radioactive but can be used as reactor fuel if separated from the remaining uranium and radioactive waste products. Fuel reprocessing refers to the process necessary to recapture usable plutonium. Waste disposal, at the present stage of technological development, refers to the storage of the very long lived and highly radioactive waste products until they detoxify sufficiently that they no longer present an environmental hazard. There are presently no physical or chemical steps which render this waste less toxic, other than simply the passage of time.

present their position and could be represented by counsel if they so desired. Written and, time permitting, oral statements would be received and incorporated into the record. All persons giving oral statements would be subject to questioning by the Commission. At the conclusion of the hearing, a transcript would be made available to the public and the record would remain open for 30 days to allow the filing of supplemental written statements. More than 40 individuals and organizations representing a wide variety of interests submitted written comments. On January 17, 1973, the Licensing Board held a planning session to schedule the appearance of witnesses and to discuss methods for compiling a record. The hearing was held on February 1 and 2, with participation by a number of groups, including the Commission's staff, the United States Environmental Protection Agency, a manufacturer of reactor equipment, a trade association from the nuclear industry, a group of electric utility companies, and a group called Consolidated National Intervenors which represented 79 groups and individuals including respondent NRDC.

After the hearing, the Commission's staff filed a supplemental document for the purpose of clarifying and revising the Environmental Survey. Then the Licensing Board forwarded its report to the Commission without rendering any decision. The Licensing Board identified as the principal procedural question the propriety of declining to use full formal adjudicatory procedures. The major substantive issue was the technical adequacy of the Environmental Survey.

In April 1974, the Commission issued a rule which adopted the second of the two proposed alternatives described above. The Commission also approved the procedures used at the hearing, and indicated that the record, including the Environmental Survey, provided an "adequate data base for the regulation adopted." Finally, the Commission ruled that to the extent the rule differed from the Appeal Board decisions in Vermont Yankee "those decisions have no further precedential significance," but that since "the environmental effects of the uranium fuel cycle have been shown to be relatively insignificant, . . . it is unnecessary to apply the amendment to applicant's environmental reports submitted prior to its effective date or to Final Environmental Statements for which Draft Environmental Statements have been circulated for comment prior to the effective date."

Respondents appealed from both the Commission's adoption of the rule and its decision to grant Vermont Yankee's license to the Court of Appeals for the District of Columbia Circuit.

C

In January 1969, petitioner Consumers Power Co. applied for a permit to construct two nuclear reactors in Midland, Mich. Consumers Power's application was examined by the Commission's staff and the ACRS. The ACRS issued reports which discussed specific problems and recommended solutions. It also made reference to "other problems" of a more generic nature and suggested that efforts should be made to resolve them with respect to these as well as all other projects. Two groups, one called Saginaw and another called Mapleton, intervened and opposed the application. Saginaw filed with the Board a number of environmental contentions, directed over 300 interrogatories to the ACRS, attempted to depose the chairman of the ACRS, and requested discovery of various ACRS documents. The Licensing Board denied the various discovery requests directed to the ACRS. Hearings were then held on numerous radiological health and safety issues. Thereafter, the Commission's staff issued a draft environmental impact statement. Saginaw submitted 119 environmental contentions which were both comments on the proposed draft statement and a statement of Saginaw's position in the upcoming hearings. The staff revised the statement and issued a final environmental statement in March 1972. Further hearings were then conducted during May and June 1972. Saginaw, however, choosing not to appear at or participate in these latter hearings, indicated that it had "no conventional findings of fact to set forth" and had not "chosen to search the record and respond to this proceeding by submitting citations of matters which we believe were proved or disproved." But the Licensing Board, recognizing its obligations to "independently consider the final balance among conflicting environmental factors in the record," nevertheless treated as contested those issues "as to which intervenors introduced affirmative evidence or engaged in substantial cross examination."

At issue now are 17 of those 119 contentions which are claimed to raise questions of "energy conservation." The Licensing Board indicated that as far as appeared from the record, the demand for the plant was made up of normal industrial and residential use. It went on to state that it was "beyond our province to inquire into whether the customary uses being made of electricity in our society are 'proper' or 'improper.'" With respect to claims that Consumers Power stimulated demand by its advertising the Licensing Board indicated that "[n]o evidence was offered on this point and absent some evidence that Applicant is creating abnormal demand, the Board did not consider the question." The Licensing Board also failed to consider the environmental effects of fuel reprocessing or disposal of radioactive wastes. The Appeal Board ultimately affirmed the Licensing Board's grant of a construction permit and the Commission declined to further review the matter. [When asked to reopen the proceedings, to consider energy conservation alternatives, the Commission declined.]

Respondents then challenged the granting of the construction permit in the Court of Appeals for the District of Columbia Circuit.

D

With respect to the challenge of Vermont Yankee's license, the court first ruled that in the absence of effective rulemaking proceedings,[13] the Commission must deal with the environmental impact of fuel reprocessing and disposal in individual licensing proceedings. The court then examined the rulemaking proceedings and, despite the fact that it appeared that the agency employed all the procedures required by 5 U.S.C. §553 (1976 ed.) and more, the court determined the proceedings to be inadequate and overturned the rule. Accordingly, the Commission's determination with respect to Vermont Yankee's license was also remanded for further proceedings.

With respect to the permit to Consumers Power, the court first held that the environmental impact statement for construction of the Midland reactors was fatally defective for failure to examine energy conservation as an alternative to a plant of this size. The court also thought the report by ACRS was inadequate,

13. In the Court of Appeals no one questioned the Commission's authority to deal with fuel cycle issues by informal rulemaking as opposed to adjudication. Neither does anyone seriously question before this Court the Commission's authority in this respect.

although it did not agree that discovery from individual ACRS members was the proper way to obtain further explication of the report. Instead, the court held that the Commission should have *sua sponte* sent the report back to the ACRS for further elucidation of the "other problems" and their resolution. Finally, the court ruled that the fuel cycle issues in this case were controlled by *NRDC v. NRC,* discussed above, and remanded for appropriate consideration of waste disposal and other unaddressed fuel cycle issues as described in that opinion.

II

A

. . . The Commission does not contend that it is not required to consider the environmental impact of the spent fuel processes when licensing nuclear power plants. . . .

Vermont Yankee will produce annually well over 100 pounds of radioactive wastes, some of which will be highly toxic. The Commission itself, in a pamphlet published by its information office, clearly recognizes that these wastes "pose the most severe potential health hazard. . . ." U.S. Atomic Energy Commission, Radioactive Wastes 12 (1965). Many of these substances must be isolated for anywhere from 600 to hundreds of thousands of years. It is hard to argue that these wastes do not constitute "adverse environmental effects which cannot be avoided should the proposal be implemented," or that by operating nuclear power plants we are not making "irreversible and irretrievable commitments of resources." 42 U.S.C. §§ 4332(2)(C)(ii), (v). As the Court of Appeals recognized, the environmental impact of the radioactive wastes produced by a nuclear power plant is analytically indistinguishable from the environmental effects of "the stack gases produced by a coal-burning power plant." For these reasons we hold that the Commission acted well within its statutory authority when it considered the back end of the fuel cycle in individual licensing proceedings.

B

We next turn to the invalidation of the fuel cycle rule. But before determining whether the Court of Appeals reached a permissible result, we must determine exactly what result it did reach, and in this case that is no mean feat. Vermont Yankee argues that the court invalidated the rule because of the inadequacy of the procedures employed in the proceedings. Respondents, on the other hand, labeling petitioner's view of the decision a "straw man," argue to this Court that the court merely held that the record was inadequate to enable the reviewing court to determine whether the agency had fulfilled its statutory obligation. But we unfortunately have not found the parties' characterization of the opinion to be entirely reliable; it appears here, as in *Orloff v. Willoughby,* 345 U.S. 83, 87 (1953), that "in this Court the parties changed positions as nimbly as if dancing a quadrille."

After a thorough examination of the opinion itself, we conclude that while the matter is not entirely free from doubt, the majority of the Court of Appeals struck down the rule because of the perceived inadequacies of the procedures employed in the rulemaking proceedings. The court first determined the intervenors' primary argument to be "that the decision to preclude 'discovery or cross-examination' denied them a meaningful opportunity to participate in the proceedings as guaranteed by due process." The court then went on to frame the issue for decision thus: "Thus, we are called upon to decide whether the procedures provided by the agency were sufficient to ventilate the issues."

The court conceded that absent extraordinary circumstances it is improper for a reviewing court to prescribe the procedural format an agency must follow, but it likewise clearly thought it entirely appropriate to "scrutinize the record as a whole to insure that genuine opportunities to participate in a meaningful way were provided. . . ." The court also refrained from actually ordering the agency to follow any specific procedures, but there is little doubt in our minds that the ineluctable mandate of the court's decision is that the procedures afforded during the hearings were inadequate. This conclusion is particularly buttressed by the fact that after the court examined the record, particularly the testimony of Dr. Pittman, and declared it insufficient, the court proceeded to discuss at some length the necessity for further procedural devices or a more "sensitive" application of those devices employed during the proceedings. *Ibid.* The exploration of the record and the statement regarding its insufficiency might initially lead one to conclude that the court was only examining the sufficiency of the evidence, but the remaining portions of the opinion dispel any doubt that this was certainly not the sole or even the principal basis of the decision. Accordingly, we feel compelled to address the opinion on its own terms, and we conclude that it was wrong.

In prior opinions we have intimated that even in a rule-making proceeding when an agency is making a "'quasi-judicial'" determination by which a very small number of persons are "'exceptionally affected, in each case upon individual grounds,'" in some circumstances additional procedures may be required in order to afford the aggrieved individuals due process.[16] *United States v. Florida East Coast R. Co.,* 410 U.S., at 242, 245, quoting from *Bi-Metallic Investment Co. v. State Board of Equalization,* 239 U.S. 441, 446 (1915). It might also be true, although we do not think the issue is presented in this case and accordingly do not decide it, that a totally unjustified departure from well-settled agency procedures of long standing might require judicial correction.

But this much is absolutely clear. Absent constitutional constraints or extremely compelling circumstances the "administrative agencies 'should be free to fashion their own rules of procedure and to pursue methods of inquiry capable of permitting them to discharge their multitudinous duties.'" *FCC v. Schreiber,* 381 U.S., at 290, quoting from *FCC v. Pottsville Broadcasting Co.,* 309 U.S., at 143. Indeed, our cases could hardly be more explicit in this regard. The Court has, as we noted in *FCC v. Schreiber, supra,* at 290, and n. 17, upheld this principle in a variety of applications, including that case where the District Court, instead of inquiring into the validity of the Federal Communications Commission's exercise of its rulemaking authority, devised procedures to be followed by the agency on the basis of its conception of how the public and private interest involved could best be served. Examining §4(j) of the Communications Act of 1934, the Court unanimously held that the Court of Appeals erred in upholding that action. And the basic reason for this decision was the Court of Appeals'

---

16. Respondent NRDC does not now argue that additional procedural devices were required under the Constitution. Since this was clearly a rulemaking proceeding in its purest form, we see nothing to support such a view. *See United States v. Florida East Coast R. Co.,* 410 U.S. 224, 244-245 (1973); *Bowles v. Willingham,* 321 U.S. 503 (1944); *Bi-Metallic Investment Co. v. State Board of Equalization,* 239 U.S. 441 (1915).

serious departure from the very basic tenet of administrative law that agencies should be free to fashion their own rules of procedure.

We have continually repeated this theme through the years, most recently in *FPC v. Transcontinental Gas Pipe Line Corp.*, 423 U.S. 326 (1976), decided just two Terms ago. In that case, in determining the proper scope of judicial review of agency action under the Natural Gas Act, we held that while a court may have occasion to remand an agency decision because of the inadequacy of the record, the agency should normally be allowed to "exercise its administrative discretion in deciding how, in light of internal organization considerations, it may best proceed to develop the needed evidence and how its prior decision should be modified in light of such evidence as develops." *Id.*, at 333. We went on to emphasize:

> "At least in the absence of substantial justification for doing otherwise, a reviewing court may not, after determining that additional evidence is requisite for adequate review, proceed by dictating to the agency the methods, procedures, and time dimension of the needed inquiry and ordering the results to be reported to the court without opportunity for further consideration on the basis of the new evidence by the agency. Such a procedure clearly runs the risk of '[propelling] the court into the domain which Congress has set aside exclusively for the administrative agency.' *SEC v. Chenery Corp.*, 332 U.S. 194, 196 (1947)." *Ibid.*

Respondent NRDC argues that §4 of the Administrative Procedure Act, 5 U.S.C. §553 (1976 ed.), merely establishes lower procedural bounds and that a court may routinely require more than the minimum when an agency's proposed rule addresses complex or technical factual issues or "Issues of Great Public Import." We have, however, previously shown that our decisions reject this view. We also think the legislative history, even the part which it cites, does not bear out its contention. The Senate Report explains what eventually became §4 thus:

> "This subsection states . . . the minimum requirements of public rule making procedure short of statutory hearing. Under it agencies might in addition confer with industry advisory committees, consult organizations, hold informal "hearings," and the like. Considerations of practicality, necessity, and public interest . . . will naturally govern the agency's determination of the extent to which public proceedings should go. Matters of great import, or those where the public submission of facts will be either useful to the agency or a protection to the public, should naturally be accorded more elaborate public procedures." S. Rep. No. 752, 79th Cong., 1st Sess., 14-15 (1945).

The House Report is in complete accord:

> "'[Uniformity] has been found possible and desirable for all classes of both equity and law actions in the courts. . . . It would seem to require no argument to demonstrate that the administrative agencies, exercising but a fraction of the judicial power may likewise operate under uniform rules of practice and procedure and that they may be required to remain within the terms of the law as to the exercise of both quasi-legislative and quasi-judicial power. . . .' [sic]
>
> "The bill is an outline of minimum essential rights and procedures. . . . It affords private parties a means of knowing what their rights are and how they may protect them. . . . [sic]

"... [The bill contains] the essentials of the different forms of administrative proceedings. ..." H. R. Rep. No. 1980, 79th Cong., 2d Sess., 9, 16-17 (1946).

And the Attorney General's Manual on the Administrative Procedure Act 31, 35 (1947), a contemporaneous interpretation previously given some deference by this Court because of the role played by the Department of Justice in drafting the legislation, further confirms that view. In short, all of this leaves little doubt that Congress intended that the discretion of the *agencies* and not that of the courts be exercised in determining when extra procedural devices should be employed.

There are compelling reasons for construing § 4 in this manner. In the first place, if courts continually review agency proceedings to determine whether the agency employed procedures which were, in the court's opinion, perfectly tailored to reach what the court perceives to be the "best" or "correct" result, judicial review would be totally unpredictable. And the agencies, operating under this vague injunction to employ the "best" procedures and facing the threat of reversal if they did not, would undoubtedly adopt full adjudicatory procedures in every instance. Not only would this totally disrupt the statutory scheme, through which Congress enacted "a formula upon which opposing social and political forces have come to rest," *Wong Yang Sung v. McGrath,* 339 U.S., at 40, but all the inherent advantages of informal rulemaking would be totally lost.

Secondly, it is obvious that the court in these cases reviewed the agency's choice of procedures on the basis of the record actually produced at the hearing, and not on the basis of the information available to the agency when it made the decision to structure the proceedings in a certain way. This sort of Monday morning quarterbacking not only encourages but almost compels the agency to conduct all rulemaking proceedings with the full panoply of procedural devices normally associated only with adjudicatory hearings.

Finally, and perhaps most importantly, this sort of review fundamentally misconceives the nature of the standard for judicial review of an agency rule. The court below uncritically assumed that additional procedures will automatically result in a more adequate record because it will give interested parties more of an opportunity to participate in and contribute to the proceedings. But informal rulemaking need not be based solely on the transcript of a hearing held before an agency. Indeed, the agency need not even hold a formal hearing. *See* 5 U.S.C. § 553(c) (1976 ed.). Thus, the adequacy of the "record" in this type of proceeding is not correlated directly to the type of procedural devices employed, but rather turns on whether the agency has followed the statutory mandate of the Administrative Procedure Act or other relevant statutes. If the agency is compelled to support the rule which it ultimately adopts with the type of record produced only after a full adjudicatory hearing, it simply will have no choice but to conduct a full adjudicatory hearing prior to promulgating every rule. In sum, this sort of unwarranted judicial examination of perceived procedural shortcomings of a rulemaking proceeding can do nothing but seriously interfere with that process prescribed by Congress. ...

In short, nothing in the APA, NEPA, the circumstances of this case, the nature of the issues being considered, past agency practice, or the statutory mandate under which the Commission operates permitted the court to review and overturn the rulemaking proceeding on the basis of the procedural devices employed (or not employed) by the Commission so long as the Commission employed at least the statutory *minima*, a matter about which there is no doubt in this case.

There remains, of course, the question of whether the challenged rule finds sufficient justification in the administrative proceedings that it should be upheld by the reviewing court. Judge Tamm, concurring in the result reached by the majority of the Court of Appeals, thought that it did not. There are also intimations in the majority opinion which suggest that the judges who joined it likewise may have thought the administrative proceedings an insufficient basis upon which to predicate the rule in question. We accordingly remand so that the Court of Appeals may review the rule as the Administrative Procedure Act provides. We have made it abundantly clear before that when there is a contemporaneous explanation of the agency decision, the validity of that action must "stand or fall on the propriety of that finding, judged, of course, by the appropriate standard of review. If that finding is not sustainable on the administrative record made, then the Comptroller's decision must be vacated and the matter remanded to him for further consideration." *Camp v. Pitts,* 411 U.S. 138, 143 (1973). *See also SEC v. Chenery Corp.,* 318 U.S. 80 (1943). The court should engage in this kind of review and not stray beyond the judicial province to explore the procedural format or to impose upon the agency its own notion of which procedures are "best" or most likely to further some vague, undefined public good.

III

A

We now turn to the Court of Appeals' holding "that rejection of energy conservation on the basis of the 'threshold test' was capricious and arbitrary," and again conclude the court was wrong. [Discussion omitted.]

B

Finally, we turn to the Court of Appeals' holding that the Licensing Board should have returned the ACRS report to ACRS for further elaboration, understandable to a layman, of the reference to other problems. . . .

We also think it worth noting that we find absolutely nothing in the relevant statutes to justify what the court did here. The Commission very well might be able to remand a report for further clarification, but there is nothing to support a court's ordering the Commission to take that step or to support a court's requiring the ACRS to give a short explanation, understandable to a layman, of each generic safety concern.

All this leads us to make one further observation of some relevance to this case. To say that the Court of Appeals' final reason for remanding is insubstantial at best is a gross understatement. Consumers Power first applied in 1969 for a construction permit — not even an operating license, just a construction permit. The proposed plant underwent an incredibly extensive review. The reports filed and reviewed literally fill books. The proceedings took years, and the actual hearings themselves over two weeks. To then nullify that effort seven years later because one report refers to other problems, which problems admittedly have been discussed at length in other reports available to the public, borders on the Kafkaesque. Nuclear energy may some day be a cheap, safe source of power or it may not. But Congress has made a choice to at least try nuclear energy, establishing a reasonable review process in which courts are to play only a limited role. The fundamental policy questions appropriately resolved in Congress and in the state legislatures are *not* subject to reexamination in the federal courts under the guise of judicial review of agency action. Time may prove wrong the decision to develop nuclear energy, but it is Congress or the States within their appropriate agencies which must eventually make that judgment. In the meantime courts should perform their appointed function. NEPA does set forth significant substantive goals for the Nation, but its mandate to the agencies is essentially procedural. It is to insure a fully informed and well-considered decision, not necessarily a decision the judges of the Court of Appeals or of this Court would have reached had they been members of the decisionmaking unit of the agency. Administrative decisions should be set aside in this context, as in every other, only for substantial procedural or substantive reasons as mandated by statute, *Consolo v. FMC,* 383 U.S. 607, 620 (1966), not simply because the court is unhappy with the result reached. And a single alleged oversight on a peripheral issue, urged by parties who never fully cooperated or indeed raised the issue below, must not be made the basis for overturning a decision properly made after an otherwise exhaustive proceeding. *Reversed and remanded.*

[Justices Blackmun and Powell did not participate. The opinion was unanimous.]

QUESTIONS

1. Note how the rule in this case was challenged both on review of the rule, and in the enforcement of the rule (in the adjudication).
2. Evaluate the *Vermont Yankee* ruling, both as a matter of law, and as a matter of administrative law policy.
3. Can the adequacy of the record really be considered totally distinct from the adequacy of the procedure without lessening rigor of substantive review?
4. Is *Nova Scotia, supra,* p. 203, still good law?
5. When *Vermont Yankee* came down, then-professor Scalia anticipated that the D.C. Circuit would not follow it. Antonin Scalia, Vermont Yankee: *The APA, the D.C. Circuit, and the Supreme Court,* 1978 Sup. Ct. Rev. 345 (1978). About twenty years after the Court's decision in *Vermont Yankee,* the D.C. Circuit considered the question of whether an administrative agency may modify a policy created via an interpretative rule by adopting a new interpretative rule amending or repealing the earlier rule. The court decided that if an agency wished to change an interpretation of one of its own regulations contained in an interpretative rule, the agency must use notice and comment rulemaking in order to do so. *See Paralyzed Veterans of America v. D. C. Arena L.P.,* 117 F.3d 579 (D.C. Cir. 1997). When the Supreme Court reviewed the D.C. Circuit's later application of this circuit rule, it held emphatically and unanimously that an agency may amend or repeal a policy established through an interpretative rule in a subsequent interpretative rule (or in a subsequent adjudicatory proceeding). *See Perez v. Mortgage Bankers Ass'n,* 135 S. Ct. 1135 (2014). Justice Sonya Sotomayor explained that "[t]he *Paralyzed Veterans* doctrine is contrary to the clear text of the APA's rulemaking provisions,

and it improperly imposes on agencies an obligation beyond the 'maximum procedural requirements' specified in the APA, *Vermont Yankee Nuclear Power Corp. v. Natural Resources Defense Council, Inc.*, 435 U. S. 519, 524 (1978)." *Id.* at 1206. Accordingly, absent an agency-specific restriction contained in the agency's organic act, an agency may modify an interpretative rule by simply issuing a new interpretative rule amending or repealing an earlier one. See *id.* at 1206-10.

6. *Vermont Yankee* resolved a significant dispute between two very well regarded members of the D.C. Circuit, Judges David Bazelon and Harold Leventhal. Judge Bazelon argued that judges reviewing administrative agency action should encourage agencies to adopt and follow procedures that would reliably provide rational regulations and policies—an approach that Justice Rehnquist categorically rejected in *Vermont Yankee*—whereas Leventhal espoused "hard look" review of the substance of agency decisions. For a discussion of the "Great Debate" between Judges Bazelon and Leventhal, *see infra* pp. 587-588.

7. The Supreme Court ultimately upheld the rule at issue in *Vermont Yankee* as not arbitrary or capricious. *Baltimore Gas & Elec. Co. v. NRDC,* 462 U.S. 87 (1983).

NOTE ON HYBRID RULEMAKING

Vermont Yankee makes clear that reviewing courts should not attempt to impose procedural requirements on agencies over and above those Congress sets forth in the APA or in the agency's organic statute. Thus without the requisite triggering language, federal agencies need not provide process rights in excess of those set forth in §553 (for notice and comment rulemaking) and those required by due process. Suppose, however, that Congress decides to require a procedural step not included within the general requirements of the APA. Must an agency observe a procedure mandated by Congress that exceeds the general requirements of the APA? The answer, obviously enough, is "of course!" Congress can require and has required agencies to observe procedures in excess of those set forth in the APA.

For example, Congress can impose procedural requirements on an agency for notice and comment rulemaking that go beyond the bare bones requirements of section 553, yet stop short of requiring formal, on-the-record rulemaking. *See*, e.g., 15 U.S.C. §2603(b)(5) (making APA section 553 applicable to a specific type of rulemaking under the Toxic Substances Control Act, but requiring, *inter alia,* that an opportunity be provided for "oral presentation of data, views, or arguments"); *see also* 42 U.S.C. §7607(d) (Clean Air Act). Such rulemaking has been termed "hybrid rulemaking" since it is neither purely informal nor purely formal. Congress may also be interpreted to have mandated hybrid procedures by requiring that all factual matters raised in a particular rulemaking be supported by "substantial evidence on the record." The substantial evidence test presupposes a paper record and judicial review on this paper record—absent a congressional mandate of this sort, the agency would be free to support its factual assertions with any materials available to the agency prior to the promulgation of the rule. See *AFL-CIO v. Marshall, infra,* p. 564.

NOTE ON ADDITIONAL GENERIC REQUIREMENTS FOR RULEMAKING

In addition to the procedural requirements for rulemaking that are defined in the APA and in organic statutes for so-called hybrid rulemaking, Congress has imposed two important generic requirements for agency rulemaking. The first is the Regulatory Flexibility Act of 1980, as amended by the Small Business Regulatory Enforcement Fairness Act of 1996, which is codified in the APA, 5 U.S.C. §§ 601 *et seq.* This law requires an agency to publish an initial regulatory flexibility analysis when it publishes a notice of proposed rulemaking (*see* 5 U.S.C. § 603) and a final regulatory flexibility analysis when it publishes a final rule (*see* 5 U.S.C. § 604). Section 604(a) identifies the content of the final flexibility analysis, which must contain:

(1) a succinct statement of the need for, and objectives of, the rule;

(2) a summary of the significant issues raised by the public comments in response to the initial regulatory flexibility analysis, a summary of the assessment of the agency of such issues, and a statement of any changes made in the proposed rule as a result of such comments;

(3) a description of and an estimate of the number of small entities to which the rule will apply or an explanation of why no such estimate is available;

(4) a description of the projected reporting, recordkeeping and other compliance requirements of the rule, including an estimate of the classes of small entities which will be subject to the requirement and the type of professional skills necessary for preparation of the report or record; and

(5) a description of the steps the agency has taken to minimize the significant economic impact on small entities consistent with the stated objectives of applicable statutes, including a statement of the factual, policy, and legal reasons for selecting the alternative adopted in the final rule and why each one of the other significant alternatives to the rule considered by the agency which affect the impact on small entities was rejected.

The requirement in Sections 603 and 604 that an agency prepare regulatory flexibility analyses is, however, inapplicable "to any proposed or final rule if the head of the agency certifies that the rule will not, if promulgated, have a significant economic impact on a substantial number of small entities." 5 U.S.C. § 605(b). The agency certification, "along with a statement providing the factual basis for such certification," must be published in the Federal Register. *Id.* The statute does not define when an economic impact is to be considered "significant," or the number of small entities that are to be considered "substantial." One court has held that, when deciding whether § 605(b) makes the requirement of regulatory flexibility analyses inapplicable, the agency need consider only the entities that are directly subject to the regulation, rather than entities that are indirectly affected. *See Mid-Tex Electric Cooperative, Inc. v. Federal Energy Regulatory Commission,* 773 F.2d 327, 341-43 (D.C. Cir. 1985) (Bork, J.).

Prior to the amendment of the Regulatory Flexibility Act in 1996, courts had held that the statute barred judicial review of an agency decision that the § 603 and § 604 flexibility analysis requirements were inapplicable under § 605(b). *See Thompson v. Clark,* 741 F.2d 401 (D.C. Cir. 1984) (Scalia, J.) (relying on prior language of 5 U.S.C. § 611(a)). *Accord Lehigh Valley Farmers v. Block,* 640 F. Supp.

1497 (E.D. Pa. 1986), *aff'd* 829 F.2d 409 (3d Cir. 1987). The current, amended version of § 611(a), however, provides specifically that an adversely affected small entity may have an agency's compliance with § 605(b) reviewed in court.

Section 611 does not provide much detail regarding judicial review of a claim that an agency failed to comply with the Regulatory Flexibility Act. For example, § 611(b) states opaquely that "[i]n an action for the judicial review of a rule, the regulatory flexibility analysis for such rule . . . shall constitute part of the entire record of agency action in connection with such review." Judicial review does, however, appear to be deferential. *See Allied Local and Regional Manufacturers Caucus v. U.S. E.P.A.*, 215 F.3d 61, 80-81 (D.C. Cir. 2000).

The second important generic requirement for agency rulemaking is included in the Unfunded Mandates Reform Act of 1995, codified at 2 U.S.C. §§ 1501 *et seq.* This statute includes a broad mandate that "[e]ach agency shall, unless otherwise prohibited by law, assess the effects of Federal regulatory actions on State, local, and tribal governments, and the private sector (other than to the extent that such regulations incorporate requirements specifically set forth in law)." 2 U.S.C. § 1531. In 2 U.S.C. § 1532, the act takes an approach similar to that in the Regulatory Flexibility Act and specifically requires that an agency prepare a written statement to accompany any "significant regulatory action[]":

§ 1532. Statements to accompany significant regulatory actions

(a) In general

Unless otherwise prohibited by law, before promulgating any general notice of proposed rulemaking that is likely to result in promulgation of any rule that includes any Federal mandate that may result in the expenditure by State, local, and tribal governments, in the aggregate, or by the private sector, of $100,000,000 or more (adjusted annually for inflation) in any 1 year, and before promulgating any final rule for which a general notice of proposed rulemaking was published, the agency shall prepare a written statement containing —

(1) an identification of the provision of Federal law under which the rule is being promulgated;

(2) a qualitative and quantitative assessment of the anticipated costs and benefits of the Federal mandate, including the costs and benefits to State, local, and tribal governments or the private sector, as well as the effect of the Federal mandate on health, safety, and the natural environment and such an assessment shall include —

(A) an analysis of the extent to which such costs to State, local, and tribal governments may be paid with Federal financial assistance (or otherwise paid for by the Federal Government); and

(B) the extent to which there are available Federal resources to carry out the intergovernmental mandate;

(3) estimates by the agency, if and to the extent that the agency determines that accurate estimates are reasonably feasible, of —

(A) the future compliance costs of the Federal mandate; and

(B) any disproportionate budgetary effects of the Federal mandate upon any particular regions of the nation or particular State, local, or tribal governments, urban or rural or other types of communities, or particular segments of the private sector;

(4) estimates by the agency of the effect on the national economy, such as the effect on productivity, economic growth, full employment, creation of productive jobs, and international competitiveness of United States goods and services, if and to the extent that the agency in its sole discretion determines that accurate estimates are reasonably feasible and that such effect is relevant and material; and

(5)(A) a description of the extent of the agency's prior consultation with elected representatives (under section 1534 of this title) of the affected State, local, and tribal governments;

(B) a summary of the comments and concerns that were presented by State, local, or tribal governments either orally or in writing to the agency; and

(C) a summary of the agency's evaluation of those comments and concerns.

(b) Promulgation

In promulgating a general notice of proposed rulemaking or a final rule for which a statement under subsection (a) of this section is required, the agency shall include in the promulgation a summary of the information contained in the statement.

(c) Preparation in conjunction with other statement

Any agency may prepare any statement required under subsection (a) of this section in conjunction with or as a part of any other statement or analysis, provided that the statement or analysis satisfies the provisions of subsection (a) of this section.

In addition to this requirement of a written statement, 2 U.S.C. § 1535 provides that the agency must in general adopt "the least costly, most cost-effective or least burdensome [regulatory] alternative that achieves the objectives of the rule":

§ 1535. Least burdensome option or explanation required

(a) In general

Except as provided in subsection (b) of this section, before promulgating any rule for which a written statement is required under section 1532 of this title, the agency shall identify and consider a reasonable number of regulatory alternatives and from those alternatives select the least costly, most cost-effective or least burdensome alternative that achieves the objectives of the rule, for—

(1) State, local, and tribal governments, in the case of a rule containing a Federal intergovernmental mandate; and

(2) the private sector, in the case of a rule containing a Federal private sector mandate.

(b) Exception

The provisions of subsection (a) of this section shall apply unless—

(1) the head of the affected agency publishes with the final rule an explanation of why the least costly, most cost-effective or least burdensome method of achieving the objectives of the rule was not adopted; or

(2) the provisions are inconsistent with law.

The scope of these broad requirements is limited in two respects. First, 2 U.S.C. § 1503 defines several exceptions to the applicability of the provision, including an exception for a regulation that "establishes or enforces any statutory rights that prohibit discrimination on the basis of race, color, religion, sex, national origin, age, handicap, or disability." *Id.* § 1503(2).

Second, the judicial review provision significantly limits the enforceability of the act's requirements. 2 U.S.C. § 1571. That provision first provides that a court may review an agency's compliance with the § 1532 required statement only to the extent of ensuring that the agency has not unlawfully withheld or unreasonably delayed issuance of the statement. *Id.* § 1571(a)(1)(2)(a) (referring to review under 5 U.S.C. § 706(1)). Moreover, even when § 1532 requires the preparation of a statement for a rule, "the inadequacy or failure to prepare such statement . . . shall not be used as a basis for staying, enjoining, invalidating or otherwise affecting such agency rule." *Id.* § 1571(a)(3). Finally, § 1571(a) does not provide for judicial review of agency compliance with the "least burdensome option" requirement of § 1535, and § 1571(b) states that "[e]xcept as provided in subsection (a) of this section . . . any compliance or noncompliance with the provisions of this chapter . . . shall not be subject to judicial review. . . ." *Id.* § 1571(b)(1). For an application of the judicial review provision, *see Allied Local and Regional Manufacturers Caucus v. U.S. E.P.A.,* 215 F.3d 61, 81 (D.C. Cir. 2000).

The Regulatory Flexibility Act and the Unfunded Mandates Reform Act are not the only statutes that impose generic requirements on agency rulemaking. Other statutes act in a similar, across-the-board manner but require agencies to meet particular requirements when their actions have certain types of effects. *See* National Technology Transfer and Advancement Act of 1995, 110 Stat. 775, 783 (codified at 15 U.S.C. § 272 note) (providing generally that "all Federal agencies and departments shall use technical standards that are developed or adopted by voluntary consensus standard bodies"); Paperwork Reduction Act of 1995, 109 Stat. 163 (codified at 44 U.S.C. §§ 3501 *et seq.*) (imposing requirement of prior review and approval of agency action to "conduct or sponsor the collection of information"); National Environmental Policy Act of 1969, 83 Stat. 852 (codified at 42 U.S.C. §§ 4321 *et seq.*) (requiring that agencies consider environmental impacts before acting). These latter three statutes apply to any regulatory action, rather than only to rulemaking.

QUESTIONS

1. How effective do you expect these generic requirements to be in improving agency consideration of regulatory flexibility?
2. Would you expect that the differences between the judicial review provisions for the amended Regulatory Flexibility Act and Unfunded Mandates Reform Act would have an impact on the effectiveness of the statutes? If so, which is likely to be more effective?
3. Consider the alternative approach of the 1981 MSAPA, which authorizes certain state government officials or the public to trigger preparation of a regulatory analysis. *See* § 3-105.

THEORY APPLIED PROBLEM

In July 2017, the Federal Communications Commission (FCC) issues new regulations regarding the use of "incidental" profanity on broadcast television and radio stations. Previously, the FCC had held, in a series of adjudications, that the incidental use of profanity in a live broadcast would not constitute a violation of a statutory ban against indecent broadcasts. In the Report and Order adopting the stricter policy on the application of the rule against indecent broadcasts, the FCC says that "times have changed and FCC policy must change with them." The agency offers no other explanation for its change of policy. In addition, the July 2017 regulations establish a ban on "unduly violent" content between the hours of 6 AM and midnight. In a 2001 proceeding, the Commission concluded that "it is not obvious that Congress considered violent programming to be 'indecent' when it established the rule against the broadcast of indecent and obscene materials over the airwaves, nor do we believe that regulating violent content on broadcast stations would serve the public interest." The FCC does not address (at all) the 2001 document and the policy that it established in the July 2017 Report and Order adopting the new broadcast violence regulations.

The National Association of Broadcasters files a petition for review of the new indecency regulations. The NAB's brief in support of the petition argues that the new regulations are arbitrary and capricious, and that the agency's failure to explain its departures from its prior policies makes the arbitrary and capricious nature of the regulations self-evident.

The D.C. Circuit rules in favor of the NAB and remands the Report and Order so that the FCC can better explain its rationale for modifying its policies so drastically. The court holds that the FCC must rewrite the concise general statement that explains the major issues involved in the proceeding and how the agency resolved them, or face an order vacating the rules (which, unlike a remand, would require the agency to start over from scratch).

Is the D.C. Circuit's opinion consistent with *Vermont Yankee*? Why or why not? Suppose that the D.C. Circuit also directly orders the FCC on remand to address the prior 2001 Report and Order. Would that be consistent with *Vermont Yankee*?

NOTE ON ALTERNATIVE DISPUTE RESOLUTION AND FEDERAL ADMINISTRATIVE AGENCIES

Alternative Dispute Resolution, often referred to as "ADR," encompasses several extra-judicial dispute resolution techniques, including arbitration, mediation, and negotiation. ADR has taken the civil practice of law by storm. The Federal Rules of Civil Procedure now require pre-trial conferences, essentially mediations, to attempt a pre-trial settlement of the dispute.[1] Similarly, private employers increasingly insist that would-be employees sign contracts that require the use of binding arbitration to resolve any disputes that should arise during the course of the employment relationship. *See*, e.g., *Circuit City Stores v. Adams,* 532 U.S. 105 (2001).

Proponents of ADR insist that it is quicker, cheaper, and more predictable than litigation in the public courts. They also suggest that ADR permits the

---

1. *See* Judge Patricia M. Wald, *ADR and the Courts: An Update,* 46 Duke L.J. 1445, 1445-51 (1997) (reviewing use of mandatory ADR mediations in the federal courts).

creation of specialized bodies of law and expertise in the application of this privatized law.[2] In light of these claims and the phenomenal growth of ADR in the context of civil litigation, it should not be surprising that efforts have been made to incorporate ADR principles into the federal administrative state.[3] In 1990, Congress enacted the Negotiated Rulemaking Act, 5 U.S.C. §§ 561-570, and the Administrative Dispute Resolution Act, 5 U.S.C. §§ 571-580.

The Negotiated Rulemaking Act authorizes federal administrative agencies "to establish a framework for the conduct of negotiated rulemaking, consistent with section 553 of this title, to encourage agencies to use the process when it enhances the informal rulemaking process." 5 U.S.C. § 561. Under this law, an agency may convene a "Negotiated Rulemaking Committee" to consider how best to approach a particular regulatory problem. The Negotiated Rulemaking Committee should include representatives of all interested groups, including the agency, regulated industries, and public interest organizations. The committee undertakes a study of the problem and attempts to draft a "consensus proposal" that all members of the committee pledge to support. Each member of the committee has an equally-weighted vote.

If the committee can agree to a consensus proposal, the agency will promulgate the proposal's substantive provisions in a Notice of Proposed Rulemaking, which then proceeds like any other NPRM through the notice and comment procedures of section 553. If ultimately adopted, the rule resulting from the negotiated rulemaking is subject to judicial review just like any other rule. 5 U.S.C. § 570 ("A rule which is the product of negotiated rulemaking and is subject to judicial review shall not be accorded any greater deference by a court than a rule which is the product of other rulemaking procedures").

The objective is to achieve a consensus through an informal, pre-NPRM consultative process of negotiation. Proponents of "reg neg" believe that section 553 notice and comment proceedings are too formalized and do not permit interested groups to negotiate directly with each other over acceptable regulatory terms and conditions.[4] The informal nature of the committee, coupled with the requirement of consensus, operate to create greater openness and cooperation than would exist in traditional notice and comment rulemaking proceedings.

Several potential objections exist to the use of negotiated rulemaking. First, and perhaps most importantly, negotiated rulemaking reduces the agency to the status of a single party, with a single vote. Congress delegates responsibility for administrative regulations to agencies, not private interest groups or regulated industries. The danger of agency capture, which is always present, is greatly exacerbated in negotiated rulemakings.[5] An administrative agency must pursue

---

2. *See* Lisa Bernstein, *Merchant Law in Merchant Court: Rethinking the Code's Search for Immanent Business Norms,* 144 U. Pa. L. Rev. 1765 (1996); Stephen Ware, *Default Rules from Mandatory Rules: Privatizing Law Through Arbitration,* 83 Minn. L. Rev. 703 (1998); *but cf.* Owen M. Fiss, *Against Settlement,* 93 Yale L.J. 1073, 1082-87 (1984) (arguing that resolution of legal disputes in the public courts advances important values associated with the Rule of Law); Ronald J. Krotoszynski, Jr., *The New Legal Process: Games People Play and the Quest for Legitimate Judicial Decision Making,* 77 Wash. U.L.Q. 993, 1034-47 (1999) (arguing that reform of public courts, rather than exodus, presents the best course of action for cultural minorities who distrust the basic fairness of public courts).

3. *See,* e.g., Philip J. Harter, *Negotiating Regulations: A Cure for Malaise,* 71 Geo. L.J. 1 (1982).

4. *See* Philip J. Harter, *Fear of Commitment: An Affliction of Adolescents,* 46 Duke L.J. 1389 (1997).

5. That is to say, an agency representative might feel pressured to go along with a consensus proposal, even if it does not fully or completely implement the will of Congress, or take account of considerations that Congress declared to be controlling. For discussion of such problems in the

the public interest, as defined by Congress, in the organic statute that the proposed regulations will enforce. Negotiated rulemaking, with its emphasis on consensus and equal voting rights on the committee, risks equating consensus with the public interest.

A second objection relates to speed: in cases where an industry consensus exists, it is doubtful that a pre-NPRM negotiated rulemaking proceeding will speed the issuance of rules.[6] Comments filed in such a proceeding would undoubtedly reflect the fact of consensus and the agency would be able to adopt final rules with dispatch. Thus, in "win-win" circumstances, negotiated rulemaking will inevitably delay the issuance of final (non-controversial) rules. In "win-lose" situations, where the interests of the agency, the affected industry, and public interest organizations are intractably opposed, no amount of negotiation is going to result in consensus. Environmentalists will never agree to permit drilling in the Arctic National Wildlife Refuge or on the rules that would govern such drilling, should Congress open the area to development; concurrently, the oil industry will never give up on the prospect of exploiting the oil reserves located underneath this national park. No amount of committee jawboning can produce consensus when an agency's decision will have dire financial or environmental consequences. Negotiated rulemaking will simply delay the inevitable battle to follow in the context of the notice and comment rulemaking proceedings.

For negotiated rulemaking to be of any real use, one would have to posit a middle set of cases in which things appear to present a "win-lose" question but, upon more careful consideration and reflection, can be recast into "win-win" encounters for the agency, the regulated industry, and the public interest organizations. This set of cases, although real, may be remarkably small. Accordingly, the value of negotiated rulemaking proceedings is open to some doubt. The Administrative Dispute Resolution Act presents a very different calculus. Simply put, there is every reason to believe that ADR techniques that succeed in reducing the time and cost of civil litigation could have the exact same effect on administrative adjudications. If arbitration, mediation, or negotiation can speed the resolution of disputes and lower the costs associated with administrative adjudications, it is difficult to see any principled objection to the use of these devices in matters pending before federal administrative agencies.[7]

The Administrative Dispute Resolution Act ("ADRA") authorizes all federal agencies to "use a dispute resolution proceeding for the resolution of an issue in controversy that relates to an administrative program, if the parties agree to such a proceeding." 5 U.S.C. §572(a). In turn, the ADRA defines a "dispute

---

context of a specific rulemaking, *see* William Funk, *When Smoke Gets in Your Eyes: Regulatory Negotiation and the Public Interest — EPA's Woodstove Standards,* 18 Envtl. L. 55 (1987). For more general (and trenchant) critiques of "reg neg," *see* William Funk, *Bargaining Toward the New Millennium: Regulatory Negotiation and the Subversion of the Public Interest,* 46 Duke L.J. 1351 (1997); Susan Rose-Ackerman, *Consensus Versus Incentives: A Skeptical Look at Regulatory Negotiation,* 1994 Duke L.J. 1206.

6. *See* Cary Coglianese, *Assessing Consensus: The Promise and Performance of Negotiated Rulemaking,* 46 Duke L.J. 1255 (1997).

7. Of course, this presumes that no party defending its interests in an adverse proceeding with a federal agency would be forced to relinquish its procedural rights under the APA in favor of some sort of ADR proceeding. As it happens, a party may not be forced to use ADR techniques under the Administrative Dispute Resolution Act. *See* 5 U.S.C. §572(c) ("Alternative means of dispute resolution authorized under this subchapter are voluntary procedures which supplement rather than limit other agency dispute resolution techniques"); *id.* at §575(a)(1) ("Arbitration may be used as an alternative means of dispute resolution whenever all parties consent").

resolution proceeding" as encompassing "any process in which an alternative means of dispute resolution is used to resolve an issue in controversy in which a neutral is appointed and specified parties participate." § 571(6). The definition of "administrative program" includes "a Federal function which involves the protection of the public interest and the determination of rights, privileges, and obligations of private persons through rule making, adjudication, licensing, or investigation, as those terms are used in [the APA]." § 571(2).

ADRA specifically authorizes the use of binding arbitration to resolve pending administrative disputes and removes judicial review of arbitral awards from the APA. Instead, federal courts are to review such awards under the highly deferential standards set forth in the Federal Arbitration Act. § 581(a). ADRA sets forth the rules governing the selection of arbitrators, the conduct of arbitral proceedings, and the enforcement of arbitral awards. §§ 575-580.

Because ADRA proceedings are entirely voluntary, it is difficult to find much fault with the incorporation of ADR techniques as a means of streamlining adjudication of administrative disputes.[8] It is therefore unsurprising that most of the scholarly commentary, both pro and con, relates to the use of ADR techniques in the context of rulemaking.

E. MUST AN AGENCY PROMULGATE RULES?

SEC v. CHENERY CORP. (CHENERY II)
332 U.S. 194 (1947)

Mr. Justice Murphy delivered the opinion of the Court.

This case is here for the second time. In *[Chenery I]*, we held that an order of the Securities and Exchange Commission could not be sustained on the grounds upon which that agency acted. We therefore directed that the case be remanded to the Commission for such further proceedings as might be appropriate. On remand, the Commission reexamined the problem, recast its rationale and reached the same result. The issue now is whether the Commission's action is proper in light of the principles established in our prior decision.

When the case was first here, we emphasized a simple but fundamental rule of administrative law. That rule is to the effect that a reviewing court, in dealing with a determination or judgment which an administrative agency alone is authorized to make, must judge the propriety of such action solely by the grounds invoked by the agency. If those grounds are inadequate or improper, the court is powerless to affirm the administrative action by substituting what it considers to be a more adequate or proper basis. To do so would propel the court into the domain which Congress has set aside exclusively for the administrative agency.

We also emphasized in our prior decision an important corollary of the foregoing rule. If the administrative action is to be tested by the basis upon which it purports to rest, that basis must be set forth with such clarity as to be understandable. It will not do for a court to be compelled to guess at the theory

---

8. See Wald, *supra*, n.1, at 1451-56 (reviewing favorably use of agency-sponsored ADR in administrative disputes that would otherwise trigger more formal adjudicatory proceedings).

underlying the agency's action; nor can a court be expected to chisel that which must be precise from what the agency has left vague and indecisive. In other words, "We must know what a decision means before the duty becomes ours to say whether it is right or wrong."

Applying this rule and its corollary, the Court was unable to sustain the Commission's original action. The Commission had been dealing with the reorganization of the Federal Water Service Corporation (Federal), a holding company registered under the Public Utility Holding Company Act of 1935, 49 Stat. 803. During the period when successive reorganization plans proposed by the management were before the Commission, the officers, directors and controlling stockholders of Federal purchased a substantial amount of Federal's preferred stock on the over-the-counter market. Under the fourth reorganization plan, this preferred stock was to be converted into common stock of a new corporation; on the basis of the purchases of preferred stock, the management would have received more than 10% of this new common stock. It was frankly admitted that the management's purpose in buying the preferred stock was to protect its interest in the new company. It was also plain that there was no fraud or lack of disclosure in making these purchases.

But the Commission would not approve the fourth plan so long as the preferred stock purchased by the management was to be treated on a parity with the other preferred stock. It felt that the officers and directors of a holding company in process of reorganization under the Act were fiduciaries and were under a duty not to trade in the securities of that company during the reorganization period. And so the plan was amended to provide that the preferred stock acquired by the management, unlike that held by others, was not to be converted into the new common stock; instead, it was to be surrendered at cost plus dividends accumulated since the purchase dates. As amended, the plan was approved by the Commission over the management's objections.

The Court interpreted the Commission's order approving this amended plan as grounded solely upon judicial authority. The Commission appeared to have treated the preferred stock acquired by the management in accordance with what it thought were standards theretofore recognized by courts. If it intended to create new standards growing out of its experience in effectuating the legislative policy, it failed to express itself with sufficient clarity and precision to be so understood. Hence the order was judged by the only standards clearly invoked by the Commission. On that basis, the order could not stand. The opinion pointed out that courts do not impose upon officers and directors of a corporation any fiduciary duty to its stockholders which precludes them, merely because they are officers and directors, from buying and selling the corporation's stock. Nor was it felt that the cases upon which the Commission relied established any principles of law or equity which in themselves would be sufficient to justify this order.

The opinion further noted that neither Congress nor the Commission had promulgated any general rule proscribing such action as the purchase of preferred stock by Federal's management. And the only judge-made rule of equity which might have justified the Commission's order related to fraud or mismanagement of the reorganization by the officers and directors, matters which were admittedly absent in this situation.

After the case was remanded to the Commission, Federal Water and Gas Corp. (Federal Water), the surviving corporation under the reorganization plan, made an application for approval of an amendment to the plan to provide for the issuance of new common stock of the reorganized company. This stock was to be distributed to the members of Federal's management on the basis of the shares of the old preferred stock which they had acquired during the period of reorganization, thereby placing them in the same position as the public holders of the old preferred stock. The intervening members of Federal's management joined in this request. The Commission denied the application in an order issued on February 8, 1945. That order was reversed by the Court of Appeals, which felt that our prior decision precluded such action by the Commission.

The latest order of the Commission definitely avoids the fatal error of relying on judicial precedents which do not sustain it. This time, after a thorough reexamination of the problem in light of the purposes and standards of the Holding Company Act, the Commission has concluded that the proposed transaction is inconsistent with the standards of §§ 7 and 11 of the Act. It has drawn heavily upon its accumulated experience in dealing with utility reorganizations. And it has expressed its reasons with a clarity and thoroughness that admit of no doubt as to the underlying basis of its order.

The argument is pressed upon us, however, that the Commission was foreclosed from taking such a step following our prior decision. It is said that, in the absence of findings of conscious wrongdoing on the part of Federal's management, the Commission could not determine by an order in this particular case that it was inconsistent with the statutory standards to permit Federal's management to realize a profit through the reorganization purchases. All that it could do was to enter an order allowing an amendment to the plan so that the proposed transaction could be consummated. Under this view, the Commission would be free only to promulgate a general rule outlawing such profits in future utility reorganizations; but such a rule would have to be prospective in nature and have no retroactive effect upon the instant situation.

We reject this contention, for it grows out of a misapprehension of our prior decision and of the Commission's statutory duties. We held no more and no less than that the Commission's first order was unsupportable for the reasons supplied by that agency. But when the case left this Court, the problem whether Federal's management should be treated equally with other preferred stockholders still lacked a final and complete answer. It was clear that the Commission could not give a negative answer by resort to prior judicial declarations. And it was also clear that the Commission was not bound by settled judicial precedents in a situation of this nature. Still unsettled, however, was the answer the Commission might give were it to bring to bear on the facts the proper administrative and statutory considerations, a function which belongs exclusively to the Commission in the first instance. The administrative process had taken an erroneous rather than a final turn. Hence we carefully refrained from expressing any views as to the propriety of an order rooted in the proper and relevant considerations.

When the case was directed to be remanded to the Commission for such further proceedings as might be appropriate, it was with the thought that the Commission would give full effect to its duties in harmony with the views we had expressed. This obviously meant something more than the entry of a perfunctory order giving parity treatment to the management holdings of preferred stock. The fact that the Commission had committed a legal error in its first disposition of the case certainly gave Federal's management no vested right to receive the benefits of such an order. After the remand was made, therefore, the Commission was bound to deal with the problem afresh, performing the function delegated to it by Congress. It was again charged with the duty of measuring the proposed treatment of the management's preferred stock holdings by relevant and proper standards. Only in that way could the legislative policies embodied in the Act be effectuated.

The absence of a general rule or regulation governing management trading during reorganization did not affect the Commission's duties in relation to the particular proposal before it. The Commission was asked to grant or deny effectiveness to a proposed amendment to Federal's reorganization plan whereby the management would be accorded parity treatment on its holdings. It could do that only in the form of an order, entered after a due consideration of the particular facts in light of the relevant and proper standards. That was true regardless of whether those standards previously had been spelled out in a general rule or regulation. Indeed, if the Commission rightly felt that the proposed amendment was inconsistent with those standards, an order giving effect to the amendment merely because there was no general rule or regulation covering the matter would be unjustified.

It is true that our prior decision explicitly recognized the possibility that the Commission might have promulgated a general rule dealing with this problem under its statutory rule-making powers, in which case the issue for our consideration would have been entirely different from that which did confront us. But we did not mean to imply thereby that the failure of the Commission to anticipate this problem and to promulgate a general rule withdrew all power from that agency to perform its statutory duty in this case. To hold that the Commission had no alternative in this proceeding but to approve the proposed transaction, while formulating any general rules it might desire for use in future cases of this nature, would be to stultify the administrative process. That we refuse to do.

Since the Commission, unlike a court, does have the ability to make new law prospectively through the exercise of its rule-making powers, it has less reason to rely upon *ad hoc* adjudication to formulate new standards of conduct within the framework of the Holding Company Act. The function of filling in the interstices of the Act should be performed, as much as possible, through this quasi-legislative promulgation of rules to be applied in the future. But any rigid requirement to that effect would make the administrative process inflexible and incapable of dealing with many of the specialized problems which arise. Not every principle essential to the effective administration of a statute can or should be cast immediately into the mold of a general rule. Some principles must await their own development, while others must be adjusted to meet particular, unforeseeable situations. In performing its important functions in these respects, therefore, an administrative agency must be equipped to act either by general rule or by individual order. To insist upon one form of action to the exclusion of the other is to exalt form over necessity.

In other words, problems may arise in a case which the administrative agency could not reasonably foresee, problems which must be solved despite the absence of a relevant general rule. Or the agency may not have had sufficient experience with a particular problem to warrant rigidifying its tentative judgment into a hard and fast rule. Or the problem may be so specialized and varying in nature as to be impossible of capture within the boundaries of a general rule.

In those situations, the agency must retain power to deal with the problems on a case-to-case basis if the administrative process is to be effective. There is thus a very definite place for the case-by-case evolution of statutory standards. And the choice made between proceeding by general rule or by individual, *ad hoc* litigation is one that lies primarily in the informed discretion of the administrative agency.

Hence we refuse to say that the Commission, which had not previously been confronted with the problem of management trading during reorganization, was forbidden from utilizing this particular proceeding for announcing and applying a new standard of conduct. That such action might have a retroactive effect was not necessarily fatal to its validity. Every case of first impression has a retroactive effect, whether the new principle is announced by a court or by an administrative agency. But such retroactivity must be balanced against the mischief of producing a result which is contrary to a statutory design or to legal and equitable principles. If that mischief is greater than the ill effect of the retroactive application of a new standard, it is not the type of retroactivity which is condemned by law.

And so in this case, the fact that the Commission's order might retroactively prevent Federal's management from securing the profits and control which were the objects of the preferred stock purchases may well be outweighed by the dangers inherent in such purchases from the statutory standpoint. If that is true, the argument of retroactivity becomes nothing more than a claim that the Commission lacks power to enforce the standards of the Act in this proceeding. Such a claim deserves rejection.

The problem in this case thus resolves itself into a determination of whether the Commission's action in denying effectiveness to the proposed amendment to the Federal reorganization plan can be justified on the basis upon which it clearly rests. As we have noted, the Commission avoided placing its sole reliance on inapplicable judicial precedents. Rather it has derived its conclusions from the particular facts in the case, its general experience in reorganization matters and its informed view of statutory requirements. It is those matters which are the guide for our review.

The Commission concluded that it could not find that the reorganization plan, if amended as proposed, would be "fair and equitable to the persons affected thereby" within the meaning of § 11(e) of the Act, under which the reorganization was taking place. Its view was that the amended plan would involve the issuance of securities on terms "detrimental to the public interest or the interest of investors" contrary to §§ 7(d) (6) and 7(e), and would result in an "unfair or inequitable distribution of voting power" among the Federal security holders within the meaning of § 7(e). It was led to this result "not by proof that the interveners [Federal's management] committed acts of conscious wrongdoing but by the character of the conflicting interests created by the interveners' program of stock purchases carried out while plans for reorganization were under consideration."

The Commission noted that Federal's management controlled a large multi-state utility system and that its influence permeated down to the lowest tier of operating companies. The financial, operational and accounting policies of the parent and its subsidiaries were therefore under the management's strict control. The broad range of business judgments vested in Federal's management multiplied opportunities for affecting the market price of Federal's outstanding securities and made the exercise of judgment on any matter a subject of greatest significance to investors. Added to these normal managerial powers, the Commission pointed out that a holding company management obtains special powers in the course of a voluntary reorganization under §11 (e) of the Holding Company Act. The management represents the stockholders in such a reorganization, initiates the proceeding, draws up and files the plan, and can file amendments thereto at any time. These additional powers may introduce conflicts between the management's normal interests and its responsibilities to the various classes of stockholders which it represents in the reorganization. Moreover, because of its representative status, the management has special opportunities to obtain advance information of the attitude of the Commission.

Drawing upon its experience, the Commission indicated that all these normal and special powers of the holding company management during the course of a §11(e) reorganization placed in the management's command "a formidable battery of devices that would enable it, if it should choose to use them selfishly, to affect in material degree the ultimate allocation of new securities among the various existing classes, to influence the market for its own gain, and to manipulate or obstruct the reorganization required by the mandate of the statute." In that setting, the Commission felt that a management program of stock purchase would give rise to the temptation and the opportunity to shape the reorganization proceeding so as to encourage public selling on the market at low prices. No management could engage in such a program without raising serious questions as to whether its personal interests had not opposed its duties "to exercise disinterested judgment in matters pertaining to subsidiaries' accounting, budgetary and dividend policies, to present publicly an unprejudiced financial picture of the enterprise, and to effectuate a fair and feasible plan expeditiously."

The Commission further felt that its answer should be the same even where proof of intentional wrongdoing on the management's part is lacking. Assuming a conflict of interests, the Commission thought that the absence of actual misconduct is immaterial; injury to the public investors and to the corporation may result just as readily. "Questionable transactions may be explained away, and an abuse of investors and the administrative process may be perpetrated without evil intent, yet the injury will remain." Moreover, the Commission was of the view that the delays and the difficulties involved in probing the mental processes and personal integrity of corporate officials do not warrant any distinction on the basis of evil intent, the plain fact being "that an absence of unfairness or detriment in cases of this sort would be practically impossible to establish by proof."

Turning to the facts in this case, the Commission noted the salient fact that the primary object of Federal's management in buying the preferred stock was admittedly to obtain the voting power that was accruing to that stock through the reorganization and to profit from the investment therein. That stock had been purchased in the market at prices that were depressed in relation to what the management anticipated would be, and what in fact was, the earning and asset value of its reorganization equivalent. The Commission admitted that the good faith and personal integrity of this management were not in question; but as to the management's justification of its motives, the Commission concluded that it was merely trying to "deny that they made selfish use of their powers during the period when their conflict of interest, vis-a-vis public investors, was in existence owing to their purchase program." Federal's management had thus placed itself in a position where it was "peculiarly susceptible to temptation to conduct the reorganization for personal gain rather than the public good" and where its desire to make advantageous purchases of stock could have an important influence, even though subconsciously, upon many of the decisions to be made in the course of the reorganization. Accordingly, the Commission felt that all of its general considerations of the problem were applicable to this case.

The scope of our review of an administrative order wherein a new principle is announced and applied is no different from that which pertains to ordinary administrative action. The wisdom of the principle adopted is none of our concern. Our duty is at an end when it becomes evident that the Commission's action is based upon substantial evidence and is consistent with the authority granted by Congress.

We are unable to say in this case that the Commission erred in reaching the result it did. The facts being undisputed, we are free to disturb the Commission's conclusion only if it lacks any rational and statutory foundation. In that connection, the Commission has made a thorough examination of the problem, utilizing statutory standards and its own accumulated experience with reorganization matters. In essence, it has made what we indicated in our prior opinion would be an informed, expert judgment on the problem. It has taken into account "those more subtle factors in the marketing of utility company securities that gave rise to the very grave evils which the Public Utility Holding [Company] Act of 1935 was designed to correct" and has relied upon the fact that "Abuse of corporate position, influence, and access to information may raise questions so subtle that the law can deal with them effectively only by prohibitions not concerned with the fairness of a particular transaction."

Such factors may properly be considered by the Commission in determining whether to approve a plan of reorganization of a utility holding company, or an amendment to such a plan. The "fair and equitable" rule of § 11 (e) and the standard of what is "detrimental to the public interest or the interest of investors or consumers" under § 7 (d) (6) and § 7 (e) were inserted by the framers of the Act in order that the Commission might have broad powers to protect the various interests at stake. The application of those criteria, whether in the form of a particular order or a general regulation, necessarily requires the use of informed discretion by the Commission. The very breadth of the statutory language precludes a reversal of the Commission's judgment save where it has plainly abused its discretion in these matters. Such an abuse is not present in this case.

The purchase by a holding company management of that company's securities during the course of a reorganization may well be thought to be so fraught with danger as to warrant a denial of the benefits and profits accruing to the management. The possibility that such a stock purchase program will result in detriment to the public investors is not a fanciful one. The influence that program may have upon the important decisions to be made by the management during reorganization is not inconsequential. Since the officers and directors occupy fiduciary positions during this period, their actions are to be held to a higher standard than that imposed upon the general investing public. There is thus a reasonable basis for a judgment that the benefits and profits accruing to the management from the stock purchases should be prohibited, regardless of the good faith involved. And it is a judgment that can justifiably be reached in terms of fairness and equitableness, to the end that the interests of the public, the investors and the consumers might be protected. But it is a judgment based upon public policy, a judgment which Congress has indicated is of the type for the Commission to make.

The Commission's conclusion here rests squarely in that area where administrative judgments are entitled to the greatest amount of weight by appellate courts. It is the product of administrative experience, appreciation of the complexities of the problem, realization of the statutory policies, and responsible treatment of the uncontested facts. It is the type of judgment which administrative agencies are best equipped to make and which justifies the use of the administrative process. Whether we agree or disagree with the result reached, it is an allowable judgment which we cannot disturb. *Reversed.*

[Justice Burton concurred in the result, the Chief Justice and Justice Douglas did not participate, and Justices Frankfurter and Jackson dissented.]

Mr. Justice Jackson, dissenting.

The Court by this present decision sustains the identical administrative order which only recently it held invalid. *SEC v. Chenery Corp.*, 318 U.S. 80. As the Court correctly notes, the Commission has only "recast its rationale and reached the same result." (Par. 1.) There being no change in the order, no additional evidence in the record and no amendment of relevant legislation, it is clear that there has been a shift in attitude between that of the controlling membership of the Court when the case was first here and that of those who have the power of decision on this second review.

I feel constrained to disagree with the reasoning offered to rationalize this shift. It makes judicial review of administrative orders a hopeless formality for the litigant, even where granted to him by Congress. It reduces the judicial process in such cases to a mere feint. While the opinion does not have the adherence of a majority of the full Court, if its pronouncements should become governing principles they would, in practice, put most administrative orders over and above the law.

I

The essential facts are few and are not in dispute. This corporation filed with the Securities and Exchange Commission a voluntary plan of reorganization. While the reorganization proceedings were pending sixteen officers and directors bought on the open market about $7\frac{1}{2}\%$ of the corporation's preferred stock. Both the Commission and the Court admit that these purchases were not forbidden by any law, judicial precedent, regulation or rule of the Commission. Nevertheless, the Commission has ordered these individuals to surrender their shares to the corporation at cost, plus 4% interest, and the Court now approves that order.

It is helpful, before considering whether this order is authorized by law, to reflect on what it is and what it is not. It is not conceivably a discharge of the Commission's duty to determine whether a proposed plan of reorganization would be "fair and equitable." It has nothing to do with the corporate structure, or the classes and amounts of stock, or voting rights or dividend preferences. It does not remotely affect the impersonal financial or legal factors of the plan. It is a personal deprivation denying particular persons the right to continue to own their stock and to exercise its privileges. Other persons who bought at the same time and price in the open market would be allowed to keep and convert their stock. Thus, the order is in no sense an exercise of the function of control over the terms and relations of the corporate securities.

Neither is the order one merely to regulate the future use of property. It literally takes valuable property away from its lawful owners for the benefit of other private parties without full compensation and the Court expressly approves the taking. It says that the stock owned by these persons is denied conversion along with similar stock owned by others; "instead, it was to be surrendered at cost plus dividends accumulated since the purchase dates." (Par. 5.) It should be noted that this formula was subsequently altered to read "cost plus 4% interest." That this basis was less than its value is recognized, for the Court says "That stock had been purchased in the market at prices that were depressed in relation to what the management anticipated would be, and what in fact was, the earning and asset value of its reorganization equivalent." (Par. 24.) Admittedly, the value above cost, and interest on it, simply is taken from the owners, without compensation. No such power has ever been confirmed in any administrative body.

It should also be noted that neither the Court nor the Commission purports to adjudge a forfeiture of this property as a consequence of sharp dealing or breach of trust. The Court says, "The Commission admitted that the good faith and personal integrity of this management were not in question;. . . ." (Par. 24.) And again, "It was frankly admitted that the management's purpose in buying the preferred stock was to protect its interest in the new company. It was also plain that there was no fraud or lack of disclosure in making these purchases." (Par. 4.)

II

The reversal of the position of this Court is due to a fundamental change in prevailing philosophy. The basic assumption of the earlier opinion as therein stated was, "*But before transactions otherwise legal can be outlawed or denied their usual business consequences, they must fall under the ban of some standards of conduct prescribed by an agency of government authorized to prescribe such standards. . . .*" [*Chenery I*] The basic assumption of the present opinion is stated thus: "*The absence of a general rule or regulation governing management trading during reorganization did not affect the Commission's duties in relation to the particular proposal before it.*" (Par. 13.) This puts in juxtaposition the two conflicting philosophies which produce opposite results in the same case and on the same facts. The difference between the first and the latest decision of the Court is thus simply the difference between holding that administrative orders must have a basis in law and a holding that absence of a legal basis is no ground on which courts may annul them.

As there admittedly is no law or regulation to support this order, we peruse the Court's opinion diligently to find on what grounds it is now held that the Court of Appeals, on pain of being reversed for error, was required to stamp this order with its approval. We find but one. That is the principle of judicial deference to administrative experience. That argument is five times stressed in as many different contexts, and I quote just enough to identify the instances: "The Commission," it says, "has drawn heavily upon its accumulated experience in dealing with utility reorganizations." (Par. 9.) "Rather it has derived its conclusions from the particular facts in the case, its general experience in reorganization matters and its informed view of statutory requirements." (Par. 19.) "Drawing upon its experience, the Commission indicated . . . ," etc. (Par. 22.) ". . . the Commission has made a thorough examination of the problem, utilizing statutory standards and its own accumulated experience with reorganization matters." (Par. 26.) And finally, of the order the Court says, "It is the product of administrative experience," etc. (Par. 29.)

What are we to make of this reiterated deference to "administrative experience" when in another context the Court says, "Hence, we refuse to say that the Commission, *which had not previously been confronted with the problem of management trading during reorganization,* was forbidden from utilizing this particular proceeding for announcing and applying *a new standard of conduct*"? (Par. 17.) (Emphasis supplied.)

The Court's reasoning adds up to this: The Commission must be sustained because of its accumulated experience in solving a problem with which it had never before been confronted!

Of course, thus to uphold the Commission by professing to find that it has enunciated a "new standard of conduct" brings the Court squarely against the invalidity of retroactive law-making. But the Court does not falter. "That such action might have a retroactive effect was not necessarily fatal to its validity." (Par. 17.) "But such retroactivity must be balanced against the mischief of producing a result which is contrary to a statutory design or to legal and equitable principles." (Par. 17.) Of course, if what these parties did really was condemned by "statutory design" or "legal and equitable principles," it could be stopped without resort to a new rule and there would be no retroactivity to condone. But if it had been the Court's view that some law already prohibited the purchases, it would hardly have been necessary three sentences earlier to hold that the Commission was not prohibited "from utilizing this particular proceeding for announcing and applying a *new standard of conduct*." (Par. 17.) (Emphasis supplied.)

I give up. Now I realize fully what Mark Twain meant when he said, "The more you explain it, the more I don't understand it."

III

But one does not need to comprehend the processes by which other minds reach a given result in order to estimate the practical consequences of their pronouncement upon judicial review of administrative orders. . . .

Even if the Commission had, as the Court says, utilized this case to announce a new legal standard of conduct, there would be hurdles to be cleared, but we need not dwell on them now. Because to promulgate a general rule of law, either by regulation or by case law, is something the Commission expressly declined to do. It did not previously promulgate, and it does not by this order profess to promulgate, any rule or regulation to prohibit such purchases absolutely or under stated conditions. On the other hand, its position is that no such rule or standard would be fair and equitable in all cases.

IV

Whether, as [a] matter of policy, corporate managers during reorganization should be prohibited from buying or selling its stock, is not a question for us to decide. But it is for us to decide whether, so long as no law or regulation prohibits them from buying, their purchases may be forfeited, or not, in the discretion of the Commission. If such a power exists in words of the statute or in their implication, it would be possible to point it out and thus end the case. Instead, the Court admits that there was no law prohibiting these purchases when they were made, or at any time thereafter. And, except for this decision, there is none now.

The truth is that in this decision the Court approves the Commission's assertion of power to govern the matter *without* law, power to force surrender of stock so purchased whenever it will, and power also to overlook such acquisitions if it so chooses. The reasons which will lead it to take one course as against the other remain locked in its own breast, and it has not and apparently does not intend to commit them to any rule or regulation. This administrative authoritarianism, this power to decide without law, is what the Court seems to approve in so many words: "The absence of a general rule or regulation governing management trading during reorganization did not affect the Commission's duties. . . ." (Par. 13). This seems to me to undervalue and to belittle the place of law, even in the system of administrative justice. It calls to mind Mr. Justice Cardozo's statement that "Law as a guide to conduct is reduced to the level of mere futility if it is unknown and unknowable."

V

The Court's averment concerning this order that "It is the type of judgment which administrative agencies are best equipped to make and which justifies the use of the administrative process," (Par. 29) is the first instance in which the administrative process is sustained by reliance on that disregard of law which enemies of the process have always alleged to be its principal evil. It is the first encouragement this Court has given to conscious lawlessness as a permissible rule of administrative action. This decision is an ominous one to those who believe that men should be governed by laws that they may ascertain and abide by, and which will guide the action of those in authority as well as of those who are subject to authority.

I have long urged, and still believe, that the administrative process deserves fostering in our system as an expeditious and nontechnical method of *applying law* in specialized fields. I can not agree that it be used, and I think its continued effectiveness is endangered when it is used, as a method of *dispensing with law* in those fields.

Mr. Justice Frankfurter joins in this opinion.

QUESTIONS

1. Note that there are two SEC decisions and two Supreme Court opinions. Our case is *Chenery II*. But what happened in *Chenery I*? Recall that an

appellate court can generally affirm a trial court judgment on grounds different from those relied upon by the lower court. Why should the rule regarding review of agency action be different?

2. Is *Chenery II* really consistent with *Chenery I?*

3. Does the majority in *Chenery II* adequately meet the arguments of the dissent? Is there a way in which the SEC action at issue can be characterized as *not* retroactive?

4. What advantages (in terms of public policy) does case-by-case adjudication have as compared with rulemaking? Disadvantages?

5. State agencies, unlike federal agencies, might have an obligation to use one procedural device rather than the other, at least in some circumstances. These rules can be a function of either a state APA or a specific requirement in an organic act. *See generally* Johnny C. Burris, *The Failure of the Florida Judicial Review Process to Provide Effective Incentives for Agency Rulemaking,* 18 Fla. St. U.L. Rev. 661, 690-97 (1991) (arguing that the Florida APA requires agencies to proceed via rulemaking in some instances, but that the Florida state courts have been insufficiently committed to enforcing the "rule/order dichotomy").

6. Of course, *Chenery*'s rule that an agency may choose to use either rulemaking or adjudication to establish new agency policies applies only in circumstances where Congress has not specified the procedural modality that an agency must use to implement an organic act. If Congress wishes to constrain an administrative agency's procedural discretion, it need only require than an agency use rulemaking (or, alternatively, adjudication) when establishing the policies necessary to implement a particular regulatory command. In fact, Congress routinely uses this discretionary authority to require an agency to use rulemaking to implement particular regulatory programs.

NOTE ON NLRB v. WYMAN-GORDON

In *NLRB v. Wyman-Gordon Co.*, 394 U.S. 759 (1969), a majority of the Supreme Court appeared to accept the proposition that an agency may not avoid procedural requirements for rulemaking by announcing a standard of conduct in an adjudicative proceeding if the standard of conduct is not applied to the very parties to the adjudication. There was no majority opinion, however.

The NLRB had required an employer to provide a list of its employees' names and addresses to unions seeking to organize the employees. The Board based its decision on its earlier *Excelsior* ruling, which had enunciated a general requirement that employment lists be furnished to unions, but which had not applied the requirement to the parties in *Excelsior* itself. The two premises required for reversing the NLRB's decision in *Wyman-Gordon* on judicial review were roughly as follows: (a) the *Excelsior* "rule" was improperly promulgated under the APA, and (b) if the *Excelsior* rule were improperly promulgated, then the agency decision must be reversed even if the agency could have made the same decision without relying on *Excelsior*. There was no question that (a) and (b) together would have required reversing the agency action, and Justices Douglas and Harlan so voted. 394 U.S. at 775-80 (Douglas, J., dissenting), 780-83 (Harlan, J., dissenting). Justice Fortas and three others accepted (a) but rejected (b), while Justice Black and two others accepted (b) but rejected (a). 394 U.S. at 761-69, 769-75 (Black, J., concurring in the result). The result was to uphold the agency action, despite the fact that a majority supported each of (a) and (b).

NLRB v. BELL AEROSPACE CO.
416 U.S. 267 (1974)

MR. JUSTICE POWELL delivered the opinion of the Court.

This case presents two questions: first, whether the National Labor Relations Board properly determined that all "managerial employees," except those whose participation in a labor organization would create a conflict of interest with their job responsibilities, are covered by the National Labor Relations Act; and second, whether the Board must proceed by rulemaking rather than by adjudication in determining whether certain buyers are "managerial employees." We answer both questions in the negative.

I

Respondent Bell Aerospace Co., Division of Textron, Inc. (company), operates a plant in Wheatfield, New York, where it is engaged in research and development in the design and fabrication of aerospace products. On July 30, 1970, Amalgamated Local No. 1286 of the United Automobile, Aerospace and Agricultural Implement Workers of America (union) petitioned the National Labor Relations Board (Board) for a representation election to determine whether the union would be certified as the bargaining representative of the 25 buyers in the purchasing and procurement department at the company's plant. The company opposed the petition on the ground that the buyers were "managerial employees" and thus were not covered by the Act.

The relevant facts adduced at the representation hearing are as follows. The purchasing and procurement department receives requisition orders from other departments at the plant and is responsible for purchasing all of the company's needs from outside suppliers. Some items are standardized and may be purchased "off the shelf" from various distributors and suppliers. Other items must be made to the company's specifications, and the requisition orders may be accompanied by detailed blueprints and other technical plans. Requisitions often designate a particular vendor, and in some instances the buyer must obtain approval before selecting a different one. Where no vendor is specified, the buyer is free to choose one.

Absent specific instructions to the contrary, buyers have full discretion, without any dollar limit, to select prospective vendors, draft invitations to bid, evaluate submitted bids, negotiate price and terms, and prepare purchase orders. Buyers execute all purchase orders up to $50,000. They may place or cancel orders of less than $5,000 on their own signature. On commitments in excess of $5,000, buyers must obtain the approval of a superior, with higher levels of approval required as the purchase cost increases. For the Minute Man missile project, which represents 70% of the company's sales, purchase decisions are made by a team of personnel from the engineering, quality assurance, finance, and manufacturing departments. The buyer serves as team chairman and signs the purchase order, but a representative from the pricing and negotiation department participates in working out the terms.

After the representation hearing, the Regional Director transferred the case to the Board. On May 20, 1971, the Board issued its decision holding that the company's buyers constituted an appropriate unit for purposes of collective bargaining and directing an election. Relying on its recent decision in *North Arkansas Electric Cooperative, Inc.*, the Board first stated that even though the company's buyers might be "managerial employees," they were nevertheless covered by the Act and entitled to its protections. The Board then rejected the company's alternative contention that representation should be denied because the buyers' authority to commit the company's credit, select vendors, and negotiate purchase prices would create a potential conflict of interest between the buyers as union members and the company. In essence, the company argued that buyers would be more receptive to bids from union contractors and would also influence "make or buy" decisions in favor of "make," thus creating additional work for sister unions in the plant. The Board thought, however, that any possible conflict was "unsupported conjecture" since the buyers' "discretion and latitude for independent action must take place within the confines of the general directions which the Employer has established" and that "any possible temptation to allow sympathy for sister unions to influence such decisions could effectively be controlled by the Employer."

On June 16, 1971, a representation election was conducted in which 15 of the buyers voted for the union and nine against. On August 12, the Board certified the union as the exclusive bargaining representative for the company's buyers. That same day, however, the Court of Appeals for the Eighth Circuit denied enforcement of another Board order in *NLRB v. North Arkansas Electric Coopera-tive, Inc.*, 446 F.2d 602, and held that "managerial employees" were not covered by the Act and were therefore not entitled to its protections.

Encouraged by the Eighth Circuit's decision, the company moved the Board for reconsideration of its earlier order. The Board denied the motion stating that it disagreed with the Eighth Circuit and would adhere to its own decision in *North Arkansas*. In the Board's view, Congress intended to exclude from the Act only those "managerial employees" associated with the "formulation and imple-mentation of labor relations policies." In each case, the "fundamental touch-stone" was "whether the duties and responsibilities of any managerial employee or group of managerial employees do or do not include determinations which should be made free of any conflict of interest which could arise if the person involved was a participating member of a labor organization." Turning to the present case, the Board reiterated its prior finding that the company had not shown that union organization of its buyers would create a conflict of interest in labor relations.

The company stood by its contention that the buyers, as "managerial employ-ees," were not covered by the Act and refused to bargain with the union. An unfair labor practice complaint resulted in a Board finding that the company had violated §§ 8 (a)(5) and (1) of the Act, 29 U. S. C. §§ 158 (a)(5) and (1), and an order compelling the company to bargain with the union. Subsequently, the company petitioned the United States Court of Appeals for the Second Circuit for review of the order and the Board cross-petitioned for enforcement.

The Court of Appeals denied enforcement. After reviewing the legislative history of the Taft-Hartley Act of 1947, 61 Stat. 136, and the Board's decisions in this area, the court concluded that Congress had intended to exclude all true "managerial employees" from the protection of the Act. It explained that this "exclusion embraced not only an employee 'so closely related to or aligned with management as to place the employee in a position of conflict of interest between his employer on the one hand and his fellow workers on the other' but also one who is 'formulating, determining and effectuating his employer's policies or has discretion, independent of an employer's established policy, in the performance of his duties,' *Illinois State Journal-Register, Inc. v. NLRB,* 412 F.2d 37, 41 (7 Cir. 1969)." The court added, however, that "the Board would [not] be precluded, on proper proceedings, from determining that buyers, or some types of buyers, are not true 'managerial employees' and consequently come within the protection of § 8 (a)(5) and (1)."

Turning to the merits of the present case, the court acknowledged that there was substantial evidence that the company's buyers were not sufficiently high in the managerial hierarchy to constitute true "managerial employees." Nevertheless, the court denied enforcement for two reasons. First, it was not certain that the Board's decision rested on a factual determination that these buyers were not true "managerial employees" rather than on "its new, and in our view, erroneous holding that it was free to regard *all* managerial employees as covered by the Act unless their duties met" the conflict-of-interest touchstone. Second, although the Board was not precluded from holding that buyers, or some types of buyers, were not "managerial employees," the court thought that, in view of the Board's long line of cases holding the contrary, it could not accomplish this change of position by adjudication. Rather, the Board should conduct a rule-making proceeding in conformity with § 6 of the Act, 29 U.S.C. § 156. The court therefore remanded the case to the Board for such a proceeding.

We granted the Board's petition for certiorari.

II

We begin with the question whether all "managerial employees," rather than just those in positions susceptible to conflicts of interest in labor relations, are excluded from the protections of the Act. The Board's early decisions, the legislative history of the Taft-Hartley Act of 1947, 61 Stat. 136, and subsequent Board and court decisions provide the necessary guidance for our inquiry. In examining these authorities, we draw on several established principles of statutory construction. In addition to the importance of legislative history, a court may accord great weight to the longstanding interpretation placed on a statute by an agency charged with its administration. This is especially so where Congress has re-enacted the statute without pertinent change. In these circumstances, congressional failure to revise or repeal the agency's interpretation is persuasive evidence that the interpretation is the one intended by Congress. We have also recognized that subsequent legislation declaring the intent of an earlier statute is entitled to significant weight. Application of these principles leads us to conclude, as did the Court of Appeals, that Congress intended to exclude from the protections of the Act all employees properly classified as "managerial." [Most discussion of this issue omitted here.]

D

In sum, the Board's early decisions, the purpose and legislative history of the Taft-Hartley Act of 1947, the Board's subsequent and consistent construction of the Act for more than two decades, and the decisions of the courts of appeals all point unmistakably to the conclusion that "managerial employees" are not covered by the Act. We agree with the Court of Appeals below that the Board "is not now free" to read a new and more restrictive meaning into the Act.

In view of our conclusion, the case must be remanded to permit the Board to apply the proper legal standard in determining the status of these buyers. *SEC v. Chenery Corp.*, 318 U.S. 80, 85 (1943); *FTC v. Sperry & Hutchinson Co.*, 405 U.S. 233, 249 (1972). We express no opinion as to whether these buyers fall within the category of "managerial employees."

III

The Court of Appeals also held that, although the Board was not precluded from determining that buyers or some types of buyers were not "managerial employees," it could do so only by invoking its rulemaking procedures under § 6 of the Act, 29 U.S.C. § 156.[21] We disagree.

At the outset, the precise nature of the present issue must be noted. The question is not whether the Board should have resorted to rulemaking, or in fact improperly promulgated a "rule," when in the context of the prior representation proceeding it held that the Act covers all "managerial employees" except those meeting the new "conflict of interest in labor relations" touchstone. Our conclusion that the Board applied the wrong legal standard makes consideration of that issue unnecessary. Rather, the present question is whether on remand the Board must invoke its rulemaking procedures if it determines, in light of our opinion, that these buyers are not "managerial employees" under the Act. The Court of Appeals thought that rulemaking was required because *any* Board finding that the company's buyers are not "managerial" would be

---

21. Section 6 provides:

"The Board shall have authority from time to time to make, amend, and rescind, in the manner prescribed by the Administrative Procedure Act, such rules and regulations as may be necessary to carry out the provisions of this subchapter." 29 U.S.C. § 156.

The Administrative Procedure Act (APA) defines "rule" as "the whole or a part of an agency statement of general or particular applicability and future effect designed to implement, interpret, or prescribe law or policy. . . ." 5 U.S.C. § 551 (4). The rulemaking requirements include publication in the Federal Register of notice of the proposed rulemaking and hearing; an opportunity for interested persons to participate; a statement of the basis and purpose of the proposed rule; and publication in the Federal Register of the rule as adopted.

The APA defines "adjudication" as "agency process for the formulation of an order," and "order" is defined as "the whole or a part of a final disposition whether affirmative, negative, injunctive, or declaratory in form, of an agency in a matter other than rule making but including licensing." 5 U.S.C. §§ 551 (7), (6). Proceedings for "the certification of worker representatives" are exempted from the Act's procedural requirements for an "adjudication." 5 U.S.C. §§ 554 (a)(6), 556 (a), 557 (a).

Sections 9 (c)(1) and (2) of the National Labor Relations Act (NLRA) empower the Board to investigate petitions involving questions of unit representation, to conduct hearings on such petitions, to direct representation elections, and to certify the results thereof. 29 U.S.C. §§ 159 (c)(1) and (2). Board determinations on such representation questions would appear to constitute "orders" within the meaning of the APA. *See* 5 U.S.C. §§ 551 (6), (7).

The NLRA does not specify in what instances the Board must resort to rulemaking.

contrary to its prior decisions and would presumably be in the nature of a general rule designed "to fit all cases at all times."

A similar issue was presented to this Court in its second decision in *SEC v. Chenery Corp.*, 332 U.S. 194 (1947) (*Chenery II*).[23] There, the respondent corporation argued that in an adjudicative proceeding the Commission could not apply a general standard that it had formulated for the first time in that proceeding. Rather, the Commission was required to resort instead to its rulemaking procedures if it desired to promulgate a new standard that would govern future conduct. In rejecting this contention, the Court first noted that the Commission had a statutory duty to decide the issue at hand in light of the proper standards and that this duty remained "regardless of whether those standards previously had been spelled out in a general rule or regulation." *Id.*, at 201. The Court continued:

> "The function of filling in the interstices of the [Securities] Act should be performed, as much as possible, through this quasi-legislative promulgation of rules to be applied in the future. But any rigid requirement to that effect would make the administrative process inflexible and incapable of dealing with many of the specialized problems which arise. . . . Not every principle essential to the effective administration of a statute can or should be cast immediately into the mold of a general rule. Some principles must await their own development, while others must be adjusted to meet particular, unforeseeable situations. *In performing its important functions in these respects, therefore, an administrative agency must be equipped to act either by general rule or by individual order. To insist upon one form of action to the exclusion of the other is to exalt form over necessity.*
>
> "In other words, problems may arise in a case which the administrative agency could not reasonably foresee, problems which must be solved despite the absence of a relevant general rule. Or the agency may not have had sufficient experience with a particular problem to warrant rigidifying its tentative judgment into a hard and fast rule. *Or the problem may be so specialized and varying in nature as to be impossible of capture within the boundaries of a general rule.* In those situations, the agency must retain power to deal with the problems on a case-to-case basis if the administrative process is to be effective. There is thus a very definite place for the case-by-case evolution of statutory standards." *Id.*, at 202-203. (Emphasis added.)

The Court concluded that "the choice made between proceeding by general rule or by individual, *ad hoc* litigation is one that lies primarily in the informed discretion of the administrative agency." *Id.*, at 203.

And in *NLRB v. Wyman-Gordon Co.*, 394 U.S. 759 (1969), the Court upheld a Board order enforcing an election list requirement first promulgated in an earlier adjudicative proceeding in *Excelsior Underwear Inc.*, 156 N.L.R.B. 1236 (1966). The plurality opinion of Mr. Justice Fortas, joined by The Chief Justice, Mr. Justice Stewart, and Mr. Justice White, recognized that "[a]djudicated cases may and do . . . serve as vehicles for the formulation of agency policies, which are applied and announced therein," and that such cases "generally provide a guide to action that the agency may be expected to take in future cases." *NLRB v. Wyman-Gordon Co., supra,* at 765-766. The concurring opinion of Mr. Justice Black, joined by Mr. Justice Brennan and Mr. Justice Marshall, also noted that the Board had both adjudicative and rulemaking powers and that the choice between the two was "within its informed discretion." *Id.*, at 772.

---

23. *Chenery II* did not involve § 4 of the APA, 5 U.S.C. § 553, but is nevertheless analogous.

The views expressed in *Chenery II* and *Wyman-Gordon* make plain that the Board is not precluded from announcing new principles in an adjudicative proceeding and that the choice between rulemaking and adjudication lies in the first instance within the Board's discretion. Although there may be situations where the Board's reliance on adjudication would amount to an abuse of discretion or a violation of the Act, nothing in the present case would justify such a conclusion. Indeed, there is ample indication that adjudication is especially appropriate in the instant context. As the Court of Appeals noted, "there must be tens of thousands of manufacturing, wholesale and retail units which employ buyers, and hundreds of thousands of the latter." 475 F.2d, at 496. Moreover, duties of buyers vary widely depending on the company or industry. It is doubtful whether any generalized standard could be framed which would have more than marginal utility. The Board thus has reason to proceed with caution, developing its standards in a case-by-case manner with attention to the specific character of the buyers' authority and duties in each company. The Board's judgment that adjudication best serves this purpose is entitled to great weight.

The possible reliance of industry on the Board's past decisions with respect to buyers does not require a different result. It has not been shown that the adverse consequences ensuing from such reliance are so substantial that the Board should be precluded from reconsidering the issue in an adjudicative proceeding. Furthermore, this is not a case in which some new liability is sought to be imposed on individuals for past actions which were taken in good-faith reliance on Board pronouncements. Nor are fines or damages involved here. In any event, concern about such consequences is largely speculative, for the Board has not yet finally determined whether these buyers are "managerial."

It is true, of course, that rulemaking would provide the Board with a forum for soliciting the informed views of those affected in industry and labor before embarking on a new course. But surely the Board has discretion to decide that the adjudicative procedures in this case may also produce the relevant information necessary to mature and fair consideration of the issues. Those most immediately affected, the buyers and the company in the particular case, are accorded a full opportunity to be heard before the Board makes its determination.

The judgment of the Court of Appeals is therefore affirmed in part and reversed in part, and the cause remanded to that court with directions to remand to the Board for further proceedings in conformity with this opinion.

It is so ordered.

Mr. Justice White, with whom Mr. Justice Brennan, Mr. Justice Stewart, and Mr. Justice Marshall join, dissenting in part.

I concur in Part III of the Court's opinion insofar as it holds that the Board was not required to resort to rulemaking in deciding this case, but I dissent from its holding in Part II that managerial employees as a class are not "employees" within the meaning of the National Labor Relations Act. . . .

QUESTIONS

1. Is it good policy for agencies to have the choice whether to proceed by rulemaking or adjudication? Note that Congress can, if it wants to, require an agency to proceed by one way or the other. The Federal Trade

Commission Act, for instance, had been interpreted, prior to the *National Petroleum Refiners Assn.* case, *supra*, p. 179, not to permit substantive rulemaking by an agency. On the other hand, some statutes specifically require an agency to proceed by rulemaking. For instance, the Clean Air Act, at issue in *Whitman v. American Trucking Assns., infra,* p. 366, requires the EPA to use rulemaking to set national ambient air quality standards.

2. Can *Bell Aerospace* be distinguished in future cases? If so, how?
3. Does the 1981 MSAPA give agencies the same amount of discretion to decide to pursue rulemaking or adjudication? *See* §§ 2-104(3) & (4).
4. What about a situation in which "some new liability is sought to be imposed on individuals for past actions which were taken in good-faith reliance on Board pronouncements"? Judge Friendly's dictum in *NLRB v. Majestic Weaving Co.,* 355 F.2d 854, 860 (2d Cir. 1966), in this regard seems prescient in light of subsequent doctrinal developments:

> Although courts have not generally balked at allowing administrative agencies to apply a rule newly fashioned in an adjudicative proceeding to past conduct, a decision branding as "unfair" conduct stamped "fair" at the time a party acted, raises judicial hackles [E.g., *NLRB v. Guy F. Atkinson Co.,* 195 F.2d 141 (9th Cir. 1952)] considerably more than a determination that merely brings within the agency's jurisdiction an employer previously left without, *see NLRB v. Pease Oil Co.,* 279 F.2d 135, 137-39 (2 Cir. 1960), or shortens the period in which a collective bargaining agreement may bar a new election, *see Leedom v. International Bhd. of Elec. Workers,* 278 F.2d 237, 243 (D.C. Cir. 1960), or imposes a more severe remedy for conduct already prohibited, *see NLRB v. A.P.W. Prods. Co.,* [316 F.2d 899 (2 Cir. 1963)]. And the hackles bristle still more when a financial penalty is assessed for action that might well have been avoided if the agency's changed disposition had been earlier made known, or might even have been taken in express reliance on the standard previously established. *See NLRB v. International Bhd. of Teamsters,* 225 F.2d 343 (8 Cir. 1955); *NLRB v. E & B Brewing Co.,* 276 F.2d 594, 600 (6 Cir. 1960), *cert. denied,* 366 U.S. 908 (1961).

What is an agency to do in this type of situation, when it wants to change its policy, but it would be unfair to apply the new policy to the parties before it? Can the agency simply adjudicate prospectively? This would arguably be precluded by the combined opinions of the *Wyman-Gordon* case. Is an agency forced to engage in rulemaking in this situation?

5. In Texas, the state courts have declared that, under the state APA, policies established incident to a contested adjudication constitute "*ad hoc* rules" and that the Texas APA permits state agencies to announce "ad hoc" rules incident to contested adjudications. *See* Ronald L. Beal, Ad Hoc *Rulemaking in Texas: The Scope of Judicial Review,* 42 Baylor L. Rev. 459, 460-67 (1990). Professor Beal explains that "[t]he truly remarkable aspect of an *ad hoc* rule, then, is that, while it is an exercise of legislative power, the standards are developed by a 'common law' method." *Id.* at 463. These Texas "*ad hoc* rules" appear to serve the same practical function as an adjudicative ruling serves for a federal administrative agency under the APA, in that "unlike a 'legislative' rule, an *ad hoc* rule is *not* immediately binding upon all persons with similar characteristics who are subject to the general legislation of the agency" but rather "serves as a vehicle for the formulation of agency policies

that are announced and applied in the specific case, and such rules generally provide a *guide* to action that the agency *may be expected to take in future cases.*" *Id.* at 463-64 (emphasis in the original). Does it make sense to conceptualize new agency policies created incident to adjudications as "ad hoc rules"? Or should agencies, when exercising quasi-judicial functions, simply be seen as possessing the same common law powers that a court would enjoy? The Texas approach clearly attempts to divide and compartmentalize agency legislative and adjudicative functions in ways that the federal system does not.

F. AVOIDING ADJUDICATION THROUGH RULEMAKING

HECKLER v. CAMPBELL
461 U.S. 458 (1983)

JUSTICE POWELL delivered the opinion of the Court.

The issue is whether the Secretary of Health and Human Services may rely on published medical-vocational guidelines to determine a claimant's right to Social Security disability benefits.

I

The Social Security Act defines "disability" in terms of the effect a physical or mental impairment has on a person's ability to function in the workplace. It provides disability benefits only to persons who are unable "to engage in any substantial gainful activity by reason of any medically determinable physical or mental impairment." 81 Stat. 868, as amended, 42 U.S.C. § 423(d)(1)(A). And it specifies that a person must "not only [be] unable to do his previous work but [must be unable], considering his age, education, and work experience, [to] engage in any other kind of substantial gainful work which exists in the national economy, regardless of whether such work exists in the immediate area in which he lives, or whether a specific job vacancy exists for him, or whether he would be hired if he applied for work." 42 U.S.C. § 423(d)(2)(A).

In 1978, the Secretary of Health and Human Services promulgated regulations implementing this definition. *See* 43 Fed. Reg. 55349 (1978) (codified, as amended, at 20 CFR pt. 404, subpt. P (1982)). The regulations recognize that certain impairments are so severe that they prevent a person from pursuing any gainful work. *See* 20 CFR § 404.1520(d) (1982) (referring to impairments listed at 20 CFR pt. 404, subpt. P, app. 1). A claimant who establishes that he suffers from one of these impairments will be considered disabled without further inquiry. *Ibid.* If a claimant suffers from a less severe impairment, the Secretary must determine whether the claimant retains the ability to perform either his former work or some less demanding employment. If a claimant can pursue his former occupation, he is not entitled to disability benefits. *See* § 404.1520(e). If he cannot, the Secretary must determine whether the claimant retains the capacity to pursue less demanding work. *See* § 404.1520(f)(1).

The regulations divide this last inquiry into two stages. First, the Secretary must assess each claimant's present job qualifications. The regulations direct the Secretary to consider the factors Congress has identified as relevant: physical ability, age, education, and work experience. *See* 42 U.S.C. § 423(d)(2)(A); 20 CFR § 404.1520(f) (1982). Second, she must consider whether jobs exist in the national economy that a person having the claimant's qualifications could perform. 20 CFR §§ 404.1520(f), 404.1566-404.1569 (1982).

Prior to 1978, the Secretary relied on vocational experts to establish the existence of suitable jobs in the national economy. After a claimant's limitations and abilities had been determined at a hearing, a vocational expert ordinarily would testify whether work existed that the claimant could perform. Although this testimony often was based on standardized guides, *see* 43 Fed. Reg. 9286 (1978), vocational experts frequently were criticized for their inconsistent treatment of similarly situated claimants. *See Santise v. Schweiker*, 676 F.2d 925, 930 (CA3 1982); J. Mashaw, C. Goetz, F. Goodman, W. Schwartz, P. Verkuil, & M. Carrow, Social Security Hearings and Appeals 78-79 (1978). To improve both the uniformity and efficiency[2] of this determination, the Secretary promulgated medical-vocational guidelines as part of the 1978 regulations. See 20 CFR pt. 404, subpt. P, app. 2 (1982).

These guidelines relieve the Secretary of the need to rely on vocational experts by establishing through rulemaking the types and numbers of jobs that exist in the national economy. They consist of a matrix of the four factors identified by Congress — physical ability, age, education, and work experience[3] — and set forth rules that identify whether jobs requiring specific combinations of these factors exist in significant numbers in the national economy.[4] Where a claimant's qualifications correspond to the job requirements identified by a rule,[5] the guidelines direct a conclusion as to whether work exists that the claimant could perform. If such work exists, the claimant is not considered disabled.

---

2. The Social Security hearing system is "probably the largest adjudicative agency in the western world." J. Mashaw, C. Goetz, F. Goodman, W. Schwartz, P. Verkuil, & M. Carrow, Social Security Hearings and Appeals xi (1978). Approximately 2.3 million claims for disability benefits were filed in fiscal year 1981. Department of Health and Human Services, Social Security Annual Report to the Congress for Fiscal Year 1981, pp. 32, 35 (1982). More than a quarter of a million of these claims required a hearing before an administrative law judge. *Id.*, at 38. The need for efficiency is self-evident.

3. Each of these four factors is divided into defined categories. A person's ability to perform physical tasks, for example, is categorized according to the physical exertion requirements necessary to perform varying classes of jobs — i.e., whether a claimant can perform sedentary, light, medium, heavy, or very heavy work. 20 CFR § 404.1567 (1982). Each of these work categories is defined in terms of the physical demands it places on a worker, such as the weight of objects he must lift and whether extensive movement or use of arm and leg controls is required. *Ibid.*

4. For example, Rule 202.10 provides that a significant number of jobs exist for a person who can perform light work, is closely approaching advanced age, has a limited education but who is literate and can communicate in English, and whose previous work has been unskilled.

5. The regulations recognize that the rules only describe "major functional and vocational patterns." 20 CFR pt. 404, subpt. P, app. 2, § 200.00(a) (1982). If an individual's capabilities are not described accurately by a rule, the regulations make clear that the individual's particular limitations must be considered. See app. 2, §§ 200.00(a), (d). Additionally, the regulations declare that the administrative law judge will not apply the age categories "mechanically in a borderline situation," 20 CFR § 404.1563(a) (1982), and recognize that some claimants may possess limitations that are not factored into the guidelines, see app. 2, § 200.00(e). Thus, the regulations provide that the rules will be applied only when they describe a claimant's abilities and limitations accurately.

II

In 1979, Carmen Campbell applied for disability benefits because a back condition and hypertension prevented her from continuing her work as a hotel maid. After her application was denied, she requested a hearing *de novo* before an Administrative Law Judge. He determined that her back problem was not severe enough to find her disabled without further inquiry, and accordingly considered whether she retained the ability to perform either her past work or some less strenuous job. He concluded that even though Campbell's back condition prevented her from returning to her work as a maid, she retained the physical capacity to do light work. In accordance with the regulations, he found that Campbell was 52 years old, that her previous employment consisted of unskilled jobs, and that she had a limited education. He noted that Campbell, who had been born in Panama, experienced difficulty in speaking and writing English. She was able, however, to understand and read English fairly well. Relying on the medical-vocational guidelines, the Administrative Law Judge found that a significant number of jobs existed that a person of Campbell's qualifications could perform. Accordingly, he concluded that she was not disabled.

This determination was upheld by both the Social Security Appeals Council, and the District Court for the Eastern District of New York. The Court of Appeals for the Second Circuit reversed. It accepted the Administrative Law Judge's determination that Campbell retained the ability to do light work. And it did not suggest that he had classified Campbell's age, education, or work experience incorrectly. The court noted, however, that it

> "has consistently required that 'the Secretary identify specific alternative occupations available in the national economy that would be suitable for the claimant' and that 'these jobs be supported by 'a job description clarifying the nature of the job, [and] demonstrating that the job does not require' exertion or skills not possessed by the claimant.'"

The court found that the medical-vocational guidelines did not provide the specific evidence that it previously had required. It explained that in the absence of such a showing, "the claimant is deprived of any real chance to present evidence showing that she cannot in fact perform the types of jobs that are administratively noticed by the guidelines." The court concluded that because the Secretary had failed to introduce evidence that specific alternative jobs existed, the determination that Campbell was not disabled was not supported by substantial evidence.

We granted certiorari to resolve a conflict among the Courts of Appeals. We now reverse.

III

The Secretary argues that the Court of Appeals' holding effectively prevents the use of the medical-vocational guidelines. By requiring her to identify specific alternative jobs in every disability hearing, the court has rendered the guidelines useless. An examination of both the language of the Social Security Act and its legislative history clearly demonstrates that the Secretary may proceed by regulation to determine whether substantial gainful work exists in the national economy. Campbell argues in response that the Secretary has misperceived the Court of Appeals' holding. Campbell reads the decision as requiring only that the Secretary give disability claimants concrete examples of the kinds of factual determinations that the administrative law judge will be making. This requirement does not defeat the guidelines' purpose; it ensures that they will be applied only where appropriate. Accordingly, respondent argues that we need not address the guidelines' validity.

A

The Court of Appeals held that "[i]n failing to show suitable available alternative jobs for Ms. Campbell, the Secretary's finding of 'not disabled' is not supported by substantial evidence." It thus rejected the proposition that "the guidelines provide adequate evidence of a claimant's ability to perform a specific alternative occupation," and remanded for the Secretary to put into evidence "particular types of jobs suitable to the capabilities of Ms. Campbell." The court's requirement that additional evidence be introduced on this issue prevents the Secretary from putting the guidelines to their intended use and implicitly calls their validity into question. Accordingly, we think the decision below requires us to consider whether the Secretary may rely on medical-vocational guidelines in appropriate cases.

The Social Security Act directs the Secretary to "adopt reasonable and proper rules and regulations to regulate and provide for the nature and extent of the proofs and evidence and the method of taking and furnishing the same" in disability cases. 42 U.S.C. § 405(a). As we previously have recognized, Congress has "conferred on the Secretary exceptionally broad authority to prescribe standards for applying certain sections of the [Social Security] Act." *Schweiker v. Gray Panthers,* 453 U.S. 34, 43 (1981); *see Batterton v. Francis,* 432 U.S. 416, 425 (1977). Where, as here, the statute expressly entrusts the Secretary with the responsibility for implementing a provision by regulation,[10] our review is limited to determining whether the regulations promulgated exeeded the Secretary's statutory authority and whether they are arbitrary and capricious.

We do not think that the Secretary's reliance on medical-vocational guidelines is inconsistent with the Social Security Act. It is true that the statutory scheme contemplates that disability hearings will be individualized determinations based on evidence adduced at a hearing. *See* 42 U.S.C. § 423(d)(2)(A) (specifying consideration of each individual's condition); 42 U.S.C. § 405(b) (1976 ed., Supp. V) (disability determination to be based on evidence adduced at hearing). But this does not bar the Secretary from relying on rulemaking to resolve certain classes of issues. The Court has recognized that even where an agency's enabling statute expressly requires it to hold a hearing, the agency may rely on its rulemaking authority to determine issues that do not require case-by-case consideration. *See FPC v. Texaco Inc.,* 377 U.S. 33, 41-44 (1964); *United States v. Storer Broadcasting Co.,* 351 U.S. 192, 205 (1956). A contrary

10. Since Congress amended the Social Security Act in 1954 to provide for disability benefits, Pub. L. 761, § 106, 68 Stat. 1079, it repeatedly has suggested that the Secretary promulgate regulations defining the criteria for evaluating disability. . . . While these sources do not establish the original congressional intent, they indicate that later Congresses perceived that regulations such as the guidelines would be consistent with the statute.

holding would require the agency continually to relitigate issues that may be established fairly and efficiently in a single rulemaking proceeding. See *FPC v. Texaco Inc., supra,* at 44.

The Secretary's decision to rely on medical-vocational guidelines is consistent with *Texaco* and *Storer.* As noted above, in determining whether a claimant can perform less strenuous work, the Secretary must make two determinations. She must assess each claimant's individual abilities and then determine whether jobs exist that a person having the claimant's qualifications could perform. The first inquiry involves a determination of historic facts, and the regulations properly require the Secretary to make these findings on the basis of evidence adduced at a hearing. We note that the regulations afford claimants ample opportunity both to present evidence relating to their own abilities and to offer evidence that the guidelines do not apply to them.[11] The second inquiry requires the Secretary to determine an issue that is not unique to each claimant — the types and numbers of jobs that exist in the national economy. This type of general factual issue may be resolved as fairly through rulemaking as by introducing the testimony of vocational experts at each disability hearing. *See American Airlines, Inc. v. CAB,* 359 F.2d 624, 633 ([D.C. Cir.] 1966) (en banc).

As the Secretary has argued, the use of published guidelines brings with it a uniformity that previously had been perceived as lacking. To require the Secretary to relitigate the existence of jobs in the national economy at each hearing would hinder needlessly an already overburdened agency. We conclude that the Secretary's use of medical-vocational guidelines does not conflict with the statute, nor can we say on the record before us that they are arbitrary and capricious.

B

We now consider Campbell's argument that the Court of Appeals properly required the Secretary to specify alternative available jobs. Campbell contends that such a showing informs claimants of the type of issues to be established at the hearing and is required by both the Secretary's regulation, 20 CFR § 404.944 (1982), and the Due Process Clause.

By referring to notice and an opportunity to respond, the decision below invites the interpretation given it by respondent. But we do not think that the decision fairly can be said to present the issues she raises. The Court of Appeals did not find that the Secretary failed to give sufficient notice in violation of the Due Process Clause or any statutory provision designed to implement it. *See* 42 U.S.C. § 405(b) (1976 ed., Supp. V) (requiring that disability claimants be given "reasonable notice and [an] opportunity for a hearing"). Nor did it find that the Secretary violated any duty imposed by regulation. *See* 20 CFR § 404.944 (1982) (requiring the administrative law judge to "[look] fully into the issues"). Rather the court's reference to notice and an opportunity to respond appears to be based on a principle of administrative law — that when an agency takes official or administrative notice of facts, a litigant must be given an adequate

11. Both *FPC v. Texaco Inc.,* 377 U.S. 33, 40 (1964), and *United States v. Storer Broadcasting Co.,* 351 U.S. 192, 205 (1956), were careful to note that the statutory scheme at issue allowed an individual applicant to show that the rule promulgated should not be applied to him. The regulations here provide a claimant with equal or greater protection since they state that an administrative law judge will not apply the rules contained in the guidelines when they fail to describe a claimant's particular limitations. *See* n.5, *supra.*

opportunity to respond. *See* 5 U.S.C. § 556(e); *McDaniel v. Celebrezze*, 331 F.2d 426 (CA4 1964).

This principle is inapplicable, however, when the agency has promulgated valid regulations. Its purpose is to provide a procedural safeguard: to ensure the accuracy of the facts of which an agency takes notice. But when the accuracy of those facts already has been tested fairly during rulemaking, the rulemaking proceeding itself provides sufficient procedural protection.

IV

The Court of Appeals' decision would require the Secretary to introduce evidence of specific available jobs that respondent could perform. It would limit severely her ability to rely on the medical-vocational guidelines. We think the Secretary reasonably could choose to rely on these guidelines in appropriate cases rather than on the testimony of a vocational expert in each case. Accordingly, the judgment of the Court of Appeals is *Reversed.*

[Justice Brennan filed a concurring opinion, criticizing the Administrative Law Judge's performance of his duty to inquire into the facts of the case. Justice Marshall filed an opinion agreeing that the Secretary's medical-vocational guidelines were valid, but dissenting in part on the ground that remand was warranted to examine the additional question whether the Administrative Law Judge fulfilled his obligation to "[look] fully into the issues."]

QUESTIONS

1. Note how this is the "flip side" of *Chenery* and *Bell Aerospace.* Does this violate a statutory right to a hearing?
2. What if the applicant admitted she was not disabled under the grid? Should the agency deny a hearing altogether?
3. Would the reasoning of *Campbell* extend to cases in which an agency is specifically granted "discretion" to decide certain matters? Compare the conflicting opinions of two notable judges on this question. In *Fook Hong Mak v. Immigration and Naturalization Service*, 435 F.2d 728, 730 (2d Cir. 1970), Judge Henry Friendly wrote that:

> We are unable to understand why there should be any general principle forbidding an administrator, vested with discretionary power, to determine by appropriate rulemaking that he will not use it in favor of a particular class on a case-by-case basis, if his determination is founded on considerations rationally related to the statute he is administering. The legislature's grant of discretion to accord a privilege does not imply a mandate that this must inevitably be done by examining each case rather than by identifying groups. The administrator also exercises the discretion accorded him when, after appropriate deliberation, he determines certain conduct to be so inimical to the statutory scheme that all persons who have engaged in it shall be ineligible for favorable consideration, regardless of other factors that otherwise might tend in their favor. He has then decided that one element is of such determinative negative force that no possible combination of others could justify an affirmative result. By the same token he could select one characteristic as entitling a group to

favorable treatment despite minor variables. Nothing in this offends the basic concept that like cases should be treated similarly and unlike ones differently. The administrator has simply determined that the one paramount element creates such "likeness" that other elements cannot be so legally significant as to warrant a difference in treatment. This may be an even "juster justice" than to accord different treatment because of trivial differences of fact; at least it is competent for the administrator to think so.

Judge Shirley Hufstedler took the contrary position in *Asimakopoulos v. Immigration and Naturalization Service,* 445 F.2d 1362, 1365 (9th Cir. 1971):

> Although eligibility for suspension [of deportation] does not compel the granting of the requested relief, eligibility does trigger the exercise of discretion. The standard announced in *Matter of Lee* effectively precludes the exercise of discretion in many cases in which the applicant would otherwise qualify for relief. The Board's failure to exercise discretion is reversible error. (*United States ex rel. Accardi v. Shaughnessy* (1954) 347 U.S. 260, 266-268.) Accordingly, reliance on a test that prevents the exercise of discretion is also reversible error. (*See Loza-Bedoya v. I&NS* (9th Cir. 1969) 410 F.2d 343, 346.) We do not express any opinion about the manner in which the Attorney General or his delegates should exercise the discretion committed to him.

4. From a claimant's perspective, the grids are far less desirable than having a "vocational expert," probably based in the local community or proximate to it, making an individualized determination of eligibility for disability benefits. From the agency's perspective, however, anything that will streamline proceedings has to be viewed as desirable — the Social Security Administration (SSA) must process tens of thousands of applications, and appeals, each year. Efficiency is a legitimate agency goal, and to the extent that proceedings can be streamlined, delays in obtaining benefits will be reduced (which clearly benefits eligible applicants). In 2003, the Supreme Court (unanimously) reversed a Third Circuit decision that prohibited the SSA from relying on an applicant's ability to perform her prior job as proof of ineligibility for SSA disability benefits, without any further inquiry. *Barnhart v. Thomas,* 540 U.S. 20, 26-28 (2003). Writing for the Court, Justice Scalia explained that:

> Congress could have determined that an analysis of a claimant's physical and mental capacity to do his previous work would "in the vast majority of cases" serve as an effective and efficient administrative proxy for the claimant's ability to do *some* work that does exist in the national economy. Such a proxy is useful because the step-five inquiry into whether the claimant's cumulative impairments preclude him from finding "other" work is very difficult, requiring consideration of "each of [t]he [vocational] factors and . . . an individualized assessment of each claimant's abilities and limitations," *Heckler v. Campbell,* 461 U.S. 450, 460-61 n.1 (1983). There is good reason to use a workable proxy that avoids the step-five analysis. As we have observed, "[t]he Social Security hearing system is 'probably the largest adjudicative agency in the western world.' . . . The need for efficiency is self-evident." 461 U.S., at 461 n.2 (citation omitted).

Id. at 28-29. It is true, of course, that using the ability to perform prior work as an absolute bar to SSA disability benefits leads to inaccurate disability determinations in at least some cases—the very point that led the Third Circuit to invalidate the SSA's policy in the first place. Justice Scalia responded to this concern by noting that "[t]o generalize is to be imprecise. Virtually *every* legal (or other) rule has imperfect applications in particular circumstances." *Id.* at 29. Thus, in some circumstances, a cost/benefit analysis favors efficiency over accuracy.

5.   Does the government have an obligation to address fairness concerns? If so, how does *Campbell* fare? The Supreme Court has suggested that using rulemaking to streamline administrative adjudications actually enhances, rather than degrades, the fairness of agency proceedings:

> We . . . reject Lopez's argument . . . that the agency must not make categorical exclusions, but must rely on case-by-case assessments. "[E]ven if a statutory scheme requires individualized determinations," which this scheme does not, "the decisionmaker has the authority to rely on rulemaking to resolve certain issues of general applicability unless Congress clearly expresses an intent to withhold that authority." *American Hospital Ass'n v. NLRB*, 499 U.S. 606, 612 (1991). The approach pressed by Lopez—case-by-case decisionmaking in thousands of cases each year—could invite favoritism, disunity, and inconsistency.

Lopez v. Davis, 531 U.S. 230, 243-44 (2001). Is this the correct way of framing the fairness inquiry? Surely treating similar cases in a similar way is a plausible way of defining "fairness." At the same time, however, the individual who believes that the agency wrongfully denied her claims is highly unlikely to find much solace in the notion that the agency's grids enhance the overall rationality of the benefits system.

G.   MUST AN AGENCY ADHERE TO ITS RULES?

SAMEENA, INC. v. U.S. AIR FORCE
147 F.3d 1148 (9th Cir. 1998)

D.W. NELSON, Circuit Judge: This case arises from a contractor's alleged attempts to defraud the government and the government's efforts to bar the contractor from bidding on future government projects. The appellants bring civil rights and common-law tort claims against a number of individual employees of the United States Air Force (the "Air Force") and argue that the Air Force's decision to debar them for a period of fifteen years was arbitrary and capricious, in violation of the Administrative Procedure Act ("APA"), codified in pertinent part at 5 U.S.C. § 704. The district court dismissed the claims against the individual defendants and granted summary judgment in favor of the Air Force on the APA claims. We have jurisdiction pursuant to 28 U.S.C. § 1291. Although we affirm the dismissal of the claims against the individual defendants, we reverse the district court's summary judgment because we conclude that the Department of the Air Force (the "Air Force") violated the appellants' constitutional right to due process when it denied them an evidentiary hearing, as required by 48 C.F.R. § 9.406-3(b)(2).

In February 1992, the Social Security Administration ("SSA") solicited bids from computer suppliers for a quantity of microcomputer workstations. University Systems, Inc. ("USI"), a California-based corporation of which Appellant Mirza Ali was Chief Executive Officer, submitted a proposal to the SSA in April 1992. USI's bid was deemed competitive, and USI provided the SSA with samples of its products for further evaluation.

During this process, questions arose regarding whether a mouse device included in the proposal was manufactured in compliance with the Trade Agreements Act of 1979, 19 U.S.C. §§ 2501-2582. While this matter was being investigated, it was discovered that two USI officers had submitted a fraudulent letter to the SSA. The SSA consequently eliminated USI from consideration for the workstation contract.

Subsequently, the United States Department of Health and Human Services ("HHS"), of which the SSA is part, commenced "debarment" proceedings against USI and four of its officers, including Mirza Ali, seeking to disqualify them from submitting government contract proposals for three years. On February 2, 1994, USI, Mirza Ali, and the other USI officers were debarred from government contracting through February 18, 1996.

Mirza Ali's wife, Appellant Sameena Ali, is president and sole director of Appellant Sameena Inc. ("Sameena"), which was incorporated in February 1993 by Keith Griffen, a USI officer. Each of the appellants uses aliases: Sameena Ali sometimes goes by "Sameena Ikbal." Mirza Ali sometimes goes by "Zulfiqar Eqbal." Sameena Inc. operates under the assumed name "Samtech Research, Inc." ("Samtech").

Like USI, Samtech supplied computer workstations to government agencies. In June 1995, an Alabama-based contracting squadron of the Air Force issued a contract solicitation for laptop computers. An amendment to the solicitation indicated that the buyer was V. Carol Moore.

Samtech submitted a proposal to Moore in July 1995. Included in Samtech's proposal was a certification that neither Samtech nor any of its principals was debarred or proposed for debarment at that time. The certification defined "principals" as "officers; directors; owners; partners; and persons having primary management or supervisory responsibilities within a business entity." Because the Air Force solicitation required that bidders have at least three years of experience as a government contractor, Samtech's proposal also included a list of "Government Contract Awards." Among them was a contract with the United States Department of Energy (the "DoE contract") that Sameena had obtained in 1994 through a novation from USI.

In response to a query, Samtech sent Moore a letter in September 1995 explaining that Samtech "started doing business with the Federal Government by acquiring a contract for the supply of ADP equipment to the United States Department of Energy in 1992." On further investigation, Moore discovered that the contract actually had been awarded to USI in 1992 and had only been novated to Samtech in 1994. Moore also obtained bank documents indicating that "Sameena Ikbal" and "Zulfiqar Eqbal" were authorized to make withdrawals from Samtech's accounts and were, respectively, "President/Secretary" and "Vice President" of the corporation. This information appeared to Moore to contradict the statements made in Samtech's contract proposal.

On the basis of these apparent misrepresentations, Samtech was deemed ineligible for the Air Force contract. Moreover, in December 1995, the Air Force Contracting Officer, Gladys McBride, submitted a recommendation that Samtech be debarred. McBride appended the entire administrative file to her recommendation, including an affidavit by Moore describing her investigations.

On December 26, 1995, Sameena Inc., Samtech, Sameena Ali, and Mirza Ali ("the appellants") were notified that they had been proposed for debarment (and, in Mirza Ali's case, an "extension" of debarment). The notices were accompanied by memoranda setting forth the grounds for the proposed debarments. The notices also invited the appellants to submit information and argument in opposition to the debarment.

The appellants included in their response a letter dated February 21, 1996, from an official at Samtech's bank. The letter stated that the document indicating that Zulfiqar Eqbal was Vice President of Samtech — a bank signature card — had been "corrected" after the bank was informed "that Eqbal was not a corporate officer" of Sameena or Samtech. The submission also included copies of checks written on Sameena's bank accounts. A number of these checks were signed by "Zulfiqar Eqbal" and were made out to a variety of payees, including physicians, a sports club, and Eqbal (Mirza Ali) himself. The appellants' submission also requested an evidentiary hearing on the issue of Mirza Ali's role at Samtech. Notwithstanding the submission, and without an evidentiary hearing, the Air Force issued a final decision in June 1996 to debar Sameena/Samtech and Sameena Ali — and to extend Mirza Ali's debarment — until December 2010. The debarment was based on findings that the appellants had (1) made false statements regarding Samtech's experience as a contractor, (2) provided false certifications that none of Samtech's principals was debarred, and (3) participated in a scheme to avoid the effects of USI's debarment.

On August 30, 1996, the appellants filed two complaints in the United States District Court for the Northern District of California. The first complaint, brought by Mirza Ali against HHS and against six agency employees in their individual capacities, focused on Ali's initial debarment and sought declaratory relief and damages. The second complaint, brought by Mirza Ali, Sameena Ali, and Sameena/Samtech against the Air Force and seven Air Force employees in their individual capacities, focused both on the debarment of Sameena/Samtech and Sameena Ali and on the extension of Mirza Ali's debarment.

This second complaint made substantially the same allegations as the first, even though it was directed at entirely different defendants. The appellants alleged (1) that the individual Air Force officials had conspired to violate their civil rights and had committed several common-law torts and (2) that the Air Force's decision to debar them was arbitrary and capricious and should be set aside pursuant to the APA.

In an order filed December 11, 1996, the district court dismissed the claims against the individual defendants for lack of personal jurisdiction and, alternatively, on the grounds that the appellants had failed either to plead conspiracy with sufficient particularity or to comply with the Federal Tort Claims Act, 28 U.S.C. §§ 1346(b), 2671-2680. The court also granted summary judgment to the Air Force on the APA claims. The appellants timely appeal. We affirm the district court's dismissal of the claims against the individual defendants but reverse the summary judgment in favor of the Air Force. . . .

I. The district court properly determined that the appellants failed adequately to plead conspiracy. [Analysis omitted.]

II. The district court properly dismissed the tort claims against the individual defendants. [Analysis omitted.]

III. The district court erred in granting the Air Force's motion for summary judgment.

The appellants argue that the decision to debar them was arbitrary and capricious. They appeal the district court's summary judgment in favor of the Air Force on three grounds: First, they argue that Carol Moore's declaration failed to establish that she had personal knowledge regarding the contract proposal at issue and should have been stricken from the administrative record. Second, they claim that, by the terms of the 1994 novation of the DoE contract, USI's previous two years of government contracting experience should have been "imputed" to Samtech. Finally, they contend that they had a due process right to an evidentiary hearing regarding Mirza Ali's role at Samtech. We address each of the appellants' claims in turn.

A. The district court properly rejected the appellants' request to strike Carol Moore's affidavit. [Analysis omitted.]

B. The 1994 novation did not "impute" to appellants USI's government contracting experience.

On February 13, 1994, following USI's debarment, USI, Sameena, and the DoE entered into a Novation Agreement, transferring USI's rights and obligations to Sameena. The agreement states, in pertinent part:

> The government recognizes the Transferee [Sameena] as the Transferor's [USI's] successor in interest in and to the contract. The Transferee by this Agreement becomes entitled to all rights, titles, and interests of the Transferor in and to the contract as if the Transferee were the original party to the contract.

The appellants claim that the terms of this Agreement led them "reasonably" to believe that, because they would be treated as the "original party" to the contract, the Novation "imputed the DoE contract experience entirely to Samtech." As the district court noted, however, this claim is directly belied by the appellants' earlier representations in their submission in response to the proposed debarment, in which they contended that their overstatement of government contracting experience had resulted from an "innocent" error about the date of the contract. In light of this inconsistency, the Air Force did not act arbitrarily or capriciously in refusing to attach any credibility to this claim.

C. The appellants were entitled to an evidentiary hearing.

The Supreme Court has long recognized that a federal agency is obliged to abide by the regulations it promulgates. *See Vitarelli v. Seaton*, 359 U.S. 535, 545 (1959); *Service v. Dulles*, 354 U.S. 363, 372 1152 (1957); *Accardi v. Shaughnessy*, 347 U.S. 260, 267 (1954). [Note: In *Accardi*, the Supreme Court required the Attorney General to follow his own regulation, which provided that the Board of Immigration Appeals would exercise its discretion in deciding suspension-of-deportation cases.] An agency's failure to follow its own regulations "tends to cause unjust discrimination and deny adequate notice" and consequently may result in a violation of an individual's constitutional right to due process.

NLRB v. Welcome-American Fertilizer Co., 443 F.2d 19, 20 (9th Cir. 1971); *see also United States v. Newell*, 578 F.2d 827, 834 (9th Cir. 1978). Where a prescribed procedure is intended to protect the interests of a party before the agency, "even though generous beyond the requirements that bind such agency, that procedure must be scrupulously observed." *Vitarelli*, 359 U.S. at 547 (Frankfurter, J., concurring); *see also* Note, *Violations by Agencies of Their Own Regulations*, 87 Harv. L. Rev. 629, 630 (1974) (observing that agency violations of regulations promulgated to provide parties with procedural safeguards generally have been invalidated by courts).

The Federal Acquisition Regulation ("FAR") establishes a system of uniform policies and procedures governing acquisitions by all executive agencies. *See* 48 C.F.R. § 1.101. In recognition of the "serious nature of debarment," *see* 48 C.F.R. § 9.402, the FAR sets out detailed procedures to ensure that this sanction, which is intended to safeguard the integrity of the acquisitions process, itself is applied in conformity with "principles of fundamental fairness." 48 C.F.R. § 9.406-3(b). Accordingly, the FAR provides:

> If it is found that the contractor's submission in opposition raises a genuine dispute over facts material to the proposed debarment, agencies shall also — (i) Afford the contractor an opportunity to appear with counsel, submit documentary evidence, and confront any person the agency presents.

48 C.F.R. § 9.406-3(b)(2). Thus, in the event of a genuine factual dispute, the FAR clearly establishes that a contractor facing debarment is entitled to an evidentiary hearing. The appellants claim that they raised a genuine issue of material fact with regard to Mirza Ali's position at Sameena/Samtech. They contend that Ali was mistakenly listed as Vice President of the company on the bank signature card discovered by Moore and that the February 1996 letter from the bank supports that contention. Accordingly, they claim that they were entitled under the FAR to an evidentiary hearing on the matter.

The district court rejected the appellants' claims on two grounds. First, the court found the letter from the bank to be inconclusive. The court pointed out that the letter merely acknowledged that the bank had issued a new signature card deleting Eqbal's name, and that it had made this "correction" after being informed that Zulfiqar Eqbal was not a corporate officer. The district court suggested that the letter had little probative value because it was sent after debarment proceedings against the appellants already had commenced.

Second, the district court observed that the operative factual question informing the debarment decision was not whether Ali/Eqbal was Vice President of Sameena/Samtech but, rather, whether he exercised control over the business. As the court noted, the Debarring Official found that Ali had written business-related and personal checks on Samtech's account and had stated on the telephone that he was project manager for government solicitations. Based on that evidence, the Debarring Official concluded, "It is clear that Mr. Eqbal had full authority to expend Samtech's resources and bind the company." Because the district court found that "nothing plaintiffs submitted created a dispute as to this issue," it concluded that they were not entitled to an evidentiary hearing.

The district court failed, however, to acknowledge evidence submitted by the appellants that calls into question whether Ali/Eqbal was a principal of

Sameena/Samtech. The appellants submitted evidence that Ali/Eqbal was Vice President of a Hong Kong corporation also called Samtech and that his position there had likely caused the confusion involving the signature cards. The appellants also submitted evidence indicating that Ali/Eqbal held no official position with Sameena/Samtech other than bookkeeper and that the writing of checks was consistent with that position. The appellants denied that Ali/Eqbal had represented himself to be a project manager or any other type of corporate officer. They explained that the checks made out to and signed by Eqbal were not for his personal use and were not issued at his discretion. Finally, the appellants challenged the government to produce any document indicating that Ali/Eqbal had actually acted in the capacity of a principal with regard to control over the company's decisionmaking process. Thus, although the appellants' submission does not establish that the Debarring Official acted arbitrarily or capriciously in determining that Ali/Eqbal was a principal of Samtech/Sameena, it does raise a genuine factual dispute regarding the issue.

The appellants requested an evidentiary hearing to address this question. The Debarring Official decided, however, that a hearing was unwarranted, finding the appellants' denials of the charges against them to be "unsupported by credible evidence." We do not doubt that the Air Force is in a better position than this Court to assess the credibility of the evidence offered by the appellants. We are convinced, however, that an evidentiary hearing would have been the appropriate forum in which to make such an assessment, particularly in view of the serious consequences attaching to a debarment of 15 years. The FAR states unambiguously that such a hearing "shall" be afforded if genuine factual disputes arise. Accordingly, we conclude that the Air Force violated the appellants' constitutional right to due process in failing to comply with binding regulations and that the appellants are entitled to such a hearing on remand. As Justice Frankfurter observed in a similar context, "He that takes the procedural sword shall perish with that sword." *Vitarelli,* 359 U.S. at 547 (Frankfurter, J., concurring).

CONCLUSION

For the foregoing reasons, we AFFIRM the district court's dismissal of the appellants' claims against the individual defendants. However, we REVERSE the summary judgment in favor of the Air Force and REMAND to the district court with instructions to remand this matter to the Air Force. The Air Force should hold an evidentiary hearing, pursuant to 48 C.F.R. § 9.406-3(b)(2), to address whether Mirza Ali/Zulfiqar Eqbal was a principal of Sameena/Samtech. AFFIRMED in part, REVERSED in part and REMANDED. Each party shall bear its own costs.

QUESTIONS

1. Would the contractor have been entitled to a hearing had the regulations not required one?
2. What is the source of the principle that an agency must act in accordance with its own rules? Does it make sense to rely on due process without

ascertaining whether there is a property or liberty interest and then doing a *Mathews v. Eldridge* analysis?

3. Should the principle extend to requiring an agency to comply with its substantive regulations (i.e., regulations that prescribe the conduct of regulated parties)?

4. In *American Farm Lines v. Black Ball Freight Service,* 397 U.S. 532 (1970), a motor carrier competing with American Farm Lines (AFL) protested an Interstate Commerce Commission (ICC) grant of operating authority to AFL on the ground that AFL had not complied with procedural requirements of ICC rules. The Supreme Court rejected this basis for the protest:

> The Commission is entitled to a measure of discretion in administering its own procedural rules in such a manner as it deems necessary to resolve quickly and correctly urgent transportation problems. It is argued that the rules were adopted to confer important procedural benefits upon individuals; in opposition it is said the rules were intended primarily to facilitate the development of relevant information for the Commission's use in deciding applications for temporary authority.
>
> We agree with the Commission that the rules were promulgated for the purpose of providing the "necessary information" for the Commission "to reach an informed and equitable decision" on temporary authority applications. . . . The Commission stated that requests for temporary authority would be turned down "if the applications do not *adequately* comply with [the] . . . rules." *Ibid.* (Emphasis added.) The rules were not intended primarily to confer important procedural benefits upon individuals in the face of otherwise unfettered discretion as in *Vitarelli v. Seaton,* 359 U.S. 535; nor is this a case in which an agency required by rule to exercise independent discretion has failed to so. *Accardi v. Shaughnessy,* 347 U.S. 260. . . . Thus there is no reason to exempt this case from the general principle that "[i]t is always within the discretion of a court or an administrative agency to relax or modify its procedural rules adopted for the orderly transaction of business before it when in a given case the ends of justice require it. The action of either in such a case is not reviewable except upon a showing of substantial prejudice to the complaining party."

397 U.S. at 538-39. Is the Ninth Circuit's holding in *Sameena* consistent with *American Farm Lines?*

CHAPTER

4

Role of Agencies in Three-branch Government

A. HISTORICAL INTRODUCTION

EXCERPT, JAY S. BYBEE, *AGENCY EXPERTISE, ALJ INDEPENDENCE, AND ADMINISTRATIVE COURTS: THE RECENT CHANGES IN LOUISIANA'S ADMINISTRATIVE PROCEDURE ACT*

59 *Louisiana Law Review* 431, 434-41 (1999)[1]

1. THE FIRST CENTURY: AGENCY ACCOUNTABILITY

The United States Constitution creates three departments of government — Congress, the President, and the Supreme Court — and it vests distinct powers and responsibilities in each department. Article I of the Constitution vests enumerated legislative power in a Congress, consisting of a House of Representatives and a Senate. Congress is a *collegial* body, and collegial bodies represent double-edged swords. On the one hand, no single member of Congress, neither the Speaker of the House nor the President *Pro Tempore* of the Senate may speak on behalf of their respective chambers, much less on behalf of Congress itself. Only the members of Congress, in Congress assembled, may speak for Congress as the legislative branch of government. This gives Congress a broad, representative base. On the other hand, just as no member of Congress may speak for the whole, no single member of Congress may be held accountable for the actions of Congress. Members of Congress are elected to office from their respective districts or states and stand for periodic election in order to retain those offices. They are accountable to their electorate, but no electorate of the whole elects or rejects the entire Congress. When we are unhappy with Congress we have no mechanism for wiping the slate clean, for "throwing the bums out"; we can only throw our own bum out and hope that everyone else will do the same. Having to stand for election makes our representatives and senators accountable to us, but we have no single mechanism for holding the collective body, Congress, accountable.

Article III creates "one Supreme Court, and . . . such inferior Courts as the Congress may from time to time ordain and establish." The Supreme Court, like

---

Congress, is a collegial body. We may disparage the presence and influence of a particular justice, but unless he or she can persuade four other members of the Court to join him or her, the Court, as a constitutional department exercising the judicial power of the United States, has not acted. Federal judges are appointed by the President, by and with the advice and consent of the Senate. Because of the appointment power, the President has some control over the judiciary. He has, however, no control over any individual judge, even one he appointed. Once appointed, Article III judges enjoy life tenure "during good Behavior" and receive compensation which Congress cannot diminish during their tenure in office. As members of a collegial body and as federal officers not subject to election, recall, or dismissal, federal judges are even less accountable to us than members of Congress.

Article II of the Constitution vests in a President the executive power of the United States and the responsibility to "take Care that the Laws be faithfully executed." The President is the only one of the three departments of government that is also a person. The President does not belong to a collegial body; he alone exercises the executive power. The Constitution makes the President the only principal officer of the government who must stand for general election. The Constitution provides for the removal from office of members of Congress, justices of the Supreme Court, and the President, but only in the case of the President does removal of a single individual vacate an entire constitutional department of the federal government. This structure makes the President accountable; he bears direct and full responsibility for the actions of the executive branch.

The Founders considered and rejected a proposal for a Council of Revision that would have divided the power of the executive among more than one person. Alexander Hamilton wrote in *Federalist No. 70* that unity in the executive was "conducive to energy" and that

> [d]ecision, activity, secrecy, and dispatch will generally characterize the proceedings of one man in a much more eminent degree, than the proceedings of any greater number; and in proportion as the number is increased, these qualities will be diminished.

Instead of creating a Council of Revision or a non-binding advisory council — which James Wilson thought "oftener serves to cover, than prevent malpractices" — the Framers located the executive power in a single figure. As Hamilton pointed out, "plurality in the executive . . . tends to conceal faults, and destroy responsibility." His description of the consequences of dividing authority in the executive branch sounds like modern complaints about Congress:

> It often becomes impossible, amidst mutual accusations, to determine on whom the blame or the punishment of a pernicious measure, or series of pernicious measures ought really to fall. It is shifted from one to another with so much dexterity, and under such plausible appearances, that the public opinion is left in suspense about the real author.
>
> The Constitution vests the President with the power to act decisively, but the burden of being uniquely responsible for his actions.

Congress, beginning with the very First Congress, recognized that the President could not faithfully execute the law unaided, and it created additional executive offices, bureaus and departments to assist the President in his duties. During the first century of our history, the President remained politically responsible for these agencies. Congress based its model of subordinate agencies on the model of the President as Chief Administrator. Congress created single-headed agencies such as the various offices now in the cabinet (War, State, Treasury, Commerce) and other, non-cabinet agencies (the Post Office, Office of Customs, and Office of Patents and Copyrights). These agencies each had a single titular head who alone was responsible for the actions of the agency and, in turn, remained fully accountable to the President. Thus, the first hundred years of our history are marked by reliance on single-headed agencies. It was the model of administrative decision making we knew best: the President, the governor, the mayor. We wanted our chief administrators where we could find them.

2. The Reform Period: Agency Independence

The arrival of the Industrial Revolution changed many things, not the least of which was our conception of what government could plausibly do.[28] Transportation and communication brought the coasts closer; it facilitated interstate trade, and it cast a spotlight on industry rather than agriculture. Farmers, in particular, saw their influence erode and felt at the mercy of more modern transportation. Transportation — principally the railroads — gave farmers access to markets they could not reach before. But the railroads exacted a heavy price in the form of monopoly profits. Farmers unwilling to pay the railroads' rates lost their markets to their neighbors who were.[29]

The earliest efforts to regulate railroad service belonged to the states.[30] These early Commissions often served *ad hoc* and mainly as fact-finding advisors for state legislatures.[31] When, in 1886, the Supreme Court held that the states could not regulate interstate railroad traffic within their borders, Congress stepped in and created the Interstate Commerce Commission. The ICC was the first regulatory Commission designed to address national concerns; it was also the first important multi-member Commission. During the debates over creation of the ICC, Senator Morgan of Alabama queried where the ICC fit in our governmental structure:

> Perhaps [the Commissioners] . . . are autocrats. But we ought to know what they are. . . . It is the first bill I have ever known to be brought into the Senate . . . where the authors of it were not willing to enter into a definition as to whether the powers they conferred . . . were . . . upon officers of the executive . . . , legislative . . . , or judicial department[s]. . . .

The ICC was as much a product of the industrial and scientific revolution as the problems it was created to address. The new multi-member agency was built on a new administrative model. Though it seemed to exercise executive power, the Commission, like Congress was made collegial in order to offer its scientific

---

28. *See generally* James M. Landis, The Administrative Process 7-15 (1938).

29. Robert L. Rabin, *Federal Regulation in Historical Perspective*, 38 Stan. L. Rev. 1189, 1197-1208 (1986).

30. *See* Robert E. Cushman, The Independent Regulatory Commissions 20-27 (1941).

31. *Id.* at 23. Professor Cushman notes that these fact-finding Commissions were typically composed of more than one official. *Id.*

expertise; like the judiciary, the Commission was made largely free of political pressure or reprisal.[34] What the ICC offered us was informed, dispassionate decision making. No longer did Commissioners serve at the pleasure of the President. The independent regulatory Commissions offered expertise, not political accountability.

The ICC proved so popular that it was followed by other multi-headed boards and Commissions such as the Federal Reserve Board (1913), the Federal Trade Commission (1914), the Tariff Commission (1916), the Water Power Commission (1920), the Commodities Exchange Authority (1922), the Federal Radio Commission (1927), the Federal Power Commission (1930), the Food & Drug Administration (1931), and the Federal Home Loan Bank Board (1932). With President Franklin Roosevelt's New Deal in 1932 came a whole rash of independent Commissions, including the Federal Deposit Insurance Corporation (1933), the Farm Credit Administration (1933), the Federal Communications Commission (1934), the Securities and Exchange Commission (1934), the National Labor Relations Board (1935), the Bituminous Coal Commission (1935), the Federal Maritime Administration (1936), and the Civil Aeronautics Board (1938). The Court proved very supportive of the efforts of the political branches and responded with great deference to these agencies' decisions. It was a romantic era for government generally, and in our minds we idealized the role of the independent agencies.

3. The New Reform: Back to Accountability

The 1960s saw a more cynical view of independent agencies. One significant theory suggested that when agencies became the guardians of their powerful wards, instead of a disciplining force, the agencies were "captured."[37] Thus, what we needed was not agency independence, but political accountability. During this era, Congress returned to the model of single-headed agencies. Better that agencies answer to the President than that they be formally independent of the President and (informally) answerable to industry.

Congress created a number of single-headed agencies within existing executive departments: the Federal Highway Administration (1966), the Federal Railroad Administration (1966), the National Highway Transportation Safety Administration (1970), the Occupational Safety and Health Administration (1970), and the Mine Enforcement and Safety Administration (1973). Congress also created several free-standing agencies: the Environmental Protection Agency (1970), the National Credit Union Administration (1970), and the Equal Employment Opportunity Commission (1972). Unlike the independent

---

34. See Landis, *supra* note 28, at 16-17. With the independent regulatory agencies what we wanted was expertise and scientific management. In contrast to our earlier theories of government, we were not as concerned with their political accountability. Not only did Congress create collegial Commissions, it often provided that the President could not remove Commissioners except for cause, and Congress gave the Commissioners fixed tenure and a term that ensured that the Commissioners would serve beyond the immediate term of the President who appointed them.

37. *See generally* Thomas W. Merrill, *Capture Theory and the Courts: 1967-1983,* 72 Chi. Kent L. Rev. 1039 (1997).

Commissions created during the New Deal, the new free-standing agencies were largely single-headed agencies accountable to the President.[39]

4. Modern Trend: Independent Accountability?

The modern trend looks to the best of both of these models and may yet discover the worst. Congress has created relatively few new agencies in the past years. Two represent the strangest animals yet: independent single-headed agencies — agencies that vest extraordinary power to a single, unaccountable individual. The first of these is the revamped Social Security Administration. In 1994, Congress freed the Social Security Administration from the Department of Health and Human Services. A single Commissioner will continue to head the Social Security Administration and will serve for a six-year term. The Commissioner appears to be accountable to Congress alone. No longer does the President have the power to direct the actions of the Commissioner or remove her except for "neglect of duty or malfeasance in office," and her budget requests go straight to Congress, bypassing ordinary budget review at OMB.

The second example has become, unfortunately, quite familiar to us: the Office of the Independent Counsel. The Independent Counsel operates only loosely under the guidelines of the Department of Justice and serves until the matter has been fully investigated and prosecuted to his satisfaction. Short of the Independent Counsel's gross misconduct in office, no one except Congress can remove the Independent Counsel. [Note: Congress permitted the Independent Counsel Provisions of the Ethics in Government Act to expire in 1999.]

A final hybrid we should note is the unusual jurisdictional overlap between the Occupational Safety and Health Administration (OSHA), which is a single-headed agency within the Department of Labor, and the Occupational Safety and Health Review Commission (OSHRC), a multi-headed, independent Commission. OSHA bears responsibility for promulgating regulations and bringing enforcement actions, but adjudications are held before OSHRC. An employer who contests OSHA's citation may appear before an ALJ employed by OSHRC. OSHRC reviews, in its discretion, the initial decisions of its ALJs. The lower courts initially divided [over the] question, in the event of a difference of opinion between OSHA and OSHRC, to which agency (if either) should the courts defer? In 1991, the Supreme Court held that courts should defer to OSHA, not OSHRC.[48] "[W]hen a traditional, unitary agency uses adjudication to engage in lawmaking by regulatory interpretation, it necessarily interprets regulations that it has promulgated." By contrast, the Commission exercised "nonpolicymaking adjudicatory powers typically exercised by a court in the agency-review context."

Finally, we have what appear to be multi-headed executive agencies. The Defense Base Closure and Realignment Commission made recommendations to the President on military base closures. The President either approved for closure the entire list or he disapproved the entire list and the Commission started over. The Commission gives the controversial base closure decisions an air of detached expertise, while the President becomes politically accountable for the ultimate decision.

---

39. During this period Congress also established additional independent agencies, including the Consumer Products Safety Commission (1972), the Nuclear Regulatory Commission (1974), and the Federal Energy Regulatory Commission (1977).

48. *Martin v. OSHRC,* 499 U.S. 144 (1991). . . .

NOTES

1. Chief Justice Roberts, dissenting in *City of Arlington v. FCC*, 133 S. Ct. 1863, 1878 (2013), provided the following view of the development of administrative agencies since the end of the twentieth century:

    > And the federal bureaucracy continues to grow; in the last 15 years, Congress has launched more than 50 new agencies. Compare Office of the Federal Register, United States Government Manual 1997/1998, with Office of the Federal Register, United States Government Manual 2012. And more are on the way. See, *e.g.*, Congressional Research Service, C. Copeland, New Entities Created Pursuant to the Patient Protection and Affordable Care Act 1 (2010) (The PPACA "creates, requires others to create, or authorizes dozens of new entities to implement the legislation").

2. In that same dissenting opinion, Chief Justice Roberts said the following about the separation of powers issues that will be considered in this chapter:

    > One of the principal authors of the Constitution famously wrote that the "accumulation of all powers, legislative, executive, and judiciary, in the same hands, . . . may justly be pronounced the very definition of tyranny." The Federalist No. 47, p. 324 (J. Cooke ed. 1961) (J. Madison). Although modern administrative agencies fit most comfortably within the Executive Branch, as a practical matter they exercise legislative power, by promulgating regulations with the force of law; executive power, by policing compliance with those regulations; and judicial power, by adjudicating enforcement actions and imposing sanctions on those found to have violated their rules. The accumulation of these powers in the same hands is not an occasional or isolated exception to the constitutional plan; it is a central feature of modern American government.

    City of Arlington v. FCC, 133 S. Ct. at 1877-78 (Roberts, C.J., dissenting). These concerns of the Chief Justice may be relevant as you read the materials in this chapter.

B. CONFORMING AGENCY PRACTICE TO ARTICLE III

CROWELL v. BENSON
285 U.S. 22 (1931)

CERTIORARI to review a decree which affirmed a decree of the District Court enjoining the enforcement of an award of compensation made by a deputy Commissioner under the Longshoremen's and Harbor Workers' Compensation Act.

MR. CHIEF JUSTICE HUGHES delivered the opinion of the Court.

This suit was brought in the District Court to enjoin the enforcement of an award made by petitioner Crowell, as deputy Commissioner of the United States Employees' Compensation Commission, in favor of the petitioner Knudsen and against the respondent Benson. The award was made under the Longshoremen's and Harbor Workers' Compensation Act (Act of March 4, 1927) and rested upon the finding of the deputy Commissioner that Knudsen was injured while in the employ of Benson and performing service upon the navigable waters of the United States. The complainant alleged that the award was contrary to law for the reason that Knudsen was not at the time of his injury an employee of the complainant and his claim was not "within the jurisdiction" of the deputy Commissioner. An amended complaint charged that the Act was unconstitutional upon the grounds that it violated the due process clause of the Fifth Amendment, the provision of the Seventh Amendment as to trial by jury, that of the Fourth Amendment as to unreasonable search and seizure, and the provisions of Article III with respect to the judicial power of the United States. The District Judge denied motions to dismiss and granted a hearing de novo upon the facts and the law, expressing the opinion that the Act would be invalid if not construed to permit such a hearing. The case was transferred to the admiralty docket, answers were filed presenting the issue as to the fact of employment, and the evidence of both parties having been heard, the District Court decided that Knudsen was not in the employ of the petitioner and restrained the enforcement of the award. The decree was affirmed by the Circuit Court of Appeals, and this Court granted writs of certiorari.

The question of the validity of the Act may be considered in relation to (1) its provisions defining substantive rights and (2) its procedural requirements.

First. The Act has two limitations that are fundamental. It deals exclusively with compensation in respect of disability or death resulting "from an injury occurring upon the navigable waters of the United States" if recovery "through workmen's compensation proceedings may not validly be provided by State law," and it applies only when the relation of master and servant exists. §3. "Injury," within the statute, "means accidental injury or death arising out of and in the course of employment," and the term "employer" means one "any of whose employees are employed in maritime employment, in whole or in part," upon such navigable waters. §2 (2) (4). Employers are made liable for the payment to their employees of prescribed compensation "irrespective of fault as a cause for the injury." §4. The liability is exclusive, unless the employer fails to secure payment of the compensation. §5. The employer is required to furnish appropriate medical and other treatment. §7. The compensation for temporary or permanent disability, total or partial, according to the statutory classification, and in case of the death of the employee, is fixed, being based upon prescribed percentages of average weekly wages, and the persons to whom payments are to be made are designated. §§6, 8, 9, 10. Employers must secure the payment of compensation by procuring insurance or by becoming self-insurers in the manner stipulated. §32. Failure to provide such security is a misdemeanor. §38.

As the Act relates solely to injuries occurring upon the navigable waters of the United States, it deals with the maritime law, applicable to matters that fall within the admiralty and maritime jurisdiction (Const. Art. III, §2); and the general authority of the Congress to alter or revise the maritime law which shall prevail throughout the country is beyond dispute. . . .

Second. The objections to the procedural requirements of the Act relate to the extent of the administrative authority which it confers. The administration of the Act — "except as otherwise specifically provided" — was given to the United States Employees' Compensation Commission, which was authorized to establish compensation districts, appoint deputy Commissioners, and make regulations. §§39, 40. . . .

As the claims which are subject to the provisions of the Act are governed by the Maritime law as established by the Congress and are within the admiralty juris-diction, the objection raised by the respondent's pleading as to the right to a trial by jury under the Seventh Amendment is unavailing; and that under the Fourth Amendment is neither explained nor urged. The other objections as to procedure invoke the due process clause and the provisions as to the judicial power of the United States.

(1) The contention under the due process clause of the Fifth Amendment relates to the determination of questions of fact. Rulings of the deputy Commis-sioner upon questions of law are without finality. So far as the latter are concerned, full opportunity is afforded for their determination by the Federal courts through proceedings to suspend or to set aside a compensation order, § 21 (b), by the requirement that judgment is to be entered on a supplementary order declaring default only in case the order follows the law (§ 18), and by the provision that the issue of injunction or other process in a proceeding by a beneficiary to compel obedience to a compensation order is dependent upon a determination by the court that the order was lawfully made and served. § 21 (c). Moreover, the statute contains no express limitation attempting to preclude the court, in proceedings to set aside an order as not in accordance with law, from making its own examination and determination of facts whenever that is deemed to be necessary to enforce a constitutional right properly asserted. As the statute is to be construed so as to support rather than to defeat it, no such limitation is to be implied.

Apart from cases involving constitutional rights to be appropriately enforced by proceedings in court, there can be no doubt that the Act contemplates that, as to questions of fact arising with respect to injuries to employees within the purview of the Act, the findings of the deputy Commissioner, supported by evidence and within the scope of his authority, shall be final. To hold otherwise would be to defeat the obvious purpose of the legislation to furnish a prompt, continuous, expert and inexpensive method for dealing with a class of questions of fact which are peculiarly suited to examination and determination by an administrative agency specially assigned to that task. The object is to secure within the prescribed limits of the employer's liability an immediate investiga-tion and a sound practical judgment, and the efficacy of the plan depends upon the finality of the determinations of fact with respect to the circumstances, nature, extent and consequences of the employee's injuries and the amount of compensation that should be awarded. And this finality may also be regarded as extending to the determination of the question of fact whether the injury "was occasioned solely by the intoxication of the employee or by the willful intention of the employee to injure or kill himself or another." While the exclu-sion of compensation in such cases is found in what are called "coverage" provisions of the Act (§ 3), the question of fact still belongs to the contemplated routine of administration, for the case is one of employment within the scope of the Act and the cause of the injury sustained by the employee as well as its character and effect must be ascertained in applying the provisions for compen-sation. The use of the administrative method for these purposes, assuming due notice, proper opportunity to be heard, and that findings are based upon evidence, falls easily within the principle of the decisions sustaining similar procedure against objections under the due process clauses of the Fifth and Fourteenth Amendments.

The statute provides for notice and hearing; and an award made without proper notice, or suitable opportunity to be heard, may be attacked and set aside as without validity. The objection is made that, as the deputy Commissioner is authorized to prosecute such inquiries as he may consider necessary, the award may be based wholly or partly upon an ex parte investigation and upon unknown sources of information, and that the hearing may be merely a formality. The statute, however, contemplates a public hearing and regulations are to require "a record of the hearings and other proceedings before the deputy Commissioner." § 23 (b). This implies that all proceedings by the deputy Commissioner upon a particular claim shall be appropriately set forth, and that whatever facts he may ascertain and their sources shall be shown in the record and be open to challenge and opposing evidence. Facts conceivably known to the deputy Commissioner, but not put in evidence so as to permit scrutiny and contest, will not support a compensation order. An award not supported by evidence in the record is not in accordance with law. But the fact that the deputy Commissioner is not bound by the rules of evidence which would be applicable to trials in court or by technical rules of procedure, § 23 (a), does not invalidate the proceeding, provided substantial rights of the parties are not infringed.

(2) The contention based upon the judicial power of the United States, as extended "to all cases of admiralty and maritime jurisdiction" (Const. Art. III), presents a distinct question. In *Murray's Lessee v. Hoboken Land and Improvement Co.*, 18 How. 272, 284, this Court, speaking through Mr. Justice Curtis, said: "To avoid misconstruction upon so grave a subject, we think it proper to state that we do not consider congress can either withdraw from judicial cognizance any matter which, from its nature, is the subject of a suit at the common law, or in equity, or admiralty; nor, on the other hand, can it bring under the judicial power a matter which, from its nature, is not a subject for judicial determination."

The question in the instant case, in this aspect, can be deemed to relate only to determinations of fact. The reservation of legal questions is to the same court that has jurisdiction in admiralty, and the mere fact that the court is not described as such is unimportant. Nor is the provision for injunction proceedings, § 21 (b), open to objection. The Congress was at liberty to draw upon another system of procedure to equip the court with suitable and adequate means for enforcing the standards of the maritime law as defined by the Act. By statute and rules, courts of admiralty may be empowered to grant injunctions, as in the case of limitation of liability proceedings. The Congress did not attempt to define questions of law, and the generality of the description leaves no doubt of the intention to reserve to the Federal court full authority to pass upon all matters which this Court had held to fall within that category. There is thus no attempt to interfere with, but rather provision is made to facilitate, the exercise by the court of its jurisdiction to deny effect to any administrative finding which is without evidence, or "contrary to the indisputable character of the evidence," or where the hearing is "inadequate," or "unfair," or arbitrary in any respect. *Interstate Commerce Comm. v. Louisville R. Co.*, [227 U.S. 88,] 91, 92.

As to determinations of fact, the distinction is at once apparent between cases of private right and those which arise between the Government and persons subject to its authority in connection with the performance of the constitutional functions of the executive or legislative departments. The Court referred to this distinction in *Murray's Lessee v. Hoboken Land and Improvement Co., supra,* pointing out that "there are matters, involving public rights, which may be presented in such form that the judicial power is capable of acting on them, and which are susceptible of judicial determination, but which Congress may or may not bring them within the cognizance of the courts of the United States, as it may deem proper." Thus the Congress, in exercising the powers confided to it, may establish "legislative" courts (as distinguished from "constitutional courts in which the judicial power conferred by the Constitution can be deposited") which are to form part of the government of territories or of the District of Columbia, or to serve as special tribunals "to examine and determine various matters, arising between the government and others, which from their nature do not require judicial determination and yet are susceptible of it." But "the mode of determining matters of this class is completely within congressional control. Congress may reserve to itself the power to decide, may delegate that power to executive officers, or may commit it to judicial tribunals." *Ex parte Bakelite Corp.*, 279 U.S. 438, 451. Familiar illustrations of administrative agencies created for the determination of such matters are found in connection with the exercise of the congressional power as to interstate and foreign commerce, taxation, immigration, the public lands, public health, the facilities of the post office, pensions and payments to veterans.

The present case does not fall within the categories just described but is one of private right, that is, of the liability of one individual to another under the law as defined. But in cases of that sort, there is no requirement that, in order to maintain the essential attributes of the judicial power, all determinations of fact in constitutional courts shall be made by judges. On the common law side of the Federal courts, the aid of juries is not only deemed appropriate but is required by the Constitution itself. In cases of equity and admiralty, it is historic practice to call to the assistance of the courts, without the consent of the parties, masters and Commissioners or assessors, to pass upon certain classes of questions, as, for example, to take and state an account or to find the amount of damages. While the reports of masters and Commissioners in such cases are essentially of an advisory nature, it has not been the practice to disturb their findings when they are properly based upon evidence, in the absence of errors of law, and the parties have no right to demand that the court shall redetermine the facts thus found. . . .

It may also be noted that while on an appeal in admiralty cases "the facts as well as the law would be subjected to review and retrial," this Court has recognized the power of the Congress "to limit the effect of an appeal to a review of the law as applicable to facts finally determined below."

In deciding whether the Congress, in enacting the statute under review, has exceeded the limits of its authority to prescribe procedure in cases of injury upon navigable waters, regard must be had, as in other cases where constitutional limits are invoked, not to mere matters of form but to the substance of what is required. The statute has a limited application, being confined to the relation of master and servant, and the method of determining the questions of fact, which arise in the routine of making compensation awards to employees under the Act, is necessary to its effective enforcement. The Act itself, where it applies, establishes the measure of the employer's liability, thus leaving open for determination the questions of fact as to the circumstances, nature, extent and consequences of the injuries sustained by the employee for which compensation is to be made in accordance with the prescribed standards. Findings of fact by the deputy Commissioner upon such questions are closely analogous to the findings of the amount of damages that are made, according to familiar practice, by Commissioners or assessors; and the reservation of full authority to the court to deal with matters of law provides for the appropriate exercise of the judicial function in this class of cases. For the purposes stated, we are unable to find any constitutional obstacle to the action of the Congress in availing itself of a method shown by experience to be essential in order to apply its standards to the thousands of cases involved, thus relieving the courts of a most serious burden while preserving their complete authority to insure the proper application of the law.

(3) [The Court, however, found that as to two particular factual issues, the statute should be interpreted to require judicial trial de novo. (This is the so-called "constitutional fact" doctrine.) The Court reasoned that, because the injuries had to be on navigable waters in order for Congress to have legislative power, and because a master-servant relationship was thought to be necessary for the statute to meet due process concerns, there was a constitutional requirement that a court determine the factual issues of whether the injuries occurred on navigable waters and whether there was a master-servant relationship. Justice Brandeis dissented vigorously and forcefully against this part of the Court's analysis.]

QUESTIONS

1. Why doesn't the Seventh Amendment require a jury trial?
2. What is the Court's Procedural Due Process analysis? Is it consistent with later cases like *Goldberg, Roth,* and *Eldridge* (*supra,* pp. 34-72)?
3. How is the Article III issue different from the due process issue? What interests underlie the provisions in Article III for the independence of judges?
4. Various functional reasons have been asserted to support the separation of judicial from executive power, including: (a) need for a check on enforcement abuse, (b) presumably nonpolitical judges will protect economic rights of individuals, rights of minorities, and decide more consistently. Are these interests met when agencies are permitted to adjudicate?
5. The following functional reasons have been asserted to support giving adjudicating responsibilities to agencies rather than courts: (a) less formality and speedier action, (b) greater expertise and greater consistency, and (c) avoiding the perceived hostility of the judiciary to certain legislative policies (e.g., labor organization rights). Are these interests lost if courts review facts de novo?
6. What is the distinction between legal issues and factual issues? According to the Court, what is the relevance of the distinction? Does the distinction make sense?
7. What is the distinction between public rights and private rights? According to the Court, what is the significance of the distinction? Is it a logical distinction for that purpose?
8. What is the Court's rationale for letting agencies adjudicate facts in cases of private rights?

Note: The third part of the majority opinion in *Crowell* (the constitutional fact doctrine) has not stood the test of time. It survives if at all only in very limited areas of the law (such as, arguably, First Amendment obscenity cases). See footnote 34 of the following case.

NORTHERN PIPELINE CONST. CO. v. MARATHON PIPE LINE CO.

458 U.S. 50 (1982)

[In this case the Supreme Court held that the Bankruptcy Act of 1978 violated Article III by assigning to bankruptcy judges jurisdiction over a wide variety of civil proceedings. The provision at issue extended jurisdiction to both state law and federal law claims, including causes of action owned by the debtor at the time of the petition for bankruptcy. Bankruptcy judges, appointed for 14-year terms, are clearly not Article III judges. The Act nonetheless gave them virtually all of the powers that a district judge has over a civil case, including the power to empanel a jury and to issue writs. Orders of such bankruptcy judges were appealable to an Article III court. Northern Pipeline brought a contract suit in the bankruptcy court against Marathon, after Northern had filed a petition for reorganization under the Bankruptcy Act. Marathon challenged the constitutionality of the Bankruptcy Act, and the government intervened to defend the validity of the Act. On appeal from the bankruptcy court's refusal to dismiss the claim, the district court (an Article III court) reversed and found the statutory grant of jurisdiction unconstitutional. The Supreme Court affirmed, but without a majority opinion.

Justice Brennan wrote the plurality opinion, joined only by Justices Marshall, Blackmun, and Stevens. Justice Brennan explained that the judicial power of the United States must be exercised by courts whose judges have the Article III protections of life tenure and compensation that cannot be diminished. Justice Brennan first identified and found inapplicable three recognized exceptions to the rule — territorial courts, military courts-martial, and courts adjudicating "public rights" in the sense of rights that arise "between the government and others."

Finally, in Part IV of the plurality opinion, Justice Brennan dealt with the government's alternative argument, based on *Crowell*, that the Bankruptcy Act could be upheld by viewing the bankruptcy court as an "adjunct" to the (Article III) district court. In the following excerpt, the plurality distinguished *Crowell* and *United States v. Raddatz*, 447 U.S. 667, to conclude that Congress does not have the same power to create adjuncts to adjudicate constitutionally recognized rights and state-created rights as it does to adjudicate rights that it creates, and that the grant of jurisdiction to bankruptcy courts could not be sustained as an exercise of Congress' power to create adjuncts to Art. III courts.]

Crowell involved the adjudication of congressionally created rights. But this Court has sustained the use of adjunct factfinders even in the adjudication of constitutional rights — so long as those adjuncts were subject to sufficient control by an Art. III district court. In *United States v. Raddatz* the Court upheld the 1978 Federal Magistrates Act, which permitted district court judges to refer certain pretrial motions, including suppression motions based on alleged violations of constitutional rights, to a magistrate for initial determination. The Court observed that the magistrate's proposed findings and recommendations were subject to de novo review by the district court, which was free to rehear the evidence or to call for additional evidence. Moreover, it was noted that the magistrate considered motions only upon reference from the district court, and that the magistrates were appointed, and subject to removal, by the district court. In short, the ultimate decisionmaking authority respecting all pretrial motions clearly remained with the district court. Under these circumstances, the Court held that the Act did not violate the constraints of Art. III.

Together these cases establish two principles that aid us in determining the extent to which Congress may constitutionally vest traditionally judicial functions in non-Art. III officers. First, it is clear that when Congress creates a substantive federal right, it possesses substantial discretion to prescribe the manner in which that right may be adjudicated—including the assignment to an adjunct of some functions historically performed by judges. Thus *Crowell* recognized that Art. III does not require "all determinations of fact [to] be made by judges," 285 U.S., at 51; with respect to congressionally created rights, some factual determinations may be made by a specialized factfinding tribunal designed by Congress, without constitutional bar, *id.*, at 54. Second, the functions of the adjunct must be limited in such a way that "the essential attributes" of judicial power are retained in the Art. III court. Thus in upholding the adjunct scheme challenged in *Crowell*, the Court emphasized that "the reservation of full authority to the court to deal with matters of law provides for the appropriate exercise of the judicial function in this class of cases." *Ibid.* And in refusing to invalidate the Magistrates Act at issue in *Raddatz*, the Court stressed that under the congressional scheme "[the] authority—and the responsibility—to make an informed, final determination . . . remains with the judge," 447 U.S., at 682, quoting *Mathews v. Weber*, 423 U.S. 261, 271 (1976); the statute's delegation of power was therefore permissible, since "the ultimate decision is made by the district court," 447 U.S., at 683.

These two principles assist us in evaluating the "adjunct" scheme presented in these cases. Appellants assume that Congress' power to create "adjuncts" to consider all cases related to those arising under Title 11 is as great as it was in the circumstances of *Crowell*. But while *Crowell* certainly endorsed the proposition that Congress possesses broad discretion to assign factfinding functions to an adjunct created to aid in the adjudication of congressionally created statutory rights, *Crowell* does not support the further proposition necessary to appellants' argument—that Congress possesses the same degree of discretion in assigning traditionally judicial power to adjuncts engaged in the adjudication of rights not created by Congress. Indeed, the validity of this proposition was expressly denied in *Crowell*, when the Court rejected "the untenable assumption that the constitutional courts may be deprived in all cases of the determination of facts upon evidence even though a *constitutional* right may be involved," 285 U.S., at 60-61 (emphasis added), and stated that

> "the essential independence of the exercise of the judicial power of the United States in the enforcement of *constitutional* rights requires that the Federal court should determine . . . an issue [of agency jurisdiction] upon its own record and the facts elicited before it." *Id.*, at 64 (emphasis added).[34]

. . .

---

34. *Crowell's* precise holding, with respect to the review of "jurisdictional" and "constitutional" facts that arise within ordinary administrative proceedings, has been undermined by later cases. *See St. Joseph Stock Yards Co. v. United States*, 298 U.S. 38, 53 (1936). *See generally* 4 K. Davis, *Administrative Law Treatise* §§ 29.08, 29.09 (1st ed. 1958). But the general principle of *Crowell*—distinguishing between congressionally created rights and constitutionally recognized rights—remains valid. . . .

Although *Crowell* and *Raddatz* do not explicitly distinguish between rights created by Congress and other rights, such a distinction [is] necessary in light of the delicate accommodations required by the principle of separation of powers reflected in Art. III. The constitutional system of checks and balances is designed to guard against "encroachment or aggrandizement" by Congress at the expense of the other branches of government. *Buckley v. Valeo*, 424 U.S., at 122. But when Congress creates a statutory right, it clearly has the discretion, in defining that right, to create presumptions, or assign burdens of proof, or prescribe remedies; it may also provide that persons seeking to vindicate that right must do so before particularized tribunals created to perform the specialized adjudicative tasks related to that right. Such provisions do, in a sense, affect the exercise of judicial power, but they are also incidental to Congress' power to define the right that it has created. No comparable justification exists, however, when the right being adjudicated is not of congressional creation. In such a situation, substantial inroads into functions that have traditionally been performed by the Judiciary cannot be characterized merely as incidental extensions of Congress' power to define rights that it has created. Rather, such inroads suggest unwarranted encroachments upon the judicial power of the United States, which our Constitution reserves for Art. III courts.

We hold that the Bankruptcy Act of 1978 carries the possibility of such an unwarranted encroachment. Many of the rights subject to adjudication by the Act's bankruptcy courts, like the rights implicated in *Raddatz*, are not of Congress' creation. Indeed, the cases before us, which center upon appellant Northern's claim for damages for breach of contract and misrepresentation, involve a right created by state law, a right independent of and antecedent to the reorganization petition that conferred jurisdiction upon the Bankruptcy Court. Accordingly, Congress' authority to control the manner in which that right is adjudicated, through assignment of historically judicial functions to a non-Art. III "adjunct," plainly must be deemed at a minimum. Yet it is equally plain that Congress has vested the "adjunct" bankruptcy judges with powers over Northern's state-created right that far exceed the powers that it has vested in administrative agencies that adjudicate only rights of Congress' own creation.

Unlike the administrative scheme that we reviewed in *Crowell*, the Act vests all "essential attributes" of the judicial power of the United States in the "adjunct" bankruptcy court. First, the agency in *Crowell* made only specialized, narrowly confined factual determinations regarding a particularized area of law. In contrast, the subject-matter jurisdiction of the bankruptcy courts encompasses not only traditional matters of bankruptcy, but also "all civil proceedings arising under title 11 or arising in or related to cases under title 11." 28 U.S.C. § 1471(b) (1976 ed., Supp. IV) (emphasis added). Second, while the agency in *Crowell* engaged in statutorily channeled factfinding functions, the bankruptcy courts exercise "*all* of the jurisdiction" conferred by the Act on the district courts, § 1471(c) (emphasis added). Third, the agency in *Crowell* possessed only a limited power to issue compensation orders pursuant to specialized procedures, and its orders could be enforced only by order of the district court. By contrast, the bankruptcy courts exercise all ordinary powers of district courts, including the power to preside over jury trials, 28 U.S.C. § 1480 (1976 ed., Supp. IV), the power to issue declaratory judgments, § 2201, the power to issue writs of habeas corpus, § 2256, and the power to issue any order, process, or judgment appropriate for the enforcement of the provisions of Title 11, 11 U.S.C. § 105(a)

(1976 ed., Supp. IV). Fourth, while orders issued by the agency in *Crowell* were to be set aside if "not supported by the evidence," the judgments of the bankruptcy courts are apparently subject to review only under the more deferential "clearly erroneous" standard. Finally, the agency in *Crowell* was required by law to seek enforcement of its compensation orders in the district court. In contrast, the bankruptcy courts issue final judgments, which are binding and enforceable even in the absence of an appeal. In short, the "adjunct" bankruptcy courts created by the Act exercise jurisdiction behind the facade of a grant to the district courts, and are exercising powers far greater than those lodged in the adjuncts approved in either *Crowell* or *Raddatz.* . . .

JUSTICE REHNQUIST, with whom JUSTICE O'CONNOR joins, concurring in the judgment. . . .

From the record before us, the lawsuit in which Marathon was named defendant seeks damages for each of contract, misrepresentation, and other counts which are the stuff of the traditional actions at common law tried by the courts at Westminster in 1789. There is apparently no federal rule of decision provided for any of the issues in the lawsuit; the claims of Northern arise entirely under state law. No method of adjudication is hinted, other than the traditional common-law mode of judge and jury. The lawsuit is before the Bankruptcy Court only because the plaintiff has previously filed a petition for reorganization in that court.

The cases dealing with the authority of Congress to create courts other than by use of its power under Art. III do not admit of easy synthesis. In the interval of nearly 150 years between *American Insurance Co. v. Canter,* 1 Pet. 511 (1828), and *Palmore v. United States,* 411 U.S. 389 (1973), the Court addressed the question infrequently. I need not decide whether these cases in fact support a general proposition and three tidy exceptions, as the plurality believes, or whether instead they are but landmarks on a judicial "darkling plain" where ignorant armies have clashed by night, as Justice WHITE apparently believes them to be. None of the cases has gone so far as to sanction the type of adjudication to which Marathon will be subjected against its will under the provisions of the 1978 Act. To whatever extent different powers granted under that Act might be sustained under the "public rights" doctrine of *Murray's Lessee v. Hoboken Land & Improvement Co.,* 18 How. 272 (1856), and succeeding cases, I am satisfied that the adjudication of Northern's lawsuit cannot be so sustained.

I am likewise of the opinion that the extent of review by Art. III courts provided on appeal from a decision of the bankruptcy court in a case such as Northern's does not save the grant of authority to the latter under the rule espoused in *Crowell v. Benson,* 285 U.S. 22 (1932). All matters of fact and law in whatever domains of the law to which the parties' dispute may lead are to be resolved by the bankruptcy court in the first instance, with only traditional appellate review by Art. III courts apparently contemplated. Acting in this manner the bankruptcy court is not an "adjunct" of either the district court or the court of appeals.

I would, therefore, hold so much of the Bankruptcy Act of 1978 as enables a Bankruptcy Court to entertain and decide Northern's lawsuit over Marathon's objection to be violative of Art. III of the United States Constitution. . . .

[Chief Justice Burger, Justice White, and Justice Powell dissented.]

QUESTIONS

1. What is the significance of a private right being statutorily created or not?
2. Can Congress still give any private right cases to Article I "courts"? Was *Crowell* overruled or distinguished?
3. Is it important to the result in the case that Marathon objected to the bankruptcy court's jurisdiction to decide the case?
4. How much is left of *Crowell?* Was the grant of judicial power to bankruptcy judges merely too extreme?

CFTC v. SCHOR
478 U.S. 833 (1986)

JUSTICE O'CONNOR delivered the opinion of the Court.

The question presented is whether the Commodity Exchange Act (CEA or Act), 7 U.S.C. § 1 *et seq.*, empowers the Commodity Futures Trading Commission (CFTC or Commission) to entertain state law counterclaims in reparation proceedings and, if so, whether that grant of authority violates Article III of the Constitution.

I

The CEA broadly prohibits fraudulent and manipulative conduct in connection with commodity futures transactions. In 1974, Congress "[overhauled]" the Act in order to institute a more "comprehensive regulatory structure to oversee the volatile and esoteric futures trading complex." H. R. Rep. No. 93-975, p. 1 (1974). Congress also determined that the broad regulatory powers of the CEA were most appropriately vested in an agency which would be relatively immune from the "political winds that sweep Washington." H. R. Rep. No. 93-975, at 44, 70. It therefore created an independent agency, the CFTC, and entrusted to it sweeping authority to implement the CEA.

Among the duties assigned to the CFTC was the administration of a reparations procedure through which disgruntled customers of professional commodity brokers could seek redress for the brokers' violations of the Act or CFTC regulations. Thus, § 14 of the CEA, 7 U.S.C. § 18 (1976 ed.), provides that any person injured by such violations may apply to the Commission for an order directing the offender to pay reparations to the complainant and may enforce that order in federal district court. Congress intended this administrative procedure to be an "inexpensive and expeditious" alternative to existing fora available to aggrieved customers, namely, the courts and arbitration. S. Rep. No. 95-850, p. 11 (1978). . . .

In conformance with the congressional goal of promoting efficient dispute resolution, the CFTC promulgated a regulation in 1976 which allows it to adjudicate counterclaims "aris[ing] out of the transaction or occurrence or series of transactions or occurrences set forth in the complaint." *Id.*, at 3995, 4002 (codified at 17 CFR § 12.23(b)(2) (1983)). This permissive counterclaim rule leaves the respondent in a reparations proceeding free to seek relief against the reparations complainant in other fora.

The instant dispute arose in February 1980, when respondents Schor and Mortgage Services of America, Inc., invoked the CFTC's reparations jurisdiction by filing complaints against petitioner Conti Commodity Services, Inc. (Conti), a commodity futures broker, and Richard L. Sandor, a Conti employee. Schor had an account with Conti which contained a debit balance because Schor's net futures trading losses and expenses, such as commissions, exceeded the funds deposited in the account. Schor alleged that this debit balance was the result of Conti's numerous violations of the CEA.

Before receiving notice that Schor had commenced the reparations proceeding, Conti had filed a diversity action in Federal District Court to recover the debit balance. Schor counterclaimed in this action, reiterating his charges that the debit balance was due to Conti's violations of the CEA. Schor also moved on two separate occasions to dismiss or stay the District Court action, arguing that the continuation of the federal action would be a waste of judicial resources and an undue burden on the litigants in view of the fact that "[the] reparations proceedings . . . will fully . . . resolve and adjudicate all the rights of the parties to this action with respect to the transactions which are the subject matter of this action."

Although the District Court declined to stay or dismiss the suit, Conti voluntarily dismissed the federal court action and presented its debit balance claim by way of a counterclaim in the CFTC reparations proceeding. Conti denied violating the CEA and instead insisted that the debit balance resulted from Schor's trading, and was therefore a simple debt owed by Schor.

After discovery, briefing, and a hearing, the Administrative Law Judge (ALJ) in Schor's reparations proceeding ruled in Conti's favor on both Schor's claims and Conti's counterclaims. After this ruling, Schor for the first time challenged the CFTC's statutory authority to adjudicate Conti's counterclaim. The ALJ rejected Schor's challenge, stating himself "bound by agency regulations and published agency policies." The Commission declined to review the decision and allowed it to become final, at which point Schor filed a petition for review with the Court of Appeals for the District of Columbia Circuit. Prior to oral argument, the Court of Appeals, *sua sponte,* raised the question whether CFTC could constitutionally adjudicate Conti's counterclaims in light of *Northern Pipeline Construction Co. v. Marathon Pipe Line Co.,* 458 U.S. 50 (1982), in which this Court held that "Congress may not vest in a non-Article III court the power to adjudicate, render final judgment, and issue binding orders in a traditional contract action arising under state law, without consent of the litigants, and subject only to ordinary appellate review." *Thomas v. Union Carbide Agricultural Products Co.,* 473 U.S. 568, 584 (1985).

After briefing and argument, the Court of Appeals upheld the CFTC's decision on Schor's claim in most respects, but ordered the dismissal of Conti's counterclaims on the ground that "the CFTC lacks authority (subject matter competence) to adjudicate" common law counterclaims. In support of this latter ruling, the Court of Appeals reasoned that the CFTC's exercise of jurisdiction over Conti's common law counterclaim gave rise to "[s]erious constitutional problems" under *Northern Pipeline.* The Court of Appeals therefore concluded that, under well-established principles of statutory construction, the relevant inquiry was whether the CEA was "'fairly susceptible' of [an alternative] construction," such that Article III objections, and thus unnecessary constitutional adjudication, could be avoided.

After examining the CEA and its legislative history, the court concluded that Congress had no "clearly expressed" or "explicit" intention to give the CFTC constitutionally questionable jurisdiction over state common law counterclaims. The Court of Appeals therefore "adopt[ed] the construction of the Act that avoids significant constitutional questions," reading the CEA to authorize the CFTC to adjudicate only those counterclaims alleging violations of the Act or CFTC regulations. Because Conti's counterclaims did not allege such violations, the Court of Appeals held that the CFTC exceeded its authority in adjudicating those claims, and ordered that the ALJ's decision on the claims be reversed and the claims dismissed for lack of jurisdiction. . . .

We . . . granted certiorari, and now reverse.

II

. . . Our examination of the CEA and its legislative history and purpose [omitted here] reveals that Congress plainly intended the CFTC to decide counterclaims asserted by respondents in reparations proceedings, and just as plainly delegated to the CFTC the authority to fashion its counterclaim jurisdiction in the manner the CFTC determined necessary to further the purposes of the reparations program. . . .

. . . We therefore are squarely faced with the question whether the CFTC's assumption of jurisdiction over common law counterclaims violates Article III of the Constitution.

III

Article III, § 1, directs that the "judicial Power of the United States shall be vested in one supreme Court and in such inferior Courts as the Congress may from time to time ordain and establish," and provides that these federal courts shall be staffed by judges who hold office during good behavior, and whose compensation shall not be diminished during tenure in office. Schor claims that these provisions prohibit Congress from authorizing the initial adjudication of common law counterclaims by the CFTC, an administrative agency whose adjudicatory officers do not enjoy the tenure and salary protections embodied in Article III.

Although our precedents in this area do not admit of easy synthesis, they do establish that the resolution of claims such as Schor's cannot turn on conclusory reference to the language of Article III. See, e.g., *Thomas*, 473 U.S., at 583. Rather, the constitutionality of a given congressional delegation of adjudicative functions to a non-Article III body must be assessed by reference to the purposes underlying the requirements of Article III. See, e.g., *id.*, at 590; *Northern Pipeline*, 458 U.S., at 64. This inquiry, in turn, is guided by the principle that "practical attention to substance rather than doctrinaire reliance on formal categories should inform application of Article III." *Thomas, supra*, at 587. See also *Crowell v. Benson*, 285 U.S., at 53.

A

Article III, § 1, serves both to protect "the role of the independent judiciary within the constitutional scheme of tripartite government," *Thomas, supra,* at 583, and to safeguard litigants' "right to have claims decided before judges who are free from potential domination by other branches of government." Although our cases have provided us with little occasion to discuss the nature or significance of this latter safeguard, our prior discussions of Article III, § 1's guarantee of an independent and impartial adjudication by the federal judi-ciary of matters within the judicial power of the United States intimated that this guarantee serves to protect primarily personal, rather than structural, interests.

Our precedents also demonstrate, however, that Article III does not confer on litigants an absolute right to the plenary consideration of every nature of claim by an Article III court. Moreover, as a personal right, Article III's guarantee of an impartial and independent federal adjudication is subject to waiver, just as are other personal constitutional rights that dictate the procedures by which civil and criminal matters must be tried. *See,* e.g., *Boykin v. Alabama,* 395 U.S. 238 (1969) (waiver of criminal trial by guilty plea); *Duncan v. Louisiana,* 391 U.S. 145, 158 (1968) (waiver of right to trial by jury in criminal case); Fed. Rule of Civ. Proc. 38(d) (waiver of right to trial by jury in civil cases). Indeed, the relevance of concepts of waiver to Article III challenges is demonstrated by our decision in *Northern Pipeline,* in which the absence of consent to an initial adjudication before a non-Article III tribunal was relied on as a significant factor in deter-mining that Article III forbade such adjudication.

In the instant cases, Schor indisputably waived any right he may have pos-sessed to the full trial of Conti's counterclaim before an Article III court. Schor expressly demanded that Conti proceed on its counterclaim in the reparations proceeding rather than before the District Court, and was content to have the entire dispute settled in the forum he had selected until the ALJ ruled against him on all counts; it was only after the ALJ rendered a decision to which he objected that Schor raised any challenge to the CFTC's consideration of Conti's counterclaim.

Even were there no evidence of an express waiver here, Schor's election to forgo his right to proceed in state or federal court on his claim and his decision to seek relief instead in a CFTC reparations proceeding constituted an effective waiver. Three years before Schor instituted his reparations action, a private right of action under the CEA was explicitly recognized in the Circuit in which Schor and Conti filed suit in District Court. Moreover, at the time Schor decided to seek relief before the CFTC rather than in the federal courts, the CFTC's regulations made clear that it was empowered to adjudicate all counterclaims "aris[ing] out of the same transaction or occurrence or series of transactions or occurrences set forth in the complaint." 41 Fed. Reg. 3995 (1976) (codified in 17 CFR § 12.23(b)(2) (1983)). Thus, Schor had the option of having the common law counterclaim against him adjudicated in a federal Article III court, but, with full knowledge that the CFTC would exercise jurisdiction over that claim, chose to avail himself of the quicker and less expensive proce-dure Congress had provided him. In such circumstances, it is clear that Schor effectively agreed to an adjudication by the CFTC of the entire controversy by seeking relief in this alternative forum.

B

As noted above, our precedents establish that Article III, § 1, not only preserves to litigants their interest in an impartial and independent federal adjudication of claims within the judicial power of the United States, but also serves as "an inseparable element of the constitutional system of checks and balances." *Northern Pipeline, supra,* at 58. See also *United States v. Will, supra,* at 217. Article III, § 1, safeguards the role of the Judicial Branch in our tripartite system by barring congressional attempts "to transfer jurisdiction [to non-Article III tribunals] for the purpose of emasculating" constitutional courts, *National Insurance Co. v. Tidewater Co.,* 337 U.S. 582, 644 (1949) (Vinson, C. J., dissenting), and thereby preventing "the encroachment or aggrandizement of one branch at the expense of the other." *Buckley v. Valeo,* 424 U.S. 1, 122 (1976) (*per curiam*). See *Thomas,* 473 U.S., at 582-583; *Northern Pipeline,* 458 U.S., at 57-58, 73-74, 83, 86; *id.,* at 98, 115-116 (White, J., dissenting). To the extent that this structural principle is implicated in a given case, the parties cannot by consent cure the constitutional difficulty for the same reason that the parties by consent cannot confer on federal courts subject-matter jurisdiction beyond the limitations imposed by Article III, § 2. *See,* e.g., *United States v. Griffin,* 303 U.S. 226, 229 (1938). When these Article III limitations are at issue, notions of consent and waiver cannot be dispositive because the limitations serve institutional interests that the parties cannot be expected to protect.

In determining the extent to which a given congressional decision to authorize the adjudication of Article III business in a non-Article III tribunal impermissibly threatens the institutional integrity of the Judicial Branch, the Court has declined to adopt formalistic and unbending rules. *Thomas,* 473 U.S., at 587. Although such rules might lend a greater degree of coherence to this area of the law, they might also unduly constrict Congress' ability to take needed and innovative action pursuant to its Article I powers. Thus, in reviewing Article III challenges, we have weighed a number of factors, none of which has been deemed determinative, with an eye to the practical effect that the congressional action will have on the constitutionally assigned role of the federal judiciary. *Id.,* at 590. Among the factors upon which we have focused are the extent to which the "essential attributes of judicial power" are reserved to Article III courts, and, conversely, the extent to which the non-Article III forum exercises the range of jurisdiction and powers normally vested only in Article III courts, the origins and importance of the right to be adjudicated, and the concerns that drove Congress to depart from the requirements of Article III. See, e.g., *id.,* at 587, 589-593; *Northern Pipeline, supra,* at 84-86.

An examination of the relative allocation of powers between the CFTC and Article III courts in light of the considerations given prominence in our precedents demonstrates that the congressional scheme does not impermissibly intrude on the province of the judiciary. The CFTC's adjudicatory powers depart from the traditional agency model in just one respect: the CFTC's jurisdiction over common law counterclaims. While wholesale importation of concepts of pendent or ancillary jurisdiction into the agency context may create greater constitutional difficulties, we decline to endorse an absolute prohibition on such jurisdiction out of fear of where some hypothetical "slippery slope" may deposit us. Indeed, the CFTC's exercise of this type of jurisdiction is not without precedent. Thus, in *RFC v. Bankers Trust Co.,* 318 U.S. 163, 168-171 (1943), we saw no constitutional difficulty in the initial adjudication of a state law claim by a federal agency, subject to judicial review, when that claim was ancillary to a federal law dispute. Similarly, in *Katchen v. Landy,* 382 U.S. 323 (1966), this Court upheld a bankruptcy referee's power to hear and decide state law counterclaims against a creditor who filed a claim in bankruptcy when those counterclaims arose out of the same transaction. We reasoned that, as a practical matter, requiring the trustee to commence a plenary action to recover on its counterclaim would be a "meaningless gesture." *Id.,* at 334.

In the instant cases, we are likewise persuaded that there is little practical reason to find that this single deviation from the agency model is fatal to the congressional scheme. Aside from its authorization of counterclaim jurisdiction, the CEA leaves far more of the "essential attributes of judicial power" to Article III courts than did that portion of the Bankruptcy Act found unconstitutional in *Northern Pipeline.* The CEA scheme in fact hews closely to the agency model approved by the Court in *Crowell v. Benson,* 285 U.S. 22 (1932).

The CFTC, like the agency in *Crowell,* deals only with a "particularized area of law," *Northern Pipeline, supra,* at 85, whereas the jurisdiction of the bankruptcy courts found unconstitutional in *Northern Pipeline* extended to broadly "all civil proceedings arising under title 11 or arising in or *related to* cases under title 11." 28 U.S.C. § 1471(b) (quoted in *Northern Pipeline,* 458 U.S., at 85) (emphasis added). CFTC orders, like those of the agency in *Crowell,* but unlike those of the bankruptcy courts under the 1978 Act, are enforceable only by order of the district court. See 7 U.S.C. § 18(f); *Northern Pipeline, supra,* at 85-86. CFTC orders are also reviewed under the same "weight of the evidence" standard sustained in *Crowell,* rather than the more deferential standard found lacking in *Northern Pipeline.* See 7 U.S.C. § 9; *Northern Pipeline, supra,* at 85. The legal rulings of the CFTC, like the legal determinations of the agency in *Crowell,* are subject to *de novo* review. Finally, the CFTC, unlike the bankruptcy courts under the 1978 Act, does not exercise "all ordinary powers of district courts," and thus may not, for instance, preside over jury trials or issue writs of habeas corpus. 458 U.S., at 85.

Of course, the nature of the claim has significance in our Article III analysis quite apart from the method prescribed for its adjudication. The counterclaim asserted in this litigation is a "private" right for which state law provides the rule of decision. It is therefore a claim of the kind assumed to be at the "core" of matters normally reserved to Article III courts. See, e.g., *Thomas, supra,* at 587; *Northern Pipeline,* 458 U.S., at 70-71, and n.25; *id.,* at 90 (Rehnquist, J., concurring in judgment). Yet this conclusion does not end our inquiry; just as this Court has rejected any attempt to make determinative for Article III purposes the distinction between public rights and private rights, *Thomas, supra,* at 585-586, there is no reason inherent in separation of powers principles to accord the state law character of a claim talismanic power in Article III inquiries. See, e.g., *Northern Pipeline,* 458 U.S., at 68, n.20; *id.,* at 98 (White, J., dissenting).

We have explained that "the public rights doctrine reflects simply a pragmatic understanding that when Congress selects a quasi-judicial method of resolving matters that 'could be conclusively determined by the Executive and Legislative Branches,' the danger of encroaching on the judicial powers" is less than when private rights, which are normally within the purview of the judiciary, are relegated as an initial matter to administrative adjudication. *Thomas,* 473 U.S., at 589 (quoting *Northern Pipeline, supra,* at 68). Similarly, the state law character of a claim is significant for purposes of determining the effect that an initial adjudication of those claims by a non-Article III tribunal will have on the separation of powers for the simple reason that private, common law rights were historically the types of matters subject to resolution by Article III courts. *See Northern Pipeline,* 458 U.S., at 68, n.20, 84; *id.,* at 90 (Rehnquist, J., concurring in judgment). The risk that Congress may improperly have encroached on the federal judiciary is obviously magnified when Congress "withdraw[s] from judicial cognizance any matter which, from its nature, is the subject of a suit at the common law, or in equity, or admiralty" and which therefore has traditionally been tried in Article III courts, and allocates the decision of those matters to a non-Article III forum of its own creation. *Murray's Lessee v. Hoboken Land & Improvement Co.,* 18 How. 272, 284 (1856). Accordingly, where private, common law rights are at stake, our examination of the congressional attempt to control the manner in which those rights are adjudicated has been searching. See, e.g., *Northern Pipeline,* 458 U.S., at 84; *id.,* at 90 (Rehnquist, J., concurring in judgment). In this litigation, however, "[looking] beyond form to the substance of what" Congress has done, we are persuaded that the congressional authorization of limited CFTC jurisdiction over a narrow class of common law claims as an incident to the CFTC's primary, and unchallenged, adjudicative function does not create a substantial threat to the separation of powers. *Thomas, supra,* at 589.

It is clear that Congress has not attempted to "withdraw from judicial cognizance" the determination of Conti's right to the sum represented by the debit balance in Schor's account. Congress gave the CFTC the authority to adjudicate such matters, but the decision to invoke this forum is left entirely to the parties and the power of the federal judiciary to take jurisdiction of these matters is unaffected. In such circumstances, separation of powers concerns are diminished, for it seems self-evident that just as Congress may encourage parties to settle a dispute out of court or resort to arbitration without impermissible incursions on the separation of powers, Congress may make available a quasi-judicial mechanism through which willing parties may, at their option, elect to resolve their differences. This is not to say, of course, that if Congress created a phalanx of non-Article III tribunals equipped to handle the entire business of the Article III courts without any Article III supervision or control and without evidence of valid and specific legislative necessities, the fact that the parties had the election to proceed in their forum of choice would necessarily save the scheme from constitutional attack. See, e.g., *Northern Pipeline, supra,* at 73-74. But this case obviously bears no resemblance to such a scenario, given the degree of judicial control saved to the federal courts, see *supra,* at 852-853, as well as the congressional purpose behind the jurisdictional delegation, the demonstrated need for the delegation, and the limited nature of the delegation.

When Congress authorized the CFTC to adjudicate counterclaims, its primary focus was on making effective a specific and limited federal regulatory scheme, not on allocating jurisdiction among federal tribunals. Congress intended to create an inexpensive and expeditious alternative forum through which customers could enforce the provisions of the CEA against professional brokers. Its decision to endow the CFTC with jurisdiction over such reparations claims is readily understandable given the perception that the CFTC was relatively immune from political pressures, *see* H. R. Rep. No. 93-975, pp. 44, 70 (1974), and the obvious expertise that the Commission possesses in applying the CEA and its own regulations. This reparations scheme itself is of unquestioned constitutional validity. See, e.g., *Thomas, supra,* at 589; *Northern Pipeline, supra,* at 80-81; *Crowell v. Benson,* 285 U.S. 22 (1932). It was only to ensure the effectiveness of this scheme that Congress authorized the CFTC to assert jurisdiction over common law counterclaims. Indeed, as was explained above, absent the CFTC's exercise of that authority, the purposes of the reparations procedure would have been confounded.

It also bears emphasis that the CFTC's assertion of counterclaim jurisdiction is limited to that which is necessary to make the reparations procedure workable. See 7 U.S.C. § 12a(5). The CFTC adjudication of common law counterclaims is incidental to, and completely dependent upon, adjudication of reparations claims created by federal law, and in actual fact is limited to claims arising out of the same transaction or occurrence as the reparations claim.

In such circumstances, the magnitude of any intrusion on the Judicial Branch can only be termed *de minimis*. Conversely, were we to hold that the Legislative Branch may not permit such limited cognizance of common law counterclaims at the election of the parties, it is clear that we would "defeat the obvious purpose of the legislation to furnish a prompt, continuous, expert and inexpensive method for dealing with a class of questions of fact which are peculiarly suited to examination and determination by an administrative agency specially assigned to that task." *Crowell v. Benson, supra,* at 46. See also *Thomas, supra,* at 583-584. We do not think Article III compels this degree of prophylaxis. . . .

. . . We conclude that the limited jurisdiction that the CFTC asserts over state law claims as a necessary incident to the adjudication of federal claims willingly submitted by the parties for initial agency adjudication does not contravene separation of powers principles or Article III.

C

Schor asserts that Article III, § 1, constrains Congress for reasons of federalism, as well as for reasons of separation of powers. He argues that the state law character of Conti's counterclaim transforms the central question in this litigation from whether Congress has trespassed upon the judicial powers of the Federal Government into whether Congress has invaded the prerogatives of state governments.

At the outset, we note that our prior precedents in this area have dealt only with separation of powers concerns, and have not intimated that principles of federalism impose limits on Congress' ability to delegate adjudicative functions to non-Article III tribunals. This absence of discussion regarding federalism is particularly telling in *Northern Pipeline,* where the Court based its analysis solely on the separation of powers principles inherent in Article III despite the fact that the claim sought to be adjudicated in the bankruptcy court was created by state law. See, e.g., 458 U.S., at 57-60, and n.11.

Even assuming that principles of federalism are relevant to Article III analysis, however, we are unpersuaded that those principles require the invalidation of the CFTC's counterclaim jurisdiction. The sole fact that Conti's counterclaim is resolved by a *federal* rather than a *state* tribunal could not be said to unduly impair state interests, for it is established that a federal court could, without constitutional hazard, decide a counterclaim such as the one asserted here under its ancillary jurisdiction, even if an independent jurisdictional basis for it were lacking. Given that the federal courts can and do exercise ancillary jurisdiction over counterclaims such as the one at issue here, the question becomes whether the fact that a federal agency rather than a federal Article

III court initially hears the state law claim gives rise to a cognizably greater impairment of principles of federalism.

Schor argues that those Framers opposed to diversity jurisdiction in the federal courts acquiesced in its inclusion in Article III only because they were assured that the federal judiciary would be protected by the tenure and salary provisions of Article III. He concludes, in essence, that to protect this constitutional compact, Article III should be read to absolutely preclude any adjudication of state law claims by federal decisionmakers that do not enjoy the Article III salary and tenure protections. We are unpersuaded by Schor's novel theory, which suffers from a number of flaws, the most important of which is that Schor identifies no historical support for the critical link he posits between the provisions of Article III that protect the independence of the federal judiciary and those provisions that define the extent of the judiciary's jurisdiction over state law claims.

The judgment of the Court of Appeals for the District of Columbia Circuit is reversed, and the case is remanded for further proceedings consistent with this opinion. *It is so ordered.*

JUSTICE BRENNAN, with whom JUSTICE MARSHALL joins, dissenting.

Article III, § 1, of the Constitution provides that "[t]he judicial Power of the United States, shall be vested in one supreme Court, and in such inferior Courts as the Congress may from time to time ordain and establish." It further specifies that the federal judicial power must be exercised by judges who "shall hold their Offices during good Behaviour, and [who] shall, at stated Times, receive for their Services a Compensation, which shall not be diminished during their Continuance in Office."

On its face, Article III, § 1, seems to prohibit the vesting of *any* judicial functions in either the Legislative or the Executive Branch. The Court has, however, recognized three narrow exceptions to the otherwise absolute mandate of Article III: territorial courts, *see,* e.g., *American Ins. Co. v. Canter,* 1 Pet. 511 (1828); courts-martial, *see,* e.g., *Dynes v. Hoover,* 20 How. 65 (1857); and courts that adjudicate certain disputes concerning public rights, *see,* e.g., *Murray's Lessee v. Hoboken Land & Improvement Co.,* 18 How. 272 (1856); *Ex parte Bakelite Corp.,* 279 U.S. 438 (1929); *Crowell v. Benson,* 285 U.S. 22 (1932); *Thomas v. Union Carbide Agricultural Products Co.,* 473 U.S. 568 (1985). *See generally Northern Pipeline Construction Co. v. Marathon Pipe Line Co.,* 458 U.S. 50 (1982) (opinion of BRENNAN, J.). Unlike the Court, I would limit the judicial authority of non-Article III federal tribunals to these few, long-established exceptions and would countenance no further erosion of Article III's mandate.

I

The Framers knew that "[t]he accumulation of all powers, Legislative, Executive, and Judiciary, in the same hands, whether of one, a few, or many, and whether hereditary, self-appointed, or elective, may justly be pronounced the very definition of tyranny." The Federalist No. 46, p. 334 (H. Dawson ed. 1876) (J. Madison). In order to prevent such tyranny, the Framers devised a governmental structure composed of three distinct branches — "a vigorous Legislative Branch," "a separate and wholly independent Executive Branch," and "a Judicial Branch equally independent." *Bowsher v. Synar, ante,* at 722. The separation of powers and the checks and balances that the Framers built into our tripartite form of government were intended to operate as a "self-executing safeguard against the encroachment or aggrandizement of one branch at the expense of the other." *Buckley v. Valeo,* 424 U.S. 1, 122 (1976) (*per curiam*). "The fundamental necessity of maintaining each of the three general departments of government entirely free from the control or coercive influence, direct or indirect, of either of the others, has often been stressed and is hardly open to serious question." *Bowsher, ante,* at 725 (quoting *Humphrey's Executor v. United States,* 295 U.S. 602, 629 (1935)). The federal judicial power, then, must be exercised by judges who are independent of the Executive and Legislature in order to maintain the checks and balances that are crucial to our constitutional structure.

The Framers also understood that a principal benefit of the separation of the judicial power from the legislative and executive powers would be the protection of individual litigants from decisionmakers susceptible to majoritarian pressures. Article III's salary and tenure provisions promote impartial adjudication by placing the judicial power of the United States "in a body of judges insulated from majoritarian pressures and thus able to enforce [federal law] without fear of reprisal or public rebuke." *United States v. Raddatz,* 447 U.S. 667, 704 (1980) (MARSHALL, J., dissenting). As Alexander Hamilton observed, "[t]hat inflexible and uniform adherence to the rights of the Constitution, and of individuals, which we perceive to be indispensable in the Courts of justice can certainly not be expected from Judges who hold their offices by a temporary Commission." The Federalist No. 78, p. 546 (H. Dawson ed. 1876). This is so because

> "[i]f the power of making [periodic appointments] was committed either to the Executive or Legislature, there would be danger of an improper complaisance to the branch which possessed it; if to both, there would be an unwillingness to hazard the displeasure of either; if to the People, or to persons chosen by them for the special purpose, there would be too great a disposition to consult popularity, to justify a reliance that nothing would be consulted but the Constitution and the law." *Ibid.*

"Next to permanency in office," Hamilton added, "nothing can contribute more to the independence of the Judges than a fixed provision for their support" because "*a power over a man's subsistence amounts to a power over his will.*" *Id.,* at 548 (emphasis in original). *See also United States v. Will,* 449 U.S. 200, 217-218 (1980) ("A Judiciary free from control by the Executive and the Legislature is essential if there is a right to have claims decided by judges who are free from potential domination by other branches of government"); *United States ex rel. Toth v. Quarles,* 350 U.S. 11, 16 (1955) (Black, J.) ("The provisions of Article III were designed to give judges maximum freedom from the possible coercion or influence by the executive or legislative branches of the Government").

These important functions of Article III are too central to our constitutional scheme to risk their incremental erosion. The exceptions we have recognized for territorial courts, courts-martial, and administrative courts were each based on "certain exceptional powers bestowed upon Congress by the Constitution or by historical consensus." *Northern Pipeline, supra,* at 70 (opinion of BRENNAN, J.). Here, however, there is no equally forceful reason to extend further these exceptions to situations that are distinguishable from existing precedents. . . . The Court, however, engages in just such an extension. By sanctioning the adjudication of state-law counterclaims by a federal administrative agency, the Court far exceeds the analytic framework of our precedents. . . .

II

. . . Article III's prophylactic protections were intended to prevent just this sort of abdication to claims of legislative convenience. The Court requires that the legislative interest in convenience and efficiency be weighed against the competing interest in judicial independence. In doing so, the Court pits an interest the benefits of which are immediate, concrete, and easily understood against one, the benefits of which are almost entirely prophylactic, and thus often seem remote and not worth the cost in any single case. Thus, while this balancing creates the illusion of objectivity and ineluctability, in fact the result was foreordained, because the balance is weighted against judicial independence. . . . The danger of the Court's balancing approach is, of course, that as individual cases accumulate in which the Court finds that the short-term benefits of efficiency out-weigh the long-term benefits of judicial independence, the protections of Article III will be eviscerated.

Perhaps the resolution of reparations claims such as respondents' may be accomplished more conveniently under the Court's decision than under my approach, but the Framers foreswore this sort of convenience in order to preserve freedom.

. . . The Framers established *three* coequal branches of government and intended to preserve *each* from encroachment by either of the others. The Constitution did not grant Congress the general authority to bypass the Judiciary whenever Congress deems it advisable, any more than it granted Congress the authority to arrogate to itself executive functions. . . .

And, contrary to the Court's intimations, dilution of judicial power operates to impair the protections of Article III regardless of whether Congress acted with the "good intention" of providing a more efficient dispute resolution system or with the "bad intention" of strengthening the Legislative Branch at the expense of the Judiciary.

. . . Our Constitution unambiguously enunciates a fundamental principle — that the "judicial Power of the United States" be reposed in an independent Judiciary. It is our obligation zealously to guard that independence so that our tripartite system of government remains strong and that individuals continue to be protected against decisionmakers subject to majoritarian pressures. Unfortunately, today the Court forsakes that obligation for expediency. I dissent.

QUESTIONS

1. What factors does the majority in *Schor* find relevant/dispositive?
2. Does this opinion limit *Northern Pipeline?* Overrule it? Adequately distinguish it?
3. Has the Court gotten away from relying on an "adjunct of the court" analysis?

NOTE ON THE SEVENTH AMENDMENT

The previous cases in this section considered the extent to which Article III's grant of the judicial power to federal courts limited Congress's power to grant adjudicatory power to agencies. The Court has also considered whether the seventh amendment imposes any limits on such grants.

The seventh amendment provides that: "[i]n suits at common law, where the value in controversy shall exceed twenty dollars, the right of trial by jury shall be preserved."

In a series of decisions, the Court seemed to hold that the seventh amendment simply did not apply to adjudications in administrative agencies. The first case in this series is *NLRB v. Jones & Laughlin Steel Corp.*, 301 U.S. 1 (1937), in which the Court upheld the National Labor Relations Act against constitutional challenge. The last of the company's constitutional challenges was that the Act contravened the seventh amendment, because, by allowing the agency to award lost wages, the right to a jury trial was improperly abridged. The Court quickly rejected this argument, *id.* at 48-49:

> The [seventh] amendment ... preserves the right which existed under the common law when the amendment was adopted. Thus it has no application to cases where recovery of money damages is an incident to equitable relief even though damages might have been recovered in an action at law. It does not apply where the proceeding is not in the nature of a suit at common law.
>
> The instant case is not a suit at common law or in the nature of such a suit. The proceeding is one unknown to the common law. It is a statutory proceeding. Reinstatement of the employee and payment for time lost are requirements imposed for violation of the statute and are remedies appropriate to its enforcement. The contention under the Seventh Amendment is without merit.

Almost four decades later, the Court returned to the issue of the applicability of the seventh amendment to administrative proceedings when it distinguished *Jones & Laughlin*, stating that the case did not apply to determine whether there was a right to a jury trial in a statutory civil rights action brought in federal district court. In *Curtis v. Loether*, 415 U.S. 189, 194-95 (1974), the Court stated that:

> *Jones & Laughlin* merely stands for the proposition that the Seventh Amendment is generally inapplicable in administrative proceedings, where jury trials would be incompatible with the whole concept of administrative adjudication and would substantially interfere with the NLRB's role in the statutory scheme. *Katchen v. Landy*, 382 U.S. 323 (1966), ... is to like effect. There the Court upheld, over a Seventh Amendment challenge, the Bankruptcy Act's grant of summary jurisdiction to the bankrutpcy court over the trustee's action to compel a claimant to surrender a voidable preference; the Court recognized that a bankruptcy court has been traditionally viewed as a court of equity, and that jury trials would "dismember" the statutory scheme of the Bankruptcy Act. These cases uphold congressional power to entrust enforcement of statutory rights to an administrative process or specialized court of equity free from the strictures of the Seventh Amendment. But when Congress provides for enforcement of statutory rights in an ordinary civil action in the district courts, where there is obviously no functional justification for denying the jury trial right, a jury trial must be available if the action involves rights and remedies of the sort typically enforced in an action at law.

The *Curtis v. Loether* Court then held that a jury trial was necessary for the *judicial* action at issue in that case, because "this cause of action is analogous to a number of tort actions recognized at common law. More important, the relief sought here — actual and punitive damages — is the traditional form of relief offered in the courts of law." *Id.* at 195.

In *Atlas Roofing Co. v. Occupational Safety and Health Review Commn.,* 430 U.S. 442 (1977), the Court addressed whether the seventh amendment foreclosed Congress from granting the authority to an agency to impose civil fines against a person for violating health and safety requirements. The Court held, consistent with the approach in *Curtis v. Loether,* that the seventh amendment did not apply to this administrative proceeding, *id.* at 455 (emphasis added):

> [W]hen Congress creates new statutory "public rights," it may assign their adjudication to an administrative agency with which a jury trial would be incompatible, without violating the Seventh Amendment's injunction that jury trial is to be "preserved" in "suits at common law." Congress is not required by the Seventh Amendment to choke the already crowded federal courts with new types of litigation or prevented from committing some new types of litigation to administrative agencies with special competence in the relevant field. *This is the case even if the Seventh Amendment would have required a jury where the adjudication of those rights is assigned to a federal court of law instead of an administrative agency.*

In other respects, however, the Court's language in *Atlas Roofing* suggested that Congress's authority to provide for agency adjudication independent of a jury depended on the nature of the right being adjudicated, rather than the adjudicatory body. The ambiguous nature of the Court's decision can be seen by contrasting the following two statements by the Court. One such statement was made when the Court considered:

> the assertion that the right to jury trial was never intended to depend on the identity of the forum to which Congress has chosen to submit a dispute; otherwise, it is said, Congress could utterly destroy the right to a jury trial by always providing for administrative rather than judicial resolution of the vast range of cases that now arise in the courts. The argument is well put, but it overstates the holdings of our prior cases and is in any event unpersuasive. Our prior cases support administrative factfinding in only those situations involving "public rights," e.g., where the Government is involved in its sovereign capacity under an otherwise valid statute creating enforceable public rights. Wholly private tort, contract, and property cases, as well as a vast range of other cases as well are not at all implicated.

Id. at 457-58. This language suggests that the seventh amendment has no application because the claim at issue involved public rights. The second, arguably inconsistent, statement was made near the end of the decision:

> history and our cases support the proposition that *the right to a jury trial turns not solely on the nature of the issue to be resolved but also on the forum in which it is to be resolved.* Congress found the common-law and other existing remedies for work injuries resulting from unsafe working conditions to be inadequate to protect the Nation's working men and women. It created a new cause of action, and remedies therefor, unknown to the common law, and placed their enforcement in a tribunal supplying speedy and expert resolutions of the issues involved. The Seventh Amendment is no bar to the creation of new rights or to their enforcement outside the regular courts of law.

Id. at 460-61 (emphasis added).

After this line of cases was decided, the Court decided *Schor*. The most recent case addressing the seventh amendment and agency adjudications seems to refocus the Court's doctrinal approach to the seventh amendment issue. In *Granfinanciera, S.A., v. Nordberg*, 492 U.S. 33 (1989), the Court in an opinion by Justice Brennan considered whether the seventh amendment limited Congress's power to assign for adjudication before a bankruptcy court a claim of a fraudulent transfer when the defendant in that action had no claim against the estate in bankruptcy.

> In *Atlas Roofing*, we noted that Congress may effectively supplant a common-law cause of action carrying with it a right to a jury trial with a statutory cause of action shorn of a jury trial right if that statutory cause of action inheres in, or lies against, the Federal Government in its sovereign capacity. Our case law makes plain, however, that the class of "public rights" whose adjudication Congress may assign to administrative agencies or courts of equity sitting without juries is more expansive than *Atlas Roofing's* discussion suggests. Indeed, our decisions point to the conclusion that, if a statutory cause of action is legal in nature, the question whether the Seventh Amendment permits Congress to assign its adjudication to a tribunal that does not employ juries as factfinders requires the same answer as the question whether Article III allows Congress to assign adjudication of that cause of action to a non-Article III tribunal. For if a statutory cause of action, such as respondent's right to recover a fraudulent conveyance under 11 U.S.C. § 548(a)(2), is not a "public right" for Article III purposes, then Congress may not assign its adjudication to a specialized non-Article III court lacking "the essential attributes of the judicial power." [Quoting *Crowell v. Benson*.] And if the action must be tried under the auspices of an Article III court, then the Seventh Amendment affords the parties a right to a jury trial whenever the cause of action is legal in nature. Conversely, if Congress may assign the adjudication of a statutory cause of action to a non-Article III tribunal, then the Seventh Amendment poses no independent bar to the adjudication of that action by a nonjury factfinder. In addition to our Seventh Amendment precedents, we therefore rely on our decisions exploring the restrictions Article III places on Congress' choice of adjudicative bodies to resolve disputes over statutory rights to determine whether petitioners are entitled to a jury trial.
>
> In our most recent discussion of the "public rights" doctrine as it bears on Congress' power to commit adjudication of a statutory cause of action to a non-Article III tribunal, we rejected the view that "a matter of public rights must at a minimum arise 'between the government and others.'" We held, instead, that the Federal Government need not be a party for a case to revolve around "public rights." The crucial question, in cases not involving the Federal Government, is whether "Congress, acting for a valid legislative purpose pursuant to its constitutional powers under Article I, [has] create[d] a seemingly 'private' right that is so closely integrated into a public regulatory scheme as to be a matter appropriate for agency resolution with limited involvement by the Article III judiciary." If a statutory right is not closely intertwined with a federal regulatory program Congress has power to enact, and if that right neither belongs to nor exists against the Federal Government, then it must be adjudicated by an Article III court. If the right is legal in nature, then it carries with it the Seventh Amendment's guarantee of a jury trial.

Id. at 53-54. The majority in *Granfinanciera* concluded that the fraudulent conveyance action at issue did not involve public rights and so held that the jury trial right attached because the claim also was legal in nature. The Court then presented, *id.* at 64, the following puzzling conclusion:

> We do not decide today whether the current jury trial provision—28 U.S.C. §1411—permits bankruptcy courts to conduct jury trials in fraudulent conveyance actions like the one respondent initiated. Nor do we express any view as to whether the Seventh Amendment or Article III allows jury trials in such actions to be held before non-Article III bankruptcy judges subject to the oversight provided by the district courts pursuant to the 1984 Amendments. We leave those issues for future decisions. We do hold, however, that whatever the answers to these questions, the Seventh Amendment entitles petitioners to the jury trial they requested. . . .

QUESTIONS

1. How did the majority's analysis of the Seventh Amendment's applicability to agency adjudications arguably shift in *Granfinanciera*?
2. What, if anything, does the conclusion of the Court in *Granfinanciera* tell us about whether the limits that Article III and the seventh amendment impose on Congress's delegation of adjudicative power to agencies are coextensive or how they might differ? Is the majority's conclusion defensible, or "coy" or "obtuse" (to use the characterizations of dissenting Justice White)? See 492 U.S. at 71 n.2.

STERN v. MARSHALL
564 U.S. 462 (2011)

[This case involved the bankruptcy proceeding of Vickie Lynn Marshall, better known to the public as Anna Nicole Smith. Ms. Marshall married J. Howard Marshall, whom the Court described as "a man believed to have been one of the richest people in Texas," one year before J. Howard died. Pierce Marshall, the other key player in the litigation was J. Howard's son. Shortly before J. Howard died, Ms. Marshall filed a state tort law claim against Pierce Marshall, claiming that he had tortiously interfered with J. Howard's intended gift to Ms. Marshall. After J. Howard died, Ms. Marshall filed for bankruptcy. Pierce Marshall filed a proof of claim against Ms. Marshall's estate in bankruptcy for defamation, after he had previously sought a declaration that the defamation claim was not dischargeable. She defended against the defamation claim by arguing truth, and filed a counterclaim in the bankruptcy proceeding for tortious interference, the same claim she had brought previously in Texas probate court.

The bankruptcy court granted summary judgment in favor of Ms. Marshall on the libel claim and awarded the bankruptcy estate more than $400 million in compensatory damages and $25 million in punitive damages for the tortious interference claim. Pierce Marshall then claimed that the bankruptcy court lacked jurisdiction based on statutory (the counterclaim was not a "core proceeding" as defined by the Bankruptcy Code) and constitutional (improper non-Article III adjudication) theories. Both Ms. Marshall and Pierce Marshall died during the course of the bankruptcy litigation. Stern is the Executor of Ms. Marshall's estate, while Marshall is the executrix of Pierce Marshall's estate.

The Supreme Court's decision refers to Ms. Marshall's estate as "Vickie" and to Pierce Marshall's estate as "Pierce."

The Court initially decided that Vickie's counterclaim was a "core proceeding" under the Bankruptcy Code, so the Court had to decide whether adjudication of Ms. Marshall's tort counterclaim was constitutionally permissible. Chief Justice Roberts wrote the opinion for the Court.]

III

Although we conclude that § 157(b)(2)(C) permits the Bankruptcy Court to enter final judgment on Vickie's counterclaim [as a core proceeding], Article III of the Constitution does not.

A

Article III, § 1, of the Constitution mandates that "[t]he judicial Power of the United States, shall be vested in one supreme Court, and in such inferior Courts as the Congress may from time to time ordain and establish." The same section provides that the judges of those constitutional courts "shall hold their Offices during good Behaviour" and "receive for their Services[] a Compensation[][that] shall not be diminished" during their tenure.

As its text and our precedent confirm, Article III is "an inseparable element of the constitutional system of checks and balances" that "both defines the power and protects the independence of the Judicial Branch." *Northern Pipeline*, 458 U.S., at 58 (plurality opinion). Under "the basic concept of separation of powers . . . that flow[s] from the scheme of a tripartite government" adopted in the Constitution, "the 'judicial Power of the United States' . . . can no more be shared" with another branch than "the Chief Executive, for example, can share with the Judiciary the veto power, or the Congress share with the Judiciary the power to override a Presidential veto." *United States v. Nixon*, 418 U.S. 683, 704 (1974) (quoting U.S. Const., Art. III, § 1).

In establishing the system of divided power in the Constitution, the Framers considered it essential that "the judiciary remain[] truly distinct from both the legislature and the executive." The Federalist No. 78, p. 466 (C. Rossiter ed. 1961) (A. Hamilton). As Hamilton put it, quoting Montesquieu, "'there is no liberty if the power of judging be not separated from the legislative and executive powers.'" *Ibid.* (quoting 1 Montesquieu, Spirit of Laws 181).

We have recognized that the three branches are not hermetically sealed from one another, *see Nixon v. Administrator of General Services*, 433 U.S. 425, 443 (1977), but it remains true that Article III imposes some basic limitations that the other branches may not transgress. Those limitations serve two related purposes. "Separation-of-powers principles are intended, in part, to protect each branch of government from incursion by the others. Yet the dynamic between and among the branches is not the only object of the Constitution's concern. The structural principles secured by the separation of powers protect the individual as well." *Bond v. United States*, 564 U.S. 211, 222 (2011).

Article III protects liberty not only through its role in implementing the separation of powers, but also by specifying the defining characteristics of Article III judges. The colonists had been subjected to judicial abuses at the hand of the Crown, and the Framers knew the main reasons why: because the King of Great

Britain "made Judges dependent on his Will alone, for the tenure of their offices, and the amount and payment of their salaries." The Declaration of Independence ¶ 11. The Framers undertook in Article III to protect citizens subject to the judicial power of the new Federal Government from a repeat of those abuses. By appointing judges to serve without term limits, and restricting the ability of the other branches to remove judges or diminish their salaries, the Framers sought to ensure that each judicial decision would be rendered, not with an eye toward currying favor with Congress or the Executive, but rather with the "[c]lear heads . . . and honest hearts" deemed "essential to good judges." 1 Works of James Wilson 363 (J. Andrews ed. 1896).

Article III could neither serve its purpose in the system of checks and balances nor preserve the integrity of judicial decision making if the other branches of the Federal Government could confer the Government's "judicial Power" on entities outside Article III. That is why we have long recognized that, in general, Congress may not "withdraw from judicial cognizance any matter which, from its nature, is the subject of a suit at the common law, or in equity, or admiralty." *Murray's Lessee v. Hoboken Land & Improvement Co.*, 59 U.S. 272, 18 How. 272, 284 (1856). When a suit is made of "the stuff of the traditional actions at common law tried by the courts at Westminster in 1789," *Northern Pipeline*, 458 U.S., at 90 (Rehnquist, J., concurring in judgment), and is brought within the bounds of federal jurisdiction, the responsibility for deciding that suit rests with Article III judges in Article III courts. The Constitution assigns that job — resolution of "the mundane as well as the glamorous, matters of common law and statute as well as constitutional law, issues of fact as well as issues of law" — to the Judiciary. *Id.*, at 86-87, n. 39 (plurality opinion).

B

This is not the first time we have faced an Article III challenge to a bankruptcy court's resolution of a debtor's suit. [Chief Justice Roberts summarized the plurality and concurring opinions in *Northern Pipeline, supra* p. 320, in which a majority of the Supreme Court rejected the constitutionality of bankruptcy courts, staffed with non-Article III judges, hearing and deciding state law contract claims related to a bankruptcy proceeding.]

After our decision in *Northern Pipeline*, Congress revised the statutes governing bankruptcy jurisdiction and bankruptcy judges. In the 1984 Act, Congress provided that the judges of the new bankruptcy courts would be appointed by the courts of appeals for the circuits in which their districts are located. 28 U.S.C. § 152(a). And, as we have explained, Congress permitted the newly constituted bankruptcy courts to enter final judgments only in "core" proceedings.

With respect to such "core" matters, however, the bankruptcy courts under the 1984 Act exercise the same powers they wielded under the Bankruptcy Act of 1978 (1978 Act), 92 Stat. 2549. As in *Northern Pipeline*, for example, the newly constituted bankruptcy courts are charged under § 157(b)(2)(C) with resolving "[a]ll matters of fact and law in whatever domains of the law to which" a counterclaim may lead. 458 U.S., at 91 (Rehnquist, J., concurring in judgment). As in *Northern Pipeline*, the new courts in core proceedings "issue final judgments, which are binding and enforceable even in the absence of an appeal." 458 U.S., at 85-86 (plurality opinion). And, as in *Northern Pipeline*, the district courts review the judgments of the bankruptcy courts in core proceedings only under the usual limited appellate standards. That requires marked deference to, among other things, the bankruptcy judges' findings of fact. *See* § 158(a); Fed. Rule Bkrtcy. Proc. 8013 (findings of fact "shall not be set aside unless clearly erroneous").

C

Vickie and the dissent argue that the Bankruptcy Court's entry of final judgment on her state common law counterclaim was constitutional, despite the similarities between the bankruptcy courts under the 1978 Act and those exercising core jurisdiction under the 1984 Act. We disagree. It is clear that the Bankruptcy Court in this case exercised the "judicial Power of the United States" in purporting to resolve and enter final judgment on a state common law claim, just as the court did in *Northern Pipeline*. No "public right" exception excuses the failure to comply with Article III in doing so, any more than in *Northern Pipeline*. Vickie argues that this case is different because the defendant is a creditor in the bankruptcy. But the debtors' claims in the cases on which she relies were themselves federal claims under bankruptcy law, which would be completely resolved in the bankruptcy process of allowing or disallowing claims. Here Vickie's claim is a state law action independent of the federal bankruptcy law and not necessarily resolvable by a ruling on the creditor's proof of claim in bankruptcy. *Northern Pipeline* and our subsequent decision in *Granfinanciera*, 492 U.S. 33, rejected the application of the "public rights" exception in such cases.

Nor can the bankruptcy courts under the 1984 Act be dismissed as mere adjuncts of Article III courts, any more than could the bankruptcy courts under the 1978 Act. The judicial powers the courts exercise in cases such as this remain the same, and a court exercising such broad powers is no mere adjunct of anyone.

1

[Chief Justice Roberts analyzes whether Vickie's counterclaim is within the public rights category, first recognized in *Murray's Lessee v. Hoboken Land & Improvement Co.*, 59 U.S. 272, 18 How. 272 (1856). The Court there defined when a case came within the category of private and public rights.] [The Court in *Murray's Lessee*] confirmed that Congress cannot "withdraw from judicial cognizance any matter which, from its nature, is the subject of a suit at the common law, or in equity, or admiralty." *Ibid.* [at 284.] The Court also recognized that "[a]t the same time there are matters, involving public rights, which may be presented in such form that the judicial power is capable of acting on them, and which are susceptible of judicial determination, but which congress may or may not bring within the cognizance of the courts of the United States, as it may deem proper." *Ibid.*

... The point of *Murray's Lessee* was simply that Congress may set the terms of adjudicating a suit when the suit could not otherwise proceed at all.

Subsequent decisions from this Court contrasted cases within the reach of the public rights exception — those arising "between the Government and persons subject to its authority in connection with the performance of the constitutional functions of the executive or legislative departments" — and those that were instead matters "of private right, that is, of the liability of one individual to another under the law as defined." *Crowell v. Benson*, 285 U.S. 22, 50, 51, (1932).[6]

. . . *Crowell* may well have additional significance in the context of expert administrative agencies that oversee particular substantive federal regimes, but we have no occasion to and do not address those issues today. . . .

Shortly after *Northern Pipeline*, the Court rejected the limitation of the public rights exception to actions involving the Government as a party. The Court has continued, however, to limit the exception to cases in which the claim at issue derives from a federal regulatory scheme, or in which resolution of the claim by an expert government agency is deemed essential to a limited regulatory objective within the agency's authority. In other words, it is still the case that what makes a right "public" rather than private is that the right is integrally related to particular federal government action. [The Court here discussed how the public rights doctrine was applied in *Thomas v. Union Carbide Agricultural Products Co.*, 473 U.S. 568, 571-575 (1985), *Commodity Futures Trading Commission v. Schor*, 478 U.S. 833, 836 (1986), and *Granfinanciera, S.A. v. Nordberg*, 492 U.S. 33 (1989).]

Vickie's counterclaim — like the fraudulent conveyance claim at issue in *Granfinanciera*— does not fall within any of the varied formulations of the public rights exception in this Court's cases. It is not a matter that can be pursued only by grace of the other branches, as in *Murray's Lessee*, 18 How., at 284, or one that "historically could have been determined exclusively by" those branches, *Northern Pipeline, supra*, at 68. The claim is instead one under state common law between two private parties. It does not "depend[] on the will of congress," *Murray's Lessee, supra*, at 284; Congress has nothing to do with it.

In addition, Vickie's claimed right to relief does not flow from a federal statutory scheme, as in *Thomas*, 473 U.S., at 584-585, or *Atlas Roofing*, 430 U.S., at 458. It is not "completely dependent upon" adjudication of a claim created by federal law, as in *Schor*, 478 U.S., at 856. And in contrast to the objecting party in *Schor, id.*, at 855-856, Pierce did not truly consent to resolution of Vickie's claim in the bankruptcy court proceedings. He had nowhere else to go if he wished to recover from Vickie's estate. See *Granfinanciera, supra*, at 59, n. 14 (noting that "[p]arallel reasoning [to *Schor*] is unavailable in the context of bankruptcy proceedings, because creditors lack an alternative forum to the bankruptcy court in which to pursue their claims").[8]

Furthermore, the asserted authority to decide Vickie's claim is not limited to a "particularized area of the law," as in *Crowell, Thomas*, and *Schor. Northern Pipeline*, 458 U.S., at 85 (plurality opinion). We deal here not with an agency but with a court, with substantive jurisdiction reaching any area of the *corpus juris*. See *ibid.*; *id.*, at 91 (Rehnquist, J., concurring in judgment). This is not a situation in which

6. Although the Court in *Crowell* went on to decide that the facts of the private dispute before it could be determined by a non-Article III tribunal in the first instance, subject to judicial review, the Court did so only after observing that the administrative adjudicator had only limited authority to make specialized, narrowly confined factual determinations regarding a particularized area of law and to issue orders that could be enforced only by action of the District Court. 285 U.S., at 38, 44-45, 54. In other words, the agency in *Crowell* functioned as a true "adjunct" of the District Court. That is not the case here.

8. Contrary to the claims of the dissent, Pierce did not have another forum in which to pursue his claim to recover from Vickie's prebankruptcy assets, rather than take his chances with whatever funds might remain after the Title 11 proceedings. Creditors who possess claims that do not satisfy the requirements for nondischargeability under 11 U.S.C. § 523 have no choice but to file their claims in bankruptcy proceedings if they want to pursue the claims at all. That is why, as we recognized in *Granfinanciera*, the notion of "consent" does not apply in bankruptcy proceedings as it might in other contexts.

Congress devised an "expert and inexpensive method for dealing with a class of questions of fact which are particularly suited to examination and determination by an administrative agency specially assigned to that task." *Crowell*, 285 U.S., at 46. The "experts" in the federal system at resolving common law counterclaims such as Vickie's are the Article III courts, and it is with those courts that her claim must stay.

. . . .

What is plain here is that this case involves the most prototypical exercise of judicial power: the entry of a final, binding judgment by a court with broad substantive jurisdiction, on a common law cause of action, when the action neither derives from nor depends upon any agency regulatory regime. If such an exercise of judicial power may nonetheless be taken from the Article III Judiciary simply by deeming it part of some amorphous "public right," then Article III would be transformed from the guardian of individual liberty and separation of powers we have long recognized into mere wishful thinking.

2

[The Court proceeded to distinguish this case from two decisions, *Katchen v. Landy*, 382 U.S. 323 (1966), and *Langenkamp v. Culp*, 498 U.S. 42 (1990) (*per curiam*), in which the Court had permitted bankruptcy court adjudication of counterclaims. The Court concluded that, "Vickie's claim, in contrast, is in no way derived from or dependent upon bankruptcy law; it is a state tort action that exists without regard to any bankruptcy proceeding."]

. . . Congress may not bypass Article III simply because a proceeding may have some bearing on a bankruptcy case; the question is whether the action at issue stems from the bankruptcy itself or would necessarily be resolved in the claims allowance process. Vickie has failed to demonstrate that her counterclaim falls within one of the "limited circumstances" covered by the public rights exception, particularly given our conclusion that, "even with respect to matters that arguably fall within the scope of the 'public rights' doctrine, the presumption is in favor of Art. III courts." *Northern Pipeline*, 458 U.S., at 69, n. 23, 77 n. 29 (plurality opinion).

3

Vickie additionally argues that the Bankruptcy Court's final judgment was constitutional because bankruptcy courts under the 1984 Act are properly deemed "adjuncts" of the district courts. We rejected a similar argument in *Northern Pipeline*, see 458 U.S., at 84-86 (plurality opinion); *id.*, at 91 (Rehnquist, J., concurring in judgment), and our reasoning there holds true today.

To begin, as explained above, it is still the bankruptcy court itself that exercises the essential attributes of judicial power over a matter such as Vickie's counterclaim. . . . [B]ankruptcy courts under the 1984 Act resolve "[a]ll matters of fact and law in whatever domains of the law to which" the parties' counterclaims might lead. *Id.*, at 91 (Rehnquist, J., concurring in judgment).

In addition, whereas the adjunct agency in *Crowell v. Benson* "possessed only a limited power to issue compensation orders . . . [that] could be enforced only by order of the district court," *Northern Pipeline, supra*, at 85, a bankruptcy court resolving a counterclaim under 28 U.S.C. § 157(b)(2)(C) has the power to enter "appropriate orders and judgments" — including final judgments — subject to review only if a party chooses to appeal. . . . Given that authority, a bankruptcy court can no more be deemed a mere "adjunct" of the district court than a district court can be deemed such an "adjunct" of the court of appeals. We certainly cannot accept the dissent's notion that judges who have the power to enter final, binding orders are the "functional []" equivalent of "law clerks[] and the Judiciary's administrative officials." And even were we wrong in this regard, that would only confirm that such judges should not be in the business of entering final judgments in the first place.

    . . . .

D

Finally, Vickie and her amici predict as a practical matter that restrictions on a bankruptcy court's ability to hear and finally resolve compulsory counterclaims will create significant delays and impose additional costs on the bankruptcy process. It goes without saying that "the fact that a given law or procedure is efficient, convenient, and useful in facilitating functions of government, standing alone, will not save it if it is contrary to the Constitution." *INS v. Chadha*, 462 U.S. 919, 944 (1983).

In addition, we are not convinced that the practical consequences of such limitations on the authority of bankruptcy courts to enter final judgments are as significant as Vickie and the dissent suggest. . . .

If our decision today does not change all that much, then why the fuss? Is there really a threat to the separation of powers where Congress has conferred the judicial power outside Article III only over certain counterclaims in bankruptcy? The short but emphatic answer is yes. A statute may no more lawfully chip away at the authority of the Judicial Branch than it may eliminate it entirely. . . . We cannot compromise the integrity of the system of separated powers and the role of the Judiciary in that system, even with respect to challenges that may seem innocuous at first blush.

***

Article III of the Constitution provides that the judicial power of the United States may be vested only in courts whose judges enjoy the protections set forth in that Article. We conclude today that Congress, in one isolated respect, exceeded that limitation in the Bankruptcy Act of 1984. The Bankruptcy Court below lacked the constitutional authority to enter a final judgment on a state law counterclaim that is not resolved in the process of ruling on a creditor's proof of claim. Accordingly, the judgment of the Court of Appeals is affirmed.

It is so ordered.

JUSTICE SCALIA, concurring.

I agree with the Court's interpretation of our Article III precedents, and I accordingly join its opinion. I adhere to my view, however, that — our contrary precedents notwithstanding — "a matter of public rights . . . must at a minimum arise between the government and others," *Granfinanciera, S.A. v. Nordberg*, 492 U.S. 33, 65 (1989) (SCALIA, J., concurring in part and concurring in judgment) (internal quotation marks omitted).

The sheer surfeit of factors that the Court was required to consider in this case should arouse the suspicion that something is seriously amiss with our jurisprudence in this area. I count at least seven different reasons given in the Court's opinion for concluding that an Article III judge was required to adjudicate this lawsuit. . . .

Apart from their sheer numerosity, the more fundamental flaw in the many tests suggested by our jurisprudence is that they have nothing to do with the text or tradition of Article III. . . .

Leaving aside certain adjudications by federal administrative agencies, which are governed (for better or worse) by our landmark decision in *Crowell v. Benson*, 285 U.S. 22 (1932), in my view an Article III judge is required in all federal adjudications, unless there is a firmly established historical practice to the contrary. For that reason — and not because of some intuitive balancing of benefits and harms — I agree that Article III judges are not required in the context of territorial courts, courts-martial, or true "public rights" cases. *See Northern Pipeline Constr. Co. v. Marathon Pipe Line Co.*, 458 U.S. 50, 71 (1982) (plurality opinion). . . .

JUSTICE BREYER, with whom JUSTICE GINSBURG, JUSTICE SOTOMAYOR, and JUSTICE KAGAN, join dissenting.

Pierce Marshall filed a claim in Federal Bankruptcy Court against the estate of Vickie Marshall. His claim asserted that Vickie Marshall had, through her lawyers, accused him of trying to prevent her from obtaining money that his father had wanted her to have; that her accusations violated state defamation law; and that she consequently owed Pierce Marshall damages. Vickie Marshall filed a compulsory counterclaim in which she asserted that Pierce Marshall had unlawfully interfered with her husband's efforts to grant her an *inter vivos* gift and that he consequently owed her damages.

The Bankruptcy Court adjudicated the claim and the counterclaim. In doing so, the court followed statutory procedures applicable to "core" bankruptcy proceedings. *See* 28 U.S.C. § 157(b). And ultimately the Bankruptcy Court entered judgment in favor of Vickie Marshall. The question before us is whether the Bankruptcy Court possessed jurisdiction to adjudicate Vickie Marshall's counterclaim. I agree with the Court that the bankruptcy statute, § 157(b)(2)(C), authorizes a bankruptcy court to adjudicate the counterclaim. But I do not agree with the majority about the statute's constitutionality. I believe the statute is consistent with the Constitution's delegation of the "judicial Power of the United States" to the Judicial Branch of Government. Art. III, § 1. Consequently, it is constitutional.

I

My disagreement with the majority's conclusion stems in part from my disagreement about the way in which it interprets, or at least emphasizes, certain precedents. In my view, the majority overstates the current relevance of statements this Court made in an 1856 case, *Murray's Lessee v. Hoboken Land & Improvement Co.*, 59 U.S. 272, 18 How. 272 (1856), and it overstates the importance of an analysis that did not command a Court majority in *Northern Pipeline Constr. Co. v. Marathon Pipe Line Co.*, 458 U.S. 50 (1982), and that was subsequently disavowed. At the same time, I fear the Court understates the importance of a watershed opinion widely thought to demonstrate the constitutional basis for the current authority of administrative agencies to adjudicate private disputes, namely,

Crowell v. Benson, 285 U.S. 22 (1932). And it fails to follow the analysis that this Court more recently has held applicable to the evaluation of claims of a kind before us here, namely, claims that a congressional delegation of adjudicatory authority violates separation-of-powers principles derived from Article III. *See Thomas v. Union Carbide Agricultural Products Co.*, 473 U.S. 568 (1985); *Commodity Futures Trading Comm'n v. Schor*, 478 U.S. 833 (1986).

[Justice Breyer's discussion of these decisions is omitted.]

II

A

This case law, as applied in *Thomas* and *Schor*, requires us to determine pragmatically whether a congressional delegation of adjudicatory authority to a non-Article III judge violates the separation-of-powers principles inherent in Article III. That is to say, we must determine through an examination of certain relevant factors whether that delegation constitutes a significant encroachment by the Legislative or Executive Branches of Government upon the realm of authority that Article III reserves for exercise by the Judicial Branch of Government. Those factors include (1) the nature of the claim to be adjudicated; (2) the nature of the non-Article III tribunal; (3) the extent to which Article III courts exercise control over the proceeding; (4) the presence or absence of the parties' consent; and (5) the nature and importance of the legislative purpose served by the grant of adjudicatory authority to a tribunal with judges who lack Article III's tenure and compensation protections. The presence of "private rights" does not automatically determine the outcome of the question but requires a more "searching" examination of the relevant factors. *Schor, supra,* at 854.

Insofar as the majority would apply more formal standards, it simply disregards recent, controlling precedent. *Thomas, supra,* at 587 ("[P]ractical attention to substance rather than doctrinaire reliance on formal categories should inform application of Article III"); *Schor, supra,* at 851 ("[T]he Court has declined to adopt formalistic and unbending rules" for deciding Article III cases).

B

Applying *Schor*'s approach here, I conclude that the delegation of adjudicatory authority before us is constitutional. A grant of authority to a bankruptcy court to adjudicate compulsory counterclaims does not violate any constitutional separation-of-powers principle related to Article III.

[Justice Breyer proceeded to analyze the factors identified in *Schor.* Of particular concern to him was the fifth factor.]

Fifth, the nature and importance of the legislative purpose served by the grant of adjudicatory authority to bankruptcy tribunals argues strongly in favor of constitutionality. Congress' delegation of adjudicatory powers over counterclaims asserted against bankruptcy claimants constitutes an important means of securing a constitutionally authorized end. Article I, § 8, of the Constitution explicitly grants Congress the "Power To . . . establish . . . uniform Laws on the subject of Bankruptcies throughout the United States." . . .

. . . .

Consequently a bankruptcy court's determination of such matters has more than "some bearing on a bankruptcy case." *Ante* (emphasis deleted). It plays a critical role in Congress' constitutionally based effort to create an efficient, effective federal bankruptcy system. At the least, that is what Congress concluded. We owe deference to that determination, which shows the absence of any legislative or executive motive, intent, purpose, or desire to encroach upon areas that Article III reserves to judges to whom it grants tenure and compensation protections.

Considering these factors together, I conclude that, as in *Schor*, "the magnitude of any intrusion on the Judicial Branch can only be termed *de minimis*." 478 U.S., at 856. I would similarly find the statute before us constitutional.

III

The majority predicts that as a "practical matter" today's decision does not change all that much. But I doubt that is so. . . . [U]nder the majority's holding, the federal district judge, not the bankruptcy judge, would have to hear and resolve the counterclaim.

Why is that a problem? Because these types of disputes arise in bankruptcy court with some frequency. Because the volume of bankruptcy cases is staggering, involving almost 1.6 million filings last year, compared to a federal district court docket of around 280,000 civil cases and 78,000 criminal cases. Because unlike the "related" non-core state law claims that bankruptcy courts must abstain from hearing, compulsory counterclaims involve the same factual disputes as the claims that may be finally adjudicated by the bankruptcy courts. Because under these circumstances, a constitutionally required game of jurisdictional ping-pong between courts would lead to inefficiency, increased cost, delay, and needless additional suffering among those faced with bankruptcy.

For these reasons, with respect, I dissent.

QUESTIONS

1. After the Supreme Court's decision in *Stern* regarding the constitutionality of non-Article III adjudication, what is the continuing significance, if any, of *Crowell*? Of *Schor*? Of *Granfinanciera*?
2. Does the fact that the Supreme Court's decisions rejecting the constitutionality of non-Article III adjudication have applied to the jurisdiction of the Bankruptcy Court mean that the line of cases is not applicable to agency adjudications?
3. How would Justice Scalia define the limits of permissible adjudication by non-Article III adjudicators?
4. Is Justice Breyer convincing when he criticizes the majority for not adhering to the Court's decisions in *Crowell* and *Schor*?
5. Which opinion seems consistent with a formalist approach to separation of powers analysis? With a functionalist analysis?
6. What are the potential benefits of permitting a bankruptcy court to adjudicate common law claims integrally related to a bankruptcy proceeding?

Do these potential benefits matter to Chief Justice Roberts? To Justice Scalia? To Justice Breyer?

7. Is the question of Pierce's consent to the adjudication of the claim relevant to the constitutionality of the bankruptcy court's jurisdiction? See footnote 8 of the majority decision.

8. The Supreme Court does not address in *Stern* the jury trial question.

WELLNESS INTERNATIONAL NETWORK, LTD. v. SHARIF
135 S. Ct. 1932 (2015)

Justice Sotomayor delivered the opinion of the Court.

Article III, §1, of the Constitution provides that "[t]he judicial Power of the United States, shall be vested in one supreme Court, and in such inferior Courts as the Congress may from time to time ordain and establish." Congress has in turn established 94 District Courts and 13 Courts of Appeals, composed of judges who enjoy the protections of Article III: life tenure and pay that cannot be diminished. Because these protections help to ensure the integrity and independence of the Judiciary, "we have long recognized that, in general, Congress may not withdraw from" the Article III courts "any matter which, from its nature, is the subject of a suit at the common law, or in equity, or in admiralty." *Stern v. Marshall*, 564 U.S. 462, 484 (2011) (internal quotation marks omitted).

Congress has also authorized the appointment of bankruptcy and magistrate judges, who do not enjoy the protections of Article III, to assist Article III courts in their work. The number of magistrate and bankruptcy judgeships exceeds the number of circuit and district judgeships.[1] And it is no exaggeration to say that without the distinguished service of these judicial colleagues, the work of the federal court system would grind nearly to a halt.[2]

Congress' efforts to align the responsibilities of non-Article III judges with the boundaries set by the Constitution have not always been successful. In *Northern Pipeline Constr. Co. v. Marathon Pipe Line Co.*, 458 U.S. 50 (1982) (plurality opinion), and more recently in *Stern*, this Court held that Congress violated Article III by authorizing bankruptcy judges to decide certain claims for which litigants are constitutionally entitled to an Article III adjudication. This case presents the question whether Article III allows bankruptcy judges to adjudicate such claims with the parties' consent. We hold that Article III is not violated when the parties knowingly and voluntarily consent to adjudication by a bankruptcy judge.

I

A

Before 1978, district courts typically delegated bankruptcy proceedings to "referees." Under the Bankruptcy Act of 1898, bankruptcy referees had "[s]ummary jurisdiction" over "claims involving 'property in the actual or

---

1. Congress has authorized 179 circuit judgeships and 677 district judgeships, a total of 856. The number of authorized magistrate and bankruptcy judgeships currently stands at 883: 534 full-time magistrate judgeships and 349 bankruptcy judgeships.

2. Between October 1, 2013, and September 30, 2014, for example, litigants filed 963,739 cases in bankruptcy courts — more than double the total number filed in district and circuit courts.

constructive possession of the bankruptcy court'" — that is, over the apportionment of the bankruptcy estate among creditors. They could preside over other proceedings — matters implicating the court's "plenary jurisdiction" — by consent.

In 1978, Congress enacted the Bankruptcy Reform Act, which repealed the 1898 Act and gave the newly created bankruptcy courts power "much broader than that exercised under the former referee system." The Act "[e]liminat[ed] the distinction between 'summary' and 'plenary' jurisdiction" and enabled bankruptcy courts to decide "all 'civil proceedings arising under title 11 [the Bankruptcy title] or arising in or related to cases under title 11.'" Congress thus vested bankruptcy judges with most of the "'powers of a court of equity, law, and admiralty,'" without affording them the benefits of Article III. This Court therefore held parts of the system unconstitutional in *Northern Pipeline.*

Congress responded by enacting the Bankruptcy Amendments and Federal Judgeship Act of 1984. Under that Act, district courts have original jurisdiction over bankruptcy cases and related proceedings. 28 U.S.C. §§ 1334(a), (b). But "[e]ach district court may provide that any or all" bankruptcy cases and related proceedings "shall be referred to the bankruptcy judges for the district." § 157(a). Bankruptcy judges are "judicial officers of the United States district court," appointed to 14-year terms by the courts of appeals, and subject to removal for cause. §§ 152(a)(1), (e). "The district court may withdraw" a reference to the bankruptcy court "on its own motion or on timely motion of any party, for cause shown." § 157(d).

When a district court refers a case to a bankruptcy judge, that judge's statutory authority depends on whether Congress has classified the matter as a "[c]ore proceedin[g]" or a "[n]on-core proceedin[g]," §§ 157(b)(2), (4) — much as the authority of bankruptcy referees, before the 1978 Act, depended on whether the proceeding was "summary" or "plenary." Congress identified as "[c]ore" a nonexclusive list of 16 types of proceedings, § 157(b)(2), in which it thought bankruptcy courts could constitutionally enter judgment. Congress gave bankruptcy courts the power to "hear and determine" core proceedings and to "enter appropriate orders and judgments," subject to appellate review by the district court. § 157(b)(1); *see* § 158. But it gave bankruptcy courts more limited authority in non-core proceedings: They may "hear and determine" such proceedings, and "enter appropriate orders and judgments," only "with the consent of all the parties to the proceeding." § 157(c)(2). Absent consent, bankruptcy courts in non-core proceedings may only "submit proposed findings of fact and conclusions of law," which the district courts review *de novo.* § 157(c)(1).

B

Petitioner Wellness International Network [Wellness] is a manufacturer of health and nutrition products. Wellness and respondent Sharif entered into a contract under which Sharif would distribute Wellness' products. The relationship quickly soured, and in 2005, Sharif sued Wellness in the United States District Court for the Northern District of Texas. Sharif repeatedly ignored Wellness' discovery requests and other litigation obligations, resulting in an entry of default judgment for Wellness. The District Court eventually sanctioned Sharif by awarding Wellness over $650,000 in attorney's fees. This case arises from Wellness' long-running — and so far unsuccessful — efforts to collect on that judgment.

In February 2009, Sharif filed for Chapter 7 bankruptcy in the Northern District of Illinois. The bankruptcy petition listed Wellness as a creditor. Wellness requested documents concerning Sharif's assets, which Sharif did not provide. Wellness later obtained a loan application Sharif had filed in 2002, listing more than $5 million in assets. When confronted, Sharif informed Wellness and the Chapter 7 trustee that he had lied on the loan application. The listed assets, Sharif claimed, were actually owned by the Soad Wattar Living Trust (Trust), an entity Sharif said he administered on behalf of his mother, and for the benefit of his sister. Wellness pressed Sharif for information on the Trust, but Sharif again failed to respond.

Wellness filed a five-count adversary complaint against Sharif in the Bankruptcy Court. Counts I–IV of the complaint objected to the discharge of Sharif's debts because, among other reasons, Sharif had concealed property by claiming that it was owned by the Trust. Count V of the complaint sought a declaratory judgment that the Trust was Sharif's alter ego and that its assets should therefore be treated as part of Sharif's bankruptcy estate. In his answer, Sharif admitted that the adversary proceeding was a "core proceeding" under 28 U.S.C. § 157(b) — i.e., a proceeding in which the Bankruptcy Court could enter final judgment subject to appeal. *See* §§ 157(b)(1), (2)(J). Indeed, Sharif requested judgment in his favor on all counts of Wellness' complaint and urged the Bankruptcy Court to "find that the Soad Wattar Living Trust is not property of the [bankruptcy] estate."

A familiar pattern of discovery evasion ensued. Wellness responded by filing a motion for sanctions, or, in the alternative, to compel discovery. Granting the motion to compel, the Bankruptcy Court warned Sharif that if he did not respond to Wellness' discovery requests a default judgment would be entered against him. Sharif eventually complied with some discovery obligations, but did not produce any documents related to the Trust.

In July 2010, the Bankruptcy Court issued a ruling finding that Sharif had violated the court's discovery order. It accordingly denied Sharif's request to discharge his debts and entered a default judgment against him in the adversary proceeding. And it declared, as requested by count V of Wellness' complaint, that the assets supposedly held by the Trust were in fact property of Sharif's bankruptcy estate because Sharif "treats [the Trust's] assets as his own property."

Sharif appealed to the District Court. Six weeks before Sharif filed his opening brief in the District Court, this Court decided *Stern*. In *Stern*, the Court held that Article III prevents bankruptcy courts from entering final judgment on claims that seek only to "augment" the bankruptcy estate and would otherwise "exis[t] without regard to any bankruptcy proceeding." 564 U.S., at 495, 499. Sharif did not cite *Stern* in his opening brief. Rather, after the close of briefing, Sharif moved for leave to file a supplemental brief, arguing that in light of *In re Ortiz*, 665 F.3d 906 (C.A.7 2011) — a recently issued decision interpreting *Stern* — "the bankruptcy court's order should only be treated as a report and recommendation." The District Court denied Sharif's motion for supplemental briefing as untimely and affirmed the Bankruptcy Court's judgment.

The Court of Appeals for the Seventh Circuit affirmed in part and reversed in part. 727 F.3d 751 (2013). . . . The Seventh Circuit [ ] ruled that the Bankruptcy Court lacked constitutional authority to enter final judgment on count V.

We granted certiorari, and now reverse the judgment of the Seventh Circuit.[7]

II

Our precedents make clear that litigants may validly consent to adjudication by bankruptcy courts.

A

Adjudication by consent is nothing new. Indeed, "[d]uring the early years of the Republic, federal courts, with the consent of the litigants, regularly referred adjudication of entire disputes to non-Article III referees, masters, or arbitrators, for entry of final judgment in accordance with the referee's report." Brubaker, The Constitutionality of Litigant Consent to Non-Article III Bankruptcy Adjudications, 32 Bkrtcy. L. Letter No. 12, p. 6 (Dec. 2012).

The foundational case in the modern era is *Commodity Futures Trading Comm'n v. Schor*, 478 U.S. 833 (1986). The Commodity Futures Trading Commission (CFTC), which Congress had authorized to hear customer complaints against commodities brokers, issued a regulation allowing itself to hear state-law counterclaims as well. William Schor filed a complaint with the CFTC against his broker, and the broker, which had previously filed claims against Schor in federal court, refiled them as counterclaims in the CFTC proceeding. The CFTC ruled against Schor on the counterclaims. This Court upheld that ruling against both statutory and constitutional challenges.

On the constitutional question (the one relevant here) the Court began by holding that Schor had "waived any right he may have possessed to the full trial of [the broker's] counterclaim before an Article III court." *Id.*, at 849. The Court then explained why this waiver legitimated the CFTC's exercise of authority: "[A]s a personal right, Article III's guarantee of an impartial and independent federal adjudication is subject to waiver, just as are other personal constitutional rights" — such as the right to a jury — "that dictate the procedures by which civil and criminal matters must be tried." *Id.*, at 848–849.

The Court went on to state that a litigant's waiver of his "personal right" to an Article III court is not always dispositive because Article III "not only preserves to litigants their interest in an impartial and independent federal adjudication of claims . . . , but also serves as 'an inseparable element of the constitutional system of checks and balances.' . . . To the extent that this structural principle is implicated in a given case" — but only to that extent — "the parties cannot by consent cure the constitutional difficulty. . . ." *Id.*, at 850–851.

Leaning heavily on the importance of Schor's consent, the Court found no structural concern implicated by the CFTC's adjudication of the counterclaims against him. While "Congress gave the CFTC the authority to adjudicate such matters," the Court wrote,

---

7. Because the Court concludes that the Bankruptcy Court could validly enter judgment on Wellness' claim with the parties' consent, this opinion does not address, and expresses no view on, Wellness' alternative contention that the Seventh Circuit erred in concluding the claim in count V of its complaint was a *Stern* claim.

"the decision to invoke this forum is left entirely to the parties and the power of the federal judiciary to take jurisdiction of these matters is unaffected. In such circumstances, separation of powers concerns are diminished, for it seems self-evident that just as Congress may encourage parties to settle a dispute out of court or resort to arbitration without impermissible incursions on the separation of powers, Congress may make available a quasi-judicial mechanism through which willing parties may, at their option, elect to resolve their differences." *Id.*, at 855.

The option for parties to submit their disputes to a non-Article III adjudicator was at most a "*de minimis*" infringement on the prerogative of the federal courts. *Id.*, at 856.

A few years after *Schor,* the Court decided a pair of cases — *Gomez v. United States,* 490 U.S. 858 (1989), and *Peretz v. United States,* 501 U.S. 923 (1991) — that reiterated the importance of consent to the constitutional analysis. Both cases concerned whether the Federal Magistrates Act authorized magistrate judges to preside over jury selection in a felony trial; the difference was that Peretz consented to the practice while Gomez did not. That difference was dispositive.

. . .

The lesson of *Schor, Peretz,* and the history that preceded them is plain: The entitlement to an Article III adjudicator is "a personal right" and thus ordinarily "subject to waiver," *Schor,* 478 U.S., at 848. Article III also serves a structural purpose, "barring congressional attempts 'to transfer jurisdiction [to non-Article III tribunals] for the purpose of emasculating' constitutional courts and thereby prevent[ing] 'the encroachment or aggrandizement of one branch at the expense of the other.'" *Id.,* at 850 (citations omitted). But allowing Article I adjudicators to decide claims submitted to them by consent does not offend the separation of powers so long as Article III courts retain supervisory authority over the process.

B

The question here, then, is whether allowing bankruptcy courts to decide *Stern* claims by consent would "impermissibly threate[n] the institutional integrity of the Judicial Branch." *Schor,* 478 U.S., at 851. And that question must be decided not by "formalistic and unbending rules," but "with an eye to the practical effect that the" practice "will have on the constitutionally assigned role of the federal judiciary." *Ibid.* The Court must weigh

"the extent to which the essential attributes of judicial power are reserved to Article III courts, and, conversely, the extent to which the non-Article III forum exercises the range of jurisdiction and powers normally vested only in Article III courts, the origins and importance of the right to be adjudicated, and the concerns that drove Congress to depart from the requirements of Article III." *Schor,* 478 U.S., at 851 (internal quotation marks omitted).

Applying these factors, we conclude that allowing bankruptcy litigants to waive the right to Article III adjudication of *Stern* claims does not usurp the constitutional prerogatives of Article III courts. Bankruptcy judges, like magistrate judges, "are appointed and subject to removal by Article III judges," *Peretz,* 501 U.S., at 937. They "serve as judicial officers of the United States district court," §151, and collectively "constitute a unit of the district court" for that district, [28 U.S.C.] §152(a)(1). Just as "[t]he 'ultimate decision' whether to invoke [a] magistrate [judge]'s assistance is made by the district court," *Peretz*, 501 U.S., at 937, bankruptcy courts hear matters solely on a district court's reference, §157(a), which the district court may withdraw *sua sponte* or at the request of a party, §157(d). "[S]eparation of powers concerns are diminished" when, as here, "the decision to invoke [a non-Article III] forum is left entirely to the parties and the power of the federal judiciary to take jurisdiction" remains in place. *Schor*, 478 U.S., at 855.

Furthermore, like the CFTC in *Schor*, bankruptcy courts possess no free-floating authority to decide claims traditionally heard by Article III courts. Their ability to resolve such matters is limited to "a narrow class of common law claims as an incident to the [bankruptcy courts'] primary, and unchallenged, adjudicative function." *Id.*, at 854. "In such circumstances, the magnitude of any intrusion on the Judicial Branch can only be termed *de minimis*." *Id.*, at 856.

Finally, there is no indication that Congress gave bankruptcy courts the ability to decide *Stern* claims in an effort to aggrandize itself or humble the Judiciary. As in *Peretz*, "[b]ecause 'the entire process takes place under the district court's total control and jurisdiction,' there is no danger that use of the [bankruptcy court] involves a 'congressional attemp[t] "to transfer jurisdiction [to non-Article III tribunals] for the purpose of emasculating" constitutional courts.'" 501 U.S., at 937 (citation omitted).[10]

Congress could choose to rest the full share of the Judiciary's labor on the shoulders of Article III judges. But doing so would require a substantial increase in the number of district judgeships. Instead, Congress has supplemented the capacity of district courts through the able assistance of bankruptcy judges. So long as those judges are subject to control by the Article III courts, their work poses no threat to the separation of powers.

C

Our recent decision in *Stern*, on which Sharif and the principal dissent rely heavily, does not compel a different result. That is because *Stern*—like its predecessor, *Northern Pipeline*—turned on the fact that the litigant "did not truly consent to" resolution of the claim against it in a non-Article III forum. 564 U.S., at 493.

To understand *Stern*, it is necessary to first understand *Northern Pipeline*. There, the Court considered whether bankruptcy judges "could 'constitutionally be vested with jurisdiction to decide [a] state-law contract claim' against an entity that was not otherwise part of the bankruptcy proceedings." 564 U.S., at 485. In answering that question in the negative, both the plurality and then-Justice Rehnquist, concurring in the judgment, noted that the entity in question did not consent to the bankruptcy court's adjudication of the claim. See 458 U.S., at 80, n. 31 (plurality opinion); *id.*, at 91 (opinion of Rehnquist, J.). The Court

10. The principal dissent accuses us of making Sharif's consent "'dispositive' in curing [a] structural separation of powers violation," contrary to the holding of *Schor*. Post. That argument misapprehends both *Schor* and the nature of our analysis. What *Schor* forbids is using consent to excuse an actual violation of Article III. See 478 U.S., at 850–851 ("*To the extent* that th[e] structural principle [protected by Article III] is implicated in a given case, the parties cannot by consent cure the constitutional difficulty . . ." (emphasis added)). But *Schor* confirms that consent remains highly relevant when determining, as we do here, whether a particular adjudication in fact raises constitutional concerns. See *id.*, at 855 ("separation of powers concerns are diminished" when "the decision to invoke [a non-Article III] forum is left entirely to the parties"). Thus, we do not rely on Sharif's consent to "cur[e]" a violation of Article III. His consent shows, in part, why no such violation has occurred.

confirmed in two later cases that *Northern Pipeline* turned on the lack of consent. See *Schor*, 478 U.S., at 849 ("[I]n *Northern Pipeline*, . . . the absence of consent to an initial adjudication before a non-Article III tribunal was relied on as a significant factor in determining that Article III forbade such adjudication"); *Thomas*, 473 U.S., at 584.

Stern presented the same scenario. The majority cited the dissent's observation that *Northern Pipeline* "establish[ed] only that Congress may not vest in a non-Article III court the power to adjudicate, render final judgment, and issue binding orders in a traditional contract action arising under state law, *without consent* of the litigants, and subject only to ordinary appellate review," 564 U.S., at 494 (emphasis added; internal quotation marks omitted). To which the majority responded, "Just so: Substitute 'tort' for 'contract,' and that statement directly covers this case." *Id.*; see also *id.*, at 493 (defendant litigated in the Bankruptcy Court because he "had nowhere else to go" to pursue his claim). Because *Stern* was premised on nonconsent to adjudication by the Bankruptcy Court, the "constitutional bar" it announced, see *post* (ROBERTS, C.J., dissenting), simply does not govern the question whether litigants may validly consent to adjudication by a bankruptcy court.

An expansive reading of *Stern*, moreover, would be inconsistent with the opinion's own description of its holding. The Court in *Stern* took pains to note that the question before it was "a 'narrow' one," and that its answer did "not change all that much" about the division of labor between district courts and bankruptcy courts. *Id.*, at 502; see also *id.*, at 503 (stating that Congress had exceeded the limitations of Article III "in one isolated respect"). That could not have been a fair characterization of the decision if it meant that bankruptcy judges could no longer exercise their longstanding authority to resolve claims submitted to them by consent. Interpreting *Stern* to bar consensual adjudications by bankruptcy courts would "meaningfully chang[e] the division of labor" in our judicial system, *contra*, *id.*, at 502.[11]

In sum, the cases in which this Court has found a violation of a litigant's right to an Article III decisionmaker have involved an objecting defendant forced to litigate involuntarily before a non-Article III court. The Court has never done what Sharif and the principal dissent would have us do — hold that a litigant who has the right to an Article III court may not waive that right through his consent.

D

The principal dissent warns darkly of the consequences of today's decision. . . .

Adjudication based on litigant consent has been a consistent feature of the federal court system since its inception. Reaffirming that unremarkable fact, we are confident, poses no great threat to anyone's birthrights, constitutional or otherwise.

---

11. In advancing its restrictive view of *Stern*, the principal dissent ignores the sweeping jurisprudential implications of its position. If, as the principal dissent suggests, consent is irrelevant to the Article III analysis, it is difficult to see how *Schor* and *Peretz* were not wrongly decided. But those decisions obviously remain good law. It is the principal dissent's position that breaks with our precedents. See *Plaut v. Spendthrift Farm, Inc.*, 514 U.S. 211, 231 (1995) ("[T]he proposition that legal defenses based upon doctrines central to the courts' structural independence can never be waived simply does not accord with our cases").

III

Sharif contends that to the extent litigants may validly consent to adjudication by a bankruptcy court, such consent must be express. We disagree.

Nothing in the Constitution requires that consent to adjudication by a bankruptcy court be express. Nor does the relevant statute, 28 U.S.C. § 157, mandate express consent; it states only that a bankruptcy court must obtain "the consent" — consent *simpliciter*— "of all parties to the proceeding" before hearing and determining a non-core claim. § 157(c)(2). And a requirement of express consent would be in great tension with our decision in *Roell v. Withrow*, 538 U.S. 580 (2003). . . .

The implied consent standard articulated in *Roell* supplies the appropriate rule for adjudications by bankruptcy courts under § 157. Applied in the bankruptcy context, that standard possesses the same pragmatic virtues — increasing judicial efficiency and checking gamesmanship — that motivated our adoption of it for consent-based adjudications by magistrate judges. See *id.*, at 590. It bears emphasizing, however, that a litigant's consent — whether express or implied — must still be knowing and voluntary. *Roell* makes clear that the key inquiry is whether "the litigant or counsel was made aware of the need for consent and the right to refuse it, and still voluntarily appeared to try the case" before the non-Article III adjudicator. *Ibid.*; see also *id.*, at 588, n. 5 ("notification of the right to refuse" adjudication by a non-Article III court "is a prerequisite to any inference of consent").[13]

IV

. . . [W]e leave it to the Seventh Circuit to decide on remand whether Sharif's actions evinced the requisite knowing and voluntary consent, and also whether, as Wellness contends, Sharif forfeited his *Stern* argument below.

* * *

The Court holds that Article III permits bankruptcy courts to decide *Stern* claims submitted to them by consent. The judgment of the United States Court of Appeals for the Seventh Circuit is therefore reversed, and the case is remanded for further proceedings consistent with this opinion.

It is so ordered.

[Justice Alito's concurring opinion is omitted.]

CHIEF JUSTICE ROBERTS, with whom JUSTICE SCALIA joins, and with whom JUSTICE THOMAS joins as to Part I, dissenting.

---

13. Even though the Constitution does not require that consent be express, it is good practice for courts to seek express statements of consent or nonconsent, both to ensure irrefutably that any waiver of the right to Article III adjudication is knowing and voluntary and to limit subsequent litigation over the consent issue. Statutes or judicial rules may require express consent where the Constitution does not. Indeed, the Federal Rules of Bankruptcy Procedure already require that pleadings in adversary proceedings before a bankruptcy court "contain a statement that the proceeding is core or non-core and, if non-core, that the pleader does or does not consent to entry of final orders or judgment by the bankruptcy judge." Fed. Rule Bkrtcy. Proc. 7008 (opening pleadings); see Fed. Rule Bkrtcy. Proc. 7012 (responsive pleadings). The Bankruptcy Court and the parties followed that procedure in this case.

The Bankruptcy Court in this case granted judgment to Wellness on its claim that Sharif's bankruptcy estate contained assets he purportedly held in a trust. Provided that no third party asserted a substantial adverse claim to those assets, the Bankruptcy Court's adjudication "stems from the bankruptcy itself" rather than from "the stuff of the traditional actions at common law tried by the courts at Westminster in 1789." *Stern v. Marshall,* 564 U.S. 462, 484 (2011) (internal quotation marks omitted). Article III poses no barrier to such a decision. That is enough to resolve this case.

Unfortunately, the Court brushes aside this narrow basis for decision and proceeds to the serious constitutional question whether private parties may consent to an Article III violation. In my view, they cannot. By reserving the judicial power to judges with life tenure and salary protection, Article III constitutes "an inseparable element of the constitutional system of checks and balances"—a structural safeguard that must "be jealously guarded." *Northern Pipeline Constr. Co. v. Marathon Pipe Line Co.,* 458 U.S. 50, 58, 60 (1982) (plurality opinion).

Today the Court lets down its guard. Despite our precedent directing that "parties cannot by consent cure" an Article III violation implicating the structural separation of powers, *Commodity Futures Trading Comm'n v. Schor,* 478 U.S. 833, 850–851 (1986), the majority authorizes litigants to do just that. The Court justifies its decision largely on pragmatic grounds. I would not yield so fully to functionalism. The Framers adopted the formal protections of Article III for good reasons, and "the fact that a given law or procedure is efficient, convenient, and useful in facilitating functions of government, standing alone, will not save it if it is contrary to the Constitution." *INS v. Chadha,* 462 U.S. 919, 944 (1983).

The impact of today's decision may seem limited, but the Court's acceptance of an Article III violation is not likely to go unnoticed. The next time Congress takes judicial power from Article III courts, the encroachment may not be so modest—and we will no longer hold the high ground of principle. The majority's acquiescence in the erosion of our constitutional power sets a precedent that I fear we will regret. I respectfully dissent.

I

The Court granted certiorari on two questions in this case. The first is whether the Bankruptcy Court's entry of final judgment on Wellness's claim violated Article III based on *Stern.* The second is whether an Article III violation of the kind recognized in *Stern* can be cured by consent. Because the first question can be resolved on narrower grounds, I would answer it alone.

A

. . .

With narrow exceptions, Congress may not confer power to decide federal cases and controversies upon judges who do not comply with the structural safeguards of Article III. Those narrow exceptions permit Congress to establish non-Article III courts to exercise general jurisdiction in the territories and the District of Columbia, to serve as military tribunals, and to adjudicate disputes over "public rights" such as veterans' benefits. *Northern Pipeline*, 458 U.S., at 64–70 (plurality opinion).

Our precedents have also recognized an exception to the requirements of Article III for certain bankruptcy proceedings. When the Framers gathered to draft the Constitution, English statutes had long empowered nonjudicial bankruptcy "commissioners" to collect a debtor's property, resolve claims by creditors, order the distribution of assets in the estate, and ultimately discharge the debts. This historical practice, combined with Congress's constitutional authority to enact bankruptcy laws, confirms that Congress may assign to non-Article III courts adjudications involving "the restructuring of debtor-creditor relations, which is at the core of the federal bankruptcy power." *Northern Pipeline*, 458 U.S., at 71 (plurality opinion).

. . .

In *Stern*, we faced the question whether a bankruptcy court could enter final judgment on an action defined by Congress as a "core" proceeding — an estate's counterclaim against a creditor based on state tort law. § 157(b)(2)(C). We said no. Because the tort claim neither "stem[med] from the bankruptcy itself" nor would "necessarily be resolved in the claims allowance process," it fell outside the recognized exceptions to Article III. 564 U.S., at 499. Like the contract claim in *Northern Pipeline*, the tort claim in *Stern* involved "the stuff of the traditional actions at common law tried by the courts at Westminster in 1789." *Id.*, at 484 (quoting *Northern Pipeline*, 458 U.S., at 90 (Rehnquist, J., concurring in judgment)). Congress had no power under the Constitution to assign the resolution of such a claim to a judge who lacked the structural protections of Article III.

B

. . .

In my view, Article III likely poses no barrier to the Bankruptcy Court's resolution of Wellness's claim. At its most basic level, bankruptcy is "an adjudication of interests claimed in a *res*." *Katchen v. Landy*, 382 U.S. 323, 329 (1966) (internal quotation marks omitted). Wellness asked the Bankruptcy Court to declare that assets held by Sharif are part of that *res*. Defining what constitutes the estate is the necessary starting point of every bankruptcy; a court cannot divide up the estate without first knowing what's in it. *See* 11 U.S.C. § 541(a). As the Solicitor General explains, "Identifying the property of the estate is therefore inescapably central to the restructuring of the debtor-creditor relationship."

. . .

In sum, . . . Wellness's alter ego claim alleges that assets within Sharif's actual or constructive possession belong to his estate. And unlike the breach of contract and tort claims at issue in *Northern Pipeline* and *Stern*, Wellness's claim stems not from any independent source of law but "from the bankruptcy itself." *Stern*, 564 U.S., at 499. Provided that no third party asserted a substantial adverse claim to the trust assets, Wellness's claim therefore falls within the narrow historical exception that permits a non-Article III adjudicator in certain bankruptcy proceedings. I would reverse the contrary holding by the Court of Appeals and end our inquiry there, rather than deciding a broader question that may not be necessary to the disposition of this case.

II

The Court "expresses no view" on whether Wellness's claim was a *Stern* claim. Instead, the Court concludes that the Bankruptcy Court had constitutional authority to enter final judgment on Wellness's claim either way. The majority rests its decision on Sharif's purported consent to the Bankruptcy Court's adjudication. But Sharif has no authority to compromise the structural separation of powers or agree to an exercise of judicial power outside Article III. His consent therefore cannot cure a constitutional violation.

A

[Chief Justice Roberts discusses the importance of the separation of powers established by the Constitution. He emphasizes that "[p]reserving the separation of powers is one of this Court's most weighty responsibilities." He states that "[a] branch's consent to a diminution of its constitutional powers therefore does not mitigate the harm or cure the wrong."]

B

If a branch of the Federal Government may not consent to a violation of the separation of powers, surely a private litigant may not do so. Just as a branch of Government may not consent away the individual liberty interest protected by the separation of powers, so too an individual may not consent away the institutional interest protected by the separation of powers. . . .

As the majority recognizes, the Court's most extensive discussion of litigant consent in a separation of powers case occurred in *Commodity Futures Trading Comm'n v. Schor,* 478 U.S. 833 (1986). There the Court held that Article III confers both a "personal right" that can be waived through consent and a structural component that "safeguards the role of the Judicial Branch in our tripartite system." *Id.,* at 848, 850. "To the extent that this structural principle is implicated in a given case, the parties cannot by consent cure the constitutional difficulty for the same reason that the parties by consent cannot confer on federal courts subject-matter jurisdiction beyond the limitations imposed by Article III." *Id.,* at 850–851. Thus, when "Article III limitations are at issue, notions of consent and waiver cannot be dispositive because the limitations serve institutional interests that the parties cannot be expected to protect." *Id.,* at 851.

. . .

. . . The majority points to no differences between the bankruptcy proceeding in *Stern* and the bankruptcy proceeding here, except for Sharif's purported consent. The majority thus treats consent as "dispositive" in curing the structural separation of powers violation — precisely what *Schor* said consent could not do. 478 U.S., at 851.

C

Eager to change the subject from *Stern*, the majority devotes considerable attention to defending the authority of magistrate judges, who may conduct certain proceedings with the consent of the parties under 28 U.S.C. § 636. No one here challenges the constitutionality of magistrate judges or disputes that they, like bankruptcy judges, may issue reports and recommendations that are reviewed *de novo* by Article III judges. The cases about magistrate judges cited by the majority therefore have little bearing on this case, because none of them involved a constitutional challenge to the entry of final judgment by a non-Article III actor. See *Roell v. Withrow*, 538 U.S. 580 (2003) (statutory challenge only); *Peretz v. United States*, 501 U.S. 923 (1991) (challenge to a magistrate judge's conduct of *voir dire* in a felony trial); *Gomez v. United States*, 490 U.S. 858 (1989) (same). . . .

The encroachment at issue here may seem benign enough. Bankruptcy judges are devoted professionals who strive to be fair to all sides, and litigants can be trusted to protect their own interests when deciding whether to consent. But the fact remains that Congress controls the salary and tenure of bankruptcy judges, and the Legislature's present solicitude provides no guarantee of its future restraint. *See Glidden Co. v. Zdanok*, 370 U.S. 530, 534 (1962) (plurality opinion). Once Congress knows that it can assign federal claims to judges outside Article III with the parties' consent, nothing would limit its exercise of that power to bankruptcy. Congress may consider it advantageous to allow claims to be heard before judges subject to greater legislative control in any number of areas of federal concern. As for the requirement of consent, Congress can find ways to "encourage" consent, say by requiring it as a condition of federal benefits. That has worked to expand Congress's power before. *See*, e.g., *College Savings Bank v. Florida Prepaid Postsecondary Ed. Expense Bd.*, 527 U.S. 666, 686 (1999) ("Congress may, in the exercise of its spending power, condition its grant of funds to the States upon their taking certain actions that Congress could not require them to take"); *South Dakota v. Dole*, 483 U.S. 203, 207 (1987) (same).

Legislative designs of this kind would not displace the Article III judiciary overnight. But steady erosion of Article III authority, no less than a brazen usurpation, violates the constitutional separation of powers. In a Federal Government of limited powers, one branch's loss is another branch's gain, see *PCAOB*, 561 U.S., at 500, so whether a branch aims to "arrogate power to itself" or to "impair another in the performance of its constitutional duties," the Constitution forbids the transgression all the same. *Loving*, 517 U.S., at 757. . . .

The Framers understood this danger. They warned that the Legislature would inevitably seek to draw greater power into its "impetuous vortex," The Federalist No. 48, at 309 (J. Madison), and that "power over a man's subsistence amounts to a power over his will," *id.*, No. 79, at 472 (A. Hamilton) (emphasis deleted). In response, the Framers adopted the structural protections of Article III, "establishing high walls and clear distinctions because low walls and vague distinctions will not be judicially defensible in the heat of interbranch conflict." *Plaut*, 514 U.S., at 239. As this Court once put it, invoking Frost, "Good fences make good neighbors." *Id.*, at 240.

Ultimately, however, the structural protections of Article III are only as strong as this Court's will to enforce them. In Madison's words, the "great security against a gradual concentration of the several powers in the same department consists in giving to those who administer each department the necessary constitutional means and personal motives to resist encroachments of the others." The Federalist No. 51, at 321–322 (J. Madison). The Court today declines to resist encroachment by the Legislature. Instead it holds that a single federal judge, for reasons adequate to him, may assign away our hard-won constitutional birthright so long as two private parties agree. I hope I will be wrong about the consequences of this decision for the independence of the Judicial Branch. But for now, another literary passage comes to mind: It profits the Court nothing to give its soul for the whole world . . . but to avoid *Stern* claims?

I respectfully dissent.

JUSTICE THOMAS, dissenting.

Like THE CHIEF JUSTICE, I would have remanded this case to the lower courts to determine, under the proper standard, whether Wellness' alter-ego claim is a *Stern* claim. I write separately to highlight a few questions touching on the consent issue that merit closer attention than either the Court or THE CHIEF JUSTICE gives them.

I agree with THE CHIEF JUSTICE that individuals cannot consent to violations of the Constitution, but this principle has nothing to do with whose interest the violated provision protects. Anytime the Federal Government acts in a manner inconsistent with the separation of powers, it acts in excess of its constitutional authority. That authority is carefully defined by the Constitution, and, except through Article V's amendment process, that document does not permit individuals to bestow additional power upon the Government.

. . .

Whether parties may consent to bankruptcy court adjudication of *Stern* claims is a difficult constitutional question. It turns on issues that are not adequately considered by the Court or briefed by the parties. And it cannot—and should not—be resolved through a cursory reading of *Schor*, which itself is hardly a model of careful constitutional interpretation. For these reasons, I would resolve the case on the narrow grounds set forth in Part I of THE CHIEF JUSTICE's opinion. I respectfully dissent.

QUESTIONS

1. What legal effect does the majority give to the parties' consent to adjudicate the claim? How does Chief Justice Roberts's view of the legal effect differ? See footnote 10. Which view do you find convincing? Is the majority's view of the legal effect of consent consistent with *Schor*?
2. Does *Wellness* indicate that the Court has returned to a functionalist, rather than formalist, approach to separation of powers?
3. Should the case have been decided on a narrower ground, as advocated by Chief Justice Roberts? What exception to article III adjudication does Chief Justice Roberts recognize and what is the basis for that exception?
4. Does *Wellness* have the effect of entirely undercutting the practical significance of *Stern*?

C.   THE NONDELEGATION DOCTRINE

A. L. A. SCHECHTER POULTRY CORP. v. UNITED STATES
295 U.S. 495 (1935)

MR. CHIEF JUSTICE HUGHES delivered the opinion of the Court.

Petitioners in No. 854 were convicted in the District Court of the United States for the Eastern District of New York on eighteen counts of an indictment charging violations of what is known as the "Live Poultry Code," and on an additional count for conspiracy to commit such violations. By demurrer to the indictment and appropriate motions on the trial, the defendants contended (1) that the Code had been adopted pursuant to an unconstitutional delegation by Congress of legislative power; (2) that it attempted to regulate intrastate transactions which lay outside the authority of Congress; and (3) that in certain provisions it was repugnant to the due process clause of the Fifth Amendment.

The Circuit Court of Appeals sustained the conviction on the conspiracy count and on sixteen counts for violation of the Code, but reversed the conviction on two counts which charged violation of requirements as to minimum wages and maximum hours of labor, as these were not deemed to be within the congressional power of regulation. On the respective applications of the defendants (No. 854) and of the Government (No. 864) this Court granted writs of certiorari, April 15, 1935. . . .

The defendants are slaughterhouse operators. . . . A. L. A. Schechter Poultry Corporation and Schechter Live Poultry Market are corporations conducting wholesale poultry slaughterhouse markets in Brooklyn, New York City. Joseph Schechter operated the latter corporation and also guaranteed the credits of the former corporation which was operated by Martin, Alex and Aaron Schechter. Defendants ordinarily purchase their live poultry from Commission men at the West Washington Market in New York City or at the railroad terminals serving the City, but occasionally they purchase from Commission men in Philadelphia. They buy the poultry for slaughter and resale. After the poultry is trucked to their slaughterhouse markets in Brooklyn, it is there sold, usually within twenty-four hours, to retail poultry dealers and butchers who sell directly to consumers. The poultry purchased from defendants is immediately slaughtered, prior to delivery, by shochtim in defendants' employ. Defendants do not sell poultry in interstate commerce.

The "Live Poultry Code" was promulgated under §3 of the National Industrial Recovery Act. That section authorizes the President to approve "codes of fair competition." Such a code may be approved for a trade or industry, upon application by one or more trade or industrial associations or groups, if the President finds (1) that such associations or groups "impose no inequitable restrictions on admission to membership therein and are truly representative," and (2) that such codes are not designed "to promote monopolies or to eliminate or oppress small enterprises and will not operate to discriminate against them, and will tend to effectuate the policy" of Title I of the Act. Such codes "shall not permit monopolies or monopolistic practices." As a condition of his approval, the President may "impose such conditions (including requirements for the making of reports and the keeping of accounts) for the protection of consumers, competitors, employees, and others, and in furtherance of the public interest, and may provide such exceptions to and exemptions from the provisions of such code as the President in his discretion deems necessary to effectuate the policy herein declared." Where such a code has not been approved, the President may prescribe one, either on his own motion or on complaint. Violation of any provision of a code (so approved or prescribed) "in any transaction in or affecting interstate or foreign commerce" is made a misdemeanor punishable by a fine of not more than $500 for each offense, and each day the violation continues is to be deemed a separate offense.

The "Live Poultry Code" was approved by the President on April 13, 1934. Its divisions indicate its nature and scope. The Code has eight articles entitled (1) purposes, (2) definitions, (3) hours, (4) wages, (5) general labor provisions, (6) administration, (7) trade practice provisions, and (8) general.

The declared purpose is "To effect the policies of title I of the National Industrial Recovery Act." The Code is established as "a code of fair competition for the live poultry industry of the metropolitan area in and about the City of New York." [The Code set maximum hour and minimum wage rules, prohibited the use of certain "unfair trade practices," and established record keeping requirements to facilitate enforcement of its substantive provisions.] . . .

Provision is made for administration through an "industry advisory committee," to be selected by trade associations and members of the industry, and a "code supervisor" to be appointed, with the approval of the committee, by agreement between the Secretary of Agriculture and the Administrator for Industrial Recovery. The expenses of administration are to be borne by the members of the industry proportionately upon the basis of volume of business, or such other factors as the advisory committee may deem equitable, "subject to the disapproval of the Secretary and/or Administrator." . . .

The President approved the Code by an executive order in which he found that the application for his approval had been duly made in accordance with the provisions of Title I of the National Industrial Recovery Act, that there had been due notice and hearings, that the Code constituted "a code of fair competition" as contemplated by the Act and complied with its pertinent provisions including clauses (1) and (2) of subsection (a) of § 3 of Title I; and that the Code would tend "to effectuate the policy of Congress as declared in section 1 of Title I." The executive order also recited that the Secretary of Agriculture and the Administrator of the National Industrial Recovery Act had rendered separate reports as to the provisions within their respective jurisdictions. The Secretary of Agriculture reported that the provisions of the Code "establishing standards of fair competition (a) are regulations of transactions in or affecting the current of interstate and/or foreign commerce and (b) are reasonable," and also that the Code would tend to effectuate the policy declared in Title I of the Act, as set forth in § 1. The report of the Administrator for Industrial Recovery dealt with wages, hours of labor and other labor provisions.

Of the eighteen counts of the indictment upon which the defendants were convicted, aside from the count for conspiracy, two counts charged violation of the minimum wage and maximum hour provisions of the Code, and ten counts were for violation of the requirement (found in the "trade practice provisions") of "straight killing." This requirement was really one of "straight" selling. The term "straight killing" was defined in the Code as "the practice of requiring persons purchasing poultry for resale to accept the run of any half coop, coop, or coops, as purchased by slaughterhouse operators, except for culls." The charges in the ten counts, respectively, were that the defendants in selling to retail dealers and butchers had permitted "selections of individual chickens taken from particular coops and half coops."

Of the other six counts, one charged the sale to a butcher of an unfit chicken; two counts charged the making of sales without having the poultry inspected or approved in accordance with regulations or ordinances of the City of New York; two counts charged the making of false reports or the failure to make reports relating to the range of daily prices and volume of sales for certain periods; and the remaining count was for sales to slaughterers or dealers who were without licenses required by the ordinances and regulations of the city of New York.

First. Two preliminary points are stressed by the Government with respect to the appropriate approach to the important questions presented. We are told that the provision of the statute authorizing the adoption of codes must be viewed in the light of the grave national crisis with which Congress was confronted. Undoubtedly, the conditions to which power is addressed are always to be considered when the exercise of power is challenged. Extraordinary conditions may call for extraordinary remedies. But the argument necessarily stops short of an attempt to justify action which lies outside the sphere of constitutional authority. Extraordinary conditions do not create or enlarge constitutional power. The Constitution established a national government with powers deemed to be adequate, as they have proved to be both in war and peace, but these powers of the national government are limited by the constitutional grants. Those who act under these grants are not at liberty to transcend the imposed limits because they believe that more or different power is necessary. Such assertions of extra-constitutional authority were anticipated and precluded by the explicit terms of the Tenth Amendment—"The powers not delegated to the United States by the Constitution, nor prohibited by it to the States, are reserved to the States respectively, or to the people."

The further point is urged that the national crisis demanded a broad and intensive cooperative effort by those engaged in trade and industry, and that this necessary cooperation was sought to be fostered by permitting them to initiate the adoption of codes. But the statutory plan is not simply one for voluntary effort. It does not seek merely to endow voluntary trade or industrial associations or groups with privileges or immunities. It involves the coercive exercise of the law-making power. The codes of fair competition which the statute attempts to authorize are codes of laws. If valid, they place all persons within their reach under the obligation of positive law, binding equally those who assent and those who do not assent. Violations of the provisions of the codes are punishable as crimes.

Second. The question of the delegation of legislative power. We recently had occasion to review the pertinent decisions and the general principles which govern the determination of this question. *Panama Refining Co. v. Ryan,* 293 U.S. 388. The Constitution provides that "All legislative powers herein granted shall be vested in a Congress of the United States, which shall consist of a Senate and House of Representatives." Art I, § 1. And the Congress is authorized "To make all laws which shall be necessary and proper for carrying into execution" its general powers. Art. I, § 8, par. 18. The Congress is not permitted to abdicate or to transfer to others the essential legislative functions with which it is thus vested. We have repeatedly recognized the necessity of adapting legislation to complex conditions involving a host of details with which the national legislature cannot deal directly. We pointed out in the *Panama Company* case that the Constitution has never been regarded as denying to Congress the necessary resources of flexibility and practicality, which will enable it to perform its function in laying down policies and establishing standards, while leaving to selected instrumentalities the making of subordinate rules within prescribed limits and the determination of facts to which the policy as declared by the legislature is to apply. But we said that the constant recognition of the necessity and validity of such provisions, and the wide range of administrative authority which has been developed by means of them, cannot be allowed to obscure the limitations of the authority to delegate, if our constitutional system is to be maintained. *Id.*, p. 421.

Accordingly, we look to the statute to see whether Congress has overstepped these limitations — whether Congress in authorizing "codes of fair competition" has itself established the standards of legal obligation, thus performing its essential legislative function, or, by the failure to enact such standards, has attempted to transfer that function to others.

The aspect in which the question is now presented is distinct from that which was before us in the case of the *Panama Company*. There, the subject of the statutory prohibition was defined. *National Industrial Recovery Act,* §9(c). That subject was the transportation in interstate and foreign commerce of petroleum and petroleum products which are produced or withdrawn from storage in excess of the amount permitted by state authority. The question was with respect to the range of discretion given to the President in prohibiting that transportation. *Id.*, pp. 414, 415, 430. As to the "codes of fair competition," under §3 of the Act, the question is more fundamental. It is whether there is any adequate definition of the subject to which the codes are to be addressed.

What is meant by "fair competition" as the term is used in the Act? Does it refer to a category established in the law, and is the authority to make codes limited accordingly? Or is it used as a convenient designation for whatever set of laws the formulators of a code for a particular trade or industry may propose and the President may approve (subject to certain restrictions), or the President may himself prescribe, as being wise and beneficent provisions for the government of the trade or industry in order to accomplish the broad purposes of rehabilitation, correction and expansion which are stated in the first section of Title I?

The Act does not define "fair competition." "Unfair competition," as known to the common law, is a limited concept. Primarily, and strictly, it relates to the palming off of one's goods as those of a rival trader. . . . The Federal Trade Commission Act (§5) introduced the expression "unfair methods of competition," which were declared to be unlawful. That was an expression new in the law. Debate apparently convinced the sponsors of the legislation that the words "unfair competition," in the light of their meaning at common law, were too narrow. We have said that the substituted phrase has a broader meaning, that it does not admit of precise definition, its scope being left to judicial determination as controversies arise. *Federal Trade Comm. v. Raladam Co.*, 283 U.S. 643, 648, 649; *Federal Trade Comm. v. Keppel & Bro.*, 291 U.S. 304, 310-312. What are "unfair methods of competition" are thus to be determined in particular instances, upon evidence, in the light of particular competitive conditions and of what is found to be a specific and substantial public interest. To make this possible, Congress set up a special procedure. A Commission, a quasi-judicial body, was created. Provision was made for formal complaint, for notice and hearing, for appropriate findings of fact supported by adequate evidence, and for judicial review to give assurance that the action of the Commission is taken within its statutory authority.

In providing for codes, the National Industrial Recovery Act dispenses with this administrative procedure and with any administrative procedure of an analogous character. But the difference between the code plan of the Recovery Act and the scheme of the Federal Trade Commission Act lies not only in procedure but in subject matter. We cannot regard the "fair competition" of the codes as antithetical to the "unfair methods of competition" of the Federal Trade

Commission Act. The "fair competition["] of the codes has a much broader range and a new significance. The Recovery Act provides that it shall not be construed to impair the powers of the Federal Trade Commission, but, when a code is approved, its provisions are to be the "standards of fair competition" for the trade or industry concerned, and any violation of such standards in any transaction in or affecting interstate or foreign commerce is to be deemed "an unfair method of competition" within the meaning of the Federal Trade Commission Act. §3 (b).

For a statement of the authorized objectives and content of the "codes of fair competition" we are referred repeatedly to the "Declaration of Policy" in section one of Title I of the Recovery Act. Thus, the approval of a code by the President is conditioned on his finding that it "will tend to effectuate the policy of this title." §3 (a). The President is authorized to impose such conditions "for the protection of consumers, competitors, employees, and others, and in furtherance of the public interest, and may provide such exceptions to and exemptions from the provisions of such code as the President in his discretion deems necessary to effectuate the policy herein declared." *Id.* The "policy herein declared" is manifestly that set forth in section one. That declaration embraces a broad range of objectives. Among them we find the elimination of "unfair competitive practices." But even if this clause were to be taken to relate to practices which fall under the ban of existing law, either common law or statute, it is still only one of the authorized aims described in section one. It is there declared to be "the policy of Congress" —

> to remove obstructions to the free flow of interstate and foreign commerce which tend to diminish the amount thereof; and to provide for the general welfare by promotion [sic] the organization of industry for the purpose of cooperative action among trade groups, to induce and maintain united action of labor and management under adequate governmental sanctions and supervision, to eliminate unfair competitive practices, to promote the fullest possible utilization of the present productive capacity of industries, to avoid undue restriction of production (except as may be temporarily required), to increase the consumption of industrial and agricultural products by increasing purchasing power, to reduce and relieve unemployment, to improve standards of labor, and otherwise to rehabilitate industry and to conserve natural resources.

Under §3, whatever "may tend to effectuate" these general purposes may be included in the "codes of fair competition." We think the conclusion is inescapable that the authority sought to be conferred by §3 was not merely to deal with "unfair competitive practices" which offend against existing law, and could be the subject of judicial condemnation without further legislation, or to create administrative machinery for the application of established principles of law to particular instances of violation. Rather, the purpose is clearly disclosed to authorize new and controlling prohibitions through codes of laws which would embrace what the formulators would propose, and what the President would approve, or prescribe, as wise and beneficient measures for the government of trades and industries in order to bring about their rehabilitation, correction and development, according to the general declaration of policy in section one. Codes of laws of this sort are styled "codes of fair competition."

We find no real controversy upon this point and we must determine the validity of the Code in question in this aspect. As the Government candidly says in its brief: "The words 'policy of this title' clearly refer to the 'policy' which Congress declared in the section entitled 'Declaration of Policy'—§1. All of the policies there set forth point toward a single goal—the rehabilitation of industry and the industrial recovery which unquestionably was the major policy of Congress in adopting the National Industrial Recovery Act." And that this is the controlling purpose of the Code now before us appears both from its repeated declarations to that effect and from the scope of its requirements. . . .

The Government urges that the codes will "consist of rules of competition deemed fair for each industry by representative members of that industry—by the persons most vitally concerned and most familiar with its problems." Instances are cited in which Congress has availed itself of such assistance; as, *e.g.*, in the exercise of its authority over the public domain, with respect to the recognition of local customs or rules of miners as to mining claims, or, in matters of a more or less technical nature, as in designating the standard height of drawbars. But would it be seriously contended that Congress could delegate its legislative authority to trade or industrial associations or groups so as to empower them to enact the laws they deem to be wise and beneficent for the rehabilitation and expansion of their trade or industries? Could trade or industrial associations or groups be constituted legislative bodies for that purpose because such associations or groups are familiar with the problems of their enterprises? And, could an effort of that sort be made valid by such a preface of generalities as to permissible aims as we find in section 1 of title I? The answer is obvious. Such a delegation of legislative power is unknown to our law and is utterly inconsistent with the constitutional prerogatives and duties of Congress.

The question, then, turns upon the authority which §3 of the Recovery Act vests in the President to approve or prescribe. If the codes have standing as penal statutes, this must be due to the effect of the executive action. But Congress cannot delegate legislative power to the President to exercise an unfettered discretion to make whatever laws he thinks may be needed or advisable for the rehabilitation and expansion of trade or industry.

Accordingly we turn to the Recovery Act to ascertain what limits have been set to the exercise of the President's discretion. *First,* the President, as a condition of approval, is required to find that the trade or industrial associations or groups which propose a code, "impose no inequitable restrictions on admission to membership" and are "truly representative." That condition, however, relates only to the status of the initiators of the new laws and not to the permissible scope of such laws. *Second,* the President is required to find that the code is not "designed to promote monopolies or to eliminate or oppress small enterprises and will not operate to discriminate against them." And, to this is added a proviso that the code "shall not permit monopolies or monopolistic practices." But these restrictions leave virtually untouched the field of policy envisaged by section one, and, in that wide field of legislative possibilities, the proponents of a code, refraining from monopolistic designs, may roam at will and the President may approve or disapprove their proposals as he may see fit. . . .

Nor is the breadth of the President's discretion left to the necessary implications of this limited requirement as to his findings. As already noted, the

President in approving a code may impose his own conditions, adding to or taking from what is proposed, as "in his discretion" he thinks necessary "to effectuate the policy" declared by the Act. Of course, he has no less liberty when he prescribes a code on his own motion or on complaint, and he is free to prescribe one if a code has not been approved. The Act provides for the creation by the President of administrative agencies to assist him, but the action or reports of such agencies, or of his other assistants — their recommendations and findings in relation to the making of codes — have no sanction beyond the will of the President, who may accept, modify or reject them as he pleases. Such recommendations or findings in no way limit the authority which § 3 undertakes to vest in the President with no other conditions than those there specified. And this authority relates to a host of different trades and industries, thus extending the President's discretion to all the varieties of laws which he may deem to be beneficial in dealing with the vast array of commercial and industrial activities throughout the country.

Such a sweeping delegation of legislative power finds no support in the decisions upon which the Government especially relies. By the Interstate Commerce Act, Congress has itself provided a code of laws regulating the activities of the common carriers subject to the Act, in order to assure the performance of their services upon just and reasonable terms, with adequate facilities and without unjust discrimination. Congress from time to time has elaborated its requirements, as needs have been disclosed. To facilitate the application of the standards prescribed by the Act, Congress has provided an expert body. That administrative agency, in dealing with particular cases, is required to act upon notice and hearing, and its orders must be supported by findings of fact which in turn are sustained by evidence. When the Commission is authorized to issue, for the construction, extension or abandonment of lines, a certificate of "public convenience and necessity," or to permit the acquisition by one carrier of the control of another, if that is found to be "in the public interest," we have pointed out that these provisions are not left without standards to guide determination. The authority conferred has direct relation to the standards prescribed for the service of common carriers and can be exercised only upon findings, based upon evidence, with respect to particular conditions of transportation.

Similarly, we have held that the Radio Act of 1927 established standards to govern radio communications and, in view of the limited number of available broadcasting frequencies, Congress authorized allocation and licenses. The Federal Radio Commission was created as the licensing authority, in order to secure a reasonable equality of opportunity in radio transmission and reception. The authority of the Commission to grant licenses "as public convenience, interest or necessity requires" was limited by the nature of radio communications, and by the scope, character and quality of the services to be rendered and the relative advantages to be derived through distribution of facilities. These standards established by Congress were to be enforced upon hearing, and evidence, by an administrative body acting under statutory restrictions adapted to the particular activity.

In *Hampton & Co. v. United States,* 276 U.S. 394, the question related to the "flexible tariff provision" of the Tariff Act of 1922. We held that Congress had described its plan "to secure by law the imposition of customs duties on articles of imported merchandise which should equal the difference between the cost of producing in a foreign country the articles in question and laying them down for sale in the United States, and the cost of producing and selling like or similar articles in the United States." As the differences in cost might vary from time to time, provision was made for the investigation and determination of these differences by the executive branch so as to make "the adjustments necessary to conform the duties to the standard underlying that policy and plan." *Id.*, pp. 404, 405. The Court found the same principle to be applicable in fixing customs duties as that which permitted Congress to exercise its rate-making power in interstate commerce, "by declaring the rule which shall prevail in the legislative fixing of rates" and then remitting "the fixing of such rates" in accordance with its provisions "to a rate-making body." *Id.*, p. 409. The Court fully recognized the limitations upon the delegation of legislative power. *Id.*, pp. 408-411.

To summarize and conclude upon this point: Section 3 of the Recovery Act is without precedent. It supplies no standards for any trade, industry or activity. It does not undertake to prescribe rules of conduct to be applied to particular states of fact determined by appropriate administrative procedure. Instead of prescribing rules of conduct, it authorizes the making of codes to prescribe them. For that legislative undertaking, §3 sets up no standards, aside from the statement of the general aims of rehabilitation, correction and expansion described in section one. In view of the scope of that broad declaration, and of the nature of the few restrictions that are imposed, the discretion of the President in approving or prescribing codes, and thus enacting laws for the government of trade and industry throughout the country, is virtually unfettered. We think that the code-making authority thus conferred is an unconstitutional delegation of legislative power.

Third. The question of the application of the provisions of the Live Poultry Code to intrastate transactions. [The Court found that the Code exceeded federal power in this respect.]

On both the grounds we have discussed, the attempted delegation of legislative power, and the attempted regulation of intrastate transactions which affect interstate commerce only indirectly, we hold the code provisions here in question to be invalid and that the judgment of conviction must be reversed.

Mr. Justice Cardozo, concurring.

The delegated power of legislation which has found expression in this code is not canalized within banks that keep it from overflowing. It is unconfined and vagrant, if I may borrow my own words in an earlier opinion. *Panama Refining Co. v. Ryan*, 293 U.S. 388, 440.

This court has held that delegation may be unlawful though the act to be performed is definite and single, if the necessity, time and occasion of performance have been left in the end to the discretion of the delegate. *Panama Refining Co. v. Ryan, supra.* I thought that ruling went too far. I pointed out in an opinion that there had been "no grant to the Executive of any roving Commission to inquire into evils and then, upon discovering them, do anything he pleases." 293 U.S. at p. 435. Choice, though within limits, had been given him "as to the occasion, but none whatever as to the means." *Ibid.* Here, in the case before us, is an attempted delegation not confined to any single act nor to any class or group of acts identified or described by reference to a standard. Here in effect is a roving Commission to inquire into evils and upon discovery correct them.

I have said that there is no standard, definite or even approximate, to which legislation must conform. Let me make my meaning more precise. If codes of fair competition are codes eliminating "unfair" methods of competition ascertained upon inquiry to prevail in one industry or another, there is no unlawful delegation of legislative functions when the President is directed to inquire into such practices and denounce them when discovered. For many years a like power has been committed to the Federal Trade Commission with the approval of this court in a long series of decisions. Delegation in such circumstances is born of the necessities of the occasion. The industries of the country are too many and diverse to make it possible for Congress, in respect of matters such as these, to legislate directly with adequate appreciation of varying conditions. Nor is the substance of the power changed because the President may act at the instance of trade or industrial associations having special knowledge of the facts. Their function is strictly advisory; it is the *imprimatur* of the President that begets the quality of law. *Doty v. Love, ante,* p. 64. When the task that is set before one is that of cleaning house, it is prudent as well as usual to take counsel of the dwellers.

But there is another conception of codes of fair competition, their significance and function, which leads to very different consequences, though it is one that is struggling now for recognition and acceptance. By this other conception a code is not to be restricted to the elimination of business practices that would be characterized by general acceptance as oppressive or unfair. It is to include whatever ordinances may be desirable or helpful for the well-being or prosperity of the industry affected. In that view, the function of its adoption is not merely negative, but positive; the planning of improvements as well as the extirpation of abuses. What is fair, as thus conceived, is not something to be contrasted with what is unfair or fraudulent or tricky. The extension becomes as wide as the field of industrial regulation. If that conception shall prevail, anything that Congress may do within the limits of the commerce clause for the betterment of business may be done by the President upon the recommendation of a trade association by calling it a code. This is delegation running riot. No such plenitude of power is susceptible of transfer. The statute, however, aims at nothing less, as one can learn both from its terms and from the administrative practice under it. Nothing less is aimed at by the code now submitted to our scrutiny.

The code does not confine itself to the suppression of methods of competition that would be classified as unfair according to accepted business standards or accepted norms of ethics. It sets up a comprehensive body of rules to promote the welfare of the industry, if not the welfare of the nation, without reference to standards, ethical or commercial, that could be known or predicted in advance of its adoption. One of the new rules, the source of ten counts in the indictment, is aimed at an established practice, not unethical or oppressive, the practice of selective buying. Many others could be instanced as open to the same objection if the sections of the code were to be examined one by one. The process of dissection will not be traced in all its details. Enough at this time to state what it reveals. Even if the statute itself had fixed the meaning of fair competition by way of contrast with practices that are oppressive or unfair, the code outruns the bounds of the authority conferred. What is excessive is not sporadic or superficial. It is deep-seated and pervasive. The licit and illicit sections are so combined and welded as to be incapable of severance without destructive mutilation. . . .

QUESTIONS

1. What aspect of the statute is unconstitutional? What's the constitutional harm?
2. How is the NIRA distinguished from the Federal Trade Commission Act? Are the distinctions persuasive?
3. Does Justice Cardozo have a principled position? How should the line be drawn?
4. Is delegation to a private party part of the problem? Lack of procedural safeguards?
5. Is it possible for the Congress to tell the Executive Branch to do *anything*, without at the same time giving the Executive the power to make at least *some* policy determinations that Congress could make if it wanted to?

INDUSTRIAL UNION DEPT. v. AMERICAN PETROLEUM INST.
448 U.S. 607 (1979)

MR. JUSTICE STEVENS announced the judgment of the Court and delivered an opinion, in which The CHIEF JUSTICE and MR. JUSTICE STEWART joined and in Parts I, II, III-A, III-B, III-C, and III-E of which MR. JUSTICE POWELL joined.

The Occupational Safety and Health Act of 1970 (Act), 84 Stat. 1590, 29 U.S.C. § 651 *et seq.*, was enacted for the purpose of ensuring safe and healthful working conditions for every working man and woman in the Nation. This lit-igation concerns a standard promulgated by the Secretary of Labor to regulate occupational exposure to benzene, a substance which has been shown to cause cancer at high exposure levels. The principal question is whether such a showing is a sufficient basis for a standard that places the most stringent limitation on exposure to benzene that is technologically and economically possible.

The Act delegates broad authority to the Secretary to promulgate different kinds of standards. The basic definition of an "occupational safety and health standard" is found in § 3 (8), which provides:

> "The term 'occupational safety and health standard' means a standard which requires conditions, or the adoption or use of one or more practices, means, methods, operations, or processes, reasonably necessary or appropriate to provide safe or healthful employment and places of employment." 84 Stat. 1591, 29 U.S.C. § 652 (8).

Where toxic materials or harmful physical agents are concerned, a standard must also comply with § 6 (b)(5), which provides:

> "The Secretary, in promulgating standards dealing with toxic materials or harmful physical agents under this subsection, shall set the standard which most adequately assures, to the extent feasible, on the basis of the best available evidence, that no employee will suffer material impairment of health or functional capacity even if such employee has regular exposure to the hazard dealt with by such standard for the period of his working life. Development of standards under this subsection shall be based upon research, demonstrations, experiments, and such other infor-mation as may be appropriate. In addition to the attainment of the highest degree of health and safety protection for the employee, other considerations shall be the

latest available scientific data in the field, the feasibility of the standards, and experience gained under this and other health and safety laws." 84 Stat. 1594, 29 U.S.C. § 655 (b)(5).

Wherever the toxic material to be regulated is a carcinogen, the Secretary has taken the position that no safe exposure level can be determined and that § 6 (b)(5) requires him to set an exposure limit at the lowest technologically feasible level that will not impair the viability of the industries regulated. In this case, after having determined that there is a causal connection between benzene and leukemia (a cancer of the white blood cells), the Secretary set an exposure limit on airborne concentrations of benzene of one part benzene per million parts of air (1 ppm), regulated dermal and eye contact with solutions containing benzene, and imposed complex monitoring and medical testing requirements on employers whose workplaces contain 0.5 ppm or more of benzene. 29 CFR §§ 1910.1028 (c), (e) (1979). [Occupational Safety and Health Administration (OSHA) regulations had previously established 10 ppm as the maximum exposure limit.]

. . .

In the end OSHA's rationale for lowering the permissible exposure limit to 1 ppm was based, not on any finding that leukemia has ever been caused by exposure to 10 ppm of benzene and that it will *not* be caused by exposure to 1 ppm, but rather on a series of assumptions indicating that some leukemias might result from exposure to 10 ppm and that the number of cases might be reduced by reducing the exposure level to 1 ppm. In reaching that result, the Agency first unequivocally concluded that benzene is a human carcinogen. Second, it concluded that industry had failed to prove that there is a safe threshold level of exposure to benzene below which no excess leukemia cases would occur. In reaching this conclusion OSHA rejected industry contentions that certain epidemiological studies indicating no excess risk of leukemia among workers exposed at levels below 10 ppm were sufficient to establish that the threshold level of safe exposure was at or above 10 ppm. It also rejected an industry witness' testimony that a dose-response curve could be constructed on the basis of the reported epidemiological studies and that this curve indicated that reducing the permissible exposure limit from 10 to 1 ppm would prevent at most one leukemia and one other cancer death every six years.

Third, the Agency applied its standard policy with respect to carcinogens, concluding that, in the absence of definitive proof of a safe level, it must be assumed that *any* level above zero presents *some* increased risk of cancer. As the federal parties point out in their brief, there are a number of scientists and public health specialists who subscribe to this view, theorizing that a susceptible person may contract cancer from the absorption of even one molecule of a carcinogen like benzene.

Fourth, the Agency reiterated its view of the Act, stating that it was required by § 6 (b)(5) to set the standard either at the level that has been demonstrated to be safe or at the lowest level feasible, whichever is higher. If no safe level is established, as in this case, the Secretary's interpretation of the statute automatically leads to the selection of an exposure limit that is the lowest feasible. Because of benzene's importance to the economy, no one has ever suggested that it would be feasible to eliminate its use entirely, or to try to limit exposures to the small amounts that are omnipresent. Rather, the Agency selected 1 ppm as a workable exposure level, and then determined that compliance with that level was technologically feasible and that "the economic impact of . . . [compliance] will not be such as to threaten the financial welfare of the affected firms or the general economy." It therefore held that 1 ppm was the minimum feasible exposure level within the meaning of §6 (b)(5) of the Act.

Finally, although the Agency did not refer in its discussion of the pertinent legal authority to any duty to identify the anticipated benefits of the new standard, it did conclude that some benefits were likely to result from reducing the exposure limit from 10 ppm to 1 ppm. This conclusion was based, again, not on evidence, but rather on the assumption that the risk of leukemia will decrease as exposure levels decrease. Although the Agency had found it impossible to construct a dose-response curve that would predict with any accuracy the number of leukemias that could be expected to result from exposures at 10 ppm, at 1 ppm, or at any intermediate level, it nevertheless "determined that the benefits of the proposed standard are likely to be appreciable." In light of the Agency's disavowal of any ability to determine the numbers of employees likely to be adversely affected by exposures of 10 ppm, the Court of Appeals held this finding to be unsupported by the record.

It is noteworthy that at no point in its lengthy explanation did the Agency quote or even cite §3 (8) of the Act. It made no finding that any of the provisions of the new standard were "reasonably necessary or appropriate to provide safe or healthful employment and places of employment." Nor did it allude to the possibility that any such finding might have been appropriate.

III

Our resolution of the issues in these cases turns, to a large extent, on the meaning of and the relationship between §3 (8), which defines a health and safety standard as a standard that is "reasonably necessary and appropriate to provide safe or healthful employment," and §6 (b)(5), which directs the Secretary in promulgating a health and safety standard for toxic materials to "set the standard which most adequately assures, to the extent feasible, on the basis of the best available evidence, that no employee will suffer material impairment of health or functional capacity. . . ."

In the Government's view, §3 (8)'s definition of the term "standard" has no legal significance or at best merely requires that a standard not be totally irrational. It takes the position that §6 (b)(5) is controlling and that it requires OSHA to promulgate a standard that either gives an absolute assurance of safety for each and every worker or reduces exposures to the lowest level feasible. The Government interprets "feasible" as meaning technologically achievable at a cost that would not impair the viability of the industries subject to the regulation. The respondent industry representatives, on the other hand, argue that the Court of Appeals was correct in holding that the "reasonably necessary and appropriate" language of §3 (8), along with the feasibility requirement of §6 (b)(5), requires the Agency to quantify both the costs and the benefits of a proposed rule and to conclude that they are roughly commensurate.

In our view, it is not necessary to decide whether either the Government or industry is entirely correct. For we think it is clear that §3 (8) does apply to all permanent standards promulgated under the Act and that it requires the Secretary, before issuing any standard, to determine that it is reasonably necessary and appropriate to remedy a significant risk of material health impairment. Only after the Secretary has made the threshold determination that such a risk exists with respect to a toxic substance, would it be necessary to decide whether § 6 (b)(5) requires him to select the most protective standard he can consistent with economic and technological feasibility, or whether, as respondents argue, the benefits of the regulation must be commensurate with the costs of its implementation. Because the Secretary did not make the required threshold finding in these cases, we have no occasion to determine whether costs must be weighed against benefits in an appropriate case.

[An extensive analysis of the statutory language, here omitted, concluded with the following paragraph:]

If the Government were correct in arguing that neither § 3 (8) nor § 6 (b)(5) requires that the risk from a toxic substance be quantified sufficiently to enable the Secretary to characterize it as significant in an understandable way, the statute would make such a "sweeping delegation of legislative power" that it might be unconstitutional under the Court's reasoning in *A.L.A. Schechter Poultry Corp. v. United States,* 295 U.S. 495, 539, and *Panama Refining Co. v. Ryan,* 293 U.S. 388. A construction of the statute that avoids this kind of open-ended grant should certainly be favored.

. . . .

The judgment of the Court of Appeals remanding the petition for review to the Secretary for further proceedings is affirmed. *It is so ordered.* [Chief Justice Burger and Justice Powell filed concurring opinions.]

MR. JUSTICE REHNQUIST, concurring in the judgment.

The statutory provision at the center of the present controversy, § 6(b)(5) of the Occupational Safety and Health Act of 1970, states, in relevant part, that the Secretary of Labor

> ". . . in promulgating standards dealing with toxic materials or harmful physical agents . . . shall set the standard which most adequately assures, *to the extent feasible,* on the basis of the best available evidence, that no employee will suffer material impairment of health or functional capacity even if such employee has regular exposure to the hazard dealt with by such standard for the period of his working life." 84 Stat. 1594, 29 U.S.C. § 655(b)(5) (emphasis added).

According to the Secretary, who is one of the petitioners herein, § 6(b)(5) imposes upon him an absolute duty, in regulating harmful substances like benzene for which no safe level is known, to set the standard for permissible exposure at the lowest level that "can be achieved at bearable cost with available technology." While the Secretary does not attempt to refine the concept of "bearable cost," he apparently believes that a proposed standard is economically feasible so long as its impact "will not be such as to threaten the financial welfare of the affected firms or the general economy."

Respondents reply, and the lower court agreed, that § 6(b)(5) must be read in light of another provision in the same act, § 3(8), which defines an "occupational health and safety standard" as

> ". . . a standard which requires conditions, or the adoption or use of one or more practices, means, methods, operations, or processes, reasonably necessary or

appropriate to provide safe or healthful employment and places of employment."
84 Stat. 1591, 29 U.S.C. §652(8).

According to respondents, §6 (b)(5), as tempered by §3 (8), requires the
Secretary to demonstrate that any particular health standard is justifiable on the
basis of a rough balancing of costs and benefits.

In considering these alternative interpretations, my colleagues manifest a
good deal of uncertainty, and ultimately divide over whether the Secretary
produced sufficient evidence that the proposed standard for benzene will result
in any appreciable benefits at all. This uncertainty, I would suggest, is eminently
justified, since I believe that this litigation presents the Court with what has to be
one of the most difficult issues that could confront a decisionmaker: whether the
statistical possibility of future deaths should ever be disregarded in light of the
economic costs of preventing those deaths. I would also suggest that the widely
varying positions advanced in the briefs of the parties and in the opinions of
Mr. Justice Stevens, The Chief Justice, Mr. Justice Powell, and Mr. Justice
Marshall demonstrate, perhaps better than any other fact, that Congress, the
governmental body best suited and most obligated to make the choice confronting us in this litigation, has improperly delegated that choice to the Secretary of
Labor and, derivatively, to this Court.

I

In his Second Treatise of Civil Government, published in 1690, John Locke
wrote that "[the] power of the legislative, being derived from the people by a
positive voluntary grant and institution, can be no other than what that positive
grant conveyed, which being only to make laws, and not to make legislators, the
legislative can have no power to transfer their authority of making laws and place
it in other hands." Two hundred years later, this Court expressly recognized the
existence of and the necessity for limits on Congress' ability to delegate its
authority to representatives of the Executive Branch: "That Congress cannot
delegate legislative power to the President is a principle universally recognized
as vital to the integrity and maintenance of the system of government ordained
by the Constitution." Field v. Clark, 143 U.S. 649, 692 (1892).

During the third and fourth decades of this century, this Court within a relatively short period of time struck down several Acts of Congress on the grounds
that they exceeded the authority of Congress under the Commerce Clause or
under the nondelegation principle of separation of powers, and at the same
time struck down state statutes because they violated "substantive" due process
or interfered with interstate commerce. When many of these decisions were later
overruled, the principle that Congress could not simply transfer its legislative
authority to the Executive fell under a cloud. Yet in my opinion decisions such as
Panama Refining Co. v. Ryan, 293 U.S. 388 (1935), suffer from none of the
excesses of judicial policymaking that plagued some of the other decisions of
that era. The many later decisions that have upheld congressional delegations of
authority to the Executive Branch have done so largely on the theory that Congress may wish to exercise its authority in a particular field, but because the field
is sufficiently technical, the ground to be covered sufficiently large, and the
Members of Congress themselves not necessarily expert in the area in which

they choose to legislate, the most that may be asked under the separation-of-powers doctrine is that Congress lay down the general policy and standards that animate the law, leaving the agency to refine those standards, "fill in the blanks," or apply the standards to particular cases. These decisions, to my mind, simply illustrate the above-quoted principle stated more than 50 years ago by Mr. Chief Justice Taft that delegations of legislative authority must be judged "according to common sense and the inherent necessities of the governmental co-ordination."

Viewing the legislation at issue here in light of these principles, I believe that it fails to pass muster. Read literally, the relevant portion of § 6 (b) (5) is completely precatory, admonishing the Secretary to adopt the most protective standard if he can, but excusing him from that duty if he cannot. In the case of a hazardous substance for which a "safe" level is either unknown or impractical, the language of § 6 (b) (5) gives the Secretary absolutely no indication where on the continuum of relative safety he should draw his line. Especially in light of the importance of the interests at stake, I have no doubt that the provision at issue, standing alone, would violate the doctrine against uncanalized delegations of legislative power. For me the remaining question, then, is whether additional standards are ascertainable from the legislative history or statutory context of § 6 (b) (5) or, if not, whether such a standardless delegation was justifiable in light of the "inherent necessities" of the situation.

II

One of the primary sources looked to by this Court in adding gloss to an otherwise broad grant of legislative authority is the legislative history of the statute in question. [In this part of his concurrence, Justice Rehnquist examined the legislative history in some detail, only to conclude as follows:]

In sum, the legislative history contains nothing to indicate that the language "to the extent feasible" does anything other than render what had been a clear, if somewhat unrealistic, standard largely, if not entirely, precatory. There is certainly nothing to indicate that these words, as used in § 6 (b) (5), are limited to technological and economic feasibility. When Congress has wanted to limit the concept of feasibility in this fashion, it has said so, as is evidenced in a statute enacted the same week as the provision at issue here. I also question whether the Secretary wants to assume the duties such an interpretation would impose upon him. In these cases, for example, the Secretary actually declined to adopt a standard lower than 1 ppm for some industries, not because it was economically or technologically infeasible, but rather because "different levels for different industries would result in serious administrative difficulties." 43 Fed. Reg. 5947 (1978). See also *ante,* at 650 (plurality opinion). If § 6 (b) (5) authorizes the Secretary to reject a more protective standard in the interest of administrative feasibility, I have little doubt that he could reject such standards for any reason whatsoever, including even political feasibility.

III

In prior cases this Court has looked to sources other than the legislative history to breathe life into otherwise vague delegations of legislative power. In *American Power & Light Co. v. SEC,* 329 U.S. 90, 104 (1946), for example, this Court concluded that certain seemingly vague delegations "derive[d] much meaning-ful content from the purpose of the Act, its factual background and the statutory context in which they appear." Here, however, there is little or nothing in the remaining provisions of the Occupational Safety and Health Act to provide specificity to the feasibility criterion in §6 (b)(5). It may be true, as suggested by Mr. Justice Marshall, that the Act as a whole expresses a distinct preference for safety over dollars. But that expression of preference, as I read it, falls far short of the proposition that the Secretary must eliminate marginal or insignificant risks of material harm right down to an industry's breaking point. . . .

In some cases where broad delegations of power have been examined, this Court has upheld those delegations because of the delegatee's residual author-ity over particular subjects of regulation. In *United States v. Curtiss-Wright Export Corp.,* 299 U.S. 304, 307 (1936), this Court upheld a statute authorizing the President to prohibit the sale of arms to certain countries if he found that such a prohibition would "contribute to the reestablishment of peace." This Court reasoned that, in the area of foreign affairs Congress "must often accord to the President a degree of discretion and freedom from statutory restriction which would not be admissible were domestic affairs alone involved." *Id.,* at 320. Similarly, *United States v. Mazurie,* 419 U.S. 544 (1975), upheld a broad delega-tion of authority to various Indian tribes to regulate the introduction of liquor into Indian country. According to *Mazurie* limitations on Congress' authority to delegate legislative power are "less stringent in cases where the entity exercising the delegated authority itself possesses independent authority over the subject matter." *Id.,* at 556-557. In the present cases, however, neither the Executive Branch in general nor the Secretary in particular enjoys any independent authority over the subject matter at issue.

Finally, as indicated earlier, in some cases this Court has abided by a rule of necessity, upholding broad delegations of authority where it would be "unrea-sonable and impracticable to compel Congress to prescribe detailed rules" regarding a particular policy or situation. *American Power & Light Co. v. SEC,* 329 U.S., at 105. See also *Buttfield v. Stranahan,* 192 U.S. 470, 496 (1904). But no need for such an evasive standard as "feasibility" is apparent in the present cases. In drafting §6(b)(5), Congress was faced with a clear, if difficult, choice between balancing statistical lives and industrial resources or authorizing the Secretary to elevate human life above all concerns save massive dislocation in an affected industry. That Congress recognized the difficulty of this choice is clear from the previously noted remark of Senator Saxbe, who stated that "[when] we come to saying that an employer must guarantee that such an employee is protected from any possible harm, I think it will be one of the most difficult areas we are going to have to ascertain." 116 Cong. Rec. 36522 (1970), Leg. Hist. 345. That Congress chose, intentionally or unintentionally, to pass this difficult choice on to the Secretary is evident from the spectral quality of the standard it selected and is capsulized in Senator Saxbe's unfulfilled promise that "the terms that we are passing back and forth are going to have to be identified." *Ibid.*

IV

As formulated and enforced by this Court, the nondelegation doctrine serves three important functions. First, and most abstractly, it ensures to the extent consistent with orderly governmental administration that important choices of social policy are made by Congress, the branch of our Government most responsive to the popular will. *See Arizona v. California,* 373 U.S. 546, 626 (1963) (Harlan, J., dissenting in part); *United States v. Robel,* 389 U.S. 258, 276 (1967) (BRENNAN, J., concurring in result). Second, the doctrine guarantees that, to the extent Congress finds it necessary to delegate authority, it provides the recipient of that authority with an "intelligible principle" to guide the exercise of the delegated discretion. See *J.W. Hampton & Co. v. United States,* 276 U.S., at 409; *Panama Refining Co. v. Ryan,* 293 U.S., at 430. Third, and derivative of the second, the doctrine ensures that courts charged with reviewing the exercise of delegated legislative discretion will be able to test that exercise against ascertainable standards. See *Arizona v. California, supra,* at 626 (Harlan, J., dissenting in part); *American Power & Light Co. v. SEC, supra,* at 106.

I believe the legislation at issue here fails on all three counts. The decision whether the law of diminishing returns should have any place in the regulation of toxic substances is quintessentially one of legislative policy. For Congress to pass that decision on to the Secretary in the manner it did violates, in my mind, John Locke's caveat — reflected in the cases cited earlier in this opinion — that legislatures are to make laws, not legislators. Nor, as I think the prior discussion amply demonstrates, do the provisions at issue or their legislative history provide the Secretary with any guidance that might lead him to his somewhat tentative conclusion that he must eliminate exposure to benzene as far as technologically and economically possible. Finally, I would suggest that the standard of "feasibility" renders meaningful judicial review impossible.

We ought not to shy away from our judicial duty to invalidate unconstitutional delegations of legislative authority solely out of concern that we should thereby reinvigorate discredited constitutional doctrines of the pre-New Deal era. If the nondelegation doctrine has fallen into the same desuetude as have substantive due process and restrictive interpretations of the Commerce Clause, it is, as one writer has phrased it, "a case of death by association." J. Ely, *Democracy and Distrust, A Theory of Judicial Review* 133 (1980). Indeed, a number of observers have suggested that this Court should once more take up its burden of ensuring that Congress does not unnecessarily delegate important choices of social policy to politically unresponsive administrators. Other observers, as might be imagined, have disagreed.

If we are ever to reshoulder the burden of ensuring that Congress itself make the critical policy decisions, these are surely the cases in which to do it. It is difficult to imagine a more obvious example of Congress simply avoiding a choice which was both fundamental for purposes of the statute and yet politically so divisive that the necessary decision or compromise was difficult, if not impossible, to hammer out in the legislative forge. Far from detracting from the substantive authority of Congress, a declaration that the first sentence of §6 (b)(5) of the Occupational Safety and Health Act constitutes an invalid delegation to the Secretary of Labor would preserve the authority of Congress. If Congress wishes to legislate in an area which it has not previously sought to enter, it will in today's political world undoubtedly run into opposition no matter how the legislation is formulated. But that is the very essence of legislative authority under our system. It is the hard choices, and not the filling in of the blanks, which must be made by the elected representatives of the people. When fundamental policy decisions underlying important legislation about to be enacted are to be made, the buck stops with Congress and the President insofar as he exercises his constitutional role in the legislative process.

[Justice Rehnquist concluded by arguing that the Court should "invalidate the first sentence of §6(b)(5)" thereby forcing the Secretary to choose "between setting a safe standard or setting no standard at all."]

MR. JUSTICE MARSHALL, with whom MR. JUSTICE BRENNAN, MR. JUSTICE WHITE, and MR. JUSTICE BLACKMUN join, dissenting.

In cases of statutory construction, this Court's authority is limited. If the statutory language and legislative intent are plain, the judicial inquiry is at an end. Under our jurisprudence, it is presumed that ill-considered or unwise legislation will be corrected through the democratic process; a court is not permitted to distort a statute's meaning in order to make it conform with the Justices' own views of sound social policy.

Today's decision flagrantly disregards these restrictions on judicial authority. The plurality ignores the plain meaning of the Occupational Safety and Health Act of 1970 in order to bring the authority of the Secretary of Labor in line with the plurality's own views of proper regulatory policy. The unfortunate consequence is that the Federal Government's efforts to protect American workers from cancer and other crippling diseases may be substantially impaired. . . .

QUESTIONS

1. Did Congress fail in its duty to make policy choices in this case? If so, why did it do so?
2. What should a court do in such a situation? Infer congressional intent as well as possible? Invalidate the whole statute? Adopt defaults?
3. How does Justice Rehnquist reconcile all the cases upholding vague delegations? Is it consistent with the theory of the nondelegation doctrine for him to distinguish cases where:
   a. factual background and statutory context provide specificity,
   b. there is pre-existing administrative practice,
   c. the delegatee has "residual authority," or
   d. a rule of necessity applies?
4. How did the plurality make use of the nondelegation doctrine?
5. Should the application of the nondelegation doctrine depend, at least in part, on the nature of the delegation? For an argument that it should, at least when the power to impose taxes or "user fees" has been delegated to an agency, *see* Ronald J. Krotoszynski, Jr., *Reconsidering the Nondelegation Doctrine: Universal Service, the Power to Tax, and the Ratification Doctrine*, 80 IND. L.J. 239 (2005).

NOTE ON MISTRETTA v. UNITED STATES

The Court returned to the nondelegation issue in *Mistretta v. United States*, 488 U.S. 361 (1989). All members of the Court, except Justice Scalia, joined an opinion that rejected a claim that the Sentencing Guidelines (governing the imposition of criminal penalties for federal crimes) promulgated by the United

States Sentencing Commission (composed in part of Article III judges) were unconstitutional. The Court rejected, *id.* at 379, a claim that the delegation was improper:

> The Act sets forth more than merely an "intelligible principle" or minimal standards. One court has aptly put it: "The statute outlines the policies which prompted establishment of the Commission, explains what the Commission should do and how it should do it, and sets out specific directives to govern particular situations."
>
> Developing proportionate penalties for hundreds of different crimes by a virtually limitless array of offenders is precisely the sort of intricate, labor-intensive task for which delegation to an expert body is especially appropriate. Although Congress has delegated significant discretion to the Commission to draw judgments from its analysis of existing sentencing practice and alternative sentencing models, "Congress is not confined to that method of executing its policy which involves the least possible delegation of discretion to administrative officers." We have no doubt that in the hands of the Commission "the criteria which Congress has supplied are wholly adequate for carrying out the general policy and purpose" of the Act.

In his dissent, Justice Scalia stated, *id.* at 416, that "I fully agree with the Court's rejection of petitioner's contention that the doctrine of unconstitutional delegation of legislative authority has been violated because of the lack of intelligible, congressionally prescribed standards to guide the Commission."

Justice Scalia then proceeded, however, to argue, *id.*, that:

> Precisely because the scope of delegation is largely uncontrollable by the courts, we must be particularly rigorous in preserving the Constitution's structural restrictions that deter excessive delegation. The major one, it seems to me, is that the power to make law cannot be exercised by anyone other than Congress, except in conjunction with the lawful exercise of executive or judicial power.

Under Justice Scalia's view of those "structural restrictions," the power exercised by the Sentencing Commission was the unlawful making of law, *id.* at 420-21:

> The lawmaking function of the Sentencing Commission is completely divorced from any responsibility for execution of the law or adjudication of private rights under the law. It is divorced from responsibility for execution of the law not only because the Commission is not said to be "located in the Executive Branch" . . . ; but, more importantly, because the Commission neither exercises any executive power on its own, nor is subject to the control of the President who does. The only functions it performs, apart from prescribing the law, conducting the investigations useful and necessary for prescribing the law, and clarifying the intended application of the law that it prescribes, are data collection and intragovernmental advice giving and education. These latter activities — similar to functions performed by congressional agencies and even congressional staff — neither determine nor affect private rights, and do not constitute an exercise of governmental power. And the Commission's lawmaking is completely divorced from the exercise of judicial powers since, not being a court, it has no judicial powers itself, nor is it subject to the control of any other body with judicial powers. The power to make law at issue here, in other words, is not ancillary but quite naked. The situation is no different in principle from what would exist if Congress gave the same power of

writing sentencing laws to a congressional agency such as the General Accounting Office, or to members of its staff.

QUESTIONS

1. Is Justice Scalia's proposed approach to nondelegation limits on lawmaking preferable to the long-standing "intelligible principle" approach?
2. Another serious objection exists to the Sentencing Commission: federal judges served as United States Sentencing Commissioners and then, sitting as Article III judges, also heard challenges to both specific guidelines and the guidelines system as a whole. *See* Ronald J. Krotoszynski, Jr., *On the Danger of Wearing Two Hats:* Mistretta *and* Morrison *Revisited*, 38 WM. & MARY L. REV. 417 (1997). Federal judges who served as Sentencing Commissioners did not routinely recuse themselves from challenges to their own work product, thereby at least arguably denying litigants the benefit of a truly neutral tribunal. See *id.* at 422-40.

WHITMAN v. AMERICAN TRUCKING ASS'NS
531 U.S. 457 (2001)

JUSTICE SCALIA delivered the opinion of the Court.

These cases present the following questions: (1) Whether § 109(b)(1) of the Clean Air Act (CAA) delegates legislative power to the Administrator of the Environmental Protection Agency (EPA). (2) Whether the Administrator may consider the costs of implementation in setting national ambient air quality standards (NAAQS) under § 109(b)(1). (3) Whether the Court of Appeals had jurisdiction to review the EPA's interpretation of Part D of Title I of the CAA, with respect to implementing the revised ozone NAAQS. (4) If so, whether the EPA's interpretation of that part was permissible.

I

Section 109(a) of the CAA, as added, 84 Stat. 1679, and amended, 42 U.S.C. § 7409(a), requires the Administrator of the EPA to promulgate NAAQS for each air pollutant for which "air quality criteria" have been issued under § 108, 42 U.S.C. § 7408. Once a NAAQS has been promulgated, the Administrator must review the standard (and the criteria on which it is based) "at five-year intervals" and make "such revisions . . . as may be appropriate." CAA § 109(d)(1), 42 U.S.C. § 7409(d)(1). These cases arose when, on July 18, 1997, the Administrator revised the NAAQS for particulate matter (PM) and ozone. American Trucking Associations, Inc., and its co-respondents in No. 99-1257—which include, in addition to other private companies, the States of Michigan, Ohio, and West Virginia—challenged the new standards in the Court of Appeals for the District of Columbia Circuit, pursuant to 42 U.S.C. § 7607(b)(1).

The District of Columbia Circuit accepted some of the challenges and rejected others. It agreed with the No. 99-1257 respondents (hereinafter respondents) that § 109(b)(1) delegated legislative power to the Administrator in contravention of the United States Constitution, Art. I, § 1, because it found that the EPA had interpreted the statute to provide no "intelligible principle" to guide the agency's exercise of authority. The court thought, however, that the EPA could perhaps avoid the unconstitutional delegation by adopting a restrictive construction of § 109(b)(1), so instead of declaring the section unconstitutional the court remanded the NAAQS to the agency. (On this delegation point, Judge Tatel dissented, finding the statute constitutional as written.) On the second issue that the Court of Appeals addressed, it unanimously rejected respondents' argument that the court should depart from the rule of *Lead Industries Assn., Inc. v. EPA,* 647 F.2d 1130, 1148 (CADC 1980), that the EPA may not consider the cost of implementing a NAAQS in setting the initial standard. It also rejected respondents' argument [regarding question (4) above, but rejected EPA's argument (3 above) that the court lacked jurisdiction to reach question (4)]. The Court of Appeals denied the EPA's suggestion for rehearing en banc, with five judges dissenting.

The Administrator and the EPA petitioned this Court for review of the first, third, and fourth questions described in the first paragraph of this opinion. Respondents conditionally cross-petitioned for review of the second question. We granted certiorari on both petitions [and] consolidated the cases for purposes of decision.

II

In *Lead Industries Assn., Inc. v. EPA,* the District of Columbia Circuit held that "economic considerations [may] play no part in the promulgation of ambient air quality standards under Section 109" of the CAA. In the present cases, the court adhered to that holding, as it had done on many other occasions. Respondents argue that these decisions are incorrect. We disagree; and since the first step in assessing whether a statute delegates legislative power is to determine what authority the statute confers, we address that issue of interpretation first and reach respondents' constitutional arguments in Part III, *infra.*

Section 109(b)(1) instructs the EPA to set primary ambient air quality standards "the attainment and maintenance of which . . . are requisite to protect the public health" with "an adequate margin of safety." 42 U.S.C. § 7409(b)(1). Were it not for the hundreds of pages of briefing respondents have submitted on the issue, one would have thought it fairly clear that this text does not permit the EPA to consider costs in setting the standards. The language, as one scholar has noted, "is absolute." D. Currie, *Air Pollution: Federal Law and Analysis* 4-15 (1981). The EPA, "based on" the information about health effects contained in the technical "criteria" documents compiled under § 108(a)(2), 42 U.S.C. § 7408(a)(2), is to identify the maximum airborne concentration of a pollutant that the public health can tolerate, decrease the concentration to provide an "adequate" margin of safety, and set the standard at that level. Nowhere are the costs of achieving such a standard made part of that initial calculation. Against this most natural of readings, respondents make a lengthy, spirited, but ultimately unsuccessful attack. [Here is omitted the Court's analysis and rejection of respondents' arguments that the EPA was statutorily authorized to consider implementation costs in setting NAAQS.]

It should be clear from what we have said that the canon requiring texts to be so construed as to avoid serious constitutional problems has no application here. No matter how severe the constitutional doubt, courts may choose only between reasonably available interpretations of a text. The text of § 109(b), interpreted in its statutory and historical context and with appreciation for its importance to the CAA as a whole, unambiguously bars cost considerations from the NAAQS-setting process, and thus ends the matter for us as well as the EPA. We therefore affirm the judgment of the Court of Appeals on this point.

Section 109(b)(1) of the CAA instructs the EPA to set "ambient air quality standards the attainment and maintenance of which in the judgment of the Administrator, based on [the] criteria [documents of § 108] and allowing an adequate margin of safety, are requisite to protect the public health." 42 U.S.C. § 7409(b)(1). The Court of Appeals held that this section as interpreted by the Administrator did not provide an "intelligible principle" to guide the EPA's exercise of authority in setting NAAQS. "[The] EPA," it said, "lacked any determinate criteria for drawing lines. It has failed to state intelligibly how much is too much." The court hence found that the EPA's interpretation (but not the statute itself) violated the nondelegation doctrine. We disagree.

In a delegation challenge, the constitutional question is whether the statute has delegated legislative power to the agency. Article I, § 1, of the Constitution vests "all legislative Powers herein granted . . . in a Congress of the United States." This text permits no delegation of those powers, *Loving v. United States,* 517 U.S. 748, 771 (1996); see *id.* at 776-777 (Scalia, J., concurring in part and concurring in judgment), and so we repeatedly have said that when Congress confers decisionmaking authority upon agencies *Congress* must "lay down by legislative act an intelligible principle to which the person or body authorized to [act] is directed to conform." *J.W. Hampton, Jr., & Co. v. United States,* 276 U.S. 394, 409 (1928). We have never suggested that an agency can cure an unlawful delegation of legislative power by adopting in its discretion a limiting construction of the statute. Both *Fahey v. Mallonee,* 332 U.S. 245 (1947), and *Lichter v. United States,* 334 U.S. 742 (1948), mention agency regulations in the course of their nondelegation discussions, but *Lichter* did so because a subsequent Congress had incorporated the regulations into a revised version of the statute, *ibid.,* and *Fahey* because the customary practices in the area, implicitly incorporated into the statute, were reflected in the regulations. 332 U.S. at 250. The idea that an agency can cure an unconstitutionally standardless delegation of power by declining to exercise some of that power seems to us internally contradictory. The very choice of which portion of the power to exercise — that is to say, the prescription of the standard that Congress had omitted — would *itself* be an exercise of the forbidden legislative authority. Whether the statute delegates legislative power is a question for the courts, and an agency's voluntary self-denial has no bearing upon the answer.

We agree with the Solicitor General that the text of § 109(b)(1) of the CAA at a minimum requires that "for a discrete set of pollutants and based on published air quality criteria that reflect the latest scientific knowledge, [the] EPA must establish uniform national standards at a level that is requisite to protect public health from the adverse effects of the pollutant in the ambient air." Requisite, in turn, "means sufficient, but not more than necessary." These limits on the EPA's discretion are strikingly similar to the ones we approved in *Touby v. United States,* 500 U.S. 160 (1991), which permitted the Attorney General to designate a drug as a controlled substance for purposes of criminal drug enforcement if doing so was "'necessary to avoid an imminent hazard to the public safety.'" *Id.* at 163. They also resemble the Occupational Safety and Health Act provision requiring the agency to "'set the standard which most adequately assures, to the extent feasible, on the basis of the best available evidence, that no employee will suffer any impairment of health'" — which the Court upheld in *Industrial Union Dept., AFL-CIO v. American Petroleum Institute,* 448 U.S. 607, 646 (1980), and which even then-Justice Rehnquist, who alone in that case thought the statute violated the nondelegation doctrine, see *id.* at 671 (opinion concurring in judgment), would have upheld if, like the statute here, it did not permit economic costs to be considered. *See American Textile Mfrs. Institute, Inc. v. Donovan,* 452 U.S. 490, 545 (1981) (REHNQUIST, J., dissenting).

The scope of discretion § 109(b)(1) allows is in fact well within the outer limits of our nondelegation precedents. In the history of the Court we have found the requisite "intelligible principle" lacking in only two statutes, one of which provided literally no guidance for the exercise of discretion, and the other of which conferred authority to regulate the entire economy on the basis of no more precise a standard than stimulating the economy by assuring "fair competition." *See Panama Refining Co. v. Ryan,* 293 U.S. 388 (1935); *A.L.A. Schechter Poultry Corp. v. United States,* 295 U.S. 495 (1935). We have, on the other hand, upheld the validity of § 11(b)(2) of the Public Utility Holding Company Act of 1935, 49 Stat. 821, which gave the Securities and Exchange Commission authority to modify the structure of holding company systems so as to ensure that they are not "unduly or unnecessarily complicated" and do not "unfairly or inequitably distribute voting power among security holders." *American Power & Light Co. v. SEC,* 329 U.S. 90, 104 (1946). We have approved the wartime conferral of agency power to fix the prices of commodities at a level that "'will be generally fair and equitable and will effectuate the [in some respects conflicting] purposes of the Act.'" *Yakus v. United States,* 321 U.S. 414, 420, 423-426 (1944). And we have found an "intelligible principle" in various statutes authorizing regulation in the "public interest." *See,* e.g., *National Broadcasting Co. v. United States,* 319 U.S. 190, 225-226 (1943) (FCC's power to regulate airwaves); *New York Central Securities Corp. v. United States,* 287 U.S. 12, 24-25 (1932) (ICC's power to approve railroad consolidations). In short, we have "almost never felt qualified to second-guess Congress regarding the permissible degree of policy judgment that can be left to those executing or applying the law." *Mistretta v. United States,* 488 U.S. 361, 416 (1989) (SCALIA, J., dissenting); see *id.* at 373 (majority opinion).

It is true enough that the degree of agency discretion that is acceptable varies according to the scope of the power congressionally conferred. See *Loving v. United States, supra,* at 772-773; *United States v. Mazurie,* 419 U.S. 544, 556-557 (1975). While Congress need not provide any direction to the EPA regarding the manner in which it is to define "country elevators," which are to be exempt from new-stationary-source regulations governing grain elevators, *see* § 7411(i), it must provide substantial guidance on setting air standards that affect the entire national economy. But even in sweeping regulatory schemes we have never demanded, as the Court of Appeals did here, that statutes provide a "determinate criterion" for saying "how much [of the regulated harm] is too much." In *Touby,* for example, we did not require the statute to decree how "imminent" was too imminent, or how "necessary" was necessary enough, or even — most relevant here — how "hazardous" was too hazardous. 500 U.S. at 165-167.

Similarly, the statute at issue in *Lichter* authorized agencies to recoup "excess profits" paid under wartime Government contracts, yet we did not insist that Congress specify how much profit was too much. 334 U.S. at 783-786. It is therefore not conclusive for delegation purposes that, as respondents argue, ozone and particulate matter are "nonthreshold" pollutants that inflict a continuum of adverse health effects at any airborne concentration greater than zero, and hence require the EPA to make judgments of degree. "[A] certain degree of discretion, and thus of lawmaking, inheres in most executive or judicial action." *Mistretta v. United States, supra,* at 417 (SCALIA, J., dissenting) (emphasis deleted); see 488 U.S. at 378-379 (majority opinion). Section 109(b)(1) of the CAA, which to repeat we interpret as requiring the EPA to set air quality standards at the level that is "requisite" — that is, not lower or higher than is necessary — to protect the public health with an adequate margin of safety, fits comfortably within the scope of discretion permitted by our precedent.

We therefore reverse the judgment of the Court of Appeals remanding for reinterpretation that would avoid a supposed delegation of legislative power. It will remain for the Court of Appeals — on the remand that we direct for other reasons — to dispose of any other preserved challenge to the NAAQS under the judicial-review provisions contained in 42 U.S.C. § 7607(d)(9).

IV

The final two issues on which we granted certiorari concern the EPA's authority to implement the revised ozone NAAQS in areas whose ozone levels currently exceed the maximum level permitted by that standard. [Omitted.] . . .

To summarize our holdings in these unusually complex cases: (1) The EPA may not consider implementation costs in setting primary and secondary NAAQS under § 109(b) of the CAA. (2) Section 109(b)(1) does not delegate legislative power to the EPA in contravention of Art. I, § 1, of the Constitution. (3) The Court of Appeals had jurisdiction to review the EPA's interpretation of Part D of Title I of the CAA, relating to the implementation of the revised ozone NAAQS. (4) The EPA's interpretation of that Part is unreasonable.

The judgment of the Court of Appeals is affirmed in part and reversed in part, and the cases are remanded for proceedings consistent with this opinion. It is so ordered.

JUSTICE THOMAS, concurring.

I agree with the majority that § 109's directive to the agency is no less an "intelligible principle" than a host of other directives that we have approved. I also agree that the Court of Appeals' remand to the agency to make its own corrective interpretation does not accord with our understanding of the delegation issue. I write separately, however, to express my concern that there may nevertheless be a genuine constitutional problem with § 109, a problem which the parties did not address.

The parties to this case who briefed the constitutional issue wrangled over constitutional doctrine with barely a nod to the text of the Constitution. Although this Court since 1928 has treated the "intelligible principle" requirement as the only constitutional limit on congressional grants of power to administrative agencies, *see J.W. Hampton, Jr., & Co. v. United States,* 276 U.S. 394, 409

(1928), the Constitution does not speak of "intelligible principles." Rather, it speaks in much simpler terms: "*All* legislative Powers herein granted shall be vested in a Congress." U.S. Const., Art. 1, § 1 (emphasis added). I am not convinced that the intelligible principle doctrine serves to prevent all cessions of legislative power. I believe that there are cases in which the principle is intelligible and yet the significance of the delegated decision is simply too great for the decision to be called anything other than "legislative."

As it is, none of the parties to this case has examined the text of the Constitution or asked us to reconsider our precedents on cessions of legislative power. On a future day, however, I would be willing to address the question whether our delegation jurisprudence has strayed too far from our Founders' understanding of separation of powers.

JUSTICE STEVENS, with whom JUSTICE SOUTER joins, concurring in part and concurring in the judgment.

Section 109(b)(1) delegates to the Administrator of the Environmental Protection Agency (EPA) the authority to promulgate national ambient air quality standards (NAAQS). In Part III of its opinion, the Court convincingly explains why the Court of Appeals erred when it concluded that § 109 effected "an unconstitutional delegation of legislative power." I wholeheartedly endorse the Court's result and endorse its explanation of its reasons, albeit with the following caveat.

The Court has two choices. We could choose to articulate our ultimate disposition of this issue by frankly acknowledging that the power delegated to the EPA is "legislative" but nevertheless conclude that the delegation is constitutional because adequately limited by the terms of the authorizing statute. Alternatively, we could pretend, as the Court does, that the authority delegated to the EPA is somehow not "legislative power." Despite the fact that there is language in our opinions that supports the Court's articulation of our holding, I am persuaded that it would be both wiser and more faithful to what we have actually done in delegation cases to admit that agency rulemaking authority is "legislative power."

The proper characterization of governmental power should generally depend on the nature of the power, not on the identity of the person exercising it. *See Black's Law Dictionary* 899 (6th ed. 1990) (defining "legislation" as, *inter alia,* "formulation of rules for the future"); 1 K. Davis & R. Pierce, Administrative Law Treatise § 2.3, p. 37 (3d ed. 1994) ("If legislative power means the power to make rules of conduct that bind everyone based on resolution of major policy issues, scores of agencies exercise legislative power routinely by promulgating what are candidly called 'legislative rules'"). If the NAAQS that the EPA promulgated had been prescribed by Congress, everyone would agree that those rules would be the product of an exercise of "legislative power." The same characterization is appropriate when an agency exercises rulemaking authority pursuant to a permissible delegation from Congress.

My view is not only more faithful to normal English usage, but is also fully consistent with the text of the Constitution. In Article I, the Framers vested "All legislative Powers" in the Congress, Art. I., § 1, just as in Article II they vested the "executive Power" in the President, Art. II, § 1. Those provisions do not purport to limit the authority of either recipient of power to delegate authority to others. *See Bowsher v. Synar,* 478 U.S. 714, 752 (1986) (STEVENS, J., concurring in judgment) ("Despite the statement in Article I of the Constitution that 'All legislative powers herein granted shall be vested in a Congress of the United States,' it is far from novel to acknowledge that independent agencies do indeed exercise legislative powers"); *INS v. Chadha,* 462 U.S. 919, 985-986 (1983) (WHITE, J., dissenting) ("Legislative power can be exercised by independent agencies and Executive departments . . ."); 1 Davis § 2.6, p. 66 ("The Court was probably mistaken from the outset in interpreting Article I's grant of power to Congress as an implicit limit on Congress' authority to delegate legislative power"). Surely the authority granted to members of the Cabinet and federal law enforcement agents is properly characterized as "Executive" even though not exercised by the President. Cf. *Morrison v. Olson,* 487 U.S. 654, 705-706 (1988) (SCALIA, J., dissenting) (arguing that the independent counsel exercised "executive power" unconstrained by the President).

It seems clear that an executive agency's exercise of rulemaking authority pursuant to a valid delegation from Congress is "legislative." As long as the delegation provides a sufficiently intelligible principle, there is nothing inherently unconstitutional about it. Accordingly, while I join Parts I, II, and IV of the Court's opinion, and agree with almost everything said in Part III, I would hold that when Congress enacted § 109, it effected a constitutional delegation of legislative power to the EPA.

JUSTICE BREYER, concurring in part and concurring in the judgment.

I join Parts I, III, and IV of the Court's opinion. I also agree with the Court's determination in Part II that the Clean Air Act does not permit the Environmental Protection Agency to consider the economic costs of implementation when setting national ambient air quality standards under § 109(b)(1) of the Act. But I would not rest this conclusion solely upon § 109's language or upon a presumption, such as the Court's presumption that any authority the Act grants the EPA to consider costs must flow from a "textual commitment" that is "clear." [Analysis omitted.]

Although I rely more heavily than does the Court upon legislative history and alternative sources of statutory flexibility, I reach the same ultimate conclusion. Section 109 does not delegate to the EPA authority to base the national ambient air quality standards, in whole or in part, upon three economic costs of compliance.

QUESTIONS

1. Why did the Court hold that an agency cannot come up with its own standard to avoid nondelegation doctrine concerns?
2. What does it mean to say that "the degree of agency discretion that is acceptable varies according to the scope of the power congressionally conferred" (p. 383)?
3. In light of the delegations upheld in *Industrial Union Dept., American Trucking Assns,* and the cases described on pages 383-384 (*American Power & Light Co. v. SEC, Yakus v. United States,* and *National Broadcasting Co. v. United States*), is there really anything left to the nondelegation doctrine? If so, what?
4. How would Chief Justice Rehnquist answer question 3? Justice Thomas? Justice Stevens?

5. Why can't the nondelegation doctrine be used as a canon of construction in the interpretation of statutes? Compare the plurality opinion in *American Petroleum Institute, supra* at p. 370, with the *American Trucking Assns.* opinion at p. 380. You may wish to revisit this question in light of the cases later in this book on judicial review of agency determinations of law, *infra*, pp. 524-543.

6. The nondelegation doctrine has followed different paths in the constitutional law of the various states. *See generally*, Jim Rossi, *Institutional Design and the Lingering Legacy of Antifederalist Separation of Powers Ideals in the States*, 52 Vand. L. Rev. 1167, 1191-1200 (1999). In a significant number of states, statutes are periodically struck down on nondelegation grounds. E.g., *Texas Boll Weevil Eradication Foundation, Inc. v. Lewellen*, 952 S.W.2d 454, 465-79 (Tex. 1997); *Askew v. Cross Key Waterways*, 370 So. 2d 913 (Fla. 1979). The nondelegation doctrine has lurched back and forth in Kentucky. *Compare Commonwealth v. Associated Industries of Kentucky*, 370 S.W.2d 584 (Ky. 1963) (includes treatment of what John Locke would think if he were alive in 1963) *with Miller v. Covington Development Authority*, 539 S.W.2d 1 (Ky. 1976) and *Legislative Research Commission v. Brown*, 664 S.W.2d 907, 915 (Ky. 1984)

NOTE ON THE CONGRESSIONAL DELEGATION OF POWER TO A PRIVATE ENTITY

Notwithstanding the minimally restrictive extent of the nondelegation doctrine reaffirmed in *Whitman, supra,* the Supreme Court has established a strong constitutional limit on congressional delegation when the delegation is to a private — that is, a non-governmental — regulator. In *Carter v. Carter Coal Co.*, 298 U.S. 238, 310-11 (1936), the Court concluded that the statute at issue "delegates the power to fix maximum hours of labor to a part of the producers and the miners — namely, 'the producers of more than two-thirds the annual national tonnage production for the preceding calendar year' and 'more than one-half the mine workers employed'; and to producers of more than two-thirds of the district annual tonnage during the preceding calendar year and a majority of the miners, there is delegated the power to fix minimum wages for the district or group of districts." The Court then concluded that this delegation to private parties was unconstitutional:

> The power conferred upon the majority is, in effect, the power to regulate the affairs of an unwilling minority. This is legislative delegation in its most obnoxious form; for it is not even delegation to an official or an official body, presumptively disinterested, but to private persons whose interests may be and often are adverse to the interests of others in the same business. The record shows that the conditions of competition differ among the various localities. In some, coal dealers compete among themselves. In other localities, they also compete with the mechanical production of electrical energy and of natural gas. Some coal producers favor the code; others oppose it; and the record clearly indicates that this diversity of view arises from their conflicting and even antagonistic interests. The difference between producing coal and regulating its production is, of course, fundamental. The former is a private activity; the latter is necessarily a governmental function, since, in the very nature of things, one person may not be intrusted with the power to regulate the business of another, and especially of a competitor. And a statute which attempts to confer such power undertakes an intolerable and

unconstitutional interference with personal liberty and private property. The delegation is so clearly arbitrary, and so clearly a denial of rights safeguarded by the due process clause of the Fifth Amendment, that it is unnecessary to do more than refer to decisions of this court which foreclose the question.

Id. at 311 (citations omitted).

In *Department of Transportation v. Association of American Railroads*, 135 S. Ct. 1225 (2015), the Supreme Court returned to the question of the legality of Congress's delegation of the power "to issue 'metrics and standards' that address the performance and scheduling of passenger railroad services." *Id.* at 1228. This power had been granted to "the National Railroad Passenger Corporation, most often known as Amtrak" and the Federal Railroad Administration (FRA). *Id.* The Court of Appeals for the District of Columbia decided "that, for purposes of this dispute, Amtrak is a private entity and that Congress violated nondelegation principles in its grant of joint authority to Amtrak and the FRA." *Id.*

Section 207(a) of the Passenger Rail Investment and Improvement Act (PRIIA) defined the role of Amtrak in establishing metrics and standards for railroads:

> Within 180 days after the date of enactment of this Act, the Federal Railroad Administration and Amtrak shall jointly, in consultation with the Surface Transportation Board, rail carriers over whose rail lines Amtrak trains operate, States, Amtrak employees, nonprofit employee organizations representing Amtrak employees, and groups representing Amtrak passengers, as appropriate, develop new or improve existing metrics and minimum standards for measuring the performance and service quality of intercity passenger train operations, including cost recovery, on-time performance and minutes of delay, ridership, on-board services, stations, facilities, equipment, and other services.

122 Stat. 4907, 4916. The statute also included in § 207(d) a provision addressing the possibility of a lack of agreement as to appropriate metrics and standards:

> If the development of the metrics and standards is not completed within the 180-day period required by subsection (a), any party involved in the development of those standards may petition the Surface Transportation Board to appoint an arbitrator to assist the parties in resolving their disputes through binding arbitration.

Id., at 4917.

Justice Kennedy, writing for all members of the court except Justice Thomas, concluded that Amtrak is *not* a private person subject to the *Carter Coal* limits on congressional delegation. The decision of the Court of Appeals had:

> treated as controlling Congress' statutory command that Amtrak "'is not a department, agency, or instrumentality of the United States Government.'" [721 F.3d] at 675 (quoting 49 U.S.C. § 24301(a)(3)). The Court of Appeals also relied on Congress' pronouncement that Amtrak "'shall be operated and managed as a for-profit corporation.'" 721 F.3d, at 675 (quoting § 24301(a)(2)); see also *id.*, at 677 ("Though the federal government's involvement in Amtrak is considerable, Congress has both designated it a private corporation and instructed that it be

managed so as to maximize profit. In deciding Amtrak's status for purposes of congressional delegations, these declarations are dispositive")....

135 S. Ct. at 1231.

The Court began its analysis by explaining why the "premise" of the Court of Appeals decision was "erroneous": The Court stated that "Congressional pronouncements, though instructive as to matters within Congress' authority to address, are not dispositive of Amtrak's status as a governmental entity for purposes of separation of powers analysis under the Constitution." *Id.* (citation omitted). The Court then undertook its own "independent inquiry," *id.*, and decided that Amtrak is a "governmental entity":

> Given the combination of these unique features and its significant ties to the Government, Amtrak is not an autonomous private enterprise. Among other important considerations, its priorities, operations, and decisions are extensively supervised and substantially funded by the political branches. A majority of its Board is appointed by the President and confirmed by the Senate and is understood by the Executive to be removable by the President at will. Amtrak was created by the Government, is controlled by the Government, and operates for the Government's benefit. Thus, in its joint issuance of the metrics and standards with the FRA, Amtrak acted as a governmental entity for purposes of the Constitution's separation of powers provisions. And that exercise of governmental power must be consistent with the design and requirements of the Constitution, including those provisions relating to the separation of powers.

Id. at 1232-33.

The Court accordingly vacated the Court of Appeals decision and remanded so that the lower court could consider other objections to the constitutionality of the standards and metrics provision:

> On remand, the Court of Appeals, after identifying the issues that are properly preserved and before it, will then have the instruction of the analysis set forth here. Respondent argues that the selection of Amtrak's president, who is appointed "not by the President . . . but by the other eight Board Members," "call[s] into question Amtrak's structure under the Appointments Clause"; that § 207(d)'s arbitrator provision "is a plain violation of the nondelegation principle" and the Appointments Clause requiring invalidation of § 207(a); and that Congress violated the Due Process Clause by "giv[ing] a federally chartered, nominally private, for-profit corporation regulatory authority over its own industry." Petitioners, in turn, contend that "the metrics and standards do not reflect the exercise of 'rulemaking' authority or permit Amtrak to 'regulate other private entities,'" and thus do not raise nondelegation concerns. . . .

Id. at 1234.

Justice Alito concurred in the opinion and wrote an extensive decision in which he explained why "[r]ecognition that Amtrak is part of the Federal Government raises a host of constitutional questions." *Id.* First, he raised doubts about whether members of Amtrak's board conform to the requirements of the Constitution's "Oath and Commission clauses." See *id.* at 1235. The board members may not have taken an "oath or affirmation to support the Constitution," *id.*, and may not have received a commission. *See id.* Justice Alito also raised questions about the constitutionality of the use of an "arbitrator" in the event that Amtrak and the FRA were unable to agree on metrics and standards. See *id.* at 1236-37. If the arbitrator were a private actor, there would be serious nondelegation concerns. *Id.* at 1237-38. If the arbitrator were a public actor, there would be "serious questions under the Appointments Clause." *Id.* at 1238. The last constitutional concerns raised by Justice Alito related to Amtrak's President, whose appointment by board members may have violated the Appointments Clause. *Id.* at 1239-40.

Justice Thomas concurred only in the Court's judgment. See *id.* at 1240. He devoted much of his lengthy opinion to a discussion of "how far our modern separation-of-powers jurisprudence has departed from the original meaning of the Constitution." *Id.* at 1241. Much of that discussion presented Justice Thomas's view that an original understanding of the Constitution would require a prohibition on nondelegation that depends on the function being performed by an agency:

> The function at issue here is the formulation of generally applicable rules of private conduct. Under the original understanding of the Constitution, that function requires the exercise of legislative power. By corollary, the discretion inherent in executive power does *not* comprehend the discretion to formulate generally applicable rules of private conduct.

Id. at 1242.

THEORY APPLIED PROBLEM

In the 1996 Communications Act, Congress established a new entitlement program to "universal service." Intended to benefit low-income households, schools, libraries, and rural health care providers, the new statutory universal service mandate instructs the Federal Communications Commission to create a program that will support access to communications services for these groups, without specifying the precise services to be provided. See 47 U.S.C. § 254(c) ("Universal service is an evolving level of telecommunications services that the Commission shall establish periodically under this section, taking into account advances in telecommunications and information technologies and services"). Moreover, Congress does not specify a net amount to spend on universal service or define precisely how the revenue will be collected to pay for universal service (although Congress does identify the entities that must "contribute" to providing the service). See 47 U.S.C. § 254(d) ("Every telecommunications carrier that provides interstate telecommunications services shall contribute, on an equitable and non-discriminatory basis, to the specific, predictable, and sufficient mechanisms established by the Commission to preserve and advance universal service"). Would such a statutory mandate satisfy the "intelligible principle" rule that *American Trucking* reiterates and reaffirms? Does it matter that Congress has delegated a kind of taxing authority to an agency? Should it matter? What is the best argument in favor of the proposition that the Universal Service Program satisfies the nondelegation doctrine's requirements? What is the best argument that it violates those requirements (even in the weaker modern form)?

D. THE LEGISLATIVE VETO

INS v. CHADHA
462 U.S. 919 (1983)

CHIEF JUSTICE BURGER delivered the opinion of the Court.

We granted certiorari in Nos. 80-2170 and 80-2171, and postponed consideration of the question of jurisdiction in No. 80-1832. Each presents a challenge to the constitutionality of the provision in §244(c)(2) of the Immigration and Nationality Act, 66 Stat. 216, as amended, 8 U.S.C. §1254(c)(2), authorizing one House of Congress, by resolution, to invalidate the decision of the Executive Branch, pursuant to authority delegated by Congress to the Attorney General of the United States, to allow a particular deportable alien to remain in the United States.

I

Chadha is an East Indian who was born in Kenya and holds a British passport. He was lawfully admitted to the United States in 1966 on a nonimmigrant student visa. His visa expired on June 30, 1972. On October 11, 1973, the District Director of the Immigration and Naturalization Service ordered Chadha to show cause why he should not be deported for having "remained in the United States for a longer time than permitted." Pursuant to §242(b) of the Immigration and Nationality Act (Act), 8 U.S.C. §1252(b), a deportation hearing was held before an Immigration Judge on January 11, 1974. Chadha conceded that he was deportable for overstaying his visa and the hearing was adjourned to enable him to file an application for suspension of deportation under §244(a)(1) of the Act, 8 U.S.C. §1254(a)(1). Section 244(a)(1), at the time in question, provided:

> "As hereinafter prescribed in this section, the Attorney General may, in his discretion, suspend deportation and adjust the status to that of an alien lawfully admitted for permanent residence, in the case of an alien who applies to the Attorney General for suspension of deportation and —
>
> (1) is deportable under any law of the United States except the provisions specified in paragraph (2) of this subsection; has been physically present in the United States for a continuous period of not less than seven years immediately preceding the date of such application, and proves that during all of such period he was and is a person of good moral character; and is a person whose deportation would, in the opinion of the Attorney General, result in extreme hardship to the alien or to his spouse, parent, or child, who is a citizen of the United States or an alien lawfully admitted for permanent residence."[1]

After Chadha submitted his application for suspension of deportation, the deportation hearing was resumed on February 7, 1974. On the basis of evidence

---

1. Congress delegated the major responsibilities for enforcement of the Immigration and Nationality Act to the Attorney General. 8 U.S.C. §1103(a). The Attorney General discharges his responsibilities through the Immigration and Naturalization Service, a division of the Department of Justice. *Ibid.*

adduced at the hearing, affidavits submitted with the application, and the results of a character investigation conducted by the INS, the Immigration Judge, on June 25, 1974, ordered that Chadha's deportation be suspended. The Immigration Judge found that Chadha met the requirements of §244(a)(1): he had resided continuously in the United States for over seven years, was of good moral character, and would suffer "extreme hardship" if deported.

Pursuant to §244(c)(1) of the Act, 8 U.S.C. §1254(c)(1), the Immigration Judge suspended Chadha's deportation and a report of the suspension was transmitted to Congress. Section 244(c)(1) provides:

> "Upon application by any alien who is found by the Attorney General to meet the requirements of subsection (a) of this section the Attorney General may in his discretion suspend deportation of such alien. If the deportation of any alien is suspended under the provisions of this subsection, a complete and detailed statement of the facts and pertinent provisions of law in the case shall be reported to the Congress with the reasons for such suspension. Such reports shall be submitted on the first day of each calendar month in which Congress is in session."

Once the Attorney General's recommendation for suspension of Chadha's deportation was conveyed to Congress, Congress had the power under §244(c)(2) of the Act, 8 U.S.C. §1254(c)(2), to veto[2] the Attorney General's determination that Chadha should not be deported. Section 244(c)(2) provides:

> "(2) In the case of an alien specified in paragraph (1) of subsection (a) of this subsection —
> if during the session of the Congress at which a case is reported, or prior to the close of the session of the Congress next following the session at which a case is reported, either the Senate or the House of Representatives passes a resolution stating in substance that it does not favor the suspension of such deportation, the Attorney General shall thereupon deport such alien or authorize the alien's voluntary departure at his own expense under the order of deportation in the manner provided by law. If, within the time above specified, neither the Senate nor the House of Representatives shall pass such a resolution, the Attorney General shall cancel deportation proceedings."

The June 25, 1974, order of the Immigration Judge suspending Chadha's deportation remained outstanding as a valid order for a year and a half. For reasons not disclosed by the record, Congress did not exercise the veto authority reserved to it under §244(c)(2) until the first session of the 94th Congress. This was the final session in which Congress, pursuant to §244(c)(2), could act to veto the Attorney General's determination that Chadha should not be deported. The session ended on December 19, 1975. Absent congressional action, Chadha's deportation proceedings would have been canceled after this date and his status adjusted to that of a permanent resident alien. See 8 U.S.C. §1254(d).

On December 12, 1975, Representative Eilberg, Chairman of the Judiciary Subcommittee on Immigration, Citizenship, and International Law, introduced

---

2. In constitutional terms, "veto" is used to describe the President's power under Art. I, §7, of the Constitution. *See Black's Law Dictionary* 1403 (5th ed. 1979). It appears, however, that congressional devices of the type authorized by §244(c)(2) have come to be commonly referred to as a "veto." We refer to the congressional "resolution" authorized by §244(c)(2) as a "one-House veto" of the Attorney General's decision to allow a particular deportable alien to remain in the United States.

a resolution opposing "the granting of permanent residence in the United States to [six] aliens," including Chadha. The resolution was referred to the House Committee on the Judiciary. On December 16, 1975, the resolution was discharged from further consideration by the House Committee on the Judiciary and submitted to the House of Representatives for a vote. The resolution had not been printed and was not made available to other Members of the House prior to or at the time it was voted on. So far as the record before us shows, the House consideration of the resolution was based on Representative Eilberg's statement from the floor that

> "[i]t was the feeling of the committee, after reviewing 340 cases, that the aliens contained in the resolution [Chadha and five others] did not meet these statutory requirements, particularly as it relates to hardship; and it is the opinion of the committee that their deportation should not be suspended."

The resolution was passed without debate or recorded vote. Since the House action was pursuant to § 244(c)(2), the resolution was not treated as an Art. I legislative act; it was not submitted to the Senate or presented to the President for his action.

After the House veto of the Attorney General's decision to allow Chadha to remain in the United States, the Immigration Judge reopened the deportation proceedings to implement the House order deporting Chadha. Chadha moved to terminate the proceedings on the ground that § 244(c)(2) is unconstitutional. The Immigration Judge held that he had no authority to rule on the constitutional validity of § 244(c)(2). On November 8, 1976, Chadha was ordered deported pursuant to the House action.

Chadha appealed the deportation order to the Board of Immigration Appeals, again contending that § 244(c)(2) is unconstitutional. The Board held that it had "no power to declare unconstitutional an act of Congress" and Chadha's appeal was dismissed.

Pursuant to § 106(a) of the Act, 8 U.S.C. § 1105a(a), Chadha filed a petition for review of the deportation order in the United States Court of Appeals for the Ninth Circuit. The Immigration and Naturalization Service agreed with Chadha's position before the Court of Appeals and joined him in arguing that § 244(c)(2) is unconstitutional. . . .

After full briefing and oral argument, the Court of Appeals held that the House was without constitutional authority to order Chadha's deportation; accordingly it directed the Attorney General "to cease and desist from taking any steps to deport this alien based upon the resolution enacted by the House of Representatives." 634 F.2d 408, 436 (1980). The essence of its holding was that § 244(c)(2) violates the constitutional doctrine of separation of powers.

We . . . now affirm.

II

Before we address the important question of the constitutionality of the one-House veto provision of § 244(c)(2), we first consider several challenges to the authority of this Court to resolve the issue raised. . . .

B. SEVERABILITY

Congress also contends that the provision for the one-House veto in § 244(c)(2) cannot be severed from § 244. Congress argues that if the provision for the one-House veto is held unconstitutional, all of § 244 must fall. If § 244 in its entirety is violative of the Constitution, it follows that the Attorney General has no authority to suspend Chadha's deportation under § 244(a)(1) and Chadha would be deported. From this, Congress argues that Chadha lacks standing to challenge the constitutionality of the one-House veto provision because he could receive no relief even if his constitutional challenge proves successful.

Only recently this Court reaffirmed that the invalid portions of a statute are to be severed "'[u]nless it is evident that the Legislature would not have enacted those provisions which are within its power, independently of that which is not.'" Here, however, we need not embark on that elusive inquiry since Congress itself has provided the answer to the question of severability in § 406 of the Immigration and Nationality Act, note following 8 U.S.C. § 1101, which provides:

> "If *any* particular provision of this Act, or the application thereof to *any* person or circumstance, is held invalid, *the remainder of the Act and the application of such provision to other persons or circumstances shall not be affected thereby.*" (Emphasis added.)

This language is unambiguous and gives rise to a presumption that Congress did not intend the validity of the Act as a whole, or of any part of the Act, to depend upon whether the veto clause of § 244(c)(2) was invalid. The one-House veto provision in § 244(c)(2) is clearly a "particular provision" of the Act as that language is used in the severability clause. Congress clearly intended "the remainder of the Act" to stand if "any particular provision" were held invalid. Congress could not have more plainly authorized the presumption that the provision for a one-House veto in § 244(c)(2) is severable from the remainder of § 244 and the Act of which it is a part.

[The Court reviewed "the legislative history of § 244" and determined that that history "supported" a conclusion that the legislative veto provision was severable. The Court also concluded that the determination that the provision was severable was supported by the Court's view that the administrative structure was "'fully operative' and workable."] . . . Congress' oversight of the exercise of this delegated authority is preserved since all such suspensions will continue to be reported to it under § 244(c)(1). Absent the passage of a bill to the contrary,[8] deportation proceedings will be canceled when the period specified in § 244(c)(2) has expired.[9] Clearly, § 244 survives as a workable administrative mechanism without the one-House veto.

---

8. Without the provision for one-House veto, Congress would presumably retain the power, during the time allotted in § 244(c)(2), to enact a law, in accordance with the requirements of Art. I of the Constitution, mandating a particular alien's deportation, unless, of course, other constitutional principles place substantive limitations on such action. *Cf.* Attorney General Jackson's attack on H. R. 9766, 76th Cong., 3d Sess. (1940), a bill to require the Attorney General to deport an individual alien. The Attorney General called the bill "an historical departure from an unbroken American practice and tradition. It would be the first time that an act of Congress singled out a named individual for deportation." S. Rep. No. 2031, 76th Cong., 3d Sess., pt. 1, p. 9 (1940) (reprinting Jackson's letter of June 18, 1940).

9. Without the one-House veto, § 244 resembles the "report and wait" provision approved by the Court in *Sibbach v. Wilson & Co.*, 312 U.S. 1 (1941). The statute examined in *Sibbach* provided that the newly promulgated Federal Rules of Civil Procedure "shall not take effect until they shall

We must also reject the contention that Chadha lacks standing because a consequence of his prevailing will advance the interests of the Executive Branch in a separation-of-powers dispute with Congress, rather than simply Chadha's private interests. Chadha has demonstrated "injury in fact and a substantial likelihood that the judicial relief requested will prevent or redress the claimed injury. . . ." *Duke Power Co. v. Carolina Environmental Study Group, Inc.*, 438 U.S. 59, 79 (1978). If the veto provision violates the Constitution, and is severable, the deportation order against Chadha will be canceled. Chadha therefore has standing to challenge the order of the Executive mandated by the House veto. . . .

III

A

We turn now to the question whether action of one House of Congress under § 244(c)(2) violates strictures of the Constitution. We begin, of course, with the presumption that the challenged statute is valid. Its wisdom is not the concern of the courts; if a challenged action does not violate the Constitution, it must be sustained:

> "Once the meaning of an enactment is discerned and its constitutionality determined, the judicial process comes to an end. We do not sit as a committee of review, nor are we vested with the power of veto." *Tennessee Valley Authority v. Hill*, 437 U.S. 153, 194-195 (1978).

By the same token, the fact that a given law or procedure is efficient, convenient, and useful in facilitating functions of government, standing alone, will not save it if it is contrary to the Constitution. Convenience and efficiency are not the primary objectives — or the hallmarks — of democratic government and our inquiry is sharpened rather than blunted by the fact that congressional veto provisions are appearing with increasing frequency in statutes which delegate authority to executive and independent agencies:

> "Since 1932, when the first veto provision was enacted into law, 295 congressional veto-type procedures have been inserted in 196 different statutes as follows: from 1932 to 1939, five statutes were affected; from 1940-49, nineteen statutes; between 1950-59, thirty-four statutes; and from 1960-69, forty-nine. From the year 1970 through 1975, at least one hundred sixty-three such provisions visions were included in eighty-nine laws." Abourezk, The Congressional Veto: A Contemporary Response to Executive Encroachment on Legislative Prerogatives, 52 Ind. L. Rev. [sic] 323, 324 (1977).

Justice White undertakes to make a case for the proposition that the one-House veto is a useful "political invention," and we need not challenge that assertion. We can even concede this utilitarian argument although the long-

---

have been reported to Congress by the Attorney General at the beginning of a regular session thereof and until after the close of such session." Act of June 19, 1934, ch. 651, § 2, 48 Stat. 1064. This statute did *not* provide that Congress could unilaterally veto the Federal Rules. Rather, it gave Congress the opportunity to review the Rules before they became effective and to pass legislation barring their effectiveness if the Rules were found objectionable. This technique was used by Congress when it acted in 1973 to stay, and ultimately to revise, the proposed Rules of Evidence.

range political wisdom of this "invention" is arguable. It has been vigorously debated, and it is instructive to compare the views of the protagonists. But policy arguments supporting even useful "political inventions" are subject to the demands of the Constitution which defines powers and, with respect to this subject, sets out just how those powers are to be exercised.

Explicit and unambiguous provisions of the Constitution prescribe and define the respective functions of the Congress and of the Executive in the legislative process. Since the precise terms of those familiar provisions are critical to the resolution of these cases, we set them out verbatim. Article I provides:

> "All legislative Powers herein granted shall be vested in a Congress of the United States, which shall consist of a Senate *and* House of Representatives." Art. I, § 1. (Emphasis added.)
>
> "Every Bill which shall have passed the House of Representatives *and* the Senate, *shall,* before it becomes a law, be presented to the President of the United States. . . ." Art. I, § 7, cl. 2. (Emphasis added.)
>
> "*Every* Order, Resolution, or Vote to which the Concurrence of the Senate and House of Representatives may be necessary (except on a question of Adjournment) *shall be* presented to the President of the United States; and before the Same shall take Effect, *shall be* approved by him, or being disapproved by him, *shall be* repassed by two thirds of the Senate and House of Representatives, according to the Rules and Limitations prescribed in the Case of a Bill." Art. I, § 7, cl. 3. (Emphasis added.)

These provisions of Art. I are integral parts of the constitutional design for the separation of powers. We have recently noted that "[the] principle of separation of powers was not simply an abstract generalization in the minds of the Framers: it was woven into the document that they drafted in Philadelphia in the summer of 1787." [W]e see that the purposes underlying the Presentment Clauses, Art. I, § 7, cls. 2, 3, and the bicameral requirement of Art. I, § 1, and § 7, cl. 2, guide our resolution of the important question presented in these cases. The very structure of the Articles delegating and separating powers under Arts. I, II, and III exemplifies the concept of separation of powers, and we now turn to Art. I.

B. THE PRESENTMENT CLAUSES

The records of the Constitutional Convention reveal that the requirement that all legislation be presented to the President before becoming law was uniformly accepted by the Framers. Presentment to the President and the Presidential veto were considered so imperative that the draftsmen took special pains to assure that these requirements could not be circumvented. During the final debate on Art. I, § 7, cl. 2, James Madison expressed concern that it might easily be evaded by the simple expedient of calling a proposed law a "resolution" or "vote" rather than a "bill." 2 Farrand 301-302. As a consequence, Art. I, § 7, cl. 3, *supra,* at 945-946, was added. 2 Farrand 304-305.

The decision to provide the President with a limited and qualified power to nullify proposed legislation by veto was based on the profound conviction of the Framers that the powers conferred on Congress were the powers to be most carefully circumscribed. It is beyond doubt that lawmaking was a power to be shared by both Houses and the President. In The Federalist No. 73 (H. Lodge ed. 1888), Hamilton focused on the President's role in making laws:

"If even no propensity had ever discovered itself in the legislative body to invade the rights of the Executive, the rules of just reasoning and theoretic propriety would of themselves teach us that the one ought not to be left to the mercy of the other, but ought to possess a constitutional and effectual power of self-defence." *Id.*, at 457-458.

The President's role in the lawmaking process also reflects the Framers' careful efforts to check whatever propensity a particular Congress might have to enact oppressive, improvident, or ill-considered measures. The President's veto role in the legislative process was described later during public debate on ratification:

"It establishes a salutary check upon the legislative body, calculated to guard the community against the effects of faction, precipitancy, or of any impulse unfriendly to the public good, which may happen to influence a majority of that body.
... The primary inducement to conferring the power in question upon the Executive is, to enable him to defend himself; the secondary one is to increase the chances in favor of the community against the passing of bad laws, through haste, inadvertence, or design." The Federalist No. 73, *supra,* at 458 (A. Hamilton).

The Court also has observed that the Presentment Clauses serve the important purpose of assuring that a "national" perspective is grafted on the legislative process:

"The President is a representative of the people just as the members of the Senate and of the House are, and it may be, at some times, on some subjects, that the President elected by all the people is rather more representative of them all than are the members of either body of the Legislature whose constituencies are local and not countrywide. . . ." *Myers v. United States, supra,* at 123.

C. BICAMERALISM

The bicameral requirement of Art. I, §§ 1, 7, was of scarcely less concern to the Framers than was the Presidential veto and indeed the two concepts are inter-dependent. By providing that no law could take effect without the concurrence of the prescribed majority of the Members of both Houses, the Framers reem-phasized their belief, already remarked upon in connection with the Present-ment Clauses, that legislation should not be enacted unless it has been carefully and fully considered by the Nation's elected officials. In the Constitutional Convention debates on the need for a bicameral legislature, James Wilson, later to become a Justice of this Court, commented:

"Despotism comes on mankind in different shapes. Sometimes in an Executive, sometimes in a military, one. Is there danger of a Legislative despotism? Theory & practice both proclaim it. If the Legislative authority be not restrained, there can be neither liberty nor stability; and it can only be restrained by dividing it within itself, into distinct and independent branches. In a single house there is no check, but the inadequate one, of the virtue & good sense of those who compose it." 1 Farrand 254.

Hamilton argued that a Congress comprised of a single House was antithetical to the very purposes of the Constitution. Were the Nation to adopt a Constitu-tion providing for only one legislative organ, he warned:

"[W]e shall finally accumulate, in a single body, all the most important prerogatives of sovereignty, and thus entail upon our posterity one of the most execrable forms of government that human infatuation ever contrived. Thus we should create in reality that very tyranny which the adversaries of the new Constitution either are, or affect to be, solicitous to avert." The Federalist No. 22, p. 135 (H. Lodge ed. 1888).

This view was rooted in a general skepticism regarding the fallibility of human nature later commented on by Joseph Story:

"Public bodies, like private persons, are occasionally under the dominion of strong passions and excitements; impatient, irritable, and impetuous. . . . If [a legislature] feels no check but its own will, it rarely has the firmness to insist upon holding a question long enough under its own view, to see and mark it in all its bearings and relations on society." 1 Story, *supra,* at 383-384.

These observations are consistent with what many of the Framers expressed, none more cogently than Madison in pointing up the need to divide and disperse power in order to protect liberty:

"In republican government, the legislative authority necessarily predominates. The remedy for this inconveniency is to divide the legislature into different branches; and to render them, by different modes of election and different principles of action, as little connected with each other as the nature of their common functions and their common dependence on the society will admit." The Federalist No. 51, p. 324 (H. Lodge ed. 1888) (sometimes attributed to "Hamilton or Madison" but now generally attributed to Madison).

However familiar, it is useful to recall that apart from their fear that special interests could be favored at the expense of public needs, the Framers were also concerned, although not of one mind, over the apprehensions of the smaller states. Those states feared a commonality of interest among the larger states would work to their disadvantage; representatives of the larger states, on the other hand, were skeptical of a legislature that could pass laws favoring a minority of the people. See 1 Farrand 176-177, 484-491. It need hardly be repeated here that the Great Compromise, under which one House was viewed as representing the people and the other the states, allayed the fears of both the large and small states.

We see therefore that the Framers were acutely conscious that the bicameral requirement and the Presentment Clauses would serve essential constitutional functions. The President's participation in the legislative process was to protect the Executive Branch from Congress and to protect the whole people from improvident laws. The division of the Congress into two distinctive bodies assures that the legislative power would be exercised only after opportunity for full study and debate in separate settings. The President's unilateral veto power, in turn, was limited by the power of two-thirds of both Houses of Congress to overrule a veto thereby precluding final arbitrary action of one person. It emerges clearly that the prescription for legislative action in Art. I, §§ 1, 7, represents the Framers' decision that the legislative power of the Federal Government be exercised in accord with a single, finely wrought and exhaustively considered, procedure.

IV

The Constitution sought to divide the delegated powers of the new Federal Government into three defined categories, Legislative, Executive, and Judicial, to assure, as nearly as possible, that each branch of government would confine itself to its assigned responsibility. The hydraulic pressure inherent within each of the separate Branches to exceed the outer limits of its power, even to accomplish desirable objectives, must be resisted.

Although not "hermetically" sealed from one another, the powers delegated to the three Branches are functionally identifiable. When any Branch acts, it is presumptively exercising the power the Constitution has delegated to it. When the Executive acts, he presumptively acts in an executive or administrative capacity as defined in Art. II. And when, as here, one House of Congress purports to act, it is presumptively acting within its assigned sphere.

Beginning with this presumption, we must nevertheless establish that the challenged action under § 244(c)(2) is of the kind to which the procedural requirements of Art. I, § 7, apply. Not every action taken by either House is subject to the bicameralism and presentment requirements of Art. I. Whether actions taken by either House are, in law and fact, an exercise of legislative power depends not on their form but upon "whether they contain matter which is properly to be regarded as legislative in its character and effect." S. Rep. No. 1335, 54th Cong., 2d Sess., 8 (1897).

Examination of the action taken here by one House pursuant to § 244(c)(2) reveals that it was essentially legislative in purpose and effect. In purporting to exercise power defined in Art. I, § 8, cl. 4, to "establish an uniform Rule of Naturalization," the House took action that had the purpose and effect of altering the legal rights, duties, and relations of persons, including the Attorney General, Executive Branch officials and Chadha, all outside the Legislative Branch. Section 244(c)(2) purports to authorize one House of Congress to require the Attorney General to deport an individual alien whose deportation otherwise would be canceled under § 244. The one-House veto operated in these cases to overrule the Attorney General and mandate Chadha's deportation; absent the House action, Chadha would remain in the United States. Congress has *acted* and its action has altered Chadha's status.

The legislative character of the one-House veto in these cases is confirmed by the character of the congressional action it supplants. Neither the House of Representatives nor the Senate contends that, absent the veto provision in § 244(c)(2), either of them, or both of them acting together, could effectively require the Attorney General to deport an alien once the Attorney General, in the exercise of legislatively delegated authority, had determined the alien should remain in the United States. Without the challenged provision in § 244(c)(2), this could have been achieved, if at all, only by legislation requiring deportation.[17] Similarly, a veto by one House of Congress under § 244(c)(2) cannot be justified as an attempt at amending the standards set out in § 244(a)(1), or as a repeal of § 244 as applied to Chadha. Amendment and repeal of statutes, no less than enactment, must conform with Art. I.

---

17. We express no opinion as to whether such legislation would violate any constitutional provision.

The nature of the decision implemented by the one-House veto in these cases further manifests its legislative character. After long experience with the clumsy, time-consuming private bill procedure, Congress made a deliberate choice to delegate to the Executive Branch, and specifically to the Attorney General, the authority to allow deportable aliens to remain in this country in certain specified circumstances. It is not disputed that this choice to delegate authority is precisely the kind of decision that can be implemented only in accordance with the procedures set out in Art. I. Disagreement with the Attorney General's decision on Chadha's deportation — that is, Congress' decision to deport Chadha — no less than Congress' original choice to delegate to the Attorney General the authority to make that decision, involves determinations of policy that Congress can implement in only one way: bicameral passage followed by presentment to the President. Congress must abide by its delegation of authority until that delegation is legislatively altered or revoked.[19]

Finally, we see that when the Framers intended to authorize either House of Congress to act alone and outside of its prescribed bicameral legislative role, they narrowly and precisely defined the procedure for such action. There are four provisions in the Constitution, explicit and unambiguous, by which one House may act alone with the unreviewable force of law, not subject to the President's veto:

(a) The House of Representatives alone was given the power to initiate impeachments. Art. I, § 2, cl. 5;

(b) The Senate alone was given the power to conduct trials following impeachment on charges initiated by the House and to convict following trial. Art. I, § 3, cl. 6;

(c) The Senate alone was given final unreviewable power to approve or to disapprove Presidential appointments. Art. II, § 2, cl. 2;

(d) The Senate alone was given unreviewable power to ratify treaties negotiated by the President. Art. II, § 2, cl. 2.

Clearly, when the Draftsmen sought to confer special powers on one House, independent of the other House, or of the President, they did so in explicit, unambiguous terms. These carefully defined exceptions from presentment and bicameralism underscore the difference between the legislative functions of Congress and other unilateral but important and binding one-House acts provided for in the Constitution. These exceptions are narrow, explicit, and separately justified; none of them authorize the action challenged here. On the contrary, they provide further support for the conclusion that congressional authority is not to be implied and for the conclusion that the veto provided for in § 244(c)(2) is not authorized by the constitutional design of the powers of the Legislative Branch.

Since it is clear that the action by the House under § 244(c)(2) was not within any of the express constitutional exceptions authorizing one House to act alone,

---

19. This does not mean that Congress is required to capitulate to "the accretion of policy control by forces outside its chambers." Javits & Klein, Congressional Oversight and the Legislative Veto: A Constitutional Analysis, 52 N.Y.U. L. Rev. 455, 462 (1977). The Constitution provides Congress with abundant means to oversee and control its administrative creatures. Beyond the obvious fact that Congress ultimately controls administrative agencies in the legislation that creates them, other means of control, such as durational limits on authorizations and formal reporting requirements, lie well within Congress' constitutional power.

and equally clear that it was an exercise of legislative power, that action was subject to the standards prescribed in Art. I.[22] The bicameral requirement, the Presentment Clauses, the President's veto, and Congress' power to override a veto were intended to erect enduring checks on each Branch and to protect the people from the improvident exercise of power by mandating certain prescribed steps. To preserve those checks, and maintain the separation of powers, the carefully defined limits on the power of each Branch must not be eroded. To accomplish what has been attempted by one House of Congress in this case requires action in conformity with the express procedures of the Constitution's prescription for legislative action: passage by a majority of both Houses and presentment to the President.[23]

The veto authorized by §244(c)(2) doubtless has been in many respects a convenient shortcut; the "sharing" with the Executive by Congress of its authority over aliens in this manner is, on its face, an appealing compromise. In purely practical terms, it is obviously easier for action to be taken by one House without submission to the President; but it is crystal clear from the records of the Convention, contemporaneous writings and debates, that the Framers ranked other values higher than efficiency. The records of the Convention and debates in the States preceding ratification underscore the common desire to define and limit the exercise of the newly created federal powers affecting the states and the

22. Justice Powell's position is that the one-House veto in this case is a *judicial* act and therefore unconstitutional as beyond the authority vested in Congress by the Constitution. We agree that there is a sense in which one-House action pursuant to §244(c)(2) has a judicial cast, since it purports to "review" Executive action. In this case, for example, the sponsor of the resolution vetoing the suspension of Chadha's deportation argued that Chadha "did not meet [the] statutory requirements" for suspension of deportation. To be sure, it is normally up to the courts to decide whether an agency has complied with its statutory mandate. But the attempted analogy between judicial action and the one-House veto is less than perfect. Federal courts do not enjoy a roving mandate to correct alleged excesses of administrative agencies; we are limited by Art. III to hearing cases and controversies and no justiciable case or controversy was presented by the Attorney General's decision to allow Chadha to remain in this country. We are aware of no decision, and Justice Powell has cited none, where a federal court has reviewed a decision of the Attorney General suspending deportation of an alien pursuant to the standards set out in §244(a)(1). This is not surprising, given that no party to such action has either the motivation or the right to appeal from it. As Justice White correctly notes, *post,* at 1001-1002, "the courts have not been given the authority to review whether an alien should be given permanent status; review is limited to whether the Attorney General has properly applied the statutory standards for" *denying* a request for suspension of deportation. . . . Thus, Justice Powell's statement that the one-House veto in this case is "clearly adjudicatory," simply is not supported by his accompanying assertion that the House has "assumed a function ordinarily entrusted to the federal courts." We are satisfied that the one-House veto is legislative in purpose and effect and subject to the procedures set out in Art. I.

23. Neither can we accept the suggestion that the one-House veto provision in §244(c)(2) either removes or modifies the bicameralism and presentation requirements for the enactment of future legislation affecting aliens. The explicit prescription for legislative action contained in Art. I cannot be amended by legislation. Justice White suggests that the Attorney General's action under §244(c)(1) suspending deportation is equivalent to a *proposal* for legislation and that because congressional approval is indicated "by the failure to veto, the one-House veto satisfies the requirement of bicameral approval." However, as the Court of Appeals noted, that approach "would analogize the effect of the one house disapproval to the failure of one house to vote affirmatively on a private bill." Even if it were clear that Congress entertained such an arcane theory when it enacted §244(c)(2), which Justice White does not suggest, this would amount to nothing less than an amending of Art. I. The legislative steps outlined in Art. I are not empty formalities; they were designed to assure that both Houses of Congress and the President participate in the exercise of lawmaking authority. This does not mean that legislation must always be preceded by debate; on the contrary, we have said that it is not necessary for a legislative body to "articulate its reasons for enacting a statute." But the steps required by Art. I, §§1, 7, make certain that there is an opportunity for deliberation and debate. To allow Congress to evade the strictures of the Constitution and in effect enact Executive proposals into law by mere silence cannot be squared with Art. I.

people. There is unmistakable expression of a determination that legislation by the national Congress be a step-by-step, deliberate and deliberative process.

The choices we discern as having been made in the Constitutional Convention impose burdens on governmental processes that often seem clumsy, inefficient, even unworkable, but those hard choices were consciously made by men who had lived under a form of government that permitted arbitrary governmental acts to go unchecked. There is no support in the Constitution or decisions of this Court for the proposition that the cumbersomeness and delays often encountered in complying with explicit constitutional standards may be avoided, either by the Congress or by the President. *See Youngstown Sheet & Tube Co. v. Sawyer*, 343 U.S. 579 (1952). With all the obvious flaws of delay, untidiness, and potential for abuse, we have not yet found a better way to preserve freedom than by making the exercise of power subject to the carefully crafted restraints spelled out in the Constitution.

V

We hold that the congressional veto provision in § 244(c)(2) is severable from the Act and that it is unconstitutional. Accordingly, the judgment of the Court of Appeals is *Affirmed*.

JUSTICE POWELL, concurring in the judgment.

The Court's decision, based on the Presentment Clauses, Art. I, § 7, cls. 2 and 3, apparently will invalidate every use of the legislative veto. The breadth of this holding gives one pause. Congress has included the veto in literally hundreds of statutes, dating back to the 1930's. Congress clearly views this procedure as essential to controlling the delegation of power to administrative agencies. One reasonably may disagree with Congress' assessment of the veto's utility, but the respect due its judgment as a coordinate branch of Government cautions that our holding should be no more extensive than necessary to decide these cases. In my view, the cases may be decided on a narrower ground. When Congress finds that a particular person does not satisfy the statutory criteria for permanent residence in this country it has assumed a judicial function in violation of the principle of separation of powers. Accordingly, I concur only in the judgment. . . .

On its face, the House's action appears clearly adjudicatory. The House did not enact a general rule; rather it made its own determination that six specific persons did not comply with certain statutory criteria. It thus undertook the type of decision that traditionally has been left to other branches. Even if the House did not make a *de novo* determination, but simply reviewed the Immigration and Naturalization Service's findings, it still assumed a function ordinarily entrusted to the federal courts.[8] *See* 5 U.S.C. § 704 (providing generally for judicial review

---

8. The Court reasons in response to this argument that the one-House veto exercised in this case was not judicial in nature because the decision of the Immigration and Naturalization Service did not present a justiciable issue that could have been reviewed by a court on appeal. See *ante*, at n.22. The Court notes that since the administrative agency decided the case in favor of Chadha, there was no aggrieved party who could appeal. Reliance by the Court on this fact misses the point. Even if review of the particular decision to suspend deportation is not committed to the courts, the House of Representatives assumed a function that generally is entrusted to an impartial tribunal. In my view, the Legislative Branch in effect acted as an appellate court by overruling the Service's

of final agency action). Where, as here, Congress has exercised a power "that cannot possibly be regarded as merely in aid of the legislative function of Congress," *Buckley v. Valeo,* 424 U.S., at 138, the decisions of this Court have held that Congress impermissibly assumed a function that the Constitution entrusted to another branch, see *id.,* at 138-141.

The impropriety of the House's assumption of this function is confirmed by the fact that its action raises the very danger the Framers sought to avoid — the exercise of unchecked power. In deciding whether Chadha deserves to be deported, Congress is not subject to any internal constraints that prevent it from arbitrarily depriving him of the right to remain in this country.[9] Unlike the judiciary or an administrative agency, Congress is not bound by established substantive rules. Nor is it subject to the procedural safeguards, such as the right to counsel and a hearing before an impartial tribunal, that are present when a court or an agency[10] adjudicates individual rights. The only effective constraint on Congress' power is political, but Congress is most accountable politically when it prescribes rules of general applicability. When it decides rights of specific persons, those rights are subject to "the tyranny of a shifting majority."

Chief Justice Marshall observed: "It is the peculiar province of the legislature to prescribe general rules for the government of society; the application of those rules to individuals in society would seem to be the duty of other departments." *Fletcher v. Peck,* 6 Cranch 87, 136 (1810). In my view, when Congress undertook to apply its rules to Chadha, it exceeded the scope of its constitutionally prescribed authority. I would not reach the broader question whether legislative vetoes are invalid under the Presentment Clauses.

Justice White, dissenting.

Today the Court not only invalidates § 244(c)(2) of the Immigration and Nationality Act, but also sounds the death knell for nearly 200 other statutory provisions in which Congress has reserved a "legislative veto." For this reason, the Court's decision is of surpassing importance. And it is for this reason that the Court would have been well advised to decide the cases, if possible, on the narrower grounds of separation of powers, leaving for full consideration the constitutionality of other congressional review statutes operating on such varied matters as war powers and agency rulemaking, some of which concern the independent regulatory agencies.

---

application of established law to Chadha. And unlike a court or an administrative agency, it did not provide Chadha with the right to counsel or a hearing before acting. Although the parallel is not entirely complete, the effect on Chadha's personal rights would not have been different in principle had he been acquitted of a federal crime and thereafter found by one House of Congress to have been guilty.

9. When Congress grants particular individuals relief or benefits under its spending power, the danger of oppressive action that the separation of powers was designed to avoid is not implicated. Similarly, Congress may authorize the admission of individual aliens by special Acts, but it does not follow that Congress unilaterally may make a judgment that a particular alien has no legal right to remain in this country. *See* Memorandum Concerning H. R. 9766 Entitled "An Act to Direct the Deportation of Harry Renton Bridges," reprinted in S. Rep. No. 2031, 76th Cong., 3d Sess., pt. 1, p. 8 (1940). As Attorney General Robert Jackson remarked, such a practice "would be an historical departure from an unbroken American practice and tradition."

10. We have recognized that independent regulatory agencies and departments of the Executive Branch often exercise authority that is "judicial in nature." *Buckley v. Valeo,* 424 U.S. 1, 140-141 (1976). This function, however, forms part of the agencies' execution of public law and is subject to the procedural safeguards, including judicial review, provided by the Administrative Procedure Act, *see* 5 U.S.C. § 551 *et seq.*

The prominence of the legislative veto mechanism in our contemporary political system and its importance to Congress can hardly be overstated. It has become a central means by which Congress secures the accountability of executive and independent agencies. Without the legislative veto, Congress is faced with a Hobson's choice: either to refrain from delegating the necessary authority, leaving itself with a hopeless task of writing laws with the requisite specificity to cover endless special circumstances across the entire policy landscape, or in the alternative, to abdicate its law-making function to the Executive Branch and independent agencies. To choose the former leaves major national problems unresolved; to opt for the latter risks unaccountable policymaking by those not elected to fill that role. Accordingly, over the past five decades, the legislative veto has been placed in nearly 200 statutes. The device is known in every field of governmental concern: reorganization, budgets, foreign affairs, war powers, and regulation of trade, safety, energy, the environment, and the economy.

I

The legislative veto developed initially in response to the problems of reorganizing the sprawling Government structure created in response to the Depression. The Reorganization Acts established the chief model for the legislative veto. . . . Although the reorganization authority reenacted in 1933 did not contain a legislative veto provision, the provision returned during the Roosevelt administration and has since been renewed numerous times. Over the years, the provision was used extensively. Presidents submitted 115 Reorganization Plans to Congress of which 23 were disapproved by Congress pursuant to legislative veto provisions.

. . . During World War II, Congress enacted over 30 statutes conferring powers on the Executive with legislative veto provisions. President Roosevelt accepted the veto as the necessary price for obtaining exceptional authority.

Over the quarter century following World War II, Presidents continued to accept legislative vetoes by one or both Houses as constitutional, while regularly denouncing provisions by which congressional Committees reviewed Executive activity. The legislative veto balanced delegations of statutory authority in new areas of governmental involvement: the space program, international agreements on nuclear energy, tariff arrangements, and adjustment of federal pay rates.

During the 1970's the legislative veto was important in resolving a series of major constitutional disputes between the President and Congress over claims of the President to broad impoundment, war, and national emergency powers. . . .

In the energy field, the legislative veto served to balance broad delegations in legislation emerging from the energy crisis of the 1970's. In the educational field, it was found that fragmented and narrow grant programs "inevitably lead to Executive-Legislative confrontations" because they inaptly limited the Commissioner of Education's authority. S. Rep. No. 93-763, p. 69 (1974). The response was to grant the Commissioner of Education rulemaking authority, subject to a legislative veto. In the trade regulation area, the veto preserved congressional authority over the Federal Trade Commission's broad mandate to make rules to prevent businesses from engaging in "unfair or deceptive acts or practices in commerce."

Even this brief review suffices to demonstrate that the legislative veto is more than "efficient, convenient, and useful." It is an important if not indispensable political invention that allows the President and Congress to resolve major constitutional and policy differences, assures the accountability of independent regulatory agencies, and preserves Congress' control over lawmaking. Perhaps there are other means of accommodation and accountability, but the increasing reliance of Congress upon the legislative veto suggests that the alternatives to which Congress must now turn are not entirely satisfactory.[10]

The history of the legislative veto also makes clear that it has not been a sword with which Congress has struck out to aggrandize itself at the expense of the other branches — the concerns of Madison and Hamilton. Rather, the veto has been a means of defense, a reservation of ultimate authority necessary if Congress is to fulfill its designated role under Art. I as the Nation's lawmaker. While the President has often objected to particular legislative vetoes, generally those left in the hands of congressional Committees, the Executive has more often agreed to legislative review as the price for a broad delegation of authority. To be sure, the President may have preferred unrestricted power, but that could be precisely why Congress thought it essential to retain a check on the exercise of delegated authority.

II

For all these reasons, the apparent sweep of the Court's decision today is regrettable. The Court's Art. I analysis appears to invalidate all legislative vetoes irrespective of form or subject. Because the legislative veto is commonly found as a

---

10. While Congress could write certain statutes with greater specificity, it is unlikely that this is a realistic or even desirable substitute for the legislative veto. The controversial nature of many issues would prevent Congress from reaching agreement on many major problems if specificity were required in their enactments. For example, in the deportation context, the solution is not for Congress to create more refined categorizations of the deportable aliens whose status should be subject to change. In 1979, the Immigration and Naturalization Service proposed regulations setting forth factors to be considered in the exercise of discretion under numerous provisions of the Act, but not including § 244, to ensure "fair and uniform" adjudication "under appropriate discretionary criteria." 44 Fed. Reg. 36187 (1979). The proposed rule was canceled in 1981, because "[there] is an inherent failure in any attempt to list those factors which should be considered in the exercise of discretion. It is impossible to list or foresee all of the adverse or favorable factors which may be present in a given set of circumstances." 46 Fed. Reg. 9119 (1981). Oversight hearings and congressional investigations have their purpose, but unless Congress is to be rendered a think tank or debating society, they are no substitute for the exercise of actual authority. The "delaying" procedure approved in *Sibbach v. Wilson & Co.*, 312 U.S. 1, 15 (1941), while satisfactory for certain measures, has its own shortcomings. Because a new law must be passed to restrain administrative action, Congress must delegate authority without the certain ability of being able to check its exercise.

Finally, the passage of corrective legislation after agency regulations take effect or Executive Branch officials have acted entails the drawbacks endemic to a retroactive response. "Post hoc substantive revision of legislation, the only available corrective mechanism in the absence of post-enactment review, could have serious prejudicial consequences; if Congress retroactively tampered with a price control system after prices have been set, the economy could be damaged and private rights seriously impaired; if Congress rescinded the sale of arms to a foreign country, our relations with that country would be severely strained; and if Congress reshuffled the bureaucracy after a President's reorganization proposal had taken effect, the results could be chaotic." Javits & Klein, Congressional Oversight and the Legislative Veto: A Constitutional Analysis, 52 N.Y.U. L. Rev. 455, 464 (1977) (footnote omitted).

check upon rulemaking by administrative agencies and upon broad-based policy decisions of the Executive Branch, it is particularly unfortunate that the Court reaches its decision in cases involving the exercise of a veto over deportation decisions regarding particular individuals. Courts should always be wary of striking statutes as unconstitutional; to strike an entire class of statutes based on consideration of a somewhat atypical and more readily indictable exemplar of the class is irresponsible. . . .

The reality of the situation is that the constitutional question posed today is one of immense difficulty over which the Executive and Legislative Branches — as well as scholars and judges — have understandably disagreed. That disagreement stems from the silence of the Constitution on the precise question: The Constitution does not directly authorize or prohibit the legislative veto. Thus, our task should be to determine whether the legislative veto is consistent with the purposes of Art. I and the principles of separation of powers which are reflected in that Article and throughout the Constitution. We should not find the lack of a specific constitutional authorization for the legislative veto surprising, and I would not infer disapproval of the mechanism from its absence. From the summer of 1787 to the present the Government of the United States has become an endeavor far beyond the contemplation of the Framers. Only within the last half century has the complexity and size of the Federal Government's responsibilities grown so greatly that the Congress must rely on the legislative veto as the most effective if not the only means to insure its role as the Nation's lawmaker. But the wisdom of the Framers was to anticipate that the Nation would grow and new problems of governance would require different solutions. Accordingly, our Federal Government was intentionally chartered with the flexibility to respond to contemporary needs without losing sight of fundamental democratic principles. . . .

. . . In my view, neither Art. I of the Constitution nor the doctrine of separation of powers is violated by this mechanism by which our elected Representatives preserve their voice in the governance of the Nation.

III

The Court holds that the disapproval of a suspension of deportation by the resolution of one House of Congress is an exercise of legislative power without compliance with the prerequisites for lawmaking set forth in Art. I of the Constitution. Specifically, the Court maintains that the provisions of §244(c)(2) are inconsistent with the requirement of bicameral approval, implicit in Art. I, §1, and the requirement that all bills and resolutions that require the concurrence of both Houses be presented to the President, Art. I, §7, cls. 2 and 3. . . .

The central concern of the presentment and bicameralism requirements of Art. I is that when a departure from the legal status quo is undertaken, it is done with the approval of the President and both Houses of Congress — or, in the event of a Presidential veto, a two-thirds majority in both Houses. This interest is fully satisfied by the operation of §244(c)(2). The President's approval is found in the Attorney General's action in recommending to Congress that the deportation order for a given alien be suspended. The House and the Senate indicate their approval of the Executive's action by not passing a resolution of disapproval within the statutory period. Thus, a change in the legal status quo — the deportability of the alien — is consummated only with the approval of each of the three relevant actors. The disagreement of any one of the three maintains the alien's pre-existing status: the Executive may choose not to recommend suspension; the House and Senate may each veto the recommendation. The effect on the rights and obligations of the affected individuals and upon the legislative system is precisely the same as if a private bill were introduced but failed to receive the necessary approval. "The President and the two Houses enjoy exactly the same say in what the law is to be as would have been true for each without the presence of the one-House veto, and nothing in the law is changed absent the concurrence of the President and a majority in each House." . . .

Thus understood, §244(c)(2) fully effectuates the purposes of the bicameralism and presentment requirements. I now briefly consider possible objections to the analysis.

First, it may be asserted that Chadha's status before legislative disapproval is one of nondeportation and that the exercise of the veto, unlike the failure of a private bill, works a change in the status quo. This position plainly ignores the statutory language. At no place in §244 has Congress delegated to the Attorney General any final power to determine which aliens shall be allowed to remain in the United States. Congress has retained the ultimate power to pass on such changes in deportable status. By its own terms, §244(a) states that whatever power the Attorney General has been delegated to suspend deportation and adjust status is to be exercisable only "[as] hereinafter prescribed in this section." Subsection (c) is part of that section. A grant of "suspension" does not cancel the alien's deportation or adjust the alien's status to that of a permanent resident alien. A suspension order is merely a "deferment of deportation," *McGrath v. Kristensen,* 340 U.S. 162, 168 (1950), which can mature into a cancellation of deportation and adjustment of status only upon the approval of Congress — by way of silence — under §244(c)(2). Only then does the statute authorize the Attorney General to "cancel deportation proceedings," §244(c)(2), and "record the alien's lawful admission for permanent residence. . . ."§244(d). The Immigration and Naturalization Service's action, on behalf of the Attorney General, "cannot become effective without ratification by Congress." 2 C. Gordon & H. Rosenfield, Immigration Law and Procedure §8.14, p. 8-121 (rev. ed. 1983). Until that ratification occurs, the Executive's action is simply a recommendation that Congress finalize the suspension — in itself, it works no legal change. . . .

Third, it may be objected that Congress cannot indicate its approval of legislative change by inaction. In the Court of Appeals' view, inaction by Congress "could equally imply endorsement, acquiescence, passivity, indecision, or indifference," 634 F.2d 408, 435 (1980), and the Court appears to echo this concern, *ante,* at n.23. This objection appears more properly directed at the wisdom of the legislative veto than its constitutionality. The Constitution does not and cannot guarantee that legislators will carefully scrutinize legislation and deliberate before acting. In a democracy it is the electorate that holds the legislators accountable for the wisdom of their choices. It is hard to maintain that a private bill receives any greater individualized scrutiny than a resolution of disapproval under §244(c)(2). Certainly the legislative veto is no more susceptible to this attack than the Court's increasingly common practice of according weight to the failure of Congress to disturb an Executive or independent agency's action. Earlier this Term, the Court found it important that Congress failed to act on bills proposed to overturn the Internal Revenue Service's interpretation of the requirements for tax-exempt status under § 501(c)(3) of the Internal Revenue Code. *Bob Jones University v. United States,* 461 U.S. 574, 600-601 (1983). If Congress may be said to have ratified the Internal Revenue Service's interpretation without passing new legislation, Congress may also be said to approve a suspension of deportation by the Attorney General when it fails to exercise its veto authority. The requirements of Art. I are not compromised by the congressional scheme.

IV

The Court of Appeals struck § 244(c)(2) as violative of the constitutional principle of separation of powers. It is true that the purpose of separating the authority of Government is to prevent unnecessary and dangerous concentration of power in one branch. For that reason, the Framers saw fit to divide and balance the powers of Government so that each branch would be checked by the others. Virtually every part of our constitutional system bears the mark of this judgment.

But the history of the separation-of-powers doctrine is also a history of accommodation and practicality. Apprehensions of an overly powerful branch have not led to undue prophylactic measures that handicap the effective working of the National Government as a whole. The Constitution does not contemplate total separation of the three branches of Government. *Buckley v. Valeo,* 424 U.S. 1, 121 (1976). "[A] hermetic sealing off of the three branches of Government from one another would preclude the establishment of a Nation capable of governing itself effectively." *Ibid.* . . .

This is the teaching of *Nixon v. Administrator of General Services,* 433 U.S. 425 (1977), which, in rejecting a separation-of-powers objection to a law requiring that the Administrator take custody of certain Presidential papers, set forth a framework for evaluating such claims:

> "[I]n determining whether the Act disrupts the proper balance between the coordinate branches, the proper inquiry focuses on the extent to which it prevents the Executive Branch from accomplishing its constitutionally assigned functions. *United States v. Nixon,* 418 U.S., at 711-712. Only where the potential for disruption is present must we then determine whether that impact is justified by an overriding need to promote objectives within the constitutional authority of Congress." *Id.,* at 443.

Section 244(c)(2) survives this test. The legislative veto provision does not "[prevent] the Executive Branch from accomplishing its constitutionally assigned functions." First, it is clear that the Executive Branch has no "constitutionally assigned" function of suspending the deportation of aliens. "'[O]ver no conceivable subject is the legislative power of Congress more complete than it is over' the admission of aliens." *Kleindienst v. Mandel,* 408 U.S. 753, 766 (1972), quoting *Oceanic Steam Navigation Co. v. Stranahan,* 214 U.S. 320, 339 (1909). Nor can it be said that the inherent function of the Executive Branch in executing the law is involved. The *Steel Seizure Case* resolved that the Art. II mandate for the President to execute the law is a directive to enforce the law which Congress has written. *Youngstown Sheet & Tube Co. v. Sawyer,* 343 U.S. 579 (1952). "The duty of the President to see that the laws be executed is a duty that does not go beyond the laws or require him to achieve more than Congress sees fit to leave within his power." *Myers v. United States,* 272 U.S., at 177 (Holmes, J., dissenting); *id.,* at 247 (Brandeis, J., dissenting). Here, § 244 grants the Executive only a qualified suspension authority, and it is only that authority which the President is constitutionally authorized to execute.

Moreover, the Court believes that the legislative veto we consider today is best characterized as an exercise of legislative or quasi-legislative authority. Under this characterization, the practice does not, even on the surface, constitute an infringement of executive or judicial prerogative. The Attorney General's suspension of deportation is equivalent to a proposal for legislation. The nature of the Attorney General's role as recommendatory is not altered because § 244 provides for congressional action through disapproval rather than by ratification. In comparison to private bills, which must be initiated in the Congress and which allow a Presidential veto to be overridden by a two-thirds majority in both Houses of Congress, § 244 augments rather than reduces the Executive Branch's authority. So understood, congressional review does not undermine, as the Court of Appeals thought, the "weight and dignity" that attends the decisions of the Executive Branch.

Nor does § 244 infringe on the judicial power, as Justice Powell would hold. Section 244 makes clear that Congress has reserved its own judgment as part of the statutory process. Congressional action does not substitute for judicial review of the Attorney General's decisions. The Act provides for judicial review of the refusal of the Attorney General to suspend a deportation and to transmit a recommendation to Congress. *INS v. Jong Ha Wang,* 450 U.S. 139 (1981) (*per curiam*). But the courts have not been given the authority to review whether an alien should be given permanent status; review is limited to whether the Attorney General has properly applied the statutory standards for essentially denying the alien a recommendation that his deportable status be changed by the Congress. Moreover, there is no constitutional obligation to provide any judicial review whatever for a failure to suspend deportation. . . .

I do not suggest that all legislative vetoes are necessarily consistent with separation-of-powers principles. A legislative check on an inherently executive function, for example, that of initiating prosecutions, poses an entirely different question. But the legislative veto device here — and in many other settings — is far from an instance of legislative tyranny over the Executive. It is a necessary check on the unavoidably expanding power of the agencies, both Executive and independent, as they engage in exercising authority delegated by Congress.

V

I regret that I am in disagreement with my colleagues on the fundamental questions that these cases present. But even more I regret the destructive scope of the Court's holding. It reflects a profoundly different conception of the Constitution than that held by the courts which sanctioned the modern administrative state. Today's decision strikes down in one fell swoop provisions in more laws enacted by Congress than the Court has cumulatively invalidated in its history. I fear it will now be more difficult to "[insure] that the fundamental policy decisions in our society will be made not by an appointed official but by the body immediately responsible to the people," *Arizona v. California,* 373 U.S. 546, 626 (1963) (Harlan, J., dissenting in part). I must dissent.

JUSTICE REHNQUIST, with whom JUSTICE WHITE joins, dissenting.

A severability clause creates a presumption that Congress intended the valid portion of the statute to remain in force when one part is found to be invalid. A severability clause does not, however, conclusively resolve the issue. "[T]he determination, in the end, is reached by" asking "[w]hat was the intent of the lawmakers," and "will rarely turn on the presence or absence of such a clause." Because I believe that Congress did not intend the one-House veto provision of § 244(c)(2) to be severable, I dissent.

Section 244(c)(2) is an exception to the general rule that an alien's deportation shall be suspended when the Attorney General finds that statutory criteria are met. It is severable only if Congress would have intended to permit the Attorney General to suspend deportations without it. This Court has held several times over the years that exceptions such as this are not severable because

> "by rejecting the exceptions intended by the legislature . . . the statute is made to enact what confessedly the legislature never meant. It confers upon the statute a positive operation beyond the legislative intent, and beyond what anyone can say it would have enacted in view of the illegality of the exceptions." *Spraigue v. Thompson,* 118 U.S. 90, 95 (1886).

By severing § 244(c)(2), the Court permits suspension of deportation in a class of cases where Congress never stated that suspension was appropriate. I do not believe we should expand the statute in this way without some clear indication that Congress intended such an expansion. . . .

The Court finds that the legislative history of § 244 shows that Congress intended § 244(c)(2) to be severable because Congress wanted to relieve itself of the burden of private bills. But the history elucidated by the Court shows that Congress was unwilling to give the Executive Branch permission to suspend deportation on its own. Over the years, Congress consistently rejected requests from the Executive for complete discretion in this area. Congress always insisted on retaining ultimate control, whether by concurrent resolution, as in the 1948 Act, or by one-House veto, as in the present Act. Congress has never indicated that it would be willing to permit suspensions of deportation unless it could retain some sort of veto.

It is doubtless true that Congress has the power to provide for suspensions of deportation without a one-House veto. But the Court has failed to identify any evidence that Congress intended to exercise that power. On the contrary, Congress' continued insistence on retaining control of the suspension process indicates that it has never been disposed to give the Executive Branch a free hand. By severing § 244(c)(2) the Court has "confounded" Congress' "intention" to permit suspensions of deportation "with their power to carry that intention into effect."

Because I do not believe that § 244(c)(2) is severable, I would reverse the judgment of the Court of Appeals.

QUESTIONS

1.   What is the majority's argument? Is it necessary for the majority to conclude that the action of the House of Representatives was "legislative"? Whether the action is "legislative" or not, may the House exercise such power?
2.   Is a two-house veto also unconstitutional?
3.   Evaluate the following arguments against the majority's reasoning:
     a.   The legislative veto is constitutional because the organic act creating the veto itself was passed by both Houses and signed by the President.
     b.   The legislative veto is constitutional because it works functionally like the bicameralism and presentment provided by the Constitution. Chadha's deportation (like legislation) needs lack of veto by each house (analogous to each House's approval) plus Attorney General action (analogous to Presidential approval).
     c.   If Congress can delegate quasi-legislative power to executive agencies, why can't it delegate the same power to an arm of itself?
     d.   The Constitution is interpreted loosely to permit the executive branch in effect to legislate. Why interpret the Constitution so strictly as to preclude the legislative branch in effect to execute the law? Shouldn't the strictness of construction work both ways?
4.   What is the result if agency power, granted in an organic statute that contains an unconstitutional veto provision, is exercised and there is no veto?
5.   State governments do not uniformly follow the federal rule prohibiting legislative vetoes on separation of powers grounds, even where a state constitution contains bicameralism and presentment requirements. *See* David E. Shipley, *The Status of Administrative Agencies Under the Georgia Constitution*, 40 GA. L. REV. 1109, 1129-33 (2006) (noting that the Georgia state courts have approved the use of legislative veto provisions in state laws delegating powers to state agencies). The Supreme Court of Georgia sustained the use of a legislative veto mechanism (by joint action of House and Senate standing committees) because "[r]egulations are not laws." *Albany Surgical, P.C. v. Georgia Dep't of Community Health*, 602 S.E. 2d 648, 651 (Ga. 2004). Professor Shipley argues that this decision, even if not mistaken, was poorly reasoned. Shipley, *supra*, at 1132-33, 1169.

NOTE ON STATUTORILY MANDATED CONGRESSIONAL REVIEW

In 1996, Congress enacted the Contract with America Advancement Act of 1996, Pub. L. No. 104-121. Section 251 of that statute, entitled "Congressional Review of Agency Rulemaking," added several new provisions to the APA, the most important of which is 5 U.S.C. § 801. Section 801(a)(1)(A) provides that:

Before a rule can take effect, the Federal agency promulgating such rule shall submit to each House of the Congress and to the Comptroller General a report containing —
   (i) a copy of the rule;
   (ii) a concise general statement relating to the rule, including whether it is a major rule; and
   (iii) the proposed effective date of the rule.

The APA, as amended, also identifies additional information that an agency must provide with the report to Congress. *See* 5 U.S.C. § 801(a)(1)(B). If a rule is major as defined in 5 U.S.C. § 804 (2) (providing that a rule is major if, *inter alia,* it has "an annual effect on the economy of $100,000,000 or more"), the General Accounting Office is required to provide Congress within fifteen days a report on the rule that "include[s] an assessment of the agency's compliance with" the act's reporting requirements. Section 801(a)(3) then governs the effective date of a major rule,[*] which is dependent on whether Congress enacts a joint resolution of disapproval:

> (3) A major rule relating to a report submitted under paragraph (1) shall take effect on the latest of—
> (A) the later of the date occurring 60 days after the date on which—
> (i) the Congress receives the report submitted under paragraph (1); or
> (ii) the rule is published in the Federal Register, if so published; or
> (B) if the Congress passes a joint resolution of disapproval described in section 802 relating to the rule, and the President signs a veto of such resolution, the earlier date—
> (i) on which either House of Congress votes and fails to override the veto of the President; or
> (ii) occurring 30 session days after the date on which the Congress received the veto and objections of the President; or
> (C) the date the rule would have otherwise taken effect, if not for this section (unless a joint resolution of disapproval under section 802 is enacted).

Section 802 establishes the procedures for congressional consideration of the joint resolution of disapproval, which must be enacted by both Houses of Congress and presented to the President.

Congressional review under these provisions led for the first time to the invalidation of a rule following a joint resolution of disapproval in March 2001. *See* 66 Fed. Reg. 20403 (Apr. 23, 2001). At the end of the Clinton Administration, the Department of Labor, Occupational Safety and Health Administration promulgated final regulations defining an Ergonomics Program Standard. *See* 65 Fed. Reg. 68262 (Nov. 14, 2000). Thereafter, the Senate passed a resolution of disapproval on March 6, 2001 (Cong. Rec. p. S1887), and the House passed that resolution the next day (Cong. Rec. p. H667). Newly elected President Bush signed the resolution into law as Pub. L. No. 107-5 on March 20, 2001. The agency then removed the regulations from the Code of Federal Regulations. 66 Fed. Reg. 20403 (Apr. 23, 2001).

An emerging issue is just what agency actions are subject to review under these provisions. The review requirement is triggered when there is an agency "rule," which is defined, subject to exceptions, by reference to the definition of "rule" in 5 U.S.C. § 551. *See* 5 U.S.C. § 804(3). The GAO has, however, construed the scope of the review requirement quite broadly. In *Opinion on Whether Trinity River Record of Decision Is a Rule* (May 14, 2001), the General Counsel of the GAO

---

[*] The effective date of a rule that is not major is governed by 5 U.S.C. § 801(a)(4), which provides that, "[e]xcept for a major rule, a rule shall take effect as otherwise provided by law after submission to Congress under paragraph (1)."

concluded that a Record of Decision (ROD) prepared by the Fish and Wildlife Service of the Department of the Interior was subject to congressional review. In the ROD, the agency reduced the amount of water diverted from the Trinity River. The GAO's conclusion was that:

> the Trinity ROD clearly constitutes a "rule" since its essential purpose is to set policy for the future. It is in no way concerned with the evaluation of past conduct based on evidentiary facts. While the Trinity ROD sets forth the past actions of the federal government that contributed to the current situation, it is presented as background to establish the state of the river basins leading up to the enactment of the [Central Valley Project Improvement Act (CVPIA)]. The Act then delegated to Interior the authority to determine the action necessary to restore the anadromous fishery on the Trinity River. The entire purpose of the ROD is to set a future course of action intended to achieve that purpose, as directed by the CVPIA.

Id. at 7-8. The GAO also concluded that the ROD did not fall within any exceptions to the definition of a rule. *Id.* at 8-9.

QUESTIONS

1. Is the review required by §§ 801-802 consistent with *Chadha, supra,* p. 391?
2. Can you think of reasons why these provisions might not be effective?
3. How, if at all, does the joint resolution of disapproval differ from ordinary legislation that could be enacted to undo a rule with which Congress disagreed?
4. What sort of legislative review is provided in the 1981 MSAPA? *See* 1981 MSAPA §§ 3-203 to 3-204.
5. Does the GAO view the scope of required congressional review too broadly in its understanding of the term "rule" in the APA?
6. In 2011, legislation — entitled the "Regulations From the Executive in Need of Scrutiny Act of 2011" ("REINS Act") — was introduced into both Houses of Congress to reshape the law governing congressional review of regulations. Both Houses held hearings on the legislation by the summer of 2011. Section 2 states that:

> The purpose of this Act is to increase accountability for and transparency in the federal regulatory process. Section 1 of article I of the United States Constitution grants all legislative powers to Congress. Over time, Congress has excessively delegated its constitutional charge while failing to conduct appropriate oversight and retain accountability for the content of the laws it passes. By requiring a vote in Congress, the REINS Act will result in more carefully drafted and detailed legislation, an improved regulatory process, and a legislative branch that is truly accountable to the American people for the laws imposed upon them.

If enacted, this law would provide that a "major" regulation would *not* be effective unless Congress enacted a joint resolution of approval by the seventieth day after the agency reports the regulation to Congress. The bill provides a one-time exception that allows regulation to be effective for 90 calendar days without congressional approval, if the President determines by Executive Order that the rule is:

>   (A) necessary because of an imminent threat to health or safety or other emergency;
>   (B) necessary for the enforcement of criminal laws;
>   (C) necessary for national security; or
>   (D) issued pursuant to any statute implementing an international trade agreement.

§ 3 (to be codified at 5 U.S.C. § 801(c)(2)).

The Act defines a major rule as a rule that:

>   has resulted in or is likely to result in —
>
>   (A) an annual effect on the economy of $100,000,000 or more;
>   (B) a major increase in costs or prices for consumers, individual industries, Federal, State, or local government agencies, or geographic regions; or
>   (C) significant adverse effects on competition, employment, investment, productivity, innovation, or on the ability of United States-based enterprises to compete with foreign-based enterprises in domestic and export markets.

§ 3 (to be codified at 5 U.S.C. § 804(2)).

The bill defines "agency" as the term is broadly defined in APA § 551. § 3 (to be codified at 5 U.S.C. § 804(1)). The bill defines "rule," with some qualifications, as that term is defined in APA § 551. § 3 (to be codified at 5 U.S.C. § 804(4)).

How does the role that would be played by Congress in the proposed REINS Act compare to the role Congress plays under the current congressional review statute? Is the proposed REINS Act consistent with the separation of powers?

7. The Republican Party Platform for 2016 "call[s] on Congress to begin reclaiming its constitutional powers from the bureaucratic state by requiring that major new federal regulations be approved by Congress before they can take effect, such as through the Regulation Freedom Amendment." Republican Platform 2016, at 10. The Regulation Freedom Amendment, if ratified, would provide that: "Whenever one quarter of the Members of the U.S. House or the U.S. Senate transmit to the President their written declaration of opposition to a proposed federal regulation, it shall require a majority vote of the House and Senate to adopt that regulation." *See* Patrick Gregory, RNC Platform Pushes Amendment to Curb Federal Regulations, 85 U.S.L.W. 81 (July 21, 2016).

8. Consider the following alternative ways for Congress to exercise control over the execution of the laws:
    a. sunset provisions (providing that statutory authority expires after a certain period, thus requiring an affirmative statutory extension of agency power),
    b. narrower delegations of power,

c.   budget controls (Congress needs to appropriate the money that agencies spend; agencies seek to please the congresspersons and committees that effectively control appropriations),

d.   informal contact (agencies sometimes informally agree to get the approval of particular congressional committees before taking certain actions, *see* Louis Fisher, The Politics of Shared Power 100-104 (4th ed. 1998)),

e.   "report and wait" provisions in organic statutes that delay certain actions until the Congress has a chance to pass legislation,

f.   the use of "statutory hammer" provisions in the organic statute providing that an absolute prohibition on the activity of concern will be imposed on a defined date, unless the agency promulgates sufficient requirements to regulate the activity by that date. For an example, *see* 42 U.S.C. § 6924 (conditional ban on land disposal of hazardous waste),

g.   oversight hearings (congressional hearings in which agency officials may be sufficiently grilled to take action desired by congressional committee members. For an example, see the scenario described in the *Florida East Coast Ry.* case, *supra,* p. 246),

h.   litigation brought by Members of Congress or congressional Committees. *See generally* Amanda Frost, *Congress in Court,* 59 UCLA L. Rev. 914, 942-47 (2012); Bradford C. Mank, *Does* United States v. Windsor *(the DOMA Case) Open the Door to Congressional Standing?,* 76 U. Pitt. L. Rev. 1 (2014).

Remarkably, Congress has continued to place legislative vetoes in public laws. According to Professor Louis Fisher, Congress has enacted over 400 legislative veto provisions in the 14 years following the *Chadha* decision. Fisher, *supra,* at 102.

9.   Partly in order to improve congressional oversight, Congress has enacted the Government Performance and Results Act of 1993, Pub. L. No. 103-62, which requires that agencies engage in strategic planning (5 U.S.C. § 306) and prepare annual performance plans (31 U.S.C. § 1115) and annual performance reports (31 U.S.C. § 1116). These plans and reports are now available on the Internet.

E.   EXECUTIVE POWER TO APPOINT

BUCKLEY v. VALEO
424 U.S. 1 (1976)

Per Curiam.

These appeals present constitutional challenges to the key provisions of the Federal Election Campaign Act of 1971, (Act) and related provisions of the Internal Revenue Code of 1954, all as amended in 1974.

The Court of Appeals, in sustaining the legislation in large part against various constitutional challenges, viewed it as "by far the most comprehensive reform legislation [ever] passed by Congress concerning the election of the President,

Vice-President, and members of Congress." The statutes at issue summarized in broad terms, contain the following provisions: (a) individual political contributions are limited to $1,000 to any single candidate per election, with an overall annual limitation of $25,000 by any contributor; independent expenditures by individuals and groups "relative to a clearly identified candidate" are limited to $1,000 a year; campaign spending by candidates for various federal offices and spending for national conventions by political parties are subject to prescribed limits; (b) contributions and expenditures above certain threshold levels must be reported and publicly disclosed; (c) a system for public funding of Presidential campaign activities is established by Subtitle H of the Internal Revenue Code; and (d) a Federal Election Commission is established to administer and enforce the legislation.

This suit was originally filed by appellants in the United States District Court for the District of Columbia. Plaintiffs included a candidate for the Presidency of the United States, a United States Senator who is a candidate for re-election, a potential contributor, the Committee for a Constitutional Presidency — McCarthy '76, the Conservative Party of the State of New York, the Mississippi Republican Party, the Libertarian Party, the New York Civil Liberties Union, Inc., the American Conservative Union, the Conservative Victory Fund, and Human Events, Inc. The defendants included the Secretary of the United States Senate and the Clerk of the United States House of Representatives, both in their official capacities and as ex officio members of the Federal Election Commission. The Commission itself was named as a defendant. Also named were the Attorney General of the United States and the Comptroller General of the United States.

[Omitted here are the procedural history and extensive treatment and resolution of constitutional challenges to the substantive provisions of the Federal Election Campaign Act.]

IV. The Federal Election Commission

The 1974 Amendments to the Act create an eight-member Federal Election Commission (Commission) and vest in it primary and substantial responsibility for administering and enforcing the Act. The question that we address in this portion of the opinion is whether, in view of the manner in which a majority of its members are appointed, the Commission may under the Constitution exercise the powers conferred upon it. We find it unnecessary to parse the complex statutory provisions in order to sketch the full sweep of the Commission's authority. It will suffice for present purposes to describe what appear to be representative examples of its various powers.

Chapter 14 of Title 2 makes the Commission the principal repository of the numerous reports and statements which are required by that chapter to be filed by those engaging in the regulated political activities. Its duties under § 438 (a) with respect to these reports and statements include filing and indexing, making them available for public inspection, preservation, and auditing and field investigations. It is directed to "serve as a national clearinghouse for information in respect to the administration of elections." § 438(b).

Beyond these recordkeeping, disclosure, and investigative functions, however, the Commission is given extensive rulemaking and adjudicative powers. Its duty under § 438 (a)(10) is "to prescribe suitable rules and regulations to carry out the provisions of . . . chapter [14]." Under § 437d (a)(8) the Commission is empowered to make such rules "as are necessary to carry out the provisions of this Act." Section 437d (a)(9) authorizes it to "formulate general policy with respect to the administration of this Act" and enumerated sections of Title 18's Criminal Code, as to all of which provisions the Commission "has primary jurisdiction with respect to [their] civil enforcement." § 437c (b). The Commission is authorized under § 437f (a) to render advisory opinions with respect to activities possibly violating the Act, the Title 18 sections, or the campaign funding provisions of Title 26, the effect of which is that "[n]otwithstanding any other provision of law, any person with respect to whom an advisory opinion is rendered . . . who acts in good faith in accordance with the provisions and findings [thereof] shall be presumed to be in compliance with the [statutory provision] with respect to which such advisory opinion is rendered." § 437f (b). In the course of administering the provisions for Presidential campaign financing, the Commission may authorize convention expenditures which exceed the statutory limits. 26 U.S.C. § 9008 (d)(3) (1970 ed., Supp. IV).

The Commission's enforcement power is both direct and wide ranging. . . .

The body in which this authority is reposed consists of eight members. The Secretary of the Senate and the Clerk of the House of Representatives are ex officio members of the Commission without the right to vote. Two members are appointed by the President pro tempore of the Senate "upon the recommendations of the majority leader of the Senate and the minority leader of the Senate." Two more are to be appointed by the Speaker of the House of Representatives, likewise upon the recommendations of its respective majority and minority leaders. The remaining two members are appointed by the President. Each of the six voting members of the Commission must be confirmed by the majority of both Houses of Congress, and each of the three appointing authorities is forbidden to choose both of their appointees from the same political party.

A. RIPENESS

[The Court found that the issues were ripe for court resolution.]

B. THE MERITS

Appellants urge that since Congress has given the Commission wide-ranging rulemaking and enforcement powers with respect to the substantive provisions of the Act, Congress is precluded under the principle of separation of powers from vesting in itself the authority to appoint those who will exercise such authority. Their argument is based on the language of Art. II, § 2, cl. 2, of the Constitution, which provides in pertinent part as follows:

> "[The President] shall nominate, and by and with the Advice and Consent of the Senate, shall appoint . . . all other Officers of the United States, whose Appointments are not herein otherwise provided for, and which shall be established by Law: but the Congress may by Law vest the Appointment of such inferior Officers, as they think proper, in the President alone, in the Courts of Law, or in the Heads of Departments."

Appellants' argument is that this provision is the exclusive method by which those charged with executing the laws of the United States may be chosen. Congress, they assert, cannot have it both ways. If the Legislature wishes the Commission to exercise all of the conferred powers, then its members are in fact "Officers of the United States" and must be appointed under the Appointments Clause. But if Congress insists upon retaining the power to appoint, then the members of the Commission may not discharge those many functions of the Commission which can be performed only by "Officers of the United States," as that term must be construed within the doctrine of separation of powers.

Appellee Commission and amici in support of the Commission urge that the Framers of the Constitution, while mindful of the need for checks and balances among the three branches of the National Government, had no intention of denying to the Legislative Branch authority to appoint its own officers. Congress, either under the Appointments Clause or under its grants of substantive legislative authority and the Necessary and Proper Clause in Art. I, is in their view empowered to provide for the appointment to the Commission in the manner which it did because the Commission is performing "appropriate legislative functions.". . .

1. Separation of Powers

. . . Our inquiry of necessity touches upon the fundamental principles of the Government established by the Framers of the Constitution, and all litigants and all of the courts which have addressed themselves to the matter start on common ground in the recognition of the intent of the Framers that the powers of the three great branches of the National Government be largely separate from one another.

James Madison, writing in the Federalist No. 47, defended the work of the Framers against the charge that these three governmental powers were not entirely separate from one another in the proposed Constitution. He asserted that while there was some admixture, the Constitution was nonetheless true to Montesquieu's well-known maxim that the legislative, executive, and judicial departments ought to be separate and distinct:

> "The reasons on which Montesquieu grounds his maxim are a further demonstration of his meaning. 'When the legislative and executive powers are united in the same person or body,' says he, 'there can be no liberty, because apprehensions may arise lest *the same* monarch or senate should *enact* tyrannical laws to *execute* them in a tyrannical manner.' Again: 'Were the power of judging joined with the legislative, the life and liberty of the subject would be exposed to arbitrary control, for *the judge* would then be *the legislator*. Were it joined to the executive power, *the judge* might behave with all the violence of *an oppressor*.' Some of these reasons are more fully explained in other passages; but briefly stated as they are here, they sufficiently establish the meaning which we have put on this celebrated maxim of this celebrated author."

Yet it is also clear from the provisions of the Constitution itself, and from the Federalist Papers, that the Constitution by no means contemplates total separation of each of these three essential branches of Government. The President is a participant in the lawmaking process by virtue of his authority to veto bills enacted by Congress. The Senate is a participant in the appointive process by virtue of its authority to refuse to confirm persons nominated to office by the President. The men who met in Philadelphia in the summer of 1787 were practical statesmen, experienced in politics, who viewed the principle of separation of powers as a vital check against tyranny. But they likewise saw that a hermetic sealing off of the three branches of Government from one another would preclude the establishment of a Nation capable of governing itself effectively. . . .

2. The Appointments Clause

The principle of separation of powers was not simply an abstract generalization in the minds of the Framers: it was woven into the document that they drafted in Philadelphia in the summer of 1787. Article I, §1, declares: "All legislative Powers herein granted shall be vested in a Congress of the United States." Article II, §1, vests the executive power "in a President of the United States of America," and Art. III, §1, declares that "The judicial Power of the United States, shall be vested in one supreme Court, and in such inferior Courts as the Congress may from time to time ordain and establish." The further concern of the Framers of the Constitution with maintenance of the separation of powers is found in the so-called "Ineligibility" and "Incompatibility" Clauses contained in Art. I, §6:

> "No Senator or Representative shall, during the Time for which he was elected, be appointed to any civil Office under the Authority of the United States, which shall have been created, or the Emoluments whereof shall have been increased during such time; and no Person holding any Office under the United States, shall be a Member of either House during his Continuance in Office."

It is in the context of these cognate provisions of the document that we must examine the language of Art. II, §2, cl. 2, which appellants contend provides the only authorization for appointment of those to whom substantial executive or administrative authority is given by statute. Because of the importance of its language, we again set out the provision:

> "[The President] shall nominate, and by and with the Advice and Consent of the Senate, shall appoint Ambassadors, other public Ministers and Consuls, Judges of the supreme Court, and all other Officers of the United States, whose Appointments are not herein otherwise provided for, and which shall be established by Law: but the Congress may by Law vest the Appointment of such inferior Officers, as they think proper, in the President alone, in the Courts of Law, or in the Heads of Departments."

The Appointments Clause could, of course, be read as merely dealing with etiquette or protocol in describing "Officers of the United States," but the drafters had a less frivolous purpose in mind. This conclusion is supported by language from *United States v. Germaine,* 99 U.S. 508, 509-510 (1879):

> "The Constitution for purposes of appointment very clearly divides all its officers into two classes. The primary class requires a nomination by the President and confirmation by the Senate. But foreseeing that when offices became numerous, and sudden removals necessary, this mode might be inconvenient, it was provided that, in regard to officers inferior to those specially mentioned, Congress might by

law vest their appointment in the President alone, in the courts of law, or in the heads of departments. *That all persons who can be said to hold an office under the government about to be established under the Constitution were intended to be included within one or the other of these modes of appointment there can be but little doubt."* (Emphasis supplied.)

We think that the term "Officers of the United States" as used in Art. II, defined to include "all persons who can be said to hold an office under the government" in *United States v. Germaine, supra,* is a term intended to have substantive meaning. We think its fair import is that any appointee exercising significant authority pursuant to the laws of the United States is an "Officer of the United States," and must, therefore, be appointed in the manner prescribed by §2, cl. 2, of that Article.

If "all persons who can be said to hold an office under the government about to be established under the Constitution were intended to be included within one or the other of these modes of appointment," *United States v. Germaine, supra,* it is difficult to see how the members of the Commission may escape inclusion. If a Postmaster first class, *Myers v. United States,* 272 U.S. 52 (1926), and the clerk of a district court, *Ex parte Hennen,* 13 Pet. 230 (1839), are inferior officers of the United States within the meaning of the Appointments Clause, as they are, surely the Commissioners before us are at the very least such "inferior Officers" within the meaning of that Clause.[162]

Although two members of the Commission are initially selected by the President, his nominations are subject to confirmation not merely by the Senate, but by the House of Representatives as well. The remaining four voting members of the Commission are appointed by the President pro tempore of the Senate and by the Speaker of the House. While the second part of the Clause authorizes Congress to vest the appointment of the officers described in that part in "the Courts of Law, or in the Heads of Departments," neither the Speaker of the House nor the President pro tempore of the Senate comes within this language.

The phrase "Heads of Departments," used as it is in conjunction with the phrase "Courts of Law," suggests that the Departments referred to are themselves in the Executive Branch or at least have some connection with that branch. While the Clause expressly authorizes Congress to vest the appointment of certain officers in the "Courts of Law," the absence of similar language to include Congress must mean that neither Congress nor its officers were included within the language "Heads of Departments" in this part of cl. 2.

Thus with respect to four of the six voting members of the Commission, neither the President, the head of any department, nor the Judiciary has any voice in their selection.

The Appointments Clause specifies the method of appointment only for "Officers of the United States" whose appointment is not "otherwise provided for" in the Constitution. But there is no provision of the Constitution remotely providing any alternative means for the selection of the members of the Commission or for anybody like them. Appellee Commission has argued, and

162. "Officers of the United States" does not include all employees of the United States, but there is no claim made that the Commissioners are employees of the United States rather than officers. Employees are lesser functionaries subordinate to officers of the United States, *see Auffmordt v. Hedden,* 137 U.S. 310, 327 (1890); *United States v. Germaine, supra,* whereas the Commissioners, appointed for a statutory term, are not subject to the control or direction of any other executive, judicial, or legislative authority.

the Court of Appeals agreed, that the Appointments Clause of Art. II should not be read to exclude the "inherent power of Congress" to appoint its own officers to perform functions necessary to that body as an institution. But there is no need to read the Appointments Clause contrary to its plain language in order to reach the result sought by the Court of Appeals. Article I, § 3, cl. 5, expressly authorizes the selection of the President pro tempore of the Senate, and § 2, cl. 5, of that Article provides for the selection of the Speaker of the House. Ranking nonmembers, such as the Clerk of the House of Representatives, are elected under the internal rules of each House[163] and are designated by statute as "officers of the Congress." There is no occasion for us to decide whether any of these member officers are "Officers of the United States" whose "appointment" is otherwise provided for within the meaning of the Appointments Clause, since even if they were such officers their appointees would not be. Contrary to the fears expressed by the majority of the Court of Appeals, nothing in our holding with respect to Art. II, § 2, cl. 2, will deny to Congress "all power to appoint its own inferior officers to carry out appropriate legislative functions."[165]

Appellee Commission and amici contend somewhat obliquely that because the Framers had no intention of relegating Congress to a position below that of the coequal Judicial and Executive Branches of the National Government, the Appointments Clause must somehow be read to include Congress or its officers as among those in whom the appointment power may be vested. But the debates of the Constitutional Convention, and the Federalist Papers, are replete with expressions of fear that the Legislative Branch of the National Government will aggrandize itself at the expense of the other two branches. The debates during the Convention, and the evolution of the draft version of the Constitution, seem to us to lend considerable support to our reading of the language of the Appointments Clause itself.

An interim version of the draft Constitution had vested in the Senate the authority to appoint Ambassadors, public Ministers, and Judges of the Supreme Court, and the language of Art. II as finally adopted is a distinct change in this regard. We believe that it was a deliberate change made by the Framers with the intent to deny Congress any authority itself to appoint those who were "Officers of the United States." The debates on the floor of the Convention reflect at least in part the way the change came about. [Discussion of the debates omitted here.]

Appellee Commission and amici urge that because of what they conceive to be the extraordinary authority reposed in Congress to regulate elections, this case stands on a different footing than if Congress had exercised its legislative authority in another field. There is, of course, no doubt that Congress has express authority to regulate congressional elections, by virtue of the power conferred

163. Rule II of the Rules of the House of Representatives, the earliest form of which was adopted in 1789, provides for the election by the House, at the commencement of each Congress, of a Clerk, Sergeant at Arms, Doorkeeper, Postmaster, and Chaplain, each of whom in turn is given appointment power over the employees of his department. Jefferson's Manual and Rules of the House of Representatives §§ 635-636. While there is apparently no equivalent rule on the Senate side, one of the first orders of business at the first session of the Senate, April 1789, was to elect a Secretary and a Doorkeeper. Senate Journal 10 (1st & 2d Congress 1789-1793).

165. Appellee Commission has relied for analogous support on the existence of the Comptroller General, who as a "legislative officer" had significant duties under the 1971 Act. § 308, 86 Stat. 16. But irrespective of Congress' designation, cf. 31 U.S.C. § 65(d), the Comptroller General is appointed by the President in conformity with the Appointments Clause. 31 U.S.C. § 42.

in Art. I, §4. This Court has also held that it has very broad authority to prevent corruption in national Presidential elections. *Burroughs v. United States,* 290 U.S. 534 (1934). But Congress has plenary authority in all areas in which it has substantive legislative jurisdiction, *McCulloch v. Maryland,* 4 Wheat. 316 (1819), so long as the exercise of that authority does not offend some other constitutional restriction. We see no reason to believe that the authority of Congress over federal election practices is of such a wholly different nature from the other grants of authority to Congress that it may be employed in such a manner as to offend well-established constitutional restrictions stemming from the separation of powers.

The position that because Congress has been given explicit and plenary authority to regulate a field of activity, it must therefore have the power to appoint those who are to administer the regulatory statute is both novel and contrary to the language of the Appointments Clause. Unless their selection is elsewhere provided for, all officers of the United States are to be appointed in accordance with the Clause. Principal officers are selected by the President with the advice and consent of the Senate. Inferior officers Congress may allow to be appointed by the President alone, by the heads of departments, or by the Judiciary. No class or type of officer is excluded because of its special functions. The President appoints judicial as well as executive officers. Neither has it been disputed — and apparently it is not now disputed — that the Clause controls the appointment of the members of a typical administrative agency even though its functions, as this Court recognized in *Humphrey's Executor v. United States,* 295 U.S. 602, 624 (1935), may be "predominantly quasi-judicial and quasi-legislative" rather than executive. The Court in that case carefully emphasized that although the members of such agencies were to be independent of the Executive in their day-to-day operations, the Executive was not excluded from selecting them. *Id.,* at 625-626. . . .

We are also told by appellees and amici that Congress had good reason for not vesting in a Commission composed wholly of Presidential appointees the authority to administer the Act, since the administration of the Act would undoubtedly have a bearing on any incumbent President's campaign for re-election. While one cannot dispute the basis for this sentiment as a practical matter, it would seem that those who sought to challenge incumbent Congressmen might have equally good reason to fear a Commission which was unduly responsive to Members of Congress whom they were seeking to unseat. But such fears, however rational, do not by themselves warrant a distortion of the Framers' work.

Appellee Commission and amici finally contend, and the majority of the Court of Appeals agreed with them, that whatever shortcomings the provisions for the appointment of members of the Commission might have under Art. II, Congress had ample authority under the Necessary and Proper Clause of Art. I to effectuate this result. We do not agree. The proper inquiry when considering the Necessary and Proper Clause is not the authority of Congress to create an office or a Commission, which is broad indeed, but rather its authority to provide that its own officers may make appointments to such office or Commission.

So framed, the claim that Congress may provide for this manner of appointment under the Necessary and Proper Clause of Art. I stands on no better footing than the claim that it may provide for such manner of appointment because of its substantive authority to regulate federal elections. Congress could not, merely because it concluded that such a measure was "necessary and proper" to the discharge of its substantive legislative authority, pass a bill of attainder or ex post facto law contrary to the prohibitions contained in §9 of Art. I. No more may it vest in itself, or in its officers, the authority to appoint officers of the United States when the Appointments Clause by clear implication prohibits it from doing so. . . .

3. The Commission's Powers

Thus, on the assumption that all of the powers granted in the statute may be exercised by an agency whose members have been appointed in accordance with the Appointments Clause, the ultimate question is which, if any, of those powers may be exercised by the present voting Commissioners, none of whom was appointed as provided by that Clause. Our previous description of the statutory provisions, disclosed that the Commission's powers fall generally into three categories: functions relating to the flow of necessary information — receipt, dissemination, and investigation; functions with respect to the Commission's task of fleshing out the statute — rulemaking and advisory opinions; and functions necessary to ensure compliance with the statute and rules — informal procedures, administrative determinations and hearings, and civil suits.

Insofar as the powers confided in the Commission are essentially of an investigative and informative nature, falling in the same general category as those powers which Congress might delegate to one of its own committees, there can be no question that the Commission as presently constituted may exercise them. As this Court stated in *McGrain, supra,* at 175:

> "A legislative body cannot legislate wisely or effectively in the absence of information respecting the conditions which the legislation is intended to affect or change; and where the legislative body does not itself possess the requisite information — which not infrequently is true — recourse must be had to others who do possess it. Experience has taught that mere requests for such information often are unavailing, and also that information which is volunteered is not always accurate or complete; so some means of compulsion are essential to obtain what is needed. All this was true before and when the Constitution was framed and adopted. In that period the power of inquiry — with enforcing process — was regarded and employed as a necessary and appropriate attribute of the power to legislate — indeed, was treated as inhering in it."

But when we go beyond this type of authority to the more substantial powers exercised by the Commission, we reach a different result. The Commission's enforcement power, exemplified by its discretionary power to seek judicial relief, is authority that cannot possibly be regarded as merely in aid of the legislative function of Congress. A lawsuit is the ultimate remedy for a breach of the law, and it is to the President, and not to the Congress, that the Constitution entrusts the responsibility to "take Care that the Laws be faithfully executed." Art. II, §3.

Congress may undoubtedly under the Necessary and Proper Clause create "offices" in the generic sense and provide such method of appointment to those "offices" as it chooses. But Congress' power under that Clause is inevitably bounded by the express language of Art. II, §2, cl. 2, and unless the method it provides comports with the latter, the holders of those offices will not be "Officers of the United States." They may, therefore, properly perform duties only in aid of those functions that Congress may carry out by itself, or in an area sufficiently removed from the administration and enforcement of the public law as to permit their being performed by persons not "Officers of the United States."

This Court observed more than a century ago with respect to litigation conducted in the courts of the United States:

> "Whether tested, therefore, by the requirements of the Judiciary Act, or by the usage of the government, or by the decisions of this court, it is clear that all such suits, so far as the interests of the United States are concerned, are subject to the direction, and within the control of, the Attorney-General." *Confiscation Cases*, 7 Wall. 454, 458-459 (1869).

The Court echoed similar sentiments 59 years later in *Springer v. Philippine Islands*, 277 U.S. at 202, saying:

> "Legislative power, as distinguished from executive power, is the authority to make laws, but not to enforce them or appoint the agents charged with the duty of such enforcement. The latter are executive functions. It is unnecessary to enlarge further upon the general subject, since it has so recently received the full consideration of this Court. *Myers v. United States*, 272 U.S. 52.
>
> "Not having the power of appointment, unless expressly granted or incidental to its powers, the legislature cannot engraft executive duties upon a legislative office, since that would be to usurp the power of appointment by indirection; though the case might be different if the additional duties were devolved upon an appointee of the executive."

We hold that these provisions of the Act, vesting in the Commission primary responsibility for conducting civil litigation in the courts of the United States for vindicating public rights, violate Art. II, §2, cl. 2, of the Constitution. Such functions may be discharged only by persons who are "Officers of the United States" within the language of that section.

All aspects of the Act are brought within the Commission's broad administrative powers: rulemaking, advisory opinions, and determinations of eligibility for funds and even for federal elective office itself. These functions, exercised free from day-to-day supervision of either Congress or the Executive Branch, are more legislative and judicial in nature than are the Commission's enforcement powers, and are of kinds usually performed by independent regulatory agencies or by some department in the Executive Branch under the direction of an Act of Congress. Congress viewed these broad powers as essential to effective and impartial administration of the entire substantive framework of the Act. Yet each of these functions also represents the performance of a significant governmental duty exercised pursuant to a public law. While the President may not insist that such functions be delegated to an appointee of his removable at will, *Humphrey's Executor v. United States*, 295 U.S. 602 (1935), none of them operates merely in aid of congressional authority to legislate or is sufficiently removed from the administration and enforcement of public law to allow it to be performed by the present Commission. These administrative functions may therefore be exercised only by persons who are "Officers of the United States."

It is also our view that the Commission's inability to exercise certain powers because of the method by which its members have been selected should not affect the validity of the Commission's administrative actions and determinations to this date, including its administration of those provisions, upheld today, authorizing the public financing of federal elections. The past acts of the Commission are therefore accorded de facto validity, just as we have recognized should be the case with respect to legislative acts performed by legislators held to have been elected in accordance with an unconstitutional apportionment plan. We also draw on the Court's practice in the apportionment and voting rights cases and stay, for a period not to exceed 30 days, the Court's judgment insofar as it affects the authority of the Commission to exercise the duties and powers granted it under the Act. This limited stay will afford Congress an opportunity to reconstitute the Commission by law or to adopt other valid enforcement mechanisms without interrupting enforcement of the provisions the Court sustains, allowing the present Commission in the interim to function de facto in accordance with the substantive provisions of the Act.

CONCLUSION

[The Court here summarized its resolution of the constitutional challenges to the substantive provisions of the Federal Election Campaign Act.] Finally, we hold that most of the powers conferred by the Act upon the Federal Election Commission can be exercised only by "Officers of the United States," appointed in conformity with Art. II, § 2, cl. 2, of the Constitution, and therefore cannot be exercised by the Commission as presently constituted.

MR. JUSTICE WHITE, concurring in part and dissenting in part. . . .

There is no doubt that the development of the administrative agency in response to modern legislative and administrative need has placed severe strain on the separation-of-powers principle in its pristine formulation. Any notion that the Constitution bans any admixture of powers that might be deemed legislative, executive, and judicial has had to give way. The independent agency has survived attacks from various directions: that it exercises invalidly delegated legislative power, *Sunshine Coal Co. v. Adkins*, 310 U.S. 381 (1940); that it invalidly exercises judicial power, *ibid.*, and that its functions are so executive in nature that its members must be subject to Presidential control, *Humphrey's Executor v. United States*, 295 U.S. 602 (1935). Until now, however, it has not been insisted that the commands of the Appointments Clause must also yield to permit congressional appointments of members of a major agency. With the Court, I am not convinced that we should create a broad exception to the requirements of that Clause that all officers of the United States be appointed in accordance with its terms. . . .

QUESTIONS

1. Does the Court's analysis of the Appointments Clause make sense? What about a congressional Sergeant at Arms?
2. Could this decision be explained just as well by *Chadha*?

3. What is the constitutional policy underlying the separation of legislative and executive power?

4. The meaning of the Appointments Clause in the context of inferior officers of the United States is addressed in *Morrison v. Olson*, 487 U.S. 654 (1988) (*infra* p. 455) and *Free Enterprise Fund v. Public Company Accounting Oversight Board*, 561 U.S. 477 (2010) (*infra* p. 471).

5. Is there a disconnect between the Supreme Court's rhetoric about the central importance of strictly enforcing the separation of powers and the remedial orders issued in these cases? The Supreme Court almost never invalidates the work performed by an administrative agency whose structural design violates the separation of powers. For example, in *Buckley, supra*, the Supreme Court expressly declined to void all of the FEC's work to date — despite the agency featuring unconstitutional legislative appointments of principal executive officers. See *Buckley*, 424 U.S. at 137-42. Indeed, the Supreme Court did not even require the FEC to stop making decisions after its decision invalidating legislative appointments to an Article II executive agency. See *Buckley*, 424 U.S. at 144 ("The mandate shall issue forthwith, except that our judgment is stayed, for a period not to exceed 30 days, insofar as it affects the authority of the Commission to exercise the duties and powers granted it under the Act").

    Professor Kent Barnett argues persuasively that "prevailing regulated parties [in constitutional separation of powers cases] often obtain not only an unsatisfactory judicial remedy, but one that may place them in an even worse position than the one they occupied before bringing suit." Kent Barnett, *To the Victor Goes the Toil — Remedies for Regulated Parties in Separation-of-Powers Litigation*, 92 N.C. L. Rev. 481, 483 (2014). He posits that the Supreme Court's failure to provide effective remedies in many major separation of powers cases "limits the efficacy of the very safeguards that courts purport to vindicate." *Id.* at 484. Barnett suggests that if the constitutional values at stake are crucially important, then "courts could provide more significant equitable remedies, such as requiring Congress to cure the structural defect if the agency is to continue acting or invalidating the past actions of an improperly structured agency." *Id.* at 536. Under the Supreme Court's current approach, however, "the remedies that courts have forged, by ignoring remedial values relevant to regulated parties, have often failed to match judicial paeans to the centrality of the structural norms." *Id.* at 546.

    Are minimalist remedial orders sufficient to vindicate important separation of powers values? If, as formalist jurists often claim, the separation of powers doctrine is integral to protecting individual liberty, shouldn't the remedies in major separation of powers cases reflect a stronger judicial commitment to undoing the work of unconstitutionally designed agencies? What does this tepid approach to remediating separation of powers violations say about the Supreme Court's real commitment to enforcing these constitutional rules? Does it suggest that formalist judges are more willing to "talk the talk" than they are to "walk the walk," when doing so would create serious dysfunction — and perhaps even regulatory chaos?

NLRB v. NOEL CANNING
134 S. Ct. 2550 (2014)

JUSTICE BREYER delivered the opinion of the Court.

Ordinarily the President must obtain "the Advice and Consent of the Senate" before appointing an "Office[r] of the United States." U.S. Const., Art. II, § 2, cl. 2. But the Recess Appointments Clause creates an exception. It gives the President alone the power "to fill up all Vacancies that may happen during the Recess of the Senate, by granting Commissions which shall expire at the End of their next Session." Art. II, § 2, cl. 3. We here consider three questions about the application of this Clause.

The first concerns the scope of the words "recess of the Senate." Does that phrase refer only to an inter-session recess (i.e., a break between formal sessions of Congress), or does it also include an intra-session recess, such as a summer recess in the midst of a session? We conclude that the Clause applies to both kinds of recess.

The second question concerns the scope of the words "vacancies that may happen." Does that phrase refer only to vacancies that first come into existence during a recess, or does it also include vacancies that arise prior to a recess but continue to exist during the recess? We conclude that the Clause applies to both kinds of vacancy.

The third question concerns calculation of the length of a "recess." The President made the appointments here at issue on January 4, 2012. At that time the Senate was in recess pursuant to a December 17, 2011, resolution providing for a series of brief recesses punctuated by "*pro forma* session[s]," with "no business . . . transacted," every Tuesday and Friday through January 20, 2012. S. J., 112th Cong., 1st Sess., 923 (2011) (hereinafter 2011 S. J.). In calculating the length of a recess are we to ignore the *pro forma* sessions, thereby treating the series of brief recesses as a single, month-long recess? We conclude that we cannot ignore these *pro forma* sessions.

Our answer to the third question means that, when the appointments before us took place, the Senate was in the midst of a 3-day recess. Three days is too short a time to bring a recess within the scope of the Clause. Thus we conclude that the President lacked the power to make the recess appointments here at issue.

I

The case before us arises out of a labor dispute. The National Labor Relations Board (NLRB) found that a Pepsi-Cola distributor, Noel Canning, had unlawfully refused to reduce to writing and execute a collective-bargaining agreement with a labor union. The Board ordered the distributor to execute the agreement and to make employees whole for any losses. *Noel Canning*, 358 N.L.R.B. No. 4 (2012).

The Pepsi-Cola distributor subsequently asked the Court of Appeals for the District of Columbia Circuit to set the Board's order aside. It claimed that three of the five Board members had been invalidly appointed, leaving the Board without the three lawfully appointed members necessary for it to act. See 29 U.S.C. § 160(f) (providing for judicial review); § 153(a) (providing for a 5-member Board); § 153(b) (providing for a 3-member quorum); *New Process Steel, L.P. v. NLRB*, 560 U.S. 674, 687–688 (2010) (in the absence of a lawfully appointed quorum, the Board cannot exercise its powers).

The three members in question were Sharon Block, Richard Griffin, and Terence Flynn. In 2011 the President had nominated each of them to the Board. As of January 2012, Flynn's nomination had been pending in the Senate awaiting confirmation for approximately a year. The nominations of each of the other two had been pending for a few weeks. On January 4, 2012, the President, invoking the Recess Appointments Clause, appointed all three to the Board. . . .

The Court of Appeals agreed that the appointments fell outside the scope of the Clause. . . .

We granted the Solicitor General's petition for certiorari. . . .

II

Before turning to the specific questions presented, we shall mention two background considerations that we find relevant to all three. First, *the Recess Appointments Clause sets forth a subsidiary, not a primary, method for appointing officers of the United States*. The immediately preceding Clause — Article II, Section 2, Clause 2 — provides the primary method of appointment. It says that the President "shall nominate, *and by and with the Advice and Consent of the Senate*, shall appoint Ambassadors, other public Ministers and Consuls, Judges of the supreme Court, and all other Officers of the United States" (emphasis added).

The Federalist Papers make clear that the Founders intended this method of appointment, requiring Senate approval, to be the norm (at least for principal officers). Alexander Hamilton wrote that the Constitution vests the power of *nomination* in the President alone because "one man of discernment is better fitted to analise and estimate the peculiar qualities adapted to particular offices, than a body of men of equal, or perhaps even of superior discernment." The Federalist No. 76, p. 510 (J. Cooke ed. 1961). At the same time, the need to secure Senate approval provides "an excellent check upon a spirit of favoritism in the President, and would tend greatly to preventing the appointment of unfit characters from State prejudice, from family connection, from personal attachment, or from a view to popularity." *Id.*, at 513. . . .

Thus the Recess Appointments Clause reflects the tension between, on the one hand, the President's continuous need for "the assistance of subordinates," *Myers v. United States*, 272 U.S. 52, 117 (1926), and, on the other, the Senate's practice, particularly during the Republic's early years, of meeting for a single brief session each year, see Art. I, § 4, cl. 2; Amdt. 20, § 2 (requiring the Senate to "assemble" only "once in every year"); 3 J. Story, Commentaries on the Constitution of the United States § 1551, p. 410 (1833) (it would be "burthensome to the senate, and expensive to the public" to require the Senate to be "perpetually in session"). We seek to interpret the Clause as granting the President the power to make appointments during a recess but not offering the President the authority routinely to avoid the need for Senate confirmation.

Second, *in interpreting the Clause, we put significant weight upon historical practice*. For one thing, the interpretive questions before us concern the allocation of power between two elected branches of Government. Long ago Chief Justice Marshall wrote that

> "a doubtful question, one on which human reason may pause, and the human judgment be suspended, in the decision of which the great principles of liberty are not concerned, but the respective powers of those who are equally the representatives of the people, are to be adjusted; if not put at rest by the practice of the government, ought to receive a considerable impression from that practice." *McCulloch v. Maryland*, 4 Wheat. 316, 401 (1819).

And we later confirmed that "[l]ong settled and established practice is a consideration of great weight in a proper interpretation of constitutional provisions" regulating the relationship between Congress and the President. *The Pocket Veto Case*, 279 U.S. 655, 689 (1929).

There is a great deal of history to consider here. Presidents have made recess appointments since the beginning of the Republic. Their frequency suggests that the Senate and President have recognized that recess appointments can be both necessary and appropriate in certain circumstances. We have not previously interpreted the Clause, and, when doing so for the first time in more than 200 years, we must hesitate to upset the compromises and working arrangements that the elected branches of Government themselves have reached.

III

The first question concerns the scope of the phrase "*the recess* of the Senate." Art. II, §2, cl. 3 (emphasis added). The Constitution provides for congressional elections every two years. And the 2-year life of each elected Congress typically consists of two formal 1-year sessions, each separated from the next by an "intersession recess." The Senate or the House of Representatives announces an intersession recess by approving a resolution stating that it will "adjourn *sine die*," i.e., without specifying a date to return (in which case Congress will reconvene when the next formal session is scheduled to begin).

The Senate and the House also take breaks in the midst of a session. The Senate or the House announces any such "intra-session recess" by adopting a resolution stating that it will "adjourn" to a fixed date, a few days or weeks or even months later. All agree that the phrase "the recess of the Senate" covers inter-session recesses. The question is whether it includes intra-session recesses as well.

In our view, the phrase "the recess" includes an intra-session recess of substantial length. Its words taken literally can refer to both types of recess. [Discussion of "Founding-era dictionaries" and usage omitted.]

We recognize that the word "the" in "*the* recess" might suggest that the phrase refers to the single break separating formal sessions of Congress. That is because the word "the" frequently (but not always) indicates "a particular thing." 2 Johnson 2003. But the word can also refer "to a term used generically or universally." 17 [Oxford English Dictionary] 879. The Constitution, for example, directs the Senate to choose a President *pro tempore* "in *the* Absence of the Vice-President." Art. I, §3, cl. 5 (emphasis added). . . . Reading "the" generically in this way, there is no linguistic problem applying the Clause's phrase to both kinds of recess. And, in fact, the phrase "the recess" was used to refer to intra-session recesses at the time of the founding.

The constitutional text is thus ambiguous. And we believe the Clause's purpose demands the broader interpretation. The Clause gives the President authority to make appointments during "the recess of the Senate" so that the President can ensure the continued functioning of the Federal Government when the Senate is away. The Senate is equally away during both an inter-session and an intra-session recess, and its capacity to participate in the appointments process has nothing to do with the words it uses to signal its departure.

History also offers strong support for the broad interpretation. . . .

In all, between the founding and the Great Depression, Congress took substantial intra-session breaks (other than holiday breaks) in four years: 1867, 1868, 1921, and 1929. And in each of those years the President made intra-session recess appointments.

Since 1929, and particularly since the end of World War II, Congress has shortened its inter-session breaks as it has taken longer and more frequent intra-session breaks; Presidents have correspondingly made more intra-session recess appointments. . . .

We recognize that the Senate cannot easily register opposition as a body to every governmental action that many, perhaps most, Senators oppose. But the Senate has not been silent or passive regarding the meaning of the Clause: A Senate Committee did register opposition to President Theodore Roosevelt's use of the Clause, and the Senate as a whole has legislated in an effort to discourage certain kinds of recess appointments. And yet we are not aware of any formal action it has taken to call into question the broad and functional definition of "recess" first set out in the 1905 Senate Report and followed by the Executive Branch since at least 1921. Nor has JUSTICE SCALIA identified any. All the while, the President has made countless recess appointments during intra-session recesses.

The upshot is that restricting the Clause to inter-session recesses would frustrate its purpose. It would make the President's recess-appointment power dependent on a formalistic distinction of Senate procedure. Moreover, the President has consistently and frequently interpreted the word "recess" to apply to intra-session recesses, and has acted on that interpretation. The Senate as a body has done nothing to deny the validity of this practice for at least three-quarters of a century. And three-quarters of a century of settled practice is long enough to entitle a practice to "great weight in a proper interpretation" of the constitutional provision. *The Pocket Veto Case*, 279 U.S., at 689. . . .

[The majority recognizes that intra-session recess appointments may extend for a longer period than inter-session appointments: "A recess appointment made between Congress' annual sessions would permit the appointee to serve for about a year, i.e., until the 'end' of the 'next' Senate 'session.' Art. II, § 2, cl. 3. But an intra-session appointment made at the beginning or in the middle of a formal session could permit the appointee to serve for 1 1/2; or almost 2 years (until the end of the following formal session)." Justice Breyer states in this regard that "[w]e agree that the intra-session interpretation permits somewhat longer recess appointments, but we do not agree that this consequence is 'illogical.' A President who makes a recess appointment will often also seek to make a regular appointment, nominating the appointee and securing ordinary Senate confirmation. And the Clause ensures that the President and Senate always have at least a full session to go through the nomination and confirmation process. That process may take several months. See O'Connell, Vacant Offices: Delays in Staffing Top Agency Positions, 82 S. Cal. L. Rev. 913, 967 (2009) (from 1987 to 2005 the nomination and confirmation process took an average of 236 days for noncabinet agency heads). A recess appointment that lasts somewhat longer than a year will ensure the President the continued assistance of subordinates that the Clause permits him to obtain while he and the Senate select a regular appointee. An appointment should last until the Senate has 'an opportunity to act on the subject,' Story, § 1551, at 410, and the Clause embodies a determination that a full session is needed to select and vet a replacement."]

The greater interpretive problem is determining how long a recess must be in order to fall within the Clause. Is a break of a week, or a day, or an hour too short to count as a "recess"? The Clause itself does not say. And JUSTICE SCALIA claims that this silence itself shows that the Framers intended the Clause to apply only to an inter-session recess.

We disagree. For one thing, the most likely reason the Framers did not place a textual floor underneath the word "recess" is that they did not foresee the *need* for one. They might have expected that the Senate would meet for a single session lasting at most half a year. The Federalist No. 84, at 596 (A. Hamilton). And they might not have anticipated that intra-session recesses would become lengthier and more significant than inter-session ones. The Framers' lack of clairvoyance on that point is not dispositive. Unlike JUSTICE SCALIA, we think it most consistent with our constitutional structure to presume that the Framers would have allowed intra-session recess appointments where there was a long history of such practice.

Moreover, the lack of a textual floor raises a problem that plagues both interpretations—JUSTICE SCALIA's and ours. Today a brief inter-session recess is just as possible as a brief intra-session recess. And though JUSTICE SCALIA says that the "notion that the Constitution empowers the President to make unilateral appointments every time the Senate takes a half-hour lunch break is *so absurd as to be self-refuting*," he must immediately concede (in a footnote) that the President "can make recess appointments during any break *between* sessions, *no matter how short*." Post, at n. 4 (emphasis added).

Even the Solicitor General, arguing for a broader interpretation, acknowledges that there is a lower limit applicable to both kinds of recess. He argues that the lower limit should be three days by analogy to the Adjournments Clause of the Constitution. That Clause says: "Neither House, during the Session of Congress, shall, without the Consent of the other, adjourn for more than three days." Art. I, § 5, cl. 4.

We agree with the Solicitor General that a 3-day recess would be too short. . . . The Adjournments Clause reflects the fact that a 3-day break is not a significant interruption of legislative business. As the Solicitor General says, it is constitutionally *de minimis*. A Senate recess that is so short that it does not require the consent of the House is not long enough to trigger the President's recess-appointment power.

That is not to say that the President may make recess appointments during any recess that is "more than three days." Art. I, § 5, cl. 4. The Recess Appointments Clause seeks to permit the Executive Branch to function smoothly when Congress is unavailable. And though Congress has taken short breaks for almost 200 years, and there have been many thousands of recess appointments in that time, we have not found a single example of a recess appointment made during an intra-session recess that was shorter than 10 days. . . .

In sum, we conclude that the phrase "the recess" applies to both intra-session and inter-session recesses. If a Senate recess is so short that it does not require the consent of the House, it is too short to trigger the Recess Appointments Clause. See Art. I, § 5, cl. 4. And a recess lasting less than 10 days is presumptively too short as well.

IV

The second question concerns the scope of the phrase "vacancies *that may happen* during the recess of the Senate." Art. II, § 2, cl. 3 (emphasis added). All agree that the phrase applies to vacancies that initially occur during a recess. But does it also apply to vacancies that initially occur before a recess and continue to exist during the recess? In our view the phrase applies to both kinds of vacancy.

We believe that the Clause's language, read literally, permits, though it does not naturally favor, our broader interpretation. We concede that the most natural meaning of "happens" as applied to a "vacancy" (at least to a modern ear) is that the vacancy "happens" when it initially occurs. *See* 1 Johnson 913 (defining "happen" in relevant part as meaning "[t]o fall out; to chance; to come to pass"). But that is not the only possible way to use the word. . . .

In any event, the linguistic question here is not whether the phrase can be, but whether it must be, read more narrowly. The question is whether the Clause is ambiguous. *The Pocket Veto Case*, 279 U.S., at 690. And the broader reading, we believe, is at least a permissible reading of a "'doubtful'" phrase. *Ibid.* We consequently go on to consider the Clause's purpose and historical practice.

The Clause's purpose strongly supports the broader interpretation. That purpose is to permit the President to obtain the assistance of subordinate officers when the Senate, due to its recess, cannot confirm them. . . .

While we concede that both interpretations carry with them some risk of undesirable consequences, we believe the narrower interpretation risks undermining constitutionally conferred powers more seriously and more often. It would prevent the President from making any recess appointment that arose before a recess, no matter who the official, no matter how dire the need, no matter how uncontroversial the appointment, and no matter how late in the session the office fell vacant. Overall, like Attorney General Wirt, we believe the broader interpretation more consistent with the Constitution's "reason and spirit." 1 Op. Atty. Gen., at 632.

Historical practice over the past 200 years strongly favors the broader interpretation. The tradition of applying the Clause to pre-recess vacancies dates at least to President James Madison. . . .

This power is important. . . . [W]e have enough information to believe that the Presidents since Madison have made many recess appointments filling vacancies that initially occurred prior to a recess. . . . [N]early every 19th- and 20th-century Attorney General expressing a view on the matter has agreed with William Wirt, and Presidents tend to follow the legal advice of their chief legal officers. . . . No one disputes that every President since James Buchanan has made recess appointments to pre-existing vacancies. . . .

The upshot is that the President has consistently and frequently interpreted the Recess Appointments Clause to apply to vacancies that initially occur before, but continue to exist during, a recess of the Senate. The Senate as a body has not countered this practice for nearly three-quarters of a century, perhaps longer. The tradition is long enough to entitle the practice "to great regard in determining the true construction" of the constitutional provision. *The Pocket Veto Case*, 279 U.S., at 690. And we are reluctant to upset this traditional practice where doing so would seriously shrink the authority that Presidents have believed existed and have exercised for so long.

In light of some linguistic ambiguity, the basic purpose of the Clause, and the historical practice we have described, we conclude that the phrase "all vacancies" includes vacancies that come into existence while the Senate is in session.

V

The third question concerns the calculation of the length of the Senate's "recess." On December 17, 2011, the Senate by unanimous consent adopted a resolution to convene "*pro forma* session[s]" only, with "no business . . . transacted," on every Tuesday and Friday from December 20, 2011, through January 20, 2012. 2011 S.J. 923. At the end of each *pro forma* session, the Senate would "adjourn until" the following *pro forma* session. *Ibid.* During that period, the Senate convened and adjourned as agreed. It held *pro forma* sessions on December 20, 23, 27, and 30, and on January 3, 6, 10, 13, 17, and 20; and at the end of each *pro forma* session, it adjourned until the time and date of the next. *Id.*, at 923-924.

The President made the recess appointments before us on January 4, 2012, in between the January 3 and the January 6 *pro forma* sessions. We must determine the significance of these sessions — that is, whether, for purposes of the Clause, we should treat them as periods when the Senate was in session or as periods when it was in recess. If the former, the period between January 3 and January 6 was a 3-day recess, which is too short to trigger the President's recess-appointment power. If the latter, however, then the 3-day period was part of a much longer recess during which the President did have the power to make recess appointments.

. . . [W]e conclude that when the Senate declares that it is in session and possesses the capacity, under its own rules, to conduct business, it is in session for purposes of the Clause.

Applying this standard, we find that the *pro forma* sessions were sessions for purposes of the Clause. First, the Senate said it was in session. . . .

Second, the Senate's rules make clear that during its *pro forma* sessions, despite its resolution that it would conduct no business, the Senate retained the power to conduct business. During any *pro forma* session, the Senate could have conducted business simply by passing a unanimous consent agreement. The Senate in fact conducts much of its business through unanimous consent. Senate rules presume that a quorum is present unless a present Senator questions it. And when the Senate has a quorum, an agreement is unanimously passed if, upon its proposal, no present Senator objects. It is consequently unsurprising that the Senate has enacted legislation during pro forma sessions even when it has said that no business will be transacted. Indeed, the Senate passed a bill by unanimous consent during the second *pro forma* session after its December 17 adjournment. 2011 S.J. 924. And that bill quickly became law. Pub. L. 112–78, 125 Stat. 1280. . . .

VI

The Recess Appointments Clause responds to a structural difference between the Executive and Legislative Branches: The Executive Branch is perpetually in operation, while the Legislature only acts in intervals separated by recesses. The purpose of the Clause is to allow the Executive to continue operating while the Senate is unavailable. We believe that the Clause's text, standing alone, is ambiguous. It does not resolve whether the President may make appointments during intra-session recesses, or whether he may fill pre-recess vacancies. But the broader reading better serves the Clause's structural function. Moreover, that broader reading is reinforced by centuries of history, which we are hesitant to disturb. We thus hold that the Constitution empowers the President to fill any existing vacancy during any recess — intra-session or inter-session — of sufficient length.

JUSTICE SCALIA would render illegitimate thousands of recess appointments reaching all the way back to the founding era. More than that: Calling the Clause an "anachronism," he would basically read it out of the Constitution. He performs this act of judicial excision in the name of liberty. We fail to see how excising the Recess Appointments Clause preserves freedom. In fact, Alexander Hamilton observed in the very first Federalist Paper that "the vigour of government is essential to the security of liberty." The Federalist No. 1, at 5. And the Framers included the Recess Appointments Clause to preserve the "vigour of government" at times when an important organ of Government, the United States Senate, is in recess. JUSTICE SCALIA's interpretation of the Clause would defeat the power of the Clause to achieve that objective.

The foregoing discussion should refute JUSTICE SCALIA's claim that we have "embrace[d]" an "adverse-possession theory of executive power." Instead, as in all cases, we interpret the Constitution in light of its text, purposes, and "our whole experience" as a Nation. *Missouri v. Holland*, 252 U.S. 416, 433 (1920). And we look to the actual practice of Government to inform our interpretation.

Given our answer to the last question before us, we conclude that the Recess Appointments Clause does not give the President the constitutional authority to make the appointments here at issue. Because the Court of Appeals reached the same ultimate conclusion (though for reasons we reject), its judgment is affirmed.

It is so ordered.

JUSTICE SCALIA, with whom THE CHIEF JUSTICE, JUSTICE THOMAS, and JUSTICE ALITO join, concurring in the judgment.

Except where the Constitution or a valid federal law provides otherwise, all "Officers of the United States" must be appointed by the President "by and with the Advice and Consent of the Senate." U.S. Const., Art. II, §2, cl. 2. That general rule is subject to an exception: "The President shall have Power to fill up all Vacancies that may happen during the Recess of the Senate, by granting Commissions which shall expire at the End of their next Session." *Id.*, §2, cl. 3. This case requires us to decide whether the Recess Appointments Clause authorized three appointments made by President Obama to the National Labor Relations Board in January 2012 without the Senate's consent.

To prevent the President's recess-appointment power from nullifying the Senate's role in the appointment process, the Constitution cabins that power in two significant ways. First, it may be exercised only in "the Recess of the Senate," that is, the intermission between two formal legislative sessions. Second, it may be used to fill only those vacancies that "happen during the Recess," that is, offices that become vacant during that intermission. Both conditions are clear from the Constitution's text and structure, and both were well understood at the founding. The Court of Appeals correctly held that the appointments here at issue are invalid because they did not meet either condition.

Today's Court agrees that the appointments were invalid, but for the far narrower reason that they were made during a 3-day break in the Senate's session. On its way to that result, the majority sweeps away the key textual limitations on the recess-appointment power. It holds, first, that the President can make appointments without the Senate's participation even during short breaks in the middle of the Senate's session, and second, that those appointments can fill offices that became vacant long before the break in which they were filled. The majority justifies those atextual results on an adverse-possession theory of executive authority: Presidents have long claimed the powers in question, and the Senate has not disputed those claims with sufficient vigor, so the Court should not "upset the compromises and working arrangements that the elected branches of Government themselves have reached."

The Court's decision transforms the recess-appointment power from a tool carefully designed to fill a narrow and specific need into a weapon to be wielded by future Presidents against future Senates. To reach that result, the majority casts aside the plain, original meaning of the constitutional text in deference to late-arising historical practices that are ambiguous at best. The majority's insistence on deferring to the Executive's untenably broad interpretation of the power is in clear conflict with our precedent and forebodes a diminution of this Court's role in controversies involving the separation of powers and the structure of government. I concur in the judgment only.

I. OUR RESPONSIBILITY

Today's majority disregards two overarching principles that ought to guide our consideration of the questions presented here.

First, the Constitution's core, government-structuring provisions are no less critical to preserving liberty than are the later adopted provisions of the Bill of Rights. . . .

Second and relatedly, when questions involving the Constitution's government-structuring provisions are presented in a justiciable case, it is the solemn responsibility of the Judicial Branch "'to say what the law is.'" *Zivotofsky v. Clinton*, 132 S. Ct. 1421, 1428 (2012) (quoting *Marbury v. Madison*, 1 Cranch 137, 177 (1803)). . . . [P]olicing the "enduring structure" of constitutional government when the political branches fail to do so is "one of the most vital functions of this

Court." *Public Citizen v. Department of Justice*, 491 U.S. 440, 468 (1989) (Kennedy, J., concurring in judgment).

Our decision in *Chadha* illustrates that principle. There, we held that a statutory provision authorizing one House of Congress to cancel an executive action taken pursuant to statutory authority — a so-called "legislative veto" — exceeded the bounds of Congress's authority under the Constitution. 462 U.S., at 957-959. We did not hesitate to hold the legislative veto unconstitutional even though Congress had enacted, and the President had signed, nearly 300 similar provisions over the course of 50 years. *Id.*, at 944-945. . . .

Of course, where a governmental practice has been open, widespread, and unchallenged since the early days of the Republic, the practice should guide our interpretation of an ambiguous constitutional provision. See, e.g., *Alden v. Maine*, 527 U.S. 706, 743–744 (1999). But "'[p]ast practice does not, by itself, create power.'" *Medellín v. Texas*, 552 U.S. 491, 532 (2008) (quoting *Dames & Moore v. Regan*, 453 U.S. 654, 686 (1981)). That is a necessary corollary of the principle that the political branches cannot by agreement alter the constitutional structure. Plainly, then, a self-aggrandizing practice adopted by one branch well after the founding, often challenged, and never before blessed by this Court — in other words, the sort of practice on which the majority relies in this case — does not relieve us of our duty to interpret the Constitution in light of its text, structure, and original understanding.

Ignoring our more recent precedent in this area, which is extensive, the majority relies on *The Pocket Veto Case*, 279 U.S. 655, 689 (1929), for the proposition that when interpreting a constitutional provision "regulating the relationship between Congress and the President," we must defer to the settled practice of the political branches if the provision is "'"in any respect of doubtful meaning."'" The language the majority quotes from that case was pure dictum. . . .

II. Intra-Session Breaks

The first question presented is whether "the Recess of the Senate," during which the President's recess-appointment power is active, is (a) the period between two of the Senate's formal sessions, or (b) any break in the Senate's proceedings. I would hold that "the Recess" is the gap between sessions and that the appointments at issue here are invalid because they undisputedly were made *during* the Senate's session. The Court's contrary conclusion — that "the Recess" includes "breaks in the midst of a session," — is inconsistent with the Constitution's text and structure, and it requires judicial fabrication of vague, unadministrable limits on the recess-appointment power (thus defined) that overstep the judicial role. And although the majority relies heavily on "historical practice," no practice worthy of our deference supports the majority's conclusion on this issue.

A. Plain Meaning

[Justice Scalia engaged in a lengthy analysis of the text of the Constitution, focusing on the meaning of "the Recess." In footnote 4, Justice Scalia addressed the issue of whether the President may exercise inter-session recess appointment power regardless of whether the inter-session recess has a very short duration. Justice Scalia stated that, "[i]f the Clause is given its plain meaning, the President cannot make recess appointments during the session but can make recess appointments during any break between sessions, no matter how short. *Contra* the majority, that is not a 'problem.' True, the recess-appointment power applies even during very short inter-session breaks. But inter-session breaks typically occur at most a few times a year, and the recess-appointment power is of limited utility during very short inter-session breaks since, as explained below, the President can fill only those vacancies that arise during the break. . . . [T]he requirement that there actually be a[n inter-session] recess does not involve anywhere near the level of indeterminacy entailed by the majority's requirement that the recess be long enough (or the circumstances unusual enough), as determined by a court, to trigger the recess-appointment power." Justice Scalia's analysis in this section concluded with the two paragraphs that follow.]

Even if the many questions raised by the majority's failure to articulate a standard could be answered, a larger question would remain: If the Constitution's text empowers the President to make appointments during any break in the Senate's proceedings, by what right does the majority subject the President's exercise of that power to vague, court-crafted limitations with no textual basis? The majority claims its temporal guideposts are informed by executive practice, but a President's self-restraint cannot "bind his successors by diminishing their powers." *Free Enterprise Fund*, 561 U.S., at 497.

An interpretation that calls for this kind of judicial adventurism cannot be correct. Indeed, if the Clause really did use "Recess" in its colloquial sense, then there would be no "judicially discoverable and manageable standard for resolving" whether a particular break was long enough to trigger the recess-appointment power, making that a nonjusticiable political question. *Zivotofsky*, 132 S. Ct., at 1427 (internal quotation marks omitted).

B. HISTORICAL PRACTICE

For the foregoing reasons, the Constitution's text and structure unambiguously refute the majority's freewheeling interpretation of "the Recess." It is not plausible that the Constitution uses that term in a sense that authorizes the President to make unilateral appointments during any break in Senate proceedings, subject only to hazy, atextual limits crafted by this Court centuries after ratification. The majority, however, insists that history "offers strong support" for its interpretation. The historical practice of the political branches is, of course, irrelevant when the Constitution is clear. But even if the Constitution were thought ambiguous on this point, history does not support the majority's interpretation.

[Justice Scalia presented a lengthy review of the historical practice.]

What does all this amount to? In short: Intra-session recess appointments were virtually unheard of for the first 130 years of the Republic, were deemed unconstitutional by the first Attorney General to address them, were not openly defended by the Executive until 1921, were not made in significant numbers until after World War II, and have been repeatedly criticized as unconstitutional by Senators of both parties. It is astonishing for the majority to assert that this history lends "strong support," to its interpretation of the Recess Appointments Clause. And the majority's contention that recent executive practice in this area merits deference because the Senate has not done more to oppose it is utterly divorced from our precedent. . . .

. . . In any controversy between the political branches over a separation-of-powers question, staking out a position and defending it over time is far easier for the Executive Branch than for the Legislative Branch. All Presidents have a high interest in expanding the powers of their office, since the more power the President can wield, the more effectively he can implement his political agenda; whereas individual Senators may have little interest in opposing Presidential encroachment on legislative prerogatives, especially when the encroacher is a President who is the leader of their own party. (The majority would not be able to point to a lack of "formal action" by the Senate "as a body" challenging intra-session recess appointments had the appointing President's party in the Senate not blocked such action on multiple occasions.) And when the President wants to assert a power and establish a precedent, he faces neither the collective-action problems nor the procedural inertia inherent in the legislative process. The majority's methodology thus all but guarantees the continuing aggrandizement of the Executive Branch.

III. Pre-Recess Vacancies

The second question presented is whether vacancies that "happen during the Recess of the Senate," which the President is empowered to fill with recess appointments, are (a) vacancies that arise during the recess, or (b) all vacancies that exist during the recess, regardless of when they arose. I would hold that the recess-appointment power is limited to vacancies that arise during the recess in which they are filled, and I would hold that the appointments at issue here — which undisputedly filled pre-recess vacancies — are invalid for that reason as well as for the reason that they were made during the session. The Court's contrary conclusion is inconsistent with the Constitution's text and structure, and it further undermines the balance the Framers struck between Presidential and Senatorial power. Historical practice also fails to support the majority's conclusion on this issue.

A. plain meaning

As the majority concedes, "the most natural meaning of 'happens' as applied to a 'vacancy' . . . is that the vacancy 'happens' when it initially occurs." The majority adds that this meaning is most natural "to a modern ear," but it fails to show that founding-era ears heard it differently. [Justice Scalia provided an analysis of the plain meaning of the Constitution's text, including an extended discussion of how the relevant text was understood.]

B. historical practice

For the reasons just given, it is clear that the Constitution authorizes the President to fill unilaterally only those vacancies that arise during a recess, not every vacancy that happens to exist during a recess. Again, however, the majority says "[h]istorical practice" requires the broader interpretation. And again the majority is mistaken. [Justice Scalia engaged in an extended discussion of the historical practice related to the President's recess appointment when the vacancy arose prior to the recess.]

In sum: Washington's and Adams' Attorneys General read the Constitution to restrict recess appointments to vacancies arising during the recess, and there is no evidence that any of the first four Presidents consciously departed from that reading. The contrary reading was first defended by an executive official in 1823, was vehemently rejected by the Senate in 1863, was vigorously resisted by legislation in place from 1863 until 1940, and is arguably inconsistent with legislation in place from 1940 to the present. The Solicitor General has identified only about 100 appointments that have ever been made under the broader reading, and while it seems likely that a good deal more have been made in the last few decades, there is good reason to doubt that many were made before 1940 (since the appointees could not have been compensated). I can conceive of no sane constitutional theory under which this evidence of "historical practice" — which is actually evidence of a long-simmering inter-branch conflict — would require us to defer to the views of the Executive Branch.

IV. CONCLUSION

What the majority needs to sustain its judgment is an ambiguous text and a clear historical practice. What it has is a clear text and an at-best-ambiguous historical practice. Even if the Executive could accumulate power through adverse possession by engaging in a *consistent* and *unchallenged* practice over a long period of time, the oft-disputed practices at issue here would not meet that standard. . . .

The majority replaces the Constitution's text with a new set of judge-made rules to govern recess appointments. Henceforth, the Senate can avoid triggering the President's now-vast recess-appointment power by the odd contrivance of never adjourning for more than three days without holding a *pro forma* session at which it is understood that no business will be conducted. How this new regime will work in practice remains to be seen. . . .

The real tragedy of today's decision is not simply the abolition of the Constitution's limits on the recess-appointment power and the substitution of a novel framework invented by this Court. It is the damage done to our separation-of-powers jurisprudence more generally. It is not every day that we encounter a proper case or controversy requiring interpretation of the Constitution's structural provisions. Most of the time, the interpretation of those provisions is left to the political branches — which, in deciding how much respect to afford the constitutional text, often take their cues from this Court. We should therefore take every opportunity to affirm the primacy of the Constitution's enduring principles over the politics of the moment. Our failure to do so today will resonate well beyond the particular dispute at hand. Sad, but true: The Court's embrace of the adverse-possession theory of executive power (a characterization the majority resists but does not refute) will be cited in diverse contexts, including those presently unimagined, and will have the effect of aggrandizing the Presidency beyond its constitutional bounds and undermining respect for the separation of powers.

I concur in the judgment only.

QUESTIONS

1. Justice Breyer states in the majority opinion that the Court's recognition of a broader recess appointments power for the President "will ensure the President the continued assistance of subordinates that the Clause permits him to obtain while he and the Senate select a regular appointee." 134 S. Ct. at 2565. He cites the work of Professor Anne Joseph O'Connell to explain that the nomination and confirmation "process may take several months. *See* O'Connell, Vacant Offices: Delays in Staffing Top Agency Positions, 82 S.

Cal. L. Rev. 913, 967 (2009) (from 1987 to 2005 the nomination and confirmation process took an average of 236 days for noncabinet agency heads)." Professor O'Connell states that her article "provides a systematic study of executive agency vacancies from President Carter to President George W. Bush" and that, "[b]y one measure, Senate-confirmed positions were empty (or filled by acting officials), on average, one-quarter of the time over these administrations." *Id.* at 914. Given these background facts about important agency vacancies and the time needed to fill them on a permanent basis, does the majority's decision reflect a functional approach to separation of powers? Is the majority's recognition of this broader executive authority to make recess appointments needed to ensure, in Alexander Hamilton's words, "the vigour of government"? Does the majority apply the encroachment/aggrandizement analysis to decide the Constitutional questions?

2. How clear is the text of the Constitution regarding the issue of intra-session recesses? Regarding the time when the vacancy occurs?

3. Why does Justice Scalia believe that "the adverse possession theory of executive power" favors the President over the Senate, or the legislative branch more generally?

4. Does the majority's presumptive ten-day rule apply to both inter-session and intra-session recess appointments? Would a President's inter-session recess appointments be valid under the majority's approach if the new session began a few hours, or even minutes, after the old session had concluded? Would they be valid under Justice Scalia's approach? Should the analysis focus on the fact that one session had ended before a new session had begun? Or should the practical availability of the Senate to receive and consider nominations be the controlling factor? A description of Senate nominations procedure states that "[n]ominations that are not confirmed or rejected are returned to the President at the end of a session or when the Senate adjourns or recesses for more than 30 days (Senate Rule XXXI, paragraph 6). If the President still wants a nominee considered, he must submit a new nomination to the Senate. The Senate can, however, waive this rule by unanimous consent, and it often does to allow nominations to remain 'in status quo' between the first and second sessions of a Congress or during a long recess." Elizabeth Rybicki, Senate Consideration of Presidential Nominations: Committee and Floor Procedure 11 (March 9, 2015) (Congressional Research Service Report 7-5700). Does this procedure mean that the length of inter-session recesses should be treated differently when assessing the President's recess appointments power?

F. EXECUTIVE POWER TO REMOVE

MYERS v. UNITED STATES
272 U.S. 52 (1926)

Mr. Chief Justice Taft delivered the opinion of the Court.

This case presents the question whether under the Constitution the President has the exclusive power of removing executive officers of the United States whom he has appointed by and with the advice and consent of the Senate.

Myers, appellant's intestate, was on July 21, 1917, appointed by the President, by and with the advice and consent of the Senate, to be a postmaster of the first class at Portland, Oregon, for a term of four years. On January 20, 1920, Myers' resignation was demanded. He refused the demand. On February 2, 1920, he was removed from office by order of the Postmaster General, acting by direction of the President. February 10th, Myers sent a petition to the President and another to the Senate Committee on Post Offices, asking to be heard, if any charges were filed. He protested to the Department against his removal, and continued to do so until the end of his term. He pursued no other occupation and drew compensation for no other service during the interval. On April 21, 1921, he brought this suit in the Court of Claims for his salary from the date of his removal, which, as claimed by supplemental petition filed after July 21, 1921, the end of his term, amounted to $8,838.71. In August, 1920, the President made a recess appointment of one Jones, who took office September 19, 1920.

The Court of Claims gave judgment against Myers, and this is an appeal from that judgment. . . .

By the 6th section of the Act of Congress of July 12, 1876, 19 Stat. 80, 81, c. 179, under which Myers was appointed with the advice and consent of the Senate as a first-class postmaster, it is provided that

> "Postmasters of the first, second and third classes shall be appointed and may be removed by the President by and with the advice and consent of the Senate and shall hold their offices for four years unless sooner removed or suspended according to law."

The Senate did not consent to the President's removal of Myers during his term. If this statute, in its requirement that his term should be four years unless sooner removed by the President by and with the consent of the Senate, is valid, the appellant, Myers' administratrix, is entitled to recover his unpaid salary for his full term, and the judgment of the Court of Claims must be reversed. The Government maintains that the requirement is invalid, for the reason that under Article II of the Constitution the President's power of removal of executive officers appointed by him with the advice and consent of the Senate is full and complete without consent of the Senate. If this view is sound, the removal of Myers by the President without the Senate's consent was legal and the judgment of the Court of Claims against the appellant was correct. . . . We are therefore confronted by the constitutional question and can not avoid it. . . .

. . . There is no express provision respecting removals in the Constitution, except as Section 4 of Article II provides for removal from office by impeachment. The subject was not discussed in the Constitutional Convention. . . .

The vesting of the executive power in the President was essentially a grant of the power to execute the laws. But the President alone and unaided could not execute the laws. He must execute them by the assistance of subordinates. . . . As he is charged specifically to take care that they be faithfully executed, the reasonable implication, even in the absence of express words, was that as part of his executive power he should select those who were to act for him under his direction in the execution of the laws. The further implication must be, in the absence of any express limitation respecting removals, that as his selection of administrative officers is essential to the execution of the laws by him, so must be his power of removing those for whom he can not continue to be responsible.

It was urged that the natural meaning of the term "executive power" granted the President included the appointment and removal of executive subordinates. If such appointments and removals were not an exercise of the executive power, what were they? They certainly were not the exercise of legislative or judicial power in government as usually understood. . . .

. . . A veto by the Senate — a part of the legislative branch of the Government — upon removals is a much greater limitation upon the executive branch and a much more serious blending of the legislative with the executive than a rejection of a proposed appointment. It is not to be implied. The rejection of a nominee of the President for a particular office does not greatly embarrass him in the conscientious discharge of his high duties in the selection of those who are to aid him, because the President usually has an ample field from which to select for office, according to his preference, competent and capable men. The Senate has full power to reject newly proposed appointees whenever the President shall remove the incumbents. Such a check enables the Senate to prevent the filling of offices with bad or incompetent men or with those against whom there is tenable objection.

The power to prevent the removal of an officer who has served under the President is different from the authority to consent to or reject his appointment. When a nomination is made, it may be presumed that the Senate is, or may become, as well advised as to the fitness of the nominee as the President, but in the nature of things the defects in ability or intelligence or loyalty in the administration of the laws of one who has served as an officer under the President, are facts as to which the President, or his trusted subordinates, must be better informed than the Senate, and the power to remove him may, therefore, be regarded as confined, for very sound and practical reasons, to the governmental authority which has administrative control. The power of removal is incident to the power of appointment, not to the power of advising and consenting to appointment, and when the grant of the executive power is enforced by the express mandate to take care that the laws be faithfully executed, it emphasizes the necessity for including within the executive power as conferred the exclusive power of removal. . . .

The constitutional construction that excludes Congress from legislative power to provide for the removal of superior officers finds support in the second section of Article II. By it the appointment of all officers, whether superior or inferior, by the President is declared to be subject to the advice and consent of the Senate. In the absence of any specific provision to the contrary, the power of appointment to executive office carries with it, as a necessary incident, the power of removal. Whether the Senate must concur in the removal is aside from the point we now are considering. That point is, that by the specific constitutional provision for appointment of executive officers with its necessary incident of removal, the power of appointment and removal is clearly provided for by the Constitution, and the legislative power of Congress in respect to both is excluded save by the specific exception as to inferior offices in the clause that follows, viz, "but the Congress may by law vest the appointment of such inferior officers, as they think proper, in the President alone, in the Courts of Law, or in the Heads of Departments." These words, it has been held by this Court, give to Congress the power to limit and regulate removal of such inferior officers by heads of departments when it exercises its constitutional power to lodge the power of appointment with them. Here, then, is an express provision, introduced in words of exception, for the exercise by Congress of legislative power in the matter of appointments and removals in the case of inferior executive officers. The phrase "But Congress may by law vest" is equivalent to "excepting that Congress may by law vest." By the plainest implication it excludes Congressional dealing with appointments or removals of executive officers not falling within the exception, and leaves unaffected the executive power of the President to appoint and remove them. . . .

It is argued that the denial of the legislative power to regulate removals in some way involves the denial of power to prescribe qualifications for office, or reasonable classification for promotion, and yet that has been often exercised. We see no conflict between the latter power and that of appointment and removal, provided of course that the qualifications do not so limit selection and so trench upon executive choice as to be in effect legislative designation. . . .

Made responsible under the Constitution for the effective enforcement of the law, the President needs as an indispensable aid to meet it the disciplinary influence upon those who act under him of a reserve power of removal. But it is contended that executive officers appointed by the President with the consent of the Senate are bound by the statutory law and are not his servants to do his will, and that his obligation to care for the faithful execution of the laws does not authorize him to treat them as such. The degree of guidance in the discharge of their duties that the President may exercise over executive officers varies with the character of their service as prescribed in the law under which they act. The highest and most important duties which his subordinates perform are those in which they act for him. In such cases they are exercising not their own but his discretion. This field is a very large one. It is sometimes described as political. Each head of a department is and must be the President's alter ego in the matters of that department where the President is required by law to exercise authority. . . .

In all such cases [of executive authority], the discretion to be exercised is that of the President in determining the national public interest and in directing the action to be taken by his executive subordinates to protect it. In this field his cabinet officers must do his will. He must place in each member of his official family, and his chief executive subordinates, implicit faith. The moment that he loses confidence in the intelligence, ability, judgment or loyalty of any one of them he must have the power to remove him without delay. To require him to file charges and submit them to the consideration of the Senate might make impossible that unity and coordination in executive administration essential to effective action.

The duties of the heads of departments and bureaus in which the discretion of the President is exercised and which we have described, are the most important in the whole field of executive action of the Government. There is nothing in the Constitution which permits a distinction between the removal of the head of a department or a bureau, when he discharges a political duty of the President or exercises his discretion, and the removal of executive officers engaged in the discharge of their other normal duties. The imperative reasons requiring an unrestricted power to remove the most important of his subordinates in their most important duties must, therefore, control the interpretation of the Constitution as to all appointed by him.

But this is not to say that there are not strong reasons why the President should have a like power to remove his appointees charged with other duties than those above described. The ordinary duties of officers prescribed by statute come under the general administrative control of the President by virtue of the general grant to him of the executive power, and he may properly supervise and guide their construction of the statutes under which they act in order to secure that unitary and uniform execution of the laws which Article II of the Constitution evidently contemplated in vesting general executive power in the President alone. Laws are often passed with specific provision for the adoption of regulations by a department or bureau head to make the law workable and effective. The ability and judgment manifested by the official thus empowered, as well as his energy and stimulation of his subordinates, are subjects which the President must consider and supervise in his administrative control. Finding such officers to be negligent and inefficient, the President should have the power to remove them. Of course there may be duties so peculiarly and specifically committed to the discretion of a particular officer as to raise a question whether the President may overrule or revise the officer's interpretation of his statutory duty in a particular instance. Then there may be duties of a quasi-judicial character imposed on executive officers and members of executive tribunals whose decisions after hearing affect interests of individuals, the discharge of which the President can not in a particular case properly influence or control. But even in such a case he may consider the decision after its rendition as a reason for removing the officer, on the ground that the discretion regularly entrusted to that officer by statute has not been on the whole intelligently or wisely exercised. Otherwise he does not discharge his own constitutional duty of seeing that the laws be faithfully executed. . . .

We come now to consider an argument advanced and strongly pressed on behalf of the complainant, that this case concerns only the removal of a postmaster; that a postmaster is an inferior officer. . . .

It is further pressed on us that, . . . under the legislative power given Congress with respect to such [inferior] officers, it might directly legislate as to the method of their removal without changing their method of appointment by the President with the consent of the Senate. We do not think the language of the Constitution justifies such a contention.

Section 2 of Article II, after providing that the President shall nominate and with the consent of the Senate appoint ambassadors, other public ministers, consuls, judges of the Supreme Court and all other officers of the United States whose appointments are not herein otherwise provided for, and which shall be established by law, contains the proviso "but the Congress may by law vest the appointment of such inferior officers as they think proper in the President alone, in the courts of law or in the heads of departments." . . .

The power to remove inferior executive officers, like that to remove superior executive officers, is an incident of the power to appoint them, and is in its nature an executive power. The authority of Congress given by the excepting clause to vest the appointment of such inferior officers in the heads of departments carries with it authority incidentally to invest the heads of departments with power to remove. It has been the practice of Congress to do so and this Court has recognized that power. The Court also has recognized . . . that Congress, in committing the appointment of such inferior officers to the heads of departments, may prescribe incidental regulations controlling and restricting the latter in the exercise of the power of removal. But the Court never has held, nor reasonably could hold, although it is argued to the contrary on behalf of the appellant, that the excepting clause enables Congress to draw to itself, or to either branch of it, the power to remove or the right to participate in the exercise of that power. To do this would be to go beyond the words and implications of that clause and to infringe the constitutional principle of the separation of governmental powers.

Assuming then the power of Congress to regulate removals as incidental to the exercise of its constitutional power to vest appointments of inferior officers in the heads of departments, certainly so long as Congress does not exercise that power, the power of removal must remain where the Constitution places it, with the President, as part of the executive power. . . .

It is said that, for forty years or more, postmasters were all by law appointed by the Postmaster General. This was because Congress under the excepting clause so provided. But thereafter Congress required certain classes of them to be, as they now are, appointed by the President with the consent of the Senate. This is an indication that Congress deemed appointment by the President with the consent of the Senate essential to the public welfare, and, until it is willing to vest their appointment in the head of the Department, they will be subject to removal by the President alone, and any legislation to the contrary must fall as in conflict with the Constitution. . . .

Our conclusion on the merits, sustained by the arguments before stated, is that Article II grants to the President the executive power of the Government, i.e., the general administrative control of those executing the laws, including the power of appointment and removal of executive officers — a conclusion confirmed by his obligation to take care that the laws be faithfully executed; that Article II excludes the exercise of legislative power by Congress to provide for appointments and removals, except only as granted therein to Congress in the matter of inferior offices; that Congress is only given power to provide for appointments and removals of inferior officers after it has vested, and on condition that it does vest, their appointment in other authority than the President with the Senate's consent; that the provisions of the second section of Article II, which blend action by the legislative branch, or by part of it, in the work of the executive, are limitations to be strictly construed and not to be extended by implication; that the President's power of removal is further established as an incident to his specifically enumerated function of appointment by and with the advice of the Senate, but that such incident does not by implication extend to removals the Senate's power of checking appointments; and finally that to hold otherwise would make it impossible for the President, in case of political or other differences with the Senate or Congress, to take care that the laws be faithfully executed. . . .

An argument *ab inconvenienti* has been made against our conclusion in favor of the executive power of removal by the President, without the consent of the Senate — that it will open the door to a reintroduction of the spoils system. The evil of the spoils system aimed at in the civil service law and its amendments is in respect of inferior offices. It has never been attempted to extend that law beyond them. Indeed, Congress forbids its extension to appointments confirmed by the Senate, except with the consent of the Senate. Act of January 16, 1883, 22 Stat. 403, 406, c. 27, sec. 7. Reform in the federal civil service was begun by the Civil Service Act of 1883. It has been developed from that time, so that the classified service now includes a vast majority of all the civil officers. It may still be enlarged by further legislation. The independent power of removal by the President alone, under present conditions, works no practical interference with the merit system. Political appointments of inferior officers are still maintained in one important class, that of the first, second and third class postmasters, collectors of internal revenue, marshals, collectors of customs and other officers of that kind, distributed through the country. They are appointed by the President with the consent of the Senate. It is the intervention of the Senate in their appointment, and not in their removal, which prevents their classification into the merit system. If such appointments were vested in the heads of departments to which they belong, they could be entirely removed from politics, and that is what a number of Presidents have recommended. . . . The extension of the merit system rests with Congress. . . .

For the reasons given, we must therefore hold that the provision of the law of 1876, by which the unrestricted power of removal of first class postmasters is denied to the President, is in violation of the Constitution, and invalid. This leads to an affirmance of the judgment of the Court of Claims. . . .

Judgment affirmed.

MR. JUSTICE HOLMES, dissenting.

My brothers MCREYNOLDS and BRANDEIS have discussed the question before us with exhaustive research and I say a few words merely to emphasize my agreement with their conclusion.

The arguments drawn from the executive power of the President, and from his duty to appoint officers of the United States (when Congress does not vest the appointment elsewhere), to take care that the laws be faithfully executed, and to Commission all officers of the United States, seem to me spider's webs inadequate to control the dominant facts.

We have to deal with an office that owes its existence to Congress and that Congress may abolish tomorrow. Its duration and the pay attached to it while it lasts depend on Congress alone. Congress alone confers on the President the power to appoint to it and at any time may transfer the power to other hands. With such power over its own creation, I have no more trouble in believing that Congress has power to prescribe a term of life for it free from any interference than I have in accepting the undoubted power of Congress to decree its end. I have equally little trouble in accepting its power to prolong the tenure of an incumbent until Congress or the Senate shall have assented to his removal. The duty of the President to see that the laws be executed is a duty that does not go beyond the laws or require him to achieve more than Congress sees fit to leave within his power.

The separate opinion of MR. JUSTICE MCREYNOLDS. . . .

Nothing short of language clear beyond serious disputation should be held to clothe the President with authority wholly beyond congressional control arbitrarily to dismiss every officer whom he appoints except a few judges. There are no such words in the Constitution, and the asserted inference conflicts with the heretofore accepted theory that this government is one of carefully enumerated powers under an intelligible charter. . . .

If the phrase "executive power" infolds the one now claimed, many others heretofore totally unsuspected may lie there awaiting future supposed necessity, and no human intelligence can define the field of the President's permissible activities. "A masked battery of constructive powers would complete the destruction of liberty." . . .

MR. JUSTICE BRANDEIS, dissenting.

In 1833 Mr. Justice Story, after discussing in §§ 1537-1543 of his Commentaries on the Constitution the much debated question concerning the President's power of removal, said in § 1544:

> "If there has been any aberration from the true constitutional exposition of the power of removal (which the reader must decide for himself), it will be difficult, and perhaps impracticable, after forty years' experience, to recall the practice to the correct theory. But, at all events, it will be a consolation to those who love the Union, and honor a devotion to the patriotic discharge of duty, that in regard to "inferior officers" (which appellation probably includes ninety-nine out of a hundred of the lucrative offices in the government), the remedy for any permanent abuse is still within the power of Congress, by the simple expedient of requiring the consent of the Senate to removals in such cases."

Postmasters are inferior officers. Congress might have vested their appointment in the head of the department. The Act of July 12, 1876, c. 176, § 6, 19 Stat. 78, 80, reenacting earlier legislation, provided that "postmasters of the first, second, and third classes shall be appointed and may be removed by the President by and with the advice and consent of the Senate, and shall hold their offices for four years unless sooner removed or suspended according to law." That statute has been in force unmodified for half a century. Throughout the period, it has governed a large majority of all civil offices to which appointments are made by and with the advice and consent of the Senate. May the President, having acted under the statute in so far as it creates the office and authorizes the appointment, ignore, while the Senate is in session, the provision which prescribes the condition under which a removal may take place?

It is this narrow question, and this only, which we are required to decide. We need not consider what power the President, being Commander in Chief, has over officers in the Army and the Navy. We need not determine whether the President, acting alone, may remove high political officers. . . .

The historical data submitted present a legislative practice, established by concurrent affirmative action of Congress and the President, to make consent of the Senate a condition of removal from statutory inferior, civil, executive offices to which the appointment is made for a fixed term by the President with such consent. They show that the practice has existed, without interruption, continuously for the last fifty-eight years; that, throughout this period, it has governed a great majority of all such offices; that the legislation applying the removal clause specifically to the office of postmaster was enacted more than half a century ago; and that recently the practice has, with the President's approval, been extended to several newly created offices. The data show further, that the insertion of the removal clause in acts creating inferior civil offices with fixed tenures is part of the broader legislative practice, which has prevailed since the formation of our government, to restrict or regulate in many ways both removal from and nomination to such offices. A persistent legislative practice which involves a delimitation of the respective powers of Congress and the President, and which has been so established and maintained, should be deemed tantamount to judicial construction, in the absence of any decision by any court to the contrary. . . .

QUESTIONS

1. How had Congress limited the president's removal authority over the postmaster?
2. Why does the Court hold that this limit on removal power is unconstitutional? Does the Court's decision turn on the nature of the authority delegated to and exercised by the postmaster?
3. Is the Court convincing in its claim that the decision does not raise a question about the constitutionality of civil service protections?
4. Is the unity of the executive a fundamental constitutional policy?
5. Are the dissenters' positions inconsistent with *Chadha, supra,* p. 391?

HUMPHREY'S EXECUTOR v. UNITED STATES
295 U.S. 602 (1935)

Mr. Justice Sutherland delivered the opinion of the Court.

Plaintiff brought suit in the Court of Claims against the United States to recover a sum of money alleged to be due the deceased for salary as a Federal Trade Commissioner from October 8, 1933, when the President undertook to remove him from office, to the time of his death on February 14, 1934. The court below has certified to this court two questions in respect of the power of the President to make the removal. The material facts which give rise to the questions are as follows:

William E. Humphrey, the decedent, on December 10, 1931, was nominated by President Hoover to succeed himself as a member of the Federal Trade Commission, and was confirmed by the United States Senate. He was duly Commissioned for a term of seven years expiring September 25, 1938; and, after taking the required oath of office, entered upon his duties. On July 25, 1933, President Roosevelt addressed a letter to the Commissioner asking for his resignation, on the ground "that the aims and purposes of the Administration with respect to the work of the Commission can be carried out most effectively with personnel of my own selection," but disclaiming any reflection upon the Commissioner personally or upon his services. The Commissioner replied, asking time to consult his friends. After some further correspondence upon the subject, the President on August 31, 1933, wrote the Commissioner expressing the hope that the resignation would be forthcoming and saying:

> "You will, I know, realize that I do not feel that your mind and my mind go along together on either the policies or the administering of the Federal Trade Commission, and, frankly, I think it is best for the people of this country that I should have a full confidence."

The Commissioner declined to resign; and on October 7, 1933, the President wrote him:

> "Effective as of this date you are hereby removed from the office of Commissioner of the Federal Trade Commission."

Humphrey never acquiesced in this action, but continued thereafter to insist that he was still a member of the Commission, entitled to perform its duties and receive the compensation provided by law at the rate of $10,000 per annum. Upon these and other facts set forth in the certificate, which we deem it unnecessary to recite, the following questions are certified:

"1. Do the provisions of section 1 of the Federal Trade Commission Act, stating that 'any Commissioner may be removed by the President for inefficiency, neglect of duty, or malfeasance in office,' restrict or limit the power of the President to remove a Commissioner except upon one or more of the causes named?

"If the foregoing question is answered in the affirmative, then —

"2. If the power of the President to remove a Commissioner is restricted or limited as shown by the foregoing interrogatory and the answer made thereto, is such a restriction or limitation valid under the Constitution of the United States?"

The Federal Trade Commission Act, c. 311, 38 Stat. 717; 15 U.S.C. §§ 41, 42, creates a Commission of five members to be appointed by the President by and with the advice and consent of the Senate, and § 1 provides:

"Not more than three of the Commissioners shall be members of the same politital party. The first Commissioners appointed shall continue in office for terms of three, four, five, six, and seven years, respectively, from the date of the taking effect of this Act, the term of each to be designated by the President, but their successors shall be appointed for terms of seven years, except that any person chosen to fill a vacancy shall be appointed only for the unexpired term of the Commissioner whom he shall succeed. The Commission shall choose a chairman from its own membership. No Commissioner shall engage in any other business, vocation, or employment. Any Commissioner may be removed by the President for inefficiency, neglect of duty, or malfeasance in office. . . ."

Section 5 of the act in part provides:

"That unfair methods of competition in commerce are hereby declared unlawful.

"The Commission is hereby empowered and directed to prevent persons, partnerships, or corporations, except banks, and common carriers subject to the acts to regulate commerce, from using unfair methods of competition in commerce."

In exercising this power, the Commission must issue a complaint stating its charges and giving notice of hearing upon a day to be fixed. A person, partnership, or corporation proceeded against is given the right to appear at the time and place fixed and show cause why an order to cease and desist should not be issued. There is provision for intervention by others interested. If the Commission finds the method of competition is one prohibited by the act, it is directed to make a report in writing stating its findings as to the facts, and to issue and cause to be served a cease and desist order. If the order is disobeyed, the Commission may apply to the appropriate circuit court of appeals for its enforcement. The party subject to the order may seek and obtain a review in the circuit court of appeals in a manner provided by the act.

Section 6, among other things, gives the Commission wide powers of investigation in respect of certain corporations subject to the act, and in respect of other matters, upon which it must report to Congress with recommendations.

Many such investigations have been made, and some have served as the basis of congressional legislation.

Section 7 provides:

"That in any suit in equity brought by or under the direction of the Attorney General as provided in the antitrust Acts, the court may, upon the conclusion of the testimony therein, if it shall be then of opinion that the complainant is entitled to relief, refer said suit to the Commission, as a master in chancery, to ascertain and report an appropriate form of decree therein. The Commission shall proceed upon such notice to the parties and under such rules of procedure as the court may prescribe, and upon the coming in of such report such exceptions may be filed and such proceedings had in relation thereto as upon the report of a master in other equity causes, but the court may adopt or reject such report, in whole or in part, and enter such decree as the nature of the case may in its judgment require."

First. The question first to be considered is whether, by the provisions of § 1 of the Federal Trade Commission Act already quoted, the President's power is limited to removal for the specific causes enumerated therein. . . .

. . . [I]f the intention of Congress that no removal should be made during the specified term except for one or more of the enumerated causes were not clear upon the face of the statute, as we think it is, it would be made clear by a consideration of the character of the Commission and the legislative history which accompanied and preceded the passage of the act. [Discussion omitted.]

We conclude that the intent of the act is to limit the executive power of removal to the causes enumerated, the existence of none of which is claimed here; and we pass to the second question.

Second. To support its contention that the removal provision of § 1, as we have just construed it, is an unconstitutional interference with the executive power of the President, the government's chief reliance is *Myers v. United States,* 272 U.S. 52. That case has been so recently decided, and the prevailing and dissenting opinions so fully review the general subject of the power of executive removal, that further discussion would add little of value to the wealth of material there collected. These opinions examine at length the historical, legislative and judicial data bearing upon the question, beginning with what is called "the decision of 1789" in the first Congress and coming down almost to the day when the opinions were delivered. They occupy 243 pages of the volume in which they are printed. Nevertheless, the narrow point actually decided was only that the President had power to remove a postmaster of the first class, without the advice and consent of the Senate as required by act of Congress. In the course of the opinion of the court, expressions occur which tend to sustain the government's contention, but these are beyond the point involved and, therefore, do not come within the rule of stare decisis. In so far as they are out of harmony with the views here set forth, these expressions are disapproved. . . .

The office of a postmaster is so essentially unlike the office now involved that the decision in the *Myers* case cannot be accepted as controlling our decision here. A postmaster is an executive officer restricted to the performance of executive functions. He is charged with no duty at all related to either the legislative or judicial power. The actual decision in the *Myers* case finds support in the theory that such an officer is merely one of the units in the executive department and, hence, inherently subject to the exclusive and illimitable power of removal by the Chief Executive, whose subordinate and aid he is. Putting aside dicta, which may be followed if sufficiently persuasive but which are not controlling, the necessary reach of the decision goes far enough to include all purely executive officers. It goes no farther; much less does it include an officer who occupies no place in the executive department and who exercises no part of the executive power vested by the Constitution in the President.

The Federal Trade Commission is an administrative body created by Congress to carry into effect legislative policies embodied in the statute in accordance with the legislative standard therein prescribed, and to perform other specified duties as a legislative or as a judicial aid. Such a body cannot in any proper sense be characterized as an arm or an eye of the executive. Its duties are performed without executive leave and, in the contemplation of the statute, must be free from executive control. In administering the provisions of the statute in respect of "unfair methods of competition" — that is to say in filling in and administering the details embodied by that general standard — the Commission acts in part quasi-legislatively and in part quasi-judicially. In making investigations and reports thereon for the information of Congress under § 6, in aid of the legislative power, it acts as a legislative agency. Under § 7, which authorizes the Commission to act as a master in chancery under rules prescribed by the court, it acts as an agency of the judiciary. To the extent that it exercises any executive function — as distinguished from executive power in the constitutional sense — it does so in the discharge and effectuation of its quasi-legislative or quasi-judicial powers, or as an agency of the legislative or judicial departments of the government.*

If Congress is without authority to prescribe causes for removal of members of the trade Commission and limit executive power of removal accordingly, that power at once becomes practically all-inclusive in respect of civil officers with the exception of the judiciary provided for by the Constitution. The Solicitor General, at the bar, apparently recognizing this to be true, with commendable candor, agreed that his view in respect of the removability of members of the Federal Trade Commission necessitated a like view in respect of the Interstate Commerce Commission and the Court of Claims. We are thus confronted with the serious question whether not only the members of these quasi-legislative and quasi-judicial bodies, but the judges of the legislative Court of Claims, exercising judicial power (*Williams v. United States,* 289 U.S. 553, 565-567), continue in office only at the pleasure of the President.

We think it plain under the Constitution that illimitable power of removal is not possessed by the President in respect of officers of the character of those just named. The authority of Congress, in creating quasi-legislative or quasi-judicial agencies, to require them to act in discharge of their duties independently of executive control cannot well be doubted; and that authority includes, as an appropriate incident, power to fix the period during which they shall continue in office, and to forbid their removal except for cause in the meantime. For it is quite evident that one who holds his office only during the pleasure of another, cannot be depended upon to maintain an attitude of independence against the latter's will.

---

*The provision of § 6 (d) of the act which authorizes the President to direct an investigation and report by the Commission in relation to alleged violations of the anti-trust acts, is so obviously collateral to the main design of the act as not to detract from the force of this general statement as to the character of that body.

The fundamental necessity of maintaining each of the three general departments of government entirely free from the control or coercive influence, direct or indirect, of either of the others, has often been stressed and is hardly open to serious question. So much is implied in the very fact of the separation of the powers of these departments by the Constitution; and in the rule which recognizes their essential co-equality. The sound application of a principle that makes one master in his own house precludes him from imposing his control in the house of another who is master there. James Wilson, one of the framers of the Constitution and a former justice of this court, said that the independence of each department required that its proceedings "should be free from the remotest influence, direct or indirect, of either of the other two powers." Andrews, The Works of James Wilson (1896), vol. 1, p. 367. And Mr. Justice Story in the first volume of his work on the Constitution, 4th ed., § 530, citing No. 48 of the Federalist, said that neither of the departments in reference to each other "ought to possess, directly or indirectly, an overruling influence in the administration of their respective powers."

The power of removal here claimed for the President falls within this principle, since its coercive influence threatens the independence of a Commission, which is not only wholly disconnected from the executive department, but which, as already fully appears, was created by Congress as a means of carrying into operation legislative and judicial powers, and as an agency of the legislative and judicial departments.

In the light of the question now under consideration, we have reexamined the precedents referred to in the *Myers* case, and find nothing in them to justify a conclusion contrary to that which we have reached. The so-called "decision of 1789" had relation to a bill proposed by Mr. Madison to establish an executive Department of Foreign Affairs. The bill provided that the principal officer was "to be removable from office by the President of the United States." This clause was changed to read "whenever the principal officer shall be removed from office by the President of the United States" certain things should follow, thereby, in connection with the debates, recognizing and confirming, as the court thought in the *Myers* case, the sole power of the President in the matter. We shall not discuss the subject further, since it is so fully covered by the opinions in the *Myers* case, except to say that the office under consideration by Congress was not only purely executive, but the officer one who was responsible to the President, and to him alone, in a very definite sense. A reading of the debates shows that the President's illimitable power of removal was not considered in respect of other than executive officers. And it is pertinent to observe that when, at a later time, the tenure of office for the Comptroller of the Treasury was under consideration, Mr. Madison quite evidently thought that, since the duties of that office were not purely of an executive nature but partook of the judiciary quality as well, a different rule in respect of executive removal might well apply. 1 Annals of Congress, cols. 611-612.

In *Marbury v. Madison, supra,* pp. 162, 165-166, it is made clear that Chief Justice Marshall was of opinion that a justice of the peace for the District of Columbia was not removable at the will of the President; and that there was a distinction between such an officer and officers appointed to aid the President in the performance of his constitutional duties. In the latter case, the distinction he saw was that "their acts are his acts" and his will, therefore, controls; and, by way of illustration, he adverted to the act establishing the Department of Foreign Affairs, which was the subject of the "decision of 1789."

The result of what we now have said is this: Whether the power of the President to remove an officer shall prevail over the authority of Congress to condition the power by fixing a definite term and precluding a removal except for cause, will depend upon the character of the office; the *Myers* decision, affirming the power of the President alone to make the removal, is confined to purely executive officers; and as to officers of the kind here under consideration, we hold that no removal can be made during the prescribed term for which the officer is appointed, except for one or more of the causes named in the applicable statute.

To the extent that, between the decision in the *Myers* case, which sustains the unrestrictable power of the President to remove purely executive officers, and our present decision that such power does not extend to an office such as that here involved, there shall remain a field of doubt, we leave such cases as may fall within it for future consideration and determination as they may arise.

In accordance with the foregoing, the questions submitted are answered.

Question No. 1, Yes.

Question No. 2, Yes.

[Justice McReynolds concurred in the result. No Justice dissented.]

QUESTIONS

1. Is the *Humphrey's* opinion more consistent with the real nature of agencies?
2. Or does it demonstrate the "unconstitutional" nature of agencies as a fourth branch of government?
3. Or is *Myers* fundamentally wrong? Can it be limited to cases where Congress inserted itself into the firing process in a way inconsistent with the later analysis in *Chadha, supra,* p. 391?
4. Is it necessary for agencies to have adjudicative functions?

NOTE ON BOWSHER v. SYNAR

The Court returned to the issue of the President's removal authority when it addressed the question of the constitutionality of the Balanced Budget and Emergency Deficit Control Act of 1985, Pub. L. 99-177, known popularly as the Gramm-Rudman-Hollings Act, in *Bowsher v. Synar,* 478 U.S. 714 (1986). This statute had been enacted by Congress as a last-ditch attempt to limit deficit spending by the government. A principal role in the deficit reduction scheme adopted by Congress was played by the Comptroller General, the federal official who heads the General Accounting Office.

The Court's analysis focused on the removal power question in the context of congressional authority, and the Court, *id.* at 726-27, reasoned that:

> Congress cannot reserve for itself the power of removal of an officer charged with the execution of the laws except by impeachment. To permit the execution of the laws to be vested in an officer answerable only to Congress would, in practical terms, reserve in Congress control over the execution of the laws. As the District

Court observed: "Once an officer is appointed, it is only the authority that can remove him, and not the authority that appointed him, that he must fear and, in the performance of his functions, obey." The structure of the Constitution does not permit Congress to execute the laws; it follows that Congress cannot grant to an officer under its control what it does not possess.

Our decision in *INS v. Chadha* supports this conclusion. . . . To permit an officer controlled by Congress to execute the laws would be, in essence, to permit a congressional veto. Congress could simply remove, or threaten to remove, an officer for executing the laws in any fashion found to be unsatisfactory to Congress. This kind of congressional control over the execution of the laws, *Chadha* makes clear, is constitutionally impermissible.

The Court thus had to decide under the statutory scheme for deficit reduction, first, whether the statute gave Congress removal power over the Comptroller General, and second, if Congress had such power, whether the Comptroller General exercised executive power under the statutory scheme. Regarding the first issue, the Court concluded, *id.* at 727-28, that Congress had given itself control over the Comptroller General by retaining a power of removal:

Appellants urge that the Comptroller General performs his duties independently and is not subservient to Congress. We agree with the District Court that this contention does not bear close scrutiny.

The critical factor lies in the provisions of the statute defining the Comptroller General's office relating to removability. Although the Comptroller General is nominated by the President from a list of three individuals recommended by the Speaker of the House of Representatives and the President pro tempore of the Senate, and confirmed by the Senate, he is removable only at the initiative of Congress. He may be removed not only by impeachment but also by joint resolution of Congress "at any time" resting on any one of the following bases:

(i)   permanent disability;
(ii) inefficiency;
(iii) neglect of duty;
(iv) malfeasance; or
(v)   a felony or conduct involving moral turpitude.

31 U.S.C. § 703(e)(1)(B). [Note that a joint resolution is effective only after passage by both Houses of Congress and, further, has no effect if it is vetoed by the President and both Houses fail to override the veto by a two-thirds majority. Regarding this opportunity for a Presidential veto, the Court stated that, "the Comptroller General could be removed in the face of Presidential opposition. Like the District Court, we therefore read the removal provision as authorizing removal by Congress alone." 478 U.S. at 728 n.7.]

This provision was included, as one Congressman explained in urging passage of the act, because Congress "felt that [the Comptroller General] should be brought under the sole control of Congress, so that Congress at any moment when it found he was inefficient and was not carrying on the duties of his office as he should and as the Congress expected, could remove him without the long, tedious process of a trial by impeachment."

The removal provision was an important part of the legislative scheme, as a number of Congressmen recognized. . . .

Having decided that Congress had retained the power of removal, the Court decided, *id.* at 733, that the Comptroller General had an important role in executing the law:

> The executive nature of the Comptroller General's functions under the Act is revealed in § 252(a)(3) which gives the Comptroller General the ultimate authority to determine the budget cuts to be made. Indeed, the Comptroller General commands the President himself to carry out, without the slightest variation (with exceptions not relevant to the constitutional issues presented), the directive of the Comptroller General as to the budget reductions. . . .

This analysis led to the Court's conclusion, *id.* at 734, that the statute violated the separation of powers:

> By placing the responsibility for execution of the Balanced Budget and Emergency Deficit Control Act in the hands of an officer who is subject to removal only by itself, Congress in effect has retained control over the execution of the Act and has intruded into the executive function. The Constitution does not permit such intrusion.

QUESTIONS

1. Does the Court's decision in *Synar* conflict with the Court's acceptance in *Humphrey's Executor* of the statutory limitation on the President's power to remove? Doesn't the deficit-reduction scheme retain presidential authority by allowing a presidential veto of a joint resolution calling for removal?
2. Is the result in *Synar* driven more by the Court's concern about unconstitutional excesses by Congress, than by a concern about the President's retention of all executive powers?

MORRISON v. OLSON
487 U.S. 654 (1988)

CHIEF JUSTICE REHNQUIST delivered the opinion of the Court.

This case presents us with a challenge to the independent counsel provisions of the Ethics in Government Act of 1978, 28 U.S.C. §§ 49, 591 *et seq.* (1982 ed., Supp. V). We hold today that these provisions of the Act do not violate the Appointments Clause of the Constitution, Art. II, § 2, cl. 2, or the limitations of Article III, nor do they impermissibly interfere with the President's authority under Article II in violation of the constitutional principle of separation of powers. [Note: Congress permitted the Independent Counsel provisions of the Ethics in Government Act to expire in 1999.]

I

Briefly stated, Title VI of the Ethics in Government Act (Title VI or the Act), 28 U.S.C. §§ 591-599 (1982 ed., Supp. V), allows for the appointment of an "independent counsel" to investigate and, if appropriate, prosecute certain highranking Government officials for violations of federal criminal laws. The Act requires the Attorney General, upon receipt of information that he determines is "sufficient to constitute grounds to investigate whether any person [covered by the Act] may have violated any Federal criminal law," to conduct a preliminary investigation of the matter. When the Attorney General has completed this investigation, or 90 days has elapsed, he is required to report to a special court (the Special Division) created by the Act "for the purpose of appointing independent counsels." 28 U.S.C. § 49 (1982 ed., Supp. V).[3] If the Attorney General determines that "there are no reasonable grounds to believe that further investigation is warranted," then he must notify the Special Division of this result. In such a case, "the division of the court shall have no power to appoint an independent counsel." § 592(b)(1). If, however, the Attorney General has determined that there are "reasonable grounds to believe that further investigation or prosecution is warranted," then he "shall apply to the division of the court for the appointment of an independent counsel."[4] The Attorney General's application to the court "shall contain sufficient information to assist the [court] in selecting an independent counsel and in defining that independent counsel's prosecutorial jurisdiction." § 592(d). Upon receiving this application, the Special Division "shall appoint an appropriate independent counsel and shall define that independent counsel's prosecutorial jurisdiction." § 593(b).

With respect to all matters within the independent counsel's jurisdiction, the Act grants the counsel "full power and independent authority to exercise all investigative and prosecutorial functions and powers of the Department of Justice, the Attorney General, and any other officer or employee of the Department of Justice." § 594(a). The functions of the independent counsel include conducting grand jury proceedings and other investigations, participating in civil and criminal court proceedings and litigation, and appealing any decision in any case in which the counsel participates in an official capacity. §§ 594(a)(1)-(3). Under § 594(a)(9), the counsel's powers include "initiating and conducting prosecutions in any court of competent jurisdiction, framing and signing indictments, filing informations, and handling all aspects of any case, in the name of the United States." The counsel may appoint employees, § 594(c), may request and obtain assistance from the Department of Justice, § 594(d), and may accept referral of matters from the Attorney General if the matter falls within the counsel's jurisdiction as defined by the Special Division, § 594(e). The act also states that an independent counsel "shall, except where not possible, comply with the written or other established policies of the Department of Justice respecting enforcement of the criminal laws." § 594(f). In addition, whenever a matter has been referred to an independent counsel under the act, the Attorney General and the Justice Department are required to suspend all investigations and proceedings regarding the matter. § 597(a). An independent counsel has

3. The Special Division is a division of the United States Court of Appeals for the District of Columbia Circuit. 28 U.S.C. § 49 (1982 ed., Supp. V). The court consists of three circuit court judges or justices appointed by the Chief Justice of the United States. One of the judges must be a judge of the United States Court of Appeals for the District of Columbia Circuit, and no two of the judges may be named to the Special Division from a particular court. The judges are appointed for 2-year terms, with any vacancy being filled only for the remainder of the 2-year period.

4. The Act also requires the Attorney General to apply for the appointment of an independent counsel if 90 days elapse from the receipt of the information triggering the preliminary investigation without a determination by the Attorney General that there are no reasonable grounds to believe that further investigation or prosecution is warranted. § 592(c)(1). Pursuant to § 592(f), the Attorney General's decision to apply to the Special Division for the appointment of an independent counsel is not reviewable "in any court."

"full authority to dismiss matters within [his or her] prosecutorial jurisdiction without conducting an investigation or at any subsequent time before prosecution, if to do so would be consistent" with Department of Justice policy. § 594(g).

Two statutory provisions govern the length of an independent counsel's tenure in office. The first defines the procedure for removing an independent counsel. Section 596(a)(1) provides:

> "An independent counsel appointed under this chapter may be removed from office, other than by impeachment and conviction, only by the personal action of the Attorney General and only for good cause, physical disability, mental incapacity, or any other condition that substantially impairs the performance of such independent counsel's duties."

If an independent counsel is removed pursuant to this section, the Attorney General is required to submit a report to both the Special Division and the Judiciary Committees of the Senate and the House "specifying the facts found and the ultimate grounds for such removal." § 596(a)(2). Under the current version of the Act, an independent counsel can obtain judicial review of the Attorney General's action by filing a civil action in the United States District Court for the District of Columbia. Members of the Special Division "may not hear or determine any such civil action or any appeal of a decision in any such civil action." The reviewing court is authorized to grant reinstatement or "other appropriate relief." § 596(a)(3).

The other provision governing the tenure of the independent counsel defines the procedures for "terminating" the counsel's office. Under § 596(b)(1), the office of an independent counsel terminates when he or she notifies the Attorney General that he or she has completed or substantially completed any investigations or prosecutions undertaken pursuant to the Act. In addition, the Special Division, acting either on its own or on the suggestion of the Attorney General, may terminate the office of an independent counsel at any time if it finds that "the investigation of all matters within the prosecutorial jurisdiction of such independent counsel . . . have been completed or so substantially completed that it would be appropriate for the Department of Justice to complete such investigations and prosecutions." § 596(b)(2). . . .

The proceedings in this case provide an example of how the Act works in practice. In 1982, two Subcommittees of the House of Representatives issued subpoenas directing the Environmental Protection Agency (EPA) to produce certain documents relating to the efforts of the EPA and the Land and Natural Resources Division of the Justice Department to enforce the "Superfund Law." At that time, appellee Olson was the Assistant Attorney General for the Office of Legal Counsel (OLC), appellee Schmults was Deputy Attorney General, and appellee Dinkins was the Assistant Attorney General for the Land and Natural Resources Division. Acting on the advice of the Justice Department, the President ordered the Administrator of EPA to invoke executive privilege to withhold certain of the documents on the ground that they contained "enforcement sensitive information." The Administrator obeyed this order and withheld the documents. In response, the House voted to hold the Administrator in contempt, after which the Administrator and the United States together filed a lawsuit against the House. The conflict abated in March 1983, when the administration agreed to give the House Subcommittees limited access to the documents.

The following year, the House Judiciary Committee began an investigation into the Justice Department's role in the controversy over the EPA documents. During this investigation, appellee Olson testified before a House Subcommittee on March 10, 1983. . . . In 1985, the majority members of the Judiciary Committee published a lengthy report on the Committee's investigation. The report . . . suggested that appellee Olson had given false and misleading testimony to the Subcommittee on March 10, 1983, and that appellees Schmults and Dinkins had wrongfully withheld certain documents from the Committee, thus obstructing the Committee's investigation. The Chairman of the Judiciary Committee forwarded a copy of the report to the Attorney General with a request, pursuant to 28 U.S.C. § 592(c), that he seek the appointment of an independent counsel to investigate the allegations against Olson, Schmults, and Dinkins.

. . . After consulting with other Department officials, however, the Attorney General chose to apply to the Special Division for the appointment of an independent counsel solely with respect to appellee Olson. The Attorney General accordingly requested appointment of an independent counsel to investigate whether Olson's March 10, 1983, testimony "regarding the completeness of [OLC's] response to the Judiciary Committee's request for OLC documents, and regarding his knowledge of EPA's willingness to turn over certain disputed documents to Congress, violated 18 U.S.C. § 1505, § 1001, or any other provision of federal criminal law." Attorney General Report, at 2-3. The Attorney General also requested that the independent counsel have authority to investigate "any other matter related to that allegation." *Id.*, at 11.

On April 23, 1986, the Special Division appointed James C. McKay as independent counsel to investigate "whether the testimony of . . . Olson and his revision of such testimony on March 10, 1983, violated either 18 U.S.C. § 1505 or § 1001, or any other provision of federal law." The court also ordered that the independent counsel

> "shall have jurisdiction to investigate any other allegation of evidence of violation of any Federal criminal law by Theodore Olson developed during investigations, by the Independent Counsel, referred to above, and connected with or arising out of that investigation, and Independent Counsel shall have jurisdiction to prosecute for any such violation."

McKay later resigned as independent counsel, and on May 29, 1986, the Division appointed appellant Morrison as his replacement, with the same jurisdiction. . . .

. . . [I]n May and June 1987, appellant caused a grand jury to issue and serve subpoenas *ad testificandum* and *duces tecum* on appellees. All three appellees moved to quash the subpoenas, claiming, among other things, that the independent counsel provisions of the Act were unconstitutional and that appellant accordingly had no authority to proceed. On July 20, 1987, the District Court upheld the constitutionality of the Act and denied the motions to quash. The court subsequently ordered that appellees be held in contempt pursuant to 28 U.S.C. § 1826(a) for continuing to refuse to comply with the subpoenas. The court stayed the effect of its contempt orders pending expedited appeal.

A divided Court of Appeals reversed. The majority ruled first that an independent counsel is not an "inferior Officer" of the United States for purposes of the Appointments Clause. Accordingly, the court found the Act invalid because it does not provide for the independent counsel to be nominated by the President and confirmed by the Senate, as the Clause requires for "principal" officers. The court then went on to consider several alternative grounds for its conclusion that the statute was unconstitutional. In the majority's view, the Act also violates the Appointments Clause insofar as it empowers a court of law to appoint an "inferior" officer who performs core executive functions; the Act's delegation of various powers to the Special Division violates the limitations of Article III; the Act's restrictions on the Attorney General's power to remove an independent counsel violate the separation of powers; and finally, the Act interferes with the Executive Branch's prerogative to "take care that the Laws be faithfully executed," Art. II, § 3. The dissenting judge was of the view that the Act was constitutional. Appellant then sought review by this Court, and we noted probable jurisdiction. We now reverse. . . .

III

The Appointments Clause of Article II reads as follows:

> "[The President] shall nominate, and by and with the Advice and Consent of the Senate, shall appoint Ambassadors, other public Ministers and Consuls, Judges of the supreme Court, and all other Officers of the United States, whose Appointments are not herein otherwise provided for, and which shall be established by Law: but the Congress may by Law vest the Appointment of such inferior Officers, as they think proper, in the President alone, in the Courts of Law, or in the Heads of Departments." U.S. Const., Art. II, § 2, cl. 2.

The parties do not dispute that "[t]he Constitution for purposes of appointment . . . divides all its officers into two classes." "Principal officers are selected by the President with the advice and consent of the Senate. Inferior officers Congress may allow to be appointed by the President alone, by the heads of departments, or by the Judiciary." The initial question is, accordingly, whether appellant is an "inferior" or a "principal" officer.[12] If she is the latter, as the Court of Appeals concluded, then the Act is in violation of the Appointments Clause.

The line between "inferior" and "principal" officers is one that is far from clear, and the Framers provided little guidance into where it should be drawn. We need not attempt here to decide exactly where the line falls between the two types of officers, because in our view appellant clearly falls on the "inferior officer" side of that line. Several factors lead to this conclusion.

First, appellant is subject to removal by a higher Executive Branch official. Although appellant may not be "subordinate" to the Attorney General (and the President) insofar as she possesses a degree of independent discretion to exercise the powers delegated to her under the Act, the fact that she can be removed by the Attorney General indicates that she is to some degree "inferior"

---

12. It is clear that appellant is an "officer" of the United States, not an "employee." See *Buckley*, 424 U.S., at 126, and n.162.

in rank and authority. Second, appellant is empowered by the Act to perform only certain, limited duties. An independent counsel's role is restricted primarily to investigation and, if appropriate, prosecution for certain federal crimes. Admittedly, the Act delegates to appellant "full power and independent authority to exercise all investigative and prosecutorial functions and powers of the Department of Justice," §594(a), but this grant of authority does not include any authority to formulate policy for the Government or the Executive Branch, nor does it give appellant any administrative duties outside of those necessary to operate her office. The Act specifically provides that in policy matters appellant is to comply to the extent possible with the policies of the Department. §594(f).

Third, appellant's office is limited in jurisdiction. Not only is the Act itself restricted in applicability to certain federal officials suspected of certain serious federal crimes, but an independent counsel can only act within the scope of the jurisdiction that has been granted by the Special Division pursuant to a request by the Attorney General. Finally, appellant's office is limited in tenure. There is concededly no time limit on the appointment of a particular counsel. Nonetheless, the office of independent counsel is "temporary" in the sense that an independent counsel is appointed essentially to accomplish a single task, and when that task is over the office is terminated, either by the counsel herself or by action of the Special Division. Unlike other prosecutors, appellant has no ongoing responsibilities that extend beyond the accomplishment of the mission that she was appointed for and authorized by the Special Division to undertake. In our view, these factors relating to the "ideas of tenure, duration . . . and duties" of the independent counsel, are sufficient to establish that appellant is an "inferior" officer in the constitutional sense.

This conclusion is consistent with our few previous decisions that considered the question whether a particular Government official is a "principal" or an "inferior" officer. In *United States v. Eaton,* 169 U.S. 331 (1898), for example, we approved Department of State regulations that allowed executive officials to appoint a "vice-consul" during the temporary absence of the consul, terming the "vice-consul" a "subordinate officer" notwithstanding the Appointment Clause's specific reference to "Consuls" as principal officers. As we stated: "Because the subordinate officer is charged with the performance of the duty of the superior for a limited time and under special and temporary conditions he is not thereby transformed into the superior and permanent official." *Id.,* at 343. In *Ex parte Siebold,* 100 U.S. 371 (1880), the Court found that federal "supervisor[s] of elections," who were charged with various duties involving oversight of local congressional elections, see *id.,* at 379-380, were inferior officers for purposes of the Clause. In *Go-Bart Importing Co. v. United States,* 282 U.S. 344, 352-353 (1931), we held that "United States Commissioners are inferior officers." *Id.,* at 352. These Commissioners had various judicial and prosecutorial powers, including the power to arrest and imprison for trial, to issue warrants, and to institute prosecutions under "laws relating to the elective franchise and civil rights." *Id.,* at 353, n.2. All of this is consistent with our reference in *United States v. Nixon,* 418 U.S. 683, 694, 696 (1974), to the office of Watergate Special Prosecutor—whose authority was similar to that of appellant, see *id.,* at 694, n.8—as a "subordinate officer."

This does not, however, end our inquiry under the Appointments Clause. Appellees argue that even if appellant is an "inferior" officer, the Clause does not empower Congress to place the power to appoint such an officer outside the Executive Branch. [Discussion omitted.] . . . In the light of the Act's provision making the judges of the Special Division ineligible to participate in any matters relating to an independent counsel they have appointed, 28 U.S.C. §49(f) (1982 ed., Supp. V), we do not think that appointment of the independent counsel by the court runs afoul of the constitutional limitation on "incongruous" interbranch appointments. . . .

V

We now turn to consider whether the Act is invalid under the constitutional principle of separation of powers. Two related issues must be addressed: The first is whether the provision of the Act restricting the Attorney General's power to remove the independent counsel to only those instances in which he can show "good cause," taken by itself, impermissibly interferes with the President's exercise of his constitutionally appointed functions. The second is whether, taken as a whole, the Act violates the separation of powers by reducing the President's ability to control the prosecutorial powers wielded by the independent counsel.

A

Two Terms ago we had occasion to consider whether it was consistent with the separation of powers for Congress to pass a statute that authorized a Government official who is removable only by Congress to participate in what we found to be "executive powers." *Bowsher v. Synar*, 78 U.S. 714, 730 (1986). We held in *Bowsher* that "Congress cannot reserve for itself the power of removal of an officer charged with the execution of the laws except by impeachment." *Id.*, at 726. A primary antecedent for this ruling was our 1926 decision in *Myers v. United States*, 272 U.S. 52. *Myers* had considered the propriety of a federal statute by which certain postmasters of the United States could be removed by the President only "by and with the advice and consent of the Senate." There too, Congress' attempt to involve itself in the removal of an executive official was found to be sufficient grounds to render the statute invalid. As we observed in *Bowsher*, the essence of the decision in *Myers* was the judgment that the Constitution prevents Congress from "draw[ing] to itself . . . the power to remove or the right to participate in the exercise of that power. To do this would be to go beyond the words and implications of the [Appointments Clause] and to infringe the constitutional principle of the separation of governmental powers." *Myers, supra*, at 161.

Unlike both *Bowsher* and *Myers*, this case does not involve an attempt by Congress itself to gain a role in the removal of executive officials other than its established powers of impeachment and conviction. The Act instead puts the removal power squarely in the hands of the Executive Branch; an independent counsel may be removed from office, "only by the personal action of the Attorney General, and only for good cause." §596(a)(1).[23] There is no requirement of congressional approval of the Attorney General's removal decision, though

---

23. As noted, an independent counsel may also be removed through impeachment and conviction. In addition, the Attorney General may remove a counsel for "physical disability, mental incapacity, or any other condition that substantially impairs the performance" of his or her duties. §596(a)(1).

the decision is subject to judicial review. § 596(a)(3). In our view, the removal provisions of the Act make this case more analogous to *Humphrey's Executor v. United States*, 295 U.S. 602 (1935), and *Wiener v. United States*, 357 U.S. 349 (1958), than to *Myers* or *Bowsher*. . . .

Appellees contend that *Humphrey's Executor* and *Wiener* are distinguishable from this case because they did not involve officials who performed a "core executive function." They argue that our decision in *Humphrey's Executor* rests on a distinction between "purely executive" officials and officials who exercise "quasi-legislative" and "quasi-judicial" powers. In their view, when a "purely executive" official is involved, the governing precedent is *Myers*, not *Humphrey's Executor*. See *Humphrey's Executor, supra*, at 628. And, under *Myers*, the President must have absolute discretion to discharge "purely" executive officials at will. See *Myers*, 272 U.S., at 132-134.

We undoubtedly did rely on the terms "quasi-legislative" and "quasi-judicial" to distinguish the officials involved in *Humphrey's Executor* and *Wiener* from those in *Myers*, but our present considered view is that the determination of whether the Constitution allows Congress to impose a "good cause"-type restriction on the President's power to remove an official cannot be made to turn on whether or not that official is classified as "purely executive."[27] The analysis contained in our removal cases is designed not to define rigid categories of those officials who may or may not be removed at will by the President, but to ensure that Congress does not interfere with the President's exercise of the "executive power" and his constitutionally appointed duty to "take care that the laws be faithfully executed" under Article II. *Myers* was undoubtedly correct in its holding, and in its broader suggestion that there are some "purely executive" officials who must be removable by the President at will if he is to be able to accomplish his constitutional role.[29] See 272 U.S., at 132-134. But as the Court noted in *Wiener*:

> "The assumption was short-lived that the *Myers* case recognized the President's inherent constitutional power to remove officials no matter what the relation of the executive to the discharge of their duties and no matter what restrictions Congress may have imposed regarding the nature of their tenure." 357 U.S., at 352.

At the other end of the spectrum from *Myers*, the characterization of the agencies in *Humphrey's Executor* and *Wiener* as "quasi-legislative" or "quasi-judicial" in large part reflected our judgment that it was not essential to the President's proper execution of his Article II powers that these agencies be headed up by

---

27. Indeed, this Court has never held that the Constitution prevents Congress from imposing limitations on the President's power to remove *all* executive officials simply because they wield "executive" power. *Myers* itself expressly distinguished cases in which Congress had chosen to vest the appointment of "inferior" executive officials in the head of a department. See 272 U.S., at 161-163, 164. In such a situation, we saw no specific constitutional impediment to congressionally imposed restrictions on the President's removal powers.

29. The dissent says that the language of Article II vesting the executive power of the United States in the President requires that every officer of the United States exercising any part of that power must serve at the pleasure of the President and be removable by him at will. *Post*, at 705. This rigid demarcation — a demarcation incapable of being altered by law in the slightest degree, and applicable to tens of thousands of holders of offices neither known nor foreseen by the Framers — depends upon an extrapolation from general constitutional language which we think is more than the text will bear. . . .

individuals who were removable at will.[30] We do not mean to suggest that an analysis of the functions served by the officials at issue is irrelevant. But the real question is whether the removal restrictions are of such a nature that they impede the President's ability to perform his constitutional duty, and the functions of the officials in question must be analyzed in that light.

Considering for the moment the "good cause" removal provision in isolation from the other parts of the Act at issue in this case, we cannot say that the imposition of a "good cause" standard for removal by itself unduly trammels on executive authority. There is no real dispute that the functions performed by the independent counsel are "executive" in the sense that they are law enforcement functions that typically have been undertaken by officials within the Executive Branch. As we noted above, however, the independent counsel is an inferior officer under the Appointments Clause, with limited jurisdiction and tenure and lacking policymaking or significant administrative authority. Although the counsel exercises no small amount of discretion and judgment in deciding how to carry out his or her duties under the Act, we simply do not see how the President's need to control the exercise of that discretion is so central to the functioning of the Executive Branch as to require as a matter of constitutional law that the counsel be terminable at will by the President.

Nor do we think that the "good cause" removal provision at issue here impermissibly burdens the President's power to control or supervise the independent counsel, as an executive official, in the execution of his or her duties under the Act. This is not a case in which the power to remove an executive official has been completely stripped from the President, thus providing no means for the President to ensure the "faithful execution" of the laws. Rather, because the independent counsel may be terminated for "good cause," the Executive, through the Attorney General, retains ample authority to assure that the counsel is competently performing his or her statutory responsibilities in a manner that comports with the provisions of the Act. Although we need not decide in this case exactly what is encompassed within the term "good cause" under the Act, the legislative history of the removal provision also makes clear that the Attorney General may remove an independent counsel for "misconduct." See H. R. Conf. Rep. No. 100-452, p. 37 (1987). Here, as with the provision of the Act conferring the appointment authority of the independent counsel on the special court, the congressional determination to limit the removal power of the Attorney General was essential, in the view of Congress, to establish the necessary independence of the office. We do not think that this limitation as it presently stands sufficiently deprives the President of control over the independent counsel to interfere impermissibly with his constitutional obligation to ensure the faithful execution of the laws.

B

The final question to be addressed is whether the Act, taken as a whole, violates the principle of separation of powers by unduly interfering with the role of the Executive Branch. Time and again we have reaffirmed the importance in our

---

30. The terms also may be used to describe the circumstances in which Congress might be more inclined to find that a degree of independence from the Executive, such as that afforded by a "good cause" removal standard, is necessary to the proper functioning of the agency or official. It is not difficult to imagine situations in which Congress might desire that an official performing "quasi-judicial" functions, for example, would be free of executive or political control.

constitutional scheme of the separation of governmental powers into the three coordinate branches. As we stated in *Buckley v. Valeo,* 424 U.S. 1 (1976), the system of separated powers and checks and balances established in the Constitution was regarded by the Framers as "a self-executing safeguard against the encroachment or aggrandizement of one branch at the expense of the other." *Id.,* at 122. We have not hesitated to invalidate provisions of law which violate this principle. See *id.,* at 123. On the other hand, we have never held that the Constitution requires that the three branches of Government "operate with absolute independence." . . .

We observe first that this case does not involve an attempt by Congress to increase its own powers at the expense of the Executive Branch. Cf. *Commodity Futures Trading Comm'n v. Schor,* 478 U.S., at 856. Unlike some of our previous cases, most recently *Bowsher v. Synar,* this case simply does not pose a "dange[r] of congressional usurpation of Executive Branch functions." 478 U.S., at 727; see also *INS v. Chadha,* 462 U.S. 919, 958 (1983). Indeed, with the exception of the power of impeachment — which applies to all officers of the United States — Congress retained for itself no powers of control or supervision over an independent counsel. The Act does empower certain Members of Congress to request the Attorney General to apply for the appointment of an independent counsel, but the Attorney General has no duty to comply with the request, although he must respond within a certain time limit. §592(g). Other than that, Congress' role under the Act is limited to receiving reports or other information and oversight of the independent counsel's activities, §595(a), functions that we have recognized generally as being incidental to the legislative function of Congress.

Similarly, we do not think that the Act works any *judicial* usurpation of properly executive functions. As should be apparent from our discussion of the Appointments Clause above, the power to appoint inferior officers such as independent counsel is not in itself an "executive" function in the constitutional sense, at least when Congress has exercised its power to vest the appointment of an inferior office in the "courts of Law." We note nonetheless that under the Act the Special Division has no power to appoint an independent counsel *sua sponte;* it may only do so upon the specific request of the Attorney General, and the courts are specifically prevented from reviewing the Attorney General's decision not to seek appointment, §592(f). In addition, once the court has appointed a counsel and defined his or her jurisdiction, it has no power to supervise or control the activities of the counsel. As we pointed out in our discussion of the Special Division in relation to Article III, the various powers delegated by the statute to the Division are not supervisory or administrative, nor are they functions that the Constitution requires be performed by officials within the Executive Branch. The Act does give a federal court the power to review the Attorney General's decision to remove an independent counsel, but in our view this is a function that is well within the traditional power of the Judiciary.

Finally, we do not think that the Act "impermissibly undermine[s]" the powers of the Executive Branch, *Schor, supra,* at 856, or "disrupts the proper balance between the coordinate branches [by] prevent[ing] the Executive Branch from accomplishing its constitutionally assigned functions," *Nixon v. Administrator of General Services, supra,* at 443. It is undeniable that the Act reduces the amount of control or supervision that the Attorney General and, through him, the President exercises over the investigation and prosecution of a certain class of alleged criminal activity. The Attorney General is not allowed to appoint the individual of his choice; he does not determine the counsel's jurisdiction; and his power to remove a counsel is limited. Nonetheless, the Act does give the Attorney General several means of supervising or controlling the prosecutorial powers that may be wielded by an independent counsel. Most importantly, the Attorney General retains the power to remove the counsel for "good cause," a power that we have already concluded provides the Executive with substantial ability to ensure that the laws are "faithfully executed" by an independent counsel. No independent counsel may be appointed without a specific request by the Attorney General, and the Attorney General's decision not to request appointment if he finds "no reasonable grounds to believe that further investigation is warranted" is committed to his unreviewable discretion. The Act thus gives the Executive a degree of control over the power to initiate an investigation by the independent counsel. In addition, the jurisdiction of the independent counsel is defined with reference to the facts submitted by the Attorney General, and once a counsel is appointed, the Act requires that the counsel abide by Justice Department policy unless it is not "possible" to do so. Notwithstanding the fact that the counsel is to some degree "independent" and free from executive supervision to a greater extent than other federal prosecutors, in our view these features of the Act give the Executive Branch sufficient control over the independent counsel to ensure that the President is able to perform his constitutionally assigned duties.

VI

In sum, we conclude today that it does not violate the Appointments Clause for Congress to vest the appointment of independent counsel in the Special Division; that the powers exercised by the Special Division under the Act do not violate Article III [omitted]; and that the Act does not violate the separation-of-powers principle by impermissibly interfering with the functions of the Executive Branch. The decision of the Court of Appeals is therefore *Reversed.*

JUSTICE SCALIA, dissenting.

It is the proud boast of our democracy that we have "a government of laws and not of men." . . . The Framers of the Federal Constitution similarly viewed the principle of separation of powers as the absolutely central guarantee of a just Government. In No. 47 of The Federalist, Madison wrote that "[n]o political truth is certainly of greater intrinsic value, or is stamped with the authority of more enlightened patrons of liberty." The Federalist No. 47, p. 301 (C. Rossiter ed. 1961) (hereinafter Federalist). Without a secure structure of separated powers, our Bill of Rights would be worthless, as are the bills of rights of many nations of the world that have adopted, or even improved upon, the mere words of ours.

The principle of separation of powers is expressed in our Constitution in the first section of each of the first three Articles. Article I, § 1, provides that "[a]ll legislative Powers herein granted shall be vested in a Congress of the United States, which shall consist of a Senate and House of Representatives." Article III, § 1, provides that "[t]he judicial Power of the United States, shall be vested in one Supreme Court, and in such inferior Courts as the Congress may from time to time ordain and establish." And the provision at issue here, Art. II, § 1, cl. 1, provides that "[t]he executive Power shall be vested in a President of the United States of America."

But just as the mere words of a Bill of Rights are not self-effectuating, the Framers recognized "[t]he insufficiency of a mere parchment delineation of the boundaries" to achieve the separation of powers. Federalist No. 73, p. 442 (A. Hamilton). "[T]he great security," wrote Madison, "against a gradual concentration of the several powers in the same department consists in giving to those who administer each department the necessary constitutional means and personal motives to resist encroachments of the others. The provision for defense must in this, as in all other cases, be made commensurate to the danger of attack." Federalist No. 51, pp. 321-322. Madison continued:

> "But it is not possible to give to each department an equal power of self-defense. In republican government, the legislative authority necessarily predominates. The remedy for this inconveniency is to divide the legislature into different branches; and to render them, by different modes of election and different principles of action, as little connected with each other as the nature of their common functions and their common dependence on the society will admit. . . . As the weight of the legislative authority requires that it should be thus divided, the weakness of the executive may require, on the other hand, that it should be fortified." *Id.,* at 322-323.

The major "fortification" provided, of course, was the veto power. But in addition to providing fortification, the Founders conspicuously and very consciously declined to sap the Executive's strength in the same way they had weakened the Legislature: by dividing the executive power. Proposals to have multiple executives, or a council of advisers with separate authority were rejected. See 1 M. Farrand, Records of the Federal Convention of 1787, pp. 66, 71-74, 88, 91-92 (rev. ed. 1966); 2 *id.,* at 335-337, 533, 537, 542. Thus, while "[a]ll legislative Powers herein granted shall be vested in a Congress of the United States, which shall consist of a Senate *and* House of Representatives," U.S. Const., Art. I, § 1 (emphasis added), "[t]he executive Power shall be vested in *a President of the United States,*" Art. II, § 1, cl. 1 (emphasis added).

That is what this suit is about. Power. The allocation of power among Congress, the President, and the courts in such fashion as to preserve the equilibrium the Constitution sought to establish — so that "a gradual concentration of the several powers in the same department," Federalist No. 51, p. 321 (J. Madison), can effectively be resisted. Frequently an issue of this sort will come before the Court clad, so to speak, in sheep's clothing: the potential of the asserted principle to effect important change in the equilibrium of power is not immediately evident, and must be discerned by a careful and perceptive analysis. But this wolf comes as a wolf. . . .

II

If to describe this case is not to decide it, the concept of a government of separate and coordinate powers no longer has meaning. The Court devotes most of its attention to such relatively technical details as the Appointments

Clause and the removal power, addressing briefly and only at the end of its opinion the separation of powers. As my prologue suggests, I think that has it backwards. Our opinions are full of the recognition that it is the principle of separation of powers, and the inseparable corollary that each department's "defense must . . . be made commensurate to the danger of attack," Federalist No. 51, p. 322 (J. Madison), which gives comprehensible content to the Appointments Clause, and determines the appropriate scope of the removal power. Thus, while I will subsequently discuss why our appointments and removal jurisprudence does not support today's holding, I begin with a consideration of the fountainhead of that jurisprudence, the separation and equilibration of powers. . . .

To repeat, Article II, § 1, cl. 1, of the Constitution provides:

"The executive Power shall be vested in a President of the United States."

As I described at the outset of this opinion, this does not mean *some of* the executive power, but *all of* the executive power. It seems to me, therefore, that the decision of the Court of Appeals invalidating the present statute must be upheld on fundamental separation-of-powers principles if the following two questions are answered affirmatively: (1) Is the conduct of a criminal prosecution (and of an investigation to decide whether to prosecute) the exercise of purely executive power? (2) Does the statute deprive the President of the United States of exclusive control over the exercise of that power? Surprising to say, the Court appears to concede an affirmative answer to both questions, but seeks to avoid the inevitable conclusion that since the statute vests some purely executive power in a person who is not the President of the United States it is void.

The Court concedes that "[t]here is no real dispute that the functions performed by the independent counsel are 'executive',". . . .

As for the second question, whether the statute before us deprives the President of exclusive control over that quintessentially executive activity: The Court does not, and could not possibly, assert that it does not. That is indeed the whole object of the statute. Instead, the Court points out that the President, through his Attorney General, has at least *some* control. That concession is alone enough to invalidate the statute, but I cannot refrain from pointing out that the Court greatly exaggerates the extent of that "some" Presidential control. "Most importan[t]" among these controls, the Court asserts, is the Attorney General's "power to remove the counsel for 'good cause.'" This is somewhat like referring to shackles as an effective means of locomotion. As we recognized in *Humphrey's Executor v. United States,* 295 U.S. 602 (1935) — indeed, what *Humphrey's Executor* was all about — limiting removal power to "good cause" is an impediment to, not an effective grant of, Presidential control. We said that limitation was necessary with respect to members of the Federal Trade Commission, which we found to be "an agency of the legislative and judicial departments," and "wholly disconnected from the executive department," *id.,* at 630, because "it is quite evident that one who holds his office only during the pleasure of another, cannot be depended upon to maintain an attitude of independence against the latter's will." *Id.,* at 629. What we in *Humphrey's Executor* found to be a means of eliminating Presidential control, the Court today considers the "most importan[t]" means of assuring Presidential control. Congress, of course, operated under no such illusion when it enacted this statute, describing the "good cause" limitation as "protecting the independent counsel's ability to act independently of the President's direct control" since it permits removal only for "misconduct." H. R. Conf. Rep. 100-452, p. 37 (1987).

. . . [T]he Court points out that the Act directs the independent counsel to abide by general Justice Department policy, except when not "possible." See 28 U.S.C. § 594(f) (1982 ed., Supp. V). The exception alone shows this to be an empty promise. Even without that, however, one would be hard put to come up with many investigative or prosecutorial "policies" (other than those imposed by the Constitution or by Congress through law) that are absolute. . . .

As I have said, however, it is ultimately irrelevant *how much* the statute reduces Presidential control. The case is over when the Court acknowledges, as it must, that "[i]t is undeniable that the Act reduces the amount of control or supervision that the Attorney General and, through him, the President exercises over the investigation and prosecution of a certain class of alleged criminal activity." . . .

[The independent counsel law] deeply wounds the President, by substantially reducing the President's ability to protect himself and his staff. That is the whole object of the law, of course, and I cannot imagine why the Court believes it does not succeed.

Besides weakening the Presidency by reducing the zeal of his staff, it must also be obvious that the institution of the independent counsel enfeebles him more directly in his constant confrontations with Congress, by eroding his public support. Nothing is so politically effective as the ability to charge that one's opponent and his associates are not merely wrongheaded, naive, ineffective, but, in all probability, "crooks." And nothing so effectively gives an appearance of validity to such charges as a Justice Department investigation and, even better, prosecution. . . .

In sum, this statute does deprive the President of substantial control over the prosecutory functions performed by the independent counsel, and it does substantially affect the balance of powers. That the Court could possibly conclude otherwise demonstrates both the wisdom of our former constitutional system, in which the degree of reduced control and political impairment were irrelevant, since *all* purely executive power had to be in the President; and the folly of the new system of standardless judicial allocation of powers we adopt today.

III

As I indicated earlier, the basic separation-of-powers principles I have discussed are what give life and content to our jurisprudence concerning the President's power to appoint and remove officers. The same result of unconstitutionality is therefore plainly indicated by our case law in these areas.

[Justice Scalia argues that the law violates the appointments clause.]

Because appellant is not subordinate to another officer, she is not an "inferior" officer and her appointment other than by the President with the advice and consent of the Senate is unconstitutional.

IV

[Justice Scalia then turned his attention to the President's removal power.] . . .

Since our 1935 decision in *Humphrey's Executor v. United States,* 295 U.S. 602 — which was considered by many at the time the product of an activist, anti-New Deal Court bent on reducing the power of President Franklin Roosevelt — it has been established that the line of permissible restriction upon removal of principal officers lies at the point at which the powers exercised by those officers are no longer purely executive. Thus, removal restrictions have been generally regarded as lawful for so-called "independent regulatory agencies," such as the Federal Trade Commission, *see ibid.;* 15 U.S.C. § 41, the Interstate Commerce Commission, *see* 49 U.S.C. § 10301(c) (1982 ed., Supp. IV), and the Consumer Product Safety Commission, see 15 U.S.C. § 2053(a), which engage substantially in what has been called the "quasi-legislative activity" of rulemaking, and for members of Article I courts, such as the Court of Military Appeals, see 10 U.S.C. § 867(a)(2), who engage in the "quasi-judicial" function of adjudication. It has often been observed, correctly in my view, that the line between "purely executive" functions and "quasi-legislative" or "quasi-judicial" functions is not a clear one or even a rational one. See *ante,* at 689-691; *Bowsher v. Synar,* 478 U.S. 714, 761, n.3 (1986) (WHITE, J., dissenting); *FTC v. Ruberoid Co.,* 343 U.S. 470, 487-488 (1952) (Jackson, J., dissenting). But at least it permitted the identification of certain officers, and certain agencies, whose functions were entirely within the control of the President. Congress had to be aware of that restriction in its legislation. Today, however, *Humphrey's Executor* is swept into the dustbin of repudiated constitutional principles. "[O]ur present considered view," the Court says, "is that the determination of whether the Constitution allows Congress to impose a 'good cause'-type restriction on the President's power to remove an official cannot be made to turn on whether or not that official is classified as 'purely executive.'" What *Humphrey's Executor* (and presumably *Myers*) really means, we are now told, is not that there are any "rigid categories of those officials who may or may not be removed at will by the President," but simply that Congress cannot "interefere with the President's exercise of the 'executive power' and his constitutionally appointed duty to 'take care that the laws be faithfully executed.'"

. . . As far as I can discern from the Court's opinion, it is now open season upon the President's removal power for all executive officers, with not even the superficially principled restriction of *Humphrey's Executor* as cover. The Court essentially says to the President: "Trust us. We will make sure that you are able to accomplish your constitutional role." I think the Constitution gives the President — and the people — more protection than that.

V

. . . How frightening it must be to have your own independent counsel and staff appointed, with nothing else to do but to investigate you until investigation is no longer worthwhile — with whether it is worthwhile not depending upon what such judgments usually hinge on, competing responsibilities. And to have that counsel and staff decide, with no basis for comparison, whether what you have done is bad enough, willful enough, and provable enough, to warrant an indictment. How admirable the constitutional system that provides the means to avoid such a distortion. And how unfortunate the judicial decision that has permitted it. . . .

. . . By its shortsighted action today, I fear the Court has permanently encumbered the Republic with an institution that will do it great harm.

Worse than what it has done, however, is the manner in which it has done it. A government of laws means a government of rules. Today's decision on the basic issue of fragmentation of executive power is ungoverned by rule, and hence ungoverned by law. It extends into the very heart of our most significant constitutional function the "totality of the circumstances" mode of analysis that this Court has in recent years become fond of. . . .

The ad hoc approach to constitutional adjudication has real attraction, even apart from its work-saving potential. It is guaranteed to produce a result, in every case, that will make a majority of the Court happy with the law. The law is, by definition, precisely what the majority thinks, taking all things into account, it *ought* to be. I prefer to rely upon the judgment of the wise men who constructed our system, and of the people who approved it, and of two centuries of history that have shown it to be sound. Like it or not, that judgment says, quite plainly, that "[t]he executive Power shall be vested in a President of the United States."

QUESTIONS

1. Are you persuaded by the majority's Appointments Clause analysis? In *Edmond v. United States*, 520 U.S. 651 (1997), the Court considered whether a judge of the Coast Guard Court of Criminal Appeals, whose appointment is vested by statute in the Secretary of Transportation, is an inferior officer of the United States. The Court, in an opinion written by Justice Scalia, acknowledged that two of the factors relied upon in *Morrison* to support its conclusion that the Special Prosecutor was an inferior officer (the judges were limited neither in tenure nor in jurisdiction as the Court analyzed those factors in *Morrison*) "do not hold with regard to the office of military judge at issue here." *Id.* at 661. The Court stated, however, that "*Morrison* did not purport to set forth a definitive test for whether an office is 'inferior' under the Appointments Clause." *Id.* The Court then decided, *id.* at 662-65, that the military judges were inferior officers, noting that "Generally speaking, the term 'inferior officer' connotes a relationship with some higher ranking officer or officers below the President: Whether one is an 'inferior' officer depends on whether he has a superior." The Court found it significant that the judges of the Court of Criminal Appeals had no power to render a final decision on behalf of the United States unless permitted to do so by other executive officers (administrative control by the Judge Advocate General and review of the outcome of proceedings by the Court of Appeals of the Armed Forces). If the Court had pursued this analytic approach in *Morrison,* would it have concluded that the Special Prosecutor was an inferior officer?

2. Some observers see the majority's treatment of the President's power to dismiss as a portentous change from formalistic to functionalistic analysis. Does the opinion really represent a change in approach? With which case is it inconsistent? *Myers? Humphrey's Executor? Synar?*

3. What of Justice Scalia's opinion? Why does he accept *Humphrey's Executor's* questionable distinction whether or not agencies have been given quasi-judicial and/or quasi-legislative functions? How else could Justice Scalia preserve the constitutionality of independent agencies like the FTC, the Federal Reserve Board, etc.?

4. Are such agencies constitutional? Why should they not all be under the control of the President, with presidential discharge power? Was that the Framers' scheme?

5. What limit is there now, if any, on the power of Congress to limit substantively the President's power to remove an officer? Could Congress preclude the President from removing, except for cause, the Secretary of Defense or the Secretary of Agriculture?

6. Note other ways the President can control the federal bureaucracy, even when he lacks the power to fire officials:

    a. appointment power,

    b. Department of Justice representation of independent agencies in court (almost all federal agencies are represented in court by the Department of Justice, which makes such significant determinations, for instance, as whether or not the agency may appeal an adverse district court judgment),

    c. control over introduction of legislation (the President can propose legislation reorganizing, or reducing the power of, an independent agency),

    d. influence on the budget (in the budget process, the President can propose less spending for an independent agency).

7. Note other ways agency officials can be immune from presidential power even when they *can* be discharged:

    a. independent political power or prestige (e.g., J. Edgar Hoover at the FBI, Hillary Clinton at the State Department),

    b. obscurity.

FREE ENTERPRISE FUND v. PUBLIC COMPANY ACCOUNTING OVERSIGHT BOARD

561 U.S. 477 (2010)

CHIEF JUSTICE ROBERTS delivered the opinion of the Court.

Our Constitution divided the "powers of the new Federal Government into three defined categories, Legislative, Executive, and Judicial." *INS v. Chadha*, 462 U. S. 919, 951 (1983). Article II vests "[t]he executive Power ... in a President of the United States of America," who must "take Care that the Laws be faithfully executed." Art. II, § 1, cl. 1; id., § 3. In light of "[t]he impossibility that one man should be able to perform all the great business of the State," the Constitution provides for executive officers to "assist the supreme Magistrate in discharging the duties of his trust." 30 Writings of George Washington 334 (J. Fitzpatrick ed. 1939).

Since 1789, the Constitution has been understood to empower the President to keep these officers accountable — by removing them from office, if necessary. See generally *Myers v. United States*, 272 U. S. 52 (1926). This Court has determined, however, that this authority is not without limit. In *Humphrey's Executor v.*

United States, 295 U. S. 602 (1935), we held that Congress can, under certain circumstances, create independent agencies run by principal officers appointed by the President, whom the President may not remove at will but only for good cause. Likewise, in *United States v. Perkins*, 116 U. S. 483 (1886), and *Morrison v. Olson*, 487 U. S. 654 (1988), the Court sustained similar restrictions on the power of principal executive officers — themselves responsible to the President — to remove their own inferiors. The parties do not ask us to reexamine any of these precedents, and we do not do so.

We are asked, however, to consider a new situation not yet encountered by the Court. The question is whether these separate layers of protection may be combined. May the President be restricted in his ability to remove a principal officer, who is in turn restricted in his ability to remove an inferior officer, even though that inferior officer determines the policy and enforces the laws of the United States?

We hold that such multilevel protection from removal is contrary to Article II's vesting of the executive power in the President. The President cannot "take Care that the Laws be faithfully executed" if he cannot oversee the faithfulness of the officers who execute them. Here the President cannot remove an officer who enjoys more than one level of good-cause protection, even if the President determines that the officer is neglecting his duties or discharging them improperly. That judgment is instead committed to another officer, who may or may not agree with the President's determination, and whom the President cannot remove simply because that officer disagrees with him. This contravenes the President's "constitutional obligation to ensure the faithful execution of the laws." *Id.*, at 693.

I

A

After a series of celebrated accounting debacles, Congress enacted the Sarbanes-Oxley Act of 2002 (or Act), 116 Stat. 745. Among other measures, the Act introduced tighter regulation of the accounting industry under a new Public Company Accounting Oversight Board. The Board is composed of five members, appointed to staggered 5-year terms by the Securities and Exchange Commission. It was modeled on private self-regulatory organizations in the securities industry — such as the New York Stock Exchange — that investigate and discipline their own members subject to Commission oversight. Congress created the Board as a private "nonprofit corporation," and Board members and employees are not considered Government "officer[s] or employee[s]" for statutory purposes. 15 U. S. C. §§ 7211(a), (b). The Board can thus recruit its members and employees from the private sector by paying salaries far above the standard Government pay scale. *See* §§ 7211(f)(4), 7219.

Unlike the self-regulatory organizations, however, the Board is a Government-created, Government-appointed entity, with expansive powers to govern an entire industry. Every accounting firm — both foreign and domestic — that participates in auditing public companies under the securities laws must register with the Board, pay it an annual fee, and comply with its rules and oversight. §§ 7211(a), 7212(a), (f), 7213, 7216(a)(1). The Board is charged with enforcing the Sarbanes-Oxley Act, the securities laws, the Commission's rules, its own rules, and professional accounting standards. §§ 7215(b)(1), (c)(4). . . .

The Board promulgates auditing and ethics standards, performs routine inspections of all accounting firms, demands documents and testimony, and initiates formal investigations and disciplinary proceedings. §§ 7213-7215 (2006 ed. and Supp. II). The willful violation of any Board rule is treated as a willful violation of the Securities Exchange Act of 1934, 48 Stat. 881, 15 U. S. C. § 78a et seq. — a federal crime punishable by up to 20 years' imprisonment or $25 million in fines ($5 million for a natural person). §§ 78ff(a), 7202(b)(1) (2006 ed.). And the Board itself can issue severe sanctions in its disciplinary proceedings, up to and including the permanent revocation of a firm's registration, a permanent ban on a person's associating with any registered firm, and money penalties of $15 million ($750,000 for a natural person). § 7215(c)(4). Despite the provisions specifying that Board members are not Government officials for statutory purposes, the parties agree that the Board is "part of the Government" for constitutional purposes, *Lebron v. National Railroad Passenger Corporation*, 513 U. S. 374, 397 (1995), and that its members are "'Officers of the United States'" who "exercis[e] significant authority pursuant to the laws of the United States," *Buckley v. Valeo*, 424 U. S. 1, 125-126 (1976) (*per curiam*) (quoting Art. II, § 2, cl. 2); . . . .

The Act places the Board under the SEC's oversight, particularly with respect to the issuance of rules or the imposition of sanctions (both of which are subject to Commission approval and alteration). §§ 7217(b)-(c). But the individual members of the Board — like the officers and directors of the self-regulatory organizations — are substantially insulated from the Commission's control. The Commission cannot remove Board members at will, but only "for good cause shown," "in accordance with" certain procedures. § 7211(e)(6).

Those procedures require a Commission finding, "on the record" and "after notice and opportunity for a hearing," that the Board member

"(A) has willfully violated any provision of th[e] Act, the rules of the Board, or the securities laws;

"(B) has willfully abused the authority of that member; or

"(C) without reasonable justification or excuse, has failed to enforce compliance with any such provision or rule, or any professional standard by any registered public accounting firm or any associated person thereof." § 7217(d)(3).

Removal of a Board member requires a formal Commission order and is subject to judicial review. *See* 5 U. S. C. §§ 554(a), 556(a), 557(a), (c)(B); 15 U. S. C. § 78y(a)(1). Similar procedures govern the Commission's removal of officers and directors of the private self-regulatory organizations. *See* § 78s(h)(4). The parties agree that the Commissioners cannot themselves be removed by the President except under the *Humphrey's Executor* standard of "inefficiency, neglect of duty, or malfeasance in office," 295 U. S., at 620 (internal quotation marks omitted); [citations to parties' briefs and oral argument omitted], and we decide the case with that understanding.

B

Beckstead and Watts, LLP, is a Nevada accounting firm registered with the Board. The Board inspected the firm, released a report critical of its auditing

procedures, and began a formal investigation. Beckstead and Watts and the Free
Enterprise Fund, a nonprofit organization of which the firm is a member, then
sued the Board and its members, seeking (among other things) a declaratory
judgment that the Board is unconstitutional and an injunction preventing the
Board from exercising its powers. App. 71.

Before the District Court, petitioners argued that the Sarbanes-Oxley Act
contravened the separation of powers by conferring wide-ranging executive
power on Board members without subjecting them to Presidential control.
Id., at 67-68. Petitioners also challenged the Act under the Appointments
Clause, which requires "Officers of the United States" to be appointed by the
President with the Senate's advice and consent. Art. II, § 2, cl. 2. . . . The United
States intervened to defend the Act's constitutionality. Both sides moved for
summary judgment; the District Court determined that it had jurisdiction
and granted summary judgment to respondents.

A divided Court of Appeals affirmed. . . .

. . . .

We granted certiorari. 556 U.S. 1234 (2009).

II

We first consider whether the District Court had jurisdiction. We agree with both
courts below that the statutes providing for judicial review of Commission action
did not prevent the District Court from considering petitioners' claims.

. . . .

III

We hold that the dual for-cause limitations on the removal of Board members
contravene the Constitution's separation of powers.

A

The Constitution provides that "[t]he executive Power shall be vested in a President of the United States of America." Art. II, § 1, cl. 1. As Madison stated on the
floor of the First Congress, "if any power whatsoever is in its nature Executive, it
is the power of appointing, overseeing, and controlling those who execute the
laws." 1 Annals of Cong. 463 (1789).

The removal of executive officers was discussed extensively in Congress when
the first executive departments were created. The view that "prevailed, as most
consonant to the text of the Constitution" and "to the requisite responsibility
and harmony in the Executive Department," was that the executive power
included a power to oversee executive officers through removal; because that
traditional executive power was not "expressly taken away, it remained with the
President." Letter from James Madison to Thomas Jefferson (June 30, 1789), 16
Documentary History of the First Federal Congress 893 (2004). "This Decision
of 1789 provides contemporaneous and weighty evidence of the Constitution's
meaning since many of the Members of the First Congress had taken part in
framing that instrument." *Bowsher v. Synar*, 478 U. S. 714, 723-724 (1986) (internal quotation marks omitted). And it soon became the "settled and well

understood construction of the Constitution." *Ex parte Hennen*, 13 Pet. 230, 259 (1839).

The landmark case of *Myers v. United States* reaffirmed the principle that Article II confers on the President "the general administrative control of those executing the laws." 272 U.S., at 164. It is his responsibility to take care that the laws be faithfully executed. The buck stops with the President, in Harry Truman's famous phrase. As we explained in *Myers*, the President therefore must have some "power of removing those for whom he can not continue to be responsible." *Id.*, at 117.

Nearly a decade later in *Humphrey's Executor*, this Court held that *Myers* did not prevent Congress from conferring good-cause tenure on the principal officers of certain independent agencies. That case concerned the members of the Federal Trade Commission, who held 7-year terms and could not be removed by the President except for "'inefficiency, neglect of duty, or malfeasance in office.'" 295 U.S., at 620 (quoting 15 U.S.C. § 41). The Court distinguished *Myers* on the ground that *Myers* concerned "an officer [who] is merely one of the units in the executive department and, hence, inherently subject to the exclusive and illimitable power of removal by the Chief Executive, whose subordinate and aid he is." 295 U.S., at 627. By contrast, the Court characterized the FTC as "quasi-legislative and quasi-judicial" rather than "purely executive," and held that Congress could require it "to act . . . independently of executive control." *Id.*, at 627-629. Because "one who holds his office only during the pleasure of another, cannot be depended upon to maintain an attitude of independence against the latter's will," the Court held that Congress had power to "fix the period during which [the Commissioners] shall continue in office, and to forbid their removal except for cause in the meantime." *Id.*, at 629.

Humphrey's Executor did not address the removal of inferior officers, whose appointment Congress may vest in heads of departments. If Congress does so, it is ordinarily the department head, rather than the President, who enjoys the power of removal. See *Myers, supra*, at 119, 127; *Hennen, supra*, at 259-260. This Court has upheld for-cause limitations on that power as well.

In *Perkins*, a naval cadet-engineer was honorably discharged from the Navy because his services were no longer required. 116 U.S. 483. He brought a claim for his salary under statutes barring his peacetime discharge except by a court-martial or by the Secretary of the Navy "for misconduct." Rev. Stat. §§ 1229, 1525. This Court adopted verbatim the reasoning of the Court of Claims, which had held that when Congress "'vests the appointment of inferior officers in the heads of Departments[,] it may limit and restrict the power of removal as it deems best for the public interest.'" 116 U.S., at 485. Because Perkins had not been "'dismissed for misconduct . . . [or upon] the sentence of a court-martial,'" the Court agreed that he was "'still in office and . . . entitled to [his] pay.'" *Ibid.*

We again considered the status of inferior officers in *Morrison*. That case concerned the Ethics in Government Act, which provided for an independent counsel to investigate allegations of crime by high executive officers. The counsel was appointed by a special court, wielded the full powers of a prosecutor, and was removable by the Attorney General only "'for good cause.'" 487 U.S., at 663 (quoting 28 U.S.C. § 596(a)(1)). We recognized that the independent counsel was undoubtedly an executive officer, rather than "'quasi-legislative'" or "'quasi-judicial,'" but we stated as "our present considered view" that

Congress had power to impose good-cause restrictions on her removal. 487 U. S., at 689-691. The Court noted that the statute "g[a]ve the Attorney General," an officer directly responsible to the President and "through [whom]" the President could act, "several means of supervising or controlling" the independent counsel — "[m]ost importantly . . . the power to remove the counsel for good cause." *Id.*, at 695-696 (internal quotation marks omitted). Under those circumstances, the Court sustained the statute. *Morrison* did not, however, address the consequences of more than one level of good-cause tenure — leaving the issue, as both the court and dissent below recognized, "a question of first impression" in this Court. 537 F. 3d, at 679; see *id.*, at 698 (dissenting opinion).

B

As explained, we have previously upheld limited restrictions on the President's removal power. In those cases, however, only one level of protected tenure separated the President from an officer exercising executive power. It was the President — or a subordinate he could remove at will — who decided whether the officer's conduct merited removal under the good-cause standard.

The Act before us does something quite different. It not only protects Board members from removal except for good cause, but withdraws from the President any decision on whether that good cause exists. That decision is vested instead in other tenured officers — the Commissioners — none of whom is subject to the President's direct control. The result is a Board that is not accountable to the President, and a President who is not responsible for the Board.

The added layer of tenure protection makes a difference. Without a layer of insulation between the Commission and the Board, the Commission could remove a Board member at any time, and therefore would be fully responsible for what the Board does. The President could then hold the Commission to account for its supervision of the Board, to the same extent that he may hold the Commission to account for everything else it does.

A second level of tenure protection changes the nature of the President's review. Now the Commission cannot remove a Board member at will. The President therefore cannot hold the Commission fully accountable for the Board's conduct, to the same extent that he may hold the Commission accountable for everything else that it does. The Commissioners are not responsible for the Board's actions. They are only responsible for their own determination of whether the Act's rigorous good-cause standard is met. And even if the President disagrees with their determination, he is powerless to intervene — unless that determination is so unreasonable as to constitute "inefficiency, neglect of duty, or malfeasance in office." *Humphrey's Executor*, 295 U. S., at 620 (internal quotation marks omitted).

This novel structure does not merely add to the Board's independence, but transforms it. Neither the President, nor anyone directly responsible to him, nor even an officer whose conduct he may review only for good cause, has full control over the Board. The President is stripped of the power our precedents have preserved, and his ability to execute the laws — by holding his subordinates accountable for their conduct — is impaired.

That arrangement is contrary to Article II's vesting of the executive power in the President. Without the ability to oversee the Board, or to attribute the Board's failings to those whom he can oversee, the President is no longer the judge of the Board's conduct. He is not the one who decides whether Board members are abusing their offices or neglecting their duties. He can neither ensure that the laws are faithfully executed, nor be held responsible for a Board member's breach of faith. This violates the basic principle that the President "cannot delegate ultimate responsibility or the active obligation to supervise that goes with it," because Article II "makes a single President responsible for the actions of the Executive Branch." *Clinton v. Jones*, 520 U. S. 681, 712-713 (1997) (BREYER, J., concurring in judgment).[4]

Indeed, if allowed to stand, this dispersion of responsibility could be multiplied. If Congress can shelter the bureaucracy behind two layers of good-cause tenure, why not a third? At oral argument, the Government was unwilling to concede that even five layers between the President and the Board would be too many. The officers of such an agency — safely encased within a Matryoshka doll of tenure protections — would be immune from Presidential oversight, even as they exercised power in the people's name.

Perhaps an individual President might find advantages in tying his own hands. But the separation of powers does not depend on the views of individual Presidents, see *Freytag v. Commissioner*, 501 U. S. 868, 879-880 (1991), nor on whether "the encroached-upon branch approves the encroachment," *New York v. United States*, 505 U. S. 144, 182 (1992). The President can always choose to restrain himself in his dealings with subordinates. He cannot, however, choose to bind his successors by diminishing their powers, nor can he escape responsibility for his choices by pretending that they are not his own.

The diffusion of power carries with it a diffusion of accountability. The people do not vote for the "Officers of the United States." Art. II, § 2, cl. 2. They instead look to the President to guide the "assistants or deputies . . . subject to his superintendence." The Federalist No. 72, p. 487 (J. Cooke ed. 1961) (A. Hamilton). Without a clear and effective chain of command, the public cannot "determine on whom the blame or the punishment of a pernicious measure, or series of pernicious measures ought really to fall." *Id.*, No. 70, at 476 (same). That is why the Framers sought to ensure that "those who are employed in the execution of the law will be in their proper situation, and the chain of dependence be preserved; the lowest officers, the middle grade, and the highest, will depend, as they ought, on the President, and the President on the community." 1 Annals of Cong., at 499 (J. Madison).

By granting the Board executive power without the Executive's oversight, this Act subverts the President's ability to ensure that the laws are faithfully executed — as well as the public's ability to pass judgment on his efforts. The Act's restrictions are incompatible with the Constitution's separation of powers.

c

Respondents and the dissent resist this conclusion, portraying the Board as "the kind of practical accommodation between the Legislature and the Executive

---

4. Contrary to the dissent's suggestion, the second layer of tenure protection does compromise the President's ability to remove a Board member the Commission wants to retain. Without a second layer of protection, the Commission has no excuse for retaining an officer who is not faithfully executing the law. With the second layer in place, the Commission can shield its decision from Presidential review by finding that good cause is absent — a finding that, given the Commission's own protected tenure, the President cannot easily overturn. The dissent describes this conflict merely as one of four possible "scenarios," but it is the central issue in this case: The second layer matters precisely when the President finds it necessary to have a subordinate officer removed, and a statute prevents him from doing so.

that should be permitted in a 'workable government.'" *Metropolitan Washington Airports Authority v. Citizens for Abatement of Aircraft Noise, Inc.,* 501 U. S. 252, 276 (1991) (*MWAA*) (quoting *Youngstown Sheet & Tube Co. v. Sawyer,* 343 U. S. 579, 635 (1952) (Jackson, J., concurring)). According to the dissent, Congress may impose multiple levels of for-cause tenure between the President and his subordinates when it "rests agency independence upon the need for technical expertise." The Board's mission is said to demand both "technical competence" and "apolitical expertise," and its powers may only be exercised by "technical professional experts." In this respect the statute creating the Board is, we are told, simply one example of the "vast numbers of statutes governing vast numbers of subjects, concerned with vast numbers of different problems, [that] provide for, or foresee, their execution or administration through the work of administrators organized within many different kinds of administrative structures, exercising different kinds of administrative authority, to achieve their legislatively mandated objectives."

No one doubts Congress's power to create a vast and varied federal bureaucracy. But where, in all this, is the role for oversight by an elected President? The Constitution requires that a President chosen by the entire Nation oversee the execution of the laws. And the "'fact that a given law or procedure is efficient, convenient, and useful in facilitating functions of government, standing alone, will not save it if it is contrary to the Constitution,'" for "'[c]onvenience and efficiency are not the primary objectives—or the hallmarks—of democratic government.'" *Bowsher,* 478 U. S., at 736 (quoting *Chadha,* 462 U. S., at 944).

One can have a government that functions without being ruled by functionaries, and a government that benefits from expertise without being ruled by experts. Our Constitution was adopted to enable the people to govern themselves, through their elected leaders. The growth of the Executive Branch, which now wields vast power and touches almost every aspect of daily life, heightens the concern that it may slip from the Executive's control, and thus from that of the people. This concern is largely absent from the dissent's paean to the administrative state. . . .

[T]he multilevel protection that the dissent endorses "provides a blueprint for extensive expansion of the legislative power." *MWAA,* at 277. In a system of checks and balances, "[p]ower abhors a vacuum," and one branch's handicap is another's strength, 537 F. 3d, at 695, n. 4 (Kavanaugh, J., dissenting) (internal quotation marks omitted). "Even when a branch does not arrogate power to itself," therefore, it must not "impair another in the performance of its constitutional duties." *Loving v. United States,* 517 U. S. 748, 757 (1996). Congress has plenary control over the salary, duties, and even existence of executive offices. Only Presidential oversight can counter its influence. That is why the Constitution vests certain powers in the President that "the Legislature has no right to diminish or modify." 1 Annals of Cong., at 463 (J. Madison).

The Framers created a structure in which "[a] dependence on the people" would be the "primary control on the government." The Federalist No. 51, at 349 (J. Madison). That dependence is maintained, not just by "parchment barriers," *id.,* No. 48, at 333 (same), but by letting "[a]mbition . . . counteract ambition," giving each branch "the necessary constitutional means, and personal motives, to resist encroachments of the others," *id.,* No. 51, at 349. A key "constitutional means" vested in the President—perhaps the key means—was "the power of appointing, overseeing, and controlling those who execute the laws." 1 Annals of Cong., at 463. And while a government of "opposite and rival interests" may sometimes inhibit the smooth functioning of administration, The Federalist No. 51, at 349, "[t]he Framers recognized that, in the long term, structural protections against abuse of power were critical to preserving liberty." *Bowsher, supra*, at 730.

Calls to abandon those protections in light of "the era's perceived necessity," *New York*, 505 U. S., at 187, are not unusual. Nor is the argument from bureaucratic expertise limited only to the field of accounting. The failures of accounting regulation may be a "pressing national problem," but "a judiciary that licensed extraconstitutional government with each issue of comparable gravity would, in the long run, be far worse." *Id.*, at 187-188. Neither respondents nor the dissent explains why the Board's task, unlike so many others, requires more than one layer of insulation from the President — or, for that matter, why only two. The point is not to take issue with for-cause limitations in general; we do not do that. The question here is far more modest. We deal with the unusual situation, never before addressed by the Court, of two layers of for-cause tenure. And though it may be criticized as "elementary arithmetical logic," two layers are not the same as one.

The President has been given the power to oversee executive officers; he is not limited, as in Harry Truman's lament, to "persuad[ing]" his unelected subordinates "to do what they ought to do without persuasion." In its pursuit of a "workable government," Congress cannot reduce the Chief Magistrate to a cajoler-in-chief.

D

The United States concedes that some constraints on the removal of inferior executive officers might violate the Constitution. It contends, however, that the removal restrictions at issue here do not.

To begin with, the Government argues that the Commission's removal power over the Board is "broad," and could be construed as broader still, if necessary to avoid invalidation. But the Government does not contend that simple disagreement with the Board's policies or priorities could constitute "good cause" for its removal. Nor do our precedents suggest as much. . . . Indeed, this case presents an even more serious threat to executive control than an "ordinary" dual for-cause standard. Congress enacted an unusually high standard that must be met before Board members may be removed. A Board member cannot be removed except for willful violations of the Act, Board rules, or the securities laws; willful abuse of authority; or unreasonable failure to enforce compliance — as determined in a formal Commission order, rendered on the record and after notice and an opportunity for a hearing. § 7217(d)(3); see § 78y(a). The Act does not even give the Commission power to fire Board members for violations of other laws that do not relate to the Act, the securities laws, or the Board's authority. . . .

The rigorous standard that must be met before a Board member may be removed was drawn from statutes concerning private organizations like the New York Stock Exchange. Cf. §§ 78s(h)(4), 7217(d)(3). While we need not decide the question here, a removal standard appropriate for limiting Government control over private bodies may be inappropriate for officers wielding the executive power of the United States.

Alternatively, respondents portray the Act's limitations on removal as irrelevant, because — as the Court of Appeals held — the Commission wields "at-will removal power over Board *functions* if not Board members." 537 F. 3d, at 683 (emphasis added). The Commission's general "oversight and enforcement authority over the Board," §7217(a), is said to "blun[t] the constitutional impact of for-cause removal," 537 F. 3d, at 683, and to leave the President no worse off than "if Congress had lodged the Board's functions in the SEC's own staff," PCAOB Brief 15.

Broad power over Board functions is not equivalent to the power to remove Board members. The Commission may, for example, approve the Board's budget, §7219(b), issue binding regulations, §§7202(a), 7217(b)(5), relieve the Board of authority, §7217(d)(1), amend Board sanctions, §7217(c), or enforce Board rules on its own, §§7202(b)(1), (c). But altering the budget or powers of an agency as a whole is a problematic way to control an inferior officer. . . . The Commission cannot wield a free hand to supervise individual members if it must destroy the Board in order to fix it.

[T]he Act nowhere gives the Commission effective power to start, stop, or alter individual Board investigations, executive activities typically carried out by officials within the Executive Branch. . . .

Finally, respondents suggest that our conclusion is contradicted by the past practice of Congress. But the Sarbanes-Oxley Act is highly unusual in committing substantial executive authority to officers protected by two layers of for-cause removal — including at one level a sharply circumscribed definition of what constitutes "good cause," and rigorous procedures that must be followed prior to removal. . . .

. . . We do not decide the status of other Government employees, nor do we decide whether "lesser functionaries subordinate to officers of the United States" must be subject to the same sort of control as those who exercise "significant authority pursuant to the laws." *Buckley, supra*, at 126, and n. 162.

Nor do the employees referenced by the dissent enjoy the same significant and unusual protections from Presidential oversight as members of the Board. Senior or policymaking positions in government may be excepted from the competitive service to ensure Presidential control, see 5 U. S. C. §§2302(a)(2)(B), 3302, 7511(b)(2), and members of the Senior Executive Service may be reassigned or reviewed by agency heads (and entire agencies may be excluded from that Service by the President), *see*, e.g., §§3132(c), 3395(a), 4312(d), 4314(b)(3), (c)(3); cf. §2302(a)(2)(B)(ii). While the full extent of that authority is not before us, any such authority is of course wholly absent with respect to the Board. Nothing in our opinion, therefore, should be read to cast doubt on the use of what is colloquially known as the civil service system within independent agencies.[10]

. . . .

10. For similar reasons, our holding also does not address that subset of independent agency employees who serve as administrative law judges. *See*, e.g., 5 U. S. C. §§556(c), 3105. Whether administrative law judges are necessarily "Officers of the United States" is disputed. *See*, e.g., *Landry v. FDIC*, 204 F. 3d 1125 (CADC 2000). And unlike members of the Board, many administrative law judges of course perform adjudicative rather than enforcement or policymaking functions, see §§554(d), 3105, or possess purely recommendatory powers. The Government below refused to identify either "civil service tenure-protected employees in independent agencies" or administrative law judges as "precedent for the PCAOB." 537 F. 3d 667, 699, n. 8 (CADC 2008) (Kavanaugh, J., dissenting).

. . . The only issue in this case is whether Congress may deprive the President of adequate control over the Board, which is the regulator of first resort and the primary law enforcement authority for a vital sector of our economy. We hold that it cannot.

IV

Petitioners' complaint argued that the Board's "freedom from Presidential oversight and control" rendered it "and all power and authority exercised by it" in violation of the Constitution. We reject such a broad holding. Instead, we agree with the Government that the unconstitutional tenure provisions are severable from the remainder of the statute.

. . . .

The Sarbanes-Oxley Act remains "'fully operative as a law'" with these tenure restrictions excised. *New York*, 505 U. S., at 186. We therefore must sustain its remaining provisions "[u]nless it is evident that the Legislature would not have enacted those provisions . . . independently of that which is [invalid]." *Ibid.* Though this inquiry can sometimes be "elusive," *Chadha*, 462 U. S., at 932, the answer here seems clear: The remaining provisions are not "incapable of functioning independently," *Alaska Airlines*, 480 U. S., at 684, and nothing in the statute's text or historical context makes it "evident" that Congress, faced with the limitations imposed by the Constitution, would have preferred no Board at all to a Board whose members are removable at will. *Ibid.*

. . . .

V

Petitioners raise three more challenges to the Board under the Appointments Clause. None has merit.

First, petitioners argue that Board members are principal officers requiring Presidential appointment with the Senate's advice and consent. We held in *Edmond v. United States*, 520 U.S. 651, 662-663 (1997), that "[w]hether one is an 'inferior' officer depends on whether he has a superior," and that "'inferior officers' are officers whose work is directed and supervised at some level" by other officers appointed by the President with the Senate's consent. In particular, we noted that "[t]he power to remove officers" at will and without cause "is a powerful tool for control" of an inferior. *Id.*, at 664. As explained above, the statutory restrictions on the Commission's power to remove Board members are unconstitutional and void. Given that the Commission is properly viewed, under the Constitution, as possessing the power to remove Board members at will, and given the Commission's other oversight authority, we have no hesitation in concluding that under *Edmond* the Board members are inferior officers whose appointment Congress may permissibly vest in a "Hea[d] of Departmen[t]."

But, petitioners argue, the Commission is not a "Departmen[t]" like the "Executive departments" (e.g., State, Treasury, Defense) listed in 5 U. S. C. § 101. In *Freytag*, 501 U. S., at 887, n. 4, we specifically reserved the question whether a "principal agenc[y], such as . . . the Securities and Exchange

Commission," is a "Departmen[t]" under the Appointments Clause. Four Justices, however, would have concluded that the Commission is indeed such a "Departmen[t]," see *id.*, at 918 (SCALIA, J., concurring in part and concurring in judgment), because it is a "free-standing, self-contained entity in the Executive Branch," *id.*, at 915.

Respondents urge us to adopt this reasoning as to those entities not addressed by our opinion in *Freytag*, and we do. Respondents' reading of the Appointments Clause is consistent with the common, near-contemporary definition of a "department" as a "separate allotment or part of business; a distinct province, in which a class of duties are allotted to a particular person." 1 N. Webster, American Dictionary of the English Language (1828) (def. 2) (1995 facsimile ed.). It is also consistent with the early practice of Congress, which in 1792 authorized the Postmaster General to appoint "an assistant, and deputy postmasters, at all places where such shall be found necessary," § 3, 1 Stat. 234 — thus treating him as the "Hea[d] of [a] Departmen[t]" without the title of Secretary or any role in the President's Cabinet. And it is consistent with our prior cases, which have never invalidated an appointment made by the head of such an establishment. See *Freytag, supra*, at 917; cf. *Burnap v. United States*, 252 U. S. 512, 515 (1920); *United States v. Germaine*, 99 U. S. 508, 511 (1879). Because the Commission is a freestanding component of the Executive Branch, not subordinate to or contained within any other such component, it constitutes a "Departmen[t]" for the purposes of the Appointments Clause.

But petitioners are not done yet. They argue that the full Commission cannot constitutionally appoint Board members, because only the Chairman of the Commission is the Commission's "Hea[d]." . . .

As a constitutional matter, we see no reason why a multimember body may not be the "Hea[d]" of a "Departmen[t]" that it governs. The Appointments Clause necessarily contemplates collective appointments by the "Courts of Law," Art. II, § 2, cl. 2, and each House of Congress, too, appoints its officers collectively, see Art. I, § 2, cl. 5; *id.*, § 3, cl. 5. Petitioners argue that the Framers vested the nomination of principal officers in the President to avoid the perceived evils of collective appointments, but they reveal no similar concern with respect to inferior officers, whose appointments may be vested elsewhere, including in multimember bodies. Practice has also sanctioned the appointment of inferior officers by multimember agencies. We conclude that the Board members have been validly appointed by the full Commission.

. . . .

* * *

The Constitution that makes the President accountable to the people for executing the laws also gives him the power to do so. That power includes, as a general matter, the authority to remove those who assist him in carrying out his duties. Without such power, the President could not be held fully accountable for discharging his own responsibilities; the buck would stop somewhere else. Such diffusion of authority "would greatly diminish the intended and necessary responsibility of the chief magistrate himself." The Federalist No. 70, at 478.

While we have sustained in certain cases limits on the President's removal power, the Act before us imposes a new type of restriction — two levels of protection from removal for those who nonetheless exercise significant executive power. Congress cannot limit the President's authority in this way.

The judgment of the United States Court of Appeals for the District of Columbia Circuit is affirmed in part and reversed in part, and the case is remanded for further proceedings consistent with this opinion.

It is so ordered.

JUSTICE BREYER, with whom JUSTICE STEVENS, JUSTICE GINSBURG, and JUSTICE SOTOMAYOR join, dissenting.

The Court holds unconstitutional a statute providing that the Securities and Exchange Commission can remove members of the Public Company Accounting Oversight Board from office only for cause. It argues that granting the "inferior officer[s]" on the Accounting Board "more than one level of good-cause protection . . . contravenes the President's 'constitutional obligation to ensure the faithful execution of the laws.'" I agree that the Accounting Board members are inferior officers. But in my view the statute does not significantly interfere with the President's "executive Power." Art. II, § 1. It violates no separation-of-powers principle. And the Court's contrary holding threatens to disrupt severely the fair and efficient administration of the laws. I consequently dissent.

I

A

The legal question before us arises at the intersection of two general constitutional principles. On the one hand, Congress has broad power to enact statutes "necessary and proper" to the exercise of its specifically enumerated constitutional authority. Art. I, § 8, cl. 18. As Chief Justice Marshall wrote for the Court nearly 200 years ago, the Necessary and Proper Clause reflects the Framers' efforts to create a Constitution that would "endure for ages to come." *McCulloch v. Maryland*, 4 Wheat. 316, 415 (1819). . . .

On the other hand, the opening sections of Articles I, II, and III of the Constitution separately and respectively vest "all legislative Powers" in Congress, the "executive Power" in the President, and the "judicial Power" in the Supreme Court (and such "inferior Courts as Congress may from time to time ordain and establish"). In doing so, these provisions imply a structural separation-of-powers principle. *See*, e.g., *Miller v. French*, 530 U. S. 327, 341-342 (2000). And that principle, along with the instruction in Article II, § 3 that the President "shall take Care that the Laws be faithfully executed," limits Congress' power to structure the Federal Government. . . .

[T]he question presented lies at the intersection of two sets of conflicting, broadly framed constitutional principles. And no text, no history, perhaps no precedent provides any clear answer.

B

When previously deciding this kind of nontextual question, the Court has emphasized the importance of examining how a particular provision, taken in context, is likely to function. . . .

The functional approach required by our precedents recognizes this administrative complexity and, more importantly, recognizes the various ways presidential power operates within this context—and the various ways in which a removal provision might affect that power. . . . If the President seeks to regulate through impartial adjudication, then insulation of the adjudicator from removal at will can help him achieve that goal. And to free a technical decisionmaker from the fear of removal without cause can similarly help create legitimacy with respect to that official's regulatory actions by helping to insulate his technical decisions from nontechnical political pressure.

. . . .

Thus, here, as in similar cases, we should decide the constitutional question in light of the provision's practical functioning in context. And our decision should take account of the Judiciary's comparative lack of institutional expertise.

II

A

It is more specific than "for cause"

To what extent then is the Act's "for cause" provision likely, as a practical matter, to limit the President's exercise of executive authority? In practical terms no "for cause" provision can, in isolation, define the full measure of executive power. This is because a legislative decision to place ultimate administrative authority in, say, the Secretary of Agriculture rather than the President, the way in which the statute defines the scope of the power the relevant administrator can exercise, the decision as to who controls the agency's budget requests and funding, the relationships between one agency or department and another, as well as more purely political factors (including Congress' ability to assert influence) are more likely to affect the President's power to get something done. . . .

But even if we put all these other matters to the side, we should still conclude that the "for cause" restriction before us will not restrict presidential power significantly. For one thing, the restriction directly limits, not the President's power, but the power of an already independent agency. The Court seems to have forgotten that fact when it identifies its central constitutional problem: According to the Court, the President "is powerless to intervene" if he has determined that the Board members' "conduct merit[s] removal" because "[t]hat decision is vested instead in other tenured officers — the Commissioners — none of whom is subject to the President's direct control." But so long as the President is legitimately foreclosed from removing the Commissioners except for cause (as the majority assumes), nullifying the Commission's power to remove Board members only for cause will not resolve the problem the Court has identified: The President will still be "powerless to intervene" by removing the Board members if the Commission reasonably decides not to do so.

. . . .

[T]he statute provides the Commission with full authority and virtually comprehensive control over all of the Board's functions. . . .

[T]he Commission's control over the Board's investigatory and legal functions is virtually absolute. Moreover, the Commission has general supervisory powers over the Accounting Board itself: It controls the Board's budget, §§ 7219(b), (d)(1); it can assign to the Board any "duties or functions" that it "determines are necessary or appropriate," § 7211(c)(5); it has full "oversight and enforcement authority over the Board," § 7217(a), *including the authority to inspect the Board's activities whenever it believes it "appropriate" to do so,* § 7217(d)(2) (emphasis added). And it can censure the Board or its members, as well as remove the members from office, if the members, for example, fail to enforce the Act, violate any provisions of the Act, or abuse the authority granted to them under the Act, § 7217(d)(3).

What is left? The Commission's inability to remove a Board member whose perfectly reasonable actions cause the Commission to overrule him with great frequency? What is the practical likelihood of that occurring, or, if it does, of the President's serious concern about such a matter? Everyone concedes that the President's control over the Commission is constitutionally sufficient. *See Humphrey's Executor*, 295 U. S. 602. And if the President's control over the Commission is sufficient, and the Commission's control over the Board is virtually absolute, then, as a practical matter, the President's control over the Board should prove sufficient as well.

B

At the same time, Congress and the President had good reason for enacting the challenged "for cause" provision. First and foremost, the Board adjudicates cases. *See* 15 U. S.C. § 7215. This Court has long recognized the appropriateness of using "for cause" provisions to protect the personal independence of those who even only sometimes engage in adjudicatory functions. . . .

Moreover, in addition to their adjudicative functions, the Accounting Board members supervise, and are themselves, technical professional experts. See § 7211(e)(1) (requiring that Board members "have a demonstrated" technical "understanding of the responsibilities" and "obligations of accountants with respect to the preparation and issuance of audit reports"). [T]his Court has recognized the constitutional legitimacy of a justification that rests agency independence upon the need for technical expertise.

. . . .

In sum, Congress and the President could reasonably have thought it prudent to insulate the adjudicative Board members from fear of purely politically based removal. . . .

C

Where a "for cause" provision is so unlikely to restrict presidential power and so likely to further a legitimate institutional need, precedent strongly supports its constitutionality. . . . Here, the removal restriction may somewhat diminish the Commission's ability to control the Board, but it will have little, if any, negative effect in respect to the President's ability to control the Board, let alone to coordinate the Executive Branch. Indeed, given *Morrison*, where the Court upheld a restriction that significantly interfered with the President's important historic power to control criminal prosecutions, a "'purely executive'" function, 487 U. S., at 687-689, the constitutionality of the present restriction would seem to follow *a fortiori*.

. . . .

In sum, the Court's prior cases impose functional criteria that are readily met here. Once one goes beyond the Court's elementary arithmetical logic (*i.e.*, "one plus one is greater than one") our precedent virtually dictates a holding that the challenged "for cause" provision is constitutional.

D

We should ask one further question. Even if the "for cause" provision before us does not itself significantly interfere with the President's authority or aggrandize Congress' power, is it nonetheless necessary to adopt a bright-line rule forbidding the provision lest, through a series of such provisions, each itself upheld as reasonable, Congress might undercut the President's central constitutional role? The answer to this question is that no such need has been shown. Moreover, insofar as the Court seeks to create such a rule, it fails. And in failing it threatens a harm that is far more serious than any imaginable harm this "for cause" provision might bring about.

[Justice Breyer engages in a lengthy review of the administrative positions that he claims are rendered constitutionally suspect by the Court's decision. His discussion relates to the broad range of inferior officers, the place of career appointees in the Senior Executive Service, the status of administrative law judges, and the status of Commissioned officers in the military. Officials in the last three categories may only be removed for cause and they are often supervised by officials who also may be removed only for cause.]

[N]otwithstanding the majority's assertions to the contrary, the potential consequences of today's holding are worrying. The upshot, I believe, is a legal dilemma. To interpret the Court's decision as applicable only in a few circumstances will make the rule less harmful but arbitrary. To interpret the rule more broadly will make the rule more rational, but destructive.

III

One last question: How can the Court simply assume without deciding that the SEC Commissioners themselves are removable only "for cause?" See *ante*, at 5 ("[W]e decide the case with th[e] *understanding*" "that the Commissioners cannot themselves be removed by the President except" for cause (emphasis added))....

It is certainly not obvious that the SEC Commissioners enjoy "for cause" protection. Unlike the statutes establishing the 48 federal agencies listed in Appendix A [omitted] the statue that established the Commission says nothing about removal. It is silent on the question. As far as its text is concerned, the President's authority to remove the Commissioners is no different from his authority to remove the Secretary of State or the Attorney General. See *Shurtleff*, 189 U. S., at 315 ("To take away th[e] power of removal . . . would require very clear and explicit language. It should not be held to be taken away by mere inference or implication"). Nor is the absence of a "for cause" provision in the statute that created the Commission likely to have been inadvertent. Congress created the Commission during the 9-year period after this Court decided *Myers*, and thereby cast serious doubt on the constitutionality of all "for cause" removal provisions, but before it decided *Humphrey's Executor*, which removed any doubt in respect to the constitutionality of making Commissioners of independent agencies removable only for cause. In other words, Congress created the SEC at a time when, under this Court's precedents, it would have been unconstitutional to make the Commissioners removable only for cause....

The Court then, by assumption, reads into the statute books a "for cause removal" phrase that does not appear in the relevant statute and which Congress probably did not intend to write. And it does so in order to strike down, not to uphold, another statute. This is not a statutory construction that seeks to avoid a constitutional question, but its opposite. *See Ashwander v. TVA*, 297 U. S. 288, 347 (1936) (Brandeis, J., concurring) ("It is not the habit of the Court to decide questions of a constitutional nature unless absolutely necessary to a decision of the case" (internal quotation marks omitted)); *NLRB v. Catholic Bishop of Chicago*, 440 U. S. 490, 500 (1979) ("[A]n Act of Congress ought not to be construed to violate the Constitution if any other possible construction remains available").

I do not need to decide whether the Commissioners are in fact removable only "for cause" because I would uphold the Accounting Board's removal provision as constitutional regardless. But were that not so, a determination that the silent SEC statute means no more than it says would properly avoid the determination of unconstitutionality that the Court now makes.

* * *

In my view the Court's decision is wrong — very wrong. . . . [I]t will undermine the President's authority. And it will create an obstacle, indeed pose a serious threat, to the proper functioning of that workable Government that the Constitution seeks to create — in provisions this Court is sworn to uphold.

With respect I dissent.

QUESTIONS

1. Do the separation of powers concerns raised by the majority relate to the for-cause removal condition applicable to the SEC? How much Presidential control is lost by the second level of for-cause removal of the officers comprising the Board? Is this an example of the Court choking on the flea (a second level of protection) after swallowing the elephant (the first level of protection)?

2. Has the majority effectively reversed the decision in *Morrison* by concluding that an encroachment upon Executive power caused by the Legislature has the effect of aggrandizing legislative power, even in the absence of Congress's retention of a formal role in the agency's structure or processes? Has the *Free Enterprise Fund* Court now done to *Morrison* what Justice Scalia accused the *Humphrey's Executor* Court of having done to *Myers?* In *PHH Corp. v. Consumer Financial Protection Bureau*, 839 F.3d 1 (D.C. Cir. 2016), the court held that the Consumer Financial Protection Bureau (CFPB) "is unconstitutionally structured because it is an independent agency headed by a single Director." *Id.* at 36. The agency was independent because the CFPB Director could only be removed by the President for cause. Judge Kavanaugh writing for the panel stated that "the independent counsel experiment ended with nearly universal consensus that the experiment had been a mistake and that Justice Scalia had been right back in 1988 to view the independent counsel system as an unconstitutional departure from historical practice and a serious threat to individual liberty." *Id.* at 20. The court held that the for-cause provision was severable and determined that the CFPB conforms to the Constitution if the Director serves at the will of the President. *Id.* at 39.

3. Does the decision in *Free Enterprise Fund* signal a return to formalism in separation of powers analysis and a rejection of the functional approach taken in *Schor* and *Morrison*?

4. Has the majority, in deciding that the Director of the Board is an inferior officer, adopted the analytic approach of *Edmond*, rather than of *Morrison*?

5. In resolving the Appointments Clause issue for an inferior officer, the majority construed the term "Department" broadly, relying on Justice Scalia's concurring opinion in *Freytag v. Commissioner of Internal Revenue*, 501 U.S. 868 (1991). There, the Court considered the constitutionality of federal statutes that created the Tax Court as an Article I court, and that authorized the Chief Judge of the Tax Court to appoint and assign "Special Trial Judges" to hear and prepare findings in Tax Court proceedings. Justice Blackmun, speaking for a majority that included Justices White, Marshall, Stevens, and Chief Justice Rehnquist, held that even though the Tax Court was not a court created by Article III, it was a sufficient "Court of Law" for Appointments Clause purposes, and therefore violated no constitutional measures when it appointed an "inferior officer." The majority held that the Appointments Clause does not limit "Courts of Law" to courts created under Article III. The Court pointed to a long-standing tradition of Article I legislative courts having the power to appoint clerks who were "inferior officers." The Supreme Court rejected the claim that the Chief Judge is a "Head of a Department," because he is not a "Cabinet-level department" head—Cabinet-level department heads in contrast are "subject to the exercise of political oversight and share the President's accountability to the people."

   Justice Scalia, in a concurring opinion joined by Justices O'Connor, Kennedy, and Souter, disagreed with the majority's contention that Article I courts may be "Courts of Law" for Appointment Clause purposes. Justice Scalia pointed out that Article I courts are created and maintained by Congress. Unlike Article III courts, which are protected separate entities from Congress pursuant to Article III, Article I judges are not independent from the other branches and could fall victim to political forces. Justice Scalia concurred in the judgment, however, because he found the Chief Judge of the Tax Court to be a "Head of Department," contrary to the majority's reasoning. Was the *Free Enterprise Fund* Court correct in adopting the reasoning of Justice Scalia's concurring opinion?

6. The majority in footnote 5 stated that it was not addressing the issue of whether an administrative law judge is an (inferior) officer of the United States, rather than an employee. The Court there cited *Landry v. FDIC*, 204 F.3d 1125 (D.C. Cir. 2000). Landry had argued that the FDIC's method for appointing ALJs violated the Appointments Clause, on the theory that the FDIC, which appointed the ALJs, was not a "department." Judge Williams's majority opinion found that an FDIC ALJ is not an officer because, unlike the special trial judge in *Freytag*, the FDIC ALJ had no power to make a final decision. "[T]he ALJs here can never render the decision of the FDIC." *Id.* at 1133. In a separate opinion, Judge Randolph concluded that an ALJ could not be distinguished from the special trial judge in *Freytag* and so was an officer of the United States. *Id.* at 1141. Judge Randolph nevertheless

concurred because he concluded that the error was harmless. *Id.* at 1144. Five Justices now sitting on the Supreme Court have suggested that an ALJ is an officer of the United States, rather than an employee. See *Free Enterprise Fund*, 561 U.S., at 542-43 (Breyer J., dissenting, joined by Stevens, Ginsburg & Sotomayor, JJ.); *Freytag*, 501 U.S. at 910 (Scalia, J., concurring in part and concurring in the judgment, joined by O'Connor, Kennedy & Souter, JJ.). (Thanks to Professor Kent Barnett for providing this insight and these sources.) In light of the Court's principal holding in *Free Enterprise Fund*, what would be the legal consequences of a conclusion that ALJs are officers of the United States? Professor Barnett addresses this issue in his article, Kent Barnett, *Resolving the ALJ Quandry*, 66 Vand. L. Rev. 797 (2013).The issue of the permissibility of the appointment of bankruptcy judges is addressed in Tuan Samahon, *Are Bankruptcy Judges Unconstitutional?*, 60 Hastings L.J. 233 (2008).

7. In the view of Justice Breyer, what are the benefits of providing good-cause removal protection for Board members?

8. Did the majority's assumption that Commissioners of the SEC could only be removed for cause give rise to a constitutional issue that could have been avoided by a decision that the SEC Commissioners were removable at will? Was it appropriate for the majority to assume that SEC Commissioners are removable only for cause?

THEORY APPLIED PROBLEM

This problem is based on an article by Professor Kent Barnett, *The Consumer Financial Protection Bureau's Appointment with Trouble*, 60 Am. U.L. Rev. 1459 (2011). There, Professor Barnett discusses a constitutional issue associated with the Consumer Financial Protection Bureau (CFPB), which Congress created in the Dodd — Frank Wall Street Reform and Consumer Protection Act of 2010, Pub. L. No. 111-203, 124 Stat. 1376, 1964 (2010) (codified at 12 U.S.C. § 5491). The statute provides that "[t]here is established in the Federal Reserve System, an independent bureau to be known as the '[CFPB]', which shall regulate the offering and provision of consumer financial products or services under the Federal consumer financial laws. The Bureau shall be considered an Executive agency, as defined in section 105 of Title 5." 12 U.S.C. § 5491(a). "Although 'established in' the Federal Reserve, the Bureau has nearly complete autonomy from the Governors of the Federal Reserve." Barnett, *supra*, at 1461-62 (footnote omitted).

The Director is "the head of the Bureau," *id.* § 5491(b)(1), and "shall be appointed by the President, by and with the advice and consent of the Senate." Id. § 5491(b)(2). With regard to removal, the statute provides that "[t]he President may remove the Director for inefficiency, neglect of duty, or malfeasance in office." *Id.* § 5491(c)(3).

The statute also "establishe[s] the position of Deputy Director, who shall — (A) be appointed by the Director; and (B) serve as acting Director in the absence or unavailability of the Director." *Id.* § 5491(b)(5). Is this method of appointing the Deputy Director of the CFPB constitutional?

G. THE ROLE OF THE PRESIDENT IN IMPLEMENTING STATUTES

1. *Presidential Signing Statements*

Presidential statements explaining their understanding of legislation enacted by Congress have been issued from the time of President James Monroe. *See* Report of the American Bar Association Task Force on Presidential Signing Statements and the Separation of Powers Doctrine 7 (2006) (available at http://www.aba-net.org/media/docs/signstatereport.pdf) (hereafter ABA Task Force Report). Since the administration of President Reagan, these presidential signing statements have been issued more frequently. President Reagan issued 71 such statements, President George H.W. Bush issued 146 statements, and President Clinton issued 105 statements. See *id.* at 13. President George W. Bush issued statements that challenged more than 800 provisions enacted by Congress, while all signing statements issued prior to the George W. Bush administration had included a total of fewer than 600 challenges. See *id.* at 14 and n.52.

President Obama issued a total of 14 signing statements during the first two years of his administration. *See* The American Presidency Project (http://www.presidency.ucsb.edu/signingstatements.php#axzz1S12Am2yf). Soon after taking office, President Obama published the following memorandum discussing signing statements:

March 9, 2009
Memorandum for the Heads of Executive Departments and Agencies
SUBJECT: Presidential Signing Statements

For nearly two centuries, Presidents have issued statements addressing constitutional or other legal questions upon signing bills into law (signing statements). Particularly since omnibus bills have become prevalent, signing statements have often been used to ensure that concerns about the constitutionality of discrete statutory provisions do not require a veto of the entire bill.

In recent years, there has been considerable public discussion and criticism of the use of signing statements to raise constitutional objections to statutory provisions. There is no doubt that the practice of issuing such statements can be abused. Constitutional signing statements should not be used to suggest that the President will disregard statutory requirements on the basis of policy disagreements. At the same time, such signing statements serve a legitimate function in our system, at least when based on well-founded constitutional objections. In appropriately limited circumstances, they represent an exercise of the President's constitutional obligation to take care that the laws be faithfully executed, and they promote a healthy dialogue between the executive branch and the Congress.

With these considerations in mind and based upon advice of the Department of Justice, I will issue signing statements to address constitutional concerns only when it is appropriate to do so as a means of discharging my constitutional responsibilities. In issuing signing statements, I shall adhere to the following principles:

1. The executive branch will take appropriate and timely steps, whenever practicable, to inform the Congress of its constitutional concerns about pending

legislation. Such communication should facilitate the efforts of the executive branch and the Congress to work together to address these concerns during the legislative process, thus minimizing the number of occasions on which I am presented with an enrolled bill that may require a signing statement.

2. Because legislation enacted by the Congress comes with a presumption of constitutionality, I will strive to avoid the conclusion that any part of an enrolled bill is unconstitutional. In exercising my responsibility to determine whether a provision of an enrolled bill is unconstitutional, I will act with caution and restraint, based only on interpretations of the Constitution that are well-founded.

3. To promote transparency and accountability, I will ensure that signing statements identify my constitutional concerns about a statutory provision with sufficient specificity to make clear the nature and basis of the constitutional objection.

4. I will announce in signing statements that I will construe a statutory provision in a manner that avoids a constitutional problem only if that construction is a legitimate one.

To ensure that all signing statements previously issued are followed only when consistent with these principles, executive branch departments and agencies are directed to seek the advice of the Attorney General before relying on signing statements issued prior to the date of this memorandum as the basis for disregarding, or otherwise refusing to comply with, any provision of a statute.

This memorandum is not intended to, and does not, create any right or benefit, substantive or procedural, enforceable at law or in equity by any party against the United States, its departments, agencies, or entities, its officers, employees, or agents, or any other person.

This memorandum shall be published in the Federal Register.

BARACK OBAMA
Statement on Signing the Department of Defense and Full-Year Continuing Appropriations Act, 2011
April 15, 2011

Today I have signed into law H.R. 1473, the "Department of Defense and Full-Year Continuing Appropriations Act, 2011."

Section 1112 of the Act bars the use of funds for the remainder of fiscal year 2011 to transfer Guantanamo detainees into the United States, and section 1113 bars the use of funds for the remainder of fiscal year 2011 to transfer detainees to the custody or effective control of foreign countries unless specified conditions are met. Section 1112 represents the continuation of a dangerous and unprecedented challenge to critical executive branch authority to determine when and where to prosecute Guantanamo detainees, based on the facts and the circumstances of each case and our national security interests. The prosecution of terrorists in Federal court is a powerful tool in our efforts to protect the Nation and must be among the options available to us. Any attempt to deprive the executive branch of that tool undermines our Nation's counterterrorism efforts and has the potential to harm our national security.

With respect to section 1113 of the Act, the restrictions on the transfer of detainees to the custody or effective control of foreign countries interfere with the authority of the executive branch to make important and consequential foreign policy and national security determinations regarding whether and under what circumstances such transfers should occur in the context of an ongoing armed conflict. We must have the ability to act swiftly and to have broad flexibility in conducting our negotiations with foreign countries. The executive branch has sought and obtained from countries that are prospective recipients of Guantanamo detainees assurances that they will take or have taken measures reasonably designed to be effective in preventing, or ensuring against, returned detainees taking action to threaten the United States or engage in terrorist activities. Consistent with existing statutes, the executive branch has kept the Congress informed about these assurances and notified the Congress prior to transfers. Requiring the executive branch to certify to additional conditions would hinder the conduct of delicate negotiations with foreign countries and therefore the effort to conclude detainee transfers in accord with our national security.

Despite my continued strong objection to these provisions, I have signed this Act because of the importance of avoiding a lapse in appropriations for the Federal Government, including our military activities, for the remainder of fiscal year 2011.

Nevertheless, my Administration will work with the Congress to seek repeal of these restrictions, will seek to mitigate their effects, and will oppose any attempt to extend or expand them in the future.

Section 2262 of the Act would prohibit the use of funds for several positions that involve providing advice directly to the President. The President has well-established authority to supervise and oversee the executive branch, and to obtain advice in furtherance of this supervisory authority. The President also has the prerogative to obtain advice that will assist him in carrying out his constitutional responsibilities, and do so not only from executive branch officials and employees outside the White House, but also from advisers within it.

Legislative efforts that significantly impede the President's ability to exercise his supervisory and coordinating authorities or to obtain the views of the appropriate senior advisers violate the separation of powers by undermining the President's ability to exercise his constitutional responsibilities and take care that the laws be faithfully executed. Therefore, the executive branch will construe section 2262 not to abrogate these Presidential prerogatives.

BARACK OBAMA
The White House,
April 15, 2011.

QUESTIONS

1. At the 2006 Annual Meeting of the American Bar Association, the House of Delegates adopted a policy to "'oppose[], as contrary to the rule of law and our constitutional system of separation of powers, the misuse of presidential

signing statements' that claim the authority or state an 'intention to disregard or decline to enforce all or part of a law the president has signed, or to interpret such a law in a manner inconsistent with the clear intent of Congress.'" Statement of Karen J. Mathis, President of the American Bar Association, Before the House Committee on the Judiciary 1 (Jan. 31, 2007) (available at http://www.abanet.org/poladv/letters/antiterror/2007jan31_signingstmts_t.pdf). Has a President misused a signing statement if the President signs a bill into law and then states that she will not enforce the specific provisions that she believes to be unconstitutional? Should a President instead follow the recommendation of the ABA Task Force that the President should veto a bill if the President believes that all or part of the bill is unconstitutional?

2. Is President Obama's signing statement consistent with the guidelines for the use of signing statements that he outlined in the March 2009 Memorandum?

3. Does the President have the authority to control how agencies will implement statutes enacted by Congress?

2. *Presidential Review of Agency Rulemaking*

NOTE ON PRESIDENTIAL REVIEW OF AGENCY RULEMAKING

Excerpt, Richard H. Pildes & Cass R. Sunstein, *Reinventing the Regulatory State*, 62 U. Chi. L. Rev. 1, 11-16 (1995).[1]

Almost since the birth of the modern administrative agency, American presidents have struggled to assert more centralized control over the regulatory state. Indeed, a recent study asserts that "the history of the presidency in the twentieth century has been the history of presidents' attempts to gain control of the sprawling federal bureaucracy." Typically, these attempts have generated sharp congressional resistance.

The first step in this direction can probably be traced to President Theodore Roosevelt's creation, in 1903, of a Commission designed to study the scientific work done by government agencies in order to recommend more efficient coordination. The results presaged those of similar reform efforts to follow. The Commission recommended that the thirty scientific agencies be consolidated into one, in order to minimize duplication and inefficiency. Roosevelt forwarded this recommendation to Congress, which declined to act on it.

Roosevelt then created a second Commission, the Keep Commission, to study a broader array of administrative reforms. In some ways a precursor of Vice President Gore's recent National Performance Review, the Keep Commission found that many civil servants were underemployed and resistant to new technologies, such as typewriters and adding machines. It also concluded that the system of supply acquisition was hopelessly chaotic. The Keep Commission forwarded eleven formal reform proposals to Congress. When it did so, the century's first major battle between Congress and the White House over control of administration was joined. Congress not only declined to act on any of the proposals, but also expressed outrage at the Executive's effort to seize "an

---

1. Reproduced with the permission of Richard Pildes, Cass Sunstein, and the University of Chicago Law Review.

authority previously the exclusive and unchallenged domain of Congress." In addition, Congress prohibited the use of government funds for such Commissions in the future and even refused to appropriate funds to publish the Keep Commission's report.

At Congress's invitation, President Taft attempted to centralize and coordinate the budgetary process. Although Congress rejected Taft's particular proposals, by 1921 Congress granted the President effective oversight control of agency fiscal requests by enacting the Budget and Accounting Act. This was an extraordinary development, in many ways a precursor of current efforts to centralize the regulatory process. For the first time, the President would be given statutory authority to submit an annual budget to Congress. Wilson's wartime presidency aggressively set into motion the vision of a more managerial presidency.

In the period after the war, the ideas of consolidation and efficiency-motivated reorganization swept the business community. Congress eventually followed suit in 1932 with the Government Reorganization Act, which granted the President unilateral authority, subject to legislative veto, to reorganize the administrative branch. Franklin Roosevelt's Brownlow Commission revived Wilson's famous distinction between policy and administration; the Commission saw "policy" as the joint domain of the President and Congress, whereas "administration," it asserted, must be under the direct and exclusive command of the President. Despite an initial congressional outcry, most of the Committee's proposals were enacted. A key reform, with lasting consequences, was the creation of the Executive Office of the President.

In 1949, the Hoover Commission produced yet another effort to create a more coordinated and managerial presidency. It issued 277 specific proposals for reorganizing and consolidating agencies. More than half of these were adopted via statute or executive order, with the purpose of creating a "clear line of command from the top to the bottom, and a return line of responsibility and accountability from the bottom to the top."

The most direct precursor to the current structure of executive oversight of regulation was the Nixon Administration's system of "Quality of Life" reviews. Nixon's response to the expanding administrative bureaucracy was to create a "counter-bureaucracy" in the White House. He doubled the executive office staff, created the modern OMB, and established the Domestic Council (chaired by a top aide, John Ehrlichman). The Council met with representatives of different departments having jurisdiction over a problem and tried to develop coordinated policy positions for presidential approval. In the "Quality of Life" review process, agencies were required to submit significant rules to OMB in advance of publication in the Federal Register. OMB's principal duty was to circulate the agency draft to other agencies for review and comment. Although the process was intended to apply to all agencies, only EPA and OSHA were actually subject to the reviewing process. OMB's goal was rarely substantive; it served instead a coordinating function.

President Ford continued the interagency review process and added to it a process designed to control the effects of regulation on inflation. Most important, the Council on Wage and Price Stability ("CWPS") reviewed regulations to assess these effects. In addition, OMB promulgated a circular to agencies arguing that the inflationary impact of a proposed rule could best be assessed through a quantitative cost-benefit comparison. The Council's role was principally technical, consultative, and advisory. It was understood that the relevant agency might well persist in the face of CWPS disagreement. Despite often antagonistic relationships between the agencies and CWPS, many observers believed that CWPS enhanced both public participation and the agencies' analytical capabilities. Congress ultimately enacted a statute allowing CWPS to participate in rule making and to explore adverse effects on inflation.

President Carter built on the Ford precedent through a successor to CWPS, the Regulatory Analysis Review Group ("RARG"). RARG consisted of representatives from major agencies, OMB, CWPS, and the Council of Economic Advisors. The purpose of this fifteen-agency group was to conduct interagency review of cost-effectiveness analyses, which were required of "significant" rules from relevant agencies. Notably, the Executive Order establishing the RARG review process did not require cost-benefit analysis. In fact RARG reviewed relatively few rules, though the President did resolve a few highly controversial issues.

All of these efforts were designed to increase interagency dialogue, coordination, and analytical precision, as well as to reduce regulatory costs. But a decisive step came within a week of President Reagan's inauguration, with the formal creation of a mechanism for OMB review of major regulations. The most important of the new innovations, contained in Executive Order 12291, were (1) a set of substantive principles for all agencies to follow, "to the extent permitted by law," including a commitment to cost-benefit analysis; (2) a requirement that a Regulatory Impact Analysis, including a cost-benefit analysis, accompany all "major" rules; and (3) a formal mechanism for OMB oversight, with a general understanding that OMB had some (undefined) substantive control. President Reagan considered subjecting the independent agencies to the new Order, but ultimately declined to do so, partly because of concerns about legal authority, but mostly because of fears of an adverse congressional reaction. The independent agencies were asked voluntarily to comply with Executive Order 12291, but not one of them formally acknowledged their willingness to do so.

Executive Order 12291 proved extremely controversial. Nonetheless, President Reagan expanded on the basic idea four years later with Executive Order 12498.[2] [T]hat Order established a requirement that agencies submit "annual regulatory plans" to OMB for review. The result is an annual publication, the Regulatory Program of the United States, which contains a discussion of all proposed actions that might be either costly or controversial. Executive Order 12498 served to increase the authority of agency heads over their staffs by exposing proposals to top-level review at an early stage. But it also increased the authority of OMB by allowing OMB supervision over basic plans and by making it hard for agencies to proceed without OMB preclearance.

The Bush Administration continued the Reagan procedures. Its principal innovation was the Council on Competitiveness, chaired by the Vice President. The Council engaged in occasional review of agency rules, operating as a kind of supervisor of OMB itself. It also set out a number of principles and proposals for regulatory reform.

President Clinton's Executive Order 12866 is the latest step in this process. . . . From the recent evidence, it seems clear that presidential oversight of the regulatory process, though relatively new, has become a permanent

---

2. Authors' note: Professors Sunstein and Pildes had stated earlier in this article, 62 U. Chi. L. Rev. at 2, that the two executive orders promulgated by President Reagan represented "[p]robably the most important development in administrative law in the 1980s."

part of the institutional design of American government. This new institutional arrangement has occurred for reasons parallel to the development of a centralized budget in the 1920s. Any president is likely to seek assurance that an unwieldy federal bureaucracy conforms its actions to his or her basic principles. Any president is likely to be concerned about excessive public and private costs. And any president is likely to want to be able to coordinate agency activity so as to ensure consistency and coherence and to guard against the imposition of conflicting duties on people who must comply with the law. The result of these forces is that a centralizing and rationalizing body, housed within OMB and devoted to regulation, has emerged as an enduring, major, but insufficiently appreciated part of the national government.

REGULATORY PLANNING AND REVIEW
Executive Order 12866 of September 30, 1993

[When Barack Obama became President in 2009, he issued Executive Order 13497. This was one of President Obama's first Executive Orders, issued on January 30, 2009. This order fully restored President Clinton's Executive Order establishing Regulatory Planning and Review through the Office of Information and Regulatory Affairs in the Office of Management and Budget. Executive Order 13497 "revoked" Executive Order 13258 of February 26, 2002, and Executive Order 13422 of January 18, 2007. President George W. Bush had issued those two Executive Orders to amend the Clinton Executive Order and reshape review within the Executive Branch. An edited version of the restored Executive Order 12866 follows.]

. . . With this Executive order, the Federal Government begins a program to reform and make more efficient the regulatory process. The objectives of this Executive order are to enhance planning and coordination with respect to both new and existing regulations; to reaffirm the primacy of Federal agencies in the regulatory decision-making process; to restore the integrity and legitimacy of regulatory review and oversight; and to make the process more accessible and open to the public. In pursuing these objectives, the regulatory process shall be conducted so as to meet applicable statutory requirements and with due regard to the discretion that has been entrusted to the Federal agencies.

Accordingly, by the authority vested in me as President by the Constitution and the laws of the United States of America, it is hereby ordered as follows:

SECTION 1. STATEMENT OF REGULATORY PHILOSOPHY AND PRINCIPLES

(a) The Regulatory Philosophy. Federal agencies should promulgate only such regulations as are required by law, are necessary to interpret the law, or are made necessary by compelling public need, such as material failures of private markets to protect or improve the health and safety of the public, the environment, or the well-being of the American people. In deciding whether and how to regulate, agencies should assess all costs and benefits of available regulatory alternatives, including the alternative of not regulating. Costs and benefits shall be understood to include both quantifiable measures (to the fullest extent that these can be usefully estimated) and qualitative measures of costs and benefits that are difficult to quantify, but nevertheless essential to consider. Further, in choosing among alternative regulatory approaches, agencies should select those approaches that maximize net benefits (including potential economic, environmental, public health and safety, and other advantages; distributive impacts; and equity), unless a statute requires another regulatory approach. . . .

Section 2. Organization

An efficient regulatory planning and review process is vital to ensure that the Federal Government's regulatory system best serves the American people.

(a) The Agencies. Because Federal agencies are the repositories of significant substantive expertise and experience, they are responsible for developing regulations and assuring that the regulations are consistent with applicable law, the President's priorities, and the principles set forth in this Executive order.

(b) The Office of Management and Budget. Coordinated review of agency rulemaking is necessary to ensure that regulations are consistent with applicable law, the President's priorities, and the principles set forth in this Executive order, and that decisions made by one agency do not conflict with the policies or actions taken or planned by another agency. The Office of Management and Budget (OMB) shall carry out that review function. Within OMB, the Office of Information and Regulatory Affairs (OIRA) is the repository of expertise concerning regulatory issues, including methodologies and procedures that affect more than one agency, this Executive order, and the President's regulatory policies. To the extent permitted by law, OMB shall provide guidance to agencies and assist the President, the Vice President, and other regulatory policy advisors to the President in regulatory planning and shall be the entity that reviews individual regulations, as provided by this Executive order.

(c) The Vice President. The Vice President is the principal advisor to the President on, and shall coordinate the development and presentation of recommendations concerning, regulatory policy, planning, and review, as set forth in this Executive order. . . .

Section 3. Definitions

For purposes of this Executive order:

. . . (b) "Agency," unless otherwise indicated, means any authority of the United States that is an "agency" under 44 U.S.C. 3502(1),[1] other than

---

1. 44 U.S. § 3502(1) provides that:

(1) the term "agency" means any executive department, military department, Government corporation, Government controlled corporation, or other establishment in the executive branch of the Government (including the Executive Office of the President), or any independent regulatory agency, but does not include —

(A) the Government Accountability Office;
(B) Federal Election Commission;
(C) the governments of the District of Columbia and of the territories and possessions of the United States, and their various subdivisions; or
(D) Government-owned contractor-operated facilities, including laboratories engaged in national defense research and production activities[.]

those considered to be independent regulatory agencies, as defined in 44 U.S.C. 3502(10).[2]

(c) "Director" means the Director of OMB.

(d) "Regulation" or "rule" means an agency statement of general applicability and future effect, which the agency intends to have the force and effect of law, that is designed to implement, interpret, or prescribe law or policy or to describe the procedure or practice requirements of an agency. It does not, however, include:

(1) Regulations or rules issued in accordance with the formal rulemaking provisions of 5 U.S.C. 556, 557;

(2) Regulations or rules that pertain to a military or foreign affairs function of the United States, other than procurement regulations and regulations involving the import or export of non-defense articles and services;

(3) Regulations or rules that are limited to agency organization, management, or personnel matters; or

(4) Any other category of regulations exempted by the Administrator of OIRA.

(e) "Regulatory action" means any substantive action by an agency (normally published in the Federal Register) that promulgates or is expected to lead to the promulgation of a final rule or regulation, including notices of inquiry, advance notices of proposed rulemaking, and notices of proposed rulemaking.

(f) "Significant regulatory action" means any regulatory action that is likely to result in a rule that may:

(1) Have an annual effect on the economy of $100 million or more or adversely affect in a material way the economy, a sector of the economy, productivity, competition, jobs, the environment, public health or safety, or State, local, or tribal governments or communities;

(2) Create a serious inconsistency or otherwise interfere with an action taken or planned by another agency;

(3) Materially alter the budgetary impact of entitlements, grants, user fees, or loan programs or the rights and obligations of recipients thereof; or

(4) Raise novel legal or policy issues arising out of legal mandates, the President's priorities, or the principles set forth in this Executive order.

Section 4. Planning Mechanism

In order to have an effective regulatory program, to provide for coordination of regulations, to maximize consultation and the resolution of potential conflicts at an early stage, to involve the public and its State, local, and tribal officials in

2. This provision, currently codified at 44 U.S.C. § 3502(5) following amendment of § 3502, provides the following:

(5) the term "independent regulatory agency" means the Board of Governors of the Federal Reserve System, the Commodity Futures Trading Commission, the Consumer Product Safety Commission, the Federal Communications Commission, the Federal Deposit Insurance Corporation, the Federal Energy Regulatory Commission, the Federal Housing Finance Board, the Federal Maritime Commission, the Federal Trade Commission, the Interstate Commerce Commission, the Mine Enforcement Safety and Health Review Commission, the National Labor Relations Board, the Nuclear Regulatory Commission, the Occupational Safety and Health Review Commission, the Postal Regulatory Commission, the Securities and Exchange Commission, and any other similar agency designated by statute as a Federal independent regulatory agency or Commission[.]

regulatory planning, and to ensure that new or revised regulations promote the President's priorities and the principles set forth in this Executive order, these procedures shall be followed, to the extent permitted by law:

(a) Agencies' Policy Meeting. Early in each year's planning cycle, the Vice President shall convene a meeting of the Advisors and the heads of agencies to seek a common understanding of priorities and to coordinate regulatory efforts to be accomplished in the upcoming year.

(b) Unified Regulatory Agenda. For purposes of this subsection, the term "agency" or "agencies" shall also include those considered to be independent regulatory agencies, as defined in 44 U.S.C. 3502(10). Each agency shall prepare an agenda of all regulations under development or review, at a time and in a manner specified by the Administrator of OIRA. The description of each regulatory action shall contain, at a minimum, a regulation identifier number, a brief summary of the action, the legal authority for the action, any legal deadline for the action, and the name and telephone number of a knowledgeable agency official. . . .

(c) The Regulatory Plan. For purposes of this subsection, the term "agency" or "agencies" shall also include those considered to be independent regulatory agencies, as defined in 44 U.S.C. 3502(10).

(1) As part of the Unified Regulatory Agenda, beginning in 1994, each agency shall prepare a Regulatory Plan (Plan) of the most important significant regulatory actions that the agency reasonably expects to issue in proposed or final form in that fiscal year or thereafter. The Plan shall be approved personally by the agency head and shall contain at a minimum: [The Executive Order lists six required components, including "[a] statement of the need for each [planned significant regulatory] action and, if applicable, how the action will reduce risks to public health, safety, or the environment, as well as how the magnitude of the risk addressed by the action relates to other risks within the jurisdiction of the agency;"]

(2) Each agency shall forward its Plan to OIRA by June 1st of each year.

(3) Within 10 calendar days after OIRA has received an agency's Plan, OIRA shall circulate it to other affected agencies, the Advisors, and the Vice President.

(4) An agency head who believes that a planned regulatory action of another agency may conflict with its own policy or action taken or planned shall promptly notify, in writing, the Administrator of OIRA, who shall forward that communication to the issuing agency, the Advisors, and the Vice President.

(5) If the Administrator of OIRA believes that a planned regulatory action of an agency may be inconsistent with the President's priorities or the principles set forth in this Executive order or may be in conflict with any policy or action taken or planned by another agency, the Administrator of OIRA shall promptly notify, in writing, the affected agencies, the Advisors, and the Vice President. . . .

(d) Regulatory Working Group. Within 30 days of the date of this Executive order, the Administrator of OIRA shall convene a Regulatory Working Group ("Working Group"), which shall consist of representatives of the heads of each agency that the Administrator determines to have significant domestic regulatory responsibility, the Advisors, and the Vice President. The Administrator of OIRA shall chair the Working Group and shall periodically advise the Vice President on the activities of the Working Group. . . .

Section 5. Existing Regulations

[The Executive Order requires agencies to review periodically "existing significant regulations to determine whether any such regulations should be modified or eliminated so as to make the agency's regulatory program more effective in achieving the regulatory objectives, less burdensome, or in greater alignment with the President's priorities and the principles set forth in this Executive order." The Executive Order also gives the Vice President authority to "identify for review" existing regulations.]

Section 6. Centralized Review of Regulations

The guidelines set forth below shall apply to all regulatory actions, for both new and existing regulations, by agencies other than those agencies specifically exempted by the Administrator of OIRA:

(a) Agency Responsibilities. . . .

(3) In addition to adhering to its own rules and procedures and to the requirements of the Administrative Procedure Act, the Regulatory Flexibility Act, the Paperwork Reduction Act, and other applicable law, each agency shall develop its regulatory actions in a timely fashion and adhere to the following procedures with respect to a regulatory action:

(A) Each agency shall provide OIRA, at such times and in the manner specified by the Administrator of OIRA, with a list of its planned regulatory actions, indicating those which the agency believes are significant regulatory actions within the meaning of this Executive order. Absent a material change in the development of the planned regulatory action, those not designated as significant will not be subject to review under this section unless, within 10 working days of receipt of the list, the Administrator of OIRA notifies the agency that OIRA has determined that a planned regulation is a significant regulatory action within the meaning of this Executive order. The Administrator of OIRA may waive review of any planned regulatory action designated by the agency as significant, in which case the agency need not further comply with subsection (a)(3)(B) or subsection (a)(3)(C) of this section.

(B) For each matter identified as, or determined by the Administrator of OIRA to be, a significant regulatory action, the issuing agency shall provide to OIRA:

(i) The text of the draft regulatory action, together with a reasonably detailed description of the need for the regulatory action and an explanation of how the regulatory action will meet that need; and

(ii) An assessment of the potential costs and benefits of the regulatory action, including an explanation of the manner in which the regulatory action is consistent with a statutory mandate and, to the extent permitted by law, promotes the President's priorities and avoids undue interference with State, local, and tribal governments in the exercise of their governmental functions.

(C) For those matters identified as, or determined by the Administrator of OIRA to be, a significant regulatory action within the scope of section 3(f)(1), the agency shall also provide to OIRA the following additional information developed as part of the agency's decision-making process (unless prohibited by law):

(i) An assessment, including the underlying analysis, of benefits anticipated from the regulatory action (such as, but not limited to, the promotion of the efficient functioning of the economy and private markets, the enhancement of health and safety, the protection of the natural environment, and the elimination or reduction of discrimination or bias) together with, to the extent feasible, a quantification of those benefits;

(ii) An assessment, including the underlying analysis, of costs anticipated from the regulatory action (such as, but not limited to, the direct cost both to the government in administering the regulation and to businesses and others in complying with the regulation, and any adverse effects on the efficient functioning of the economy, private markets (including productivity, employment, and competitiveness), health, safety, and the natural environment), together with, to the extent feasible, a quantification of those costs; and

(iii) An assessment, including the underlying analysis, of costs and benefits of potentially effective and reasonably feasible alternatives to the planned regulation, identified by the agencies or the public (including improving the current regulation and reasonably viable nonregulatory actions), and an explanation why the planned regulatory action is preferable to the identified potential alternatives. . . .

(E) After the regulatory action has been published in the Federal Register or otherwise issued to the public, the agency shall:

(i) Make available to the public the information set forth in subsections (a)(3)(B) and (C);

(ii) Identify for the public, in a complete, clear, and simple manner, the substantive changes between the draft submitted to OIRA for review and the action subsequently announced; and

(iii) Identify for the public those changes in the regulatory action that were made at the suggestion or recommendation of OIRA . . . .

(b) OIRA Responsibilities. The Administrator of OIRA shall provide meaningful guidance and oversight so that each agency's regulatory actions are consistent with applicable law, the President's priorities, and the principles set forth in this Executive order and do not conflict with the policies or actions of another agency. OIRA shall, to the extent permitted by law, adhere to the following guidelines:

(1) OIRA may review only actions identified by the agency or by OIRA as significant regulatory actions under subsection (a)(3)(A) of this section.

(2) OIRA shall waive review or notify the agency in writing of the results of its review within the following time periods:

(A) For any notices of inquiry, advance notices of proposed rulemaking, or other preliminary regulatory actions prior to a Notice of Proposed Rulemaking, within 10 working days after the date of submission of the draft action to OIRA;

(B) For all other regulatory actions, within 90 calendar days after the date of submission of the information set forth in subsections (a)(3)(B) and (C) of this section, unless OIRA has previously reviewed this information and, since that review, there has been no material change in the facts and circumstances upon which the regulatory action is based, in which case, OIRA shall complete its review within 45 days; and

(C) The review process may be extended (1) once by no more than 30 calendar days upon the written approval of the Director and (2) at the request of the agency head.

(3) For each regulatory action that the Administrator of OIRA returns to an agency for further consideration of some or all of its provisions, the Administrator of OIRA shall provide the issuing agency a written explanation for such return, setting forth the pertinent provision of this Executive order on which OIRA is relying. If the agency head disagrees with some or all of the bases for the return, the agency head shall so inform the Administrator of OIRA in writing.

(4) [The Executive Order identifies specific public disclosure requirements "to ensure greater openness, accessibility, and accountability in the regulatory review process. . . ." One set of requirements is the following:]

(C) OIRA shall maintain a publicly available log that shall contain, at a minimum, the following information pertinent to regulatory actions under review:

(i) The status of all regulatory actions, including if (and if so, when and by whom) Vice Presidential and Presidential consideration was requested; . . .

(iii) The dates and names of individuals involved in all substantive oral communications, including meetings and telephone conversations, between OIRA personnel and any person not employed by the executive branch of the Federal Government, and the subject matter discussed during such communications. . . .

SECTION 7. RESOLUTION OF CONFLICTS

To the extent permitted by law, disagreements or conflicts between or among agency heads or between OMB and any agency that cannot be resolved by the Administrator of OIRA shall be resolved by the President, or by the Vice President acting at the request of the President, with the relevant agency head (and, as appropriate, other interested government officials). . . .

At the end of this review process, the President, or the Vice President acting at the request of the President, shall notify the affected agency and the Administrator of OIRA of the President's decision with respect to the matter.

SECTION 8. PUBLICATION

Except to the extent required by law, an agency shall not publish in the Federal Register or otherwise issue to the public any regulatory action that is subject to review under section 6 of this Executive order until (1) the Administrator of OIRA notifies the agency that OIRA has waived its review of the action or has completed its review without any requests for further consideration, or (2) the applicable time period in section 6(b)(2) expires without OIRA having notified the agency that it is returning the regulatory action for further consideration under section 6(b)(3), whichever occurs first. . . .

SECTION 9. AGENCY AUTHORITY

Nothing in this order shall be construed as displacing the agencies' authority or responsibilities, as authorized by law.

SECTION 10. JUDICIAL REVIEW

Nothing in this Executive order shall affect any otherwise available judicial review of agency action. This Executive order is intended only to improve the internal management of the Federal Government and does not create any right or benefit, substantive or procedural, enforceable at law or equity by a party against the United States, its agencies or instrumentalities, its officers or employees, or any other person.

SECTION 11. REVOCATIONS

Executive Orders Nos. 12291 and 12498 [the relevant Reagan Administration Executive Orders]; all amendments to those Executive orders; all guidelines issued under those orders; and any exemptions from those orders heretofore granted for any category of rule are revoked.

QUESTIONS

1. In *Sierra Club v. Costle,* 657 F.2d 298, 408 (D.C. Cir. 1981) (footnote omitted), the court stated that "it is always possible that undisclosed Presidential prodding may direct an outcome that is factually based on the record, but different from the outcome that would have obtained in the absence of Presidential involvement. In such a case, it would be true that the political process did affect the outcome in a way the courts could not police. But we do not believe that Congress intended that the courts convert informal rulemaking into a rarified technocratic process, unaffected by political considerations or the presence of Presidential power." Scholars have varied opinions about the advisability and permissibility of the President's politically-motivated involvement in agency decision making. Professor Nina Mendelson, for instance, has noted that "Presidents have been claiming ever-increasing power to supervise decisions traditionally developed primarily in the agencies" and that such "oversight could displace agency expertise either in the context of a particular decision or in an agency's determination of which issues deserve top priority," Nina A. Mendelson, *Another Word on the President's Statutory Authority Over Agency Action,* 79 Fordham L. Rev. 2455, 2479 (2010-2011). Professor Mendelson contends that "[i]t is . . . unclear whether the President ought to be the 'decider' of a difficult question delegated by Congress to the executive branch or whether an executive agency official should make the final call. In my view, that may depend on the question's content—whether it is primarily technical or one of value. It also may depend on the processes used in the agency, the White House,

or both." *Id.* at 2485. Mendelson further argues that "[t]he lack of adequate transparency [undermines both] the appropriateness of presidential influence and . . . the legitimacy of agency decision making." Nina Mendelson, *Disclosing "Political" Oversight of Agency Decision Making*, 108 Mich. L. Rev. 1127, 1159 (2010). On the other hand, Professor Kathryn Watts argues that "what count as 'valid' reasons under arbitrary and capricious review should be expanded to include certain political influences from the President, other executive officials, and members of Congress, so long as the political influences are openly and transparently disclosed in the agency's rulemaking record." Kathryn A. Watts, *Proposing a Place for Politics in Arbitrary and Capricious Review*, 119 Yale L.J. 2, 8 (2009).

2. Is the section 6 requirement of review of regulations by OIRA constitutional? With regard to the legality of requiring centralized review of executive agency rulemaking, *see Environmental Defense Fund v. Thomas*, 627 F. Supp. 566 (D.D.C. 1986) (requirement of OMB review does not excuse executive agency from complying with statutory deadline for promulgation of regulations).

3. Identify how the executive order treats independent agencies with regard to review of rulemaking and planning for rulemaking. Are the regulations promulgated by independent agencies subject to review by OIRA? *See* sections 3(b) and 6. Professors Pildes and Sunstein describe the planning provision (section 4) as "bold and dramatic, simply because it is unprecedented" in its application to independent agencies. Richard H. Pildes & Cass R. Sunstein, *Reinventing the Regulatory State*, 62 U. Chi. L. Rev. 1, 29 (1995). Professor Sunstein served for nearly three years as the Administrator of OIRA under President Obama.

4. In Executive Order 13563 (Jan. 18, 2011), President Obama acted to "supplement[] and reaffirm[] the principles, structures and definitions" included in Executive Order 12866. Section 6 of the new executive order provides for "Retrospective Analyses of Existing Rules" and requires each agency to submit plans describing how it "will periodically review its existing significant regulations to determine whether any such regulations should be modified, streamlined, expanded, or repealed so as to make the agency's regulatory program more effective or less burdensome in achieving the regulatory objectives." Section 7(a) of the executive order states that "'agency' shall have the meaning set forth in section 3(b) of Executive Order 12866." In an explanatory memorandum of February 2, 2011, Administrator Sunstein stated that "Executive Order 13563 is designed to affirm and to supplement Executive Order 12866; it adds to and amplifies the provisions of Executive Order 12866, rather than displacing or qualifying them." With regard to independent agencies, Administrator Sunstein stated that "Executive Order 13563 does not apply to independent agencies, but such agencies are encouraged to give consideration to all of its provisions, consistent with their legal authority. In particular, such agencies are encouraged to consider undertaking, on a voluntary basis, retrospective analysis of existing rules."

On July 11, 2011, President Obama issued Executive Order 13579, "Regulation and Independent Regulatory Agencies." Section 1(b) of this executive order stated that "Executive Order 13563 of January 18, 2011, 'Improving Regulation and Regulatory Review,' directed to executive agencies, was meant to produce a regulatory system that protects 'public health, welfare, safety, and our environment while promoting economic growth, innovation, competitiveness, and job creation.' Independent regulatory agencies, no less than executive agencies, should promote that goal." Section 1(c) then stated that "Executive Order 13563 set out general requirements directed to executive agencies concerning public participation, integration and innovation, flexible approaches, and science. To the extent permitted by law, independent regulatory agencies should comply with these provisions as well." Finally, with respect to agency review of existing regulations, Section 2(b) stated that, "[w]ithin 120 days of the date of this order, each independent regulatory agency should develop and release to the public a plan, consistent with law and reflecting its resources and regulatory priorities and processes, under which the agency will periodically review its existing significant regulations to determine whether any such regulations should be modified, streamlined, expanded, or repealed so as to make the agency's regulatory program more effective or less burdensome in achieving the regulatory objectives." Does this executive order raise constitutional concerns regarding the President's relation to independent agencies?

5.   Note that the presidential review process has consistently focused on agency rulemaking to the exclusion of agency adjudication. At least when presidential involvement in an adjudication occurs in private, it may be barred. In *Portland Audubon Soc. v. Endangered Species Comm.*, 984 F.2d 1534, 1546 (9th Cir. 1993), the court stated that "[i]t is a fundamental precept of administrative law that when an agency performs a quasi-judicial (or a quasi-legislative) function its independence must be protected. There is no presidential prerogative to influence quasi-judicial administrative agency proceedings through behind-the-scenes lobbying." That court also held that, in the case of a formal APA adjudication, "the President and his staff are covered by section 557's prohibition [against ex parte contacts] and are not free to attempt to influence the decision-making processes of the Committee through ex parte communications." Does the OMB review process for regulations create incentives for agencies to develop regulatory policy by adjudication, rather than by rulemaking? President George W. Bush, whose changes to Executive Order 12866 were revoked by President Obama, had provided OIRA with the authority to review "significant guidance documents." Would you expect that this broader scope of the executive order would be significant?

6.   Is it anomalous that the President is apparently not required to comply with § 553 of the APA when promulgating the executive orders summarized and reproduced in this note? The Supreme Court has held that the President does not come within the definition of "agency" in the judicial review provisions of the APA. *Franklin v. Massachusetts*, 505 U.S. 788, 800-01 (1992). *See also Armstrong v. Bush*, 924 F.2d 282 (D.C. Cir. 1991) ("A conclusion that the President is not an 'agency' under the APA is also supported by the long-standing practice of the executive branch. . . . [T]he President has never been thought to have to comply with APA rulemaking procedures when issuing executive orders").

7.   How does the executive review required by Executive Order 12866 compare to the executive review provided by 1981 MSAPA § 3-202?

CHAPTER
5

Judicial Review

A. SCOPE OF REVIEW OF FACT

NLRB v. UNIVERSAL CAMERA CORP.
179 F.2d 749 (2d Cir. 1950)

On petition of the National Labor Relations Board for an order, "enforcing" an order of the Board to "cease and desist from discharging . . . any employee because he has filed charges or given testimony under the Act"; to "offer one, Imre Chairman, immediate and full reinstatement to his former, or a substantially equivalent, position"; to make him "whole for any loss of pay he has suffered because of the Respondent's discrimination against him"; and to post an appropriate notice.

Before L. HAND, CHIEF JUDGE, and SWAN and FRANK, CIRCUIT JUDGES. HAND, C.J.

This case arises upon a petition to enforce an order of the Labor Board, whose only direction that we need consider was to reinstate with back pay a "supervisory employee," named Chairman, whom the respondent discharged on January 24, 1944, avowedly for insubordination. If the Board was right, the discharge was in fact for giving testimony hostile to the respondent at a hearing conducted by the Board to determine who should be the representative of the respondent's "maintenance employees." Chairman was an assistant engineer, whose duties were to supervise the "maintenance employees," and he testified at the hearing in favor of their being recognized as a separate bargaining unit. The respondent opposed the recognition of such a unit, and several of its officers testified to that effect, among whom were Shapiro, the vice-president, Kende, the chief engineer, and Politzer, the "plant engineer." The examiner, who heard the witnesses, was not satisfied that the respondent's motive in discharging Chairman was reprisal for his testimony; but on review of the record a majority of the Board found the opposite, and on August 31, 1948, ordered Chairman's reinstatement. The respondent argues (1) that the majority's findings are subject to a more searching review under the New Act than under the Old; [and] (2) that in the case at bar the findings cannot be supported, because they are not supported by "substantial evidence". . . .

The substance of the evidence was as follows. On November 30, 1943, Chairman and Kende testified at the hearing upon representation, after which Kende told Chairman that he had "perjured" himself; and on the stand in the proceeding at bar Kende testified that Chairman "was either ignorant of the true facts regarding the organization within the company . . . or . . . he was deliberately lying, not in one instance, but in many instances, all afternoon"; and "that there was definite doubt regarding his suitability for a supervisory position of that nature." The examiner believed the testimony of Chairman that two other employees, Goldson and Politzer, had cautioned him that the respondent would take it against him, if he testified for the "maintenance employees"; and Kende swore that he told another employee, Weintraub — the personnel manager — that he thought that Chairman was a Communist. After Politzer reported to him on December second or third that this was a mistake, Kende told him to keep an eye on Chairman. From all this it is apparent that at the beginning of December Kende was hostile to Chairman; but he took no steps at that time to discharge him.

Nothing material happened until the very end of that month, when Chairman and Weintraub got into a quarrel, about disciplining a workman, named Kollisch. Chairman swore that Weintraub demanded that he discharge Kollisch for loafing; and Weintraub swore that he only demanded that Chairman put Kollisch to work. In any event high words followed; Chairman told Weintraub that he was drunk; Weintraub brought up a plant guard to put Chairman out of the premises, and the quarrel remained hot, until one, Zicarelli, a union steward, succeeded in getting the two men to patch up an apparent truce. Two days later Weintraub saw Politzer and told him that he had heard that Politzer was looking into Chairman's statement that Weintraub was drunk, and on this account Weintraub asked Politzer to discharge Chairman. Politzer testified that he answered that Chairman was going to resign soon anyway, and this the examiner believed. He did not, however, believe Politzer's further testimony that Chairman had in fact told Politzer that he was going to resign; he thought that Politzer either was mistaken in so supposing, or that he had made up the story in order to quiet Weintraub. Probably his reason for not believing this part of Politzer's testimony was that he accepted Chairman's testimony that ten days later Politzer intimated to Chairman that it would be well for him to resign, and Chairman refused. Whatever the reason, Weintraub did not, after his talk with Politzer, press the matter until January 24, 1944, when, learning that Chairman was still in the factory, he went again to Politzer and asked why this was. When Politzer told him that Chairman had changed his mind, Weintraub insisted that he must resign anyway, and, upon Politzer's refusal to discharge him, they together went to Kende. Weintraub repeated his insistence that Chairman must go, giving as the reason that his accusation of drunkenness had undermined Weintraub's authority, Kende took Weintraub's view and Politzer wrote out an order of dismissal. No one testified that at this interview, or any time after December first, any of the three mentioned Chairman's testimony at the representation hearing.

As we have said, the examiner was not satisfied that the Board had proved that Chairman's testimony at the representation proceeding had been an actuating cause of his discharge; but, not only did the majority of the Board reverse his ruling as to that, but they also overruled his finding that Politzer had told Weintraub on January first that Chairman was going to resign. They then found that Kende and Weintraub had agreed to bring about Chairman's discharge, at some undefined time after December first, because of Chairman's testimony; and that Weintraub's complaint on January 24 was a cover for affecting that purpose.

Whether these findings were justified is the first, and indeed the only important, question of fact; and as a preliminary point arises the extent of our review.

This has been the subject of so much uncertainty that we shall not try to clarify it; but we must decide what change, if any, the amendment of 1947 has made. Section 10(e) now reads that the findings "shall be conclusive" "if supported by substantial evidence on the record considered as a whole"; and the original was merely that they should be conclusive, "if supported by evidence." . . . The most probable intent in adding the phrase, "on the record considered as a whole," was to overrule what Congress apparently supposed — perhaps rightly — had been the understanding of some courts: i.e. that, if any passage could be found in the testimony to support a finding, the review was to stop, no matter how much other parts of the testimony contradicted, or outweighed, it. That the words throughout section ten were chosen with deliberation and care is evident from the changes in Sec. 10(c), apparently intended to confine the Board to the record before it, and in Sec. 10(b), restricting it in the admission of evidence to Rule 43(a) of the Federal Rules of Civil Procedure, 28 U.S.C.A. It appears to us that, had it been intended to set up a new measure of review by the courts, the matter would not have been left so at large. We cannot agree that our review has been "broadened"; we hold that no more was done than to make definite what was already implied.

Just what that review was is another and much more difficult matter — particularly, when it comes to deciding how to treat a reversal by the Board of a finding of one of its own examiners. Obviously no printed record preserves all the evidence, on which any judicial officer bases his findings; and it is principally on that account that upon an appeal from the judgment of a district court, a court of appeals will hesitate to reverse. Its position must be: "No matter what you saw of the witnesses and what else you heard than these written words, we are satisfied from them alone that you were clearly wrong. Nothing which could have happened that is not recorded, could have justified your conclusion in the face of what is before us." That gives such findings great immunity, which the Rules extend even to the findings of masters, when reviewed by a district judge. The standing of an examiner's findings under the Labor Relations Act is not plain; but it appears to us at least clear that they were not intended to be as unassailable as a master's. The old Act provided for "examiners"; but they did not have to make reports, and, although Sec. 10(c) of the New Act requires them to do that, it does not undertake to say how persuasive their findings are to be. On the other hand, Sec. 8(a) of the Administrative Procedure Act provides that "on appeal from or review of" the decision of an "officer" who has presided at a hearing, "the agency shall . . . have all the powers which it would have in making the initial decision." It is clear that these words apply to the decisions of the "agency" upon the evidence; but nothing is said as to what effect the "agency" must give to the "officer's" findings; except that, if the text be read literally, it could be argued that the "agency" was to disregard it. The reports in Congress do not help very much. The Senate Report merely said that the findings "would be of consequence, for example, to the extent that material facts in any case depend on the determination of the credibility of witnesses as shown by their demeanor or conduct at the hearing." The House Report was the same, in *ipsissimis verbis*, although it did add that "in a broad sense the agencies reviewing powers are to be compared with that of courts under Sec. 10(a) of the bill." That would have made them as conclusive upon an "agency" as the "agency's" findings are upon a court; and it is safe to say that the words will not bear so much. When the same question came up under the Old Act, the courts left the answer equally uncertain. The Seventh Circuit in *A.E. Staley Manufacturing Company v. National Labor Relations Board* said that, "where it" (the Board) "reaches a conclusion opposite to that of an Examiner, we think the report of the latter has a bearing on the question of substantial support and materially detracts therefrom"; and that has in substance received the approval of the Eighth Circuit, and of the Sixth, as well as a recent reaffirmation by the Seventh itself. All this leaves the question in confusion. On the one hand we are not to assume that the Board must accept the finding, unless what is preserved in the record makes it "clearly erroneous." That would assimilate examiners to masters, and, if that had been intended, we should expect a plainer statement. On the other hand, the decisions we have cited certainly do mean that, when the Board reverses a finding, it shall count in the court's review of the Board's substituted finding; the case does not then come up as it does, when the testimony has been taken by deposition. On the whole we find ourselves unable to apply so impalpable a standard without bringing greater perplexity into a subject already too perplexing. The weight to be given to another person's conclusion from evidence that has disappeared, depends altogether upon one's confidence in his judicial powers. The decision of a child of ten would count for nothing; that of an experienced master would count for much. Unless we are to set up some canon, universally applicable, like that of Rule 53(e)(2), each case in this statute will depend upon what competence the Board ascribes to the examiner in question. Section 4(a) provides that he shall be an employee of the Board, which will therefore have means of informing itself about his work. We hold that, although the Board would be wrong in totally disregarding his findings, it is practically impossible for a court, upon review of those findings which the Board itself substitutes, to consider the Board's reversal as a factor in the court's own decision. This we say, because we cannot find any middle ground between doing that and treating such a reversal as error, whenever it would be such, if done by a judge to a master in equity.

The foregoing discussion is relevant in the case at bar for the following reason. One ground why the evidence failed to convince the examiner of any agreement between Kende and Weintraub to discharge Chairman, was that he thought it quite as likely that the quarrel between Weintraub and Chairman at the end of December still rankled in Weintraub's mind, and induced him to insist upon Chairman's discharge on January 24, 1944. It became important in this view to explain why Weintraub waited for over three weeks; and this the examiner did explain because he believed that Politzer had told Weintraub that Chairman was going to resign. When the majority of the Board refused to accept this finding, they concluded that, since this left Weintraub's delay unexplained, his motive was to be related back to the quarrel of Kende and Chairman on November 30. We should feel obliged in our turn to reverse the reversal of this finding, if we were dealing with the finding of a judge who had reversed the finding of a master, because the reasons given do not seem to us enough to overbear the evidence which the record did not preserve and which may have convinced the examiner. These were (1) that the examiner did not believe all that Politzer had said; and (2) that the finding was "irreconcilable with the other related facts and all the other evidence bearing on Politzer's behavior and attitude." It is no reason for refusing to accept everything that a witness says, because you do not believe all of it; nothing is more common in all kinds of judicial decisions than to believe some and not all. Nor can we find "other related facts" which were "irreconcilable" with believing that Politzer told Weintraub that Chairman was going to resign. Indeed Chairman himself swore that on January 11, Politzer suggested to him that he resign, which affirmatively serves to confirm the examiner's finding that Politzer told Weintraub that Chairman would resign in order to placate him. However, as we have said, we think that we are altogether to disregard this as a factor in our review, which we should confine to the bare record; and on that we cannot say that Politzer's testimony had to be believed, in the face of Chairman's denial that he ever told him that he would resign.

There remains the question whether, with this explanation of Weintraub's delay missing, there was "substantial evidence" that the cause of Chairman's discharge was his testimony; and on that the Board had the affirmative; so that it is not enough that Kende and Weintraub might have agreed to find a means of getting rid of Chairman, or that Kende unassisted might have been awaiting an opportunity. Once more, if this was the finding of a judge, we should be in doubt whether it was sufficiently supported. When Weintraub went to Politzer on January 24, 1944, with his complaint at Chairman's continued presence in the factory, and when the two went to Kende because Politzer would not discharge Chairman, if Weintraub was acting in accordance with an agreement between Kende and himself, he was concealing the facts from Politzer. So too was Kende at the ensuing interview; indeed, we must assume that the two had arranged beforehand to keep Politzer in the dark, else Weintraub could scarcely have relied upon Kende to play his part. This appears to us to be constructed substantially out of whole cloth, so improbable is it that they should have gone to such devious means to deceive Politzer. On the other hand, although it is possible that Kende had been waiting for a proper occasion, independently of Weintraub, and that he seized upon Weintraub's complaint, being secretly actuated by his old grievance, we do not read the majority's decision as distinctly indicating that they meant so to find. But, if they did, unless we assume that Weintraub's complaint was trumped up ad hoc, to deceive Politzer, it becomes the merest guess that Kende did not find it alone a sufficient reason for his action, and reverted to his concealed spite.

Nevertheless, in spite of all this we shall direct the Board's order to be enforced. If by special verdict a jury had made either the express finding of the majority that there was an agreement between Kende and Weintraub, or the alternate finding, if there be one, that Kende without Weintraub's concurrence used Weintraub's complaint as an excuse, we should not reverse the verdict; and we understand our function in cases of this kind to be the same. Such a verdict would be within the bounds of rational entertainment. When all is said, Kende had been greatly outraged at Chairman's testimony; he then did propose to get him out of the factory; he still thought at the hearings that he was unfit to remain; and he had told Weintraub to keep watch on him. We cannot say that, with all these circumstances before him, no reasonable person could have concluded that Chairman's testimony was one of the causes of his discharge, little as it would have convinced us, were we free to pass upon the evidence in the first instance. . . .

An enforcement order will issue.

Swan, Circuit Judge (dissenting).

In *National Labor Relations Board v. A. Sartorius & Co.*, 2 Cir., 140 F.2d 203, 205 we said that "if an administrative agency ignores all the evidence given by one side in a controversy and with studied design gives credence to the testimony of the other side, the findings would be arbitrary and not in accord with the legal requirement." I think that is what the majority of the board has done in the case at bar. I would reverse its finding of motive and deny enforcement of the order.

UNIVERSAL CAMERA CORP. v. NLRB
340 U.S. 474 (1951)

Mr. Justice Frankfurter delivered the opinion of the Court.

The essential issue raised by this case . . . is the effect of the Administrative Procedure Act and the legislation colloquially known as the Taft-Hartley Act on the duty of Courts of Appeals when called upon to review orders of the National Labor Relations Board.

The Court of Appeals for the Second Circuit granted enforcement of an order directing, in the main, that petitioner reinstate with back pay an employee found to have been discharged because he gave testimony under the Wagner Act and cease and desist from discriminating against any employee who files charges or gives testimony under that Act. The court below, Judge Swan dissenting, decreed full enforcement of the order. . . .

I

Want of certainty in judicial review of Labor Board decisions partly reflects the intractability of any formula to furnish definiteness of content for all the impalpable factors involved in judicial review. But in part doubts as to the nature of the reviewing power and uncertainties in its application derive from history, and to that extent an elucidation of this history may clear them away.

The Wagner Act provided: "The findings of the Board as to the facts, if supported by evidence, shall be conclusive." Act of July 5, 1935, § 10(e), 49 Stat. 449, 454, 29 U.S.C. § 160(e). This Court read "evidence" to mean "substantial evidence," *Washington, V. & M. Coach Co. v. Labor Board*, 301 U.S. 142, and we said that "substantial evidence is more than a mere scintilla. It means such relevant evidence as a reasonable mind might accept as adequate to support a conclusion." *Consolidated Edison Co. v. Labor Board*, 305 U.S. 197, 229. Accordingly, it "must do more than create a suspicion of the existence of the fact to be established. . . . it must be enough to justify, if the trial were to a jury, a refusal to direct a verdict when the conclusion sought to be drawn from it is one of fact for the jury." *Labor Board v. Columbian Enameling & Stamping Co.*, 306 U.S. 292, 300.

The very smoothness of the "substantial evidence" formula as the standard for reviewing the evidentiary validity of the Board's findings established its currency. But the inevitably variant applications of the standard to conflicting evidence soon brought contrariety of views and in due course bred criticism. Even though the whole record may have been canvassed in order to determine whether the evidentiary foundation of a determination by the Board was "substantial," the phrasing of this Court's process of review readily lent itself to the notion that it was enough that the evidence supporting the Board's result was "substantial" when considered by itself. It is fair to say that by imperceptible steps regard for the fact-finding function of the Board led to the assumption that the requirements of the Wagner Act were met when the reviewing court could find in the record evidence which, when viewed in isolation, substantiated the Board's findings. *Compare Labor Board v. Waterman Steamship Corp.*, 309 U.S. 206; *Labor Board v. Bradford Dyeing Assn.*, 310 U.S. 318; and *see Labor Board v. Nevada Consolidated Copper Corp.*, 316 U.S. 105. This is not to say that every member of this Court was consciously guided by this view or that the Court ever explicitly avowed this practice as doctrine. What matters is that the belief justifiably arose that the Court had so construed the obligation to review.

Criticism of so contracted a reviewing power reinforced dissatisfaction felt in various quarters with the Board's administration of the Wagner Act in the years preceding the war. The scheme of the Act was attacked as an inherently unfair fusion of the functions of prosecutor and judge. Accusations of partisan bias were not wanting. The "irresponsible admission and weighing of hearsay, opinion, and emotional speculation in place of factual evidence" was said to be a "serious menace." No doubt some, perhaps even much, of the criticism was baseless and some surely was reckless. What is here relevant, however, is the climate of opinion thereby generated and its effect on Congress. Protests against "shocking injustices" and intimations of judicial "abdication" with which some courts granted enforcement of the Board's orders stimulated pressures for legislative relief from alleged administrative excesses.

The strength of these pressures was reflected in the passage in 1940 of the Walter-Logan Bill. It was vetoed by President Roosevelt, partly because it imposed unduly rigid limitations on the administrative process, and partly because of the investigation into the actual operation of the administrative process then being conducted by an experienced committee appointed by the Attorney General. It is worth noting that despite its aim to tighten control over administrative determinations of fact, the Walter-Logan Bill contented itself with the conventional formula that an agency's decision could be set aside if "the findings of fact are not supported by substantial evidence."

The final report of the Attorney General's Committee was submitted in January, 1941. The majority concluded that "dissatisfaction with the existing standards as to the scope of judicial review derives largely from dissatisfaction with the fact-finding procedures now employed by the administrative bodies." Departure from the "substantial evidence" test, it thought, would either create unnecessary uncertainty or transfer to courts the responsibility for ascertaining and assaying matters the significance of which lies outside judicial competence. Accordingly, it recommended against legislation embodying a general scheme of judicial review.

Three members of the Committee registered a dissent. Their view was that the "present system or lack of system of judicial review" led to inconsistency and uncertainty. They reported that under a "prevalent" interpretation of the "substantial evidence" rule "if what is called 'substantial evidence' is found anywhere in the record to support conclusions of fact, the courts are said to be obliged to sustain the decision without reference to how heavily the countervailing evidence may preponderate — unless indeed the stage of arbitrary decision is reached. Under this interpretation, the courts need to read only one side of the case and, if they find any evidence there, the administrative action is to be sustained and the record to the contrary is to be ignored."

Their view led them to recommend that Congress enact principles of review applicable to all agencies not excepted by unique characteristics. One of these principles was expressed by the formula that judicial review could extend to "findings, inferences, or conclusions of fact unsupported, upon the whole record, by substantial evidence." So far as the history of this movement for enlarged review reveals, the phrase "upon the whole record" makes its first appearance in this recommendation of the minority of the Attorney General's Committee. This evidence of the close relationship between the phrase and the criticism out of which it arose is important, for the substance of this formula for judicial review found its way into the statute books when Congress with unquestioning — we might even say uncritical — unanimity enacted the Administrative Procedure Act.[15]

One is tempted to say "uncritical" because the legislative history of that Act hardly speaks with that clarity of purpose which Congress supposedly furnishes courts in order to enable them to enforce its true will. On the one hand, the sponsors of the legislation indicated that they were reaffirming the prevailing "substantial evidence" test. But with equal clarity they expressed disapproval of the manner in which the courts were applying their own standard. The committee reports of both houses refer to the practice of agencies to rely upon "suspicion, surmise, implications, or plainly incredible evidence," and indicate that courts are to exact higher standards "in the exercise of their independent judgment" and on consideration of "the whole record."

Similar dissatisfaction with too restricted application of the "substantial evidence" test is reflected in the legislative history of the Taft-Hartley Act. The bill as reported to the House provided that the "findings of the Board as to the facts shall be conclusive unless it is made to appear to the satisfaction of the court either (1) that the findings of fact are against the manifest weight of the evidence, or (2) that the findings of fact are not supported by substantial evidence." The bill left the House with this provision. Early committee prints in the Senate provided for review by "weight of the evidence" or "clearly erroneous" standards. But, as the Senate Committee Report relates, "it was finally decided to conform the statute to the corresponding section of the Administrative Procedure Act where the substantial evidence test prevails. In order to clarify any ambiguity in that statute, however, the committee inserted the words

---

15. 60 Stat. 237, 5 U.S.C. § 1001 *et seq.* The form finally adopted reads as follows:

"SEC. 10. Except so far as (1) statutes preclude judicial review or (2) agency action is by law committed to agency discretion — . . .

"(e) SCOPE OF REVIEW. — So far as necessary to decision and where presented the reviewing court shall decide all relevant questions of law, interpret constitutional and statutory provisions, and determine the meaning or applicability of the terms of any agency action. It shall (A) compel agency action unlawfully withheld or unreasonably delayed; and (B) hold unlawful and set aside agency action, findings, and conclusions found to be (1) arbitrary, capricious, an abuse of discretion, or otherwise not in accordance with law; (2) contrary to constitutional right, power, privilege, or immunity; (3) in excess of statutory jurisdiction, authority, or limitations, or short of statutory right; (4) without observance of procedure required by law; (5) unsupported by substantial evidence in any case subject to the requirements of sections 7 and 8 or otherwise reviewed on the record of an agency hearing provided by statute; or (6) unwarranted by the facts to the extent that the facts are subject to trial de novo by the reviewing court. In making the foregoing determinations the court shall review the *whole* record or such portions thereof as may be cited by any party, and due account shall be taken of the rule of prejudicial error." 60 Stat. 243-244, 5 U.S.C. § 1009(e). (Italics ours.)

'questions of fact, if supported by substantial evidence *on the record considered as a whole. . . .*'"[21]

This phraseology was adopted by the Senate. The House conferees agreed. They reported to the House: "It is believed that the provisions of the conference agreement relating to the courts' reviewing power will be adequate to preclude such decisions as those in *NLRB v. Nevada Consol. Copper Corp.* (316 U.S. 105) and in the *Wilson, Columbia Products, Union Pacific Stages, Hearst, Republic Aviation*, and *Le Tourneau*, etc. cases, *supra*, without unduly burdening the courts." The Senate version became the law.

It is fair to say that in all this Congress expressed a mood. And it expressed its mood not merely by oratory but by legislation. As legislation that mood must be respected, even though it can only serve as a standard for judgment and not as a body of rigid rules assuring sameness of application. Enforcement of such broad standards implies subtlety of mind and solidity of judgment. But it is not for us to question that Congress may assume such qualities in the federal judiciary.

From the legislative story we have summarized, two concrete conclusions do emerge. One is the identity of aim of the Administrative Procedure Act and the Taft-Hartley Act regarding the proof with which the Labor Board must support a decision. The other is that now Congress has left no room for doubt as to the kind of scrutiny which a Court of Appeals must give the record before the Board to satisfy itself that the Board's order rests on adequate proof.

It would be mischievous word-playing to find that the scope of review under the Taft-Hartley Act is any different from that under the Administrative Procedure Act. The Senate Committee which reported the review clause of the Taft-Hartley Act expressly indicated that the two standards were to conform in this regard, and the wording of the two Acts is for purposes of judicial administration identical. And so we hold that the standard of proof specifically required of the Labor Board by the Taft-Hartley Act is the same as that to be exacted by courts reviewing every administrative action subject to the Administrative Procedure Act.

Whether or not it was ever permissible for courts to determine the substantiality of evidence supporting a Labor Board decision merely on the basis of evidence which in and of itself justified it, without taking into account contradictory evidence or evidence from which conflicting inferences could be drawn, the new legislation definitively precludes such a theory of review and bars its practice. The substantiality of evidence must take into account whatever in the record fairly detracts from its weight. This is clearly the significance of the requirement in both statutes that courts consider the whole record. Committee reports and the adoption in the Administrative Procedure Act of the minority views of the Attorney General's Committee demonstrate that to enjoin

21. S. Rep. No. 105, 80th Cong., 1st Sess. 26-27, reprinted in 1 Legislative History 432-433. The Committee did not explain what the ambiguity might be; and it is to be noted that the phrase it italicized is indistinguishable in content from the requirement of § 10(e) of the Administrative Procedure Act that "the court shall review the whole record or such portions thereof as may be cited by any party. . . ."

Senator Taft gave this explanation to the Senate of the meaning of the section: "In the first place, the evidence must be substantial; in the second place, it must still look substantial when viewed in the light of the entire record. That does not go so far as saying that a decision can be reversed on the weight of the evidence. It does not go quite so far as the power given to a circuit court of appeals to review a district-court decision, but it goes a great deal further than the present law, and gives the court greater opportunity to reverse an obviously unjust decision on the part of the National Labor Relations Board." 93 Cong. Rec. 3839, reprinted in 2 Legislative History 1014.

such a duty on the reviewing court was one of the important purposes of the movement which eventuated in that enactment.

To be sure, the requirement for canvassing "the whole record" in order to ascertain substantiality does not furnish a calculus of value by which a reviewing court can assess the evidence. Nor was it intended to negative the function of the Labor Board as one of those agencies presumably equipped or informed by experience to deal with a specialized field of knowledge, whose findings within that field carry the authority of an expertness which courts do not possess and therefore must respect. Nor does it mean that even as to matters not requiring expertise a court may displace the Board's choice between two fairly conflicting views, even though the court would justifiably have made a different choice had the matter been before it *de novo*. Congress has merely made it clear that a reviewing court is not barred from setting aside a Board decision when it cannot conscientiously find that the evidence supporting that decision is substantial, when viewed in the light that the record in its entirety furnishes, including the body of evidence opposed to the Board's view.

There remains, then, the question whether enactment of these two statutes has altered the scope of review other than to require that substantiality be determined in the light of all that the record relevantly presents. A formula for judicial review of administrative action may afford grounds for certitude but cannot assure certainty of application. Some scope for judicial discretion in applying the formula can be avoided only by falsifying the actual process of judging or by using the formula as an instrument of futile casuistry. It cannot be too often repeated that judges are not automata. The ultimate reliance for the fair operation of any standard is a judiciary of high competence and character and the constant play of an informed professional critique upon its work.

Since the precise way in which courts interfere with agency findings cannot be imprisoned within any form of words, new formulas attempting to rephrase the old are not likely to be more helpful than the old. There are no talismanic words that can avoid the process of judgment. The difficulty is that we cannot escape, in relation to this problem, the use of undefined defining terms.

Whatever changes were made by the Administrative Procedure and Taft-Hartley Acts are clearly within this area where precise definition is impossible. Retention of the familiar "substantial evidence" terminology indicates that no drastic reversal of attitude was intended.

But a standard leaving an unavoidable margin for individual judgment does not leave the judicial judgment at large even though the phrasing of the standard does not wholly fence it in. The legislative history of these Acts demonstrates a purpose to impose on courts a responsibility which has not always been recognized. Of course it is a statute and not a committee report which we are interpreting. But the fair interpretation of a statute is often "the art of proliferating a purpose," revealed more by the demonstrable forces that produced it than by its precise phrasing. The adoption in these statutes of the judicially-constructed "substantial evidence" test was a response to pressures for stricter and more uniform practice, not a reflection of approval of all existing practices. To find the change so elusive that it cannot be precisely defined does not mean it may be ignored. We should fail in our duty to effectuate the will of Congress if we denied recognition to expressed Congressional disapproval of the finality accorded to Labor Board findings by some decisions of this and lower courts, or even of the atmosphere which may have favored those decisions.

We conclude, therefore, that the Administrative Procedure Act and the Taft-Hartley Act direct that courts must now assume more responsibility for the reasonableness and fairness of Labor Board decisions than some courts have shown in the past. Reviewing courts must be influenced by a feeling that they are not to abdicate the conventional judicial function. Congress has imposed on them responsibility for assuring that the Board keeps within reasonable grounds. That responsibility is not less real because it is limited to enforcing the requirement that evidence appear substantial when viewed, on the record as a whole, by courts invested with the authority and enjoying the prestige of the Courts of Appeals. The Board's findings are entitled to respect; but they must nonetheless be set aside when the record before a Court of Appeals clearly precludes the Board's decision from being justified by a fair estimate of the worth of the testimony of witnesses or its informed judgment on matters within its special competence or both.

From this it follows that enactment of these statutes does not require every Court of Appeals to alter its practice. Some — perhaps a majority — have always applied the attitude reflected in this legislation. To explore whether a particular court should or should not alter its practice would only divert attention from the application of the standard now prescribed to a futile inquiry into the nature of the test formerly used by a particular court. Our power to review the correctness of application of the present standard ought seldom to be called into action. Whether on the record as a whole there is substantial evidence to support agency findings is a question which Congress has placed in the keeping of the Courts of Appeals. This Court will intervene only in what ought to be the rare instance when the standard appears to have been misapprehended or grossly misapplied.

                                        II

Our disagreement with the view of the court below that the scope of review of Labor Board decisions is unaltered by recent legislation does not of itself, as we have noted, require reversal of its decision. The court may have applied a standard of review which satisfies the present Congressional requirement.

The decision of the Court of Appeals is assailed on two grounds. It is said (1) that the court erred in holding that it was barred from taking into account the report of the examiner on questions of fact insofar as that report was rejected by the Board, and (2) that the Board's order was not supported by substantial evidence on the record considered as a whole, even apart from the validity of the court's refusal to consider the rejected portions of the examiner's report.

The latter contention is easily met. It is true that two of the earlier decisions of the court below were among those disapproved by Congress. But this disapproval, we have seen, may well have been caused by unintended intimations of judicial phrasing. And in any event, it is clear from the court's opinion in this case that it in fact did consider the "record as a whole," and did not deem itself merely the judicial echo of the Board's conclusion. The testimony of the company's witnesses was inconsistent, and there was clear evidence that the complaining employee had been discharged by an officer who was at one time influenced against him because of his appearance at the Board hearing. On such a record we could not say that it would be error to grant enforcement.

The first contention, however, raises serious questions to which we now turn.

III

The Court of Appeals deemed itself bound by the Board's rejection of the examiner's findings because the court considered these findings not "as unassailable as a master's."[24] 179 F.2d at 752. They are not. Section 10(c) of the Labor Management Relations Act provides that "If upon the preponderance of the testimony taken the Board shall be of the opinion that any person named in the complaint has engaged in or is engaging in any such unfair labor practice, then the Board shall state its findings of fact. . . ." 61 Stat. 147, 29 U.S.C. (Supp. III) § 160(c). The responsibility for decision thus placed on the Board is wholly inconsistent with the notion that it has power to reverse an examiner's findings only when they are "clearly erroneous." Such a limitation would make so drastic a departure from prior administrative practice that explicitness would be required.

The Court of Appeals concluded from this premise "that, although the Board would be wrong in totally disregarding his findings, it is practically impossible for a court, upon review of those findings which the Board itself substitutes, to consider the Board's reversal as a factor in the court's own decision. This we say, because we cannot find any middle ground between doing that and treating such a reversal as error, whenever it would be such, if done by a judge to a master in equity." Much as we respect the logical acumen of the Chief Judge of the Court of Appeals, we do not find ourselves pinioned between the horns of his dilemma.

We are aware that to give the examiner's findings less finality than a master's and yet entitle them to consideration in striking the account, is to introduce another and an unruly factor into the judgmatical process of review. But we ought not to fashion an exclusionary rule merely to reduce the number of imponderables to be considered by reviewing courts.

The Taft-Hartley Act provides that "The findings of the Board with respect to questions of fact if supported by substantial evidence on the record considered as a whole shall be conclusive." 61 Stat. 148, 29 U.S.C. (Supp. III) § 160(e). Surely an examiner's report is as much a part of the record as the complaint or the testimony. According to the Administrative Procedure Act, "All decisions (including initial, recommended, or tentative decisions) shall become a part of the record. . . ." § 8(b), 60 Stat. 242, 5 U.S.C. § 1007(b). We found that this Act's provision for judicial review has the same meaning as that in the Taft-Hartley Act. The similarity of the two statutes in language and purpose also requires that the definition of "record" found in the Administrative Procedure Act be construed to be applicable as well to the term "record" as used in the Taft-Hartley Act.

It is therefore difficult to escape the conclusion that the plain language of the statutes directs a reviewing court to determine the substantiality of evidence on the record including the examiner's report. The conclusion is confirmed by the indications in the legislative history that enhancement of the status and function of the trial examiner was one of the important purposes of the movement for administrative reform.

---

24. Rule 53(e)(2), Fed. Rules Civ. Proc., gives finality to the findings of a master unless they are clearly erroneous. . . . [This rule was more recently amended, in 2003, so that clearly erroneous review applies only when stipulated by the parties. F.R. Civ. P. 53(g).]

This aim was set forth by the Attorney General's Committee on Administrative Procedure:

> In general, the relationship upon appeal between the hearing Commissioner and the agency ought to a considerable extent to be that of trial court to appellate court. Conclusions, interpretations, law, and policy should, of course, be open to full review. On the other hand, on matters which the hearing Commissioner, having heard the evidence and seen the witnesses, is best qualified to decide, the agency should be reluctant to disturb his findings unless error is clearly shown.

Apparently it was the Committee's opinion that these recommendations should not be obligatory. For the bill which accompanied the Final Report required only that hearing officers make an initial decision which would become final in the absence of further agency action, and that agencies which differed on the facts from their examiners give reasons and record citations supporting their conclusion. This proposal was further moderated by the Administrative Procedure Act. It permits agencies to use examiners to record testimony but not to evaluate it, and contains the rather obscure provision that an agency which reviews an examiner's report has "all the powers which it would have in making the initial decision."

But this refusal to make mandatory the recommendations of the Attorney General's Committee should not be construed as a repudiation of them. Nothing in the statutes suggests that the Labor Board should not be influenced by the examiner's opportunity to observe the witnesses he hears and sees and the Board does not. Nothing suggests that reviewing courts should not give to the examiner's report such probative force as it intrinsically commands. To the contrary, §11 of the Administrative Procedure Act contains detailed provisions designed to maintain high standards of independence and competence in examiners. Section 10(c) of the Labor Management Relations Act requires that examiners "shall issue . . . a proposed report, together with a recommended order." Both statutes thus evince a purpose to increase the importance of the role of examiners in the administrative process. High standards of public administration counsel that we attribute to the Labor Board's examiners both due regard for the responsibility which Congress imposes on them and the competence to discharge it.

The committee reports also make it clear that the sponsors of the legislation thought the statutes gave significance to the findings of examiners. Thus, the Senate Committee responsible for the Administrative Procedure Act explained in its report that examiners' decisions "would be of consequence, for example, to the extent that material facts in any case depend on the determination of credibility of witnesses as shown by their demeanor or conduct at the hearing." The House Report reflects the same attitude; and the Senate Committee Report on the Taft-Hartley Act likewise indicates regard for the responsibility devolving on the examiner.

We do not require that the examiner's findings be given more weight than in reason and in the light of judicial experience they deserve. The "substantial evidence" standard is not modified in any way when the Board and its examiner disagree. We intend only to recognize that evidence supporting a conclusion may be less substantial when an impartial, experienced examiner who has observed the witnesses and lived with the case has drawn conclusions different from the Board's than when he has reached the same conclusion. The findings of the examiner are to be considered along with the consistency and inherent probability of testimony. The significance of his report, of course, depends largely on the importance of credibility in the particular case. To give it this significance does not seem to us materially more difficult than to heed the other factors which in sum determine whether evidence is "substantial."

The direction in which the law moves is often a guide for decision of particular cases, and here it serves to confirm our conclusion. However halting its progress, the trend in litigation is toward a rational inquiry into truth, in which the tribunal considers everything "logically probative of some matter requiring to be proved." Thayer, A Preliminary Treatise on Evidence, 530; *Funk v. United States,* 290 U.S. 371. This Court has refused to accept assumptions of fact which are demonstrably false, *United States v. Provident Trust Co.,* 291 U.S. 272, even when agreed to by the parties, *Swift & Co. v. Hocking Valley R. Co.,* 243 U.S. 281. Machinery for discovery of evidence has been strengthened; the boundaries of judicial notice have been slowly but perceptibly enlarged. It would reverse this process for courts to deny examiners' findings the probative force they would have in the conduct of affairs outside a courtroom.

We therefore remand the cause to the Court of Appeals. On reconsideration of the record it should accord the findings of the trial examiner the relevance that they reasonably command in answering the comprehensive question whether the evidence supporting the Board's order is substantial. But the court need not limit its reexamination of the case to the effect of that report on its decision. We leave it free to grant or deny enforcement as it thinks the principles expressed in this opinion dictate. *Judgment vacated and cause remanded.*

MR. JUSTICE BLACK and MR. JUSTICE DOUGLAS concur with parts I and II of this opinion but as to part III agree with the opinion of the court below.

QUESTIONS

1. What is the factual issue? How do we know that it is an issue of fact (and not an issue of law)?
2. What is the proper scope of review according to the Court? Where does it come from? How does the federal APA qualify the applicability of substantial evidence review?
3. What would be the scope of review of facts in cases not subject to §§ 556 and 557 and where the organic act does not provide for a "substantial evidence" scope of review? In *Assn. of Data Processing v. Bd. of Governors,* 745 F.2d 677, 683-84 (D.C. Cir. 1984), then-Judge Scalia offered the following solution to this puzzle:

> The "scope of review" provisions of the APA, 5 U.S.C. § 706(2), are cumulative. Thus, an agency action which is supported by the required substantial evidence may in another regard be "arbitrary, capricious, an abuse of discretion, or otherwise not in accordance with law" — for example, because it is an abrupt and unexplained departure from agency precedent. Paragraph (A) of subsection 706(2) — the "arbitrary or capricious" provision — is a catchall, picking up administrative misconduct not covered by the other more specific

paragraphs. Thus, in those situations where paragraph (E) has no application (informal rulemaking, for example, which is not governed by §§ 556 and 557 to which paragraph (E) refers), paragraph (A) takes up the slack, so to speak, enabling the courts to strike down, as arbitrary, agency action that is devoid of needed factual support. When the arbitrary or capricious standard is performing that function of assuring factual support, there is no substantive difference between what it requires and what would be required by the substantial evidence test, since it is impossible to conceive of a "nonarbitrary" factual judgment supported only by evidence that is not substantial in the APA sense — i.e., not "'enough to justify, if the trial were to a jury, a refusal to direct a verdict when the conclusion sought to be drawn . . . is one of fact for the jury,'" *Illinois Central R.R. v. Norfolk & Western Ry.*, 385 U.S. 57, 66 (1966) (quoting *NLRB v. Columbian Enameling & Stamping Co.*, 306 U.S. 292, 300 (1939)).

This view of the review of agency fact findings under the arbitrary and capricious standard has been adopted by at least one other court. *See Olenhouse v. Commodity Credit Corp.*, 42 F.3d 1560, 1575 (10th Cir. 1994).

4. Recall *Crowell v. Benson, supra*, p. 314. Is this a case of "private rights" under *Crowell*? Is *Universal Camera* a constitutional case? *Compare* APA § 706(2)(E).

5. What are the horns of Judge Hand's dilemma? *See* F.R. Civ. P. 52(a), 53, and footnote 24 of the opinion.

6. Should deference be to the agency or the hearing examiner? Why? Should it depend on nature of issue?

7. Is "substantial evidence" review more or less deferential than "clearly erroneous" review? See footnote 21 of opinion. Why should this be? In *Dickinson v. Zurko*, 527 U.S. 150 (1999), the Supreme Court decided that the scope of judicial review of decisions of the Patent and Trademark Office was the APA's substantial evidence standard, rather than the clearly erroneous standard that the PTO claimed had traditionally applied. The Court included the following comment about the "subtle" difference in these review standards:

> The upshot in terms of judicial review is some practical difference in outcome depending upon which standard is used. The court/agency standard, as we have said, is somewhat less strict that the court/court standard. But the difference is a subtle one — so fine that (apart from the present case) we have failed to uncover a single instance in which a reviewing court conceded that use of one standard rather than the other would in fact have produced a different outcome. Cf. *International Brotherhood of Electrical Workers v. NLRB*, 448 F.2d 1127, 1142 (D.C. Cir. 1971) (Leventhal, J., dissenting) (wrongly believing — and correcting himself — that he had found the "case dreamed of by law school professors" where the agency's findings, though "clearly erroneous" were "nevertheless" supported by "substantial evidence").
>
> The difficulty of finding such a case may in part reflect the basic similarity of the reviewing task, which requires judges to apply logic and experience to an evidentiary record, whether that record was made in a court or by an agency. It may in part reflect the difficulty of attempting to capture in a form of words intangible factors such as judicial confidence in the fairness of the factfinding process. *Universal Camera*, [340 U.S.] at 489; Jaffe, Judicial Review: "Substantial Evidence on the Whole Record," 64 Harv. L. Rev. 1233, 1245 (1951). It may in part reflect the comparatively greater importance of case-specific factors, such

as a finding's dependence upon agency expertise or the presence of internal agency review, which factors will often prove more influential in respect to outcome than will the applicable standard of review.

  Id. at 162-63.

8. In *T-Mobile South, LLC v. City of Roswell*, 135 S. Ct. 808 (2015), Justice Soto-mayor, writing for the Court majority, discussed how a statutory "substantial evidence" standard affected the need for an agency, this time a state agency, to provide reasons for its decision. She wrote that "[i]n order to determine whether a locality's denial was supported by substantial evidence, as Congress directed, courts must be able to identify the reason or reasons why the locality denied the application." *Id.* at 814 (citation omitted). She reiterated later in the opinion that, "[b]y employing the term 'substantial evidence,' Congress thus invoked, among other things, our recognition that 'the orderly functioning of the process of [substantial-evidence] review requires that the grounds upon which the administrative agency acted be clearly disclosed,' and that 'courts cannot exercise their duty of [substantial-evidence] review unless they are advised of the considerations underlying the action under review.'" *Id.* at 815 (citations omitted). When she summarized the agency's obligation to provide reasons, she sought to limit the burden for agencies: "the statutory text and structure, and the concepts that Congress imported into the statutory framework, all point clearly toward the conclusion that localities must provide reasons when they deny cell phone tower siting applications. We stress, however, that these reasons need not be elaborate or even sophisticated, but rather . . . simply clear enough to enable judicial review." *Id.*

9. Does 1981 MSAPA § 5-116(c)(7) provide for the same or a different standard of review? Is that provision's application limited only to on-the-record decisions?

B.   SCOPE OF REVIEW OF LAW

CABINET FOR HUMAN RESOURCES v. JEWISH HOSPITAL HEALTHCARE SVCS.

932 S.W.2d 388 (Ky. App. 1996)

SCHRODER, Judge:

This is an appeal from an order of the Franklin Circuit Court reversing a decision of the Interim Office of Health Planning and Certification which ruled that appellee Hospital needed to obtain a Certificate of Need in order to add a sixth cardiac catheterization laboratory. We agree with the lower court's interpretation of KRS 216B.061 and KRS 216B.015(20) as it applies to the facts of this case. Thus, we affirm.

In January of 1994, appellee, Jewish Hospital in Louisville filed an application for a Certificate of Need to add a sixth cardiac catheterization laboratory to its five duly approved cardiac catheterization laboratories already in operation. Jewish Hospital requested nonsubstantive review status under 902 KAR

20:004E section 9(d), which authorizes expedited review under certain circumstances, but was denied by appellant, the Interim Office of Health Planning and Certification (Interim Office).

In December of 1994, Jewish Hospital wrote the Interim Office a letter withdrawing its application for a Certificate of Need. In the letter, the Hospital asserted it was not required to obtain a Certificate of Need for a sixth cardiac catheterization lab according to a recent decision in a similar case in the Franklin Circuit Court interpreting KRS 216B.061(1)(d) and KRS 216B.015(20). The Interim Office thereafter advised Jewish Hospital that it was maintaining its position that a Certificate of Need was required and that its reliance on the other case was misplaced since it was on appeal to the Court of Appeals.

On December 22, 1994, Jewish Hospital wrote the Interim Office informing them that its plans to add the sixth cardiac catheterization lab were going forward and that the lab was expected to open on or about April 30, 1995. The Interim Office then issued a Notice for a Show Cause Hearing and an Order to Appeal. After said hearing, the hearing officer for the Interim Office issued a final decision and order on March 7, 1995 ordering Jewish Hospital to immediately cease and desist any construction or planning associated with the sixth cardiac catheterization lab unless it obtained a Certificate of Need and further ordered Jewish Hospital to pay $10,000 in fines for willfully violating the provisions of Chapter 216B. The Hospital then appealed to the Franklin Circuit Court which reversed the order of the Interim Office. This appeal by the Interim Office followed.

KRS 216B.061(1) sets out the circumstances when a Certificate of Need is required:

> (1) Unless otherwise provided in this chapter, no person shall do any of the following without first obtaining a certificate of need: . . .
> (d) Make a substantial change in a health service. . . .

As it relates to the present case, KRS 216B.015(20)(a) defines a "substantial change in a health service" as follows:

> [T]he addition of a health service for which there are review criteria and standards in the state health plan; . . . .

The sole issue before us is whether the lower court erred in concluding that the addition of a sixth cardiac catheterization lab does not constitute "the addition of a health service." As to questions of fact or the exercise of discretion by an administrative agency, judicial review is limited to whether the agency's decision was supported by substantial evidence or whether the decision was arbitrary or unreasonable. However, statutory construction is a matter of law for the courts, and a reviewing court is not bound by an administrative body's interpretation of a statute. Contrary to appellant's position, the issue in the present case is clearly one of law.

KRS 446.080(4) ["All words and phrases shall be construed according to the common and approved usage of language, but technical words and phrases, and such others as may have acquired a peculiar and appropriate meaning in the law, shall be construed according to such meaning"] requires this Court to give statutory language its plain, ordinary meaning. The cardinal rule of statutory construction is that the intention of the legislature should be ascertained and given effect. In our view, the addition of a health service necessarily connotes that the health service be one which is new to the facility. If the legislature meant to require Certificates of Need for additional services which are already in existence, the language of KRS 216B.015(20)(a) would have read, "the addition to a health service . . .".

In the instant case, Jewish Hospital is merely increasing the quantity of cardiac catheterization labs and, to our knowledge, is not adding to, or even changing, the scope of services it already provides. Accordingly, the lower court did not err in concluding that Jewish Hospital did not "make a substantial change in a health service" within the meaning of KRS 216B.061(1) and KRS 216B.015(20). . . .

For the reasons stated above, the judgment of the Franklin Circuit Court is affirmed. All concur.

QUESTIONS

1. How is the issue raised in this case different in nature from the issue in *Universal Camera*?
2. Why shouldn't the court accept the agency interpretation of the statute? Is *Marbury v. Madison* relevant here?
3. Distinguish carefully between a determination whether a record can be upheld on review, which determination is legal in nature, and an original agency determination that is being reviewed, which may be factual in nature. For instance, in a typical "substantial evidence" review by a district court of a purely factual issue in a Social Security disability claim, the Supreme Court need not defer to the court of appeals and the court of appeals need not defer to the district court. Instead, the appellate courts review de novo the trial court's *legal* determination that there is substantial evidence to support the agency's *factual* determination.

SKIDMORE v. SWIFT & CO.
323 U.S. 134 (1944)

MR. JUSTICE JACKSON delivered the opinion of the Court.

Seven employees of the Swift and Company packing plant at Fort Worth, Texas, brought an action under the Fair Labor Standards Act to recover overtime, liquidated damages, and attorneys' fees, totalling approximately $77,000. The District Court rendered judgment denying this claim wholly, and the Circuit Court of Appeals for the Fifth Circuit affirmed.

It is not denied that the daytime employment of these persons was working time within the Act. Two were engaged in general fire-hall duties and maintenance of firefighting equipment of the Swift plant. The others operated elevators or acted as relief men in fire duties. They worked from 7:00 A.M. to 3:30 P.M., with a half-hour lunch period, five days a week. They were paid weekly salaries.

Under their oral agreement of employment, however, petitioners undertook to stay in the fire hall on the Company premises, or within hailing distance, three and a half to four nights a week. This involved no task except to answer alarms, either because of fire or because the sprinkler was set off for some other reason. No fires occurred during the period in issue, the alarms were rare, and the time required for their answer rarely exceeded an hour. For each alarm answered the employees were paid in addition to their fixed compensation an agreed amount, fifty cents at first, and later sixty-four cents. The Company provided a brick fire hall equipped with steam heat and air-conditioned rooms. It provided sleeping quarters, a pool table, a domino table, and a radio. The men used their time in sleep or amusement as they saw fit, except that they were required to stay in or close by the fire hall and be ready to respond to alarms. It is stipulated that "they agreed to remain in the fire hall and stay in it or within hailing distance, subject to call, in event of fire or other casualty, but were not required to perform any specific tasks during these periods of time, except in answering alarms." The trial court found the evidentiary facts as stipulated; it made no findings of fact as such as to whether under the arrangement of the parties and the circumstances of this case, which in some respects differ from those of the *Armour* case, the fire-hall duty or any part thereof constituted working time. It said, however, as a "conclusion of law" that "the time plaintiffs spent in the fire hall subject to call to answer fire alarms does not constitute hours worked, for which overtime compensation is due them under the Fair Labor Standards Act, as interpreted by the Administrator and the Courts," and in its opinion observed, "of course we know pursuing such pleasurable occupations or performing such personal chores, does not constitute work." The Circuit Court of Appeals affirmed.

For reasons set forth in the *Armour* case decided herewith we hold that no principle of law found either in the statute or in Court decisions precludes waiting time from also being working time. We have not attempted to, and we cannot, lay down a legal formula to resolve cases so varied in their facts as are the many situations in which employment involves waiting time. Whether in a concrete case such time falls within or without the Act is a question of fact to be resolved by appropriate findings of the trial court. This involves scrutiny and construction of the agreements between the particular parties, appraisal of their practical construction of the working agreement by conduct, consideration of the nature of the service, and its relation to the waiting time, and all of the surrounding circumstances. Facts may show that the employee was engaged to wait, or they may show that he waited to be engaged. His compensation may cover both waiting and task, or only performance of the task itself. Living quarters may in some situations be furnished as a facility of the task and in another as a part of its compensation. The law does not impose an arrangement upon the parties. It imposes upon the courts the task of finding what the arrangement was.

We do not minimize the difficulty of such an inquiry where the arrangements of the parties have not contemplated the problem posed by the statute. But it does not differ in nature or in the standards to guide judgment from that which frequently confronts courts where they must find retrospectively the effect of contracts as to matters which the parties failed to anticipate or explicitly to provide for.

Congress did not utilize the services of an administrative agency to find facts and to determine in the first instance whether particular cases fall within or without the Act. Instead, it put this responsibility on the courts. But it did create the office of Administrator, impose upon him a variety of duties, endow him with powers to inform himself of conditions in industries and employments subject to the Act, and put on him the duties of bringing injunction actions to restrain violations. Pursuit of his duties has accumulated a considerable experience in the problems of ascertaining working time in employments involving periods of inactivity and a knowledge of the customs prevailing in reference to their solution. From these he is obliged to reach conclusions as to conduct without the law, so that he should seek injunctions to stop it, and that within the law, so that he has no call to interfere. He has set forth his views of the application of the Act under different circumstances in an interpretative bulletin and in informal rulings. They provide a practical guide to employers and employees as to how the office representing the public interest in its enforcement will seek to apply it. Wage and Hour Division, Interpretative Bulletin No. 13.

The Administrator thinks the problems presented by inactive duty require a flexible solution, rather than the all-in or all-out rules respectively urged by the parties in this case, and his Bulletin endeavors to suggest standards and examples to guide in particular situations. In some occupations, it says, periods of inactivity are not properly counted as working time even though the employee is subject to call. Examples are an operator of a small telephone exchange where the switchboard is in her home and she ordinarily gets several hours of uninterrupted sleep each night; or a pumper of a stripper well or watchman of a lumber camp during the off season, who may be on duty twenty-four hours a day but ordinarily "has a normal night's sleep, has ample time in which to eat his meals, and has a certain amount of time for relaxation and entirely private pursuits." Exclusion of all such hours the Administrator thinks may be justified. In general, the answer depends "upon the degree to which the employee is free to engage in personal activities during periods of idleness when he is subject to call and the number of consecutive hours that the employee is subject to call without being required to perform active work." "Hours worked are not limited to the time spent in active labor but include time given by the employee to the employer. . . ."

The facts of this case do not fall within any of the specific examples given, but the conclusion of the Administrator, as expressed in the brief amicus curiae, is that the general tests which he has suggested point to the exclusion of sleeping and eating time of these employees from the work-week and the inclusion of all other on-call time: although the employees were required to remain on the premises during the entire time, the evidence shows that they were very rarely interrupted in their normal sleeping and eating time, and these are pursuits of a purely private nature which would presumably occupy the employees' time whether they were on duty or not and which apparently could be pursued adequately and comfortably in the required circumstances; the rest of the time is different because there is nothing in the record to suggest that, even though pleasurably spent, it was spent in the ways the men would have chosen had they been free to do so.

There is no statutory provision as to what, if any, deference courts should pay to the Administrator's conclusions. And, while we have given them notice, we have had no occasion to try to prescribe their influence. The rulings of this

Administrator are not reached as a result of hearing adversary proceedings in which he finds facts from evidence and reaches conclusions of law from findings of fact. They are not, of course, conclusive, even in the cases with which they directly deal, much less in those to which they apply only by analogy. They do not constitute an interpretation of the Act or a standard for judging factual situations which binds a district court's processes, as an authoritative pronouncement of a higher court might do. But the Administrator's policies are made in pursuance of official duty, based upon more specialized experience and broader investigations and information than is likely to come to a judge in a particular case. They do determine the policy which will guide applications for enforcement by injunction on behalf of the Government. Good administration of the Act and good judicial administration alike require that the standards of public enforcement and those for determining private rights shall be at variance only where justified by very good reasons. The fact that the Administrator's policies and standards are not reached by trial in adversary form does not mean that they are not entitled to respect. This Court has long given considerable and in some cases decisive weight to Treasury Decisions and to interpretative regulations of the Treasury and of other bodies that were not of adversary origin.

We consider that the rulings, interpretations and opinions of the Administrator under this Act, while not controlling upon the courts by reason of their authority, do constitute a body of experience and informed judgment to which courts and litigants may properly resort for guidance. The weight of such a judgment in a particular case will depend upon the thoroughness evident in its consideration, the validity of its reasoning, its consistency with earlier and later pronouncements, and all those factors which give it power to persuade, if lacking power to control.

The courts in the *Armour* case weighed the evidence in the particular case in the light of the Administrator's rulings and reached a result consistent therewith. The evidence in this case in some respects, such as the understanding as to separate compensation for answering alarms, is different. Each case must stand on its own facts. But in this case, although the District Court referred to the Administrator's Bulletin, its evaluation and inquiry were apparently restricted by its notion that waiting time may not be work, an understanding of the law which we hold to be erroneous. Accordingly, the judgment is reversed and the cause remanded for further proceedings consistent herewith. Reversed.

QUESTIONS

1. What is the legal issue? How do we know that it is an "issue of law" (as opposed to an issue of fact)?
2. Is the agency interpretation binding as law?
3. What is the relevance of the agency interpretation?
4. What *theory* for deference to the agency can we infer from the weight-determining factors that the Court lists?
5. In particular, why give greater weight to agency interpretations that have been consistent?
6. Should a court give greater weight to agency interpretations that are more contemporaneous with passage of the statute?

CHEVRON U.S.A. v. NRDC
467 U.S. 837 (1984)

JUSTICE STEVENS delivered the opinion of the Court.

In the Clean Air Act Amendments of 1977, Pub. L. 95-95, 91 Stat. 685, Congress enacted certain requirements applicable to States that had not achieved the national air quality standards established by the Environmental Protection Agency (EPA) pursuant to earlier legislation. The amended Clean Air Act required these "nonattainment" States to establish a permit program regulating "new or modified major stationary sources" of air pollution. Generally, a permit may not be issued for a new or modified major stationary source unless several stringent conditions are met. The EPA regulation promulgated to implement this permit requirement allows a State to adopt a plantwide definition of the term "stationary source."[2] Under this definition, an existing plant that contains several pollution-emitting devices may install or modify one piece of equipment without meeting the permit conditions if the alteration will not increase the total emissions from the plant. The question presented by these cases is whether EPA's decision to allow States to treat all of the pollution-emitting devices within the same industrial grouping as though they were encased within a single "bubble" is based on a reasonable construction of the statutory term "stationary source."

I

The EPA regulations containing the plantwide definition of the term stationary source were promulgated on October 14, 1981. Respondents filed a timely petition for review in the United States Court of Appeals for the District of Columbia Circuit pursuant to 42 U.S.C. § 7607(b)(1). The Court of Appeals set aside the regulations.

The court observed that the relevant part of the amended Clean Air Act "does not explicitly define what Congress envisioned as a 'stationary source,' to which the permit program . . . should apply," and further stated that the precise issue was not "squarely addressed in the legislative history." In light of its conclusion that the legislative history bearing on the question was "at best contradictory," it reasoned that "the purposes of the non-attainment program should guide our decision here." Based on two of its precedents concerning the applicability of the bubble concept to certain Clean Air Act programs, the court stated that the bubble concept was "mandatory" in programs designed merely to maintain existing air quality, but held that it was "inappropriate" in programs enacted to improve air quality. Since the purpose of the permit program — its "*raison d'etre*," in the court's view — was to improve air quality, the court held that the bubble concept was inapplicable in these cases under its prior precedents. It

---

2. "(i) 'Stationary source' means any building, structure, facility, or installation which emits or may emit any air pollutant subject to regulation under the Act."

"(ii) 'Building, structure, facility, or installation' means all of the pollutant-emitting activities which belong to the same industrial grouping, are located on one or more contiguous or adjacent properties, and are under the control of the same person (or persons under common control) except the activities of any vessel." 40 CFR §§ 51.18(j)(1)(i) and (ii) (1983).

therefore set aside the regulations embodying the bubble concept as contrary to law. We granted certiorari to review that judgment, and we now reverse.

The basic legal error of the Court of Appeals was to adopt a static judicial definition of the term "stationary source" when it had decided that Congress itself had not commanded that definition. Respondents do not defend the legal reasoning of the Court of Appeals. Nevertheless, since this Court reviews judgments, not opinions, we must determine whether the Court of Appeals' legal error resulted in an erroneous judgment on the validity of the regulations.

II

When a court reviews an agency's construction of the statute which it administers, it is confronted with two questions. First, always, is the question whether Congress has directly spoken to the precise question at issue. If the intent of Congress is clear, that is the end of the matter; for the court, as well as the agency, must give effect to the unambiguously expressed intent of Congress.[9] If, however, the court determines Congress has not directly addressed the precise question at issue, the court does not simply impose its own construction on the statute, as would be necessary in the absence of an administrative interpretation. Rather, if the statute is silent or ambiguous with respect to the specific issue, the question for the court is whether the agency's answer is based on a permissible construction of the statute.[11]

"The power of an administrative agency to administer a congressionally created . . . program necessarily requires the formulation of policy and the making of rules to fill any gap left, implicitly or explicitly, by Congress." If Congress has explicitly left a gap for the agency to fill, there is an express delegation of authority to the agency to elucidate a specific provision of the statute by regulation. Such legislative regulations are given controlling weight unless they are arbitrary, capricious, or manifestly contrary to the statute. Sometimes the legislative delegation to an agency on a particular question is implicit rather than explicit. In such a case, a court may not substitute its own construction of a statutory provision for a reasonable interpretation made by the administrator of an agency.

We have long recognized that considerable weight should be accorded to an executive department's construction of a statutory scheme it is entrusted to administer, and the principle of deference to administrative interpretations

> "has been consistently followed by this Court whenever decision as to the meaning or reach of a statute has involved reconciling conflicting policies, and a full understanding of the force of the statutory policy in the given situation has depended upon more than ordinary knowledge respecting the matters subjected to agency regulations. *See,* e.g., *National Broadcasting Co. v. United States,* 319 U.S. 190; *Labor Board v. Hearst Publications, Inc.,* 322 U.S. 111; *Republic Aviation Corp. v.*

---

9. The judiciary is the final authority on issues of statutory construction and must reject administrative constructions which are contrary to clear congressional intent. If a court, employing traditional tools of statutory construction, ascertains that Congress had an intention on the precise question at issue, that intention is the law and must be given effect.

11. The court need not conclude that the agency construction was the only one it permissibly could have adopted to uphold the construction, or even the reading the court would have reached if the question initially had arisen in a judicial proceeding.

Labor Board, 324 U.S. 793; *Securities & Exchange Comm'n v. Chenery Corp.*, 332 U.S. 194; *Labor Board v. Seven-Up Bottling Co.*, 344 U.S. 344.

"...If this choice represents a reasonable accommodation of conflicting policies that were committed to the agency's care by the statute, we should not disturb it unless it appears from the statute or its legislative history that the accommodation is not one that Congress would have sanctioned." *United States v. Shimer*, 367 U.S. 374, 382, 383 (1961).

In light of these well-settled principles it is clear that the Court of Appeals misconceived the nature of its role in reviewing the regulations at issue. Once it determined, after its own examination of the legislation, that Congress did not actually have an intent regarding the applicability of the bubble concept to the permit program, the question before it was not whether in its view the concept is "inappropriate" in the general context of a program designed to improve air quality, but whether the Administrator's view that it is appropriate in the context of this particular program is a reasonable one. Based on the examination of the legislation and its history which follows, we agree with the Court of Appeals that Congress did not have a specific intention on the applicability of the bubble concept in these cases, and conclude that the EPA's use of that concept here is a reasonable policy choice for the agency to make.

[In Sections III and IV of its opinion, the Court summarized the history of the development of the Clean Air Act, initially enacted in its present structure in 1970. The Court stated that statute had:

directed the EPA to promulgate National Ambient Air Quality Standards (NAAQS's) and §110 directed the States to develop plans (SIP's) to implement the standards within specified deadlines. In addition, §111 provided that major new sources of pollution would be required to conform to technology-based performance standards; the EPA was directed to publish a list of categories of sources of pollution and to establish new source performance standards (NSPS) for each. Section 111(e) prohibited the operation of any new source in violation of a performance standard.

Section 111(a) defined the terms that are to be used in setting and enforcing standards of performance for new stationary sources. It provided:

For purposes of this section: ...
    (3) The term "stationary source" means any building, structure, facility, or installation which emits or may emit any air pollutant. 84 Stat. 1683.

In describing the implementation of the 1970 Act, the Court stated that, "[i]n 1974, [EPA] issued NSPS's for the nonferrous smelting industry that provided that the standards would not apply to the modification of major smelting units if their increased emissions were offset by reductions in other portions of the same plant."

The Court's summary focused particular attention on portions of the Act adopted in 1977 to address the fact that many areas had been unable to attain the NAAQS by the original statutory deadlines. As a result of the 1977 Amendments, major new sources locating in such nonattainment areas had to obtain a special permit and meet stringent regulatory requirements. The Court included the following discussion:

The 1977 Amendments contain no specific reference to the "bubble concept." Nor do they contain a specific definition of the term "stationary source," though they did not disturb the definition of "stationary source" contained in § 111(a)(3), applicable by the terms of the Act to the NSPS program. Section 302(j), however, defines the term "major stationary source" as follows:

"(j) Except as otherwise expressly provided, the terms "major stationary source" and "major emitting facility" mean any stationary facility or source of air pollutants which directly emits, or has the potential to emit, one hundred tons per year or more of any air pollutant (including any major emitting facility or source of fugitive emissions of any such pollutant, as determined by rule by the Administrator)." 91 Stat. 770.

V

The legislative history of the portion of the 1977 Amendments dealing with nonattainment areas does not contain any specific comment on the "bubble concept" or the question whether a plantwide definition of a stationary source is permissible under the permit program. . . .

VI

As previously noted, prior to the 1977 Amendments, the EPA had adhered to a plantwide definition of the term "source" under a NSPS program. . . .

In August 1980, . . . the EPA adopted a regulation that, in essence, applied the basic reasoning of the Court of Appeals in these cases. The EPA took particular note of the two then-recent Court of Appeals decisions, which had created the bright-line rule that the "bubble concept" should be employed in a program designed to maintain air quality but not in one designed to enhance air quality. Relying heavily on those cases, EPA adopted a dual definition of "source" for nonattainment areas that required a permit whenever a change in either the entire plant, or one of its components, would result in a significant increase in emissions even if the increase was completely offset by reductions elsewhere in the plant. The EPA expressed the opinion that this interpretation was "more consistent with congressional intent" than the plantwide definition because it "would bring in more sources or modifications for review," but its primary legal analysis was predicated on the two Court of Appeals decisions.

In 1981 a new administration took office and initiated a "Government-wide reexamination of regulatory burdens and complexities." In the context of that review, the EPA reevaluated the various arguments that had been advanced in connection with the proper definition of the term "source" and concluded that the term should be given the same definition in both nonattainment areas and PSD areas.

In explaining its conclusion, the EPA first noted that the definitional issue was not squarely addressed in either the statute or its legislative history and therefore that the issue involved an agency "judgment as how to best carry out the Act." It then set forth several reasons for concluding that the plantwide definition was more appropriate. It pointed out that the dual definition "can act as a disincentive to new investment and modernization by discouraging modifications to existing facilities" and "can actually retard progress in air pollution control by discouraging replacement of older, dirtier processes or pieces of equipment with new, cleaner ones." Moreover, the new definition "would simplify EPA's rules by using the same definition of 'source' for [the attainment program], nonattainment new source review and the construction moratorium. This reduces confusion and inconsistency." Finally, the agency explained that additional requirements that remained in place would accomplish the fundamental purposes of achieving attainment with NAAQS's as expeditiously as possible. These conclusions were expressed in a proposed rulemaking in August 1981 that was formally promulgated in October.

VII

In this Court respondents expressly reject the basic rationale of the Court of Appeals' decision. That court viewed the statutory definition of the term "source" as sufficiently flexible to cover either a plantwide definition, a narrower definition covering each unit within a plant, or a dual definition that could apply to both the entire "bubble" and its components. It interpreted the policies of the statute, however, to mandate the plantwide definition in programs designed to maintain clean air and to forbid it in programs designed to improve air quality. Respondents place a fundamentally different construction on the statute. They contend that the text of the Act requires the EPA to use a dual definition — if either a component of a plant, or the plant as a whole, emits over 100 tons of pollutant, it is a major stationary source. They thus contend that the EPA rules adopted in 1980, insofar as they apply to the maintenance of the quality of clean air, as well as the 1981 rules which apply to nonattainment areas, violate the statute.

STATUTORY LANGUAGE

The definition of the term "stationary source" in § 111(a)(3) refers to "any building, structure, facility, or installation" which emits air pollution. This definition is applicable only to the NSPS program by the express terms of the statute; the text of the statute does not make this definition applicable to the permit program. Petitioners therefore maintain that there is no statutory language even relevant to ascertaining the meaning of stationary source in the permit program aside from § 302(j), which defines the term "major stationary source." We disagree with petitioners on this point.

The definition in § 302(j) tells us what the word "major" means — a source must emit at least 100 tons of pollution to qualify — but it sheds virtually no light on the meaning of the term "stationary source." It does equate a source with a facility — a "major emitting facility" and a "major stationary source" are synonymous under § 302(j). The ordinary meaning of the term "facility" is some collection of integrated elements which has been designed and constructed to achieve some purpose. Moreover, it is certainly no affront to common English usage to take a reference to a major facility or a major source to connote an entire plant as opposed to its constituent parts. Basically, however, the language of § 302(j) simply does not compel any given interpretation of the term "source."

Respondents recognize that, and hence point to § 111(a)(3). Although the definition in that section is not literally applicable to the permit program, it sheds as much light on the meaning of the word "source" as anything in the statute. As respondents point out, use of the words "building, structure, facility, or installation," as the definition of source, could be read to impose the permit conditions on an individual building that is a part of a plant. A "word may have a character of its own not to be submerged by its association." *Russell Motor Car Co. v. United States*, 261 U.S. 514, 519 (1923). On the other hand, the meaning of a word must be ascertained in the context of achieving particular objectives, and the words associated with it may indicate that the true meaning of the series is to convey a common idea. The language may reasonably be interpreted to impose the requirement on any discrete, but integrated, operation which pollutes. This gives meaning to all of the terms — a single building, not part of a larger operation, would be covered if it emits more than 100 tons of pollution, as would any facility, structure, or installation. Indeed, the language itself implies a "bubble concept" of sorts: each enumerated item would seem to be treated as if it were encased in a bubble. While respondents insist that each of these terms must be given a discrete meaning, they also argue that § 111(a)(3) defines "source" as that term is used in § 302(j). The latter section, however, equates a source with a facility, whereas the former defines "source" as a facility, among other items.

We are not persuaded that parsing of general terms in the text of the statute will reveal an actual intent of Congress. We know full well that this language is not dispositive; the terms are overlapping and the language is not precisely directed to the question of the applicability of a given term in the context of a larger operation. To the extent any congressional "intent" can be discerned from this language, it would appear that the listing of overlapping, illustrative terms was intended to enlarge, rather than to confine, the scope of the agency's power to regulate particular sources in order to effectuate the policies of the Act.

LEGISLATIVE HISTORY

In addition, respondents argue that the legislative history and policies of the Act foreclose the plantwide definition, and that the EPA's interpretation is not entitled to deference because it represents a sharp break with prior interpretations of the Act.

Based on our examination of the legislative history, we agree with the Court of Appeals that it is unilluminating. . . .

Our review of the EPA's varying interpretations of the word "source" — both before and after the 1977 Amendments — convinces us that the agency primarily responsible for administering this important legislation has consistently interpreted it flexibly — not in a sterile textual vacuum, but in the context of implementing policy decisions in a technical and complex arena. The fact that the agency has from time to time changed its interpretation of the term "source" does not, as respondents argue, lead us to conclude that no deference should be accorded the agency's interpretation of the statute. An initial agency interpretation is not instantly carved in stone. On the contrary, the agency, to engage in informed rulemaking, must consider varying interpretations and the wisdom of its policy on a continuing basis. Moreover, the fact that the agency has adopted different definitions in different contexts adds force to the argument that the definition itself is flexible, particularly since Congress has never indicated any disapproval of a flexible reading of the statute.

Significantly, it was not the agency in 1980, but rather the Court of Appeals that read the statute inflexibly to command a plantwide definition for programs designed to maintain clean air and to forbid such a definition for programs designed to improve air quality. The distinction the court drew may well be a sensible one, but our labored review of the problem has surely disclosed that it is not a distinction that Congress ever articulated itself, or one that the EPA found in the statute before the courts began to review the legislative work product. We conclude that it was the Court of Appeals, rather than Congress or any of the decisionmakers who are authorized by Congress to administer this legislation, that was primarily responsible for the 1980 position taken by the agency.

POLICY

The arguments over policy that are advanced in the parties' briefs create the impression that respondents are now waging in a judicial forum a specific policy battle which they ultimately lost in the agency and in the 32 jurisdictions opting for the "bubble concept," but one which was never waged in the Congress. Such policy arguments are more properly addressed to legislators or administrators, not to judges.

In these cases the Administrator's interpretation represents a reasonable accommodation of manifestly competing interests and is entitled to deference: the regulatory scheme is technical and complex, the agency considered the matter in a detailed and reasoned fashion, and the decision involves reconciling conflicting policies. Congress intended to accommodate both interests, but did not do so itself on the level of specificity presented by these cases. Perhaps that body consciously desired the Administrator to strike the balance at this level, thinking that those with great expertise and charged with responsibility for administering the provision would be in a better position to do so; perhaps it simply did not consider the question at this level; and perhaps Congress was unable to forge a coalition on either side of the question, and those on each side decided to take their chances with the scheme devised by the agency. For judicial purposes, it matters not which of these things occurred.

Judges are not experts in the field, and are not part of either political branch of the Government. Courts must, in some cases, reconcile competing political interests, but not on the basis of the judges' personal policy preferences. In contrast, an agency to which Congress has delegated policymaking responsibilities may, within the limits of that delegation, properly rely upon the incumbent administration's views of wise policy to inform its judgments. While agencies are not directly accountable to the people, the Chief Executive is, and it is entirely appropriate for this political branch of the Government to make such policy choices — resolving the competing interests which Congress itself either inadvertently did not resolve, or intentionally left to be resolved by the agency charged with the administration of the statute in light of everyday realities.

When a challenge to an agency construction of a statutory provision, fairly conceptualized, really centers on the wisdom of the agency's policy, rather than whether it is a reasonable choice within a gap left open by Congress, the challenge must fail. In such a case, federal judges — who have no constituency — have a duty to respect legitimate policy choices made by those who do. The responsibilities for assessing the wisdom of such policy choices and resolving the struggle between competing views of the public interest are not judicial ones: "Our Constitution vests such responsibilities in the political branches." *TVA v. Hill*, 437 U.S. 153, 195 (1978). We hold that the EPA's definition of the term "source" is a permissible construction of the statute which seeks to accommodate progress in reducing air pollution with economic growth. "The Regulations which the Administrator has adopted provide what the agency could allowably view as . . . [an] effective reconciliation of these twofold ends. . . ." *United States v. Shimer,* 367 U.S., at 383.

The judgment of the Court of Appeals is reversed. *It is so ordered.* [Justices Marshall, Rehnquist, and O'Connor did not participate in the decision.]

QUESTIONS

1. Does this case involve review of a legal issue, a factual issue, or an exercise of discretion?
2. How does the Court's analysis differ from that of the Kentucky court in *Jewish Hospital?* From a public policy standpoint, which standard is preferable?
3. Do you think the Kentucky Court of Appeals would have reached a different conclusion in *Jewish Hospital* if it had applied the *Chevron* doctrine? Does 1981 MSAPA § 5-116(c)(4) endorse or foreclose the application of *Chevron*-type deference?
4. Does an agency need to be consistent in its interpretation to warrant court deference under *Chevron?*
5. What arguments remain for litigants challenging agency action as contrary to the organic statute? Can public policy arguments be used at all?
6. Why should statutory ambiguity lead to deference to the agency? Is that what Congress would want? Is there a difference between (a) Congress having a single intent poorly expressed and (b) Congress intending to let the executive give concreteness to a vague provision? Why should the Court generally presume the latter?
7. Should *Chevron* deference apply to constitutional interpretation? To one agency's interpretation of statutes that apply to many agencies? To an agency's interpretation of whether language in its organic statute triggers formal adjudication under APA § 554? (For an affirmative answer to the last question, *see Chemical Waste Management v. EPA,* 873 F.2d 1477 (D.C. Cir. 1989).)
8. How is the *Chevron* theory different from the *Skidmore* theory?
9. The Court in footnote 9 states that "[i]f a court, employing traditional tools of statutory construction, ascertains that Congress had an intention on the precise question at issue, that intention is the law and must be given effect." Did the *Chevron* Court believe that those "traditional tools" included legislative history? In *I.N.S. v. Cardoza-Fonseca,* 480 U.S. 421, 452-53 (1987), Justice Scalia, writing only for himself, concurred in the Court's judgment, because he rejected the majority's consideration of legislative history, which he believed to reflect "an ill-advised deviation from the venerable principle that if the language of a statute is clear, that language must be given effect — at least in the absence of a patent absurdity." *Id.* at 452 (citations omitted). This disagreement within the Court remains to this day. Compare *Zuni Public School District No. 89 v. Department of Education,* 550 U.S. 81, 90 (2007) ("Considerations other than [statutory] language provide us with unusually strong indications that Congress intended to leave the Secretary free to use the calculation method before us and that the Secretary's chosen method is a reasonable one") with *id.* at 108 (Scalia, J., dissenting) ("today's decision is nothing other than the elevation of judge-

supposed legislative intent over clear statutory text. The plain language of the federal Impact Aid statute clearly and unambiguously forecloses the Secretary of Education's preferred methodology for determining whether a State's school-funding system is equalized. Her selection of that methodology is therefore entitled to zero deference under *Chevron*"). Justice Scalia was joined in the *Zuni Public School* dissent by Chief Justice Roberts and Justice Thomas in claiming that the Court must rely on the meaning of the statute's text, rather than on legislative intent.

10. How clear must the intent of Congress be in order to meet the first step of *Chevron* and be "the end of the matter"? The next case deals with that question. If Congress cannot help writing ambiguous statutes because of the vicissitudes of the legislative process, then *Chevron* has enormous significance in its resulting assignment of extensive discretion to the administrative agencies. But if reviewing courts find most statutes *not* to be ambiguous at Step 1, then *Chevron*'s potential for freeing agencies to interpret statutes as they see fit is a great deal more limited.

MCI TELECOMMUNICATIONS CORP. v. AT&T CO.
512 U.S. 218 (1994)

Justice Scalia delivered the opinion of the Court.

Section 203(a) of Title 47 of the United States Code requires communications common carriers to file tariffs with the Federal Communications Commission, and § 203(b) authorizes the Commission to "modify" any requirement of § 203. These cases present the question whether the Commission's decision to make tariff filing optional for all nondominant long-distance carriers is a valid exercise of its modification authority.

[In Section I, the Court recited the history of the FCC's use of filed tariffs to regulate interstate telephone call charges.]

II

Section 203 of the Communications Act contains both the filed rate provisions of the Act and the Commission's disputed modification authority. It provides in relevant part:

"(a) Filing; public display.
   "Every common carrier, except connecting carriers, shall, within such reasonable time as the Commission shall designate, file with the Commission and print and keep open for public inspection schedules showing all charges . . . , whether such charges are joint or separate, and showing the classifications, practices, and regulations affecting such charges. . . .
"(b) Changes in schedule; discretion of Commission to modify requirements.
   "(1) No change shall be made in the charges, classifications, regulations, or practices which have been so filed and published except after one hundred and twenty days notice to the Commission and to the public, which shall be published in such form and contain such information as the Commission may by regulations prescribe.
   "(2) The Commission may, in its discretion and for good cause shown, modify any requirement made by or under the authority of this section either in

> particular instances or by general order applicable to special circumstances or conditions except that the Commission may not require the notice period specified in paragraph (1) to be more than one hundred and twenty days. . . ."

The dispute between the parties turns on the meaning of the phrase "modify any requirement" in § 203(b)(2). Petitioners argue that it gives the Commission authority to make even basic and fundamental changes in the scheme created by that section. We disagree. The word "modify" — like a number of other English words employing the root "mod-" (deriving from the Latin word for "measure"), such as "moderate," "modulate," "modest," and "modicum" — has a connotation of increment or limitation. Virtually every dictionary we are aware of says that "to modify" means to change moderately or in minor fashion. *See*, e.g., Random House Dictionary of the English Language 1236 (2d ed. 1987) ("to change somewhat the form or qualities of; alter partially; amend"); Webster's Third New International Dictionary 1452 (1981) ("to make minor changes in the form or structure of: alter without transforming"); 9 Oxford English Dictionary 952 (2d ed. 1989) ("[t]o make partial changes in; to change (an object) in respect of some of its qualities; to alter or vary without radical transformation"); Black's Law Dictionary 1004 (6th ed. 1990) ("[t]o alter; to change in incidental or subordinate features; enlarge; extend; amend; limit; reduce").

In support of their position, petitioners cite dictionary definitions contained in, or derived from, a single source, Webster's Third New International Dictionary 1452 (1981) (Webster's Third), which includes among the meanings of "modify," "to make a basic or important change in." Petitioners contend that this establishes sufficient ambiguity to entitle the Commission to deference in its acceptance of the broader meaning, which in turn requires approval of its permissive detariffing policy. *See Chevron U.S.A. Inc. v. Natural Resources Defense Council, Inc.*, 467 U.S. 837, 843 (1984). In short, they contend that the courts must defer to the agency's choice among available dictionary definitions, citing *National Railroad Passenger Corporation v. Boston & Maine Corp.*, 503 U.S. 407, 418 (1992).

. . . But what petitioners demand that we accept as creating an ambiguity here is a rarity even rarer than that: a meaning set forth in a single dictionary (and, as we say, its progeny) which not only *supplements* the meaning contained in all other dictionaries, but *contradicts* one of the meanings contained in virtually all other dictionaries. Indeed, contradicts one of the alternative meanings contained in the out-of-step dictionary itself — for as we have observed, Webster's Third itself defines "modify" to connote *both* (specifically) major change *and* (specifically) minor change. It is hard to see how that can be. When the word "modify" has come to mean *both* "to change in some respects" *and* "to change fundamentally" it will in fact mean *neither* of those things. It will simply mean "to change," and some adverb will have to be called into service to indicate the great or small degree of the change.

If that is what the peculiar Webster's Third definition means to suggest has happened — and what petitioners suggest by appealing to Webster's Third — we simply disagree. "Modify," in our view, connotes moderate change. It might be good English to say that the French Revolution "modified" the status of the French nobility — but only because there is a figure of speech called understatement and a literary device known as sarcasm. And it might be unsurprising to discover a 1972 White House press release saying that "the Administration is modifying its position with regard to prosecution of the war in Vietnam"—but only because press agents tend to impart what is nowadays called "spin." Such intentional distortions, or simply careless or ignorant misuse, must have formed the basis for the usage that Webster's Third, and Webster's Third alone, reported. It is perhaps gilding the lily to add this: In 1934, when the Communications Act became law—the most relevant time for determining a statutory term's meaning, *see Perrin v. United States*, 444 U.S. 37, 42-45 (1979)—Webster's Third was not yet even contemplated. To our knowledge *all* English dictionaries provided the narrow definition of "modify," including those published by G. & C. Merriam Company. *See* Webster's New International Dictionary 1577 (2d ed. 1934); Webster's Collegiate Dictionary 628 (4th ed. 1934). We have not the slightest doubt that is the meaning the statute intended.

Beyond the word itself, a further indication that the § 203(b)(2) authority to "modify" does not contemplate fundamental changes is the sole exception to that authority which the section provides. One of the requirements of § 203 is that changes to filed tariffs can be made only after 120 days' notice to the Commission and the public. § 203(b)(1). The *only* exception to the Commission's § 203(b)(2) modification authority is as follows: "except that the Commission may not require the notice period specified in paragraph (1) to be more than one hundred and twenty days." Is it conceivable that the statute is indifferent to the Commission's power to eliminate the tariff-filing requirement entirely for all except one firm in the long-distance sector, and yet strains out the gnat of extending the waiting period for tariff revision beyond 120 days? We think not. The exception is not as ridiculous as a Lilliputian in London only because it is to be found in Lilliput: in the small-scale world of "modifications," it is a big deal.

Since an agency's interpretation of a statute is not entitled to deference when it goes beyond the meaning that the statute can bear, *see*, e.g., *Pittston Coal Group v. Sebben*, 488 U.S. 105, 113 (1988); *Chevron*, 467 U.S., at 842-843, the Commission's permissive detariffing policy can be justified only if it makes a less than radical or fundamental change in the Act's tariff-filing requirement. The Commission's attempt to establish that no more than that is involved greatly understates the extent to which its policy deviates from the filing requirement, and greatly undervalues the importance of the filing requirement itself. . . .

Much of the rest of the Communications Act subchapter applicable to Common Carriers, *see* 47 U.S.C. §§ 201-228, and the Act's Procedural and Administrative Provisions, 47 U.S.C. §§ 401-416, are premised upon the tariff-filing requirement of § 203. For example, § 415 defines "over-charges" (which customers are entitled to recover) by reference to the filed rate. *See* § 415(g). The provisions allowing customers and competitors to challenge rates as unreasonable or as discriminatory, *see* 47 U.S.C. §§ 204, 206-208, 406, would not be susceptible of effective enforcement if rates were not publicly filed. See *Maislin, supra*, at 132. Rate filings are, in fact, the essential characteristic of a rate-regulated industry. It is highly unlikely that Congress would leave the determination of whether an industry will be entirely, or even substantially, rate-regulated to agency discretion—and even more unlikely that it would achieve that through such a subtle device as permission to "modify" rate-filing requirements.

Bearing in mind, then, the enormous importance to the statutory scheme of the tariff-filing provision, we turn to whether what has occurred here can be considered a mere "modification." . . . What we have here, in reality, is a fundamental revision of the statute, changing it from a scheme of rate regulation in long-distance common-carrier communications to a scheme of rate regulation only where effective competition does not exist. That may be a good idea, but it was not the idea Congress enacted into law in 1934. . . .

. . . As we noted earlier this Term, there is considerable "debate in other forums about the wisdom of the filed rate doctrine," *Security Services, Inc. v. Kmart Corp.*, 511 U.S. 431, 440 (1994), and, more broadly, about the value of continued regulation of the telecommunications industry. But our estimations, and the Commission's estimations, of desirable policy cannot alter the meaning of the Federal Communications Act of 1934. For better or worse, the Act establishes a rate-regulation, filed-tariff system for common-carrier communications, and the Commission's desire "to 'increase competition' cannot provide [it] authority to alter the well-established statutory filed rate requirements," *Maislin*, 497 U.S., at 135. As we observed in the context of a dispute over the filed-rate doctrine more than 80 years ago, "such considerations address themselves to Congress, not to the courts," *Armour Packing*, 209 U.S., at 82.

We do not mean to suggest that the tariff-filing requirement is so inviolate that the Commission's existing modification authority does not reach it at all. Certainly the Commission can modify the form, contents, and location of required filings, and can defer filing or perhaps even waive it altogether in limited circumstances. But what we have here goes well beyond that. It is effectively the introduction of a whole new regime of regulation (or of free-market competition), which may well be a better regime but is not the one that Congress established.

The judgment of the Court of Appeals is *Affirmed.*

JUSTICE STEVENS, with whom JUSTICE BLACKMUN and JUSTICE SOUTER join, dissenting.

The communications industry has an unusually dynamic character. In 1934, Congress authorized the Federal Communications Commission (FCC or Commission) to regulate "a field of enterprise the dominant characteristic of which was the rapid pace of its unfolding." *National Broadcasting Co. v. United States*, 319 U.S. 190, 219 (1943). The Communications Act of 1934 (Act) gives the FCC unusually broad discretion to meet new and unanticipated problems in order to fulfill its sweeping mandate "to make available, so far as possible, to all the people of the United States, a rapid, efficient, Nation-wide and world-wide wire and radio communication service with adequate facilities at reasonable charges." 47 U.S.C. § 151. This Court's consistent interpretation of the Act has afforded the Commission ample leeway to interpret and apply its statutory powers and responsibilities. *See*, e.g., *United States v. Southwestern Cable Co.*, 392 U.S. 157, 172-173 (1968); *FCC v. Pottsville Broadcasting Co.*, 309 U.S. 134, 138 (1940). The Court today abandons that approach in favor of a rigid literalism that deprives the FCC of the flexibility Congress meant it to have in order to implement the core policies of the Act in rapidly changing conditions. . . .

III

Although the majority observes that further relaxation of tariff-filing requirements might more effectively enhance competition, it does not take issue with
the Commission's conclusions that mandatory filing of tariff schedules serves no
useful purpose and is actually counter-productive in the case of carriers who lack
market power. As the Commission had noted in its prior detariffing orders, see,
e.g., 84 F.C.C. 2d, at 479-480, if a nondominant carrier sought to charge inflated
rates, "customers would simply move to other carriers." Moreover, an absence of
market power will ordinarily preclude firms of any kind from engaging in price
discrimination. *See*, e.g., L. Sullivan, Law of Antitrust 89 (1977) ("A firm will not
discriminate unless it has market power"); 9 P. Areeda, Anti-trust Law ¶ 1711a,
pp. 119-120 (1991). The Commission plausibly concluded that any slight
enforcement benefits a tariff-filing requirement might offer were outweighed
by the burdens it would put on new entrants and consumers. Thus, the sole
question for us is whether the FCC's policy, however sensible, is nonetheless
inconsistent with the Act.

In my view, each of the Commission's detariffing orders was squarely within its
power to "modify any requirement" of § 203. Section 203(b)(2) plainly confers
at least some discretion to modify the general rule that carriers file tariffs, for it
speaks of "*any* requirement."[2] Section 203(c) of the Act, ignored by the Court,
squarely supports the FCC's position; it prohibits carriers from providing service
without a tariff "*unless otherwise provided by or under authority of this Act.*" Section
203(b)(2) is plainly one provision that "otherwise provides," and thereby
authorizes, service without a filed schedule. The FCC's authority to modify
§ 203's requirements in "particular instances" or by "general order applicable
to special circumstances or conditions" emphasizes the expansive character of
the Commission's authority: modifications may be narrow or broad, depending
upon the Commission's appraisal of current conditions. From the vantage of a
Congress seeking to regulate an almost completely monopolized industry, the
advent of competition is surely a "special circumstance or condition" that might
legitimately call for different regulatory treatment.

The only statutory exception to the Commission's modification authority
provides that it may not extend the 120-day notice period set out in
§ 203(b)(1). *See* § 203(b)(2). The Act thus imposes a specific limit on the Commission's authority to *stiffen* that regulatory imposition on carriers, but does not
confine the Commission's authority to *relax* it. It was no stretch for the FCC to
draw from this single, unidirectional statutory limitation on its modification
authority the inference that its authority is otherwise unlimited.

According to the Court, the term "modify," as explicated in all but the most
unreliable dictionaries, *ante* at n.3, rules out the Commission's claimed authority
to relieve nondominant carriers of the basic obligation to file tariffs. Dictionaries
can be useful aides in statutory interpretation, but they are no substitute for
close analysis of what words mean as used in a particular statutory content. . . .

The filed tariff provisions of the Communications Act are not ends in themselves, but are merely one of several procedural *means* for the Commission to
ensure that carriers do not charge unreasonable or discriminatory rates. See 84

2. Section 203(b)(2) must do more than merely allow the Commission to dictate the form and
contents of tariff filings, for § 203(b)(1) separately grants it that authority.

F.C.C. 2d, at 483. The Commission has reasonably concluded that this particular means of enforcing the statute's substantive mandates will prove counterproductive in the case of nondominant long-distance carriers. Even if the 1934 Congress did not define the scope of the Commission's modification authority with perfect scholarly precision, this is surely a paradigm case for judicial deference to the agency's interpretation, particularly in a statutory regime so obviously meant to maximize administrative flexibility.[7] Whatever the best reading of § 203(b)(2), the Commission's reading cannot in my view be termed unreasonable. It is informed (as ours is not) by a practical understanding of the role (or lack thereof) that filed tariffs play in the modern regulatory climate and in the telecommunications industry. Since 1979, the FCC has sought to adapt measures originally designed to control monopoly power to new market conditions. It has carefully and consistently explained that mandatory tariff-filing rules frustrate the core statutory interest in rate reasonableness. The Commission's use of the "discretion" expressly conferred by § 203(b)(2) reflects "a reasonable accommodation of manifestly competing interests and is entitled to deference: the regulatory scheme is technical and complex, the agency considered the matter in a detailed and reasoned fashion, and the decision involves reconciling conflicting policies." *Chevron U.S.A. v. Natural Resources Defense Council, Inc.*, 467 U.S. 837, 865 (1984) (footnotes omitted). The FCC has permissibly interpreted its § 203(b)(2) authority in service of the goals Congress set forth in the Act. We should sustain its eminently sound, experience-tested, and uncommonly well-explained judgment.

I respectfully dissent.

QUESTIONS

1. Is Justice Scalia's reliance on dictionary definitions of the word "modify" persuasive? If this is the proper way to approach *Chevron* questions, does the doctrine really represent a form of heightened judicial deference?
2. Should administrative agencies be free to "update" antiquated statutes without congressional approval, as Justice Stevens implicitly suggests? Or, rather, should the burden of inertia to update outdated statutes rest on Congress? In this regard, one should note that Congress relaxed the FCC's obligation to require tariff filings from long distance carriers in the Telecommunications Act of 1996. Which way does this fact cut?
3. Who has the better argument — Justice Scalia or Justice Stevens? Does the social and economic cost associated with retaining outdated or outmoded regulatory models justify a lawmaking model in which agencies and courts, in tandem, revise statutes without any input from Congress?

---

7. The majority considers it unlikely that Congress would have conferred power on the Commission to exempt carriers from the supposedly pivotal rate-filing obligation. But surely such a delegation is not out of place in a statute that also empowers the FCC, for example, to decide what the "public convenience, interest, or necessity" requires, see, *e.g.*, 47 U.S.C. § 303, and to "prescribe such rules and regulations as may be necessary in the public interest," § 201(b); see also § 154(i). The Court's rigid reading of § 202(b)(2) is out of step with our prior recognition that the 1934 Act was meant to be a "supple instrument for the exercise of discretion by the expert body which Congress has charged to carry out its legislative policy." *FCC v. Pottsville Broadcasting Co.*, 309 U.S. 134, 138 (1940).

4. Is Justice Scalia's approach "formalist" or "functionalist" in nature? What about Justice Stevens's?

5. Does the Court make use of any canons of construction in deciding that the agency acted unlawfully? Is the use of canons consistent with *Chevron*? One commentator has written that the canons of construction "are best understood as falling into two discrete categories: descriptive canons and normative canons." Stephen F. Ross, *Where Have You Gone, Karl Llewellyn? Should Congress Turn Its Lonely Eyes to You?*, 45 VAND. L. REV. 561, 563 (1992). Professor Ross stated that "[d]escriptive canons are principles that involve predictions as to what the legislature must have meant, or probably meant, by employing particular statutory language. . . . Rules of syntax or grammar, principles that statutory provisions should be read to avoid internal inconsistency or conflict with other enactments, . . . are examples of descriptive canons." *Id.* In contrast to the descriptive canons, "normative canons are principles, created in the federal system exclusively by judges, that do not purport to describe accurately what Congress actually intended or what the words of a statute mean, but rather direct courts to construe any ambiguity in a particular way in order to further some policy objective." Ross, *supra*, at 563 (footnote omitted). Should the application of "normative" canons render an ambiguous statute sufficiently clear that a court need not reach Step 2 of *Chevron*? The Supreme Court has applied arguably "normative" canons to decline to defer to an agency interpretation of a statute. *See Immigration and Naturalization Service v. St. Cyr*, 533 U.S. 289, 320 n.45 (2001) ("The INS argues that we should extend deference under [*Chevron*] to the BIA's interpretation of [the statute] as applying to all deportation proceedings initiated after [the statute's] effective date. We only defer, however, to agency interpretations of statutes that, applying the normal 'tools of statutory construction,' are ambiguous. . . . Because a statute that is ambiguous with respect to retroactive application is construed under our precedent to be unambiguously prospective, there is, for *Chevron* purposes, no ambiguity in such a statute for an agency to resolve"); *Solid Waste Agency of Northern Cook County (SWANCC) v. United States Army Corps of Engineers*, 531 U.S. 159, 174 (2001) ("We thus read the statute as written to avoid the significant constitutional and federalism questions raised by respondents' interpretation, and therefore reject the request for administrative deference"). Should the Court distinguish between descriptive and normative canons in its application of step 1 of the *Chevron* doctrine, given that the doctrine purports to leave policy-making decisions unresolved by Congress to agencies rather than courts?

6. Does the use of canons of construction determine whether an agency should receive *Chevron* deference when two statutes impose obligations on the agency that appear to conflict directly? In *National Ass'n of Home Builders v. Defenders of Wildlife*, 551 U.S. 644, 666 (2007), the majority, in an opinion written by Justice Alito, concluded that:

> We must therefore read §7(a)(2) of the [Endangered Species Act (ESA)] against the statutory backdrop of the many mandatory agency directives whose operation it would implicitly abrogate or repeal if it were construed as broadly as the Ninth Circuit did below. When §7(a)(2) is read this way, we are left with a fundamental ambiguity that is not resolved by the statutory text.

An agency cannot simultaneously obey the differing mandates set forth in § 7(a)(2) of the ESA and § 402(b) of the [Clean Water Act], and consequently the statutory language — read in light of the canon against implied repeals — does not itself provide clear guidance as to which command must give way.

In this situation, it is appropriate to look to the implementing agency's expert interpretation, which cabins § 7(a)(2)'s application to "actions in which there is discretionary Federal involvement or control." 50 CFR § 402.03. This reading harmonizes the statutes by applying § 7(a)(2) to guide agencies' existing discretionary authority, but not reading it to override express statutory mandates.

UNITED STATES v. MEAD CORP.
533 U.S. 218 (2001)

JUSTICE SOUTER delivered the opinion of the Court.

The question is whether a tariff classification ruling by the United States Customs Service deserves judicial deference. The Federal Circuit rejected Customs's invocation of *Chevron U.S.A. Inc. v. Natural Resources Defense Council, Inc.,* 467 U.S. 837 (1984), in support of such a ruling, to which it gave no deference. We agree that a tariff classification has no claim to judicial deference under *Chevron,* there being no indication that Congress intended such a ruling to carry the force of law, but we hold that under *Skidmore v. Swift & Co.,* 323 U.S. 134 (1944), the ruling is eligible to claim respect according to its persuasiveness.

I

A

Imports are taxed under the Harmonized Tariff Schedule of the United States (HTSUS), 19 U.S.C. § 1202. Title 19 U.S.C. § 1500(b) provides that Customs "shall, under rules and regulations prescribed by the Secretary [of the Treasury] . . . fix the final classification and rate of duty applicable to . . . merchandise" under the HTSUS. Section 1502(a) provides that

> "the Secretary of the Treasury shall establish and promulgate such rules and regulations not inconsistent with the law (including regulations establishing procedures for the issuance of binding rulings prior to the entry of the merchandise concerned), and may disseminate such information as may be necessary to secure a just, impartial, and uniform appraisement of imported merchandise and the classification and assessment of duties thereon at the various ports of entry."[1]

See also § 1624 (general delegation to Secretary to issue rules and regulations for the admission of goods).

The Secretary provides for tariff rulings before the entry of goods by regulations authorizing "ruling letters" setting tariff classifications for particular imports. 19 CFR § 177.8 (2000). A ruling letter

---

1. The statutory term "ruling" is defined by regulation as "a written statement . . . that interprets and applies the provisions of the Customs and related laws to a specific set of facts." 19 CFR § 177.1(d)(1) (2000).

"represents the official position of the Customs Service with respect to the particular transaction or issue described therein and is binding on all Customs Service personnel in accordance with the provisions of this section until modified or revoked. In the absence of a change of practice or other modification or revocation which affects the principle of the ruling set forth in the ruling letter, that principle may be cited as authority in the disposition of transactions involving the same circumstances." § 177.9(a).

After the transaction that gives it birth, a ruling letter is to "be applied only with respect to transactions involving articles identical to the sample submitted with the ruling request or to articles whose description is identical to the description set forth in the ruling letter." § 177.9(b)(2). As a general matter, such a letter is "subject to modification or revocation without notice to any person, except the person to whom the letter was addressed," § 177.9(c), and the regulations consequently provide that "no other person should rely on the ruling letter or assume that the principles of that ruling will be applied in connection with any transaction other than the one described in the letter," *ibid.* Since ruling letters respond to transactions of the moment, they are not subject to notice and comment before being issued, may be published but need only be made "available for public inspection," 19 U.S.C. § 1625(a), and, at the time this action arose, could be modified without notice and comment under most circumstances, 19 CFR § 177.10(c) (2000). A broader notice-and-comment requirement for modification of prior rulings was added by statute in 1993, and took effect after this case arose.

Any of the 46 port-of-entry Customs offices may issue ruling letters, and so may the Customs Headquarters Office, in providing "advice or guidance as to the interpretation or proper application of the Customs and related laws with respect to a specific Customs transaction [which] may be requested by Customs Service field offices . . . at any time, whether the transaction is prospective, current, or completed," 19 CFR § 177.11(a) (2000). Most ruling letters contain little or no reasoning, but simply describe goods and state the appropriate category and tariff. A few letters, like the Headquarters ruling at issue here, set out a rationale in some detail.

B

Respondent, the Mead Corporation, imports "day planners," three-ring binders with pages having room for notes of daily schedules and phone numbers and addresses, together with a calendar and suchlike. The tariff schedule on point falls under the HTSUS heading for "registers, account books, notebooks, order books, receipt books, letter pads, memorandum pads, diaries and similar articles," HTSUS subheading 4820.10, which comprises two subcategories. Items in the first, "diaries, notebooks and address books, bound; memorandum pads, letter pads and similar articles," were subject to a tariff of 4.0% at the time in controversy. Objects in the second, covering "other" items, were free of duty.

Between 1989 and 1993, Customs repeatedly treated day planners under the "other" HTSUS subheading. In January 1993, however, Customs changed its position, and issued a Headquarters ruling letter classifying Mead's day planners as "Diaries . . . , bound" subject to tariff under subheading 4820.10.20. That letter was short on explanation, but after Mead's protest, Customs Headquarters issued a new letter, carefully reasoned but never published, reaching the same conclusion. This letter considered two definitions of "diary" from the Oxford English Dictionary, the first covering a daily journal of the past day's events, the second a book including "printed dates for daily memoranda and jottings; also . . . calendars. . . ." Customs concluded that "diary" was not confined to the first, in part because the broader definition reflects commercial usage and hence the "commercial identity of these items in the marketplace." As for the definition of "bound," Customs concluded that HTSUS was not referring to "bookbinding," but to a less exact sort of fastening described in the Harmonized Commodity Description and Coding System Explanatory Notes to Heading 4820, which spoke of binding by "reinforcements or fittings of metal, plastics, etc."

Customs rejected Mead's further protest of the second Headquarters ruling letter, and Mead filed suit in the Court of International Trade (CIT). The CIT granted the Government's motion for summary judgment, adopting Customs's reasoning without saying anything about deference.

Mead then went to the United States Court of Appeals for the Federal Circuit. While the case was pending there this Court decided *United States v. Haggar Apparel Co.*, 526 U.S. 380 (1999), holding that Customs regulations receive the deference described in *Chevron.* The appeals court requested briefing on the impact of *Haggar,* and the Government argued that classification rulings, like Customs regulations, deserve *Chevron* deference.

The Federal Circuit, however, reversed the CIT and held that Customs classification rulings should not get *Chevron* deference, owing to differences from the regulations at issue in *Haggar.* Rulings are not preceded by notice and comment as under the Administrative Procedure Act (APA), 5 U.S.C. §553, they "do not carry the force of law and are not, like regulations, intended to clarify the rights and obligations of importers beyond the specific case under review." The appeals court thought classification rulings had a weaker *Chevron* claim even than Internal Revenue Service interpretive rulings, to which that court gives no deference; unlike rulings by the IRS, Customs rulings issue from many locations and need not be published.

The Court of Appeals accordingly gave no deference at all to the ruling classifying the Mead day planners and rejected the agency's reasoning as to both "diary" and "bound." It thought that planners were not diaries because they had no space for "relatively extensive notations about events, observations, feelings, or thoughts" in the past. And it concluded that diaries "bound" in subheading 4810.10.20 presupposed "unbound" diaries, such that treating ring-fastened diaries as "bound" would leave the "unbound diary" an empty category.

We granted certiorari in order to consider the limits of *Chevron* deference owed to administrative practice in applying a statute. We hold that administrative implementation of a particular statutory provision qualifies for *Chevron* deference when it appears that Congress delegated authority to the agency generally to make rules carrying the force of law, and that the agency interpretation claiming deference was promulgated in the exercise of that authority. Delegation of such authority may be shown in a variety of ways, as by an agency's power to engage in adjudication or notice-and-comment rulemaking, or by some other indication of a comparable congressional intent. The Customs ruling at issue here fails to qualify, although the possibility that it deserves some deference under *Skidmore* leads us to vacate and remand.

II

A

When Congress has "explicitly left a gap for an agency to fill, there is an express delegation of authority to the agency to elucidate a specific provision of the statute by regulation," *Chevron*, and any ensuing regulation is binding in the courts unless procedurally defective, arbitrary or capricious in substance, or manifestly contrary to the statute.[6] But whether or not they enjoy any express delegation of authority on a particular question, agencies charged with applying a statute necessarily make all sorts of interpretive choices, and while not all of those choices bind judges to follow them, they certainly may influence courts facing questions the agencies have already answered. "The well-reasoned views of the agencies implementing a statute 'constitute a body of experience and informed judgment to which courts and litigants may properly resort for guidance,'" *Bragdon v. Abbott*, 524 U.S. 624, 642 (1998) (quoting *Skidmore*, 323 U.S. at 139-140), and "we have long recognized that considerable weight should be accorded to an executive department's construction of a statutory scheme it is entrusted to administer. . . ." *Chevron, supra*, at 844 (footnote omitted); *see also Ford Motor Credit Co. v. Milhollin*, 444 U.S. 555, 565 (1980); *Zenith Radio Corp. v. United States*, 437 U.S. 443, 450 (1978). The fair measure of deference to an agency administering its own statute has been understood to vary with circumstances, and courts have looked to the degree of the agency's care, its consistency, formality,[9] and relative expertness, and to the persuasiveness of the agency's position, see *Skidmore, supra*. The approach has produced a spectrum of judicial responses, from great respect at one end, *see*, e.g., *Aluminum Co. of America v. Central Lincoln Peoples' Util. Dist.*, 467 U.S. 380, 389-390 (1984) ("substantial deference" to administrative construction), to near indifference at the other, *see*, e.g., *Bowen v. Georgetown Univ. Hospital*, 488 U.S. 204, 212-213 (1988) (interpretation advanced for the first time in a litigation brief). Justice Jackson summed things up in *Skidmore v. Swift & Co.*:

> "The weight [accorded to an administrative] judgment in a particular case will depend upon the thoroughness evident in its consideration, the validity of its reasoning, its consistency with earlier and later pronouncements, and all those factors which give it power to persuade, if lacking power to control." 323 U.S. at 140.

Since 1984, we have identified a category of interpretive choices distinguished by an additional reason for judicial deference. This Court in *Chevron* recognized that Congress not only engages in express delegation of specific interpretive authority, but that "sometimes the legislative delegation to an agency on a particular question is implicit." 467 U.S. at 844. Congress, that is, may not have expressly delegated authority or responsibility to implement a particular provision or fill a particular gap. Yet it can still be apparent from the agency's generally conferred authority and other statutory circumstances that Congress would expect the agency to be able to speak with the force of law when it

---

6. Assuming in each case, of course, that the agency's exercise of authority is constitutional, *see* 5 U.S.C. § 706(2)(B), and does not exceed its jurisdiction, *see* § 706(2)(C).

9. *See*, e.g., *Reno v. Koray*, 515 U.S. 50, 61 (1995) (internal agency guideline that is not "subject to the rigors of the [APA], including public notice and comment," is entitled only to "some deference" (internal quotation marks omitted)).

addresses ambiguity in the statute or fills a space in the enacted law, even one about which "Congress did not actually have an intent" as to a particular result. When circumstances implying such an expectation exist, a reviewing court has no business rejecting an agency's exercise of its generally conferred authority to resolve a particular statutory ambiguity simply because the agency's chosen resolution seems unwise, but is obliged to accept the agency's position if Congress has not previously spoken to the point at issue and the agency's interpretation is reasonable, *see id.;* cf. 5 U.S.C. § 706(2) (a reviewing court shall set aside agency action, findings, and conclusions found to be "arbitrary, capricious, an abuse of discretion, or otherwise not in accordance with law").

We have recognized a very good indicator of delegation meriting *Chevron* treatment in express congressional authorizations to engage in the process of rulemaking or adjudication that produces regulations or rulings for which deference is claimed. *See,* e.g., *EEOC v. Arabian American Oil Co.,* 499 U.S. 244, 257 (1991) (no *Chevron* deference to agency guideline where congressional delegation did not include the power to "promulgate rules or regulations" (quoting *General Elec. Co. v. Gilbert,* 429 U.S. 125, 141 (1976)); see also *Christensen v. Harris County,* 529 U.S. 576, 596-597 (2000) (BREYER, J., dissenting) (where it is in doubt that Congress actually intended to delegate particular interpretive authority to an agency, *Chevron* is "inapplicable"). It is fair to assume generally that Congress contemplates administrative action with the effect of law when it provides for a relatively formal administrative procedure tending to foster the fairness and deliberation that should underlie a pronouncement of such force.[11] Thus, the overwhelming number of our cases applying *Chevron* deference have reviewed the fruits of notice-and-comment rulemaking or formal adjudication. That said, and as significant as notice-and-comment is in pointing to *Chevron* authority, the want of that procedure here does not decide the case, for we have sometimes found reasons for *Chevron* deference even when no such administrative formality was required and none was afforded, see, *e.g., NationsBank of N.C., N.A. v. Variable Annuity Life Ins. Co.,* 513 U.S. 251, 256-257, 263 (1995).[13] The fact that the tariff classification here was not a product of such formal process does not alone, therefore, bar the application of *Chevron.*

There are, nonetheless, ample reasons to deny *Chevron* deference here. The authorization for classification rulings, and Customs's practice in making them, present a case far removed not only from notice-and-comment process, but from any other circumstances reasonably suggesting that Congress ever thought of classification rulings as deserving the deference claimed for them here.

---

11. *See* Merrill & Hickman, *Chevron's* Domain, 89 Geo. L.J. 833, 872 (2001) ("If *Chevron* rests on a presumption about congressional intent then *Chevron* should apply only where Congress would want *Chevron* to apply. In delineating the types of delegations of agency authority that trigger *Chevron* deference, it is therefore important to determine whether a plausible case can be made that Congress would want such a delegation to mean that agencies enjoy primary interpretational authority").

13. In *NationsBank of N.C., N.A. v. Variable Annuity Life Ins. Co.,* 513 U.S. 251, 256-257 (1995), we quoted longstanding precedent concluding that "the Comptroller of the Currency is charged with the enforcement of banking laws to an extent that warrants the invocation of [the rule of deference] with respect to his deliberative conclusions as to the meaning of these laws" (internal quotation marks omitted). See also 1 M. Malloy, Banking Law and Regulation § 1.3.1, p. 1.41 (1996) (stating that the Comptroller is given "personal authority" under the National Bank Act).

B

No matter which angle we choose for viewing the Customs ruling letter in this case, it fails to qualify under *Chevron*. On the face of the statute, to begin with, the terms of the congressional delegation give no indication that Congress meant to delegate authority to Customs to issue classification rulings with the force of law. We are not, of course, here making any global statement about Customs's authority, for it is true that the general rulemaking power conferred on Customs, *see* 19 U.S.C. § 1624, authorizes some regulation with the force of law, or "legal norms," as we put it in *Haggar*, 526 U.S. at 391. It is true as well that Congress had classification rulings in mind when it explicitly authorized, in a parenthetical, the issuance of "regulations establishing procedures for the issuance of binding rulings prior to the entry of the merchandise concerned," 19 U.S.C. § 1502(a). The reference to binding classifications does not, however, bespeak the legislative type of activity that would naturally bind more than the parties to the ruling, once the goods classified are admitted into this country. And though the statute's direction to disseminate "information" necessary to "secure" uniformity, 19 U.S.C. § 1502(a), seems to assume that a ruling may be precedent in later transactions, precedential value alone does not add up to *Chevron* entitlement; interpretive rules may sometimes function as precedents, and they enjoy no *Chevron* status as a class. In any event, any precedential claim of a classification ruling is counterbalanced by the provision for independent review of Customs classifications by the CIT, see 28 U.S.C. §§ 2638-2640; the scheme for CIT review includes a provision that treats classification rulings on par with the Secretary's rulings on "valuation, rate of duty, marking, restricted merchandise, entry requirements, drawbacks, vessel repairs, or similar matters," § 1581(h); see § 2639(b). It is hard to imagine a congressional understanding more at odds with the *Chevron* regime.[16]

It is difficult, in fact, to see in the agency practice itself any indication that Customs ever set out with a lawmaking pretense in mind when it undertook to make classifications like these. Customs does not generally engage in notice-and-comment practice when issuing them, and their treatment by the agency makes it clear that a letter's binding character as a ruling stops short of third parties; Customs has regarded a classification as conclusive only as between itself and the importer to whom it was issued, 19 CFR § 177.9(c) (2000), and even then only until Customs has given advance notice of intended change, §§ 177.9(a), (c). Other importers are in fact warned against assuming any right of detrimental reliance. § 177.9(c).

Indeed, to claim that classifications have legal force is to ignore the reality that 46 different Customs offices issue 10,000 to 15,000 of them each year. Any suggestion that rulings intended to have the force of law are being churned out at a rate of 10,000 a year at an agency's 46 scattered offices is simply self-refuting. Although the circumstances are less startling here, with a Headquarters letter in issue, none of the relevant statutes recognizes this category of rulings as separate or different from others; there is thus no indication that a more potent delegation might have been understood as going to Headquarters

16. Although Customs's decision "is presumed to be correct" on review, 28 U.S.C. § 2639(a)(1), the CIT "may consider any new ground" even if not raised below, § 2638, and "shall make its determinations upon the basis of the record made before the court," rather than that developed by Customs, § 2640(a); see generally *Haggar Apparel*, 526 U.S. at 391.

even when Headquarters provides developed reasoning, as it did in this instance.

Nor do the amendments to the statute made effective after this case arose disturb our conclusion. The new law requires Customs to provide notice-and-comment procedures only when modifying or revoking a prior classification ruling or modifying the treatment accorded to substantially identical transactions, 19 U.S.C. § 1625(c); and under its regulations, Customs sees itself obliged to provide notice-and-comment procedures only when "changing a practice" so as to produce a tariff increase, or in the imposition of a restriction or prohibition, or when Customs Headquarters determines that "the matter is of sufficient importance to involve the interests of domestic industry," 19 CFR §§ 177.10(c)(1)(2) (2000). The statutory changes reveal no new congressional objective of treating classification decisions generally as rulemaking with force of law, nor do they suggest any intent to create a *Chevron* patchwork of classification rulings, some with force of law, some without.

In sum, classification rulings are best treated like "interpretations contained in policy statements, agency manuals, and enforcement guidelines." *Christensen,* 529 U.S. at 587. They are beyond the *Chevron* pale.

C

To agree with the Court of Appeals that Customs ruling letters do not fall within *Chevron* is not, however, to place them outside the pale of any deference whatever. *Chevron* did nothing to eliminate *Skidmore*'s holding that an agency's interpretation may merit some deference whatever its form, given the "specialized experience and broader investigations and information" available to the agency, 323 U.S. at 139, and given the value of uniformity in its administrative and judicial understandings of what a national law requires, *id.*, at 140.

There is room at least to raise a *Skidmore* claim here, where the regulatory scheme is highly detailed, and Customs can bring the benefit of specialized experience to bear on the subtle questions in this case: whether the daily planner with room for brief daily entries falls under "diaries," when diaries are grouped with "notebooks and address books, bound; memorandum pads, letter pads and similar articles," HTSUS subheading 4820.10.20; and whether a planner with a ring binding should qualify as "bound," when a binding may be typified by a book, but also may have "reinforcements or fittings of metal, plastics, etc.," Harmonized Commodity Description and Coding System Explanatory Notes to Heading 4820, p. 687. A classification ruling in this situation may therefore at least seek a respect proportional to its "power to persuade," *Skidmore, supra,* at 140; see also *Christensen,* 529 U.S. at 587; *id.,* at 595 (STEVENS, J., dissenting); *id.,* at 596-597 (BREYER, J., dissenting). Such a ruling may surely claim the merit of its writer's thoroughness, logic and expertness, its fit with prior interpretations, and any other sources of weight.

D

Underlying the position we take here, like the position expressed by Justice Scalia in dissent, is a choice about the best way to deal with an inescapable feature of the body of congressional legislation authorizing administrative action. That feature is the great variety of ways in which the laws invest the Government's administrative arms with discretion, and with procedures for exercising it, in giving meaning to Acts of Congress. Implementation of a statute may occur in formal adjudication or the choice to defend against judicial challenge; it may occur in a central board or office or in dozens of enforcement agencies dotted across the country; its institutional lawmaking may be confined to the resolution of minute detail or extend to legislative rulemaking on matters intentionally left by Congress to be worked out at the agency level.

Although we all accept the position that the Judiciary should defer to at least some of this multifarious administrative action, we have to decide how to take account of the great range of its variety. If the primary objective is to simplify the judicial process of giving or withholding deference, then the diversity of statutes authorizing discretionary administrative action must be declared irrelevant or minimized. If, on the other hand, it is simply implausible that Congress intended such a broad range of statutory authority to produce only two varieties of administrative action, demanding either *Chevron* deference or none at all, then the breadth of the spectrum of possible agency action must be taken into account. Justice Scalia's first priority over the years has been to limit and simplify. The Court's choice has been to tailor deference to variety. This acceptance of the range of statutory variation has led the Court to recognize more than one variety of judicial deference, just as the Court has recognized a variety of indicators that Congress would expect *Chevron* deference.[18]

Our respective choices are repeated today. Justice Scalia would pose the question of deference as an either-or choice. On his view that *Chevron* rendered *Skidmore* anachronistic, when courts owe any deference it is *Chevron* deference that they owe. Whether courts do owe deference in a given case turns, for him, on whether the agency action (if reasonable) is "authoritative." The character of the authoritative derives, in turn, not from breadth of delegation or the agency's procedure in implementing it, but is defined as the "official" position of an agency, and may ultimately be a function of administrative persistence alone.

The Court, on the other hand, said nothing in *Chevron* to eliminate *Skidmore's* recognition of various justifications for deference depending on statutory circumstances and agency action; *Chevron* was simply a case recognizing that even without express authority to fill a specific statutory gap, circumstances pointing to implicit congressional delegation present a particularly insistent call for deference. Indeed, in holding here that *Chevron* left *Skidmore* intact and applicable where statutory circumstances indicate no intent to delegate general authority to make rules with force of law, or where such authority was not invoked, we hold nothing more than we said last Term in response to the particular statutory circumstances in *Christensen*, to which Justice Scalia then took exception, see 529 U.S. at 589, just as he does again today.

We think, in sum, that Justice Scalia's efforts to simplify ultimately run afoul of Congress's indications that different statutes present different reasons for considering respect for the exercise of administrative authority or deference to it. Without being at odds with congressional intent much of the time, we believe that judicial responses to administrative action must continue to differentiate between *Chevron* and *Skidmore*, and that continued recognition of

---

18. It is, of course, true that the limit of *Chevron* deference is not marked by a hard-edged rule. But *Chevron* itself is a good example showing when *Chevron* deference is warranted, while this is a good case showing when it is not. Judges in other, perhaps harder, cases will make reasoned choices between the two examples, the way courts have always done.

Skidmore is necessary for just the reasons Justice Jackson gave when that case was decided.[19]

Since the *Skidmore* assessment called for here ought to be made in the first instance by the Court of Appeals for the Federal Circuit or the Court of International Trade, we go no further than to vacate the judgment and remand the case for further proceedings consistent with this opinion. It is so ordered.

JUSTICE SCALIA, dissenting.

Today's opinion makes an avulsive change in judicial review of federal administrative action. Whereas previously a reasonable agency application of an ambiguous statutory provision had to be sustained so long as it represented the agency's authoritative interpretation, henceforth such an application can be set aside unless "it appears that Congress delegated authority to the agency generally to make rules carrying the force of law," as by giving an agency "power to engage in adjudication or notice-and-comment rulemaking, or . . . some other [procedure] indicating comparable congressional intent," and "the agency interpretation claiming deference was promulgated in the exercise of that authority."[1] What was previously a general presumption of authority in agencies to resolve ambiguity in the statutes they have been authorized to enforce has been changed to a presumption of no such authority, which must be overcome by affirmative legislative intent to the contrary. And whereas previously, when agency authority to resolve ambiguity did not exist the court was free to give the statute what it considered the best interpretation, henceforth the court must supposedly give the agency view some indeterminate amount of so-called *Skidmore* deference. We will be sorting out the consequences of the *Mead* doctrine, which has today replaced the *Chevron* doctrine, for years to come. I would adhere to our established jurisprudence, defer to the reasonable interpretation the Customs Service has given to the statute it is charged with enforcing, and reverse the judgment of the Court of Appeals.

I

Only five years ago, the Court described the *Chevron* doctrine as follows: "We accord deference to agencies under *Chevron* . . . because of a presumption that Congress, when it left ambiguity in a statute meant for implementation by an

---

19. Surely Justice Jackson's practical criteria, along with *Chevron's* concern with congressional understanding, provide more reliable guideposts than conclusory references to the "authoritative" or "official." Even if those terms provided a true criterion, there would have to be something wrong with a standard that accorded the status of substantive law to every one of 10,000 "official" customs classifications rulings turned out each year from over 46 offices placed around the country at the Nation's entryways. Justice Scalia tries to avoid that result by limiting what is "authoritative" or "official" to a pronouncement that expresses the "judgment of central agency management, approved at the highest level," as distinct from the pronouncements of "underlings," *post,* at n.5. But that analysis would not entitle a Headquarters ruling to *Chevron* deference; the "highest level" at Customs is the source of the regulation at issue in *Haggar,* the Commissioner of Customs with the approval of the Secretary of the Treasury. 526 U.S. at 386. The Commissioner did not issue the Headquarters ruling. What Justice Scalia has in mind here is that because the Secretary approved the Government's position in its brief to this Court, *Chevron* deference is due. But if that is so, *Chevron* deference was not called for until sometime after the litigation began, when central management at the highest level decided to defend the ruling, and the deference is not to the classification ruling as such but to the brief. This explains why the Court has not accepted Justice Scalia's position.

1. It is not entirely clear whether the formulation newly minted by the Court today extends to both formal and informal adjudication, or simply the former.

agency, understood that the ambiguity would be resolved, first and foremost, by the agency, and desired the agency (rather than the courts) to possess whatever degree of discretion the ambiguity allows," *Smiley v. Citibank (South Dakota), N.A.*, 517 U.S. 735, 740-741 (1996). Today the Court collapses this doctrine, announcing instead a presumption that agency discretion does not exist unless the statute, expressly or impliedly, says so. While the Court disclaims any hard-and-fast rule for determining the existence of discretion-conferring intent, it asserts that "a very good indicator [is] express congressional authorizations to engage in the process of rulemaking or adjudication that produces regulations or rulings for which deference is claimed." Only when agencies act through "adjudication[,] notice-and-comment rulemaking, or . . . some other [procedure] indicating comparable congressional intent [whatever that means]" is *Chevron* deference applicable — because these "relatively formal administrative procedures [designed] to foster . . . fairness and deliberation" bespeak (according to the Court) congressional willingness to have the agency, rather than the courts, resolve statutory ambiguities. Once it is determined that *Chevron* deference is not in order, the uncertainty is not at an end — and indeed is just beginning. Litigants cannot then assume that the statutory question is one for the courts to determine, according to traditional interpretive principles and by their own judicial lights. No, the Court now resurrects, in full force, the pre-*Chevron* doctrine of *Skidmore* deference, whereby "the fair measure of deference to an agency administering its own statute . . . varies with circumstances," including "the degree of the agency's care, its consistency, formality, and relative expertness, and . . . the persuasiveness of the agency's position." The Court has largely replaced *Chevron*, in other words, with that test most beloved by a court unwilling to be held to rules (and most feared by litigants who want to know what to expect): th' ol' "totality of the circumstances" test.

The Court's new doctrine is neither sound in principle nor sustainable in practice.

A

As to principle: The doctrine of *Chevron* — that all *authoritative* agency interpretations of statutes they are charged with administering deserve deference — was rooted in a legal presumption of congressional intent, important to the division of powers between the Second and Third Branches. When, *Chevron* said, Congress leaves an ambiguity in a statute that is to be administered by an executive agency, it is presumed that Congress meant to give the agency discretion, within the limits of reasonable interpretation, as to how the ambiguity is to be resolved. By committing enforcement of the statute to an agency rather than the courts, Congress committed its initial and primary interpretation to that branch as well.

There is some question whether *Chevron* was faithful to the text of the Administrative Procedure Act (APA), which it did not even bother to cite. But it was in accord with the origins of federal-court judicial review. Judicial control of federal executive officers was principally exercised through the prerogative writ of mandamus. *See* L. Jaffe, Judicial Control of Administrative Action 166, 176-177 (1965). That writ generally would not issue unless the executive officer was acting plainly beyond the scope of his authority.

> "The questions mooted before the Secretary and decided by him were whether the fund is a tribal fund, whether the tribe is still existing and whether the distribution of the annuities is to be confined to members of the tribe. . . . These are all

questions of law the solution of which requires a construction of the act of 1889 and other related acts. A reading of these acts shows that they fall short of plainly requiring that any of the questions be answered in the negative and that in some aspects they give color to the affirmative answers of the Secretary. That the construction of the acts insofar as they have a bearing on the first and third questions is sufficiently uncertain to involve the exercise of judgment and discretion is rather plain. . . .

"From what has been said it follows that the case is not one in which mandamus will lie." *Wilbur v. United States ex rel. Kadrie*, 281 U.S. 206, 221-222 (1930).

Statutory ambiguities, in other words, were left to reasonable resolution by the Executive.

The basis in principle for today's new doctrine can be described as follows: The background rule is that ambiguity in legislative instructions to agencies is to be resolved not by the agencies but by the judges. Specific congressional intent to depart from this rule must be found — and while there is no single touchstone for such intent it can generally be found when Congress has authorized the agency to act through (what the Court says is) relatively formal procedures such as informal rulemaking and formal (and informal?) adjudication, and when the agency in fact employs such procedures. The Court's background rule is contradicted by the origins of judicial review of administrative action. But in addition, the Court's principal criterion of congressional intent to supplant its background rule seems to me quite implausible. There is no necessary connection between the formality of procedure and the power of the entity administering the procedure to resolve authoritatively questions of law. The most formal of the procedures the Court refers to — formal adjudication — is modeled after the process used in trial courts, which of course are not generally accorded deference on questions of law. The purpose of such a procedure is to produce a closed record for determination and review of the facts — which implies nothing about the power of the agency subjected to the procedure to resolve authoritatively questions of law.

As for informal rulemaking: While formal adjudication procedures are *prescribed* (either by statute or by the Constitution), *see* 5 U.S.C. §§ 554, 556, informal rulemaking is more typically *authorized* but not required. Agencies with such authority are free to give guidance through rulemaking, but they may proceed to administer their statute case-by-case, "making law" as they implement their program (not necessarily through formal adjudication). *See NLRB v. Bell Aerospace Co.*, 416 U.S. 267, 290-295 (1974); *SEC v. Chenery Corp.*, 332 U.S. 194, 202-203 (1947). Is it likely — or indeed even plausible — that Congress meant, when such an agency chooses rulemaking, to accord the administrators of that agency, *and their successors*, the flexibility of interpreting the ambiguous statute now one way, and later another; but, when such an agency chooses case-by-case administration, to eliminate all future agency discretion by having that same ambiguity resolved authoritatively (and forever) by the courts? Surely that makes no sense. It is also the case that certain significant categories of rules — those involving grant and benefit programs, for example, are exempt from the requirements of informal rulemaking. *See* 5 U.S.C. § 553(a)(2). Under the Court's novel theory, when an agency takes advantage of that exemption its rules will be deprived of *Chevron* deference, i.e., authoritative effect. Was this either the plausible intent of the APA rulemaking exemption, or the plausible intent of the Congress that established the grant or benefit program?

Some decisions that are neither informal rulemaking nor formal adjudication are required to be made personally by a Cabinet Secretary, without any prescribed procedures. *See*, e.g., *United States v. Giordano*, 416 U.S. 505, 508 (1974) (involving application of 18 U.S.C. § 2516 (1970 ed.), requiring wiretap applications to be authorized by "the Attorney General, or any Assistant Attorney General specially designated by the Attorney General"). Is it conceivable that decisions specifically committed to these high-level officers are meant to be accorded no deference, while decisions by an administrative law judge left in place without further discretionary agency review, *see* 5 U.S.C. § 557(b), are authoritative? This seems to me quite absurd, and not at all in accord with any plausible actual intent of Congress.

B

As for the practical effects of the new rule:

(1) The principal effect will be protracted confusion. As noted above, the one test for *Chevron* deference that the Court enunciates is wonderfully imprecise: whether "Congress delegated authority to the agency generally to make rules carrying the force of law, . . . as by . . . adjudication[,] notice-and-comment rulemaking, or . . . some other [procedure] indicating comparable congressional intent." But even this description does not do justice to the utter flabbiness of the Court's criterion, since, in order to maintain the fiction that the new test is really just the old one, applied consistently throughout our case law, the Court must make a virtually open-ended exception to its already imprecise guidance: . . .

(2) Another practical effect of today's opinion will be an artificially induced increase in informal rulemaking. . . . Agencies will now have high incentive to rush out barebones, ambiguous rules construing statutory ambiguities, which they can then in turn further clarify through informal rulings entitled to judicial respect.

(3) Worst of all, the majority's approach will lead to the ossification of large portions of our statutory law. . . . [Justice Scalia's concerns and the development of law in this area are addressed in the note that follows this case.]

(4) And finally, the majority's approach compounds the confusion it creates by breathing new life into the anachronism of *Skidmore*, which sets forth a sliding scale of deference owed an agency's interpretation of a statute that is dependent "upon the thoroughness evident in [the agency's] consideration, the validity of its reasoning, its consistency with earlier and later pronouncements, and all those factors which give it power to persuade, if lacking power to control"; in this way, the appropriate measure of deference will be accorded the "body of experience and informed judgment" that such interpretations often embody, 323 U.S., at 140. Justice Jackson's eloquence notwithstanding, the rule of *Skidmore* deference is an empty truism and a trifling statement of the obvious: A judge should take into account the well-considered views of expert observers.

It was possible to live with the indeterminacy of *Skidmore* deference in earlier times. But in an era when federal statutory law administered by federal agencies is pervasive, and when the ambiguities (intended or unintended) that those statutes contain are innumerable, totality-of-the-circumstances *Skidmore* deference is a recipe for uncertainty, unpredictability, and endless litigation. To condemn a vast body of agency action to that regime (all except rulemaking, formal (and informal?) adjudication, and whatever else might now and then be included within today's intentionally vague formulation of affirmative congressional intent to "delegate") is irresponsible.

II

The Court's pretense that today's opinion is nothing more than application of our prior case law does not withstand analysis. It is, to be sure, impossible to demonstrate that any of our cases contradicts the rule of decision that the Court prescribes, because the Court prescribes none. More precisely, it at one and the same time (1) renders meaningless its newly announced requirement that there be an affirmative congressional intent to have ambiguities resolved by the administering agency, and (2) ensures that no prior decision can possibly be cited which contradicts that requirement, by simply announcing that all prior decisions according *Chevron* deference exemplify the multifarious ways in which that congressional intent can be manifested: "As significant as notice-and-comment is in pointing to *Chevron* authority, the want of that procedure here does not decide the case, for we have sometimes found reasons for *Chevron* deference even when no such administrative formality was required and none was afforded."[4]

The principles central to today's opinion have no antecedent in our jurisprudence. *Chevron*, the case that the opinion purportedly explicates, made no mention of the "relatively formal administrative procedures," that the Court today finds the best indication of an affirmative intent by Congress to have ambiguities resolved by the administering agency. Which is not so remarkable, since *Chevron* made no mention of any *need* to find such an affirmative intent; it said that in the event of statutory ambiguity agency authority to clarify was to be *presumed*. And our cases have followed that prescription.

. . .

III

To decide the present case, I would adhere to the original formulation of *Chevron*. "The power of an administrative agency to administer a congressionally created . . . program necessarily requires the formulation of policy and the making of rules to fill any gap left, implicitly or explicitly, by Congress." We accordingly presume — and our precedents have made clear to Congress that we

---

4. As a sole, teasing example of those "sometimes" the Court cites *NationsBank of N.C., N.A. v. Variable Annuity Life Ins. Co.*, 513 U.S. 251 (1995), explaining in a footnote that our "longstanding precedent" evinced a tradition of great deference to the "deliberative conclusions" of the Comptroller of the Currency as to the meaning of the banking laws the Comptroller is charged with enforcing. *Ante*, at n.13. How is it that a tradition of great judicial deference to the agency head provides affirmative indication of congressional intent to delegate authority to resolve statutory ambiguities challenges the intellect and the imagination. If the point is that Congress must have been aware of that tradition of great deference when it enacted the law at issue, the same could be said of the Customs Service, and indeed of *all* agencies. Indeed, since our opinion in *Chevron* Congress must have been aware that we would defer to *all* authoritative agency resolutions of statutory ambiguities. Needless to say, *NationsBank* itself makes no mention of any such affirmative indication, because it was never the law. The many other cases that contradict the Court's new rule will presumably be explained, like *NationsBank*, as other "modes" of displaying affirmative congressional intent. If a tradition of judicial deference can be called that with a straight face, what cannot be?

presume — that, absent some clear textual indication to the contrary, "Congress, when it left ambiguity in a statute meant for implementation by an agency, understood that the ambiguity would be resolved, first and foremost, by the agency, and desired the agency (rather than the courts) to possess whatever degree of discretion the ambiguity allows," *Smiley*, 517 U.S. at 740-741 (citing *Chevron, supra*, at 843-844). *Chevron* sets forth an across-the-board presumption, which operates as a background rule of law against which Congress legislates: Ambiguity means Congress intended agency discretion. Any resolution of the ambiguity by the administering agency that is authoritative — that represents the official position of the agency — must be accepted by the courts if it is reasonable.
. . .

There is no doubt that the Customs Service's interpretation represents the authoritative view of the agency. Although the actual ruling letter was signed by only the Director of the Commercial Rulings Branch of Customs Headquarters' Office of Regulations and Rulings, the Solicitor General of the United States has filed a brief, cosigned by the General Counsel of the Department of the Treasury, that represents the position set forth in the ruling letter to be the official position of the Customs Service. No one contends that it is merely a "post hoc rationalization" or an "agency litigating position wholly unsupported by regulations, rulings, or administrative practice."[6]

The *authoritativeness* of the agency ruling may not be a bright-line standard — but it is infinitely brighter than the line the Court asks us to draw today, between a statute such as the one at issue in *NationsBank* that (according to the Court) *does* display an "affirmative intent" to "delegate" interpretive authority, and innumerable indistinguishable statutes that (according to the Court) do *not*. And, most important of all, it is a line that focuses attention on the right question: not whether Congress "affirmatively intended" to delegate interpretive authority (if it entrusted administration of the statute to an agency, it did, because that is how our system works); but whether it is truly the agency's considered view, or just the opinions of some underlings, that are at issue.

There is also no doubt that the Customs Service's interpretation is a reasonable one, whether or not judges would consider it the best. I will not belabor this point, since the Court evidently agrees: An interpretation that was unreasonable would not merit the remand that the Court decrees for consideration of *Skidmore* deference.

---

6. The Court's parting shot, that "there would have to be something wrong with a standard that accorded the status of substantive law to every one of 10,000 'official' customs classifications rulings turned out each year from over 46 offices placed around the country at the Nation's entryways," *ante*, at n.19, misses the mark. I do not disagree. The "authoritativeness" of an agency interpretation does not turn upon whether it has been enunciated by someone who is actually employed by the agency. It must represent the judgment of central agency management, approved at the highest levels. I would find that condition to have been satisfied when, a ruling having been attacked in court, the general counsel of the agency has determined that it should be defended. If one thinks that that does not impart sufficient authoritativeness, then surely the line has been crossed when, as here, the General Counsel of the agency and the Solicitor General of the United States have assured this Court that the position represents the agency's authoritative view. (Contrary to the Court's suggestion, there would be nothing bizarre about the fact that this latter approach would entitle the ruling to deference here, though it would not have been entitled to deference in the lower courts. Affirmation of the official agency position before this court — if that is thought necessary — is no different from the agency's issuing a new rule after the Court of Appeals determination. It establishes a new legal basis for the decision, which this Court must take into account (or remand for that purpose), even though the Court of Appeals could not. *See Thorpe v. Housing Authority of Durham*, 393 U.S. 268, 282 (1969); *see also United States v. Schooner Peggy*, 5 U.S. 103 (1801)).

IV

Finally, and least importantly, even were I to accept the Court's revised version of *Chevron* as a correct statement of the law, I would still accord deference to the tariff classification ruling at issue in this case. For the case is indistinguishable, in that regard, from *NationsBank of N.C., N.A. v. Variable Annuity Life Ins. Co.*, 513 U.S. 251 (1995), which the Court acknowledges as an instance in which *Chevron* deference is warranted notwithstanding the absence of formal adjudication, notice-and-comment rulemaking, or comparable "administrative formality," *ante*, at 11. Here, as in *NationsBank*, there is a tradition of great deference to the opinions of the agency head. . . . And here, as in *NationsBank*, the agency interpretation in question is officially that of the agency head. Consequently, even on the Court's own terms, the Customs ruling at issue in this case should be given *Chevron* deference. . . .

For the reasons stated, I respectfully dissent from the Court's judgment. I would uphold the Customs Service's construction of Subheading 4820.10.20 of the Harmonized Tariff Schedule of the United States, 19 U.S.C. § 1202, and would reverse the contrary decision of the Court of Appeals. I dissent even more vigorously from the reasoning that produces the Court's judgment, and that makes today's decision one of the most significant opinions ever rendered by the Court dealing with the judicial review of administrative action. Its consequences will be enormous, and almost uniformly bad.

QUESTIONS

1. Do both the majority and Justice Scalia agree that the *Chevron* rule is in essence a canon of construction (i.e., a rule for interpreting the meaning of a statute)?
2. What is the logical foundation for such a canon? In other words, why assume that Congress would want the *Chevron* doctrine?
3. After *Mead Corp.*, how do we tell whether *Chevron* deference applies to agency determinations of law?
4. *Mead* makes the applicability of *Chevron* deference dependent on congressional delegation of lawmaking power to an agency and the agency's exercise of that delegated authority. In *Adams Fruit Co. v. Barrett*, 494 U.S. 638, 649-50 (1990), the Court's analysis foreshadowed the reasoning in *Mead* regarding the importance of agency authority to promulgate rules:

> A precondition to deference under *Chevron* is a congressional delegation of administrative authority. No such delegation regarding AWPA's [Agricultural Worker Protection Act's] enforcement provisions is evident in the statute. Rather, Congress established an enforcement scheme independent of the Executive and provided aggrieved farmworkers with direct recourse to federal court where their rights under the statute are violated. . . .
>
> Congress clearly envisioned, indeed expressly mandated, a role for the Department of Labor in administering the statute by requiring the Secretary [of Labor] to promulgate standards implementing AWPA's motor vehicle provisions. This delegation, however, does not empower the Secretary to regulate the scope of the judicial power vested by the statute. Although agency determinations within the scope of delegated authority are entitled to

deference, it is fundamental "that an agency may not bootstrap itself into an area in which it has no jurisdiction." *Federal Maritime Comm'n v. Seatrain Lines, Inc.*, 411 U.S. 726, 745 (1973). . . .

More recently, in *Gonzales v. Oregon*, 546 U.S. 243 (2006), the Court declined to accord *Chevron* deference to an agency because, the Court concluded, Congress had not delegated relevant lawmaking authority to the Attorney General. See *id.* at 258-68. *Cf. King v. Burwell, infra* p. 609 (declining to find regulatory authority delegated to the I.R.S.).

5. Is the degree of formality of an agency's process a logical basis to draw a line between (a) assuming that Congress meant ambiguity to be a delegation of lawmaking power to the agency and (b) assuming that Congress meant ambiguity to be a delegation of such power to the courts?

6. Why is the Court reluctant to apply *Chevron* to very informal agency decisions? Can this reluctance be tied to Congressional intent?

7. If the agency counsel know that agency members would prefer a particular interpretation of an ambiguous organic statute, should they advise the agency to engage in rulemaking rather than case-by-case adjudication? If so, does the *Mead Corp.* case effectively restrict the discretion preserved in *Chenery II, supra*, p. 275, and *Bell Aerospace, supra*, p. 287? Is that bad?

8. Even if Justice Scalia is correct that informal agency actions should get *Chevron* deference, isn't there room for *Skidmore* deference at the first step of *Chevron*? Why is Justice Scalia totally opposed to *Skidmore*?

9. In two recent cases, the Court viewed *Skidmore* to be applicable, but declined to give any deference to the agency, because of the conditions on deference defined by *Skidmore*. In *Young v. United Parcel Service, Inc.*, 135 S. Ct. 1338, 1351-52 (2015), the Court declined, based on "difficulties . . . of timing, consistency and thoroughness of consideration," to defer to agency guidelines. In *University of Texas Southwestern Medical Center v. Nassar*, 133 S. Ct. 2517, 2533 (2013), the Court held that the agency's "explanations [in guidelines] lack the persuasive force that is a necessary precondition to deference under *Skidmore*."

NOTE ON MEAD CORP. *AND THE OSSIFICATION OF ADMINISTRATIVE LAW*

In Justice Scalia's view, 533 U.S. at 247-50, the "worst of all" of the "practical effects" of the *Mead Corp.* decision is:

the ossification of large portions of our statutory law. Where *Chevron* applies, statutory ambiguities remain ambiguities subject to the agency's ongoing clarification. They create a space, so to speak, for the exercise of continuing agency discretion. As *Chevron* itself held, the Environmental Protection Agency can interpret "stationary source" to mean a single smokestack, can later replace that interpretation with the "bubble concept" embracing an entire plant, and if that proves undesirable can return again to the original interpretation. 467 U.S., at 853-859, 865-866. For the indeterminately large number of statutes taken out of *Chevron* by today's decision, however, ambiguity (and hence flexibility) will cease with the first judicial resolution. *Skidmore* deference gives the agency's current position some vague and uncertain amount of respect, but it does not, like *Chevron*, leave the matter within the control of the Executive Branch for the future. Once the court has spoken, it becomes unlawful for the agency to take a contradictory position; the statute now says what the court has prescribed. *See Neal v. United States*, 516 U.S. 284, 295 (1996); *Lechmere, Inc. v. NLRB*, 502 U.S. 527, 536-537 (1992); *Maislin Industries, U.S., Inc. v. Primary Steel, Inc.*, 497 U.S. 116, 131 (1990). It will be bad enough when this ossification occurs as a result of judicial determination (under today's new principles) that there is no affirmative indication of congressional intent to "delegate"; but it will be positively bizarre when it occurs simply because of an agency's failure to act by rulemaking (rather than informal adjudication) before the issue is presented to the courts.

One might respond that such ossification would not result if the agency were simply to readopt its interpretation, after a court reviewing it under *Skidmore* had rejected it, by repromulgating it through one of the *Chevron*-eligible procedural formats approved by the Court today. Approving this procedure would be a landmark abdication of judicial power. It is worlds apart from *Chevron* proper, where the court does not purport to give the statute a judicial interpretation — except in identifying the scope of the statutory ambiguity, as to which the court's judgment is final and irreversible. (Under *Chevron* proper, when the agency's authoritative interpretation comes within the scope of that ambiguity — and the court therefore approves it — the agency will not be "overruling" the court's decision when it later decides that a different interpretation (still within the scope of the ambiguity) is preferable.) By contrast, under this view, the reviewing court will not be holding the agency's authoritative interpretation within the scope of the ambiguity; but will be holding that the agency has not used the "delegation-conferring" procedures, and that the court must therefore interpret the statute on its own — but subject to reversal if and when the agency uses the proper procedures.

One is reminded of Justice Jackson's words in *Chicago & Southern Air Lines, Inc. v. Waterman S.S. Corp.*, 333 U.S. 103, 113 (1948):

> "The court below considered that after it reviewed the Board's order its judgment would be submitted to the President, that his power to disapprove would apply after as well as before the court acts, and hence that there would be no chance of a deadlock and no conflict of function. But if the President may completely disregard the judgment of the court, it would be only because it is one the courts were not authorized to render. Judgments within the powers vested in courts by the Judiciary Article of the Constitution may not lawfully be revised, overturned or refused faith and credit by another Department of Government."

I know of no case, in the entire history of the federal courts, in which we have allowed a judicial interpretation of a statute to be set aside by an agency-or have allowed a lower court to render an interpretation of a statute subject to correction by an agency. As recently as 1996, we rejected an attempt to do precisely that. In *Chapman v. United States*, 500 U.S. 453 (1991), we had held that the weight of the blotter paper bearing the lysergic acid diethylamide (LSD) must be counted for purposes of determining whether the quantity crossed the 10-gram threshold of 21 U.S.C. § 841(b)(1)(A)(v) imposing a minimum sentence of 10 years. At that time the United States Sentencing Commission applied a similar approach under the Sentencing Guidelines, but had taken no position regarding the meaning of the statutory provision. The Commission later changed its Guidelines approach, and, according to the petitioner in *Neal v. United States*, 516 U.S. 284 (1996), made clear its view that the statute bore that meaning as well. The petitioner argued that we should defer to that new approach. We would have none of it.

"Were we, for argument's sake, to adopt petitioner's view that the Commission intended the commentary as an interpretation of §841(b)(1), and that the last sentence of the commentary states the Commission's view that the dose-based method is consistent with the term 'mixture or substance' in the statute, he still would not prevail. The Commission's dose-based method cannot be squared with *Chapman*. . . . In these circumstances, we need not decide what, if any, deference is owed the Commission in order to reject its alleged contrary interpretation. Once we have determined a statute's meaning, we adhere to our ruling under the doctrine of *stare decisis*, and we assess an agency's later interpretation of the statute against that settled law." *Id.*, at 294-295 (citations omitted).

There is, in short, no way to avoid the ossification of federal law that today's opinion sets in motion. What a court says is the law after according *Skidmore* deference will be the law forever, beyond the power of the agency to change even through rulemaking.

A majority of the Court, in an opinion authored by Justice Thomas, addressed the ossification issue in *National Cable & Telecommunications Ass'n v. Brand X Internet Services*, 545 U.S. 967, 981-82 (2005), and reached a conclusion at odds with the view of Justice Scalia:

The [Ninth Circuit] Court of Appeals declined to apply *Chevron* because it thought the Commission's interpretation of the Communications Act foreclosed by the conflicting construction of the Act [the Ninth Circuit Court of Appeals] had adopted in [*AT & T Corp. v. Portland*, 216 F.3d 871 (9th Cir. 2000)]. See 345 F.3d, at 1127-1132. It based that holding on the assumption that *Portland*'s construction overrode the Commission's, regardless of whether *Portland* had held the statute to be unambiguous. 345 F.3d, at 1131. That reasoning was incorrect.

A court's prior judicial construction of a statute trumps an agency construction otherwise entitled to *Chevron* deference only if the prior court decision holds that its construction follows from the unambiguous terms of the statute and thus leaves no room for agency discretion. This principle follows from *Chevron* itself. *Chevron* established a "presumption that Congress, when it left ambiguity in a statute meant for implementation by an agency, understood that the ambiguity would be resolved, first and foremost, by the agency, and desired the agency (rather than the courts) to possess whatever degree of discretion the ambiguity allows." *Smiley*, 517 U.S. at 740-741. Yet allowing a judicial precedent to foreclose an agency from interpreting an ambiguous statute, as the Court of Appeals assumed it could, would allow a court's interpretation to override an agency's. *Chevron*'s premise is that it is for agencies, not courts, to fill statutory gaps. See 467 U.S., at 843-844, and n. 11. The better rule is to hold judicial interpretations contained in precedents to the same demanding *Chevron* step one standard that applies if the court is reviewing the agency's construction on a blank slate: Only a judicial precedent holding that the statute unambiguously forecloses the agency's interpretation, and therefore contains no gap for the agency to fill, displaces a conflicting agency construction.

A contrary rule would produce anomalous results. It would mean that whether an agency's interpretation of an ambiguous statute is entitled to *Chevron* deference would turn on the order in which the interpretations issue: If the court's construction came first, its construction would prevail, whereas if the agency's came first, the agency's construction would command *Chevron* deference. Yet whether Congress has delegated to an agency the authority to interpret a statute does not depend on the order in which the judicial and administrative constructions occur. The Court of Appeals' rule, moreover, would "lead to the ossification of large portions of our statutory law," *Mead, supra*, at 247 (SCALIA, J., dissenting), by precluding agencies from revising unwise judicial constructions of ambiguous statutes. Neither *Chevron* nor the doctrine of *stare decisis* requires these haphazard results.

The dissent answers that allowing an agency to override what a court believes to be the best interpretation of a statute makes "judicial decisions subject to reversal by Executive officers." It does not. Since *Chevron* teaches that a court's opinion as to the best reading of an ambiguous statute an agency is charged with administering is not authoritative, the agency's decision to construe that statute differently from a court does not say that the court's holding was legally wrong. Instead, the agency may, consistent with the court's holding, choose a different construction, since the agency remains the authoritative interpreter (within the limits of reason) of such statutes. In all other respects, the court's prior ruling remains binding law (for example, as to agency interpretations to which *Chevron* is inapplicable). The precedent has not been "reversed" by the agency, any more than a federal court's interpretation of a State's law can be said to have been "reversed" by a state court that adopts a conflicting (yet authoritative) interpretation of state law.

The Court of Appeals derived a contrary rule from a mistaken reading of this Court's decisions. It read *Neal v. United States*, 516 U.S. 284(1996), to establish that a prior judicial construction of a statute categorically controls an agency's contrary construction. 345 F.3d, at 1131-1132; .... *Neal* established no such proposition. *Neal* declined to defer to a construction adopted by the United States Sentencing Commission that conflicted with one the Court previously had adopted in *Chapman v. United States*, 500 U.S. 453 (1991). *Neal, supra*, at 290-295. *Chapman*, however, had held the relevant statute to be unambiguous. See 500 U.S., at 463 (declining to apply the rule of lenity given the statute's clear language). Thus, *Neal* established only that a precedent holding a statute to be unambiguous forecloses a contrary agency construction. That limited holding accorded with this Court's prior decisions, which had held that a court's interpretation of a statute trumps an agency's under the doctrine of *stare decisis* only if the prior court holding "determined a statute's *clear* meaning." *Maislin Industries, U.S., Inc. v. Primary Steel, Inc.*, 497 U.S. 116, 131 (1990) (emphasis added); see also *Lechmere, Inc. v. NLRB*, 502 U.S. 527, 536-537 (1992). Those decisions allow a court's prior interpretation of a statute to override an agency's interpretation only if the relevant court decision held the statute unambiguous.

Against this background, the Court of Appeals erred in refusing to apply *Chevron* to the Commission's interpretation of the definition of "telecommunications service," 47 U.S.C. § 153(46). Its prior decision in *Portland* held only that the best reading of § 153(46) was that cable modem service was a "telecommunications service," not that it was the only permissible reading of the statute. See 216 F.3d, at 877-880. Nothing in *Portland* held that the Communications Act unambiguously required treating cable Internet providers as telecommunications carriers. Instead, the court noted that it was "not presented with a case involving potential deference to an administrative agency's statutory construction pursuant to the *Chevron* doctrine," *id.*, at 876; and the court invoked no other rule of construction (such as the rule of lenity) requiring it to conclude that the statute was unambiguous to reach its judgment. Before a judicial construction of a statute, whether contained in a precedent or not, may trump an agency's, the court must hold that the statute unambiguously requires the court's construction. *Portland* did not do so.

As the dissent points out, it is not logically necessary for us to reach the question whether the Court of Appeals misapplied *Chevron* for us to decide whether the Commission acted lawfully. Nevertheless, it is no "great mystery" why we are reaching the point here. There is genuine confusion in the lower courts over the interaction between the *Chevron* doctrine and *stare decisis* principles, as the petitioners informed us at the certiorari stage of this litigation. The point has been briefed. And not reaching the point could undermine the purpose of our grant of certiorari: to settle authoritatively whether the Commission's Declaratory Ruling is lawful. Were we to uphold the Declaratory Ruling without reaching the *Chevron* point, the Court of Appeals could once again strike down the Commission's rule based on its *Portland* decision. *Portland* (at least arguably) could compel the Court of Appeals once again to reverse the Commission despite our decision, since our conclusion that it is reasonable to read the Communications Act to classify cable modem service solely as an "information service" leaves untouched *Portland*'s holding that the Commission's interpretation is not the best reading of the statute. . . .

Justice Scalia, 545 U.S. at 1016-20, was alone in his dissent in *Brand X Internet Services*, and address the question of ossification:[1]

The Court today moves to solve th[e ossification] problem of its own creation by inventing yet another breathtaking novelty: judicial decisions subject to reversal by Executive officers.

Imagine the following sequence of events: FCC action is challenged as *ultra vires* under the governing statute; the litigation reaches all the way to the Supreme Court of the United States. The Solicitor General sets forth the FCC's official position (approved by the Commission) regarding interpretation of the statute. Applying *Mead*, however, the Court denies the agency position *Chevron* deference, finds that the best interpretation of the statute contradicts the agency's position, and holds the challenged agency action unlawful. The agency promptly conducts a rulemaking, and adopts a rule that comports with its earlier position-in effect disagreeing with the Supreme Court concerning the best interpretation of the statute. According to today's opinion, the agency is thereupon free to take the action that the Supreme Court found unlawful.

This is not only bizarre. It is probably unconstitutional. . . .

Of course, like *Mead* itself, today's novelty in belated remediation of *Mead* creates many uncertainties to bedevil the lower courts. A court's interpretation is conclusive, the Court says, only if it holds that interpretation to be "the only permissible reading of the statute," and not if it merely holds it to be "the best reading." Does this mean that in future statutory-construction cases involving agency-administered statutes courts must specify (presumably in dictum) which of the two they are holding? And what of the many cases decided in the past, before this dictum's requirement was established? Apparently, silence on the point means that the court's decision is subject to agency reversal: "Before a judicial construction of a statute, whether contained in a precedent or not, may trump an agency's, the court must hold that the statute unambiguously requires the court's construction." . . . How much extra work will it entail for each court confronted with an agency-administered statute to determine whether it has reached, not only the right ("best") result, but "the only permissible" result? Is the standard for "unambiguous" under the Court's new agency-reversal rule the same as the standard for "unambiguous" under step one of *Chevron*? (If so, of course, every case that reaches step two of Chevron will be agency-reversible.) Does the "unambiguous"

1. In his concurring opinion, Justice Stevens, who had joined the majority opinion rejecting Justice Scalia's views on ossification, expressed the following "caveat": the majority "correctly explains why a court of appeals' interpretation of an ambiguous provision in a regulatory statute does not foreclose a contrary reading by the agency. That explanation would not necessarily be applicable to a decision by this Court that would presumably remove any pre-existing ambiguity." *Brand X Internet Services*, 545 U.S. at 1003.

dictum produce *stare decisis* effect even when a court is affirming, rather than reversing, agency action-so that in the future the agency must adhere to that affirmed interpretation? If so, does the victorious agency have the right to appeal a Court of Appeals judgment in its favor, on the ground that the text in question is in fact not (as the Court of Appeals held) unambiguous, so the agency should be able to change its view in the future?

It is indeed a wonderful new world that the Court creates, one full of promise for administrative-law professors in need of tenure articles and, of course, for litigators. I would adhere to what has been the rule in the past: When a court interprets a statute without *Chevron* deference to agency views, its interpretation (whether or not asserted to rest upon an unambiguous text) is the law. . . .

QUESTIONS

1. What insights does the dispute about ossification provide into the question of the locus of lawmaking authority that drives the disagreement about *Mead*'s limit on the application of *Chevron* deference?
2. Is Justice Scalia correct in his view that the majority approach in *Brand X Internet Services* has violated the separation of powers by subjecting judicial decisions to review by members of the executive branch?

DECKER v. NORTHWEST ENVIRONMENTAL DEFENSE CENTER

133 S. Ct. 1326 (2013)

JUSTICE KENNEDY delivered the opinion of the Court.

These cases present the question whether the Clean Water Act (Act) and its implementing regulations require permits before channeled stormwater runoff from logging roads can be discharged into the navigable waters of the United States. Under the statute and its implementing regulations, a permit is required if the discharges are deemed to be "associated with industrial activity." 33 U.S.C. § 1342(p)(2)(B). The Environmental Protection Agency (EPA), with the responsibility to enforce the Act, has issued a regulation defining the term "associated with industrial activity" to cover only discharges "from any conveyance that is used for collecting and conveying storm water and that is directly related to manufacturing, processing or raw materials storage areas at an industrial plant." 40 C.F.R. § 122.26(b)(14) (2006). The EPA interprets its regulation to exclude the type of stormwater discharges from logging roads at issue here. For reasons now to be explained, the Court concludes the EPA's determination is a reasonable interpretation of its own regulation; and, in consequence, deference is accorded to the interpretation under *Auer v. Robbins*, 519 U.S. 452, 461 (1997).

I

A

[The Court provided the legal history related to the question of whether the "channeled stormwater runoff" was subject to the Act's permit requirement for point sources. The Act was first enacted as law in 1972, but was amended in 1987 in relevant part because of permitting difficulties encountered by the EPA.] In 1987, Congress responded to these problems and adopted various stormwater-related amendments to the Act. § 405, 101 Stat. 69, 33 U.S.C. § 1342(p).

The 1987 amendments exempt from the NPDES permitting scheme most "discharges composed entirely of stormwater." § 1342(p)(1). The general exemption, however, does not extend to all stormwater discharges. As relevant here, Congress directed the EPA to continue to require permits for stormwater discharges "associated with industrial activity." § 1342(p)(2)(B). The statute does not define that term, but the EPA adopted a regulation (hereinafter Industrial Stormwater Rule) in which it defined ["stormwater discharges 'associated with industrial activity'"] as

> "the discharge from any conveyance that is used for collecting and conveying storm water and that is directly related to manufacturing, processing or raw materials storage areas at an industrial plant. The term does not include discharges from facilities or activities excluded from the NPDES program under this part 122. For the categories of industries identified in this section, the term includes, but is not limited to, storm water discharges from . . . immediate access roads and rail lines used or traveled by carriers of raw materials, manufactured products, waste material, or by-products used or created by the facility. . . ." 40 C.F.R. § 122.26(b)(14) (2006).

The Industrial Stormwater Rule also specified that, with one exception not relevant here, "[f]acilities classified as Standard Industrial Classificatio[n] 24" are "considered to be engaging in 'industrial activity' for purposes of paragraph (b)(14)." *Ibid.* The Standard Industrial Classifications are a system used by federal agencies to categorize firms engaged in different types of business activity. Standard Industrial Classification 24 identifies industries involved in the field of "Lumber and Wood Products." This includes the "Logging" industry, defined as "[e]stablishments primarily engaged in cutting timber and in producing . . . primary forest or wood raw materials." *Ibid.*

On November 30, 2012—three days before the instant cases were argued in this Court—the EPA issued its final version of an amendment to the Industrial Stormwater Rule. The amendment was the agency's response to the Court of Appeals' ruling now under review. The amended version seeks to clarify the types of facilities within Standard Industrial Classification 24 that are deemed to be engaged in industrial activity for purposes of the rule. The amended Industrial Stormwater Rule does not cover all facilities within Standard Industrial Classification 24. It limits covered stormwater discharges to

> "[f]acilities classified within Standard Industrial Classification 24, Industry Group 241 that are rock crushing, gravel washing, log sorting, or log storage facilities operated in connection with silvicultural activities . . . and Industry Groups 242 through 249." 77 Fed. Reg. 72974 (2012).

It should be noted, by way of explanation, that an Industry Group is a subcategory of businesses within a Standard Industrial Classification. Industry Group 241 is "Logging," while Industry Groups 242 through 245 are, respectively, "Sawmills and Planing Mills," "Millwork, Veneer, Plywood, and Structural Wood," "Wood Containers," and "Wood Buildings and Mobile Homes."

Industry Group 249 is "Miscellaneous Wood Products." Industry Groups 246 through 248 are blank categories.

It is fair to say the purpose of the amended regulation is to bring within the NPDES permit process only those logging operations that involve the four types of activity (rock crushing, gravel washing, log sorting, and log storage facilities) that are defined as point sources by the explicit terms of the [Industrial Stormwater] Rule.

Up to this stage in the litigation, of course, the cases have been concerned with the Industrial Stormwater Rule before the amendment adopted on November 30, 2012. The amended regulation will determine whether from this point forward NPDES permits will be required for the stormwater discharges at issue. . . .

B

At issue are discharges of channeled stormwater runoff from two logging roads in Oregon's Tillamook State Forest, lying in the Pacific Coast Range about 40 miles west of Portland. Petitioner Georgia–Pacific West, along with other logging and paper-products companies, has a contract with the State of Oregon to harvest timber from the forest. It uses the roads for that purpose. When it rains (which it does often in the mountains of northwest Oregon, averaging in some areas more than 100 inches per year), water runs off the graded roads into a system of ditches, culverts, and channels that discharge the water into nearby rivers and streams. The discharges often contain large amounts of sediment, in the form of dirt and crushed gravel from the roads. There is evidence that this runoff can harm fish and other aquatic organisms.

In September 2006, respondent Northwest Environmental Defense Center (NEDC) filed suit in the United States District Court for the District of Oregon. It invoked the Clean Water Act's citizen-suit provision, 33 U.S.C. § 1365, and named as defendants certain firms involved in logging and paper-products operations (including petitioner Georgia–Pacific West), as well as state and local governments and officials (including the State Forester of Oregon, who is now petitioner Doug Decker). The suit alleged that the defendants caused discharges of channeled stormwater runoff into two waterways — the South Fork Trask River and the Little South Fork Kilchis River. The defendants had not obtained NPDES permits, and so, the suit alleged, they had violated the Act.

The District Court dismissed the action for failure to state a claim. . . . The Court of Appeals for the Ninth Circuit reversed. . . .

This Court granted certiorari.

II

[Discussion of federal court jurisdiction under the Clean Water Act is omitted.]

III

The substantive question of the necessity for an NPDES permit under the earlier rule now must be addressed. Under the Act, petitioners were required to secure NPDES permits for the discharges of channeled stormwater runoff only if the discharges were "associated with industrial activity," 33 U.S.C. § 1342(p)(2)(B), as that statutory term is defined in the preamendment version of the Industrial Stormwater Rule, 40 C.F.R. § 122.26(b)(14) (2006). Otherwise, the discharges fall within the Act's general exemption of "discharges composed entirely of stormwater" from the NPDES permitting scheme. 33 U.S.C. § 1342(p)(1).

NEDC first contends that the statutory term "associated with industrial activity" unambiguously covers discharges of channeled stormwater runoff from logging roads. *See Chevron U.S.A. Inc. v. Natural Resources Defense Council, Inc.,* 467 U.S. 837, 842–843 (1984). That view, however, overlooks the multiple definitions of the terms "industrial" and "industry." These words can refer to business activity in general, yet so too can they be limited to "economic activity concerned with the processing of raw materials and manufacture of goods in factories." Oxford Dict. 887. The latter definition does not necessarily encompass outdoor timber harvesting. The statute does not foreclose more specific definition by the agency, since it provides no further detail as to its intended scope.

Somewhat more plausible is NEDC's claim that the preamendment version of the Industrial Stormwater Rule unambiguously required a permit for the discharges at issue. NEDC reasons that under the rule, "[f]or the categories of industries identified in this section," NPDES permits are required for, among other things, "storm water discharges from . . . immediate access roads . . . used or traveled by carriers of raw materials." 40 C.F.R. § 122.26(b)(14) (2006). Yet this raises the question whether logging is a "categor[y] of industr[y]" identified by the section. The regulation goes on to identify a list of "categories of facilities" that "are considered to be engaging in 'industrial activity' for purposes" of the Industrial Stormwater Rule. *Ibid.* In the earlier version of the regulation, this list included "[f]acilities classified as Standard Industrial Classificatio[n] 24," which encompasses "Logging." *Ibid.* Hence, NEDC asserts, logging is among the categories of industries for which "storm water discharges from . . . immediate access roads . . . used or traveled by carriers of raw materials" required NPDES permits under the earlier version of the Industrial Stormwater Rule. § 122.26(b)(14). NEDC further notes, in support of its reading of the regulation, that modern logging is a large-scale, highly mechanized enterprise, using sophisticated harvesting machines weighing up to 20 tons.

The EPA takes a different view. It concludes that the earlier regulation invoked Standard Industrial Classification 24 "'to regulate traditional *industrial* sources such as sawmills.'" Brief for United States as *Amicus Curiae* 24–25. It points to the regulation's reference to "facilities" and the classification's reference to "establishments," which suggest industrial sites more fixed and permanent than outdoor timber-harvesting operations. *Ibid.* This reading is reinforced by the Industrial Stormwater Rule's definition of discharges associated with industrial activity as discharges "from any conveyance that is used for collecting and conveying storm water and that is directly related to manufacturing, processing or raw materials storage areas at an industrial plant." 40 C.F.R. § 122.26(b)(14) (2006). This language lends support to the EPA's claim that the regulation does not cover temporary, outdoor logging installations. It was reasonable for the agency to conclude that the conveyances at issue are "directly related" only to the harvesting of raw materials, rather than to "manufacturing," "processing," or "raw materials storage areas." See Oxford Dict. 1066 (manufacturing is "mak[ing] (something) on a large scale using machinery"); *id.*, at 1392 (processing is "perform[ing] a series of mechanical or chemical operations on (something) in order to change or preserve it"). In addition, even if logging as a general matter is a type of economic activity within the regulation's scope, a reasonable interpretation of the regulation could still require the discharges to be related in a direct way to operations "at an industrial plant" in order to be subject to NPDES permitting.

NEDC resists this conclusion, noting that elsewhere in the Industrial Stormwater Rule the EPA has required NPDES permits for stormwater discharges associated with other types of outdoor economic activity. *See* § 122.26(b)(14)(iii) (mining); § 122.26(b)(14)(v) (landfills receiving industrial waste); § 122.26(b)(14)(x) (large construction sites). The EPA reasonably could conclude, however, that these types of activities tend to be more fixed and permanent than timber-harvesting operations are and have a closer connection to traditional industrial sites. In light of the language of the regulation just discussed, moreover, the inclusion of these types of economic activity in the Industrial Stormwater Rule need not be read to mandate that all stormwater discharges related to these activities fall within the rule, just as the inclusion of logging need not be read to extend to all discharges from logging sites. The regulation's reach may be limited by the requirement that the discharges be "directly related to manufacturing, processing or raw materials storage areas at an industrial plant." § 122.26(b)(14).

It is well established that an agency's interpretation need not be the only possible reading of a regulation — or even the best one — to prevail. When an agency interprets its own regulation, the Court, as a general rule, defers to it "unless that interpretation is 'plainly erroneous or inconsistent with the regulation.'" *Chase Bank USA, N.A. v. McCoy,* 131 S. Ct. 871, 880 (2011) (quoting *Auer,* 519 U.S., at 461). The EPA's interpretation is a permissible one. Taken together, the regulation's references to "facilities," "establishments," "manufacturing," "processing," and an "industrial plant" leave open the rational interpretation that the regulation extends only to traditional industrial buildings such as factories and associated sites, as well as other relatively fixed facilities.

There is another reason to accord *Auer* deference to the EPA's interpretation: there is no indication that its current view is a change from prior practice or a post hoc justification adopted in response to litigation. *See Christopher v. Smith-Kline Beecham Corp.,* 132 S. Ct. 2156, 2166–2167 (2012). The opposite is the case. The agency has been consistent in its view that the types of discharges at issue here do not require NPDES permits.

The EPA's decision exists against a background of state regulation with respect to stormwater runoff from logging roads. The State of Oregon has made an extensive effort to develop a comprehensive set of best practices to manage stormwater runoff from logging roads. . . . In exercising the broad discretion the Clean Water Act gives the EPA in the realm of stormwater runoff, the agency could reasonably have concluded that further federal regulation in this area would be duplicative or counterproductive. Indeed, Congress has given express instructions to the EPA to work "in consultation with State and local officials" to alleviate stormwater pollution by developing the precise kind of best management practices Oregon has established here. 33 U.S.C. § 1342(p)(6).

* * *

. . . For the reasons stated, the judgment of the Court of Appeals is reversed, and the cases are remanded for proceedings consistent with this opinion.

It is so ordered.

JUSTICE BREYER took no part in the consideration or decision of these cases.

CHIEF JUSTICE ROBERTS, with whom JUSTICE ALITO joins, concurring.

The opinion concurring in part and dissenting in part raises serious questions about the principle set forth in *Bowles v. Seminole Rock & Sand Co.*, 325 U.S. 410 (1945), and *Auer v. Robbins*, 519 U.S. 452 (1997). It may be appropriate to reconsider that principle in an appropriate case. But this is not that case.

. . .

The issue is a basic one going to the heart of administrative law. Questions of *Seminole Rock* and *Auer* deference arise as a matter of course on a regular basis. The bar is now aware that there is some interest in reconsidering those cases, and has available to it a concise statement of the arguments on one side of the issue.

I would await a case in which the issue is properly raised and argued. The present cases should be decided as they have been briefed and argued, under existing precedent.

JUSTICE SCALIA, concurring in part and dissenting in part.

I join Parts I and II of the Court's opinion. . . . I do not join Part III. The Court there gives effect to a reading of EPA's regulations that is not the most natural one, simply because EPA says that it believes the unnatural reading is right. It does this, moreover, even though the agency has vividly illustrated that it can write a rule saying precisely what it means — by doing *just that* while these cases were being briefed.

Enough is enough.

I

For decades, and for no good reason, we have been giving agencies the authority to say what their rules mean, under the harmless-sounding banner of "defer[ring] to an agency's interpretation of its own regulations." *Talk America, Inc. v. Michigan Bell Telephone Co.*, 131 S. Ct. 2254, 2265 (2011) (SCALIA, J., concurring). This is generally called *Seminole Rock* or *Auer* deference.

Two terms ago, in my separate concurrence in *Talk America*, I expressed doubts about the validity of this practice. In that case, however, the agency's interpretation of the rule was also the fairest one, and no party had asked us to reconsider *Auer*. Today, however, the Court's deference to the agency makes the difference (note the Court's defensive insistence that the agency's interpretation need not be "the best one"). And respondent has asked us, if necessary, to "'reconsider *Auer*.'" I believe that it is time to do so. This is especially true because the circumstances of these cases illustrate *Auer*'s flaws in a particularly vivid way.

The canonical formulation of *Auer* deference is that we will enforce an agency's interpretation of its own rules unless that interpretation is "plainly erroneous or inconsistent with the regulation." *Seminole Rock, supra,* at 414.

But of course whenever the agency's interpretation of the regulation is different from the fairest reading, it is in that sense "inconsistent" with the regulation. Obviously, that is not enough, or there would be nothing for *Auer* to do. In practice, *Auer* deference is *Chevron* deference applied to regulations rather than statutes. The agency's interpretation will be accepted if, though not the fairest reading of the regulation, it is a plausible reading—within the scope of the ambiguity that the regulation contains.

Our cases have not put forward a persuasive justification for *Auer* deference. The first case to apply it, *Seminole Rock*, offered no justification whatever—just the *ipse dixit* that "the administrative interpretation . . . becomes of controlling weight unless it is plainly erroneous or inconsistent with the regulation." 325 U.S., at 414. Our later cases provide two principal explanations, neither of which has much to be said for it. See generally Stephenson & Pogoriler, *Seminole Rock*'s Domain, 79 Geo. Wash. L. Rev. 1449, 1454–1458 (2011). First, some cases say that the agency, as the drafter of the rule, will have some special insight into its intent when enacting it. E.g., *Martin v. Occupational Safety and Health Review Comm'n*, 499 U.S. 144, 150–153 (1991). The implied premise of this argument—that what we are looking for is the agency's intent in adopting the rule—is false. There is true of regulations what is true of statutes. As Justice Holmes put it: "[w]e do not inquire what the legislature meant; we ask only what the statute means." The Theory of Legal Interpretation, 12 Harv. L. Rev. 417, 419 (1899). Whether governing rules are made by the national legislature or an administrative agency, we are bound by what they say, not by the unexpressed intention of those who made them.

The other rationale our cases provide is that the agency possesses special expertise in administering its "'complex and highly technical regulatory program.'" *See*, e.g., *Thomas Jefferson Univ. v. Shalala*, 512 U.S. 504, 512 (1994). That is true enough, and it leads to the conclusion that agencies and not courts should make regulations. But it has nothing to do with who should interpret regulations—unless one believes that the purpose of interpretation is to make the regulatory program work in a fashion that the current leadership of the agency deems effective. Making regulatory programs effective is the purpose of rulemaking, in which the agency uses its "special expertise" to formulate the best rule. But the purpose of interpretation is to determine the fair meaning of the rule—to "say what the law is," *Marbury v. Madison*, 1 Cranch 137, 177 (1803). Not to make policy, but to determine what policy has been made and promulgated by the agency, to which the public owes obedience. Indeed, since the leadership of agencies (and hence the policy preferences of agencies) changes with Presidential administrations, an agency head can only be sure that the application of his "special expertise" to the issue addressed by a regulation *will be given effect* if we adhere to predictable principles of textual interpretation rather than defer to the "special expertise" of his successors. If we take agency enactments as written, the Executive has a stable background against which to write its rules and achieve the policy ends it thinks best.

Another conceivable justification for *Auer* deference, though not one that is to be found in our cases, is this: If it is reasonable to defer to agencies regarding the meaning of statutes that Congress enacted, as we do per *Chevron*, it is *a fortiori* reasonable to defer to them regarding the meaning of regulations *that they themselves crafted*. To give an agency less control over the meaning of its own regulations than it has over the meaning of a congressionally enacted statute seems quite odd.

But it is not odd at all. The theory of *Chevron* (take it or leave it) is that when Congress gives an agency authority to administer a statute, including authority to issue interpretive regulations, it implicitly accords the agency a degree of discretion, which the courts must respect, regarding the meaning of the statute. *See Smiley v. Citibank (South Dakota), N.A.*, 517 U.S. 735, 740–741 (1996). While the implication of an agency power to clarify the statute is reasonable enough, there is surely no congressional implication that the agency can resolve ambiguities in its own regulations. For that would violate a fundamental principle of separation of powers — that the power to write a law and the power to interpret it cannot rest in the same hands. "When the legislative and executive powers are united in the same person . . . there can be no liberty; because apprehensions may arise, lest the same monarch or senate should enact tyrannical laws, to execute them in a tyrannical manner." Montesquieu, Spirit of the Laws bk. XI, ch. 6, pp. 151–152 (O. Piest ed., T. Nugent transl. 1949). Congress cannot enlarge its own power through *Chevron* — whatever it leaves vague in the statute will be worked out *by someone else*. *Chevron* represents a presumption about who, as between the Executive and the Judiciary, that someone else will be. (The Executive, by the way — the competing political branch — is the less congenial repository of the power as far as Congress is concerned.) So Congress's incentive is to speak as clearly as possible on the matters it regards as important.

But when an agency interprets its *own* rules — that is something else. Then the power to prescribe is augmented by the power to interpret; and the incentive is to speak vaguely and broadly, so as to retain a "flexibility" that will enable "clarification" with retroactive effect. "It is perfectly understandable" for an agency to "issue vague regulations" if doing so will "maximiz[e] agency power." *Thomas Jefferson Univ., supra*, at 525 (THOMAS, J., dissenting). Combining the power to prescribe with the power to interpret is not a new evil: Blackstone condemned the practice of resolving doubts about "the construction of the Roman laws" by "stat[ing] the case to the emperor in writing, and tak[ing] his opinion upon it." 1 W. Blackstone, Commentaries on the Laws of England 58 (1765). And our Constitution did not mirror the British practice of using the House of Lords as a court of last resort, due in part to the fear that he who has "agency in passing bad laws" might operate in the "same spirit" in their interpretation. The Federalist No. 81, pp. 543–544 (J. Cooke ed. 1961). *Auer* deference encourages agencies to be "vague in framing regulations, with the plan of issuing 'interpretations' to create the intended new law without observance of notice and comment procedures." Anthony, The Supreme Court and the APA: Sometimes They Just Don't Get It, 10 Admin. L.J. Am. U. 1, 11–12 (1996). *Auer* is not a logical corollary to *Chevron* but a dangerous permission slip for the arrogation of power. See *Talk America*, 131 S. Ct., at 2266 (SCALIA, J., concurring); Manning, Constitutional Structure and Judicial Deference to Agency Interpretations of Agency Rules, 96 Colum. L. Rev. 612 (1996).

It is true enough that *Auer* deference has the same beneficial pragmatic effect as *Chevron* deference: The country need not endure the uncertainty produced by divergent views of numerous district courts and courts of appeals as to what is the fairest reading of the regulation, until a definitive answer is finally provided, years later, by this Court. The agency's view can be relied upon, unless it is, so to speak, beyond the pale. But the duration of the uncertainty produced by a vague regulation need not be as long as the uncertainty produced by a vague statute. For as soon as an interpretation uncongenial to the agency is pronounced by a district court, the agency can begin the process of amending the regulation to make its meaning entirely clear. The circumstances of this case demonstrate the point. While these cases were being briefed before us, EPA issued a rule designed to respond to the Court of Appeals judgment we are reviewing. See 77 Fed. Reg. 72974 (2012) (to be codified in 40 C.F.R. pt. 122, sub pt. B). It did so (by the standards of such things) relatively quickly: The decision below was handed down in May 2011, and in December 2012 the EPA published an amended rule setting forth in unmistakable terms the position it argues here. And there is another respect in which a lack of *Chevron*-type deference has less severe pragmatic consequences for rules than for statutes. In many cases, when an agency believes that its rule permits conduct that the text arguably forbids, it can simply exercise its discretion not to prosecute. That is not possible, of course, when, as here, a party harmed by the violation has standing to compel enforcement.

In any case, however great may be the efficiency gains derived from *Auer* deference, beneficial effect cannot justify a rule that not only has no principled basis but contravenes one of the great rules of separation of powers: He who writes a law must not adjudge its violation.

II

I would therefore resolve these cases by using the familiar tools of textual interpretation to decide: Is what the petitioners did here proscribed by the fairest reading of the regulations? What they did was to channel stormwater runoff from logging roads without a permit. To decide whether that was permissible we must answer one, and possibly two, questions: First, was the stormwater discharged from a "point source"? If not, no permit was required. But if so, we face the second question: Were the stormwater discharges exempt from the permit requirement because they were not "associated with industrial activity"? The fairest reading of the statute and regulations is that these discharges were from point sources, and were associated with industrial activity. . . .

Because the fairest reading of the agency's rules proscribes the conduct at issue in these cases, I would affirm the judgment below. It is time for us to presume (to coin a phrase) that an agency says in a rule what it means, and means in a rule what it says there.

QUESTIONS

1. What theory supports court deference to agency interpretations of its own (legislative) regulations? Who better than the agency knows what the agency's rules mean?
2. What form does the interpretation of the agency regulations take in *Decker*? Given this form, should a Court give *Chevron*-like deference to the interpretation?
3. Justice Scalia wrote the opinion for the Court in *Auer v. Robbins*, 519 U.S. 452 (1997), which accepted post-*Chevron* the rule that a court must defer to an

agency's interpretation of its own regulations, a rule first established in
Bowles v. Seminole Rock & Sand Co., 325 U.S. 410 (1945). What is the separation of powers argument that Justice Scalia now presents to challenge the
application of *Auer* deference? Is *Chevron* deference subject to the same
argument? In his dissent in *Michigan v. EPA*, 135 S. Ct. 2699, 2712 (2015),
Justice Thomas opined that:

> *Chevron* deference is premised on "a presumption that Congress, when it left
> ambiguity in a statute meant for implementation by an agency, understood
> that the ambiguity would be resolved, first and foremost, by the agency, and
> desired the agency (rather than the courts) to possess whatever degree of
> discretion the ambiguity allows." *Smiley v. Citibank (South Dakota), N. A.*, 517
> U.S. 735, 740–741 (1996). We most often describe Congress' supposed choice
> to leave matters to agency discretion as an allocation of interpretive authority.
> *See*, e.g., *National Cable & Telecommunications Assn. v. Brand X Internet Services*,
> 545 U.S. 967, 983 (2005) (referring to the agency as "the authoritative inter-
> preter (within the limits of reason) of [ambiguous] statutes"). But we
> sometimes treat that discretion as though it were a form of legislative
> power. See, e.g., *United States v. Mead Corp.*, 533 U.S. 218, 229 (2001) (noting
> that the agency "speak[s] with the force of law when it addresses ambiguity in
> the statute or fills a space in the enacted law" even when "'Congress did not
> actually have an intent' as to a particular result"). Either way, *Chevron* defer-
> ence raises serious separation-of-powers questions.

Justice Thomas expressed similar concerns about the constitutionality of
Chevron deference in his concurring opinion in *Cuozzo Speed Technologies,
LLC v. Lee*, 136 S. Ct. 2131, 2148 (2016).

4. Why should an agency's interpretation of its own regulations be denied *Auer*
   deference because the interpretation "is a change from prior practice or a
   post hoc justification adopted in response to litigation" (citing *Christopher v.
   SmithKline Beecham Corp.*, 132 S. Ct. 2156, 2166–2167 (2012))? This is a new
   limit on the application of *Auer* deference. In an earlier decision, *Long Island
   Health Care at Home v. Coke*, 551 U.S. 158, 170 (2007), the Supreme Court
   deferred to an agency interpretation of its own regulation, even though that
   interpretation had changed. The Court stated that: "we conceded that the
   Department may have interpreted these regulations differently at different
   times in their history. But as long as interpretive changes create no unfair
   surprise . . . the change in interpretation alone presents no separate ground
   for disregarding the Department's present interpretation." *Id.* (citations
   omitted).

5. If *Auer* deference is not owed to an agency's interpretation of its own regulations, does the agency still receive the benefit of *Skidmore* deference? In
   SmithKline Beecham Corp., 132 S. Ct., at 2168-69, the Court held that *Skidmore*
   deference does apply in this circumstance. That deference would be limited if,
   as in *SmithKline Beecham Corp.*, the Court declined *Auer* deference because the
   agency had changed its interpretation of the regulations. See *id.* at 2169-70.

6. Is the application of *Auer* deference in *Decker* consistent with *Mead Corp.*? If
   Auer deference is equivalent to *Chevron* deference, has Congress intended
   the application of such deference because the agency has received law making power from Congress and has acted in the exercise of that power?

7. Do the facts of the case, which involved the agency's revision of its regulations to conform to its preferred interpretation of the previous version of the regulations, show that *Auer* deference has limited utility and that rejecting this type of deference would not harm the effectiveness of agencies? Moreover, is there a strong argument that *Auer* deference undermines APA notice and comment requirements?

8. In *Gonzales v. Oregon*, 546 U.S. 243, 257 (2006), the Supreme Court held that it would not accord *Auer* deference to the Attorney General's interpretation of a "parroting regulation" — that is, a regulation that "just repeats two statutory phrases and attempts to summarize the others." *Id.* at 257. The Supreme Court reasoned that "[a]n agency does not acquire special authority to interpret its own words when, instead of using its expertise and experience to formulate a regulation, it has elected merely to paraphrase the statutory language." *Id.* Is this exception to the application of deference proper?

9. For a consideration of *Auer* deference, *see* Michael P. Healy, *The Past, Present and Future of* Auer *Deference:* Mead, *Form and Function in Judicial Review of Agency Interpretations of Regulations*, 62 U. Kan. L. Rev. 633-93 (2014).

NOTE ON AGENCY NONACQUIESCENCE IN COURT OF APPEALS DECISIONS

The practical question of whether a party ought to follow the law as laid down in one judicial circuit, when the law of other circuits differs, assumes legal importance when the party is an administrative agency. The issue has been very controversial.

Federal administrative agencies operate in every state of the union, enforcing myriad statutory and regulatory mandates. Consider, for example, the Environmental Protection Agency. The EPA enjoys ultimate responsibility for the enforcement of federal laws enacted to protect the quality of the natural environment, including air, water, and soil. The EPA's regulatory duties require it to maintain a national enforcement presence; regardless of an industrial facility's physical location, the EPA must ensure that the facility complies with applicable federal environmental laws and regulations.

Congress has divided the nation into twelve geographic districts for purposes of allocating responsibility for initial appellate jurisdiction over federal cases — including review of agency action. Each of the twelve federal U.S. Circuit Courts of Appeals hears appeals in cases arising within its territory.[1] Because of this, agencies from time to time will find it necessary to litigate the same question in different courts of appeals. *See, e.g., United States v. Stauffer Chemical Co.*, 464 U.S. 165 (1984). Decisions from outside the U.S. Circuit Court of Appeals charged with deciding a pending case have merely persuasive, not full precedential, value. Accordingly, an agency might convince one reviewing court to accept its position on a particular matter, even if another reviewing court in a different

---

1. There are actually thirteen such courts — the United States Court of Appeals for the Federal Circuit hears certain tax, trade, patents matters in addition to cases brought against the federal government in the Court of Claims. The Federal Circuit, unlike the other twelve Circuit Courts of Appeals, has a jurisdiction defined exclusively by subject matter rather than geography.

part of the country has already rejected it. When this happens, a "circuit split" comes into existence.

An agency that believes a Court of Appeals has wrongly rejected its view of a particular matter might wish to relitigate the claim in another Court of Appeals. In other words, the agency might well refuse to give up in pressing its view of the matter. When an agency refuses to accept a Circuit Court's reading of a statute or regulation, the agency has engaged in an act of "inter-circuit nonacquiescence."

If the local U.S. Court of Appeals has not yet ruled on a particular question of law, it is perfectly appropriate for an administrative agency to stick to its guns. The U.S. Government should not be required to appeal every minor case that it loses to the Supreme Court in order to preserve its legal position in more important cases. The Supreme Court so held in *United States v. Mendoza*, 464 U.S. 154 (1984). Unsurprisingly, this kind of nonacquiescence has not provoked much serious criticism.

The problem of nonacquiescence gets decidedly more complicated when an agency refuses to follow a court of appeals decision for cases arising within the same Circuit that established the adverse precedent. This is called "intra-circuit nonacquiescence." Such acquiescence is most defensible when a particular agency action may be reviewed by more than one court of appeals. Many organic statutes so provide. Because the agency cannot necessarily control the location in which a party files its petition for review, the agency may disregard a binding precedent of the local court of appeals in which the enforcement action takes place on the theory that judicial review of the action might occur someplace else.

Suppose that the Second Circuit holds that an EPA interpretation of the Clean Air Act is impermissible and invalidates regulations based on the agency's unlawful interpretation of the relevant statutory language. Suppose further that the reviewing court voids regulations imposing limits on a specific kind of particulate emission commonly associated with certain kinds of industrial production. An industrial plant in New York, a state within the jurisdiction of the United States Court of Appeals for the Second Circuit, operates a facility in a fashion that results in particulate emissions that exceed those permitted under the EPA's regulations.

The organic statute in question authorizes the EPA to bring enforcement actions against polluters in either the location in which the facility is located or in the United States Court of Appeals for the District of Columbia Circuit. The EPA, in theory, could bring its enforcement action in the D.C. Circuit, a jurisdiction that does not yet have a precedent on point, rather than in the Second Circuit. In this sense, then, the EPA's decision to apply regulations that the Second Circuit invalidated might not be entirely unreasonable. On these facts, the agency could make a good faith argument that it was engaged in inter-circuit, and not intra-circuit, nonacquiescence.

Some agencies, including the Social Security Administration, have taken nonacquiescence a step further. In cases where a would-be claimant seeks to obtain SSA benefits, the SSA has applied regulations invalidated in the locality where the claim arises and the claimant lives. The argument for intra-circuit nonacquiescence runs as follows. If we assume that the agency had the right to continue to litigate the issue involved in different circuits, considerations of equal treatment warrant consistent application of agency regulations *across the country*, with exceptions only for successful litigants.

The difficulty that results, however, is that only those benefit applicants with the wherewithal to seek judicial review of the agency's denial would receive the benefits to which they have a legal entitlement under the local court of appeals's binding legal interpretation of the program rules. And even with respect to those with the wherewithal, such nonacquiescence results in repetitive litigation. Some court of appeals judges have expressed outrage about the practice in the most forceful terms. E.g., *Hillhouse v. Harris*, 715 F.2d 428, 430 (8th Cir. 1983) (McMILLIAN, J., concurring) ("if the Secretary persists in pursuing her nonacquiescence in this circuit's decisions, I will seek to bring contempt proceedings against the Secretary both in her official and individual capacities"); *Ithaca College v. NLRB*, 623 F.2d 224 (2nd Cir. 1980) ("The Board cites no contrary authority except its own consistent practice of refusing to follow the law of the circuit unless it coincides with the Board's views. This is intolerable if the rule of law is to prevail"); *Lopez v. Heckler*, 713 F.2d 1432, 1441 (9th Cir. 1983) (PREGERSON, J., concurring).

The District of Columbia Circuit recently addressed the concerns about nonacquiescence by a federal agency. In *Heartland Plymouth Court MI, LLC, v. National Labor Relations Board*, 2016 WL 548145, at *4 (D.C. Cir. 2016), the court stated that:

> Our approval of nonacquiescence presumed its stated virtue: opposing adverse circuit decisions permits the Board to bring national labor law questions to Supreme Court resolution. Indeed, when our Court discussed different forms of agency nonacquiescence in *Johnson v. United States Railroad Retirement Board*, 969 F.2d 1082 (D.C. Cir. 1992), it predicated the method's acceptability upon the agency redressing a circuit's conflicting interpretation, *not defying* it *ad infinitum*. *See id.* at 1092 ("When an agency honestly believes a circuit court has misinterpreted the law, there are two places it can go to correct the error: Congress or the Supreme Court").
>
> To that end, nonacquiescence allows for an issue's "percolation" among the circuits; generating a circuit split that can improve the likelihood of *certiorari* being granted. But, nonacquiescence is justifiable only as a means to judicial finality, not agency aggrandizement. As we said in *Johnson*, nonacquiescence is divorced from its purpose when an agency asserts it with no stated intention of seeking *certiorari*.
>
> Achieving judicial finality through national uniformity requires nonacquiescence to rest on certain conditions. First, as explained above, any nonacquiescence depends upon the agency actually seeking Supreme Court review of adverse decisions. Second, nonacquiescence requires candor in its application. The agency should clearly assert its nonacquiescence, specifying its arguments against adverse precedent to preserve them for Supreme Court review. These two conditions characterize proper nonacquiescence.

Judge Millett dissented. Although Judge Millett credited the majority's "concern that an agency's persistent defiance of uniform and settled circuit precedent could ignite a separation-of-powers firestorm," she argued that "a bad-faith award of all the fees that Heartland incurred in this appeal" was not warranted. *Id.* at *10.

For an extended discussion of the various permutations of agency nonacquiescence, *see* Samuel Estreicher & Richard L. Revesz, *Nonacquiescence by Federal Administrative Agencies*, 98 Yale L.J. 679 (1989). *See also* Dan T. Coenen, *The Constitutional Case Against Intracircuit Nonacquiescence*, 75 Minn. L. Rev. 1339 (1991).

NOTE ON DISTINGUISHING QUESTIONS OF FACT AND LAW

Although a reviewing court typically defers to an agency determination regarding either fact or law, the theory and scope of the deference differ. Litigants and courts struggle in distinguishing questions of fact from questions of law. For example, consider this paragraph from Justice Jackson's opinion for the Court in *Skidmore v. Swift & Co., supra* p. 525 (emphasis added):

> For reasons set forth in the *Armour* case decided herewith we hold that no principle of law found either in the statute or in Court decisions precludes waiting time from also being working time. We have not attempted to, and we cannot, lay down a legal formula to resolve cases so varied in their facts as are the many situations in which employment involves waiting time. *Whether in a concrete case such time falls within or without the Act is a question of fact to be resolved by appropriate findings of the trial court.* This involves scrutiny and construction of the agreements between the particular parties, appraisal of their practical construction of the working agreement by conduct, consideration of the nature of the service, and its relation to the waiting time, and all of the surrounding circumstances. Facts may show that the employee was engaged to wait, or they may show that he waited to be engaged. His compensation may cover both waiting and task, or only performance of the task itself. Living quarters may in some situations be furnished as a facility of the task and in another as a part of its compensation. The law does not impose an arrangement upon the parties. It imposes upon the courts the task of finding what the arrangement was.

Do you agree with Justice Jackson that the question "[w]hether in a concrete case [] time falls within or without the act is a question of fact to be resolved by appropriate findings of the trial court"? For a discussion of the distinction in the partially analogous context of appellate review of trial court determinations, *see Indmar Prods. v. Comm'r*, 444 F.3d 771, 784-88 (6th Cir. 2006) (ROGERS, J., concurring).

QUESTIONS

1. Which side in a judicial review case is likely to argue that a question is one of fact, and which side is likely to argue that a question is one of law?
2. Should there be a separately conceptualized scope of review for "mixed questions of law and fact"?
3. Or should a reviewing court try to break down every issue into its factual and legal components?
4. In view of the deference required by *Chevron* and *Skidmore*, does it really make much difference whether a "mixed" question is determined to be one of fact or of law?
5. In two cases — *N.L.R.B. v. Curtin Matheson Scientific, Inc.*, 494 U.S. 775 (1990) and *Allentown Mack Sales and Service, Inc. v. N.L.R.B.*, 522 U.S. 359 (1998) — the Supreme Court considered the relationship between the review of a question of law and review of a question of fact. In *Curtin Matheson*, the Court considered the agency's decision to forgo the use of a presumption about a lack of union support among replacement workers as a legal issue, the resolution of which was consistent with the purposes of the statute,

specifically the promotion of labor peace and the union's ability to strike. See *id.* at 794-95. The Court suggested that the agency's use of a presumption that replacement workers are opposed to the union may also be reasonable. See *id.* at 794 n.12. The majority, in short, treated the agency decision not to use a presumption as a substantive interpretation of the statute. Chief Justice Rehnquist, in his concurring opinion, stated that the majority had not considered the fact question of whether, independent of the use of a presumption, there was sufficient evidence on the record of a lack of union support among employees, including replacement workers. Justice Blackmun argued in his dissent that the agency had acted unlawfully because it had not explained adequately the reasons for its change in the use of a presumption about anti-union sentiment — a critique of the agency's decision making process, rather than the substance of the decision. Justice Scalia, joined by Justices O'Connor and Kennedy, concluded that the agency had acted unlawfully because its decision that the employer lacked good-faith reasonable doubt about the union's majority status was not supported by substantial evidence. Justice Scalia accordingly viewed the case as involving a question of fact, rather than law or decision making process. See *id.* at 813 ("The Board's framing of the question presented, like its opinion in this case, invites us to confuse fact-finding with policymaking. The Court should not so readily have accepted the invitation"); *id.* at 818 (the Board "did not purport to be deciding the case on the assumption that the union lacked majority support. It found respondent guilty of an unfair labor practice on the ground that there was, *in fact*, no reasonable doubt of the union's majority status; and it is exclusively *that* finding which respondent challenged, both here and in the Fifth Circuit. If we permitted the Board's order to be enforced on the quite different ground that it does not matter whether respondent had a reasonable, good-faith doubt, we not only would be making for the Board a decision it has not yet reached, but also would be depriving respondent of judicial review of that decision" (footnote omitted; emphasis in original)).

In *Allentown Mack*, the Supreme Court was sharply divided in its review of an NLRB adjudication in which the agency had determined that Allentown Mack — a successor owner of a company — had engaged in an unfair labor practice because it had conducted an internal poll of employee support for a union without demonstrating that it had the requisite objective good-faith reasonable doubt. A majority of the Court decided that the agency had not committed a legal error in establishing the good-faith reasonable doubt standard, but had committed a factual error. Justice Scalia, however, was the only Justice who reached both these conclusions. Four Justices, who joined a concurring and dissenting opinion by Chief Justice Rehnquist, concluded both that the NLRB's good-faith reasonable doubt standard was unlawful and that the fact-finding failed to meet the substantial evidence standard. The other four Justices, who joined a concurring and dissenting opinion by Justice Breyer, concluded that both the NLRB's standard and its fact-finding were proper.

After summarizing the record evidence, Justice Scalia concluded for the Court that "[g]iving fair weight to Allentown's circumstantial evidence, we think it quite impossible for a rational fact-finder to avoid the conclusion that Allentown had reasonable, good-faith grounds to doubt — to be uncertain about — the union's retention of majority support." *Id.* at 371. He then echoed the concerns that he had raised in his *Curtin Matheson* dissent, this time presenting them in a majority opinion:

> The Board can, of course, forthrightly and explicitly adopt counterfactual evidentiary presumptions (which are in effect substantive rules of law) as a way of furthering particular legal or policy goals — for example, the Board's irrebuttable presumption of majority support for the union during the year following certification. The Board might also be justified in forthrightly and explicitly adopting a rule of evidence that categorically excludes certain testimony on policy grounds, without reference to its inherent probative value. (Such clearly announced rules of law or of evidentiary exclusion would of course be subject to judicial review for their reasonableness and their compatibility with the Act.) That is not the sort of Board action at issue here, however, but rather the Board's allegedly systematic undervaluation of certain evidence, or allegedly systematic exaggeration of what the evidence must prove. When the Board purports to be engaged in simple factfinding, unconstrained by substantive presumptions or evidentiary rules of exclusion, it is not free to prescribe what inferences from the evidence it will accept and reject, but must draw all those inferences that the evidence fairly demands. "Substantial evidence" review exists precisely to ensure that the Board achieves minimal compliance with this obligation, which is the foundation of all honest and legitimate adjudication.

Id. at 378-79.

What is the distinction that Justice Scalia is making between the agency's adoption of presumptions and its finding of facts?

C. SCOPE OF REVIEW OF EXERCISES OF DISCRETION

CITIZENS TO PRESERVE OVERTON PARK v. VOLPE
401 U.S. 402 (1971)

Opinion of the Court by MR. JUSTICE MARSHALL, announced by MR. JUSTICE STEWART.

The growing public concern about the quality of our natural environment has prompted Congress in recent years to enact legislation designed to curb the accelerating destruction of our country's natural beauty. We are concerned in this case with §4(f) of the Department of Transportation Act of 1966, as amended, and §18(a) of the Federal-Aid Highway Act of 1968, 23 U.S.C. §138 (1964 ed., Supp. V) (hereafter §138). These statutes prohibit the Secretary of Transportation from authorizing the use of federal funds to finance the construction of highways through public parks if a "feasible and prudent" alternative route exists. If no such route is available, the statutes allow him to approve construction through parks only if there has been "all possible planning to minimize harm" to the park.

Petitioners, private citizens as well as local and national conservation organizations, contend that the Secretary has violated these statutes by authorizing the expenditure of federal funds for the construction of a six-lane interstate highway through a public park in Memphis, Tennessee. Their claim was rejected by the District Court, which granted the Secretary's motion for summary judgment, and the Court of Appeals for the Sixth Circuit affirmed. After oral argument, this Court granted a stay that halted construction and, treating the application for the stay as a petition for certiorari, granted review. We now reverse the judgment below and remand for further proceedings in the District Court.

Overton Park is a 342-acre city park located near the center of Memphis. The park contains a zoo, a nine-hole municipal golf course, an outdoor theater, nature trails, a bridle path, an art academy, picnic areas, and 170 acres of forest. The proposed highway, which is to be a six-lane, high-speed, expressway, will sever the zoo from the rest of the park. Although the roadway will be depressed below ground level except where it crosses a small creek, 26 acres of the park will be destroyed. The highway is to be a segment of Interstate Highway I-40, part of the National System of Interstate and Defense Highways. I-40 will provide Memphis with a major east-west expressway which will allow easier access to downtown Memphis from the residential areas on the eastern edge of the city.

Although the route through the park was approved by the Bureau of Public Roads in 1956 and by the Federal Highway Administrator in 1966, the enactment of §4(f) of the Department of Transportation Act prevented distribution of federal funds for the section of the highway designated to go through Overton Park until the Secretary of Transportation determined whether the requirements of §4(f) had been met. Federal funding for the rest of the project was, however, available; and the state acquired a right-of-way on both sides of the park. In April 1968, the Secretary announced that he concurred in the judgment of local officials that I-40 should be built through the park. And in September 1969 the State acquired the right-of-way inside Overton Park from the city. Final approval for the project — the route as well as the design — was not announced until November 1969, after Congress had reiterated in §138 of the Federal-Aid Highway Act that highway construction through public parks was to be restricted. Neither announcement approving the route and design of I-40 was accompanied by a statement of the Secretary's factual findings. He did not indicate why he believed there were no feasible and prudent alternative routes or why design changes could not be made to reduce the harm to the park.

Petitioners contend that the Secretary's action is invalid without such formal findings and that the Secretary did not make an independent determination but merely relied on the judgment of the Memphis City Council. They also contend that it would be "feasible and prudent" to route I-40 around Overton Park either to the north or to the south. And they argue that if these alternative routes are not "feasible and prudent," the present plan does not include "all possible" methods for reducing harm to the park. Petitioners claim that I-40 could be built under the park by using either of two possible tunneling methods, and they claim that, at a minimum, by using advanced drainage techniques the expressway could be depressed below ground level along the entire route through the park including the section that crosses the small creek.

Respondents argue that it was unnecessary for the Secretary to make formal findings, and that he did, in fact, exercise his own independent judgment which was supported by the facts. In the District Court, respondents introduced affidavits, prepared specifically for this litigation, which indicated that the Secretary had made the decision and that the decision was supportable. These affidavits were contradicted by affidavits introduced by petitioners, who also sought to take the deposition of a former Federal Highway Administrator who had participated in the decision to route I-40 through Overton Park.

The District Court and the Court of Appeals found that formal findings by the Secretary were not necessary and refused to order the deposition of the former Federal Highway Administrator because those courts believed that probing of the mental processes of an administrative decisionmaker was prohibited. And, believing that the Secretary's authority was wide and reviewing courts' authority narrow in the approval of highway routes, the lower courts held that the affidavits contained no basis for a determination that the Secretary had exceeded his authority.

We agree that formal findings were not required. But we do not believe that in this case judicial review based solely on litigation affidavits was adequate.

A threshold question — whether petitioners are entitled to any judicial review — is easily answered. Section 701 of the Administrative Procedure Act, 5 U.S.C. § 701 (1964 ed., Supp. V), provides that the action of "each authority of the Government of the United States," which includes the Department of Transportation, is subject to judicial review except where there is a statutory prohibition on review or where "agency action is committed to agency discretion by law." In this case, there is no indication that Congress sought to prohibit judicial review and there is most certainly no "showing of 'clear and convincing evidence' of a . . . legislative intent" to restrict access to judicial review.

Similarly, the Secretary's decision here does not fall within the exception for action "committed to agency discretion." This is a very narrow exception. The legislative history of the Administrative Procedure Act indicates that it is applicable in those rare instances where "statutes are drawn in such broad terms that in a given case there is no law to apply." S. Rep. No. 752, 79th Cong., 1st Sess., 26 (1945).

Section 4(f) of the Department of Transportation Act and § 138 of the Federal-Aid Highway Act are clear and specific directives. Both the Department of Transportation Act and the Federal-Aid Highway Act provide that the Secretary "shall not approve any program or project" that requires the use of any public parkland "unless (1) there is no feasible and prudent alternative to the use of such land, and (2) such program includes all possible planning to minimize harm to such park. . . ." 23 U.S.C. § 138 (1964 ed., Supp. V); 49 U.S.C. § 1653(f) (1964 ed., Supp. V). This language is a plain and explicit bar to the use of federal funds for construction of highways through parks — only the most unusual situations are exempted.

Despite the clarity of the statutory language, respondents argue that the Secretary has wide discretion. They recognize that the requirement that there be no "feasible" alternative route admits of little administrative discretion. For this exemption to apply the Secretary must find that as a matter of sound engineering it would not be feasible to build the highway along any other route. Respondents argue, however, that the requirement that there be no other "prudent" route requires the Secretary to engage in a wide-ranging balancing of competing interests. They contend that the Secretary should weigh the detriment resulting from the destruction of parkland against the cost of other routes, safety considerations, and other factors, and determine on the basis of the importance that he attaches to these other factors whether, on balance, alternative feasible routes would be "prudent."

But no such wide-ranging endeavor was intended. It is obvious that in most cases considerations of cost, directness of route, and community disruption will indicate that parkland should be used for highway construction whenever possible. Although it may be necessary to transfer funds from one jurisdiction to another, there will always be a smaller outlay required from the public purse when parkland is used since the public already owns the land and there will be no need to pay for right-of-way. And since people do not live or work in parks, if a highway is built on parkland no one will have to leave his home or give up his business. Such factors are common to substantially all highway construction. Thus, if Congress intended these factors to be on an equal footing with preservation of parkland there would have been no need for the statutes.

Congress clearly did not intend that cost and disruption of the community were to be ignored by the Secretary. But the very existence of the statutes indicates that protection of parkland was to be given paramount importance. The few green havens that are public parks were not to be lost unless there were truly unusual factors present in a particular case or the cost or community disruption resulting from alternative routes reached extraordinary magnitudes. If the statutes are to have any meaning, the Secretary cannot approve the destruction of parkland unless he finds that alternative routes present unique problems.

Plainly, there is "law to apply" and thus the exemption for action "committed to agency discretion" is inapplicable. But the existence of judicial review is only the start: the standard for review must also be determined. For that we must look to § 706 of the Administrative Procedure Act, 5 U.S.C. § 706 (1964 ed., Supp. V), which provides that a "reviewing court shall . . . hold unlawful and set aside agency action, findings, and conclusions found" not to meet six separate standards. In all cases agency action must be set aside if the action was "arbitrary, capricious, an abuse of discretion, or otherwise not in accordance with law" or if the action failed to meet statutory, procedural, or constitutional requirements. 5 U.S.C. §§ 706 (2)(A), (B), (C), (D) (1964 ed., Supp. V). In certain narrow, specifically limited situations, the agency action is to be set aside if the action was not supported by "substantial evidence." And in other equally narrow circumstances the reviewing court is to engage in a de novo review of the action and set it aside if it was "unwarranted by the facts." 5 U.S.C. §§ 706 (2)(E), (F) (1964 ed., Supp. V).

Petitioners argue that the Secretary's approval of the construction of I-40 through Overton Park is subject to one or the other of these latter two standards of limited applicability. First, they contend that the "substantial evidence" standard of § 706 (2)(E) must be applied. In the alternative, they claim that § 706 (2)(F) applies and that there must be a de novo review to determine if the Secretary's action was "unwarranted by the facts." Neither of these standards is, however, applicable.

Review under the substantial-evidence test is authorized only when the agency action is taken pursuant to a rulemaking provision of the Administrative Procedure Act itself, 5 U.S.C. § 553 (1964 ed., Supp. V), or when the agency action is based on a public adjudicatory hearing. See 5 U.S.C. §§ 556, 557 (1964 ed., Supp. V). The Secretary's decision to allow the expenditure of federal funds to build I-40 through Overton Park was plainly not an exercise of a rulemaking function. And the only hearing that is required by either the Administrative

Procedure Act or the statutes regulating the distribution of federal funds for highway construction is a public hearing conducted by local officials for the purpose of informing the community about the proposed project and eliciting community views on the design and route. 23 U.S.C. § 128 (1964 ed., Supp. V). The hearing is nonadjudicatory, quasi-legislative in nature. It is not designed to produce a record that is to be the basis of agency action — the basic requirement for substantial-evidence review.

Petitioners' alternative argument also fails. De novo review of whether the Secretary's decision was "unwarranted by the facts" is authorized by § 706 (2) (F) in only two circumstances. First, such de novo review is authorized when the action is adjudicatory in nature and the agency factfinding procedures are inadequate. And, there may be independent judicial factfinding when issues that were not before the agency are raised in a proceeding to enforce nonadjudicatory agency action. Neither situation exists here.

Even though there is no de novo review in this case and the Secretary's approval of the route of I-40 does not have ultimately to meet the substantial-evidence test, the generally applicable standards of § 706 require the reviewing court to engage in a substantial inquiry. Certainly, the Secretary's decision is entitled to a presumption of regularity. But that presumption is not to shield his action from a thorough, probing, in-depth review.

The court is first required to decide whether the Secretary acted within the scope of his authority. This determination naturally begins with a delineation of the scope of the Secretary's authority and discretion. As has been shown, Congress has specified only a small range of choices that the Secretary can make. Also involved in this initial inquiry is a determination of whether on the facts the Secretary's decision can reasonably be said to be within that range. The reviewing court must consider whether the Secretary properly construed his authority to approve the use of parkland as limited to situations where there are no feasible alternative routes or where feasible alternative routes involve uniquely difficult problems. And the reviewing court must be able to find that the Secretary could have reasonably believed that in this case there are no feasible alternatives or that alternatives do involve unique problems.

Scrutiny of the facts does not end, however, with the determination that the Secretary has acted within the scope of his statutory authority. Section 706 (2)(A) requires a finding that the actual choice made was not "arbitrary, capricious, an abuse of discretion, or otherwise not in accordance with law." 5 U.S.C. § 706 (2)(A) (1964 ed., Supp. V). To make this finding the court must consider whether the decision was based on a consideration of the relevant factors and whether there has been a clear error of judgment. Although this inquiry into the facts is to be searching and careful, the ultimate standard of review is a narrow one. The court is not empowered to substitute its judgment for that of the agency.

The final inquiry is whether the Secretary's action followed the necessary procedural requirements. Here the only procedural error alleged is the failure of the Secretary to make formal findings and state his reason for allowing the highway to be built through the park. Undoubtedly, review of the Secretary's action is hampered by his failure to make such findings, but the absence of formal findings does not necessarily require that the case be remanded to the

Secretary. Neither the Department of Transportation Act nor the Federal-Aid Highway Act requires such formal findings. Moreover, the Administrative Procedure Act requirements that there be formal findings in certain rulemaking and adjudicatory proceedings do not apply to the Secretary's action here. See 5 U.S.C. §§ 553 (a) (2), 554 (a) (1964 ed., Supp. V). And, although formal findings may be required in some cases in the absence of statutory directives when the nature of the agency action is ambiguous, those situations are rare. Plainly, there is no ambiguity here; the Secretary has approved the construction of I-40 through Overton Park and has approved a specific design for the project. . . .

. . . The lower courts based their review on the litigation affidavits that were presented. These affidavits were merely "post hoc" rationalizations, which have traditionally been found to be an inadequate basis for review. And they clearly do not constitute the "whole record" compiled by the agency: the basis for review required by § 706 of the Administrative Procedure Act.

Thus it is necessary to remand this case to the District Court for plenary review of the Secretary's decision. That review is to be based on the full administrative record that was before the Secretary at the time he made his decision. But since the bare record may not disclose the factors that were considered or the Secretary's construction of the evidence it may be necessary for the District Court to require some explanation in order to determine if the Secretary acted within the scope of his authority and if the Secretary's action was justifiable under the applicable standard.

The court may require the administrative officials who participated in the decision to give testimony explaining their action. Of course, such inquiry into the mental processes of administrative decisionmakers is usually to be avoided. And where there are administrative findings that were made at the same time as the decision, . . . there must be a strong showing of bad faith or improper behavior before such inquiry may be made. But here there are no such formal findings and it may be that the only way there can be effective judicial review is by examining the decisionmakers themselves.

The District Court is not, however, required to make such an inquiry. It may be that the Secretary can prepare formal findings . . . that will provide an adequate explanation for his action. Such an explanation will, to some extent, be a "post hoc rationalization" and thus must be viewed critically. If the District Court decides that additional explanation is necessary, that court should consider which method will prove the most expeditious so that full review may be had as soon as possible.

Reversed and remanded. [JUSTICE DOUGLAS took no part in the consideration or decision of this case.]

QUESTIONS AND NOTE

1. Into what category does the administrative action being reviewed in *Overton Park* fall?
2. What purpose is served by the court's review under the arbitrary or capricious standard? Does the standard allow a court to hold an agency action unlawful because the court disagrees with the substance of the action?
3. We will discuss the reviewability issues raised in *Overton Park* in connection with our consideration of *Webster v. Doe, infra,* p. 635.

NOTE ON JUDICIAL SUPPLEMENTATION OF THE AGENCY RECORD

In *Camp v. Pitts*, 411 U.S. 138, 142 (1973) (*per curiam*), the Supreme Court stated that, when a court applies the APA arbitrary and capricious review standard, "the focal point for judicial review should be the administrative record already in existence, not some new record made initially in the reviewing court."

Challengers to administrative action may nevertheless seek to supplement the informal agency record claiming that this general rule should not apply because of special circumstances. The court in *IMS, P.C., v. Alvarez*, 129 F.3d 618, 623-24 (D.C. Cir. 1997), rejected a request to supplement the record for the reasons that follow:

> It is a widely accepted principle of administrative law that the courts base their review of an agency's actions on the materials that were before the agency at the time its decision was made. *See Puerto Rico Higher Educ. Assistance Corp. v. Riley*, 10 F.3d 847, 850-51 (D.C. Cir. 1993) ("We base our review of the Department's actions on the materials that were before the Department at the time its decision was made") (citation omitted); *Walter O. Boswell Mem'l Hosp. v. Heckler*, 749 F.2d 788, 792 (D.C. Cir. 1984) ("If a court is to review an agency's action fairly, it should have before it neither more nor less information than did the agency when it made its decision"). As the Supreme Court noted in 1985, "The task of the reviewing court is to apply the appropriate APA standard of review, 5 U.S.C. § 706, to the agency decision based on the record the agency presents to the reviewing court." *Florida Power & Light Co. v. Lorion*, 470 U.S. 729, 743-44 (1985) (citing *Citizens to Preserve Overton Park v. Volpe*, 401 U.S. 402 (1971)). . . . It is not necessary that the agency hold a formal hearing in compiling its record, for "[t]he APA specifically contemplates judicial review on the basis of the agency record compiled in the course of informal agency action in which a hearing has not occurred." *Florida Power*, 470 U.S. at 744.
>
> Both parties agree that the affidavits submitted by IMS were not available to the [Small Business Administration] at the time it made its decision regarding IMS's participation term. IMS claims, however, that the district court should have considered the affidavits as part of the administrative record because they merely elaborated on details already included in the record. In addition, IMS argues that "even if the affidavits constituted extraneous evidence, they still should have been considered by the Court under various exceptions which permit supplementation of the administrative record."
>
> We find no legal support for IMS's assertions. Even if IMS were correct in its claim that information that elaborates on details already in the record could be considered by the court, the affidavits in question could not be considered because they provide significant new information about the circumstances surrounding the 1987 contract that is not available in the administrative record. Moreover, the affidavits do not appear to fall within any of the accepted exceptions to the principle that the court cannot consider information that falls outside the agency record. As the district court concluded, IMS has not demonstrated that the agency failed to examine all relevant factors or to adequately explain its grounds for decision, or that the agency acted in bad faith or engaged in improper behavior in reaching its decision. This is not a case where the agency failed "to explain administrative action [so] as to frustrate effective judicial review." *Pitts*, 411 U.S. at 142-43. Nor has IMS made the "strong showing of bad faith or improper behavior" required to justify supplementing the record. *Citizens to Preserve Overton Park v. Volpe*, 401 U.S. 402, 420 (1971).

The affidavits contain information that should have been submitted to the agency before this dispute reached the courts. To allow the affidavits to be considered now would be to permit ex post supplementation of the record, which is not consistent with the prevailing standards of agency review. *See AT&T Info. Sys. v. General Serv. Admin.*, 810 F.2d 1233, 1236 (D.C. Cir. 1987) ("we have repeatedly applied [the rule against supplementing the agency record] to bar introduction of litigation affidavits to supplement the administrative record") (citations omitted); *Walter O. Boswell Mem'l Hosp.*, 749 F.2d at 793 (noting that the court had struck portions of an amicus brief that discussed affidavits not available to the agency at the time of its decision). As this court held in *Walter O. Boswell Memorial Hospital v. Heckler*, if the parties to a case "wish to contest the merits of the case by referring or submitting to the District Court any material that does not appear in the . . . administrative record, they may do so only by joint stipulation." *Id.* at 794.

QUESTIONS

1. What policies support the strong limit on the introduction of evidence in court to supplement the administrative record?
2. What policies support the exceptions to the bar against record supplementation identified in IMS? For another common-sense exception, *see Valley Citizens for a Safe Environment v. Aldridge*, 886 F.2d 458, 460 (1st Cir. 1989) (Breyer, J.) ("a reviewing court might want additional testimony by experts, simply to help it understand matters in the agency record; indeed, it might ask for additional factual evidence as an aid to understanding. However desirable this kind of evidentiary supplementation as an aid to understanding highly technical, environmental matters, its use is discretionary with the reviewing court"). Should the ability to supplement a record depend on whether the available judicial review is in a district court or a court of appeals? See *Valley Citizens, supra* ("the degree to which a party is, or is not, legally free to build a new record ought not to reflect simply the happenstance of which level of reviewing court a particular jurisdictional statute selects"). Compare record supplementation under the APA with the specific provisions on supplementing the agency record included in 1981 MSAPA § 5-114.

NOTE ON THE ARBITRARY OR CAPRICIOUS STANDARD AND "HARD LOOK" REVIEW

In *Greater Boston Television Corp. v. FCC*, 444 F.2d 841, 851-53 (D.C. Cir. 1970), Judge Harold Leventhal, writing prior to the Supreme Court decision in *Overton Park*, described judicial review of agency discretion in the following famous terms:

Assuming consistency with law and the legislative mandate, the agency has latitude not merely to find facts and make judgments, but also to select the policies deemed in the public interest. The function of the court is to assure that the agency has given reasoned consideration to all the material facts and issues. This calls for insistence that the agency articulate with reasonable clarity its reasons for decision, and identify the significance of the crucial facts, a course that tends to assure that the agency's policies effectuate general standards, applied without unreasonable discrimination. As for the particular subject of comparative hearings, the findings must cover all the substantial differences between the applicants and the ultimate conclusion must be based on a composite consideration of the findings as to each applicant.

Its supervisory function calls on the court to intervene not merely in case of procedural inadequacies, or bypassing of the mandate in the legislative charter, but more broadly if the court becomes aware, especially from a combination of danger signals, that the agency has not really taken a "hard look" at the salient problems, and has not genuinely engaged in reasoned decision-making. If the agency has not shirked this fundamental task, however, the court exercises restraint and affirms the agency's action even though the court would on its own account have made different findings or adopted different standards. Nor will the court upset a decision because of errors that are not material, there being room for the doctrine of harmless error. If satisfied that the agency has taken a hard look at the issues with the use of reasons and standards, the court will uphold its findings, though of less than ideal clarity, if the agency's path may reasonably be discerned, though of course the court must not be left to guess as to the agency's findings or reasons.

The process thus combines judicial supervision with a salutary principle of judicial restraint, an awareness that agencies and courts together constitute a "partnership" in furtherance of the public interest, and are "collaborative instrumentalities of justice." The court is in a real sense part of the total administrative process, and not a hostile stranger to the office of first instance. This collaborative spirit does not undercut, it rather underlines the court's rigorous insistence on the need for conjunction of articulated standards and reflective findings, in furtherance of evenhanded application of law, rather than impermissible whim, improper influence, or misplaced zeal. Reasoned decision promotes results in the public interest by requiring the agency to focus on the values served by its decision, and hence releasing the clutch of unconscious preference and irrelevant prejudice. It furthers the broad public interest of enabling the public to repose confidence in the process as well as the judgments of its decision-makers.

Judge Leventhal thus sought to employ judicial review to ensure that the *agency* had taken the required hard look. Judicial review under the APA's arbitrary and capricious standard however also came to be understood as dictating a hard look by the *court* at the agency's action, as the D.C. Circuit summarized in *National Lime Assn. v. EPA*, 627 F.2d 416, 451 n.126 (D.C. Cir. 1980):

As originally articulated the words "hard look" described the agency's responsibility and not the court's. However, the phrase subsequently evolved to connote the rigorous standard of judicial review applied to increasingly utilized informal rulemaking proceedings or to other decisions made upon less than a full trial-type record. Judge Leventhal himself used the phrase in this sense in *Maryland-Nat'l Capital Park and Planning Comm'n v. United States Postal Serv.*, 487 F.2d 1029, 1037-38 and n.4 (D.C. Cir. 1973). The etymological evolution of the phrase "hard look" and of other capsule descriptions of standards stated on judicial review of administrative decisions is in no small part attributable to the shifting meaning of "informal rulemaking." The transformation in informal rulemaking proceedings in turn can be traced to the more rigorous standards of review applied.

As originally conceived, "notice and comment" rulemaking provided a scant "record" for review. The statutorily required rationale consisted merely in "a concise general statement of (the rule's) basis and purpose." 5 U.S.C. § 553(c) (1976). The cumbersomeness of rulemaking "on the record" and its attendant delays prompted increased provision for the more flexible and expedient "notice and comment" rules in areas in urgent need of regulation. *See* Pedersen, *Formal Records and Informal Rulemaking*, 85 Yale L.J. 38, 39 (1975) (hereinafter cited as Pedersen). [Authors' note: For cases and notes related to this legal development, see pp. 194-214, *supra.*]

The sheer massiveness of impact of the urgent regulations issued under the new rulemaking provisions and the diffidence of judges in the face of highly technical regulatory schemes prompted the courts to require the agencies to develop a more complete record and a more clearly articulated rationale to facilitate review for arbitrariness and caprice. *See Kennecott Copper Corp. v. EPA*, 462 F.2d 846, 849-50 (D.C. Cir. 1972) (remand of national secondary ambient air quality standards to EPA for additional rationale); K. Davis, *Administrative Law of the Seventies*, § 29.01-6 (1976); Stewart, *Vermont Yankee and the Evolution of Administrative Procedure*, 91 Harv. L. Rev. 1805, 1812-13 (1978); Nathanson, *Probing the Mind of the Administrator: Hearing Variations and Standards of Judicial Review Under the Administrative Procedure Act and Other Federal Statutes*, 75 Colum. L. Rev. 721, 746-70 (1975). . . . As these newly-required records and rationales became more routinely available, the "hard look" taken began to appear more judicial than administrative, blurring the original meaning of that phrase. The availability for judicial review of substantial administrative records has also generated both confusion and controversy over the applicable standard of review under the Administrative Procedure Act. *See generally* DeLong, *Informal Rulemaking and the Integration of Law and Policy*, 65 Va. L. Rev. 257, 284-89 (1979); Auerbach, *Informal Rulemaking: A Proposed Relationship Between Administrative Procedures and Judicial Review*, 72 Nw. U. L. Rev. 15 (1977); Pedersen, at 46-49.

The "hard look" approach to judicial review advocated by Judge Leventhal may be contrasted with the approach urged by his colleague on the D.C. Circuit — Judge David Bazelon. Judge Bazelon was very skeptical of the ability of generalist judges to understand adequately difficult issues of science or highly technical problems; he advocated the use of process to establish procedures that, if followed, would likely ensure the rationality of an agency's work product. *See Ethyl Corp. v. EPA*, 541 F.2d 1, 67 (D.C. Cir. 1976) (en banc) (Bazelon, C.J., concurring); *see also NRDC v. NRC*, 547 F.2d 633, 657 (D.C. Cir. 1976) (Bazelon, C.J., concurring), *rev'd sub nom., Vermont Yankee Nuclear Power Corp v. NRDC*, 435 U.S. 519 (1978). In Judge Bazelon's view, judges should "establish a decision-making process which assures a reasoned decision that can be held up to the scrutiny of the scientific community and the public." *International Harvester Co. v. Ruckelshaus*, 478 F.2d 615, 652 (D.C. Cir. 1973) (Bazelon, C.J., concurring). The debate between the two judges raged during the 1970s and was finally resolved — in Judge Leventhal's favor — by the Supreme Court in *Vermont Yankee*, see *supra* pp. 256-257. Reviewing courts, contrary to Judge Bazelon's suggestion, are emphatically *not* free to impose particular procedural requirements on administrative agencies (beyond enforcing those set forth in the APA or in the agency's organic act or regulations). Even so, there are aspects of judicial review of administrative action that reflect and incorporate Judge Bazelon's concerns with the quality of process. *See* Ronald J. Krotoszynski, Jr., *"History Belongs to the Winners": The Bazelon-Leventhal Debate and the Continuing Relevance of the Process/Substance Dichotomy in Judicial Review of Agency Action*, 58 ADMIN. L. REV. 995, 1012-15 (2006).

QUESTIONS

1. Are judges better at process than substance, as Judge Bazelon argued? Do most judges have enough scientific or technical expertise to evaluate whether a record supports a particular design requirement for bolts used in a nuclear power plant? If judges are not well suited to making such determinations, was Judge Bazelon correct to insist that reviewing courts rely on process to ensure that agencies reach rational outcomes?

2. If judges must engage in "hard look" review of the substance of an agency's decision, rather than consider whether more process would likely lead to a good outcome, how can generalist judges best equip themselves for this task? Is there a risk that judges might be too deferential to agencies when questions turn on difficult scientific or technical matters? Or perhaps fail to be sufficiently deferential when science provides only a probabalistic answer (i.e., the matter cannot be resolved without significant uncertainty remaining about the correct answer)?

3. If Congress knows about the limits of generalist judges and nevertheless permits agencies to conduct informal rulemakings or adjudications to make policy, is the best answer that ultimate responsibility lies with the legislative, not judicial, branch? Judge Leventhal's position was that judges must enforce the statutes that Congress actually writes, not the statutes that judges might wish Congress had written.

MOTOR VEHICLE MFRS. ASS'N v. STATE FARM MUT. AUTO. INS. CO.
463 U.S. 29 (1983)

JUSTICE WHITE delivered the opinion of the Court.

The development of the automobile gave Americans unprecedented freedom to travel, but exacted a high price for enhanced mobility. Since 1929, motor vehicles have been the leading cause of accidental deaths and injuries in the United States. In 1982, 46,300 Americans died in motor vehicle accidents and hundreds of thousands more were maimed and injured. While a consensus exists that the current loss of life on our highways is unacceptably high, improving safety does not admit to easy solution. In 1966, Congress decided that at least part of the answer lies in improving the design and safety features of the vehicle itself. But much of the technology for building safer cars was undeveloped or untested. Before changes in automobile design could be mandated, the effectiveness of these changes had to be studied, their costs examined, and public acceptance considered. This task called for considerable expertise and Congress responded by enacting the National Traffic and Motor Vehicle Safety Act of 1966 (Act). The Act, created for the purpose of "reduc[ing] traffic accidents and deaths and injuries to persons resulting from traffic accidents," 15 U.S.C. § 1381, directs the Secretary of Transportation or his delegate to issue motor vehicle safety standards that "shall be practicable, shall meet the need for motor vehicle safety, and shall be stated in objective terms." 15 U.S.C. § 1392(a) (1976 ed., Supp. V). In issuing these standards, the Secretary is directed to consider "relevant available motor vehicle safety data," whether the proposed standard "is reasonable, practicable and appropriate" for the particular type of motor vehicle, and the "extent to which such standards will contribute to carrying out the purposes" of the Act. 15 U.S.C. §§ 1392(f)(1), (3), (4).

The Act also authorizes judicial review under the provisions of the Administrative Procedure Act (APA), 5 U.S.C. § 706, of all "orders establishing, amending, or revoking a Federal motor vehicle safety standard," 15 U.S.C. § 1392(b). Under this authority, we review today whether NHTSA acted arbitrarily and capriciously in revoking the requirement in Motor Vehicle Safety Standard 208 that new motor vehicles produced after September 1982 be equipped with passive restraints to protect the safety of the occupants of the vehicle in the event of a collision. Briefly summarized, we hold that the agency failed to present an adequate basis and explanation for rescinding the passive restraint requirement and that the agency must either consider the matter further or adhere to or amend Standard 208 along lines which its analysis supports.

I

The regulation whose rescission is at issue bears a complex and convoluted history. Over the course of approximately 60 rulemaking notices, the requirement has been imposed, amended, rescinded, reimposed, and now rescinded again.

As originally issued by the Department of Transportation in 1967, Standard 208 simply required the installation of seatbelts in all automobiles. It soon became apparent that the level of seatbelt use was too low to reduce traffic injuries to an acceptable level. The Department therefore began consideration of "passive occupant restraint systems" — devices that do not depend for their effectiveness upon any action taken by the occupant except that necessary to operate the vehicle. Two types of automatic crash protection emerged: automatic seatbelts and airbags. The automatic seatbelt is a traditional safety belt, which when fastened to the interior of the door remains attached without impeding entry or exit from the vehicle, and deploys automatically without any action on the part of the passenger. The airbag is an inflatable device concealed in the dashboard and steering column. It automatically inflates when a sensor indicates that deceleration forces from an accident have exceeded a preset minimum, then rapidly deflates to dissipate those forces. The lifesaving potential of these devices was immediately recognized, and in 1977, after substantial on-the-road experience with both devices, it was estimated by NHTSA that passive restraints could prevent approximately 12,000 deaths and over 100,000 serious injuries annually.

In 1969, the Department formally proposed a standard requiring the installation of passive restraints, thereby commencing a lengthy series of proceedings. In 1970, the agency revised Standard 208 to include passive protection requirements, and in 1972, the agency amended the Standard to require full passive protection for all front seat occupants of vehicles manufactured after August 15, 1975. In the interim, vehicles built between August 1973 and August 1975 were to carry either passive restraints or lap and shoulder belts coupled with an "ignition interlock" that would prevent starting the vehicle if the belts were not connected. On review, the agency's decision to require passive restraints was found to be supported by "substantial evidence" and upheld.

In preparing for the upcoming model year, most car makers chose the "ignition interlock" option, a decision which was highly unpopular, and led Congress to amend the Act to prohibit a motor vehicle safety standard from requiring or permitting compliance by means of an ignition interlock or a continuous buzzer designed to indicate that safety belts were not in use. The 1974 Amendments also provided that any safety standard that could be satisfied by a system other than seatbelts would have to be submitted to Congress where it could be vetoed by concurrent resolution of both Houses.

The effective date for mandatory passive restraint systems was extended for a year until August 31, 1976. But in June 1976, Secretary of Transportation William T. Coleman, Jr., initiated a new rulemaking on the issue. After hearing testimony and reviewing written comments, Coleman extended the optional alternatives indefinitely and suspended the passive restraint requirement. Although he found passive restraints technologically and economically feasible, the Secretary based his decision on the expectation that there would be widespread public resistance to the new systems. He instead proposed a demonstration project involving up to 500,000 cars installed with passive restraints, in order to smooth the way for public acceptance of mandatory passive restraints at a later date.

Coleman's successor as Secretary of Transportation disagreed. Within months of assuming office, Secretary Brock Adams decided that the demonstration project was unnecessary. He issued a new mandatory passive restraint regulation, known as Modified Standard 208. The Modified Standard mandated the phasing in of passive restraints beginning with large cars in model year 1982 and extending to all cars by model year 1984. The two principal systems that would satisfy the Standard were airbags and passive belts; the choice of which system to install was left to the manufacturers. In *Pacific Legal Foundation v. Department of Transportation*, 593 F.2d 1338 (1979), the Court of Appeals upheld Modified Standard 208 as a rational, nonarbitrary regulation consistent with the agency's mandate under the Act. The Standard also survived scrutiny by Congress, which did not exercise its authority under the legislative veto provision of the 1974 Amendments.

Over the next several years, the automobile industry geared up to comply with Modified Standard 208. As late as July 1980, NHTSA reported:

> "On the road experience in thousands of vehicles equipped with air bags and automatic safety belts has confirmed agency estimates of the life-saving and injury-preventing benefits of such systems. When all cars are equipped with automatic crash protection systems, each year an estimated 9,000 more lives will be saved, and tens of thousands of serious injuries will be prevented." NHTSA, Automobile Occupant Crash Protection, Progress Report No. 3, p. 4; App. in No. 81-2220 (CADC), p. 1627 (hereinafter App.).

In February 1981, however, Secretary of Transportation Andrew Lewis reopened the rulemaking due to changed economic circumstances and, in particular, the difficulties of the automobile industry. Two months later, the agency ordered a one-year delay in the application of the Standard to large cars, extending the deadline to September 1982, and at the same time, proposed the possible rescission of the entire Standard. After receiving written comments and holding public hearings, NHTSA issued a final rule (Notice 25) that rescinded the passive restraint requirement contained in Modified Standard 208.

II

In a statement explaining the rescission, NHTSA maintained that it was no longer able to find, as it had in 1977, that the automatic restraint requirement would produce significant safety benefits. This judgment reflected not a change of opinion on the effectiveness of the technology, but a change in plans by the automobile industry. In 1977, the agency had assumed that airbags would be installed in 60% of all new cars and automatic seatbelts in 40%. By 1981 it became apparent that automobile manufacturers planned to install the automatic seatbelts in approximately 99% of the new cars. For this reason, the lifesaving potential of airbags would not be realized. Moreover, it now appeared that the overwhelming majority of passive belts planned to be installed by manufacturers could be detached easily and left that way permanently. Passive belts, once detached, then required "the same type of affirmative action that is the stumbling block to obtaining high usage levels of manual belts." For this reason, the agency concluded that there was no longer a basis for reliably predicting that the Standard would lead to any significant increased usage of restraints at all.

In view of the possibly minimal safety benefits, the automatic restraint requirement no longer was reasonable or practicable in the agency's view. The requirement would require approximately $1 billion to implement and the agency did not believe it would be reasonable to impose such substantial costs on manufacturers and consumers without more adequate assurance that sufficient safety benefits would accrue. In addition, NHTSA concluded that automatic restraints might have an adverse effect on the public's attitude toward safety. Given the high expense and limited benefits of detachable belts, NHTSA feared that many consumers would regard the Standard as an instance of ineffective regulation, adversely affecting the public's view of safety regulation and, in particular, "poisoning . . . popular sentiment toward efforts to improve occupant restraint systems in the future."

State Farm Mutual Automobile Insurance Co. and the National Association of Independent Insurers filed petitions for review of NHTSA's rescission of the passive restraint Standard. The United States Court of Appeals for the District of Columbia Circuit held that the agency's rescission of the passive restraint requirement was arbitrary and capricious. . . .

III

Unlike the Court of Appeals, we do not find the appropriate scope of judicial review to be the "most troublesome question" in these cases. Both the Act and the 1974 Amendments concerning occupant crash protection standards indicate that motor vehicle safety standards are to be promulgated under the informal rulemaking procedures of the Administrative Procedure Act. 5 U.S.C. § 553. The agency's action in promulgating such standards therefore may be set aside if found to be "arbitrary, capricious, an abuse of discretion, or otherwise not in accordance with law." 5 U.S.C. § 706(2)(A). We believe that the rescission or modification of an occupant-protection standard is subject to the same test. Section 103(b) of the Act, 15 U.S.C. § 1392(b), states that the procedural and judicial review provisions of the Administrative Procedure Act "shall apply to all orders establishing, amending, or revoking a Federal motor vehicle safety standard," and suggests no difference in the scope of judicial review depending upon the nature of the agency's action.

Petitioner Motor Vehicle Manufacturers Association (MVMA) disagrees, contending that the rescission of an agency rule should be judged by the same standard a court would use to judge an agency's refusal to promulgate a rule in the first place—a standard petitioner believes considerably narrower than the traditional arbitrary-and-capricious test. We reject this view. The Act expressly equates orders "revoking" and "establishing" safety standards; neither that Act nor the APA suggests that revocations are to be treated as refusals to promulgate standards. Petitioner's view would render meaningless Congress' authorization for judicial review of orders revoking safety rules. Moreover, the revocation of an extant regulation is substantially different than a failure to act. Revocation constitutes a reversal of the agency's former views as to the proper course. A "settled course of behavior embodies the agency's informed judgment that, by pursuing that course, it will carry out the policies committed to it by Congress. There is, then, at least a presumption that those policies will be carried out best if the settled rule is adhered to." *Atchison, T. & S. F. R. Co. v. Wichita Bd. of Trade*, 412 U.S. 800, 807-808 (1973). Accordingly, an agency changing its course by rescinding a rule is obligated to supply a reasoned analysis for the change beyond that which may be required when an agency does not act in the first instance.

In so holding, we fully recognize that "[r]egulatory agencies do not establish rules of conduct to last forever," *American Trucking Assns., Inc. v. Atchison, T. & S. F. R. Co.*, 387 U.S. 397, 416 (1967), and that an agency must be given ample latitude to "adapt their rules and policies to the demands of changing circumstances." *Permian Basin Area Rate Cases*, 390 U.S. 747, 784 (1968). But the forces of change do not always or necessarily point in the direction of deregulation. In the abstract, there is no more reason to presume that changing circumstances require the rescission of prior action, instead of a revision in or even the extension of current regulation. If Congress established a presumption from which judicial review should start, that presumption—contrary to petitioners' views—is not against safety regulation, but against changes in current policy that are not justified by the rulemaking record. While the removal of a regulation may not entail the monetary expenditures and other costs of enacting a new standard, and, accordingly, it may be easier for an agency to justify a deregulatory action, the direction in which an agency chooses to move does not alter the standard of judicial review established by law.

The Department of Transportation accepts the applicability of the "arbitrary and capricious" standard. It argues that under this standard, a reviewing court may not set aside an agency rule that is rational, based on consideration of the relevant factors, and within the scope of the authority delegated to the agency by the statute. We do not disagree with this formulation.[9] The scope of review under the "arbitrary and capricious" standard is narrow and a court is not to substitute its judgment for that of the agency. Nevertheless, the agency must examine the relevant data and articulate a satisfactory explanation for its action

---

9. The Department of Transportation suggests that the arbitrary-and-capricious standard requires no more than the minimum rationality a statute must bear in order to withstand analysis under the Due Process Clause. We do not view as equivalent the presumption of constitutionality afforded legislation drafted by Congress and the presumption of regularity afforded an agency in fulfilling its statutory mandate.

including a "rational connection between the facts found and the choice made." *Burlington Truck Lines, Inc. v. United States*, 371 U.S. 156, 168 (1962). In reviewing that explanation, we must "consider whether the decision was based on a consideration of the relevant factors and whether there has been a clear error of judgment." *Bowman Transportation, Inc. v. Arkansas-Best Freight System, Inc., supra,* at 285; *Citizens to Preserve Overton Park v. Volpe, supra,* at 416. Normally, an agency rule would be arbitrary and capricious if the agency has relied on factors which Congress has not intended it to consider, entirely failed to consider an important aspect of the problem, offered an explanation for its decision that runs counter to the evidence before the agency, or is so implausible that it could not be ascribed to a difference in view or the product of agency expertise. The reviewing court should not attempt itself to make up for such deficiencies; we may not supply a reasoned basis for the agency's action that the agency itself has not given. *SEC v. Chenery Corp.,* 332 U.S. 194, 196 (1947). We will, however, "uphold a decision of less than ideal clarity if the agency's path may reasonably be discerned." *Bowman Transportation, Inc. v. Arkansas-Best Freight System, Inc., supra,* at 286. *See also Camp v. Pitts,* 411 U.S. 138, 142-143 (1973) (*per curiam*). For purposes of these cases, it is also relevant that Congress required a record of the rulemaking proceedings to be compiled and submitted to a reviewing court, 15 U.S.C. § 1394, and intended that agency findings under the Act would be supported by "substantial evidence on the record considered as a whole." S. Rep. No. 1301, 89th Cong., 2d Sess., 8 (1966); H. R. Rep. No. 1776, 89th Cong., 2d Sess., 21 (1966)....

V

The ultimate question before us is whether NHTSA's rescission of the passive restraint requirement of Standard 208 was arbitrary and capricious. We conclude, as did the Court of Appeals, that it was. We also conclude, but for somewhat different reasons, that further consideration of the issue by the agency is therefore required. We deal separately with the rescission as it applies to airbags and as it applies to seatbelts.

A

The first and most obvious reason for finding the rescission arbitrary and capricious is that NHTSA apparently gave no consideration whatever to modifying the Standard to require that airbag technology be utilized. Standard 208 sought to achieve automatic crash protection by requiring automobile manufacturers to install either of two passive restraint devices: airbags or automatic seatbelts. There was no suggestion in the long rulemaking process that led to Standard 208 that if only one of these options were feasible, no passive restraint standard should be promulgated. Indeed, the agency's original proposed Standard contemplated the installation of inflatable restraints in all cars. Automatic belts were added as a means of complying with the Standard because they were believed to be as effective as airbags in achieving the goal of occupant crash protection. At that time, the passive belt approved by the agency could not be detached. Only later, at a manufacturer's behest, did the agency approve of the detachability feature — and only after assurances that the feature would not compromise the safety benefits of the restraint. Although it was then foreseen that 60% of the new cars would contain airbags and 40% would have automatic seatbelts, the ratio between the two was not significant as long as the passive belt would also assure greater passenger safety.

The agency has now determined that the detachable automatic belts will not attain anticipated safety benefits because so many individuals will detach the mechanism. Even if this conclusion were acceptable in its entirety, standing alone it would not justify any more than an amendment of Standard 208 to disallow compliance by means of the one technology which will not provide effective passenger protection. It does not cast doubt on the need for a passive restraint standard or upon the efficacy of airbag technology. In its most recent rulemaking, the agency again acknowledged the lifesaving potential of the airbag:

> "The agency has no basis at this time for changing its earlier conclusions in 1976 and 1977 that basic air bag technology is sound and has been sufficiently demonstrated to be effective in those vehicles in current use. . . ." NHTSA Final Regulatory Impact Analysis (RIA) XI-4 (Oct. 1981).

Given the effectiveness ascribed to airbag technology by the agency, the mandate of the Act to achieve traffic safety would suggest that the logical response to the faults of detachable seatbelts would be to require the installation of airbags. At the very least this alternative way of achieving the objectives of the Act should have been addressed and adequate reasons given for its abandonment. But the agency not only did not require compliance through airbags, it also did not even consider the possibility in its 1981 rulemaking. Not one sentence of its rulemaking statement discusses the airbags-only option. Because, as the Court of Appeals stated, "NHTSA's . . . analysis of airbags was nonexistent," 680 F.2d, at 236, what we said in *Burlington Truck Lines, Inc. v. United States*, 371 U.S., at 167, is apropos here:

> "There are no findings and no analysis here to justify the choice made, no indication of the basis on which the [agency] exercised its expert discretion. We are not prepared to and the Administrative Procedure Act will not permit us to accept such . . . practice. . . . Expert discretion is the lifeblood of the administrative process, but "unless we make the requirements for administrative action strict and demanding, *expertise*, the strength of modern government, can become a monster which rules with no practical limits on its discretion." *New York v. United States*, 342 U.S. 882, 884 (dissenting opinion)."

We have frequently reiterated that an agency must cogently explain why it has exercised its discretion in a given manner, *Atchison, T. & S. F. R. Co. v. Wichita Bd. of Trade*, 412 U.S., at 806; *FTC v. Sperry & Hutchinson Co.*, 405 U.S. 233, 249 (1972); *NLRB v. Metropolitan Life Ins. Co.*, 380 U.S. 438, 443 (1965); and we reaffirm this principle again today.

The automobile industry has opted for the passive belt over the airbag, but surely it is not enough that the regulated industry has eschewed a given safety device. For nearly a decade, the automobile industry waged the regulatory equivalent of war against the airbag and lost—the inflatable restraint was proved sufficiently effective. Now the automobile industry has decided to employ a seatbelt system which will not meet the safety objectives of Standard 208. This hardly constitutes cause to revoke the Standard itself. Indeed, the Act was necessary because the industry was not sufficiently responsive to safety concerns. The Act intended that safety standards not depend on current technology and could be "technology-forcing" in the sense of inducing the development of superior safety design. If, under the statute, the agency should not defer to the industry's failure to develop safer cars, which it surely should not do, *a fortiori* it may not revoke a safety standard which can be satisfied by current technology simply because the industry has opted for an ineffective seatbelt design.

Although the agency did not address the mandatory airbag option and the Court of Appeals noted that "airbags seem to have none of the problems that NHTSA identified in passive seatbelts," petitioners recite a number of difficulties that they believe would be posed by a mandatory airbag standard. These range from questions concerning the installation of airbags in small cars to that of adverse public reaction. But these are not the agency's reasons for rejecting a mandatory airbag standard. Not having discussed the possibility, the agency submitted no reasons at all. The short — and sufficient — answer to petitioners' submission is that the courts may not accept appellate counsel's *post hoc* rationalizations for agency action. *Burlington Truck Lines, Inc. v. United States*, 371 U.S., at 168. It is well established that an agency's action must be upheld, if at all, on the basis articulated by the agency itself. *Ibid.; SEC v. Chenery Corp.*, 332 U.S., at 196; *American Textile Mfrs. Institute, Inc. v. Donovan*, 452 U.S. 490, 539 (1981).

Petitioners also invoke our decision in *Vermont Yankee Nuclear Power Corp. v. Natural Resources Defense Council, Inc.*, 435 U.S. 519 (1978), as though it were a talisman under which any agency decision is by definition unimpeachable. Specifically, it is submitted that to require an agency to consider an airbags-only alternative is, in essence, to dictate to the agency the procedures it is to follow. Petitioners both misread *Vermont Yankee* and misconstrue the nature of the remand that is in order. In *Vermont Yankee*, we held that a court may not impose additional procedural requirements upon an agency. We do not require today any specific procedures which NHTSA must follow. Nor do we broadly require an agency to consider all policy alternatives in reaching decision. It is true that rulemaking "cannot be found wanting simply because the agency failed to include every alternative device and thought conceivable by the mind of man . . . regardless of how uncommon or unknown that alternative may have been. . . ." *Id.*, at 551. But the airbag is more than a policy alternative to the passive restraint Standard; it is a technological alternative within the ambit of the existing Standard. We hold only that given the judgment made in 1977 that airbags are an effective and cost-beneficial life-saving technology, the mandatory passive restraint rule may not be abandoned without any consideration whatsoever of an airbags-only requirement.

B

Although the issue is closer, we also find that the agency was too quick to dismiss the safety benefits of automatic seatbelts. NHTSA's critical finding was that, in light of the industry's plans to install readily detachable passive belts, it could not reliably predict "even a 5 percentage point increase as the minimum level of expected usage increase." The Court of Appeals rejected this finding because there is "not one iota" of evidence that Modified Standard 208 will fail to increase nationwide seatbelt use by at least 13 percentage points, the level of increased usage necessary for the Standard to justify its cost. Given the lack of probative evidence, the court held that "only a well justified refusal to seek more evidence could render rescission non-arbitrary."

Petitioners object to this conclusion. In their view, "substantial uncertainty" that a regulation will accomplish its intended purpose is sufficient reason, without more, to rescind a regulation. We agree with petitioners that just as an agency reasonably may decline to issue a safety standard if it is uncertain about its efficacy, an agency may also revoke a standard on the basis of serious uncertainties if supported by the record and reasonably explained. Rescission of the passive restraint requirement would not be arbitrary and capricious simply because there was no evidence in direct support of the agency's conclusion. It is not infrequent that the available data do not settle a regulatory issue, and the agency must then exercise its judgment in moving from the facts and probabilities on the record to a policy conclusion. Recognizing that policymaking in a complex society must account for uncertainty, however, does not imply that it is sufficient for an agency to merely recite the terms "substantial uncertainty" as a justification for its actions. As previously noted, the agency must explain the evidence which is available, and must offer a "rational connection between the facts found and the choice made." Generally, one aspect of that explanation would be a justification for rescinding the regulation before engaging in a search for further evidence.

In these cases, the agency's explanation for rescission of the passive restraint requirement is *not* sufficient to enable us to conclude that the rescission was the product of reasoned decisionmaking. To reach this conclusion, we do not upset the agency's view of the facts, but we do appreciate the limitations of this record in supporting the agency's decision. We start with the accepted ground that if used, seatbelts unquestionably would save many thousands of lives and would prevent tens of thousands of crippling injuries. Unlike recent regulatory decisions we have reviewed, *Industrial Union Dept. v. American Petroleum Institute*, 448 U.S. 607 (1980); *American Textile Mfrs. Institute, Inc. v. Donovan*, 452 U.S. 490 (1981), the safety benefits of wearing seatbelts are not in doubt, and it is not challenged that were those benefits to accrue, the monetary costs of implementing the Standard would be easily justified. We move next to the fact that there is no direct evidence in support of the agency's finding that detachable automatic belts cannot be predicted to yield a substantial increase in usage. The empirical evidence on the record, consisting of surveys of drivers of automobiles equipped with passive belts, reveals more than a doubling of the usage rate experienced with manual belts.[16] Much of the agency's rulemaking statement — and much of the controversy in these cases — centers on the conclusions that should be drawn from these studies. The agency maintained that the doubling of seatbelt usage in these studies could not be extrapolated to an across-the-board mandatory standard because the passive seatbelts were guarded by ignition interlocks and purchasers of the tested cars are somewhat atypical.[17] Respondents insist these studies demonstrate that Modified Standard 208 will

16. Between 1975 and 1980, Volkswagen sold approximately 350,000 Rabbits equipped with detachable passive seatbelts that were guarded by an ignition interlock. General Motors sold 8,000 1978 and 1979 Chevettes with a similar system, but eliminated the ignition interlock on the 13,000 Chevettes sold in 1980. NHTSA found that belt usage in the Rabbits averaged 34% for manual belts and 84% for passive belts. RIA, at IV-52. For the 1978-1979 Chevettes, NHTSA calculated 34% usage for manual belts and 72% for passive belts. On 1980 Chevettes, the agency found these figures to be 31% for manual belts and 70% for passive belts.

17. "NHTSA believes that the usage of automatic belts in Rabbits and Chevettes would have been substantially lower if the automatic belts in those cars were not equipped with a use-inducing device inhibiting detachment." Notice 25, 46 Fed. Reg. 53422 (1981).

substantially increase seatbelt usage. We believe that it is within the agency's discretion to pass upon the generalizability of these field studies. This is precisely the type of issue which rests within the expertise of NHTSA, and upon which a reviewing court must be most hesitant to intrude.

But accepting the agency's view of the field tests on passive restraints indicates only that there is no reliable real-world experience that usage rates will substantially increase. To be sure, NHTSA opines that "it cannot reliably predict even a 5 percentage point increase as the minimum level of expected increased usage." But this and other statements that passive belts will not yield substantial increases in seatbelt usage apparently take no account of the critical difference between detachable automatic belts and current manual belts. A detached passive belt does require an affirmative act to reconnect it, but — unlike a manual seatbelt — the passive belt, once reattached, will continue to function automatically unless again disconnected. Thus, inertia — a factor which the agency's own studies have found significant in explaining the current low usage rates for seatbelts — works in *favor* of, not *against*, use of the protective device. Since 20% to 50% of motorists currently wear seatbelts on some occasions, there would seem to be grounds to believe that seatbelt use by occasional users will be substantially increased by the detachable passive belts. Whether this is in fact the case is a matter for the agency to decide, but it must bring its expertise to bear on the question.

The agency is correct to look at the costs as well as the benefits of Standard 208. The agency's conclusion that the incremental costs of the requirements were no longer reasonable was predicated on its prediction that the safety benefits of the regulation might be minimal. Specifically, the agency's fears that the public may resent paying more for the automatic belt systems is expressly dependent on the assumption that detachable automatic belts will not produce more than "negligible safety benefits." When the agency reexamines its findings as to the likely increase in seatbelt usage, it must also reconsider its judgment of the reasonableness of the monetary and other costs associated with the Standard. In reaching its judgment, NHTSA should bear in mind that Congress intended safety to be the pre-eminent factor under the Act:

> "The Committee intends that safety shall be the overriding consideration in the issuance of standards under this bill. The Committee recognizes . . . that the Secretary will necessarily consider reasonableness of cost, feasibility and adequate lead-time." S. Rep. No. 1301, 89th Cong., 2d Sess., 6 (1966).
>
> "In establishing standards the Secretary must conform to the requirement that the standard be practicable. This would require consideration of all relevant factors, including technological ability to achieve the goal of a particular standard as well as consideration of economic factors.
>
> "Motor vehicle safety is the paramount purpose of this bill and each standard must be related thereto." H. R. Rep. No. 1776, 89th Cong., 2d Sess., 16 (1966).

The agency also failed to articulate a basis for not requiring nondetachable belts under Standard 208. It is argued that the concern of the agency with the easy detachability of the currently favored design would be readily solved by a continuous passive belt, which allows the occupant to "spool out" the belt and create the necessary slack for easy extrication from the vehicle. The agency did not separately consider the continuous belt option, but treated it together with the ignition interlock device in a category it titled "Option of Adopting Use-Compelling Features." The agency was concerned that use-compelling devices would "complicate the extrication of [an] occupant from his or her car." "[T]o require that passive belts contain use-compelling features," the agency observed, "could be counterproductive [, given] . . . widespread, latent and irrational fear in many members of the public that they could be trapped by the seat belt after a crash." In addition, based on the experience with the ignition interlock, the agency feared that use-compelling features might trigger adverse public reaction.

By failing to analyze the continuous seatbelts option in its own right, the agency has failed to offer the rational connection between facts and judgment required to pass muster under the arbitrary-and-capricious standard. We agree with the Court of Appeals that NHTSA did not suggest that the emergency release mechanisms used in nondetachable belts are any less effective for emergency egress than the buckle release system used in detachable belts. In 1978, when General Motors obtained the agency's approval to install a continuous passive belt, it assured the agency that nondetachable belts with spool releases were as safe as detachable belts with buckle releases. NHTSA was satisfied that this belt design assured easy extricability: "[t]he agency does not believe that the use of [such] release mechanisms will cause serious occupant egress problems. . . ." While the agency is entitled to change its view on the acceptability of continuous passive belts, it is obligated to explain its reasons for doing so.

The agency also failed to offer any explanation why a continuous passive belt would engender the same adverse public reaction as the ignition interlock, and, as the Court of Appeals concluded, "every indication in the record points the other way." We see no basis for equating the two devices: the continuous belt, unlike the ignition interlock, does not interfere with the operation of the vehicle. More importantly, it is the agency's responsibility, not this Court's, to explain its decision.

VI

"An agency's view of what is in the public interest may change, either with or without a change in circumstances. But an agency changing its course must supply a reasoned analysis. . . ." *Greater Boston Television Corp. v. FCC*, 444 F.2d 841, 852 (1970) (footnote omitted), *cert. denied*, 403 U.S. 923 (1971). We do not accept all of the reasoning of the Court of Appeals but we do conclude that the agency has failed to supply the requisite "reasoned analysis" in this case. Accordingly, we vacate the judgment of the Court of Appeals and remand the cases to that court with directions to remand the matter to the NHTSA for further consideration consistent with this opinion. *So ordered.*

JUSTICE REHNQUIST, with whom the CHIEF JUSTICE, JUSTICE POWELL, and JUSTICE O'CONNOR join, concurring in part and dissenting in part.

I join Parts I, II, III, IV, and V-A of the Court's opinion. In particular, I agree that, since the airbag and continuous spool automatic seatbelt were explicitly approved in the Standard the agency was rescinding, the agency should explain why it declined to leave those requirements intact. In this case, the agency gave no explanation at all. Of course, if the agency can provide a rational explanation, it may adhere to its decision to rescind the entire Standard.

I do not believe, however, that NHTSA's view of detachable automatic seat-belts was arbitrary and capricious. The agency adequately explained its decision to rescind the Standard insofar as it was satisfied by detachable belts.

The statute that requires the Secretary of Transportation to issue motor vehicle safety standards also requires that "[e]ach such . . . standard shall be practicable [and] shall meet the need for motor vehicle safety." The Court rejects the agency's explanation for its conclusion that there is substantial uncertainty whether requiring installation of detachable automatic belts would substantially increase seatbelt usage. The agency chose not to rely on a study showing a substantial increase in seatbelt usage in cars equipped with automatic seatbelts *and* an ignition interlock to prevent the car from being operated when the belts were not in place *and* which were voluntarily purchased with this equipment by consumers. *See ante,* at n.16. It is reasonable for the agency to decide that this study does not support any conclusion concerning the effect of automatic seat-belts that are installed in all cars whether the consumer wants them or not and are not linked to an ignition interlock system.

The Court rejects this explanation because "there would seem to be grounds to believe that seatbelt use by occasional users will be substantially increased by the detachable passive belts," and the agency did not adequately explain its rejection of these grounds. It seems to me that the agency's explanation, while by no means a model, is adequate. The agency acknowledged that there would probably be some increase in belt usage, but concluded that the increase would be small and not worth the cost of mandatory detachable automatic belts. The agency's obligation is to articulate a "rational connection between the facts found and the choice made." I believe it has met this standard.

The agency explicitly stated that it will increase its educational efforts in an attempt to promote public understanding, acceptance, and use of passenger restraint systems. It also stated that it will "initiate efforts with automobile man-ufacturers to ensure that the public will have [automatic crash protection] tech-nology available. If this does not succeed, the agency will consider regulatory action to assure that the last decade's enormous advances in crash protection technology will not be lost."

The agency's changed view of the standard seems to be related to the election of a new President of a different political party. It is readily apparent that the responsible members of one administration may consider public resistance and uncertainties to be more important than do their counterparts in a previous administration. A change in administration brought about by the people casting their votes is a perfectly reasonable basis for an executive agency's reappraisal of the costs and benefits of its programs and regulations. As long as the agency remains within the bounds established by Congress, it is entitled to assess admin-istrative records and evaluate priorities in light of the philosophy of the administration.

QUESTIONS

1.   What scope of review is applied in this case? Where did it come from?
2.   According to the Court, under what circumstances will an agency's action "normally" be considered arbitrary or capricious? Can you relate each listed circumstance to checking agency decision making that is *based on*

invalid or inappropriate reasons? What reasons are most clearly invalid or inappropriate? Will the court's suspicion that invalid reasons may be operating affect its application of the elements of the scope of review? What might such reasons be in this case?

3. Who is in a better position to evaluate the studies referred to in the record, the agency or the court?

4. Was rejection of the continuous spool option really arbitrary and capricious?

5. Was rejection of the "airbag only" option really arbitrary and capricious?

6. Is this just second-guessing? Does it give too much power to courts?

7. What do you think of Justice Rehnquist's argument regarding the legitimacy of policy changes resulting from a presidential election?

8. When you compare *Airbags* and *Vermont Yankee, supra,* p. 256, is there an argument that the Court has it backwards (i.e., to scrutinize substantive decisions but not procedural decisions)?

9. The Supreme Court returned to the question of whether an agency's change in policy, accomplished on this occasion in the adjudicatory context, survived review under the arbitrary or capricious standard. In *FCC v. Fox Television Stations, Inc.*, 556 U.S. 502 (2009), the Supreme Court reviewed the FCC's decision to modify its indecency standard, to permit the imposition of penalties for the use of fleeting expletives by broadcasters. Prior to this change, the FCC had required that expletives be used repetitively to result in legal violations. See *id.* at 507. Justice Scalia, writing for five Justices, held, *id.* at 514-16, that changes in agency positions are *not* reviewed more closely under the arbitrary or capricious standard:

> In overturning the Commission's judgment, the Court of Appeals here relied in part on Circuit precedent requiring a more substantial explanation for agency action that changes prior policy. The Second Circuit has interpreted the Administrative Procedure Act and our opinion in *State Farm* as requiring agencies to make clear "'why the original reasons for adopting the [displaced] rule or policy are no longer dispositive'" as well as "'why the new rule effectuates the statute as well as or better than the old rule.'" 489 F.3d, at 456-457 (quoting *New York Council, Assn. of Civilian Technicians v. FLRA*, 757 F.2d 502, 508 (C.A.2 1985); emphasis deleted). The Court of Appeals for the District of Columbia Circuit has similarly indicated that a court's standard of review is "heightened somewhat" when an agency reverses course. *NAACP v. FCC*, 682 F.2d 993, 998 (1982).
>
> We find no basis in the Administrative Procedure Act or in our opinions for a requirement that all agency change be subjected to more searching review. The Act mentions no such heightened standard. And our opinion in *State Farm* neither held nor implied that every agency action representing a policy change must be justified by reasons more substantial than those required to adopt a policy in the first instance. That case, which involved the rescission of a prior regulation, said only that such action requires "a reasoned analysis for the change beyond that which may be required when an agency *does not act* in the first instance." 463 U.S., at 42 (emphasis added). Treating failures to act and rescissions of prior action differently for purposes of the standard of review makes good sense, and has basis in the text of the statute, which likewise treats the two separately. It instructs a reviewing court to "compel agency action unlawfully withheld or unreasonably delayed," 5 U.S.C. §706(1), and to "hold unlawful and set aside agency

action, findings, and conclusions found to be [among other things] . . . arbitrary [or] capricious," § 706(2)(A). The statute makes no distinction, however, between initial agency action and subsequent agency action undoing or revising that action.

To be sure, the requirement that an agency provide reasoned explanation for its action would ordinarily demand that it display awareness that it is changing position. An agency may not, for example, depart from a prior policy *sub silentio* or simply disregard rules that are still on the books. *See United States v. Nixon*, 418 U.S. 683, 696 (1974). And of course the agency must show that there are good reasons for the new policy. But it need not demonstrate to a court's satisfaction that the reasons for the new policy are better than the reasons for the old one; it suffices that the new policy is permissible under the statute, that there are good reasons for it, and that the agency believes it to be better, which the conscious change of course adequately indicates. This means that the agency need not always provide a more detailed justification than what would suffice for a new policy created on a blank slate. Sometimes it must — when, for example, its new policy rests upon factual findings that contradict those which underlay its prior policy; or when its prior policy has engendered serious reliance interests that must be taken into account. *Smiley v. Citibank (South Dakota), N. A.*, 517 U.S. 735, 742 (1996). It would be arbitrary or capricious to ignore such matters. In such cases it is not that further justification is demanded by the mere fact of policy change; but that a reasoned explanation is needed for disregarding facts and circumstances that underlay or were engendered by the prior policy.

The Court concluded that the agency decision did not violate the arbitrary or capricious standard. See 556 U.S. at 517-18.

10. Does the 1981 MSAPA define more clearly the standard of review of an agency's exercise of discretion? *See* § 5-116(c)(8).

NOTE ON THE RELATIONSHIP BETWEEN ARBITRARY OR CAPRICIOUS REVIEW AND CHEVRON *STEP 2 ANALYSIS*

The analysis of reasonableness required by Step 2 of *Chevron* may perhaps best be thought of as arbitrary-or-capricious review. In *National Association of Regulatory Utility Commissioners v. Interstate Commerce Commission*, 41 F.3d 721, 726-29 (D.C. Cir. 1994) (invalidating several aspects of the Interstate Commerce Commission's "single-state registration" regulations, which changed the system under which interstate motor carriers register with the states through which they operate their vehicles), the D.C. Circuit reasoned:

The statute is silent as to whether the registration state or the carrier is to make the copies of the registration receipts that must be kept in each truck. The Commission accordingly argues that under [*Chevron*] we are obliged to defer to its regulations as a permissible interpretation of the statute. Perhaps because neither the wording of the statute nor the legislative history explicitly addresses the question of the assignment of copying responsibility, petitioners frame their arguments in terms of an arbitrary and capricious challenge rather than a claim of agency misinterpretation of the statute. Yet petitioners emphasize that the "Commission's analysis of congressional intent makes no sense" — because it assumes that "Congress did not intend, or was indifferent, that the [single-state system] be enforced." Implicitly then, if not directly, petitioners are arguing as well that the Commission has impermissibly interpreted the statute (*Chevron* Step II). This is not surprising; the inquiry at the second step of *Chevron* overlaps analytically with a court's task under the Administrative Procedure Act (APA), 5 U.S.C. § 706(2)(A), in determining whether agency action is arbitrary and capricious (unreasonable). *But cf. Continental Air Lines v. Department of Transp.*, 843 F.2d 1444, 1452 (D.C. Cir. 1988) (although *Chevron*'s second step "sounds closely akin to plain vanilla arbitrary-and-capricious style review, ... interpreting a statute is quite a different enterprise than policy-making"). Whether an agency action is to be judged as reasonable, in accordance with the APA's general arbitrary and capricious standard, or whether it is to be examined as a permissible interpretation of the statute vel non depends, at least theoretically, on the scope of the specific congressional delegation implicated. The range of delegations extends from, at one end, a statute that simply charges an agency to act (e.g., to grant licenses) in the public interest to, at the other end, a painstakingly detailed and focused command. When Congress' instructions are conveyed at a high level of generality, an agency is not likely to consider its action as an "interpretation" of the authorizing statute, nor is that action likely to be challenged as a "misinterpretation." (Yet even then, the agency would be expected to assert that a particular decision was shaped by the general policy concerns that animated the legislation.) When, on the other hand, the statute is quite specific, agency action normally is evaluated in terms of how faithfully it follows the more detailed direction; in such cases the question is more obviously whether the agency permissibly interpreted the statute. In any event, the more an agency purports to rely on Congress' policy choice — as set forth in specific legislation — than on the agency's generally conferred discretion, the more the question before the court is logically treated as an issue of statutory interpretation, to be judged by *Chevron* standards. . . .

The Commission has, in our view, acted unreasonably whether one considers the case as one involving a question of *Chevron* Step II statutory interpretation or a garden variety arbitrary and capricious review or, as we do, a case that overlaps both administrative law concepts.

QUESTIONS

1. Do you agree with the D.C. Circuit that arbitrary or capricious review "overlaps" with the Step 2 *Chevron* analysis? For a discussion of the relationship between the *Chevron* and *Skidmore* deference regimes and arbitrary or capricious review, *see* Michael P. Healy, *Reconciling* Chevron, Mead, *and the Review of Agency Discretion: Source of Law and the Standards of Judicial Review of Administrative Action*, 19 Geo. Mason L. Rev. 1 (2011).

2. Has the Supreme Court in *Mead Corp., supra*, accepted the equivalence of *Chevron* Step 2 and arbitrary-or-capricious review, at least in dictum? See p. 547, *supra*. Despite the dictum in *Mead Corp.*, recent decisions of the Supreme Court provide examples of the uncertain relationship between arbitrary or capricious review and *Chevron* review. In *Michigan v. EPA*, 135 S. Ct. 2699, 2704 (2015), the Court reviewed the legality of a regulation imposing limits on "emissions of hazardous air pollutants from power plants." Justice Scalia, writing for the Court, held that the agency had acted unlawfully when it failed to consider the costs of the regulation in the initial decision to regulate emissions from these sources. The agency omitted the consideration of costs notwithstanding the relevant terms of the Clean Air Act, which provided that the agency "'shall regulate'" the power plant emissions, if the agency "'finds . . . regulation is appropriate and

necessary after considering the results of [a required] study.'" *Id.* at 2705 (quoting 42 U.S.C. §7412(n)(1)(A)). The Court referred specifically to *Chevron*'s "deferential standard," but decided that the "EPA strayed far beyond those bounds when it read §7412(n)(1) to mean that it could ignore cost when deciding whether to regulate power plants." *Id.* at 2707. Justice Scalia concluded that, "[a]lthough this term [i.e., 'appropriate'] leaves agencies with flexibility, an agency may not 'entirely fai[l] to consider an important aspect of the problem' when deciding whether regulation is appropriate. *State Farm, supra*, at 43." *Id.* Because the statute itself may define the matters that are important for the agency to consider when taking action, *State Farm*'s arbitrary or capricious review is closely connected to the meaning of a statute: "Read naturally in the present context, the phrase 'appropriate and necessary' requires at least some attention to cost. One would not say that it is even rational, never mind 'appropriate,' to impose billions of dollars in economic costs in return for a few dollars in health or environmental benefits." *Id.* Justice Scalia stated later in the decision that: "*Chevron* allows agencies to choose among competing reasonable interpretations of a statute; it does not license interpretive gerrymanders under which an agency keeps parts of statutory context it likes while throwing away parts it does not." *Id.* at 2708. The Court's holding is stated as an application of *Chevron* review: "We hold that EPA interpreted §7412(n)(1)(A) unreasonably when it deemed cost irrelevant to the decision to regulate power plants." *Id.* at 2712. Do you think that the Court should have employed the arbitrary or capricious standard because the agency failed to consider an important factor? Is this actually a *Chevron* Step 1 decision? Does it matter which standard applies?

3. In *Encino Motorcars, LLC v. Navarro*, 136 S. Ct. 2117 (2016), the Court decided that a legislative rulemaking defining the term "salesman" in the Federal Labor Standards Act received no deference under Step 2 of *Chevron*. The Court stated the proposition that "[a]n arbitrary and capricious regulation . . . is itself unlawful and receives no *Chevron* deference. See *Mead Corp., supra*, at 227." 136 S. Ct. at 2126. The Court decided that, because the agency "said almost nothing" to explain the change of position contained in the regulation, *id.* at 2127, the agency had failed under the *Fox Television* standard. See *id.* The Court then stated its conclusion: "This lack of reasoned explication for a regulation that is inconsistent with the Department's longstanding earlier position results in a rule that cannot carry the force of law. See 5 U.S.C. §706(2)(A); *State Farm, supra*, at 42-43. It follows that this regulation does not receive *Chevron* deference in the interpretation of the relevant statute." 136 S. Ct. at 2127. Is this just another way of saying that Step 2 of *Chevron* looks to whether the agency decision is arbitrary or capricious?

4. In *Verizon Communications, Inc. v. FCC*, 535 U.S. 467 (2002), the Justices disagreed about the application of Step 2 of *Chevron*. Justice Souter's majority opinion mentioned *State Farm* only in a footnote, *id.* at 502 n.20, while Justice Breyer's dissent relied explicitly on *State Farm*. 535 U.S. at 541-42 (BREYER, J., dissenting).

AFL-CIO v. MARSHALL

617 F.2d 636 (D.C. Cir. 1979)

BAZELON, Senior Circuit Judge: These consolidated petitions for review challenge a new permanent health standard limiting occupational exposure to cotton dust which was promulgated by regulations on June 19, 1978 by the Occupational Safety and Health Administration of the Department of Labor (OSHA), under section 6(b)(5) of the Occupational Safety and Health Act of 1970 (the Act). OSHA's action, which rests on its determination that occupational exposure to cotton dust presents a material health hazard to workers, is attacked by three groups of petitioners: (1) representatives of the cotton textile industry and (2) non-textile industries who claim that the standard is unwarranted and infeasible; and (3) their employee unions, who attack two provisions of the standard as too lax, but support the rest. These very divergent claims reflect the wide variety of conflicting interests that make OSHA's task a difficult one. On direct review, we uphold the standard except for its application to the cottonseed oil industry which we remand for clarification or reconsideration.

To assist a proper understanding of the issues, we discuss (I) the history and context of the agency's action; (II) the nature of our review under the Act; (III) the claims of the textile industry; (IV) the claims of the non-textile industries; and (V) challenges to a few technical provisions of the standard. . . .

I

. . . C. THE OSHA STANDARD

On the basis of the massive rulemaking record, OSHA promulgated the cotton standard in an effort to reduce the health risks to cotton workers. Part of the standard sets "permissible exposure limits" (PELs) for each manufacturing operation and industry that exposes workers to cotton dust. Thus, OSHA set (1) 200 micrograms per cubic meter (200 $\mu g/m^3$) as the PEL for lint-free respirable cotton dust in yard manufacturing; (2) 750 $\mu g/m^3$ for slashing and weaving operations in the cotton industry; and (3) 500 $\mu g/m^3$ for all other processes in the cotton industry and for all non-textile industries that expose workers to cotton dust.

Implementation of the standard depends primarily on the adoption of engineering and work practice controls by employers. OSHA established a four-year implementation period during which employers are expected to achieve compliance. If an employer establishes that the required controls are infeasible, he can obtain an administrative variance from the standard, but he must make respirators available to protect his employees until he achieves compliance. The standard also requires employers to monitor employees' exposure to cotton dust, to provide medical surveillance and employee education, and to post warning signs about the health risks.

Before examining petitioners' objections, we consider the limits of our review.

II. SCOPE OF REVIEW

The Occupational Safety and Health Act of 1970 is one of a number of recent Congressional statutes that designates the stringent "substantial evidence" test for judicial review of notice-and-comment rulemaking. The explicit language of the Act, its legislative history, and its application by the courts confirm that regulations promulgated under the Act are to be upheld on review if supported by "substantial evidence on the record considered as a whole."

The substantial evidence test provides for more rigorous scrutiny than the usual "arbitrary and capricious" test applicable to informal rulemaking. Although Congress required this more rigorous judicial review, it nevertheless delegated unusually broad discretionary authority to regulate against possible harms.[47] We have already resolved this seeming anomaly in *Industrial Union Dep't v. Hodgson*, 499 F.2d 467 (D.C. Cir. 1974). There we concluded that the reviewing court's task under the Act is to provide a careful check on the agency's determinations without substituting its judgment for that of the agency.[48] Congress apparently created an "uneasy partnership" between the agency and the reviewing court to check extravagant exercises of the agency's authority to regulate risk. Our role in this partnership is to ensure that the regulations resulted from a process of reasoned decisionmaking consistent with the agency's mandate from Congress. By statute, this process must include notice to interested parties of issues presented in the proposed rule. The agency must also provide opportunities for these parties to offer contrary evidence and arguments.

OSHA adopted additional procedures to improve its decision-making process. A qualified hearing examiner must preside at oral hearings on proposed standards. A verbatim transcript of the hearing is required, and cross-examination is permitted. These procedures, which were followed in this case, transform OSHA's action into "hybrid" rulemaking, and produce a record more susceptible to rigorous judicial review than the more usual informal rulemaking record.[56]

The tasks of this reviewing court are thus to ensure that the agency has (1) acted within the scope of its authority; (2) followed the procedures required by statute and by its own regulations; (3) explicated the bases for its decision; (4) adduced substantial evidence in the record to support its determinations.

The meaning of "substantial evidence" in this context is problematic. Factual proof about particular health risks may not be substantial in the traditional sense simply because the medical and scientific communities do not yet completely understand the nature of threatening diseases. To protect workers from

---

47. The substantial evidence test was adopted in the Act apparently as a compromise when the House relinquished its advocacy of formal agency proceedings and adopted the Senate's informal rulemaking provision. *See* H. R. Rep. No. 91-1765, 91st Cong., 2d Sess. 36 (1970), *reprinted* in Legis. Hist. at 1189. See also *Industrial Union Dep't v. Hodgson*, 499 F.2d at 473; *Assoc. Indus. v. Dep't of Labor*, 487 F.2d at 348-49 (discussing legislative history of scope of review provision).

48. In *Industrial Union Dep't v. Hodgson*, this court construed the substantial evidence review in terms of the demands to be made by the reviewing court:

> What we are entitled to at all events is a careful identification by the Secretary, when his proposed standards are challenged, of the reasons why he chooses to follow one course rather than another. Where that choice purports to be based on the existence of certain determinable facts, the Secretary must, in form as well as substance, find those facts from evidence in the record. By the same token, when the Secretary is obliged to make policy judgments where no factual certainties exist or where facts alone do not provide the answer, he should so state and go on to identify the considerations he found persuasive.

499 F.2d at 475-76.

56. In describing the additional procedures, the agency noted a congressional expectation that the rulemaking would be on the basis of a record "to which a substantial evidence test, where pertinent, may be applied."

material health impairments, OSHA must rely on predictions of possible future events and extrapolations from limited data. It may have to fill gaps in knowledge with policy considerations. Congress recognized this problem by authorizing the agency to promulgate rules on the basis of the "best available evidence." OSHA's mandate necessarily requires it to act — even if information is incomplete — when the best available evidence indicates a serious threat to the health of workers. Thus, a court entrusted with the rigorous "substantial evidence" review must examine not only OSHA's factual support, but also the "judgment calls" and reasoning that contribute to its final decision. Otherwise, an agency's claim of ignorance would clothe it with unreviewable discretion.

Therefore, the reviewing court must examine both factual evidence and the agency's policy considerations set forth in the record. To facilitate this review of the record, the agency must pinpoint the factual evidence and the policy considerations upon which it relied. This requires explication of the assumptions underlying predictions or extrapolations, and of the basis for its resolution of conflicts and ambiguities. In enforcing these requirements, the court does not reach out to resolve controversies over technical data. Instead, it seeks to ensure public accountability. Explicit explanation for the basis of the agency's decision not only facilitates proper judicial review but also provides the opportunity for effective peer review, legislative oversight, and public education. This requirement is in the best interest of everyone, including the decision-makers themselves. If the decision-making process is open and candid, it will inspire more confidence in those who are affected. Further, by opening the process to public scrutiny and criticism, we reduce the risk that important information will be overlooked or ignored. Instructed by these ends, this court on review will "combine supervision with restraint."

[In a lengthy opinion, the court proceeded to uphold the standard except for its application to the cottonseed oil industry, as to which the court was unable to ascertain the basis for the agency's determination that the standard was economically feasible.]

QUESTIONS AND NOTE

1. Has the D.C. Circuit done a good job of giving meaning to the "substantial evidence" standard for review of agency exercises of discretion?
2. Is the procedural aspect of the D.C. Circuit analysis inconsistent with *Vermont Yankee, supra*, p. 256?
3. For another example of the application of a statutorily mandated "substantial evidence" scope applied to an informal rulemaking, *see Corrosion Proof Fittings v. EPA*, 947 F.2d 1201 (5th Cir. 1991), holding that the substantial evidence standard required more rigorous judicial review than the arbitrary and capricious standard.

NOTE ON HARMLESS ERROR IN THE ADMINISTRATIVE PROCESS

Judge Leventhal in the excerpt from *Greater Boston Television Corp. v. FCC*, 444 F.2d 841, 851-53 (D.C. Cir. 1970), quoted at *supra* p. 586, stated that a "court [will not] upset a[n administrative agency] decision because of errors that are not material, there being room for the doctrine of harmless error." Section 706 of the APA specifically provides that, when a court reviews an agency's action, "due account shall be taken of the rule of prejudicial error." The Supreme Court recently relied on this provision in deciding that an agency action was not arbitrary or capricious:

> We are not persuaded that this statement [in the Federal Register that is inconsistent with the final agency decision] constitutes the type of error that requires a remand. By the time the Federal Register statement was issued, the EPA had already consulted with the FWS about the Arizona application, and the question whether that consultation had been required, as opposed to voluntarily undertaken by the agency, was simply not germane to the final agency transfer decision. The Federal Register statement, in short, was dictum, and it had no bearing on the final agency action that respondents challenge. Mindful of Congress' admonition that in reviewing agency action, "due account shall be taken of the rule of prejudicial error," 5 U.S.C. § 706, we do not believe that this stray statement, which could have had no effect on the underlying agency action being challenged, requires that we further delay the transfer of permitting authority to Arizona by remanding to the agency for clarification. *See also PDK Labs., Inc. v. United States Drug Enforcement Admin.*, 362 F.3d 786, 799 (C.A.D.C. 2004) ("In administrative law, as in federal civil and criminal litigation, there is a harmless error rule").

National Ass'n of Home Builders v. Defenders of Wildlife, 551 U.S. 644, 659-660 (2007) (footnote omitted).

THEORY APPLIED PROBLEM

In 1990, Congress enacted the Children's Television Act (codified at 47 U.S.C. §§ 303a & 303b) (the "CTA"). The CTA includes substantive provisions that limit the amount of advertising time aired during children's programming to 12.5 minutes per half hour on weekdays and 10.5 minutes per half hour on weekends. *See* 47 U.S.C. § 303a(b). In addition, the CTA seeks to ensure that commercial television broadcasters meet the "educational and informational" programming needs of children. The law requires the Federal Communications Commission (the "Commission") to ensure that broadcasters comply with their responsibilities.

In 1991, the Commission issued a Notice of Proposed Rulemaking containing proposed rules implementing the CTA. The proposed rules simply codified the commercial time limits into the Code of Federal Regulations. With respect to the requirement that commercial broadcasters meet the educational and informational needs of children, the Commission admonished broadcasters to do a better job in this area and required them to report on their efforts when seeking renewal of their station licenses. After carefully reviewing the language of the CTA and its legislative history, the Commission expressly rejected requiring television broadcasters to air a minimum amount of educational or informational children's programming. In addition, the Commission declined to adopt a definition of such programming, leaving it to broadcasters to identify such programming as they thought best.

Between 1991 and 1994, commercial television broadcasters seeking renewal of their station licenses made some unusual claims regarding their compliance efforts with the CTA's programming requirements. Many stations claimed that programs such as "Gilligan's Island," "Green Acres," and "The Jetsons" constituted educational or "pro-social" informational children's programming. Moreover, the total amount of educational or informational children's television programming aired on most commercial television stations actually *decreased* from 1991 to 1994.

In 1994, under heavy pressure from children's advocates, the Commission issued a new Notice of Proposed Rulemaking. In this NPRM, the Commission proposed quantitative and qualitative standards for enforcing the CTA. Specifically, the Commission proposed requiring every commercial television station to show at least three hours per week of educational or informational children's programming. In addition, the Commission adopted a definition of such programming that mandated that the programming be broadcast during particular hours of the day, be regularly scheduled, be program length, have a defined educational or informational objective, be identified as CTA-compliant programming, and meet the educational or informational needs of the children comprising the intended audience.

In explaining its change of position, the Commission stated that neither the language of the CTA nor the legislative history expressly prohibited the adoption of quantitative and qualitative standards for enforcing its provisions. Given the abject failure of the 1991 implementing regulations, the Commission argued that its new approach was necessary in order to achieve Congress's objectives.

The Commission observed all the procedural requirements set forth in section 553 of the APA, including publication of the proposed rules, an opportunity for public comment, a concise explanatory statement, and compliance with the timing requirements for informal rulemaking. Commission staff reviewed the comments and prepared summaries of their content for the five Commissioners. The Commissioners never actually read the actual comments; at least two of them did not bother to read the staff summaries. All five Commissioners spoke with staff about the proposed rules. These staff members had read the comments or the summaries of them. All five Commissioners participated in the decision to adopt the rules, which carried by a margin of 3 to 2. One of the two Commissioners who failed to read either the comments or the staff summary voted in favor of the new rules and the other voted against them.

A second Commissioner in the majority was something of a maverick. During the pendency of these proceedings, she gave numerous public speeches and interviews, during which she accused commercial television broadcasters of "poisoning the minds of the nation's youth" and "polluting the airwaves with filth." She vowed "to teach these vile corporate cretins a lesson that they won't soon forget" and promised "to put some real teeth into the CTA." She also refused to attend meetings with representatives of the broadcasting industry during the pendency of the rulemaking proceedings. During the vote, she stated that, "with this vote, we take the first small step in forcing television broadcasters to accept some measure of accountability. In my view, these rules do not go far enough in bringing these irresponsible predators to book."

You work as a staff lawyer for the National Association of Broadcasters (the "NAB"). Henry Baumann, the NAB's general counsel, asks you to determine whether the NAB could bring a successful challenge to the new regulations implementing the CTA. He asks you to disregard any potential First Amendment objections and to focus exclusively on potential APA problems and/or problems grounded in procedural due process.

D. REVIEW OF SCOPE OF REVIEW

KING v. BURWELL
135 S. Ct. 2480 (2015)

CHIEF JUSTICE ROBERTS delivered the opinion of the Court.

The Patient Protection and Affordable Care Act adopts a series of interlocking reforms designed to expand coverage in the individual health insurance market. First, the Act bars insurers from taking a person's health into account when deciding whether to sell health insurance or how much to charge. Second, the Act generally requires each person to maintain insurance coverage or make a payment to the Internal Revenue Service. And third, the Act gives tax credits to certain people to make insurance more affordable.

In addition to those reforms, the Act requires the creation of an "Exchange" in each State — basically, a marketplace that allows people to compare and purchase insurance plans. The Act gives each State the opportunity to establish its own Exchange, but provides that the Federal Government will establish the Exchange if the State does not.

This case is about whether the Act's interlocking reforms apply equally in each State no matter who establishes the State's Exchange. Specifically, the question presented is whether the Act's tax credits are available in States that have a Federal Exchange.

I

A

The Patient Protection and Affordable Care Act, 124 Stat. 119, grew out of a long history of failed health insurance reform. In the 1990s, several States began experimenting with ways to expand people's access to coverage. One common approach was to impose a pair of insurance market regulations — a "guaranteed issue" requirement, which barred insurers from denying coverage to any person because of his health, and a "community rating" requirement, which barred insurers from charging a person higher premiums for the same reason. Together, those requirements were designed to ensure that anyone who wanted to buy health insurance could do so.

The guaranteed issue and community rating requirements achieved that goal, but they had an unintended consequence: They encouraged people to wait until they got sick to buy insurance. Why buy insurance coverage when you are healthy, if you can buy the same coverage for the same price when you become ill? This consequence — known as "adverse selection" — led to a second: Insurers were forced to increase premiums to account for the fact that, more and more, it was the sick rather than the healthy who were buying insurance.

And that consequence fed back into the first: As the cost of insurance rose, even more people waited until they became ill to buy it.

This led to an economic "death spiral." As premiums rose higher and higher, and the number of people buying insurance sank lower and lower, insurers began to leave the market entirely. As a result, the number of people without insurance increased dramatically.

This cycle happened repeatedly during the 1990s. For example, in 1993, the State of Washington reformed its individual insurance market by adopting the guaranteed issue and community rating requirements. Over the next three years, premiums rose by 78 percent and the number of people enrolled fell by 25 percent. By 1999, 17 of the State's 19 private insurers had left the market, and the remaining two had announced their intention to do so. . . .

In 1996, Massachusetts adopted the guaranteed issue and community rating requirements and experienced similar results. But in 2006, Massachusetts added two more reforms: The Commonwealth required individuals to buy insurance or pay a penalty, and it gave tax credits to certain individuals to ensure that they could afford the insurance they were required to buy. The combination of these three reforms — insurance market regulations, a coverage mandate, and tax credits — reduced the uninsured rate in Massachusetts to 2.6 percent, by far the lowest in the Nation.

B

The Affordable Care Act adopts a version of the three key reforms that made the Massachusetts system successful. First, the Act adopts the guaranteed issue and community rating requirements. The Act provides that "each health insurance issuer that offers health insurance coverage in the individual . . . market in a State must accept every . . . individual in the State that applies for such coverage." 42 U.S.C. § 300gg–1(a). The Act also bars insurers from charging higher premiums on the basis of a person's health. § 300gg.

Second, the Act generally requires individuals to maintain health insurance coverage or make a payment to the IRS. 26 U.S.C. § 5000A. Congress recognized that, without an incentive, "many individuals would wait to purchase health insurance until they needed care." 42 U.S.C. § 18091(2)(I). So Congress adopted a coverage requirement to "minimize this adverse selection and broaden the health insurance risk pool to include healthy individuals, which will lower health insurance premiums." *Ibid.* In Congress's view, that coverage requirement was "essential to creating effective health insurance markets." *Ibid.* Congress also provided an exemption from the coverage requirement for anyone who has to spend more than eight percent of his income on health insurance. 26 U.S.C. §§ 5000A(e)(1)(A), (e)(1)(B)(ii).

Third, the Act seeks to make insurance more affordable by giving refundable tax credits to individuals with household incomes between 100 percent and 400 percent of the federal poverty line. § 36B. Individuals who meet the Act's requirements may purchase insurance with the tax credits, which are provided in advance directly to the individual's insurer. 42 U.S.C. §§ 18081, 18082.

These three reforms are closely intertwined. As noted, Congress found that the guaranteed issue and community rating requirements would not work without the coverage requirement. § 18091(2)(I). And the coverage requirement would not work without the tax credits. The reason is that, without the tax credits, the cost of buying insurance would exceed eight percent of income for a large number of individuals, which would exempt them from the coverage requirement. Given the relationship between these three reforms, the Act provided that they should take effect on the same day—January 1, 2014.

C

In addition to those three reforms, the Act requires the creation of an "Exchange" in each State where people can shop for insurance, usually online. 42 U.S.C. § 18031(b)(1). An Exchange may be created in one of two ways. First, the Act provides that "[e]ach State shall . . . establish an American Health Benefit Exchange . . . for the State." *Ibid.* Second, if a State nonetheless chooses not to establish its own Exchange, the Act provides that the Secretary of Health and Human Services "shall . . . establish and operate such Exchange within the State." § 18041(c)(1).

The issue in this case is whether the Act's tax credits are available in States that have a Federal Exchange rather than a State Exchange. The Act initially provides that tax credits "shall be allowed" for any "applicable taxpayer." 26 U.S.C. § 36B(a). The Act then provides that the amount of the tax credit depends in part on whether the taxpayer has enrolled in an insurance plan through "an Exchange *established by the State* under section 1311 of the Patient Protection and Affordable Care Act [hereinafter 42 U.S.C. § 18031]." 26 U.S.C. §§ 36B(b)-(c) (emphasis added).

The IRS addressed the availability of tax credits by promulgating a rule that made them available on both State and Federal Exchanges. 77 Fed. Reg. 30378 (2012). As relevant here, the IRS Rule provides that a taxpayer is eligible for a tax credit if he enrolled in an insurance plan through "an Exchange," 26 CFR § 1.36B–2 (2013), which is defined as "an Exchange serving the individual market . . . regardless of whether the Exchange is established and operated by a State . . . or by HHS," 45 CFR § 155.20 (2014). At this point, 16 States and the District of Columbia have established their own Exchanges; the other 34 States have elected to have HHS do so.

D

Petitioners are four individuals who live in Virginia, which has a Federal Exchange. They do not wish to purchase health insurance. In their view, Virginia's Exchange does not qualify as "an Exchange established by the State under [42 U.S.C. § 18031]," so they should not receive any tax credits. That would make the cost of buying insurance more than eight percent of their income, which would exempt them from the Act's coverage requirement. 26 U.S.C. § 5000A(e)(1).

Under the IRS Rule, however, Virginia's Exchange would qualify as "an Exchange established by the State under [42 U.S.C. § 18031]," so petitioners would receive tax credits. That would make the cost of buying insurance less than eight percent of petitioners' income, which would subject them to the Act's coverage requirement. The IRS Rule therefore requires petitioners to either buy health insurance they do not want, or make a payment to the IRS.

Petitioners challenged the IRS Rule in Federal District Court. The District Court dismissed the suit. . . . The Court of Appeals for the Fourth Circuit affirmed. 759 F.3d 358 (2014). The Fourth Circuit viewed the Act as "ambiguous and subject to at least two different interpretations." *Id.*, at 372. The court therefore deferred to the IRS's interpretation under *Chevron U.S.A. Inc. v. Natural Resources Defense Council, Inc.*, 467 U.S. 837 (1984). 759 F.3d, at 376.

The same day that the Fourth Circuit issued its decision, the Court of Appeals for the District of Columbia Circuit vacated the IRS Rule in a different case, holding that the Act "unambiguously restricts" the tax credits to State Exchanges. *Halbig v. Burwell*, 758 F.3d 390, 394 (2014). We granted certiorari in the present case.

II

The Affordable Care Act addresses tax credits in what is now Section 36B of the Internal Revenue Code. That section provides: "In the case of an applicable taxpayer, there shall be allowed as a credit against the tax imposed by this subtitle . . . an amount equal to the premium assistance credit amount." 26 U.S.C. § 36B(a). Section 36B then defines the term "premium assistance credit amount" as "the sum of the *premium assistance amounts* determined under paragraph (2) with respect to all *coverage months* of the taxpayer occurring during the taxable year." § 36B(b)(1) (emphasis added). Section 36B goes on to define the two italicized terms—"premium assistance amount" and "coverage month"—in part by referring to an insurance plan that is enrolled in through "an Exchange established by the State under [42 U.S.C. § 18031]." 26 U.S.C. §§ 36B(b)(2)(A), (c)(2)(A)(i).

The parties dispute whether Section 36B authorizes tax credits for individuals who enroll in an insurance plan through a Federal Exchange. . . .

When analyzing an agency's interpretation of a statute, we often apply the two-step framework announced in *Chevron*, 467 U.S. 837. Under that framework, we ask whether the statute is ambiguous and, if so, whether the agency's interpretation is reasonable. *Id.*, at 842-843. This approach "is premised on the theory that a statute's ambiguity constitutes an implicit delegation from Congress to the agency to fill in the statutory gaps." *FDA v. Brown & Williamson Tobacco Corp.*, 529 U.S. 120, 159 (2000). "In extraordinary cases, however, there may be reason to hesitate before concluding that Congress has intended such an implicit delegation." *Ibid.*

This is one of those cases. The tax credits are among the Act's key reforms, involving billions of dollars in spending each year and affecting the price of health insurance for millions of people. Whether those credits are available on Federal Exchanges is thus a question of deep "economic and political significance" that is central to this statutory scheme; had Congress wished to assign that question to an agency, it surely would have done so expressly. *Utility Air Regulatory Group v. EPA*, 134 S. Ct. 2427, 2444 (2014) (quoting *Brown & Williamson*, 529 U.S., at 160). It is especially unlikely that Congress would have delegated this decision to the IRS, which has no expertise in crafting health insurance policy of this sort. See *Gonzales v. Oregon*, 546 U.S. 243, 266-267 (2006). This is not a case for the IRS.

It is instead our task to determine the correct reading of Section 36B. If the statutory language is plain, we must enforce it according to its terms. *Hardt v. Reliance Standard Life Ins. Co.*, 560 U.S. 242, 251 (2010). But oftentimes the "meaning—or ambiguity—of certain words or phrases may only become evident when placed in context." *Brown & Williamson*, 529 U.S., at 132. So when deciding whether the language is plain, we must read the words "in their context and with a view to their place in the overall statutory scheme." *Id.*, at 133 (internal quotation marks omitted). Our duty, after all, is "to construe statutes, not isolated provisions." *Graham County Soil and Water Conservation Dist. v. United States ex rel. Wilson*, 559 U.S. 280, 290 (2010) (internal quotation marks omitted).

A

We begin with the text of Section 36B. As relevant here, Section 36B allows an individual to receive tax credits only if the individual enrolls in an insurance plan through "an Exchange established by the State under [42 U.S.C. § 18031]." In other words, three things must be true: First, the individual must enroll in an insurance plan through "an Exchange." Second, that Exchange must be "established by the State." And third, that Exchange must be established "under [42 U.S.C. § 18031]." We address each requirement in turn.

First, all parties agree that a Federal Exchange qualifies as "an Exchange" for purposes of Section 36B. Section 18031 provides that "[e]ach State shall . . . establish an American Health Benefit Exchange . . . for the State." § 18031(b)(1). Although phrased as a requirement, the Act gives the States "flexibility" by allowing them to "elect" whether they want to establish an Exchange. § 18041(b). If the State chooses not to do so, Section 18041 provides that the Secretary "shall . . . establish and operate *such Exchange* within the State." § 18041(c)(1) (emphasis added).

By using the phrase "such Exchange," Section 18041 instructs the Secretary to establish and operate the *same* Exchange that the State was directed to establish under Section 18031. In other words, State Exchanges and Federal Exchanges are equivalent — they must meet the same requirements, perform the same functions, and serve the same purposes. . . . A Federal Exchange therefore counts as "an Exchange" under Section 36B.

Second, we must determine whether a Federal Exchange is "established by the State" for purposes of Section 36B. At the outset, it might seem that a Federal Exchange cannot fulfill this requirement. After all, the Act defines "State" to mean "each of the 50 States and the District of Columbia" — a definition that does not include the Federal Government. 42 U.S.C. § 18024(d). But when read in context, "with a view to [its] place in the overall statutory scheme," the meaning of the phrase "established by the State" is not so clear. *Brown & Williamson*, 529 U.S., at 133 (internal quotation marks omitted).

After telling each State to establish an Exchange, Section 18031 provides that all Exchanges "shall make available qualified health plans to qualified individuals." 42 U.S.C. § 18031(d)(2)(A). Section 18032 then defines the term "qualified individual" in part as an individual who "resides in the State that established the Exchange." § 18032(f)(1)(A). And that's a problem: If we give the phrase "the State that established the Exchange" its most natural meaning, there would be no "qualified individuals" on Federal Exchanges. But the Act clearly contemplates that there will be qualified individuals on every Exchange. As we just mentioned, the Act requires all Exchanges to "make available qualified health plans to qualified individuals" — something an Exchange could not do if there were no such individuals. § 18031(d)(2)(A). And the Act tells the Exchange, in deciding which health plans to offer, to consider "the interests of qualified individuals . . . in the State or States in which such Exchange operates" — again, something the Exchange could not do if qualified individuals did not exist. § 18031(e)(1)(B). This problem arises repeatedly throughout the Act.[1]

These provisions suggest that the Act may not always use the phrase "established by the State" in its most natural sense. Thus, the meaning of that phrase may not be as clear as it appears when read out of context.

Third, we must determine whether a Federal Exchange is established "under [42 U.S.C. § 18031]." This too might seem a requirement that a Federal Exchange cannot fulfill, because it is Section 18041 that tells the Secretary when to "establish and operate such Exchange." But here again, the way different provisions in the statute interact suggests otherwise.

The Act defines the term "Exchange" to mean "an American Health Benefit Exchange established under section 18031." § 300gg-91(d)(21). If we import that definition into Section 18041, the Act tells the Secretary to "establish and operate such 'American Health Benefit Exchange established under section 18031.'"...

This interpretation of "under [42 U.S.C. § 18031]" fits best with the statutory context. All of the requirements that an Exchange must meet are in Section 18031, so it is sensible to regard all Exchanges as established under that provision....

The upshot of all this is that the phrase "an Exchange established by the State under [42 U.S.C. § 18031]" is properly viewed as ambiguous. The phrase may be limited in its reach to State Exchanges. But it is also possible that the phrase refers to all Exchanges—both State and Federal—at least for purposes of the tax credits. If a State chooses not to follow the directive in Section 18031 that it establish an Exchange, the Act tells the Secretary to establish "such Exchange." § 18041. And by using the words "such Exchange," the Act indicates that State and Federal Exchanges should be the same. But State and Federal Exchanges would differ in a fundamental way if tax credits were available only on State Exchanges—one type of Exchange would help make insurance more affordable by providing billions of dollars to the States' citizens; the other type of Exchange would not.

The conclusion that Section 36B is ambiguous is further supported by several provisions that assume tax credits will be available on both State and Federal Exchanges....

Petitioners and the dissent respond that the words "established by the State" would be unnecessary if Congress meant to extend tax credits to both State and Federal Exchanges. But "our preference for avoiding surplusage constructions is not absolute." *Lamie v. United States Trustee*, 540 U.S. 526, 536 (2004). And specifically with respect to this Act, rigorous application of the canon does not seem a particularly useful guide to a fair construction of the statute.

The Affordable Care Act contains more than a few examples of inartful drafting....

---

1. The dissent argues that one would "naturally read instructions about qualified individuals to be inapplicable to the extent a particular Exchange has no such individuals." But the fact that the dissent's interpretation would make so many parts of the Act "inapplicable" to Federal Exchanges is precisely what creates the problem. It would be odd indeed for Congress to write such detailed instructions about customers on a State Exchange, while having nothing to say about those on a Federal Exchange.

... After reading Section 36B along with other related provisions in the Act, we cannot conclude that the phrase "an Exchange established by the State under [Section 18031]" is unambiguous.

B

Given that the text is ambiguous, we must turn to the broader structure of the Act to determine the meaning of Section 36B. "A provision that may seem ambiguous in isolation is often clarified by the remainder of the statutory scheme . . . because only one of the permissible meanings produces a substantive effect that is compatible with the rest of the law." *United Sav. Assn. of Tex. v. Timbers of Inwood Forest Associates, Ltd.*, 484 U.S. 365, 371 (1988). Here, the statutory scheme compels us to reject petitioners' interpretation because it would destabilize the individual insurance market in any State with a Federal Exchange, and likely create the very "death spirals" that Congress designed the Act to avoid. See *New York State Dept. of Social Servs. v. Dublino*, 413 U.S. 405, 419-420 (1973) ("We cannot interpret federal statutes to negate their own stated purposes.").

As discussed above, Congress based the Affordable Care Act on three major reforms: first, the guaranteed issue and community rating requirements; second, a requirement that individuals maintain health insurance coverage or make a payment to the IRS; and third, the tax credits for individuals with household incomes between 100 percent and 400 percent of the federal poverty line. In a State that establishes its own Exchange, these three reforms work together to expand insurance coverage. The guaranteed issue and community rating requirements ensure that anyone can buy insurance; the coverage requirement creates an incentive for people to do so before they get sick; and the tax credits — it is hoped — make insurance more affordable. Together, those reforms "minimize . . . adverse selection and broaden the health insurance risk pool to include healthy individuals, which will lower health insurance premiums." 42 U.S.C. § 18091(2)(I).

Under petitioners' reading, however, the Act would operate quite differently in a State with a Federal Exchange. As they see it, one of the Act's three major reforms — the tax credits — would not apply. And a second major reform — the coverage requirement — would not apply in a meaningful way. As explained earlier, the coverage requirement applies only when the cost of buying health insurance (minus the amount of the tax credits) is less than eight percent of an individual's income. 26 U.S.C. §§ 5000A(e)(1)(A), (e)(1)(B)(ii). So without the tax credits, the coverage requirement would apply to fewer individuals. And it would be a lot fewer. In 2014, approximately 87 percent of people who bought insurance on a Federal Exchange did so with tax credits, and virtually all of those people would become exempt. If petitioners are right, therefore, only one of the Act's three major reforms would apply in States with a Federal Exchange.

The combination of no tax credits and an ineffective coverage requirement could well push a State's individual insurance market into a death spiral. . . .

It is implausible that Congress meant the Act to operate in this manner. See *National Federation of Independent Business v. Sebelius*, 132 S. Ct. 2566, 2674 (2012) (SCALIA, KENNEDY, THOMAS, and ALITO, JJ., dissenting) ("Without the federal subsidies . . . the exchanges would not operate as Congress intended and may not operate at all"). Congress made the guaranteed issue and community rating requirements applicable in every State in the Nation. But those requirements only work when combined with the coverage requirement and the tax credits. So it stands to reason that Congress meant for those provisions to apply in every State as well.

Petitioners respond that Congress was not worried about the effects of withholding tax credits from States with Federal Exchanges because "Congress evidently believed it was offering states a deal they would not refuse." . . .

Section 18041 refutes the argument that Congress believed it was offering the States a deal they would not refuse. That section provides that, if a State elects not to establish an Exchange, the Secretary "shall . . . establish and operate such Exchange within the State." 42 U.S.C. § 18041(c)(1)(A). The whole point of that provision is to create a federal fallback in case a State chooses not to establish its own Exchange. Contrary to petitioners' argument, Congress did not believe it was offering States a deal they would not refuse — it expressly addressed what would happen if a State did refuse the deal.

C

Finally, the structure of Section 36B itself suggests that tax credits are not limited to State Exchanges. Section 36B(a) initially provides that tax credits "shall be allowed" for any "applicable taxpayer." Section 36B(c)(1) then defines an "applicable taxpayer" as someone who (among other things) has a household income between 100 percent and 400 percent of the federal poverty line. Together, these two provisions appear to make anyone in the specified income range eligible to receive a tax credit. . . .

We have held that Congress "does not alter the fundamental details of a regulatory scheme in vague terms or ancillary provisions." *Whitman v. American Trucking Assns., Inc.*, 531 U.S. 457, 468 (2001). But in petitioners' view, Congress made the viability of the entire Affordable Care Act turn on the ultimate ancillary provision: a sub-sub-sub section of the Tax Code. We doubt that is what Congress meant to do. Had Congress meant to limit tax credits to State Exchanges, it likely would have done so in the definition of "applicable taxpayer" or in some other prominent manner. It would not have used such a winding path of connect-the-dots provisions about the amount of the credit.

D

Petitioners' arguments about the plain meaning of Section 36B are strong. But while the meaning of the phrase "an Exchange established by the State under [42 U.S.C. § 18031]" may seem plain "when viewed in isolation," such a reading turns out to be "untenable in light of [the statute] as a whole." *Department of Revenue of Ore. v. ACF Industries, Inc.*, 510 U.S. 332, 343 (1994). In this instance, the context and structure of the Act compel us to depart from what would otherwise be the most natural reading of the pertinent statutory phrase.

Reliance on context and structure in statutory interpretation is a "subtle business, calling for great wariness lest what professes to be mere rendering becomes creation and attempted interpretation of legislation becomes legislation itself." *Palmer v. Massachusetts*, 308 U.S. 79, 83 (1939). For the reasons we have given, however, such reliance is appropriate in this case, and leads us to conclude that Section 36B allows tax credits for insurance purchased on any Exchange created under the Act. Those credits are necessary for the Federal Exchanges to function like their State Exchange counterparts, and to avoid the type of calamitous result that Congress plainly meant to avoid.

* * *

In a democracy, the power to make the law rests with those chosen by the people. Our role is more confined — "to say what the law is." *Marbury v. Madison,* 1 Cranch 137, 177 (1803). That is easier in some cases than in others. But in every case we must respect the role of the Legislature, and take care not to undo what it has done. A fair reading of legislation demands a fair understanding of the legislative plan.

Congress passed the Affordable Care Act to improve health insurance markets, not to destroy them. If at all possible, we must interpret the Act in a way that is consistent with the former, and avoids the latter. Section 36B can fairly be read consistent with what we see as Congress's plan, and that is the reading we adopt.

The judgment of the United States Court of Appeals for the Fourth Circuit is *Affirmed.*

JUSTICE SCALIA, with whom JUSTICE THOMAS and JUSTICE ALITO join, dissenting.

The Court holds that when the Patient Protection and Affordable Care Act says "Exchange established by the State" it means "Exchange established by the State or the Federal Government." That is of course quite absurd, and the Court's 21 pages of explanation make it no less so.

I

The Patient Protection and Affordable Care Act makes major reforms to the American health-insurance market. It provides, among other things, that every State "shall . . . establish an American Health Benefit Exchange" — a marketplace where people can shop for health-insurance plans. 42 U.S.C. § 18031(b)(1). And it provides that if a State does not comply with this instruction, the Secretary of Health and Human Services must "establish and operate such Exchange within the State." § 18041(c)(1).

A separate part of the Act — housed in § 36B of the Internal Revenue Code — grants "premium tax credits" to subsidize certain purchases of health insurance made on Exchanges. The tax credit consists of "premium assistance amounts" for "coverage months." 26 U.S.C. § 36B(b)(1). An individual has a coverage month only when he is covered by an insurance plan "that was enrolled in through an Exchange established by the State under [§ 18031]." § 36B(c)(2)(A). And the law ties the size of the premium assistance amount to the premiums for health plans which cover the individual "and which were enrolled in through an Exchange established by the State under [§ 18031]." § 36B(b)(2)(A). The premium assistance amount further depends on the cost of certain other insurance plans "offered through the same Exchange." § 36B(b)(3)(B)(i).

This case requires us to decide whether someone who buys insurance on an Exchange established by the Secretary gets tax credits. You would think the answer would be obvious — so obvious there would hardly be a need for the Supreme Court to hear a case about it. In order to receive any money under § 36B, an individual must enroll in an insurance plan through an "Exchange established by the State." The Secretary of Health and Human Services is not a State. So an Exchange established by the Secretary is not an Exchange established by the State—which means people who buy health insurance through such an Exchange get no money under § 36B.

Words no longer have meaning if an Exchange that is not established by a State is "established by the State." It is hard to come up with a clearer way to limit tax credits to state Exchanges than to use the words "established by the State." And it is hard to come up with a reason to include the words "by the State" other than the purpose of limiting credits to state Exchanges. "[T]he plain, obvious, and rational meaning of a statute is always to be preferred to any curious, narrow, hidden sense that nothing but the exigency of a hard case and the ingenuity and study of an acute and powerful intellect would discover." *Lynch v. Alworth–Stephens Co.*, 267 U.S. 364, 370 (1925) (internal quotation marks omitted). Under all the usual rules of interpretation, in short, the Government should lose this case. But normal rules of interpretation seem always to yield to the overriding principle of the present Court: The Affordable Care Act must be saved. . . .

The Court's decision reflects the philosophy that judges should endure whatever interpretive distortions it takes in order to correct a supposed flaw in the statutory machinery. That philosophy ignores the American people's decision to give Congress "[a]ll legislative Powers" enumerated in the Constitution. Art. I, § 1. They made Congress, not this Court, responsible for both making laws and mending them. This Court holds only the judicial power— the power to pronounce the law as Congress has enacted it. We lack the prerogative to repair laws that do not work out in practice, just as the people lack the ability to throw us out of office if they dislike the solutions we concoct. We must always remember, therefore, that "[o]ur task is to apply the text, not to improve upon it." *Pavelic & LeFlore v. Marvel Entertainment Group, Div. of Cadence Industries Corp.*, 493 U.S. 120, 126 (1989). . . .

QUESTIONS

1. Despite the fact that the Court does not defer to the IRS's interpretation of the Affordable Care Act, the Court decides that the statute provides for the payment of subsidies to qualified taxpayers who obtain insurance through the Federal exchange, as well as through a State exchange. Why does the court decline to give *Chevron* deference to the agency interpretation, which was included in a rulemaking? Although the Court does not cite *Mead Corp.*, is the Court actually applying the *Mead Corp.* analysis? If this decision is an application of *Mead Corp.*, does the Court's analysis change our understanding of that analysis? If the decision in *King* is an application of *Mead Corp.*, what does the case indicate about when the *Mead Corp.* analysis is applied? Is this analysis conducted before the *Chevron* Step 1 analysis (i.e., at Step 0), or after the Court decides that the statute has no clear meaning (i.e., at Step 1.5)? Is the *Mead Corp.* analysis more appropriate at Step 0 or at Step 1.5?

2. Does the Court conclude that the statute has a clear meaning about the availability of subsidies for individuals purchasing insurance offered by the Federal exchange? What is the elephants in mouseholes canon and how does the Court use this canon to interpret the statute? Is the Court using the canon in *King* in the same way that Justice O'Connor used the

canon in *Brown & Williamson*? This canon implements the rule that the agency may interpret a statute in a way that permits an exercise of great administrative power only if the statute expressly grants such significant power to the agency. See *Brown & Williamson, supra* p. 15. An agency may *not* rely on a court's deference to the agency's interpretation of an ambiguous statute when the agency exercises great administrative power, because, as the canon colorfully provides, Congress does not hide policy elephants in the mouseholes of minor statutory provisions. The Court in *King* holds early in its decision that the delegation of great power to an agency must be clear before the agency will receive *Chevron* deference to its exercise of great power. (The Court later deploys the elephants in mouseholes canon when the Court itself interprets the Affordable Care Act.) Is there a practical difference between declining to defer to an agency's exercise of great administrative authority and concluding at Step 1 of *Chevron* that the statute does not permit the agency's exercise of great power because the statute did not clearly delegate such power?

3. In *City of Arlington v. F.C.C.*, 133 S. Ct. 1863 (2013), Justice Scalia, writing for the Court's majority, held that *Chevron* deference applies to an agency interpretation that it has regulatory jurisdiction to exercise regulatory authority. Chief Justice Roberts in his dissent in *City of Arlington* viewed the question presented by the case to be "whether the authority of administrative agencies should be augmented even further, to include not only broad power to give definitive answers to questions left to them by Congress, but also the same power to decide when Congress has given them that power." *Id.* at 1879. The Chief Justice declared that, "before a court may grant such [*Chevron*] deference, it must on its own decide whether Congress — the branch vested with law making authority under the Constitution — has in fact delegated to the agency law making power over the ambiguity at issue." *Id.* at 1880. Does Chief Justice Roberts, now writing for the majority in *King*, effectively win the debate about deference that he seemed to have lost in *City of Arlington*?

4. If a President were elected who opposed the Affordable Care Act, could the IRS, relying on *Brand X Internet Services, supra* p. 560, change its interpretation of the statute to prevent individuals from receiving subsidies if the individuals purchased health insurance in a state that had no State exchange and instead made use of the Federal exchange?

E. CAUSE OF ACTION, REVIEWABILITY, JURISDICTION, IMMUNITY

NOTE ON JUDICIAL REVIEW AS A CIVIL ACTION

It is helpful to remember that judicial review of agency action is in many respects a civil court action. We may compare it for the moment to a garden-variety tort action. In a tort action we are used to distinguishing among whether there is a cause of action (e.g., whether the elements of negligence are met), whether the court has jurisdiction (e.g., in federal court, whether there is diversity and the required amount in controversy), and whether the defendant has an immunity based on the defendant's status (e.g., spousal, charitable, or workers' compensation immunity). While these issues may interrelate (e.g., court jurisdiction may depend on the nature of the cause of action), it is often helpful to think of them as distinct issues. The same is true in administrative law.

"Cause of action" (reviewability)

The black letter for finding a "cause of action," at least in federal administrative law, is found in the federal APA §§ 703 and 704.

[5 U.S.C. § 703] "The form of proceeding for judicial review is the special statutory review proceeding relevant to the subject matter in a court specified by statute . . ." When an organic statute provides that an agency action is reviewable in court, then the "cause of action" is statutorily provided, and resort to common law writs is unnecessary.

[5 U.S.C. § 703 continued] "or, in the absence or inadequacy thereof, any applicable form of legal action, including actions for declaratory judgments or writs of prohibitory or mandatory injunction or habeas corpus, in a court of competent jurisdiction." Common law writs that may provide a cause of action to review administrative action include mandamus and habeas corpus. Of course the common law requirements of such writs must be met. Mandamus (familiar to you from your study of *Marbury v. Madison*, 5 U.S. 137 (1803)), for instance lies only to require ministerial, not discretionary, acts. E.g., *Decatur v. Spaulding*, 39 U.S. 497, 515 (1840); *see* Rogers, *A Fresh Look at Agency Discretion*, 57 Tulane L. Rev. 776, 780-87 (1983). And habeas lies only where the person bringing the action is in custody in some sense, as for instance in challenges to military reserve obligations. *See Strait v. Laird*, 406 U.S. 341 (1972). If no common law writ is applicable, an important alternative is a suit in equity, typically in the form of a suit for injunctive relief. Of course injunction suits must meet the requirements that equity jurisprudence imposes, e.g., "clean hands," no adequate remedy at law, etc.

[5 U.S.C. § 703 last sentence] "Except to the extent that prior, adequate, and exclusive opportunity for judicial review is prohibited by law, agency action is subject to judicial review in civil or criminal proceedings for judicial enforcement." An important additional way for regulated parties to get court review of agency action is to wait for the agency itself to go to court to enforce a statutory or regulatory provision. In defending the court action, the regulated party gets court review. A good example is the *Nova Scotia Food Products Corp.* case, *supra*, p. 203. Only when an organic statute gives "prior, adequate, and exclusive" opportunity for pre-enforcement review is the wait-for-enforcement option unavailable. See *Yakus v. United States*, 321 U.S. 414, 427-31 (1944) and Note on Statutory Time Limits, *infra*, p. 739.

[5 U.S.C. § 704] "Agency action made reviewable by statute and final agency action for which there is no adequate remedy in a court are subject to judicial review." Finally, if none of the above causes of action provides an "adequate remedy," the APA *itself* provides a cause of action, as long as the agency action is "final." The finality requirement is treated *infra* at pp. 729 *et seq.*

The foregoing suggests that a good lawyer can generally meet the requirement of asserting the elements of a "cause of action" to review agency action, at least where the action is "final." Another way of stating this is to say that agency action is presumed to be judicially reviewable.

[5 U.S.C. § 701] "This chapter applies . . . except to the extent that (1) statutes preclude judicial review; or (2) agency action is committed to agency discretion by law." What *may* keep agency action from being reviewable, however, is one of two important overarching exceptions to judicial review. These are reflected in the first sentence of *the APA chapter on judicial review.* Agency action is not reviewable when there is an applicable statutory preclusion of review, or when the agency action is "committed to agency discretion by law." When either of these is present, then the "causes of action" described above fall by the wayside. This chapter of this book, dealing with judicial review, starts out with cases on the scope of these two exceptions to the general judicial reviewability of agency actions (*Johnson v. Robison* and *Webster v. Doe*).

In contrast to the federal APA, the 1981 MSAPA "establishes the exclusive means of judicial review of agency action," § 5-101, while providing that "[i]f the relief available under . . . this Act is not equal or substantially equivalent to the relief otherwise available under law, the relief otherwise available and the related procedures supersede and supplement this Act to the extent necessary for their effectuation." § 5-101(3).

Court jurisdiction

The question of whether a court has subject-matter jurisdiction is distinct from the question of whether an agency action is reviewable. State statutory jurisdictional provisions control state court review of state agencies, of course, and in the absence thereof, state courts of general jurisdiction may hear cases seeking review of state agency action. The 1981 MSAPA establishes the jurisdiction of the reviewing court. § 5-104. Federal court subject matter jurisdiction in administrative law cases, on the other hand, is not provided by the APA. *Califano v. Sanders*, 430 U.S. 99 (1977). And the federal courts are not courts of general jurisdiction. But federal court jurisdiction is typically not a problem, since challenges to federal agency action inherently involve federal law, and federal question jurisdiction is generally available under 28 U.S.C. § 1331, if not under some more specific jurisdictional provision. If a specific court (e.g., a court of appeals) is designated in the organic statute, such a provision itself typically provides the jurisdiction, and generally such a jurisdictional provision is exclusive. That is, if an organic statute provides for judicial review of a particular action in the court of appeals, a district court lacks jurisdiction. E.g., *Whitney National Bank v. Bank of New Orleans & Trust Co.*, 379 U.S. 411, 419-23 (1965).

Sovereign immunity

Sovereign immunity is a doctrine analytically distinct from court jurisdiction, although sovereign immunity is often referred to as "jurisdictional." It is impossible to describe in a short note the vagaries of the immunities of the various states in their own courts. The law with respect to the immunity of the United States in federal courts is however nicely captured in APA § 702. The 1976 amendment to § 702 was intended to codify and simplify a complex body of sovereign immunity case law, which you are accordingly spared.

[5 U.S.C. § 702] "An action in a court of the United States seeking relief other than money damages and stating a claim that an agency or an officer or employee thereof acted or failed to act in an official capacity or under color of legal authority shall not be dismissed nor relief therein be denied on the ground that it is against the United States or that the United States is an indispensable party." This language constitutes a statutory waiver of sovereign immunity, thereby eliminating the defense altogether to the extent that the waiver applies. The important qualifier is contained in the words "other than money damages." If money damages are sought against the government, then the United States retains its sovereign immunity, subject to some other statutory waiver. (Two important examples of such waivers, albeit qualified and limited, permitting money damage suits against the United States are the Federal Tort Claims Act and the Tucker Act.) But where a litigant seeks injunctive or declaratory relief, or reversal of an agency determination, for instance, to discontinue benefits or deny a license, sovereign immunity should not be a problem.

[5 U.S.C. § 702 last sentence] "Nothing herein (1) affects other limitations on judicial review or the power or duty of the court to dismiss any action or deny relief on any other appropriate legal or equitable ground. . . ." The House and Senate committee reports explaining this provision list several doctrines that are not affected by this statutory waiver of immunity:

> These grounds [i.e., other grounds for dismissal that are preserved] include, but are not limited to, the following: (1) extraordinary relief should not be granted because of the hardship to the defendant or to the public ("balancing the equities") or because the plaintiff has an adequate remedy at law; (2) action committed to agency discretion; (3) express or implied preclusion of judicial review; (4) standing; (5) ripeness; (6) failure to exhaust administrative remedies; and (7) an exclusive alternative remedy.

H. R. Rep. No. 94-1656, 94th Cong., 2d Sess. 12 (1976), *reprinted in* 1976 U.S.C.C.A.N. 6121, 6132; S. Rep. No. 94-996, 94th Cong., 2d Sess. 11 (1976). Cases involving these alternative hurdles to judicial review take up much of this last chapter of this book.

[5 U.S.C. § 702 last sentence concluded] "Nothing herein . . . (2) confers authority to grant relief if any other statute that grants consent to suit expressly or impliedly forbids the relief which is sought." As an example, the Tucker Act waiver of immunity for contract suits against the government contains implicit limits on specific relief, and APA § 702 does not change that law. H. R. Rep. No. 94-1656, 94th Cong., 2d Sess. 13 (1976), *reprinted in* 1976 U.S.C.C.A.N. 6121, 6133; S. Rep. No. 94-996, 94th Cong., 2d Sess. 12 (1976).

NOTE ON MONEY DAMAGE SUITS

Most of the rest of the chapter that follows this note deals with cases seeking to reverse or modify agency action, not suits for money damages resulting from decisions that for practical purposes can no longer be changed. Suits for damages can only indirectly be called "judicial review of agency action," but of course the possibility of money damage suits can have a great effect on what agencies do.

A whole host of difficult issues are raised by suits for money damages. The topic sometimes falls between the cracks of a law school curriculum. The subject could reasonably be presented in a course in advanced torts, in a course on federal jurisdiction, in a more specialized course, or in an administrative law course. This book leaves extensive treatment for other courses. This note, however, is intended to alert the student to the types of issues raised, and to orient the student with regard to the differences between money damage suits and "judicial review" to change agency determinations. The cases that follow this note are almost entirely *not* money damage suits, but rather cases that fall in the latter category.

Any discussion of suits for money damages against the government or governmental officials first requires an understanding of the differences among suits against the government, suits against officials in their official capacity, and suits against officials in their individual capacity.

A suit against the government would be styled, for instance, *Doe v. United States* or *Doe v. Department of Commerce.* Generally speaking, such suits are not permitted unless the government has waived its *sovereign immunity* (as discussed in the previous note). When there is such a waiver, generally by statute, a money judgment runs against the treasury of the government. Federal examples are the Federal Tort Claims Act, which waives the immunity of the United States for tort suits, subject to significant qualifications and exceptions, and the Tucker Act, which permits contract suits against the United States. See F, below. Government attorneys (e.g., the U.S. Attorney's Office or the state attorney general's office) represent the defendant government in such suits.

Even when governments are immune from suits for damages, there is the possibility that the government may not be immune from a suit for prospective (e.g., injunctive) relief. Though such a suit might be styled as a suit against the government pursuant to a statutory waiver such as that contained in APA, 5 U.S.C. § 702, such suits generally are brought against particular officials in their *official capacity.* A suit for injunction is a garden-variety APA suit for judicial review of agency action. It is defended by government attorneys. A defendant in his or her official capacity is whoever holds the office. Thus, if an office changes hands during the pendency of the suit, the name of the defendant changes but the case moves on as before. In the *American Trucking* case in this book for instance (see p. 380), EPA Administrator Whitman's name was used by the Supreme Court in its style of the case even though she took office after oral argument. Any injunction that is issued in such a case continues to run against the holder of the office, whether or not that person was around when the judgment was entered.[1]

It makes little sense to speak of a suit for *damages* against an official in his or her *official* capacity. If a plaintiff wants money damages from the government treasury, the plaintiff will sue the government. In suits for money damages, unlike suits seeking only prospective injunctive relief, a plaintiff cannot circumvent the general Eleventh Amendment rule against imposing liability on states, state entities, or state officers by suing a state officer in his or her official capacity. *See Edelman v. Jordan,* 415 U.S. 651, 663-71 (1974) (11th Amendment immunity of states); 5 U.S.C. § 702 (federal government immunity).

---

1. In addition, injunction suits brought under 42 U.S.C. § 1983 against state officials in federal court may be (and often are) brought against those officials in their official capacity even though the so-called stripping doctrine is used to get around 11th Amendment immunity of states in federal court. That is, even though the officer is stripped of his or her status as a state officer by his or her allegedly unconstitutional action for 11th Amendment purposes (*see Ex parte Young,* 209 U.S. 123 (1908)), the injunction if entered would run against whoever holds the office, not the particular individual who held the office at the time of suit.

In contrast, a suit against a government official in his or her *individual capacity* seeks the private assets of the individual office holder. This is in many respects a legally different person from the official capacity defendant. Service on one is not necessarily service on the other. The individual capacity defendant engages his or her own private counsel, although the government agency may provide representation by a government attorney. Most importantly, at least in concept, the individual capacity defendant must pay any judgment out of his or her own pocketbook. When the official leaves office, the suit against an individual capacity defendant continues against the same named individual.

The remainder of this note deals with suits for *money damages only*, against governments and against individual capacity government defendants.

A. STATE COURT; STATE GOVERNMENT DEFENDANT

Suits against state governments in state courts are typically subject to common law *sovereign immunity*, unless abolished by the state courts or waived by the state legislature. Such suits require careful examination of state laws waiving the immunity of the state, which of course vary from state to state.

B. STATE COURT; INDIVIDUAL CAPACITY DEFENDANT

Suits against individual capacity state government defendants in state court based on state law are subject to the state law of *official immunity*. The law of particular states in this regard is beyond the scope of this brief note. (For violations of federal law, 42 U.S.C. § 1983 may be invoked in state court. See *Howlett v. Rose*, 496 U.S. 356 (1990), and E below.)

C. FEDERAL COURT; STATE GOVERNMENT DEFENDANT

Suits for damages against a state in federal court are barred by the *sovereign immunity* preserved by the Eleventh Amendment (actually an Eleventh Amendment gloss on Article III). *Hans v. Louisiana*, 134 U.S. 1 (1890); *Edelman v. Jordan*, 415 U.S. 651 (1974). The only recognized exception is where Congress has explicitly provided for money judgments against states *and* in doing so Congress has relied on its power to enforce the 14th Amendment. *Fitzpatrick v. Bitzer*, 427 U.S. 445 (1976); *Seminole Tribe v. Florida*, 517 U.S. 44 (1996).

D. FEDERAL COURT; INDIVIDUAL CAPACITY STATE OFFICER DEFENDANT; STATE TORT LAW

If a state officer is sued in his or her individual capacity in federal court for a state common law tort, jurisdiction would have to be based on diversity (28 U.S.C. § 1332) and the state law of official immunity referred to in B would apply under *Erie R.R. v. Tompkins*, 304 U.S. 64 (1938).

E. FEDERAL COURT; INDIVIDUAL CAPACITY STATE OFFICER DEFENDANT; FEDERAL LAW VIOLATION

If the individual capacity state officer is sued for violation of federal constitutional or statutory law, a federal cause of action is provided by 42 U.S.C. § 1983. *Monroe v. Pape*, 365 U.S. 167 (1961); *Maine v. Thiboutot*, 448 U.S. 1 (1980). Subject matter jurisdiction is provided by 28 U.S.C. § 1331 or § 1343.

The big issue here is *official immunity*. The theory of official immunity is that without it administrators will not act vigorously in the public interest, for fear of lawsuits. *Gregoire v. Biddle*, 177 F.2d 579 (2d Cir. 1949) (Hand, J.). The law of official immunity is for practical purposes the same for both § 1983 suits against state officers and for so-called *Bivens* suits against individual capacity federal officers, described in H below. *Butz v. Economou*, 438 U.S. 478, 500-501 (1978). Judges and prosecutors are *absolutely immune* from suit, as long as they are not acting wholly outside of their judicial or prosecutorial functions. *Pierson v. Ray*, 386 U.S. 547, 553-55 (1967) (judges); *Imbler v. Pachtman*, 424 U.S. 409 (1976) (prosecutors). In part, the theory is that court proceedings and appeals adequately correct for illegal actions by such officers. This absolute immunity has been extended to administrative agency officers who act in judicial or prosecutorial capacities (e.g., administrative law judges). *Economou, supra*, 438 U.S. at 508-17. Most other state or federal officials have only *qualified* immunity. *Scheuer v. Rhodes*, 416 U.S. 232 (1974). That is, they are immune from suit if they have a good faith, reasonable belief that their actions are legal. The standard sounds subjective, but has become significantly objectified, so that the immunity can be determined on summary judgment rather than only after trial. *Harlow v. Fitzgerald*, 457 U.S. 800, 815-19 (1982). Summary judgment for the defendant is warranted if the defendant did not violate "clearly established" statutory or constitutional rights of which a reasonable person would have known. *Id.* at 817-18; *Davis v. Scherer*, 468 U.S. 183 (1984).

F. FEDERAL COURT; FEDERAL GOVERNMENT DEFENDANT

Like the states under the Eleventh Amendment, the United States government enjoys *sovereign immunity*. Federal courts generally cannot award money damages from the U.S. Treasury unless Congress has waived the immunity of the United States. The two most important statutory waivers of sovereign immunity are the Tucker Act, 28 U.S.C. § 1491, and the Federal Tort Claims Act, 28 U.S.C. §§ 2671-2680; *id.* § 1346(b). The Tucker Act waives immunity for contract claims, but when such claims are for more than $10,000, they must be brought in a special set of federal courts (the Court of Federal Claims, an Article I court, appealable to the U.S. Court of Appeals for the Federal Circuit, an Article III court). The Federal Tort Claims Act waives federal sovereign immunity for tort suits, subject to important conditions and significant exceptions. Prior presentation of an administrative claim is required (28 U.S.C. § 2675), jury trials are not permitted (28 U.S.C. § 2402), punitive damages are not permitted (28 U.S.C. § 2674), and the waiver of immunity does not extend to strict liability claims (*Laird v. Nelms*, 406 U.S. 797 (1972)) or to many intentional torts (28 U.S.C. § 2680(h)).

One important exception to the waiver of immunity is for exercises of discretionary functions. 28 U.S.C. § 2680(a). That is, immunity is preserved for exercises of discretionary functions. Just what amounts to an exercise of a discretionary function can present a difficult issue. *Compare United States v. VARIG Airlines*, 467 U.S. 797 (1984), and *United States v. Gaubert*, 499 U.S. 315 (1991), with *Berkovitz v. United States*, 486 U.S. 531 (1988). The language of the discretionary function exception suggests that it serves the purpose of channeling garden-variety judicial review of agency action out of the tort context. *See* Rogers, *supra*, 57 Tulane L. Rev. at 813-22. Thus, the paradigm situation for application of the discretionary function exception would be a negligence suit based on the negligent failure of an agency to find certain facts. If the agency acted without substantial evidence, or abused its discretion, judicial review is appropriate under the APA, but not via a tort suit under the Federal Tort Claims Act.

G. FEDERAL COURT; INDIVIDUAL CAPACITY FEDERAL OFFICER DEFENDANT; COMMON LAW TORTS

In the case of suits against individual capacity federal officials for common law torts, such as defamation, the courts originally provided absolute official immunity for discretionary actions, even if malicious, within the outer perimeter of the officer's official duties. *Barr v. Matteo*, 360 U.S. 564 (1969). When the Supreme Court put some limits on this immunity in *Westfall v. Erwin*, 484 U.S. 292 (1988), Congress responded with the so-called Westfall Act, 28 U.S.C. § 2679(b)-(d). Under the Westfall Act, if the Attorney General determines that the official was acting within the scope of his office or employment, the individual capacity defendant is dismissed from suit and a Federal Tort Claims Act suit is substituted, subject to the conditions and exceptions applicable under the Federal Tort Claims Act. 28 U.S.C. § 2679(d).

H. FEDERAL COURT; INDIVIDUAL CAPACITY FEDERAL OFFICER DEFENDANT; FEDERAL LAW VIOLATION

The Supreme Court has found implied causes of action against individual-capacity federal officials for constitutional violations — *Bivens v. Six Unknown Fed. Narcotics Agents*, 403 U.S. 388 (1971) (4th Amendment), *Davis v. Passman*, 442 U.S. 228 (1979) (5th Amendment due process), and *Carlson v. Green*, 446 U.S. 14 (1980) (8th Amendment) — but not where the type of case involves "special factors counselling hesitation" — *Bush v. Lucas*, 462 U.S. 367 (1983) (civil servant suing supervisor), and *Chappell v. Wallace*, 462 U.S. 296 (1983) (naval personnel suing superior officers). The Westfall Act does not apply to such constitutional claims. 28 U.S.C. § 2679(b)(2). When there is a cause of action, the key issue again is *official immunity*, and the law in that regard is described in E, above. The President is absolutely immune for official actions while President, *Nixon v. Fitzgerald*, 457 U.S. 731 (1982), but not for unofficial conduct before he was President, *Clinton v. Jones*, 520 U.S. 681 (1997).

I. MUNICIPAL GOVERNMENT LIABILITY

Municipalities do not enjoy 11th Amendment immunity and under state law may not enjoy governmental immunity. Municipalities are subject to § 1983 suits for damages, but they are not subject to a regime of respondeat superior. Instead, they must pay damages for their employee's violations of federal law only if the illegal action was taken pursuant to official municipal policy. *Monell v. Dept. of Social Services*, 436 U.S. 658 (1978). Drawing this distinction has generated significant litigation. *See, e.g., Canton v. Harris*, 489 U.S. 378, 388-92 (1989) (claim based on city's inadequate training of police must show that failure to train "reflects deliberate indifference to the constitutional rights of [city's] inhabitants"); *Pembaur v. Cincinnati*, 475 U.S. 469 (1986) (a single action can be governmental policy if by an official responsible for establishing final policy).

JOHNSON v. ROBISON
415 U.S. 361 (1974)

MR. JUSTICE BRENNAN delivered the opinion of the Court.

A draftee accorded Class I-O conscientious objector status and completing performance of required alternative civilian service does not qualify under 38

U.S.C. § 1652(a)(1) as a "veteran who . . . served on active duty" (defined in 38 U.S.C. § 101 (21) as "full-time duty in the Armed Forces"), and is therefore not an "eligible veteran" entitled under 38 U.S.C. § 1661(a) to veterans' educational benefits provided by the Veterans' Readjustment Benefits Act of 1966. Appellants, the Veterans' Administration and the Administrator of Veterans' Affairs, for that reason, denied the application for educational assistance of appellee Robison, a conscientious objector who filed his application after he satisfactorily completed two years of alternative civilian service at the Peter Bent Brigham Hospital, Boston. Robison thereafter commenced this class action in the United States District Court for the District of Massachusetts, seeking a declaratory judgment that 38 U.S.C. §§ 101 (21), 1652(a)(1), and 1661(a), read together, violated the First Amendment's guarantee of religious freedom and the Fifth Amendment's guarantee of equal protection of the laws. Appellants moved to dismiss the action on the ground, among others, that the District Court lacked jurisdiction because of 38 U.S.C. § 211(a) which prohibits judicial review of decisions of the Administrator.[5] The District Court denied the motion, and, on the merits, rejected appellee's First Amendment claim, but sustained the equal protection claim and entered a judgment declaring "that 38 U.S.C. §§ 1652(a)(1) and 1661(a) defining 'eligible veteran' and providing for entitlement to educational assistance are unconstitutional and that 38 U.S.C. § 101 (21) defining 'active duty' is unconstitutional with respect to chapter 34 of Title 38, United States Code, 38 U.S.C. §§ 1651-1697, conferring Veterans' Educational Assistance, for the reason that said sections deny plaintiff and members of his class due process of law in violation of the Fifth Amendment to the Constitution of the United States. . . ." We postponed consideration of the question of jurisdiction in light of § 211(a) to the hearing on the merits. . . . We hold, in agreement with the District Court, that § 211(a) is inapplicable to this action and therefore that appellants' motion to dismiss for lack of jurisdiction of the subject matter was properly denied. On the merits, we agree that appellee's First Amendment claim is without merit but disagree that §§ 1652(a)(1), 1661 (a), and 101 (21) violate the Fifth Amendment and therefore reverse the judgment of the District Court.

I

We consider first appellants' contention that § 211(a) bars federal courts from deciding the constitutionality of veterans' benefits legislation. Such a construction would, of course, raise serious questions concerning the constitutionality of § 211(a), and in such case "it is a cardinal principle that this Court will first ascertain whether a construction of the statute is fairly possible by which the [constitutional] question[s] may be avoided." *United States v. Thirty-seven Photographs*, 402 U.S. 363, 369 (1971).

---

5. Title 38 U.S.C. § 211 (a) provides:

"(a) On and after October 17, 1940, except as provided in sections 775, 784, and as to matters arising under chapter 37 of this title, the decisions of the Administrator on any question of law or fact under any law administered by the Veterans' Administration providing benefits for veterans and their dependents or survivors shall be final and conclusive and no other official or any court of the United States shall have power or jurisdiction to review any such decision by an action in the nature of mandamus or otherwise."

Plainly, no explicit provision of § 211 (a) bars judicial consideration of appellee's constitutional claims. That section provides that "the *decisions* of the Administrator on any question of law or fact *under* any law administered by the Veterans' Administration providing benefits for veterans . . . shall be final and conclusive and no . . . court of the United States shall have power or jurisdiction to review any such decision. . . ." (Emphasis added.) The prohibitions would appear to be aimed at review only of those decisions of law or fact that arise in the *administration* by the Veterans' Administration of a *statute* providing benefits for veterans. A decision of law or fact "under" a statute is made by the Administrator in the interpretation or application of a particular provision of the statute to a particular set of facts. Appellee's constitutional challenge is not to any such decision of the *Administrator*, but rather to a decision of *Congress* to create a statutory class entitled to benefits that does not include I-O conscientious objectors who performed alternative civilian service. Thus, as the District Court stated: "The questions of law presented in these proceedings arise under the Constitution, not under the statute whose validity is challenged." This construction is also supported by the administrative practice of the Veterans' Administration. "When faced with a problem of statutory construction, this Court shows great deference to the interpretation given the statute by the officers or agency charged with its administration." *Udall v. Tallman*, 380 U.S. 1, 16 (1965). The Board of Veterans' Appeals expressly disclaimed authority to decide constitutional questions in *Appeal of Sly*, C-27 593 725 (May 10, 1972). There the Board, denying a claim for educational assistance by a I-O conscientious objector, held that "this decision does not reach the issue of the constitutionality of the pertinent laws as this matter is not within the jurisdiction of this Board." *Sly* thus accepts and follows the principle that "adjudication of the constitutionality of congressional enactments has generally been thought beyond the jurisdiction of administrative agencies. *See Public Utilities Comm'n v. United States*, 355 U.S. 534, 539 (1958); *Engineers Public Service Co. v. SEC*, 138 F.2d 936, 952-953 (D.C. Cir. 1943), dismissed as moot, 332 U.S. 788." *Oestereich v. Selective Service Board*, 393 U.S. 233, 242 (1968) (Harlan, J., concurring in result); *see* Jaffe, Judicial Review: Question of Law, 69 Harv. L. Rev. 239, 271-275 (1955). Nor does the legislative history accompanying the 1970 amendment of § 211 (a) demonstrate a congressional intention to bar judicial review even of constitutional questions. No-review clauses similar to § 211 (a) have been a part of veterans' benefits legislation since 1933. While the legislative history accompanying these precursor no-review clauses is almost nonexistent, the Administrator, in a letter written in 1952 in connection with a revision of the clause under consideration by the Subcommittee of the House Committee on Veterans' Affairs, comprehensively explained the policies necessitating the no-review clause and identified two primary purposes: (1) to insure that veterans' benefits claims will not burden the courts and the Veterans' Administration with expensive and time-consuming litigation, and (2) to insure that the technical and complex determinations and applications of Veterans' Administration policy connected with veterans' benefits decisions will be adequately and uniformly made.

The legislative history of the 1970 amendment indicates nothing more than a congressional intent to preserve these two primary purposes. Before amendment, the no-review clause made final "the decisions of the Administrator on any question of law or fact *concerning a claim for benefits or payments* under [certain] law[s] administered by the Veterans' Administration" (emphasis added), 38 U.S.C. § 211(a) (1964 ed.), 71 Stat. 92. In a series of decisions, e.g., *Wellman v. Whittier*, 259 F.2d 163 (D.C. Cir. 1958); *Thompson v. Gleason*, 317 F.2d 901 (D.C. Cir. 1962); and *Tracy v. Gleason*, 379 F.2d 469 (D.C. Cir. 1967), the Court of Appeals for the District of Columbia Circuit interpreted the term "claim" as a limitation upon the reach of § 211(a), and as a consequence held that the judicial review of actions by the Administrator *subsequent* to an original grant of benefits was not barred.

Congress perceived this judicial interpretation as a threat to the dual purposes of the no-review clause. First, the interpretation would lead to an inevitable increase in litigation with consequent burdens upon the courts and the Veterans' Administration. In its House Report, the Committee on Veterans' Affairs stated that "since the decision in the *Tracy* case — and as the result of that decision and the *Wellman* and *Thompson* decisions — suits in constantly increasing numbers have been filed in the U.S. District Court for the District of Columbia by plaintiffs seeking a resumption of terminated benefits." H. R. Rep. No. 91-1166, p. 10 (1970). This same concern over the rising number of court cases was expressed by the Administrator in a letter to the Committee:

> "The *Wellman*, *Thompson*, and *Tracy* decisions have not been followed in any of the other 10 Federal judicial circuits throughout the country. Nevertheless, soon after the *Tracy* decision, suits in the nature of mandamus or for declaratory judgment commenced to be filed in the U.S. District Court for the District of Columbia in constantly increasing numbers by plaintiffs seeking resumption of terminated benefits. As of March 8, 1970, 353 suits of this type had been filed in the District of Columbia circuit. . . .
>
> "The scope of the *Tracy* decision and the decisions upon which it is based is so broad that it could well afford a basis for judicial review of millions of decisions terminating or reducing many types of benefits provided under laws administered by the Veterans' Administration. Such review might even extend to the decisions of predecessor agencies made many years ago." *Id.*, at 21, 24.

Second, Congress was concerned that the judicial interpretation of § 211(a) would involve the courts in day-to-day determination and interpretation of Veterans' Administration policy. The House Report states that the cases already filed in the courts in response to *Wellman*, *Thompson*, and *Tracy*

> "involve a large variety of matters — a 1930's termination of a widow's pension payments under a statute then extant, because of her open and notorious adulterous cohabitation; invalid marriage to a veteran; severance of a veteran's service connection for disability compensation; reduction of such compensation because of lessened disability . . . [and] suits . . . brought by [Filipino] widows of World War II servicemen seeking restoration of death compensation or pension benefits terminated after the Administrator raised a presumption of their remarriage on the basis of evidence gathered through field examination. Notwithstanding the 1962 endorsement by the Congress of the Veterans' Administrations [*sic*] administrative presumption of remarriage rule, most of [the suits brought by Filipino widows] have resulted in judgments adverse to the Government." *Id.*, at 10.

The Administrator voiced similar concerns, stating that "it seems obvious that suits similar to the several hundred already filed can — and undoubtedly will — subject nearly every aspect of our benefit determinations to judicial review, including rating decisions, related Veterans' Administration regulations,

Administrator's decisions, and various adjudication procedures." Letter to the Committee on Veterans' Affairs 23-24. Thus, the 1970 amendment was enacted to overrule the interpretation of the Court of Appeals for the District of Columbia Circuit, and thereby restore vitality to the two primary purposes to be served by the no-review clause. Nothing whatever in the legislative history of the 1970 amendment, or predecessor no-review clauses, suggests any congressional intent to preclude judicial cognizance of constitutional challenges to veterans' benefits legislation. Such challenges obviously do not contravene the purposes of the no-review clause, for they cannot be expected to burden the courts by their volume, nor do they involve technical considerations of Veterans' Administration policy. We therefore conclude, in agreement with the District Court, that a construction of § 211(a) that does not extend the prohibitions of that section to actions challenging the constitutionality of laws providing benefits for veterans is not only "fairly possible" but is the most reasonable construction, for neither the text nor the scant legislative history of § 211(a) provides the "clear and convincing" evidence of congressional intent required by this Court before a statute will be construed to restrict access to judicial review. *See Abbott Laboratories v. Gardner,* 387 U.S. 136, 141 (1967).

II

[The Court proceeded to reject Robison's claims on the merits. Justice Douglas dissented.]

QUESTIONS

1. Compare the statutory language with the Court's interpretation of it. Is this interpretation a stretch? a long one? If so, what is driving such a stretch? Could Congress constitutionally prohibit the court review sought in this case?
2. In the absence of a constitutional issue on the merits, is there any constitutional difficulty with precluding judicial review of veterans' benefit determinations, when the determination is essentially a factual one? A legal one?
3. In *Cuozzo Speed Technologies, LLC v. Lee,* 136 S. Ct. 2131, 2142 (2016), the Supreme Court held that review of portions of the plaintiff's claims was precluded by statute, notwithstanding "the 'strong presumption' in favor of judicial review." *Id.* at 2140. The Court limited its holding, stating that "we need not, and do not, decide the precise effect of § 314(d) on appeals that implicate constitutional questions." 136 S. Ct. at 2141.

BOWEN v. MICHIGAN ACADEMY OF FAMILY PHYSICIANS
476 U.S. 667 (1986)

JUSTICE STEVENS delivered the opinion of the Court.

The question presented in this case is whether Congress, in either § 1395ff or § 1395ii of Title 42 of the United States Code, barred judicial review of regulations promulgated under Part B of the Medicare program.

Respondents, who include an association of family physicians and several individual doctors, filed suit to challenge the validity of 42 CFR § 405.504(b) (1985), which authorizes the payment of benefits in different amounts for similar physicians' services. The District Court held that the regulation contravened several provisions of the statute governing the Medicare program:

> "There is no basis to justify the segregation of allopathic family physicians from all other types of physicians. Such segregation is not rationally related to any legitimate purpose of the Medicare statute. To lump MDs who are family physicians, but who have chosen not to become board certified family physicians for whatever motive, with chiropractors, dentists, and podiatrists for the purpose of determining Medicare reimbursement defies all reason."

Because it ruled in favor of respondents on statutory grounds, the District Court did not reach their constitutional claims. The Court of Appeals agreed with the District Court that the Secretary's regulation was "obvious[ly] inconsist[ent] with the plain language of the Medicare statute" and held that "this regulation is irrational and is invalid." Like the District Court, it too declined to reach respondents' constitutional claims.

The Secretary of Health and Human Services has not sought review of the decision on the merits invalidating the regulation. Instead, he renews the contention, rejected by both the District Court and the Court of Appeals, that Congress has forbidden judicial review of all questions affecting the amount of benefits payable under Part B of the Medicare program. Because the question is important and has divided the Courts of Appeals, we granted the petition for a writ of certiorari. We now affirm.

I

We begin with the strong presumption that Congress intends judicial review of administrative action. From the beginning "our cases [have established] that judicial review of a final agency action by an aggrieved person will not be cut off unless there is persuasive reason to believe that such was the purpose of Congress." *Abbott Laboratories v. Gardner*, 387 U.S. 136, 140 (1967) (citing cases). *See generally* L. Jaffe, Judicial Control of Administrative Action 339-353 (1965). In *Marbury v. Madison*, 1 Cranch 137, 163 (1803), a case itself involving review of executive action, Chief Justice Marshall insisted that "[the] very essence of civil liberty certainly consists in the right of every individual to claim the protection of the laws." Later, in the lesser known but nonetheless important case of *United States v. Nourse*, 9 Pet. 8, 28-29 (1835), the Chief Justice noted the traditional observance of this right and laid the foundation for the modern presumption of judicial review:

> "It would excite some surprise if, in a government of laws and of principle, furnished with a department whose appropriate duty it is to decide questions of right, not only between individuals, but between the government and individuals; a ministerial officer might, at his discretion, issue this powerful process . . . leaving to the debtor no remedy, no appeal to the laws of his country, if he should believe the claim to be unjust. But this anomaly does not exist; this imputation cannot be cast on the legislature of the United States."

Committees of both Houses of Congress have endorsed this view. In undertaking the comprehensive rethinking of the place of administrative agencies in a regime of separate and divided powers that culminated in the passage of the Administrative Procedure Act (APA), 5 U.S.C. §§ 551-559, 701-706, the Senate Committee on the Judiciary remarked:

> "Very rarely do statutes withhold judicial review. It has never been the policy of Congress to prevent the administration of its own statutes from being judicially confined to the scope of authority granted or to the objectives specified. Its policy could not be otherwise, for in such a case statutes would in effect be blank checks drawn to the credit of some administrative officer or board." S. Rep. No. 752, 79th Cong., 1st Sess., 26 (1945).

The Committee on the Judiciary of the House of Representatives agreed that Congress ordinarily intends that there be judicial review, and emphasized the clarity with which a contrary intent must be expressed:

> "The statutes of Congress are not merely advisory when they relate to administrative agencies, any more than in other cases. To preclude judicial review under this bill a statute, if not specific in withholding such review, must upon its face give clear and convincing evidence of an intent to withhold it. The mere failure to provide specially by statute for judicial review is certainly no evidence of intent to withhold review." *Ibid.*

Taking up the language in the House Committee Report, Justice Harlan reaffirmed the Court's holding in *Rusk v. Cort*, 369 U.S. 367, 379-380 (1962), that "only upon a showing of 'clear and convincing evidence' of a contrary legislative intent should the courts restrict access to judicial review." *Abbott Laboratories v. Gardner*, 387 U.S., at 141 (citations omitted). This standard has been invoked time and again when considering whether the Secretary has discharged "the heavy burden of overcoming the strong presumption that Congress did not mean to prohibit all judicial review of his decision," *Dunlop v. Bachowski*, 421 U.S. 560, 567 (1975).

Subject to constitutional constraints, Congress can, of course, make exceptions to the historic practice whereby courts review agency action. The presumption of judicial review is, after all, a presumption, and "like all presumptions used in interpreting statutes, may be overcome by," *inter alia*, "specific language or specific legislative history that is a reliable indicator of congressional intent," or a specific congressional intent to preclude judicial review that is "'fairly discernible' in the detail of the legislative scheme." *Block v. Community Nutrition Institute*, 467 U.S. 340, 349, 351 (1984).[4]

In this case, the Government asserts that two statutory provisions remove the Secretary's regulation from review under the grant of general federal-question jurisdiction found in 28 U.S.C. § 1331. First, the Government contends that 42

---

4. "The congressional intent necessary to overcome the presumption may also be inferred from contemporaneous judicial construction barring review and the congressional acquiescence in it, *see*, e.g., *Ludecke v. Watkins*, 335 U.S. 160 (1948), or from the collective import of legislative and judicial history behind a particular statute, *see*, e.g., *Heikkila v. Barber*, 345 U.S. 229 (1953). More important for purposes of this case, the presumption favoring judicial review of administrative action may be overcome by inferences of intent drawn from the statutory scheme as a whole. *See*, e.g., *Morris v. Gressette*, 432 U.S. 491 (1977); *Switchmen v. National Mediation Board*, 320 U.S. 297 (1943)." *Block v. Community Nutrition Institute*, 467 U.S., at 349.

U.S.C. § 1395ff(b) (1982 ed., Supp. II), which authorizes "Appeal by individuals," impliedly forecloses administrative or judicial review of any action taken under Part B of the Medicare program by failing to authorize such review while simultaneously authorizing administrative and judicial review of "any determination . . . as to . . . the amount of benefits under part A," § 1395ff(b)(1)(C). Second, the Government asserts that 42 U.S.C. § 1395ii (1982 ed., Supp. II), which makes applicable 42 U.S.C. § 405(h) (1982 ed., Supp. II), of the Social Security Act to the Medicare program, expressly precludes all administrative or judicial review not otherwise provided in that statute. We find neither argument persuasive.

II

Section 1395ff on its face is an explicit authorization of judicial review, not a bar.[5] As a general matter, "[t]he mere fact that some acts are made reviewable should not suffice to support an implication of exclusion as to others. The right to review is too important to be excluded on such slender and indeterminate evidence of legislative intent." *Abbott Laboratories v. Gardner*, 387 U.S., at 141 (quoting L. Jaffe, Judicial Control of Administrative Action 357 (1965)).

In the Medicare program, however, the situation is somewhat more complex. Under Part B of that program, which is at issue here, the Secretary contracts with private health insurance carriers to provide benefits for which individuals voluntarily remit premiums. This optional coverage, which is federally subsidized, supplements the mandatory institutional health benefits (such as coverage for hospital expenses) provided by Part A. Subject to an amount-in-controversy requirement, individuals aggrieved by delayed or insufficient payment with respect to benefits payable under Part B are afforded an "opportunity for a fair hearing by the *carrier*," 42 U.S.C. § 1395u(b)(3)(C) (emphasis added); in comparison, and subject to a like amount-in-controversy requirement, a similarly aggrieved individual under Part A is entitled "to a hearing thereon by the *Secretary* . . . and to judicial review," 42 U.S.C. §§ 1395ff(b)(1)(C), (b)(2) (1982 ed. and Supp. II). "In the context of the statute's precisely drawn provisions," we

---

5. The pertinent text of § 1395ff reads as follows:

"a. Entitlement to and amount of benefits
"The determination of whether an individual is entitled to benefits under part A or part B, and the determination of the amount of benefits under part A, shall be made by the Secretary in accordance with regulations prescribed by him.
"b. Appeal by individuals
    "(1) Any individual dissatisfied with any determination under subsection (a) of this section as to —
    "(A) whether he meets the conditions of section 426 or section 426a of this title [which set forth eligibility requirements to be satisfied before an individual is permitted to participate in Part A of the Medicare program], or
    "(B) whether he is eligible to enroll and has enrolled pursuant to the provisions of part B of [the Medicare program] . . . , or,
    "(C) the amount of the benefits under part A (including a determination where such amount is determined to be zero)

"shall be entitled to a hearing thereon by the Secretary to the same extent as is provided in section 405(b) of this title and to judicial review of the Secretary's final decision after such hearing as is provided in section 405(g) of this title."

held in *United States v. Erika, Inc.*, 456 U.S. 201, 208 (1982), that the failure "to authorize further review for determinations of the amount of Part B awards . . . provides persuasive evidence that Congress deliberately intended to foreclose further review of such claims." Not limiting our consideration to the statutory text, we investigated the legislative history which "confirm[ed] this view," *ibid.*, and disclosed a purpose to "'avoid overloading the courts'" with "'trivial matters,'" a consequence which would "'unduly ta[x]'" the federal court system with "'little real value'" to be derived by participants in the program, *id.*, at 210, n.13 (quoting 118 Cong. Rec. 33992 (1972) (remarks of Sen. Bennett)).

Respondents' federal-court challenge to the validity of the Secretary's regulation is not foreclosed by §1395ff as we construed that provision in *Erika.* The reticulated statutory scheme, which carefully details the forum and limits of review of "any determination . . . of . . . the amount of benefits under part A," 42 U.S.C. §1395ff(b)(1)(C) (1982 ed., Supp. II), and of the "amount of . . . payment" of benefits under Part B, 42 U.S.C. §1395u(b)(3)(C), simply does not speak to challenges mounted against the *method* by which such amounts are to be determined rather than the *determinations* themselves. As the Secretary has made clear, "the legality, constitutional or otherwise, of any provision of the act or regulations relevant to the Medicare Program" is not considered in a "fair hearing" held by a carrier to resolve a grievance related to a determination of the amount of a Part B award. As a result, an attack on the validity of a regulation is not the kind of administrative action that we described in *Erika* as an "amount determination" which decides "the amount of the Medicare payment to be made on a particular claim" and with respect to which the act impliedly denies judicial review. 456 U.S., at 208.

That Congress did not preclude review of the method by which Part B awards are computed (as opposed to the computation) is borne out by the very legislative history we found persuasive in *Erika.* The Senate Committee Report on the original 1965 legislation reveals an intention to preclude "judicial review of a determination concerning the *amount of benefits* under part B where claims will probably be for substantially smaller amounts than under part A." S. Rep. No. 404, 89th Cong., 1st Sess., 54-55 (1965) (emphasis added). The Report makes plain that "carriers, not the Secretary, would review beneficiary complaints regarding the *amount of benefits.*" *Ibid.* (emphasis added). *Accord*, H. R. Rep. No. 213, 89th Cong., 1st Sess., 47 (1965) ("Under the supplementary plan [Part B], carriers, not the Secretary, would review beneficiary complaints regarding the *amount of benefits*" (emphasis added)). The legislative history of the pertinent 1972 amendment likewise reveals that judicial review was precluded only as to controversies regarding determinations of amounts of benefits. The Conference Report on the 1972 amendment explains that "there is no authorization for an appeal to the Secretary or for judicial review on matters *solely involving amounts of benefits under Part B.*" H. R. Conf. Rep. No. 92-1605, p. 61 (1972) (emphasis added). Senator Bennett's introductory explanation to the amendment confirms that preclusion of judicial review of Part B awards — designed "to avoid overloading the courts with quite minor matters" — embraced only "decisions on a claim for payment for a given service." 118 Cong. Rec. 33992 (1972). The Senator feared that "[i]f judicial review is made available where any claim is denied, as some court decisions have held, the resources of the Federal court system would be unduly taxed and little real value would be derived by the enrollees. The proposed amendment would merely clarify the original intent of the law and prevent the overloading of the courts with trivial matters because the intent is considered unclear." *Ibid.* As we found in *Erika,* 456 U.S., at 206, Congress has precluded judicial review only "of adverse hearing officer determinations of the amount of Part B payments."

Careful analysis of the governing statutory provisions and their legislative history thus reveals that Congress intended to bar judicial review only of determinations of the amount of benefits to be awarded under Part B. Congress delegated this task to carriers who would finally determine such matters in conformity with the regulations and instructions of the Secretary. We conclude, therefore, that those matters which Congress did *not* leave to be determined in a "fair hearing" conducted by the carrier — including challenges to the validity of the Secretary's instructions and regulations — are not impliedly insulated from judicial review by 42 U.S.C. § 1395ff (1982 ed. and Supp. II).

[In part III the Court also rejected the government's argument against judicial review based on the Medicare Act's incorporation of a review-precluding provision of Title II of the Social Security Act. The Court stated, *inter alia,* that "We ordinarily presume that Congress intends the executive to obey its statutory commands and, accordingly, that it expects the courts to grant relief when an executive agency violates such a command. That presumption has not been surmounted here."]

The judgment of the Court of Appeals is *Affirmed.*

QUESTIONS

1. Is *Erika* overruled by *Bowen?*
2. How is this case different from *Erika?*

WEBSTER v. DOE
486 U.S. 592 (1988)

CHIEF JUSTICE REHNQUIST delivered the opinion of the Court.

Section 102(c) of the National Security Act of 1947, 61 Stat. 498, as amended, provides that:

> "[T]he Director of Central Intelligence may, in his discretion, terminate the employment of any officer or employee of the Agency whenever he shall deem such termination necessary or advisable in the interests of the United States. . . ." 50 U.S.C. § 403(c).

In this case we decide whether, and to what extent, the termination decisions of the Director under § 102(c) are judicially reviewable.

I

Respondent John Doe was first employed by the Central Intelligence Agency (CIA or Agency) in 1973 as a clerk-typist. He received periodic fitness reports that consistently rated him as an excellent or outstanding employee. By 1977, respondent had been promoted to a position as a covert electronics technician.

In January 1982, respondent voluntarily informed a CIA security officer that he was a homosexual. Almost immediately, the Agency placed respondent on paid administrative leave pending an investigation of his sexual orientation and conduct. On February 12 and again on February 17, respondent was extensively questioned by a polygraph officer concerning his homosexuality and possible security violations. Respondent denied having sexual relations with any foreign nationals and maintained that he had not disclosed classified information to any of his sexual partners. After these interviews, the officer told respondent that the polygraph tests indicated that he had truthfully answered all questions. The polygraph officer then prepared a five-page summary of his interviews with respondent, to which respondent was allowed to attach a two-page addendum.

On April 14, 1982, a CIA security agent informed respondent that the Agency's Office of Security had determined that respondent's homosexuality posed a threat to security, but declined to explain the nature of the danger. Respondent was then asked to resign. When he refused to do so, the Office of Security recommended to the CIA Director (petitioner's predecessor) that respondent be dismissed. After reviewing respondent's records and the evaluations of his subordinates, the Director "deemed it necessary and advisable in the interests of the United States to terminate [respondent's] employment with this Agency pursuant to section 102(c) of the National Security Act. . . ." Respondent was also advised that, while the CIA would give him a positive recommendation in any future job search, if he applied for a job requiring a security clearance the Agency would inform the prospective employer that it had concluded that respondent's homosexuality presented a security threat.

Respondent then filed an action against petitioner in the United States District Court for the District of Columbia. Respondent's amended complaint asserted a variety of statutory and constitutional claims against the Director. Respondent alleged that the Director's decision to terminate his employment violated the Administrative Procedure Act (APA), 5 U.S.C. § 706, because it was arbitrary and capricious, represented an abuse of discretion, and was reached without observing the procedures required by law and CIA regulations. He also complained that the Director's termination of his employment deprived him of constitutionally protected rights to property, liberty, and privacy in violation of the First, Fourth, Fifth, and Ninth Amendments. Finally, he asserted that his dismissal transgressed the procedural due process and equal protection of the laws guaranteed by the Fifth Amendment. Respondent requested a declaratory judgment that the Director had violated the APA and the Constitution, and asked the District Court for an injunction ordering petitioner to reinstate him to the position he held with the CIA prior to his dismissal. As an alternative remedy, he suggested that he be returned to paid administrative leave and that petitioner be ordered to reevaluate respondent's employment termination and provide a statement of the reasons for any adverse final determination. Respondent sought no monetary damages in his amended complaint.

Petitioner moved to dismiss respondent's amended complaint on the ground that § 102(c) of the National Security Act (NSA) precludes judicial review of the Director's termination decisions under the provisions of the APA set forth in 5 U.S.C. §§ 701, 702, and 706 (1982 ed., Supp. IV). Section 702 provides judicial review to any "person suffering legal wrong because of agency action, or adversely affected or aggrieved by agency action within the meaning of a relevant statute." The section further instructs that "an action in a court of the United States seeking relief other than money damages and stating a claim that an agency or an officer or employee thereof acted or failed to act in an official capacity or under color of legal authority shall not be dismissed nor relief therein be denied on the ground that it is against the United States or that the United States is an indispensable party." The scope of judicial review under § 702, however, is circumscribed by § 706, and its availability at all is predicated on satisfying the requirements of § 701, which provides:

> "(a) This chapter applies, according to the provisions thereof, except to the extent that —
> "(1) statutes preclude judicial review; or
> "(2) agency action is committed to agency discretion by law."

The District Court denied petitioner's motion to dismiss, and granted respondent's motion for partial summary judgment. The court determined that the APA provided judicial review of petitioner's termination decisions made under § 102(c) of the NSA, and found that respondent had been unlawfully discharged because the CIA had not followed the procedures described in its own regulations. The District Court declined, however, to address respondent's constitutional claims. Respondent was ordered reinstated to administrative leave status, and the Agency was instructed to reconsider his case using procedures that would supply him with the reasons supporting any termination decision and provide him with an opportunity to respond.

A divided panel of the Court of Appeals for the District of Columbia Circuit vacated the District Court's judgment and remanded the case for further proceedings. The Court of Appeals first decided that judicial review under the APA of the Agency's decision to terminate respondent was not precluded by §§ 701(a)(1) or (a)(2). Turning to the merits, the Court of Appeals found that, while an agency must normally follow its own regulations, the CIA regulations cited by respondent do not limit the Director's discretion in making termination decisions. Moreover, the regulations themselves state that, with respect to terminations pursuant to § 102(c), the Director need not follow standard discharge procedures, but may direct that an employee "be separated immediately and without regard to any suggested procedural steps." The majority thus concluded that the CIA regulations provide no independent source of procedural or substantive protection.

The Court of Appeals went on to hold that respondent must demonstrate that the Director's action was an arbitrary and capricious exercise of his power to discharge employees under § 102(c). Because the record below was unclear on certain points critical to respondent's claim for relief, the Court of Appeals remanded the case to District Court for a determination of the reason for the Director's termination of respondent. We granted certiorari to decide the question whether the Director's decision to discharge a CIA employee under § 102(c) of the NSA is judicially reviewable under the APA.

II

The APA's comprehensive provisions, set forth in 5 U.S.C. §§ 701-706 (1982 ed. and Supp. IV), allow any person "adversely affected or aggrieved" by agency action to obtain judicial review thereof, so long as the decision challenged represents a "final agency action for which there is no other adequate remedy in a court." Typically, a litigant will contest an action (or failure to act) by an agency on the ground that the agency has neglected to follow the statutory directives of Congress. Section 701(a), however, limits application of the entire APA to situations in which judicial review is not precluded by statute, *see* § 701(a)(1), and the agency action is not committed to agency discretion by law, *see* § 701(a)(2).

In *Citizens to Preserve Overton Park, Inc. v. Volpe*, 401 U.S. 402 (1971), this Court explained the distinction between §§ 701(a)(1) and (a)(2). Subsection (a)(1) is concerned with whether Congress expressed an intent to prohibit judicial review; subsection (a)(2) applies "in those rare instances where 'statutes are drawn in such broad terms that in a given case there is no law to apply.'" 401 U.S. at 410 (citing S. Rep. No. 752, 79th Cong., 1st Sess., 26 (1945)).

We further explained what it means for an action to be "committed to agency discretion by law" in *Heckler v. Chaney*, 470 U.S. 821 (1985). *Heckler* required the Court to determine whether the Food and Drug Administration's decision not to undertake an enforcement proceeding against the use of certain drugs in administering the death penalty was subject to judicial review. We noted that, under § 701(a)(2), even when Congress has not affirmatively precluded judicial oversight, "review is not to be had if the statute is drawn so that a court would have no meaningful standard against which to judge the agency's exercise of discretion." 470 U.S. at 830. Since the statute conferring power on the Food and Drug Administration to prohibit the unlawful misbranding or misuse of drugs provided no substantive standards on which a court could base its review, we found that enforcement actions were committed to the complete discretion of the FDA to decide when and how they should be pursued.

Both *Overton Park* and *Heckler* emphasized that § 701(a)(2) requires careful examination of the statute on which the claim of agency illegality is based (the Federal-Aid Highway Act of 1968 in *Overton Park* and the Federal Food, Drug, and Cosmetic Act in *Heckler*). In the present case, respondent's claims against the CIA arise from the Director's asserted violation of § 102(c) of the NSA. As an initial matter, it should be noted that § 102(c) allows termination of an Agency employee whenever the Director "shall *deem* such termination necessary or advisable in the interests of the United States" (emphasis added), not simply when the dismissal *is* necessary or advisable to those interests. This standard fairly exudes deference to the Director, and appears to us to foreclose the application of any meaningful judicial standard of review. Short of permitting cross-examination of the Director concerning his views of the Nation's security and whether the discharged employee was inimical to those interests, we see no basis on which a reviewing court could properly assess an Agency termination decision. The language of § 102(c) thus strongly suggests that its implementation was "committed to agency discretion by law."

So too does the overall structure of the NSA. Passed shortly after the close of the Second World War, the NSA created the CIA and gave its Director the responsibility "for protecting intelligence sources and methods from unauthorized disclosure." Section 102(c) is an integral part of that statute, because the Agency's efficacy, and the Nation's security, depend in large measure on the reliability and trustworthiness of the Agency's employees. As we recognized in

Snepp v. United States, 444 U.S. 507 (1980), employment with the CIA entails a high degree of trust that is perhaps unmatched in Government service. . . .

We thus find that the language and structure of § 102(c) indicate that Congress meant to commit individual employee discharges to the Director's discretion, and that § 701(a)(2) accordingly precludes judicial review of these decisions under the APA. We reverse the Court of Appeals to the extent that it found such terminations reviewable by the courts.

III

In addition to his claim that the Director failed to abide by the statutory dictates of § 102(c), respondent also alleged a number of constitutional violations in his amended complaint. Respondent charged that petitioner's termination of his employment deprived him of property and liberty interests under the Due Process Clause of the Fifth Amendment, denied him equal protection of the laws, and unjustifiably burdened his right to privacy. Respondent asserts that he is entitled, under the APA, to judicial consideration of these claimed violations.[7]

We share the confusion of the Court of Appeals as to the precise nature of respondent's constitutional claims. It is difficult, if not impossible, to ascertain from the amended complaint whether respondent contends that his termination, based on *his* homosexuality, is constitutionally impermissible, or whether he asserts that a more pervasive discrimination policy exists in the CIA's employment practices regarding *all* homosexuals. This ambiguity in the amended complaint is no doubt attributable in part to the inconsistent explanations respondent received from the Agency itself regarding his termination. Prior to his discharge, respondent had been told by two CIA security officers that his homosexual activities themselves violated CIA regulations. In contrast, the Deputy General Counsel of the CIA later informed respondent that homosexuality was merely a security concern that did not inevitably result in termination, but instead was evaluated on a case-by-case basis.

Petitioner maintains that, no matter what the nature of respondent's constitutional claims, judicial review is precluded by the language and intent of § 102(c). In petitioner's view, all Agency employment termination decisions, even those based on policies normally repugnant to the Constitution, are given over to the absolute discretion of the Director, and are hence unreviewable under the APA. We do not think § 102(c) may be read to exclude review of constitutional claims. We emphasized in *Johnson v. Robison*, 415 U.S. 361 (1974), that where Congress intends to preclude judicial review of constitutional claims its intent to do so must be clear. *Id.*, at 373-374. In *Weinberger v. Salfi*, 422 U.S. 749 (1975), we reaffirmed that view. We require this heightened showing in part to avoid the "serious constitutional question" that would arise if a federal

7. We understand that petitioner concedes that the Agency's failure to follow its own regulations can be challenged under the APA as a violation of § 102(c). *See Service v. Dulles*, 354 U.S. 363 (1957) (recognizing the right of federal courts to review an agency's actions to ensure that its own regulations have been followed); *Sampson v. Murray*, 415 U.S. 61, 71 (1974) (stating that "federal courts do have authority to review the claim of a discharged governmental employee that the agency effectuating the discharge has not followed administrative regulations"). The Court of Appeals, however, found that the CIA's own regulations plainly protect the discretion granted the Director by § 102(c), and that the regulations "provid[e] no independent source of procedural or substantive protections." Thus, since petitioner prevailed on this ground below and does not seek further review of the question here, we do not reach that issue.

statute were construed to deny any judicial forum for a colorable constitutional claim. *See Bowen v. Michigan Academy of Family Physicians*, 476 U.S. 667, 681, n.12 (1986).

Our review of § 102(c) convinces us that it cannot bear the preclusive weight petitioner would have it support. As detailed above, the section does commit employment termination decisions to the Director's discretion, and precludes challenges to these decisions based upon the statutory language of § 102(c). A discharged employee thus cannot complain that his termination was not "necessary or advisable in the interests of the United States," since that assessment is the Director's alone. Subsections (a)(1) and (a)(2) of § 701, however, remove from judicial review only those determinations specifically identified by Congress or "committed to agency discretion by law." Nothing in § 102(c) persuades us that Congress meant to preclude consideration of colorable constitutional claims arising out of the actions of the Director pursuant to that section; we believe that a constitutional claim based on an individual discharge may be reviewed by the District Court. We agree with the Court of Appeals that there must be further proceedings in the District Court on this issue.

Petitioner complains that judicial review even of constitutional claims will entail extensive "rummaging around" in the Agency's affairs to the detriment of national security. But petitioner acknowledges that Title VII claims attacking the hiring and promotion policies of the Agency are routinely entertained in federal court, and the inquiry and discovery associated with those proceedings would seem to involve some of the same sort of rummaging. Furthermore, the District Court has the latitude to control any discovery process which may be instituted so as to balance respondent's need for access to proof which would support a colorable constitutional claim against the extraordinary needs of the CIA for confidentiality and the protection of its methods, sources, and mission.

Petitioner also contends that even if respondent has raised a colorable constitutional claim arising out of his discharge, Congress in the interest of national security may deny the courts the authority to decide the claim and to order respondent's reinstatement if the claim is upheld. For the reasons previously stated, we do not think Congress meant to impose such restrictions when it enacted § 102(c) of the NSA. Even without such prohibitory legislation from Congress, of course, traditional equitable principles requiring the balancing of public and private interests control the grant of declaratory or injunctive relief in the federal courts. On remand, the District Court should thus address respondent's constitutional claims and the propriety of the equitable remedies sought.

The judgment of the Court of Appeals is affirmed in part, reversed in part, and the case is remanded for further proceedings consistent with this opinion.

It is so ordered.

[JUSTICE KENNEDY did not participate in the decision.]

JUSTICE O'CONNOR, concurring in part and dissenting in part.

I agree that the Administrative Procedure Act (APA) does not authorize judicial review of the employment decisions referred to in § 102(c) of the National Security Act of 1947. Because § 102(c) does not provide a meaningful standard for judicial review, such decisions are clearly "committed to agency discretion by law" within the meaning of the provision of the APA set forth in 5 U.S.C. § 701 (a)(2). I do not understand the Court to say that the exception in § 701(a)(2) is necessarily or fully defined by reference to statutes "drawn in such broad terms that in a given case there is no law to apply." *See Citizens to Preserve Overton Park, Inc. v. Volpe*, 401 U.S. 402, 410 (1971). Accordingly, I join Parts I and II of the Court's opinion.

I disagree, however, with the Court's conclusion that a constitutional claim challenging the validity of an employment decision covered by §102(c) may nonetheless be brought in a federal district court. Whatever may be the exact scope of Congress' power to close the lower federal courts to constitutional claims in other contexts, I have no doubt about its authority to do so here. The functions performed by the Central Intelligence Agency and the Director of Central Intelligence lie at the core of "the very delicate, plenary and exclusive power of the President as the sole organ of the federal government in the field of international relations." *United States v. Curtiss-Wright Export Corp.*, 299 U.S. 304, 320 (1936). The authority of the Director of Central Intelligence to control access to sensitive national security information by discharging employees deemed to be untrustworthy flows primarily from this constitutional power of the President, and Congress may surely provide that the inferior federal courts are not used to infringe on the President's constitutional authority. Section 102(c) plainly indicates that Congress has done exactly that, and the Court points to nothing in the structure, purpose, or legislative history of the National Security Act that would suggest a different conclusion. Accordingly, I respectfully dissent from the Court's decision to allow this lawsuit to go forward.

JUSTICE SCALIA, dissenting.

I agree with the Court's apparent holding in Part II of its opinion, that the Director's decision to terminate a CIA employee is "committed to agency discretion by law" within the meaning of 5 U.S.C. §701(a)(2). But because I do not see how a decision can, either practically or legally, be both unreviewable and yet reviewable for constitutional defect, I regard Part III of the opinion as essentially undoing Part II. I therefore respectfully dissent from the judgment of the Court.

I

Before proceeding to address Part III of the Court's opinion, which I think to be in error, I must discuss one significant element of the analysis in Part II. Though I subscribe to most of that analysis, I disagree with the Court's description of what is required to come within subsection (a)(2) of §701, which provides that judicial review is unavailable "to the extent that . . . agency action is committed to agency discretion by law." The Court's discussion suggests that the Court of Appeals below was correct in holding that this provision is triggered only when there is "no law to apply." Our precedents amply show that "commit[ment] to agency discretion by law" includes, but is not limited to, situations in which there is "no law to apply."

The Court relies for its "no law to apply" formulation upon our discussion in *Heckler v. Chaney*, 470 U.S. 821 (1985) — which, however, did not apply that as the sole criterion of §701(a)(2)'s applicability, but to the contrary discussed the subject action's "general unsuitability" for review, and adverted to "tradition, case law, and sound reasoning." 470 U.S. at 831. Moreover, the only supporting authority for the "no law to apply" test cited in *Chaney* was our observation in *Citizens to Preserve Overton Park, Inc. v. Volpe*, 401 U.S. 402 (1971), that "the legislative history of the Administrative Procedure Act indicates that [§ 701(a)(2)] is applicable in those rare instances where 'statutes are drawn in such broad terms that in a given case there is no law to apply.' S. Rep. No. 752, 79th Cong., 1st Sess., 26 (1945)," *id.*, at 410. Perhaps *Overton Park* discussed only the "no law to apply" factor because that was the only basis for nonreviewability that was even arguably applicable. It surely could not have believed that factor to be exclusive, for that would contradict the very legislative history, both cited and quoted in the opinion, from which it had been derived, which read in full: "The basic exception of matters committed to agency discretion would apply even if not stated at the outset [of the judicial review Chapter]. If, *for example*, statutes are drawn in such broad terms that in a given case there is no law to apply, courts of course have no statutory question to review." S. Rep. No. 752, 79th Cong., 1st Sess., 26 (1945) (emphasis added).

The "no law to apply" test can account for the nonreviewability of certain issues, but falls far short of explaining the full scope of the areas from which the courts are excluded. For the fact is that there is no governmental decision that is not subject to a fair number of legal constraints precise enough to be susceptible of judicial application. . . .

The key to understanding the "committed to agency discretion *by law*" provision of § 701(a)(2) lies in contrasting it with the "*statutes* preclude judicial review" provision of § 701(a)(1). Why "statutes" for preclusion, but the much more general term "law" for commission to agency discretion? The answer is, as we implied in *Chaney*, that the latter was intended to refer to "the 'common law' of judicial review of agency action," 470 U.S. at 832 — a body of jurisprudence that had marked out, with more or less precision, certain issues and certain areas that were beyond the range of judicial review. That jurisprudence included principles ranging from the "political question" doctrine, to sovereign immunity (including doctrines determining when a suit against an officer would be deemed to be a suit against the sovereign), to official immunity, to prudential limitations upon the courts' equitable powers, to what can be described no more precisely than a traditional respect for the functions of the other branches reflected in the statement in *Marbury v. Madison*, 5 U.S. 137, 1 Cranch 137, 170-171 (1803), that "where the head of a department acts in a case, in which executive discretion is to be exercised; in which he is the mere organ of executive will; it is again repeated, that any application to a court to control, in any respect, his conduct, would be rejected without hesitation." Only if all that "common law" were embraced within § 701(a)(2) could it have been true that, as was generally understood, "the intended result of [§ 701(a)] is to restate the existing law as to the area of reviewable agency action." Attorney General's Manual on the Administrative Procedure Act 94 (1947). Because that is the meaning of the provision, we have continued to take into account for purposes of determining reviewability, post-APA as before, not only the text and structure of the statute under which the agency acts, but such factors as whether the decision involves "a sensitive and inherently discretionary judgment call," *Department of Navy v. Egan*, 484 U.S. 518, 527 (1988), whether it is the sort of decision that has traditionally been nonreviewable, *ICC v. Locomotive Engineers*, 482 U.S. 270, 282 (1987); *Chaney*, *supra*, at 832, and whether review would have "disruptive practical consequences," *see Southern R. Co. v. Seaboard Allied Milling Corp.*, 442 U.S. 444, 457 (1979). This explains the seeming contradiction between § 701(a)(2)'s disallowance of review to the extent that action is "committed to agency discretion," and § 706's injunction that a court shall set aside agency action that constitutes "an abuse of discretion." Since, in the former provision, "committed to agency discretion by law" means "of the sort that is traditionally unreviewable," it operates to keep certain categories of agency action out of the courts; but when agency action is appropriately in the courts, abuse of discretion is of course grounds for reversal.

All this law, shaped over the course of centuries and still developing in its application to new contexts, cannot possibly be contained within the phrase "no law to apply." It is not surprising, then, that although the Court recites the test it does not really apply it. Like other opinions relying upon it, this one essentially announces the test, declares victory and moves on. It is not really true "'that a court would have no meaningful standard against which to judge the agency's exercise of discretion,'" *ante*, at 600, quoting *Chaney*, 470 U.S. at 830. The standard set forth in § 102(c) of the National Security Act of 1947, 50 U.S.C. § 403(c), "necessary or advisable in the interests of the United States," at least excludes dismissal out of personal vindictiveness, or because the Director wants to give the job to his cousin. Why, on the Court's theory, is respondent not entitled to assert the presence of such excesses, under the "abuse of discretion" standard of § 706?

If and when this Court does come to consider the reviewability of a dismissal such as the present one on the ground that it violated the agency's regulations — a question the Court avoids today, see *ante*, at n.7 — the difference between the "no law to apply" test and what I consider the correct test will be crucial. Perhaps a dismissal in violation of the regulations can be reviewed, but not simply because the regulations provide a standard that makes review possible. Thus, I agree with the Court's holding in Part II of its opinion (though, as will soon appear, that holding seems to be undone by its holding in Part III), but on different reasoning.

II

Before taking the reader through the terrain of the Court's holding that respondent may assert constitutional claims in this suit, I would like to try to clear some of the underbrush, consisting primarily of the Court's ominous warning that "[a] 'serious constitutional question' . . . would arise if a federal statute were construed to deny any judicial forum for a colorable constitutional claim." *Ante*, at 603, quoting from *Bowen v. Michigan Academy of Family Physicians*, 476 U.S. 667, 681, n.12 (1986).

[Justice Scalia's analysis of this issue is omitted.]

I think it entirely beyond doubt that if Congress intended, by the APA in 5 U.S.C. § 701(a)(2), to exclude judicial review of the President's decision (through the Director of Central Intelligence) to dismiss an officer of the Central Intelligence Agency, that disposition would be constitutionally permissible.

III

I turn, then, to whether that executive action is, within the meaning of § 701(a)(2), "committed to agency discretion by law." My discussion of this point can be brief, because the answer is compellingly obvious. Section 102(c) of the National Security Act of 1947, 61 Stat. 498, states:

> "*Notwithstanding . . . the provisions of any other law*, the Director of Central Intelligence, *may, in his discretion*, terminate the employment of any officer or employee of the Agency *whenever he shall deem* such termination necessary or advisable in the interests of the United States. . . ." 50 U.S.C. § 403(c) (emphasis added).

Further, as the Court declares, § 102(c) is an "integral part" of the National Security Act, which throughout exhibits "extraordinary deference to the Director." Given this statutory text, and given (as discussed above) that the area to which the text pertains is one of predominant executive authority and of traditional judicial abstention, it is difficult to conceive of a statutory scheme that more clearly reflects that "commit[ment] to agency discretion by law" to which § 701(a)(2) refers.

. . . .

Today's result . . . will have ramifications far beyond creation of the world's only secret intelligence agency that must litigate the dismissal of its agents. If constitutional claims can be raised in this highly sensitive context, it is hard to imagine where they cannot. The assumption that there are any executive decisions that cannot be hauled into the courts may no longer be valid. Also obsolete may be the assumption that we are capable of preserving a sensible common law of judicial review.

I respectfully dissent.

NOTE ON HECKLER v. CHANEY *AND* MASSACHUSETTS v. EPA

The issue of whether agency action is "committed to agency discretion" tends to arise in areas where the executive branch has traditionally had very broad discretion, e.g., military, diplomacy, or national security cases, like *Webster v. Doe.* Another area where the executive branch has traditionally enjoyed broad discretion is when it acts as a prosecutor. When a party seeks review of an agency action that is analogous to deciding whether to prosecute a crime, the "committed to agency discretion" issue is likely to arise.

The leading example of this type of case is *Heckler v. Chaney*, 470 U.S. 821 (1985). Chaney and others, sentenced to death by lethal injection, requested the Food and Drug Administration (FDA) to take enforcement action against the unapproved use of drugs as a means of capital punishment. The FDA refused. The FDA questioned its own jurisdiction and, in the alternative, exercised its "inherent discretion to decline to pursue certain enforcement matters." The plaintiffs sought judicial review of the FDA decision in federal court. The Supreme Court, overturning a decision of the D.C. Circuit, held that the FDA's exercise of its enforcement discretion was "committed to agency discretion" and thus not judicially reviewable.

The opinion by Justice Rehnquist first answered several questions about § 701(a)(2):

> [C]ommentators have pointed out that construction of § (a)(2) is further complicated by the tension between a literal reading of § (a)(2), which exempts from

judicial review those decisions committed to agency "discretion," and the primary scope of review prescribed by § 706(2)(A) — whether the agency's action was "arbitrary, capricious, or an abuse of discretion." How is it, they ask, that an action committed to agency discretion can be unreviewable and yet courts still can review agency actions for abuse of that discretion? *See* 5 K. Davis, Administrative Law § 28:6 (1984); Berger, Administrative Arbitrariness and Judicial Review, 65 Colum. L. Rev. 55, 58 (1965). The APA's legislative history provides little help on this score. Mindful, however, of the common-sense principle of statutory construction that sections of a statute generally should be read "to give effect, if possible, to every clause . . . ," we think there is a proper construction of § (a)(2) which satisfies each of these concerns.

This Court first discussed § (a)(2) in *Citizens to Preserve Overton Park v. Volpe*, 401 U.S. 402 (1971). That case dealt with the Secretary of Transportation's approval of the building of an interstate highway through a park in Memphis, Tennessee. The relevant federal statute provided that the Secretary "shall not approve" any program or project using public parkland unless the Secretary first determined that no feasible alternatives were available. Interested citizens challenged the Secretary's approval under the APA, arguing that he had not satisfied the substantive statute's requirements. This Court first addressed the "threshold question" of whether the agency's action was at all reviewable. After setting out the language of § 701(a), the Court stated:

In this case, there is no indication that Congress sought to prohibit judicial review and there is most certainly no "showing of 'clear and convincing evidence' of a . . . legislative intent" to restrict access to judicial review. *Abbott Laboratories v. Gardner*, 387 U.S. 136, 141 (1967). . . . "Similarly, the Secretary's decision here does not fall within the exception for action 'committed to agency discretion.' This is a very narrow exception. . . . The legislative history of the Administrative Procedure Act indicates that it is applicable in those rare instances where 'statutes are drawn in such broad terms that in a given case there is no law to apply.' S. Rep. No. 752, 79th Cong., 1st Sess., 26 (1945)." *Overton Park, supra*, at 410 (footnote omitted).

The above quote answers several of the questions raised by the language of § 701(a), although it raises others. First, it clearly separates the exception provided by § (a)(1) from the § (a)(2) exception. The former applies when Congress has expressed an intent to preclude judicial review. The latter applies in different circumstances; even where Congress has not affirmatively precluded review, review is not to be had if the statute is drawn so that a court would have no meaningful standard against which to judge the agency's exercise of discretion. In such a case, the statute ("law") can be taken to have "committed" the decisionmaking to the agency's judgment absolutely. This construction avoids conflict with the "abuse of discretion" standard of review in § 706 — if no judicially manageable standards are available for judging how and when an agency should exercise its discretion, then it is impossible to evaluate agency action for "abuse of discretion."

470 U.S. at 829-30.

The Court went on to find a presumption against reviewability of agency refusals to take enforcement steps:

This Court has recognized on several occasions over many years that an agency's decision not to prosecute or enforce, whether through civil or criminal process, is a decision generally committed to an agency's absolute discretion. This recognition of the existence of discretion is attributable in no small part to the general unsuitability for judicial review of agency decisions to refuse enforcement.

The reasons for this general unsuitability are many. First, an agency decision not to enforce often involves a complicated balancing of a number of factors which are peculiarly within its expertise. Thus, the agency must not only assess whether a violation has occurred, but whether agency resources are best spent on this violation or another, whether the agency is likely to succeed if it acts, whether the particular enforcement action requested best fits the agency's overall policies, and, indeed, whether the agency has enough resources to undertake the action at all. An agency generally cannot act against each technical violation of the statute it is charged with enforcing. The agency is far better equipped than the courts to deal with the many variables involved in the proper ordering of its priorities. Similar concerns animate the principles of administrative law that courts generally will defer to an agency's construction of the statute it is charged with implementing, and to the procedures it adopts for implementing that statute.

In addition to these administrative concerns, we note that when an agency refuses to act it generally does not exercise its coercive power over an individual's liberty or property rights, and thus does not infringe upon areas that courts often are called upon to protect. Similarly, when an agency does act to enforce, that action itself provides a focus for judicial review, inasmuch as the agency must have exercised its power in some manner. The action at least can be reviewed to determine whether the agency exceeded its statutory powers. Finally, we recognize that an agency's refusal to institute proceedings shares to some extent the characteristics of the decision of a prosecutor in the Executive Branch not to indict—a decision which has long been regarded as the special province of the Executive Branch, inasmuch as it is the Executive who is charged by the Constitution to "take Care that the Laws be faithfully executed." U.S. Const., Art. II, § 3.

We of course only list the above concerns to facilitate understanding of our conclusion that an agency's decision not to take enforcement action should be presumed immune from judicial review under § 701(a)(2). For good reasons, such a decision has traditionally been "committed to agency discretion," and we believe that the Congress enacting the APA did not intend to alter that tradition. . . . Thus, in establishing this presumption in the APA, Congress did not set agencies free to disregard legislative direction in the statutory scheme that the agency administers. Congress may limit an agency's exercise of enforcement power if it wishes, either by setting substantive priorities, or by otherwise circumscribing an agency's power to discriminate among issues or cases it will pursue. How to determine when Congress has done so is the question left open by *Overton Park*.

470 U.S. at 831-33. The Court then found nothing in the enforcement provisions of the FDA's organic statute, or in an agency policy statement, that circumscribed the agency's enforcement discretion. The Court concluded:

The FDA's decision not to take the enforcement actions requested by respondents is therefore not subject to judicial review under the APA. The general exception to reviewability provided by § 701(a)(2) for action "committed to agency discretion" remains a narrow one, *see Citizens to Preserve Overton Park v. Volpe*, 401 U.S. 402 (1971), but within that exception are included agency refusals to institute investigative or enforcement proceedings, unless Congress has indicated otherwise. In so holding, we essentially leave to Congress, and not to the courts, the decision as to whether an agency's refusal to institute proceedings should be judicially reviewable. No colorable claim is made in this case that the agency's refusal to institute proceedings violated any constitutional rights of respondents, and we do not address the issue that would be raised in such a case. Cf. *Johnson v. Robison*, 415 U.S. 361, 366 (1974); *Yick Wo v. Hopkins*, 118 U.S. 356, 372-374 (1886). The fact that the drugs involved in this case are ultimately to be used in imposing the death penalty must not lead this Court or other courts to import profound differences of opinion over the meaning of the Eighth Amendment to the United States Constitution into the domain of administrative law.

470 U.S. at 838.

The unavailability of judicial review of an agency decision not to take an enforcement action may be distinguished from the reviewability of other agency decisions not to act. Section 553(e) of the APA provides that "[e]ach agency shall give an interested person the right to petition for the issuance, amendment, or repeal of a rule." Section 555(e) requires an agency to give "[p]rompt notice" of the denial of a formal request for action. *See id.* ("Prompt notice shall be given of the denial in whole or in part of a written application, petition, or other request of an interested person made in connection with any agency proceeding. Except in affirming a prior denial or when the denial is self-explanatory, the notice shall be accompanied by a brief statement of the grounds for denial.") Of course, this requirement does not mean that an agency must grant the requested relief. A short letter thanking the petitioner for her concerns would probably satisfy the requirements of section 555(e). Thus, a federal administrative agency is not free to ignore completely a formal request for action, even though it might have no obligation to act favorably on the request.

Is an agency decision to deny a request for the promulgation of regulations subject to judicial review and, if it is, what standard of review applies? In *Massachusetts v. Environmental Protection Agency*, 549 U.S. 497 (2007), "private organizations filed a rulemaking petition asking EPA to regulate 'greenhouse gas emissions from new motor vehicles under §202 of the Clean Air Act.'" *Id.* at 510 (footnote omitted). Almost four years later, "EPA entered an order denying the rulemaking petition. The agency gave two reasons for its decision: (1) that contrary to the opinions of its former general counsels, the Clean Air Act does not authorize EPA to issue mandatory regulations to address global climate change, and (2) that even if the agency had the authority to set greenhouse gas emission standards, it would be unwise to do so at this time." *Id.* at 511 (citations omitted).

Several parties sought judicial review of the EPA's denial of the petition for rulemaking. Justice Stevens wrote the majority opinion for the Court, holding that the agency decision declining to promulgate a regulation was reviewable under a deferential standard of review:

> The scope of our review of the merits of the statutory issues is narrow. As we have repeated time and again, an agency has broad discretion to choose how best to marshal its limited resources and personnel to carry out its delegated responsibilities. *See Chevron U.S.A. Inc. v. Natural Resources Defense Council, Inc.*, 467 U.S. 837, 842-845 (1984). That discretion is at its height when the agency decides not to bring an enforcement action. Therefore, in *Heckler v. Chaney*, 470 U.S. 821 (1985), we held that an agency's refusal to initiate enforcement proceedings is not ordinarily subject to judicial review. Some debate remains, however, as to the rigor with which we review an agency's denial of a petition for rulemaking.
>
> . . . In contrast to nonenforcement decisions, agency refusals to initiate rulemaking "are less frequent, more apt to involve legal as opposed to factual analysis, and subject to special formalities, including a public explanation." They moreover arise out of denials of petitions for rulemaking which (at least in the circumstances here) the affected party had an undoubted procedural right to file in the first instance.

Refusals to promulgate rules are thus susceptible to judicial review, though such review is "extremely limited" and "highly deferential." *National Customs Brokers & Forwarders Assn. of America, Inc. v. United States*, 883 F.2d 93, 96 (C.A.D.C.1989).

. . . We therefore "may reverse any such action found to be . . . arbitrary, capricious, an abuse of discretion, or otherwise not in accordance with law." § 7607(d)(9) [the Clean Air Act standard of review provision].

549 U.S. at 527-28.

When the Court applied this standard, it concluded first that, contrary to the conclusion of the EPA, the statute permitted the regulation of greenhouse gases as pollutants under the CAA. See *id.* at 528-32.

The majority also rejected the EPA's alternate rationale for declining to regulate greenhouse gases, notwithstanding the deferential standard of review:

The alternative basis for EPA's decision — that even if it does have statutory authority to regulate greenhouse gases, it would be unwise to do so at this time — rests on reasoning divorced from the statutory text. While the statute does condition the exercise of EPA's authority on its formation of a "judgment," 42 U.S.C. § 7521(a)(1), that judgment must relate to whether an air pollutant "cause[s], or contribute[s] to, air pollution which may reasonably be anticipated to endanger public health or welfare," *ibid.* Put another way, the use of the word "judgment" is not a roving license to ignore the statutory text. It is but a direction to exercise discretion within defined statutory limits.

If EPA makes a finding of endangerment, the Clean Air Act requires the Agency to regulate emissions of the deleterious pollutant from new motor vehicles. *Ibid.* (stating that "[EPA] shall by regulation prescribe . . . standards applicable to the emission of any air pollutant from any class or classes of new motor vehicles"). EPA no doubt has significant latitude as to the manner, timing, content, and coordination of its regulations with those of other agencies. But once EPA has responded to a petition for rulemaking, its reasons for action or inaction must conform to the authorizing statute. Under the clear terms of the Clean Air Act, EPA can avoid taking further action only if it determines that greenhouse gases do not contribute to climate change or if it provides some reasonable explanation as to why it cannot or will not exercise its discretion to determine whether they do. *Ibid.* To the extent that this constrains agency discretion to pursue other priorities of the Administrator or the President, this is the congressional design.

EPA has refused to comply with this clear statutory command. Instead, it has offered a laundry list of reasons not to regulate. For example, EPA said that a number of voluntary Executive Branch programs already provide an effective response to the threat of global warming, 68 Fed. Reg. 52932, that regulating greenhouse gases might impair the President's ability to negotiate with "key developing nations" to reduce emissions, *id.*, at 52931, and that curtailing motor-vehicle emissions would reflect "an inefficient, piecemeal approach to address the climate change issue," *ibid.*

Although we have neither the expertise nor the authority to evaluate these policy judgments, it is evident they have nothing to do with whether greenhouse gas emissions contribute to climate change. Still less do they amount to a reasoned justification for declining to form a scientific judgment. In particular, while the President has broad authority in foreign affairs, that authority does not extend to the refusal to execute domestic laws. In the Global Climate Protection Act of 1987, Congress authorized the State Department — not EPA — to formulate United States foreign policy with reference to environmental matters relating to climate. See § 1103(c), 101 Stat. 1409. EPA has made no showing that it issued the ruling in question here after consultation with the State Department. Congress did direct EPA to consult with other agencies in the formulation of its policies and rules, but the State Department is absent from that list. § 1103(b).

Nor can EPA avoid its statutory obligation by noting the uncertainty surrounding various features of climate change and concluding that it would therefore be better not to regulate at this time. *See* 68 Fed. Reg. 52930–52931. If the scientific uncertainty is so profound that it precludes EPA from making a reasoned judgment as to whether greenhouse gases contribute to global warming, EPA must say so. That EPA would prefer not to regulate greenhouse gases because of some residual uncertainty — which, contrary to JUSTICE SCALIA's apparent belief, is in fact all that it said, see 68 Fed. Reg. 52929–52930 ("We do not believe . . . that it would be either effective or appropriate for EPA *to establish [greenhouse gas] standards for motor vehicles* at this time" (emphasis added)) — is irrelevant. The statutory question is whether sufficient information exists to make an endangerment finding.

In short, EPA has offered no reasoned explanation for its refusal to decide whether greenhouse gases cause or contribute to climate change. Its action was therefore "arbitrary, capricious, . . . or otherwise not in accordance with law." 42 U.S.C. § 7607(d)(9)(A). We need not and do not reach the question whether on remand EPA must make an endangerment finding, or whether policy concerns can inform EPA's actions in the event that it makes such a finding. Cf. *Chevron U.S.A. Inc. v. Natural Resources Defense Council, Inc.*, 467 U.S. 843–844. We hold only that EPA must ground its reasons for action or inaction in the statute.

Id. at 532-35.

Justice Scalia's dissent focused on the discretion that Congress gave to the EPA by providing that the Administrator should exercise his or her "judgment":

The provision of law at the heart of this case is § 202(a)(1) of the Clean Air Act (CAA or Act), which provides that the Administrator of the Environmental Protection Agency (EPA) "shall by regulation prescribe . . . standards applicable to the emission of any air pollutant from any class or classes of new motor vehicles or new motor vehicle engines, which *in his judgment* cause, or contribute to, air pollution which may reasonably be anticipated to endanger public health or welfare." 42 U.S.C. § 7521(a)(1) (emphasis added). As the Court recognizes, the statute "condition[s] the exercise of EPA's authority on its formation of a 'judgment.'" There is no dispute that the Administrator has made no such judgment in this case.

The question thus arises: Does anything require the Administrator to make a "judgment" whenever a petition for rulemaking is filed? Without citation of the statute or any other authority, the Court says yes. Why is that so? When Congress wishes to make private action force an agency's hand, it knows how to do so. See, e.g., Brock v. Pierce County, 476 U.S. 253, 254–255 (1986) (discussing the Comprehensive Employment and Training Act (CETA), 92 Stat. 1926, 29 U.S.C. § 816(b) (1976 ed., Supp. V), which "provide[d] that the Secretary of Labor 'shall' issue a final determination as to the misuse of CETA funds by a grant recipient within 120 days after receiving a complaint alleging such misuse"). Where does the CAA say that the EPA Administrator is required to come to a decision on this question whenever a rulemaking petition is filed? The Court points to no such provision because none exists.

Instead, the Court invents a multiple-choice question that the EPA Administrator must answer when a petition for rulemaking is filed. The Administrator must exercise his judgment in one of three ways: (a) by concluding that the pollutant does cause, or contribute to, air pollution that endangers public welfare (in which case EPA is required to regulate); (b) by concluding that the pollutant does not cause, or contribute to, air pollution that endangers public welfare (in which case EPA is not required to regulate); or (c) by "provid[ing] some reasonable explanation as to why it cannot or will not exercise its discretion to determine whether" greenhouse gases endanger public welfare (in which case EPA is not required to regulate).

I am willing to assume, for the sake of argument, that the Administrator's discretion in this regard is not entirely unbounded — that if he has no reasonable basis for deferring judgment he must grasp the nettle at once. The Court, however, with no basis in text or precedent, rejects all of EPA's stated "policy judgments" as not "amount[ing] to a reasoned justification," effectively narrowing the universe of potential reasonable bases to a single one: Judgment can be delayed only if the Administrator concludes that "the scientific uncertainty is [too] profound." The Administrator is precluded from concluding for other reasons "that it would . . . be better not to regulate at this time." Such other reasons — perfectly valid reasons — were set forth in the Agency's statement.

The Court dismisses this [EPA] analysis as "rest[ing] on reasoning divorced from the statutory text." [Citation to majority opinion omitted.] "While the statute does condition the exercise of EPA's authority on its formation of a 'judgment,' . . . that judgment must relate to whether an air pollutant 'cause[s], or contribute[s] to, air pollution which may reasonably be anticipated to endanger public health or welfare.'" [Citation to majority opinion omitted.] True but irrelevant. When the Administrator makes a judgment whether to regulate greenhouse gases, that judgment must relate to whether they are air pollutants that "cause, or contribute to, air pollution which may reasonably be anticipated to endanger public health or welfare." 42 U.S.C. § 7521(a)(1). But the statute says *nothing at all* about the reasons for which the Administrator may *defer* making a judgment — the permissible reasons for deciding not to grapple with the issue at the present time. Thus, the various "policy" rationales that the Court criticizes are not "divorced from the statutory text," except in the sense that the statutory text is silent, as texts are often silent about permissible reasons for the exercise of agency discretion. The reasons EPA gave are surely considerations executive agencies *regularly* take into account (and *ought* to take into account) when deciding whether to consider entering a new field: the impact such entry would have on other Executive Branch programs and on foreign policy. There is no basis in law for the Court's imposed limitation.

EPA's interpretation of the discretion conferred by the statutory reference to "its judgment" is not only reasonable, it is the most natural reading of the text. The Court nowhere explains why this interpretation is incorrect, let alone why it is not entitled to deference under *Chevron U.S.A. Inc. v. Natural Resources Defense Council, Inc.*, 467 U.S. 837 (1984). As the Administrator acted within the law in declining to make a "judgment" for the policy reasons above set forth, I would uphold the decision to deny the rulemaking petition on that ground alone.

Id. at 549-53 (footnote omitted).

Justice Scalia concluded his dissent by again contending that the Court should have deferred to the EPA:

> . . . This is a straightforward administrative-law case, in which Congress has passed a malleable statute giving broad discretion, not to us but to an executive agency. No matter how important the underlying policy issues at stake, this Court has no business substituting its own desired outcome for the reasoned judgment of the responsible agency.

Id. at 560.

QUESTIONS

1. How are APA § 701(a)(1) and (a)(2) different?
2. *Webster* focuses on the language and intent of APA § 701(a) in deciding whether judicial review is available, while neither *Johnson v. Robison* nor *Bowen v. Michigan Academy* discuss it. Why is the APA featured in *Webster* but not in the other cases?
3. Can you reconcile the formal language of § 701(a)(2) and § 706(2)(A)? Compare Justice Scalia's reconciliation in dissent in *Webster* with that of Justice Rehnquist for the majority in *Heckler v. Chaney.*
4. Can the same agency decision be both committed to agency discretion, and *not* committed to agency discretion, depending on the basis for the challenge to the decision? Who gets the better of this argument, the majority or the dissents?
5. What is the constitutional issue that the *Webster v. Doe* Court seeks to avoid? Is Justice Scalia correct in his suggestion that this constitutional issue is easy to resolve?
6. Is Justice Stevens convincing in distinguishing *Heckler v. Chaney* from *Massachusetts v. EPA* regarding reviewability? Is Justice Scalia convincing in describing the breadth of discretion granted to the EPA by the Clean Air Act because of the statute's reference to "judgment"?

F. STANDING

1. *Article III Standing*

LUJAN v. DEFENDERS OF WILDLIFE
504 U.S. 555 (1992)

Justice Scalia delivered the opinion of the Court with respect to Parts I, II, III-A, and IV, and an opinion with respect to Part III-B, in which the Chief Justice, Justice White, and Justice Thomas join.

This case involves a challenge to a rule promulgated by the Secretary of the Interior interpreting § 7 of the Endangered Species Act of 1973 (ESA), 87 Stat. 892, as amended, 16 U.S.C. § 1536, in such fashion as to render it applicable only to actions within the United States or on the high seas. The preliminary issue, and the only one we reach, is whether respondents here, plaintiffs below, have standing to seek judicial review of the rule.

I

The ESA, 87 Stat. 884, as amended, 16 U.S.C. §§ 1531 *et seq.*, seeks to protect species of animals against threats to their continuing existence caused by man. The ESA instructs the Secretary of the Interior to promulgate by regulation a list of those species which are either endangered or threatened under enumerated criteria, and to define the critical habitat of these species. 16 U.S.C. §§ 1533, 1536. Section 7(a)(2) of the act then provides, in pertinent part:

> "Each Federal agency shall, in consultation with and with the assistance of the Secretary [of the Interior], insure that any action authorized, funded, or carried out by such agency . . . is not likely to jeopardize the continued existence of any endangered species or threatened species or result in the destruction or adverse modification of habitat of such species which is determined by the Secretary, after consultation as appropriate with affected States, to be critical." 16 U.S.C. § 1536(a)(2).

In 1978, the Fish and Wildlife Service (FWS) and the National Marine Fisheries Service (NMFS), on behalf of the Secretary of the Interior and the Secretary of Commerce respectively, promulgated a joint regulation stating that the obligations imposed by § 7(a)(2) extend to actions taken in foreign nations. 43 Fed. Reg. 874 (1978). The next year, however, the Interior Department began to reexamine its position. A revised joint regulation, reinterpreting § 7(a)(2) to require consultation only for actions taken in the United States or on the high seas, was proposed in 1983, and promulgated in 1986.

Shortly thereafter, respondents, organizations dedicated to wildlife conservation and other environmental causes, filed this action against the Secretary of the Interior, seeking a declaratory judgment that the new regulation is in error as to the geographic scope of § 7(a)(2) and an injunction requiring the Secretary to promulgate a new regulation restoring the initial interpretation. The District Court granted the Secretary's motion to dismiss for lack of standing. The Court of Appeals for the Eighth Circuit reversed by a divided vote. On remand, . . . [t]he District Court . . . granted respondents' merits motion, and ordered the Secretary to publish a revised regulation. The Eighth Circuit affirmed. We granted certiorari.

II

While the Constitution of the United States divides all power conferred upon the Federal Government into "legislative Powers," Art. I, § 1, "[t]he executive Power," Art. II, § 1, and "[t]he judicial Power," Art. III, § 1, it does not attempt to define those terms. To be sure, it limits the jurisdiction of federal courts to "Cases" and "Controversies," but an executive inquiry can bear the name "case" (the Hoffa case) and a legislative dispute can bear the name "controversy" (the Smoot-Hawley controversy). Obviously, then, the Constitution's central mechanism of separation of powers depends largely upon common understanding of what activities are appropriate to legislatures, to executives, and to courts. In The Federalist No. 48, Madison expressed the view that "it is not infrequently a question of real nicety in legislative bodies whether the operation of a particular measure will, or will not, extend beyond the legislative sphere," whereas "the executive power [is] restrained within a narrower compass and . . . more simple in its nature," and "the judiciary [is] described by landmarks still less uncertain." The Federalist No. 48, p. 256 (Carey and McClellan eds. 1990). One of those landmarks, setting apart the "Cases" and "Controversies" that are of the justiciable sort referred to in Article III—

"serv[ing] to identify those disputes which are appropriately resolved through the judicial process," *Whitmore v. Arkansas*, 495 U.S. 149, 155 (1990) — is the doctrine of standing. Though some of its elements express merely prudential considerations that are part of judicial self-government, the core component of standing is an essential and unchanging part of the case-or-controversy requirement of Article III.

Over the years, our cases have established that the irreducible constitutional minimum of standing contains three elements. First, the plaintiff must have suffered an "injury in fact" — an invasion of a legally protected interest which is (a) concrete and particularized, see *id.*, at 756; *Warth v. Seldin*, 422 U.S. 490, 508 (1975); *Sierra Club v. Morton*, 405 U.S. 727, 740-741, n.16 (1972);[1] and (b) "actual or imminent, not 'conjectural' or 'hypothetical,'" *Whitmore, supra*, at 155 (quoting *Los Angeles v. Lyons*, 461 U.S. 95, 102 (1983)). Second, there must be a causal connection between the injury and the conduct complained of — the injury has to be "fairly . . . trace[able] to the challenged action of the defendant, and not . . . th[e] result [of] the independent action of some third party not before the court." *Simon v. Eastern Ky. Welfare Rights Organization*, 426 U.S. 26, 41-42 (1976). Third, it must be "likely," as opposed to merely "speculative," that the injury will be "redressed by a favorable decision." *Id.*, at 38, 43.

The party invoking federal jurisdiction bears the burden of establishing these elements. Since they are not mere pleading requirements but rather an indispensable part of the plaintiff's case, each element must be supported in the same way as any other matter on which the plaintiff bears the burden of proof, i.e., with the manner and degree of evidence required at the successive stages of the litigation. At the pleading stage, general factual allegations of injury resulting from the defendant's conduct may suffice, for on a motion to dismiss we "presume that general allegations embrace those specific facts that are necessary to support the claim." In response to a summary judgment motion, however, the plaintiff can no longer rest on such "mere allegations," but must "set forth" by affidavit or other evidence "specific facts," Fed. Rule Civ. Proc. 56(e), which for purposes of the summary judgment motion will be taken to be true. And at the final stage, those facts (if controverted) must be "supported adequately by the evidence adduced at trial."

When the suit is one challenging the legality of government action or inaction, the nature and extent of facts that must be averred (at the summary judgment stage) or proved (at the trial stage) in order to establish standing depends considerably upon whether the plaintiff is himself an object of the action (or forgone action) at issue. If he is, there is ordinarily little question that the action or inaction has caused him injury, and that a judgment preventing or requiring the action will redress it. When, however, as in this case, a plaintiff's asserted injury arises from the government's allegedly unlawful regulation (or lack of regulation) of *someone else*, much more is needed. In that circumstance, causation and redressability ordinarily hinge on the response of the regulated (or regulable) third party to the government action or inaction — and perhaps on the response of others as well. The existence of one or more of the essential elements of standing "depends on the unfettered choices made by independent actors not before the courts and whose exercise of broad and legitimate

---

1. By particularized, we mean that the injury must affect the plaintiff in a personal and individual way.

discretion the courts cannot presume either to control or to predict," and it becomes the burden of the plaintiff to adduce facts showing that those choices have been or will be made in such manner as to produce causation and permit redressability of injury. Thus, when the plaintiff is not himself the object of the government action or inaction he challenges, standing is not precluded, but it is ordinarily "substantially more difficult" to establish.

III

We think the Court of Appeals failed to apply the foregoing principles in denying the Secretary's motion for summary judgment. Respondents had not made the requisite demonstration of (at least) injury and redressability.

A

Respondents' claim to injury is that the lack of consultation with respect to certain funded activities abroad "increas[es] the rate of extinction of endangered and threatened species." Complaint ¶ 5. Of course, the desire to use or observe an animal species, even for purely esthetic purposes, is undeniably a cognizable interest for purpose of standing. See, e.g., *Sierra Club v. Morton*, 405 U.S. at 734. "But the 'injury in fact' test requires more than an injury to a cognizable interest. It requires that the party seeking review be himself among the injured." *Id.*, at 734-735. To survive the Secretary's summary judgment motion, respondents had to submit affidavits or other evidence showing, through specific facts, not only that listed species were in fact being threatened by funded activities abroad, but also that one or more of respondents' members would thereby be "directly" affected apart from their "'special interest' in the subject." *Id.*, at 735, 739. See generally *Hunt v. Washington State Apple Advertising Comm'n*, 432 U.S. 333, 343 (1977).

With respect to this aspect of the case, the Court of Appeals focused on the affidavits of two Defenders' members—Joyce Kelly and Amy Skilbred. Ms. Kelly stated that she traveled to Egypt in 1986 and "observed the traditional habitat of the endangered Nile crocodile there and intend[s] to do so again, and hope[s] to observe the crocodile directly," and that she "will suffer harm in fact as the result of [the] American . . . role . . . in overseeing the rehabilitation of the Aswan High Dam on the Nile . . . and [in] develop[ing] . . . Egypt's . . . Master Water Plan." Ms. Skilbred averred that she traveled to Sri Lanka in 1981 and "observed th[e] habitat" of "endangered species such as the Asian elephant and the leopard" at what is now the site of the Mahaweli project funded by the Agency for International Development (AID), although she "was unable to see any of the endangered species"; "this development project," she continued, "will seriously reduce endangered, threatened, and endemic species habitat including areas that I visited . . . [, which] may severely shorten the future of these species"; that threat, she concluded, harmed her because she "intend[s] to return to Sri Lanka in the future and hope[s] to be more fortunate in spotting at least the endangered elephant and leopard." When Ms. Skilbred was asked at a subsequent deposition if and when she had any plans to return to Sri Lanka, she reiterated that "I intend to go back to Sri Lanka," but confessed that she had no current plans: "I don't know [when]. There is a civil war going on right now. I don't know. Not next year, I will say. In the future."

We shall assume for the sake of argument that these affidavits contain facts showing that certain agency-funded projects threaten listed species — though that is questionable. They plainly contain no facts, however, showing how damage to the species will produce "imminent" injury to Mses. Kelly and Skilbred. That the women "had visited" the areas of the projects before the projects commenced proves nothing. As we have said in a related context, "Past exposure to illegal conduct does not in itself show a present case or controversy regarding injunctive relief . . . if unaccompanied by any continuing, present adverse effects." *Lyons*, 461 U.S. at 102 (quoting *O'Shea v. Littleton*, 414 U.S. 488, 495-496 (1974)). And the affiants' profession of an "intent" to return to the places they had visited before — where they will presumably, this time, be deprived of the opportunity to observe animals of the endangered species — is simply not enough. Such "some day" intentions — without any description of concrete plans, or indeed even any specification of *when* the some day will be — do not support a finding of the "actual or imminent" injury that our cases require.[2]

Besides relying upon the Kelly and Skilbred affidavits, respondents propose a series of novel standing theories. The first, inelegantly styled "ecosystem nexus," proposes that any person who uses *any part* of a "contiguous ecosystem" adversely affected by a funded activity has standing even if the activity is located a great distance away. This approach, as the Court of Appeals correctly observed, is inconsistent with our opinion in *National Wildlife Federation*, which held that a plaintiff claiming injury from environmental damage must use the area affected by the challenged activity and not an area roughly "in the vicinity" of it. 497 U.S. at 887-889; see also *Sierra Club*, 405 U.S. at 735. It makes no difference that the general-purpose section of the ESA states that the Act was intended in part "to provide a means whereby the ecosystems upon which endangered species and threatened species depend may be conserved," 16 U.S.C. § 1531(b). To say that the Act protects ecosystems is not to say that the Act creates (if it were possible) rights of action in persons who have not been injured in fact, that is, persons who use portions of an ecosystem not perceptibly affected by the unlawful action in question.

---

2. The dissent acknowledges the settled requirement that the injury complained of be, if not actual, then at least *imminent*, but it contends that respondents could get past summary judgment because "a reasonable finder of fact could conclude . . . that . . . Kelly or Skilbred will soon return to the project sites." This analysis suffers either from a factual or from a legal defect, depending on what the "soon" is supposed to mean. If "soon" refers to the standard mandated by our precedents — that the injury be "imminent," *Whitmore v. Arkansas*, 495 U.S. 149, 155 (1990) — we are at a loss to see how, as a factual matter, the standard can be met by respondents' mere profession of an intent, some day, to return. But if, as we suspect, "soon" means nothing more than "in this lifetime," then the dissent has undertaken quite a departure from our precedents. Although "imminence" is concededly a somewhat elastic concept, it cannot be stretched beyond its purpose, which is to ensure that the alleged injury is not too speculative for Article III purposes — that the injury is "*certainly* impending," *id.*, at 158 (emphasis added). It has been stretched beyond the breaking point when, as here, the plaintiff alleges only an injury at some indefinite future time, and the acts necessary to make the injury happen are at least partly within the plaintiff's own control. . . .

Our insistence upon these established requirements of standing does not mean that we would, as the dissent contends, "demand . . . detailed descriptions" of damages, such as a "nightly schedule of attempted activities" from plaintiffs alleging loss of consortium. That case and the others posited by the dissent all involve *actual* harm; the existence of standing is clear, though the precise extent of harm remains to be determined at trial. Where there is no actual harm, however, its imminence (though not its precise extent) must be established.

Respondents' other theories are called, alas, the "animal nexus" approach, whereby anyone who has an interest in studying or seeing the endangered animals anywhere on the globe has standing; and the "vocational nexus" approach, under which anyone with a professional interest in such animals can sue. Under these theories, anyone who goes to see Asian elephants in the Bronx Zoo, and anyone who is a keeper of Asian elephants in the Bronx Zoo, has standing to sue because the Director of the Agency for International Development (AID) did not consult with the Secretary regarding the AID-funded project in Sri Lanka. This is beyond all reason. Standing is not "an ingenious academic exercise in the conceivable," *United States v. Students Challenging Regulatory Agency Procedures (SCRAP)*, 412 U.S. 669, 688 (1973), but as we have said requires, at the summary judgment stage, a factual showing of perceptible harm. It is clear that the person who observes or works with a particular animal threatened by a federal decision is facing perceptible harm, since the very subject of his interest will no longer exist. It is even plausible — though it goes to the outermost limit of plausibility — to think that a person who observes or works with animals of a particular species in the very area of the world where that species is threatened by a federal decision is facing such harm, since some animals that might have been the subject of his interest will no longer exist, see *Japan Whaling Assn. v. American Cetacean Society*, 478 U.S. 221, 231, n.4 (1986). It goes beyond the limit, however, and into pure speculation and fantasy, to say that anyone who observes or works with an endangered species, anywhere in the world, is appreciably harmed by a single project affecting some portion of that species with which he has no more specific connection.

B

Besides failing to show injury, respondents failed to demonstrate redressability. Instead of attacking the separate decisions to fund particular projects allegedly causing them harm, respondents chose to challenge a more generalized level of Government action (rules regarding consultation), the invalidation of which would affect all overseas projects. This programmatic approach has obvious practical advantages, but also obvious difficulties insofar as proof of causation or redressability is concerned. As we have said in another context, "suits challenging, not specifically identifiable Government violations of law, but the particular programs agencies establish to carry out their legal obligations . . . [are], even when premised on allegations of several instances of violations of law, . . . rarely if ever appropriate for federal-court adjudication." *Allen*, 468 U.S. at 759-760.

The most obvious problem in the present case is redressability. Since the agencies funding the projects were not parties to the case, the District Court could accord relief only against the Secretary: He could be ordered to revise his regulation to require consultation for foreign projects. But this would not remedy respondents' alleged injury unless the funding agencies were bound by the Secretary's regulation, which is very much an open question. . . . The short of the matter is that redress of the only injury in fact respondents complain of requires action (termination of funding until consultation) by the individual funding agencies; and any relief the District Court could have provided in this suit against the Secretary was not likely to produce that action.

A further impediment to redressability is the fact that the agencies generally supply only a fraction of the funding for a foreign project. AID, for example, has provided less than 10% of the funding for the Mahaweli project. Respondents have produced nothing to indicate that the projects they have named will either be suspended, or do less harm to listed species, if that fraction is eliminated. As in *Simon*, 426 U.S., at 43-44, it is entirely conjectural whether the non-agency activity that affects respondents will be altered or affected by the agency activity they seek to achieve. There is no standing.

IV

The Court of Appeals found that respondents had standing for an additional reason: because they had suffered a "procedural injury." The so-called "citizen-suit" provision of the ESA provides, in pertinent part, that "any person may commence a civil suit on his own behalf (A) to enjoin any person, including the United States and any other governmental instrumentality or agency . . . who is alleged to be in violation of any provision of this chapter." 16 U.S.C. § 1540(g). The court held that, because § 7(a)(2) requires interagency consultation, the citizen-suit provision creates a "procedural right" to consultation in all "persons" — so that *anyone* can file suit in federal court to challenge the Secretary's (or presumably any other official's) failure to follow the assertedly correct consultative procedure, notwithstanding his or her inability to allege any discrete injury flowing from that failure. To understand the remarkable nature of this holding one must be clear about what it does *not* rest upon: This is not a case where plaintiffs are seeking to enforce a procedural requirement the disregard of which could impair a separate concrete interest of theirs (e.g., the procedural requirement for a hearing prior to denial of their license application, or the procedural requirement for an environmental impact statement before a federal facility is constructed next door to them).[7] Nor is it simply a case where concrete injury has been suffered by many persons, as in mass fraud or mass tort situations. Nor, finally, is it the unusual case in which Congress has created a concrete private interest in the outcome of a suit against a private party for the Government's benefit, by providing a cash bounty for the victorious plaintiff. Rather, the court held that the injury-in-fact requirement had been satisfied by congressional conferral upon *all* persons of an abstract, self-contained, noninstrumental "right" to have the Executive observe the procedures required by law. We reject this view.

We have consistently held that a plaintiff raising only a generally available grievance about government — claiming only harm to his and every citizen's interest in proper application of the Constitution and laws, and seeking relief that no more directly and tangibly benefits him than it does the public at large —

---

7. There is this much truth to the assertion that "procedural rights" are special: The person who has been accorded a procedural right to protect his concrete interests can assert that right without meeting all the normal standards for redressability and immediacy. Thus, under our case law, one living adjacent to the site for proposed construction of a federally licensed dam has standing to challenge the licensing agency's failure to prepare an environmental impact statement, even though he cannot establish with any certainty that the statement will cause the license to be withheld or altered, and even though the dam will not be completed for many years. (That is why we do not rely, in the present case, upon the Government's argument that, *even if* the other agencies were obliged to consult with the Secretary, they might not have followed his advice.) What respondents' "procedural rights" argument seeks, however, is quite different from this: standing for persons who have no concrete interests affected — persons who live (and propose to live) at the other end of the country from the dam.

does not state an Article III case or controversy. For example, in *Fairchild v. Hughes*, 258 U.S. 126, 129-130 (1922), we dismissed a suit challenging the propriety of the process by which the Nineteenth Amendment was ratified. Justice Brandeis wrote for the Court:

> "[This is] not a case within the meaning of . . . Article III. . . . Plaintiff has [asserted] only the right, possessed by every citizen, to require that the Government be administered according to law and that the public moneys be not wasted. Obviously this general right does not entitle a private citizen to institute in the federal courts a suit. . . ." *Ibid.*

In *Massachusetts v. Mellon*, 262 U.S. 447 (1923), we dismissed for lack of Article III standing a taxpayer suit challenging the propriety of certain federal expenditures. We said:

> "The party who invokes the power [of judicial review] must be able to show not only that the statute is invalid but that he has sustained or is immediately in danger of sustaining some direct injury as the result of its enforcement, and not merely that he suffers in some indefinite way in common with people generally. . . . Here the parties plaintiff have no such case. . . . [T]heir complaint . . . is merely that officials of the executive department of the government are executing and will execute an act of Congress asserted to be unconstitutional; and this we are asked to prevent. To do so would be not to decide a judicial controversy, but to assume a position of authority over the governmental acts of another and coequal department, an authority which plainly we do not possess." *Id.* at 488-489.

In *Ex parte Levitt*, 302 U.S. 633 (1937), we dismissed a suit contending that Justice Black's appointment to this Court violated the Ineligibility Clause, Art. I, § 6, cl. 2. "It is an established principle," we said, "that to entitle a private individual to invoke the judicial power to determine the validity of executive or legislative action he must show that he has sustained or is immediately in danger of sustaining a direct injury as the result of that action and it is not sufficient that he has merely a general interest common to all members of the public." 302 U.S. at 634. *See also Doremus v. Board of Ed. of Hawthorne*, 342 U.S. 429, 433-434 (1952) (dismissing taxpayer action on the basis of *Mellon*).

More recent cases are to the same effect. In *United States v. Richardson*, 418 U.S. 166 (1974), we dismissed for lack of standing a taxpayer suit challenging the Government's failure to disclose the expenditures of the Central Intelligence Agency, in alleged violation of the constitutional requirement, Art. I, § 9, cl. 7, that "a regular Statement and Account of the Receipts and Expenditures of all public Money shall be published from time to time." We held that such a suit rested upon an impermissible "generalized grievance," and was inconsistent with "the framework of Article III" because "the impact on [plaintiff] is plainly undifferentiated and 'common to all members of the public.'" *Richardson, supra*, at 171, 176-177. And in *Schlesinger v. Reservists Comm. to Stop the War*, 418 U.S. 208 (1974), we dismissed for the same reasons a citizen-taxpayer suit contending that it was a violation of the Incompatibility Clause, Art. I, § 6, cl. 2, for Members of Congress to hold Commissions in the military Reserves. We said that the challenged action, "standing alone, would adversely affect only the generalized interest of all citizens in constitutional governance. . . . We reaffirm *Levitt* in holding that standing to sue may not be predicated upon an interest of th[is] kind. . . ." *Schlesinger, supra*, at 217, 220. . . .

To be sure, our generalized-grievance cases have typically involved Government violation of procedures assertedly ordained by the Constitution rather than the Congress. But there is absolutely no basis for making the Article III inquiry turn on the source of the asserted right. Whether the courts were to act on their own, or at the invitation of Congress, in ignoring the concrete injury requirement described in our cases, they would be discarding a principle fundamental to the separate and distinct constitutional role of the Third Branch — one of the essential elements that identifies those "Cases" and "Controversies" that are the business of the courts rather than of the political branches. "The province of the court," as Chief Justice Marshall said in *Marbury v. Madison*, 5 U.S. 137, 1 Cranch 137, 170, "is, solely, to decide on the rights of individuals." Vindicating the *public* interest (including the public interest in Government observance of the Constitution and laws) is the function of Congress and the Chief Executive. The question presented here is whether the public interest in proper administration of the laws (specifically, in agencies' observance of a particular, statutorily prescribed procedure) can be converted into an individual right by a statute that denominates it as such, and that permits all citizens (or, for that matter, a subclass of citizens who suffer no distinctive concrete harm) to sue. If the concrete injury requirement has the separation-of-powers significance we have always said, the answer must be obvious: To permit Congress to convert the undifferentiated public interest in executive officers' compliance with the law into an "individual right" vindicable in the courts is to permit Congress to transfer from the President to the courts the Chief Executive's most important constitutional duty, to "take Care that the Laws be faithfully executed," Art. II, § 3. It would enable the courts, with the permission of Congress, "to assume a position of authority over the governmental acts of another and co-equal department," *Massachusetts v. Mellon*, 262 U.S. at 489, and to become "virtually continuing monitors of the wisdom and soundness of Executive action." *Allen, supra*, at 760 (quoting *Laird v. Tatum*, 408 U.S. 1, 15 (1972)). . . .

Nothing in this contradicts the principle that "the . . . injury required by Art. III may exist solely by virtue of 'statutes creating legal rights, the invasion of which creates standing.'" *Warth*, 422 U.S. at 500 (quoting *Linda R.S. v. Richard D.*, 410 U.S. 614, 617, n.3 (1973)). Both of the cases used by *Linda R.S.* as an illustration of that principle involved Congress' elevating to the status of legally cognizable injuries concrete, *de facto* injuries that were previously inadequate in law (namely, injury to an individual's personal interest in living in a racially integrated community, *see Trafficante v. Metropolitan Life Ins. Co.*, 409 U.S. 205, 208-212 (1972), and injury to a company's interest in marketing its product free from competition, *see Hardin v. Kentucky Utilities Co.*, 390 U.S. 1, 6 (1968)). As we said in *Sierra Club*, "[Statutory] broadening [of] the categories of injury that may be alleged in support of standing is a different matter from abandoning the requirement that the party seeking review must himself have suffered an injury." 405 U.S. at 738. Whether or not the principle set forth in *Warth* can be extended beyond that distinction, it is clear that in suits against the Government, at least, the concrete injury requirement must remain. . . .

We hold that respondents lack standing to bring this action and that the Court of Appeals erred in denying the summary judgment motion filed by the United

States. The opinion of the Court of Appeals is hereby reversed, and the cause is remanded for proceedings consistent with this opinion. *It is so ordered.*

JUSTICE KENNEDY, with whom JUSTICE SOUTER joins, concurring in part and concurring in the judgment.

Although I agree with the essential parts of the Court's analysis, I write separately to make several observations.

I agree with the Court's conclusion in Part III-A that, on the record before us, respondents have failed to demonstrate that they themselves are "among the injured." *Sierra Club v. Morton*, 405 U.S. 727, 735 (1972). This component of the standing inquiry is not satisfied unless

> "[p]laintiffs . . . demonstrate a 'personal stake in the outcome.' . . . Abstract injury is not enough. The plaintiff must show that he 'has sustained or is immediately in danger of sustaining some direct injury' as the result of the challenged official conduct and the injury or threat of injury must be both 'real and immediate' not 'conjectural' or 'hypothetical.'" *Los Angeles v. Lyons*, 461 U.S. 95, 101-102 (1983) (citations omitted).

While it may seem trivial to require that Mses. Kelly and Skilbred acquire airline tickets to the project sites or announce a date certain upon which they will return, this is not a case where it is reasonable to assume that the affiants will be using the sites on a regular basis, see *Sierra Club v. Morton, supra*, at 735, n.8, nor do the affiants claim to have visited the sites since the projects commenced. With respect to the Court's discussion of respondents' "ecosystem nexus," "animal nexus," and "vocational nexus" theories, I agree that on this record respondents' showing is insufficient to establish standing on any of these bases. I am not willing to foreclose the possibility, however, that in different circumstances a nexus theory similar to those proffered here might support a claim to standing. *See Japan Whaling Assn. v. American Cetacean Society*, 478 U.S. 221, 231, n.4 (1986) ("[R]espondents . . . undoubtedly have alleged a sufficient 'injury in fact' in that the whale watching and studying of their members will be adversely affected by continued whale harvesting"). . . .

I also join Part IV of the Court's opinion with the following observations. As Government programs and policies become more complex and far reaching, we must be sensitive to the articulation of new rights of action that do no have clear analogs in our common-law tradition. Modern litigation has progressed far from the paradigm of Marbury suing Madison to get his Commission, *Marbury v. Madison*, 1 Cranch 137 (1803), or Ogden seeking an injunction to halt Gibbons' steamboat operations, *Gibbons v. Ogden*, 9 Wheat. 1 (1824). In my view, Congress has the power to define injuries and articulate chains of causation that will give rise to a case or controversy where none existed before, and I do not read the Court's opinion to suggest a contrary view. *See Warth v. Seldin*, 422 U.S. 490, 500 (1975). In exercising this power, however, Congress must at the very least identify the injury it seeks to vindicate and relate the injury to the class of persons entitled to bring suit. The citizen-suit provision of the Endangered Species Act does not meet these minimal requirements, because while the statute purports to confer a right on "any person . . . to enjoin . . . the United States and any other governmental instrumentality or agency . . . who is alleged to be in violation of any provision of this chapter," it does not of its own force establish that there is an injury in "any person" by virtue of any "violation." 16 U.S.C. § 1540(g)(1)(A).

The Court's holding that there is an outer limit to the power of Congress to confer rights of action is a direct and necessary consequence of the case and controversy limitations found in Article III. I agree that it would exceed those limitations if, at the behest of Congress and in the absence of any showing of concrete injury, we were to entertain citizen suits to vindicate the public's non-concrete interest in the proper administration of the laws. While it does not matter how many persons have been injured by the challenged action, the party bringing suit must show that the action injures him in a concrete and personal way. This requirement is not just an empty formality. It preserves the vitality of the adversarial process by assuring both that the parties before the court have an actual, as opposed to professed, stake in the outcome, and that "the legal questions presented . . . will be resolved, not in the rarified atmosphere of a debating society, but in a concrete factual context conducive to a realistic appreciation of the consequences of judicial action." *Valley Forge Christian College v. Americans United for Separation of Church and State, Inc.*, 454 U.S. 464, 472 (1982). . . .

With these observations, I concur in Parts I, II, III-A, and IV of the Court's opinion and in the judgment of the Court.

JUSTICE STEVENS, concurring in the judgment.

Because I am not persuaded that Congress intended the consultation requirement in § 7(a)(2) of the Endangered Species Act of 1973 (ESA), 16 U.S.C. § 1536(a)(2), to apply to activities in foreign countries, I concur in the judgment of reversal. I do not, however, agree with the Court's conclusion that respondents lack standing because the threatened injury to their interest in protecting the environment and studying endangered species is not "imminent." Nor do I agree with the plurality's additional conclusion that respondents' injury is not "redressable" in this litigation.

I

In my opinion a person who has visited the critical habitat of an endangered species has a professional interest in preserving the species and its habitat, and intends to revisit them in the future has standing to challenge agency action that threatens their destruction. Congress has found that a wide variety of endangered species of fish, wildlife, and plants are of "aesthetic, ecological, educational, historical, recreational, and scientific value to the Nation and its people." 16 U.S.C. § 1531(a)(3). Given that finding, we have no license to demean the importance of the interest that particular individuals may have in observing any species or its habitat, whether those individuals are motivated by esthetic enjoyment, an interest in professional research, or an economic interest in preservation of the species. Indeed, this Court has often held that injuries to such interests are sufficient to confer standing, and the Court reiterates that holding today.

The Court nevertheless concludes that respondents have not suffered "injury in fact" because they have not shown that the harm to the endangered species will produce "imminent" injury to them. I disagree. An injury to an individual's interest in studying or enjoying a species and its natural habitat occurs when someone (whether it be the Government or a private party) takes action that harms that species and habitat. In my judgment, therefore, the "imminence" of such an injury should be measured by the timing and the likelihood of the threatened environmental harm, rather than — as the Court seems to suggest, *ante*, at n.2 — by the time that might elapse between the present and the time when the individuals would visit the area if no such injury should occur. . . .

If respondents are genuinely interested in the preservation of the endangered species and intend to study or observe these animals in the future, their injury will occur as soon as the animals are destroyed. Thus the only potential source of "speculation" in this case is whether respondents' intent to study or observe the animals is genuine. In my view, Joyce Kelly and Amy Skilbred have introduced sufficient evidence to negate petitioner's contention that their claims of injury are "speculative" or "conjectural." . . .

II

Although I believe that respondents have standing, I nevertheless concur in the judgment of reversal because I am persuaded that the Government is correct in its submission that § 7(a)(2) does not apply to activities in foreign countries. . . . [Justices Blackmun and O'Connor dissented, arguing that plaintiffs had "raised genuine issues of fact — sufficient to survive summary judgment — both as to injury and as to redressability" and questioning "the Court's breadth of language in rejecting standing for 'procedural' injuries."]

QUESTIONS

1. Why shouldn't the Constitution be read to permit the courts to stop any government action that is illegal?
2. Should someone who is denied a property interest by the government without procedural due process be out of court if he or she cannot show likelihood of success on the merits of his or her entitlement claim? Is this case really different from that situation?
3. Can injury-in-fact, causation, and redressability all be considered aspects of the single question does the plaintiff get something if he or she wins?
4. Can Congress provide that some plaintiffs have standing even though they cannot show injury in fact?

FEDERAL ELECTION COMMISSION v. AKINS
524 U.S. 11 (1998)

JUSTICE BREYER delivered the opinion of the Court.

The Federal Election Commission (FEC) has determined that the American Israel Public Affairs Committee (AIPAC) is not a "political committee" as defined by the Federal Election Campaign Act of 1971, 2 U.S.C. § 431(4) (FECA), and, for that reason, the Commission has refused to require AIPAC to make disclosures regarding its membership, contributions, and expenditures that FECA would otherwise require. We hold that respondents, a group of voters, have standing to challenge the Commission's determination in court, and we remand this case for further proceedings.

I

In light of our disposition of this case, we believe it necessary to describe its procedural background in some detail. As commonly understood, the Federal Election Campaign Act seeks to remedy any actual or perceived corruption of the political process in several important ways. . . .

This case concerns requirements in the Act that extend beyond the[] better-known contribution and expenditure limitations. In particular the Act imposes extensive recordkeeping and disclosure requirements upon groups that fall within the Act's definition of a "political committee." Those groups must register with the FEC, appoint a treasurer, keep names and addresses of contributors, track the amount and purpose of disbursements, and file complex FEC reports that include lists of donors giving in excess of $200 per year (often, these donors may be the group's members), contributions, expenditures, and any other disbursements irrespective of their purposes. §§ 432-434.

. . . The Act states that a "political committee" includes "*any* committee, club, association or other group of persons which receives" more than $1,000 in "contributions" or "which makes" more than $1,000 in "expenditures" in any given year. § 431(4)(A).

This broad definition, however, is less universally encompassing than at first it may seem, for later definitional subsections limit its scope. The Act defines the key terms "contribution" and "expenditure" as covering only those contributions and expenditures that are made "for the purpose of influencing any election for Federal office." §§ 431(8)(A)(i), (9)(A)(i). Moreover, the Act sets forth detailed categories of disbursements, loans, and assistance-in-kind that do not count as a "contribution" or an "expenditure," even when made for election-related purposes. §§ 431(8)(B), (9)(B). In particular, assistance given to help a particular candidate will not count toward the $1,000 "expenditure" ceiling that qualifies an organization as a "political committee" if it takes the form of a "communication" by an organization "to its members" — as long as the organization at issue is a "membership organization or corporation" and it is not "organized primarily for the purpose of influencing the nomination . . . or electio[n], of any individual." § 431(9)(B)(iii).

This case arises out of an effort by respondents, a group of voters with views often opposed to those of AIPAC, to persuade the FEC to treat AIPAC as a "political committee." Respondents filed a complaint with the FEC, stating that AIPAC had made more than $1,000 in qualifying "expenditures" per year, and thereby became a "political committee." They added that AIPAC had violated the FEC provisions requiring "political committee[s]" to register and to make public the information about members, contributions, and expenditures to which we have just referred. Respondents also claimed that AIPAC had violated § 441b of FECA, which prohibits corporate campaign "contribution[s]" and "expenditure[s]." They asked the FEC to find that AIPAC had violated the Act, and, among other things, to order AIPAC to make public the information that FECA demands of a "political committee."

AIPAC asked the FEC to dismiss the complaint. AIPAC described itself as an issue-oriented organization that seeks to maintain friendship and promote goodwill between the United States and Israel. AIPAC conceded that it lobbies elected officials and disseminates information about candidates for public office. But in responding to the § 441b charge, AIPAC denied that it had made the kinds of "expenditures" that matter for FECA purposes (i.e., the kinds of election-related expenditures that corporations cannot make, and which count as the kind of expenditures that, when they exceed $1,000, qualify a group as a "political committee").

To put the matter more specifically: AIPAC focused on certain "expenditures" that respondents had claimed were election-related, such as the costs of meetings with candidates, the introduction of AIPAC members to candidates, and the distribution of candidate position papers. AIPAC said that its spending on such activities, even if election-related, fell within a relevant exception. They amounted, said AIPAC, to communications by a membership organization with its members, which the Act exempts from its definition of "expenditures," § 431(9)(B)(iii). In AIPAC's view, these communications therefore did not violate § 441b's corporate expenditure prohibition. (And, if AIPAC was right, those expenditures would not count towards the $1,000 ceiling on "expenditures" that might transform an ordinary issue-related group into a "political committee." § 431(4))....

The FEC [] held that AIPAC was not subject to the disclosure requirements.... In the FEC's view, the Act's definition of "political committee" includes only those organizations that have as a "major purpose" the nomination or election of candidates. AIPAC, it added, was fundamentally an issue-oriented lobbying organization, not a campaign-related organization, and hence AIPAC fell outside the definition of a "political committee" regardless. The FEC consequently dismissed respondents' complaint.

Respondents filed a petition in Federal District Court seeking review of the FEC's determination dismissing their complaint. *See* §§ 437g(8)(A), 437g(8)(C). The District Court granted summary judgment for the FEC, and a divided panel of the Court of Appeals affirmed. The en banc Court of Appeals reversed, however, on the ground that the FEC's "major purpose" test improperly interpreted the Act's definition of a "political committee."...

II

The Solicitor General argues that respondents lack standing to challenge the FEC's decision not to proceed against AIPAC. He claims that ... respondents have not shown that they "suffe[r] injury in fact," that their injury is "fairly traceable" to the FEC's decision, or that a judicial decision in their favor would "redres[s]" the injury. In his view, respondents' District Court petition consequently failed to meet Article III's demand for a "case" or "controversy."...

[We do not] agree with the FEC or the dissent that Congress lacks the constitutional power to authorize federal courts to adjudicate this lawsuit. Article III, of course, limits Congress' grant of judicial power to "cases" or "controversies." That limitation means that respondents must show, among other things, an "injury in fact" — a requirement that helps assure that courts will not "pass upon . . . abstract, intellectual problems," but adjudicate "concrete, living contest[s] between adversaries." In our view, respondents here have suffered a genuine "injury in fact."

The "injury in fact" that respondents have suffered consists of their inability to obtain information — lists of AIPAC donors (who are, according to AIPAC, its members), and campaign-related contributions and expenditures — that, on respondents' view of the law, the statute requires that AIPAC make public. There is no reason to doubt their claim that the information would help them (and others to whom they would communicate it) to evaluate candidates for public office, especially candidates who received assistance from AIPAC, and to evaluate the role that AIPAC's financial assistance might play in a specific election. Respondents' injury consequently seems concrete and particular. Indeed, this Court has previously held that a plaintiff suffers an "injury in fact" when the plaintiff fails to obtain information which must be publicly disclosed pursuant to a statute. *Public Citizen v. Department of Justice*, 491 U.S. 440, 449 (1989) (failure to obtain information subject to disclosure under Federal Advisory Committee Act "constitutes a sufficiently distinct injury to provide standing to sue"). *See also Havens Realty Corp. v. Coleman*, 455 U.S. 363, 373-374 (1982) (deprivation of information about housing availability constitutes "specific injury" permitting standing).

The dissent refers to *United States v. Richardson*, 418 U.S. 166 (1974), a case in which a plaintiff sought information (details of Central Intelligence Agency expenditures) to which, he said, the Constitution's Accounts Clause, Art. I, §9, cl. 7, entitled him. The Court held that the plaintiff there lacked Article III standing. The dissent says that *Richardson* and this case are "indistinguishable." But as the parties' briefs suggest — for they do not mention *Richardson* — that case does not control the outcome here.

Richardson's plaintiff claimed that a statute permitting the CIA to keep its expenditures nonpublic violated the Accounts Clause, which requires that "a regular Statement and Account of the Receipts and Expenditures of all public Money shall be published from time to time." The Court held that the plaintiff lacked standing because there was "no 'logical nexus' between the [plaintiff's] asserted status of taxpayer and the claimed failure of the Congress to require the Executive to supply a more detailed report of the [CIA's] expenditures."

In this case, however, the "logical nexus" inquiry is not relevant. Here, there is no constitutional provision requiring the demonstration of the "nexus" the Court believed must be shown in *Richardson* and *Flast* [*v. Cohen*]. Rather, there is a statute which, as we previously pointed out, does seek to protect individuals such as respondents from the kind of harm they say they have suffered, i.e., failing to receive particular information about campaign-related activities.

The fact that the Court in *Richardson* focused upon taxpayer standing, not voter standing, places that case at still a greater distance from the case before us. We are not suggesting, as the dissent implies, that *Richardson* would have come out differently if only the plaintiff had asserted his standing to sue as a voter, rather than as a taxpayer. Faced with such an assertion, the *Richardson* court would simply have had to consider whether "the Framers . . . ever imagined that general directives [of the Constitution] . . . would be subject to enforcement by an individual citizen." But since that answer (like the answer to whether there was taxpayer standing in *Richardson*) would have rested in significant part upon the Court's view of the Accounts Clause, it still would not control our answer in this case. All this is to say that the legal logic which critically determined *Richardson*'s outcome is beside the point here.

The FEC's strongest argument is its contention that this lawsuit involves only a "generalized grievance." (Indeed, if *Richardson* is relevant at all, it is because of its broad discussion of this matter, not its basic rationale.) The Solicitor General points out that respondents' asserted harm (their failure to obtain information) is one which is "shared in substantially equal measure by all or a large class of citizens." This Court, he adds, has often said that "generalized grievance[s]" are not the kinds of harms that confer standing. Whether styled as a constitutional or prudential limit on standing, the Court has sometimes determined that where large numbers of Americans suffer alike, the political process, rather than the judicial process, may provide the more appropriate remedy for a widely shared grievance.

The kind of judicial language to which the FEC points, however, invariably appears in cases where the harm at issue is not only widely shared, but is also of an abstract and indefinite nature—for example, harm to the "common concern for obedience to law." . . . Cf. *Lujan, supra*, at 572-578 (injury to interest in seeing that certain procedures are followed not normally sufficient by itself to confer standing); *Frothingham*, 262 U.S. 447 at 488 (party may not merely assert that "he suffers in some indefinite way in common with people generally"); *Perkins v. Lukens Steel Co.*, 310 U.S. 113, 125 (1940) (plaintiffs lack standing because they have failed to show injury to "a particular right of their own, as distinguished from the public's interest in the administration of the law"). The abstract nature of the harm—for example, injury to the interest in seeing that the law is obeyed—deprives the case of the concrete specificity that characterized those controversies which were "the traditional concern of the courts at Westminster," and which today prevents a plaintiff from obtaining what would, in effect, amount to an advisory opinion.

Often the fact that an interest is abstract and the fact that it is widely shared go hand in hand. But their association is not invariable, and where a harm is concrete, though widely shared, the Court has found "injury in fact." See *Public Citizen*, 491 U.S. at 449-450 ("The fact that other citizens or groups of citizens might make the same complaint after unsuccessfully demanding disclosure . . . does not lessen [their] asserted injury"). Thus the fact that a political forum may be more readily available where an injury is widely shared (while counseling against, say, interpreting a statute as conferring standing) does not, by itself, automatically disqualify an interest for Article III purposes. Such an interest, where sufficiently concrete, may count as an "injury in fact." This conclusion seems particularly obvious where (to use a hypothetical example) large numbers of individuals suffer the same common-law injury (say, a widespread mass tort), or where large numbers of voters suffer interference with voting rights conferred by law. We conclude that similarly, the informational injury at issue here, directly related to voting, the most basic of political rights, is sufficiently concrete and specific such that the fact that it is widely shared does not deprive Congress of constitutional power to authorize its vindication in the federal courts.

Respondents have also satisfied the remaining two constitutional standing requirements. The harm asserted is "fairly traceable" to the FEC's decision about which respondents complain. Of course, as the FEC points out, it is possible that even had the FEC agreed with respondents' view of the law, it would still have decided in the exercise of its discretion not to require AIPAC to produce the information. But that fact does not destroy Article III "causation," for we cannot know that the FEC would have exercised its prosecutorial discretion in this way. Agencies often have discretion about whether or not to take a particular action. Yet those adversely affected by a discretionary agency decision generally have standing to complain that the agency based its decision upon an improper legal ground. If a reviewing court agrees that the agency misinterpreted the law, it will set aside the agency's action and remand the case — even though the agency (like a new jury after a mistrial) might later, in the exercise of its lawful discretion, reach the same result for a different reason. Thus respondents' "injury in fact" is "fairly traceable" to the FEC's decision not to issue its complaint, even though the FEC might reach the same result exercising its discretionary powers lawfully. For similar reasons, the courts in this case can "redress" respondents' "injury in fact."

Finally, the FEC argues that we should deny respondents standing because this case involves an agency's decision not to undertake an enforcement action — an area generally not subject to judicial review. In *Heckler*, this Court noted that agency enforcement decisions "have traditionally been 'committed to agency discretion,'" and concluded that Congress did not intend to alter that tradition in enacting the APA. *Heckler*, 470 U.S. 821, 832. We deal here with a statute that explicitly indicates the contrary.

In sum, respondents, as voters, have satisfied both prudential and constitutional standing requirements. They may bring this petition for a declaration that the FEC's dismissal of their complaint was unlawful. *See* 2 U.S.C. § 437g(8)(A). . . .

For these reasons, the decision of the Court of Appeals is vacated, and the case is remanded for further proceedings consistent with this opinion.

It is so ordered.

JUSTICE SCALIA, with whom JUSTICE O'CONNOR and JUSTICE THOMAS join, dissenting.

The provision of law at issue in this case is an extraordinary one, conferring upon a private person the ability to bring an Executive agency into court to compel its enforcement of the law against a third party. Despite its liberality, the Administrative Procedure Act does not allow such suits, since enforcement action is traditionally deemed "committed to agency discretion by law." 5 U.S.C. § 701(a)(2); *Heckler v. Chaney*, 470 U.S. 821, 827-835 (1985). If provisions such as the present one were commonplace, the role of the Executive Branch in our system of separated and equilibrated powers would be greatly reduced, and that of the Judiciary greatly expanded. . . .

In *Richardson*, we dismissed for lack of standing a suit whose "aggrievement" was precisely the "aggrievement" respondents assert here: the Government's unlawful refusal to place information within the public domain. The only difference, in fact, is that the aggrievement there was more direct, since the Government already had the information within its possession, whereas here the respondents seek enforcement action that will bring information within the Government's possession and *then* require the information to be made public. The plaintiff in *Richardson* challenged the Government's failure to disclose the expenditures of the Central Intelligence Agency (CIA), in alleged violation of the constitutional requirement, Art. I, § 9, cl. 7, that "a regular Statement and

Account of the Receipts and Expenditures of all public Money shall be published from time to time." We held that such a claim was a nonjusticiable "generalized grievance" because "the impact on [plaintiff] is plainly undifferentiated and common to all members of the public."

It was alleged in *Richardson* that the Government had denied a right conferred by the Constitution, whereas respondents here assert a right conferred by statute — but of course "there is absolutely no basis for making the Article III inquiry turn on the source of the asserted right." The Court today distinguishes *Richardson* on a different basis — a basis that reduces it from a landmark constitutional holding to a curio. According to the Court, "*Richardson* focused upon taxpayer standing, . . . not voter standing." In addition to being a silly distinction, given the weighty governmental purpose underlying the "generalized grievance" prohibition — *viz.*, to avoid "something in the nature of an Athenian democracy or a New England town meeting to oversee the conduct of the National Government by means of lawsuits in federal courts" — this is also a distinction that the Court in *Richardson* went out of its way explicitly to eliminate. It is true enough that the narrow question presented in *Richardson* was "[w]hether a federal taxpayer has standing." But the *Richardson* Court did not hold only, as the Court today suggests, that the plaintiff failed to qualify for the exception to the rule of no taxpayer standing established by the "logical nexus" test of *Flast v. Cohen*, 392 U.S. 83 (1968). The plaintiff's complaint in Richardson had also alleged that he was "'a member of the electorate,'" and he asserted injury in that capacity as well. The *Richardson* opinion treated that as fairly included within the taxpayer-standing question, or at least as plainly indistinguishable from it:

> "The respondent's claim is that without detailed information on CIA expenditures — and hence its activities — he cannot intelligently follow the actions of Congress or the Executive, *nor can he properly fulfill his obligations as a member of the electorate in voting for candidates seeking national office.*
> "*This is surely the kind of a generalized grievance described in both Frothingham and Flast* since the impact on him is plainly undifferentiated and common to all members of the public." (Emphasis added.)

If *Richardson* left voter-standing unaffected, one must marvel at the unaccustomed ineptitude of the American Civil Liberties Union Foundation, which litigated *Richardson*, in not immediately refiling with an explicit voter-standing allegation. Fairly read, and applying a fair understanding of its important purposes, *Richardson* is indistinguishable from the present case.

The Court's opinion asserts that our language disapproving generalized grievances "invariably appears in cases where the harm at issue is not only widely shared, but is also of an abstract and indefinite nature." "Often," the Court says, "the fact that an interest is abstract and the fact that it is widely shared go hand in hand. But their association is not invariable, and where a harm is concrete, though widely shared, the Court has found 'injury in fact.'" If that is so — if concrete generalized grievances (like concrete particularized grievances) are OK, and abstract generalized grievances (like abstract particularized grievances) are bad — one must wonder why we ever *developed* the superfluous distinction between generalized and particularized grievances at all. But of course the Court is wrong to think that generalized grievances have only concerned us when they are abstract. One need go no further than *Richardson* to prove that — unless the Court believes that deprivation of information is an abstract injury, in which event this case could be disposed of on that much broader ground.

What is noticeably lacking in the Court's discussion of our generalized-grievance jurisprudence is all reference to two words that have figured in it prominently: "particularized" and "undifferentiated." "Particularized" means that "the injury must affect the plaintiff in a personal and individual way." If the effect is "undifferentiated and common to all members of the public," the plaintiff has a "generalized grievance" that must be pursued by political rather than judicial means. These terms explain why it is a gross oversimplification to reduce the concept of a generalized grievance to nothing more than "the fact that [the grievance] is widely shared," thereby enabling the concept to be dismissed as a standing principle by such examples as "large numbers of individuals suffer[ing] the same common-law injury (say, a widespread mass tort), or . . . large numbers of voters suffer[ing] interference with voting rights conferred by law." The exemplified injuries are widely shared, to be sure, but each individual suffers a particularized and differentiated harm. One tort victim suffers a burnt leg, another a burnt arm — or even if both suffer burnt arms they are *different* arms. One voter suffers the deprivation of his franchise, another the deprivation of *hers*. With the generalized grievance, on the other hand, the injury or deprivation is not only widely shared but it is *undifferentiated*. The harm caused to Mr. Richardson by the alleged disregard of the State-ment-of-Accounts Clause was precisely the same as the harm caused to everyone else: unavailability of a description of CIA expenditures. Just as the (more indirect) harm caused to Mr. Akins by the allegedly unlawful failure to enforce FECA is precisely the same as the harm caused to everyone else: unavailability of a description of AIPAC's activities.

The Constitution's line of demarcation between the Executive power and the judicial power presupposes a common understanding of the type of interest needed to sustain a "case or controversy" against the Executive in the courts. A system in which the citizenry at large could sue to compel Executive compliance with the law would be a system in which the courts, rather than the President, are given the primary responsibility to "take Care that the Laws be faithfully executed," Art. II, § 3. We do not have such a system because the common understanding of the interest necessary to sustain suit has included the requirement, affirmed in *Richardson,* that the complained-of injury be particularized and differentiated, rather than common to all the electorate. When the Executive can be directed by the courts, at the instance of any voter, to remedy a deprivation which affects the entire electorate in precisely the same way — and particularly when that deprivation (here, the unavailability of information) is one inseverable part of a larger enforcement scheme — there has occurred a shift of political responsibility to a branch designed not to protect the public at large but to protect individual rights. "To permit Congress to convert the undifferentiated public interest in executive officers' compliance with the law into an 'individual right' vindicable in the courts is to permit Congress to transfer from the President to the courts the Chief Executive's most important constitutional duty. . . ." If today's decision is correct, it is within the power of Congress to authorize any interested person to manage (through the courts) the Executive's enforcement of any law that includes a requirement for the filing and public availability of a piece of paper. This is not the system we have had, and is not the system we should desire. . . .

Because this statute should not be interpreted to confer upon the entire electorate the power to invoke judicial direction of prosecutions, and because if it is so interpreted the statute unconstitutionally transfers from the Executive to the courts the responsibility to "take Care that the Laws be faithfully executed," Art. II, § 3, I respectfully dissent.

QUESTIONS

1. What constitutional injury in fact does the Court conclude that the plaintiffs have shown in this case?
2. Does the Court's decision in this case mean that Congress has the power to define a constitutionally sufficient injury in fact by defining a legal requirement and providing a citizen's suit if the requirement is violated?

NOTE ON STANDING IN QUI TAM ACTIONS

In *Defenders of Wildlife*, the Court distinguished the plaintiffs' lack of an informational injury in fact with "the unusual case in which Congress has created a concrete private interest in the outcome of a suit against a private party for the Government's benefit, by providing a cash bounty for the victorious plaintiff." One statutory context in which Congress has provided for such a bounty is an action brought under the False Claims Act ("FCA"), 31 U.S.C. §§ 3729-3733. This is "the most frequently used of a handful of extant laws creating a form of civil action known as *qui tam*." *Vermont Agency of Natural Resources v. United States*, 529 U.S. 765, 768 (2000). In that case, the Court had to decide whether a private claimant had standing under Article III to bring the action claiming that the defendant had violated federal law and seeking to recover a bounty. The defendant claimed that there was no injury in fact because the injury had been suffered by the United States. The Court rejected this argument, concluding that the claimant met the requirements of Article III:

> There is no doubt . . . that as to th[e] . . . bounty he will receive if the suit is successful—a *qui tam* relator [i.e., claimant] has a "concrete private interest in the outcome of [the] suit." But the same might be said of someone who has placed a wager upon the outcome. An interest unrelated to injury in fact is insufficient to give a plaintiff standing. The interest must consist of obtaining compensation for, or preventing, the violation of a legally protected right. A *qui tam* relator has suffered no such invasion—indeed, the "right" he seeks to vindicate does not even fully materialize until the litigation is completed and the relator prevails. This is not to suggest that Congress cannot define new legal rights, which in turn will confer standing to vindicate an injury caused to the claimant. As we have held in another context, however, an interest that is merely a "byproduct" of the suit itself cannot give rise to a cognizable injury in fact for Article III standing purposes. See *Steel Co.*, [523 U.S.] at 107 ("[A] plaintiff cannot achieve standing to litigate a substantive issue by bringing suit for the cost of bringing suit").
>
> We believe, however, that adequate basis for the relator's suit for his bounty is to be found in the doctrine that the assignee of a claim has standing to assert the injury in fact suffered by the assignor. The FCA can reasonably be regarded as

effecting a partial assignment of the Government's damages claim. Although we have never expressly recognized "representational standing" on the part of assignees, we have routinely entertained their suits. We conclude, therefore, that the United States' injury in fact suffices to confer standing on respondent Stevens.

We are confirmed in this conclusion by the long tradition of *qui tam* actions in England and the American Colonies. That history is particularly relevant to the constitutional standing inquiry since, as we have said elsewhere, Article III's restriction of the judicial power to "Cases" and "Controversies" is properly understood to mean "cases and controversies of the sort traditionally amenable to, and resolved by, the judicial process." . . .

We think this history well nigh conclusive with respect to the question before us here: whether *qui tam* actions were "cases and controversies of the sort traditionally amenable to, and resolved by, the judicial process." When combined with the theoretical justification for relator standing discussed earlier, it leaves no room for doubt that a *qui tam* relator under the FCA has Article III standing.

529 U.S. at 772-78.

QUESTIONS

1. In *Defenders of Wildlife*, Justice Scalia claimed that the Constitution barred the litigation of generalized grievances in order to ensure that the executive branch retained its constitutional power to execute the laws:

   > If the concrete injury requirement has the separation-of-powers significance we have always said, the answer must be obvious: To permit Congress to convert the undifferentiated public interest in executive officers' compliance with the law into an "individual right" vindicable in the courts is to permit Congress to transfer from the President to the courts the Chief Executive's most important constitutional duty, to "take Care that the Laws be faithfully executed," Art. II, § 3.

   504 U.S. at 576-77. In *Vermont Agency of Natural Resources*, the Court decided that a private party had standing to bring a *qui tam* action. Does the constitutional permissibility of the *qui tam* action significantly undercut the separation of powers concerns raised in *Defenders of Wildlife*, given that Congress can effectively evade the generalized grievance issue by providing a bounty?

2. Does the Court's decision in this case mean that Congress has the power to define a constitutionally sufficient injury in fact by defining a legal requirement and providing for a *qui tam* action and bounty if the requirement is violated?

NOTE ON REDRESSABILITY

In two recent cases involving claims brought under environmental citizen suits, the Court has considered the redressability part of the "triad of injury in fact, causation, and redressability [that] comprises the core of Article III's case-or-controversy requirement." *Steel Co. v. Citizens for a Better Env't*, 523 U.S. 83, 103-04 (1998). In *Steel Co.* the plaintiff's citizen suit claimed that the defendant had violated the Emergency Planning and Community Right-to-Know Act of 1986 (EPCRA) by failing to prepare required reports on its inventory of hazardous substances and release of toxic substances. After receiving the required notice of the plaintiff's planned citizen suit, the defendant issued the required reports prior to the filing of the complaint. The Court assumed that the plaintiff had demonstrated injury in fact, but held that the plaintiff lacked standing because none of the forms of relief it had sought would redress the injury caused by the defendant's filing of its unlawfully late reports.

The form of relief that the Court analyzed most closely regarding redressability was the plaintiff's request for the civil penalties that the statute imposed for statutory violations. Justice Scalia's opinion for the majority relied upon, this time in the redressability context, the principle that the Constitution does not permit adjudication based on a generalized grievance. Because the civil penalties available under the statute would be paid to the federal government, rather than to the plaintiff, the Court stated that "[i]n requesting them, . . . respondent seeks not remediation of its own injury — reimbursement for the costs it incurred as a result of the late filing — but vindication of the rule of law — the 'undifferentiated public interest' in faithful execution of EPCRA." 523 U.S. at 106.

Although the Court then referred to Justice Stevens's contention in his concurring opinion that the civil penalties provided by the statute are adequate redress because of their deterrent effect, the Court's analysis, *id.* at 106-07, actually rejected only his claim that such penalties are adequate redress because of the "psychic satisfaction" they yield:

> JUSTICE STEVENS thinks it is enough that respondent will be gratified by seeing petitioner punished for its infractions and that the punishment will deter the risk of future harm. If that were so, our holdings in *Linda R.S. v. Richard D.*, and *Simon v. Eastern Ky. Welfare Rights Organization*, are inexplicable. Obviously, such a principle would make the redressability requirement vanish. By the mere bringing of his suit, every plaintiff demonstrates his belief that a favorable judgment will make him happier. But although a suitor may derive great comfort and joy from the fact that the United States Treasury is not cheated, that a wrongdoer gets his just deserts, or that the nation's laws are faithfully enforced, that psychic satisfaction is not an acceptable Article III remedy because it does not redress a cognizable Article III injury. Relief that does not remedy the injury suffered cannot bootstrap a plaintiff into federal court; that is the very essence of the redressability requirement.

The Court returned to the redressability requirement in *Friends of the Earth, Inc., v. Laidlaw Envtl. Services (TOC), Inc.*, 528 U.S. 167 (2000). The factual context of the claim in *Laidlaw* differed significantly from *Steel Co.* because the Court, based on the plaintiffs' proof and the Clean Water Act citizen suit provision, assumed that there was a reasonable threat that future injuries would result from the statutory violations proved by the plaintiffs.

In this context of the threat of future permit violations, the Court concluded, *id.* at 185-86, that civil money penalties payable to the United States provide reasonable deterrence against future violations and accordingly redress injuries that result from violations:

> It can scarcely be doubted that, for a plaintiff who is injured or faces the threat of future injury due to illegal conduct ongoing at the time of suit, a sanction that

effectively abates that conduct and prevents its recurrence provides a form of redress. Civil penalties can fit that description. To the extent that they encourage defendants to discontinue current violations and deter them from committing future ones, they afford redress to citizen plaintiffs who are injured or threatened with injury as a consequence of ongoing unlawful conduct.

2. Non-Article III Standing

NOTE ON THE LAW OF STATUTORY STANDING BEFORE THE SUPREME COURT DECISION IN DATA PROCESSING

By the middle of the twentieth century, Supreme Court decisions had established that a party has statutory standing to bring a claim in two circumstances. First, a party has a right to bring a claim based on a claimed violation of a statute when the statute provides a legal right to the claimant that the claimant believes has been violated. This principle was defined by several decisions, the most prominent of which were *Edward Hines Yellow Pine Trustees v. United States*, 263 U.S. 143, 148 (1923), the *Chicago Junction Case*, 264 U.S. 258 (1924), and *Alabama Power Co. v. Ickes*, 302 U.S. 464 (1938). Second, a party may bring a claim of a statutory violation when Congress has expressly granted a right of review to a party aggrieved by the claimed statutory violation. This principle was defined by two decisions: *ICC v. Oregon-Washington R.R.*, 288 U.S. 14 (1933), and the better known *FCC v. Sanders Bros. Radio Station*, 309 U.S. 470 (1940). Establishing statutory standing based on a legal right or legal interest will often involve inferential reasoning about the interests protected by a statute, while a party's ability to assert a statutory claim as an aggrieved party will involve the application of an express statutory provision providing a party aggrieved by an agency action with a right of action in court.

The next critical step in the development of the modern law of statutory standing was the enactment in 1946 of the APA. *See* Administrative Procedure Act, ch. 324, 60 Stat. 237 (1946) (codified as amended at 5 U.S.C. §§ 551 et seq. (2012)). In that statute, Congress addressed the issue of a person's statutory standing by including the following language: "A person suffering legal wrong because of agency action, or adversely affected or aggrieved by agency action within the meaning of a relevant statute, is entitled to judicial review thereof. . . ." 5 U.S.C. § 702. Although the language of the text is hardly perfect, it does make it clear by the use of the disjunctive "or" that the "entitle[ment] to judicial review" may be grounded in either "suffering legal wrong" or being "adversely affected or aggrieved by agency action within the meaning of a relevant statute." The last phrase is unfortunately obscure, and would have been clearer if it had read, "adversely affected or aggrieved by agency action if a relevant statute grants review to a party in such a case."

The text of section 702 accordingly provides for statutory standing to challenge an agency's action for either of the two reasons that had been recognized by the Supreme Court for such standing: a party suffering legal injury or a party "aggrieved" by an agency action and granted statutory standing to sue by another statute. The legislative history of the APA confirms this understanding of the intent of those who developed the statute:

> The Attorney General advised the Senate Committee on the Judiciary of his understanding that [the first sentence of APA § 702] was a restatement of existing law. More specifically he indicated his understanding that [the first sentence of APA § 702] preserved the rules developed by the courts in such cases as *Alabama Power . . . Chicago Junction . . .* and *Sanders Bros. . . .* This construction of [the first sentence of APA § 702] was not questioned or contradicted in the legislative history.

Attorney General's Manual on the Administrative Procedure Act 96 (1947).

In sum, the APA simply codified the understanding of statutory standing that had emerged by the first half of the twentieth century. That understanding was that a party had statutory standing to sue when a statute gave the party a legal interest that the government had injured or when the text of a statute gave any aggrieved party the right to sue. Section 702 had not therefore itself granted statutory standing, but looked to statutory standing being determined by a statute either creating a legal interest or granting standing expressly to any aggrieved party.

This summary provides context for understanding *Association of Data Processing Service Organizations, Inc. v. Camp,* 397 U.S. 150 (1970), the case that follows. When the court of appeals decided the case, its reasoning reflected the bases for statutory standing summarized in this note:

> '(A) plaintiff may challenge alleged illegal competition when as complainant it pursues (1) a legal interest by reason of public charter or contract, . . . (2) a legal interest by reason of statutory protection, . . . or (3) a "public interest" in which Congress has recognized the need for review of administrative action and plaintiff is significantly involved to have standing to represent the public. . . . '

Id. at 152-53 (quoting 406 F.2d, at 842-43) (footnote omitted).

The first rationale of the court of appeals did not relate to statutory standing, but instead reflected a common-law rationale. The second rationale required that a plaintiff had standing to sue under a statute only when the statute gave the party a legal interest. The third rationale was based on Congress allowing broad review by granting any aggrieved party the right to bring an action.

In its review of this court of appeals decision, the Supreme Court defined a new test for determining whether a party has statutory standing.

ADPSO v. CAMP ("DATA PROCESSING")
397 U.S. 150 (1970)

Mr. Justice Douglas delivered the opinion of the Court.

Petitioners sell data processing services to businesses generally. In this suit they seek to challenge a ruling by respondent Comptroller of the Currency that, as an incident to their banking services, national banks, including respondent American National Bank & Trust Company, may make data processing services available to other banks and to bank customers. The District Court dismissed the complaint for lack of standing of petitioners to bring the suit. The Court of Appeals affirmed. The case is here on a petition for writ of certiorari which we granted.

Generalizations about standing to sue are largely worthless as such. One generalization is, however, necessary and that is that the question of standing in the federal courts is to be considered in the framework of Article III which restricts judicial power to "cases" and "controversies." As we recently stated in *Flast v. Cohen*, 392 U.S. 83, 101, "In terms of Article III limitations on federal court jurisdiction, the question of standing is related only to whether the dispute sought to be adjudicated will be presented in an adversary context and in a form historically viewed as capable of judicial resolution." *Flast* was a *taxpayer's* suit. The present is a *competitor's* suit. And while the two have the same Article III starting point, they do not necessarily track one another.

The first question is whether the plaintiff alleges that the challenged action has caused him injury in fact, economic or otherwise. There can be no doubt but that petitioners have satisfied this test. The petitioners not only allege that competition by national banks in the business of providing data processing services might entail some future loss of profits for the petitioners, they also allege that respondent American National Bank & Trust Company was performing or preparing to perform such services for two customers for whom petitioner Data Systems, Inc., had previously agreed or negotiated to perform such services. The petitioners' suit was brought not only against the American National Bank & Trust Company, but also against the Comptroller of the Currency. The Comptroller was alleged to have caused petitioners injury in fact by his 1966 ruling which stated:

> "Incidental to its banking services, a national bank may make available its data processing equipment or perform data processing services on such equipment for other banks and bank customers." Comptroller's Manual for National Banks ¶ 3500 (October 15, 1966).

The Court of Appeals viewed the matter differently, stating:

> "[A] plaintiff may challenge alleged illegal competition when as complainant it pursues(1) a legal interest by reason of public charter or contract, . . . (2) a legal interest by reason of statutory protection, . . . or (3) a 'public interest' in which Congress has recognized the need for review of administrative action and plaintiff is significantly involved to have standing to represent the public. . . ." 406 F.2d, at 842-843.[1]

Those tests were based on prior decisions of this Court, such as *Tennessee Power Co. v. TVA*, 306 U.S. 118, where private power companies sought to enjoin TVA from operating, claiming that the statutory plan under which it was created was unconstitutional. The Court denied the competitors' standing, holding that they did not have that status "unless the right invaded is a legal right, — one of property, one arising out of contract, one protected against tortious invasion, or one founded on a statute which confers a privilege." *Id.*, at 137-138.

---

1. The first two tests applied by the Court of Appeals required a showing of a "legal interest." But the existence or non-existence of a "legal interest" is a matter quite distinct from the problem of standing. The third test mentioned by the Court of Appeals, which rests on an explicit provision in a regulatory statute conferring standing and is commonly referred to in terms of allowing suits by "private attorneys general," is inapplicable to the present case. *See FCC v. Sanders Bros. Radio Station*, 309 U.S. 470.

The "legal interest" test goes to the merits. The question of standing is different. It concerns, apart from the "case" or "controversy" test, the question whether the interest sought to be protected by the complainant is arguably within the zone of interests to be protected or regulated by the statute or constitutional guarantee in question. Thus the Administrative Procedure Act grants standing to a person "aggrieved by agency action within the meaning of a relevant statute." 5 U.S.C. § 702 (1964 ed., Supp. IV). That interest, at times, may reflect "aesthetic, conservational, and recreational" as well as economic values. *Scenic Hudson Preservation Conf. v. FPC*, 354 F.2d 608, 616; *Office of Communication of United Church of Christ v. FCC*, 359 F.2d 994, 1000-1006. A person or a family may have a spiritual stake in First Amendment values sufficient to give standing to raise issues concerning the Establishment Clause and the Free Exercise Clause. *Abington School District v. Schempp*, 374 U.S. 203. We mention these non-economic values to emphasize that standing may stem from them as well as from the economic injury on which petitioners rely here. Certainly he who is "likely to be financially" injured, *FCC v. Sanders Bros. Radio Station*, 309 U.S. 470, 477, may be a reliable private attorney general to litigate the issues of the public interest in the present case.

Apart from Article III jurisdictional questions, problems of standing, as resolved by this Court for its own governance, have involved a "rule of self-restraint." *Barrows v. Jackson*, 346 U.S. 249, 255. Congress can, of course, resolve the question one way or another, save as the requirements of Article III dictate otherwise. *Muskrat v. United States*, 219 U.S. 346.

Where statutes are concerned, the trend is toward enlargement of the class of people who may protest administrative action. The whole drive for enlarging the category of aggrieved "persons" is symptomatic of that trend. In a closely analogous case we held that an existing entrepreneur had standing to challenge the legality of the entrance of a newcomer into the business, because the established business was allegedly protected by a valid city ordinance that protected it from unlawful competition. *Chicago v. Atchison, T. & S. F. R. Co.*, 357 U.S. 77, 83-84. In that tradition was *Hardin v. Kentucky Utilities Co.*, 390 U.S. 1, which involved a section of the TVA Act designed primarily to protect, through area limitations, private utilities against TVA competition. We held that no explicit statutory provision was necessary to confer standing, since the private utility bringing suit was within the class of persons that the statutory provision was designed to protect.

It is argued that the *Chicago* case and the *Hardin* case are relevant here because of §4 of the Bank Service Corporation Act of 1962, 76 Stat. 1132, 12 U.S.C. §1864, which provides:

> "No bank service corporation may engage in any activity other than the performance of bank services for banks."

The Court of Appeals for the First Circuit held in *Arnold Tours, Inc. v. Camp*, 408 F.2d 1147, 1153, that by reason of §4 a data processing company has standing to contest the legality of a national bank performing data processing services for other banks and bank customers:

> "Section 4 had a broader purpose than regulating only the service corporations. It was also a response to the fears expressed by a few senators, that without such a

prohibition, the bill would have enabled "banks to engage in a nonbanking activity," S. Rep. No. 2105, [87th Cong., 2d Sess., 7-12] (Supplemental views of Senators Proxmire, Douglas, and Neuberger), and thus constitute "a serious exception to the accepted public policy which strictly limits banks to banking." (Supplemental views of Senators Muskie and Clark). We think Congress has provided the sufficient statutory aid to standing even though the competition may not be the precise kind Congress legislated against."

We do not put the issue in those words, for they implicate the merits. We do think, however, that § 4 arguably brings a competitor within the zone of interests protected by it. . . .

We read § 701 (a) as sympathetic to the issue presented in this case. As stated in the House Report:

"The statutes of Congress are not merely advisory when they relate to administrative agencies, any more than in other cases. To preclude judicial review under this bill a statute, if not specific in withholding such review, must upon its face give clear and convincing evidence of an intent to withhold it. The mere failure to provide specially by statute for judicial review is certainly no evidence of intent to withhold review." H. R. Rep. No. 1980, 79th Cong., 2d Sess., 41.

There is no presumption against judicial review and in favor of administrative absolutism (*see Abbott Laboratories v. Gardner*, 387 U.S. 136, 140), unless that purpose is fairly discernible in the statutory scheme. We find no evidence that Congress in either the Bank Service Corporation Act or the National Bank Act sought to preclude judicial review of administrative rulings by the Comptroller as to the legitimate scope of activities available to national banks under those statutes. Both Acts are clearly "relevant" statutes within the meaning of § 702. The Acts do not in terms protect a specified group. But their general policy is apparent; and those whose interests are directly affected by a broad or narrow interpretation of the Acts are easily identifiable. It is clear that petitioners, as competitors of national banks which are engaging in data processing services, are within that class of "aggrieved" persons who, under § 702, are entitled to judicial review of "agency action."

Whether anything in the Bank Service Corporation Act or the National Bank Act gives petitioners a "legal interest" that protects them against violations of those Acts, and whether the actions of respondents did in fact violate either of those Acts, are questions which go to the merits and remain to be decided below.

We hold that petitioners have standing to sue and that the case should be remanded for a hearing on the merits. *Reversed and remanded.*

QUESTIONS

1. Is Justice Douglas convincing in his rejection in footnote 1 of the applicability of the two types of statutory standing recognized by the Supreme Court prior to the enactment of the APA, which was intended to codify the pre-existing law? Regarding the legal interest basis for statutory standing, Justice Douglas's position that the existence of a legal interest is *not* a proper basis for recognizing a party's statutory standing to sue is simply incorrect. Regarding the type of statutory standing that the Court had recognized

prior to the APA in *ICC v. Oregon-Washington R.R., 288 U.S. 14* (1933), and *FCC v. Sanders Bros. Radio Station*, 309 U.S. 470 (1940) (mentioned in the Note that precedes *Data Processing, supra* p. 673), Justice Douglas stated in footnote 1 that such standing, which "rests on an explicit provision in a regulatory statute conferring standing and is commonly referred to in terms of allowing suits by 'private attorneys general,' is inapplicable to the present case." Justice Douglas provided no explanation for this "inapplicab[ility]." Presumably, the explanation was that the statute governing the activities of the Comptroller did not include a provision granting a right to judicial review for "any aggrieved party."

2. Having rejected the long-standing, conventional tests for statutory standing that had been applied by the court of appeals, Justice Douglas fashioned a new "arguably within the zone of interests" test. Where does this test come from? Is the test entirely of Justice Douglas's own making?

3. Justice Douglas's conclusion that "the Administrative Procedure Act grants standing to a person 'aggrieved by agency action within the meaning of a relevant statute'" is contrary to the position of the Attorney General's Manual, *supra* p. 674. Consider whether this is a defensible interpretation of § 702 of the APA. The key first sentence of § 702 provides that "[a] person suffering legal wrong because of agency action, or adversely affected or aggrieved by agency action within the meaning of a relevant statute, is entitled to judicial review thereof." By rejecting the legal interest test and establishing an "arguably within the zone of interests" test, is the Court giving effect to the statutory text? Does the text mention a "zone of interests"? To the extent that a party that is "arguably within the zone of interests to be protected or regulated by the statute or constitutional guarantee in question" now has statutory standing, is there any legal effect for the part of § 702 that recognizes statutory standing for a party who "suffer[s] legal wrong because of agency action," or is this part of the statute now superfluous?

4. What does "arguably" mean in this context? "Zone"?

5. Is the scope of standing defined by the zone of interests test broader or narrower than the scope of standing defined by the 1981 MSAPA § 5-106?

NOTE ON AGENCY CAPTURE AND THE AVAILABILITY OF JUDICIAL REVIEW

The Court's decision in the *Data Processing* case identifying an APA "zone of interests" test looks inconsistent with the earlier Supreme Court decisions that Congress had apparently codified when it enacted the statute. The novel nature of the Court's analysis is even more apparent if you consider the court of appeals decision in the *Data Processing* case. In its decision, the Eighth Circuit had applied the theory of the earlier Supreme Court decisions, and had determined that the plaintiff had no legal interest and could not rely on a congressional grant of *Sanders Brothers* standing in the organic statute. What then explains the Court's new approach to non-Article III standing under the APA?

Professor Thomas W. Merrill has suggested that the Court's decision to allow broader standing under the APA reflected acceptance of "capture theory" by the judiciary. *See* Thomas W. Merrill, *Capture Theory and the Courts: 1967-1983*, Chi.-Kent L. Rev. 1039, 1076 (1997). Professor Merrill argues that, during the

1967-1983 period, courts came to believe that agencies had been captured by the industries and businesses that they regulated and that the judiciary needed to exert greater control over agencies in order to ensure adequate protection of the public interest. See *id.* at 1067 ("There is little question that the period from roughly 1967 to 1983 was characterized by widespread disillusionment with agencies, focusing in particular on the problem of capture").

Although Justice Douglas made no reference to capture theory in the *Data Processing* decision, strong support for Professor Merrill's argument can be found in a later opinion of Justice Douglas. In *Sierra Club v. Morton*, 405 U.S. 727 (1972), the Supreme Court concluded that the Sierra Club, an organization dedicated to the preservation of the natural environment, did not have standing under Article III to challenge an agency decision permitting the development of the Mineral King area adjoining Sequoia National Park. The Court accepted that the Sierra Club had identified a cognizable injury-in-fact, when it alleged that the government-permitted development "would destroy or otherwise adversely affect the scenery, natural and historic objects and wildlife of the park and would impair the enjoyment of the park for future generations." It concluded, however, that standing was not present because "[t]he alleged injury will be felt directly only by those who use Mineral King and Sequoia National Park, and for whom the aesthetic and recreational values of the area will be lessened by the highway and ski resort. The Sierra Club failed to allege that it or its members would be affected in any of their activities or pastimes by the Disney development." Having failed to win Supreme Court approval of a broadened approach to *constitutional* standing for public interest groups two years after *Data Processing,* Justice Douglas made explicit reference to the need for judicial review to police the effects of agency capture:

> The Solicitor General . . . takes a wholly different approach. He considers the problem in terms of "government by the Judiciary." With all respect, the problem is to make certain that the inanimate objects, which are the very core of America's beauty, have spokesmen before they are destroyed. It is, of course, true that most of them are under the control of a federal or state agency. The standards given those agencies are usually expressed in terms of the "public interest." Yet "public interest" has so many differing shades of meaning as to be quite meaningless on the environmental front. . . .
>
> Yet the pressures on agencies for favorable action one way or the other are enormous. The suggestion that Congress can stop action which is undesirable is true in theory; yet even Congress is too remote to give meaningful direction and its machinery is too ponderous to use very often. The federal agencies of which I speak are not venal or corrupt. But they are notoriously under the control of powerful interests who manipulate them through advisory committees, or friendly working relations, or who have that natural affinity with the agency which in time develops between the regulator and the regulated. As early as 1894, Attorney General Olney predicted that regulatory agencies might become "industry-minded," as illustrated by his forecast concerning the Interstate Commerce Commission:
>
> "The Commission . . . is, or can be made, of great use to the railroads. It satisfies the popular clamor for a government supervision of railroads, at the same time that that supervision is almost entirely nominal. Further, the older such a Commission gets to be, the more inclined it will be found to take the business and railroad view of things." M. Josephson, The Politicos 526 (1938).
>
> Years later a court of appeals observed, "the recurring question which has plagued public regulation of industry (is) whether the regulatory agency is unduly

oriented toward the interests of the industry it is designed to regulate, rather than the public interest it is designed to protect." *Moss v. CAB*, 430 F.2d 891, 893 (D.C. Cir.). . . . *But see* Jaffe, The Federal Regulatory Agencies In Perspective: Administrative Limitations In A Political Setting, 11 B.C. Ind. & Com. L. Rev. 565 (1970) (labels "industry-mindedness" as "devil" theory).

The Forest Service — one of the federal agencies behind the scheme to despoil Mineral King — has been notorious for its alignment with lumber companies, although its mandate from Congress directs it to consider the various aspects of multiple use in its supervision of the national forests.

The voice of the inanimate object, therefore, should not be stilled. That does not mean that the judiciary takes over the managerial functions from the federal agency. It merely means that before these priceless bits of Americana (such as a valley, an alpine meadow, a river, or a lake) are forever lost or are so transformed as to be reduced to the eventual rubble of our urban environment, the voice of the existing beneficiaries of these environmental wonders should be heard.

Perhaps they will not win. Perhaps the bulldozers of "progress" will plow under all the aesthetic wonders of this beautiful land. That is not the present question. The sole question is, who has standing to be heard?

405 U.S. at 745-51 (Douglas, J., dissenting). Justice Douglas supported his capture argument with the following footnote:

The federal budget annually includes about $75 million for underwriting about 1,500 advisory committees attached to various regulatory agencies. These groups are almost exclusively composed of industry representatives appointed by the President or by Cabinet members. Although public members may be on these committees, they are rarely asked to serve. Senator Lee Metcalf warns: "Industry advisory committees exist inside most important federal agencies, and even have offices in some. Legally, their function is purely as kibitzer, but in practice many have become internal lobbies — printing industry handouts in the Government Printing Office with taxpayers' money, and even influencing policies. Industry committees perform the dual function of stopping government from finding out about corporations while at the same time helping corporations get inside information about what government is doing. Sometimes, the same company that sits on an advisory council that obstructs or turns down a government questionnaire is precisely the company which is withholding information the government needs in order to enforce a law." Metcalf, The Vested Oracles; How Industry Regulates Government, 3 The Washington Monthly, July 1971, p. 45. . . .

The web spun about administrative agencies by industry representatives does not depend, of course, solely upon advisory committees for effectiveness. See Elman, Administrative Reform of the Federal Trade Commission, 59 Geo. L.J. 777, 788 (1971); Johnson, A New Fidelity to the Regulatory Ideal, 59 Geo. L.J. 869, 874, 906 (1971); R. Berkman & K. Viscusi, Damming The West, The Ralph Nader Study Group Report On The Bureau of Reclamation 155 (1971); R. Fellmeth, The Interstate Commerce Omission, The Ralph Nader Study Group Report on the Interstate Commerce Commission and Transportation 15-39 and *passim* (1970); J. Turner, The Chemical Feast, The Ralph Nader Study Group Report on Food Protection and the Food and Drug Administration *passim* (1970); Massel, The Regulatory Process, 26 Law & Contemp. Prob. 181, 189 (1961); J. Landis, Report on Regulatory Agencies to the President-Elect 13, 69 (1960).

405 U.S. at 746-47 n.6 (Douglas, J., dissenting).

QUESTIONS

1. When standing is present, is judicial review likely to be effective in protecting against the effects of capture and ensuring that agencies act in the public interest? Professor Merrill argues that the period since 1983 has been marked by the emergence of public choice theory, see 72 Chi.-Kent L. Rev. at 1068-73, which has given rise to "deep skepticism about all government institutions, combined with very little sense that judges have any tools that allow them to do something about it." *Id.* at 1073-74.

2. If courts wished to develop other legal doctrines in an effort to control agency capture, what might those doctrines be? More stringent standards of judicial review, including a limitation on the application of *Chevron* deference? *See* Einer R. Elhauge, *Does Interest Group Theory Justify More Intrusive Judicial Review*, 101 Yale L.J. 31, 34 (1991) ("interest group theory does not establish (as it must to justify more intrusive judicial review) that the litigation process is, overall, less defective than the political process"). *Cf. Elizabeth Blackwell Health Center for Women v. Knoll*, 61 F.3d 170, 195-96 (3d Cir. 1995) (Nygaard, J., dissenting) ("The argument [of *Chevron* deference] is that agencies, which at least in theory are indirectly responsive to majoritarian pressure, are more legitimate policy makers than Article III courts. . . . It is no secret, however, that what is true in theory may be less so in practice; because of superior expertise and 'agency capture,' actual agency action may be less majoritarian than we might hope. *See* Sanford N. Caust-Ellenbogen, *Blank Checks: Restoring the Balance of Powers in the Post-*Chevron *Era*, 32 B.C. L. Rev. 757, 814 (1991). Even so, it is reasonable in such circumstances to favor the policy choices of agency heads rather than judges"). A more inclusive definition of persons "arguably within the zone of interests"? *Compare Federation for Am. Immigration v. Reno*, 93 F.3d 897, 902 (D.C. Cir. 1996) with *id.* at 906 n.4 (Rogers, J., dissenting). *See also Wood v. General Motors Corp.*, 865 F.2d 395, 418-19 (1st Cir. 1988) (rejecting capture theory as a basis for construing a statute in the absence of positive evidence in legislative history).

AIR COURIER CONFERENCE v. POSTAL WORKERS
498 U.S. 517 (1990)

CHIEF JUSTICE REHNQUIST delivered the opinion of the Court.

This case requires us to decide whether postal employees are within the "zone of interests" of the group of statutes known as the Private Express Statutes (PES), so that they may challenge the action of the United States Postal Service in suspending the operation of the PES with respect to a practice of private courier services called "international remailing." We hold that they are not.

Since its establishment, the United States Postal Service has exercised a monopoly over the carriage of letters in and from the United States. The postal monopoly is codified in the PES, 18 U.S.C. §§ 1693-1699 and 39 U.S.C. §§ 601-606. The monopoly was created by Congress as a revenue protection measure for the Postal Service to enable it to fulfill its mission. It prevents private competitors from offering service on low-cost routes at prices below those of the Postal Service, while leaving the Service with high-cost routes and insufficient means to fulfill its mandate of providing uniform rates and service to patrons in all areas, including those that are remote or less populated.

A provision of the PES allows the Postal Service to "suspend [the PES restrictions] upon any mail route where the public interest requires the suspension." 39 U.S.C. § 601(b). In 1979, the Postal Service suspended the PES restrictions for "extremely urgent letters," thereby allowing overnight delivery of letters by private courier services. 39 CFR § 320.6(1990); 44 Fed. Reg. 61178(1979). Private courier services, including members of petitioner-intervenor Air Courier Conference of America, relied on that suspension to engage in a practice called "international remailing." This entails bypassing the Postal Service and using private courier systems to deposit with foreign postal systems letters destined for foreign addresses. Believing this international remailing was a misuse of the urgent-letter suspension, the Postal Service issued a proposed modification and clarification of its regulation in order to make clear that the suspension for extremely urgent letters did not cover this practice. 50 Fed. Reg. 41462 (1985). The comments received in response to the proposed rule were overwhelmingly negative and focused on the perceived benefits of international remailing: Lower cost, faster delivery, greater reliability, and enhanced ability of United States companies to remain competitive in the international market. Because of the vigorous opposition to the proposed rule, the Postal Service agreed to reconsider its position and instituted a rulemaking "to remove the cloud" over the validity of the international remailing services. 51 Fed. Reg. 9852, 9853 (1986). After receiving additional comments and holding a public meeting on the subject, on June 17, 1986, the Postal Service issued a proposal to suspend operation of the PES for international remailing. *Id.*, at 21929-21932. Additional comments were received, and after consideration of the record it had compiled, the Postal Service issued a final rule suspending the operation of the PES with respect to international remailing. *Id.*, at 29637.

Respondents, the American Postal Workers Union, AFL-CIO, and the National Association of Letter Carriers, AFL-CIO (Unions), sued in the United States District Court for the District of Columbia, challenging the international remailing regulation pursuant to the judicial review provisions of the Administrative Procedure Act (APA), 5 U.S.C. § 702. They claimed that the rulemaking record was inadequate to support a finding that the suspension of the PES for international remailing was in the public interest. Petitioner Air Courier Conference of America (ACCA) intervened. On December 20, 1988, the District Court granted summary judgment in favor of the Postal Service and ACCA. The Unions appealed to the Court of Appeals for the District of Columbia Circuit, and that court vacated the grant of summary judgment. It held that the Unions satisfied the zone-of-interests requirement for APA review under *Clarke v. Securities Industry Assn.*, 479 U.S. 388 (1987), and that the Postal Service's regulation was arbitrary and capricious because it relied on too narrow an interpretation of "the public interest." In determining that the Unions' interest in employment opportunities was protected by the PES, the Court of Appeals noted that the PES were reenacted as part of the Postal Reorganization Act (PRA), Pub. L. 91-375, 84 Stat. 719, codified at 39 U.S.C. § 101 *et seq.* The Court of Appeals found that a "key impetus" and "principal purpose" of the PRA was "to implement various labor reforms that would improve pay, working conditions and labor-management relations for postal employees." Reasoning that "[t]he Unions' asserted interest is embraced directly by the labor reform provisions of the PRA," and that "[t]he PES constitute the linchpin in a statutory scheme concerned with maintaining an effective, financially viable Postal Service," the court concluded that "[t]he interplay between the PES and the entire PRA persuades us that there is an 'arguable' or 'plausible' relationship between the purposes of the PES and the interests of the Union[s]." The Court of Appeals also held that "the revenue protective purposes of the PES, standing alone, plausibly relate to the Unions' interest in preventing the reduction of employment opportunities," since "postal workers benefit from the PES's function in ensuring a sufficient revenue base" for the Postal Service's activities.

Addressing the merits of the Unions' challenge to the suspension order, the Court of Appeals held that it was arbitrary and capricious because the Postal Service had applied § 601(b)'s public interest test too narrowly by considering only the benefits of the international remail rule to the small segment of the Postal Service's consumer base that engages in international commerce. We granted certiorari and we now reverse.

The United States Postal Service, nominally a respondent, argues along with ACCA that the Unions do not have standing to challenge the Postal Service's suspension of the PES for international remailing. . . .

To establish standing to sue under the APA, respondents must establish that they have suffered a legal wrong because of the challenged agency action, or are adversely affected or "aggrieved by agency action within the meaning of a relevant statute." 5 U.S.C. § 702. Once they have shown that they are adversely affected, i.e., have suffered an "injury in fact," *see Allen v. Wright*, 468 U.S. 737, 751 (1984), the Unions must show that they are within the zone of interests sought to be protected through the PES. *Lujan v. National Wildlife Federation*, 497 U.S. 871 (1990); *Clarke v. Securities Industry Assn.*, 479 U.S. 388 (1987); *Association of Data Processing Service Organizations, Inc. v. Camp*, 397 U.S. 150 (1970). Specifically, "the plaintiff must establish that the injury he complains of (his aggrievement, or the adverse effect upon him) falls within the 'zone of interests' sought to be protected by the statutory provision whose violation forms the legal basis for his complaint." *Lujan, supra*, at 883 (citing *Clarke, supra*, at 396-397).

The District Court found that the Unions had satisfied the injury-in-fact test because increased competition through international remailing services might have an adverse effect on employment opportunities of postal workers. This finding of injury in fact was not appealed. The question before us, then, is whether the adverse effect on the employment opportunities of postal workers resulting from the suspension is within the zone of interests encompassed by the PES — the statutes which the Unions assert the Postal Service has violated in promulgating the international remailing rule.

The Court of Appeals found that the Unions had standing because "the revenue protective purposes of the PES, standing alone, plausibly relate to the Unions' interest in preventing the reduction of employment opportunities." This view is mistaken, for it conflates the zone-of-interests test with injury in fact. In *Lujan*, this Court gave the following example illustrating how injury in fact does not necessarily mean one is within the zone of interests to be protected by a given statute:

"[T]he failure of an agency to comply with a statutory provision requiring 'on the record' hearings would assuredly have an adverse effect upon the company that has the contract to record and transcribe the agency's proceedings; but since the provision was obviously enacted to protect the interests of the parties to the proceedings and not those of the reporters, that company would not be 'adversely affected within the meaning' of the statute." 497 U.S., at 883.

We must inquire, then, as to Congress' intent in enacting the PES in order to determine whether postal workers were meant to be within the zone of interests protected by those statutes. The particular language of the statutes provides no support for respondents' assertion that Congress intended to protect jobs with the Postal Service. In fact, the provisions of 18 U.S.C. § 1696(c), allowing private conveyance of letters if done on a one-time basis or without compensation, and 39 U.S.C. § 601(a), allowing letters to be carried out of the mails if certain procedures are followed, indicate that the congressional concern was not with opportunities for postal workers but with the receipt of necessary revenues for the Postal Service.

Nor does the history of this legislation — such as it is — indicate that the PES were intended for the benefit of postal workers. When the first statutes limiting private carriage of letters on post roads were enacted in 1792, the Post Office offered no pickup or delivery services. *See* C. Scheele, A Short History of the Mail Service 66, 91 (1970). Statutory authority to employ letter carriers was not enacted until two years later and was largely ignored until the late 1820's. *Id.*, at 66. The 1792 restrictions on private carriage protected the Government's capital investment in the post roads, not the jobs of as yet virtually nonexistent postal employees. In 1825 and 1827, Acts were passed prohibiting the private carriage of letters through the use of stages or other vehicles, packet boats, or other vessels, § 19, ch. 64 of Act of March 3, 1825, 4 Stat. 107, and foot and horse posts, § 3, ch. 61 of Act of March 2, 1827, 4 Stat. 238. Postal employees cannot have been within the zone of interests of either the 1824 or 1827 Acts; those Acts targeted transportation of mail which even then was contracted out to private carriers. See W. Fuller, The American Mail: Enlarger of the Common Life 150 (1972).

Congress' consideration of the 1845 Act was the only occasion on which the postal monopoly was the subject of substantial debate. The 1845 statute, entitled "An Act to reduce the rates of postage, to limit the use and correct the abuse of the franking privilege, and for the prevention of frauds on the revenues of the Post Office Department," 5 Stat. 732, was the result of three circumstances, none of which involved the interests of postal employees. First, the Post Office Department continued to run substantial deficits in spite of high postage rates. H. R. Rep. No. 477, 28th Cong., 1st Sess., 2-3, 5 (1844). Second, high postal rates enabled private expresses to make substantial inroads into the domestic market for delivery of letters and the 1825 and 1827 Acts proved unsuccessful in prosecuting them. Third, inauguration of the "penny post" in England quadrupled use of the mails, and it was thought that a substantial reduction in American postal rates would have the dual virtues of driving private expresses out of business and increasing mail volume of the Post Office. This, in turn, would help reduce the Post Office's deficit.

The legislative history of the sections of the Act limiting private carriage of letters shows a two-fold purpose. First, the Postmaster General and the States most distant from the commercial centers of the Northeast believed that the postal monopoly was necessary to prevent users of faster private expresses from taking advantage of early market intelligence and news of international affairs that had not yet reached the general populace through the slower mails. S. Doc. No. 66, 28th Cong., 2d Sess., 3-4 (1845). Second, it was thought to be the duty of the Government to serve outlying, frontier areas, even if it meant doing so below cost. H. R. Rep. No. 477, *supra*, at 2-3. Thus, the revenue protection provisions were not seen as an end in themselves, nor in any sense as a means of ensuring certain levels of public employment, but rather were seen as the means to achieve national integration and to ensure that all areas of the Nation were equally served by the Postal Service.

The PES enable the Postal Service to fulfill its responsibility to provide service to all communities at a uniform rate by preventing private courier services from competing selectively with the Postal Service on its most profitable routes. If competitors could serve the lower cost segment of the market, leaving the Postal Service to handle the high-cost services, the Service would lose lucrative portions of its business, thereby increasing its average unit cost and requiring higher prices to all users.[5] *See* Report of the President's Commission on Postal Organization, Towards Postal Excellence, 94th Cong., 2d Sess., 129 (Comm. Print 1968). The postal monopoly, therefore, exists to ensure that postal services will be provided to the citizenry at large, and not to secure employment for postal workers.

The Unions' claim on the merits is that the Postal Service has failed to comply with the mandate of 39 U.S.C. § 601(b) that the PES be suspended only if the public interest requires. The foregoing discussion has demonstrated that the PES were not designed to protect postal employment or further postal job opportunities, but the Unions argue that the courts should look beyond the PES to the entire 1970 PRA in applying the zone-of-interests test. The Unions argue that because one of the purposes of the labor-management provisions of the PRA was to stabilize labor-management relations within the Postal Service, and because the PES is the "linchpin" of the Postal Service, employment opportunities of postal workers are arguably within the zone of interests covered by the PES. The Unions rely upon our opinion in *Clarke v. Securities Industry Assn.*, 479 U.S. 388 (1987), to support this contention.

Clarke is the most recent in a series of cases in which we have held that competitors of regulated entities have standing to challenge regulations. *Clarke, supra; Investment Co. Institute v. Camp*, 401 U.S. 617 (1971); *Association of Data Processing Service Organizations, Inc. v. Camp*, 397 U.S. 150 (1970). In *Clarke*, we said that "we are not limited to considering the statute under which respondents sued, but may consider any provision that helps us to understand Congress' overall purposes in the National Bank Act." 479 U.S., at 401. This statement, like all others in our opinions, must be taken in the context in which it was made. In the next paragraph of the opinion, the Court pointed out that 12 U.S.C. § 36, which the plaintiffs in that case claimed had been misinterpreted by the Comptroller, was itself "a limited exception to the otherwise applicable requirement

5. The PES are competition statutes that regulate the conduct of competitors of the Postal Service. The postal employees for whose benefit the Unions have brought suit here are not competitors of either the Postal Service or remailers. Employees have generally been denied standing to enforce competition laws because they lack competitive and direct injury. *See, e.g., Adams v. Pan American World Airways, Inc.*, 828 F.2d 24 (D.C. Cir. 1987), *cert. denied sub nom. Union de Transports Aeriens v. Beckman*, 485 U.S. 934 (1988) (former airline employees denied standing to assert antitrust claim against airline that allegedly drove their former employer out of business); *Curtis v. Campbell-Taggart, Inc.*, 687 F.2d 336 (CA10), *cert. denied*, 459 U.S. 1090 (1982) (employees of corporation injured by anticompetitive conduct denied standing under anti-trust laws).

of [12 U.S.C.] § 81," limiting the places at which a national bank could transact business to its headquarters and any "branches" permitted by § 36. Thus the zone-of-interests test was to be applied not merely in the light of § 36, which was the basis of the plaintiffs' claim on the merits, but also in the light of § 81, to which § 36 was an exception.

The situation in the present case is quite different. The only relationship between the PES, upon which the Unions rely for their claim on the merits, and the labor-management provisions of the PRA, upon which the Unions rely for their standing, is that both were included in the general codification of postal statutes embraced in the PRA. The statutory provisions enacted and reenacted in the PRA are spread over some 65 pages in the United States Code and take up an entire title of that volume. We said in *Lujan* that "the relevant statute [under the APA] of course, is the statute whose violation is the gravamen of the complaint." 497 U.S., at 886. To adopt petitioners' contention would require us to hold that the "relevant statute" in this case is the PRA, with all of its various provisions united only by the fact that they deal with the Postal Service. But to accept this level of generality in defining the "relevant statute" could deprive the zone-of-interests test of virtually all meaning.

Unlike the two sections of the National Bank Act discussed in *Clarke, supra*, none of the provisions of the PES have any integral relationship with the labor-management provisions of the PRA. When it enacted the PRA, Congress made no substantive changes to those portions of the PES codified in the Criminal Code, 18 U.S.C. §§ 1693-1699; Congress readopted without change those portions of the PES codified in the Postal Service Code, 39 U.S.C. §§ 601-606; and Congress required the Postal Service to conduct a 2-year study and reevaluation of the PES before deciding whether those laws should be modified or repealed.

None of the documents constituting the PRA legislative history suggest that those concerned with postal reforms saw any connection between the PES and the provisions of the PRA dealing with labor-management relations. The Senate and House Reports simply note that the proposed bills continue existing law without change and require the Postal Service to conduct a study of the PES. The Court of Appeals referred to the PES as the "linchpin" of the Postal Service, which it may well be; but it stretches the zone-of-interests test too far to say that because of that fact those who a different part of the PRA was designed to benefit may challenge a violation of the PES.

It would be a substantial extension of our holdings in *Clarke, supra, Data Processing, supra*, and *Investment Co. Institute, supra*, to allow the Unions in this case to leapfrog from their asserted protection under the labor-management provisions of the PRA to their claim on the merits under the PES. We decline to make that extension, and hold that the Unions do not have standing to challenge the Postal Service's suspension of the PES to permit private couriers to engage in international remailing. We therefore do not reach the merits of the Unions' claim that the suspension was not in the public interest. The judgment of the Court of Appeals is Reversed.

QUESTIONS

1. After years of abeyance, does the "zone of interests" test now have bite?
2. How is the "zone of interests" test here any different from the legal interest test?

NCUA v. FIRST NAT'L & TRUST CO.

522 U.S. 479 (1998)

Justice Thomas delivered the opinion of the Court, except as to footnote 6. [Justice Scalia joined the opinion, except as to footnote 6.]

Section 109 of the Federal Credit Union Act (FCUA), 48 Stat. 1219, 12 U.S.C. § 1759, provides that "federal credit union membership shall be limited to groups having a common bond of occupation or association, or to groups within a well-defined neighborhood, community, or rural district." Since 1982, the National Credit Union Administration (NCUA), the agency charged with administering the FCUA, has interpreted § 109 to permit federal credit unions to be composed of multiple unrelated employer groups, each having its own common bond of occupation. In this case, respondents, five banks and the American Bankers Association, have challenged this interpretation on the ground that § 109 unambiguously requires that the same common bond of occupation unite every member of an occupationally defined federal credit union. We granted certiorari to answer two questions. First, do respondents have standing under the Administrative Procedure Act to seek federal court review of the NCUA's interpretation? Second, under the analysis set forth in *Chevron U.S.A. Inc. v. Natural Resources Defense Council, Inc.*, 467 U.S. 837 (1984), is the NCUA's interpretation permissible? We answer the first question in the affirmative and the second question in the negative. We therefore affirm.

I

A

In 1934, during the Great Depression, Congress enacted the FCUA, which authorizes the chartering of credit unions at the national level and provides that federal credit unions may, as a general matter, offer banking services only to their members. Section 109 of the FCUA, which has remained virtually unaltered since the FCUA's enactment, expressly restricts membership in federal credit unions. In relevant part, it provides:

> "Federal credit union membership shall consist of the incorporators and such other persons and incorporated and unincorporated organizations, to the extent permitted by rules and regulations prescribed by the Board, as may be elected to membership and as such shall each, subscribe to at least one share of its stock and pay the initial installment thereon and a uniform entrance fee if required by the board of directors; *except that Federal credit union membership shall be limited to groups having a common bond of occupation or association, or to groups within a well-defined neighborhood, community, or rural district.*" 12 U.S.C. § 1759 (emphasis added).

Until 1982, the NCUA and its predecessors consistently interpreted § 109 to require that the same common bond of occupation unite every member of an occupationally defined federal credit union. In 1982, however, the NCUA reversed its longstanding policy in order to permit credit unions to be composed of multiple unrelated employer groups. *See* IRPS 82-1, 47 Fed. Reg. 16775 (1982). It thus interpreted § 109's common bond requirement to apply only to each employer group in a multiple-group credit union, rather than to every member of that credit union. *See* IRPS 82-3, 47 Fed. Reg. 26808 (1982). Under the NCUA's new interpretation, all of the employer groups in a multiple-group credit union had to be located "within a well-defined area," *ibid.*, but the NCUA later revised this requirement to provide that each employer group could be located within "an area surrounding the [credit union's] home or a branch office that can be reasonably served by the [credit union] as determined by NCUA." IRPS 89-1, 54 Fed. Reg. 31170 (1989). Since 1982, therefore, the NCUA has permitted federal credit unions to be composed of wholly unrelated employer groups, each having its own distinct common bond.

B

After the NCUA revised its interpretation of § 109, petitioner AT&T Family Federal Credit Union (ATTF) expanded its operations considerably by adding unrelated employer groups to its membership. As a result, ATTF now has approximately 110,000 members nationwide, only 35% of whom are employees of AT&T and its affiliates. The remaining members are employees of such diverse companies as the Lee Apparel Company, the Coca-Cola Bottling Company, the Ciba-Geigy Corporation, the Duke Power Company, and the American Tobacco Company.

In 1990, after the NCUA approved a series of amendments to ATTF's charter that added several such unrelated employer groups to ATTF's membership, respondents brought this action. Invoking the judicial review provisions of the Administrative Procedure Act (APA), 5 U.S.C. § 702, respondents claimed that the NCUA's approval of the charter amendments was contrary to law because the members of the new groups did not share a common bond of occupation with ATTF's existing members, as respondents alleged § 109 required. ATTF and petitioner Credit Union National Association were permitted to intervene in the case as defendants. . . .

The Court of Appeals for the District of Columbia Circuit [below] concluded that respondents' interests were sufficiently congruent with the interests of § 109's intended beneficiaries that respondents were "suitable challengers" to the NCUA's chartering decision; therefore, their suit could proceed.

The Court of Appeals [also held under *Chevron* that] Congress had indeed spoken directly to the precise question at issue and had unambiguously indicated that the same common bond of occupation must unite members of a federal credit union composed of multiple employer groups. The Court of Appeals reasoned that because the concept of a "common bond" is implicit in the term "group," the term "common bond" would be surplusage if it applied only to the members of each constituent "group" in a multiple-group federal credit union. It further noted that the NCUA had not interpreted § 109's geographical limitation to allow federal credit unions to comprise groups from multiple unrelated "neighborhood[s], communit[ies], or rural district[s]" and stated that the occupational limitation should not be interpreted differently. The NCUA's revised interpretation of § 109 was therefore impermissible. Because of the importance of the issues presented, we granted certiorari.

II

Respondents claim a right to judicial review of the NCUA's chartering decision under § 10(a) of the APA, which provides:

"A person suffering legal wrong because of agency action, or adversely affected or aggrieved by agency action within the meaning of a relevant statute, is entitled to judicial review thereof." 5 U.S.C. § 702.

We have interpreted § 10(a) of the APA to impose a prudential standing requirement in addition to the requirement, imposed by Article III of the Constitution, that a plaintiff have suffered a sufficient injury-in-fact. *See*, e.g., *Association of Data Processing Service Organizations, Inc. v. Camp*, 397 U.S. 150, 152 (1970) (*Data Processing*).[4] For a plaintiff to have prudential standing under the APA, "the interest sought to be protected by the complainant [must be] arguably within the zone of interests to be protected or regulated by the statute . . . in question." *Id.*, at 153.

Based on four of our prior cases finding that competitors of financial institutions have standing to challenge agency action relaxing statutory restrictions on the activities of those institutions, we hold that respondents' interest in limiting the markets that federal credit unions can serve is arguably within the zone of interests to be protected by § 109. Therefore, respondents have prudential standing under the APA to challenge the NCUA's interpretation.

A

Although our prior cases have not stated a clear rule for determining when a plaintiff's interest is "arguably within the zone of interests" to be protected by a statute, they nonetheless establish that we should not inquire whether there has been a congressional intent to benefit the would-be plaintiff. In *Data Processing*, *supra*, the Office of the Comptroller of the Currency (the Comptroller) had interpreted the National Bank Act's incidental powers clause, Rev. Stat. § 5136, 12 U.S.C. § 24 Seventh, to permit national banks to perform data processing services for other banks and bank customers. The plaintiffs, a data processing corporation and its trade association, alleged that this interpretation was impermissible because providing data processing services was not, as was required by the statute, "[an] incidental powe[r] . . . necessary to carry on the business of banking." See 397 U.S. at 157, n.2.

In holding that the plaintiffs had standing, we stated that § 10(a) of the APA required only that "the interest sought to be protected by the complainant [be] arguably within the zone of interests to be protected or regulated by the statute . . . in question." *Id.*, at 153. In determining that the plaintiffs' interest met this requirement, we noted that although the relevant federal statutes — the National Bank Act, 12 U.S.C. § 24 Seventh, and the Bank Service Corporation Act, 76 Stat. 1132, 12 U.S.C. § 1864 — did not "in terms protect a specified group[,] . . . their general policy is apparent; and those whose interests are directly affected by a broad or narrow interpretation of the Acts are easily identifiable." *Data Processing*, 397 U.S. at 157. "As competitors of national banks

---

4. In this case, it is not disputed that respondents have suffered an injury in fact because the NCUA's interpretation allows persons who might otherwise be their customers to be members, and therefore customers, of ATTF.

which are engaging in data processing services," the plaintiffs were within that class of "aggrieved persons" entitled to judicial review of the Comptroller's interpretation. *Ibid.*

Less than a year later, we applied the "zone of interests" test in *Arnold Tours, Inc. v. Camp*, 400 U.S. 45 (1970) (*Arnold Tours*) (*per curiam*) [a case similar in many respects to *Data Processing*].

A year later, we decided *Investment Company Institute v. Camp*, 401 U.S. 617 (1971) (*ICI*). In that case, an investment company trade association and several individual investment companies alleged that the Comptroller had violated, inter alia, § 21 of the Glass-Steagall Act[5] by permitting national banks to establish and operate what in essence were early versions of mutual funds. We held that the plaintiffs, who alleged that they would be injured by the competition resulting from the Comptroller's action, had standing under the APA and stated that the case was controlled by *Data Processing. See* 401 U.S. at 621. Significantly, we found unpersuasive Justice Harlan's argument in dissent that the suit should be dismissed because "neither the language of the pertinent provisions of the Glass-Steagall Act nor the legislative history evinced any congressional concern for the interests of petitioners and others like them in freedom from competition." 401 U.S. at 640.

Our fourth case in this vein was *Clarke v. Securities Industry Assn.*, 479 U.S. 388 (1987) (*Clarke*). There, a securities dealers trade association sued the Comptroller, this time for authorizing two national banks to offer discount brokerage services both at their branch offices and at other locations inside and outside their home States. See *id.*, at 391. The plaintiff contended that the Comptroller's action violated the McFadden Act, which permits national banks to carry on the business of banking only at authorized branches, and to open new branches only in their home States and only to the extent that state-chartered banks in that State can do so under state law. See *id.*, at 391-392.

We again held that the plaintiff had standing under the APA. Summarizing our prior holdings, we stated that although the "zone of interests" test "denies a right of review if the plaintiff's interests are . . . marginally related to or inconsistent with the purposes implicit in the statute," *id.*, at 399, "there need be no indication of congressional purpose to benefit the would-be plaintiff," *id.*, at 399-400 (citing *ICI*). We then determined that by limiting the ability of national banks to do business outside their home States, "Congress had shown a concern to keep national banks from gaining a monopoly control over credit and money." *Id.*, at 403. The interest of the securities dealers in preventing national banks from expanding into the securities markets directly implicated this concern because offering discount brokerage services would allow national banks "access to more money, in the form of credit balances, and enhanced opportunities to lend money, *viz.*, for margin purchases." *Ibid.* The case was thus analogous to *Data Processing* and *ICI:* "In those cases the question was what activities banks could engage in at all; here, the question is what activities banks can engage in without regard to the limitations imposed by state branching law." 479 U.S. at 403.

---

5. Under § 21 of the Glass-Steagall Act, it is unlawful "[f]or any person, firm, [or] corporation . . . engaged in the business of issuing . . . securities, to engage at the same time to any extent whatever in the business of receiving deposits." § 21 of the Banking Act of 1933, 48 Stat. 189, 12 U.S.C. § 378(a).

B

Our prior cases, therefore, have consistently held that for a plaintiff's interests to be arguably within the "zone of interests" to be protected by a statute, there does not have to be an "indication of congressional purpose to benefit the would-be plaintiff." *Id.*, at 399-400 (citing *ICI*); see also *Arnold Tours, supra*, at 46 (citing *Data Processing*). The proper inquiry is simply "whether the interest sought to be protected by the complainant is *arguably* within the zone of interests to be protected . . . by the statute." *Data Processing*, 397 U.S. at 153 (emphasis added). Hence in applying the "zone of interests" test, we do not ask whether, in enacting the statutory provision at issue, Congress specifically intended to benefit the plaintiff. Instead, we first discern the interests "arguably . . . to be protected" by the statutory provision at issue; we then inquire whether the plaintiff's interests affected by the agency action in question are among them.

Section 109 provides that "federal credit union membership shall be limited to groups having a common bond of occupation or association, or to groups within a well-defined neighborhood, community, or rural district." 12 U.S.C. § 1759. By its express terms, § 109 limits membership in every federal credit union to members of definable "groups." Because federal credit unions may, as a general matter, offer banking services only to members, *see*, e.g., 12 U.S.C. §§ 1757(5)-(6), § 109 also restricts the markets that every federal credit union can serve. Although these markets need not be small, they unquestionably are limited. The link between § 109's regulation of federal credit union membership and its limitation on the markets that federal credit unions can serve is unmistakable. Thus, even if it cannot be said that Congress had the specific purpose of benefiting commercial banks, one of the interests "arguably . . . to be protected" by § 109 is an interest in limiting the markets that federal credit unions can serve.[6] This interest is precisely the interest of respondents affected by the NCUA's interpretation of § 109. As competitors of federal credit unions, respondents certainly have an interest in limiting the markets that federal credit unions can serve, and the NCUA's interpretation has affected that interest by allowing federal credit unions to increase their customer base.[7]

---

6. The legislative history of § 109, upon which petitioners so heavily rely, supports this conclusion. . . . The legislative history thus confirms that § 109 was thought to reinforce the cooperative nature of credit unions, which in turn was believed to promote their safety and soundness and allow access to credit to persons otherwise unable to borrow. Because, by its very nature, a cooperative institution must serve a limited market, the legislative history of § 109 demonstrates that one of the interests "arguably . . . to be protected" by § 109 is an interest in limiting the markets that federal credit unions can serve.

7. Contrary to the dissent's contentions, our formulation does not "eviscerat[e]" or "abolis[h]" the zone of interests requirement. Nor can it be read to imply that in order to have standing under the APA, a plaintiff must merely have an interest in enforcing the statute in question. The test we have articulated — discerning the interests "arguably . . . to be protected" by the statutory provision at issue and inquiring whether the plaintiff's interests affected by the agency action in question are among them — differs only as a matter of semantics from the formulation that the dissent has accused us of "eviscerating" or "abolishing," *see post* (stating that the plaintiff must establish that "the injury he complains of . . . falls within the zone of interests sought to be protected by the statutory provision whose violation forms the legal basis for his complaint") (internal quotations and citation omitted). Our only disagreement with the dissent lies in the application of the zone of interests test. Because of the unmistakable link between § 109's express restriction on credit union membership and the limitation on the markets that federal credit unions can serve, there is objectively "some indication in the statute," that respondents' interest is "arguably within the zone of interests to be protected" by § 109. Hence respondents are more than merely incidental beneficiaries of § 109's effects on competition.

Section 109 cannot be distinguished from the statutory provisions at issue in *Clarke, ICI, Arnold Tours,* and *Data Processing.* Although in *Clarke* the McFadden Act appeared to be designed to protect only the interest of state banks in parity of treatment with national banks, we nonetheless determined that the statute also limited "the extent to which [national] banks [could] engage in the discount brokerage business and hence limited the competitive impact on non-bank discount brokerage houses." *Clarke,* 479 U.S. at 403. Accordingly, although Congress did not intend specifically to protect securities dealers, one of the interests "arguably . . . to be protected" by the statute was an interest in restricting national bank market power. The plaintiff securities dealers, as competitors of national banks, had that interest, and that interest had been affected by the interpretation of the McFadden Act they sought to challenge, because that interpretation had allowed national banks to expand their activities and serve new customers. See *ibid.*

Similarly, in *ICI,* even though in enacting the Glass-Steagall Act, Congress did not intend specifically to benefit investment companies and may have sought only to protect national banks and their depositors, one of the interests "arguably . . . to be protected" by the statute was an interest in restricting the ability of national banks to enter the securities business. The investment company plaintiffs, as competitors of national banks, had that interest, and that interest had been affected by the Comptroller's interpretation allowing national banks to establish mutual funds.

So too, in *Arnold Tours* and *Data Processing,* although in enacting the National Bank Act and the Bank Service Corporation Act, Congress did not intend specifically to benefit travel agents and data processors and may have been concerned only with the safety and soundness of national banks, one of the interests "arguably . . . to be protected" by the statutes was an interest in preventing national banks from entering other businesses' product markets. As competitors of national banks, travel agents and data processors had that interest, and that interest had been affected by the Comptroller's interpretations opening their markets to national banks. . . .

C

Petitioners attempt to distinguish this case principally on the ground that there is no evidence that Congress, when it enacted the FCUA, was at all concerned with the competitive interests of commercial banks, or indeed at all concerned with competition. Indeed, petitioners contend that the very reason Congress passed the FCUA was that "banks were simply not in the picture" as far as small borrowers were concerned, and thus Congress believed it necessary to create a new source of credit for people of modest means.

The difficulty with this argument is that similar arguments were made unsuccessfully in each of *Data Processing, Arnold Tours, ICI,* and *Clarke.* . . .

In each case, we declined to accept the Comptroller's argument. In *Data Processing,* we considered it irrelevant that the statutes in question "d[id] not in terms protect a specified group," because "their general policy [was] apparent[,] and those whose interests [were] directly affected by a broad or narrow interpretation of [the statutes] [were] easily identifiable." 397 U.S. at 157. In *Arnold Tours,* we similarly believed it irrelevant that Congress had shown no concern for the competitive position of travel agents in enacting the statutes in question. See 400 U.S. at 46. In *ICI,* we were unmoved by Justice Harlan's comment in dissent that the Glass-Steagall Act was passed *in spite* of its positive effects on the competitive position of investment banks. See 401 U.S. at 640 (Harlan, J., dissenting). And in *Clarke*, we did not debate whether the Congress that enacted the McFadden Act was concerned about the competitive position of securities dealers. See 479 U.S. at 403. The provisions at issue in each of these cases, moreover, could be said merely to be safety-and-soundness provisions, enacted only to protect national banks and their depositors and without a concern for competitive effects. We nonetheless did not hesitate to find standing.

We therefore cannot accept petitioners' argument that respondents do not have standing because there is no evidence that the Congress that enacted § 109 was concerned with the competitive interests of commercial banks. To accept that argument, we would have to reformulate the "zone of interests" test to require that Congress have specifically intended to benefit a particular class of plaintiffs before a plaintiff from that class could have standing under the APA to sue. We have refused to do this in our prior cases, and we refuse to do so today.

Petitioners also mistakenly rely on our decision in *Air Courier Conference v. Postal Workers*, 498 U.S. 517 (1991). In *Air Courier*, we held that the interest of Postal Service employees in maximizing employment opportunities was not within the "zone of interests" to be protected by the postal monopoly statutes, and hence those employees did not have standing under the APA to challenge a Postal Service regulation suspending its monopoly over certain international operations. See *id.*, at 519. We stated that the purposes of the statute were solely to increase the revenues of the Post Office and to ensure that postal services were provided in a manner consistent with the public interest, see *id.*, at 526-27. Only those interests, therefore, and not the interests of Postal Service employees in their employment, were "arguably within the zone of interests to be protected" by the statute. Cf. *Lujan v. National Wildlife Federation*, 497 U.S. 871, 883 (1990) (stating that an agency reporting company would not have prudential standing to challenge an agency's failure to comply with a statutory mandate to conduct hearings on the record). We further noted that although the statute in question regulated competition, the interests of the plaintiff employees had nothing to do with competition. See *Air Courier, supra*, at 528, n.5 (stating that "employees have generally been denied standing to enforce competition laws because they lack competitive and direct injury"). In this case, not only do respondents have "competitive and direct injury," 498 U.S. at 528, n.5, but, as the foregoing discussion makes clear, they possess an interest that is "arguably . . . to be protected" by § 109.

Respondents' interest in limiting the markets that credit unions can serve is "arguably within the zone of interests to be protected" by § 109. Under our precedents, it is irrelevant that in enacting the FCUA, Congress did not specifically intend to protect commercial banks. Although it is clear that respondents' objectives in this action are not eleemosynary in nature, under our prior cases that too is beside the point.

III

Turning to the merits, we must judge the permissibility of the NCUA's current interpretation of § 109 by employing the analysis set forth in *Chevron U.S.A. Inc. v. Natural Resources Defense Council, Inc.*, 467 U.S. 837 (1984). Under that analysis, we first ask whether Congress has "directly spoken to the precise question at issue. If the intent of Congress is clear, that is the end of the matter; for the court, as well as the agency, must give effect to the unambiguously expressed intent of Congress." *Id.*, at 842-843. If we determine that Congress has not directly spoken to the precise question at issue, we then inquire whether the agency's interpretation is reasonable. See *id.*, at 843-844. Because we conclude that Congress has made it clear that the same common bond of occupation must unite each member of an occupationally defined federal credit union, we hold that the NCUA's contrary interpretation is impermissible under the first step of *Chevron.*

As noted, § 109 requires that "[f]ederal credit union membership shall be limited to groups having a common bond of occupation or association, or to groups within a well-defined neighborhood, community, or rural district." Respondents contend that because § 109 uses the article "a" — "i.e., one" — in conjunction with the noun "common bond," the "natural reading" of § 109 is that all members in an occupationally defined federal credit union must be united by one common bond. Petitioners reply that because § 109 uses the plural noun "groups," it permits multiple groups, each with its own common bond, to constitute a federal credit union.

Like the Court of Appeals, we do not think that either of these contentions, standing alone, is conclusive. The article "a" could be thought to convey merely that one bond must unite only the members of each group in a multiple-group credit union, and not all of the members in the credit union taken together. Similarly, the plural word "groups" could be thought to refer not merely to multiple groups in a particular credit union, but rather to every single "group" that forms a distinct credit union under the FCUA. Nonetheless, as the Court of Appeals correctly recognized, additional considerations compel the conclusion that the same common bond of occupation must unite all of the members of an occupationally defined federal credit union.

First, the NCUA's current interpretation makes the phrase "common bond" surplusage when applied to a federal credit union made up of multiple unrelated employer groups, because each "group" in such a credit union already has its own "common bond." To use the facts of this case, the employees of AT&T and the employees of the American Tobacco Company each already had a "common bond" before being joined together as members of ATTF. The former were bonded because they worked for AT&T, and the latter were bonded because they worked for the American Tobacco Company. If the phrase "common bond" is to be given any meaning when these employees are joined together, a different "common bond" — one extending to each and every employee considered together — must be found to unite them. Such a "common bond" exists when employees of different subsidiaries of the same company are joined together in a federal credit union; it does not exist, however, when employees of unrelated companies are so joined. Put another way, in the multiple employer group context, the NCUA has read the statute as though it merely stated that "federal credit union membership shall be limited to occupational groups," but that is simply not what the statute provides.

Second, the NCUA's interpretation violates the established canon of construction that similar language contained within the same section of a statute must be accorded a consistent meaning. Section 109 consists of two parallel clauses: Federal credit union membership is limited "to groups having a common bond of occupation or association, *or* to groups within a well-defined neighborhood, community, or rural district." 12 U.S.C. §1759 (emphasis added). The NCUA concedes that even though the second limitation permits geographically defined credit unions to have as members more than one "group," all of the groups must come from the same "neighborhood, community, or rural district." The reason that the NCUA has never interpreted, and does not contend that it *could* interpret, the geographical limitation to allow a credit union to be composed of members from an unlimited number of unrelated geographic units, is that to do so would render the geographical limitation meaningless. Under established principles of statutory interpretation, we must interpret the occupational limitation in the same way. . . .

Finally, by its terms, §109 requires that membership in federal credit unions "shall be limited." The NCUA's interpretation — under which a common bond of occupation must unite only the members of each unrelated employer group — has the potential to read these words out of the statute entirely. The NCUA has not contested that, under its current interpretation, it would be permissible to grant a charter to a conglomerate credit union whose members would include the employees of every company in the United States. Nor can it: Each company's employees would be a "group," and each such "group" would have its own "common bond of occupation." Section 109, however, cannot be considered a *limitation* on credit union membership if at the same time it permits such a *limitless* result.

For the foregoing reasons, we conclude that the NCUA's current interpretation of §109 is contrary to the unambiguously expressed intent of Congress and is thus impermissible under the first step of *Chevron*. The judgment of the Court of Appeals is therefore *Affirmed*.

JUSTICE O'CONNOR, with whom JUSTICE STEVENS, JUSTICE SOUTER, and JUSTICE BREYER join, dissenting.

In determining that respondents have standing under the zone-of-interests test to challenge the National Credit Union Administration's (NCUA's) interpretation of the "common bond" provision of the Federal Credit Union Act (FCUA), 12 U.S.C. §1759, the Court applies the test in a manner that is contrary to our decisions and, more importantly, that all but eviscerates the zone-of-interests requirement. In my view, under a proper conception of the inquiry, "the interest sought to be protected by" respondents in this case is not "arguably within the zone of interests to be protected" by the common bond provision. Accordingly, I respectfully dissent.

I

Respondents brought this suit under §10(a) of the Administrative Procedure Act (APA), 5 U.S.C. §702. To establish their standing to sue here, respondents must demonstrate that they are "adversely affected or aggrieved by agency action within the meaning of a relevant statute." *Ibid.; see Air Courier Conference v. Postal Workers*, 498 U.S. 517 (1991); *Lujan v. National Wildlife Federation*, 497 U.S. 871, 882-883 (1990). The two aspects of that requirement correspond to the familiar concepts in standing doctrine of "injury in fact" under Article III of the Constitution and "zone of interests" under our prudential standing principles. *See*, e.g., *Bennett v. Spear*, 520 U.S. 154 (1997). . . .

... [I]n *Data Processing*, where the plaintiffs—like respondents here—alleged competitive injury to their commercial interest, we found that the plaintiffs had standing because "their commercial interest was sought to be protected by the ... provision which they alleged had been violated." *Bennett, supra,* at 176 (discussing *Data Processing*).

The Court adopts a quite different approach to the zone-of-interests test today, eschewing any assessment of whether the common bond provision was intended to protect respondents' commercial interest. The Court begins by observing that the terms of the common bond provision—"[f]ederal credit union membership shall be limited to groups having a common bond of occupation or association, or to groups within a well-defined neighborhood, community, or rural district," 12 U.S.C. § 1759—expressly limit membership in federal credit unions to persons belonging to certain "groups." Then, citing other statutory provisions that bar federal credit unions from serving nonmembers, *see* §§ 1757(5)-(6), the Court reasons that one interest sought to be protected by the common bond provision "is an interest in limiting the markets that federal credit unions can serve." The Court concludes its analysis by observing simply that respondents, "[a]s competitors of federal credit unions, ... certainly have [that] interest ... , and the NCUA's interpretation has affected that interest."

Under the Court's approach, every litigant who establishes injury in fact under Article III will automatically satisfy the zone-of-interests requirement, rendering the zone-of-interests test ineffectual. See *Air Courier, supra,* at 524 ("mistake" to "conflate the zone-of-interests test with injury in fact"). That result stems from the Court's articulation of the relevant "interest." In stating that the common bond provision protects an "interest in limiting the markets that federal credit unions can serve," the Court presumably uses the term "markets" in the sense of *customer* markets, as opposed to, for instance, product markets: The common bond requirement and the provisions prohibiting credit unions from serving nonmembers combine to limit the customers a credit union can serve, not the services a credit union can offer.

With that understanding, the Court's conclusion that respondents "have" an interest in "limiting the [customer] markets that federal credit unions can serve" means little more than that respondents "have" an interest in enforcing the statute. The common bond requirement limits a credit union's membership, and hence its customer base, to certain groups, 12 U.S.C. § 1759, and in the Court's view, it is enough to establish standing that respondents "have" an interest in limiting the customers a credit union can serve. The Court's additional observation that respondents' interest has been "affected" by the NCUA's interpretation adds little to the analysis; agency interpretation of a statutory restriction will of course affect a party who has an interest in the restriction. Indeed, a party presumably will bring suit to vindicate an interest only if the interest has been affected by the challenged action. The crux of the Court's zone-of-interests inquiry, then, is simply that the plaintiff must "have" an interest in enforcing the pertinent statute.

A party, however, will invariably have an interest in enforcing a statute when he can establish injury in fact caused by an alleged violation of that statute. An example we used in *National Wildlife Federation* illustrates the point. There, we hypothesized a situation involving "the failure of an agency to comply with a statutory provision requiring 'on the record' hearings." That circumstance "would assuredly have an adverse effect upon the company that has the contract to record and transcribe the agency's proceedings," and so the company would establish injury in fact. But the company would not satisfy the zone-of-interests test, because "the provision was obviously enacted to protect the interests of the parties to the proceedings and not those of the reporters." Under the Court's approach today, however, the reporting company would have standing under the zone-of-interests test: Because the company is injured by the failure to comply with the requirement of on-the-record hearings, the company would certainly "have" an interest in enforcing the statute.

Our decision in *Air Courier*, likewise cannot be squared with the Court's analysis in this case. *Air Courier* involved a challenge by postal employees to a decision of the Postal Service suspending its statutory monopoly over certain international mailing services. The postal employees alleged a violation of the Private Express Statutes (PES) — the provisions that codify the Service's postal monopoly — citing as their injury in fact that competition from private mailing companies adversely affected their employment opportunities. 498 U.S. at 524. We concluded that the postal employees did not have standing under the zone-of-interests test, because "the PES were not designed to protect postal employment or further postal job opportunities." *Id.*, at 528. As with the example from *National Wildlife Federation*, though, the postal employees would have established standing under the Court's analysis in this case: The employees surely "had" an interest in enforcing the statutory monopoly given that suspension of the monopoly caused injury to their employment opportunities.

In short, requiring simply that a litigant "have" an interest in enforcing the relevant statute amounts to hardly any test at all. That is why our decisions have required instead that a party "establish that the *injury he complains of . . .* falls within the 'zone of interests' sought to be protected by the statutory provision" in question. *National Wildlife Federation, supra,* at 883 (emphasis added); see *Bennett*, 520 U.S., at 176. In *Air Courier*, for instance, after noting that the asserted injury in fact was "an adverse effect on employment opportunities of postal workers," we characterized "[t]he question before us" as "whether the adverse effect on the employment opportunities of postal workers . . . is within the zone of interests encompassed by the PES." 498 U.S. at 524; see also *National Wildlife Federation, supra,* 497 U.S. 871 at 885-886 (noting that asserted injury is to the plaintiffs' interests in "recreational use and aesthetic enjoyment," and finding those particular interests "are among the *sorts* of interests [the] statutes were specifically designed to protect"). . . .

II

Contrary to the Court's suggestion, its application of the zone-of-interests test in this case is not in concert with the approach we followed in a series of cases in which the plaintiffs, like respondents here, alleged that agency interpretation of a statute caused competitive injury to their commercial interests. In each of those cases, we focused, as in *Bennett, Air Courier,* and *National Wildlife Federation,* on whether competitive injury to the plaintiff's commercial interest fell within the zone of interests protected by the relevant statute.

The earliest of the competitor standing decisions was *Association of Data Processing Service Organizations, Inc. v. Camp,* 397 U.S. 150 (1970), in which we first formulated the zone-of-interests requirement. There, an association of data processors challenged a decision of the Comptroller of the Currency allowing national banks to provide data processing services. The data processors alleged violation of, among other statutes, §4 of the Bank Service Corporation Act of 1962, 76 Stat. 1132, which provided that "[n]o bank service corporation may engage in any activity other than the performance of bank services." 397 U.S. at 154-155. We articulated the applicable test as "whether the interest sought to be protected by the complainant is arguably within the zone of interests to be protected or regulated by the statute . . . in question." *Id.*, at 153.

In answering that question, we assessed whether the injury asserted by the plaintiffs was to an interest arguably within the zone of interests protected by the relevant statute. The data processors, like respondents here, asserted "economic injury" from the "competition by national banks in the business of providing data processing services." *Id.*, at 152, 154. We concluded that the data processors' "commercial interest was sought to be protected by the anti-competition limitation contained in §4," *Bennett, supra*, at 176 (discussing *Data Processing*), explaining that the provision "arguably brings a competitor within the zone of interests protected by it," 397 U.S. at 156. . . .

In each of the competitor standing cases, though, we found that Congress had enacted an "anti-competition limitation," see *Bennett*, 520 U.S., at 176 (discussing *Data Processing*), or, alternatively, that Congress had "legislated against . . . competition," see *Clarke, supra*, at 403; *ICI, supra*, at 620-621, and accordingly, that the plaintiff-competitor's "commercial interest was sought to be protected by the anti-competition limitation" at issue, *Bennett, supra*, at 176. We determined, in other words, that "the injury [the plaintiff] complain[ed] of . . . [fell] within the zone of interests sought to be protected by the [relevant] statutory provision." *National Wildlife Federation*, 497 U.S. at 883. The Court fails to undertake that analysis here.

III

Applying the proper zone-of-interests inquiry to this case, I would find that competitive injury to respondents' commercial interests does not arguably fall within the zone of interests sought to be protected by the common bond provision. The terms of the statute do not suggest a concern with protecting the business interests of competitors. The common bond provision limits "[f]ederal credit union membership . . . to groups having a common bond of occupation or association, or to groups within a well-defined neighborhood, community, or rural district." 12 U.S.C. §1759. And the provision is framed as an exception to the preceding clause, which confers membership on "incorporators and such other persons and incorporated and unincorporated organizations . . . as may be elected . . . and as such shall each, subscribe to at least one share of its stock and pay the initial installment thereon and a uniform entrance fee." *Ibid.* The language suggests that the common bond requirement is an internal organizational principle concerned primarily with defining membership in a way that secures a financially sound organization. There is no indication in the text of the provision or in the surrounding language that the membership limitation was even arguably designed to protect the commercial interests of competitors.

Nor is there any nontextual indication to that effect. Significantly, the operation of the common bond provision is much different from the statutes at issue in *Clarke, ICI*, and *Data Processing.* Those statutes evinced a congressional intent to legislate against competition, e.g., *Clarke, supra,* at 403, because they imposed direct restrictions on banks generally, specifically barring their entry into certain markets. In *Data Processing* and *ICI*, "the question was what activities banks could engage in at all," and in *Clarke*, "the question [was] what activities banks [could] engage in without regard to the limitations imposed by state branching law." 479 U.S. at 403.

The operation of the common bond provision does not likewise denote a congressional desire to legislate against competition. First, the common bond requirement does not purport to restrict credit unions from becoming large, nationwide organizations, as might be expected if the provision embodied a congressional concern with the competitive consequences of credit union growth. *See* Brief for Petitioner NCUA 25-26 (Navy Federal Credit Union has 1.6 million members; American Airlines Federal Credit Union has 157,000 members); *see also* S. Rep. No. 555, 73d Cong., 2d Sess., 2 (1934) (citing "employees of the United States Government" as a "specific group with a common bond of occupation or association").

More tellingly, although the common bond provision applies to all credit unions, the restriction operates against credit unions individually: The common bond requirement speaks only to whether a *particular* credit union's membership can include a given group of customers, not to whether credit unions in *general* can serve that group. Even if a group of would-be customers does not share the requisite bond with a particular credit union, nothing in the common bond provision prevents that same group from joining a different credit union that is within the same "neighborhood, community, or rural district" or with whose members the group shares an adequate "occupation[al] or association[al]" connection. 12 U.S.C. §1759. Also, the group could conceivably form its own credit union. In this sense, the common bond requirement does not limit credit unions collectively from serving any customers, nor does it bar any customers from being served by credit unions.

In *Data Processing, ICI*, and *Clarke*, by contrast, the statutes operated against national banks generally, prohibiting all banks from competing in a particular market: Banks in general were barred from providing a specific type of service (*Data Processing* and *ICI*), or from providing services at a particular location (*Clarke*). Thus, whereas in *Data Processing* customers could not obtain data processing services from any national bank, and in *Clarke* customers outside of the permissible branching area likewise could not obtain financial services from any national bank, in this case customers who lack an adequate bond with the members of a particular credit union can still receive financial services from a *different* credit union. Unlike the statutes in *Data Processing, ICI*, and *Clarke*, then, the common bond provision does not erect a competitive boundary excluding credit unions from any identifiable market.

The circumstances surrounding the enactment of the FCUA also indicate that Congress did not intend to legislate against competition through the common bond provision. As the Court explains, *ante*, at n.6, the FCUA was enacted in the shadow of the Great Depression; Congress thought that the ability of credit unions to "come through the depression without failures, when banks have failed so notably, is a tribute to the worth of cooperative credit and indicates clearly the great potential value of rapid national credit union extension." S. Rep. No. 555, *supra*, at 3-4. Credit unions were believed to enable the general public, which had been largely ignored by banks, to obtain credit at reasonable rates. See *id.*, at 2-3; *First Nat'l Bank & Trust Co. v. National Credit Union Administration*, 988 F.2d 1272, 1274 (CADC), *cert. denied*, 510 U.S. 907 (1993). The common bond requirement "was seen as the cement that united credit union members in a cooperative venture, and was, therefore, thought important to credit unions' continued success." 988 F.2d at 1276. "Congress assumed implicitly that a common bond amongst members would ensure both that those making lending decisions would know more about applicants and that borrowers would be more reluctant to default." *Ibid.*; see *ante*, at n.6; A. Burger & T. Dacin, Field of Membership: An Evolving Concept 7-8 (2d ed. 1992).

The requirement of a common bond was thus meant to ensure that each credit union remains a cooperative institution that is economically stable and responsive to its members' needs. As a principle of internal governance designed to secure the viability of individual credit unions in the interests of the membership, the common bond provision was in no way designed to impose a restriction on all credit unions in the interests of institutions that might one day become competitors. "Indeed, the very notion seems anomalous, because Congress' general purpose was to encourage the proliferation of credit unions, which were expected to provide service to those would-be customers that banks disdained."

That the common bond requirement would later come to be viewed by competitors as a useful tool for curbing a credit union's membership should not affect the zone-of-interests inquiry. The pertinent question under the zone-of-interests test is whether Congress *intended* to protect certain interests through a particular provision, not whether, irrespective of congressional intent, a provision may have the *effect* of protecting those interests. See *Clarke*, 479 U.S. at 394 (the "matter [is] basically one of interpreting congressional intent"); *id.*, at 400; 988 F.2d at 1276 ("To be sure, as time passed — as credit unions flourished and competition among consumer lending institutions intensified — bankers began to see the common bond requirement as a desirable limitation on credit union expansion. . . . But that fact, assuming it is true, hardly serves to illuminate the intent of the Congress that first enacted the common bond requirement in 1934"). Otherwise, competitors could bring suits challenging the interpretation of a host of provisions in the FCUA that might have the unintended effect of furthering their competitive interest, such as restrictions on the loans credit unions can make or on the sums credit unions can borrow. *See* 12 U.S.C. §§ 1757(5), (6).

In this light, I read our decisions as establishing that there must at least be *some* indication in the statute, beyond the mere fact that its enforcement has the effect of incidentally benefiting the plaintiff, from which one can draw an inference that the plaintiff's injury arguably falls within the zone of interests sought to be protected by that statute. The provisions we construed in *Clarke*, *ICI*, and *Data Processing*, allowed such an inference: Where Congress legislates against competition, one can properly infer that the statute is at least arguably intended to protect competitors from injury to their commercial interest, even if that is not the statute's principal objective. . . . Accordingly, "[t]here [was] sound reason to infer" in those cases "that Congress intended [the] class [of plaintiffs] to be relied upon to challenge agency disregard of the law." *Clarke, supra,* at 403 (internal quotation marks omitted).

The same cannot be said of respondents in this case, because neither the terms of the common bond provision, nor the way in which the provision operates, nor the circumstances surrounding its enactment, evince a congressional desire to legislate against competition. This, then, is a case where "the plaintiff's interests are so marginally related to or inconsistent with the purposes implicit in the statute that it cannot reasonably be assumed that Congress intended to permit the suit." 479 U.S. at 399. The zone-of-interests test "seeks to exclude those plaintiffs whose suits are more likely to frustrate than to further statutory objectives," *id.,* at 397, n.12, and one can readily envision circumstances in which the interests of competitors, who have the incentive to suppress credit union expansion in all circumstances, would be at odds with the statute's general aim of supporting the growth of credit unions that are cohesive and hence financially stable.

The Court's attempt to distinguish *Air Courier* is instructive in this regard. The Court observes that here, unlike in *Air Courier,* the plaintiffs suffer "competitive and direct injury." 498 U.S. at 528, n.5. But the lack of competitive injury was pertinent in *Air Courier* because the statutes alleged to have been violated — the PES — were "competition statutes that regulate the conduct of competitors." *Ibid.* The common bond provision, for all the noted reasons, is not a competition law, and so the mere presence of "competitive and direct injury" should not establish standing. Thus, while in *Air Courier* "the statute in question regulated competition [but] the interests of the plaintiff employees had nothing to do with competition," here, the common bond provision does not regulate competition but the interests of the plaintiff have *everything* to do with competition. In either case, the plaintiff's injury is at best "marginally related" to the interests sought to be protected by the statute, and the most that can be said is that the provision has the incidental effect of benefiting the plaintiffs. That was not enough to establish standing in *Air Courier,* and it should not suffice here.

IV

Prudential standing principles "are 'founded in concern about the proper — and properly limited — role of the courts in a democratic society.'" The zone-of-interests test is an integral part of the prudential standing inquiry, and we ought to apply the test in a way that gives it content. The analysis the Court undertakes today, in my view, leaves the zone-of-interests requirement a hollow one. As with the example in *National Wildlife Federation,* where the reporting company suffered injury from the alleged statutory violation, but the injury to the company's commercial interest was not within the zone of interests protected by the statute, here, too, respondents suffer injury from the NCUA's interpretation of the common bond requirement, but the injury to their commercial interest is not within the zone of interests protected by the provision. Applying the zone-of-interests inquiry as it has been articulated in our decisions, I conclude that respondents have failed to establish standing. I would therefore vacate the judgment of the Court of Appeals and remand the case with instructions that it be dismissed.

QUESTIONS

1. In their opinions, both Justice Thomas, *supra* p. 689, and Justice O'Connor, *supra* p. 701, refer to the zone of interests test as reflecting a "prudential" limit defined by the judiciary on a party's standing under the APA to bring an action. This view that the judiciary may limit standing beyond the limits on standing defined by Article III is also evident in Justice Douglas's opinion for the Court in *Data Processing, supra.* Justice Douglas stated that "[a]part from Article III jurisdictional questions, problems of standing, as resolved by this Court for its own governance, have involved a 'rule of self-restraint.' *Barrows v. Jackson*, 346 U.S. 249, 255." *Data Processing*, 397 U.S., at 154. Justice Brennan dissented from this view, arguing that a plaintiff has standing when the party has met the requirements of Article III standing, *id.* at 168, and that the only remaining question is a statutory determination that Congress has authorized the claimant to bring the action. See *id.* at 169 n. 2.

    Justice Scalia, writing for a unanimous Court in *Lexmark Int'l, Inc. v. Static Control Components, Inc.*, 134 S. Ct. 1377 (2014), specifically opined about the proper terminology to be used when considering whether a party meeting the irreducible minimum requirements of Article III standing may bring a statutory claim in federal court. Justice Scalia began the Court's analysis of this issue "by clarifying the nature of the question at issue in this case," *id.* at 1386, which "[t]he parties' briefs treat[ed] . . . as one of 'prudential standing.'" *Id.* The Court, despite consistently using that same terminology in its earlier decisions, found "that label misleading." *Id.*

    The Court then held that the proper inquiry in determining whether a claimant who has Article III standing may bring a claim in federal court is entirely a question of statutory construction:

    > we ask whether [the claimant] has a cause of action under the statute. That question requires us to determine the meaning of the congressionally enacted provision creating a cause of action. In doing so, we apply traditional principles of statutory interpretation. We do not ask whether in our judgment Congress should have authorized Static Control's suit, but whether Congress in fact did so. Just as a court cannot apply its independent policy judgment to recognize a cause of action that Congress has denied, it cannot limit a cause of action that Congress has created merely because "prudence" dictates.

    Id. at 1387-88 (footnote and citation omitted). Justice Scalia accordingly decided that labeling this issue as one of "statutory standing" constitutes "an improvement over the language of 'prudential standing,' since it correctly places the focus on the statute." *Id.* at 1387 n. 4. In *Lexmark Intl.*, Justice Scalia did acknowledge that the statutory standing label "is misleading, since the absence of a valid (as opposed to arguable) cause of action does not implicate subject-matter jurisdiction, i.e., the court's statutory or constitutional power to adjudicate the case." 134 S. Ct. at 1387 n.4 (citations and internal quotations omitted).

    Although the Supreme Court's apparent preference for the term "statutory standing" avoids the questionable provenance of judicial "prudence" as a basis for limiting federal court power, the term "statutory standing" has its own limits. A non-Article III standing argument generally involves an inquiry into whether the legal basis for the plaintiff's claim (sufficiently or arguably) protects the interests of parties like the plaintiff. When the legal basis of the claim is a statutory provision, it makes some sense to categorize the inquiry (as to whom the statute protects) as "statutory." But what about when the legal basis for the suit is a constitutional provision (for instance in the case of a court reporter who challenges the absence of transcribed hearings on Due Process grounds), or a regulation? The inquiry is not under Article III, but also not really statutory. It is true that a statute may be required to permit review when the constitutional or regulatory provision does not protect the plaintiff's interest, but that appears not to be the sense in which Justice Scalia meant that the question was "statutory."

2. Is the zone of interests test gone again?
3. Can *Air Courier* really be distinguished from the facts of *NCUA*?
4. Is there a special rule for competitors?
5. Is the majority affected by the perceived clear illegality of the agency action, along with the absence of any other means of court review?
6. Suppose that, although Congress did not intend to benefit banks when it enacted the common-bond requirement in 1934, Congress's subsequent failure to repeal that requirement was motivated by a congressional desire to protect banks from competition from credit unions. Can the purpose of a statute in a coherent zone-of-interests analysis include Congress' reasons for *not repealing* the statute long after it has been passed?

3. Review of Standing Law

BENNETT v. SPEAR
520 U.S. 154 (1997)

Justice Scalia delivered the opinion of the [unanimous] Court.

This is a challenge to a biological opinion issued by the Fish and Wildlife Service in accordance with the Endangered Species Act of 1973 (ESA) concerning the operation of the Klamath Irrigation Project by the Bureau of Reclamation, and the project's impact on two varieties of endangered fish. The question for decision is whether the petitioners, who have competing economic and other interests in Klamath Project water, have standing to seek judicial review of the biological opinion under the citizen-suit provision of the ESA, § 1540(g)(1), and the Administrative Procedure Act (APA), 5 U.S.C. § 701 *et seq.*

I

The ESA requires the Secretary of the Interior to promulgate regulations listing those species of animals that are "threatened" or "endangered" under specified criteria, and to designate their "critical habitat." 16 U.S.C. § 1533. The ESA further requires each federal agency to "insure that any action authorized, funded, or carried out by such agency . . . is not likely to jeopardize the continued existence of any endangered species or threatened species or result in the destruction or adverse modification of habitat of such species which is determined by the Secretary . . . to be critical." § 1536(a)(2). If an agency determines that action it proposes to take may adversely affect a listed species, it must engage in formal consultation with the Fish and Wildlife Service, as delegate of the Secretary, *ibid.;* 50 CFR § 402.14 (1995), after which the Service must provide the agency with a written statement (the Biological Opinion) explaining how the proposed action will affect the species or its habitat, 16 U.S.C. § 1536(b)(3)(A). If the Service concludes that the proposed action will "jeopardize the continued existence of any [listed] species or result in the destruction or adverse modification of [critical habitat]," § 1536(a)(2), the Biological Opinion must outline any "reasonable and prudent alternatives" that the Service believes will avoid that consequence, § 1536(b)(3)(A). Additionally, if the Biological Opinion concludes that the agency action will not result in jeopardy or adverse habitat modification, or if it offers reasonable and prudent alternatives to avoid that consequence, the Service must provide the agency with a written statement (known as the "Incidental Take Statement") specifying the "impact of such incidental taking on the species," any "reasonable and prudent measures that the [Service] considers necessary or appropriate to minimize such impact," and setting forth "the terms and conditions . . . that must be complied with by the Federal agency . . . to implement [those measures]." § 1536(b)(4).

The Klamath Project, one of the oldest federal reclamation schemes, is a series of lakes, rivers, dams and irrigation canals in northern California and southern Oregon. The project was undertaken by the Secretary of the Interior pursuant to the Reclamation Act of 1902, 32 Stat. 388, as amended, 43 U.S.C. § 371 *et seq.*, and the Act of Feb. 9, 1905, 33 Stat. 714, and is administered by the Bureau of Reclamation, which is under the Secretary's jurisdiction. In 1992, the Bureau notified the Service that operation of the project might affect the Lost River Sucker *(Deltistes luxatus)* and Shortnose Sucker *(Chasmistes brevirostris),* species of fish that were listed as endangered in 1988, *see* 53 Fed. Reg. 27130-27133 (1988). After formal consultation with the Bureau in accordance with 50 CFR § 402.14 (1995), the Service issued a Biological Opinion which concluded that the "long-term operation of the Klamath Project was likely to jeopardize the continued existence of the Lost River and shortnose suckers." The Biological Opinion identified "reasonable and prudent alternatives" the Service believed would avoid jeopardy, which included the maintenance of minimum water levels on Clear Lake and Gerber reservoirs. The Bureau later notified the Service that it intended to operate the project in compliance with the Biological Opinion.

Petitioners, two Oregon irrigation districts that receive Klamath Project water and the operators of two ranches within those districts, filed the present action against the director and regional director of the Service and the Secretary of the Interior. Neither the Bureau nor any of its officials is named as defendant. The complaint asserts that the Bureau "has been following essentially the same procedures for storing and releasing water from Clear Lake and Gerber reservoirs throughout the twentieth century"; that "[t]here is no scientifically or commercially available evidence indicating that the populations of endangered suckers in Clear Lake and Gerber reservoirs have declined, are declining, or will decline as a result" of the Bureau's operation of the Klamath Project; that "[t]here is no commercially or scientifically available evidence indicating that the restrictions on lake levels imposed in the Biological Opinion will have any beneficial effect on the . . . populations of suckers in Clear Lake and Gerber reservoirs"; and that the Bureau nonetheless "will abide by the restrictions imposed by the Biological Opinion."

Petitioners' complaint included three claims for relief that are relevant here. The first and second claims allege that the Service's jeopardy determination with respect to Clear Lake and Gerber reservoirs, and the ensuing imposition of minimum water levels, violated § 7 of the ESA, 16 U.S.C. § 1536. The third claim is that the imposition of minimum water elevations constituted an implicit determination of critical habitat for the suckers, which violated § 4 of the ESA, 16 U.S.C. § 1533(b)(2), because it failed to take into consideration the designation's economic impact. Each of the claims also states that the relevant action violated the APA's prohibition of agency action that is "arbitrary, capricious, an abuse of discretion, or otherwise not in accordance with law." 5 U.S.C. § 706(2)(A).

The complaint asserts that petitioners' use of the reservoirs and related waterways for "recreational, aesthetic and commercial purposes, as well as for their primary sources of irrigation water" will be "irreparably damaged" by the actions complained of, and that the restrictions on water delivery "recommended" by the Biological Opinion "adversely affect plaintiffs by substantially reducing the quantity of available irrigation water." In essence, petitioners claim a competing interest in the water the Biological Opinion declares necessary for the preservation of the suckers.

The District Court dismissed the complaint for lack of jurisdiction. It concluded that petitioners did not have standing because their "recreational, aesthetic, and commercial interests . . . do not fall within the zone of interests sought to be protected by ESA." *Id.*, at 28. The Court of Appeals for the Ninth Circuit affirmed. *Bennett v. Plenert*, 63 F.3d 915 (1995). It held that the "zone of interests" test limits the class of persons who may obtain judicial review not only under the APA, but also under the citizen-suit provision of the ESA, 16 U.S.C. § 1540(g), and that "only plaintiffs who allege an interest in the *preservation* of endangered species fall within the zone of interests protected by the ESA," 63 F.3d at 919 (emphasis in original). We granted certiorari. 517 U.S. 1102 (1996).

In this Court, petitioners raise two questions: first, whether the prudential standing rule known as the "zone of interests" test applies to claims brought under the citizen-suit provision of the ESA; and second, if so, whether petitioners have standing under that test notwithstanding that the interests they seek to vindicate are economic rather than environmental. In this Court, the Government has made no effort to defend the reasoning of the Court of Appeals. Instead, it advances three alternative grounds for affirmance: (1) that petitioners fail to meet the standing requirements imposed by Article III of the Constitution; (2) that the ESA's citizen-suit provision does not authorize judicial review of the types of claims advanced by petitioners; and (3) that judicial review is unavailable under the APA because the Biological Opinion does not constitute final agency action.

II

We first turn to the question the Court of Appeals found dispositive: whether petitioners lack standing by virtue of the zone-of-interests test. Although petitioners contend that their claims lie both under the ESA and the APA, we look first at the ESA because it may permit petitioners to recover their litigation costs, *see* 16 U.S.C. § 1540(g)(4), and because the APA by its terms independently authorizes review only when "there is no other adequate remedy in a court," 5 U.S.C. § 704.

The question of standing "involves both constitutional limitations on federal-court jurisdiction and prudential limitations on its exercise." *Warth v. Seldin*, 422 U.S. 490, 498 (1975) (citing *Barrows v. Jackson*, 346 U.S. 249 (1953)). To satisfy the "case" or "controversy" requirement of Article III, which is the "irreducible constitutional minimum" of standing, a plaintiff must, generally speaking, demonstrate that he has suffered "injury in fact," that the injury is "fairly traceable" to the actions of the defendant, and that the injury will likely be redressed by a favorable decision. *Lujan v. Defenders of Wildlife*, 504 U.S. 555, 560-561 (1992); *Valley Forge Christian College v. Americans United for Separation of Church and State, Inc.*, 454 U.S. 464, 471-472 (1982). In addition to the immutable requirements of Article III, "the federal judiciary has also adhered to a set of prudential principles that bear on the question of standing." *Id.*, at 474-475. Like their constitutional counterparts, these "judicially self-imposed limits on the exercise of federal jurisdiction," *Allen v. Wright*, 468 U.S. 737, 751 (1984), are "founded in concern about the proper — and properly limited — role of the courts in a democratic society," *Warth, supra*, at 498; but unlike their constitutional counterparts, they can be modified or abrogated by Congress, see 422 U.S. at 501. Numbered among these prudential requirements is the doctrine of particular concern in this case: that a plaintiff's grievance must arguably fall within the zone of interests protected or regulated by the statutory provision or constitutional guarantee invoked in the suit. See *Allen, supra*, at 751; *Valley Forge, supra*, at 474-475.

The "zone of interests" formulation was first employed in *Association of Data Processing Service Organizations, Inc. v. Camp*, 397 U.S. 150 (1970). There, certain data processors sought to invalidate a ruling by the Comptroller of the Currency authorizing national banks to sell data processing services on the ground that it violated, inter alia, § 4 of the Bank Service Corporation Act of 1962, 76 Stat. 1132, which prohibited bank service corporations from engaging in "any activity other than the performance of bank services for banks." The Court of Appeals had held that the banks' data-processing competitors were without standing to challenge the alleged violation of § 4. In reversing, we stated the applicable prudential standing requirement to be "whether the interest sought to be protected by the complainant is arguably within the zone of interests to be protected or regulated by the statute or constitutional guarantee in question." *Data Processing, supra*, at 153. *Data Processing*, and its companion case, *Barlow v. Collins*, 397 U.S. 159 (1970), applied the zone-of-interests test to suits under the APA, but later cases have applied it also in suits not involving review of federal administrative action, see *Dennis v. Higgins*, 498 U.S. 439, 449 (1991), and have specifically listed it among other prudential standing requirements of general application, see, e.g., *Allen, supra*, at 751; *Valley Forge, supra*, at 474-475. We have made clear, however, that the breadth of the zone of interests varies according to the provisions of law at issue, so that what comes within the zone of interests of a statute for purposes of obtaining judicial review of administrative action under the "generous review provisions" of the APA may not do so for other purposes, *Clarke v. Securities Industry Assn.*, 479 U.S. 388, 400, n.16 (1987) (quoting *Data Processing, supra*, at 156).

Congress legislates against the background of our prudential standing doctrine, which applies unless it is expressly negated. *See Block v. Community Nutrition Institute*, 467 U.S. 340, 345-348 (1984). The first question in the present case is whether the ESA's citizen-suit provision, set forth in pertinent part in the margin,[2] negates the zone-of-interests test (or, perhaps more accurately, expands the zone of interests). We think it does. The first operative portion of the provision says that "any person may commence a civil suit" — an authorization of remarkable breadth when compared with the language Congress ordinarily uses. Even in some other environmental statutes, Congress has used more restrictive formulations, such as "[any person] having an interest which is or may be adversely affected," 33 U.S.C. § 1365(g) (Clean Water Act); *see also* 30 U.S.C. § 1270(a) (Surface Mining Control and Reclamation Act) (same); "[a]ny person suffering legal wrong," 15 U.S.C. § 797(b)(5) (Energy Supply and Environmental Coordination Act); or "any person having a valid legal interest which is or may be adversely affected . . . whenever such action constitutes a case or controversy," 42 U.S.C. § 9124(a) (Ocean Thermal Energy Conversion Act). And in contexts other than the environment, Congress has often been even more restrictive. In statutes concerning unfair trade practices and other commercial matters, for example, it has authorized suit only by "[a]ny person injured in his business or property," 7 U.S.C. § 2305(c); see also 15 U.S.C. § 72 (same), or only by "competitors, customers, or subsequent purchasers," § 298(b).

Our readiness to take the term "any person" at face value is greatly augmented by two interrelated considerations: that the overall subject matter of this legislation is the environment (a matter in which it is common to think all persons have an interest) and that the obvious purpose of the particular

---

2. "(1) Except as provided in paragraph (2) of this subsection any person may commence a civil suit on his own behalf—

"(A) to enjoin any person, including the United States and any other governmental instrumentality or agency (to the extent permitted by the eleventh amendment to the Constitution), who is alleged to be in violation of any provision of this chapter or regulation issued under the authority thereof; or. . . .
"(C) against the Secretary where there is alleged a failure of the Secretary to perform any act or duty under section 1533 of this title which is not discretionary with the Secretary.

"The district courts shall have jurisdiction, without regard to the amount in controversy or the citizenship of the parties, to enforce any such provision or regulation, or to order the Secretary to perform such act or duty, as the case may be. . . .

"(2)(A) No action may be commenced under subparagraph (1)(A) of this section—
"(i) prior to sixty days after written notice of the violation has been given to the Secretary, and to any alleged violator of any such provision or regulation;
"(ii) if the Secretary has commenced action to impose a penalty pursuant to subsection (a) of this section; or
"(iii) if the United States has commenced and is diligently prosecuting a criminal action . . . to redress a violation of any such provision or regulation. . . .
"(3)(B) In any such suit under this subsection in which the United States is not a party, the Attorney General, at the request of the Secretary, may intervene on behalf of the United States as a matter of right.
"(4) The court, in issuing any final order in any suit brought pursuant to paragraph (1) of this subsection, may award costs of litigation (including reasonable attorney and expert witness fees) to any party, whenever the court determines such award is appropriate." 16 U.S.C. § 1540(g).

provision in question is to encourage enforcement by so-called "private attorneys general" — evidenced by its elimination of the usual amount-in-controversy and diversity-of-citizenship requirements, its provision for recovery of the costs of litigation (including even expert witness fees), and its reservation to the Government of a right of first refusal to pursue the action initially and a right to intervene later. Given these factors, we think the conclusion of expanded standing follows *a fortiori* from our decision in *Trafficante v. Metropolitan Life Ins. Co.*, 409 U.S. 205 (1972), which held that standing was expanded to the full extent permitted under Article III by § 810(a) of the Civil Rights Act of 1968, 82 Stat. 85, 42 U.S.C. § 3610(a) (1986 ed.), that authorized "[a]ny person who claims to have been injured by a discriminatory housing practice" to sue for violations of the act. There also we relied on textual evidence of a statutory scheme to rely on private litigation to ensure compliance with the act. See 409 U.S., at 210-211. The statutory language here is even clearer, and the subject of the legislation makes the intent to permit enforcement by every man even more plausible.

It is true that the plaintiffs here are seeking to prevent application of environmental restrictions rather than to implement them. But the "any person" formulation applies to all the causes of action authorized by § 1540(g) — not only to actions against private violators of environmental restrictions, and not only to actions against the Secretary asserting underenforcement under § 1533, but also to actions against the Secretary asserting overenforcement under § 1533. As we shall discuss below, the citizen-suit provision does favor environmentalists in that it covers all private violations of the ESA but not all failures of the Secretary to meet his administrative responsibilities; but there is no textual basis for saying that its expansion of standing requirements applies to environmentalists alone. The Court of Appeals therefore erred in concluding that petitioners lacked standing under the zone-of-interests test to bring their claims under the ESA's citizen-suit provision.

III

The Government advances several alternative grounds upon which it contends we may affirm the dismissal of petitioners' suit. Because the District Court and the Court of Appeals found the zone-of-interests ground to be dispositive, these alternative grounds were not reached below. A respondent is entitled, however, to defend the judgment on any ground supported by the record. [Editor's note: Compare this principle with that of *Chenery I, supra*, pp. 274-76.] The asserted grounds were raised below, and have been fully briefed and argued here; we deem it an appropriate exercise of our discretion to consider them now rather than leave them for disposition on remand.

A

The Government's first contention is that petitioners' complaint fails to satisfy the standing requirements imposed by the "case" or "controversy" provision of Article III. This "irreducible constitutional minimum" of standing requires: (1) that the plaintiff have suffered an "injury in fact" — an invasion of a judicially cognizable interest which is (a) concrete and particularized and (b) actual or imminent, not conjectural or hypothetical; (2) that there be a causal connection between the injury and the conduct complained of—the injury must be fairly traceable to the challenged action of the defendant, and not the result of the independent action of some third party not before the court; and (3) that it be likely, as opposed to merely speculative, that the injury will be redressed by a favorable decision. *Defenders of Wildlife,* 504 U.S. at 560-561.

Petitioners allege, among other things, that they currently receive irrigation water from Clear Lake, that the Bureau "will abide by the restrictions imposed by the Biological Opinion," and that "[t]he restrictions on lake levels imposed in the Biological Opinion adversely affect [petitioners] by substantially reducing the quantity of available irrigation water." The Government contends, first, that these allegations fail to satisfy the "injury in fact" element of Article III standing because they demonstrate only a diminution in the *aggregate* amount of available water, and do not necessarily establish (absent information concerning the Bureau's water allocation practices) that the *petitioners* will receive less water. This contention overlooks, however, the proposition that each element of Article III standing "must be supported in the same way as any other matter on which the plaintiff bears the burden of proof, i.e., with the manner and degree of evidence required at the successive stages of the litigation." *Defenders of Wildlife, supra,* at 561. Thus, while a plaintiff must "set forth" by affidavit or other evidence "specific facts," to survive a motion for summary judgment, Fed. Rule Civ. Proc. 56(e), and must ultimately support any contested facts with evidence adduced at trial, "[a]t the pleading stage, general factual allegations of injury resulting from the defendant's conduct may suffice, for on a motion to dismiss we 'presum[e] that general allegations embrace those specific facts that are necessary to support the claim.'" *Defenders of Wildlife, supra,* at 561 (quoting *Lujan v. National Wildlife Federation,* 497 U.S. 871, 889 (1990)). Given petitioners' allegation that the amount of available water will be reduced and that they will be adversely affected thereby, it is easy to presume specific facts under which petitioners will be injured—for example, the Bureau's distribution of the reduction pro rata among its customers. The complaint alleges the requisite injury in fact.

The Government also contests compliance with the second and third Article III standing requirements, contending that any injury suffered by petitioners is neither "fairly traceable" to the Service's Biological Opinion, nor "redressable" by a favorable judicial ruling, because the "action agency" (the Bureau) retains ultimate responsibility for determining whether and how a proposed action shall go forward. *See* 50 CFR § 402.15(a) (1995) ("Following the issuance of a biological opinion, the Federal agency shall determine whether and in what manner to proceed with the action in light of its section 7 obligations and the Service's biological opinion"). "If the petitioners have suffered injury," the Government contends, "the proximate cause of their harm is an (as yet unidentified) decision by the Bureau regarding the volume of water allocated to petitioners, not the biological opinion itself." This wrongly equates injury "fairly traceable" to the defendant with injury as to which the defendant's actions are the very last step in the chain of causation. While, as we have said, it does not suffice if the injury complained of is "th[e] result [of] the *independent* action of some third party not before the court," *Defenders of Wildlife, supra,* 504 U.S. at 560-561 (emphasis added) (quoting *Simon v. Eastern Ky. Welfare Rights Organization,* 426 U.S. 26, 41-42 (1976)), that does not exclude injury produced by determinative or coercive effect upon the action of someone else.

By the Government's own account, while the Service's Biological Opinion theoretically serves an "advisory function," 51 Fed. Reg. 19928 (1986), in reality it has a powerful coercive effect on the action agency:

> "The statutory scheme ... presupposes that the biological opinion will play a central role in the action agency's decisionmaking process, and that it will typically be based on an administrative record that is fully adequate for the action agency's decision insofar as ESA issues are concerned. ... [A] federal agency that chooses to deviate from the recommendations contained in a biological opinion bears the burden of 'articulat[ing] in its administrative record its reasons for disagreeing with the conclusions of a biological opinion,' 51 Fed. Reg. 19,956 (1986). In the government's experience, action agencies very rarely choose to engage in conduct that the Service has concluded is likely to jeopardize the continued existence of a listed species."

What this concession omits to say, moreover, is that the action agency must not only articulate its reasons for disagreement (which ordinarily requires species and habitat investigations that are not within the action agency's expertise), but that it runs a substantial risk if its (inexpert) reasons turn out to be wrong. A Biological Opinion of the sort rendered here alters the legal regime to which the action agency is subject. When it "offers reasonable and prudent alternatives" to the proposed action, a Biological Opinion must include a so-called "Incidental Take Statement"—a written statement specifying, among other things, those "measures that the [Service] considers necessary or appropriate to minimize [the action's impact on the affected species]" and the "terms and conditions ... that must be complied with by the Federal agency ... to implement [such] measures." 16 U.S.C. § 1536(b)(4). Any taking that is in compliance with these terms and conditions "shall not be considered to be a prohibited taking of the species concerned." § 1536(o)(2). Thus, the Biological Opinion's Incidental Take Statement constitutes a permit authorizing the action agency to "take" the endangered or threatened species so long as it respects the Service's "terms and conditions." The action agency is technically free to disregard the Biological Opinion and proceed with its proposed action, but it does so at its own peril (and that of its employees), for "any person" who knowingly "takes" an endangered or threatened species is subject to substantial civil and criminal penalties, including imprisonment. *See* §§ 1540(a) and (b) (authorizing civil fines of up to $25,000 per violation and criminal penalties of up to $50,000 and imprisonment for one year); *see also Babbitt v. Sweet Home Chapter, Communities for Great Ore.*, 515 U.S. 687 (1995) (upholding interpretation of the term "take" to include significant habitat degradation).

The Service itself is, to put it mildly, keenly aware of the virtually determinative effect of its biological opinions. The Incidental Take Statement at issue in the present case begins by instructing the reader that any taking of a listed species is prohibited unless "such taking is in compliance with this incidental take statement," and warning that "the measures described below are nondiscretionary, and must be taken by [the Bureau]." Given all of this, and given petitioners' allegation that the Bureau had, until issuance of the Biological Opinion, operated the Klamath Project in the same manner throughout the twentieth century, it is not difficult to conclude that petitioners have met their burden—which is relatively modest at this stage of the litigation—of alleging that their injury is "fairly traceable" to the Service's Biological Opinion and that it will "likely" be redressed — i.e., the Bureau will not impose such water level restrictions — if the Biological Opinion is set aside.

B

Next, the Government contends that the ESA's citizen-suit provision does not authorize judicial review of petitioners' claims. The relevant portions of that provision provide that

> "any person may commence a civil suit on his own behalf—
> "(A) to enjoin any person, including the United States and any other governmental instrumentality or agency . . . who is alleged to be in violation of any provision of this chapter or regulation issued under the authority thereof; or. . . .
> "(C) against the Secretary [of Commerce or the Interior] where there is alleged a failure of the Secretary to perform any act or duty under section 1533 of this title which is not discretionary with the Secretary." 16 U.S.C. § 1540(g)(1).

The Government argues that judicial review is not available under subsection (A) because the Secretary is not "in violation" of the ESA, and under subsection (C) because the Secretary has not failed to perform any nondiscretionary duty under § 1533.

1

Turning first to subsection (C): that it covers only violations of § 1533 is clear and unambiguous. Petitioners' first and second claims, which assert that the Secretary has violated § 1536, are obviously not reviewable under this provision. However, as described above, the third claim alleges that the Biological Opinion implicitly determines critical habitat without complying with the mandate of § 1533(b)(2) that the Secretary "take into consideration the economic impact, and any other relevant impact, of specifying any particular area as critical habitat." This claim does come within subsection (C). [Discussion omitted.]

2

Having concluded that petitioners' § 1536 claims are not reviewable under subsection (C), we are left with the question whether they are reviewable under subsection (A), which authorizes injunctive actions against any person "who is alleged to be in violation" of the ESA or its implementing regulations. [Discussion omitted.] Viewed in the context of the entire statute, § 1540(g)(1)(A)'s reference to any "violation" of the ESA cannot be interpreted to include the Secretary's maladministration of the Act. Petitioners' claims are not subject to judicial review under § 1540(g)(1)(A).

IV

The foregoing analysis establishes that the principal statute invoked by petitioners, the ESA, does authorize review of their § 1533 claim, but does not support their claims based upon the Secretary's alleged failure to comply with § 1536. To complete our task, we must therefore inquire whether these § 1536 claims may nonetheless be brought under the Administrative Procedure

Act, which authorizes a court to "set aside agency action, findings, and conclusions found to be . . . arbitrary, capricious, an abuse of discretion, or otherwise not in accordance with law," 5 U.S.C. § 706.

A

No one contends (and it would not be maintainable) that the causes of action against the Secretary set forth in the ESA's citizen-suit provision are exclusive, supplanting those provided by the APA. The APA, by its terms, provides a right to judicial review of all "final agency action for which there is no other adequate remedy in a court," 5 U.S.C. § 704, and applies universally "except to the extent that — (1) statutes preclude judicial review; or (2) agency action is committed to agency discretion by law," § 701(a). Nothing in the ESA's citizen-suit provision expressly precludes review under the APA, nor do we detect anything in the statutory scheme suggesting a purpose to do so. And any contention that the relevant provision of 16 U.S.C. § 1536(a)(2) is discretionary would fly in the face of its text, which uses the imperative "shall."

In determining whether the petitioners have standing under the zone-of-interests test to bring their APA claims, we look not to the terms of the ESA's citizen-suit provision, but to the substantive provisions of the ESA, the alleged violations of which serve as the gravamen of the complaint. See *National Wildlife Federation*, 497 U.S. at 886. The classic formulation of the zone-of-interests test is set forth in *Data Processing*, 397 U.S. at 153: "whether the interest sought to be protected by the complainant is arguably within the zone of interests to be protected or regulated by the statute or constitutional guarantee in question." The Court of Appeals concluded that this test was not met here, since petitioners are neither directly regulated by the ESA nor seek to vindicate its overarching purpose of species preservation. That conclusion was error.

Whether a plaintiff's interest is "arguably . . . protected . . . by the statute" within the meaning of the zone-of-interests test is to be determined not by reference to the overall purpose of the Act in question (here, species preservation), but by reference to the particular provision of law upon which the plaintiff relies. It is difficult to understand how the Ninth Circuit could have failed to see this from our cases. In *Data Processing* itself, for example, we did not require that the plaintiffs' suit vindicate the overall purpose of the Bank Service Corporation Act of 1962, but found it sufficient that their commercial interest was sought to be protected by the anti-competition limitation contained in § 4 of the Act — the specific provision which they alleged had been violated. See *Data Processing, supra*, 397 U.S. at 155-156. As we said with the utmost clarity in *National Wildlife Federation*, "the plaintiff must establish that the injury he complains of . . . falls within the 'zone of interests' sought to be protected *by the statutory provision whose violation forms the legal basis for his complaint.*" *National Wildlife Federation, supra*, at 883 (emphasis added). See also *Air Courier Conference v. Postal Workers*, 498 U.S. 517, 523-524 (1991) (same).

In the claims that we have found not to be covered by the ESA's citizen-suit provision, petitioners allege a violation of § 7 of the ESA, 16 U.S.C. § 1536, which requires, *inter alia*, that each agency "use the best scientific and commercial data available," § 1536(a)(2). Petitioners contend that the available scientific and commercial data show that the continued operation of the Klamath Project will not have a detrimental impact on the endangered suckers, that the imposition of minimum lake levels is not necessary to protect the fish, and that by issuing a Biological Opinion which makes unsubstantiated findings to the contrary the defendants have acted arbitrarily and in violation of § 1536(a)(2). The obvious purpose of the requirement that each agency "use the best scientific and commercial data available" is to ensure that the ESA not be implemented haphazardly, on the basis of speculation or surmise. While this no doubt serves to advance the ESA's overall goal of species preservation, we think it readily apparent that another objective (if not indeed the primary one) is to avoid needless economic dislocation produced by agency officials zealously but unintelligently pursuing their environmental objectives. That economic consequences are an explicit concern of the act is evidenced by § 1536(h), which provides exemption from § 1536(a)(2)'s no-jeopardy mandate where there are no reasonable and prudent alternatives to the agency action and the benefits of the agency action clearly outweigh the benefits of any alternatives. We believe the "best scientific and commercial data" provision is similarly intended, at least in part, to prevent uneconomic (because erroneous) jeopardy determinations. Petitioners' claim that they are victims of such a mistake is plainly within the zone of interests that the provision protects.

[Part IV. B., rejecting the Government's argument that the Biological Opinion did not constitute "final agency action," is reproduced below at p. 619.]

The Court of Appeals erred in affirming the District Court's dismissal of petitioners' claims for lack of jurisdiction. Petitioners' complaint alleges facts sufficient to meet the requirements of Article III standing, and none of their ESA claims is precluded by the zone-of-interests test. Petitioners' § 1533 claim is reviewable under the ESA's citizen-suit provision, and petitioners' remaining claims are reviewable under the APA.

The judgment of the Court of Appeals is reversed, and the case is remanded for further proceedings consistent with this opinion. *It is so ordered.*

QUESTIONS

1. Can you reconcile *Bennett* with *Defenders of Wildlife, supra,* p. 651 Does standing depend on whether one is a property owner or an environmentalist?
2. The Court's discussion in *Bennett* accepted the very broad extent of standing recognized in *Trafficante.* Although the *Trafficante* Court did not cite *Sanders Brothers,* the Court concluded that Congress had granted statutory standing to any person who has Article III standing through the use of the statutory term "aggrieved." In *Thompson v. North American Stainless, LP,* 562 U.S. 170 (2011), the Supreme Court interpreted the scope of statutory standing granted by the Civil Rights Act of 1964, which permitted those "aggrieved" by unlawful employment activities to bring an action in federal court. *See* 42 U.S.C. §§ 2000e–5(f)(1) (providing that "a civil action may be brought . . . by the person claiming to be aggrieved"). The Court declined to find that Congress had imposed no statutory standing limits. See 562 U.S., at 177 ("the term 'aggrieved' must be construed more narrowly than the outer boundaries of Article III"). The Court instead concluded

that the provision triggered the application of the zone of interests test. See *id.* at 178 ("We hold that the term 'aggrieved' in Title VII incorporates this [zone of interests] test, enabling suit by any plaintiff with an interest 'arguably [sought] to be protected by the statutes,' while excluding plaintiffs who might technically be injured in an Article III sense but whose interests are unrelated to the statutory prohibitions in Title VII" (citation omitted)). The Court reached this conclusion despite the fact that the statutory provision had been enacted after *Sanders Brothers* and six years before the Supreme Court's unexpected interpretation of the "aggrieved" language in § 701 of the APA in *Data Processing*.

3. In *Lexmark Int'l, Inc. v. Static Control Components, Inc.*, 134 S. Ct. 1377 (2014), the Court considered whether a company could pursue a counterclaim that the counterclaim defendant had violated section 43(a) of the Lanham Act by its false advertising. *See id.* at 1384. The Lanham Act provision is codified at 15 U.S.C. § 1125(a). Congress had provided in that section that an action claiming a violation may be brought "in a civil action by any person who believes that he or she is or is likely to be damaged by such act." *Id.* This text was enacted in 1946. Ch. 540 (July 5, 1946), Tit. VIII § 43, 60 Stat. 441. The Court held that the zone of interests test "applies to *all* statutorily created causes of action," 134 S. Ct. at 1388, "'unless [the test] is expressly negated.'" *Id.* (citation omitted). When the Court applied this presumption to the Lanham Act provision, the Court concluded that "[t]he zone-of-interests test is therefore an appropriate tool for determining who may invoke the cause of action in § 1125(a)." *Id.* at 1388-89 (footnote omitted). Given the breadth of the Lanham Act provision quoted above, Congress will be able to accomplish the negation of the zone-of-interest test only if it enacts statutory text that is even clearer and broader than the quite clear and exceptionally broad text of § 1125(a). Should the zone of interests test, first described in 1970, have applied when this Lanham Act provision was enacted in 1946, just after the enactment of the APA?

   The Court also decided in *Lexmark Int'l* that, when applying the zone of interests test, the Court will require that the plaintiff show that the injury complained of was proximately caused by the violation of the statute:

   > [W]e generally presume that a statutory cause of action is limited to plaintiffs whose injuries are proximately caused by violations of the statute. For centuries, it has been a well established principle of [the common] law, that in all cases of loss, we are to attribute it to the proximate cause, and not to any remote cause. That venerable principle reflects the reality that the judicial remedy cannot encompass every conceivable harm that can be traced to alleged wrongdoing. Congress, we assume, is familiar with the common-law rule and does not mean to displace it *sub silentio*. We have thus construed federal causes of action in a variety of contexts to incorporate a requirement of proximate causation. No party disputes that it is proper to read § 1125(a) as containing such a requirement, its broad language notwithstanding.

   134 S. Ct. at 1390. Is the Court's resolution of the question of statutory standing in *Lexmark Int'l* consistent with Congress's grant of a right of action in the Lanham Act? Does the Court's requirement that a plaintiff show a

proximately caused injury to come within the zone of interests of the Lanham Act suggest that the Court will begin to impose a proximate cause requirement in an APA case?

THEORY APPLIED PROBLEM

The Bureau of Prisons (BOP), an agency within the U.S. Department of Justice, has the authority to assign federal prisoners to the facilities in which they must serve their terms of confinement. The scope of the BOP's discretion to designate where a prisoner will be incarcerated is defined by 18 U.S.C. § 3621(b). That provision provides the following:

> The Bureau of Prisons shall designate the place of the prisoner's imprisonment. The Bureau may designate any available penal or correctional facility that meets minimum standards of health and habitability established by the Bureau, whether maintained by the Federal Government or otherwise and whether within or without the judicial district in which the person was convicted, that the Bureau determines to be appropriate and suitable, considering —
> 1. the resources of the facility contemplated;
> 2. the nature and circumstances of the offense;
> 3. the history and characteristics of the prisoner;
> 4. any statement by the court that imposed the sentence —
>   A. concerning the purposes for which the sentence to imprisonment was determined to be warranted; or
>   B. recommending a type of penal or correctional facility as appropriate; and
> 5. any pertinent policy statement issued by the Sentencing Commission pursuant to section 994(a)(2) of title 28.
>
> In designating the place of imprisonment or making transfers under this subsection, there shall be no favoritism given to prisoners of high social or economic status. The Bureau may at any time, having regard for the same matters, direct the transfer of a prisoner from one penal or correctional facility to another. The Bureau shall make available appropriate substance abuse treatment for each prisoner the Bureau determines has a treatable condition of substance addiction or abuse.

Community Correction Inc. (CCI) operates community correction facilities, which offer private places of incarceration for federal inmates. CCI's facilities had been receiving federal inmates pursuant to a DOJ interpretation of § 3621(b), which provided that the BOP had unfettered discretion to order federal prisoners to be confined at any facility appropriate for incarceration, including privately operated facilities. CCI's facilities were viewed as appropriate for the incarceration of federal inmates.

The DOJ has now changed its interpretation of § 3621(b) to impose significant limits on when the BOP may place federal prisoners in CCI's facilities. Under this new interpretation, CCI is receiving greatly reduced numbers of federal inmates at its facilities.

CCI believes that the new DOJ interpretation of § 3621(b) is arbitrary or capricious. Analyze whether CCI has constitutional and zone-of-interests standing to assert its claim of illegality under the APA.

G. RIPENESS

ABBOTT LABORATORIES v. GARDNER
387 U.S. 136 (1967)

MR. JUSTICE HARLAN delivered the opinion of the Court.

In 1962 Congress amended the Federal Food, Drug, and Cosmetic Act to require manufacturers of prescription drugs to print the "established name" of the drug "prominently and in type at least half as large as that used thereon for any proprietary name or designation for such drug," on labels and other printed material, § 502(e)(1)(B), 21 U.S.C. § 352(e)(1)(B). The "established name" is one designated by the Secretary of Health, Education, and Welfare pursuant to § 502(e)(2) of the Act, 21 U.S.C. § 352(e)(2); the "proprietary name" is usually a trade name under which a particular drug is marketed. The underlying purpose of the 1962 amendment was to bring to the attention of doctors and patients the fact that many of the drugs sold under familiar trade names are actually identical to drugs sold under their "established" or less familiar trade names at significantly lower prices. The Commissioner of Food and Drugs, exercising authority delegated to him by the Secretary published proposed regulations designed to implement the statute. After inviting and considering comments submitted by interested parties the Commissioner promulgated the following regulation for the "efficient enforcement" of the Act, § 701(a), 21 U.S.C. § 371(a):

> "If the label or labeling of a prescription drug bears a proprietary name or designation for the drug or any ingredient thereof, the established name, if such there be, corresponding to such proprietary name or designation, shall accompany each appearance of such proprietary name or designation." 21 CFR § 1.104(g)(1).

A similar rule was made applicable to advertisements for prescription drugs, 21 CFR § 1.105 (b)(1). The present action was brought by a group of 37 individual drug manufacturers and by the Pharmaceutical Manufacturers Association, of which all the petitioner companies are members, and which includes manufacturers of more than 90% of the Nation's supply of prescription drugs. They challenged the regulations on the ground that the Commissioner exceeded his authority under the statute by promulgating an order requiring labels, advertisements, and other printed matter relating to prescription drugs to designate the established name of the particular drug involved every time its trade name is used anywhere in such material.

The District Court, on cross motions for summary judgment, granted the declaratory and injunctive relief sought, finding that the statute did not sweep so broadly as to permit the Commissioner's "every time" interpretation. The Court of Appeals for the Third Circuit reversed without reaching the merits of the case. It held first that under the statutory scheme provided by the Federal Food, Drug, and Cosmetic Act pre-enforcement[2] review of these regulations was unauthorized and therefore beyond the jurisdiction of the District Court.

---

2. That is, a suit brought by one before any attempted enforcement of the statute or regulation against him.

Second, the Court of Appeals held that no "actual case or controversy" existed and, for that reason, that no relief under the Administrative Procedure Act, 5 U.S.C. §§ 701-704, or under the Declaratory Judgment Act, 28 U.S.C. § 2201, was in any event available. . . .

I

The first question we consider is whether Congress by the Federal Food, Drug, and Cosmetic Act intended to forbid pre-enforcement review of this sort of regulation promulgated by the Commissioner. The question is phrased in terms of "prohibition" rather than "authorization" because a survey of our cases shows that judicial review of a final agency action by an aggrieved person will not be cut off unless there is persuasive reason to believe that such was the purpose of Congress. Early cases in which this type of judicial review was entertained have been reinforced by the enactment of the Administrative Procedure Act, which embodies the basic presumption of judicial review to one "suffering legal wrong because of agency action, or adversely affected or aggrieved by agency action within the meaning of a relevant statute," 5 U.S.C. § 702, so long as no statute precludes such relief or the action is not one committed by law to agency discretion, 5 U.S.C. § 701(a). The Administrative Procedure Act provides specifically not only for review of "[a]gency action made reviewable by statute" but also for review of "final agency action for which there is no other adequate remedy in a court," 5 U.S.C. § 704. The legislative material elucidating that seminal act manifests a congressional intention that it cover a broad spectrum of administrative actions, and this Court has echoed that theme by noting that the Administrative Procedure Act's "generous review provisions" must be given a "hospitable" interpretation. Again in *Rusk v. Cort, supra,* at 379-380, the Court held that only upon a showing of "clear and convincing evidence" of a contrary legislative intent should the courts restrict access to judicial review. *See also* Jaffe, Judicial Control of Administrative Action 336-359 (1965).

Given this standard, we are wholly unpersuaded that the statutory scheme in the food and drug area excludes this type of action. The Government relies on no explicit statutory authority for its argument that pre-enforcement review is unavailable, but insists instead that because the statute includes a specific procedure for such review of certain enumerated kinds of regulations, not encompassing those of the kind involved here, other types were necessarily meant to be excluded from any pre-enforcement review. The issue, however, is not so readily resolved; we must go further and inquire whether in the context of the entire legislative scheme the existence of that circumscribed remedy evinces a congressional purpose to bar agency action not within its purview from judicial review. As a leading authority in this field has noted, "The mere fact that some acts are made reviewable should not suffice to support an implication of exclusion as to others. The right to review is too important to be excluded on such slender and indeterminate evidence of legislative intent." Jaffe, *supra,* at 357.

In this case the Government has not demonstrated such a purpose; indeed, a study of the legislative history shows rather conclusively that the specific review provisions were designed to give an additional remedy and not to cut down more traditional channels of review. . . .

This conclusion is strongly buttressed by the fact that the Act itself, in §701(f)(6), states, "The remedies provided for in this subsection shall be in addition to and not in substitution for any other remedies provided by law." . . .

We conclude that nothing in the Food, Drug, and Cosmetic Act itself precludes this action.

II

A further inquiry must, however, be made. The injunctive and declaratory judgment remedies are discretionary, and courts traditionally have been reluctant to apply them to administrative determinations unless these arise in the context of a controversy "ripe" for judicial resolution. Without undertaking to survey the intricacies of the ripeness doctrine it is fair to say that its basic rationale is to prevent the courts, through avoidance of premature adjudication, from entangling themselves in abstract disagreements over administrative policies, and also to protect the agencies from judicial interference until an administrative decision has been formalized and its effects felt in a concrete way by the challenging parties. The problem is best seen in a twofold aspect, requiring us to evaluate both the fitness of the issues for judicial decision and the hardship to the parties of withholding court consideration.

As to the former factor, we believe the issues presented are appropriate for judicial resolution at this time. First, all parties agree that the issue tendered is a purely legal one: whether the statute was properly construed by the Commissioner to require the established name of the drug to be used *every time* the proprietary name is employed.[16] Both sides moved for summary judgment in the District Court, and no claim is made here that further administrative proceedings are contemplated. It is suggested that the justification for this rule might vary with different circumstances, and that the expertise of the Commissioner is relevant to passing upon the validity of the regulation. This of course is true, but the suggestion overlooks the fact that both sides have approached this case as one purely of congressional intent, and that the Government made no effort to justify the regulation in factual terms.

Second, the regulations in issue we find to be "final agency action" within the meaning of §10 of the Administrative Procedure Act, 5 U.S.C. §704, as construed in judicial decisions. An "agency action" includes any "rule," defined by the Act as "an agency statement of general or particular applicability and future effect designed to implement, interpret, or prescribe law or policy," §§2(c), 2(g), 5 U.S.C. §§551(4), 551(13). The cases dealing with judicial review of administrative actions have interpreted the "finality" element in a pragmatic way. Thus in *Columbia Broadcasting System v. United States*, 316 U.S. 407, a suit under the Urgent Deficiencies Act, 38 Stat. 219, this Court held reviewable a regulation of the Federal Communications Commission setting forth certain proscribed contractual arrangements between chain broadcasters and local stations. The FCC did not have direct authority to regulate these contracts, and its rule asserted only that it would not license stations which maintained such contracts with the networks. Although no license had in fact been denied or

---

16. While the "every time" issue has been framed by the parties in terms of statutory *compulsion*, we think that its essentially legal character would not be different had it been framed in terms of statutory *authorization* for the requirement.

revoked, and the FCC regulation could properly be characterized as a statement only of its intentions, the Court held that "Such regulations have the force of law before their sanctions are invoked as well as after. When, as here, they are promulgated by order of the Commission and the expected conformity to them causes injury cognizable by a court of equity, they are appropriately the subject of attack. . . ." 316 U.S., at 418-419.

Two more recent cases have taken a similarly flexible view of finality. In *Frozen Food Express v. United States*, 351 U.S. 40, at issue was an Interstate Commerce Commission order specifying commodities that were deemed to fall within the statutory class of "agricultural commodities." Vehicles carrying such commodities were exempt from ICC supervision. An action was brought by a carrier that claimed to be transporting exempt commodities, but which the ICC order had not included in its terms. Although the dissenting opinion noted that this ICC order had no authority except to give notice of how the Commission interpreted the Act and would have effect only if and when a particular action was brought against a particular carrier, and argued that "judicial intervention [should] be withheld until administrative action has reached its complete development," 351 U.S., at 45, the Court held the order reviewable.

Again, in *United States v. Storer Broadcasting Co.*, 351 U.S. 192, the Court held to be a final agency action within the meaning of the Administrative Procedure Act an FCC regulation announcing a Commission policy that it would not issue a television license to an applicant already owning five such licenses, even though no specific application was before the Commission. The Court stated: "The process of rulemaking was complete. It was final agency action . . . by which Storer claimed to be 'aggrieved.'" 351 U.S., at 198.

We find decision in the present case following *a fortiori* from these precedents. The regulation challenged here, promulgated in a formal manner after announcement in the Federal Register and consideration of comments by interested parties is quite clearly definitive. There is no hint that this regulation is informal, *see Helco Products Co. v. McNutt*, 137 F.2d 681, or only the ruling of a subordinate official, see *Swift & Co. v. Wickham*, 230 F. Supp. 398, 409, *aff'd*, 364 F.2d 241, or tentative. It was made effective upon publication, and the Assistant General Counsel for Food and Drugs stated in the District Court that compliance was expected.

The Government argues, however, that the present case can be distinguished from cases like *Frozen Food Express* on the ground that in those instances the agency involved could implement its policy directly, while here the Attorney General must authorize criminal and seizure actions for violations of the statute. In the context of this case, we do not find this argument persuasive. These regulations are not meant to advise the Attorney General, but purport to be directly authorized by the statute. Thus, if within the Commissioner's authority, they have the status of law and violations of them carry heavy criminal and civil sanctions. Also, there is no representation that the Attorney General and the Commissioner disagree in this area; the Justice Department is defending this very suit. It would be adherence to a mere technicality to give any credence to this contention. Moreover, the agency does have direct authority to enforce this regulation in the context of passing upon applications for clearance of new drugs, §505, 21 U.S.C. §355, or certification of certain antibiotics, §507, 21 U.S.C. §357.

This is also a case in which the impact of the regulations upon the petitioners is sufficiently direct and immediate as to render the issue appropriate for judicial review at this stage. These regulations purport to give an authoritative interpretation of a statutory provision that has a direct effect on the day-to-day business of all prescription drug companies; its promulgation puts petitioners in a dilemma that it was the very purpose of the Declaratory Judgment Act to ameliorate. As the District Court found on the basis of uncontested allegations, "Either they must comply with the every time requirement and incur the costs of changing over their promotional material and labeling or they must follow their present course and risk prosecution." The regulations are clear-cut, and were made effective immediately upon publication; as noted earlier the agency's counsel represented to the District Court that immediate compliance with their terms was expected. If petitioners wish to comply they must change all their labels, advertisements, and promotional materials; they must destroy stocks of printed matter; and they must invest heavily in new printing type and new supplies. The alternative to compliance — continued use of material which they believe in good faith meets the statutory requirements, but which clearly does not meet the regulation of the Commissioner — may be even more costly. That course would risk serious criminal and civil penalties for the unlawful distribution of "misbranded" drugs.

It is relevant at this juncture to recognize that petitioners deal in a sensitive industry, in which public confidence in their drug products is especially important. To require them to challenge these regulations only as a defense to an action brought by the Government might harm them severely and unnecessarily. Where the legal issue presented is fit for judicial resolution, and where a regulation requires an immediate and significant change in the plaintiffs' conduct of their affairs with serious penalties attached to noncompliance, access to the courts under the Administrative Procedure Act and the Declaratory Judgment Act must be permitted, absent a statutory bar or some other unusual circumstance, neither of which appears here.

The Government does not dispute the very real dilemma in which petitioners are placed by the regulation, but contends that "mere financial expense" is not a justification for pre-enforcement judicial review. It is of course true that cases in this Court dealing with the standing of particular parties to bring an action have held that a possible financial loss is not by itself a sufficient interest to sustain a judicial challenge to governmental action. But there is no question in the present case that petitioners have sufficient standing as plaintiffs: the regulation is directed at them in particular; it requires them to make significant changes in their everyday business practices; if they fail to observe the Commissioner's rule they are quite clearly exposed to the imposition of strong sanctions. . . .

The Government further contends that the threat of criminal sanctions for noncompliance with a judicially untested regulation is unrealistic; the Solicitor General has represented that if court enforcement becomes necessary, "the Department of Justice will proceed only civilly for an injunction . . . or by condemnation." We cannot accept this argument as a sufficient answer to petitioners' petition. This action at its inception was properly brought and this subsequent representation of the Department of Justice should not suffice to defeat it.

Finally, the Government urges that to permit resort to the courts in this type of case may delay or impede effective enforcement of the Act. We fully recognize the important public interest served by assuring prompt and unimpeded administration of the Pure Food, Drug, and Cosmetic Act, but we do not find the Government's argument convincing. First, in this particular case, a pre-enforcement challenge by nearly all prescription drug manufacturers is calculated to speed enforcement. If the Government prevails, a large part of the industry is bound by the decree; if the Government loses, it can more quickly revise its regulation.

The Government contends, however, that if the Court allows this consolidated suit, then nothing will prevent a multiplicity of suits in various jurisdictions challenging other regulations. The short answer to this contention is that the courts are well equipped to deal with such eventualities. The venue transfer provision, 28 U.S.C. § 1404(a), may be invoked by the Government to consolidate separate actions. Or, actions in all but one jurisdiction might be stayed pending the conclusion of one proceeding. A court may even in its discretion dismiss a declaratory judgment or injunctive suit if the same issue is pending in litigation elsewhere. In at least one suit for a declaratory judgment, relief was denied with the suggestion that the plaintiff intervene in a pending action elsewhere.

Further, the declaratory judgment and injunctive remedies are equitable in nature, and other equitable defenses may be interposed. If a multiplicity of suits are undertaken in order to harass the Government or to delay enforcement, relief can be denied on this ground alone. The defense of laches could be asserted if the Government is prejudiced by a delay. And courts may even refuse declaratory relief for the nonjoinder of interested parties who are not, technically speaking, indispensable.

In addition to all these safeguards against what the Government fears, it is important to note that the institution of this type of action does not by itself stay the effectiveness of the challenged regulation. There is nothing in the record to indicate that petitioners have sought to stay enforcement of the "every time" regulation pending judicial review. *See* 5 U.S.C. § 705. If the agency believes that a suit of this type will significantly impede enforcement or will harm the public interest, it need not postpone enforcement of the regulation and may oppose any motion for a judicial stay on the part of those challenging the regulation. *Ibid.* It is scarcely to be doubted that a court would refuse to postpone the effective date of an agency action if the Government could show, as it made no effort to do here, that delay would be detrimental to the public health or safety. *See Associated Securities Corp. v. SEC*, 283 F.2d 773, 775, where a stay was denied because "the petitioners . . . [had] not sustained the burden of establishing that the requested stays will not be harmful to the public interest . . ."; *see Eastern Air Lines v. CAB*, 261 F.2d 830; cf. *Scripps-Howard Radio v. FCC*, 316 U.S. 4, 10-11; 5 U.S.C. § 705.

Lastly, although the Government presses us to reach the merits of the challenge to the regulation in the event we find the District Court properly entertained this action, we believe the better practice is to remand the case to the Court of Appeals for the Third Circuit to review the District Court's decision that the regulation was beyond the power of the Commissioner. *Reversed and remanded.* [Justices Fortas and Clark dissented.]

TOILET GOODS ASS'N v. GARDNER
387 U.S. 158 (1967)

Mr. Justice Harlan delivered the opinion of the Court.

Petitioners in this case are the Toilet Goods Association, an organization of cosmetics manufacturers accounting for some 90% of annual American sales in this field, and 39 individual cosmetics manufacturers and distributors. They brought this action in the United States District Court for the Southern District of New York seeking declaratory and injunctive relief against the Secretary of Health, Education, and Welfare and the Commissioner of Food and Drugs, on the ground that certain regulations promulgated by the Commissioner exceeded his statutory authority under the Color Additive Amendments to the Federal Food, Drug, and Cosmetic Act, 74 Stat. 397, 21 U.S.C. §§ 321-376. The District Court held that the Act did not prohibit this type of preenforcement suit, that a case and controversy existed, that the issues presented were justiciable, and that no reasons had been presented by the Government to warrant declining jurisdiction on discretionary grounds. . . . The Court of Appeals affirmed the judgment of the District Court that jurisdiction to hear the suit existed as to three of the challenged regulations, but sustained the Government's contention that judicial review was improper as to a fourth.

Each side below sought review here from the portions of the Court of Appeals' decision adverse to it, the Government as petitioner in *Gardner v. Toilet Goods Assn.*, No. 438, and the Toilet Goods Association and other plaintiffs in the present case. . . . The two *Toilet Goods* cases were set and argued together with *Abbott Laboratories.*

In our decisions reversing the judgment in *Abbott Laboratories* and affirming the judgment in *Gardner v. Toilet Goods Assn.*, both decided today, we hold that nothing in the Food, Drug, and Cosmetic Act, 52 Stat. 1040, as amended, bars a pre-enforcement suit under the Administrative Procedure Act, 5 U.S.C. §§ 701-704 (1964 ed., Supp. II), and the Declaratory Judgment Act, 28 U.S.C. § 2201. We nevertheless agree with the Court of Appeals that judicial review of this particular regulation in this particular context is inappropriate at this stage because, applying the standards set forth in *Abbott Laboratories v. Gardner*, the controversy is not presently ripe for adjudication.

The regulation in issue here was promulgated under the Color Additive Amendments of 1960, 74 Stat. 397, 21 U.S.C. §§ 321-376, a statute that revised and somewhat broadened the authority of the Commissioner to control the ingredients added to foods, drugs, and cosmetics that impart color to them. The Commissioner of Food and Drugs, exercising power delegated by the Secretary, 22 Fed. Reg. 1051, 25 Fed. Reg. 8625, under statutory authority "to promulgate regulations for the efficient enforcement" of the Act, § 701(a), 21 U.S.C. § 371 (a), issued the following regulation after due public notice, 26 Fed. Reg. 679, and consideration of comments submitted by interested parties:

"(a) When it appears to the Commissioner that a person has: . . .
"(4) Refused to permit duly authorized employees of the Food and Drug Administration free access to all manufacturing facilities, processes, and formulae involved in the manufacture of color additives and intermediates from which such color additives are derived;

"he may immediately suspend certification service to such person and may continue such suspension until adequate corrective action has been taken." 28 Fed. Reg. 6445-6446; 21 CFR § 8.28.[1]

The petitioners maintain that this regulation is an impermissible exercise of authority, that the FDA has long sought congressional authorization for free access to facilities, processes, and formulae, but that Congress has always denied the agency this power except for prescription drugs. § 704, 21 U.S.C. § 374. Framed in this way, we agree with petitioners that a "legal" issue is raised, but nevertheless we are not persuaded that the present suit is properly maintainable.

In determining whether a challenge to an administrative regulation is ripe for review a twofold inquiry must be made: first to determine whether the issues tendered are appropriate for judicial resolution, and second to assess the hardship to the parties if judicial relief is denied at that stage.

As to the first of these factors, we agree with the Court of Appeals that the legal issue as presently framed is not appropriate for judicial resolution. This is not because the regulation is not the agency's considered and formalized determination, for we are in agreement with petitioners that under this Court's decisions in *Frozen Food Express v. United States*, 351 U.S. 40, and *United States v. Storer Broadcasting Co.*, 351 U.S. 192, there can be no question that this regulation — promulgated in a formal manner after notice and evaluation of submitted comments — is a "final agency action" under § 10 of the Administrative Procedure Act, 5 U.S.C. § 704. *See Abbott Laboratories v. Gardner, ante.* Also, we recognize the force of petitioners' contention that the issue as they have framed it presents a purely legal question: whether the regulation is totally beyond the agency's power under the statute, the type of legal issue that courts have occasionally dealt with without requiring a specific attempt at enforcement, *Columbia Broadcasting System v. United States*, 316 U.S. 407; cf. *Pierce v. Society of Sisters*, 268 U.S. 510, or exhaustion of administrative remedies.

These points which support the appropriateness of judicial resolution are, however, outweighed by other considerations. The regulation serves notice only that the Commissioner *may* under certain circumstances order inspection of certain facilities and data, and that further certification of additives *may* be refused to those who decline to permit a duly authorized inspection until they have complied in that regard. At this juncture we have no idea whether or when such an inspection will be ordered and what reasons the Commissioner will give to justify his order. The statutory authority asserted for the regulation is the power to promulgate regulations "for the efficient enforcement" of the Act, § 701(a). Whether the regulation is justified thus depends not only, as petitioners appear to suggest, on whether Congress refused to include a specific section of the Act authorizing such inspections, although this factor is to be sure a highly relevant one, but also on whether the statutory scheme as a whole justified promulgation of the regulation. *See Wong Yang Sung v. McGrath*, 339

1. The Color Additive Amendments provide for listings of color additives by the Secretary "if and to the extent that such additives are suitable and safe. . . ." § 706(b)(1), 21 U.S.C. § 376(b)(1). The Secretary is further authorized to provide "for the certification, with safe diluents or without diluents, of batches of color additives. . . ." § 706(c), 21 U.S.C. § 376(c). A color additive is "deemed unsafe" unless it is either from a certified batch or exempted from the certification requirement, § 706(a), 21 U.S.C. § 376(a). A cosmetic containing such an "unsafe" additive is deemed to be adulterated, § 601(e), 21 U.S.C. § 361(e), and is prohibited from interstate commerce. § 301(a), 21 U.S.C. § 331(a).

U.S. 33, 47. This will depend not merely on an inquiry into statutory purpose, but concurrently on an understanding of what types of enforcement problems are encountered by the FDA, the need for various sorts of supervision in order to effectuate the goals of the Act, and the safeguards devised to protect legitimate trade secrets (*see* 21 CFR § 130.14(c)). We believe that judicial appraisal of these factors is likely to stand on a much surer footing in the context of a specific application of this regulation than could be the case in the framework of the generalized challenge made here.

We are also led to this result by considerations of the effect on the petitioners of the regulation, for the test of ripeness, as we have noted, depends not only on how adequately a court can deal with the legal issue presented, but also on the degree and nature of the regulation's present effect on those seeking relief. The regulation challenged here is not analogous to those . . . where the impact of the administrative action could be said to be felt immediately by those subject to it in conducting their day-to-day affairs.

This is not a situation in which primary conduct is affected — when contracts must be negotiated, ingredients tested or substituted, or special records compiled. This regulation merely states that the Commissioner may authorize inspectors to examine certain processes or formulae; no advance action is required of cosmetics manufacturers, who since the enactment of the 1938 Act have been under a statutory duty to permit reasonable inspection of a "factory, warehouse, establishment, or vehicle and all pertinent equipment, finished and unfinished materials; containers, and labeling therein." § 704(a). Moreover, no irremediable adverse consequences flow from requiring a later challenge to this regulation by a manufacturer who refuses to allow this type of inspection. Unlike the other regulations challenged in this action, in which seizure of goods, heavy fines, adverse publicity for distributing "adulterated" goods, and possible criminal liability might penalize failure to comply, a refusal to admit an inspector here would at most lead only to a suspension of certification services to the particular party, a determination that can then be promptly challenged through an administrative procedure,[2] which in turn is reviewable by a court. Such review will provide an adequate forum for testing the regulation in a concrete situation.

It is true that the administrative hearing will deal with the "factual basis" of the suspension, from which petitioners infer that the Commissioner will not entertain and consider a challenge to his statutory authority to promulgate the regulation. Whether or not this assumption is correct, given the fact that only minimal, if any, adverse consequences will face petitioners if they challenge the regulation in this manner, we think it wiser to require them to exhaust this administrative process through which the factual basis of the inspection order will certainly be aired and where more light may be thrown on the Commissioner's statutory and practical justifications for the regulation. Judicial review will then be available, and a court at that juncture will be in a better position to

2. We recognize that a denial of certification might under certain circumstances cause inconvenience and possibly hardship, depending upon such factors as how large a supply of certified additives the particular manufacturer may have, how rapidly the administrative hearing and judicial review are conducted, and what temporary remedial or protective provisions, such as compliance with a reservation pending litigation, might be available to a manufacturer testing the regulation. In the context of the present case we need only say that such inconvenience is speculative and we have been provided with no information that would support an assumption that much weight should be attached to this possibility.

deal with the question of statutory authority. Administrative Procedure Act § 10(e)(B)(3), 5 U.S.C. § 706(2)(C).

For these reasons the judgment of the Court of Appeals is *Affirmed.*

MR. JUSTICE FORTAS, with whom the CHIEF JUSTICE and MR. JUSTICE CLARK join, concurring in [*Toilet Goods*], and dissenting in [*Abbott Labs* and a companion case]. . . .

With all respect, I submit that established principles of jurisprudence, solidly rooted in the constitutional structure of our Government, require that the courts should not intervene in the administrative process at this stage, under these facts and in this gross, shotgun fashion. . . . In none of these cases is judicial interference warranted at this stage, in this fashion, and to test — on a gross, free-wheeling basis — whether the content of these regulations is within the statutory intendment. The contrary is dictated by a proper regard for the purpose of the regulatory statute and the requirements of effective administration; and by regard for the salutary rule that courts should pass upon concrete, specific questions in a particularized setting rather than upon a general controversy divorced from particular facts.

The Court . . . has opened Pandora's box. Federal injunctions will now threaten programs of vast importance to the public welfare. The Court's holding here strikes at programs for the public health. The dangerous precedent goes even further. It is cold comfort — it is little more than delusion — to read in the Court's opinion that "It is scarcely to be doubted that a court would refuse to postpone the effective date of an agency action if the Government could show . . . that delay would be detrimental to the public health or safety." Experience dictates, on the contrary, that it can hardly be hoped that some federal judge somewhere will not be moved as the Court is here, by the cries of anguish and distress of those regulated, to grant a disruptive injunction.

The difference between the majority and me in these cases is not with respect to the existence of jurisdiction to enjoin, but to the definition of occasions on which such jurisdiction may be invoked. . . . I believe that [the Court's] approach improperly and unwisely gives individual federal district judges a roving Commission to halt the regulatory process, and to do so on the basis of abstractions and generalities instead of concrete fact situations, and that it impermissibly broadens the license of the courts to intervene in administrative action by means of a threshold suit for injunction rather than by the method provided by statute.

The Administrative Procedure Act and fundamental principles of our jurisprudence insist that there must be some type of effective judicial review of final, substantive agency action which seriously affects personal or property rights. But, "[a]ll constitutional questions aside, it is for Congress to determine how the rights which it creates shall be enforced. . . . In such a case the specification of one remedy normally excludes another." Where Congress has provided a method of review, the requisite showing to induce the courts otherwise to bring a governmental program to a halt may not be made by a mere showing of the impact of the regulation and the customary hardships of interim compliance. At least in cases where the claim is of erroneous action rather than the lack of jurisdiction or denial of procedural due process, a suit for injunctive or declaratory relief will not lie absent a clear demonstration that the type of review available under the statute would not be "adequate," that the controversies are otherwise "ripe" for judicial decision, and that no public interest exists which offsets the private values which the litigation seeks to vindicate. As I shall discuss, no such showing is or can be made here.

I

Since enactment of the Federal Food, Drug, and Cosmetic Act in 1938, the mechanism for judicial review of agency actions under its provisions has been well understood. Except for specific types of agency regulations and actions to which I shall refer, judicial review has been confined to enforcement actions instituted by the Attorney General on recommendation of the agency. As the recurrent debate over this technique demonstrates, this restricted avenue for challenge has been deemed necessary because of the direct and urgent relationship of the field of regulation to the public health. It is this avenue that applies with respect to the regulations at issue in the present cases.

The scheme of the Act, in this respect, is as follows: "Prohibited acts" are listed in § 301, 52 Stat. 1042, as amended, 21 U.S.C. § 331. Subsequent sections authorize the Attorney General to institute three types of proceedings. First, he may apply to the district courts of the United States for injunctive relief. If an injunction is violated, jury trial is assured on demand of the accused. Second, the Attorney General may institute libel proceedings in the district courts and seek orders for seizure of any misbranded or adulterated food, drug, device, or cosmetic. Third, criminal prosecution is authorized for violations, but before the Secretary may report a violation to the Attorney General for criminal prosecution, he must afford the affected person an opportunity to present his views.

The present regulations concededly would be reviewable in the course of any of the above proceedings. Apart from these general provisions, the Act contains specific provisions for administrative hearing and review in the courts of appeals with respect to regulations issued under certain, enumerated provisions of the Act—not including those here involved. . . .

I submit that if we are to judge and not to legislate policy, we should implement and not contradict the program laid out by the Congress. Congress did not intend that the regulations at issue in this case might be challenged in gross, apart from a specific controversy, or in the district courts, or by injunction or declaratory judgment action. . . .

The Court is in error, I submit, in its approach to this problem; and, as I shall attempt to show, it is in error in its decision that, even given this permissive approach to the use of judicial injunctive power, these controversies are "ripe" or appropriate for decision.

II

I come then to the questions whether the review otherwise available under the statute is "adequate," whether the controversies are "ripe" or appropriate for review in terms of the evaluation of the competing private and public interests. I discuss these together because the questions of adequacy and ripeness or appropriateness for review are interrelated. I again note that no constitutional issues are raised, and, indeed, no issues as to the authority of the agency to issue regulations of the general sort involved. The only issue is whether that authority was properly exercised.

There is, of course, no abstract or mechanical method for determining the adequacy of review provisions. Where personal status or liberties are involved, the courts may well insist upon a considerable ease of challenging administrative orders or regulations. But in situations where a regulatory scheme designed to protect the public is involved, this Court has held that postponement of the opportunity to obtain judicial relief in the interest of avoiding disruption of the regulatory plan is entirely justifiable. *Ewing v. Mytinger & Casselberry*, 339 U.S. 594 (1950); cf. *Myers v. Bethlehem Shipbuilding Corp.*, 303 U.S. 41 (1938). The *Ewing* case dramatically illustrates the point. It involves the same statute and enforcement plan as are now before us. Appellee filed suit in the United States District Court to restrain enforcement of the provision of the Food, Drug, and Cosmetic Act which authorizes multiple seizure of misbranded products. Appellee claimed that the provision was unconstitutional under the Due Process Clause, and that the agency had acted arbitrarily "in instituting" (through the Attorney General) multiple seizures without affording appellee an opportunity for hearing as to whether there was "probable cause" for the seizures. A three-judge district court was convened. It held for appellee on both issues and granted an injunction. This Court reversed on the grounds that no hearing is necessary for the administrative determination of probable cause, and that, in any event, the District Court had no jurisdiction to review that determination. [Further discussion of *Ewing* omitted.]

I submit that this Court's action in Nos. 39 and 438 sharply departs from *Ewing* and from the principles of judicial restraint and respect for congressional enactments and administrative agencies which have to this day been fundamental to our jurisprudence. The Court refers in passing to the injunctions here as "traditional avenues of judicial relief." But there is nothing "traditional" about the courts providing injunctive relief against agency action in situations where the Congress has prescribed another avenue which is available to the plaintiffs. Eloquent testimony of this is the paucity of pertinent precedents.

. . . .

The Court, however, moved by petitioners' claims as to the expense and inconvenience of compliance and the risks of deferring challenge by noncompliance, decrees that the manufacturers may have their suit for injunction at this time and reverses the Third Circuit. The Court says that this confronts the manufacturer with a "real dilemma." But the fact of the matter is that the dilemma is no more than citizens face in connection with countless statutes and with the rules of the SEC, FTC, FCC, ICC, and other regulatory agencies. This has not heretofore been regarded as a basis for injunctive relief unless Congress has so provided. The overriding fact here is — or should be — that the public interest in avoiding the delay in implementing Congress' program far outweighs the private interest; and that the private interest which has so impressed the Court is no more than that which exists in respect of most regulatory statutes or agency rules. Somehow, the Court has concluded that the damage to petitioners if they have to engage in the required redesign and reprint of their labels and printed materials without threshold review outweighs the damage to the public of deferring during the tedious months and years of litigation a cure for the possible danger and asserted deceit of peddling plain medicine under fancy trademarks and for fancy prices which, rightly or wrongly, impelled the Congress to enact this legislation. I submit that a much stronger showing is necessary than the expense and trouble of compliance and the risk of defiance. Actually, if the Court refused to permit this shotgun assault, experience and reasonably sophisticated common sense show that there would be orderly compliance without the disaster so dramatically predicted by the industry, reasonable adjustments by the agency in real hardship cases, and where extreme intransigence involving substantial violations occurred, enforcement actions in which legality of the regulation would be tested in specific, concrete situations. I respectfully submit that this would be the correct and appropriate result. Our refusal to respond to the vastly overdrawn cries of distress would reflect not only healthy skepticism, but our regard for a proper relationship between the courts on the one hand and Congress and the administrative agencies on the other. It would represent a reasonable solicitude for the purposes and programs of the Congress. And it would reflect appropriate modesty as to the competence of the courts. The courts cannot properly — and should not — attempt to judge in the abstract and generally whether this regulation is within the statutory scheme. Judgment as to the "every time" regulation should be made only in light of specific situations, and it may differ depending upon whether the FDA seeks to enforce it as to doctors' circulars, pamphlets for patients, labels, etc.

I submit, therefore, that this invitation to the courts to rule upon the legality of these regulations in these actions for injunction and declaratory relief should be firmly rejected. . . . In short, the parties have an "adequate remedy" to test the regulations; these controversies are not "ripe" for judicial decision; and it is not appropriate that the courts should respond to the call for this private relief at disproportionate burden to the public interest. With all respect, we should refuse to accept the invitation to abandon the traditional insistence of the courts upon specific, concrete facts, and instead entertain this massive onslaught in which it will be utterly impossible to make the kind of discrete judgments which are within judicial competence. With all respect, we should not permit the administration of a law of the Congress to be disrupted by this nonadjudicable mass assault.

QUESTIONS

1. Identify three considerations (two "factors," with two considerations in the first factor) that the Supreme Court looks at to determine whether a case is ripe. What interests do the three considerations serve? For a more recent application of these factors, *see Ohio Forestry Assn. v. Sierra Club*, 523 U.S. 726 (1998) (holding *not* ripe a challenge to a U.S. Forest Service plan for the Wayne National Forest, where the plan set logging goals, selected the areas of the forest suited to timber production, and determined which methods of timber harvest were appropriate, but did not itself authorize the cutting of any trees).
2. What is the legal basis for finding that a case is not ripe?
3. How does the Court resolve each of the three considerations in distinguishing *Toilet Goods* from *Abbott Labs*?
4. Does Justice Fortas's dissent have persuasive force? Does it reflect a very trusting view of administrative agencies? For a recent reprise of the ideas

in Justice Fortas's dissent, *see* Frank Cross, *Shattering the Fragile Case for Judicial Review of Rulemaking,* 85 Va. L. Rev. 1243 (1999).

5. In *Lexmark Int'l, Inc. v. Static Control Components, Inc.,* 134 S. Ct. 1377 (2014), Justice Scalia wrote the opinion for a unanimous Court. In that decision, Justice Scalia questioned whether a court may limit federal court jurisdiction when the Constitution and a federal statute give a party the right to bring a statutory action: "Just as a court cannot apply its independent policy judgment to recognize a cause of action that Congress has denied, *see Alexander v. Sandoval,* 532 U.S. 275, 286-287 (2001), it cannot limit a cause of action that Congress has created merely because 'prudence' dictates." 134 S. Ct. at 1388. Does this rule against the application of prudential limits on federal causes of action bring into question the continued viability of *Abbott Laboratories?*

6. Contrast the approach to ripeness taken in 1981 MSAPA §§ 5-102 to 5-103. Should the irreparability of harm to an affected party have a greater impact in the determination of ripeness than the Supreme Court approach permits?

H. FINALITY

UNITED STATES ARMY CORPS OF ENGINEERS v. HAWKES CO.

136 S. Ct. 1807 (2016)

CHIEF JUSTICE ROBERTS delivered the opinion of the Court.

The Clean Water Act regulates the discharge of pollutants into "the waters of the United States." 33 U.S.C. §§ 1311(a), 1362(7), (12). Because it can be difficult to determine whether a particular parcel of property contains such waters, the U.S. Army Corps of Engineers will issue to property owners an "approved jurisdictional determination" stating the agency's definitive view on that matter. *See* 33 CFR § 331.2 and pt. 331, App. C (2015). The question presented is whether that determination is final agency action judicially reviewable under the Administrative Procedure Act, 5 U.S.C. § 704.

I

A

The Clean Water Act prohibits "the discharge of any pollutant" without a permit into "navigable waters," which it defines, in turn, as "the waters of the United States." 33 U.S.C. §§ 1311(a), 1362(7), (12). During the time period relevant to this case, the U.S. Army Corps of Engineers defined the waters of the United States to include land areas occasionally or regularly saturated with water — such as "mudflats, sandflats, wetlands, sloughs, prairie potholes, wet meadows, [and] playa lakes" — the "use, degradation or destruction of which could affect interstate or foreign commerce." 33 CFR § 328.3(a)(3) (2012). The Corps has applied that definition to assert jurisdiction over "270–to–300 million acres of swampy lands in the United States — including half of Alaska and an area the size of California in the lower 48 States." *Rapanos v. United States*, 547 U.S. 715, 722 (2006) (plurality opinion).

It is often difficult to determine whether a particular piece of property contains waters of the United States, but there are important consequences if it does. The Clean Water Act imposes substantial criminal and civil penalties for discharging any pollutant into waters covered by the Act without a permit from the Corps. *See* 33 U.S.C. §§ 1311(a), 1319(c), (d), 1344(a). The costs of obtaining such a permit are significant. For a specialized "individual" permit of the sort at issue in this case, for example, one study found that the average applicant "spends 788 days and $271,596 in completing the process," without "counting costs of mitigation or design changes." *Rapanos*, 547 U.S., at 721. Even more readily available "general" permits took applicants, on average, 313 days and $28,915 to complete. *Ibid. See generally* 33 CFR § 323.2(h) (limiting "general" permits to activities that "cause only minimal individual and cumulative environmental impacts").

The Corps specifies whether particular property contains "waters of the United States" by issuing "jurisdictional determinations" (JDs) on a case-by-case basis. § 331.2. JDs come in two varieties: "preliminary" and "approved." *Ibid.* While preliminary JDs merely advise a property owner "that there *may* be waters of the United States on a parcel," approved JDs definitively "stat[e] the presence or absence" of such waters. *Ibid.* (emphasis added). Unlike preliminary JDs, approved JDs can be administratively appealed and are defined by regulation to "constitute a Corps final agency action." §§ 320.1(a)(6), 331.2. They are binding for five years on both the Corps and the Environmental Protection Agency, which share authority to enforce the Clean Water Act.

B

Respondents are three companies engaged in mining peat in Marshall County, Minnesota. Peat is an organic material that forms in waterlogged grounds, such as wetlands and bogs. It is widely used for soil improvement and burned as fuel. It can also be used to provide structural support and moisture for smooth, stable greens that leave golfers with no one to blame but themselves for errant putts. At the same time, peat mining can have significant environmental and ecological impacts, and therefore is regulated by both federal and state environmental protection agencies, see, e.g., Minn. Stat. § 103G.231 (2014).

Respondents own a 530–acre tract near their existing mining operations. The tract includes wetlands, which respondents believe contain sufficient high quality peat, suitable for use in golf greens, to extend their mining operations for 10 to 15 years.

In December 2010, respondents applied to the Corps for a Section 404 permit for the property. A Section 404 permit authorizes "the discharge of dredged or fill material into the navigable waters at specified disposal sites." 33 U.S.C. § 1344(a). Over the course of several communications with respondents, Corps officials signaled that the permitting process would be very expensive and take years to complete. The Corps also advised respondents that, if they wished to pursue their application, they would have to submit numerous assessments of various features of the property, which respondents estimate would cost more than $100,000.

In February 2012, in connection with the permitting process, the Corps issued an approved JD stating that the property contained "water of the United States" because its wetlands had a "significant nexus" to the Red River of the North, located some 120 miles away. Respondents appealed the JD to the Corps' Mississippi Valley Division Commander, who remanded for further factfinding. On remand, the Corps reaffirmed its original conclusion and issued a revised JD to that effect.

Respondents then sought judicial review of the revised JD under the Administrative Procedure Act (APA). The District Court dismissed for want of subject matter jurisdiction, holding that the revised JD was not "final agency action for which there is no other adequate remedy in a court," as required by the APA prior to judicial review, 5 U.S.C. § 704. The Court of Appeals for the Eighth Circuit reversed, and we granted certiorari.

II

The Corps contends that the revised JD is not "final agency action" and that, even if it were, there are adequate alternatives for challenging it in court. We disagree at both turns.

A

In *Bennett v. Spear*, 520 U.S. 154 (1997), we distilled from our precedents two conditions that generally must be satisfied for agency action to be "final" under the APA. "First, the action must mark the consummation of the agency's decisionmaking process — it must not be of a merely tentative or interlocutory nature. And second, the action must be one by which rights or obligations have been determined, or from which legal consequences will flow."[2]

The Corps does not dispute that an approved JD satisfies the first *Bennett* condition. Unlike preliminary JDs — which are "advisory in nature" and simply indicate that "there may be waters of the United States" on a parcel of property, 33 CFR § 331.2 — an approved JD clearly "mark[s] the consummation" of the Corps' decisionmaking process on that question, *Bennett*, 520 U.S., at 178 (internal quotation marks omitted). It is issued after extensive factfinding by the Corps regarding the physical and hydrological characteristics of the property, and is typically not revisited if the permitting process moves forward. Indeed, the Corps itself describes approved JDs as "final agency action," *see* 33 CFR § 320.1(a)(6), and specifies that an approved JD "will remain valid for a period of five years," Corps, Regulatory Guidance Letter No. 05–02, § 1(a), p. 1 (June 14, 2005) (2005 Guidance Letter).

The Corps may revise an approved JD within the five-year period based on "new information." 2005 Guidance Letter § 1(a), at 1. That possibility, however, is a common characteristic of agency action, and does not make an otherwise definitive decision nonfinal. By issuing respondents an approved JD, the Corps for all practical purposes "has ruled definitively" that respondents' property contains jurisdictional waters.

The definitive nature of approved JDs also gives rise to "direct and appreciable legal consequences," thereby satisfying the second prong of *Bennett*. Consider the effect of an approved JD stating that a party's property does *not* contain

---

2. Because we determine that a JD satisfies both prongs of *Bennett*, we need not consider respondents' argument that an agency action that satisfies only the first may also constitute final agency action.

jurisdictional waters — a "negative" JD, in Corps parlance. As noted, such a JD will generally bind the Corps for five years. Under a longstanding memorandum of agreement between the Corps and EPA, it will also be "binding on the Government and represent the Government's position in any subsequent Federal action or litigation concerning that final determination." Memorandum of Agreement §§ IV–C–2, VI–A. A negative JD thus binds the two agencies authorized to bring civil enforcement proceedings under the Clean Water Act, *see* 33 U.S.C. § 1319, creating a five-year safe harbor from such proceedings for a property owner. Additionally, although the property owner may still face a citizen suit under the Act, such a suit — unlike actions brought by the Government — cannot impose civil liability for wholly past violations. See §§ 1319(d), 1365(a). In other words, a negative JD both narrows the field of potential plaintiffs and limits the potential liability a landowner faces for discharging pollutants without a permit. Each of those effects is a "legal consequence[]" satisfying the second *Bennett* prong.

It follows that affirmative JDs have legal consequences as well: They represent the denial of the safe harbor that negative JDs afford. See 5 U.S.C. § 551(13) (defining "agency action" to include an agency "rule, order, license, sanction, relief, or the equivalent," or the "denial thereof"). Because "legal consequences . . . flow" from approved JDs, they constitute final agency action. *Bennett*, 520 U.S., at 178 (internal quotation marks omitted).

This conclusion tracks the "pragmatic" approach we have long taken to finality. *Abbott Laboratories v. Gardner*, 387 U.S. 136, 149 (1967). For example, in *Frozen Food Express v. United States*, 351 U.S. 40 (1956), we considered the finality of an order specifying which commodities the Interstate Commerce Commission believed were exempt by statute from regulation, and which it believed were not. Although the order "had no authority except to give notice of how the Commission interpreted" the relevant statute, and "would have effect only if and when a particular action was brought against a particular carrier," *Abbott*, 387 U.S., at 150, we held that the order was nonetheless immediately reviewable, *Frozen Food*, 351 U.S., at 44–45. The order, we explained, "warns every carrier, who does not have authority from the Commission to transport those commodities, that it does so at the risk of incurring criminal penalties." *Id.*, at 44. So too here, while no administrative or criminal proceeding can be brought for failure to conform to the approved JD itself, that final agency determination not only deprives respondents of a five-year safe harbor from liability under the Act, but warns that if they discharge pollutants onto their property without obtaining a permit from the Corps, they do so at the risk of significant criminal and civil penalties.

B

Even if final, an agency action is reviewable under the APA only if there are no adequate alternatives to APA review in court. 5 U.S.C. § 704. The Corps contends that respondents have two such alternatives: either discharge fill material without a permit, risking an EPA enforcement action during which they can argue that no permit was required, or apply for a permit and seek judicial review if dissatisfied with the results.

Neither alternative is adequate. As we have long held, parties need not await enforcement proceedings before challenging final agency action where such proceedings carry the risk of "serious criminal and civil penalties." *Abbott*, 387 U.S., at 153. If respondents discharged fill material without a permit, in the mistaken belief that their property did not contain jurisdictional waters, they would expose themselves to civil penalties of up to $37,500 for each day they violated the Act, to say nothing of potential criminal liability. *See* 33 U.S.C. §§ 1319(c), (d). Respondents need not assume such risks while waiting for EPA to "drop the hammer" in order to have their day in court.

Nor is it an adequate alternative to APA review for a landowner to apply for a permit and then seek judicial review in the event of an unfavorable decision. As Corps officials indicated in their discussions with respondents, the permitting process can be arduous, expensive, and long. See *Rapanos*, 547 U.S., at 721 (plurality opinion). On top of the standard permit application that respondents were required to submit, *see* 33 CFR § 325.1(d) (detailing contents of permit application), the Corps demanded that they undertake, among other things, a "hydrogeologic assessment of the rich fen system including the mineral/ nutrient composition and pH of the groundwater; groundwater flow spatially and vertically; discharge and recharge areas"; a "functional/resource assessment of the site including a vegetation survey and identification of native fen plan communities across the site"; an "inventory of similar wetlands in the general area (watershed), including some analysis of their quality"; and an "inventory of rich fen plant communities that are within sites of High and Outstanding Biodiversity Significance in the area." Respondents estimate that undertaking these analyses alone would cost more than $100,000. And whatever pertinence all this might have to the issuance of a permit, none of it will alter the finality of the approved JD, or affect its suitability for judicial review. The permitting process adds nothing to the JD.

The Corps nevertheless argues that Congress made the "evident[ ]" decision in the Clean Water Act that a coverage determination would be made "as part of the permitting process, and that the property owner would obtain any necessary judicial review of that determination at the conclusion of that process." But as the Corps acknowledges, the Clean Water Act makes no reference to standalone [sic] jurisdictional determinations, so there is little basis for inferring anything from it concerning the reviewability of such distinct final agency action. And given "the APA's presumption of reviewability for all final agency action," *Sackett*, 132 S. Ct., at 1373, "[t]he mere fact" that permitting decisions are "reviewable should not suffice to support an implication of exclusion as to other[ ]" agency actions, such as approved JDs, *Abbott*, 387 U.S., at 141 (internal quotation marks omitted); see also *Sackett*, 132 S. Ct., at 1373 ("[I]f the express provision of judicial review in one section of a long and complicated statute were alone enough to overcome the APA's presumption of reviewability . . . , it would not be much of a presumption at all").

Finally, the Corps emphasizes that seeking review in an enforcement action or at the end of the permitting process would be the only available avenues for obtaining review "[i]f the Corps had never adopted its practice of issuing standalone jurisdictional determinations upon request." True enough. But such a "count your blessings" argument is not an adequate rejoinder to the assertion of a right to judicial review under the APA.

The judgment of the Court of Appeals for the Eighth Circuit is affirmed.

It is so ordered.

[Justice Kennedy's concurring opinion, joined by Justices Thomas and Alito, is omitted.]

JUSTICE KAGAN, concurring.

I join the Court's opinion in full. I write separately to note that for me, unlike for JUSTICE GINSBURG (opinion concurring in part and concurring in judgment), the memorandum of agreement between the Army Corps of Engineers and the Environmental Protection Agency is central to the disposition of this case. For an agency action to be final, "the action must be one by which rights or obligations have been determined, or from which legal consequences will flow." *Bennett v. Spear*, 520 U.S. 154, 178 (1997). As the Court states, the memorandum of agreement establishes that jurisdictional determinations (JDs) are "binding on the Government and represent the Government's position in any subsequent Federal action or litigation concerning that final determination." A negative JD thus prevents the Corps and EPA — the two agencies with authority to enforce the Clean Water Act — from bringing a civil action against a property owner for the JD's entire 5-year lifetime. The creation of that safe harbor, which binds the agencies in any subsequent litigation, is a "direct and appreciable legal consequence[ ]" satisfying the second prong of *Bennett*, 520 U.S., at 178.

JUSTICE GINSBURG, concurring in part and concurring in the judgment.

I join the Court's opinion, save for its reliance upon the Memorandum of Agreement between the Army Corps of Engineers and the Environmental Protection Agency. The Court received scant briefing about this memorandum, and the United States does not share the Court's reading of it. But the JD at issue is "definitive," not "informal" or "tentative," *Abbott Laboratories v. Gardner*, 387 U.S. 136, 151 (1967), and has "an immediate and practical impact," *Frozen Food Express v. United States*, 351 U.S. 40, 44, (1956). Accordingly, I agree with the Court that the JD is final.

QUESTIONS

1. What law makes judicial review depend on finality?
2. Why is the issue of finality less important to the availability of judicial review under the 1981 MSAPA than under the federal APA? *See* §§ 5-102 to 5-103. Does the test for finality under the MSAPA differ from the test for APA finality?
3. What policies support the finality requirement?

NOTE ON BENNETT v. SPEAR

In *Bennett v. Spear, supra* p. 703, the Court rejected the Government's contention that the Biological Opinion challenged in that case did not constitute "final agency action," reasoning as follows:

> The Government contends that petitioners may not obtain judicial review under the APA on the theory that the Biological Opinion does not constitute "final agency action," 5 U.S.C. § 704, because it does not conclusively determine the manner in which Klamath Project water will be allocated:
> "Whatever the practical likelihood that the [Bureau] would adopt the reasonable and prudent alternatives (including the higher lake levels) identified by the Service, the Bureau was not legally obligated to do so. Even if the Bureau decided to adopt the higher lake levels, moreover, nothing in the biological opinion would

constrain the [Bureau's] discretion as to how the available water should be allocated among potential users."

This confuses the question of whether the Secretary's action is final with the separate question of whether the petitioners' harm is "fairly traceable" to the Secretary's action (a question we have already resolved against the Government, see *supra*, at Part III-A). As a general matter, two conditions must be satisfied for agency action to be "final": First, the action must mark the "consummation" of the agency's decisionmaking process — it must not be of a merely tentative or interlocutory nature. And second, the action must be one by which "rights or obligations have been determined," or from which "legal consequences will flow." It is uncontested that the first requirement is met here; and the second is met because, as we have discussed above, the Biological Opinion and accompanying Incidental Take Statement alter the legal regime to which the action agency is subject, authorizing it to take the endangered species if (but only if) it complies with the prescribed conditions. In this crucial respect the present case is different from the cases upon which the Government relies, *Franklin v. Massachusetts*, 505 U.S. 788 (1992), and *Dalton v. Specter*, 511 U.S. 462 (1994). In the former case, the agency action in question was the Secretary of Commerce's presentation to the President of a report tabulating the results of the decennial census; our holding that this did not constitute "final agency action" was premised on the observation that the report carried "no direct consequences" and served "more like a tentative recommendation than a final and binding determination." And in the latter case, the agency action in question was submission to the President of base closure recommendations by the Secretary of Defense and the Defense Base Closure and Realignment Commission; our holding that this was not "final agency action" followed from the fact that the recommendations were in no way binding on the President, who had absolute discretion to accept or reject them. Unlike the reports in *Franklin* and *Dalton*, which were purely advisory and in no way affected the legal rights of the relevant actors, the Biological Opinion at issue here has direct and appreciable legal consequences.

NOTE ON THE FINALITY OF AGENCY INACTION

The issue of whether there is a final agency action may arise when an agency has failed to act and the party desiring action is aggrieved by the inaction. As the court discussed in *Cobell v. Norton*, 240 F.3d 1081 (D.C. Cir. 2001), agency inaction will in some circumstances amount to final agency action reviewable under the APA.

The plaintiffs in the *Cobell* litigation claimed that the Department of the Interior had violated its obligations as trustee for the beneficiaries of Individual Indian Money ("IIM") trust accounts. The IIM accounts were established as a result of the Indian Reorganization Act of 1934 ("IRA"), 48 Stat. 984 (codified as amended at 25 U.S.C. §§ 461 *et seq.*), which ended the prior policy of allotment of Indian lands and reaffirmed a trust relationship between the United States and Native Americans. Some of the aspects of this trust relationship were the subject of legislation in 1994, which the court summarized, 240 F.3d at 1090, as follows:

In 1994, Congress enacted the Indian Trust Fund Management Reform Act ("1994 Act"), Pub. L. No. 103-412 (1994). This law recognized the federal government's preexisting trust responsibilities. It further identified some of the Interior Secretary's duties to ensure "proper discharge of the trust responsibilities of the United States." 25 U.S.C. § 162a(d). These "include (but are not limited to) the following":

Providing adequate systems for accounting for and reporting trust fund balances;

Providing adequate controls over receipts and disbursements;

Providing periodic, timely reconciliations to assure the accuracy of accounts;

"Preparing and supplying . . . periodic statements of . . . account performance" and balances to account holders; and

Establishing consistent, written policies and procedures for trust fund management and accounting.

The 1994 Act also

created the Office of the Special Trustee for American Indians ("OST") "to provide for more effective management of, and accountability for the proper discharge of, the Secretary's trust responsibilities" and ensure proper reform measures are implemented. 25 U.S.C. § 4042(b)(1). The Special Trustee ("ST") is a sub-cabinet level officer appointed by the President and confirmed by the Senate who reports directly to the Interior Secretary. *Id.* § 4042(b). The ST is required to develop a "comprehensive strategic plan" for trust management reform and an appropriate reform timetable to ensure "proper and efficient discharge of the Secretary's trust responsibilities." *Id.* § 4043(a)(1). The ST is also to oversee a "fair and accurate accounting" of the trust accounts and submit annual reports to Congress. *Id.* §§ 4043(b)(2)(A) and (j). Despite these responsibilities, the ST only has "general oversight" responsibilities; decision-making authority for IIM trust management remains with the Secretary of the Interior. *Id.* § 4043(b)(1).

The first ST under the Act was Paul Homan. In April 1997, Homan submitted a "strategic plan" to the Secretary and Congress pursuant to the 1994 Act. Among other things, the plan called for the reorganization of Indian trust fund management and the centralization of record-keeping, changes that may have required legislative authorization. The Interior Secretary opted to implement portions of the strategic plan, including the upgrade of computer systems, the clean-up of trust records, and the elimination of processing backlogs. The Secretary's plan, known as the High Level Implementation Plan ("HLIP"), was issued in July 1998. As drafted, the HLIP consisted of twelve "subprojects" which focus on ensuring the accuracy of information regarding the IIM trust accounts and developing uniform policies and procedures to guide trust management in the future. These subprojects included data cleanup, clearing probate backlogs, improving records management, and establishing internal controls to prevent future mismanagement.

240 F.3d at 1090-91.

In June 1996, the plaintiffs brought a class action suit "'to compel performance of trust obligations.' They alleged that the federal government's trustee-delegates, including the Secretaries of the Interior and Treasury, breached the fiduciary duties owed to plaintiffs by mismanaging the IIM trust accounts." *Id.* at 1092-93. In its appeal of an adverse decision of the district court, the Interior Department claimed that the court lacked jurisdiction because the plaintiffs were not seeking review of a final agency action. The court rejected this argument:

Where a federal court has jurisdiction to hear challenges to an agency action it also has jurisdiction over claims of unreasonable delay. *See Telecommunications Research and Action Center v. FCC,* 750 F.2d 70, 75 (D.C. Cir. 1984). As this court has noted in the past, where "an agency is under an unequivocal statutory duty to act, failure so to act constitutes, in effect, an affirmative act that triggers 'final agency action' review." *Sierra Club v. Thomas*, 828 F.2d 783, 793 (D.C. Cir. 1987); *see also Public Citizen Health Research Group v. Commissioner*, 740 F.2d 21, 32 (D.C. Cir. 1984). Were it otherwise, agencies could effectively prevent judicial review of their policy determinations by simply refusing to take final action.

In the case at bar, it is clear that the federal government has been under an obligation to discharge the fiduciary duties owed to IIM trust beneficiaries for decades. It is also clear that refusing to hear plaintiffs' claims could unduly prejudice their rights as trust beneficiaries. The district court's findings of fact, largely unchallenged by the government, make clear that insofar as the federal government owes trust beneficiaries a duty to maintain records and provide an accounting, delaying review is tantamount to denying review altogether. The district court further concluded that appellants' extensive delay in discharging their fiduciary duties was unreasonable. In such circumstances, federal courts may exercise jurisdiction to compel agency action "unlawfully withheld or unreasonably denied." 5 U.S.C. § 706.

Even assuming, as appellants argue, that the 1994 Act effectively reset the clock for a finding of unreasonable delay, appellants' "reasonable time to discharge" its fiduciary obligations "has expired." *Cobell V*, 91 F. Supp.2d. at 48. The district court's judgment came down over six years after passage of the 1994 Act. During that time, deadlines were missed, documents destroyed, and, in the words of the district court, appellants had yet to progress much beyond planting the "seed" for discharging their fiduciary obligations. See *id.* at 20. Courts owe substantial deference to agency prerogatives in fulfilling their legal obligations, especially where Congress intervenes to address longstanding problems, as it did with the 1994 Act. But this does not require courts to turn a blind eye when government officials fail to discharge their duties.

As a general rule, Section 706 of the APA "leaves in the courts the discretion to decide whether agency delay is unreasonable." *Forest Guardians v. Babbitt*, 174 F.3d 1178, 1190 (10th Cir. 1999). The legal standard used to determine whether agency delay is unreasonable is a question of law to be reviewed de novo by this court. However, the factual findings that underlie that determination are only to be overturned if the district court's findings are clearly erroneous.

For good reason, courts are reluctant to upset existing agency priorities, unless the delay is "egregious." See *Telecommunications Research and Action Center*, 750 F.2d at 79. An agency's own timetable for performing its duties in the absence of a statutory deadline is due "considerable deference." *Sierra Club v. Gorsuch*, 715 F.2d 653, 658 (D.C. Cir. 1983). Moreover, "a finding that delay is unreasonable does not, alone, justify judicial intervention." *In re Barr Labs., Inc.*, 930 F.2d 72, 75 (D.C. Cir. 1991).

In reviewing an unreasonable delay claim, this court considers four factors:

> First, "the court should ascertain the length of time that has elapsed since the agency came under a duty to act." . . . Second, "the reasonableness of the delay must be judged 'in the context of the statute' which authorizes the agency's action." . . . Third, the court must examine the consequences of the agency's delay. . . . Finally, the court should give due consideration in the balance to "any plea of administrative error, administrative convenience, practical difficulty in carrying out a legislative mandate, or need to prioritize in the face of limited resources."

In re International Chemical Workers Union, 958 F.2d 1144, 1149 (D.C. Cir. 1992) (citations omitted).

Considering the first two factors, it is beyond question that the government has delayed fulfilling its trust obligations for many years. The district court specifically found that IIM trust beneficiaries have been denied their rights—in particular their right to an accounting—for decades. See *Cobell V*, 91 F. Supp. 2d at 47 (noting that IIM beneficiaries have waited "a century" for "an accurate accounting" which is the "most basic fiduciary duty"). That Congress enacted its own remedial statute to address this unconscionable delay does not mitigate the egregious amount of time plaintiffs have waited for, as discussed below, the 1994 Act is not the source of plaintiffs' rights. Rather, it is designed to help rectify the government's longstanding failure. Given the record before it, the district court reasonably concluded that absent court intervention, discharge of the government's fiduciary obligations may yet be far off.

Appellants note that the 1994 statute provides no deadlines for the reforms at issue. Failure to provide a statutory timetable may indicate that Congress sought to leave the timing of reform to agency discretion. But the lack of a timetable does not give government officials carte blanche to ignore their legal obligations. This is particularly true where, as here, the act of outlining specific steps toward reform was enacted against a background of agency delay dating back many years.

The district court noted that the consequences of further agency delay are potentially quite severe. Documents necessary for a proper accounting and reconciliation have been lost or destroyed, and the district court found little reason to believe that this would change in the near future. "The longer defendants delay in creating the plans necessary to render an accounting, the greater the chance that plaintiffs will never receive an actual accounting of their own trust money." *Cobell V*, 91 F. Supp. 2d at 47. Given that many plaintiffs rely upon their IIM trust accounts for their financial well-being, the injury from delay could cause irreparable harm to plaintiffs' interests as IIM trust beneficiaries. Thus it seems that "the interests at stake are not merely economic interests in [an administrative scheme], but personal interests in life and health." *Public Citizen Health Research Group v. Auchter*, 702 F.2d 1150, 1156 (D.C. Cir. 1983) (citation omitted).

Concern for "administrative convenience" certainly counsels against interfering with the government's reform priorities. *See Grand Canyon Air Tour Coalition v. FAA*, 154 F.3d 455, 476 (D.C. Cir. 1998) ("Although the APA gives courts the authority to 'compel agency action unlawfully withheld or unreasonably delayed,' we are acutely aware of the limits of our institutional competence in the highly technical area at issue in this case." (citations omitted)). Yet neither a lack of sufficient funds nor administrative complexity, in and of themselves, justify extensive delay, nor can the government claim that it has become subject to unreasonable expectations. Federal officials were aware of their fiduciary obligations long before the passage of the 1994 Act—let alone the initiation of this action—and yet little progress has been made in discharging those duties. What little progress the government has made appears more due to the litigation than diligence in discharging its fiduciary obligations. For these reasons, we find no basis for disturbing the district court's conclusion that appellants unreasonably delayed the discharge of their fiduciary obligations, nor for upsetting the district court's exercise of jurisdiction under 5 U.S.C. § 706 on this basis.

240 F.3d at 1095-97.

The claims at issue in the *Cobell* litigation were ultimately settled by section 101 of the Claims Resolution Act of 2010, Pub. L. No. 111-291 (Dec. 8, 2010), 124 Stat. 3064, 3066 (2010). That statute "authorized, ratified, and confirmed" the settlement reached by the parties. *Id.* The *New York Times* reported that the "$3.4 billion settlement over mismanaged Indian royalties . . . represents the largest settlement ever approved against the United States government." "Judge Approves $3.4 Billion in Indian Royalties Settlement," N.Y. Times, June 20, 2011, at A18.

QUESTIONS

1. Of what relevance is the existence of congressionally mandated deadlines to a court's decision that agency inaction may be reviewed as a final agency action?
2. What types of agency inaction will result in the availability of judicial review? Must an agency have a nondiscretionary duty to take action of a particular type? Will an agency's decision not to take enforcement action be subject to review as a final action under the APA? *See Heckler v. Chaney*, 470 U.S. 821 (1985), holding that an agency's decision not to take enforcement action should be presumed immune from judicial review, but distinguishing *Dunlop v. Bachowski*, 421 U.S. 560 (1975), as a case where the presumption was overcome by statutory language providing guidelines for the exercise of enforcement power.

NOTE ON STATUTORY TIME LIMITS ON JUDICIAL REVIEW OF AGENCY ACTION

While litigants must consider whether doctrines of ripeness and finality mean that a legal claim against an agency is premature, they must also consider whether the claim must be asserted before it becomes untimely. The APA addresses the issue only by negative inference: "[e]xcept to the extent that prior, adequate, and exclusive opportunity for judicial review is provided by law, agency action is subject to judicial review in civil or criminal proceedings for judicial enforcement." 5 U.S.C. § 703. The APA thus permits a party to withhold a challenge to the lawfulness of agency action until the party is subjected to an enforcement action, except when an organic statute directs that the challenge must be brought at an earlier time. Examples of such statutory provisions are plentiful. The Clean Air Act, for example, establishes the following conditions on judicial review of the EPA's actions under that statute:

(b) Judicial review

(1) A petition for review of action of the Administrator in promulgating any national primary or secondary ambient air quality standard, any emission standard or requirement under section 7412 of this title, any standard of performance or requirement under section 7411 of this title, . . . or any other nationally applicable regulations promulgated, or final action taken, by the Administrator under this chapter may be filed only in the United States Court of Appeals for the District of Columbia. . . . *Any petition for review under this subsection shall be filed within sixty days from the date notice of such promulgation, approval, or action appears in the Federal Register, except that if such petition is based solely on grounds arising after such sixtieth day, then any petition for review under this subsection shall be filed within sixty days after such grounds arise.* The filing of a petition for reconsideration by the Administrator of any otherwise final rule or action shall not affect the finality of such rule or action for purposes of judicial review nor extend the time within which a petition for

judicial review of such rule or action under this section may be filed, and shall not postpone the effectiveness of such rule or action.

(2) Action of the Administrator with respect to which review could have been obtained under paragraph (1) shall not be subject to judicial review in civil or criminal proceedings for enforcement. Where a final decision by the Administrator defers performance of any nondiscretionary statutory action to a later time, any person may challenge the deferral pursuant to paragraph (1).

42 U.S.C. § 7607(b) (emphasis added). For other examples of time limits for review defined by organic statutes, *see* 42 U.S.C. 9613(a) (the Comprehensive Environmental Response, Compensation and Liability Act) ("Review of any regulation promulgated under this chapter may be had upon application by any interested person only in the Circuit Court of Appeals of the United States for the District of Columbia. Any such application shall be made within ninety days from the date of promulgation of such regulations. Any matter with respect to which review could have been obtained under this subsection shall not be subject to judicial review in any civil or criminal proceeding for enforcement or to obtain damages or recovery of response costs"); 28 U.S.C. § 2344 (the Hobbs Act) ("On the entry of a final order reviewable under this chapter, the agency shall promptly give notice thereof by service or publication in accordance with its rules. Any party aggrieved by the final order may, within 60 days after its entry, file a petition to review the order in the court of appeals wherein venue lies"). *See also,* e.g., 42 U.S.C. § 6976(a)(1) (the Resource Conservation and Recovery Act). For time limits on review established by the 1981 MSAPA, *see* § 5-108.

When applying these time limits on judicial review, courts typically hold that the failure to bring an action within the defined time limit bars later judicial review. *See,* e.g., *Pan American Grain Mfg. Co. v. United States Environmental Protection Agency,* 95 F.3d 101 (1st Cir. 1996) (applying Clean Air Act provision); *Kelley v. Selin,* 42 F.3d 1501, 1515 n.3 (6th Cir. 1995) (applying Hobbs Act provision); *Ackels v. United States Environmental Protection Agency,* 7 F.3d 862, 869 (9th Cir. 1993) (applying Clean Water Act provision). In order for the untimely claim to be barred, however, two requirements generally apply. First, the agency action at issue must have put the party whose claim would be barred on notice of the content and effect of the agency action. In *RCA Global Communications, Inc. v. FCC,* 758 F.2d 722 (D.C. Cir. 1985), the agency argued that a party's statutory challenge to an agency action was barred because the statutory time limit on judicial review had passed and the party had not raised its challenge within that time period. The court rejected this argument:

> The argument founders on the erroneous assumption that the Commission's prior order had confronted the issue presented in this appeal at all, much less disposed of the question with sufficient clarity to put RCA on notice that failure to pursue its claim would bar subsequent review in this court. The Commission's entirely private view that two utterly opaque footnotes in a lengthy opinion disposed of the statutory question and now preclude this appeal comports with neither elemental fairness nor our precedent. Although statutory time limitations on judicial review of agency action are jurisdictional, *see Nat'l Bank of Davis v. Office of Comptroller of Currency,* 725 F.2d 1390, 1391 n.1 (D.C. Cir. 1984) (*per curiam*), self-evidently the calendar does not run until the agency has decided a question in a manner that reasonably puts aggrieved parties on notice of the rule's content. None of the cases

in this circuit even remotely suggest the contrary. Indeed, even if we were to conclude that *Natural Resources Defense Council v. NRC,* [666 F.2d 595 (D.C. Cir. 1981)], the case principally relied on by the Commission, is applicable in the circumstances of this case, that decision would provide no support for the FCC's position. In that decision the court recognized that participants in rulemaking may not later complain of the rule's invalidity "*on grounds fully known to them at the time of [its] issuance.*" 666 F.2d at 602-603 (emphasis added). *See also Outward Continental N. Pacific Freight Conf. v. FMC,* 385 F.2d 981, 982-983 n.3 (D.C. Cir. 1967) (*per curiam*).

Id. at 730.

The second requirement that courts impose before they will bar a claim for failure to adhere to a statutory time limit on judicial review is that judicial review must have been ripe during the statutory review period. In *Baltimore Gas & Elec. Co. v. ICC,* 672 F.2d 146 (D.C. Cir. 1982), the claimant challenged an agency action within the statutorily-defined sixty-day limit on petitions for review, despite the fact that the agency action admittedly caused no present harm to the claimant, to eliminate the risk that the limitations period would bar a later claim. The court held that the claim was not ripe for review and opined that a subsequent claim raised after the sixty-day period would not be barred:

The ICC's interpretation of Section 229(c) calls for no change in BG&E's conduct of its affairs. The Commission's order, since it lacks current impact on BG&E and others similarly situated, is inappropriate for judicial review at this stage. [Citation to *Abbott Laboratories, supra*]. The ICC's opinion, we stress, does present a question ultimately appropriate for judicial determination. But that determination must abide a developed case properly timed. At this juncture, the future impact of Section 229(c) on BG&E remains speculative; the ICC's interpretation is not yet felt by this shipper "in a concrete way." If and when the traffic of BG&E or any other shipper warrants recourse to Section 229(c), as BG&E reads that provision, appropriate proceedings may be instituted before the Commission, and the Commission's disposition of that controversy will be subject to judicial review.

   Pending the development of such a controversy, BG&E need not fear preclusion by reason of the 60-day stipulation in 28 U.S.C. § 2344. A time limitation on petitions for judicial review, it should be apparent, can run only against challenges ripe for review. *See Investment Company Institute v. Board of Governors of the Federal Reserve System,* 551 F.2d 1270, 1280-81 (D.C. Cir. 1977). In the event that BG&E, at some future date, should have a ripe case fitting within its interpretation of Section 229(c), it can file a complaint with the Commission and, if the complaint is rejected, seek our review within 60 days of that Commission order. In the course of that review, the Commission's interpretation of Section 229 would be subject to our scrutiny. *See Geller v. FCC,* 610 F.2d 973, 977-78 (D.C. Cir. 1979) (*per curiam*); *Functional Music, Inc. v. FCC,* 274 F.2d 543, 546 (D.C. Cir. 1958), *cert. denied,* 361 U.S. 813 (1959).

Id. at 149-50. *See also Illinois EPA v. United States EPA,* 947 F.2d 283, 288-89 (7th Cir. 1991).

If a party had adequate notice and failed to bring a ripe action within the time period for judicial review defined in the organic statute, the claim may nevertheless be reviewed by a court, if an exception to review preclusion is present. The most important such exception applies when an agency has reopened its consideration of the matter that gave rise to the claim of illegality. This reopening exception was addressed by the court in *National Assn. of Mnfrs. (NAM) v. U.S. Dep't of the Interior*, 134 F.3d 1095, 1104-06 (D.C. Cir. 1998):

> While an agency need not subject settled policy or established statutory interpretation to renewed legal challenge whenever it revises a regulation, "the period for seeking judicial review may be made to run anew when the agency in question by some new promulgation creates the opportunity for renewed comment and objection." *Ohio v. EPA*, 838 F.2d 1325, 1329 (D.C. Cir.1988) [hereinafter *Ohio I*]. Thus, in *Ohio I* we held that, although the petitioner had an opportunity to comment on the relevant provision in the original regulation, it was not barred from challenging the provision in the revised regulation because the agency had republished the provision, explained it anew and responded to at least one comment directed to it. *Id.* at 1328-29; see also [*Kennecott Utah Copper Co. v. DOI*, 88 F.3d 1191, 1213 (D.C. Cir. 1996)] ("[J]udicial review of longstanding regulation is not barred when an agency reopens an issue covered in, or changes its interpretation of, that regulation; e.g., if an agency in the course of a rulemaking proceeding solicits comments on a pre-existing regulation or otherwise indicates its willingness to reconsider such a regulation by inviting and responding to comments, then a new review period is triggered"). However, "[t]he 'reopening rule' of [*Ohio I*] is not a license for bootstrap procedures by which petitioners can comment on matters other than those actually at issue, goad an agency into a reply, and then sue on the grounds that the agency had re-opened the issue." *American Iron & Steel Inst. v. EPA*, 886 F.2d 390, 398 (D.C. Cir. 1989), *cert. denied*, 497 U.S. 1003 (1990). Thus, "when the agency merely responds to an unsolicited comment by reaffirming its prior position, that response does not create a new opportunity for review." *Kennecott*, 88 F.3d at 1213.
>
> Moreover, "the appropriate way to challenge a longstanding regulation on the ground that it is 'violative of statute' is ordinarily 'by filing a petition for amendment or rescission of the agency's regulations, and challenging the denial of that petition.'" Id. at 1214 (quoting *Public Citizen v. Nuclear Regulatory Commn.*, 901 F.2d 147, 152 (D.C. Cir.), *cert. denied*, 498 U.S. 992 (1990)). But "where an agency reiterates a rule or policy in such a way as to render the rule or policy subject to renewed challenge on any substantive grounds, a coordinate challenge that such a rule or policy is contrary to law" need not proceed by amendment or rescission petition. *Public Citizen*, 901 F.2d at 152-53. In such circumstances, to require that an administrative petition precede the "coordinate challenge" to the lawfulness of the agency's provision "would be a waste of time and resources." *Kennecott*, 88 F.3d at 1214.

For other applications of this reopening exception, *see Edison Electric Institute v. United States EPA*, 996 F.2d 326 (D.C. Cir. 1993); *Association of American Railroads v. ICC*, 846 F.2d 1465 (D.C. Cir. 1988).

Another exception to the rule that a claim is barred when it is not brought within the time period defined by a statute arises when changed circumstances result in a claim that was not present during the statutory time period. This exception was found to be a narrow one in *RSR Corp. v. EPA*, 102 F.3d 1266, 1269-70 (D.C. Cir. 1997):

> RSR argues that this case comes within an exception to the timeliness rule. RSR points to [*Eagle-Picher Indus., Inc. v. EPA (Eagle-Picher I)*, 759 F.2d 905 (D.C. Cir. 1985)], where we stated that exceptions to a statutory time bar "occasionally may be justified in the light of changed circumstances giving rise to a new cause of action beyond the statutory period for review." *Id.* at 909. We characterized this

exception, derived from *Geller v. FCC*, 610 F.2d 973 (D.C. Cir. 1979), as covering "a case in which events occur or information becomes available after the statutory review period expires that essentially create a challenge that did not previously exist." *Eagle-Picher I*, 759 F.2d at 913.

RSR asserts that the "numerous recent studies" bring this case within the *Geller* exception. We emphatically reject this contention. The *Geller* exception is extremely narrow. As we stated in *Eagle-Picher I*, "[w]e have entertained untimely claims only in a limited number of exceptional circumstances." *Id.* at 911. The narrowness of the *Geller* exception can be seen from *Geller* itself: in that case, the sole basis of the challenged regulation had "long since evaporated;" the court held that the agency was required to reexamine its regulations, despite the statutory deadline, in light of the "abnormal circumstances" of the case. See *Geller*, 610 F.2d at 979-80.

If we were to allow petitioner's challenge based on the "new studies" (whose meaning is not undisputed), . . . the *Geller* exception would swallow the rule. . . . If petitioners could repeatedly challenge the [Hazard Ranking System], "EPA would be forced, contrary to the will of Congress, to defend the [Hazard Ranking System] repeatedly, wasting both time and funds that would be better spent cleaning up hazardous wastes that threaten human health and the environment." *Eagle-Picher I*, 759 F.2d at 916-17. Creating a "new studies" exception to section 113(a) would have precisely this effect.

The danger of a broad *Geller* exception can be seen in this case. Here, the relevance of the new studies is ambiguous: RSR argues that the new studies clearly undermine the lead HTF [Human Toxicities Factor] value, but EPA counters that the studies address an entirely different issue. Under the broad reading of the *Geller* exception offered by petitioner, however, even these ambiguous data could force EPA to reassess the [Hazard Ranking System]. We reject petitioner's invitation to broaden the scope of the *Geller* exception. If we were to permit this challenge, we have little doubt that industry groups would be encouraged to develop "new studies" in every instance. The result would be to eviscerate the [Hazard Ranking System].

The proper place for RSR to raise its "new studies" argument is in a petition for a rulemaking. This avenue protects both the [Hazard Ranking System] and those challenging the [Hazard Ranking System]. On the one hand, EPA is given the leeway that Congress intended, as a denial of a rulemaking petition is subject to extremely narrow review, *see WWHT, Inc. v. FCC*, 656 F.2d 807, 818-19 (D.C. Cir. 1981) ("It is only in the rarest and most compelling of circumstances that this court has acted to overturn an agency judgment not to institute rulemaking"). On the other hand, if the new studies in fact remove the factual premise on which the HTF value is based, we do not see how EPA could ignore this information. *See id.* at 819 ("[A]n agency may be forced by a reviewing court to institute rulemaking proceedings if a significant factual predicate of a prior decision on the subject . . . has been removed").

QUESTIONS

1. Assuming that an organic statute does not prescribe any time limit for judicial review and the APA applies, will a party be able to litigate each and every objection to the agency action "in civil or criminal proceedings for judicial enforcement," 5 U.S.C. § 703? For example, would a court review in the enforcement proceeding a claim that the regulation forming the basis for the enforcement cannot be enforced because it was not adopted in

accordance with §553 (notice-and-comment rulemaking)? See *Nova Scotia Food Products, supra*, p. 203, and *Vermont Yankee, supra*, p. 256.

2. Assuming that a party has not raised an objection to an agency action within the time limit defined by an organic statute, would a court decline to consider a claim that the agency action is unconstitutional? (*Yakus v. United States*, 321 U.S. 414 (1944), suggests that the answer to this question is yes, but the case has been heavily criticized. E.g., Henry M. Hart, Jr., *The Power of Congress to Limit the Jurisdiction of Federal Courts: An Exercise in Dialectic*, 66 Harv. L. Rev. 1362, 1379-80 (1953). *Compare Johnson v. Robison, supra*, p. 626.)

3. If a party has failed to comply with applicable time limits for judicial review and judicial review is barred, what mechanism may the party employ to bring the issue before a court? If the party employs this mechanism, how does the nature of the court's review differ from its review of a timely challenge to the agency action?

I. EXHAUSTION OF ADMINISTRATIVE REMEDIES

MYERS v. BETHLEHEM SHIPBUILDING CORP.
303 U.S. 41 (1938)

Mr. Justice Brandeis delivered the [unanimous] opinion of the Court.

The question for decision is whether a federal district court has equity jurisdiction to enjoin the National Labor Relations Board from holding a hearing upon a complaint filed by it against an employer alleged to be engaged in unfair labor practices prohibited by National Labor Relations Act. The Circuit Court of Appeals for the First Circuit held in these cases that the District Court possesses such jurisdiction; and granted preliminary injunctions. . . .

The declared purpose of the National Labor Relations Act is to diminish the causes of labor disputes burdening and obstructing interstate and foreign commerce; and its provisions are applicable only to such commerce. In order to protect it the Act seeks to promote collective bargaining; confers upon employees engaged in such commerce the right to form, and join in, labor organizations; defines acts of an employer which shall be deemed unfair labor practice; and confers upon the Board certain limited powers with a view to preventing such practices. If a charge is made to the Board that a person "has engaged in or is engaging in any . . . unfair labor practice," and it appears that a proceeding in respect thereto should be instituted, a complaint stating the charge is to be filed, and a hearing is to be held thereon upon notice to the person complained of.

The Industrial Union of Marine and Shipbuilding Workers of America, Local No. 5, made to the Board a charge that the Bethlehem Shipbuilding Corporation, Ltd., was engaging in unfair labor practices at its plant in Quincy, Massachusetts, for the production, sale and distribution of boats, ships, and marine equipment. Upon that charge the Board filed, on April 13, 1936, a complaint which alleged, among other things, that the company dominates and interferes in the manner described "with a labor organization known as Plan of Representation of Employees in Plants of the Bethlehem Shipbuilding Corporation,

Ltd."; that such action leads to strikes interfering with interstate commerce; and that "the aforesaid acts of respondent constitute unfair labor practices affecting commerce, within the meaning of Section 8, subdivisions (1) and (2) and Section 2, subdivisions (6) and (7) of said [National Labor Relations] Act."

The complaint alleged, specifically:

> "The respondent in the course and conduct of its business causes and has continuously caused large quantities of the raw materials used in the production of its boats, ships and marine equipment to be purchased and transported in interstate commerce from and through states of the United States other than the State of Massachusetts to the Fore River Plant in the State of Massachusetts, and causes and has continuously caused the boats, ships and marine equipment produced by it to be sold and transported in interstate commerce from the Fore River Plant in the State of Massachusetts to, into and through states of the United States other than the State of Massachusetts, all of the aforesaid constituting a continuous flow of trade, traffic and commerce among the several states."

The Board duly notified the Corporation that a hearing on the complaint would be held on April 27, 1936, at Boston, Massachusetts, in accordance with Rules and Regulations of the Board, a copy of which was annexed to the notice; and that the Corporation "will have the right to appear, in person or otherwise, and give testimony."

On that day the Corporation filed, in the federal court for Massachusetts, the bill in equity, herein numbered 181, against A. Howard Myers, Acting Regional Director for the First Region, National Labor Relations Board, Edmund J. Blake, its Regional Attorney for the First Region, and Daniel M. Lyons, Trial Examiner, to enjoin them from holding "a hearing for the purpose of determining whether or not the plaintiff has engaged at its Fore River Plant in any so-called unfair labor practices under the National Labor Relations Act, and from having any proceedings or taking any action whatsoever, at any time or times, with respect thereto." There were prayers for a restraining order, an interlocutory injunction and a permanent injunction; and, also, a prayer that the court declare that the National Labor Relations Act and "defendants' actions and proposed actions thereunder" violate the Federal Constitution. . . .

. . . [T]he District Court issued a restraining order and an order of notice to show cause why a preliminary injunction should not issue. [T]he defendants filed a motion to dismiss the bill of complaint and also a return to the order to show cause. [T]he District Court issued the preliminary injunction; and the decrees therefor are still in effect. They were affirmed by the Circuit Court of Appeals for the First Circuit on February 12, 1937. . . .

We are of opinion that the District Court was without power to enjoin the Board from holding the hearings.

First. There is no claim by the Corporation that the statutory provisions and the rules of procedure prescribed for such hearings are illegal; or that the Corporation was not accorded ample opportunity to answer the complaint of the Board; or that opportunity to introduce evidence on the allegations made will be denied. The claim is that the provisions of the Act are not applicable to the Corporation's business at the Fore River Plant, because the operations conducted there are not carried on, and the products manufactured are not sold, in interstate or foreign commerce; that, therefore, the Corporation's relations with its employees at the plant cannot burden or interfere with such commerce; that hearings would, at best, be futile; and that the holding of them would result in irreparable damage to the Corporation, not only by reason of their direct cost and the loss of time of its officials and employees, but also because the hearings would cause serious impairment of the good will and harmonious relations existing between the Corporation and its employees, and thus seriously impair the efficiency of its operations.

Second. The District Court is without jurisdiction to enjoin hearings because the power "to prevent any person from engaging in any unfair practice affecting commerce," has been vested by Congress in the Board and the Circuit Court of Appeals, and Congress has declared: "This power shall be exclusive, and shall not be affected by any other means of adjustment or prevention that has been or may be established by agreement, code, law, or otherwise." The grant of that exclusive power is constitutional, because the Act provided for appropriate procedure before the Board and in the review by the Circuit Court of Appeals an adequate opportunity to secure judicial protection against possible illegal action on the part of the Board. No power to enforce an order is conferred upon the Board. To secure enforcement, the Board must apply to a Circuit Court of Appeals for its affirmance. And until the Board's order has been affirmed by the appropriate Circuit Court of Appeals, no penalty accrues for disobeying it. The independent right to apply to a Circuit Court of Appeals to have an order set aside is conferred upon any party aggrieved by the proceeding before the Board. The Board is even without power to enforce obedience to its subpoena to testify or to produce written evidence. To enforce obedience it must apply to a District Court; and to such an application appropriate defence may be made.

As was said in *National Labor Relations Board v. Jones & Laughlin Steel Corp.*, 301 U.S. 1, 46, 47, the procedural provisions,

> "do not offend against the constitutional requirements governing the creation and action of administrative bodies. *See Interstate Commerce Commission v. Louisville & Nashville R. Co.*, 227 U.S. 88, 91. The Act establishes standards to which the Board must conform. There must be complaint, notice and hearing. The Board must receive evidence and make findings. The findings as to the facts are to be conclusive, but only if supported by evidence. The order of the Board is subject to review by the designated court, and only when sustained by the court may the order be enforced. Upon that review all questions of the jurisdiction of the Board and the regularity of its proceedings, all questions of constitutional right or statutory authority, are open to examination by the court. We construe the procedural provisions as affording adequate opportunity to secure judicial protection against arbitrary action in accordance with the well-settled rules applicable to administrative agencies set up by Congress to aid in the enforcement of valid legislation."

It is true that the Board has jurisdiction only if the complaint concerns interstate or foreign commerce. Unless the Board finds that it does, the complaint must be dismissed. And if it finds that interstate or foreign commerce is involved, but the Circuit Court of Appeals concludes that such finding was without adequate evidence to support it, or otherwise contrary to law, the Board's petition to enforce it will be dismissed, or the employer's petition to have it set aside will be granted. Since the procedure before the Board is appropriate and the judicial review so provided is adequate, Congress had power to vest exclusive jurisdiction in the Board and the Circuit Court of Appeals.

Third. The Corporation contends that, since it denies that interstate or foreign commerce is involved and claims that a hearing would subject it to irreparable damage, rights guaranteed by the Federal Constitution will be denied unless it be held that the District Court has jurisdiction to enjoin the holding of a hearing by the Board. So to hold would, as the Government insists, in effect substitute the District Court for the Board as the tribunal to hear and determine what Congress declared the Board exclusively should hear and determine in the first instance. The contention is at war with the long settled rule of judicial administration that no one is entitled to judicial relief for a supposed or threatened injury until the prescribed administrative remedy has been exhausted.[9] That rule has been repeatedly acted on in cases where, as here, the contention is made that the administrative body lacked power over the subject matter.

Obviously, the rule requiring exhaustion of the administrative remedy cannot be circumvented by asserting that the charge on which the complaint rests is groundless and that the mere holding of the prescribed administrative hearing would result in irreparable damage. Lawsuits also often prove to have been groundless; but no way has been discovered of relieving a defendant from the necessity of a trial to establish the fact. . . .

Decrees for preliminary injunction reversed with direction to dismiss the bills.

[JUSTICE CARDOZO did not participate.]

QUESTIONS

1. What policies support the administrative exhaustion requirement?
2. What is the legal basis for the administrative exhaustion requirement, according to the Court?

McCARTHY v. MADIGAN
503 U.S. 140 (1992)

[The Supreme Court held in this case that a federal prisoner need not resort to an internal grievance procedure promulgated by the Federal Bureau of Prisons before he could initiate a so-called "Bivens" suit against prison officials for money damages. (*Bivens v. Six Unknown Fed. Narcotics Agents*, 403 U.S. 388 (1971), permits suits against federal agents for money damages for violations of constitutional rights.) The *McCarthy* holding was later statutorily overruled (i.e., exhaustion in this context is now required). *See Booth v. Churner*, 532 U.S. 731 (2001). The *McCarthy* opinion contains a handy overview of the federal law up until 1992 regarding the requirement of exhaustion of administrative remedies.]

---

9. The rule has been most frequently applied in equity where relief by injunction was sought. But because the rule is one of judicial administration — not merely a rule governing the exercise of discretion — it is applicable to proceedings at law as well as suits in equity.

II

The doctrine of exhaustion of administrative remedies is one among related doctrines — including abstention, finality, and ripeness — that govern the timing of federal-court decision making. Of "paramount importance" to any exhaustion inquiry is congressional intent. Where Congress specifically mandates, exhaustion is required. But where Congress has not clearly required exhaustion, sound judicial discretion governs. *McGee v. United States*, 402 U.S. 479, 483, n.6. See also *Patsy*, 457 U.S. at 518 (White, J., concurring in part) ("Exhaustion is 'a rule of judicial administration,' . . . and unless Congress directs otherwise, rightfully subject to crafting by judges"). Nevertheless, even in this field of judicial discretion, appropriate deference to Congress' power to prescribe the basic procedural scheme under which a claim may be heard in a federal court requires fashioning of exhaustion principles in a manner consistent with congressional intent and any applicable statutory scheme.

A

This Court long has acknowledged the general rule that parties exhaust prescribed administrative remedies before seeking relief from the federal courts. *See*, e.g., *Myers v. Bethlehem Shipbuilding Corp.*, 303 U.S. 41, 50-51, and n.9 (1938) (discussing cases as far back as 1898). Exhaustion is required because it serves the twin purposes of protecting administrative agency authority and promoting judicial efficiency.

As to the first of these purposes, the exhaustion doctrine recognizes the notion, grounded in deference to Congress' delegation of authority to coordinate branches of Government, that agencies, not the courts, ought to have primary responsibility for the programs that Congress has charged them to administer. Exhaustion concerns apply with particular force when the action under review involves exercise of the agency's discretionary power or when the agency proceedings in question allow the agency to apply its special expertise. *McKart v. United States*, 395 U.S. 185, 194 (1969). The exhaustion doctrine also acknowledges the commonsense notion of dispute resolution that an agency ought to have an opportunity to correct its own mistakes with respect to the programs it administers before it is haled into federal court. Correlatively, exhaustion principles apply with special force when "frequent and deliberate flouting of administrative processes" could weaken an agency's effectiveness by encouraging disregard of its procedures. *McKart v. United States*, 395 U.S. at 195.

As to the second of the purposes, exhaustion promotes judicial efficiency in at least two ways. When an agency has the opportunity to correct its own errors, a judicial controversy may well be mooted, or at least piecemeal appeals may be avoided. And even where a controversy survives administrative review, exhaustion of the administrative procedure may produce a useful record for subsequent judicial consideration, especially in a complex or technical factual context.

B

Notwithstanding these substantial institutional interests, federal courts are vested with a "virtually unflagging obligation" to exercise the jurisdiction given them. "We have no more right to decline the exercise of jurisdiction which is given, than to usurp that which is not given." *Cohens v. Virginia*, 19

U.S. 264 (1821). Accordingly, this Court has declined to require exhaustion in some circumstances even where administrative and judicial interests would counsel otherwise. In determining whether exhaustion is required, federal courts must balance the interest of the individual in retaining prompt access to a federal judicial forum against countervailing institutional interests favoring exhaustion. "[A]dministrative remedies need not be pursued if the litigant's interests in immediate judicial review outweigh the government's interests in the efficiency or administrative autonomy that the exhaustion doctrine is designed to further." *West v. Bergland*, 611 F.2d 710, 715 (CA8 1979). Application of this balancing principle is "intensely practical," *Bowen v. City of New York*, 476 U.S. at 484, citing *Mathews v. Eldridge*, 424 U.S. 319, 331, n.11 (1976), because attention is directed to both the nature of the claim presented and the characteristics of the particular administrative procedure provided.

C

This Court's precedents have recognized at least three broad sets of circumstances in which the interests of the individual weigh heavily against requiring administrative exhaustion. First, requiring resort to the administrative remedy may occasion undue prejudice to subsequent assertion of a court action. Such prejudice may result, for example, from an unreasonable or indefinite time-frame for administrative action. *See Gibson v. Berryhill*, 411 U.S. 564, 575, n.14, (1973) (administrative remedy deemed inadequate "most often . . . because of delay by the agency"). *See also Coit Independence Joint Venture v. FSLIC*, 489 U.S. at 587 ("Because the Bank Board's regulations do not place a reasonable time limit on FSLIC's consideration of claims, Coit cannot be required to exhaust those procedures"); *Walker v. Southern R. Co.*, 385 U.S. 196, 198 (1966) (possible delay of 10 years in administrative proceedings makes exhaustion unnecessary); *Smith v. Illinois Bell Telephone Co.*, 270 U.S. 587, 591-592 (1926) (claimant "is not required indefinitely to await a decision of the rate-making tribunal before applying to a federal court for equitable relief"). Even where the administrative decision making schedule is otherwise reasonable and definite, a particular plaintiff may suffer irreparable harm if unable to secure immediate judicial consideration of his claim. *Bowen v. City of New York*, 476 U.S. at 483 (disability-benefit claimants "would be irreparably injured were the exhaustion requirement now enforced against them"); *Aircraft & Diesel Equipment Corp. v. Hirsch*, 331 U.S. 752, 773 (1947) ("impending irreparable injury flowing from delay incident to following the prescribed procedure" may contribute to finding that exhaustion is not required). By the same token, exhaustion principles apply with less force when an individual's failure to exhaust may preclude a defense to criminal liability. *Moore v. East Cleveland*, 431 U.S. 494, 497, n.5 (1977) (plurality opinion); *McKart v. United States*, 395 U.S. at 197.

Second, an administrative remedy may be inadequate "because of some doubt as to whether the agency was empowered to grant effective relief." *Gibson v. Berryhill*, 411 U.S. at 575, n.14. For example, an agency, as a preliminary matter, may be unable to consider whether to grant relief because it lacks institutional competence to resolve the particular type of issue presented, such as the constitutionality of a statute. In a similar vein, exhaustion has not been required where the challenge is to the adequacy of the agency procedure itself, such that "the question of the adequacy of the administrative remedy . . . [is] for all practical purposes identical with the merits of [the plaintiff's] lawsuit."

Alternatively, an agency may be competent to adjudicate the issue presented, but still lack authority to grant the type of relief requested. *McNeese v. Board of Ed. for Community Unit School Dist. 187*, 373 U.S. 668, 675 (1963) (students seeking to integrate public school need not file complaint with school superintendent because the "Superintendent himself apparently has no power to order corrective action" except to request the Attorney General to bring suit); *Montana National Bank of Billings v. Yellowstone County*, 276 U.S. 499, 505 (1928) (taxpayer seeking refund not required to exhaust where "any such application [would have been] utterly futile since the county board of equalization was powerless to grant any appropriate relief" in face of prior controlling court decision).

Third, an administrative remedy may be inadequate where the administrative body is shown to be biased or has otherwise predetermined the issue before it. *Gibson v. Berryhill*, 411 U.S. at 575, n.14; *Houghton v. Shafer*, 392 U.S. 639, 640 (1968) (in view of Attorney General's submission that the challenged rules of the prison were "validly and correctly applied to petitioner," requiring administrative review through a process culminating with the Attorney General "would be to demand a futile act"); *Association of National Advertisers, Inc. v. FTC*, 627 F.2d 1151, 1156-1157 (1979) (bias of Federal Trade Commission chairman), *cert. denied*, 447 U.S. 921 (1980). See also *Patsy v. Florida International University*, 634 F.2d 900, 912-913 (CA5 1981) (*en banc*) (administrative procedures must "not be used to harass or otherwise discourage those with legitimate claims"), *rev'd* on other grounds *sub nom. Patsy v. Board of Regents of Florida*, 457 U.S. 496 (1982).

. . .

DARBY v. CISNEROS

509 U.S. 137 (1993)

JUSTICE BLACKMUN delivered the opinion of the Court. The CHIEF JUSTICE, JUSTICE SCALIA, and JUSTICE THOMAS join all but Part III of this opinion.

This case presents the question whether federal courts have the authority to require that a plaintiff exhaust available administrative remedies before seeking judicial review under the Administrative Procedure Act (APA), 5 U.S.C. § 701 *et seq.*, where neither the statute nor agency rules specifically mandate exhaustion as a prerequisite to judicial review. At issue is the relationship between the judicially created doctrine of exhaustion of administrative remedies and the statutory requirements of § 10(c) of the APA.

I

Petitioner R. Gordon Darby is a self-employed South Carolina real estate developer who specializes in the development and management of multifamily rental projects. In the early 1980s, he began working with Lonnie Garvin, Jr., a mortgage banker, who had developed a plan to enable multifamily developers to obtain single-family mortgage insurance from respondent Department of Housing and Urban Development (HUD). Respondent Secretary of HUD (Secretary) is authorized to provide single-family mortgage insurance under

§ 203(b) of the National Housing Act, 48 Stat. 1252, as amended, 12 U.S.C. § 1709(b). Although HUD also provides mortgage insurance for multifamily projects under § 207 of the National Housing Act, 12 U.S.C. § 1713, the greater degree of oversight and control over such projects makes it less attractive for investors than the single-family mortgage insurance option.

The principal advantage of Garvin's plan was that it promised to avoid HUD's "Rule of Seven." This rule prevented rental properties from receiving single-family mortgage insurance if the mortgagor already had financial interests in seven or more similar rental properties in the same project or subdivision. See 24 CFR § 203.42(a) (1992). Under Garvin's plan, a person seeking financing would use straw purchasers as mortgage-insurance applicants. Once the loans were closed, the straw purchasers would transfer title back to the development company. Because no single purchaser at the time of purchase would own more than seven rental properties within the same project, the Rule of Seven appeared not to be violated. HUD employees in South Carolina apparently assured Garvin that his plan was lawful and that he thereby would avoid the limitation of the Rule of Seven.

Darby obtained financing for three separate multi-unit projects, and, through Garvin's plan, Darby obtained single-family mortgage insurance from HUD. Although Darby successfully rented the units, a combination of low rents, falling interest rates, and a generally depressed rental market forced him into default in 1988. HUD became responsible for the payment of over $6.6 million in insurance claims.

HUD had become suspicious of Garvin's financing plan as far back as 1983. In 1986, HUD initiated an audit but concluded that neither Darby nor Garvin had done anything wrong or misled HUD personnel. Nevertheless, in June 1989, HUD issued a limited denial of participation (LDP) that prohibited petitioners for one year from participating in any program in South Carolina administered by respondent Assistant Secretary of Housing. Two months later, the Assistant Secretary notified petitioners that HUD was also proposing to debar them from further participation in all HUD procurement contracts and in any nonprocurement transaction with any federal agency.

Petitioners' appeals of the LDP and of the proposed debarment were consolidated, and an Administrative Law Judge (ALJ) conducted a hearing on the consolidated appeals in December 1989. The judge issued an "Initial Decision and Order" in April 1990, finding that the financing method used by petitioners was "a sham which improperly circumvented the Rule of Seven." The ALJ concluded, however, that most of the relevant facts had been disclosed to local HUD employees, that petitioners lacked criminal intent, and that Darby himself "genuinely cooperated with HUD to try [to] work out his financial dilemma and avoid foreclosure." In light of these mitigating factors, the ALJ concluded that an indefinite debarment would be punitive and that it would serve no legitimate purpose; good cause existed, however, to debar petitioners for a period of 18 months.

Under HUD regulations,

"The hearing officer's determination shall be final unless, pursuant to 24 CFR part 26, the Secretary or the Secretary's designee, within 30 days of receipt of a request decides as a matter of discretion to review the finding of the hearing officer. The 30 day period for deciding whether to review a determination may be extended upon written notice of such extension by the Secretary or his designee. Any party may request such a review in writing within 15 days of receipt of the hearing officer's determination." 24 CFR § 24.314(c) (1992).

Neither petitioners nor respondents sought further administrative review of the ALJ's "Initial Decision and Order."

On May 31, 1990, petitioners filed suit in the United States District Court for the District of South Carolina. They sought an injunction and a declaration that the administrative sanctions were imposed for purposes of punishment, in violation of HUD's own debarment regulations, and therefore were "not in accordance with law" within the meaning of § 10(e)(B)(1) of the APA, 5 U.S.C. § 706(2)(A).

Respondents moved to dismiss the complaint on the ground that petitioners, by forgoing the option to seek review by the Secretary, had failed to exhaust administrative remedies. The District Court denied respondents' motion to dismiss, reasoning that the administrative remedy was inadequate and that resort to that remedy would have been futile. In a subsequent opinion, the District Court granted petitioners' motion for summary judgment, concluding that the "imposition of debarment in this case encroached too heavily on the punitive side of the line, and for those reasons was an abuse of discretion and not in accordance with the law."

The Court of Appeals for the Fourth Circuit reversed. It recognized that neither the National Housing Act nor HUD regulations expressly mandate exhaustion of administrative remedies prior to filing suit. The court concluded, however, that the District Court had erred in denying respondents' motion to dismiss, because there was no evidence to suggest that further review would have been futile or that the Secretary would have abused his discretion by indefinitely extending the time limitations for review. . . .

II

Section 10(c) of the APA bears the caption "Actions reviewable." It provides in its first two sentences that judicial review is available for "final agency action for which there is no other adequate remedy in a court," and that "preliminary, procedural, or intermediate agency action . . . is subject to review on the review of the final agency action." The last sentence of § 10(c) reads:

> "Except as otherwise expressly required by statute, agency action otherwise final is final for the purposes of this section whether or not there has been presented or determined an application for a declaratory order, for any form of reconsideration, or, unless the agency otherwise requires by rule and provides that the action meanwhile is inoperative, for an appeal to superior agency authority." 5 U.S.C. § 704.

Petitioners argue that this provision means that a litigant seeking judicial review of a final agency action under the APA need not exhaust available administrative remedies unless such exhaustion is expressly required by statute or agency rule. According to petitioners, since § 10(c) contains an explicit exhaustion provision, federal courts are not free to require further exhaustion as a matter of judicial discretion.

Respondents contend that § 10(c) is concerned solely with timing, that is, when agency actions become "final," and that Congress had no intention to interfere with the courts' ability to impose conditions on the timing of their exercise of jurisdiction to review final agency actions. Respondents concede that petitioners' claim is "final" under § 10(c), for neither the National Housing Act nor applicable HUD regulations require that a litigant pursue further administrative appeals prior to seeking judicial review. However, even though nothing in § 10(c) precludes judicial review of petitioners' claim, respondents argue that federal courts remain free under the APA to impose appropriate exhaustion requirements.

We have recognized that the judicial doctrine of exhaustion of administrative remedies is conceptually distinct from the doctrine of finality:

> "[T]he finality requirement is concerned with whether the initial decision maker has arrived at a definitive position on the issue that inflicts an actual, concrete injury; the exhaustion requirement generally refers to administrative and judicial procedures by which an injured party may seek review of an adverse decision and obtain a remedy if the decision is found to be unlawful or otherwise inappropriate." *Williamson County Regional Planning Comm'n v. Hamilton Bank of Johnson City*, 473 U.S. 172, 193 (1985).

Whether courts are free to impose an exhaustion requirement as a matter of judicial discretion depends, at least in part, on whether Congress has provided otherwise, for "of 'paramount importance' to any exhaustion inquiry is congressional intent," *McCarthy v. Madigan*, 503 U.S. 140, 144 (1992), quoting *Patsy v. Board of Regents of Florida*, 457 U.S. 496, 501 (1982). We therefore must consider whether § 10(c), by providing the conditions under which agency action becomes "final for the purposes of" judicial review, limits the authority of courts to impose additional exhaustion requirements as a prerequisite to judicial review.

It perhaps is surprising that it has taken over 45 years since the passage of the APA for this Court definitively to address this question. Professor Davis noted in 1958 that § 10(c) had been almost completely ignored in judicial opinions, *see* 3 K. Davis, Administrative Law Treatise § 20.08, p. 101 (1958); he reiterated that observation 25 years later, noting that the "provision is relevant in hundreds of cases and is customarily overlooked." 4 K. Davis, Administrative Law Treatise § 26.12, pp. 468-469 (2d ed. 1983). Only a handful of opinions in the Courts of Appeals have considered the effect of § 10(c) on the general exhaustion doctrine.

This Court has had occasion, however, to consider § 10(c) in other contexts. . . .

While some dicta in these cases might be claimed to lend support to petitioners' interpretation of § 10(c), the text of the APA leaves little doubt that petitioners are correct. Under § 10(a) of the APA, "[a] person suffering legal wrong because of agency action, or adversely affected or aggrieved by agency action within the meaning of a relevant statute, *is entitled to judicial review thereof.*" 5 U.S.C. § 702 (emphasis added). Although § 10(a) provides the general right to judicial review of agency actions under the APA, § 10(c) establishes when such review is available. When an aggrieved party has exhausted all administrative remedies expressly prescribed by statute or agency rule, the agency action is "final for the purposes of this section" and therefore "subject to judicial review" under the first sentence. While federal courts may be free to apply, where appropriate, other prudential doctrines of judicial administration to limit the scope and timing of judicial review, § 10(c), by its very terms, has limited the availability of the doctrine of exhaustion of administrative remedies to that which the statute or rule clearly mandates.

The last sentence of § 10(c) refers explicitly to "any form of reconsideration" and "an appeal to superior agency authority." Congress clearly was concerned with making the exhaustion requirement unambiguous so that aggrieved parties would know precisely what administrative steps were required before judicial review would be available. If courts were able to impose additional exhaustion requirements beyond those provided by Congress or the agency, the last sentence of § 10(c) would make no sense. To adopt respondents' reading would transform § 10(c) from a provision designed to "remove obstacles to judicial review of agency action," into a trap for unwary litigants. Section 10(c) explicitly requires exhaustion of all intra-agency appeals mandated either by statute or by agency rule; it would be inconsistent with the plain language of § 10(c) for courts to require litigants to exhaust optional appeals as well.

III

Recourse to the legislative history of § 10(c) is unnecessary in light of the plain meaning of the statutory text. Nevertheless, we consider that history briefly because both sides have spent much of their time arguing about its implications. . . .

In a statement appended to a letter dated October 19, 1945, to the Judiciary Committee, Attorney General Tom C. Clark set forth his understanding of the effect of § 10(c):

> "This subsection states (subject to the provisions of section 10(a)) the acts which are reviewable under section 10. It is intended to state existing law. The last sentence makes it clear that the doctrine of exhaustion of administrative remedies with respect to finality of agency action is intended to be applied only (1) where expressly required by statute . . . or (2) where the agency's rules require that decisions by subordinate officers must be appealed to superior agency authority before the decision may be regarded as final for purposes of judicial review." Id., at 44, Leg. Hist. 230.

Respondents place great weight on the Attorney General's statement that § 10(c) "is intended to state existing law." That law, according to respondents, "plainly permitted federal courts to require exhaustion of adequate administrative remedies." We cannot agree with this categorical pronouncement. With respect to the exhaustion of motions for administrative reconsideration or rehearing, the trend in pre-APA cases was in the opposite direction. . . .

Respondents in effect concede that the trend in the law prior to the enactment of the APA was to require exhaustion of motions for administrative reconsideration or rehearing only when explicitly mandated by statute. Respondents argue, however, that the law governing the exhaustion of administrative appeals prior to the APA was significantly different from § 10(c) as petitioners would have us interpret it. Respondents rely on *United States v. Sing Tuck*, 194 U.S. 161

(1904), in which the Court considered whether, under the relevant statute, an aggrieved party had to appeal an adverse decision by the Inspector of Immigration to the Secretary of Commerce and Labor before judicial review would be available. It recognized that the relevant statute "points out a mode of procedure which must be followed before there can be a resort to the courts," *id.*, at 167, and that a party must go through "the preliminary sifting process provided by the statutes," *id.*, at 170. *Accord, Chicago, M., St. P. & P. R. Co. v. Risty*, 276 U.S. 567, 574-575 (1928).

Nothing in this pre-APA history, however, supports respondents' argument that initial decisions that were "final" for purposes of judicial review were nonetheless unreviewable unless and until an administrative appeal was taken. The pre-APA cases concerning judicial review of federal agency action stand for the simple proposition that, until an administrative appeal was taken, the agency action was unreviewable because it was not yet "final." This is hardly surprising, given the fact that few, if any, administrative agencies authorized hearing officers to make final agency decisions prior to the enactment of the APA. *See* Federal Administrative Law Developments — 1971, 1972 Duke L.J. 115, 295, n.22 ("[P]rior to the passage of the APA, the existing agencies ordinarily lacked the authority to make binding determinations at a level below that of the agency board or Commission, so that section 10(c) would be expected to affect the exhaustion doctrine in only a very limited number of instances").

The purpose of § 10(c) was to permit agencies to require an appeal to "superior agency authority" before an examiner's initial decision became final. This was necessary because, under § 8(a), initial decisions could become final agency decisions in the absence of an agency appeal. *See* 5 U.S.C. § 557(b). Agencies may avoid the finality of an initial decision, first, by adopting a rule that an agency appeal be taken before judicial review is available, and, second, by providing that the initial decision would be "inoperative" pending appeal. Otherwise, the initial decision becomes final and the aggrieved party is entitled to judicial review. . . .

IV

We noted just last Term in a non-APA case that

> "appropriate deference to Congress' power to prescribe the basic procedural scheme under which a claim may be heard in a federal court requires fashioning of exhaustion principles in a manner consistent with congressional intent and any applicable statutory scheme." *McCarthy v. Madigan*, 503 U.S. at 144 (1992).

Appropriate deference in this case requires the recognition that, with respect to actions brought under the APA, Congress effectively codified the doctrine of exhaustion of administrative remedies in § 10(c). Of course, the exhaustion doctrine continues to apply as a matter of judicial discretion in cases not governed by the APA. But where the APA applies, an appeal to "superior agency authority" is a prerequisite to judicial review *only* when expressly required by statute or when an agency rule requires appeal before review and the administrative action is made inoperative pending that review. Courts are not free to impose an exhaustion requirement as a rule of judicial administration where the agency action has already become "final" under § 10(c).

The judgment of the Court of Appeals is reversed, and the case is remanded for further proceedings consistent with this opinion. *It is so ordered.*

QUESTIONS

1. Does this case represent a major change from the law as described in *McCarthy v. Madigan*? *Compare* 1981 MSAPA § 5-107, which imposes a presumptive requirement that a party exhaust administrative remedies prior to seeking judicial review.

2. Consider a federal statute or regulation that provides that an initial decision is final unless reviewed by a certain agency appellate body. Without more, can a court ever require exhaustion of the agency appeal process? What if the agency is merely turning down an application for benefits?

3. Does the *Darby* holding unduly burden agencies or courts?

4. Does this case render all the more important the distinction set out in *Socal* between finality and exhaustion?

5. Is an administrative remedy exhausted if the remedy is no longer available to the claimant because review by the agency was not sought in a timely manner? The Court in *Woodford v. Ngo*, 548 U.S. 81 (2006), reviewed whether a state prisoner could gain federal court review of a challenge to the conditions of confinement in state prison. The federal statute foreclosed federal court review "until such administrative remedies as are available are exhausted." 42 U.S.C. § 1997e(a). The Court construed the exhaustion requirement in light of the understanding of exhaustion in administrative law and determined that Congress intended that federal court review would be available only when there had been "proper exhaustion":

> Because exhaustion requirements are designed to deal with parties who do not want to exhaust, administrative law creates an incentive for these parties to do what they would otherwise prefer not to do, namely, to give the agency a fair and full opportunity to adjudicate their claims. Administrative law does this by requiring proper exhaustion of administrative remedies, which "means using all steps that the agency holds out, and doing so properly (so that the agency addresses the issues on the merits)." [citation] This Court has described the doctrine as follows: "[A]s a general rule . . . courts should not topple over administrative decisions unless the administrative body not only has erred, but has erred against objection *made at the time appropriate under its practice."* *United States v. L.A. Tucker Truck Lines, Inc.*, 344 U.S. 33, 37 (1952) (emphasis added). . . . Proper exhaustion demands compliance with an agency's deadlines and other critical procedural rules because no adjudicative system can function effectively without imposing some orderly structure on the course of its proceedings.

Id. at 90-91.

Is this notion of "proper exhaustion" consistent with the exceptions to the exhaustion requirement discussed in *McCarthy v. Madigan*?

NOTE ON SIMS v. APFEL

A person whose claim for Social Security benefits is denied by an administrative law judge (ALJ) must in most cases, before seeking judicial review of that denial, request that the Social Security Appeals Council review his claim. In *Sims v. Apfel*, 530 U.S. 103 (2000), the Supreme Court held that a claimant pursuing judicial review had not waived issues that he did not include in that request. The Court recognized that so-called "issue exhaustion," generally required by statute or regulation, may also be judicially imposed. Justice Thomas, writing for four justices, refused to impose the requirement, however, largely because of the nonadversarial nature of Social Security administrative procedures. Justice O'Connor, providing the fifth vote to dispense with an issue-exhaustion requirement, relied primarily on the misleading nature of the Social Security forms with respect to the need to raise specific issues before the appeals council. Four dissenting justices, including the two former administrative law professors (Breyer and Scalia), found issue exhaustion to be most forcefully required where, as they found in *Sims*, the issues not raised on administrative appeal "significantly depend[] upon specialized agency knowledge or practice."

J. JUDICIAL REMEDIES FOR UNLAWFUL AGENCY ACTION

Chenery I, supra pp. 275-276, stands for the core administrative law principle that, when Congress has delegated law-making authority to an agency, the agency should be permitted to exercise that authority—even when the authority is exercised in the context of reconsidering a matter that a court determines the agency got wrong the first time. Thus, following a judicial determination that an agency has committed an error in its decision making, the court will remand the matter at issue to be reconsidered by the agency.

Chenery I, however, does not resolve the issue of the status of the agency decision that has been determined to be unlawful and that had led to the remand to the agency for reconsideration. The significance of this issue is most pronounced when the action at issue is a rulemaking that is intended to have broad effect. Two possible resolutions are most apparent: the agency decision is allowed to stand while the agency reconsiders the matter, or the agency decision is vacated and of no legal effect while the matter is reconsidered. Section 706(2) (emphasis added) of the APA arguably speaks to this issue, although its clarity is debatable:

The reviewing court shall—
    (1) compel agency action unlawfully withheld or unreasonably delayed; and
    (2) *hold unlawful and set aside agency action*, findings, and conclusions found to be—
        A. arbitrary, capricious, an abuse of discretion, or otherwise not in accordance with law;
        B. contrary to constitutional right, power, privilege, or immunity;
        C. in excess of statutory jurisdiction, authority, or limitations, or short of statutory right;
        D. without observance of procedure required by law;

E. unsupported by substantial evidence in a case subject to sections 556 and
557 of this title or otherwise reviewed on the record of an agency hearing
provided by statute; or

F. unwarranted by the facts to the extent that the facts are subject to trial de
novo by the reviewing court.

Although a claim has been made that § 706(2) mandates that a court vacate an
agency decision prior to remand, *see Natural Resources Defense Council v. E.P.A.*,
489 F.3d 1250, 1262 (D.C. Cir. 2007) (Randolph, J., concurring) ("In cases
governed by the Administrative Procedure Act, I have long believed that the
law requires us to vacate the unlawful agency rule" (citing § 706(2)), the D.C.
Circuit's approach to remedies is that, when remanding to the agency, the court
has discretion to vacate the agency action:

> Under circuit precedent, the decision to remand or vacate hinges upon [the]
> court's assessment of "the seriousness of the . . . deficiencies (and thus the extent
> of doubt whether the agency chose correctly) and the disruptive consequences of
> an interim change that may itself be changed." *Allied-Signal, Inc. v. U.S. Nuclear
> Regulatory Comm'n*, 988 F.2d 146, 150-51 (D.C. Cir.1993) (citations omitted).

Chamber of Commerce of U.S. v. S.E.C., 443 F.3d 890, 908 (D.C. Cir. 2006).

In a recent case, judges of the D.C. Circuit Court of Appeals disagreed about
the proper remedy following a determination of agency illegality. *See Natural
Resources Defense Council, supra.* In his concurring opinion, Judge Randolph
argued that an important advantage of vacating an agency's decision is that
the agency will then be required to seek a stay from the court in the event
that it has concerns about the effect of vacating the decision. *Id.* at 1263; see
Honeywell International, Inc. v. E.P.A., 374 F.3d 1363, 1375 (D.C. Cir. 2004) (Randolph, J., concurring). Agency concerns, which would be raised and litigated
when the agency seeks a stay, will typically relate to the impact on the public
interest of wiping away the agency action. See, e.g., 489 F.3d at 1265-66 (Rogers,
J., concurring in part and dissenting in part) (arguing that vacating agency
regulation establishing standards for emissions of hazardous air pollutants
unduly risks harm to public health). An alternate approach—taken by the
court in *Chamber of Commerce of U.S., supra*—is to order vacation of the agency
action but to withhold issuance of the mandate for a defined period of time.
During that time period, the agency may seek a stay or attempt to complete its
own reconsideration of the matter that has been remanded. See 443 F.3d at 909.
See also Natural Resources Defense Council, 489 F.3d at 1262 ("To remedy the
resulting lack of standards [due to the vacatur], any party 'may file a motion to
delay issuance of the mandate to request either that the current standards
remain in place or that EPA be allowed reasonable time to develop interim
standards.'" (citation omitted)).

The default provision of the APA may, of course, be supplemented by or
superseded by the terms of an agency's organic act. *See Honeywell International,
Inc. v. E.P.A.*, 393 F.3d 1315 (D.C. Cir. 2005) (declining to decide whether
§ 307(d)(9) of the Clean Air Act compels court to vacate rulemakings determined to be unlawful, because rulemaking at issue was properly vacated as a
discretionary matter).

QUESTIONS

1. Assuming that § 706(2) is ambiguous regarding the remedy to be ordered by a court when the court determines that an agency has acted unlawfully, can an agency interpret the provision by rulemaking to establish that a court is not permitted to vacate the agency decision following remand?
2. As the note indicates, when a court decides whether to vacate the agency decision, the court considers whether the agency is likely to adhere to its initial decision following remand. Is a court's discussion of this consideration likely to affect an agency's decision following remand in a way that undermines the *Chenery* principle?
3. For more extended analyses of the issue of judicial remedies, *see* Ronald M. Levin, *"Vacation" at Sea: Judicial Remedies and Equitable Discretion in Administrative Law*, 53 Duke L.J. 291 (2003); Kristina Daugirdas, *Note, Evaluating Remand Without Vacatur: A New Judicial Remedy for Defective Agency Rulemakings*, 80 N.Y.U. L. Rev. 278 (2005).

APPENDIX

A

The Constitution of the United States

WE THE PEOPLE — of the United States, in Order to form a more perfect Union, establish Justice, insure domestic Tranquility, provide for the common defence, promote the general Welfare, and secure the Blessings of Liberty to ourselves and our Posterity, do ordain and establish this Constitution for the United States of America.

ARTICLE I

Section 1. All legislative Powers herein granted shall be vested in a Congress of the United States, which shall consist of a Senate and House of Representatives.

Section 2. The House of Representatives shall be composed of Members chosen every second Year by the People of the several States, and the Electors in each State shall have the Qualifications requisite for Electors of the most numerous Branch of the State Legislature.

No Person shall be a Representative who shall not have attained to the Age of twenty five Years, and been seven Years a Citizen of the United States, and who shall not, when elected, be an Inhabitant of that State in which he shall be chosen.

Representatives and direct Taxes shall be apportioned among the several States which may be included within this Union, according to their respective Numbers, which shall be determined by adding to the whole Number of free Persons, including those bound to Service for a Term of Years, and excluding Indians not taxed, three fifths of all other Persons. The actual Enumeration shall be made within three Years after the first Meeting of the Congress of the United States, and within every subsequent Term of ten Years, in such Manner as they shall by Law direct. The Number of Representatives shall not exceed one for every thirty Thousand, but each State shall have at Least one Representative; and until such enumerations shall be made, the State of New Hampshire shall be entitled to chuse three, Massachusetts eight, Rhode-Island and Providence Plantations one, Connecticut five, New-York six, New Jersey four, Pennsylvania eight, Delaware one, Maryland six, Virginia ten, North Carolina five, South Carolina five, and Georgia three.

When vacancies happen in the Representation from any State, the Executive Authority thereof shall issue Writs of Election to fill such Vacancies.

The House of Representatives shall chuse their speaker and other Officers; and shall have the sole Power of Impeachment.

Section 3. The Senate of the United States shall be composed of two Senators from each State, chosen by the Legislature thereof, for six Years; and each Senator shall have one Vote.

Immediately after they shall be assembled in Consequence of the first Election, they shall be divided as equally as may be into three Classes. The Seats of the Senators of the first Class shall be vacated at the Expiration of the second Year, of the second Class at the Expiration of the fourth Year, and of the third Class at the Expiration of the sixth Year, so that one third may be chosen every second Year; and if Vacancies happen by Resignation, or otherwise, during the Recess of the Legislature of any State, the Executive thereof may make temporary Appointments until the next Meeting of the Legislature, which shall then fill such Vacancies.

No Person shall be a Senator who shall not have attained to the Age of thirty Years, and been nine Years a Citizen of the United States, and who shall not, when elected, be an Inhabitant of that State for which he shall be chosen.

The Vice President of the United States shall be President of the Senate, but shall have no Vote, unless they be equally divided.

The Senate shall chuse their other Officers, and also a President pro tempore, in the Absence of the Vice President, or when he shall exercise the Office of President of the United States.

The Senate shall have the sole Power to try all Impeachments. When sitting for that Purpose, they shall be on Oath or Affirmation. When the President of the United States is tried, the Chief Justice shall preside: And no Person shall be convicted without the concurrence of two thirds of the Members present. Judgment in Cases of Impeachment shall not extend further than to removal from Office, and disqualification to hold and enjoy any Office of honor, Trust or Profit under the United States: but the Party convicted shall nevertheless be liable and subject to Indictment, Trial, Judgment and Punishment, according to law.

Section 4. The Times, Places and Manner of holding Elections for Senators and Representatives, shall be prescribed in each State by the Legislature thereof; but the Congress may at any time by Law make or alter such Regulations, except as to the Places of chusing Senators.

The Congress shall assemble at least once in every Year, and such Meeting shall be on the first Monday in December, unless they shall by Law appoint a different Day.

Section 5. Each House shall be the Judge of the Elections, Returns and Qualifications of its own Members, and a Majority of each shall constitute a Quorum to do business; but a smaller Number may adjourn from day to day, and may be authorized to compel the Attendance of absent Members, in such Manner, and under such Penalties as each House may provide.

Each House may determine the Rules of its Proceedings, punish its Members for disorderly Behaviour, and, with the Concurrence of two thirds, expel a Member.

Each House shall keep a Journal of its Proceedings, and from time to time publish the same, excepting such Parts as may in their Judgment require Secrecy; and the years and Nays of the Members of either House on any question shall, at the Desire of one fifth of those Present, be entered on the Journal.

Neither House, during the Session of Congress, shall, without the Consent of the other, adjourn for more than three days, nor to any other place than that in which the two Houses shall be sitting.

Section 6. The Senators and Representatives shall receive a Compensation for their Services, to be ascertained by Law, and paid out of the Treasury of the United States. They shall in all Cases, except Treason, Felony and Breach of the Peace, be privileged from Arrest during their Attendance at the Session of their respective Houses, and in going to and returning from the same; and for any Speech or Debate in either House, they shall not be questioned in any other Place.

No Senator or Representative shall, during the Time for which he was elected, be appointed to any civil Office under the Authority of the United States, which shall have been created, or the Emoluments whereof shall have been encreased during such time; and no Person holding any Office under the United States, shall be a Member of either House during his Continuance in Office.

Section 7. All Bills for raising Revenue shall originate in the House of Representatives; but the Senate may propose or concur with Amendments as on other Bills.

Every Bill which shall have passed the House of Representatives and the Senate, shall, before it become a Law, be presented to the President of the United States; If he approve he shall sign it, but if not he shall return it, with his Objections to that House in which it shall have originated, who shall enter the Objections at large on their Journal, and proceed to reconsider it. If after such Reconsideration two thirds of that House shall agree to pass the Bill, it shall be sent, together with the Objections, to the other House, by which it shall likewise be reconsidered, and if approved by two thirds of that House, it shall become a Law. But in all such Cases the Votes of both Houses shall be determined by yeas and Nays, and the Names of the Persons voting for and against the Bill shall be entered on the Journal of each House respectively. If any Bill shall not be returned by the President within ten Days (Sundays excepted) after it shall have been presented to him, the Same shall be a Law, in like Manner as if he had signed it, unless the Congress by their Adjournment prevent its Return, in which Case it shall not be a Law.

Every Order, Resolution, or Vote to which the Concurrence of the Senate and House of Representatives may be necessary (except on a question of Adjournment) shall be presented to the President of the United States; and before the Same shall take Effect, shall be approved by him, or being disapproved by him, shall be repassed by two thirds of the Senate and House of Representatives, according to the Rules and Limitations prescribed in the Case of a Bill.

Section 8. The Congress shall have Power To lay and collect Taxes, Duties, Imposts and Excises, to pay the Debts and provide for the common Defence and general Welfare of the United States; but all duties, Imposts and Excises shall be uniform throughout the United States;

To borrow Money on the Credit of the United States;

To regulate Commerce with foreign Nations, and among the several States, and with the Indian Tribes;

To establish an uniform Rule of Naturalization, and uniform Laws on the subject of Bankruptcies throughout the United States;

To coin Money, regulate the Value thereof, and of foreign Coin, and fix the Standard of Weights and Measures;

To provide for the Punishment of counterfeiting the Securities and current Coin of the United States;

To establish Post Offices and post Roads;

To promote the Progress of Science and useful Arts, by securing for limited Times to Authors and Inventors exclusive Right to their respective Writings and Discoveries;

To constitute Tribunals inferior to the supreme Court;

To define and punish Piracies and Felonies committed on the high Seas, and Offences against the Law of Nations;

To declare War, grant Letters of Marque and Reprisal, and make rules concerning Captures on Land and Water;

To raise and support Armies, but no Appropriation of Money to that Use shall be for a longer Term than two Years;

To provide and maintain a Navy;

To make rules for the Government and Regulation of the land and naval Forces;

To provide for calling forth the Militia to execute the Laws of the Union, suppress Insurrections and repel Invasions;

To provide for organizing, arming, and disciplining, the Militia, and for governing such Part of them as may be employed in the Service of the United States, reserving to the States respectively, the Appointment of the Officers, and the Authority of training the Militia according to the discipline prescribed by Congress;

To exercise exclusive Legislation in all Cases whatsoever, over such District (not exceeding ten Miles square), as may, by Cession of particular States, and the Acceptance of Congress, become the Seat of the Government of the United States, and to exercise like Authority over all Places purchased by the Consent of the Legislature of the State in which the Same shall be for the Erection of Forts, Magazines, Arsenals, dock-Yards, and other needful Buildings; — And

To make all Laws which shall be necessary and proper for carrying into Execution the foregoing Powers, and all other Powers vested by this Constitution in the Government of the United States, or in any Department or Officer thereof.

Section 9. The Migration or Importation of such Persons as any of the States now existing shall think proper to admit, shall not be prohibited by the Congress prior to the Year one thousand eight hundred and eight, but a Tax or duty may be imposed on such Importation, not exceeding ten dollars for each Person.

The Privilege of the Writ of Habeas Corpus shall not be suspended, unless when in Cases of Rebellion or Invasion the public Safety may require it.

No Bill of Attainder or ex post facto Law shall be passed.

No Capitation, or other direct, Tax shall be laid, unless in Proportion to the Census or Enumeration herein before directed to be taken.

No Tax or Duty shall be laid on Articles exported from any State.

No Preference shall be given by any Regulation of Commerce or Revenue to the Ports of one State over those of another: nor shall Vessels bound to, or from, one State, be obliged to enter, clear, or pay Duties in another.

No money shall be drawn from the Treasury, but in Consequence of Appropriations made by Law; and a regular Statement and Account of the Receipts and Expenditures of all public Money shall be published from time to time.

No Title of Nobility shall be granted by the United States: And no Person holding any Office of Profit or Trust under them, shall, without the Consent of the Congress, accept of any present, Emolument, Office, or Title, of any kind whatever, from any King, Prince, or foreign State.

Section 10. No State shall enter into any Treaty, Alliance, or Confederation; grant Letters of Marque and Reprisal; coin Money; emit Bills of Credit; make any Thing but gold and silver Coin a Tender in Payment of Debts; pass any Bill of Attainder, ex post facto Law, or Law impairing the Obligation of Contracts, or grant any Title of Nobility.

No State shall, without the Consent of the Congress, lay any Imposts or Duties on Imports or Exports, except what may be absolutely necessary for executing it's inspection Laws: and the net Produce of all Duties and Imposts, laid by any State on Imports or Exports, shall be for the Use of the Treasury of the United States; and all such Laws shall be subject to the Revision and Controul of the Congress.

No State shall, without the Consent of Congress, lay any Duty of Tonnage, keep Troops, or Ships of War in time of Peace, enter into any Agreement or Compact with another State, or with a foreign Power, or engage in War, unless actually invaded, or in such imminent Danger as will not admit of delay.

ARTICLE II

Section 1. The executive Power shall be vested in a President of the United States of America. He shall hold his Office during the Term of four Years, and, together with the Vice President, chosen for the same Term, be elected, as follows

Each State shall appoint, in such Manner as the Legislature thereof may direct, a Number of Electors, equal to the whole Number of Senators and Representatives to which the State may be entitled in the Congress: but no Senator or Representative, or Person holding an Office of Trust or Profit under the United States, shall be appointed an Elector.

The Electors shall meet in their respective States, and vote by Ballot for two Persons, of whom one at least shall not be an Inhabitant of the same State with themselves. And they shall make a List of all the Persons voted for, and of the Number of Votes for each; which List they shall sign and certify, and transmit sealed to the Seat of the Government of the United States, directed to the President of the Senate. The President of the Senate shall, in the Presence of the Senate and House of Representatives, open all the Certificates, and the Votes shall then be counted. The Person having the greatest Number of Votes shall be the President, if such Number be a Majority of the whole Number of Electors appointed; and if there be more than one who have such Majority, and have an equal Number of Votes, then the House of Representatives shall immediately chuse by Ballot one of them for President: and if no Person have a Majority, then from the five highest on the List the said House shall in like Manner chuse the President. But in chusing the President, the Votes shall be taken by States, the Representation from each State having one Vote; A quorum for this Purpose shall consist of a Member or Members from two thirds of the States, and a Majority of all the States shall be necessary to a Choice. In every Case, after the Choice of the President, the Person having the greatest Number of Votes of the Electors shall be the Vice President. But if there should remain two or more who have equal Votes, the Senate shall chuse from them by Ballot the Vice President.

The Congress may determine the Time of chusing the Electors, and the Day on which they shall give their Votes; which Day shall be the same throughout the United States.

No Person except a natural born Citizen, or a Citizen of the United States, at the time of the Adoption of this Constitution, shall be eligible to the Office of President; neither shall any Person be eligible to that Office who shall not have attained to the Age of thirty five Years, and been fourteen Years a Resident within the United States.

In Case of the Removal of the President from Office, or of his Death, Resignation, or Inability to discharge the Powers and Duties of the said Office, the Same shall devolve on the Vice President, and the Congress may by Law provide for the Case of Removal, Death, Resignation or Inability, both of the President and Vice President, declaring what Officer shall then act as President, and such Officer shall act accordingly, until the Disability be removed, or a President shall be elected.

The President shall, at stated Times, receive for his Services, a Compensation, which shall neither be encreased nor diminished during the Period for which he shall have been elected, and he shall not receive within that Period any other Emolument from the United States, or any of them.

Before he enter on the Execution of his Office, he shall take the following Oath or Affirmation: — "I do solemnly swear (or affirm) that I will faithfully execute the Office of President of the United States, and will to the best of my Ability, preserve, protect and defend the Constitution of the United States."

Section 2. The President shall be Commander in Chief of the Army and Navy of the United States, and of the Militia of the several States, when called into the actual Service of the United States; he may require the Opinion, in writing, of the principal Officer in each of the executive Departments, upon any Subject relating to the Duties of their respective Offices, and he shall have Power to grant Reprieves and Pardons for Offences against the United States, except in Cases of Impeachment.

He shall have Power, by and with the Advice and Consent of the Senate, to make Treaties, provided two thirds of the Senators present concur; and he shall nominate, and by and with the Advice and Consent of the Senate, shall appoint Ambassadors, other public Ministers and Consuls, Judges of the supreme Court, and all other Officers of the United States, whose Appointments are not herein otherwise provided for, and which shall be established by Law: but the Congress may by Law vest the Appointment of such inferior Officers, as they think proper, in the President alone, in the Courts of Law, or in the Heads of Departments.

The President shall have Power to fill up all Vacancies that may happen during the Recess of the Senate, by granting Commissions which shall expire at the End of their next Session.

Section 3. He shall from time to time give to the Congress Information of the State of the Union, and recommend to their Consideration such Measures as he shall judge necessary and expedient; he may, on extraordinary Occasions, convene both Houses, or either of them, and in Case of Disagreement between them, with Respect to the Time of Adjournment, he may adjourn them to such Time as he shall think proper; he shall receive Ambassadors and other public Ministers; he shall take Care that the Laws be faithfully executed, and shall Commission all the Officers of the United States.

Section 4. The President, Vice President and all civil Officers of the United States, shall be removed from Office on Impeachment for, and Conviction of, Treason, Bribery, or other High Crimes and Misdemeanors.

ARTICLE III

Section 1. The judicial Power of the United States, shall be vested in one supreme Court, and in such inferior Courts as the Congress may from time to time ordain and establish. The Judges, both of the supreme and inferior Courts, shall hold their Offices during good Behaviour, and shall, at stated Times, receive for their Services, a Compensation, which shall not be diminished during their Continuance in Office.

Section 2. The judicial Power shall extend to all Cases, in Law and Equity, arising under this Constitution, the Laws of the United States, and Treaties made, or which shall be made, under their Authority; — to all Cases affecting Ambassadors, other public Ministers and Consuls; — to all Cases of admiralty and maritime Jurisdiction; — to Controversies to which the United States shall be a Party; — to Controversies between two or more States; between a State and Citizens of another State; — between Citizens of different States; — between Citizens of the same State claiming Lands under Grants of different States, and between a State, or the Citizens thereof, and foreign States, Citizens or Subjects.

In all Cases affecting Ambassadors, other public Ministers and Consuls, and those in which a State shall be Party, the supreme Court shall have original Jurisdiction. In all the other Cases before mentioned, the supreme Court shall have appellate Jurisdiction, both as to Law and Fact, with such Exceptions, and under such Regulations as the Congress shall make.

The Trial of all Crimes, except in Cases of Impeachment, shall be by Jury; and such Trial shall be held in the State where the said Crimes shall have been committed; but when not committed within any State, the Trial shall be at such Place or Places as the Congress may by Law have directed.

Section 3. Treason against the United States, shall consist only in levying War against them, or in adhering to their Enemies, giving them Aid and Comfort.

No Person shall be convicted of Treason unless on the Testimony of two Witnesses to the same overt Act, or on Confession in open Court.

The Congress shall have Power to declare the Punishment of Treason, but no Attainder of Treason shall work Corruption of Blood, or Forfeiture except during the Life of the Person attainted.

ARTICLE IV

Section 1. Full Faith and Credit shall be given in each State to the public Acts, Records, and judicial Proceedings of every other State. And the Congress may by general Laws prescribe the Manner in which such Acts, Records and Proceedings shall be proved, and the Effect thereof.

Section 2. The Citizens of each State shall be entitled to all Privileges and Immunities of Citizens in the several States.

A Person charged in any State with Treason, Felony, or other Crime, who shall flee from Justice, and be found in another State, shall on Demand of the executive Authority of the State from which he fled, be delivered up, to be removed to the State having Jurisdiction of the Crime.

No person held to Service or Labour in one State, under the Laws thereof, escaping into another, shall, in Consequence of any Law or Regulation therein, be discharged from such Service or Labour, but shall be delivered up on Claim of the Party to whom such Service or Labour may be due.

Section 3. New States may be admitted by the Congress into this Union; but no new State shall be formed or erected within the Jurisdiction of any other State; nor any State be formed by the Junction of two or more States, or Parts of States, without the Consent of the Legislatures of the States concerned as well as of the Congress.

The Congress shall have Power to dispose of and make all needful Rules and Regulations respecting the Territory or other Property belonging to the United States; and nothing in this Constitution shall be so construed as to Prejudice any Claims of the United States, or of any particular State.

Section 4. The United States shall guarantee to every State in this Union a Republican Form of Government, and shall protect each of them against Invasion; and on Application of the Legislature, or of the Executive (when the Legislature cannot be convened) against domestic Violence.

ARTICLE V

The Congress, whenever two thirds of both Houses shall deem it necessary, shall propose Amendments to this Constitution, or, on the Application of the Legislatures of two thirds of the several States, shall call a Convention for proposing Amendments, which, in either Case, shall be valid to all Intents and Purposes, as Part of this Constitution, when ratified by the Legislatures of three fourths of the several States, or by Conventions in three fourths thereof, as the one or the other Mode of Ratification may be proposed by the Congress; Provided that no

Amendment which may be made prior to the Year One thousand eight hundred and eight shall in any Manner affect the first and fourth Clauses in the Ninth Section of the first Article; and that no State, without its Consent, shall be deprived of its equal Suffrage in the Senate.

ARTICLE VI

All Debts contracted and Engagements entered into, before the Adoption of this Constitution, shall be as valid against the United States under this Constitution, as under the Confederation.

This Constitution, and the Laws of the United States which shall be made in Pursuance thereof; and all Treaties made, or which shall be made, under the Authority of the United States, shall be the supreme Law of the Land; and the Judges in every State shall be bound thereby, any Thing in the Constitution or Laws of any State to the Contrary notwithstanding.

The Senators and Representatives before mentioned, and the Members of the several State Legislatures, and all executive and judicial Officers, both of the United States and of the several States, shall be bound by Oath or Affirmation, to support this Constitution; but no religious Test shall ever be required as a Qualification to any Office or public Trust under the United States.

ARTICLE VII

The Ratification of the Conventions of nine States, shall be sufficient for the Establishment of this Constitution between the States so ratifying the Same.

Done in Convention by the Unanimous Consent of the States present the Seventeenth Day of September in the Year of our Lord one thousand seven hundred and Eighty seven and of the Independence of the United States of America the Twelfth. . . .

AMENDMENTS

(The first 10 Amendments were ratified December 15, 1791, and form what is known as the Bill of Rights)

AMENDMENT 1
Congress shall make no law respecting an establishment of religion, or prohibiting the free exercise thereof; or abridging the freedom of speech, or of the press; or the right of the people peaceably to assemble, and to petition the Government for a redress of grievances.

AMENDMENT 2
A well regulated Militia, being necessary to the security of a free State, the right of the people to keep and bear Arms, shall not be infringed.

AMENDMENT 3
No Soldier shall, in time of peace be quartered in any house, without the consent of the Owner, nor in time of war, but in a manner to be prescribed by law.

AMENDMENT 4

The right of the people to be secure in their persons, houses, papers, and effects, against unreasonable searches and seizures, shall not be violated, and no Warrants shall issue, but upon probable cause, supported by Oath or affirmation, and particularly describing the place to be searched, and the persons or things to be seized.

AMENDMENT 5

No person shall be held to answer for a capital, or otherwise infamous crime, unless on a presentment or indictment of a Grand Jury, except in cases arising in the land or naval forces, or in the Militia, when in actual service in time of War or public danger; nor shall any person be subject for the same offence to be twice put in jeopardy of life or limb; nor shall be compelled in any criminal case to be a witness against himself, nor be deprived of life, liberty, or property, without due process of law; nor shall private property be taken for public use, without just compensation.

AMENDMENT 6

In all criminal prosecutions, the accused shall enjoy the right to a speedy and public trial, by an impartial jury of the State and district wherein the crime shall have been committed, which district shall have been previously ascertained by law, and to be informed of the nature and cause of the accusation; to be confronted with the witnesses against him; to have compulsory process for obtaining witnesses in his favor, and to have the Assistance of Counsel for his defence.

AMENDMENT 7

In Suits at common law, where the value in controversy shall exceed twenty dollars, the right of trial by jury shall be preserved, and no fact tried by a jury, shall be otherwise re-examined in any Court of the United States, than according to the rules of the common law.

AMENDMENT 8

Excessive bail shall not be required, nor excessive fines imposed, nor cruel and unusual punishments inflicted.

AMENDMENT 9

The enumeration in the Constitution, of certain rights, shall not be construed to deny or disparage others retained by the people.

AMENDMENT 10

The powers not delegated to the United States by the Constitution, nor prohibited by it to the States, are reserved to the States respectively, or to the people.

AMENDMENT 11
(Ratified February 7, 1795)

The Judicial power of the United States shall not be construed to extend to any suit in law or equity, commenced or prosecuted against one of the United States by Citizens of another State, or by Citizens or Subjects of any Foreign State.

AMENDMENT 12
(Ratified July 27, 1804)

The Electors shall meet in their respective states, and vote by ballot for President and Vice-President, one of whom, at least, shall not be an inhabitant of the same state with themselves; they shall name in their ballots the person voted for as President, and in distinct ballots the person voted for as Vice-President, and they shall make distinct lists of all persons voted for as President, and of all persons voted for as Vice-President, and of the number of votes for each, which lists they shall sign and certify, and transmit sealed to the seat of the government of the United States, directed to the President of the Senate; — The President of the Senate shall, in the presence of the Senate and House of Representatives, open all the certificates and the votes shall then be counted; — The person having the greatest number of votes for President, shall be the President, if such number be a majority of the whole number of Electors appointed; and if no person have such majority, then from the persons having the highest numbers not exceeding three on the list of those voted for as President, the House of Representatives shall choose immediately, by ballot, the President. But in choosing the President, the votes shall be taken by states, the representation from each state having one vote; a quorum for this purpose shall consist of a member or members from two-thirds of the states, and a majority of all the states shall be necessary to a choice. And if the House of Representatives shall not choose a President whenever the right of choice shall devolve upon them, before the fourth day of March next following, then the Vice-President shall act as President, as in the case of the death or other constitutional disability of the President. — The person having the greatest number of votes as Vice-President, shall be the Vice-President, if such number be a majority of the whole number of Electors appointed, and if no person have a majority, then from the two highest numbers on the list, the Senate shall choose the Vice-President; a quorum for the purpose shall consist of two-thirds of the whole number of Senators, and a majority of the whole number shall be necessary to a choice. But no person constitutionally ineligible to the office of President shall be eligible to that of Vice-President of the United States.

AMENDMENT 13
(Ratified December 6, 1865)

Section 1. Neither slavery nor involuntary servitude, except as a punishment for crime whereof the party shall have been duly convicted, shall exist within the United States, or any place subject to their jurisdiction.

Section 2. Congress shall have power to enforce this article by appropriate legislation.

AMENDMENT 14
(Ratified July 9, 1868)

Section 1. All persons born or naturalized in the United States, and subject to the jurisdiction thereof, are citizens of the United States and of the State wherein they reside. No State shall make or enforce any law which shall abridge the privileges or immunities of citizens of the United States; nor shall any State deprive any person of life, liberty, or property, without due process of law; nor deny to any person within its jurisdiction the equal protection of the laws.

Section 2. Representatives shall be apportioned among the several States according to their respective numbers, counting the whole number of persons in each State, excluding Indians not taxed. But when the right to vote at any election for the choice of electors for President and Vice President of the United States, Representatives in Congress, the Executive and Judicial officers of a State, or the members of the Legislature thereof, is denied to any of the male inhabitants of such State, being twenty-one years of age, and citizens of the United States, or in any way abridged, except for participation in rebellion, or other crime, the basis of representation therein shall be reduced in the proportion which the number of such male citizens shall bear to the whole number of male citizens twenty-one years of age in such State.

Section 3. No person shall be a Senator or Representative in Congress, or elector of President and Vice President, or hold any office, civil or military, under the United States, or under any State, who, having previously taken an oath, as a member of Congress, or as an officer of the United States, or as a member of any State legislature, or as an executive or judicial officer of any State, to support the Constitution of the United States, shall have engaged in insurrection or rebellion against the same, or given aid or comfort to the enemies thereof. But Congress may by a vote of two-thirds of each House, remove such disability.

Section 4. The validity of the public debt of the United States, authorized by law, including debts incurred for payment of pensions and bounties for services in suppressing insurrection or rebellion, shall not be questioned. But neither the United States nor any State shall assume or pay any debt or obligation incurred in aid of insurrection or rebellion against the United States, or any claim for the loss or emancipation of any slave; but all such debts, obligations and claims shall be held illegal and void.

Section 5. The Congress shall have power to enforce, by appropriate legislation, the provisions of this article.

AMENDMENT 15
(Ratified February 3, 1870)

Section 1. The right of citizens of the United States to vote shall not be denied or abridged by the United States or by any State on account of race, color, or previous condition of servitude.

Section 2. The Congress shall have power to enforce this article by appropriate legislation.

AMENDMENT 16
(Ratified February 3, 1913)

The Congress shall have power to lay and collect taxes on incomes, from whatever source derived, without apportionment among the several States, and without regard to any census or enumeration.

AMENDMENT 17
(Ratified April 8, 1913)

The Senate of the United States shall be composed of two Senators from each State, elected by the people thereof for six years; and each Senator shall have one vote. The electors in each State shall have the qualifications requisite for electors of the most numerous branch of the State legislatures.

When vacancies happen in the representation of any State in the Senate, the executive authority of such State shall issue writs of election to fill such vacancies: Provided, That the legislature of any State may empower the executive thereof to make temporary appointments until the people fill the vacancies by election as the legislature may direct.

This amendment shall not be so construed as to affect the election or term of any Senator chosen before it becomes valid as part of the Constitution.

AMENDMENT 18
(Ratified January 16, 1919. Repealed December 5, 1933 by Amendment 21)

Section 1. After one year from the ratification of this article the manufacture, sale, or transportation of intoxicating liquors within, the importation thereof into, or the exportation thereof from the United States and all territory subject to the jurisdiction thereof for beverage purposes is hereby prohibited.

Section 2. The Congress and the several States shall have concurrent power to enforce this article by appropriate legislation.

Section 3. This article shall be inoperative unless it shall have been ratified as an amendment to the Constitution by the legislatures of the several States as provided in the Constitution, within seven years from the date of the submission hereof to the States by the Congress.

AMENDMENT 19
(Ratified August 18, 1920)

The right of citizens of the United States to vote shall not be denied or abridged by the United States or by any State on account of sex.

Congress shall have power to enforce this article by appropriate legislation.

AMENDMENT 20
(Ratified January 23, 1933)

Section 1. The terms of the President and Vice President shall end at noon on the 20th day of January, and the terms of Senators and Representatives at noon on the 3d day of January, of the years in which such terms would have ended if this article had not been ratified; and the terms of their successors shall then begin.

Section 2. The Congress shall assemble at least once in every year, and such meeting shall begin at noon on the 3d day of January, unless they shall by law appoint a different day.

Section 3. If, at the time fixed for the beginning of the term of the President, the President elect shall have died, the Vice President elect shall become President. If a President shall not have been chosen before the time fixed for the beginning of his term, or if the President elect shall have failed to qualify, then the Vice President elect shall act as President until a President shall have qualified; and the Congress may by law provide for the case wherein neither a President elect nor a Vice President elect shall have qualified, declaring who shall then act as President, or the manner in which one who is to act shall be selected, and such person shall act accordingly until a President or Vice President shall have qualified.

Section 4. The Congress may by law provide for the case of the death of any of the persons from whom the House of Representatives may choose a President whenever the right of choice shall have devolved upon them, and for the case of the death of any of the persons from whom the Senate may choose a Vice President whenever the right of choice shall have devolved upon them.

Section 5. Sections 1 and 2 shall take effect on the 15th day of October following the ratification of this article.

Section 6. This article shall be inoperative unless it shall have been ratified as an amendment to the Constitution by the legislatures of three-fourths of the several States within seven years from the date of its submission.

AMENDMENT 21
(Ratified December 5, 1933)

Section 1. The eighteenth article of amendment to the Constitution of the United States is hereby repealed.

Section 2. The transportation or importation into any State, Territory, or possession of the United States for delivery or use therein of intoxicating liquors, in violation of the laws thereof, is hereby prohibited.

Section 3. This article shall be inoperative unless it shall have been ratified as an amendment to the Constitution by conventions in the several States, as provided in the Constitution, within seven years from the date of the submission hereof to the States by the Congress.

AMENDMENT 22
(Ratified February 27, 1951)

Section 1. No person shall be elected to the office of the President more than twice, and no person who has held the office of President, or acted as President, for more than two years of a term to which some other person was elected President shall be elected to the office of the President more than once. But this Article shall not apply to any person holding the office of President when this Article was proposed by the Congress, and shall not prevent any person who may be holding the office of President, or acting as President, during the term within which this Article becomes operative from holding the office of President or acting as President during the remainder of such term.

Section 2. This article shall be inoperative unless it shall have been ratified as an amendment to the Constitution by the legislatures of three-fourths of the several States within seven years from the date of its submission to the States by the Congress.

AMENDMENT 23
(Ratified March 29, 1961)

Section 1. The District constituting the seat of Government of the United States shall appoint in such manner as the Congress may direct:

A number of electors of President and Vice President equal to the whole number of Senators and Representatives in Congress to which the District would be entitled if it were a State, but in no event more than the least populous State; they shall be in addition to those appointed by the States, but they shall be considered, for the purposes of the election of President and Vice President, to be electors appointed by a State; and they shall meet in the District and perform such duties as provided by the twelfth article of amendment.

Section 2. The Congress shall have power to enforce this article by appropriate legislation.

AMENDMENT 24
(Ratified January 23, 1964)

Section 1. The right of citizens of the United States to vote in any primary or other election for President or Vice President, for electors for President or Vice President, or for Senator or Representative in Congress, shall not be denied or abridged by the United States or any State by reason of failure to pay any poll tax or other tax.

Section 2. The Congress shall have power to enforce this article by appropriate legislation.

AMENDMENT 25
(Ratified February 10, 1967)

Section 1. In case of the removal of the President from office or of his death or resignation, the Vice President shall become President.

Section 2. Whenever there is a vacancy in the office of the Vice President, the President shall nominate a Vice President who shall take office upon confirmation by a majority vote of both Houses of Congress.

Section 3. Whenever the President transmits to the President pro tempore of the Senate and the Speaker of the House of Representatives his written declaration that he is unable to discharge the powers and duties of his office, and until he transmits to them a written declaration to the contrary, such powers and duties shall be discharged by the Vice President as Acting President.

Section 4. Whenever the Vice President and a majority of either the principal officers of the executive departments or of such other body as Congress may by law provide, transmit to the President pro tempore of the Senate and the Speaker of the House of Representatives their written declaration that the President is unable to discharge the powers and duties of his office, the Vice

President shall immediately assume the powers and duties of the office as Acting President.

Thereafter, when the President transmits to the President pro tempore of the Senate and the Speaker of the House of Representatives his written declaration that no inability exists, he shall resume the powers and duties of his office unless the Vice President and a majority of either the principal officers of the executive department or of such other body as Congress may by law provide, transmit within four days to the President pro tempore of the Senate and the Speaker of the House of Representatives their written declaration that the President is unable to discharge the powers and duties of his office. Thereupon Congress shall decide the issue, assembling within forty-eight hours for that purpose if not in session. If the Congress, within twenty-one days after receipt of the latter written declaration, or, if Congress is not in session, within twenty-one days after Congress is required to assemble, determines by two-thirds vote of both Houses that the President is unable to discharge the powers and duties of his office, the Vice President shall continue to discharge the same as Acting President; otherwise, the President shall resume the powers and duties of his office.

AMENDMENT 26
(Ratified July 1, 1971)

Section 1. The right of citizens of the United States, who are eighteen years of age or older, to vote shall not be denied or abridged by the United States or by any State on account of age.

Section 2. The Congress shall have the power to enforce this article by appropriate legislation.

AMENDMENT 27
(Ratified May 7, 1992)

No law, varying the compensation for the services of the Senators and Representatives, shall take effect, until an election of Representatives shall have intervened.

APPENDIX

B

The Administrative Procedure Act
(Selected Provisions)

TITLE 5 — GOVERNMENT ORGANIZATION AND EMPLOYEES

§ 504. Costs and Fees of Parties

[This section codifies part of Pub. L. No. 96-481 (1980), and provides generally that "[a]n agency that conducts an adversary adjudication shall award, to a prevailing party other than the United States, fees and other expenses incurred by that party in connection with that proceeding, unless the adjudicative officer of the agency finds that the position of the agency was substantially justified or that special circumstances make an award unjust. . . ."]

§ 551. Definitions

For the purpose of this subchapter —

(1) "agency" means each authority of the Government of the United States, whether or not it is within or subject to review by another agency, but does not include —

(A) the Congress;

(B) the courts of the United States;

(C) the governments of the territories or possessions of the United States;

(D) the government of the District of Columbia; or except as to the requirements of section 552 of this title —

(E) agencies composed of representatives of the parties or of representatives of organizations of the parties to the disputes determined by them;

(F) courts martial and military commissions;

(G) military authority exercised in the field in time of war or in occupied territory; or

(H) functions conferred by sections 1738, 1739, 1743, and 1744 of title 12; subchapter II of chapter 471 of title 49; or sections 1884, 1891-1902, and former section 1641(b)(2), of title 50, appendix;

(2) "person" includes an individual, partnership, corporation, association, or public or private organization other than an agency;

(3) "party" includes a person or agency named or admitted as a party, or properly seeking and entitled as of right to be admitted as a party, in an agency proceeding, and a person or agency admitted by an agency as a party for limited purposes;

(4) "rule" means the whole or a part of an agency statement of general or particular applicability and future effect designed to implement, interpret, or prescribe law or policy or describing the organization, procedure, or practice requirements of an agency and includes the approval or prescription for the future of rates, wages, corporate or financial structures or reorganizations thereof, prices, facilities, appliances, services or allowances therefor or of valuations, costs, or accounting, or practices bearing on any of the foregoing;

(5) "rule making" means agency process for formulating, amending, or repealing a rule;

(6) "order" means the whole or a part of a final disposition, whether affirmative, negative, injunctive, or declaratory in form, of an agency in a matter other than rule making but including licensing;

(7) "adjudication" means agency process for the formulation of an order;

(8) "license" includes the whole or a part of an agency permit, certificate, approval, registration, charter, membership, statutory exemption or other form of permission;

(9) "licensing" includes agency process respecting the grant, renewal, denial, revocation, suspension, annulment, withdrawal, limitation, amendment, modification, or conditioning of a license;

(10) "sanction" includes the whole or a part of an agency—

(A) prohibition, requirement, limitation, or other condition affecting the freedom of a person;

(B) withholding of relief;

(C) imposition of penalty or fine;

(D) destruction, taking, seizure, or withholding of property;

(E) assessment of damages, reimbursement, restitution, compensation, costs, charges, or fees;

(F) requirement, revocation, or suspension of a license; or

(G) taking other compulsory or restrictive action;

(11) "relief" includes the whole or a part of an agency—

(A) grant of money, assistance, license, authority, exemption, exception, privilege, or remedy;

(B) recognition of a claim, right, immunity, privilege, exemption, or exception; or

(C) taking of other action on the application or petition of, and beneficial to, a person;

(12) "agency proceeding" means an agency process as defined by paragraphs (5), (7), and (9) of this section;

(13) "agency action" includes the whole or a part of an agency rule, order, license, sanction, relief, or the equivalent or denial thereof, or failure to act; and

(14) "ex parte communication" means an oral or written communication not on the public record with respect to which reasonable prior notice to all parties is not given, but it shall not include requests for status reports on any matter or proceeding covered by this subchapter.

§ 552. Public Information; Agency Rules, Opinions, Orders, Records, and Proceedings

[This section, which includes the Freedom of Information Act of 1966 (FOIA), Pub. L. No. 89-487, as amended, is omitted.]

[§ 552a. The Privacy Protection Act is omitted.]

§ 552b. Open Meetings

[This section, which includes the Government in the Sunshine Act, Pub. L. No. 94-409, as amended, is omitted.]

§ 553. Rule Making

(a) This section applies, according to the provisions thereof, except to the extent that there is involved —
    (1) a military or foreign affairs function of the United States; or
    (2) a matter relating to agency management or personnel or to public property, loans, grants, benefits, or contracts.
(b) General notice of proposed rule making shall be published in the Federal Register, unless persons subject thereto are named and either personally served or otherwise have actual notice thereof in accordance with law. The notice shall include —
    (1) a statement of the time, place, and nature of public rule making proceedings;
    (2) reference to the legal authority under which the rule is proposed; and
    (3) either the terms or substance of the proposed rule or a description of the subjects and issues involved.
Except when notice or hearing is required by statute, this subsection does not apply —
    (A) to interpretative rules, general statements of policy, or rules of agency organization, procedure, or practice; or
    (B) when the agency for good cause finds (and incorporates the finding and a brief statement of reasons therefor in the rules issued) that notice and public procedure thereon are impracticable, unnecessary, or contrary to the public interest.
(c) After notice required by this section, the agency shall give interested persons an opportunity to participate in the rule making through submission of written data, views, or arguments with or without opportunity for oral presentation. After consideration of the relevant matter presented, the agency shall incorporate in the rules adopted a concise general statement of their basis and purpose. When rules are required by statute to be made on the record after opportunity for an agency hearing, sections 556 and 557 of this title apply instead of this subsection.
(d) The required publication or service of a substantive rule shall be made not less than 30 days before its effective date, except —
    (1) a substantive rule which grants or recognizes an exemption or relieves a restriction;
    (2) interpretative rules and statements of policy; or

(3) as otherwise provided by the agency for good cause found and published with the rule.

(e) Each agency shall give an interested person the right to petition for the issuance, amendment, or repeal of a rule.

§ 554.   Adjudications

(a) This section applies, according to the provisions thereof, in every case of adjudication required by statute to be determined on the record after opportunity for an agency hearing, except to the extent that there is involved—

(1) a matter subject to a subsequent trial of the law and the facts de novo in a court;

(2) the selection or tenure of an employee, except a[n] administrative law judge appointed under section 3105 of this title;

(3) proceedings in which decisions rest solely on inspections, tests, or elections;

(4) the conduct of military or foreign affairs functions;

(5) cases in which an agency is acting as an agent for a court; or

(6) the certification of worker representatives.

(b) Persons entitled to notice of an agency hearing shall be timely informed of—

(1) the time, place, and nature of the hearing;

(2) the legal authority and jurisdiction under which the hearing is to be held; and

(3) the matters of fact and law asserted.

When private persons are the moving parties, other parties to the proceeding shall give prompt notice of issues controverted in fact or law; and in other instances agencies may by rule require responsive pleading. In fixing the time and place for hearings, due regard shall be had for the convenience and necessity of the parties or their representatives.

(c) The agency shall give all interested parties opportunity for—

(1) the submission and consideration of facts, arguments, offers of settlement, or proposals of adjustment when time, the nature of the proceeding, and the public interest permit; and

(2) to the extent that the parties are unable so to determine a controversy by consent, hearing and decision on notice and in accordance with sections 556 and 557 of this title.

(d) The employee who presides at the reception of evidence pursuant to section 556 of this title shall make the recommended decision or initial decision required by section 557 of this title, unless he becomes unavailable to the agency. Except to the extent required for the disposition of ex parte matters as authorized by law, such an employee may not—

(1) consult a person or party on a fact in issue, unless on notice and opportunity for all parties to participate; or

(2) be responsible to or subject to the supervision or direction of an employee or agent engaged in the performance of investigative or prosecuting functions for an agency. An employee or agent engaged in the performance of investigative or prosecuting functions for an agency in a case may not, in that or a factually related case, participate or advise in the decision, recommended decision, or agency review pursuant to section

557 of this title, except as witness or counsel in public proceedings. This subsection does not apply —

> (A) in determining applications for initial licenses;
>
> (B) to proceedings involving the validity or application of rates, facilities, or practices of public utilities or carriers; or
>
> (C) to the agency or a member or members of the body comprising the agency.

(e) The agency, with like effect as in the case of other orders, and in its sound discretion, may issue a declaratory order to terminate a controversy or remove uncertainty.

§ 555. Ancillary Matters

(a) This section applies, according to the provisions thereof, except as otherwise provided by this subchapter.

(b) A person compelled to appear in person before an agency or representative thereof is entitled to be accompanied, represented, and advised by counsel or, if permitted by the agency, by other qualified representative. A party is entitled to appear in person or by or with counsel or other duly qualified representative in an agency proceeding. So far as the orderly conduct of public business permits, an interested person may appear before an agency or its responsible employees for the presentation, adjustment, or determination of an issue, request, or controversy in a proceeding, whether interlocutory, summary, or otherwise, or in connection with an agency function. With due regard for the convenience and necessity of the parties or their representatives and within a reasonable time, each agency shall proceed to conclude a matter presented to it. This subsection does not grant or deny a person who is not a lawyer the right to appear for or represent others before an agency or in an agency proceeding.

(c) Process, requirement of a report, inspection, or other investigative act or demand may not be issued, made, or enforced except as authorized by law. A person compelled to submit data or evidence is entitled to retain or, on payment of lawfully prescribed costs, procure a copy or transcript thereof, except that in a nonpublic investigatory proceeding the witness may for good cause be limited to inspection of the official transcript of his testimony.

(d) Agency subpenas authorized by law shall be issued to a party on request and, when required by rules of procedure, on a statement or showing of general relevance and reasonable scope of the evidence sought. On contest, the court shall sustain the subpena or similar process or demand to the extent that it is found to be in accordance with law. In a proceeding for enforcement, the court shall issue an order requiring the appearance of the witness or the production of the evidence or data within a reasonable time under penalty of punishment for contempt in case of contumacious failure to comply.

(e) Prompt notice shall be given of the denial in whole or in part of a written application, petition, or other request of an interested person made in connection with any agency proceeding. Except in affirming a prior denial or when the denial is self-explanatory, the notice shall be accompanied by a brief statement of the grounds for denial.

§ 556.   Hearings; Presiding Employees; Powers and Duties; Burden of Proof; Evidence; Record as Basis of Decision

(a) This section applies, according to the provisions thereof, to hearings required by section 553 or 554 of this title to be conducted in accordance with this section.

(b) There shall preside at the taking of evidence —

(1) the agency;

(2) one or more members of the body which comprises the agency; or

(3) one or more administrative law judges appointed under section 3105 of this title.

This subchapter does not supersede the conduct of specified classes of proceedings, in whole or in part, by or before boards or other employees specially provided for by or designated under statute. The functions of presiding employees and of employees participating in decisions in accordance with section 557 of this title shall be conducted in an impartial manner. A presiding or participating employee may at any time disqualify himself. On the filing in good faith of a timely and sufficient affidavit of personal bias or other disqualification of a presiding or participating employee, the agency shall determine the matter as a part of the record and decision in the case.

(c) Subject to published rules of the agency and within its powers, employees presiding at hearings may —

(1) administer oaths and affirmations;

(2) issue subpenas authorized by law;

(3) rule on offers of proof and receive relevant evidence;

(4) take depositions or have depositions taken when the ends of justice would be served;

(5) regulate the course of the hearing;

(6) hold conferences for the settlement or simplification of the issues by consent of the parties or by the use of alternative means of dispute resolution as provided in subchapter IV of this chapter;

(7) inform the parties as to the availability of one or more alternative means of dispute resolution, and encourage use of such methods;

(8) require the attendance at any conference held pursuant to paragraph (6) of at least one representative of each party who has authority to negotiate concerning resolution of issues in controversy;

(9) dispose of procedural requests or similar matters;

(10) make or recommend decisions in accordance with section 557 of this title; and

(11) take other action authorized by agency rule consistent with this subchapter.

(d) Except as otherwise provided by statute, the proponent of a rule or order has the burden of proof. Any oral or documentary evidence may be received, but the agency as a matter of policy shall provide for the exclusion of irrelevant, immaterial, or unduly repetitious evidence. A sanction may not be imposed or rule or order issued except on consideration of the whole record or those parts thereof cited by a party and supported by and in accordance with the reliable, probative, and substantial evidence. The agency may, to the extent consistent with the interests of justice and the policy of the underlying statutes administered by the agency, consider a violation of section 557(d) of this title sufficient grounds for a decision adverse to a party who has knowingly committed such violation or knowingly caused such violation to occur. A party is entitled to present his case or defense by oral or documentary evidence, to submit rebuttal evidence, and to conduct such cross-examination as may be required for a full and true disclosure of the facts. In rule making or determining claims for money or benefits or applications for initial licenses an agency may, when a party will not be prejudiced thereby, adopt procedures for the submission of all or part of the evidence in written form.

(e) The transcript of testimony and exhibits, together with all papers and requests filed in the proceeding, constitutes the exclusive record for decision in accordance with section 557 of this title and, on payment of lawfully prescribed costs, shall be made available to the parties. When an agency decision rests on official notice of a material fact not appearing in the evidence in the record, a party is entitled, on timely request, to an opportunity to show the contrary.

§ 557. Initial Decisions; Conclusiveness; Review by Agency; Submissions by Parties; Contents of Decisions; Record

(a) This section applies, according to the provisions thereof, when a hearing is required to be conducted in accordance with section 556 of this title.

(b) When the agency did not preside at the reception of the evidence, the presiding employee or, in cases not subject to section 554(d) of this title, an employee qualified to preside at hearings pursuant to section 556 of this title, shall initially decide the case unless the agency requires, either in specific cases or by general rule, the entire record to be certified to it for decision. When the presiding employee makes an initial decision, that decision then becomes the decision of the agency without further proceedings unless there is an appeal to, or review on motion of, the agency within time provided by rule. On appeal from or review of the initial decision, the agency has all the powers which it would have in making the initial decision except as it may limit the issues on notice or by rule. When the agency makes the decision without having presided at the reception of the evidence, the presiding employee or an employee qualified to preside at hearings pursuant to section 556 of this title shall first recommend a decision, except that in rule making or determining applications for initial licenses—

(1) instead thereof the agency may issue a tentative decision or one of its responsible employees may recommend a decision; or

(2) this procedure may be omitted in a case in which the agency finds on the record that due and timely execution of its functions imperatively and unavoidably so requires.

(c) Before a recommended, initial, or tentative decision, or a decision on agency review of the decision of subordinate employees, the parties are entitled to a reasonable opportunity to submit for the consideration of the employees participating in the decisions—

(1) proposed findings and conclusions; or

(2) exceptions to the decisions or recommended decisions of subordinate employees or to tentative agency decisions; and

(3) supporting reasons for the exceptions or proposed findings or conclusions. The record shall show the ruling on each finding, conclusion, or

exception presented. All decisions, including initial, recommended, and tentative decisions, are a part of the record and shall include a statement of—

(A) findings and conclusions, and the reasons or basis therefor, on all the material issues of fact, law, or discretion presented on the record; and

(B) the appropriate rule, order, sanction, relief, or denial thereof.

(d)(1) In any agency proceeding which is subject to subsection (a) of this section, except to the extent required for the disposition of ex parte matters as authorized by law—

(A) no interested person outside the agency shall make or knowingly cause to be made to any member of the body comprising the agency, administrative law judge, or other employee who is or may reasonably be expected to be involved in the decisional process of the proceeding, an ex parte communication relevant to the merits of the proceeding;

(B) no member of the body comprising the agency, administrative law judge, or other employee who is or may reasonably be expected to be involved in the decisional process of the proceeding, shall make or knowingly cause to be made to any interested person outside the agency an ex parte communication relevant to the merits of the proceeding;

(C) a member of the body comprising the agency, administrative law judge, or other employee who is or may reasonably be expected to be involved in the decisional process of such proceeding who receives, or who makes or knowingly causes to be made, a communication prohibited by this subsection shall place on the public record of the proceeding:

(i) all such written communications;

(ii) memoranda stating the substance of all such oral communications; and

(iii) all written responses, and memoranda stating the substance of all oral responses, to the materials described in clauses (i) and (ii) of this subparagraph;

(D) upon receipt of a communication knowingly made or knowingly caused to be made by a party in violation of this subsection, the agency, administrative law judge, or other employee presiding at the hearing may, to the extent consistent with the interests of justice and the policy of the underlying statutes, require the party to show cause why his claim or interest in the proceeding should not be dismissed, denied, disregarded, or otherwise adversely affected on account of such violation; and

(E) the prohibitions of this subsection shall apply beginning at such time as the agency may designate, but in no case shall they begin to apply later than the time at which a proceeding is noticed for hearing unless the person responsible for the communication has knowledge that it will be noticed, in which case the prohibitions shall apply beginning at the time of his acquisition of such knowledge.

(2) This subsection does not constitute authority to withhold information from Congress.

§ 558. Imposition of Sanctions; Determination of Applications for Licenses; Suspension, Revocation, and Expiration of Licenses

(a) This section applies, according to the provisions thereof, to the exercise of a power or authority.

(b) A sanction may not be imposed or a substantive rule or order issued except within jurisdiction delegated to the agency and as authorized by law.

(c) When application is made for a license required by law, the agency, with due regard for the rights and privileges of all the interested parties or adversely affected persons and within a reasonable time, shall set and complete proceedings required to be conducted in accordance with sections 556 and 557 of this title or other proceedings required by law and shall make its decision. Except in cases of willfulness or those in which public health, interest, or safety requires otherwise, the withdrawal, suspension, revocation, or annulment of a license is lawful only if, before the institution of agency proceedings therefor, the licensee has been given —

(1) notice by the agency in writing of the facts or conduct which may warrant the action; and

(2) opportunity to demonstrate or achieve compliance with all lawful requirements.

When the licensee has made timely and sufficient application for a renewal or a new license in accordance with agency rules, a license with reference to an activity of a continuing nature does not expire until the application has been finally determined by the agency.

§ 559. Effect on Other Laws; Effect of Subsequent Statute

This subchapter, chapter 7, and sections 1305, 3105, 3344, 4301(2)(E), 5372, and 7521 of this title, and the provisions of section 5335(a)(B) of this title that relate to administrative law judges, do not limit or repeal additional requirements imposed by statute or otherwise recognized by law. Except as otherwise required by law, requirements or privileges relating to evidence or procedure apply equally to agencies and persons. Each agency is granted the authority necessary to comply with the requirements of this subchapter through the issuance of rules or otherwise. Subsequent statute may not be held to supersede or modify this subchapter, chapter 7, sections 1305, 3105, 3344, 4301(2)(E), 5372, or 7521 of this title, or the provisions of section 5335(a)(B) of this title that relate to administrative law judges, except to the extent that it does so expressly.

§ 601. Definitions

For purposes of this chapter —

(1) the term "agency" means an agency as defined in section 551(1) of this title;

(2) the term "rule" means any rule for which the agency publishes a general notice of proposed rulemaking pursuant to section 553(b) of this title, or any other law, including any rule of general applicability governing Federal grants to State and local governments for which the agency provides an opportunity for notice and public comment, except that the term "rule" does not include a rule of particular applicability relating to rates, wages, corporate or financial structures or reorganizations thereof, prices, facilities, appliances, services, or allowances therefor or to valuations, costs or accounting, or practices relating to such rates, wages, structures, prices, appliances, services, or allowances;

(3) the term "small business" has the same meaning as the term "small business concern" under section 3 of the Small Business Act, unless an

agency, after consultation with the Office of Advocacy of the Small Business Administration and after opportunity for public comment, establishes one or more definitions of such term which are appropriate to the activities of the agency and publishes such definition(s) in the Federal Register;

(4) the term "small organization" means any not-for-profit enterprise which is independently owned and operated and is not dominant in its field, unless an agency establishes, after opportunity for public comment, one or more definitions of such term which are appropriate to the activities of the agency and publishes such definition(s) in the Federal Register;

(5) the term "small governmental jurisdiction" means governments of cities, counties, towns, townships, villages, school districts, or special districts, with a population of less than fifty thousand, unless an agency establishes, after opportunity for public comment, one or more definitions of such term which are appropriate to the activities of the agency and which are based on such factors as location in rural or sparsely populated areas or limited revenues due to the population of such jurisdiction, and publishes such definition(s) in the Federal Register;

(6) the term "small entity" shall have the same meaning as the terms "small business", "small organization" and "small governmental jurisdiction" defined in paragraphs (3), (4) and (5) of this section; and

(7) the term "collection of information" —

(A) means the obtaining, causing to be obtained, soliciting, or requiring the disclosure to third parties or the public, of facts or opinions by or for an agency, regardless of form or format, calling for either —

(i) answers to identical questions posed to, or identical reporting or recordkeeping requirements imposed on, 10 or more persons, other than agencies, instrumentalities, or employees of the United States; or

(ii) answers to questions posed to agencies, instrumentalities, or employees of the United States which are to be used for general statistical purposes; and

(B) shall not include a collection of information described under section 3518(c)(1) of title 44, United States Code.

(8) Recordkeeping requirement. — The term "recordkeeping requirement" means a requirement imposed by an agency on persons to maintain specified records.

§ 602.   Regulatory Agenda

(a) During the months of October and April of each year, each agency shall publish in the Federal Register a regulatory flexibility agenda which shall contain —

(1) a brief description of the subject area of any rule which the agency expects to propose or promulgate which is likely to have a significant economic impact on a substantial number of small entities;

(2) a summary of the nature of any such rule under consideration for each subject area listed in the agenda pursuant to paragraph (1), the objectives and legal basis for the issuance of the rule, and an approximate schedule for completing action on any rule for which the agency has issued a general notice of proposed rulemaking, and

(3) the name and telephone number of an agency official knowledgeable concerning the items listed in paragraph (1).

(b) Each regulatory flexibility agenda shall be transmitted to the Chief Counsel for Advocacy of the Small Business Administration for comment, if any.

(c) Each agency shall endeavor to provide notice of each regulatory flexibility agenda to small entities or their representatives through direct notification or publication of the agenda in publications likely to be obtained by such small entities and shall invite comments upon each subject area on the agenda.

(d) Nothing in this section precludes an agency from considering or acting on any matter not included in a regulatory flexibility agenda, or requires an agency to consider or act on any matter listed in such agenda.

§ 603.   Initial Regulatory Flexibility Analysis

(a) Whenever an agency is required by section 553 of this title, or any other law, to publish general notice of proposed rulemaking for any proposed rule, or publishes a notice of proposed rulemaking for an interpretative rule involving the internal revenue laws of the United States, the agency shall prepare and make available for public comment an initial regulatory flexibility analysis. Such analysis shall describe the impact of the proposed rule on small entities. The initial regulatory flexibility analysis or a summary shall be published in the Federal Register at the time of the publication of general notice of proposed rulemaking for the rule. The agency shall transmit a copy of the initial regulatory flexibility analysis to the Chief Counsel for Advocacy of the Small Business Administration. In the case of an interpretative rule involving the internal revenue laws of the United States, this chapter applies to interpretative rules published in the Federal Register for codification in the Code of Federal Regulations, but only to the extent that such interpretative rules impose on small entities a collection of information requirement.

(b) Each initial regulatory flexibility analysis required under this section shall contain —

(1) a description of the reasons why action by the agency is being considered;

(2) a succinct statement of the objectives of, and legal basis for, the proposed rule;

(3) a description of and, where feasible, an estimate of the number of small entities to which the proposed rule will apply;

(4) a description of the projected reporting, recordkeeping and other compliance requirements of the proposed rule, including an estimate of the classes of small entities which will be subject to the requirement and the type of professional skills necessary for preparation of the report or record;

(5) an identification, to the extent practicable, of all relevant Federal rules which may duplicate, overlap or conflict with the proposed rule.

(c) Each initial regulatory flexibility analysis shall also contain a description of any significant alternatives to the proposed rule which accomplish the stated objectives of applicable statutes and which minimize any significant economic impact of the proposed rule on small entities. Consistent with the stated objectives of applicable statutes, the analysis shall discuss significant alternatives such as —

(1) the establishment of differing compliance or reporting requirements or timetables that take into account the resources available to small entities;

(2) the clarification, consolidation, or simplification of compliance and reporting requirements under the rule for such small entities;

(3) the use of performance rather than design standards; and

(4) an exemption from coverage of the rule, or any part thereof, for such small entities.

(d)(1) For a covered agency, as defined in section 609(d)(2), each initial regulatory flexibility analysis shall include a description of—

(A) any projected increase in the cost of credit for small entities;

(B) any significant alternatives to the proposed rule which accomplish the stated objectives of applicable statutes and which minimize any increase in the cost of credit for small entities; and

(C) advice and recommendations of representatives of small entities relating to issues described in subparagraphs (A) and (B) and subsection (b).

(2) A covered agency, as defined in section 609(d)(2), shall, for purposes of complying with paragraph (1)(C) —

(A) identify representatives of small entities in consultation with the Chief Counsel for Advocacy of the Small Business Administration; and

(B) collect advice and recommendations from the representatives identified under subparagraph (A) relating to issues described in sub-paragraphs (A) and (B) of paragraph (1) and subsection (b).

§ 604.   Final Regulatory Flexibility Analysis

(a) When an agency promulgates a final rule under section 553 of this title, after being required by that section or any other law to publish a general notice of proposed rulemaking, or promulgates a final interpretative rule involving the internal revenue laws of the United States as described in section 603(a), the agency shall prepare a final regulatory flexibility analysis. Each final regulatory flexibility analysis shall contain —

(1) a succinct statement of the need for, and objectives of, the rule;

(2) a summary of the significant issues raised by the public comments in response to the initial regulatory flexibility analysis, a summary of the assess-ment of the agency of such issues, and a statement of any changes made in the proposed rule as a result of such comments;

(3) a description of and an estimate of the number of small entities to which the rule will apply or an explanation of why no such estimate is available;

(4) a description of the projected reporting, recordkeeping and other compliance requirements of the rule, including an estimate of the classes of small entities which will be subject to the requirement and the type of professional skills necessary for preparation of the report or record;

(5) a description of the steps the agency has taken to minimize the sig-nificant economic impact on small entities consistent with the stated objec-tives of applicable statutes, including a statement of the factual, policy, and legal reasons for selecting the alternative adopted in the final rule and why

each one of the other significant alternatives to the rule considered by the agency which affect the impact on small entities was rejected;

(6) a description of the steps the agency has taken to minimize the significant economic impact on small entities consistent with the stated objectives of applicable statutes, including a statement of the factual, policy, and legal reasons for selecting the alternative adopted in the final rule and why each one of the other significant alternatives to the rule considered by the agency which affect the impact on small entities was rejected; and

[sic] for a covered agency, as defined in section 609(d)(2), a description of the steps the agency has taken to minimize any additional cost of credit for small entities.

(b) The agency shall make copies of the final regulatory flexibility analysis available to members of the public and shall publish in the Federal Register such analysis or a summary thereof.

§ 605. Avoidance of Duplicative or Unnecessary Analyses

(a) Any Federal agency may perform the analyses required by sections 602, 603, and 604 of this title in conjunction with or as a part of any other agenda or analysis required by any other law if such other analysis satisfies the provisions of such sections.

(b) Sections 603 and 604 of this title shall not apply to any proposed or final rule if the head of the agency certifies that the rule will not, if promulgated, have a significant economic impact on a substantial number of small entities. If the head of the agency makes a certification under the preceding sentence, the agency shall publish such certification in the Federal Register at the time of publication of general notice of proposed rulemaking for the rule or at the time of publication of the final rule, along with a statement providing the factual basis for such certification. The agency shall provide such certification and statement to the Chief Counsel for Advocacy of the Small Business Administration.

(c) In order to avoid duplicative action, an agency may consider a series of closely related rules as one rule for the purposes of sections 602, 603, 604 and 610 of this title.

§ 606. Effect on Other Law

The requirements of sections 603 and 604 of this title do not alter in any manner standards otherwise applicable by law to agency action.

§ 607. Preparation of Analyses

In complying with the provisions of sections 603 and 604 of this title, an agency may provide either a quantifiable or numerical description of the effects of a proposed rule or alternatives to the proposed rule, or more general descriptive statements if quantification is not practicable or reliable.

§ 608. Procedure for Waiver or Delay of Completion

(a) An agency head may waive or delay the completion of some or all of the requirements of section 603 of this title by publishing in the Federal Register, not later than the date of publication of the final rule, a written finding, with reasons therefor, that the final rule is being promulgated in response to an emergency that makes compliance or timely compliance with the provisions of section 603 of this title impracticable.

(b) Except as provided in section 605(b), an agency head may not waive the requirements of section 604 of this title. An agency head may delay the completion of the requirements of section 604 of this title for a period of not more than one hundred and eighty days after the date of publication in the Federal Register of a final rule by publishing in the Federal Register, not later than such date of publication, a written finding, with reasons therefor, that the final rule is being promulgated in response to an emergency that makes timely compliance with the provisions of section 604 of this title impracticable. If the agency has not prepared a final regulatory analysis pursuant to section 604 of this title within one hundred and eighty days from the date of publication of the final rule, such rule shall lapse and have no effect. Such rule shall not be repromulgated until a final regulatory flexibility analysis has been completed by the agency.

§ 609.   Procedures for Gathering Comments

(a) When any rule is promulgated which will have a significant economic impact on a substantial number of small entities, the head of the agency promulgating the rule or the official of the agency with statutory responsibility for the promulgation of the rule shall assure that small entities have been given an opportunity to participate in the rulemaking for the rule through the reasonable use of techniques such as —

(1) the inclusion in an advanced notice of proposed rulemaking, if issued, of a statement that the proposed rule may have a significant economic effect on a substantial number of small entities;

(2) the publication of general notice of proposed rulemaking in publications likely to be obtained by small entities;

(3) the direct notification of interested small entities;

(4) the conduct of open conferences or public hearings concerning the rule for small entities including soliciting and receiving comments over computer networks; and

(5) the adoption or modification of agency procedural rules to reduce the cost or complexity of participation in the rulemaking by small entities.

(b) Prior to publication of an initial regulatory flexibility analysis which a covered agency is required to conduct by this chapter —

(1) a covered agency shall notify the Chief Counsel for Advocacy of the Small Business Administration and provide the Chief Counsel with information on the potential impacts of the proposed rule on small entities and the type of small entities that might be affected;

(2) not later than 15 days after the date of receipt of the materials described in paragraph (1), the Chief Counsel shall identify individuals representative of affected small entities for the purpose of obtaining advice and recommendations from those individuals about the potential impacts of the proposed rule;

(3) the agency shall convene a review panel for such rule consisting wholly of full time Federal employees of the office within the agency responsible for carrying out the proposed rule, the Office of Information

and Regulatory Affairs within the Office of Management and Budget, and the Chief Counsel;

(4) the panel shall review any material the agency has prepared in connection with this chapter, including any draft proposed rule, collect advice and recommendations of each individual small entity representative identified by the agency after consultation with the Chief Counsel, on issues related to subsections 603(b), paragraphs (3), (4) and (5) and 603(c);

(5) not later than 60 days after the date a covered agency convenes a review panel pursuant to paragraph (3), the review panel shall report on the comments of the small entity representatives and its findings as to issues related to subsections 603(b), paragraphs (3), (4) and (5) and 603(c), provided that such report shall be made public as part of the rulemaking record; and

(6) where appropriate, the agency shall modify the proposed rule, the initial regulatory flexibility analysis or the decision on whether an initial regulatory flexibility analysis is required.

(c) An agency may in its discretion apply subsection (b) to rules that the agency intends to certify under subsection 605(b), but the agency believes may have a greater than de minimis impact on a substantial number of small entities.

(d) For purposes of this section, the term "covered agency" means—

(1) the Environmental Protection Agency;

(2) the Consumer Financial Protection Bureau of the Federal Reserve System; and

(3) the Occupational Safety and Health Administration of the Department of Labor.

(e) The Chief Counsel for Advocacy, in consultation with the individuals identified in subsection (b)(2), and with the Administrator of the Office of Information and Regulatory Affairs within the Office of Management and Budget, may waive the requirements of subsections (b)(3), (b)(4), and (b)(5) by including in the rulemaking record a written finding, with reasons therefor, that those requirements would not advance the effective participation of small entities in the rulemaking process. For purposes of this subsection, the factors to be considered in making such a finding are as follows:

(1) In developing a proposed rule, the extent to which the covered agency consulted with individuals representative of affected small entities with respect to the potential impacts of the rule and took such concerns into consideration.

(2) Special circumstances requiring prompt issuance of the rule.

(3) Whether the requirements of subsection (b) would provide the individuals identified in subsection (b)(2) with a competitive advantage relative to other small entities.

§ 610. Periodic Review of Rules

(a) Within one hundred and eighty days after the effective date of this chapter, each agency shall publish in the Federal Register a plan for the periodic review of the rules issued by the agency which have or will have a significant economic impact upon a substantial number of small entities. Such plan may be amended by the agency at any time by publishing the revision in the Federal Register. The purpose of the review shall be to determine whether such rules should be continued without change, or should be amended or rescinded, consistent with the stated objectives of applicable statutes, to minimize any significant economic impact of the rules upon a substantial number of such small entities. The plan shall provide for the review of all such agency rules existing on the effective date of this chapter within ten years of that date and for the review of such rules adopted after the effective date of this chapter within ten years of the publication of such rules as the final rule. If the head of the agency determines that completion of the review of existing rules is not feasible by the established date, he shall so certify in a statement published in the Federal Register and may extend the completion date by one year at a time for a total of not more than five years.

(b) In reviewing rules to minimize any significant economic impact of the rule on a substantial number of small entities in a manner consistent with the stated objectives of applicable statutes, the agency shall consider the following factors —

(1) the continued need for the rule;

(2) the nature of complaints or comments received concerning the rule from the public;

(3) the complexity of the rule;

(4) the extent to which the rule overlaps, duplicates or conflicts with other Federal rules, and, to the extent feasible, with State and local governmental rules; and

(5) the length of time since the rule has been evaluated or the degree to which technology, economic conditions, or other factors have changed in the area affected by the rule.

(c) Each year, each agency shall publish in the Federal Register a list of the rules which have a significant economic impact on a substantial number of small entities, which are to be reviewed pursuant to this section during the succeeding twelve months. The list shall include a brief description of each rule and the need for and legal basis of such rule and shall invite public comment upon the rule.

§ 611. Judicial Review

(a)(1) For any rule subject to this chapter, a small entity that is adversely affected or aggrieved by final agency action is entitled to judicial review of agency compliance with the requirements of sections 601, 604, 605(b), 608(b), and 610 in accordance with chapter 7. Agency compliance with sections 607 and 609(a) shall be judicially reviewable in connection with judicial review of section 604.

(2) Each court having jurisdiction to review such rule for compliance with section 553, or under any other provision of law, shall have jurisdiction to review any claims of noncompliance with sections 601, 604, 605(b), 608(b), and 610 in accordance with chapter 7. Agency compliance with sections 607 and 609(a) shall be judicially reviewable in connection with judicial review of section 604.

(3)(A) A small entity may seek such review during the period beginning on the date of final agency action and ending one year later, except that where a provision of law requires that an action challenging a final agency action be commenced before the expiration of one year, such lesser period shall apply to an action for judicial review under this section.

(B) In the case where an agency delays the issuance of a final regulatory flexibility analysis pursuant to section 608(b) of this chapter, an action for judicial review under this section shall be filed not later than—

(i) one year after the date the analysis is made available to the public, or

(ii) where a provision of law requires that an action challenging a final agency regulation be commenced before the expiration of the 1-year period, the number of days specified in such provision of law that is after the date the analysis is made available to the public.

(4) In granting any relief in an action under this section, the court shall order the agency to take corrective action consistent with this chapter and chapter 7, including, but not limited to—

(A) remanding the rule to the agency, and

(B) deferring the enforcement of the rule against small entities unless the court finds that continued enforcement of the rule is in the public interest.

(5) Nothing in this subsection shall be construed to limit the authority of any court to stay the effective date of any rule or provision thereof under any other provision of law or to grant any other relief in addition to the requirements of this section.

(b) In an action for the judicial review of a rule, the regulatory flexibility analysis for such rule, including an analysis prepared or corrected pursuant to paragraph (a)(4), shall constitute part of the entire record of agency action in connection with such review.

(c) Compliance or noncompliance by an agency with the provisions of this chapter shall be subject to judicial review only in accordance with this section.

(d) Nothing in this section bars judicial review of any other impact statement or similar analysis required by any other law if judicial review of such statement or analysis is otherwise permitted by law.

§ 612.   Reports and Intervention Rights

(a) The Chief Counsel for Advocacy of the Small Business Administration shall monitor agency compliance with this chapter and shall report at least annually thereon to the President and to the Committees on the Judiciary and Small Business of the Senate and House of Representatives.

(b) The Chief Counsel for Advocacy of the Small Business Administration is authorized to appear as amicus curiae in any action brought in a court of the United States to review a rule. In any such action, the Chief Counsel is authorized to present his or her views with respect to compliance with this chapter, the adequacy of the rulemaking record with respect to small entities and the effect of the rule on small entities.

(c) A court of the United States shall grant the application of the Chief Counsel for Advocacy of the Small Business Administration to appear in any such action for the purposes described in subsection (b).

§ 701. Application; Definitions

(a) This chapter applies, according to the provisions thereof, except to the extent that —

(1) statutes preclude judicial review; or

(2) agency action is committed to agency discretion by law.

(b) For the purpose of this chapter —

(1) "agency" means each authority of the Government of the United States, whether or not it is within or subject to review by another agency, but does not include —

(A) the Congress;

(B) the courts of the United States;

(C) the governments of the territories or possessions of the United States;

(D) the government of the District of Columbia;

(E) agencies composed of representatives of the parties or of representatives of organizations of the parties to the disputes determined by them;

(F) courts martial and military commissions;

(G) military authority exercised in the field in time of war or in occupied territory; or

(H) functions conferred by sections 1738, 1739, 1743, and 1744 of title 12; subchapter II of chapter 471 of title 49; or sections 1884, 1891-1902, and former section 1641(b)(2), of title 50, appendix; and

(2) "person," "rule," "order," "license," "sanction," "relief," and "agency action" have the meanings given them by section 551 of this title.

§ 702. Right of Review

A person suffering legal wrong because of agency action, or adversely affected or aggrieved by agency action within the meaning of a relevant statute, is entitled to judicial review thereof. An action in a court of the United States seeking relief other than money damages and stating a claim that an agency or an officer or employee thereof acted or failed to act in an official capacity or under color of legal authority shall not be dismissed nor relief therein be denied on the ground that it is against the United States or that the United States is an indispensable party. The United States may be named as a defendant in any such action, and a judgment or decree may be entered against the United States: Provided, That any mandatory or injunctive decree shall specify the Federal officer or officers (by name or by title), and their successors in office, personally responsible for compliance. Nothing herein (1) affects other limitations on judicial review or the power or duty of the court to dismiss any action or deny relief on any other appropriate legal or equitable ground; or (2) confers authority to grant relief if any other statute that grants consent to suit expressly or impliedly forbids the relief which is sought.

§ 703. Form and Venue of Proceeding

The form of proceeding for judicial review is the special statutory review proceeding relevant to the subject matter in a court specified by statute or, in the absence or inadequacy thereof, any applicable form of legal action, including actions for declaratory judgments or writs of prohibitory or mandatory injunction or habeas corpus, in a court of competent jurisdiction. If no special statutory review proceeding is applicable, the action for judicial review may be brought against the United States, the agency by its official title, or the appropriate officer. Except to the extent that prior, adequate, and exclusive opportunity for judicial review is provided by law, agency action is subject to judicial review in civil or criminal proceedings for judicial enforcement.

§ 704. Actions Reviewable

Agency action made reviewable by statute and final agency action for which there is no other adequate remedy in a court are subject to judicial review. A preliminary, procedural, or intermediate agency action or ruling not directly reviewable is subject to review on the review of the final agency action. Except as otherwise expressly required by statute, agency action otherwise final is final for the purposes of this section whether or not there has been presented or determined an application for a declaratory order, for any form of reconsideration, or, unless the agency otherwise requires by rule and provides that the action meanwhile is inoperative, for an appeal to superior agency authority.

§ 705. Relief Pending Review

When an agency finds that justice so requires, it may postpone the effective date of action taken by it, pending judicial review. On such conditions as may be required and to the extent necessary to prevent irreparable injury, the reviewing court, including the court to which a case may be taken on appeal from or on application for certiorari or other writ to a reviewing court, may issue all necessary and appropriate process to postpone the effective date of an agency action or to preserve status or rights pending conclusion of the review proceedings.

§ 706. Scope of Review

To the extent necessary to decision and when presented, the reviewing court shall decide all relevant questions of law, interpret constitutional and statutory provisions, and determine the meaning or applicability of the terms of an agency action. The reviewing court shall —

(1) compel agency action unlawfully withheld or unreasonably delayed; and

(2) hold unlawful and set aside agency action, findings, and conclusions found to be —

(A) arbitrary, capricious, an abuse of discretion, or otherwise not in accordance with law;

(B) contrary to constitutional right, power, privilege, or immunity;

(C) in excess of statutory jurisdiction, authority, or limitations, or short of statutory right;

(D) without observance of procedure required by law;

(E) unsupported by substantial evidence in a case subject to sections 556 and 557 of this title or otherwise reviewed on the record of an agency hearing provided by statute; or

(F) unwarranted by the facts to the extent that the facts are subject to trial de novo by the reviewing court.

In making the foregoing determinations, the court shall review the whole record or those parts of it cited by a party, and due account shall be taken of the rule of prejudicial error.

§801.   Congressional Review

(a)(1) (A) Before a rule can take effect, the Federal agency promulgating such rule shall submit to each House of the Congress and to the Comptroller General a report containing—

(i) a copy of the rule;

(ii) a concise general statement relating to the rule, including whether it is a major rule; and

(iii) the proposed effective date of the rule.

(B) On the date of the submission of the report under subparagraph (A), the Federal agency promulgating the rule shall submit to the Comptroller General and make available to each House of Congress—

(i) a complete copy of the cost-benefit analysis of the rule, if any;

(ii) the agency's actions relevant to sections 603, 604, 605, 607, and 609;

(iii) the agency's actions relevant to sections 202, 203, 204, and 205 of the Unfunded Mandates Reform Act of 1995; and

(iv) any other relevant information or requirements under any other Act and any relevant Executive orders.

(C) Upon receipt of a report submitted under subparagraph (A), each House shall provide copies of the report to the chairman and ranking member of each standing committee with jurisdiction under the rules of the House of Representatives or the Senate to report a bill to amend the provision of law under which the rule is issued.

(2)(A) The Comptroller General shall provide a report on each major rule to the committees of jurisdiction in each House of the Congress by the end of 15 calendar days after the submission or publication date as provided in section 802(b)(2). The report of the Comptroller General shall include an assessment of the agency's compliance with procedural steps required by paragraph (1)(B).

(B) Federal agencies shall cooperate with the Comptroller General by providing information relevant to the Comptroller General's report under subparagraph (A).

(3) A major rule relating to a report submitted under paragraph (1) shall take effect on the latest of—

(A) the later of the date occurring 60 days after the date on which—

(i) the Congress receives the report submitted under paragraph (1); or

(ii) the rule is published in the Federal Register, if so published;

(B) if the Congress passes a joint resolution of disapproval described in section 802 relating to the rule, and the President signs a veto of such resolution, the earlier date—

(i) on which either House of Congress votes and fails to override the veto of the President; or

(ii) occurring 30 session days after the date on which the Congress received the veto and objections of the President; or

(C) the date the rule would have otherwise taken effect, if not for this section (unless a joint resolution of disapproval under section 802 is enacted).

(4) Except for a major rule, a rule shall take effect as otherwise provided by law after submission to Congress under paragraph (1).

(5) Notwithstanding paragraph (3), the effective date of a rule shall not be delayed by operation of this chapter beyond the date on which either House of Congress votes to reject a joint resolution of disapproval under section 802.

(b)(1) A rule shall not take effect (or continue), if the Congress enacts a joint resolution of disapproval, described under section 802, of the rule.

(2) A rule that does not take effect (or does not continue) under paragraph (1) may not be reissued in substantially the same form, and a new rule that is substantially the same as such a rule may not be issued, unless the reissued or new rule is specifically authorized by a law enacted after the date of the joint resolution disapproving the original rule.

(c)(1) Notwithstanding any other provision of this section (except subject to paragraph (3)), a rule that would not take effect by reason of subsection (a)(3) may take effect, if the President makes a determination under paragraph (2) and submits written notice of such determination to the Congress.

(2) Paragraph (1) applies to a determination made by the President by Executive order that the rule should take effect because such rule is —

(A) necessary because of an imminent threat to health or safety or other emergency;

(B) necessary for the enforcement of criminal laws;

(C) necessary for national security; or

(D) issued pursuant to any statute implementing an international trade agreement.

(3) An exercise by the President of the authority under this subsection shall have no effect on the procedures under section 802 or the effect of a joint resolution of disapproval under this section.

(d)(1) In addition to the opportunity for review otherwise provided under this chapter, in the case of any rule for which a report was submitted in accordance with subsection (a)(1)(A) during the period beginning on the date occurring —

(A) in the case of the Senate, 60 session days, or

(B) in the case of the House of Representatives, 60 legislative days, before the date the Congress adjourns a session of Congress through the date on which the same or succeeding Congress first convenes its next session, section 802 shall apply to such rule in the succeeding session of Congress.

(2)(A) In applying section 802 for purposes of such additional review, a rule described under paragraph (1) shall be treated as though —

(i) such rule were published in the Federal Register (as a rule that shall take effect) on —

(I) in the case of the Senate, the 15th session day, or

(II) in the case of the House of Representatives, the 15th legislative day, after the succeeding session of Congress first convenes; and

(ii) a report on such rule were submitted to Congress under subsection (a)(1) on such date.

(B) Nothing in this paragraph shall be construed to affect the requirement under subsection (a)(1) that a report shall be submitted to Congress before a rule can take effect.

(3) A rule described under paragraph (1) shall take effect as otherwise provided by law (including other subsections of this section).

(e)(1) For purposes of this subsection, section 802 shall also apply to any major rule promulgated between March 1, 1996, and the date of the enactment of this chapter.

(2) In applying section 802 for purposes of Congressional review, a rule described under paragraph (1) shall be treated as though —

(A) such rule were published in the Federal Register on the date of enactment of this chapter; and

(B) a report on such rule were submitted to Congress under subsection (a)(1) on such date.

(3) The effectiveness of a rule described under paragraph (1) shall be as otherwise provided by law, unless the rule is made of no force or effect under section 802.

(f) Any rule that takes effect and later is made of no force or effect by enactment of a joint resolution under section 802 shall be treated as though such rule had never taken effect.

(g) If the Congress does not enact a joint resolution of disapproval under section 802 respecting a rule, no court or agency may infer any intent of the Congress from any action or inaction of the Congress with regard to such rule, related statute, or joint resolution of disapproval.

§ 802. Congressional Disapproval Procedure

(a) For purposes of this section, the term "joint resolution" means only a joint resolution introduced in the period beginning on the date on which the report referred to in section 801(a)(1)(A) is received by Congress and ending 60 days thereafter (excluding days either House of Congress is adjourned for more than 3 days during a session of Congress), the matter after the resolving clause of which is as follows: "That Congress disapproves the rule submitted by _____ the relating to _____, and such rule shall have no force or effect." (The blank spaces being appropriately filled in.)

(b)(1) A joint resolution described in subsection (a) shall be referred to the committees in each House of Congress with jurisdiction.

(2) For purposes of this section, the term "submission or publication date" means the later of the date on which —

(A) the Congress receives the report submitted under section 801(a)(1); or

(B) the rule is published in the Federal Register, if so published.

(c) In the Senate, if the committee to which is referred a joint resolution described in subsection (a) has not reported such joint resolution (or an identical joint resolution) at the end of 20 calendar days after the submission or publication date defined under subsection (b)(2), such committee may be discharged from further consideration of such joint resolution upon a petition supported in writing by 30 Members of the Senate, and such joint resolution shall be placed on the calendar.

(d)(1) In the Senate, when the committee to which a joint resolution is referred has reported, or when a committee is discharged (under subsection (c)) from further consideration of a joint resolution described in subsection (a), it is at any time thereafter in order (even though a previous motion to the same effect has been disagreed to) for a motion to proceed to the consideration of the joint resolution, and all points of order against the joint resolution (and against consideration of the joint resolution) are waived. The motion is not subject to amendment, or to a motion to postpone, or to a motion to proceed to the consideration of other business. A motion to reconsider the vote by which the motion is agreed to or disagreed to shall not be in order. If a motion to proceed to the consideration of the joint resolution is agreed to, the joint resolution shall remain the unfinished business of the Senate until disposed of.

(2) In the Senate, debate on the joint resolution, and on all debatable motions and appeals in connection therewith, shall be limited to not more than 10 hours, which shall be divided equally between those favoring and those opposing the joint resolution. A motion further to limit debate is in order and not debatable. An amendment to, or a motion to postpone, or a motion to proceed to the consideration of other business, or a motion to recommit the joint resolution is not in order.

(3) In the Senate, immediately following the conclusion of the debate on a joint resolution described in subsection (a), and a single quorum call at the conclusion of the debate if requested in accordance with the rules of the Senate, the vote on final passage of the joint resolution shall occur.

(4) Appeals from the decisions of the Chair relating to the application of the rules of the Senate to the procedure relating to a joint resolution described in subsection (a) shall be decided without debate.

(e) In the Senate the procedure specified in subsection (c) or (d) shall not apply to the consideration of a joint resolution respecting a rule —

(1) after the expiration of the 60 session days beginning with the applicable submission or publication date, or

(2) if the report under section 801(a)(1)(A) was submitted during the period referred to in section 801(d)(1), after the expiration of the 60 session days beginning on the 15th session day after the succeeding session of Congress first convenes.

(f) If, before the passage by one House of a joint resolution of that House described in subsection (a), that House receives from the other House a joint resolution described in subsection (a), then the following procedures shall apply:

(1) The joint resolution of the other House shall not be referred to a committee.

(2) With respect to a joint resolution described in subsection (a) of the House receiving the joint resolution —

(A) the procedure in that House shall be the same as if no joint resolution had been received from the other House; but

(B) the vote on final passage shall be on the joint resolution of the other House.

(g) This section is enacted by Congress —

(1) as an exercise of the rulemaking power of the Senate and House of Representatives, respectively, and as such it is deemed a part of the rules of each House, respectively, but applicable only with respect to the procedure to be followed in that House in the case of a joint resolution described in subsection (a), and it supersedes other rules only to the extent that it is inconsistent with such rules; and

(2) with full recognition of the constitutional right of either House to change the rules (so far as relating to the procedure of that House) at any time, in the same manner, and to the same extent as in the case of any other rule of that House.

§ 803.   Special Rule on Statutory, Regulatory, and Judicial Deadlines

(a) In the case of any deadline for, relating to, or involving any rule which does not take effect (or the effectiveness of which is terminated) because of enactment of a joint resolution under section 802, that deadline is extended until the date 1 year after the date of enactment of the joint resolution. Nothing in this subsection shall be construed to affect a deadline merely by reason of the postponement of a rule's effective date under section 801(a).

(b) The term "deadline" means any date certain for fulfilling any obligation or exercising any authority established by or under any Federal statute or regulation, or by or under any court order implementing any Federal statute or regulation.

§ 804.   Definitions

For purposes of this chapter —

(1) The term "Federal agency" means any agency as that term is defined in section 551(1).

(2) The term "major rule" means any rule that the Administrator of the Office of Information and Regulatory Affairs of the Office of Management and Budget finds has resulted in or is likely to result in —

(A) an annual effect on the economy of $100,000,000 or more;

(B) a major increase in costs or prices for consumers, individual industries, Federal, State, or local government agencies, or geographic regions; or

(C) significant adverse effects on competition, employment, investment, productivity, innovation, or on the ability of United States-based enterprises to compete with foreign-based enterprises in domestic and export markets. The term does not include any rule promulgated under the Telecommunications Act of 1996 and the amendments made by that Act.

(3) The term "rule" has the meaning given such term in section 551, except that such term does not include —

(A) any rule of particular applicability, including a rule that approves or prescribes for the future rates, wages, prices, services, or allowances therefor, corporate or financial structures, reorganizations, mergers, or acquisitions thereof, or accounting practices or disclosures bearing on any of the foregoing;

(B) any rule relating to agency management or personnel; or

(C) any rule of agency organization, procedure, or practice that does not substantially affect the rights or obligations of non-agency parties.

§ 805. Judicial Review

No determination, finding, action, or omission under this chapter shall be subject to judicial review.

APPENDIX

C

Uniform Law Commissioners' Model State Administrative Procedure Act (1981)[1] (Selected Provisions)

ARTICLE I. GENERAL PROVISIONS

§ 1-101. [Short Title].

This Act may be cited as the [state] Administrative Procedure Act.

§ 1-102. [Definitions].

As used in this Act:

(1) "Agency" means a board, commission, department, officer, or other administrative unit of this State, including the agency head, and one or more members of the agency head or agency employees or other persons directly or indirectly purporting to act on behalf or under the authority of the agency head. The term does not include the [legislature] or the courts [, or the governor] [, or the governor in the exercise of powers derived directly and exclusively from the constitution of this State]. The term does not include a political subdivision of the state or any of the administrative units of a political subdivision, but it does include a board, commission, department, officer, or other administrative unit created or appointed by joint or concerted action of an agency and one or more political subdivisions of the state or any of their units. To the extent it purports to exercise authority subject to any provision of this Act, an administrative unit otherwise qualifying as an "agency" must be treated as a separate agency even if the unit is located within or subordinate to another agency.

(2) "Agency action" means:

(i) the whole or a part of a rule or an order;

(ii) the failure to issue a rule or an order; or

(iii) an agency's performance of, or failure to perform, any other duty, function, or activity, discretionary or otherwise.

(3) "Agency head" means an individual or body of individuals in whom the ultimate legal authority of the agency is vested by any provision of law.

1. © 1981, National Conference of Commissioners on Uniform State Laws, reprinted with permission.

(4) "License" means a franchise, permit, certification, approval, registration, charter, or similar form of authorization required by law.

(5) "Order" means an agency action of particular applicability that determines the legal rights, duties, privileges, immunities, or other legal interests of one or more specific persons. [The term does not include an "executive order" issued by the governor pursuant to Section 1-104 or 3-202.]

(6) "Party to agency proceedings," or "party" in context so indicating, means:

(i) a person to whom the agency action is specifically directed; or

(ii) a person named as a party to an agency proceeding or allowed to intervene or participate as a party in the proceeding.

(7) "Party to judicial review or civil enforcement proceedings," or "party" in context so indicating, means:

(i) a person who files a petition for judicial review or civil enforcement or

(ii) a person named as a party in a proceeding for judicial review or civil enforcement or allowed to participate as a party in the proceeding.

(8) "Person" means an individual, partnership, corporation, association, governmental subdivision or unit thereof, or public or private organization or entity of any character, and includes another agency.

(9) "Provision of law" means the whole or a part of the federal or state constitution, or of any federal or state (i) statute, (ii) rule of court, (iii) executive order, or (iv) rule of an administrative agency.

(10) "Rule" means the whole or a part of an agency statement of general applicability that implements, interprets, or prescribes (i) law or policy, or (ii) the organization, procedure, or practice requirements of an agency. The term includes the amendment, repeal, or suspension of an existing rule.

(11) "Rule making" means the process for formulation and adoption of a rule. . . .

ARTICLE II. PUBLIC ACCESS TO AGENCY LAW AND POLICY

§ 2-104.   [Required Rule Making].

In addition to other rule-making requirements imposed by law, each agency shall:

(1) adopt as a rule a description of the organization of the agency which states the general course and method of its operations and where and how the public may obtain information or make submissions or requests;

(2) adopt rules of practice setting forth the nature and requirements of all formal and informal procedures available to the public, including a description of all forms and instructions that are to be used by the public in dealing with the agency; [and]

(3) as soon as feasible and to the extent practicable, adopt rules, in addition to those otherwise required by this Act, embodying appropriate standards, principles, and procedural safeguards that the agency will apply to the law it administers [; and] [.]

[(4) as soon as feasible and to the extent practicable, adopt rules to supersede principles of law or policy lawfully declared by the agency as the basis for its decisions in particular cases.] . . .

ARTICLE III. RULE MAKING

CHAPTER I. ADOPTION AND EFFECTIVENESS OF RULES

§ 3-103.   [Notice of Proposed Rule Adoption].

(a) At least [30] days before the adoption of a rule an agency shall cause notice of its contemplated action to be published in the [administrative bulletin]. The notice of proposed rule adoption must include:

(1) a short explanation of the purpose of the proposed rule;

(2) the specific legal authority authorizing the proposed rule;

(3) subject to Section 2-101(e), the text of the proposed rule;

(4) where, when, and how persons may present their views on the proposed rule; and

(5) where, when, and how persons may demand an oral proceeding on the proposed rule if the notice does not already provide for one.

(b) Within [3] days after its publication in the [administrative bulletin], the agency shall cause a copy of the notice of proposed rule adoption to be mailed to each person who has made a timely request to the agency for a mailed copy of the notice. An agency may charge persons for the actual cost of providing them with mailed copies.

§ 3-104.   [Public Participation].

(a) For at least [30] days after publication of the notice of proposed rule adoption, an agency shall afford persons the opportunity to submit in writing, argument, data, and views on the proposed rule.

(b)(1) An agency shall schedule an oral proceeding on a proposed rule if, within [20] days after the published notice of proposed rule adoption, a written request for an oral proceeding is submitted by [the administrative rules review committee,] [the administrative rules counsel,] a political subdivision, an agency, or [25] persons. At that proceeding, persons may present oral argument, data, and views on the proposed rule.

(2) An oral proceeding on a proposed rule, if required, may not be held earlier than [20] days after notice of its location and time is published in the [administrative bulletin].

(3) The agency, a member of the agency, or another presiding officer designated by the agency, shall preside at a required oral proceeding on a proposed rule. If the agency does not preside, the presiding official shall prepare a memorandum for consideration by the agency summarizing the contents of the presentations made at the oral proceeding. Oral proceedings must be open to the public and be recorded by stenographic or other means.

(4) Each agency shall issue rules for the conduct of oral rule-making proceedings. Those rules may include provisions calculated to prevent undue repetition in the oral proceedings.

§ 3-105.   [Regulatory Analysis].

(a) An agency shall issue a regulatory analysis of a proposed rule if, within [20] days after the published notice of proposed rule adoption, a written request for the analysis is filed in the office of the [secretary of state] by [the administrative rules review committee, the governor, a political subdivision, an agency, or [300] persons signing the request]. The [secretary of state] shall immediately forward to the agency a certified copy of the filed request.

(b) Except to the extent that the written request expressly waives one or more of the following, the regulatory analysis must contain:

(1) a description of the classes of persons who probably will be affected by the proposed rule, including classes that will bear the costs of the proposed rule and classes that will benefit from the proposed rule;

(2) a description of the probable quantitative and qualitative impact of the proposed rule, economic or otherwise, upon affected classes of persons;

(3) the probable costs to the agency and to any other agency of the implementation and enforcement of the proposed rule and any anticipated effect on state revenues;

(4) a comparison of the probable costs and benefits of the proposed rule to the probable costs and benefits of inaction;

(5) a determination of whether there are less costly methods or less intrusive methods for achieving the purpose of the proposed rule; and

(6) a description of any alternative methods for achieving the purpose of the proposed rule that were seriously considered by the agency and the reasons why they were rejected in favor of the proposed rule.

(c) Each regulatory analysis must include quantification of the data to the extent practicable and must take account of both short-term and long-term consequences.

(d) A concise summary of the regulatory analysis must be published in the [administrative bulletin] at least [10] days before the earliest of:

(1) the end of the period during which persons may make written submissions on the proposed rule;

(2) the end of the period during which an oral proceeding may be requested; or

(3) the date of any required oral proceeding on the proposed rule.

(e) The published summary of the regulatory analysis must also indicate where persons may obtain copies of the full text of the regulatory analysis and where, when, and how persons may present their views on the proposed rule and demand an oral proceeding thereon if one is not already provided.

(f) If the agency has made a good faith effort to comply with the requirements of subsections (a) through (c), the rule may not be invalidated on the ground that the contends of the regulatory analysis are insufficient or inaccurate.

§ 3-106.   [Time and Manner of Rule Adoption].

(a) An agency may not adopt a rule until the period for making written submissions and oral presentations has expired.

(b) Within [180] days after the later of (i) the publication of the notice of proposed rule adoption, or (ii) the end of oral proceedings thereon, an agency shall adopt a rule pursuant to the rule-making proceeding or terminate the proceeding by publication of a notice to that effect in the [administrative bulletin].

(c) Before the adoption of a rule, an agency shall consider the written submissions, oral submissions or any memorandum summarizing oral submissions, and any regulatory analysis, provided for by this Chapter.

(d) Within the scope of its delegated authority, an agency may use its own experience, technical competence, specialized knowledge, and judgment in the adoption of a rule.

§ 3-107.   [Variance Between Adopted Rule and Published Notice of Proposed Rule Adoption].

(a) An agency may not adopt a rule that is substantially different from the proposed rule contained in the published notice of proposed rule adoption. However, an agency may terminate a rule-making proceeding and commence a new rule-making proceeding for the purpose of adopting a substantially different rule.

(b) In determining whether an adopted rule is substantially different from the published proposed rule upon which it is required to be based, the following must be considered:

(1) the extent to which all persons affected by the adopted rule should have understood that the published proposed rule would affect their interests;

(2) the extent to which the subject matter of the adopted rule or the issues determined by that rule are different from the subject matter or issues involved in the published proposed rule; and

(3) the extent to which the effects of the adopted rule differ from the effects of the published proposed rule had it been adopted instead.

§ 3-108.   [General Exemption from Public Rule-making Procedures].

(a) To the extent an agency for good cause finds that any requirements of Sections 3-103 through 3-107 are unnecessary, impracticable, or contrary to the public interest in the process of adopting a particular rule, those requirements do not apply. The agency shall incorporate the required finding and a brief statement of its supporting reasons in each rule adopted in reliance upon this subsection.

(b) In an action contesting a rule adopted under subsection (a), the burden is upon the agency to demonstrate that any omitted requirements of Sections 3-103 through 3-107 were impracticable, unnecessary, or contrary to the public interest in the particular circumstances involved.

(c) Within [2] years after the effective date of a rule adopted under subsection (a), the [administrative rules review committee or the governor] may request the agency to hold a rule-making proceeding thereon according to the requirements of Sections 3-103 through 3-107. The request must be in writing and filed in the office of the [secretary of state]. The [secretary of state] shall immediately forward to the agency and to the [administrative rules editor] a certified copy of the request. Notice of the filing of the request must be published in the next issue of the [administrative bulletin]. The rule in question ceases to be effective [180] days after the request is filed. However, an agency, after the filing of the request, may subsequently adopt an identical rule in a rule-making proceeding conducted pursuant to the requirements of Sections 3-103 through 3-107.

§ 3-109.   [Exemption for Certain Rules].

(a) An agency need not follow the provisions of Sections 3-103 through 3-108 in the adoption of a rule that only defines the meaning of a statute or other provision of law or precedent if the agency does not possess delegated authority to bind the courts to any extent with its definition. A rule adopted under this subsection must include a statement that it was adopted under this subsection when it is published in the [administrative bulletin], and there must be an indication to that effect adjacent to the rule when it is published in the [administrative code].

(b) A reviewing court shall determine wholly de novo the validity of a rule within the scope of subsection (a) that is adopted without complying with the provisions of Sections 3-103 through 3-108.

§ 3-110.   [Concise Explanatory Statement].

(a) At the time it adopts a rule, an agency shall issue a concise explanatory statement containing:

(1) its reasons for adopting the rule; and

(2) an indication of any change between the text of the proposed rule contained in the published notice of proposed rule adoption and the text of the rule as finally adopted, with the reasons for any change.

(b) Only the reasons contained in the concise explanatory statement may be used by any party as justifications for the adoption of the rule in any proceeding in which its validity is at issue.

§ 3-111.   [Contents, Style, and Form of Rule].

(a) Each rule adopted by an agency must contain the text of the rule and:

(1) the date the agency adopted the rule;

(2) a concise statement of the purpose of the rule;

(3) a reference to all rules repealed, amended, or suspended by the rule;

(4) a reference to the specific statutory or other authority authorizing adoption of the rule;

(5) any findings required by any provision of law as a prerequisite to adoption or effectiveness of the rule; and

(6) the effective date of the rule if other than that specified in Section 3-115(a).

[(b) To the extent feasible, each rule should be written in clear and concise language understandable to persons who may be affected by it.]

(c) An agency may incorporate, by reference in its rules and without publishing the incorporated matter in full, all or any part of a code, standard, rule, or regulation that has been adopted by an agency of the United States or of this state, another state, or by a nationally recognized organization or association, if incorporation of its text in agency rules would be unduly cumbersome, expensive, or otherwise inexpedient. The reference in the agency rules must fully identify the incorporated matter by location, date, and otherwise, [and must state that the rule does not include any later amendments or editions of the incorporated matter]. An agency may incorporate by reference such matter in its rules only if the agency, organization, or association originally issuing that matter makes copies of it readily available to the public. The rules must state where copies of the incorporated matter are available at cost from the agency issuing the rule, and where copies are available from the agency of the United States, this State, another state, or the organization or association originally issuing that matter.

(d) In preparing its rules pursuant to this Chapter, each agency shall follow the uniform numbering system, form, and style prescribed by the [administrative rules editor].

§ 3-112.   [Agency Rule-making Record].

(a) An agency shall maintain an official rule-making record for each rule it (i) proposes by publication in the [administrative bulletin] of a notice of proposed rule adoption, or (ii) adopts. The record and materials incorporated by reference must be available for public inspection.

(b) The agency rule-making record must contain:

(1) copies of all publications in the [administrative bulletin] with respect to the rule or the proceeding upon which the rule is based;

(2) copies of any portions of the agency's public rule-making docket containing entries relating to the rule or the proceeding upon which the rule is based;

(3) all written petitions, requests, submissions, and comments received by the agency and all other written materials considered by the agency in connection with the formulation, proposal, or adoption of the rule or the proceeding upon which the rule is based;

(4) any official transcript of oral presentations made in the proceeding upon which the rule is based or, if not transcribed, any tape recording or stenographic record of those presentations, and any memorandum prepared by a presiding official summarizing the contents of those presentations;

(5) a copy of any regulatory analysis prepared for the proceeding upon which the rule is based;

(6) a copy of the rule and explanatory statement filed in the office of the [secretary of state];

(7) all petitions for exceptions to, amendments of, or repeal or suspension of, the rule;

(8) a copy of any request filed pursuant to Section 3-108(c);

[(9) a copy of any objection to the rule filed by the [administrative rules review committee] pursuant to Section 3-204(d) and the agency's response;] and

(10) a copy of any filed executive order with respect to the rule.

(c) Upon judicial review, the record required by this section constitutes the official agency rule-making record with respect to a rule. Except as provided in Section 3-110(b) or otherwise required by a provision of law, the agency rule-making record need not constitute the exclusive basis for agency action on that rule or for judicial review thereof.

§ 3-113. [Invalidity of Rules Not Adopted According to Chapter; Time Limitation].

(a) A rule adopted after [date] is invalid unless adopted in substantial compliance with the provisions of Sections 3-102 through 3-108 and Sections 3-110 through 3-112. However, inadvertent failure to mail a notice of proposed rule adoption to any person as required by Section 3-103(b) does not invalidate a rule.

(b) An action to contest the validity of a rule on the grounds of its non-compliance with any provision of Sections 3-102 through 3-108 or Sections 3-110 through 3-112 must be commenced within [2] years after the effective date of the rule.

§ 3-114. [Filing of Rules].

(a) An agency shall file in the office of the [secretary of state] each rule it adopts and all rules existing on the effective date of this Act that have not previously been filed. The filing must be done as soon after adoption of the rule as is practicable. At the time of filing, each rule adopted after the effective date of this Act must have attached to it the explanatory statement required by Section 3-110. The [secretary of state] shall affix to each rule and statement a certification of the time and date of filing and keep a permanent register open to public inspection of all filed rules and attached explanatory statements. In filing a rule, each agency shall use a standard form prescribed by the [secretary of state].

(b) The [secretary of state] shall transmit to the [administrative rules editor], [administrative rules counsel], and to the members of the [administrative rules review committee] a certified copy of each filed rule as soon after its filing as is practicable.

§ 3-115. [Effective Date of Rules].

(a) Except to the extent subsection (b) or (c) provides otherwise, each rule adopted after the effective date of this Act becomes effective [30] days after the later of (i) its filing in the office of the [secretary of state] or (ii) its publication and indexing in the [administrative bulletin].

(b)(1) A rule becomes effective on a date later than that established by subsection (a) if a later date is required by another statute or specified in the rule.

(2) A rule may become effective immediately upon its filing or on any subsequent date earlier than that established by subsection (a) if the agency establishes such an effective date and finds that:

(i) it is required by constitution, statute, or court order;

(ii) the rule only confers a benefit or removes a restriction on the public or some segment thereof;

(iii) the rule only delays the effective date of another rule that is not yet effective; or

(iv) the earlier effective date is necessary because of imminent peril to the public health, safety, or welfare.

(3) The finding and a brief statement of the reasons therefor required by paragraph (2) must be made a part of the rule. In any action contesting the

effective date of a rule made effective under paragraph (2), the burden is on the agency to justify its finding.

(4) Each agency shall make a reasonable effort to make known to persons who may be affected by it a rule made effective before publication and indexing under this subsection.

(c) This section does not relieve an agency from compliance with any provision of law requiring that some or all of its rules be approved by other designated officials or bodies before they become effective.

§ 3-116.   [Special Provision for Certain Classes of Rules].

Except to the extent otherwise provided by any provision of law, Sections 3-102 through 3-115 are inapplicable to:

(1) a rule concerning only the internal management of an agency which does not directly and substantially affect the procedural or substantive rights or duties of any segment of the public;

(2) a rule that establishes criteria or guidelines to be used by the staff of an agency in performing audits, investigations, or inspections, settling commercial disputes, negotiating commercial arrangements, or in the defense, prosecution, or settlement of cases, if disclosure of the criteria or guidelines would:

(i) enable law violators to avoid detection;

(ii) facilitate disregard of requirements imposed by law; or

(iii) give a clearly improper advantage to persons who are in an adverse position to the state;

(3) a rule that only establishes specific prices to be charged for particular goods or services sold by an agency;

(4) a rule concerning only the physical servicing, maintenance, or care of agency owned or operated facilities or property;

(5) a rule relating only to the use of a particular facility or property owned, operated, or maintained by the state or any of its subdivisions, if the substance of the rule is adequately indicated by means of signs or signals to persons who use the facility or property;

(6) a rule concerning only inmates of a correctional or detention facility, students enrolled in an educational institution, or patients admitted to a hospital, if adopted by that facility, institution, or hospital;

(7) a form whose contents or substantive requirements are prescribed by rule or statute, and instructions for the execution or use of the form;

(8) an agency budget; [or]

(9) an opinion of the attorney general [; or] [.]

(10) [the terms of a collective bargaining agreement.]

§ 3-117.   [Petition For Adoption of Rule].

Any person may petition an agency requesting the adoption of a rule. Each agency shall prescribe by rule the form of the petition and the procedure for its submission, consideration, and disposition. Within [60] days after submission of a petition, the agency shall either (i) deny the petition in writing, stating its reasons therefor, (ii) initiate rule-making proceedings in accordance with this Chapter, or (iii) if otherwise lawful, adopt a rule.

CHAPTER II. REVIEW OF AGENCY RULES

§ 3-201.   [Review by Agency].

At least [annually], each agency shall review all of its rules to determine whether any new rule should be adopted. In conducting that review, each agency shall prepare a written report summarizing its findings, its supporting reasons, and any proposed course of action. For each rule, the [annual] report must include, at least once every [7] years, a concise statement of:

(1) the rule's effectiveness in achieving its objectives, including a summary of any available data supporting the conclusions reached;

(2) criticisms of the rule received during the previous [7] years, including a summary of any petitions for waiver of the rule tendered to the agency or granted by it; and

(3) alternative solutions to the criticisms and the reasons they were rejected or the changes made in the rule in response to those criticisms and the reasons for the changes. A copy of the [annual] report must be sent to the [administrative rules review committee and the administrative rules counsel] and be available for public inspection.

[§ 3-202.   [Review by Governor; Administrative Rules Counsel].

(a) To the extent the agency itself would have authority, the governor may rescind or suspend all or a severable portion of a rule of an agency. In exercising this authority, the governor shall act by an executive order that is subject to the provisions of this Act applicable to the adoption and effectiveness of a rule.

(b) The governor may summarily terminate any pending rule-making proceeding by an executive order to that effect, stating therein the reasons for the action. The executive order must be filed in the office of the [secretary of state], which shall promptly forward a certified copy to the agency and the [administrative rules editor]. An executive order terminating a rule-making proceeding becomes effective on [the date it is filed] and must be published in the next issue of the [administrative bulletin].

(c) There is created, within the office of the governor, an [administrative rules counsel] to advise the governor in the execution of the authority vested under this Article. The governor shall appoint the [administrative rules counsel] who shall serve at the pleasure of the governor.]

[§ 3-203.   [Administrative Rules Review Committee].

There is created the ["administrative rules review committee"] of the [legislature]. The committee must be [bipartisan] and composed of [3] senators appointed by the [president of the senate] and [3] representatives appointed by the [speaker of the house]. Committee members must be appointed within [30] days after the convening of a regular legislative session. The term of office is [2] years while a member of the [legislature] and begins on the date of appointment to the committee. While a member of the [legislature], a member of the committee whose term has expired shall serve until a successor is appointed. A vacancy on the committee may be filled at any time by the original appointing authority for the remainder of the term. The committee shall choose a chairman from its membership for a [2]-year term and may employ staff it considers advisable.]

§ 3-204.   [Review by Administrative Rules Review Committee].

(a) The [administrative rules review committee] shall selectively review possible, proposed, or adopted rules and prescribe appropriate committee procedures for that purpose. The committee may receive and investigate complaints from members of the public with respect to possible, proposed, or adopted rules and hold public proceedings on those complaints.

(b) Committee meetings must be open to the public. Subject to procedures established by the committee, persons may present oral argument, data, or views at those meetings. The committee may require a representative of an agency whose possible, proposed, or adopted rule is under examination to attend a committee meeting and answer relevant questions. The committee may also communicate to the agency its comments on any possible, proposed, or adopted rule and require the agency to respond to them in writing. Unless impracticable, in advance of each committee meeting notice of the time and place of the meeting and the specific subject matter to be considered must be published in the [administrative bulletin].

(c) The committee may recommend enactment of a statute to improve the operation of an agency. The committee may also recommend that a particular rule be superseded in whole or in part by statute. The [speaker of the house and the president of the senate] shall refer those recommendations to the appropriate standing committees. This subsection does not preclude any committee of the legislature from reviewing a rule on its own motion or recommending that it be superseded in whole or in part by statute.

[(d)(1) If the committee objects to all or some portion of a rule because the committee considers it to be beyond the procedural or substantive authority delegated to the adopting agency, the committee may file that objection in the office of the [secretary of state]. The filed objection must contain a concise statement of the committee's reasons for its action.]

(2) The [secretary of state] shall affix to each objection a certification of the date and time of its filing and as soon thereafter as practicable shall transmit a certified copy thereof to the agency issuing the rule in question, the [administrative rules editor, and the administrative rules counsel]. The [secretary of state] shall also maintain a permanent register open to public inspection of all objections by the committee.

(3) The [administrative rules editor] shall publish and index an objection filed pursuant to this subsection in the next issue of the [administrative bulletin] and indicate its existence adjacent to the rule in question when that rule is published in the [administrative code]. In case of a filed objection by the committee to a rule that is subject to the requirements of Section 2-101(g), the agency shall indicate the existence of that objection adjacent to the rule in the official compilation referred to in that subsection.

(4) Within [14] days after the filing of an objection by the committee to a rule, the issuing agency shall respond in writing to the committee. After receipt of the response, the committee may withdraw or modify its objection.

[(5) After the filing of an objection by the committee that is not subsequently withdrawn, the burden is upon the agency in any proceeding for judicial review or for enforcement of the rule to establish that the whole or portion of the rule objected to is within the procedural and substantive authority delegated to the agency.]

(6) The failure of the [administrative rules review committee] to object to a rule is not an implied legislative authorization of its procedural or substantive validity.]

(e) The committee may recommend to an agency that it adopt a rule. [The committee may also require an agency to publish notice of the committee's recommendation as a proposed rule of the agency and to allow public participation thereon, according to the provisions of Sections 3-103 through 3-104. An agency is not required to adopt the proposed rule.]

(f) The committee shall file an annual report with the [presiding officer] of each house and the governor.

ARTICLE IV. ADJUDICATIVE PROCEEDINGS

CHAPTER I. AVAILABILITY OF ADJUDICATIVE PROCEEDINGS; APPLICATIONS; LICENSES

§ 4-101.   [Adjudicative Proceedings; When Required; Exceptions].

(a) An agency shall conduct an adjudicative proceeding as the process for formulating and issuing an order, unless the order is a decision:

(1) to issue or not to issue a complaint, summons, or similar accusation;

(2) to initiate or not to initiate an investigation, prosecution, or other proceeding before the agency, another agency, or a court; or

(3) under Section 4-103, not to conduct an adjudicative proceeding.

(b) This Article applies to rule-making proceedings only to the extent that another statute expressly so requires.

§ 4-102.   [Adjudicative Proceedings; Commencement].

(a) An agency may commence an adjudicative proceeding at any time with respect to a matter within the agency's jurisdiction.

(b) An agency shall commence an adjudicative proceeding upon the application of any person, unless:

(1) the agency lacks jurisdiction of the subject matter;

(2) resolution of the matter requires the agency to exercise discretion within the scope of Section 4-101(a);

(3) a statute vests the agency with discretion to conduct or not to conduct an adjudicative proceeding before issuing an order to resolve the matter and, in the exercise of that discretion, the agency has determined not to conduct an adjudicative proceeding;

(4) resolution of the matter does not require the agency to issue an order that determines the applicant's legal rights, duties, privileges, immunities, or other legal interests;

(5) the matter was not timely submitted to the agency; or

(6) the matter was not submitted in a form substantially complying with any applicable provision of law.

(c) An application for an agency to issue an order includes an application for the agency to conduct appropriate adjudicative proceedings, whether or not the applicant expressly requests those proceedings.

(d) An adjudicative proceeding commences when the agency or a presiding officer:

(1) notifies a party that a pre-hearing conference, hearing, or other stage of an adjudicative proceeding will be conducted; or

(2) begins to take action on a matter that appropriately may be determined by an adjudicative proceeding, unless this action is:

(i) an investigation for the purpose of determining whether an adjudicative proceeding should be conducted; or

(ii) a decision which, under Section 4-101(a), the agency may make without conducting an adjudicative proceeding.

§ 4-103.   [Decision Not to Conduct Adjudicative Proceeding].

If an agency decides not to conduct an adjudicative proceeding in response to an application, the agency shall furnish the applicant a copy of its decision in writing, with a brief statement of the agency's reasons and of any administrative review available to the applicant.

§ 4-104.   [Agency Action on Applications].

(a) Except to the extent that the time limits in this subsection are inconsistent with limits established by another statute for any stage of the proceedings, an agency shall process an application for an order, other than a declaratory order, as follows:

(1) Within [30] days after receipt of the application, the agency shall examine the application, notify the applicant of any apparent errors or omissions, request any additional information the agency wishes to obtain and is permitted by law to require, and notify the applicant of the name, official title, mailing address and telephone number of an agency member or employee who may be contacted regarding the application.

(2) Except in situations governed by paragraph (3), within [90] days after receipt of the application or of the response to a timely request made by the agency pursuant to paragraph (1), the agency shall:

(i) approve or deny the application, in whole or in part, on the basis of emergency or summary adjudicative proceedings, if those proceedings are available under this Act for disposition of the matter;

(ii) commence a formal adjudicative hearing or a conference adjudicative hearing in accordance with this Act; or

(iii) dispose of the application in accordance with Section 4-103.

(3) If the application pertains to subject matter that is not available when the application is filed but may be available in the future, including an application for housing or employment at a time no vacancy exists, the agency may proceed to make a determination of eligibility within the time provided in paragraph (2). If the agency determines that the applicant is eligible, the agency shall maintain the application on the agency's list of

eligible applicants as provided by law and, upon request, shall notify the applicant of the status of the application.

(b) If a timely and sufficient application has been made for renewal of a license with reference to any activity of a continuing nature, the existing license does not expire until the agency has taken final action upon the application for renewal or, if the agency's action is unfavorable, until the last day for seeking judicial review of the agency's action or a later date fixed by the reviewing court.

§ 4-105.   [Agency Action Against Licensees].

An agency may not revoke, suspend, modify, annul, withdraw, or amend a license unless the agency first gives notice and an opportunity for an appropriate adjudicative proceeding in accordance with this Act or other statute. This section does not preclude an agency from (i) taking immediate action to protect the public interest in accordance with Section 4-501 or (ii) adopting rules, otherwise within the scope of its authority, pertaining to a class of licensees, including rules affecting the existing licenses of a class of licensees.

CHAPTER II. FORMAL ADJUDICATIVE HEARING

§ 4-201.   [Applicability].

An adjudicative proceeding is governed by this chapter, except as otherwise provided by:

(1) a statute other than this Act;

(2) a rule that adopts the procedures for the conference adjudicative hearing or summary adjudicative proceeding in accordance with the standards provided in this Act for those proceedings;

(3) Section 4-501 pertaining to emergency adjudicative proceedings; or

(4) Section 2-103 pertaining to declaratory proceedings.

§ 4-202.   [Presiding Officer, Disqualification, Substitution].

(a) The agency head, one or more members of the agency head, one or more administrative law judges assigned by the office of administrative hearings in accordance with Section 4-301 [, or, unless prohibited by law, one or more other persons designated by the agency head], in the discretion of the agency head, may be the presiding officer.

(b) Any person serving or designated to serve alone or with others as presiding officer is subject to disqualification for bias, prejudice, interest, or any other cause provided in this Act or for which a judge is or may be disqualified.

(c) Any party may petition for the disqualification of a person promptly after receipt of notice indicating that the person will preside or promptly upon discovering facts establishing grounds for disqualification, whichever is later.

(d) A person whose disqualification is requested shall determine whether to grant the petition, stating facts and reasons for the determination.

(e) If a substitute is required for a person who is disqualified or becomes unavailable for any other reason, the substitute must be appointed by:

(1) the governor, if the disqualified or unavailable person is an elected official; or

(2) the appointing authority, if the disqualified or unavailable person is an appointed official.

(f) Any action taken by a duly-appointed substitute for a disqualified or unavailable person is as effective as if taken by the latter.

§ 4-203.   [Representation].

(a) Any party may participate in the hearing in person or, if the party is a corporation or other artificial person, by a duly authorized representative.

(b) Whether or not participating in person, any party may be advised and represented at the party's own expense by counsel or, if permitted by law, other representative.

§ 4-204.   [Pre-hearing Conference — Availability, Notice].

The presiding officer designated to conduct the hearing may determine, subject to the agency's rules, whether a pre-hearing conference will be conducted. If the conference is conducted:

(1) The presiding officer shall promptly notify the agency of the determination that a pre-hearing conference will be conducted. The agency shall assign or request the office of administrative hearings to assign a presiding officer for the pre-hearing conference, exercising the same discretion as is provided by Section 4-202 concerning the selection of a presiding officer for a hearing.

(2) The presiding officer for the pre-hearing conference shall set the time and place of the conference and give reasonable written notice to all parties and to all persons who have filed written petitions to intervene in the matter. The agency shall give notice to other persons entitled to notice under any provision of law.

(3) The notice must include:

(i) the names and mailing addresses of all parties and other persons to whom notice is being given by the presiding officer;

(ii) the name, official title, mailing address, and telephone number of any counsel or employee who has been designated to appear for the agency;

(iii) the official file or other reference number, the name of the proceeding, and a general description of the subject matter;

(iv) a statement of the time, place, and nature of the pre-hearing conference;

(v) a statement of the legal authority and jurisdiction under which the pre-hearing conference and the hearing are to be held;

(vi) the name, official title, mailing address and telephone number of the presiding officer for the pre-hearing conference;

(vii) a statement that at the pre-hearing conference the proceeding, without further notice, may be converted into a conference adjudicative hearing or a summary adjudicative proceeding for disposition of the matter as provided by this Act; and

(viii) a statement that a party who fails to attend or participate in a pre-hearing conference, hearing, or other state of an adjudicative proceeding may be held in default under this Act.

(4) The notice may include any other matter that the presiding officer considers desirable to expedite the proceedings. . . .

§ 4-207.   [Pleadings, Briefs, Motions, Service].

(a) The presiding officer, at appropriate stages of the proceedings, shall give all parties full opportunity to file pleadings, motions, objections and offers of settlement.

(b) The presiding officer, at appropriate stages of the proceedings, may give all parties full opportunity to file briefs, proposed findings of fact and conclusions of law, and proposed initial or final orders.

(c) A party shall serve copies of any filed item on all parties, by mail or any other means prescribed by agency rule.

§ 4-208.   [Default].

(a) If a party fails to attend or participate in a pre-hearing conference, hearing, or other stage of an adjudicative proceeding, the presiding officer may serve upon all parties written notice of a proposed default order, including a statement of the grounds.

(b) Within [7] days after service of a proposed default order, the party against whom it was issued may file a written motion requesting that the proposed default order be vacated and stating the grounds relied upon. During the time within which a party may file a written motion under this subsection, the presiding officer may adjourn the proceedings or conduct them without the participation of the party against whom a proposed default order was issued, having due regard for the interests of justice and the orderly and prompt conduct of the proceedings.

(c) The presiding officer shall either issue or vacate the default order promptly after expiration of the time within which the party may file a written motion under subsection (b).

(d) After issuing a default order, the presiding officer shall conduct any further proceedings necessary to complete the adjudication without the participation of the party in default and shall determine all issues in the adjudication, including those affecting the defaulting party.

§ 4-209.   [Intervention].

(a) The presiding officer shall grant a petition for intervention if:

(1) the petition is submitted in writing to the presiding officer, with copies mailed to all parties named in the presiding officer's notice of the hearing, at least [3] days before the hearing;

(2) the petition states facts demonstrating that the petitioner's legal rights, duties, privileges, immunities, or other legal interests may be substantially affected by the proceeding or that the petitioner qualifies as an intervener under any provision of law; and

(3) the presiding officer determines that the interests of justice and the orderly and prompt conduct of the proceedings will not be impaired by allowing the intervention.

(b) The presiding officer may grant a petition for intervention at any time, upon determining that the intervention sought is in the interests of justice and will not impair the orderly and prompt conduct of the proceedings.

(c) If a petitioner qualifies for intervention, the presiding officer may impose conditions upon the intervener's participation in the proceedings, either at the time that intervention is granted or at any subsequent time. Conditions may include:

(1) limiting the intervener's participation to designated issues in which the intervener has a particular interest demonstrated by the petition;

(2) limiting the intervener's use of discovery, cross-examination, and other procedures so as to promote the orderly and prompt conduct of the proceedings; and

(3) requiring 2 or more interveners to combine their presentations of evidence and argument, cross-examination, discovery, and other participation in the proceedings.

(d) The presiding officer, at least [24 hours] before the hearing, shall issue an order granting or denying each pending petition for intervention, specifying any conditions, and briefly stating the reasons for the order. The presiding officer may modify the order at any time, stating the reasons for the modification. The presiding officer shall promptly give notice of an order granting, denying, or modifying intervention to the petitioner for intervention and to all parties.

§ 4-210.   [Subpoenas, Discovery and Protective Orders].

(a) The presiding officer [at the request of any party shall, and upon the presiding officer's own motion,] may issue subpoenas, discovery orders and protective orders, in accordance with the rules of civil procedure.

(b) Subpoenas and orders issued under this section may be enforced pursuant to the provisions of this Act on civil enforcement of agency action.

§ 4-211.   [Procedure at Hearing].

At a hearing:

(1) The presiding officer shall regulate the course of the proceedings in conformity with any pre-hearing order.

(2) To the extent necessary for full disclosure of all relevant facts and issues, the presiding officer shall afford to all parties the opportunity to respond, present evidence and argument, conduct cross-examination, and submit rebuttal evidence, except as restricted by a limited grant of intervention or by the pre-hearing order.

(3) The presiding officer may give nonparties an opportunity to present oral or written statements. If the presiding officer proposes to consider a statement by a nonparty, the presiding officer shall give all parties an opportunity to challenge or rebut it and, on motion of any party, the presiding officer shall require the statement to be given under oath or affirmation.

(4) The presiding officer may conduct all or part of the hearing by telephone, television, or other electronic means, if each participant in the hearing has an opportunity to participate in, to hear, and, if technically feasible, to see the entire proceeding while it is taking place.

(5) The presiding officer shall cause the hearing to be recorded at the agency's expense. The agency is not required, at its expense, to prepare a transcript, unless required to do so by a provision of law. Any party, at the party's expense, may cause a reporter approved by the agency to prepare a transcript from the agency's record, or cause additional recordings to be

made during the hearing if the making of the additional recordings does not cause distraction or disruption.

(6) The hearing is open to public observation, except for the parts that the presiding officer states to be closed pursuant to a provision of law expressly authorizing closure. To the extent that a hearing is conducted by telephone, television, or other electronic means, and is not closed, the availability of public observation is satisfied by giving members of the public an opportunity, at reasonable times, to hear or inspect the agency's record, and to inspect any transcript obtained by the agency.

§ 4-212.   [Evidence, Official Notice].

(a) Upon proper objection, the presiding officer shall exclude evidence that is irrelevant, immaterial, unduly repetitious, or excludable on constitutional or statutory grounds or on the basis of evidentiary privilege recognized in the courts of this state. In the absence of proper objection, the presiding officer may exclude objectionable evidence. Evidence may not be excluded solely because it is hearsay.

(b) All testimony of parties and witnesses must be made under oath or affirmation.

(c) Statements presented by nonparties in accordance with Section 4-211(3) may be received as evidence.

(d) Any part of the evidence may be received in written form if doing so will expedite the hearing without substantial prejudice to the interests of any party.

(e) Documentary evidence may be received in the form of a copy or excerpt. Upon request, parties must be given an opportunity to compare the copy with the original if available.

(f) Official notice may be taken of (i) any fact that could be judicially noticed in the courts of this State, (ii) the record of other proceedings before the agency, (iii) technical or scientific matters within the agency's specialized knowledge, and (iv) codes or standards that have been adopted by an agency of the United States, of this State or of another state, or by a nationally recognized organization or association. Parties must be notified before or during the hearing, or before the issuance of any initial or final order that is based in whole or in part on facts or material noticed, of the specific facts or material noticed and the source thereof, including any staff memoranda and data, and be afforded an opportunity to contest and rebut the facts or material so noticed.

§ 4-213.   [Ex parte Communications].

(a) Except as provided in subsection (b) or unless required for the disposition of ex parte matters specifically authorized by statute, a presiding officer serving in an adjudicative proceeding may not communicate, directly or indirectly, regarding any issue in the proceeding, while the proceeding is pending, with any party, with any person who has a direct or indirect interest in the outcome of the proceeding, or with any person who presided at a previous stage of the proceeding, without notice and opportunity for all parties to participate in the communication.

(b) A member of a multi-member panel of presiding officers may communicate with other members of the panel regarding a matter pending before the panel, and any presiding officer may receive aid from staff assistants if the assistants do not (i) receive ex parte communications of a type that the presiding officer would be prohibited from receiving or (ii) furnish, augment, diminish, or modify the evidence in the record.

(c) Unless required for the disposition of ex parte matters specifically authorized by statute, no party to an adjudicative proceeding, and no person who has a direct or indirect interest in the outcome of the proceeding or who presided at a previous stage of the proceeding, may communicate, directly or indirectly, in connection with any issue in that proceeding, while the proceeding is pending, with any person serving as presiding officer, without notice and opportunity for all parties to participate in the communication.

(d) If, before serving as presiding officer in an adjudicative proceeding, a person receives an ex parte communication of a type that could not properly be received while serving, the person, promptly after starting to serve, shall disclose the communication in the manner prescribed in subsection (e).

(e) A presiding officer who receives an ex parte communication in violation of this section shall place on the record of the pending matter all written communications received, all written responses to the communications, and a memorandum stating the substance of all oral communications received, all responses made, and the identity of each person from whom the presiding officer received an ex parte communication, and shall advise all parties that these matters have been placed on the record. Any party desiring to rebut the ex parte communication must be allowed to do so, upon requesting the opportunity for rebuttal within [10] days after notice of the communication.

(f) If necessary to eliminate the effect of an ex parte communication received in violation of this section, a presiding officer who receives the communication may be disqualified and the portions of the record pertaining to the communication may be sealed by protective order.

(g) The agency shall, and any party may, report any willful violation of this section to appropriate authorities for any disciplinary proceedings provided by law. In addition, each agency by rule may provide for appropriate sanctions, including default, for any violations of this section.

§ 4-214. [Separation of Functions].

(a) A person who has served as investigator, prosecutor or advocate in an adjudicative proceeding or in its pre-adjudicative stage may not serve as presiding officer or assist or advise a presiding officer in the same proceeding.

(b) A person who is subject to the authority, direction, or discretion of one who has served as investigator, prosecutor, or advocate in an adjudicative proceeding or in its pre-adjudicative stage may not serve as presiding officer or assist or advise a presiding officer in the same proceeding.

(c) A person who has participated in a determination of probable cause or other equivalent preliminary determination in an adjudicative proceeding may serve as presiding officer or assist or advise a presiding officer in the same proceeding, unless a party demonstrates grounds for disqualification in accordance with Section 4-202.

(d) A person may serve as presiding officer at successive stages of the same adjudicative proceeding, unless a party demonstrates grounds for disqualification in accordance with Section 4-202.

§ 4-215.   [Final Order, Initial Order].

(a) If the presiding officer is the agency head, the presiding officer shall render a final order.

(b) If the presiding officer is not the agency head, the presiding officer shall render an initial order, which becomes a final order unless reviewed in accordance with Section 4-216.

(c) A final order or initial order must include, separately stated, findings of fact, conclusions of law, and policy reasons for the decision if it is an exercise of the agency's discretion, for all aspects of the order, including the remedy prescribed and, if applicable, the action taken on a petition for stay of effectiveness. Findings of fact, if set forth in language that is no more than mere repetition or paraphrase of the relevant provision of law, must be accompanied by a concise and explicit statement of the underlying facts of record to support the findings. If a party has submitted proposed findings of fact, the order must include a ruling on the proposed findings. The order must also include a statement of the available procedures and time limits for seeking reconsideration or other administrative relief. An initial order must include a statement of any circumstances under which the initial order, without further notice, may become a final order.

(d) Findings of fact must be based exclusively upon the evidence of record in the adjudicative proceeding and on matters officially noticed in that proceeding. Findings must be based upon the kind of evidence on which reasonably prudent persons are accustomed to rely in the conduct of their serious affairs and may be based upon such evidence even if it would be inadmissible in a civil trial. The presiding officer's experience, technical competence, and specialized knowledge may be utilized in evaluating evidence.

(e) If a person serving or designated to serve as presiding officer becomes unavailable, for any reason, before rendition of the final order or initial order, a substitute presiding officer must be appointed as provided in Section 4-202. The substitute presiding officer shall use any existing record and may conduct any further proceedings appropriate in the interests of justice.

(f) The presiding officer may allow the parties a designated amount of time after conclusion of the hearing for the submission of proposed findings.

(g) A final order or initial order pursuant to this section must be rendered in writing within [90] days after conclusion of the hearing or after submission of proposed findings in accordance with subsection (f) unless this period is waived or extended with the written consent of all parties or for good cause shown.

(h) The presiding officer shall cause copies of the final order or initial order to be delivered to each party and to the agency head.

§ 4-216.   [Review of Initial Order; Exceptions to Reviewability].

(a) The agency head, upon its own motion may, and upon appeal by any party shall, review an initial order, except to the extent that:

(1) a provision of law precludes or limits agency review of the initial order; or

(2) the agency head, in the exercise of discretion conferred by a provision of law,

(i) determines to review some but not all issues, or not to exercise any review,

(ii) delegates its authority to review the initial order to one or more persons, or

(iii) authorizes one or more persons to review the initial order, subject to further review by the agency head.

(b) A petition for appeal from an initial order must be filed with the agency head, or with any person designated for this purpose by rule of the agency, within [10] days after rendition of the initial order. If the agency head on its own motion decides to review an initial order, the agency head shall give written notice of its intention to review the initial order within [10] days after its rendition. The [10]-day period for a party to file a petition for appeal or for the agency head to give notice of its intention to review an initial order on the agency head's own motion is tolled by the submission of a timely petition for reconsideration of the initial order pursuant to Section 4-218, and a new [10]-day period starts to run upon disposition of the petition for reconsideration. If an initial order is subject both to a timely petition for reconsideration and to a petition for appeal or to review by the agency head on its own motion, the petition for reconsideration must be disposed of first, unless the agency head determines that action on the petition for reconsideration has been unreasonably delayed.

(c) The petition for appeal must state its basis. If the agency head on its own motion gives notice of its intent to review an initial order, the agency head shall identity the issues that it intends to review.

(d) The presiding officer for the review of an initial order shall exercise all the decision-making power that the presiding officer would have had to render a final order had the presiding officer presided over the hearing, except to the extent that the issues subject to review are limited by a provision of law or by the presiding officer upon notice to all parties.

(e) The presiding officer shall afford each party an opportunity to present briefs and may afford each party an opportunity to present oral argument.

(f) Before rendering a final order, the presiding officer may cause a transcript to be prepared, at the agency's expense, of such portions of the proceeding under review as the presiding officer considers necessary.

(g) The presiding officer may render a final order disposing of the proceeding or may remand the matter for further proceedings with instructions to the person who rendered the initial order. Upon remanding a matter, the presiding officer may order such temporary relief as is authorized and appropriate.

(h) A final order or an order remanding the matter for further proceedings must be rendered in writing within [60] days after receipt of briefs and oral argument unless that period is waived or extended with the written consent of all parties or for good cause shown.

(i) A final order or an order remanding the matter for further proceedings under this section must identify any difference between this order and the initial order and must include, or incorporate by express reference to the initial order, all the matters required by Section 4-215(c).

(j) The presiding officer shall cause copies of the final order or order remanding the matter for further proceedings to be delivered to each party and to the agency head.

§ 4-217.   [Stay].

A party may submit to the presiding officer a petition for stay of effectiveness of an initial or final order within [7] days after its rendition unless otherwise provided by statute or stated in the initial or final order. The presiding officer may take action on the petition for stay, either before or after the effective date of the initial or final order.

§ 4-218.   [Reconsideration].

Unless otherwise provided by statute or rule:

(1) Any party, within [10] days after rendition of an initial or final order, may file a petition for reconsideration, stating the specific grounds upon which relief is requested. The filing of the petition is not a prerequisite for seeking administrative or judicial review.

(2) The petition must be disposed of by the same person or persons who rendered the initial or final order, if available.

(3) The presiding officer shall render a written order denying the petition, granting the petition and dissolving or modifying the initial or final order, or granting the petition and setting the matter for further proceedings. The petition may be granted, in whole or in part, only if the presiding officer states, in the written order, findings of fact, conclusions of law, and policy reasons for the decision if it is an exercise of the agency's discretion, to justify the order. The petition is deemed to have been denied if the presiding officer does not dispose of it within [20] days after the filing of the petition.

§ 4-219.   [Review by Superior Agency].

If, pursuant to statute, an agency may review the final order of another agency, the review is deemed to be a continuous proceeding as if before a single agency. The final order of the first agency is treated as an initial order and the second agency functions as though it were reviewing an initial order in accordance with Section 4-216.

§ 4-220.   [Effectiveness of Orders].

(a) Unless a later date is stated in a final order or a stay is granted, a final order is effective [10] days after rendition, but:

(1) a party may not be required to comply with a final order unless the party has been served with or has actual knowledge of the final order;

(2) a nonparty may not be required to comply with a final order unless the agency has made the final order available for public inspection and copying or the nonparty has actual knowledge of the final order.

(b) Unless a later date is stated in an initial order or a stay is granted, the time when an initial order becomes a final order in accordance with Section 4-215 is determined as follows:

(1) when the initial order is rendered, if administrative review is unavailable;

(2) when the agency head renders an order stating, after a petition for appeal has been filed, that review will not be exercised, if discretion is available to make a determination to this effect; or

(3) [10] days after rendition of the initial order, if no party has filed a petition for appeal and the agency head has not given written notice of its intention to exercise review.

(c) Unless a later date is stated in an initial order or a stay is granted, an initial order that becomes a final order in accordance with subsection (b) and Section 4-215 is effective [10] days after becoming a final order, but:

(1) a party may not be required to comply with the final order unless the party has been served with or has actual knowledge of the initial order or of an order stating that review will not be exercised; and

(2) a nonparty may not be required to comply with the final order unless the agency has made the initial order available for public inspection and copying or the nonparty has actual knowledge of the initial order or of an order stating that review will not be exercised.

(d) This section does not preclude an agency from taking immediate action to protect the public interest in accordance with Section 4-501.

§ 4-221.   [Agency Record].

(a) An agency shall maintain an official record of each adjudicative proceeding under this Chapter.

(b) The agency record consists only of:

(1) notices of all proceedings;

(2) any pre-hearing order;

(3) any motions, pleadings, briefs, petitions, requests, and intermediate rulings;

(4) evidence received or considered;

(5) a statement of matters officially noticed;

(6) proffers of proof and objections and rulings thereon;

(7) proposed findings, requested orders, and exceptions;

(8) the record prepared for the presiding officer at the hearing, together with any transcript of all or part of the hearing considered before final disposition of the proceeding;

(9) any final order, initial order, or order on reconsideration;

(10) staff memoranda or data submitted to the presiding officer, unless prepared and submitted by personal assistants and not inconsistent with Section 4-213(b); and

(11) matters placed on the record after an ex parte communication.

(c) Except to the extent that this Act or another statute provides otherwise, the agency record constitutes the exclusive basis for agency action in adjudicative proceedings under this Chapter and for judicial review thereof.

CHAPTER III. OFFICE OF ADMINISTRATIVE HEARINGS

§ 4-301.   [Office of Administrative Hearings — Creation, Powers, Duties].

(a) There is created the office of administrative hearings within the [Department of _____], to be headed by a director appointed by the governor [and confirmed by the senate].

(b) The office shall employ administrative law judges as necessary to conduct proceedings required by this Act or other provision of law. [Only a person admitted to practice law in [this State] [a jurisdiction in the United States] may be employed as an administrative law judge.]

(c) If the office cannot furnish one of its administrative law judges in response to an agency request, the director shall designate in writing a full-time employee of an agency other than the requesting agency to serve as administrative law judge for the proceeding, but only with the consent of the employing agency. The designee must possess the same qualifications required of administrative law judges employed by the office.

(d) The director may furnish administrative law judges on a contract basis to any governmental entity to conduct any proceeding not subject to this Act.

(e) The office may adopt rules:

(1) to establish further qualifications for administrative law judges, procedures by which candidates will be considered for employment, and the manner in which public notice of vacancies in the staff of the office will be given;

(2) to establish procedures for agencies to request and for the director to assign administrative law judges; however, an agency may neither select nor reject any individual administrative law judge for any proceeding except in accordance with this Act;

(3) to establish procedures and adopt forms, consistent with this Act, the model rules of procedure, and other provisions of law, to govern administrative law judges;

(4) to establish standards and procedures for the evaluation, training, promotion, and discipline of administrative law judges; and

(5) to facilitate the performance of the responsibilities conferred upon the office by this Act.

(f) The director may:

(1) maintain a staff of reporters and other personnel; and

(2) implement the provisions of this section and rules adopted under its authority.

CHAPTER IV. CONFERENCE ADJUDICATIVE HEARING

§ 4-401.   [Conference Adjudicative Hearing — Applicability].

A conference adjudicative hearing may be used if its use in the circumstances does not violate any provision of law and the matter is entirely within one or more categories for which the agency by rule had adopted this chapter [; however, those categories may include only the following:

(1) a matter in which there is no disputed issue of material fact; or

(2) a matter in which there is a disputed issue of material fact, if the matter involves only:

(i) a monetary amount of not more than [$1,000];

(ii) a disciplinary sanction against a prisoner;

(iii) a disciplinary sanction against a student which does not involve expulsion from an academic institution or suspension for more than [10] days;

(iv) a disciplinary sanction against a public employee which does not involve discharge from employment or suspension for more than [10] days;

(v) a disciplinary sanction against a licensee which does not involve revocation, suspension, annulment, withdrawal, or amendment of a license; or
(vi). . . .]

§ 4-402.   [Conference Adjudicative Hearing — Procedures].

The procedures of this Act pertaining to formal adjudicative hearings apply to a conference adjudicative hearing, except to the following extent:
(1) If a matter is initiated as a conference adjudicative hearing, no prehearing conference may be held.
(2) The provisions of Section 4-210 do not apply to conference adjudicative hearings insofar as those provisions authorize the issuance and enforcement of subpoenas and discovery orders, but do apply to conference adjudicative hearings insofar as those provisions authorize the presiding officer to issue protective orders at the request of any party or upon the presiding officer's motion.
(3) Paragraphs (1), (2) and (3) of Section 4-211 do not apply; but,
(i) the presiding officer shall regulate the course of the proceedings,
(ii) only the parties may testify and present written exhibits, and
(iii) the parties may offer comments on the issues.

§ 4-403.   [Conference Adjudicative Hearing — Proposed Proof].

(a) If the presiding officer has reason to believe that material facts are in dispute, the presiding officer may require any party to state the identity of the witnesses or other sources through whom the party would propose to present proof if the proceeding were converted to a formal adjudicative hearing, but if disclosure of any fact, allegation, or source is privileged or expressly prohibited by any provision of law, the presiding officer may require the party to indicate that confidential facts, allegations, or sources are involved, but not to disclose the confidential facts, allegations, or sources.

(b) If a party has reason to believe that essential facts must be obtained in order to permit an adequate presentation of the case, the party may inform the presiding officer regarding the general nature of the facts and the sources from whom the party would propose to obtain those facts if the proceeding were converted to a formal adjudicative hearing.

CHAPTER V. EMERGENCY AND SUMMARY ADJUDICATIVE PROCEEDINGS

§ 4-501.   [Emergency Adjudicative Proceedings].

(a) An agency may use emergency adjudicative proceedings in a situation involving an immediate danger to the public health, safety, or welfare requiring immediate agency action.

(b) The agency may take only such action as is necessary to prevent or avoid the immediate danger to the public health, safety, or welfare that justifies use of emergency adjudication.

(c) The agency shall render an order, including a brief statement of findings of fact, conclusions of law, and policy reasons for the decision if it is an exercise of the agency's discretion, to justify the determination of an immediate danger and the agency's decision to take the specific action.

(d) The agency shall give such notice as is practicable to persons who are required to comply with the order. The order is effective when rendered.

(e) After issuing an order pursuant to this section, the agency shall proceed as quickly as feasible to complete any proceedings that would be required if the matter did not involve an immediate danger.

(f) The agency record consists of any documents regarding the matter that were considered or prepared by the agency. The agency shall maintain these documents as its official record.

(g) Unless otherwise required by a provision of law, the agency record need not constitute the exclusive basis for agency action in emergency adjudicative proceedings or for judicial review thereof.

§ 4-502.   [Summary Adjudicative Proceedings — Applicability].

An agency may use summary adjudicative proceedings if:

(1) the use of those proceedings in the circumstances does not violate any provision of law;

(2) the protection of the public interest does not require the agency to give notice and an opportunity to participate to persons other than the parties; and

(3) the matter is entirely within one or more categories for which the agency by rule has adopted this section and Sections 4-503 to 4-506 [; however, those categories may include only the following:

(i) a monetary amount of not more than [$100];

(ii) a reprimand, warning, disciplinary report, or other purely verbal sanction without continuing impact against a prisoner, student, public employee, or licensee;

(iii) the denial of an application after the applicant has abandoned the application;

(iv) the denial of an application for admission to an educational institution or for employment by an agency;

(v) the denial, in whole or in part, of an application if the applicant has an opportunity for administrative review in accordance with Section 4-504;

(vi) a matter that is resolved on the sole basis of inspections, examinations, or tests;

(vii) the acquisition, leasing, or disposal of property or the procurement of goods or services by contract;

(viii) any matter having only trivial potential impact upon the affected parties; and

(ix). . . .]

§ 4-503.   [Summary Adjudicative Proceedings — Procedures].

(a) The agency head, one or more members of the agency head, one or more administrative law judges assigned by the office of administrative hearings in accordance with Section 4-301 [, or, unless prohibited by law, one or more other persons designated by the agency head], in the discretion of the agency head, may be the presiding officer. Unless prohibited by law, a person exercising authority over the matter is the presiding officer.

(b) If the proceeding involves a monetary matter or a reprimand, warning, disciplinary report, or other sanction:

(1) the presiding officer, before taking action, shall give each party an opportunity to be informed of the agency's view of the matter and to explain the party's view of the matter; and

(2) the presiding officer, at the time any unfavorable action is taken, shall give each party a brief statement of findings of fact, conclusions of law, and policy reasons for the decision if it is an exercise of the agency's discretion, to justify the action, and a notice of any available administrative review.

(c) An order rendered in a proceeding that involves a monetary matter must be in writing. An order in any other summary adjudicative proceeding may be oral or written.

(d) The agency, by reasonable means, shall furnish to each party notification of the order in a summary adjudicative proceeding. Notification must include at least a statement of the agency's action and a notice of any available administrative review.

§ 4-504. [Administrative Review of Summary Adjudicative Proceedings — Applicability].

Unless prohibited by any provision of law, an agency, on its own motion, may conduct administrative review of an order resulting from summary adjudicative proceedings, and shall conduct this review upon the written or oral request of a party if the agency receives the request within [10] days after furnishing notification under Section 4-503(d).

§ 4-505. [Administrative Review of Summary Adjudicative Proceedings — Procedures].

Unless otherwise provided by statute [or rule]:

(1) An agency need not furnish notification of the pendency of administrative review to any person who did not request the review, but the agency may not take any action on review less favorable to any party than the original order without giving that party notice and an opportunity to explain that party's view of the matter.

(2) The reviewing officer, in the discretion of the agency head, may be any person who could have presided at the summary adjudicative proceeding, but the reviewing officer must be one who is authorized to grant appropriate relief upon review.

(3) The reviewing officer shall give each party an opportunity to explain the party's view of the matter unless the party's view is apparent from the written materials in the file submitted to the reviewing officer. The reviewing officer shall make any inquiries necessary to ascertain whether the proceeding must be converted to a conference adjudicative hearing or a formal adjudicative hearing.

(4) The reviewing officer may render an order disposing of the proceeding in any manner that was available to the presiding officer at the summary adjudicative proceeding or the reviewing officer may remand the matter for further proceedings, with or without conversion to a conference adjudicative hearing or a formal adjudicative hearing.

(5) If the order under review is or should have been in writing, the order on review must be in writing, including a brief statement of findings of fact, conclusions of law, and policy reasons for the decision if it is an exercise of the agency's discretion, to justify the order, and a notice of any further available administrative review.

(6) A request for administrative review is deemed to have been denied if the reviewing officer does not dispose of the matter or remand it for further proceedings within [20] days after the request is submitted.

§ 4-506. [Agency Record of Summary Adjudicative Proceedings and Administrative Review].

(a) The agency record consists of any documents regarding the matter that were considered or prepared by the presiding officer for the summary adjudicative proceeding or by the reviewing officer for any review. The agency shall maintain these documents as its official record.

(b) Unless otherwise required by a provision of law, the agency record need not constitute the exclusive basis for agency action in summary adjudicative proceedings or for judicial review thereof.

ARTICLE V. JUDICIAL REVIEW AND CIVIL ENFORCEMENT

CHAPTER I. JUDICIAL REVIEW

§ 5-101. [Relationship Between This Act and Other Law on Judicial Review and Other Judicial Remedies].

This Act establishes the exclusive means of judicial review of agency action, but:

(1) The provisions of this Act for judicial review do not apply to litigation in which the sole issue is a claim for money damages or compensation and the agency whose action is at issue does not have statutory authority to determine the claim.

(2) Ancillary procedural matters, including intervention, class actions, consolidation, joinder, severance, transfer, protective orders, and other relief from disclosure of privileged or confidential material, are governed, to the extent not inconsistent with this Act, by other applicable law.

(3) If the relief available under other sections of this Act is not equal or substantially equivalent to the relief otherwise available under law, the relief otherwise available and the related procedures supersede and supplement this Act to the extent necessary for their effectuation. The applicable provisions of this Act and other law must be combined to govern a single proceeding or, if the court orders, 2 or more separate proceedings, with or without transfer to other courts, but no type of relief may be sought in a combined proceeding after expiration of the time limit for doing so.

§ 5-102. [Final Agency Action Reviewable].

(a) A person who qualifies under this Act regarding (i) standing (Section 5-106), (ii) exhaustion of administrative remedies (Section 5-107), and (iii) time for filing the petition for review (Section 5-108), and other applicable provisions of law regarding bond, compliance, and other pre-conditions is entitled to judicial review of final agency action, whether or not the person has sought judicial review of any related non-final agency action.

(b) For purposes of this section and Section 5-103:

(1) "Final agency action" means the whole or a part of any agency action other than non-final agency action;

(2) "Non-final agency action" means the whole or a part of an agency determination, investigation, proceeding, hearing, conference, or other process that the agency intends or is reasonably believed to intend to be preliminary, preparatory, procedural, or intermediate with regard to subsequent agency action of that agency or another agency.

§ 5-103.   [Non-final Agency Action Reviewable].

A person is entitled to judicial review of non-final agency action only if:

(1) it appears likely that the person will qualify under Section 5-102 for judicial review of the related final agency action; and

(2) postponement of judicial review would result in an inadequate remedy or irreparable harm disproportionate to the public benefit derived from postponement.

§ 5-104.   [Jurisdiction, Venue]. [ALTERNATIVE A].

(a) The [trial court of general jurisdiction] shall conduct judicial review.

(b) Venue is in the [district] [that includes the state capital] [where the petitioner resides or maintains a principal place of business] unless otherwise provided by law.

§ 5-104.   [Jurisdiction, Venue]. [ALTERNATIVE B].

(a) The [appellate court] shall conduct judicial review.

(b) Venue is in the [district][that includes the state capital][where the petitioner resides or maintains a principal place of business] unless otherwise provided by law.

(c) If evidence is to be adduced in the reviewing court in accordance with Section 5-114(a), the court shall appoint a [referee, master, trial court judge] for this purpose, having due regard for the convenience of the parties.

§ 5-105.   [Form of Action].

Judicial review is initiated by filing a petition for review in [the appropriate] court. A petition may seek any type of relief available under Sections 5-101(3) and 5-117.

§ 5-106.   [Standing].

(a) The following persons have standing to obtain judicial review of final or non-final agency action:

(1) a person to whom the agency action is specifically directed;

(2) a person who was a party to the agency proceedings that led to the agency action;

(3) if the challenged agency action is a rule, a person subject to that rule;

(4) a person eligible for standing under another provision of law; or

(5) a person otherwise aggrieved or adversely affected by the agency action. For purposes of this paragraph, no person has standing as one otherwise aggrieved or adversely affected unless:

(i) the agency action has prejudiced or is likely to prejudice that person;

(ii) that person's asserted interests are among those that the agency was required to consider when it engaged in the agency action challenged; and

(iii) a judgment in favor of that person would substantially eliminate or redress the prejudice to that person caused or likely to be caused by the agency action.

[(b) A standing committee of the legislature which is required to exercise general and continuing oversight over administrative agencies and procedures may petition for judicial review of any rule or intervene in any litigation arising from agency action.]

§ 5-107.   [Exhaustion of Administrative Remedies].

A person may file a petition for judicial review under this Act only after exhausting all administrative remedies available within the agency whose action is being challenged and within any other agency authorized to exercise administrative review, but:

(1) a petitioner for judicial review of a rule need not have participated in the rule-making proceeding upon which that rule is based, or have petitioned for its amendment or repeal;

(2) a petitioner for judicial review need not exhaust administrative remedies to the extent that this Act or any other statute states that exhaustion is not required; or

(3) the court may relieve a petitioner of the requirement to exhaust any or all administrative remedies, to the extent that the administrative remedies are inadequate, or requiring their exhaustion would result in irreparable harm disproportionate to the public benefit derived from requiring exhaustion.

§ 5-108.   [Time for Filing Petition for Review].

Subject to other requirements of this Act or of another statute:

(1) A petition for judicial review of a rule may be filed at any time, except as limited by Section 3-113(b).

(2) A petition for judicial review of an order is not timely unless filed within [30] days after rendition of the order, but the time is extended during the pendency of the petitioner's timely attempts to exhaust administrative remedies, if the attempts are not clearly frivolous or repetitious.

(3) A petition for judicial review of agency action other than a rule or order is not timely unless filed within [30] days after the agency action, but the time is extended:

(i) during the pendency of the petitioner's timely attempts to exhaust administrative remedies, if the attempts are not clearly frivolous or repetitious; and

(ii) during any period that the petitioner did not know and was under no duty to discover, or did not know and was under a duty to discover but could not reasonably have discovered, that the agency had taken the action or that the agency action had a sufficient effect to confer standing upon the petitioner to obtain judicial review under this Act. . . .

§ 5-114.   [New Evidence Taken by Court or Agency Before Final Disposition].

(a) The court [(if Alternative B of Section 5-104 is adopted), assisted by a referee, master, trial court judge as provided in Section 5-104(c),] may receive evidence, in addition to that contained in the agency record for judicial review, only if it relates to the validity of the agency action at the time it was taken and is needed to decide disputed issues regarding:

(1) improper constitution as a decision-making body, or improper motive or grounds for disqualification, of those taking the agency action;

(2) unlawfulness of procedure or of decision-making process; or

(3) any material fact that was not required by any provision of law to be determined exclusively on an agency record of a type reasonably suitable for judicial review.

(b) The court may remand a matter to the agency, before final disposition of a petition for review, with directions that the agency conduct fact-finding and other proceedings the court considers necessary and that the agency take such further action on the basis thereof as the court directs, if:

(1) the agency was required by this Act or any other provision of law to base its action exclusively on a record of a type reasonably suitable for judicial review, but the agency failed to prepare or preserve an adequate record;

(2) the court finds that (i) new evidence has become available that relates to the validity of the agency action at the time it was taken, that one or more of the parties did not know and was under no duty to discover, or did not know and was under a duty to discover but could not reasonably have discovered, until after the agency action, and (ii) the interests of justice would be served by remand to the agency;

(3) the agency improperly excluded or omitted evidence from the record; or

(4) a relevant provision of law changed after the agency action and the court determines that the new provision may control the outcome. . . .

§ 5-116.   [Scope of Review; Grounds for Invalidity].

(a) Except to the extent that this Act or another statute provides otherwise:

(1) The burden of demonstrating the invalidity of agency action is on the party asserting invalidity; and

(2) The validity of agency action must be determined in accordance with the standards of review provided in this section, as applied to the agency action at the time it was taken.

(b) The court shall make a separate and distinct ruling on each material issue on which the court's decision is based.

(c) The court shall grant relief only if it determines that a person seeking judicial relief has been substantially prejudiced by any one or more of the following:

(1) The agency action, or the statute or rule on which the agency action is based, is unconstitutional on its face or as applied.

(2) The agency has acted beyond the jurisdiction conferred by any provision of law.

(3) The agency has not decided all issues requiring resolution.

(4) The agency has erroneously interpreted or applied the law.

(5) The agency has engaged in an unlawful procedure or decision-making process, or has failed to follow prescribed procedure.

(6) The persons taking the agency action were improperly constituted as a decision-making body, motivated by an improper purpose, or subject to disqualification.

(7) The agency action is based on a determination of fact, made or implied by the agency, that is not supported by evidence that is substantial when viewed in light of the whole record before the court, which includes the agency record for judicial review, supplemented by any additional evidence received by the court under this Act.

(8) The agency action is:

(i) outside the range of discretion delegated to the agency by any provision of law;

(ii) agency action, other than a rule, that is inconsistent with a rule of the agency; [or]

(iii) agency action, other than a rule, that is inconsistent with the agency's prior practice unless the agency justifies the inconsistency by stating facts and reasons to demonstrate a fair and rational basis for the inconsistency. [; or][.]

(iv) [otherwise unreasonable, arbitrary or capricious.] . . .

TABLE OF CASES

(Principal cases and cases for which there is a substantial explanatory note are in bold.)

INDEX